国际文化法文件汇编

Documents on International Cultural Law

中英文对照 ⊙ In Chinese & English Edition

中共中央宣传部政策法规研究室
中国社会科学院法学研究所 编

学习出版社

出版说明

为适应全面推进依法治国的要求，提高文化建设法制化水平，帮助宣传文化工作者更好地学习掌握文化法律法规，也为文化立法工作者提供一手参考资料，近两年来，我们在有关部门和单位的大力支持下，系统收集整理国内外文化立法方面的资料，开展了文化立法资料库建设，已编辑出版了《宣传文化法规汇编》、《地方文化法规汇编》、《与宣传文化相关的法律法规条文汇编》等。这本《国际文化法文件汇编》是我们委托中国社会科学院法学所对50余件“国际文化条约和协议”进行收集翻译、汇编而成，是资料库中的新成果。

文化定义非常广泛，本书立足我国实际，以我国宣传文化主管部门职责范围为基准，确定“文化”的内涵外延，并以此为依据收录文件。本书收录的国际文化法文件均与文化直接相关，对于与文化有一定关系但非以文化问题为主要内容的国际法文件基本未予收录，因此将书名定为“国际文化法文件汇编”。

本书分综合，大众传媒、文学艺术与文化产业，公共文化服务，文物与文化遗产保护，著作权保护五个部分，收录了与文化密切相关的55个国际法文件。在收录的文件中，公约（Covenant，Convention）、条约（Convention，Treaty）、协定（Agreement）、议定书（Protocol）具有法律约束力，宣言（Declaration）和建议（Commendation）没有直接的法律约束力，属于国际法上的“软法”范畴。本书采取中英文对照的方式，同时汇编了相关文件的中文和英文版本。英文文件已有中译本的，尽量采用，译文含义不清之处，根据原文予以校核；无中译本的，由课题组组织翻译，为尊重译者的劳动，以脚注形式注明译者的姓名和单位。本书收集的文件截止时间为2013年6月。

参与本书收集编译以及研究课题组成员名单如下：

冯　军　中国社会科学院法学研究所研究员、教授、博士生导师，中国社会科学院文化法制研究中心主任，课题组负责人。

陈欣新　中国社会科学院法学研究所传媒信息法研究室主任，研究员、教授，中国科学院文化法制研究中心副主任。

谢增毅　中国社会科学院法学研究所科研组织与外事处处长，副研究员、副教授、法学博士。

陈根发　中国社会科学院法学研究所传媒信息法研究室副主任，中国社会科学院文化法制研究中心副主任，副研究员、副教授、法学博士。

沈卫利　中国社会科学院法学研究所传媒信息法研

究室副研究员、副教授。

吴　峻　中国社会科学院法学研究所传媒信息法研究室助理研究员，瑞士苏黎世大学法学博士。

郑文明　首都经济贸易大学传播学系副主任、副教授、法学博士。

杨会永　郑州大学法学院副教授、法学博士。

汪　梦　西南政法大学法学院讲师，意大利博洛尼亚大学法学博士后。

吴晓丹　中国社会科学院国际法研究所博士后，意大利米兰大学法学博士。

吴峻博士收集、整理本书中英文资料，并翻译多份英文文献。首都经济贸易大学郑文明博士、中央广播电视大学谢军博士，以及首都经济贸易大学传播学系法学院的部分同学参与本书校对工作。全书由冯军研究员审阅、修改和定稿。

在本书出版印发之际，谨向付出辛劳、作出贡献的各位同志表示衷心感谢！

编　者

2013 年 11 月 26 日

目　　录

第一部分　综　　合
Part I　General

第二部分 大众传媒、文学艺术与文化产业
Part II Mass Media，Literature & Arts，Cultural Industry

第三部分 公共文化服务
Part III Service for Public Culture

第四部分 文物与文化遗产保护
Part IV Protection of Antique and Cultural Heritage

第五部分　著作权保护
Part V　Protection of Copyrights

第一部分　综　合

Part I　General

经济、社会和文化权利国际公约

（1966年12月16日第二十一届联合国大会第2200A号决议通过，1976年1月3日生效。1997年10月27日我国正式签署该公约。2001年2月28日第九届全国人大常委会第二十次会议作出批准决定。同年3月27日向联合国秘书长交存批准书）

序　言

鉴于按照《联合国宪章》所确立的原则，对人类大家庭所有成员固有尊严及其平等和不可剥夺的权利的承认，是世界自由、正义与和平的基础；

鉴于这些权利来源于人类固有的尊严；

鉴于按照《世界人权宣言》，人类享受免于恐惧和贫困之自由的理想，只有在人人得以行使其公民权利和政治权利以及经济、社会和文化权利时，才能实现；

鉴于各国根据《联合国宪章》负有促进对人权和自由的普遍尊重与遵行的义务；

鉴于人人都应当对他人和社会负有为增进和遵行本公约所确认的各项权利而奋斗的义务；

本公约缔约各国，兹同意下述各条：

第一章

第一条

一、各民族享有自决权。他们凭这种权利自由决定他们的政治地位，并自由谋求他们的经济、社会和文化的发展。

二、各民族得为他们自己的所有人民自由处置他们的天然财富和资源，但不得损害其根据国际经济合作、互利原则以及国际法而产生的任何义务。在任何情况下不得剥夺一个民族维持其生存的手段。

三、本公约缔约各国，包括那些负责管理非自治领土和托管领土的国家，应在符合联合国宪章规定的条件下，促进自决权的实现，并尊重这种权利。

第二章

第二条

一、本公约缔约各国应采取措施，在其可用资源的最大限度内，独自或通过国际援助与合作，特别是国际经济和技术方面的援助与合作，采用一切适当的方法，尤其是采用立法措施，以保证本公约确认的权利逐步得到充分的实现。

二、本公约缔约各国应当确保本公约所宣布的各项权利在行使时不会受到诸如种族、肤色、性别、语言、宗教、政治或其他见解、国籍或社会出身、财产、出生或其他身份方面的歧视。

三、发展中国家，在适当顾及人权及其国民经济的情况下，得决定它们对非本国国民享受本公约中所确认的经济权利，给予何种程度的保障。

第三条　本公约缔约各国应当确保男子和妇女在本公约所载一切经济、社会及文化权利方面享有平等的权利。

第四条　本公约缔约各国承认，对于本公约确认的各项权利，各国在作相应规定时，可以通过法律予以限制，但这类限制不得与其所限权利的性质相冲突，并且只能为了促进民主社会总体福利的目的。

第五条

一、本公约中的任何部分不得解释为隐示任何国家、团体或个人有权利从事任何旨在破坏本公约所确认的任何权利或自由或对它们加以较本公约所规定的范围更广的限制的活动或行为。

二、对于在任何国家中依据法律、惯例、条例或习惯而被承认或存在的任何基本人权，不得借口本公约未予承认或只在较小范围上予以承认而予以限制或克减。

第三章

第六条

一、本公约缔约各国承认工作权，包括人人应有机会凭其自由选择和接受的工作谋生的权利，并将采取适当措施对这一权利予以保障。

二、本公约缔约各国为充分实现这一权利而采取的措施应包括技术的和职业的指导和训练，以及在保障个人基本政治和经济自由的条件下达到稳定的经济、社会和文化的发展和充分的生产就业的计划、政策和技术。

第七条　本公约缔约各国承认人人有权享受公正和良好的工作条件，特别要保证：

（甲）最低限度给予所有工人以下列报酬：

（1）公平的工资和同工同酬而没有任何歧视，特别是保证妇女享受不差于男子所享受的工作条件，并享受同工同酬；

（2）保证他们自己和他们的家庭过上符合本公约规定的体面生活；

（乙）安全和卫生的工作条件；

（丙）人人在其行业中享有适当的提级的同等机会，除资历和能力的考虑外，不受其他考虑的限制；

（丁）休息、休闲和合理限制工作时间，定期带薪休假以及公共假日加班报偿。

第八条

一、本公约缔约各国确认保障：

（甲）人人有权组织工会和参加他所选择的工会，以促进和保护他的经济和社会利益；这个权利只受有关工会的规章的限制。对这一权利的行使，不得加以除法律所规定及在民主社会中为了国家安全或公共秩序的利益或为保护他人的权利和自由所必需的限制以外的任何限制；

（乙）工会有权建立全国性的协会或联合会，有权组织或参加国际工会组织；

（丙）工会有权自由地进行工作，不受除法律所规定及在民主社会中为了国家安全或公共秩序的利益或为保护他人的权利和自由所需要的限制以外的任何限制；

（丁）有权罢工，但应按照各个国家的法律行使此项权利。

二、本条不应禁止各国对军队或警察或国家行政机关成员行使上述权利加以合法的限制。

三、本条并不授权关于结社自由和保护结社权利的1948年《国际劳工组织公约》的缔约国通过立法或法律适用损害该公约确认的各项保障。

第九条

本公约缔约各国承认人人有权享受社会保障，包括社会保险。

第十条

本公约缔约各国承认：

一、对作为社会自然和基本组织单元的家庭，特别是对于家庭的建立和家庭负有照看和教育未独立儿童的责任时，应给予尽可能广泛的保护和协助。结婚必须经男女双方自由同意。

二、对母亲，在产前和产后的合理期间，应给以特别保护。在此期间，对有工作的母亲应给以带薪休假或有适当社会保障福利的休假。

三、应为一切儿童和青少年采取特殊的保护和协助措施，不得因出身或其他条件而有任何歧视。应予儿童和青少年保护免受经济和社会的剥削。雇佣他们做对他们的道德或健康有害或对生命有危险的工作或做足以妨害他们正常发育的工作，依法应受惩罚。各国应规定限定的年龄，凡雇佣这个年龄以下的童工，应予禁止和依法予以惩罚。

第十一条

一、本公约缔约各国承认人人有权为他自己和家庭获得相当的生活水准，包括足够的食物、衣着和住房，并能不断改进生活条件。各缔约国将采取适当的措施保证实现这一权利，并承认为此而实行基于自愿同意的国际合作的重要性。

二、本公约缔约各国确认人人享有免于饥饿的基本权利，为此应各自采取必要的措施或经由国际合作采取必要的措施，包括具体的计划在内：

（甲）通过充分利用科技知识、传播营养知识以及建立或改革能够使自然资源得到最有效开发利用的农业制度，改进粮食的生产、保存及分配方法；

（乙）兼顾粮食进口国和出口国面临的问题，保证世界粮食供应根据需要公平分配。

第十二条

一、本公约缔约各国承认人人有权享有能达到的最高的体质和心理健康的标准。

二、本公约缔约各国为充分实现这一权利而采取的措施应包括为实现下列目标而采取的必要措施：

（甲）减低死胎率和婴儿死亡率，以及使儿童得到健康的发育；

（乙）全面改善环境卫生和工业卫生；

（丙）预防、治疗和控制传染病、地方病、职业病以及其他的疾病；

（丁）创造保证人人在患病时能够得到医疗服务和医疗照顾的条件。

第十三条

一、本公约缔约各国承认，人人享有接受教育的权利。各国同意，教育应鼓励人的个性和尊严的充分发展，加强对人权和基本自由的尊重，并应使所有的人能够在自由社会中进行有效的社会参与，促进各民族之间和各种族、人种或宗教团体之间的了解、容忍和友谊，以及促进联合国维护和平的各项活动。

二、本公约缔约各国承认，为了充分实现这一权利：

（甲）初等教育应属义务性质并一律免费；

（乙）各种形式的中等教育，包括中等技术和职业教育，应以一切适当方法，普遍设立，并对一切人开放，特别要逐渐做到免费；

（丙）高等教育应根据成绩，以一切适当方法，对一切人平等开放，特别要逐渐做到免费；

（丁）对那些未受到或未完成初等教育的人的基础教育，应尽可能加以鼓励或推进；

（戊）各级学校的制度，应积极加以发展；适当的奖学金制度，应予设置；教员的物质条件，应不断加以改善。

三、本公约缔约各国保证尊重父母和（如适用时）法定监护人的下列自由：为他们的孩子选择非公立的但系符合于国家所可能规定或批准的最低教育标准的学校，并保证他们的孩子能按照他们自己的信仰接受宗教和道德教育。

四、本条的任何部分不得解释为干涉个人或团体设立及管理教育机构的自由，但以遵守本条第一款所述各项原则以及此等机构实施的教育必须符合国家所可能规定的最低标准。

第十四条

本公约任何缔约国在参加本公约时尚未做到在其本土或其他在其管辖下的领土实施免费、义务性初等教育的，应当在两年之内制定和采取一个逐步实行的详细的行动计划，其中应当规定在合理的年限内全面实现义务教育免费的原则。

第十五条

一、本公约缔约各国承认人人有权：

（甲）参加文化生活；

（乙）享受科学进步及其应用所产生的利益；

（丙）对其本人的任何科学、文学或艺术作品所产生的精神上和物质上的利益，享受被保护的权利。

二、本公约缔约各国为充分实现这一权利而采取的措施应包括为保存、发展和传播科学和文化所必需的措施。

三、本公约缔约各国应当尊重进行科学研究和创造性活动所不可缺少的自由。

四、本公约缔约各国认同在科学和文化领域进行鼓励和发展国际接触和合作的益处。

第四章

第十六条

一、本公约缔约各国应当依照本公约本部分的规定提交关于其在遵行本公约所承认的权利方面所采取的措施和所取得的进展的报告。

二、（甲）所有的报告应提交给联合国秘书长；联合国秘书长应将报告副本转交经济与社会理事会按照本公约的规定审议；

（乙）本公约任何缔约国，同时是联合国某个专门机构的成员国者，其所提交的报告或其中某部分，倘若按照该专门机构的组织法规定与该机构职责范围内的事项有关，联合国秘书长应同时将报告副本或其中的有关部分转交该专门机构。

第十七条

一、本公约缔约各国应按照经济与社会理事会于本公约生效后一年内经与本公约缔约各国和有关专门机构进行咨商后所制订的方案，分批提交报告。

二、报告得指出影响本公约义务履行的因素和困难。

三、有关材料先前已由缔约国提交联合国或联合国相关专门机构的，缔约国不必再次提交，但需提供关于该材料详细出处的说明。

第十八条

基于根据《联合国宪章》所承担的保障人权和基本自由的责任，经济与社会理事会得安排有关专门机构报告他们在各自职权范围内推进本公约所取得的进展。报告应包括相关专门机构为推进本公约的施行而作出决定和提出建议的细节。

第十九条

经济与社会理事会得将各国按照第十六条和第十七条规定提交的关于人权的报告和各专门机构按照第十八条的规定提交的关于人权的报告转交人权委员会以供研究和提出一般建议或在适当时候参考。

第二十条

本公约缔约各国以及有关的专门机构得就第十九条中规定的任何一般建议或就人权委员会任何报告中的此种一般建议或其中所提及的任何文件，向经济与社会理事会提出意见。

第二十一条

经济与社会理事会得随时向联合国大会提交有关本公约实施的一般性建议的报告，以及从本公约各缔约国和各专门机构收到的关于其在普遍遵行本公约所承认的权利方面所采取措施和所取得进展的材料的摘要。

第二十二条

经济与社会理事会得提请从事技术援助的其他联合国机构和它们的辅助机构以及有关的专门机构对本公约本部分所提到的各种报告所引起的任何事项予以注意，这些事项可能帮助这些机构在他们各自的权限内决定是否需要采取有助于促进本公约的逐步切实履行的国际措施。

第二十三条

本公约缔约各国同意为实现本公约所承认的权利而采取的国际行动应包括签订公约、提出建议、进行技术援助，以及为磋商和研究的目的同有关国家政府共同召开区域会议和技术会议等方法。

第二十四条

本公约的任何部分不得解释为有损联合国宪章和各专门机构组织法在本公约所涉及事项方面有关联合国组织和各专门机构的责任的规定。

第二十五条

本公约中任何部分不得解释为有损各民族充分、自由地享受和利用其自然财富与资源的固有权利。

第五章

第二十六条

一、本公约开放给联合国任何会员国或其专门机构的任何会员国、国际法院规约的任何当事国以及经联合国大会邀请为本公约缔约国的任何其他国家签署。

二、本公约须经批准。批准书应交存联合国秘书长。

三、本公约应开放给本条第一款所述的任何国家加入。

四、加入应向联合国秘书长交存加入书。

五、联合国秘书长应将每一批准书或加入书的交存通知已经签署或加入本公约的所有国家。

第二十七条

一、本公约应自第三十五件批准书或加入书交存联合国秘书长之日起三个月后生效。

二、对于在第三十五件批准书或加入书交存后批准或加入本公约的国家，本公约应自该国交存其批准书或加入书之日起三个月后生效。

第二十八条

本公约的规定应扩及联邦国家的所有部分，没有任何限制和例外。

第二十九条

一、本公约的任何缔约国均得提出对本公约的修正案，并将其提交联合国秘书长。秘书长应立即将提出的修正案转告本公约各缔约国，同时请他们通知秘书长是否赞成召开缔约国家会议以审议该提案并对其进行表决。在至少有三分之一缔约国赞成召开这一会议的情况下，应在联合国秘书长主持下召开此会议。出席会议并投票的多数缔约国所通过的任何修正案，应提交联合国大会批准。

二、此等修正案由联合国大会批准并被本公约缔约国的三分之二多数按照他们各自的宪法程序加以接受后，即行生效。

三、此等修正案生效时，对接受该修正案的各缔约国有拘束力，其他缔约国仍受本公约的条款和他们接受的任何以前的修正案的拘束。

第三十条

除按照第二十六条第五款作出的通知外，联合国秘书长应将下列事项通知同条第一款所述的所有国家：

（甲）按照第二十六条规定所作的签署、批准和加入；

（乙）本公约按照第二十七条规定生效的日期，以及对本公约的任何修正案按照第二十九条规定生效的日期。

第三十一条

一、本公约应交存联合国档案库，其中文、英文、法文、俄文、西班牙文各文本具有同等效力。

二、联合国秘书长应将本公约的正式副本分送第二十六条所指的所有国家。

International Covenant on Economic, Social and Cultural Rights

Adopted and opened for signature, ratification and accession by General Assembly resolution 2200A (XXI) of 16 December 1966 entry into force 3 January 1976, in accordance with article 27

Preamble

The States Parties to the present Covenant,

Considering that, in accordance with the principles proclaimed in the Charter of the United Nations, recognition of the inherent dignity and of the equal and inalienable rights of all members of the human family is the foundation of freedom, justice and peace in the world,

Recognizing that these rights derive from the inherent dignity of the human person,

Recognizing that, in accordance with the Universal Declaration of Human Rights, the ideal of free human beings enjoying freedom from fear and want can only be achieved if conditions are created whereby everyone may enjoy his economic, social and cultural rights, as well as his civil and political rights,

Considering the obligation of States under the Charter of the United Nations to promote universal respect for, and observance of, human rights and freedoms,

Realizing that the individual, having duties to other individuals and to the community to which he belongs, is under a responsibility to strive for the promotion and observance of the rights recognized in the present Covenant,

Agree upon the following articles:

PART I

Article 1

1. All peoples have the right of self - determination. By virtue of that right they freely determine their political status and freely pursue their economic, social and cultural development.

2. All peoples may, for their own ends, freely dispose of their natural wealth and resources without prejudice to any obligations arising out of international economic co - operation, based upon the principle of mutual benefit, and international law. In no case may a people be deprived of its own means of subsistence.

3. The States Parties to the present Covenant, including those having responsibility for the administration of Non - Self - Governing and Trust Territories, shall promote the realization of the right of self - determination, and shall respect that right, in conformity with the provisions of the Charter of the United Nations.

PART II

Article 2

1. Each State Party to the present Covenant undertakes to take steps, individually and through international assistance and co - operation, especially economic and technical, to the maximum of its available resources, with a view to achieving progressively the full realization of the rights recognized in the present Covenant by all appropriate means, including particularly the adoption of legislative measures.

2. The States Parties to the present Covenant undertake to guarantee that the rights enunciated in the present Covenant will be exercised without discrimination of any kind as to race, colour, sex, language, religion, political or other opinion, national or social origin, property, birth or other status.

3. Developing countries, with due regard to human rights and their national economy, may determine to what extent they would guarantee the economic rights recognized in the present Covenant to non - nationals.

Article 3

The States Parties to the present Covenant undertake to ensure the equal right of men and women to the enjoyment of all economic, social and cultural rights set forth in the present Covenant.

Article 4

The States Parties to the present Covenant recognize that, in the enjoyment of those rights provided by the State in conformity with the present Covenant, the State may subject such rights only to such limitations as are determined by law only in so far as this may be compatible with the nature of these rights and solely for the purpose of promoting the general welfare in a democratic society.

Article 5

1. Nothing in the present Covenant may be interpreted as implying for any State, group or person any right to engage in any activity or to perform any act aimed at the destruction of any of the rights or freedoms recognized herein, or at their limitation to a greater extent than is provided for in the present Covenant.

2. No restriction upon or derogation from any of the fundamental human rights recognized or existing in any country in virtue of law, conventions, regulations or custom shall be admitted on the pretext that the present Covenant does not recognize such rights or that it recognizes them to a lesser extent.

PART III

Article 6

1. The States Parties to the present Covenant recognize the right to work, which includes the right of everyone to the opportunity to gain his living by work which he freely chooses or accepts, and will take appropriate steps to safeguard this right.

2. The steps to be taken by a State Party to the present Covenant to achieve the full realization of this right shall include technical and vocational guidance and training programmes, policies and techniques to achieve steady economic, social and cultural development and full and productive employment under conditions safeguarding fundamental political and economic freedoms to the individual.

Article 7

The States Parties to the present Covenant recognize the right of everyone to the enjoyment of just and favourable conditions of work which ensure, in particular:

(a) Remuneration which provides all workers, as a minimum, with:

(i) Fair wages and equal remuneration for work of equal value without distinction of any kind, in particular women being guaranteed conditions of work not inferior to those enjoyed by men, with equal pay for equal work;

(ii) A decent living for themselves and their families in accordance with the provisions of the present Covenant;

(b) Safe and healthy working conditions;

(c) Equal opportunity for everyone to be promoted in his employment to an appropriate higher level, subject to no considerations other than those of seniority and competence;

(d) Rest, leisure and reasonable limitation of working hours and periodic holidays with pay, as well as remuneration for public holidays

Article 8

1. The States Parties to the present Covenant undertake to ensure:

(a) The right of everyone to form trade unions and join the trade union of his choice, subject only to the rules of the organization concerned, for the promotion and protection of his economic and social interests. No restrictions may be placed on the exercise of this right other than those prescribed by law and which are necessary in a democratic society in the interests of national security or public order or for the protection of the rights and freedoms of others;

(b) The right of trade unions to establish national federations or confederations and the right of the latter to form or join international trade - union organizations;

(c) The right of trade unions to function freely subject to no limitations other than those prescribed by law and which are necessary in a democratic society in the interests of national security or public order or for the protection of the rights and freedoms of others;

(d) The right to strike, provided that it is exercised in conformity with the laws of the particular country.

2. This article shall not prevent the imposition of lawful restrictions on the exercise of these rights by members of the armed forces or of the police or of the administration of the State.

3. Nothing in this article shall authorize States Parties to the International Labour Organisation Convention of 1948 concerning Freedom of Association and Protection of the Right to Organize to take legislative measures which would prejudice, or apply the law in such a manner as would prejudice, the guarantees provided for in that Convention.

Article 9

The States Parties to the present Covenant recognize the right of everyone to social security, including social insurance.

Article 10

The States Parties to the present Covenant recognize that:

1. The widest possible protection and assistance should be accorded to the family, which is the natural and fundamental group unit of society, particularly for its establishment and while it is responsible for the care and education of dependent children. Marriage must be entered into with the free consent of the intending spouses.

2. Special protection should be accorded to mothers during a reasonable period before and after childbirth. During such period working mothers should be accorded paid leave or leave with adequate social security benefits.

3. Special measures of protection and assistance should be taken on behalf of all children and young persons without any discrimination for reasons of parentage or other conditions. Children and young persons should be protected from economic and social exploitation. Their employment in work harmful to their morals or health or dangerous to life or likely to hamper their normal development should be punishable by law. States should also set age limits below which the paid employment of child labour should be prohibited and punishable by law.

Article 11

1. The States Parties to the present Covenant recognize the right of everyone to an adequate standard of living for himself and his family, including adequate food, clothing and housing, and to the continuous improvement of living conditions. The States Parties will take appropriate steps to ensure the realization of this right, recognizing to this effect the essential importance of international co - operation based on free consent.

2. The States Parties to the present Covenant, recognizing the fundamental

right of everyone to be free from hunger, shall take, individually and through international co - operation, the measures, including specific programmes, which are needed:

(a) To improve methods of production, conservation and distribution of food by making full use of technical and scientific knowledge, by disseminating knowledge of the principles of nutrition and by developing or reforming agrarian systems in such a way as to achieve the most efficient development and utilization of natural resources;

(b) Taking into account the problems of both food - importing and food - exporting countries, to ensure an equitable distribution of world food supplies in relation to need.

Article 12

1. The States Parties to the present Covenant recognize the right of everyone to the enjoyment of the highest attainable standard of physical and mental health.

2. The steps to be taken by the States Parties to the present Covenant to achieve the full realization of this right shall include those necessary for:

(a) The provision for the reduction of the stillbirth - rate and of infant mortality and for the healthy development of the child;

(b) The improvement of all aspects of environmental and industrial hygiene;

(c) The prevention, treatment and control of epidemic, endemic, occupational and other diseases;

(d) The creation of conditions which would assure to all medical service and medical attention in the event of sickness.

Article 13

1. The States Parties to the present Covenant recognize the right of everyone to education. They agree that education shall be directed to the full development of the human personality and the sense of its dignity, and shall strengthen the respect for human rights and fundamental freedoms. They further agree that education shall enable all persons to participate effectively in a free society, promote understanding, tolerance and friendship among all nations and all racial, ethnic or religious groups, and further the activities of the United Nations for the maintenance of peace.

2. The States Parties to the present Covenant recognize that, with a view to achieving the full realization of this right:

(a) Primary education shall be compulsory and available free to all;

(b) Secondary education in its different forms, including technical and vocational secondary education, shall be made generally available and accessible to all by every appropriate means, and in particular by the progressive introduction of free education;

(c) Higher education shall be made equally accessible to all, on the basis of capacity, by every appropriate means, and in particular by the progressive introduction of free education;

(d) Fundamental education shall be encouraged or intensified as far as possible for those persons who have not received or completed the whole period of their primary education;

(e) The development of a system of schools at all levels shall be actively pursued, an adequate fellowship system shall be established, and the material conditions of teaching staff shall be continuously improved.

3. The States Parties to the present Covenant undertake to have respect for the liberty of parents and, when applicable, legal guardians to choose for their children schools, other than those established by the public authorities, which conform to such minimum educational standards as may be laid down or approved by the State and to ensure the religious and moral education of their children in conformity with their own convictions.

4. No part of this article shall be construed so as to interfere with the liberty of individuals and bodies to establish and direct educational institutions, subject always to the observance of the principles set forth in paragraph I of this article and to the requirement that the education given in such institutions shall conform to such minimum standards as may be laid down by the State.

Article 14

Each State Party to the present Covenant which, at the time of becoming a Party, has not been able to secure in its metropolitan territory or other territories under its jurisdiction compulsory primary education, free of charge, undertakes, within two years, to work out and adopt a detailed plan of action for the progressive implementation, within a reasonable number of years, to be fixed in the plan, of the principle of compulsory education free of charge for all.

Article 15

1. The States Parties to the present Covenant recognize the right of everyone:

(a) To take part in cultural life;

(b) To enjoy the benefits of scientific progress and its applications;

(c) To benefit from the protection of the moral and material interests resulting from any scientific, literary or artistic production of which he is the author.

2. The steps to be taken by the States Parties to the present Covenant to achieve the full realization of this right shall include those necessary for the conservation, the development and the diffusion of science and culture.

3. The States Parties to the present Covenant undertake to respect the freedom indispensable for scientific research and creative activity.

4. The States Parties to the present Covenant recognize the benefits to be derived from the encouragement and development of international contacts and co - operation in the scientific and cultural fields.

PART IV

Article 16

1. The States Parties to the present Covenant undertake to submit in conformity with this part of the Covenant reports on the measures which they have adopted and the progress made in achieving the observance of the rights recognized herein.

2.

(a) All reports shall be submitted to the Secretary - General of the United Nations, who shall transmit copies to the Economic and Social Council for consideration in accordance with the provisions of the present Covenant;

(b) The Secretary - General of the United Nations shall also transmit to the specialized agencies copies of the reports, or any relevant parts therefrom, from States Parties to the present Covenant which are also members of these specialized agencies in so far as these reports, or parts therefrom, relate to any matters which fall within the responsibilities of the said agencies in accordance with their constitutional instruments.

Article 17

1. The States Parties to the present Covenant shall furnish their reports in sta-

ges, in accordance with a programme to be established by the Economic and Social Council within one year of the entry into force of the present Covenant after consultation with the States Parties and the specialized agencies concerned.

2. Reports may indicate factors and difficulties affecting the degree of fulfillment of obligations under the present Covenant.

3. Where relevant information has previously been furnished to the United Nations or to any specialized agency by any State Party to the present Covenant, it will not be necessary to reproduce that information, but a precise reference to the information so furnished will suffice.

Article 18

Pursuant to its responsibilities under the Charter of the United Nations in the field of human rights and fundamental freedoms, the Economic and Social Council may make arrangements with the specialized agencies in respect of their reporting to it on the progress made in achieving the observance of the provisions of the present Covenant falling within the scope of their activities. These reports may include particulars of decisions and recommendations on such implementation adopted by their competent organs.

Article 19

The Economic and Social Council may transmit to the Commission on Human Rights for study and general recommendation or, as appropriate, for information the reports concerning human rights submitted by States in accordance with articles 16 and 17, and those concerning human rights submitted by the specialized agencies in accordance with article 18.

Article 20

The States Parties to the present Covenant and the specialized agencies concerned may submit comments to the Economic and Social Council on any general recommendation under article 19 or reference to such general recommendation in any report of the Commission on Human Rights or any documentation referred to therein.

Article 21

The Economic and Social Council may submit from time to time to the General Assembly reports with recommendations of a general nature and a summary of the information received from the States Parties to the present Covenant and the specialized agencies on the measures taken and the progress made in achieving general observance of the rights recognized in the present Covenant.

Article 22

The Economic and Social Council may bring to the attention of other organs of the United Nations, their subsidiary organs and specialized agencies concerned with furnishing technical assistance any matters arising out of the reports referred to in this part of the present Covenant which may assist such bodies in deciding, each within its field of competence, on the advisability of international measures likely to contribute to the effective progressive implementation of the present Covenant.

Article 23

The States Parties to the present Covenant agree that international action for the achievement of the rights recognized in the present Covenant includes such methods as the conclusion of conventions, the adoption of recommendations, the furnishing of technical assistance and the holding of regional meetings and technical meetings for the purpose of consultation and study organized in conjunction with the Governments concerned.

Article 24

Nothing in the present Covenant shall be interpreted as impairing the provisions of the Charter of the United Nations and of the constitutions of the specialized agencies which define the respective responsibilities of the various organs of the United Nations and of the specialized agencies in regard to the matters dealt with in the present Covenant.

Article 25

Nothing in the present Covenant shall be interpreted as impairing the inherent right of all peoples to enjoy and utilize fully and freely their natural wealth and resources.

PART V

Article 26

1. The present Covenant is open for signature by any State Member of the United Nations or member of any of its specialized agencies, by any State Party to

the Statute of the International Court of Justice, and by any other State which has been invited by the General Assembly of the United Nations to become a party to the present Covenant.

2. The present Covenant is subject to ratification. Instruments of ratification shall be deposited with the Secretary - General of the United Nations.

3. The present Covenant shall be open to accession by any State referred to in paragraph 1 of this article.

4. Accession shall be effected by the deposit of an instrument of accession with the Secretary - General of the United Nations.

5. The Secretary - General of the United Nations shall inform all States which have signed the present Covenant or acceded to it of the deposit of each instrument of ratification or accession.

Article 27

1. The present Covenant shall enter into force three months after the date of the deposit with the Secretary - General of the United Nations of the thirty - fifth instrument of ratification or instrument of accession.

2. For each State ratifying the present Covenant or acceding to it after the deposit of the thirty - fifth instrument of ratification or instrument of accession, the present Covenant shall enter into force three months after the date of the deposit of its own instrument of ratification or instrument of accession.

Article 28

The provisions of the present Covenant shall extend to all parts of federal States without any limitations or exceptions.

Article 29

1. Any State Party to the present Covenant may propose an amendment and file it with the Secretary - General of the United Nations. The Secretary - General shall thereupon communicate any proposed amendments to the States Parties to the present Covenant with a request that they notify him whether they favour a conference of States Parties for the purpose of considering and voting upon the proposals. In the event that at least one third of the States Parties favours such a conference, the Secretary - General shall convene the conference under the auspices of the United Nations. Any amendment adopted by a majority of the States Parties present and voting at the conference shall be submitted to the General Assembly of the United

Nations for approval.

2. Amendments shall come into force when they have been approved by the General Assembly of the United Nations and accepted by a two - thirds majority of the States Parties to the present Covenant in accordance with their respective constitutional processes.

3. When amendments come into force they shall be binding on those States Parties which have accepted them, other States Parties still being bound by the provisions of the present Covenant and any earlier amendment which they have accepted.

Article 30

Irrespective of the notifications made under article 26, paragraph 5, the Secretary - General of the United Nations shall inform all States referred to in paragraph I of the same article of the following particulars:

(a) Signatures, ratifications and accessions under article 26;

(b) The date of the entry into force of the present Covenant under article 27 and the date of the entry into force of any amendments under article 29.

Article 31

1. The present Covenant, of which the Chinese, English, French, Russian and Spanish texts are equally authentic, shall be deposited in the archives of the United Nations.

2. The Secretary - General of the United Nations shall transmit certified copies of the present Covenant to all States referred to in article 26.

关于实施《经济、社会和文化权利国际公约》的林堡原则*

（联合国经济社会理事会 1986 年 6 月 6 日通过）

第一部分：缔约国义务的性质和范围

A. 概述

1. 经济、社会及文化权利是国际人权法的固有组成部分。他们是若干法律文件中特定公约义务的对象，该特定公约具体而言，就是《国际经济、社会和文化权利公约》。

2. 《经济、社会和文化权利国际公约》及《公民权利和政治权利国际公约》及其选择性议定书于 1976 年生效。这两部公约进一步阐明了《世界人权宣言》，它们与《世界人权宣言》共同构成《国际人权法案》。

3. 人权及基本自由不可分割、相互依存，因此，在实施、促进和保护时应对公民权利、政治权利与经济、社会和文化权利同等重视并作为紧迫事项予以考虑。

4. 《经济、社会和文化权利国际公约》（以下简称“《公约》”）应根据《维也纳条约法公约》（《1969 年维也纳公约》）结合条约的对象、目的、通常含义、起草过程以及相关惯例，作出善意解释。

5. 实施《公约》并监督缔约国取得的进展时，应考虑联合国机构、国家间组织（包括人权领域联合国工作组及特派调查员）及相关专门机构的经验。

6. 经济、社会和文化权利可以在各种不同的政治背景下得以实现。对其

---

* 中国社会科学院法学研究所吴峻译。

全部落实并无单一路径可循。无论在市场经济、非市场经济，还是集中制、非集中制的政治结构中，都有成功和失败记录在案。

7. 缔约国在任何时候都要对其在《公约》项下接受的义务予以善意履行。

8. 虽然对《公约》所承认的权利予以完全落实需要采取渐进方式，但可以即时在法律中实施一些权利，而其他权利则可以逐渐在法律中予以落实。

9. 非政府组织可以发挥重要作用以促进《公约》的实施。应相应地在国际及国际层面促使其发挥这种作用。

10. 缔约国就履行其在《公约》项下的义务向国际社会及其人民负责。

11. 一致性的全国行动以促使社会的全部阶层完全参与其中，对于推动实现经济、社会和文化权利而言必不可少。在包括制定、实施及事后重审在内的所有阶段，都须得到广泛的参与。

12. 对是否遵守《公约》的监督应当本着合作及对话的精神加以进行。为此目的，在审议缔约国报告时，经济、社会和文化权利小组委员会（以下简称“小组委员会”）应当分析阻碍实现《公约》所确认权利的因素，并在可能的情形下提出解决方案。这种方法不应排除在得到充足信息的支持下得出结论：缔约国未能遵守《公约》项下的义务。

13. 所有监督《公约》的机构在评估缔约国遵守《公约》情况时都应对法律面前不歧视及平等原则予以特别关注。

14. 鉴于渐进落实《公约》所规定权利的意义，应当尤其关注提高贫穷或其他弱势群体生活水平的措施，其中应考虑到可能需要采取特殊措施保护本地人群及少数族群的文化权利。

15. 评估国际社会在实现《公约》目的的努力时，应考虑国际经济关系的趋向。

B.《公约》第二部分相关内容的解释原则

第二条第一款：“采取措施……采用一切适当方法，尤其是采用立法措施”

16. 所有缔约国家都有义务立即采取措施以完全落实《公约》所规定的权利。

17. 缔约各国须在国家层面利用包括立法、行政、司法、经济、社会及教育措施在内的、符合权利性质的所有适当方式履行其在《公约》项下的义务。

18. 仅仅凭借立法措施对于履行《公约》项下的义务，并不足够。然而，需要注意的是，第二条第一款通常在现有法律违反《公约》项下承担义务的情形下要求采取相关立法措施。

19．缔约各国须规定包括适当情形下司法救济方式在内的有效救济方式。

20．在特定缔约国适用某项手段的适当性由该缔约国予以认定，并须接受联合国经济及社会理事会在小组委员会协助下进行的审议。该等审议不影响根据《联合国宪章》所确定机构的职权。

“逐步达到权利的充分实现。”

21．“逐渐达到权利的充分实现”这一义务要求缔约各国尽快迅速行动，达到权利的充分实现。在任何情形下，这都不能被解释为隐含着缔约国有权无限期推迟确保权利全部达成的努力。相反，所有缔约国均有义务立即考虑采取措施以履行其在《公约》项下的义务。

22．《公约》项下的一些义务要求缔约各国马上予以完全实施，例如《公约》第二条第二款的禁止歧视之规定。

23．逐步实施条约之义务独立于资源之增加而存在：它要求有效使用现有资源。

24．条约的逐步实施不仅通过增加自然资源予以实现，而且通过开发使得人人都能实现《公约》项下权利的社会资源予以实现。

“可用资源的最大限度”

25．缔约各国有义务确保对所有人最低限度协助权的尊重，无论其经济发展水平。

26．“可用资源”系指一国内部资源及通过国际合作及协助而来自于国际社会的资源。

27．在认定是否采取足够措施实现《公约》项下所承认权利时，须关注现有能力公平及有效的使用和开发。

28．在使用可用资源时，为确保满足每个人的生存需要和提供基本服务，对本公约中与此相关的权利应当给予适当的优先考虑。

“各自采取措施或经由国际援助和合作，特别是经济和技术方面的援助和合作”

29．根据《联合国宪章》第五十五条及第五十六条和本《公约》的规定，国际合作和援助应将所有人权及基本自由，无论涉及经济、社会及文化权利还是公民权利和政治权利，均作为优先事项。

30．国际合作及援助须旨在建立使本《公约》规定的权利和自由可以完全达成的社会及国际秩序。

31．无论其政治、经济及社会制度之间有何不同，缔约国之间应当彼此合作，以推动国际社会、经济及文化的发展，尤其是发展中国家的经济增长。任何缔约国均不应因这些方面的差异而受到歧视。

32. 缔约国各方须采取措施通过国际援助及合作的方式达成本《公约》项下的权利。

33. 国际合作和援助须基于缔约各国主权平等原则，并以达成本《公约》规定的权利为目标。

34. 根据本《公约》第二条第一款规定进行国际合作及援助时，须关注国际组织的作用和非政府组织的贡献。

第二条第二款：不歧视

35. 第二条第二款应予立即适用，对此缔约各国给予明确保证。为此，该条款应受到司法审查及其他救济程序的保障。

36. 第二条第二款描述的歧视情形并非穷尽。

37. 在成为本《公约》缔约国后，缔约国须在法律上立即废除影响享受经济、社会及文化权利的任何歧视性法律、行政法规及做法（包括不予行为及要求予以一定行为的情形）。

38. 因资源匮乏或者过剩而引起的经济、社会和文化权利在享有上的不平等属于事实歧视。对于此种事实歧视应尽快予以消除。

39. 为使特定群体或个人平等地享有经济、社会和文化权利而必须采取特殊措施对其加以特殊保护，以使其获得充分发展的，此种特殊保护措施不应视为歧视，但这类特殊措施不得导致在不同群体间实行不同权利的后果，并且在达到目标后不得继续采用。

40. 第二条第二款要求缔约各国禁止私人及机构在任何公共生活领域实施歧视性做法。

41. 适用第二条第二款规定时，应对包括《消除任何形式种族歧视的宣言》及《消除一切形式种族歧视国际公约》在内的所有相关国际文件及该《公约》项下监督委员会（消除种族歧视委员会）的活动予以适当关注。

第二条第三款：发展中国家的非本国公民

42. 作为一项一般规则，本《公约》对本国及非本国公民平等适用。

43. 第二条第三款的目的是为了终结殖民地时期特定的非本国经济群体的主导地位。基于此，对第二条第三款规定的例外情形应当予以严格解释。

44. 上述严格解释应特别适用于对“经济权利”和“发展中国家”这两个概念的解释。“发展中国家”是指已经取得独立，并且符合联合国对发展中国家适当分类的国家。

第三条：男女平等权

45. 适用第三条时，应当对《消除对妇女一切形式歧视公约》及《消除对妇女一切形式歧视宣言》及其他相关文件及该《公约》项下监督委员会（消除对妇女歧视委员会）的活动予以合理注意。

第四条：限制

46. 第四条主要旨在保护个人权利，而不是允许国家施加限制。

47. 本条不是为了对影响人的生计和生存以及人的自我完善的各项权利进行限制。

“法律所确定”

48. 除非由普遍适用的国内法规定，不得对经济、社会及文化权利的行使予以限制，且该等国内法须与《公约》相符且在限制适用时有效。

49. 对经济、社会及文化权利的行使予以限制的法律不得专断、不合理或具歧视性。

50. 对经济、社会及文化权利的行使予以限制的法律规定须清楚并可以被每个人所查阅。

51. 为防止违法或滥用法律对经济、社会及文化权利的限制性规定，法律须规定足够的保障及有效救济方式。

“促进总体福利”

52. 该术语须解释为意在促进全体人民的福利。

“民主社会中”

53. “民主社会中”这一表述须被解释为对该等限制的适用予以进一步限制。

54. 施加限制的国家须承担举证责任，证明该等限制并未损害社会的民主运作。

“不得与其所限权利的性质相冲突”

56. “不得与其所限权利的性质相冲突”这一限制要求在解释或适用一项限制时不得损害相关权利的核心内容。

57. 第五条第一款强调国家并无一般性的隐含或剩余权利在法律明确规定的范围以外施加限制。法律中的任何条款均不得解释为损害“得到确认的任何权利或自由”。另外，第五条旨在确保《公约》中的任何内容都不得解释为损害各民族充分及自由地享有并行使其天然财富和自然财产和资源的固有权利。

第五条

58. 第五条第二款的目的在于确保《公约》中的任何条款均不得解释为

影响已经生效或可能生效的、给予被保护人员更多优越待遇的国内法或任何双边或多边条约、公约或协定。第五条第二款也不得解释为缔约国可根据其承担的国内或国际义务，对被保护的人权给予更大程度的限制。

C.《公约》第三部分相关内容的解释原则

第八条　法律所规定

59. 请见第四条同义术语“法律所确定”的解释原则。

“民主社会所必需”

60. 除了适用第四条“在民主社会中”这一表述的解释原则之外，第八条对缔约国针对工会权利予以限制的权力施加更大的约束。它要求对工会权利的限制确实是必需的。“必需”一词意味着此类限制必须符合以下要求：这就要求该等限制的确是需要的。“需要”这个术语隐含着该等限制：

（a）回应公众或社会的迫切需求；

（b）追求合法目标；

（c）与该等目标相称。

61. 对一项限制是否属于“必需”进行的评估，应当建立在客观考虑的基础上。

“国家安全”

62. 国家安全，仅在国家面临武力或武力威胁，为保护国家生存、领土完整或政治上独立的情况下，方可成为对特定权利采取限制措施的正当理由。

63. 国家安全，不能成为为防范对法律和秩序的地方性或相对孤立的威胁，而对权利施以限制的正当理由。

64. 不得以国家安全作为对权利施以模糊不清或专断限制的托辞。仅在具备防止滥用权力的充分保障和有效救济手段的情况下，方可以国家安全为由对权利予以限制。

65. 对经济、社会及文化权利的体系化违反将真正地损害国家安全，并可能损害国际和平及安全。对此等体系化违反负有责任的国家，不得以国家安全为由，为其目的在于压制反对意见或对其人民予以镇压的任何措施寻找依据。

“公共秩序”

66.《公约》中使用的“公共秩序”这一术语可以被定义为确保社会运作的成套规则或社会所赖以存在的一系列基本原则。对经济、社会及文化权利予以尊重就是公共秩序的一部分。

67. 公共秩序须根据以公共秩序为由加以限制的特定经济、社会和文化权利的具体情况予以解释。

68. 负责维护公共秩序的国家机关或机构须在其行使职权时接受议会、法院或其他法定独立机构监督。

“他人的权利和自由”

69. 可以用来对本公约规定的权利和自由予以限制的“他人的权利和自由”的范围，比本公约确认的权利和自由的范围更为广泛。

D. 违反经济、社会及文化权利

70. 缔约国未能遵守本《公约》所规定义务的，构成国际法上对本《公约》的违反。

71. 在判断缔约国是否遵守本公约的规定时，必须注意公约赋予缔约国在一定范围内选择实现目标之手段的自由裁量权，同时还须注意那些超出缔约国合理控制的范围，对其实施本公约的能力造成不利影响的因素。

72. 一个缔约国如有下述情形，将构成对本公约的违反：

——未能采取《公约》要求采取的措施；

——未能立即消除其负有义务消除的障碍，以便即刻实现相关权利；

——故意在其有能力做到的情形下，不满足国际公认的最低限度的履约标准；

——不按照《公约》规定对《公约》所确认的有关权利予以限制；

——故意阻碍或叫停权利实现进程，除非其行为在《公约》所允许限度之内，或其行为是由于资源缺乏或不可抗力；

——未能按照《公约》要求提交报告。

73. 根据国际法，《公约》缔约各国有权表达意见，认为其他缔约国未能履行其《公约》项下的义务，并提请该缔约国注意。由此可能产生的任何争议须根据和平解决争议的相关国际法规则的规定予以解决。

第二部分：根据《公约》第四部分对缔约国报告及国际合作的审议

A. 缔约国准备及提交报告

74. 本《公约》第四部分所规定监督机制的有效性很大程度上有赖于缔约国报告的水平和时效性。因此，要求各缔约国政府认真准备报告。为此目的，各缔约国政府应当建立足够的内部程序与相关政府部门及机构进行协商、收集相关数据、培训职员、获取背景文件并征询与相关非政府组织及国际机构的意见。

75. 通过落实 1984 年国际主要人权监督机构的主席们在其向联合国大会提交的报告中建议的有关咨询服务和技术援助方案的有关内容，可使本公约第十六条规定的各项报告的准备工作获益。

76. 缔约各国应将其报告义务视为在公众中就其为实现经济、社会及文化权利所确定的目标和制定的政策进行广泛讨论的机会。为此目的，应当将报告予以广泛公布，如应在报告的起草阶段即予公布。准备报告也是审核相关国内政策是否足够反映了每一项权利的范围及内容，并明确实现该权利需要采取哪些方式的一次机会。

77. 鼓励缔约各国认真考虑相关非政府组织参与报告准备工作的可行性。

78. 就实施《公约》所采取的法律措施进行报告时，缔约各方不应仅仅就相关法律规定进行描述。在适当情形下，应该写明其为保障权利实现而适用的司法救济、行政程序和其他措施，以及与这些救济渠道和程序相关的具体做法。

79. 缔约国报告中应载有量化信息，以便说明权利实际受到保护的程度。对数字信息及预算分配和开支信息进行说明的方式应当有助于评估对《公约》义务的遵守情形。该等目标及指数应当在适当情形下适用基于国际合作所确立的标准，以便提高缔约国在报告中提供数据的相关度和可比性。

80. 必要时，政府应该进行或委托进行研究，以使其得以矫正误差，获取有关在落实公约权利方面取得成绩和存在阻碍的真实信息。

81. 缔约国报告应该指明通过国际合作可以取得更多成就的领域，并提出有助于达成该目标的有关经济和技术合作项目的建议。

82. 为了确保缔约国与评估其是否遵守《公约》规定的机构之间实现实质对话，缔约国应当指定对报告内容充分熟识的代表参与对话。

B. 经济、社会和文化权利委员会的作用

83. 委员会获得授权协助联合国经济与社会理事会行使其《公约》赋予的职责。委员会的作用尤其表现在它对缔约国报告的审议并提出一般性的建议和意见上，包括对缔约国提出如何更充分履行公约义务的意见和建议。经济和社会理事会作出的以独立专家组成的委员会代替其会议期间工作小组的决定有利于对缔约国的履约行为进行更为有效的监督。

84. 为使委员会充分履行其职责，联合国经济与社会理事会应当保证委员会有足够的开会时间，迫切需要为委员会配备必要的职员和设施，以使其能够有效行使经济与社会理事会第 1985/17 号决议赋予委员会的各项职能。

85. 为应对《公约》涵盖的各种复杂问题，委员会可以考虑将特定职权授予其成员。例如，可以建立起草小组以准备一般意义上的初始文本或推荐性意见，或对收到的信息予以总结；可以委任特派调查员协助委员会的工作，尤其是就特定议题准备报告并为该目的与缔约国、专门机构及有关专家进行磋商；起草可以帮助缔约国克服其履行《公约》义务所遇困难的有关经济及技术援助项目的建议。

86. 委员会应根据本《公约》第二十二，二十三条的规定与联合国其他机构、专门机构以及其他相关组织一起探讨为促进《公约》进一步落实而采取新的国际措施的可行性。

87. 委员会应当审视现行六年一个报告周期的合理性，由于报告过程中的延误，造成一个报告周期内不同阶段提交的报告不得不同时接受审议。委员会还应当对帮助缔约国准备其报告的指南进行复审，并提出必要的修改建议。

88. 委员会应当考虑邀请缔约国对选定的议题提出意见，以使其与委员会之间进行直接及持续的对话。

89. 委员会应当充分关注在对是否遵守《公约》规定义务进行评估过程中涉及的方法问题。在有关指数有助于衡量实施公约权利所取得的进展时，对这些指数的参考和引用有利于对根据公约提交的报告进行评估。委员会应对专门机构提出的指数予以适当关注，并在发现指数与实情存在差异时，经与有关专门机构协调，开展或推动对指数的进一步研究。

90. 在委员会认为有关缔约国提供的信息不足以对其取得的成就及遇到的困难进行实质性评估时，应要求其提供补充信息，必要时明确提出其希望缔约国回应的具体议题或问题。

91. 在根据第 1985/17 号 ECOSOC 决议准备报告时，小组委员会应该在“其报告考虑总结”之外考虑将其在审议过程中的专题议题加以强调。

C. 委员会与专门机构及其他国际组织之间的关系

92. 应将委员会的建立视为在委员会与专门机构及其他国际组织间发展积极、互惠关系的机会。

93. 当根据本公约第十八条的规定所作的安排能够增大专门机构对委员

会工作的贡献时，经济与社会理事会应当考虑作出这样的安排，鉴于不同的专门机构彼此之间在推进经济、社会和文化权利时的工作方式的不相同，根据公约第十八条所作的安排应当具有适当的灵活性。

94. 专门机构与委员会就共同关心的问题开展对话，对于根据本公约第四部分的规定，对公约的履行予以适当监督而言，是十分必要的。双方的协商对话尤其应当围绕建立评估公约实施状况的指标体系；起草缔约国提交报告的指南；以及根据公约第十八条的规定，为专门机构提交报告作出安排等问题进行。还应当考虑在专门机构内部制定相关程序。专门机构的代表参加委员会的会议极具价值。

95. 委员会成员如能够拜访有关专门机构，通过个人交往了解该等机构有关落实《公约》规定权利的项目，并就与该等机构进行合作的可能领域进行探讨，将十分有益。

96. 应当在委员会与国际金融机构及发展机构间发起协商，以交换信息，就涉及落实《公约》所承认权利的现有资源分配进行交流。该等交流应当考虑到国际经济援助对缔约国为实施《公约》所做出的努力的影响，并应考虑根据《公约》第二十二条进行技术和经济合作的可行性。

97. 联合国人权委员会，除履行本公约第十九条赋予它的职责之外，还应在审议其涉及经济、社会和文化权利的议程时，顾及经济、社会和文化权利委员会的工作。

98.《经济、社会与文化权利国际公约》与《公民权利和政治权利国际条约》密切相关。虽然对大多数权利而言，可以清楚地界定出它们属于两个公约中某个公约的架构之中，两个公约中均予规定的若干权利和条款并不容易作出区分。此外，两个公约的一些规定和条款是一致的。重要的就是要在经济、社会和文化权利委员会与人权委员会之间确立协商性的安排。

99. 鉴于其他国际法律文件对《公约》的相关性，对于在各个监督机构间建立有效协商机制安排的需要，经济与社会理事会应当早作考虑。

100. 应督促涉及经济、社会及文化权利落实的国际及区域政府间组织采取合适的措施推进《公约》的实施。

101. 因为联合国经济与社会理事会委员会是经济和社会理事会的附属机构，应督促对经济与社会理事会具有协商地位的非政府组织参加并跟进委员会的会议，并在适当情形下根据联合国经济与社会理事会第1296（XLIV）号决议提交信息。

102. 委员会应当与政府间组织和非政府组织及研究机构合作，建立一套大家认可的体系，以记录、存储与经济、社会及文化权利国际文件有关的案例法及其他解释性材料，并提供查阅。

103. 作为本公约第二十三条所推荐的措施之一，建议定期举行研讨会，检审委员会的工作以及缔约国在落实经济、社会及文化权利方面取得的进展。

Limburg Principles on the Implementation of the International Covenant on Economic, Social and Cultural Rights

Part I: THE NATURE AND SCOPE OF STATES PARTIES´OBLIGATIONS

A. General Observations

1. Economic, social and cultural rights are an integral part of international human rights law. They are the subject of specific treaty obligations in various international instruments, notably the International Covenant on Economic, Social and Cultural Rights.

2. The International Covenant on Economic, Social and Cultural Rights, together with the International Covenant on Civil and Political Rights and the Optional Protocol, entered into force in 1976. The Covenants serve to elaborate the Universal Declaration of Human Rights: these instruments constitute the International Bill of Human Rights.

3. As human rights and fundamental freedoms are indivisible and interdependent, equal attention and urgent consideration should be given to the implementation, promotion and protection of both civil and political, and economic, social and cultural rights.

4. The International Covenant on Economic, Social and Cultural Rights (hereafter the Covenant) should, in accordance with the Vienna Convention on the Law of Treaties (vienna 1969), be interpreted in good faith, taking into account the object and purpose, the ordinary meaning, the preparatory work and the relevant practice.

5. The experience of the relevant specialized agencies as well as of United Nations bodies and intergovernmental organizations, including the United Nations working groups and special rapporteurs in the field of human rights, should be taken into account in the implementation of the Covenant and in monitoring States parties' achievements.

6. The achievement of economic, social and cultural rights may be realized in a variety of political settings. There is no single road to their full realization. Successes and failures have been registered in both market and non - market economies, in both centralized and decentralized political structures.

7. States Parties must at all times act in good faith to fulfil the obligations they have accepted under the Covenant.

8. Although the full realization of the rights recognized in the Covenant is to be attained progressively, the application of some rights can be made justiciable immediately while other rights can become justiciable over time.

9. Non - governmental organizations can play an important role in promoting the implementation of the Covenant. This role should accordingly be facilitated at the national as well as the international level.

10. States Parties are accountable both to the international community and to their own people for their compliance with the obligations under the Covenant.

11. A concerted national effort to invoke the full participation of all sectors of society is, therefore, indispensable to achieving progress in realizing economic, social and cultural rights. Popular participation is required at all stages, including the formulation, application and review of national policies.

12. The supervision of compliance with the Covenant should be approached in a spirit of co - operation and dialogue. To this end, in considering the reports of States parties, the Committee on Economic, Social and Cultural Rights, hereinafter called "the Committee", should analyze the causes and factors impeding the realization of the rights covered under the Covenant and, where possible, indicate solutions. This approach should not preclude a finding, where the information available warrants such a conclusion, that a State party has failed to comply with its obligations under the Covenant.

13. All organs monitoring the Covenant should pay special attention to the principles of non - discrimination and equality before the law when assessing

States parties' compliance with the Covenant.

14. Given the significance for development of the progressive realization of the rights set forth in the Covenant, particular attention should be given to measures to improve the standard of living of the poor and other disadvantaged groups, taking into account that special measures may be required to protect cultural rights of indigenous peoples and minorities.

15. Trends in international economic relations should be taken into account in assessing the efforts of the international community to achieve the Covenant's objectives.

B. Interpretative Principles specifically relating to Part II of the Covenant

Article 2 (1): "*to take steps... by all appropriate means, including particularly the adoption of legislation*"

16. All States parties have an obligation to begin immediately to take steps towards full realization of the rights contained in the Covenant.

17. At the national level States parties shall use all appropriate means, including legislative, administrative, judicial, economic, social and educational measures, consistent with the nature of the rights in order to fulfil their obligations under the Covenant.

18. Legislative measures alone are not sufficient to fulfil the obligations of the Covenant. It should he noted, however, that article 2 (1) would often require legislative action to be taken in cases where existing legislation is in violation of the obligations assumed under the Covenant.

19. States parties shall provide for effective remedies including, where appropriate, judicial remedies.

20. The appropriateness of the means to be applied in a particular State shall be determined by that State party, and shall be subject to review by the United Nations Economic and Social Council, with the assistance of the Committee. Such review shall be without prejudice to the competence of the other organs established pursuant to the Charter of the United Nations.

"*to achieve progressively the full realization of the rights*"

21. The obligation "to achieve progressively the full realization of the rights" requires States parties to move as expeditiously as possible towards the realization

of the rights. Under no circumstances shall this be interpreted as implying for States the right to deter indefinitely efforts to ensure full realization. On the contrary all States parties have the obligation to begin immediately to take steps to fulfil their obligations under the Covenant.

22. Some obligations under the Covenant require immediate implementation in full by all States parties, such as the prohibition of discrimination in article 2 (2) of the Covenant.

23. The obligation of progressive achievement exists independently of the increase in resources; it requires effective use of resources available.

24. Progressive implementation can be effected not only by increasing resources, but also by the development of societal resources necessary for the realization by everyone of the rights recognized in the Covenant.

"*to the maximum of its available resources*"

25. States parties are obligated. regardless of the level of economic development, to ensure respect for minimum subsistence rights for all.

26. "Its available resources" refers to both the resources within a State and those available from the international community through international co - operation and assistance.

27. In determining whether adequate measures have been taken for the realization of the rights recognized in the Covenant attention shall be paid to equitable and effective use of and access to the available resources.

28. In the use of the available resources due priority shall be given to the realization of rights recognized in the Covenant, mindful of the need to assure to everyone the satisfaction of subsistence requirements as well as the provision of essential services.

"*individually and through international assistance and co – operation especially economic and technical*"

29. International co - operation and assistance pursuant to the Charter of the United Nations (arts. 55 and 56) and the Covenant shall have in view as a matter of priority the realization of all human rights and fundamental freedoms, economic, social and cultural as well as civil and political.

30. International co - operation and assistance must be directed towards the establishment of a social and international order in which the rights and freedoms

set forth in the Covenant can be fully realized (*cf.* article 28 Universal Declaration of Human Rights).

31. Irrespective of differences in their political, economic and social systems, States shall co - operate with one another to promote international social, economic and cultural progress, in particular the economic growth of developing countries, free from discrimination based on such differences.

32. States parties shall take steps by international means to assist and co - operate in the realization of the rights recognized by the Covenant.

33. International co - operation and assistance shall be based on the sovereign equality of States and be aimed at the realization of the rights contained in the Covenant.

34. In undertaking international co - operation and assistance pursuant to article 2 (1) the role of international organizations and the contribution of non - governmental organizations shall be kept in mind.

Article 2 (2): *Non – discrimination*

35. Article 2 (2) calls for immediate application and involves an explicit guarantee on behalf of the States parties. It should, therefore, be made subject to judicial review and other recourse procedures.

36. The grounds of discrimination mentioned in article 2 (2) are not exhaustive.

37. Upon becoming a party to the Covenant States shall eliminate *de jure* discrimination by abolishing without delay any discriminatory laws, regulations and practices (including acts of omission as well as commission) affecting the enjoyment of economic, social and cultural rights.

38. *De facto* discrimination occurring as a result of the unequal enjoyment of economic, social and cultural rights, on account of a lack of resources or otherwise, should be brought to an end as speedily as possible.

39. Special measures taken for the sole purpose of securing adequate advancement of certain groups or individuals requiring such protection as may be necessary in order to ensure to such groups or individuals equal enjoyment of economic, social and cultural rights shall not be deemed discrimination, provided, however, that such measures do not, as a consequence, lead to the maintenance of separate rights to different groups and that such measures shall not be continued after their intended objectives have been achieved.

40. Article 2 (2) demands from States parties that they prohibit private persons and bodies from practising discrimination in any field of public life.

41. In the application of article 2 (2) due regard should be paid to all relevant international instruments including the Declaration and Convention on the Elimination of all Forms of Racial Discrimination as well as to the activities of the supervisory committee (CERD) under the said Convention.

Article 2 (3): *Non – nationals in developing countries*

42. As a general rule the Covenant applies equally to nationals and non - nationals.

43. The purpose of article 2 (3) was to end the domination of certain economic groups of non - nationals during colonial times. In the light of this the exception in article 2 (3) should be interpreted narrowly.

44. This narrow interpretation of article 2 (3) refers in particular to the notion of economic rights and to the notion of developing countries. The latter notion refers to those countries which have gained independence and which fall within the appropriate United Nations classifications of developing countries.

Article 3: *Equal rights for men and women*

45. In the application of article 3 due regard should be paid to the Declaration and Convention on the Elimination of All Forms of Discrimination against Women and other relevant instruments and the activities of the supervisory committee (CEDAW) under the said Convention.

Article 4: *Limitations*

46. Article 4 was primarily intended to be protective of the rights of individuals rather than permissive of the imposition of limitations by the State.

47. The article was not meant to introduce limitations on rights affecting the subsistence or survival of the individual or integrity of the person.

"*determined by law*"

48. No limitation on the exercise of economic, social and cultural rights shall be made unless provided for by national law of general application which is consistent with the Covenant and is in force at the time the limitation is applied.

49. Laws imposing limitations on the exercise of economic, social and cultural rights shall not be arbitrary or unreasonable or discriminatory.

50. Legal rules limiting the exercise of economic, social and cultural rights

shall be clear and accessible to everyone.

51. Adequate safeguards and effective remedies shall be provided by law against illegal or abusive imposition on application of limitations on economic, social and cultural rights.

"promoting the general welfare"

52. This term shall be construed to mean furthering the well - being of the people as a whole.

"in a democratic society"

53. The expression "in a democratic society" shall be interpreted as imposing a further restriction on the application of limitations.

54. The burden is upon a State imposing limitations to demonstrate that the limitations do not impair the democratic functioning of the society.

55. While there is no single model of a democratic society, a society which recognizes and respects the human rights set forth in the United Nations Charter and the Universal Declaration of Human Rights may be viewed as meeting this definition.

"compatible with the nature of these rights"

56. The restriction "compatible with the nature of these rights" requires that a limitation shall not be interpreted or applied so as to jeopardize the essence of the right concerned.

57. Article 5 (1) underlines the fact that there is no general, implied or residual right for a State to impose limitations beyond those which are specifically provided for in the law. None of the provisions in the law may be interpreted in such a way as to destroy "any of the rights or freedoms recognized". In addition article 5 is intended to ensure that nothing in the Covenant shall be interpreted as impairing the inherent right of all peoples to enjoy and utilize fully and freely their natural wealth and resources.

Article 5

58. The purpose of article 5 (2) is to ensure that no provision in the Covenant shall be interpreted to prejudice the provisions of domestic law or any bilateral or multilateral treaties, conventions or agreements which are already in force, or may come into force, under which more favourable treatment would be accorded to the persons protected. Neither shall article 5 (2) be interpreted to restrict the exercise of

any human right protected to a greater extent by national or international obligations accepted by the State party .

C. Interpretative Principles specifically relating to Part III of the Covenant

Article 8: "*prescribed by law*"

59. See the interpretative principles under the synonymous term "determined by law" in article 4.

"*necessary in a democratic society*"

60. In addition to the interpretative principles listed under article 4 concerning the phrase "in a democratic society", article 8 imposes a greater restraint upon a State party which is exercising limitations on trade union rights. It requires that such a limitation is indeed necessary. The term "necessary" implies that the limitation:

(a) responds to a pressing public or social need;

(b) pursues a legitimate aim; and

(c) is proportional to that aim.

61. Any assessment as to the necessity of a limitation shall be based upon objective considerations.

"*national security*"

62. National security may be invoked to justify measures limiting certain rights only when they are taken to protect the existence of the nation or its territorial integrity or political independence against force or threat of force.

63. National security cannot be invoked as a reason for imposing limitations to prevent merely local or relatively isolated threats to law and order.

64. National security cannot be used as a pretext for imposing vague or arbitrary limitations and may be invoked only when there exist adequate safeguards and effective remedies against abuse.

65. The systematic violation of economic, social and cultural rights undermines true national security and may jeopardize international peace and security. A State responsible for such violation shall not invoke national security as a justification for measures aimed at suppressing opposition to such violation or at perpetrating repressive practices against its population.

"*public order (ordre public)*"

66. The expression "public order (ordre public)" as used in the Covenant may be defined as the sum of rules which ensures the functioning of society or the set of fundamental principles on which a society is founded. Respect for economic, social and cultural rights is part of public order (ordre public).

67. Public order (ordre public) shall be interpreted in the context of the purpose of the particular economic, social and cultural rights which are limited on this ground.

68. State organs or agents responsible for the maintenance of public order (ordre public) shall be subject to controls in the exercise of their power through the parliament, courts, or other competent independent bodies.

"*rights and freedoms of others*"

69. The scope of the rights and freedoms of others that may act as a limitation upon rights in the Covenant extends beyond the rights and freedoms recognized in the Covenant.

D. Violations of Economic, Social and Cultural Rights

70. A failure by a State party to comply with an obligation contained in the Covenant is, under international law, a violation of the Covenant.

71. In determining what amounts to a failure to comply, it must be borne in mind that the Covenant affords to a State party a margin of discretion in selecting the means for carrying out its objects, and that factors beyond its reasonable control may adversely affect its capacity to implement particular rights.

72. A State party will be in violation of the Covenant, *inter alia*, if:

- it fails to take a step which it is required to take by the Covenant;
- it fails to remove promptly obstacles which it is under a duty to remove to permit the immediate fulfilment of a right;
- it fails to implement without delay a right which it is required by the Covenant to provide immediately;
- it wilfully fails to meet a generally accepted international minimum standard of achievement, which is within its powers to meet;
- it applies a limitation to a right recognized in the Covenant other than in accordance with the Covenant;
- it deliberately retards or halts the progressive realization of a right, unless

it is acting within a limitation permitted by the Covenant or it does so due to a lack of available resources or *force majeure*;

- it fails to submit reports as required under the Covenant.

73. In accordance with international law each State party to the Covenant has the right to express the view that another State party is not complying with its obligations under the Covenant and to bring this to the attention of that State party. Any dispute that may thus arise shall be settled in accordance with the relevant rules of international law relating to the peaceful settlement of disputes.

Part II: CONSIDERATION OF STATES PARTIES´ REPORTS AND INTERNATIONAL CO - OPERATION UNDER PART IV OF THE COVENANT

A. Preparation and submission of reports by States parties

74. The effectiveness of the supervisory machinery provided in Part IV of the Covenant depends largely upon the quality and timeliness of reports by States parties. Governments are therefore urged to make their reports as meaningful as possible. For this purpose they should develop adequate internal procedures for consultations with the competent government departments and agencies, compilation of relevant data, training of staff, acquisition of background documentation, and consultation with relevant non - governmental and international institutions.

75. The preparation of reports under article 16 of the Covenant could be facilitated by the implementation of elements of the programme of advisory services and technical assistance as proposed by the chairmen of the main human rights supervisory organs in their 1984 report to the General Assembly (United Nations Doc. A39/484).

76. States parties should view their reporting obligations as an opportunity for broad public discussion on goals and policies designed to realize economic, social and cultural rights. For this purpose wide publicity should be given to the reports, if possible in draft. The preparation of reports should also be an occasion to review

the extent to which relevant national policies adequately reflect the scope and content of each right, and to specify the means by which it is to be realized.

77. States parties are encouraged to examine the possibility of involving non-governmental organizations in the preparation of their reports.

78. In reporting on legal steps taken to give effect to the Covenant, States parties should not merely describe any relevant legislative provisions. They should specify, as appropriate, the judicial remedies, administrative procedures and other measures they have adopted for enforcing those rights and the practice under those remedies and procedures.

79. Quantitative information should be included in the reports of States parties in order to indicate the extent to which the rights are protected in fact. Statistical information and information on budgetary allocations and expenditures should be presented in such a way as to facilitate the assessment of the compliance with Covenant obligations. States parties should, where possible, adopt clearly defined targets and indicators in implementing the Covenant. Such targets and indicators should, as appropriate, be based on criteria established through international co-operation in order to increase the relevance and comparability of data submitted by States parties in their reports.

80. Where necessary, governments should conduct or commission studies to enable them to fill gaps in information regarding progress made and difficulties encountered in achieving the observance of the Covenant rights.

81. Reports by States parties should indicate the areas where more progress could be achieved through international co-operation and suggest economic and technical co-operation programmes that might be helpful toward that end.

82. In order to ensure a meaningful dialogue between the States parties and the organs assessing their compliance with the provisions of the Covenant, States parties should designate representatives who are fully familiar with the issues raised in the report.

B. Role of the Committee on Economic, Social and Cultural Rights

83. The Committee has been entrusted with assisting the Economic and Social Council in the substantive tasks assigned to it by the Covenant. In particular, its role is to consider States parties reports and to make suggestions and recommenda-

tions of a general nature, including suggestions and recommendations as to fuller compliance with the Covenant by States parties. The decision of the Economic and Social Council to replace its sessional Working Group by a Committee of independent experts should lead to a more effective supervision of the implementation by States Parties.

84. In order to enable it to discharge fully its responsibilities the Economic and Social Council should ensure that sufficient sessions are provided to the Committee. It is imperative that the necessary staff and facilities for the effective performance of the Committee's functions be provided, in accordance with ECOSOC resolution 1985/17.

85. In order to address the complexity of the substantive issues covered by the Covenant, the Committee might consider delegating certain tasks to its members. For example, drafting groups could be established to prepare preliminary formulations or recommendations of a general nature or summaries of the information received. Rapporteurs could be appointed to assist the work of the Committee in particular to prepare reports on specific topics and for that purpose consult States parties, specialized agencies and relevant experts and to draw up proposals regarding economic and technical assistance projects that could help overcome difficulties States parties have encountered in fulfilling their Covenant obligations.

86. The Committee should, pursuant to articles 22 and 23 of the Covenant, explore with other organs of the United Nations, specialized agencies and other concerned organizations, the possibilities of taking additional international measures likely to contribute to the progressive implementation of the Covenant.

87. The Committee should reconsider the current six - year cycle of reporting in view of the delays which have led to simultaneous consideration of reports submitted under different phases of the cycle. The Committee should also review the guidelines for States parties to assist them in preparing reports and propose any necessary modifications.

88. The Committee should consider inviting States parties to comment on selected topics leading to a direct and sustained dialogue with the Committee.

89. The Committee should devote adequate attention to the methodological issues involved in assessing compliance with the obligations contained in the Covenant. Reference to indicators, in so far as they may help measure progress made in

the achievement of certain rights, may be useful in evaluating reports submitted under the Covenant. The Committee should take due account of the indicators selected by or in the framework of the specialized agencies and draw upon or promote additional research, in consultation with the specialized agencies concerned, where gaps have been identified.

90. Whenever the Committee is not satisfied that the information provided by a State party is adequate for a meaningful assessment of progress achieved and difficulties encountered it should request supplementary information, specifying as necessary the precise issues or questions it would like the State Party to address.

91. In preparing its reports under ECOSOC resolution 1985/17, the Committee should consider, in addition to the "summary of its consideration of the reports", highlighting thematic issues raised during its deliberations.

C. Relations between the Committee and Specialized Agencies, and other international organs

92. The establishment of the Committee should be seen as an opportunity to develop a positive and mutually beneficial relationship between the Committee and the specialized agencies and other international organs.

93. New arrangements under article 18 of the Covenant should be considered where they could enhance the contribution of the specialized agencies to the work of the Committee. Given that the working methods with regard to the implementation of economic, social and cultural rights vary from one specialized agency to another, flexibility is appropriate in making such arrangements under article 18.

94. It is essential for the proper supervision of the implementation of the Covenant under Part IV that a dialogue be developed between the specialized agencies and the Committee with respect to matters of common interest. In particular consultations should address the need for developing indicators for assessing compliance with the Covenant; drafting guidelines for the submission of reports by States parties; making arrangements for submission of reports by the specialized agencies under article 18. Consideration should also be given to any relevant procedures adopted in the agencies. Participation of their representatives in meetings of the Committee would be very valuable.

95. It would be useful if Committee members could visit specialized agencies

concerned, learn through personal contact about programmes of the agencies relevant to the realization of the rights contained in the Covenant and discuss the possible areas of collaboration with those agencies.

96. Consultations should be initiated between the Committee and international financial institutions and development agencies to exchange information and share ideas on the distribution of available resources in relation to the realization of the rights recognized in the Covenant. These exchanges should consider the impact of international economic assistance on efforts by States parties to implement the Covenant and possibilities of technical and economic co - operation under article 22 of the Covenant.

97. The Commission on Human Rights, in addition to its responsibilities under article 19 of the Covenant, should take into account the work of the Committee in its consideration of items on its agenda relating to economic, social and cultural rights.

98. The Covenant on Economic, Social and Cultural Rights is related to the Covenant on Civil and Political Rights. Although most rights can clearly be delineated as falling within the framework of one or other Covenant, there are several rights and provisions referred to in both instruments which are not susceptible to clear differentiation. Both Covenants moreover share common provisions and articles. It is important that consultative arrangements be established between the Economic, Social and Cultural Rights Committee and the Human Rights Committee.

99. Given the relevance of other international legal instruments to the Covenant, early consideration should be given by the Economic and Social Council to the need for developing effective consultative arrangements between the various supervisory bodies.

100. International and regional intergovernmental organizations concerned with the realization of economic, social and cultural rights are urged to develop measures, as appropriate, to promote the implementation of the Covenant.

101. As the Committee is a subsidiary organ of the Economic and Social Council, non - governmental organizations enjoying consultative status with the Economic and Social Council are urged to attend and follow the meetings of the Committee and, when appropriate, to submit information in accordance with ECOSOC resolution 1296 (XLIV).

102. The Committee should develop, in co - operation with intergovernmental organizations and non - governmental organizations as well as research institutes an agreed system for recording, storing and making accessible case law and other interpretative material relating to international instruments on economic, social and cultural rights.

103. As one of the measures recommended in article 23 it is recommended that seminars be held periodically to review the work of the Committee and the progress made in the realization of economic, social and cultural rights by States parties.

保护和促进文化表现形式多样性公约

（2005 年 10 月 20 日联合国教育、科学及文化组织第三十三届会议通过。我国于 2007 年 1 月 30 日递交批准书）

序　言

联合国教育、科学及文化组织大会于 2005 年 10 月 3 日至 21 日在巴黎举行第三十三届会议：

（一）确认文化多样性是人类的一项基本特性；

（二）认识到文化多样性是人类的共同遗产，应当为了全人类的利益对其加以珍爱和维护；

（三）意识到文化多样性创造了一个多姿多彩的世界，它使人类有了更多的选择，得以提高自己的能力和形成价值观，并因此成为各社区、各民族和各国可持续发展的一股主要推动力；

（四）忆及在民主、宽容、社会公正以及各民族和各文化间相互尊重的环境中繁荣发展起来的文化多样性对于地方、国家和国际层面的和平与安全是不可或缺的；

（五）颂扬文化多样性对充分实现《世界人权宣言》和其他世界公认的文件主张的人权和基本自由所具有的重要意义；

（六）强调需要把文化作为一个战略要素纳入国家和国际发展政策，以及国际发展合作之中，同时也要特别考虑强调消除贫困的《联合国千年宣言》（2000 年）；

（七）考虑到文化在不同时间和空间具有多样形式，这种多样性体现为人类各民族和各社会文化特征和文化表现形式的独特性和多元性；

（八）承认作为非物质和物质财富来源的传统知识的重要性，特别是原住民知识体系的重要性，其对可持续发展的积极贡献，及其得到充分保护和促进的需要；

（九）认识到需要采取措施保护文化表现形式连同其内容的多样性，特别是当文化表现形式有可能遭到灭绝或受到严重损害时；

（十）强调文化对社会凝聚力的重要性，尤其是对提高妇女的社会地位、发挥其社会作用所具有的潜在影响力；

（十一）意识到文化多样性通过思想的自由交流得到加强，通过文化间的不断交流和互动得到滋养；

（十二）重申思想、表达和信息自由以及传媒多样性使各种文化表现形式得以在社会中繁荣发展；

（十三）认识到文化表现形式，包括传统文化表现形式的多样性，是个人和各民族能够表达并同他人分享自己的思想和价值观的重要因素；

（十四）忆及语言多样性是文化多样性的基本要素之一，并重申教育在保护和促进文化表现形式中发挥着重要作用；

（十五）考虑到文化活力的重要性，包括对少数民族和原住民人群中的个体的重要性，这种重要的活力体现为创造、传播、销售及获取其传统文化表现形式的自由，以有益于他们自身的发展；

（十六）强调文化互动和文化创造力对滋养和革新文化表现形式所发挥的关键作用，它们也会增强那些为社会整体进步而参与文化发展的人们所发挥的作用；

（十七）认识到知识产权对支持文化创造的参与者具有重要意义；

（十八）确信传递着文化特征、价值观和意义的文化活动、产品与服务具有经济和文化双重性质，故不应视为仅具商业价值；

（十九）注意到信息和传播技术飞速发展所推动的全球化进程为加强各种文化互动创造了前所未有的条件，但同时也对文化多样性构成挑战，尤其是可能在富国与穷国之间造成种种失衡；

（二十）意识到联合国教科文组织肩负的特殊使命，即确保对文化多样性的尊重以及建议签订有助于推动通过语言和图像进行自由思想交流的各种国际协定；

根据联合国教科文组织通过的有关文化多样性和行使文化权利的各种国际文件的条款，特别是2001 年通过的《世界文化多样性宣言》，于2005 年10 月 20 日通过本公约。

第一章　目标与指导原则

第一条　目标

本公约的目标是：

（一）保护和促进文化表现形式的多样性；

（二）以互利的方式为各种文化的繁荣发展和自由互动创造条件；

（三）鼓励不同文化间的对话，以保证世界上的文化交流更广泛和均衡，促进不同文化间的相互尊重与和平文化建设；

（四）加强文化的互动性，本着在各民族间架设桥梁的精神开展文化互动；

（五）促进地方、国家和国际层面对文化表现形式多样性的尊重，并提高对其价值的认识；

（六）确认文化与发展之间的联系对所有国家，特别是对发展中国家的重要性，并支持为确保承认这种联系的真正价值而在国内和国际采取的行动；

（七）承认文化活动、产品与服务具有传递文化特征、价值观和意义的特殊性；

（八）重申各国拥有在其领土上维持、采取和实施他们认为合适的保护和促进文化表现形式多样性的政策和措施的主权；

（九）本着伙伴精神，加强国际合作与团结，特别是要提高发展中国家保护和促进文化表现形式多样性的能力。

第二条　指导原则

一、尊重人权和基本自由原则

只有确保人权，以及表达、信息和交流等基本自由，并确保个人可以选择文化表现形式，才能保护和促进文化多样性。任何人都不得援引本公约的规定侵犯《世界人权宣言》规定的或受到国际法保障的人权和基本自由，或限制其适用范围。

二、主权原则

根据《联合国宪章》和国际法原则，各国拥有在其境内采取保护和促进文化表现形式多样性措施和政策的主权。

三、所有文化同等尊严和尊重原则

保护与促进文化表现形式多样性的前提是承认所有文化，包括少数民族和原住民的文化在内，具有同等尊严，并应受到同等尊重。

四、国际团结与合作原则

国际合作与团结的目的应当是使各个国家，尤其是发展中国家都有能力在地方、国家和国际层面上创建和加强其文化表现手段，包括其新兴的或成熟的文化产业。

五、经济和文化发展互补原则

文化是发展的主要推动力之一，所以文化的发展与经济的发展同样重要，且所有个人和民族都有权参与两者的发展并从中获益。

六、可持续发展原则

文化多样性是个人和社会的一种财富。保护、促进和维护文化多样性是当代和后代的可持续发展的一项基本要求。

七、平等享有原则

平等享有全世界丰富多样的文化表现形式，所有文化享有各种表现形式和传播手段，是增进文化多样性和促进相互理解的要素。

八、开放和平衡原则

在采取措施维护文化表现形式多样性时，各国应寻求以适当的方式促进向世界其他文化开放，并确保这些措施符合本公约的目标。

第二章　适用范围

第三条　公约的适用范围

本公约适用于缔约方采取的有关保护和促进文化表现形式多样性的政策和措施。

第三章　定　义

第四条　定义

在本公约中，应作如下理解：

（一）文化多样性

“文化多样性”指各群体和社会借以表现其文化的多种不同形式。这些表现形式在他们内部及他们之间传承。

文化多样性不仅体现在人类文化遗产通过丰富多彩的文化表现形式来表达、弘扬和传承的多种方式，也体现在借助各种方式和技术进行的艺术创造、生产、传播、销售和消费的多种方式。

（二）文化内容

“文化内容”指源于文化特征或表现文化特征的象征意义、艺术特色和文化价值。

（三）文化表现形式

“文化表现形式”指个人、群体和社会创造的具有文化内容的表现形式。

（四）文化活动、产品与服务

“文化活动、产品与服务”是指从其具有的特殊属性、用途或目的考虑时，体现或传达文化表现形式的活动、产品与服务，无论他们是否具有商业价值。文化活动可能以自身为目的，也可能是为文化产品与服务的生产提供帮助。

（五）文化产业

“文化产业”指生产和销售上述第（四）项所述的文化产品或服务的产业。

（六）文化政策和措施

“文化政策和措施”指地方、国家、区域或国际层面上针对文化本身或为了对个人、群体或社会的文化表现形式产生直接影响的各项政策和措施，包括与创作、生产、传播、销售和享有文化活动、产品与服务相关的政策和措施。

（七）保护

名词“保护”意指为保存、保障和加强文化表现形式多样性而采取的措施。

动词“保护”意指采取这类措施。

（八）文化互动性

“文化互动性”指不同文化的存在与平等互动，以及通过对话和相互尊重产生共同文化表现形式的可能性。

第四章　缔约方的权利和义务

第五条　权利和义务的一般规则

一、缔约方根据《联合国宪章》、国际法原则及国际公认的人权文书，重申拥有为实现本公约的宗旨而制定和实施其文化政策、采取措施以保护和促进文化表现形式多样性及加强国际合作的主权。

二、当缔约方在其境内实施政策和采取措施以保护和促进文化表现形式的多样性时，这些政策和措施应与本公约的规定相符。

第六条 缔约方在本国的权利

一、各缔约方可在第四条第（六）项所定义的文化政策和措施范围内，根据自身的特殊情况和需求，在其境内采取措施保护和促进文化表现形式的多样性。

二、这类措施可包括：

（一）为了保护和促进文化表现形式的多样性所采取的管理性措施；

（二）以适当方式在本国境内的所有文化活动、产品与服务中为本国的文化活动、产品与服务提供创作、生产、传播、销售和享有的机会的措施，包括规定上述活动、产品与服务所使用的语言；

（三）为国内独立的文化产业和非正规产业部门活动能有效获取生产、传播和销售文化活动、产品与服务的手段采取的措施；

（四）提供公共财政资助的措施；

（五）鼓励非营利组织以及公共和私人机构、艺术家及其他文化专业人员发展和促进思想、文化表现形式、文化活动、产品与服务的自由交流和流通，以及在这些活动中激励创新精神和积极进取精神的措施；

（六）建立并适当支持公共机构的措施；

（七）培育并支持从事文化表现形式创新活动的艺术家和其他人员的措施；

（八）旨在加强媒体多样性的措施，包括运用公共广播服务。

第七条 促进文化表现形式的措施

一、缔约方应努力在其境内创造环境，鼓励个人和社会群体：

（一）创作、生产、传播、销售和获取他们自己的文化表现形式，同时对妇女及不同社会群体，包括少数民族和原住民的特殊情况和需求给予应有的重视；

（二）获取本国境内及世界其他国家的各种不同的文化表现形式。

二、缔约方还应努力承认艺术家、参与创作活动的其他人员、文化界以及支持他们工作的有关组织的重要贡献，以及他们在培育文化表现形式多样性方面的核心作用。

第八条 保护文化表现形式的措施

一、在不影响第五条和第六条规定的前提下，缔约一方可以确定其领土上哪些文化表现形式属于面临消亡危险、受到严重威胁、或是需要紧急保护的情况。

二、缔约方可通过与本公约的规定相符的方式，采取一切恰当的措施保护处于第一款所述情况下的文化表现形式。

三、缔约方应向政府间委员会报告应对这类紧急情况所采取的所有措施，该委员会则可以对此提出合适的建议。

第九条　信息共享和透明度

缔约方应：

（一）在联合国教科文组织四年一度的报告中，提供其在本国境内和国际层面为保护和促进文化表现形式多样性所采取措施的适当信息；

（二）指定一处联络点，负责共享有关本公约的信息；

（三）共享和交流有关保护和促进文化表现形式多样性的信息。

第十条　教育和公众认知

缔约方应：

（一）鼓励和提高对保护和促进文化表现形式多样性重要意义的理解，尤其是通过教育和提高公众认知的计划；

（二）为实现本条的宗旨与其他缔约方和相关国际组织及地区组织开展合作；

（三）通过制定文化产业方面的教育、培训和交流计划，致力于鼓励创作和提高生产能力，但所采取的措施不能对传统生产形式产生负面影响。

第十一条　公民社会的参与

缔约方承认公民社会在保护和促进文化表现形式多样性方面的重要作用。缔约方应鼓励公民社会积极参与其为实现本公约各项目标所作的努力。

第十二条　促进国际合作

缔约方应致力于加强双边、区域和国际合作，创造有利于促进文化表现形式多样性的条件，同时特别考虑第八条和第十七条所述情况，以便着重：

（一）促进缔约方之间开展文化政策和措施的对话；

（二）通过开展专业和国际文化交流及有关成功经验的交流，增强公共文化部门战略管理能力；

（三）加强与公民社会、非政府组织和私人部门及其内部的伙伴关系，以鼓励和促进文化表现形式的多样性；

（四）提倡应用新技术，鼓励发展伙伴关系以加强信息共享和文化理解，促进文化表现形式的多样性；

（五）鼓励缔结共同生产和共同销售的协定。

第十三条 将文化纳入可持续发展

缔约方应致力于将文化纳入其各级发展政策，创造有利于可持续发展的条件，并在此框架内完善与保护和促进文化表现形式多样性相关的各个环节。

第十四条 为发展而合作

缔约方应致力于支持为促进可持续发展和减轻贫困而开展的合作，尤其要关注发展中国家的特殊需要，主要通过以下途径来推动形成富有活力的文化部门：

（一）通过以下方式加强发展中国家的文化产业：

1. 建立和加强发展中国家文化生产和销售能力；

2. 推动其文化活动、产品与服务，更多地进入全球市场和国际销售网络；

3. 促使形成有活力的地方市场和区域市场；

4. 尽可能在发达国家采取适当措施，为发展中国家的文化活动、产品与服务进入这些国家提供方便；

5. 尽可能支持发展中国家艺术家的创作，促进他们的流动；

6. 鼓励发达国家与发展中国家之间开展适当的协作，特别是在音乐和电影领域。

（二）通过在发展中国家开展信息、经验和专业知识交流以及人力资源培训，加强公共和私人部门的能力建设，尤其是在战略管理能力、政策制定和实施、文化表现形式的促进和推广、中小企业和微型企业的发展、技术的应用及技能开发与转让等方面。

（三）通过采取适当的鼓励措施来推动技术和专门知识的转让，尤其是在文化产业和文化企业领域。

（四）通过以下方式提供财政支持：

1. 根据第十八条的规定设立文化多样性国际基金；

2. 提供官方发展援助，必要时包括提供技术援助，以激励和支持创作；

3. 提供其他形式的财政援助，比如提供低息贷款、赠款以及其他资金机制。

第十五条 协作安排

缔约方应鼓励在公共、私人部门和非营利组织之间及其内部发展伙伴关系，以便与发展中国家合作，增强他们在保护和促进文化表现形式多样性方面的能力。这类新型伙伴关系应根据发展中国家的实际需求，注重基础设施建设、人力资源开发和政策制定，以及文化活动、产品与服务的交流。

第十六条 对发展中国家的优惠待遇

发达国家应通过适当的机构和法律框架，为发展中国家的艺术家和其他文化专业人员及从业人员，以及那里的文化产品和文化服务提供优惠待遇，促进与这些国家的文化交流。

第十七条 在文化表现形式受到严重威胁情况下的国际合作

在第八条所述情况下，缔约方应开展合作，相互提供援助，特别要援助发展中国家。

第十八条 文化多样性国际基金

一、兹建立“文化多样性国际基金”（以下简称基金）。

二、根据教科文组织《财务条例》，此项基金为信托基金。

三、基金的资金来源为：

（一）缔约方的自愿捐款；

（二）教科文组织大会为此划拨的资金；

（三）其他国家、联合国系统组织和计划署、其他地区和国际组织、公共和私人部门以及个人的捐款、赠款和遗赠；

（四）基金产生的利息；

（五）为基金组织募捐或其他活动的收入；

（六）基金条例许可的所有其他资金来源。

四、政府间委员会应根据缔约方大会确定的指导方针决定基金资金的使用。

五、对已获政府间委员会批准的具体项目，政府间委员会可以接受为实现这些项目的整体目标或具体目标而提供的捐款及其他形式的援助。

六、捐赠不得附带任何与本公约目标不相符的政治、经济或其他条件。

七、缔约方应努力定期为实施本公约提供自愿捐款。

第十九条 信息交流、分析和传播

一、缔约方同意，就有关文化表现形式多样性以及对其保护和促进方面的先进经验的数据收集和统计，开展信息交流和共享专业知识。

二、教科文组织应利用秘书处现有的机制，促进各种相关的信息、统计数据和先进经验的收集、分析和传播。

三、教科文组织还应建立一个文化表现形式领域内各类部门和政府组织、私人及非营利组织的数据库，并更新其内容。

四、为了便于收集数据，教科文组织应特别重视申请援助的缔约方的能力建设和专业知识积累。

五、本条涉及的信息收集应作为第九条规定的信息搜集的补充。

第五章　与其他法律文件的关系

第二十条　与其他条约的关系：相互支持，互为补充和互不隶属

一、缔约方承认，他们应善意履行其在本公约及其为缔约方的其他所有条约中的义务。因此，在本公约不隶属于其他条约的情况下：

（一）缔约方应促使本公约与其为缔约方的其他条约相互支持；

（二）缔约方解释和实施其为缔约方的其他条约或承担其他国际义务时，应考虑到本公约的相关规定。

二、本公约的任何规定不得解释为变更缔约方在其为缔约方的其他条约中的权利和义务。

第二十一条　国际磋商与协调

缔约方承诺在其他国际场合倡导本公约的宗旨和原则。为此，缔约方在需要时应进行相互磋商，并牢记这些目标与原则。

第六章　公约的机构

第二十二条　缔约方大会

一、应设立一个缔约方大会。缔约方大会应为本公约的全会和最高权力机构。

二、缔约方大会每两年一次，尽可能与联合国教科文组织大会同期举行。缔约方大会作出决定，或政府间委员会收到至少三分之一缔约方的请求，缔约方大会可召开特别会议。

三、缔约方大会应通过自己的议事规则。

四、缔约方大会的职能应主要包括以下方面：

（一）选举政府间委员会的成员；

（二）接受并审议由政府间委员会转交的缔约方报告；

（三）核准政府间委员会根据缔约方大会的要求拟订的操作指南；

（四）采取其认为有必要的其他措施来推进本公约的目标。

第二十三条　政府间委员会

一、应在联合国教科文组织内设立“保护与促进文化表现形式多样性政府间委员会”（以下简称政府间委员会）。政府间委员会由缔约方大会在本公

约根据其第二十九条规定生效后选出的18个本公约缔约国的代表组成，任期四年。

二、政府间委员会每年举行一次会议。

三、政府间委员会根据缔约方大会的授权和在其指导下运作并向其负责。

四、一旦公约缔约方数目达到50个，政府间委员会的成员应增至24名。

五、政府间委员会成员的选举应遵循公平的，合理的代表性以及轮换的原则。

六、在不影响本公约赋予它的其他职责的前提下，政府间委员会的职责如下：

（一）促进本公约目标，鼓励并监督公约的实施；

（二）应缔约方大会要求，起草并提交缔约方大会核准履行和实施公约条款的操作指南；

（三）向缔约方大会转交公约缔约方的报告，并随附评论及报告内容概要；

（四）根据公约的有关规定，特别是第八条规定，对公约缔约方提请关注的情况提出适当的建议；

（五）建立磋商程序和其他机制，以在其他国际场合倡导本公约的目标和原则；

（六）执行缔约方大会可能要求的其他任务。

七、政府间委员会根据其议事规则，可随时邀请公共或私人组织或个人参加就具体问题举行的磋商会议。

八、政府间委员会应制定并提交缔约方大会核准自己的议事规则。

第二十四条　联合国教科文组织秘书处

一、联合国教科文组织秘书处应为本公约的有关机构提供协助。

二、秘书处编制缔约方大会和政府间委员会的文件及其会议的议程，协助实施会议的决定，并报告缔约方大会决定的实施情况。

第七章　最后条款

第二十五条　争端的解决

一、公约缔约方之间关于本公约的解释或实施产生的争端，应通过谈判寻求解决。

二、如果有关各方不能通过谈判达成一致，可共同寻求第三方斡旋或要求第三方调停。

三、如果没有进行斡旋或调停，或者协商、斡旋或调停均未能解决争端，一方可根据本公约附件所列的程序要求调解。相关各方应善意考虑调解委员会为解决争端提出的建议。

四、任何缔约方均可在批准、接受、核准或加入本公约时，声明不承认上述调解程序。任何发表这一声明的缔约方，可随时通知教科文组织总干事，宣布撤回该声明。

第二十六条 会员国批准、接受、核准或加入

一、联合国教科文组织会员国依据各自的宪法程序批准、接受、核准或加入本公约。

二、批准书、接受书、核准书或加入书应交联合国教科文组织总干事保存。

第二十七条 加入

一、所有非联合国教科文组织会员国，但为联合国或其任何一个专门机构成员的国家，经联合国教科文组织大会邀请，均可加入本公约。

二、任何经联合国承认享有充分内部自治，并有权处理本公约范围内的事宜，包括有权就这些事宜签署协议，但按联合国大会第1514（XV）号决议没有完全独立的地区，也可以加入本公约。

三、对区域经济一体化组织适用如下规定：

（一）任何一个区域经济一体化组织均可加入本公约，除以下各项规定外，这类组织应以与缔约国相同的方式，完全受本公约规定的约束；

（二）如果这类组织的一个或数个成员国也是本公约的缔约国，该组织与这一或这些成员国应确定在履行公约规定的义务上各自承担的责任。责任的分担应在完成第（三）项规定的书面通知程序后生效，该组织与成员国无权同时行使公约规定的权利。此外，经济一体化组织在其权限范围内，行使与其参加本公约的成员国数目相同的表决权。如果其任何一个成员国行使其表决权，此类组织则不应行使表决权，反之亦然。

（三）同意按照第（二）项规定分担责任的区域经济一体化组织及其一个或数个成员国，应按以下方式将所建议的责任分担通知各缔约方：

1. 该组织在加入书内，应具体声明对本公约管辖事项责任的分担；

2. 在各自承担的责任变更时，该经济一体化组织应将拟议的责任变更通知保管人，保管人应将此变更通报各缔约方。

（四）已成为本公约缔约国的区域经济一体化组织的成员国在其没有明

确声明或通知保管人将管辖权转给该组织的所有领域，应被推定为仍然享有管辖权。

（五）“区域经济一体化组织”，系指由作为联合国或其任何一个专门机构成员国的主权国家组成的组织，这些国家已将其在本公约所辖领域的权限转移给该组织，并且该组织已按其内部程序获得适当授权成为本公约的缔约方。

四、加入书应交存联合国教科文组织总干事处。

第二十八条　联络点

在成为本公约缔约方时，每一缔约方应指定第九条所述的联络点。

第二十九条　生效

一、本公约在第三十份批准书、接受书、核准书或加入书交存之日起的三个月后生效，但只针对在该日或该日之前交存批准书、接受书、核准书或加入书的国家或区域经济一体化组织。对其他缔约方，本公约则在其批准书、接受书、核准书或加入书交存之日起的三个月之后生效。

二、就本条而言，一个区域经济一体化组织交存的任何文书不得在该组织成员国已交存文书之外另行计算。

第三十条　联邦制或非单一立宪制

鉴于国际协定对无论采取何种立宪制度的缔约方具有同等约束力，对实行联邦制或非单一立宪制的缔约方实行下述规定：

（一）对于在联邦或中央立法机构的法律管辖下实施的本公约各项条款，联邦或中央政府的义务与非联邦国家的缔约方的义务相同；

（二）对于在构成联邦，但按照联邦立宪制无须采取立法手段的单位，如州、成员国、省或行政区的法律管辖下实施的本公约各项条款，联邦政府须将这些条款连同其关于采用这些条款的建议一并通知各个州、成员国、省或行政区等单位的主管当局。

第三十一条　退约

一、本公约各缔约方均可宣布退出本公约。

二、退约决定须以书面形式通知，有关文件交存联合国教科文组织总干事处。

三、退约在收到退约书十二个月后开始生效。退约国在退约生效之前的财政义务不受任何影响。

第三十二条　保管职责

联合国教科文组织总干事作为本公约的保管人，应将第二十六条和第二十七条规定的所有批准书、接受书、核准书或加入书和第三十一条规定的退约书的交存情况通告本组织各会员国、第二十七条提到的非会员国和区域经济一体化组织以及联合国。

第三十三条　修正

一、本公约缔约方可通过给总干事的书面函件，提出对本公约的修正。总干事应将此类函件周知全体缔约方。如果通知发出的六个月内对上述要求做出积极反应的成员国不少于半数，总干事则可将公约修正建议提交下一届缔约方大会进行讨论或通过。

二、对公约的修正须经出席并参加表决的缔约方三分之二多数票通过。

三、对本公约的修正一旦获得通过，须交各缔约方批准、接受、核准或加入。

四、对于批准、接受、核准或加入修正案的缔约方来说，本公约修正案在三分之二的缔约方递交本条第三款所提及的文件之日起三个月后生效。此后，对任何批准、接受、核准或加入该公约修正案的缔约方来说，在其递交批准书、接受书、核准书或加入书之日起三个月之后，本公约修正案生效。

五、第三款及第四款所述程序不适用第二十三条所述政府间委员会成员国数目的修改。该类修改一经通过即生效。

六、在公约修正案按本条第四款生效之后加入本公约的那些第二十七条所指的国家或区域经济一体化组织，如未表示异议，则应：

（一）被视为经修正的本公约的缔约方；

（二）但在与不受修正案约束的任何缔约方的关系中，仍被视为未经修正的公约的缔约方。

第三十四条　有效文本

本公约用阿拉伯文、中文、英文、法文、俄文和西班牙文制定，六种文本具有同等效力。

第三十五条　登记

根据《联合国宪章》第一百零二条的规定，本公约将应联合国教科文组织总干事的要求交联合国秘书处登记。

附件：

调解程序

第一条 调解委员会

应争议一方的请求成立调解委员会。除非各方另有约定，委员会应由5名成员组成，有关各方各指定其中2名，受指定的成员再共同选定1名主席。

第二条 委员会成员

如果争议当事方超过两方，利益一致的各方应共同协商指定代表自己的委员会成员。如果两方或更多方利益各不相同，或对是否拥有一致利益无法达成共识，则各方应分别指定代表自己的委员会成员。

第三条 成员的任命

在提出成立调解委员会请求之日起的两个月内，如果某一方未指定其委员会成员，联合国教科文组织总干事可在提出调解请求一方的要求下，在随后的两个月内做出任命。

第四条 委员会主席

如果调解委员会在最后一名成员获得任命后的两个月内未选定主席，联合国教科文组织总干事可在一方要求下，在随后的两个月内指定一位主席。

第五条 决定

调解委员会根据其成员的多数表决票做出决定。除非争议各方另有约定，委员会应确定自己的议事规则。委员会应就解决争议提出建议，争议各方应善意考虑委员会提出的建议。

第六条 分歧

对是否属于调解委员会的权限出现分歧时，由委员会作出决定。

Convention on the Protection and Promotion of the Diversity of Cultural Expressions

Paris, 20 October 2005

The General Conference of the United Nations Educational, Scientific and Cultural Organization, meeting in Paris from 3 to 21 October 2005 at its 33rd session,

Affirming that cultural diversity is a defining characteristic of humanity,

Conscious that cultural diversity forms a common heritage of humanity and should be cherished and preserved for the benefit of all, *Being aware* that cultural diversity creates a rich and varied world, which increases the range of choices and nurtures human capacities and values, and therefore is a mainspring for sustainable development for communities, peoples and nations,

Recalling that cultural diversity, flourishing within a framework of democracy, tolerance, social justice and mutual respect between peoples and cultures, is indispensable for peace and security at the local, national and international levels, *Celebrating* the importance of cultural diversity for the full realization of human rights and fundamental freedoms proclaimed in the Universal Declaration of Human Rights and other universally recognized instruments,

Emphasizing the need to incorporate culture as a strategic element in national and international development policies, as well as in international development co-operation, taking into account also the United Nations Millennium Declaration (2000) with its special emphasis on poverty eradication,

Taking into account that culture takes diverse forms across time and space and that this diversity is embodied in the uniqueness and plurality of the identities and cultural expressions of the peoples and societies making up humanity, *Recognizing* the importance of traditional knowledge as a source of intangible and material wealth, and in particular the knowledge systems of indigenous peoples, and its positive contribution to sustainable development, as well as the need for its adequate protection and promotion, *Recognizing* the need to take measures to protect the diversity of cultural expressions, including their contents, especially in situations where cultural expressions may be threatened by the possibility of extinction or serious impairment,

Emphasizing the importance of culture for social cohesion in general, and in particular its potential for the enhancement of the status and role of women in society, *Being aware* that cultural diversity is strengthened by the free flow of ideas, and that it is nurtured by constant exchanges and interaction between cultures,

Reaffirming that freedom of thought, expression and information, as well as diversity of the media, enable cultural expressions to flourish within societies,

Recognizing that the diversity of cultural expressions, including traditional cultural expressions, is an important factor that allows individuals and peoples to express and to share with others their ideas and values,

Recalling that linguistic diversity is a fundamental element of cultural diversity, and reaffirming the fundamental role that education plays in the protection and promotion of cultural expressions, *Taking into account* the importance of the vitality of cultures, including for persons belonging to minorities and indigenous peoples, as manifested in their freedom to create, disseminate and distribute their traditional cultural expressions and to have access thereto, so as to benefit them for their own development,

Emphasizing the vital role of cultural interaction and creativity, which nurture and renew cultural expressions and enhance the role played by those involved in the development of culture for the progress of society at large,

Recognizing the importance of intellectual property rights in sustaining those involved in cultural creativity, *Being convinced* that cultural activities, goods and services have both an economic and a cultural nature, because they convey identities, values and meanings, and must therefore not be treated as solely having commercial value,

Noting that while the processes of globalization, which have been facilitated by the rapid development of information and communication technologies, afford unprecedented conditions for enhanced interaction between cultures, they also represent a challenge for cultural diversity, namely in view of risks of imbalances between rich and poor countries, *Being aware* of UNESCO's specific mandate to ensure respect for the diversity of cultures and to recommend such international agreements as may be necessary to promote the free flow of ideas by word and image,

Referring to the provisions of the international instruments adopted by UNESCO relating to cultural diversity and the exercise of cultural rights, and in particular the Universal Declaration on Cultural Diversity of 2001, *Adopts* this Convention on 20 October 2005.

I. Objectives and guiding principles

Article 1 – Objectives

The objectives of this Convention are:

(a) to protect and promote the diversity of cultural expressions;

(b) to create the conditions for cultures to flourish and to freely interact in a mutually beneficial manner;

(c) to encourage dialogue among cultures with a view to ensuring wider and balanced cultural exchanges in the world in favour of intercultural respect and a culture of peace;

(d) to foster interculturality in order to develop cultural interaction in the spirit of building bridges among peoples;

(e) to promote respect for the diversity of cultural expressions and raise awareness of its value at the local, national and international levels;

(f) to reaffirm the importance of the link between culture and development for all countries, particularly for developing countries, and to support actions undertaken nationally and internationally to secure recognition of the true value of this link;

(g) to give recognition to the distinctive nature of cultural activities, goods and services as vehicles of identity, values and meaning;

(h) to reaffirm the sovereign rights of States to maintain, adopt and implement policies and measures that they deem appropriate for the protection and promotion of the diversity of cultural expressions on their territory;

(i) to strengthen international cooperation and solidarity in a spirit of partnership with a view, in particular, to enhancing the capacities of developing countries in order to protect and promote the diversity of cultural expressions.

Article 2 – Guiding principles

1. Principle of respect for human rights and fundamental freedoms

Cultural diversity can be protected and promoted only if human rights and fundamental freedoms, such as freedom of expression, information and communication, as well as the ability of individuals to choose cultural expressions, are guaranteed. No one may invoke the provisions of this Convention in order to infringe human rights and fundamental freedoms as enshrined in the Universal Declaration of Human Rights or guaranteed by international law, or to limit the scope thereof.

2. Principle of sovereignty

States have, in accordance with the Charter of the United Nations and the principles of international law, the sovereign right to adopt measures and policies to protect and promote the diversity of cultural expressions within their territory.

3. Principle of equal dignity of and respect for all cultures

The protection and promotion of the diversity of cultural expressions presuppose the recognition of equal dignity of and respect for all cultures, including the cultures of persons belonging to minorities and indigenous peoples.

4. Principle of international solidarity and cooperation

International cooperation and solidarity should be aimed at enabling countries, especially developing countries, to create and strengthen their means of cultural expression, including their cultural industries, whether nascent or established, at the local, national and international levels.

5. Principle of the complementarity of economic and cultural aspects of development

Since culture is one of the mainsprings of development, the cultural aspects of development are as important as its economic aspects, which individuals and peoples have the fundamental right to participate in and enjoy.

6. Principle of sustainable development

Cultural diversity is a rich asset for individuals and societies. The protection, promotion and maintenance of cultural diversity are an essential requirement for sustainable development for the benefit of present and future generations.

7. Principle of equitable access

Equitable access to a rich and diversified range of cultural expressions from all over the world and access of cultures to the means of expressions and dissemination constitute important elements for enhancing cultural diversity and encouraging mutual understanding.

8. Principle of openness and balance

When States adopt measures to support the diversity of cultural expressions, they should seek to promote, in an appropriate manner, openness to other cultures of the world and to ensure that these measures are geared to the objectives pursued under the present Convention.

II. Scope of application

Article 3 – Scope of application

This Convention shall apply to the policies and measures adopted by the Parties related to the protection and promotion of the diversity of cultural expressions.

III. Definitions

Article 4 – Definitions

For the purposes of this Convention, it is understood that:

1. Cultural diversity

"Cultural diversity" refers to the manifold ways in which the cultures of groups and societies find expression. These expressions are passed on within and among groups and societies.

Cultural diversity is made manifest not only through the varied ways in which the cultural heritage of humanity is expressed, augmented and transmitted through the variety of cultural expressions, but also through diverse modes of artistic creation, production, dissemination, distribution and enjoyment, whatever the means and technologies used.

2. Cultural content

"Cultural content" refers to the symbolic meaning, artistic dimension and cultural values that originate from or express cultural identities.

3. Cultural expressions

"Cultural expressions" are those expressions that result from the creativity of individuals, groups and societies, and that have cultural content.

4. Cultural activities, goods and services

"Cultural activities, goods and services" refers to those activities, goods and services, which at the time they are considered as a specific attribute, use or purpose, embody or convey cultural expressions, irrespective of the commercial value they may have. Cultural activities may be an end in themselves, or they may contribute to the production of cultural goods and services.

5. Cultural industries

"Cultural industries" refers to industries producing and distributing cultural goods or services as defined in paragraph 4 above.

6. Cultural policies and measures

"Cultural policies and measures" refers to those policies and measures relating to culture, whether at the local, national, regional or international level that are either focused on culture as such or are designed to have a direct effect on cultural expressions of individuals, groups or societies, including on the creation, production, dissemination, distribution of and access to cultural activities, goods and services.

7. Protection

"Protection" means the adoption of measures aimed at the preservation, safeguarding and enhancement of the diversity of cultural expressions.

"Protect" means to adopt such measures.

8. Interculturality

"Interculturality" refers to the existence and equitable interaction of diverse cultures and the possibility of generating shared cultural expressions through dialogue and mutual respect.

IV. Rights and obligations of Parties

Article 5 – General rule regarding rights and obligations

1. The Parties, in conformity with the Charter of the United Nations, the prin-

ciples of international law and universally recognized human rights instruments, reaffirm their sovereign right to formulate and implement their cultural policies and to adopt measures to protect and promote the diversity of cultural expressions and to strengthen international cooperation to achieve the purposes of this Convention.

2. When a Party implements policies and takes measures to protect and promote the diversity of cultural expressions within its territory, its policies and measures shall be consistent with the provisions of this Convention.

Article 6 – Rights of parties at the national level

1. Within the framework of its cultural policies and measures as defined in Article 4. 6 and taking into account its own particular circumstances and needs, each Party may adopt measures aimed at protecting and promoting the diversity of cultural expressions within its territory.

2. Such measures may include the following:

(a) regulatory measures aimed at protecting and promoting diversity of cultural expressions;

(b) measures that, in an appropriate manner, provide opportunities for domestic cultural activities, goods and services among all those available within the national territory for the creation, production, dissemination, distribution and enjoyment of such domestic cultural activities, goods and services, including provisions relating to the language used for such activities, goods and services;

(c) measures aimed at providing domestic independent cultural industries and activities in the informal sector effective access to the means of production, dissemination and distribution of cultural activities, goods and services;

(d) measures aimed at providing public financial assistance;

(e) measures aimed at encouraging non - profit organizations, as well as public and private institutions and artists and other cultural professionals, to develop and promote the free exchange and circulation of ideas, cultural expressions and cultural activities, goods and services, and to stimulate both the creative and entrepreneurial spirit in their activities;

(f) measures aimed at establishing and supporting public institutions, as appropriate;

(g) measures aimed at nurturing and supporting artists and others involved in the creation of cultural expressions;

(h) measures aimed at enhancing diversity of the media, including through public service broadcasting.

Article 7 – Measures to promote cultural expressions

1. Parties shall endeavour to create in their territory an environment which encourages individuals and social groups:

(a) to create, produce, disseminate, distribute and have access to their own cultural expressions, paying due attention to the special circumstances and needs of women as well as various social groups, including persons belonging to minorities and indigenous peoples;

(b) to have access to diverse cultural expressions from within their territory as well as from other countries of the world.

2. Parties shall also endeavour to recognize the important contribution of artists, others involved in the creative process, cultural communities, and organizations that support their work, and their central role in nurturing the diversity of cultural expressions.

Article 8 – Measures to protect cultural expressions

1. Without prejudice to the provisions of Articles 5 and 6, a Party may determine the existence of special situations where cultural expressions on its territory are at risk of extinction, under serious threat, or otherwise in need of urgent safeguarding.

2. Parties may take all appropriate measures to protect and preserve cultural expressions in situations referred to in paragraph 1 in a manner consistent with the provisions of this Convention.

3. Parties shall report to the Intergovernmental Committee referred to in Article 23 all measures taken to meet the exigencies of the situation, and the Committee may make appropriate recommendations.

Article 9 – Information sharing and transparency

Parties shall:

(a) provide appropriate information in their reports to UNESCO every four years on measures taken to protect and promote the diversity of cultural expressions within their territory and at the international level;

(b) designate a point of contact responsible for information sharing in relation to this Convention;

(c) share and exchange information relating to the protection and promotion of the diversity of cultural expressions.

Article 10 – Education and public awareness

Parties shall:

(a) encourage and promote understanding of the importance of the protection and promotion of the diversity of cultural expressions, inter alia, through educational and greater public awareness programmes;

(b) cooperate with other Parties and international and regional organizations in achieving the purpose of this article;

(c) endeavour to encourage creativity and strengthen production capacities by setting up educational, training and exchange programmes in the field of cultural industries. These measures should be implemented in a manner which does not have a negative impact on traditional forms of production.

Article 11 – Participation of civil society

Parties acknowledge the fundamental role of civil society in protecting and promoting the diversity of cultural expressions. Parties shall encourage the active participation of civil society in their efforts to achieve the objectives of this Convention.

Article 12 – Promotion of international cooperation

Parties shall endeavour to strengthen their bilateral, regional and international cooperation for the creation of conditions conducive to the promotion of the diversity of cultural expressions, taking particular account of the situations referred to in Articles 8 and 17, notably in order to:

(a) facilitate dialogue among Parties on cultural policy;

(b) enhance public sector strategic and management capacities in cultural public sector institutions, through professional and international cultural exchanges and sharing of best practices;

(c) reinforce partnerships with and among civil society, non - governmental organizations and the private sector in fostering and promoting the diversity of cultural expressions;

(d) promote the use of new technologies, encourage partnerships to enhance information sharing and cultural understanding, and foster the diversity of cultural expressions;

(e) encourage the conclusion of co - production and co - distribution agreements.

Article 13 – Integration of culture in sustainable development

Parties shall endeavour to integrate culture in their development policies at all levels for the creation of conditions conducive to sustainable development and, within this framework, foster aspects relating to the protection and promotion of the diversity of cultural expressions.

Article 14 – Cooperation for development

Parties shall endeavour to support cooperation for sustainable development and poverty reduction, especially in relation to the specific needs of developing countries, in order to foster the emergence of a dynamic cultural sector by, inter alia, the following means:

(a) the strengthening of the cultural industries in developing countries through:

(i) creating and strengthening cultural production and distribution capacities in developing countries;

(ii) facilitating wider access to the global market and international distribution networks for their cultural activities, goods and services;

(iii) enabling the emergence of viable local and regional markets;

(iv) adopting, where possible, appropriate measures in developed countries with a view to facilitating access to their territory for the cultural activities, goods and services of developing countries;

(v) providing support for creative work and facilitating the mobility, to the extent possible, of artists from the developing world;

(vi) encouraging appropriate collaboration between developed and developing countries in the areas, inter alia, of music and film;

(b) capacity - building through the exchange of information, experience and expertise, as well as the training of human resources in developing countries, in the public and private sector relating to, inter alia, strategic and management capacities, policy development and implementation, promotion and distribution of cultural expressions, small - , medium - and micro - enterprise development, the use of technology, and skills development and transfer;

(c) technology transfer through the introduction of appropriate incentive measures for the transfer of technology and know - how, especially in the areas of cultural industries and enterprises;

(d) financial support through:

(i) the establishment of an International Fund for Cultural Diversity as provided in Article 18;

(ii) the provision of official development assistance, as appropriate, including technical assistance, to stimulate and support creativity;

(iii) other forms of financial assistance such as low interest loans, grants and other funding mechanisms.

Article 15 – Collaborative arrangements

Parties shall encourage the development of partnerships, between and within the public and private sectors and non - profit organizations, in order to cooperate with developing countries in the enhancement of their capacities in the protection and promotion of the diversity of cultural expressions. These innovative partnerships shall, according to the practical needs of developing countries, emphasize the further development of infrastructure, human resources and policies, as well as the exchange of cultural activities, goods and services.

Article 16 – Preferential treatment for developing countries

Developed countries shall facilitate cultural exchanges with developing countries by granting, through the appropriate institutional and legal frameworks, preferential treatment to artists and other cultural professionals and practitioners, as well as cultural goods and services from developing countries.

Article 17 – International cooperation in situations of serious threat to cultural expressions

Parties shall cooperate in providing assistance to each other, and, in particular to developing countries, in situations referred to under Article 8.

Article 18 – International Fund for Cultural Diversity

1. An International Fund for Cultural Diversity, hereinafter referred to as "the Fund", is hereby established.

2. The Fund shall consist of funds - in - trust established in accordance with the Financial Regulations of UNESCO.

3. The resources of the Fund shall consist of:

(a) voluntary contributions made by Parties;

(b) funds appropriated for this purpose by the General Conference of UNESCO;

(c) contributions, gifts or bequests by other States; organizations and programmes of the United Nations system, other regional or international organizations; and public or private bodies or individuals;

(d) any interest due on resources of the Fund;

(e) funds raised through collections and receipts from events organized for the benefit of the Fund;

(f) any other resources authorized by the Fund's regulations.

4. The use of resources of the Fund shall be decided by the Intergovernmental Committee on the basis of guidelines determined by the Conference of Parties referred to in Article 22.

5. The Intergovernmental Committee may accept contributions and other forms of assistance for general and specific purposes relating to specific projects, provided that those projects have been approved by it.

6. No political, economic or other conditions that are incompatible with the objectives of this Convention may be attached to contributions made to the Fund.

7. Parties shall endeavour to provide voluntary contributions on a regular basis towards the implementation of this Convention.

Article 19 – Exchange, analysis and dissemination of information

1. Parties agree to exchange information and share expertise concerning data collection and statistics on the diversity of cultural expressions as well as on best practices for its protection and promotion.

2. UNESCO shall facilitate, through the use of existing mechanisms within the Secretariat, the collection, analysis and dissemination of all relevant information, statistics and best practices.

3. UNESCO shall also establish and update a data bank on different sectors and governmental, private and non - profit organizations involved in the area of cultural expressions.

4. To facilitate the collection of data, UNESCO shall pay particular attention to capacity - building and the strengthening of expertise for Parties that submit a request for such assistance.

5. The collection of information identified in this Article shall complement the

information collected under the provisions of Article 9.

V. Relationship to other instruments

Article 20 – Relationship to other treaties: mutual supportiveness, complementarity and non – subordination

1. Parties recognize that they shall perform in good faith their obligations under this Convention and all other treaties to which they are parties. Accordingly, without subordinating this Convention to any other treaty,

(a) they shall foster mutual supportiveness between this Convention and the other treaties to which they are parties; and

(b) when interpreting and applying the other treaties to which they are parties or when entering into other international obligations, Parties shall take into account the relevant provisions of this Convention.

2. Nothing in this Convention shall be interpreted as modifying rights and obligations of the Parties under any other treaties to which they are parties.

Article 21 – International consultation and coordination

Parties undertake to promote the objectives and principles of this Convention in other international forums. For this purpose, Parties shall consult each other, as appropriate, bearing in mind these objectives and principles.

VI. Organs of the Convention

Article 22 – Conference of Parties

1. A Conference of Parties shall be established. The Conference of Parties shall be the plenary and supreme body of this Convention.

2. The Conference of Parties shall meet in ordinary session every two years, as far as possible, in conjunction with the General Conference of UNESCO. It may meet in extraordinary session if it so decides or if the Intergovernmental Committee receives a request to that effect from at least one - third of the Parties.

3. The Conference of Parties shall adopt its own rules of procedure.

4. The functions of the Conference of Parties shall be, inter alia:

(a) to elect the Members of the Intergovernmental Committee;

(b) to receive and examine reports of the Parties to this Convention transmitted by the Intergovernmental Committee;

(c) to approve the operational guidelines prepared upon its request by the Intergovernmental Committee;

(d) to take whatever other measures it may consider necessary to further the objectives of this Convention.

Article 23 – Intergovernmental Committee

1. An Intergovernmental Committee for the Protection and Promotion of the Diversity of Cultural Expressions, hereinafter referred to as "the Intergovernmental Committee", shall be established within UNESCO. It shall be composed of representatives of 18 States Parties to the Convention, elected for a term of four years by the Conference of Parties upon entry into force of this Convention pursuant to Article 29.

2. The Intergovernmental Committee shall meet annually.

3. The Intergovernmental Committee shall function under the authority and guidance of and be accountable to the Conference of Parties.

4. The Members of the Intergovernmental Committee shall be increased to 24 once the number of Parties to the Convention reaches 50.

5. The election of Members of the Intergovernmental Committee shall be based on the principles of equitable geographical representation as well as rotation.

6. Without prejudice to the other responsibilities conferred upon it by this Convention, the functions of the Intergovernmental Committee shall be:

(a) to promote the objectives of this Convention and to encourage and monitor the implementation thereof;

(b) to prepare and submit for approval by the Conference of Parties, upon its request, the operational guidelines for the implementation and application of the provisions of the Convention;

(c) to transmit to the Conference of Parties reports from Parties to the Convention, together with its comments and a summary of their contents;

(d) to make appropriate recommendations to be taken in situations brought to its attention by Parties to the Convention in accordance with relevant provisions of the Convention, in particular Article 8;

(e) to establish procedures and other mechanisms for consultation aimed at promoting the objectives and principles of this Convention in other international forums;

(f) to perform any other tasks as may be requested by the Conference of Parties.

7. The Intergovernmental Committee, in accordance with its Rules of Procedure, may invite at any time public or private organizations or individuals to participate in its meetings for consultation on specific issues.

8. The Intergovernmental Committee shall prepare and submit to the Conference of Parties, for approval, its own Rules of Procedure.

Article 24 – UNESCO Secretariat

1. The organs of the Convention shall be assisted by the UNESCO Secretariat.

2. The Secretariat shall prepare the documentation of the Conference of Parties and the Intergovernmental Committee as well as the agenda of their meetings and shall assist in and report on the implementation of their decisions.

VII. Final clauses

Article 25 – Settlement of disputes

1. In the event of a dispute between Parties to this Convention concerning the interpretation or the application of the Convention, the Parties shall seek a solution by negotiation.

2. If the Parties concerned cannot reach agreement by negotiation, they may jointly seek the good offices of, or request mediation by, a third party.

3. If good offices or mediation are not undertaken or if there is no settlement by negotiation, good offices or mediation, a Party may have recourse to conciliation in accordance with the procedure laid down in the Annex of this Convention. The Parties shall consider in good faith the proposal made by the Conciliation Commission for the resolution of the dispute.

4. Each Party may, at the time of ratification, acceptance, approval or accession, declare that it does not recognize the conciliation procedure provided for above. Any Party having made such a declaration may, at any time, withdraw this declaration by notification to the Director - General of UNESCO.

Article 26 – Ratification, acceptance, approval or accession by Member States

1. This Convention shall be subject to ratification, acceptance, approval or

accession by Member States of UNESCO in accordance with their respective constitutional procedures.

2. The instruments of ratification, acceptance, approval or accession shall be deposited with the Director - General of UNESCO.

Article 27 – Accession

1. This Convention shall be open to accession by all States not Members of UNESCO but members of the United Nations, or of any of its specialized agencies, that are invited by the General Conference of UNESCO to accede to it.

2. This Convention shall also be open to accession by territories which enjoy full internal self - government recognized as such by the United Nations, but which have not attained full independence in accordance with General Assembly resolution 1514 (XV), and which have competence over the matters governed by this Convention, including the competence to enter into treaties in respect of such matters.

3. The following provisions apply to regional economic integration organizations:

(a) This Convention shall also be open to accession by any regional economic integration organization, which shall, except as provided below, be fully bound by the provisions of the Convention in the same manner as States Parties;

(b) In the event that one or more Member States of such an organization is also Party to this Convention, the organization and such Member State or States shall decide on their responsibility for the performance of their obligations under this Convention. Such distribution of responsibility shall take effect following completion of the notification procedure described in subparagraph (c). The organization and the Member States shall not be entitled to exercise rights under this Convention concurrently. In addition, regional economic integration organizations, in matters within their competence, shall exercise their rights to vote with a number of votes equal to the number of their Member States that are Parties to this Convention. Such an organization shall not exercise its right to vote if any of its Member States exercises its right, and vice - versa;

(c) A regional economic integration organization and its Member State or States which have agreed on a distribution of responsibilities as provided in subparagraph (b) shall inform the Parties of any such proposed distribution of responsibilities in the following manner:

(i) in their instrument of accession, such organization shall declare with specificity, the distribution of their responsibilities with respect to matters governed by the Convention;

(ii) in the event of any later modification of their respective responsibilities, the regional economic integration organization shall inform the depositary of any such proposed modification of their respective responsibilities; the depositary shall in turn inform the Parties of such modification;

(d) Member States of a regional economic integration organization which become Parties to this Convention shall be presumed to retain competence over all matters in respect of which transfers of competence to the organization have not been specifically declared or informed to the depositary;

(e) "Regional economic integration organization" means an organization constituted by sovereign States, members of the United Nations or of any of its specialized agencies, to which those States have transferred competence in respect of matters governed by this Convention and which has been duly authorized, in accordance with its internal procedures, to become a Party to it.

4. The instrument of accession shall be deposited with the Director - General of UNESCO.

Article 28 – Point of contact

Upon becoming Parties to this Convention, each Party shall designate a point of contact as referred to in Article 9.

Article 29 – Entry into force

1. This Convention shall enter into force three months after the date of deposit of the thirtieth instrument of ratification, acceptance, approval or accession, but only with respect to those States or regional economic integration organizations that have deposited their respective instruments of ratification, acceptance, approval, or accession on or before that date. It shall enter into force with respect to any other Party three months after the deposit of its instrument of ratification, acceptance, approval or accession.

2. For the purposes of this Article, any instrument deposited by a regional economic integration organization shall not be counted as additional to those deposited by Member States of the organization.

Article 30 – Federal or non – unitary constitutional systems

Recognizing that international agreements are equally binding on Parties regardless of their constitutional systems, the following provisions shall apply to Parties which have a federal or non - unitary constitutional system:

(a) with regard to the provisions of this Convention, the implementation of which comes under the legal jurisdiction of the federal or central legislative power, the obligations of the federal or central government shall be the same as for those Parties which are not federal States;

(b) with regard to the provisions of the Convention, the implementation of which comes under the jurisdiction of individual constituent units such as States, counties, provinces, or cantons which are not obliged by the constitutional system of the federation to take legislative measures, the federal government shall inform, as necessary, the competent authorities of constituent units such as States, counties, provinces or cantons of the said provisions, with its recommendation for their adoption.

Article 31 – Denunciation

1. Any Party to this Convention may denounce this Convention.

2. The denunciation shall be notified by an instrument in writing deposited with the Director - General of UNESCO.

3. The denunciation shall take effect 12 months after the receipt of the instrument of denunciation. It shall in no way affect the financial obligations of the Party denouncing the Convention until the date on which the withdrawal takes effect.

Article 32 – Depositary functions

The Director - General of UNESCO, as the depositary of this Convention, shall inform the Member States of the Organization, the States not members of the Organization and regional economic integration organizations referred to in Article 27, as well as the United Nations, of the deposit of all the instruments of ratification, acceptance, approval or accession provided for in Articles 26 and 27, and of the denunciations provided for in Article 31.

Article 33 – Amendments

1. A Party to this Convention may, by written communication addressed to the Director - General, propose amendments to this Convention. The Director - General shall circulate such communication to all Parties. If, within six months from

the date of dispatch of the communication, no less than one half of the Parties reply favourably to the request, the Director - General shall present such proposal to the next session of the Conference of Parties for discussion and possible adoption.

2. Amendments shall be adopted by a two - thirds majority of Parties present and voting.

3. Once adopted, amendments to this Convention shall be submitted to the Parties for ratification, acceptance, approval or accession.

4. For Parties which have ratified, accepted, approved or acceded to them, amendments to this Convention shall enter into force three months after the deposit of the instruments referred to in paragraph 3 of this Article by two - thirds of the Parties. Thereafter, for each Party that ratifies, accepts, approves or accedes to an amendment, the said amendment shall enter into force three months after the date of deposit by that Party of its instrument of ratification, acceptance, approval or accession.

5. The procedure set out in paragraphs 3 and 4 shall not apply to amendments to Article 23 concerning the number of Members of the Intergovernmental Committee. These amendments shall enter into force at the time they are adopted.

6. A State or a regional economic integration organization referred to in Article 27 which becomes a Party to this Convention after the entry into force of amendments in conformity with paragraph 4 of this Article shall, failing an expression of different intention, be considered to be:

(a) Party to this Convention as so amended; and

(b) a Party to the unamended Convention in relation to any Party not bound by the amendments.

Article 34 – Authoritative texts

This Convention has been drawn up in Arabic, Chinese, English, French, Russian and Spanish, all six texts being equally authoritative.

Article 35 – Registration

In conformity with Article 102 of the Charter of the United Nations, this Convention shall be registered with the Secretariat of the United Nations at the request of the Director - General of UNESCO.

ANNEX

Conciliation Procedure

Article 1 – Conciliation Commission

A Conciliation Commission shall be created upon the request of one of the Parties to the dispute. The Commission shall, unless the Parties otherwise agree, be composed of five members, two appointed by each Party concerned and a President chosen jointly by those members.

Article 2 – Members of the Commission

In disputes between more than two Parties, Parties in the same interest shall appoint their members of the Commission jointly by agreement. Where two or more Parties have separate interests or there is a disagreement as to whether they are of the same interest, they shall appoint their members separately.

Article 3 – Appointments

If any appointments by the Parties are not made within two months of the date of the request to create a Conciliation Commission, the Director - General of UNESCO shall, if asked to do so by the Party that made the request, make those appointments within a further two - month period.

Article 4 – President of the Commission

If a President of the Conciliation Commission has not been chosen within two months of the last of the members of the Commission being appointed, the Director - General of UNESCO shall, if asked to do so by a Party, designate a President within a further two - month period.

Article 5 – Decisions

The Conciliation Commission shall take its decisions by majority vote of its members. It shall, unless the Parties to the dispute otherwise agree, determine its own procedure. It shall render a proposal for resolution of the dispute, which the Parties shall consider in good faith.

Article 6 – Disagreement

A disagreement as to whether the Conciliation Commission has competence shall be decided by the Commission.

世界文化多样性宣言

（2001 年 11 月 2 日联合国教科文组织通过）

大会重视充分实现《世界人权宣言》和其他普遍认同的文件中宣布的人权和基本自由，铭记 1966 年有关公民权利和政治权利以及有关经济、社会和文化权利的两个国际公约；

忆及《联合国教科文组织章程》序言确认“……人类尊严需要传播文化，并为争取正义、自由与和平对人类进行教育，所有国家必须按照互助的精神履行神圣的义务”；

还忆及《联合国教科文组织章程》第一条特别规定联合国教科文组织的其中一项宗旨是，建议“订立必要的国际协定，以便运用文字和图像进行思想的自由交流”；

参照联合国教科文组织颁布的国际条约中涉及文化多样性和行使文化权利的各项条款；

重申应该把文化视为显示某个社会或某个社会群体精神与物质，智力与感情的不同特点的总和；除了文学和艺术外，文化还应包括生活方式、共处的方式、价值观体系、传统和信仰；

注意到文化是当代有关身份认同、社会凝聚力和知识经济发展问题辩论的焦点；

确认在相互信任和理解的气氛下，尊重文化多样性，宽容、对话和合作是国际和平与安全的最佳保证之一；

希望在承认文化多样性，认识到人类是一个统一整体和发展文化间交流的基础上开展更广泛的团结互助；

认为尽管受到信息和传播新技术迅速发展推动的全球化进程对文化多样性是一种挑战，但它也为各种文化和文明之间进行新的对话创造了条件；

认识到联合国教科文组织在联合国系统中担负着保护和促进丰富的文化多样性的特殊职责；

宣布下述原则并通过本宣言：

特性、多样性和多元化

第 1 条　文化多样性——人类的共同遗产

文化在不同的时代和不同的地方具有不同的形式。这种多样性体现在显示构成人类各群体和各社会特性的独创性和多样性中。文化的多样性是交流、革新和创新的源泉，它对人类来讲就像生物多样性对维持生物平衡一样必不可少。从这个意义上讲，文化多样性是人类的共同遗产，为了当代人和子孙后代的利益应当予以承认和肯定。

第 2 条　从文化多样性到文化多元化

在日益走向多样化的当今社会中，必须确保具有多元、丰富多彩和充满活力的文化特性的个人和群体的和睦相处和共同生活的愿望。主张所有公民融入和参与的政策是增强社会凝聚力、民间社会活力和维护和平的可靠保障。因此，文化多元化是对文化多样性客观现实的政治回应。文化多元化是民主范畴内不可分割的一部分，它有利于文化交流，也有利于充实公众生活的创造能力的充分发挥。

第 3 条　文化多样性——发展的因素

文化多样性增加了每个人选择的机会；它是发展的源泉之一，它不仅是促进经济增长的因素，而且也是达到令人满意的智力、情感、道德和精神要求的手段。

文化多样性与人权

第 4 条　人权——文化多样性的保障

捍卫文化多样性是伦理的迫切需要，它与尊重人的尊严密不可分。它要求人们必须尊重人权和基本自由，特别是要尊重少数人群体和土著人的权利。任何人不得以文化多样性为由，损害受国际法保护的人权或限制其范围。

第 5 条　文化权利——文化多样性的有利条件

文化权利是人权的一个组成部分，它们是普遍的、不可分割和相互依存的。富有创造力的多样性的发挥要求充分实现《世界人权宣言》第 27 条和《经济、社会和文化权利国际公约》第 13 条和第 15 条规定的文化权利。因此，每个人都应该能用其选择的语言，特别是用自己的母语来表达自己的思想、进行创作和传播自己的作品；每个人都有权接受充分尊重其文化特性的良好教育和培训；每个人都应当能够参加其选择的文化生活和从事自己的文化活动，然而必须在尊重人权和基本自由的范围内。

第 6 条 面向所有人可以获取的文化多样性

在保障思想通过文字和图像自由交流的同时，务必使所有的文化都能表达自己和宣传自己。言论自由、传媒多元化、语言多元化、平等享有各种艺术表现、科学和技术知识，包括数字化形式的知识，以及所有文化在表达和传播手段中有表现的机会等，都是文化多样性的可靠保证。

文化多样性与创作

第 7 条 文化遗产——创作的源泉

每项创作都来源于文化传统，但也在同其他文化传统的交流中得到充分发展。因此，各种形式的文化遗产都应该作为人类经验和愿望的见证得到保护、开发利用和代代相传，以支持多样性的创作和建立各种文化之间的真正对话。

第 8 条 文化产品和文化服务——不同于一般的商品

面对目前为创作和革新开辟了广阔前景的经济和技术的发展变化，应该特别注意创作意愿的多样性，公正地考虑作者和艺术家的权利，以及文化产品和文化服务的特殊性，因为它们体现的是特性、价值和观念，不应把其视为一般的商品或消费品。

第 9 条 文化政策——创作的催化剂

文化政策应当在确保思想和作品自由交流的同时，利用那些有能力在地方和世界一级发挥作用的文化产业创造有利于生产和传播多样化文化产品和文化服务的条件。每个国家都应在遵守国际义务的前提下，制订本国的文化政策，并采取其认为最为合适的行动手段，即不管是行动上给予支持还是制订必要的规章制度来实施这一政策。

文化多样性与国际团结

第 10 条 增强世界范围的创作和传播能力

面对目前世界上文化产品的流通和交流存在失衡的现象，必须加强国际合作和国际团结，使所有国家，尤其是发展中国家和转型国家能够创办一些有活力、在本国和国际上具有竞争力的文化产业。

第 11 条 建立公共部门、私营部门和民间社会之间的合作伙伴关系

单靠市场的力量不可能保证文化多样性的保护和发展，文化多样性是人类可持续发展的保证。为此，必须重申在与私营部门和民间社会的合作伙伴

关系中公共政策具有首要作用。

第 12 条　联合国教科文组织的作用

联合国教科文组织根据其职责和职能，负责：

（1）促进各政府间组织在制定发展战略时考虑本宣言中陈述的原则；

（2）充任各国、各政府间组织和国际非政府组织、民间社会和私营部门之间为共同确定有利于文化多样性的概念、目标和政策所需要的联系与协商机构；

（3）继续在其与本宣言有关的各主管领域中开展制定准则的行动、提高认识的行动和发挥能力的行动；

（4）为实施行动计划提供便利，制订行动计划的主要方针作为本宣言的附件。

Universal Declaration on Cultural Diversity

2 November 2001

The General Conference,

Committedto the full implementation of the human rights and fundamental freedoms proclaimed in the Universal Declaration of Human Rights and other universally recognized legal instruments, such as the two International Covenants of 1966 relating respectively to civil and political rights and to economic, social and cultural rights,

Recalling that the Preamble to the Constitution of UNESCO affirms "that the wide diffusion of culture, and the education of humanity for justice and liberty and peace are indispensable to the dignity of man and constitute a sacred duty which all the nations must fulfil in a spirit of mutual assistance and concern",

Further recalling Article I of the Constitution, which assigns to UNESCO among other purposes that of recommending "such international agreements as may be necessary to promote the free flow of ideas by word and image",

Referring to the provisions relating to cultural diversity and the exercise of cultural rights in the international instruments enacted by UNESCO,

Reaffirming that culture should be regarded as the set of distinctive spiritual, material, intellectual and emotional features of society or a social group, and that it encompasses, in addition to art and literature, lifestyles, ways of living together, value systems, traditions and beliefs,

Noting that culture is at the heart of contemporary debates about identity, social cohesion, and the development of a knowledge - based economy,

Affirming that respect for the diversity of cultures, tolerance, dialogue and cooperation, in a climate of mutual trust and understanding are among the best guarantees of international peace and security,

Aspiring to greater solidarity on the basis of recognition of cultural diversity, of awareness of the unity of humankind, and of the development of intercultural exchanges,

Considering that the process of globalization, facilitated by the rapid development of new information and communication technologies, though representing a challenge for cultural diversity, creates the conditions for renewed dialogue among cultures and civilizations,

Aware of the specific mandate which has been entrusted to UNESCO, within the United Nations system, to ensure the preservation and promotion of the fruitful diversity of cultures,

Proclaims the following principles and adopts the present Declaration:

IDENTITY, DIVERSITY AND PLURALISM

Article 1 – Cultural diversity: the common heritage of humanity

Culture takes diverse forms across time and space. This diversity is embodied in the uniqueness and plurality of the identities of the groups and societies making up humankind. As a source of exchange, innovation and creativity, cultural diversity is as necessary for humankind as biodiversity is for nature. In this sense, it is the common heritage of humanity and should be recognized and affirmed for the benefit of present and future generations.

Article 2 – From cultural diversity to cultural pluralism

In our increasingly diverse societies, it is essential to ensure harmonious interaction among people and groups with plural, varied and dynamic cultural identities as well as their willingness to live together. Policies for the inclusion and participation of all citizens are guarantees of social cohesion, the vitality of civil society and peace. Thus defined, cultural pluralism gives policy expression to the reality of cultural diversity. Indissociable from a democratic framework, cultural pluralism is conducive to cultural exchange and to the flourishing of creative capacities that sustain public life.

Article 3 – Cultural diversity as a factor in development

Cultural diversity widens the range of options open to everyone; it is one of the roots of development, understood not simply in terms of economic growth, but also as a means to achieve a more satisfactory intellectual, emotional, moral and spiritual existence.

CULTURAL DIVERSITY AND HUMAN RIGHTS

Article 4 – Human rights as guarantees of cultural diversity

The defence of cultural diversity is an ethical imperative, inseparable from respect for human dignity. It implies a commitment to human rights and fundamental freedoms, in particular the rights of persons belonging to minorities and those of indigenous peoples. No one may invoke cultural diversity to infringe upon human rights guaranteed by international law, nor to limit their scope.

Article 5 – Cultural rights as an enabling environment for cultural diversity

Cultural rights are an integral part of human rights, which are universal, indivisible and interdependent. The flourishing of creative diversity requires the full implementation of cultural rights as defined in Article 27 of the Universal Declaration of Human Rights and in Articles 13 and 15 of the International Covenant on Economic, Social and Cultural Rights. All persons have therefore the right to express themselves and to create and disseminate their work in the language of their choice, and particularly in their mother tongue; all persons are entitled to quality education and training that fully respect their cultural identity; and all persons have the right to participate in the cultural life of their choice and conduct their own cultural practices, subject to respect for human rights and fundamental freedoms.

Article 6 – Towards access for all to cultural diversity

While ensuring the free flow of ideas by word and image care should be exercised so that all cultures can express themselves and make themselves known. Freedom of expression, media pluralism, multilingualism, equal access to art and to scientific and technological knowledge, including in digital form, and the possibility for all cultures to have access to the means of expression and dissemination are the guarantees of cultural diversity.

CULTURAL DIVERSITY AND CREATIVITY

Article 7 – Cultural heritage as the wellspring of creativity

Creation draws on the roots of cultural tradition, but flourishes in contact with other cultures. For this reason, heritage in all its forms must be preserved, enhanced and handed on to future generations as a record of human experience and aspirations, so as to foster creativity in all its diversity and to inspire genuine dialogue among cultures.

Article 8 – Cultural goods and services: commodities of a unique kind

In the face of present - day economic and technological change, opening up vast prospects for creation and innovation, particular attention must be paid to the diversity of the supply of creative work, to due recognition of the rights of authors and artists and to the specificity of cultural goods and services which, as vectors of identity, values and meaning, must not be treated as mere commodities or consumer goods.

Article 9 – Cultural policies as catalysts of creativity

While ensuring the free circulation of ideas and works, cultural policies must create conditions conducive to the production and dissemination of diversified cultural goods and services through cultural industries that have the means to assert themselves at the local and global level. It is for each State, with due regard to its international obligations, to define its cultural policy and to implement it through the means it considers fit, whether by operational support or appropriate regulations.

CULTURAL DIVERSITY AND INTERNATIONAL SOLIDARITY

Article 10 – Strengthening capacities for creation and dissemination worldwide

In the face of current imbalances in flows and exchanges of cultural goods at the global level, it is necessary to reinforce international cooperation and solidarity aimed at enabling all countries, especially developing countries and countries in transition, to establish cultural industries that are viable and competitive at national and international level.

Article 11 – Building partnerships between the public sector, the private sector and civil society

Market forces alone cannot guarantee the preservation and promotion of cultural diversity, which is the key to sustainable human development. From this perspective, the pre - eminence of public policy, in partnership with the private sector and civil society, must be reaffirmed.

Article 12 – The role of UNESCO

UNESCO, by virtue of its mandate and functions, has the responsibility to:

(a) promote the incorporation of the principles set out in the present Declaration into the development strategies drawn up within the various intergovernmental bodies;

(b) serve as a reference point and a forum where States, international governmental and nongovernmental organizations, civil society and the private sector may join together in elaborating concepts, objectives and policies in favour of cultural diversity;

(c) pursue its activities in standard - setting, awareness raising and capacity - building in the areas related to the present Declaration within its fields of competence;

(d) facilitate the implementation of the Action Plan, the main lines of which are appended to the present Declaration.

国际文化合作原则宣言*

（1966年11月4日联合国教科文组织通过）

联合国教育、科学及文化组织大会于1966年11月4日本组织成立二十周年纪念日在巴黎举行第十四次全体会议。

考虑到本组织章程宣布“由于战争源于人的意念，因此必须从人的思想深处保卫和平”，以及为不使维护和平的努力归于失败，必须将和平建立在人类的共同认识和伦理基础之上；

考虑到本组织章程同时指出，人类有关正义和自由的教育和文化的普及对于维护人的尊严不可或缺，这是所有国家基于互相帮助和互相关心的精神必须履行的神圣职责；

考虑到本组织成员国认同对真理的追求，以及思想和知识的自由交流，一致同意和决心发展和丰富其人民之间通信交流的方式。鉴于技术进步尽管有助于知识和思想的发展与传播，但对人类生活方式和民族习惯的轻视仍然构成不同国家间建立友谊，开展和平合作以及人类进步的障碍；

考虑到不断为联合国大会所重申的《世界人权宣言》、《儿童权利宣言》、《赋予殖民地国家和人民独立宣言》、《联合国消除一切形式种族歧视宣言》、《在青年中促进和平理想、增进不同民族间相互理解和尊重宣言》以及《反对干预各国内政、维护各国主权和独立宣言》的精神和有关规定；

基于本组织头二十年的实践和经验，坚信加强国际文化合作必须坚定维护本组织的原则；

为使各国负责文化活动的政府、机构、组织、团体、单位接受国际公认原则的指导，为落实本组织章程规定的通过增进世界各国人民之间的教育、科学和文化关系而促进《联合国宪章》确立的和平与福利目标之实现的相关意图，兹通过并宣布本宣言如下：

---

* 中国社会科学院法学研究所吴峻译。

第一条

一、各种文化都具有尊严和价值，必须予以尊重和保存。

二、每一个民族都有发展其文化的权利和义务。

三、所有文化都属于全人类共同遗产的一部分，其种类繁多，彼此互异，互为影响。

第二条

为在技术进步与人类智慧和道德进步之间建立和谐的平衡关系，各国应共同努力同步开发各文化领域。

第三条

国际文化合作的范围应包括有关教育、科学和文化的智力和创造活动的所有方面。

第四条

无论是双边或多边，地区的还是世界性的，各种形式的国际文化合作应以下列各点为目的：

一、传播知识、启发才能和提高文化；

二、发展各国人民之间的和平关系和友谊并增进对彼此生活方式的了解；

三、继续执行本宣言序言部分所回顾的各个联合国宣言所确定的原则；

四、使人人能够获得知识，享受各国人民的艺术和文学，分享世界各地的科技进步以及这些进步所产生的利益，并对文化生活的提高作出贡献；

五、提高世界各地人民精神生活和物质生活水平。

第五条

文化合作是所有民族和所有国家的权利和义务，他们应当互相分享彼此的知识和技能。

第六条

国际合作在通过其本身良好行动促进所有文化提高的同时，应尊重每一文化的特殊性质。

第七条

一、在最自由的交换和讨论的基础上广泛传播思想和知识，是创造性活动、追求真理和发展人格所必要的。

二、在文化合作中，应以那些有助于创造友好与和平气氛的思想和价值为重点。在态度和意见表达上，应避免任何敌意色彩。在提供及传播信息时，应力求保证其真实性。

第八条

文化合作的进行，应当是为了所有从事该项合作的国家的共同利益。文化合作所引起的交换，其安排应体现广泛互惠的精神。

第九条

文化合作应对各国人民之间建立稳定的、长久的关系作出贡献，使这种关系尽可能少受国际生活中可能产生的紧张的影响。

第十条

文化合作应特别注意青年的道德和智力教育，培养其友好、全球认知与和平精神，并应促进各国强化人才培养意识，在各领域，对正在成长的一代加强培训，培育英才。

第十一条

一、各国在其文化关系上，应考虑联合国的各项原则。他们在寻求达成国际合作时，应尊重各国的主权平等，并应避免干涉实属任何国家国内管辖范围的事项。

二、本宣言各项原则的执行应适当考虑到各项人权和基本自由。

Declaration of Principles of International Cultural Co – operation

4 November 1966

The General Conference of the United Nations Educational, Scientific and Cultural Organization, met in Paris for its fourteenth session, this fourth day of November 1966, being the twentieth anniversary of the foundation of the Organization,

Recalling that the Constitution of the Organization declares that `since wars begin in the minds of men, it is in the minds of men that the defenses of peace must be constructed' and that the peace must be founded, if it is not to fail, upon the intellectual and moral solidarity of mankind,

Recalling that the Constitution also states that the wide diffusion of culture and the education of humanity for justice and liberty and peace are indispensable to the dignity of man and constitute a sacred duty which all the nations must fulfill in a spirit of mutual assistance and concern,

Considering that the Organization's Member States, believing in the pursuit of truth and the free exchange of ideas and knowledge, have agreed and determined to develop and to increase the means of communication between their peoples,

Considering that, despite the technical advances which facilitate the development and dissemination of knowledge and ideas, ignorance of the way of life and customs of peoples still presents an obstacle to friendship among the nations, to peaceful co - operation and to the progress of mankind,

Taking account of the Universal Declaration of Human Rights, the Declaration of the Rights of the Child, the Declaration on the Granting of Independence to Colonial Countries and Peoples, the United Nations Declaration on the Elimination of all Forms of Racial Discrimination, the Declaration on the Promotion among Youth of the Ideals of Peace, Mutual Respect and Understanding between Peoples, and the Declaration on the Inadmissibility of Intervention in the Domestic Affairs of States and the Protection of their Independence and Sovereignty, proclaimed successively by the General Assembly of the United Nations,

Convinced by the experience of the Organization's first twenty years that, if international cultural co - operation is to be strengthened its principles require to be affirmed,

Proclaims this Declaration of the principles of international cultural co - operation, to the end that governments, authorities, organizations, associations and institutions responsible for cultural activities may constantly be guided by these principles; and for the purpose, as set out in the Constitution of the Organization, of advancing, through the educational, scientific and cultural relations of the peoples of the world, the objectives of peace and welfare that are defined in the Charter of the United Nations

Article I

1. Each culture has a dignity and value which must be respected and preserved.

2. Every people has the right and the duty to develop its culture.

3. In their rich variety and diversity, and in the reciprocal influences they exert on one another, all cultures form part of the common heritage belonging to all mankind.

Article II

Nations shall endeavour to develop the various branches of culture side by side and, as far as possible, simultaneously, so as to establish a harmonious balance between technical progress and the intellectual and moral advancement of mankind.

Article III

International cultural co - operation shall cover all aspects of intellectual and creative activities relating to education, science and culture.

Article IV

The aims of international cultural co - operation in its various forms, bilateral or multilateral; regional or universal, shall be:

1. To spread knowledge, to stimulate talent and to enrich cultures;

2. To develop peaceful relations and friendship among the peoples and bring about a better understanding of each other's way of life;

3. To contribute to the application of the principles set out in the United Nations Declarations that are recalled in the Preamble to this Declaration;

4. To enable, everyone to have access to knowledge, to enjoy the arts and literature f all peoples, to share in advances made in science in all parts of the world and in the resulting benefits, and to contribute to the enrichment of cultural life;

5. To raise the level of the spiritual and material life of man in all parts of the world.

Article V

Cultural co - operation is a right and a duty for all peoples and all nations, which should share with one another their knowledge and skills.

Article VI

International co - operation, while promoting the enrichment of all cultures through its beneficent action, shall respect the distinctive character of each.

Article VII

1. Broad dissemination of ideas and knowledge, based on the freest exchange and discussion, is essential to creative activity, the pursuit of truth and the development of the personality.

2. In cultural co - operation, stress shall be laid on ideas and values conducive to the creation of a climate of friendship and peace. Any mark of hostility in attitudes and in expression of opinion shall be avoided. Every effort shall be made, in presenting and disseminating information, to ensure its authenticity.

Article VIII

Cultural co - operation shall be carried on for the mutual benefit of all the nations practicing it. Exchanges to which it gives rise shall be arranged in a spirit of broad reciprocity.

Article IX

Cultural co - operation shall contribute to the establishment of stable, long - term relations between peoples, which - should be subjected as little as possible to the strains which may arise in international life.

Article X

Cultural co - operation shall be specially concerned with the moral and intellectual education of young people in a spirit of friendship, international understanding and peace and shall foster awareness among States of the need to stimulate talent and promote the training of the rising generations in the most varied sectors.

Article XI

1. In their cultural relations, States shall bear in mind the principles of the United Nations. In seeking to achieve international co - operation, they shall respect the sovereign equality of States and shall refrain from intervention in matters which are essentially within the domestic jurisdiction of any State.

2. The principles of this Declaration shall be applied with due regard for human rights and fundamental freedoms.

文化政策墨西哥宣言*

（世界文化政策大会 1982 年 8 月 6 日于墨西哥城通过）

最近世界发生了深刻的变化。科技进步改变了人类在世界中的位置及其社会关系的性质。教育和文化的意义越发显著，范围愈发宽广，对于个人与社会的发展是真正至关重要的。

虽然目前对话的机会越来越多，但国际社会也面临严重的经济困难，众多冲突及严峻局势也威胁着和平及安全。

因此，在各国间建立更紧密的合作关系变得更为迫切，以确保国与国之间对彼此权利互相尊重，并确保个人和民族可以自由行使自己的基本权利及其自决权。比之前更为紧迫的是，要通过教育、科学及文化的手段在每一个人的思想中贯彻“保卫和平”的理念，而这也是联合国教科文组织章程所确立的概念。

值世界文化政策大会于墨西哥城召开之际，国际社会决定采取措施加强各民族之间的交流并加深人员之间的理解。

因此，为表达对人类文化和精神目标终极融合的信念，大会同意：

就其最广泛的意义而言，现在可以说文化已经成为社会或社会群体独特的精神、物质、智力和情感特征的综合体。它不仅包括艺术和文字，也包括生活方式、人类的基本权利、价值体系、风俗习惯及信仰；

文化使得人能够进行反思。文化使得我们个体才能称之为人、理性生命，能够做出深入的判断并作出严肃的道德承诺。正是通过文化，我们在价值观之间进行区分并作出自己的选择。正是通过文化，人才可以进行自我表达，承认自己的不足，对其成就进行质疑，不知疲倦地寻求新的意义并创作出超越极限的作品。

因此，本次大会郑重同意以下适用于文化政策的原则：

---

* 中国社会科学院法学研究所吴峻译。

文化认同

1. 由于每个民族的风俗习惯及表达方式是其证明自己存在性的最有效方式，所以每一种文化都代表着独到的、不可代替的价值体系。

2. 因此，对文化认同的主张有助于民族的解放。反之，任何形式的主导都构成对身份认同的拒绝和削弱。

3. 文化认同是一种财富，通过促使每个民族、每个团体从自己的过去汲取营养、从外部开放吸收与自己特点相一致的动力而促进自我创造，从而丰富了人类的可能性。

4. 所有文化构成了人类的共同财产。民族的文化认同通过与传统及外部价值的互动而不断更新和丰富自身。文化是思想与经验的交流，也是对其他价值体系与传统的鉴赏；孤立只能使得文化萎缩和死亡。

5. 任何单一文化都不可能对普遍原则进行抽象推定：它来自于所有民族对其文化认同进行确认而产生的经验。文化认同与文化多样性密不可分。

6. 特殊之处并没有阻碍而是促进了普遍价值的交流，增强了各民族在一起的凝聚力。因此，只要不同传统并存下对不同文化认同予以承认，就构成了文化多样性最核心的内容。

7. 国际社会认为其有义务保留及保护每一民族的文化认同。

8. 非常有必要制定保护、促进并丰富每一民族文化认同及文化遗产的文化政策，该等文化政策应确立对少数文化及世界上其他民族的文化予以鉴赏的绝对尊重。对任何团体的文化予以忽视和毁弃就使得全人类蒙受损失。

9. 必须承认所有文化的平等的地位及尊严，每个民族或文化共同体都有确认及保留其文化认同并使之得到其他民族尊重的权利。

发展过程中的文化意义

10. 文化对发展进程有着根本性的意义，有助于国家的独立、主权及认同。很多时候增长被量化，没有体现其中必要的质量内涵，即人的精神和文化渴望的满足。真正的发展宗旨是使得每一个个人都能继续其幸福和自我实现。

11. 使发展人性化是至关重要的，其最终目的就是使得个人作为人类一员享有尊严并承担其对社会的责任。对于每个人及每个民族而言，发展也意味着就学习和相互间交流获取信息和机会。

12. 如果要使男女均有机会提高其份额，则发展的进程需要进行调整。

13. 越来越多的人追求一个更好的世界。他们并不仅仅追求基本需求的满足，还追求人类的发展、自身的幸福及与其他民族结伴生活的可能。其目标不限于生产、利润或消费本身，而是要实现个人和集体的潜力完全挖掘，并实现环境的保护。

14．发展要以人为本。

15．任何文化政策都需使得发展恢复到其本质的人性意义。为此需要采取新方式。这就需要在文化和教育层面进行发掘。

16．唯有将文化因素作为发展战略内在部分方能确保发展的均衡性；因此，应该从一个社会历史、社会及文化层面对有关战略进行设计。

文化与民主

17．《世界人权宣言》第27条宣称："每个人都有权利自由参与社会的文化生活、欣赏艺术及分享科学发展及其成果。"成员国须采取必要步骤实现这一目标。

18．文化来源于社会整体并应对之予以回馈，无论文化的创作还是其成果的享受，都不得成为精英阶层的特权。文化民主的基础是个人和社会在文化产品的创作、文化生活的决策及文化的传播及欣赏方面进行最大程度的参与。

19．其首要目的就是通过教育和文化的机会平等为民主开辟新的渠道。

20．有必要在区域和行政管理方面推进文化生活的分散化，确保负责文化行动的机构更能完全感受社会在文化事项方面的偏好、选择及需要。因此，关键就是要为公共机构与文化机构之间提供更多交流的机会。

21．文化民主的计划首先就要求对娱乐和艺术活动的开放进行分散化。民主文化政策将会规定由社会各阶层及全体人民都能享受卓越的文化。

22．为确保全民对文化生活的共同参与，要求消除基于社会背景及地位、教育、民族、年龄、语言、性别、宗教信仰、健康等方面的不平等，以及因属于特定种族、少数民族或者边缘群体而产生的不平等。

文化遗产

23．一个民族的文化遗产包括其艺术家、建筑家、音乐家、作家及科学家的作品，也包括无名艺术家的作品、民族精神表达及赋予生活以意义的价值体系。它包括该等民族通过有形和无形的作品表达其创造性的作品：语言、仪式、信仰、历史遗迹及纪念碑、文学艺术作品、档案馆及图书馆。

24．由于社会是通过创造动力之源的价值而对自己予以认可的，因此，每一个民族都有权利和义务去保卫和保留其文化遗产。

25．由于鲁莽、城镇化和工业化进程和技术应用使得文化遗产时常蒙受损失和毁坏。更令人难以接受的是殖民、武装冲突、外部占领及外部价值观强加于人所带来的损害。所有这些造成了民族内部联系的割裂及其记忆的消除。因此，对一个民族的文化遗产予以保留和利用将使其能够保护自己的主权和独立，以便确认和促进其文化认同。

26. 将非法转移的艺术品归还于其来源国是民族之间关系的基本原则。可以对目前的国际文件、协定和决议予以加强，以增强其在这方面的有效性。

文艺、智力创造与艺术教育

27. 文化繁荣与民族独立及个人自由密不可分。意见及表达自由对于艺术家及知识分子的创造行为至关重要。

28. 必须确立文化及社会条件，以促进、激励并保证文艺和智力创造，并使之不受政治、意识形态、经济及社会的歧视。

29. 教育的发展和促进不仅仅意味着制定具体计划，以培育艺术鉴赏力并对从事创造及传播的群体或机构予以扶持，还意味着对有助于使得公众发现艺术和智力创造，对社会重要作用的活动予以鼓励。

文化与教育、科学及通讯的关系

30. 为了在科技发展与人类的智力及道德进步之间取得平衡，社会总体发展就需要在文化、教育、科学和通讯领域实行相辅相成的政策。

31. 教育是适于传播国家及普遍价值的理想方式，应在促进汲取科技知识的同时又不损害个人的能力和价值。

32. 目前，需要基本及创新性的教育，这不仅需要启蒙和传播知识，还要求训练和更新知识体系；它有助于学生了解其所处时代和环境的现实情况；它有助于人格的全面发展；它对自律、尊重他人、社会及国际中的团结进行训练；它使得人具有组织性和劳动力，并使得其可以生产必要的商品和服务；它最后还会鼓励创新并激励创造。

33. 有必要鼓励使用本国语言对知识进行交流。

34. 识字水平对于每个民族的文化发展而言至关重要。

35. 科学及技术教学之要务应设计为文化进程，以发展民众的批判意识，并应根据民众的需要将之作为教育的基础部分。

36. 信息、思想及知识的自由流动及广泛和平衡的传播是信息及通讯世界新秩序原则之一。对所有国家而言，这意味着不但有权接受也有权传播文化、教育、科学及技术信息。

37. 现代通讯媒体应促进各国文化潮流的客观信息得以传播，但不得对各国创作自由及文化认同构成损害。

38. 过去几年科技的发展扩张了文化产业。无论其组织形式为何，这些产业都在文化产品的分销方面起着重要的作用。然而，在其国际活动中，它们通常无视社会的传统价值，促成了与发展实际需要无关的希望和热望。另外，尤其在发展中国家本国文化产业的缺乏构成了文化依附的缘由，并导致了疏离局面的产生。

39．因此，关键要鼓励在不存在文化产业的国家建立文化产业，可以通过双边和多边的扶持项目予以实施，总要确保文化商品的生产与分销符合每个社会的综合发展趋势。

40．现代通讯媒体对当今的教育和文化传播都发挥着基础性的作用。因此，社会需要发掘使用新的生产及通讯技术的方法和方式，以实现个人与集体的真正发展，并通过保护其主权及捍卫世界和平而促进各国的独立。

文化活动的规划、管理及资助

41．真正发展的关键条件就是文化。社会必须对文化活动的规划、管理及资助进行大力工作。为此目的，必须对每一个社会的需要及困境进行考虑，须永远保证文化创作在精神及内容上所必需的自由。

42．如果要在成员国实现有效的文化发展，须增加相关的预算分配并应用多种来源以尽可能多地募集资金。同样，也要采取更多的措施以培训文化规划及管理领域的人员。

国际文化合作

43．在文化交流和撞击基础上使思想和知识实现最大范围的传播对于人的创作活动、个人及社会的全面发展至关重要。

44．要在各国间营造尊重、信任、对话及和平的环境，其前提条件就是在区域内部、区域、区域间及国际层面就文化事项进行更充分的合作和理解。如果没有削弱或消除目前的紧张局势及冲突、不停止军备竞赛并削减军备，就不可能充分实现这种环境。

45．本届大会庄严确认联合国教科文组织第 14 届会议所通过《国际文化合作原则宣言》中确定的价值和效力。

46．国际文化合作须基于对文化认同的尊重、对所有文化尊严和价值的承认，并须基于国家独立、主权和不干涉原则。因此，在国家之间的合作关系中，应避免一种文化对另一种文化出现一切形式的附属和替代。关键要对文化交流和合作进行进一步平衡，以便那些尤其在特定发展中国家并不出名的文化能在更广的范围散播到所有国家。

47．文化、科学及教育交流应巩固和平、促进对人权的尊重，并有助于消除殖民主义、新殖民主义、种族主义、种族隔离及所有形式的侵略、奴役及干涉。同样的，文化合作应有助于实现一个促进军备裁减的环境，以便将用于军备的人力及财力用于建设性的用途，诸如文化、科学及技术发展项目等。

48. 国际文化合作需要在跨领域的背景下得以多样化发展，并须特别关注对文化服务合格人员的培训。

49. 应特别鼓励在发展中国家之间进行文化合作，以便其他文化和其他发展经验的知识能够丰富该等国家的生活。

50. 大会再次确认，教育和文化因素对于建立国际经济新秩序而言至关重要。

联合国教科文组织

51. 在一个被种种危机及不同文明文化价值的纷争所撕裂的世界里，成员国和联合国教科文组织秘书处须进一步努力，以保存这种价值，并采取进一步的行动促进人类的发展。

52. 这种情形下，联合国教科文组织章程中确认的目标至关重要。

53. 世界文化政策大会吁请联合国教科文组织继续并加强其工作，增进各民族国家之间的接触，继续追求其崇高使命，以在多样性的人类之中实现四海之内皆兄弟的古老梦想。

54. 国际社会在本次大会上聚会，支持了贝尼多·华莱士的座右铭："国与国之间等同于人与人之间的关系，和平就意味着对他人权利的尊重。"

Mexico City Declaration on Cultural Policies

Mexico City, 26 July - 6 August 1982

The world has undergone profound changes in recent years. The progress of science and technology has changed man's place in the world and the nature of his social relations. Education and culture, whose significance and scope have been considerably extended, are essential for the genuine development of the individual and society.

Despite today's increased opportunities for dialogue, the community of nations is also faced with serious economic difficulties, inequality between nations is growing, and many conflicts and grave tensions are threatening peace and security.

It is therefore now more urgent than ever to establish closer collaboration among nations, to guarantee respect for the rights of others and to ensure the exercise of the fundamental freedoms of man and of peoples, and of their right to self-determination. More than ever it is urgent to construct 'defences of peace' in the mind of each individual, inter alia through education, science and culture, as affirmed in the Constitution of UNESCO.

By gathering in Mexico City on the occasion of the World Conference on Cultural Policies, the international community has decided to contribute effectively to the closer communion of peoples and to greater understanding among men.

Therefore, expressing trust in the ultimate convergence of the cultural and spiritual goals of mankind, the Conference agrees:

that in its widest sense, culture may now be said to be the whole complex of distinctive spiritual, material, intellectual and emotional features that characterize a society or social group. It includes not only the arts and letters, but also modes of life, the fundamental rights of the human being, value systems, traditions and beliefs;

that it is culture that gives man the ability to reflect upon himself. It is culture that makes us specifically human, rational beings, endowed with a critical judgment and a sense of moral commitment. It is through culture that we discern values and make choices. It is through culture that man expresses himself, becomes aware of himself, recognizes his incompleteness, questions his own achievements, seeks untiringly for new meanings and creates works through which he transcends his limitations.

Consequently, the Conference solemnly agrees that the following principles should govern cultural policies:

CULTURAL IDENTITY

1. Every culture represents a unique and irreplaceable body of values since each people's traditions and forms of expression are its most effective means of demonstrating its presence in the world.

2. The assertion of cultural identity therefore contributes to the liberation of peoples. Conversely, any form of domination constitutes a denial or an impairment of that identity.

3. Cultural identity is a treasure that vitalizes mankind's possibilities of self-fulfilment by moving every people and every group to seek nurture in its past, to welcome contributions from outside that are compatible with its own characteristics, and so to continue the process of its own creation. 4. All cultures form part of the common heritage of mankind. The cultural identity of a people is renewed and enriched through contact with the traditions and values of others. Culture is dialogue, the exchange of ideas and experience and the appreciation of other values and traditions; it withers and dies in isolation.

5. The universal cannot be postulated in the abstract by any single culture: it emerges from the experience of all the world's peoples as each affirms its own identity. Cultural identity and cultural diversity are inseparable.

6. Special characteristics do not hinder, but rather enrich the communion of the universal values that unite peoples. Hence recognition of the presence of a variety of cultural identities wherever various traditions exist side by side constitutes the very essence of cultural pluralism.

7. The international community considers it its duty to ensure that the cultural identity of each people is preserved and protected.

8. All of this points to the need for cultural policies that will protect, stimulate and enrich each people's identity and cultural heritage, and establish absolute respect for and appreciation of cultural minorities and the other cultures of the world. The neglect or destruction of the culture of any group is a loss to mankind as a whole.

9. The equality and dignity of all cultures must be recognized, as must the right of each people and cultural community to affirm and preserve its cultural identity and have it respected by others.

CULTURAL DIMENSION OF DEVELOPMENT

10. Culture constitutes a fundamental dimension of the development process and helps to strengthen the independence, sovereignty and identity of nations. Growth has frequently been conceived in quantitative terms, without taking into account its necessary qualitative dimension, namely the satisfaction of man's spiritual and cultural aspirations. The aim of genuine development is the continuing well - being and fulfilment of each and every individual.

11. It is vital to humanize development, the ultimate goal of which is the individual in his dignity as a human being and his responsibility to society. Development implies for every individual and every people access to information and opportunities to learn and to communicate with others.

12. If all men and women are to be given the opportunity to improve their lot the course of development must be continually adjusted.

13. Steadily increasing numbers of men and women are seeking a better world. They do not only seek the satisfaction of basic needs but also the development of human beings, their well - being and their possibilities of living together in fellowship with all peoples. Their objective is not production, profit or consumption per se, but the full realization of their potential, both individual and collective, and the preservation of nature.

14. Man is the origin and the goal of development.

15. Any cultural policy should restore to development its profound, human significance. New models are required. And it is in the sphere of culture and education that they are to be found.

16. Balanced development can only be ensured by making cultural factors an integral part of the strategies designed to achieve it; consequently, these strategies should always be devised in the light of the historical, social and cultural context of each society.

CULTURE AND DEMOCRACY

17. Article 27 of the Universal Declaration of Human Rights proclaims that ' everyone has the right freely to participate in the cultural life of the community, to enjoy the arts and to share in scientific advancement and its benefits'. States must take the necessary steps to attain this objective.

18. Culture springs from the community as a whole and should return to it; neither the production of culture nor the enjoyment of its benefits should be the privilege of élites. Cultural democracy is based on the broadest possible participation by the individual and society in the creation of cultural goods, in decision - making concerning cultural life and in the dissemination and enjoyment of culture.

19. The aim, above all, should be to open up new channels for democracy through equality of opportunity in education and culture.

20. It is necessary to bring about a geographical and administrative decentralization of cultural life and ensure that the institutions responsible for cultural action are more fully aware of the preferences, options and needs of society in cultural matters. It is essential, therefore, that more opportunities should be provided for contact between the public and cultural bodies.

21. A programme for the democratization of culture calls, in the first place, for the decentralization of access to leisure pursuits and the arts. A democratic cultural policy will provide for enjoyment of artistic excellence by all communities and the whole population.

22. The participation of all individuals in cultural life requires the elimination of inequalities based, inter alia, on social background and status, education, nationality, age, language, sex, religious beliefs, health or the fact of belonging to ethnic, minority or fringe groups.

CULTURAL HERITAGE

23. The cultural heritage of a people includes the works of its artists, architects, musicians, writers and scientists and also the work of anonymous artists, expressions of the people's spirituality, and the body of values which give mean-

ing to life. It includes both tangible and intangible works through which the creativity of that people finds expression: languages, rites, beliefs, historic places and monuments, literature, works of art, archives and libraries.

24. Every people therefore has a right and a duty to defend and preserve its cultural heritage, since societies recognize themselves through the values in which they find a source of creative inspiration.

25. The cultural heritage has frequently suffered damage or destruction as a result of thoughtlessness as well as of the processes of urbanization, industrialization and technological penetration. But even more intolerable is the damage caused to the cultural heritage by colonialism, armed conflict, foreign occupation and the imposition of alien values. A11 these have the effect of severing a people's links with and obliterating the memory of its past. Preservation and appreciation of its cultural heritage therefore enable a people to defend its sovereignty and independence, and hence affirm and promote its cultural identity.

26. The restitution to their countries of origin of works illicitly removed from them is a basic principle of cultural relations between peoples. Existing international instruments, agreements and resolutions could be strengthened to increase their effectiveness in this respect.

ARTISTIC AND INTELLECTUAL CREATION AND ART EDUCATION

27. The flowering of culture is inseparable both from the independence of peoples and from individual freedom. Freedom of opinion and expression is essential for the creative activities of artists and intellectuals alike.

28. Social and cultural conditions must be established which will facilitate, stimulate and guarantee artistic and intellectual creation without political, ideological, economic or social discrimination.

29. The development and promotion of art education imply not only the formulation of specific programmes designed to foster artistic appreciation and support groups or institutions engaged in creation and dissemination, but also the encouragement of activities that will stimulate public awareness of the social importance of art and intellectual creation.

RELATIONSHIP OF CULTURE WITH EDUCATION, SCIENCE AND COMMUNICATION

30. The overall development of society calls for complementary policies in the

fields of culture, education, science and communication with a view to the establishment of a harmonious balance between technological progress and the intellectual and moral advancement of mankind.

31. Education is ideally suited to the transmission of national and universal cultural values and should foster the assimilation of scientific and technological knowledge without detriment to each people's capacities and values.

32. At the present time, integral, innovative education is required that not only informs and transmits, but also trains and renews; that helps students to become aware of the realities of their times and of their environment, that assists in the full development of the personality; that provides training in self - discipline, respect for others, and social and international solidarity; that equips people for organization and productivity and for the production of truly necessary goods and services; and finally, that encourages renovation and stimulates creativity.

33. It is necessary to encourage the use of national languages to communicate knowledge.

34. Literacy is an essential condition for each people's cultural development.

35. Science and technology teaching should be conceived above all as a cultural process which develops critical awareness, and should be made an integral part of education systems in accordance with the development needs of peoples.

36. A free flow and a wider and more balanced dissemination of information, ideas and knowledge, which are among the principles of a new world information and communication order, imply for all nations the right not only to receive but also to transmit cultural, educational, scientific and technical information.

37. The modern communication media should facilitate objective information on cultural trends in the various countries, without detriment to the freedom of creativity and cultural identity of nations.

38. The technological progress of the last few years has led to the expansion of cultural industries. Whatever their mode of organization, these industries play an important role in the distribution of cultural goods. However, in their international activities they often disregard the traditional values of society and kindle hopes and aspirations which are not in keeping with the actual needs of its development. Furthermore, the absence of national cultural industries may, particularly in developing countries, constitute a source of cultural dependence and give rise

to alienation.

39. It is consequently essential to encourage the establishment of cultural industries in countries where they do not exist, through bilateral and multilateral assistance programmes, always ensuring that the production and distribution of cultural goods is in keeping with the integrated development of each society.

40. The modern communication media are now fulfilling a basic role in education and the spreading of culture. Society therefore has to find ways and means of using new production and communication technologies to achieve genuine individual and collective development and to promote the independence of nations by preserving their sovereignty and strengthening peace in the world.

PLANNING, ADMINISTRATION AND FINANCING OF CULTURAL ACTIVITIES

41. Culture is the essential condition for genuine development. Society must make substantial efforts with respect to the planning, administration and financing of cultural activities. For this purpose account must be taken of the needs and problems of each society, always guaranteeing the freedom necessary for cultural creation, as regards both its spirit and its content.

42. If cultural development in the Member States is to be effective, the corresponding budget allocations must be increased and funds from a variety of sources must be employed as far as possible. Similarly, more must be done to train staff in the fields of cultural planning and administration.

INTERNATIONAL CULTURAL CO-OPERATION

43. The widest possible dissemination of ideas and knowledge on the basis of cultural exchanges and encounters is essential to man's creative activity and to the full development of the individual and of society.

44. More extensive sub-regional, regional, interregional and international co-operation and understanding in cultural matters are pre-conditions for the achievement of a climate of respect, confidence, dialogue and peace among the nations. Such a climate cannot be fully achieved without reducing and eliminating current tensions and conflicts and without halting the arms race and achieving disarmament.

45. The Conference solemnly reaffirms the value and validity of the Declaration of the Principles of International Cultural Co-operation, adopted at its four-

teenth session by the General Conference of the United Nations Educational, Scientific and Cultural Organization.

46. International cultural co - operation must be based on respect for cultural identity, recognition of the dignity and value of all cultures, national independence and sovereignty, and non - intervention. Consequently, in co - operative relations between nations, all forms of subordination or the replacement of one culture by another should be avoided. It is also essential to rebalance cultural interchange and co - operation in order that the less - known cultures, particularly those of certain developing countries, may be more broadly disseminated in all countries.

47. Cultural, scientific and educational exchanges should strengthen peace, promote respect for human rights, and help to eradicate colonialism, neo - colonialism, racism, apartheid and all forms of aggression, domination and interference. Similarly, cultural co - operation should help to create an international climate conducive to disarmament, so that the human resources and huge sums allocated to armaments can be used for constructive purposes, such as programmes of cultural, scientific and technological development.

48. International cultural co - operation needs to be diversified and fostered in an interdisciplinary context and with special attention to the training of qualified staff for cultural services.

49. Encouragement should be given, in particular, to co - operation among developing countries, so that knowledge of other cultures and of other experiences of development may enrich the lives of such countries.

50. The Conference reaffirms that educational and cultural factors are essential in efforts to establish a new international economic order.

UNESCO

51. In a world torn by dissensions which imperil the cultural values of the different civilizations, the Member States and Secretariat of the United Nations Educational, Scientific and Cultural Organization must increase their efforts to preserve such values and take more intensive action to further the development of mankind. The establishment of a lasting peace is essential to the very existence of human culture.

52. In this situation, the goals of UNESCO, as set out in its Constitution, acquire a capital importance.

53. The World Conference on Cultural Policies appeals to UNESCO to continue and strengthen its work to increase cultural contacts between peoples and nations and continue to pursue its lofty mission of helping men, despite their diversity, to make the ancient dream of universal brotherhood come true.

54. The international community, meeting in this Conference, endorses the motto of Benito Juárez: 'In relations between individuals as between nations, peace means respect for others' rights'.

欧洲文化公约[*]

（1954 年 12 月 19 日欧洲理事会成员国于巴黎签署，1955 年 5 月 5 日生效）

作为欧洲委员会成员的政府签字人，鉴于欧洲委员会的宗旨是为了实现其成员为保卫并落实作为其共同遗产的理念和原则而实现更紧密的团结；鉴于实现该宗旨就需要欧洲各民族彼此之间进行更深的了解；鉴于为该等目的需要的不仅是在理事会成员之间订立双边文化条约，也需要通过共同行动政策以保障及鼓励欧洲文化的发展，决议达成一般性的《欧洲文化公约》，以便在所有成员国民及其他可能加入的欧洲国家国民中推动对其他国家语言、历史及文明及其共有文明的研究，达成协定如下：

第一条

每一缔约方须采取适当措施保障并鼓励其本国对欧洲文化遗产作出贡献。

第二条

每一缔约方须尽可能地：

a. 鼓励其自己国民研究其他缔约方的历史和文明，并向该等缔约方提供设施，以促进在其领土上进行该等研究；及

b. 努力促进在其他缔约方领土上对其语言、历史及文明的研究，并向该等缔约方国民提供设施以便在其领土上进行该等研究。

第三条

缔约方须在欧洲委员会框架下彼此协商，以便就促进符合欧洲利益的文化活动采取协调一致的行动。

第四条

每个缔约方须尽力促进人员及具有文化价值物品的流动和交流，以便可以落实第二条及第三条的规定。

---

* 中国社会科学院法学研究所吴峻译。

第五条

每一缔约方须将其控制的具有欧洲文化价值的物品作为欧洲共同文化遗产的有机组成部分，须采取适当措施对其予以保护并须确保其可以对外进行合理的开放。

第六条

1. 适用现时有效《公约》条款的建议及解释须在欧洲委员会文化专家小组委员会上进行审议。

2. 根据第九条第四款加入现时有效《公约》的任何非理事会会员国可以委任一名或多名代表参与上款的会议。

3. 本条第一款所规定会议作出的结论须以推荐意见的方式提交欧洲委员会部长理事会，不产生额外花销的、文化专家小组委员会权限内的管理事项除外。

4. 欧洲委员会秘书长须就部长理事会或文化专家小组委员会可能做出的任何有关决定通告委员会成员及加入现时有效《公约》国家的政府。

5. 每一缔约国须就其因部长理事会或文化专家小组委员会的决定而对现时有效《公约》条款适用采取的任何行动以适当的方式通告欧洲委员会秘书长。

6. 适用现时有效《公约》之特定建议仅仅符合部分缔约方利益的，可以根据第七条的规定对该等建议予以进一步审议，但其落实不得使欧洲委员会负担其他开销。

第七条

为了推进对现时有效《公约》宗旨的实现，如果两个或多个缔约方希望在欧洲委员会这个场合而不是第六条第一款规定的场合进行讨论，欧洲委员会秘书长须提供他们所要求的协助。

第八条

现时有效《公约》中任何规定都不能被认定为影响：

a. 任何缔约方可能是签署方的任何现有双边文化协定的规定，或者使得任何缔约方不愿意达成任何该等协定，或者

b. 任何人有义务遵守任何缔约方国内现时有效的涉及外国人入境、居住及离境的法律和行政法规。

第九条

1. 现时有效的《公约》须开放供欧洲委员会所有成员签字。其须得到批准，批准文件须交存于欧洲委员会秘书长。

2. 一旦有三个签字国政府将其批准文件交存，现时《公约》就在该等政府间生效。

3. 对于之后批准的每一个签字国政府，其交存批准书之日即为《公约》生效之日。

4. 欧洲委员会部长理事会可以一致决定按照其认为适当的条款和条件邀请现时《公约》的非委员会成员的欧洲国家加入。任何获得邀请的国家可以通过向欧洲委员会秘书长交存批准书的方式加入。该等加入在接到批准书之日起生效。

5. 欧洲委员会秘书长须就所有交存的批准及加入文件通告所有委员会成员及任何加入国家。

第十条

任何缔约方可以明确现时《公约》适用的地域范围，但须向欧洲委员会秘书长提交声明，欧洲委员会须将之通告所有缔约方。

第十一条

1. 任何缔约方可以在现时《公约》生效五年之后的任何时间以向欧洲委员会秘书长提起书面声明的方式退出现时《公约》，欧洲委员会秘书长需将之告知其他缔约方。

2. 该等退出在欧洲委员会秘书长收到退出声明之日的六个月后对有关缔约方生效。

为以下各自政府合法授权签署的代表所见证，签署了现时《公约》。

1954 年 12 月 19 日于巴黎签署，分为英文及法文文本，两种文本有同等效力，构成唯一文本，交存于欧洲委员会档案。秘书长须将认证文本送达每一个签署方及加入国政府。

European Cultural Convention

Paris, 19. XII. 1954

The governments signatory hereto, being members of the Council of Europe,

Considering that the aim of the Council of Europe is to achieve a greater unity between its members for the purpose, among others, of safeguarding and realising the ideals and principles which are their common heritage;

Considering that the achievement of this aim would be furthered by a greater understanding of one another among the peoples of Europe;

Considering that for these purposes it is desirable not only to conclude bilateral cultural conventions between members of the Council but also to pursue a policy of common action designed to safeguard and encourage the development of European culture;

Having resolved to conclude a general European Cultural Convention designed to foster among the nationals of all members, and of such other European States as may accede thereto, the study of the languages, history and civilisation of the others and of the civilisation which is common to them all,

Have agreed as follows:

Article 1

Each Contracting Party shall take appropriate measures to safeguard and to encourage the development of its national contribution to the common cultural heritage of Europe.

Article 2

Each Contracting Party shall, insofar as may be possible:

a. encourage the study by its own nationals of the languages, history and civilisation of the other Contracting Parties and grant facilities to those Parties to promote such studies in its territory; and

b. endeavour to promote the study of its language or languages, history and civilisation in the territory of the other Contracting Parties and grant facilities to the nationals of those Parties to pursue such studies in its territory.

Article 3

The Contracting Parties shall consult with one another within the framework of the Council of Europe with a view to concerted action in promoting cultural activities of European interest.

Article 4

Each Contracting Party shall, insofar as may be possible, facilitate the movement and exchange of persons as well as of objects of cultural value so that Articles 2 and 3 may be implemented.

Article 5

Each Contracting Party shall regard the objects of European cultural value placed under its control as integral parts of the common cultural heritage of Europe, shall take appropriate measures to safeguard them and shall ensure reasonable access thereto.

Article 6

1. Proposals for the application of the provisions of the present Convention and questions relating to the interpretation thereof shall be considered at meetings of the Committee of Cultural Experts of the Council of Europe.

2. Any State not a member of the Council of Europe which has acceded to the present Convention in accordance with the provisions of paragraph 4 of Article 9 may appoint a representative or representatives to participate in the meetings provided for in the preceding paragraph.

3. The conclusions reached at the meetings provided for in paragraph 1 of this article shall be submitted in the form of recommendations to the Committee of Ministers of the Council of Europe, unless they are decisions which are within the competence of the Committee of Cultural Experts as relating to matters of an administrative nature which do not entail additional expenditure.

4. The Secretary General of the Council of Europe shall communicate to the members of the Council and to the government of any State which has acceded to the present Convention any decisions relevant thereto which may be taken by the Committee of Ministers or by the Committee of Cultural Experts.

5. Each Contracting Party shall notify the Secretary General of the Council of

Europe in due course of any action which may be taken by it for the application of the provisions of the present Convention consequent on the decisions of the Committee of Ministers or of the Committee of Cultural Experts.

6. In the event of certain proposals for the application of the present Convention being found to interest only a limited number of the Contracting Parties, such proposals may be further considered in accordance with the provisions of Article 7, provided that their implementation entails no expenditure by the Council of Europe.

Article 7

If, in order to further the aims of the present Convention, two or more Contracting Parties desire to arrange meetings at the seat of the Council of Europe other than those specified in paragraph 1 of Article 6, the Secretary General of the Council shall afford them such administrative assistance as they may require.

Article 8

Nothing in the present Convention shall be deemed to affect:

a. the provisions of any existing bilateral cultural convention to which any of the Contracting Parties may be signatory or to render less desirable the conclusion of any further such convention by any of the Contracting Parties, or

b. the obligation of any person to comply with the laws and regulations in force in the territory of any Contracting Party concerning the entry, residence and departure of foreigners.

Article 9

1. The present Convention shall be open to the signature of the members of the Council of Europe. It shall be ratified, and the instruments of ratification shall be deposited with the Secretary General of the Council of Europe.

2. As soon as three signatory governments have deposited their instruments of ratification, the present Convention shall enter into force as between those governments.

3. With respect to each signatory government ratifying subsequently, the Convention shall enter into force on the date of deposit of its instrument of ratification.

4. The Committee of Ministers of the Council of Europe may decide, by a unanimous vote, to invite, upon such terms and conditions as it deems appropriate, any European State which is not a member of the Council to accede to the present

Convention. Any State so invited may accede by depositing its instrument of accession with the Secretary General of the Council of Europe. Such accession shall take effect on the date of receipt of the said instrument.

5. The Secretary General of the Council of Europe shall notify all members of the Council and any acceding States of the deposit of all instruments of ratification and accession.

Article 10

Any Contracting Party may specify the territories to which the provisions of the present Convention shall apply by addressing to the Secretary General of the Council of Europe a declaration which shall be communicated by the latter to all the other Contracting Parties.

Article 11

1. Any Contracting Party may denounce the present Convention at any time after it has been in force for a period of five years by means of a notification in writing addressed to the Secretary General of the Council of Europe, who shall inform the other Contracting Parties.

2. Such denunciation shall take effect for the Contracting Party concerned six months after the date on which it is received by the Secretary General of the Council of Europe.

In witness whereof the undersigned, duly authorised thereto by their respective governments, have signed the present Convention.

Done at Paris this 19th day of December 1954, in the English and French languages, both texts being equally authoritative, in a single copy which shall remain deposited in the archives of the Council of Europe. The Secretary General shall transmit certified copies to each of the signatory and acceding governments.

促进美洲国家间文化关系公约*

（美洲国家组织1954年3月1日至28日在
加拉加斯召开的第10次泛美会议上签署）

派代表出席第十次泛美会议的各国政府，鉴于对美洲国家组织成员国人民和制度的更多知识和了解将会有助于实现大会召开的目的；并且美洲国家间的教授、老师及学生的交换及鼓励在对形成公共舆论拥有影响力的非政府机构中建立紧密关系就是达成该等目的的适当方式，决议：

对1936年在布宜诺斯艾利斯制定的《关于促进美洲国家间文化关系公约》进行修改并对其精神进行加强，为此目的达成以下条款：

第一条

每年成员国政府都尽量提供一个或多个奖学金，以供其他成员国研究生、教师或拥有同等资格的人士在下一学年享用。奖学金获得者应该根据本《公约》第四条规定的程序予以遴选。尽管有上述规定，其他国际条约或其他法律文件另有规定的，每一成员国政府可以发放更大数量的奖学金以资助研究。

第二条

所发放的每一奖学金须通过适当的机构涵盖奖学金发放国所指定高等教育机构的学费，及教科书、工作材料，以及为支付住宿、基本生活费用的每月补助费用及其他必要的额外开支。到指定机构的旅行费用及返回派出国的旅行费用及旅行中发生的额外旅行费用都应由奖学金获得者或指定政府承担。

第三条

有关评审委员及候选人通知的下一条规定的期间开始的至少一个月以前，每一成员国政府须告知他国准备发放奖学金的领域。

第四条

第一条规定的奖学金须在有关政府以下列方式交换评审员姓名之后方可

---

* 中国社会科学院法学研究所吴峻译。

发放：

每个成员国政府应该向每一个其他成员国政府在东道国学年开始至少六个月前提供包括第一条规定种类候选人姓名的评审委员会名单，并须提供奖学金发放国政府认为每一必要事项的有关信息，但有关政府另有协议的除外。评审委员会名单须具有充足数量的候选人，以供发放奖学金的国家从中选择。后者至少在学年开始三个月之前向提名国政府宣布奖学金的发放及可以领取奖学金的候选人。

候选人的姓名在名单出现次数不得超过两次。奖学金应当为一年期，但可以延长至两年，并可以在特别情形下延长至第三年。如果其他任何国家所建议的候选人名单并没有按照规定的日程提交，一国政府并无义务对该等候选人名单予以考虑。

第五条

如果基于任何理由有必要将奖学金获得者遣送回国，授予奖学金国家政府可以在提名国政府承担费用的情况下进行遣返。

第六条

任何高级缔约方对获取其他国家教授或专家服务抱有兴趣并对之没有具体人选的，可以通过泛美国家联盟取得。泛美国家联盟将该等请求转交予其他国家并将之答复在三个月内回馈予抱有兴趣的国家，后者然后在建议的人选中予以选择。

访问教授或专家应当全力履行其所具体承担的责任。

选派教授或专家的政府需负责每人赴其所委任职位机构的及返回派出国家的旅行费用。

每一个国家的政府须采取必要措施使得访问教授或专家可以取得与其所委任职位相匹配的薪水。派出相关教授或专家的国家政府须就其从东道国领取薪水少于其自派出国领取薪水之间的差额予以补偿。然而，在特定情形下，有关国家政府可以进行其他安排。

第七条

高级缔约方将通过其他方式、尤其是利用假期鼓励教师、艺术家、学生及其他专业人员为了文化的目的在其各自国家间进行交流。

第八条

每个国家政府须制定或建立适当的机构，或委任特定官员负责执行基于该《公约》而承担的义务。

第九条

每个高级缔约方所发布旨在促使遵守本《公约》行政条例的认证副本须送达予其他高级缔约方及泛美国家组织。

第十条

高级缔约方须每年向泛美国家联盟提交一份报告，列明政府根据本《公约》规定条款授予奖学金的人员。该报告须说明奖学金获得者的国籍及其所接受资助的金额及种类。

该报告也应载明根据其他人员交换项目或自费进行大学学习或进行类似研究而来自其他美洲国家人员的信息。

上述报告也应载明教授及专家的信息。

泛美国家联盟须将根据本条所收到报告进行编纂以供缔约方查阅。

第十一条

缔约方宣布本《公约》是基于合作的最高原则而制定，人员交换的范围根据每个国家特有情形而决定。

第十二条

本《公约》并不影响高级缔约方之前订立的相似谅解备忘录，也并不排除其未来可以订立其他该种谅解备忘录。

第十三条

本公约需开放供美洲国家组织成员国签署，并须由签署国根据其各自宪法程序予以批准。

第十四条

原始文本系以英语、法语、葡萄牙语及西班牙语写就，各语言文本具有相同的效力，须交存于泛美国家联盟，后者将认证文本交给各国政府以供批准。批准文件须交存于泛美国家联盟，后者需就该等交存通知签字各国。

第十五条

本《公约》需在批准国依据其交存各自批准文书的顺序而生效。

第十六条

本《公约》须无限期有效，但任何签字国提前一年通知后可以退出，一年期满后对于该退出国不再生效，但对其他签字国仍然有效。退出需通告予泛美国家联盟，后者须就此通知其他签字国。

为作见证，出示形式完善合法全权授权书的以下签名全权代表代表其各自政府在加拉加斯城于一九五四年三月二十九日签署本《公约》。

Convention for the Promotion of Inter – American Cultural Relations

Signed at the Tenth Inter –American Conference
Caracas, March 1 –28, 1954

The governments represented at the Tenth Inter - American Conference,

CONSIDERING:

That greater knowledge and understanding of the peoples and the institutions of the countries members of the Organization of American States will contribute to the realization of the purposes for which the Conference was convened; and

That, among the suitable means for attaining this end, are the exchange of professors, teachers, and students among the American countries and the encouragement of closer relationships among the unofficial agencies that exert an influence on the formation of public opinion,

RESOLVE:

To revise the text and strengthen the spirit of the Convention for the Promotion of Inter - American Cultural Relations, concluded at Buenos Aires in 1936, and to that end agree on the following articles:

Article 1

Every year each government shall award one or more fellowships, in so far as it may be able to do so, for the ensuing scholastic year, which may be granted to graduate students or to teachers or to other persons with equiv alent qualifications from each of the other Member States. The recipients shall be chosen in accordance with the procedure established in Article 4 of this Convention. Notwithstanding the foregoing, each government may award a greater number of fellowships for study if this has been provided in other international agreements or otherwise.

Article 2

Each fellowship shall include, through such agency as may be deemed appropriate, tuition in an institution of higher learning designated by the country awarding the fellowship, as well as textbooks, working materials, and, in addition, a monthly allowance to cover lodging, subsistence, and other necessary additional reexpenses. The expenses of traveling to the designated institution and those of returning to the country of origin and, in addition, an amount for incidental travel expenses during the journey shall be borne by the recipient or by the nominating government.

Article 3

Each government shall notify the others of the fields of study in which it is prepared to award fellowships at least one month before the period referred to in the following article for the transmission of the panels of candidates.

Article 4

The fellowships referred to in Article 1 shall be awarded after the governments concerned exchange panels of names in the following manner:

Each government shall send to each of the other governments, at least 6 months before the opening of the scholastic year in the host country, unless otherwise agreed upon by the interested governments, a panel containing the names of candidates of the categories referred to in Article 1, together with the information regarding each that the government awarding the fellow - ships deems necessary. The panel shall contain a sufficient number of names to permit the country awarding the fellowships to choose from among the candidates. The latter country shall announce the award of the fellowships and the names of the successful candidates to the nominating government at least 3 months before the opening of the scholastic year.

A candidate's name shall not appear on the panels more than twice. The fellowships shall be awarded for one year, but may be extended for a second year and, in exceptional cases, for a third. No government shall be obliged to consider the panel of names of candidates proposed by any other government if it has not been presented in accordance with the schedule indicated.

Article 5

If for any reason it becomes necessary to repatriate the recipient of a fellowship, the government awarding the fellowship may effect the repatriation at the expense of the nominating government.

Article 6

Any of the High Contracting Parties which may be interested in obtaining the services of professors or specialists from other countries and which has not chosen specific individuals may do so through the services of the Pan American Union. The Pan American Union will forward the request to the other countries and will send their replies to the interested country within three months, the latter country then choosing from among the candidates suggested. Visiting professors or specialists shall devote themselves to the duties for which they have been specifically engaged.

The government that is sending the professors or specialists shall provide the expenses of travel of each to the seat of the institution to which he has been appointed, and of return to the country of origin.

Each government shall take the necessary measures for visiting professors or specialists to receive a salary commensurate with the duties which are assigned to them. The government of the country from which the professor or specialist comes shall compensate him for any unfavorable difference between the salary which he is to receive in the host country and that which he has been receiving in the country from which he comes. However, in specific cases, the governments concerned may make other arrangements.

Article 7

The High Contracting Parties will encourage, in other ways, especially during vacation periods, the exchange, for cultural purposes, of teachers, artists, students, and other persons engaged in the professions, between their respective countries.

Article 8

Each government shall designate or create an appropriate organ, or appoint a special officer, to have responsibility for carrying out the obligations assumed by virtue of this Convention.

Article 9

Authenticated copies of the regulations issued by each of the High Contracting Parties to facilitate compliance with this Convention shall be sent to the other

High Contracting Parties and to the Pan American Union.

Article 10

The High Contracting Parties shall transmit annually to the Pan American Union a report enumerating the persons to whom fellowships have been awarded by the governments in accordance with the terms of this Convention. The report shall indicate the nationality of the recipients and the amount of money and the type of assistance which they have received.

This report should likewise include information with regard to persons who have come from other American States and are pursuing university or similar studies in accordance with other exchange - of - persons programs or at their own expense.

The reports referred to above should also include information regard - ing professors and specialists.

The Pan American Union shall compile the reports received under this Article for the information of the High Contracting Parties.

Article 11

The High Contracting Parties declare that this Convention is motivated by the highest principles of cooperation, the extent of the interchange depending upon the circumstances peculiar to each country.

Article 12

This Convention does not affect similar understandings which have been entered into previously by the High Contracting Parties, nor does it exclude the possibility of their entering into other such understandings in the future.

Article 13

This Convention shall remain open for signature by the States Members of the Organization of American States and shall be ratified by the signatory States in accordance with their respective constitutional procedures.

Article 14

The original instrument, the English, French, Portuguese, and Spanish texts of which are equally authentic, shall be deposited with the Pan American Union, which shall transmit certified copies thereof to the governments for purposes of ratification. The instruments of ratification shall be deposited with the Pan American Union, which shall notify the signatory States of such deposit.

Article 15

This Convention shall enter into force between the States that ratify it in the order in which they deposit their respective instruments of ratification.

Article 16

This Convention shall remain in force indefinitely, but may be denounced by any of the signatory States upon one year's notice, at the end of which it shall cease to be in force with respect to the denouncing State, remaining in force for the other signatory States. The denunciation shall be communicated to the Pan American Union, which shall notify the other signatory States of it.

IN WITNESS WHEREOF, the undersigned Plenipotentiaries, whose full powers have been presented and found to be in good and due form, sign this Convention, on behalf of their respective Governments, at the city of Caracas, on March twenty - eight, nineteen hundred and fifty - four.

第二部分　大众传媒、文学艺术与文化产业

Part Ⅱ　Mass Media, Literature & Arts, Cultural Industry

关于大众媒体为推动和平以及增进人权保障、反对种族隔离和煽动战争的国际共识发挥积极作用的基本原则宣言*

（1978 年 11 月 28 日联合国教科文组织大会通过）

前　言

大会

回顾本组织章程，联合国教科文组织的宗旨在于“通过教育、科学及文化来促进各国间之合作，对和平与安全作出贡献，以增进对正义、法治及人权与基本自由之普遍尊重”（第一条第一款）；为了实现该宗旨，教科文组织将努力“便于运用文字与形象促进思想之自由交流”（第一条第二款）。

进一步回顾本组织章程，联合国教科文组织成员国：“人人皆享有充分与平等受教育机会之信念，人人皆有权不受限制地寻求客观真理以及自由交流思想与知识之信念，特同意并决心发展及增进各国人民之间交往手段，并借此种手段之运用促成相互了解，达到对彼此之生活更真实、更全面认识之目的。”（前言第六项）；

回顾联合国宪章中确立的宗旨与原则；

回顾联合国大会于 1948 年通过的《世界人权宣言》，其中第 19 条规定：“人人有权享有主张和发表意见的自由；此项权利包括持有主张而不受干涉的自由；和通过任何媒介和不论国界寻求、接受和传递消息和思想的自由。”并且，联合国大会于 1966 年通过的《公民权利和政治权利国际公约》第 19 条

---

* 中国社会科学院法学研究所吴峻译。

申明了同样的原则，而其第 20 条谴责了鼓吹战争的宣传、鼓吹民族、种族或宗教仇恨的主张，任何构成煽动歧视、敌视或暴力的宣传；

回顾联合国大会于 1965 年通过的《消除一切形式种族歧视国际公约》第四条、联合国大会于 1973 年通过的《禁止并惩治种族隔离罪行国际公约》，加入该等公约的国家承诺采取即时、有效的措施消除一切形式煽动或实施种族歧视的行为，并同意禁止一切鼓励种族隔离罪行、类似种族隔离政策或措施的行为。

回顾联合国大会于 1965 年通过的《关于在青年中促进和平以及相互尊重和理解的宣言》；

回顾联合国就建立国际经济新秩序及呼吁联合国教科文组织在这方面所起的作用；

回顾教科文组织会议于 1966 年通过的《国际文化合作原则宣言》；

回顾联合国大会于 1946 年通过的第 59（I）号决议宣布："信息自由是一项基本人权，是联合国所尊崇所有自由的试金石……作为必要的组成部分，信息自由要求不滥用其特权的意愿和能力。作为一项基本原则，它要求承担无偏见追寻真相及无恶意传播知识的道德义务"；

回顾联合国大会于 1947 年通过的第 110（I1）号决议，对任何形式旨在或者可能激发或煽动任何对和平的威胁、破坏和平或侵略行为的任何宣传予以谴责；

回顾联合国大会于 1947 年通过的第 127（11）号决议，吁请成员国在其宪法程序允许的情形下采取措施，打击散布有可能影响国家间友好关系的虚假或不实报告，并回顾联合国大会就大众传媒及其在增进和平、信任及国家间友好关系方面所发挥作用而通过的其他决议；

回顾联合国教科文组织大会于 1968 年通过的第 9. 12 号决议，重申了联合国教科文组织协助消除殖民主义和种族主义的目标，并回顾大会于 1976 年通过的第 12. 1 号决议，该决议宣布，所有形式及表现的殖民主义、新殖民主义及种族主义均与联合国教科文组织的基本宗旨不符；

回顾联合国教科文组织大会于 1970 年通过的第 4. 301 号决议，涉及信息媒体为了和平及人类福祉而促进国际间理解及合作及反对为战争、种族主义、种族隔离及国家间的仇恨而进行的宣传所做贡献，并注意到大众传媒对实现这些目标所可以作出的基础性贡献；

回顾联合国教科文组织第 20 届大会通过的《种族及种族偏见宣言》；

认识到发展中国家对于建立世界更公正、更有效信息和通信秩序的愿望，认识到现代社会中信息问题的复杂性，解决问题的手段的多样性（联合国教科文组织内部关于这些问题的审议尤其说明了这一点），以及相关各方希望其愿望、观点和文化背景能够得到适当考虑的正当要求；

兹于 1978 年 11 月 28 日宣布该《关于大众媒体为推动和平以及增进人权保障、反对种族隔离和煽动战争的国际共识发挥积极作用的基本原则宣言》。

第一条

加强和平及国际间理解及促进人权、反对种族主义、种族隔离主义及反对战争煽动要求信息传播能够自由地在更广的范围内更平衡地实现。为此目的，大众传媒发挥着首要的作用。该等作用体现在使得信息更有效地反映了所涉事项种种不同方面。

第二条

1. 自由发表意见、进行表达并传递信息作为人权及基本自由的有机组成部分，是增进和平及国际间相互理解的核心要素。

2. 信息向公众开放应当以信息来源及信息渠道多样性来确保，以使得每一个人都可以校验事实的准确性，并能对事件进行客观评估。为此目的，记者须能自由报道并对信息有着最大程度的了解。同样，重要的是大众传媒须对民众及个人的关切有所回应，以促进公众对信息论述的参与。

3. 为增进和平和国际间了解，为促进人权并反对种族主义、种族隔离主义及煽动战争，全世界的大众媒体基于其角色有助于促进人权，有权使得为反对殖民主义、新殖民主义、外国占领及所有形式的种族歧视、压迫而无法在其领土内进行言论表达的人可以表达其意见。

4. 为使大众传媒能够在其活动中促进本宣言规定的原则，须使记者及其他大众传媒的代理人在其本国及海外得到可靠的保障，确保其在执业中能够得到最好的条件。

第三条

1. 大众传媒对于增进和平及国际间了解并反对种族主义、隔离主义及战争煽动都有着重要的贡献。

2. 在反对侵略战争、种族主义及其他出于包括偏见及无知而引发的侵犯人权情形中，大众传媒通过传播有关民众目的、志向、文化及需要的诸多信息，有助于消除民族间的无知和误解，使得一国民众能够体谅其他国民众的需要和愿望，确保所有国家、所有民众及所有个人的权利和尊严得到尊重，无论其种族、性别、语言、宗教或国籍为何，并使人关注诸如贫穷、营养不良及疾病等带给人类痛苦的更大罪恶，以便促使各国制定能够最好地缓解国际紧张局势及使国际争议能够得到和平和公平解决的政策。

第四条

大众传媒在对青年人就和平、公正、自由、相互尊重和理解的精神进行教育方面发挥着至关重要的作用，以便促进人权、人类及所有国家之间的平等权，并推进经济和社会进步。同样，他们对于推广青年一代的意见及志向而言也非常重要。

第五条

为尊重意见、表达及信息自由，并为了信息可以反映所有的观点，必须使那些认为已出版或传播的关于他们的信息严重影响了他们为增进和平及国际了解、促进人权或反对种族主义、种族隔离及鼓吹战争的努力的人的观点得到传播，这一点非常重要。

第六条

信息流通有助于实现公平的制度、持久的和平及发展中国家经济和政治的独立，为了在信息流通中确立新的平衡及更大的互惠性，有必要纠正来源地和目的地为发展中国家及发展中国家间的信息流动中出现的不平等性。为此目的，关键就是其大众传媒应该有条件和资源使得其可以壮大并扩张，并在其发展中国家大众传媒内部及与发达国家大众传媒间进行合作。

第七条

将作为联合国不同机构作出决议所依据的普遍接受目标及原则相关信息尽可能的广泛传播，大众传媒有效促进了和平的增进及国际间理解的深入、人权的促进及公正、平等国际经济秩序的建立。

第八条

专业组织、参与专业培训记者及大众传媒其他代表和帮助他们有责任地履行其职能的人员在制定或者确保道德准则得以实施时，应该对本宣言的原则予以特别重视。

第九条

基于本宣言的精神，国际社会应致力于为信息自由流动以及更为广泛和更为平衡的传播创造条件，为大众传媒记者及其他从业人员在行使其职能时能够得到有效保护创造条件。联合国教科文组织在这方面大有可为。

第十条

1. 在对旨在确保信息自由的宪法规定及所适用的国际文件和协定予以适当尊重的条件下，在全世界建立并维护使得组织和人员专业化参与信息的传播的条件，以便实现本宣言宗旨，必不可少。

2. 重要的是要鼓励信息自由流动并能在更广范围内实现更为平衡的传播。

3. 为此目的，各国有必要促使发展中国家的大众媒体取得足够的条件和资源以便其能发展壮大，有必要支持发展中国家之间及其与发达国家大众媒体的合作。

4. 同样的，在权利平等、互惠及尊重构成人类共同遗产之文化多样性的基础上，国家间进行双边和多边的信息交换至关重要，尤其是要鼓励及发展不同经济和社会制度国家间的信息交换。

第十一条

为使本宣言实现其全部效力，在对成员国法律和行政规定及其他义务予以适当尊重的情形下，有必要根据《世界人权宣言》的有关规定，以及联合国大会于 1966 年通过的《公民权利与政治权利国际公约》中声明的相关原则，保证大众媒体具有良好的工作条件。

Declaration on Fundamental Principles Concerning the Contribution of the Mass Media to Strengthening Peace and International Understanding, to the Promotion of Human Rights and to Countering Racialism, apartheid and incitement to war

28 November 1978

Preamble

The General Conference,

Recalling that by virtue of its Constitution the purpose of Unesco is to 'contribute to peace and security by promoting collaboration among the nations through education, science and culture in order to further universal respect for justice, for the rule of law and for the human rights and fundamental freedoms' (Art. I, 1), and that to realize this purpose the Organization will strive 'to promote the free flow of ideas by word and image' (Art. I, 2),

Further recalling that under the Constitution the Member States of UNESCO, 'believing in full and equal opportunities for education for all, in the unrestricted pursuit of objective truth, and in the free exchange of ideas and knowledge, are agreed and determined to develop and to increase the means of communication between their peoples and to employ these means for the purposes of mutual understanding and a truer and more perfect knowledge of each other's lives' (sixth preambular paragraph),

Recalling the purposes and principles of the United Nations, as specified in its Charter,

Recalling the Universal Declaration of Human Rights, adopted by the General Assembly of the United Nations in 1948 and particularly Article 19 thereof, which provides that 'everyone has the right to freedom of opinion and expression; this right includes freedom to hold opinions without interference and to seek, receive and impart information and ideas through any media and regardless of frontiers'; and the International Covenant on Civil and Political Rights, adopted by the General Assembly of the United Nations in 1966, Article 19 of which proclaims the same principles and Article 20 of which condemns incitement to war, the advocacy of national, racial or religious hatred and any form of discrimination, hostility or violence,

Recalling Article 4 of the International Convention on the Elimination of all Forms of Racial Discrimination, adopted by the General Assembly of the United Nations in 1965, and the International Convention on the Suppression and Punishment of the Crime of Apartheid, adopted by the General Assembly of the United Nations in 1973, whereby the States acceding to these Conventions undertook to adopt immediate and positive measures designed to eradicate all incitement to, or acts of, racial discrimination, and agreed to prevent any encouragement of the crime of apartheid and similar segregationist policies or their manifestations,

Recalling the Declaration on the Promotion among Youth of the Ideals of Peace, Mutual Respect and Understanding between Peoples, adopted by the General Assembly of the United Nations in 1965,

Recalling the declarations and resolutions adopted by the various organs of the United Nations concerning the establishment of a new international economic order and the role Unesco is called upon to play in this respect,

Recalling the Declaration of the Principles of International Cultural Co-operation, adopted by the General Conference of Unesco in 1966,

Recalling Resolution 59 (I) of the General Assembly of the United Nations, adopted in 1946 and declaring:

'Freedom of information is a fundamental human right and is the touchstone of all the freedoms to which the United Nations is consecrated;

Freedom of information requires as an indispensable element the willingness and capacity to employ its privileges without abuse. It requires as a basic discipline the moral obligation to seek the facts without prejudice and to spread knowledge without malicious intent; '

Recalling Resolution 110 (II) of the General Assembly of the United Nations, adopted in 1947, condemning all forms of propaganda which are designed or likely to provoke or encourage any threat to the peace, breach of the peace, or act of aggression,

Recalling resolution 127 (II), also adopted by the General Assembly in 1947, which invites Member States to take measures, within the limits of constitutional procedures, to combat the diffusion of false or distorted reports likely to injure friendly relations between States, as well as the other resolutions of the General Assembly concerning the mass media and their contribution to strengthening peace, trust and friendly relations among States,

Recalling resolution 9. 12 adopted by the General Conference of Unesco in 1968, reiterating Unesco's objective to help to eradicate colonialism and racialism, and resolution 12. 1 adopted by the General Conference in 1976, which proclaims that colonialism, neo - colonialism and racialism in all its forms and manifestations are incompatible with the fundamental aims of Unesco,

Recalling resolution 4. 301 adopted in 1970 by the General Conference of Unesco on the contribution of the information media to furthering international understanding and co - operation in the interests of peace and human welfare, and to countering propaganda on behalf of war, racialism, apartheid and hatred among nations, and aware of the fundamental contribution that mass media can make to the realization of these objectives,

Recalling the Declaration on Race and Racial Prejudice adopted by the General Conference of Unesco at its twentieth session,

Conscious of the complexity of the problems of information in modern society, of the diversity of solutions which have been offered to them, as evidenced in particular by the consideration given to them within Unesco, and of the legitimate desire of all parties concerned that their aspirations, points of view and cultural identity be taken into due consideration,

Conscious of the aspirations of the developing countries for the establishment of a new, more just and more effective world information and communication order,

Proclaims on this twenty - eighth day of November 1978 this Declaration on Fundamental Principles concerning the Contribution of the Mass Media to Strengthening Peace and International Understanding, to the Promotion of Human Rights and to Countering Racialism, Apartheid and Incitement to War.

Article I

The strengthening of peace and international understanding, the promotion of human rights and the countering of racialism, apartheid and incitement to war demand a free flow and a wider and better balanced dissemination of information. To this end, the mass media have a leading contribution to make. This contribution will be the more effective to the extent that the information reflects the different aspects of the subject dealt with.

Article II

1. The exercise of freedom of opinion, expression and information, recognized as an integral part of human rights and fundamental freedoms, is a vital factor in the strengthening of peace and international understanding.

2. Access by the public to information should be guaranteed by the diversity of the sources and means of information available to it, thus enabling each individual to check the accuracy of facts and to appraise events objectively. To this end, journalists must have freedom to report and the fullest possible facilities of access to information. Similarly, it is important that the mass media be responsive to concerns of peoples and individuals, thus promoting the participation of the public in the elaboration of information.

3. With a view to the strengthening of peace and international understanding, to promoting human rights and to countering racialism, apartheid and incitement to war, the mass media throughout the world, by reason of their role, contribute to promoting human rights, in particular by giving expression to oppressed peoples who struggle against colonialism, neo - colonialism, foreign occupation and all forms of racial discrimination and oppression and who are unable to make their voices heard within their own territories.

4. If the mass media are to be in a position to promote the principles of this Declaration in their activities, it is essential that journalists and other agents of the

mass media, in their own country or abroad, be assured of protection guaranteeing them the best conditions for the exercise of their profession.

Article III

1. The mass media have an important contribution to make to the strengthening of peace and international understanding and in countering racialism, apartheid and incitement to war.

2. In countering aggressive war, racialism, apartheid and other violations of human rights which are inter alia spawned by prejudice and ignorance, the mass media, by disseminating information on the aims, aspirations, cultures and needs of all peoples, contribute to eliminate ignorance and misunderstanding between peoples, to make nationals of a country sensitive to the needs and desires of others, to ensure the respect of the rights and dignity of all nations, all peoples and all individuals without distinction of race, sex, language, religion or nationality and to draw attention to the great evils which afflict humanity, such as poverty, malnutrition and diseases, thereby promoting the formulation by States of the policies best able to promote the reduction of international tension and the peaceful and equitable settlement of international disputes.

Article IV

The mass media have an essential part to play in the education of young people in a spirit of peace, justice, freedom, mutual respect and understanding, in order to promote human rights, equality of rights as between all human beings and all nations, and economic and social progress. Equally, they have an important role to play in making known the views and aspirations of the younger generation.

Article V

In order to respect freedom of opinion, expression and information and in order that information may reflect all points of view, it is important that the points of view presented by those who consider that the information published or disseminated about them has seriously prejudiced their effort to strengthen peace and international understanding, to promote human rights or to counter racialism, apartheid and incitement to war be disseminated.

Article VI

For the establishment of a new equilibrium and greater reciprocity in the flow of information, which will be conducive to the institution of a just and lasting peace and to the economic and political independence of the developing countries, it is necessary to correct the inequalities in the flow of information to and from developing countries, and between those countries. To this end, it is essential that their mass media should have conditions and resources enabling them to gain strength and expand, and to co - operate both among themselves and with the mass media in developed countries.

Article VII

By disseminating more widely all of the information concerning the universally accepted objectives and principles which are the bases of the resolutions adopted by the different organs of the United Nations, the mass media contribute effectively to the strengthening of peace and international understanding, to the promotion of human rights, and to the establishment of a more just and equitable international economic order.

Article VIII

Professional organizations, and people who participate in the professional training of journalists and other agents of the mass media and who assist them in performing their functions in a responsible manner should attach special importance to the principles of this Declaration when drawing up and ensuring application of their codes of ethics.

Article IX

In the spirit of this Declaration, it is for the international community to contribute to the creation of the conditions for a free flow and wider and more balanced dissemination of information, and of the conditions for the protection, in the exercise of their functions, of journalists and other agents of the mass media. Unesco is well placed to make a valuable contribution in this respect.

Article X

1. With due respect for constitutional provisions designed to guarantee freedom of information and for the applicable international instruments and agreements, it is indispensable to create and maintain throughout the world the conditions which make it possible for the organizations and persons professionally involved in the dissemination of information to achieve the objectives of this Declaration.

2. It is important that a free flow and wider and better balanced dissemination of information be encouraged.

3. To this end, it is necessary that States facilitate the procurement by the mass media in the developing countries of adequate conditions and resources enabling them to gain strength and expand, and that they support co - operation by the latter both among themselves and with the mass media in developed countries.

4. Similarly, on a basis of equality of rights, mutual advantage and respect for the diversity of the cultures which go to make up the common heritage of mankind, it is essential that bilateral and multilateral exchanges of information among all States, and in particular between those which have different economic and social systems, be encouraged and developed.

Article XI

For this Declaration to be fully effective it is necessary, with due respect for the legislative and administrative provisions and the other obligations of Member States, to guarantee the existence of favourable conditions for the operation of the mass media, in conformity with the provisions of the Universal Declaration of Human Rights and with the corresponding principles proclaimed in the International Covenant on Civil and Political Rights adopted by the General Assembly of the United Nations in 1966.

关于为信息自由流动、教育普及以及更广泛文化交流而使用卫星广播的指导原则宣言*

（联合国教科文组织1972年11月15日通过）

鉴于通讯卫星的发展能够为社会或个人接收广播电视节目确立国际通讯的新维度；鉴于根据其组织章程，联合国教科文组织的宗旨就是通过推动国家以教育、科学及文化的形式进行合作来促进和平及安全，为实现该宗旨，教科文组织将在使用各种大众通讯方式推进各民族之间相互了解及理解的工作中予以合作，并为该目的在必要时提出制定相关国际协定的建议，以促进通过文字或图像表达的思想的自由流动；鉴于《联合国宪章》在联合国宗旨及原则中明确了基于权利平等、不干涉各国内部事务原则上发展国与国友好关系、实现国际在人权及基本自由领域的合作；鉴于《世界人权宣言》宣告每个人都有权利通过任何媒介寻求、接收并发布消息和思想而不受国界的限制，人人都有权接受教育，人人都有权自由参加社会的文化生活，并有权就其为作者的任何科学、文字或艺术产品的精神和物质权益得到保护；鉴于《各国在探索与利用外层空间活动的法律原则的宣言》（1963年12月13日通过的第1962（18）号决议）及1967年《关于各国探索和利用包括月球和其他天体在内外层空间活动的原则条约》（以下简称"外层空间条约"）；鉴于联合国大会于1947年11月3日通过的第110（2）号决议谴责旨在或可能挑起或鼓动对和平进行威胁、破坏或侵略行为的宣传，像在外层空间条约序言中描述的那样，也适用于外层空间；鉴于联合国大会于1961年12月20日通过的第1721D（16）号决议宣布，卫星通讯一旦具备在全球化以及非歧视基础上应用的条件，就应当尽快开放和提供；鉴于联合国教科文组织大会第十

---

* 中国社会科学院法学研究所吴峻译。

四届大会通过了《国际文化合作原则宣言》；鉴于无线电频率是属于各国的有限自然资源，其使用适用《国际电信公约》及其《无线电法规》，分配足够的频率对于因教育、科学、文化及信息目的使用卫星广播至关重要；鉴于联合国大会于1970年12月16日通过的第2733（25）号决议建议成员国、包括广播协会在内的地区及国际组织应当在区域及其他层面促进并鼓励进行国际合作，以便使得所有参与方都可以分享区域卫星广播服务的设置与运营；鉴于同一个决议也吁请联合国教科文组织继续促进为推进教育及培训、科学和文化而使用卫星广播，并与适当政府间组织及非政府组织和广播协会进行协商，以努力解决其职权范围内的问题，联合国教科文组织1972年在巴黎召开的第十七届大会于1972年11月15日通过本《关于为信息自由流动、教育普及以及更广泛文化交流而使用卫星广播的指导原则宣言》：

第一条

对外层空间的利用适用国际法，发展卫星广播须遵循国际法的原则和规定，尤其是《联合国宪章》及外层空间条约。

第二条

1．卫星广播须尊重所有国家的主权及平等地位。

2．卫星广播须不涉足政治，其运营须合理考虑个人及非政府机构被各国及国际法承认的权利。

第三条

1．应该使得所有国家都可以不受歧视地享受到卫星广播的便利，无论其发展程度如何。

2．对卫星广播的使用应基于全球及地区的、政府间及专业方面的国际合作。

第四条

1．卫星广播提供了传播知识并在各民族间促进深入了解的新方式。

2．为实现该等可能，就要求考虑受众的需要和权利，并考虑和平、友谊及民族间合作的目标及经济、社会、文化进步的目标。

第五条

1．卫星广播用于信息自由流动的目标就是要确保在世界各民族间实现不论是发达国家还是发展中国家在内所有国家的新闻能传播到最远的范围。

2．卫星广播使得全世界都可以同时传播新闻，要求用尽一切方法确保所告知公众信息的事实准确性。新闻广播须确定为整个新闻节目承担责任的机构，在适当情形下须就特定的新闻报道说明来源。

第六条

1. 为传播教育进行卫星广播目的就是为了促进教育的推广、提供更多的教育机会、改善学校授课教育的内容，深化对教育者的培训、协助消除文盲现象，并有助于确保终身教育。

2. 每个国家都有权利决定通过卫星向其国民提供教育节目的内容，如果该等节目是同其他国家合作摄制的，有权基于自愿和平等的原则参与其规划和摄制。

第七条

1. 用于促进文化交流之卫星广播的宗旨就是通过以前所未有的规模为受众提供涉及包括艺术表演、体育及其他事件在内的社会、文化生活节目，从而密切各民族间的接触、增进互相间的了解。

2. 文化项目在进一步丰富所有文化的同时，应尊重每一个文化的特色、价值及尊严，并须尊重所有国家和民众将其文化作为人类共同遗产予以保留的权利。

第八条

应鼓励广播电视台及其国家、地区和国际协会在制作及交换方面进行合作，并在包括技术和节目人员培训的卫星广播所有其他方面进行合作。

第九条

1. 为了进一步实现前条规定的目标，成员国有必要在考虑信息自由原则的情形下事先达成或促成实现涉及向传输来源国之外其他国家的民众进行直接卫星广播的协定。

2. 传送商业广告应符合发送国与接收国之间达成的特定协定。

第十条

在准备向其他国家直接播放的节目时，须考虑接收国家法律之间的不同。

第十一条

该宣言的原则须在对人权及基本自由予以合理尊重的前提下予以适用。

Declaration of Guiding Principles on the Use of Satellite Broadcasting for the Free Flow of Information, the Spread of Education and Greater Cultural Exchange

15 November 1972

The General Conference of the United Nations Educational, Scientific and Cultural Organization meeting in Paris at its seventeenth session in 1972,

Recognizing that the development of communication satellites capable of broadcasting programmes for community or individual reception establishes a new dimension in international communication,

Recalling that under its Constitution the purpose of UNESCO is to contribute to peace and security by promoting collaboration among the nations through education, science and culture, and that, to realize this purpose, the Organization will collaborate in the work of advancing the mutual knowledge and understanding of peoples through all means of mass communication and to that end recommend such international agreements as may be necessary to promote the free flow of ideas by word and image,

Recalling that the Charter of the United Nations specifies, among the purposes and principles of the United Nations, the development of friendly relations among nations based on respect for the principle of equal rights, the non - interference in matters within the domestic jurisdiction of any State, the achievement of international co - operation and the respect for human rights and fundamental freedoms,

Bearing in mind that the Universal Declaration of Human Rights proclaims that everyone has the right to seek, receive and impart information and ideas through any media and regardless of frontiers, that everyone has the right to education and that everyone has the right freely to participate in the cultural life of the community, as well as the right to the protection of the moral and material interests resulting from any scientific, literary or artistic production of which he is the author,

Recalling the Declaration of Legal Principles Governing the Activities of States in the Exploration and Use of Outer Space (resolution 1962 (XVIII) of 13 December 1963), and the Treaty on Principles Governing the Activities of States in the Exploration and Use of Outer Space, including the Moon and Other Celestial Bodies, of 1967 (hereinafter referred to as the Outer Space Treaty),

Taking account of United Nations General Assembly resolution 110 (II) of 3 November 1947, condemning propaganda designed or likely to provoke or encourage any threat to the peace, breach of the peace or act of aggression, which resolution as stated in the preamble to the Outer Space Treaty is applicable to outer space; and the United Nations General Assembly resolution 1721 D (XVI) of 20 December 1961 declaring that communication by means of satellites should be available as soon as practicable on a global 'and non - discriminatory basis,

Bearing in mind the Declaration of the Principles of International Cultural Co - operation adopted by the General Conference of UNESCO, at its fourteenth session,

Considering that radio frequencies are a limited natural resource belonging to all nations, that their use is regulated by the International Telecommunications Convention and its Radio Regulations and that the assignment of adequate frequencies is essential to the use of satellite broadcasting for education, science, culture and information,

Noting the United Nations General Assembly resolution 2733 (XXV) of 16 December 1970 recommending that Member States, regional and international organizations, including broadcasting associations, should promote and encourage international co - operation at regional and other levels in order to allow all participating parties to share in the establishment and operation of regional satellite broadcasting services,

Noting further that the same resolution invites UNESCO to continue to promote the use of satellite broadcasting for advancement of education and training, science and culture, and in consultation with appropriate intergovernmental and non - governmental organizations and broadcasting associations, to direct its efforts towards the solution of problems falling within its mandate,

Proclaims on the 15th day of November 1972, this Declaration of Guiding Principles on the Use of Satellite Broadcasting for the Free Flow of Information, the Spread of Education and Greater Cultural Exchange:

Article I

The use of Outer Space being governed by international law, the development of satellite broadcasting shall be guided by the principles and rules of international law, in particular the Charter of the United Nations and the Outer Space Treaty.

Article II

1. Satellite broadcasting shall respect the sovereignty and equality of all States.

2. Satellite broadcasting shall be apolitical and conducted with due regard for the rights of individual persons and non - governmental entities, as recognized by States and international law.

Article III

1. The benefits of satellite broadcasting should be available to all countries without discrimination and regardless of their degree, of development.

2. The use of satellites for broadcasting should be based on international co - operation, world - wide and regional, intergovernmental and professional.

Article IV

1. Satellite broadcasting provides a new means of disseminating knowledge and promoting better understanding among peoples.

2. The fulfillment of these potentialities requires that account be taken of the needs and rights of audiences, as well as the objectives of peace, friendship, and co - operation between peoples, and of economic, social and cultural progress.

Article V

1. The objective of satellite broadcasting for the free flow of information is to ensure the widest possible dissemination, among the peoples of the world, of news of all countries, developed and developing alike.

2. Satellite broadcasting, making possible instantaneous worldwide dissemina-

tion of news, requires that every effort be made to ensure the factual accuracy of the information reaching the public. News broadcasts shall identify the body which assumes responsibility for the news programme as a whole, attributing where appropriate particular news items to their source.

Article VI

1. The objectives of satellite broadcasting for the spread of education are to accelerate the expansion of education, extend educational opportunities, improve the content of school curricula, further the training of educators, assist in the struggle against illiteracy, and help ensure life - long education.

2. Each country has the right to decide on the content of the educational programmes broadcast by satellite to its people and, in cases where such programmes are produced in co - operation with other countries, to take part in their planning and production, on a free and equal footing.

Article VII

1. The objective of satellite broadcasting for the promotion of cultural exchange is to foster greater contact and mutual understanding between peoples by permitting audiences to enjoy, on an unprecedented scale, programmes on each other's social and cultural life including artistic performances and sporting and other events.

2. Cultural programmes, while promoting the enrichment of all cultures, should respect the distinctive character, the value and the dignity of each, and the right of all countries and peoples to preserve their cultures as part of the common heritage of mankind.

Article VIII

Broadcasters and their national, regional and international associations should be encouraged to co - operate in the production and exchange of programmes and in all other aspects of satellite broadcasting including the training of technical and programme personnel.

Article IX

1. In order to further the objectives set out in the preceding articles, it is necessary that States, taking into account the principle of freedom of information, reach or promote prior agreements concerning direct satellite broadcasting to the population of countries other than the country of origin of the transmission.

2. With respect to commercial advertising, its transmission shall be subject to specific agreement between the originating and receiving countries.

Article X

In the preparation of programmes for direct broadcasting to other countries, account shall be taken of differences in the national laws of the countries of reception.

Article XI

The principles of this Declaration shall be applied with due regard for human rights and fundamental freedoms.

关于播发卫星传输节目信号的布鲁塞尔公约*

（联合国教科文组织1974年5月21日于布鲁塞尔通过）

缔约国，注意到发送卫星传送节目信号在数量及涵盖地理范围上都在日益增长，关注到并不存在阻止非授权发送商发送卫星传送节目信号的全球机制，这可能会阻碍卫星通讯的应用，认识到在这方面作者、表演者、录音制品制作商及广播电视机构相关权益的重要性，认为应该建立国际体系，规定措施，以阻止非授权发送商发送卫星传送节目信号，意识到无论如何都不得损害目前有效国际协定的效力，包括《国际电信公约》及其所附《条例》，尤其不应损害1961年10月20日所通过向表演者、录音制品制作商及广播电视机构提供保护的《罗马公约》取得更大的接受度，

达成协定如下：

第一条

为本公约之目的，

（Ⅰ）“信号”系指电子方式产生的传送节目的载体；

（Ⅱ）“节目”系指由图像、声音或两者共同构成的现场或录制材料，为最终发送的目的而体现在信号当中；

（Ⅲ）“卫星”系指在外层空间传输信号的任何装置；

（Ⅳ）“传送信号”系指任何传送节目的信号通过或者传送到卫星上；

（Ⅴ）“衍生信号”系指通过修改传送信号的技术特征，无论是否加入固定的成分，都被认为是衍生信号；

（Ⅵ）“来源机构”系指决定传送信号所承载何种节目的个人或实体；

（Ⅶ）“发送商”系指决定将衍生信号发送与普通公众或其任一部分的个人或实体；

---

* 中国社会科学院法学研究所吴峻译。

（Ⅷ）“发送”系指发送商将衍生信号发送予普通公众或其任一部分的操作。

第二条

（1）每个缔约国保证采取足够措施阻止任何发送商在或者从其领土发送未经授权的节目信号。在来源组织系另一成员国国民而所传送信号为衍生信号的，该义务须适用。

（2）在任何对第一款规定措施之适用予以时间限制的任何国家中，其期间须由国内法规定。在批准、接受或加入之时，或者在有关国内法生效或于之后修改的，在生效或修改的六个月内，须将该等期间书面通知予联合国秘书长。

（3）本条第一款规定的义务并不适用于将有权发送传送信号的发送商已经发送的衍生信号进行的发送。

第三条

本公约并不适用于来源机构意图让大众通过卫星直接接收而传送或通过其代理传送的信号。

第四条

在发送商在其领土发送未经授权传送信号时，下列情形中，第二条第一款规定的义务不得对缔约国适用：

（1）载有传送信号所承载节目的节选，构成对时事的报道，但仅仅在该等节选的告知功能是合理正当的要求，或者

（2）作为引用载有传送信号所承载节目的节选，但该等引用构成合理的做法，并且该等引用的告知功能满足合理正当的要求，

（3）在根据联合国大会成熟做法所认定发展中国家的缔约国领土内载有所传送节目，但该等发送的唯一目的就是为了教育，包括在成人教育和科学研究框架内所进行的教育。

第五条

缔约国不得在本公约对该国生效之前就被要求遵守本公约有关信号发送的规定。

第六条

本公约在任何情况下都不得解释为限制或损害国内法和国际条约中确保予以作者、表演者、录音制品制作商和广播电视机构的保护。

第七条

本公约在任何情况下都不得解释为限制任何缔约国为制止滥用垄断权而适用国内法规定的权利。

第八条

（1）除非以下第二款和第三款另有规定，不允许对本公约进行任何保留。

（2）任何缔约国国内法在1974年5月21日有规定的，可以向联合国秘书长提存书面通知，宣布须考虑以“信号系从另一缔约国传送的”语句代替第二条第一款“来源机构系另一成员国国民”的表述。

（3）

（a）在1974年5月21日限制或拒绝对以有线、线缆或其他类似通讯方式向签约公众发送传输节目信号予以保护的任何缔约国，可以向联合国秘书长提存书面通知，宣布在其国内法限制或拒绝保护的程度之内，对该等发送并不适用本公约。

（b）根据a项规定进行通知提存的任何国家，其国内法发生变动使得依据a项规定所作保留无效或其范围受到限制的，须在该等变动生效后的六个月内向联合国秘书长进行书面通告。

第九条

（1）本公约须保存于联合国秘书长处。在1975年3月31日之前，开放供联合国成员国、与联合国相关联的任何专门机构、国际原子能组织或者《国际法院规约》缔约国予以签署。

（2）本公约有待签署国予以批准或接受。其须向第一款规定的国家开放供加入。

（3）批准、接受及加入文本由联合国秘书长保存。

（4）一个国家在受本公约约束之时，就可以被理解为其能够根据其国内法实施本公约之条款。

第十条

（1）本公约在收到第五项批准、接受或加入文件三个月之后予以生效。

（2）任何国家在本公约第五项批准、接受或加入文件交存之后对本公约予以批准、接受或加入的，本公约须在交存文件三个月之后对该国生效。

第十一条

（1）任何缔约国都可以通过向联合国秘书长交存书面通知而退出本公约。

（2）退出须在收到按照第一款规定交存通知十二个月后生效。

第十二条

（1）本公约应当以英语、法语、俄语及西班牙语的单一文本形式签署，四种语言具有同等效力。

（2）在联合国教科文组织秘书长及世界知识产权组织秘书长与感兴趣国家的政府协商后，可以在阿拉伯语、荷兰语、德语、意大利语和葡萄牙语中确立官方语言。

（3）就下列事项，联合国秘书长须通知第九条第一款规定的国家、联合国教科文组织秘书长、世界知识产权组织秘书长、国际劳工组织秘书长及国际电信联盟秘书长：

（Ⅰ）本公约之签署；

（Ⅱ）批准、接受或加入文件的交存；

（Ⅲ）本公约根据第10条第一款生效的日期；

（Ⅳ）与第二条第二款或第八条第二款和第三款有关的通知交存；

（Ⅴ）退出通知的收悉。

（4）联合国秘书长须向第九条第一款规定的所有国家发送本公约两份经认证的文本。

Convention Relating to the Distribution of Programme – Carrying Signals Transmitted by Satellite

Done at Brussels on May 21, 1974

The Contracting States,

Aware that the use of satellites for the distribution of programme - carrying signals is rapidly growing both in volume and geographical coverage;

Concerned that there is no world - wide system to prevent distributors from distributing programme - carrying signals transmitted by satellite which were not intended for those distributors, and that this lack is likely to hamper the use of satellite communications;

Recognizing, in this respect, the importance of the interests of authors, performers, producers of phonograms and broadcasting organizations;

Convinced that an international system should be established under which measures would be provided to prevent distributors from distributing programme - carrying signals transmitted by satellite which were not intended for those distributors;

Conscious of the need not to impair in any way international agreements already in force, including the International Telecommunication Convention and the Radio Regulations annexed to that Convention, and in particular in no way to prejudice wider acceptance of the Rome Convention of October 26, 1961, which affords protection to performers, producers of phonograms and broadcasting organizations,

Have agreed as follows:

Article 1

For the purposes of this Convention:

(i) "signal" is an electronically - generated carrier capable of transmitting programmes;

(ii) "programme" is a body of live or recorded material consisting of images, sounds or both, embodied in signals emitted for the purpose of ultimate distribution;

(iii) "satellite" is any device in extraterrestrial space capable of transmitting sig nals;

(iv) "emitted signal" or "signal emitted" is any programme - carrying signal that goes to or passes through a satellite;

(v) "derived signal" is a signal obtained by modifying the technical characteristics of the emitted signal, whether or not there have been one or more intervening fixations;

(vi) "originating organization" is the person or legal entity that decides what programme the emitted signals will carry;

(vii) "distributor" is the person or legal entity that decides that the transmission of the derived signals to the general public or any section thereof should take place;

(viii) "distribution" is the operation by which a distributor transmits derived signals to the general public or any section thereof.

Article 2

(1) Each Contracting State undertakes to take adequate measures to prevent the distribution on or from its territory of any programme - carrying signal by any distributor for whom the signal emitted to or passing through the satellite is not intended. This obligation shall apply where the originating organization is a national of another Contracting State and where the signal distributed is a derived signal.

(2) In any Contracting State in which the application of the measures referred to in paragraph (1) is limited in time, the duration thereof shall be fixed by its domestic law. The Secretary - General of the United Nations shall be notified in writing of such duration at the time of ratification, acceptance or accession, or if the domestic law comes into force or is changed thereafter, within six months of the coming into force of that law or of its modification.

(3) The obligation provided for in paragraph (1) shall not apply to the distribution of derived signals taken from signals which have already been distributed by a

distributor for whom the emitted signals were intended.

Article 3

This Convention shall not apply where the signals emitted by or on behalf of the originating organization are intended for direct reception from the satellite by the general public.

Article 4

No Contracting State shall be required to apply the measures referred to in Article 2 (1) where the signal distributed on its territory by a distributor for whom the emitted signal is not intended

(i) carries short excerpts of the programme carried by the emitted signal, consisting of reports of current events, but only to the extent justified by the informatory purpose of such excerpts, or

(ii) carries, as quotations, short excerpts of the programme carried by the emitted signal, provided that such quotations are compatible with fair practice and are justified by the informatory purpose of such quotations, or

(iii) carries, where the said territory is that of a Contracting State regarded as a developing country in conformity with the established practice of the General Assembly of the United Nations, a programme carried by the emitted signal, provided that the distribution is solely for the purpose of teaching, including teaching in the framework of adult education, or scientific research.

Article 5

No Contracting State shall be required to apply this Convention with respect to any signal emitted before this Convention entered into force for that State.

Article 6

This Convention shall in no way be interpreted to limit or prejudice the protection secured to authors, performers, producers of phonograms, or broadcasting organizations, under any domestic law or international agreement.

Article 7

This Convention shall in no way be interpreted as limiting the right of any Contracting State to apply its domestic law in order to prevent abuses of monopoly.

Article 8

(1) Subject to paragraphs (2) and (3), no reservation to this Convention shall be permitted.

(2) Any Contracting State whose domestic law, on May 21, 1974, so provides may, by a written notification deposited with the Secretary - General of the United Nations, declare that, for its purposes, the words "where the originating organization is a national of another Contracting State" appearing in Article 2 (1) shall be considered as if they were replaced by the words "where the signal is emitted from the territory of another Contracting State."

(3) (a) Any Contracting State which, on May 21, 1974, limits or denies protection with respect to the distribution of programme - carrying signals by means of wires, cable or other similar communications channels to subscribing members of the public may, by a written notification deposited with the Secretary - General of the United Nations, declare that, to the extent that and as long as its domestic law limits or denies protection, it will not apply this Convention to such distributions.

(b) Any State that has deposited a notification in accordance with subparagraph (a) shall notify the Secretary - General of the United Nations in writing, within six months of their coming into force, of any changes in its domestic law whereby the reservation under that subparagraph becomes inapplicable or more limited in scope.

Article 9

(1) This Convention shall be deposited with the Secretary - General of the United Nations. It shall be open until March 31, 1975, for signature by any State that is a member of the United Nations, any of the Specialized Agencies brought into relationship with the United Nations, or the International Atomic Energy Agency, or is a party to the Statute of the International Court of Justice.

(2) This Convention shall be subject to ratification or acceptance by the signatory States. It shall be open for accession by any State referred to in paragraph (1).

(3) Instruments of ratification, acceptance or accession shall be deposited with the Secretary - General of the United Nations.

(4) It is understood that, at the time a State becomes bound by this Convention, it will be in a position in accordance with its domestic law to give effect to the provisions of the Convention.

Article 10

(1) This Convention shall enter into force three months after the deposit of the

fifth instrument of ratification, acceptance or accession.

(2) For each State ratifying, accepting or acceding to this Convention after the deposit of the fifth instrument of ratification, acceptance or accession, this Convention shall enter into force three months after the deposit of its instrument.

Article 11

(1) Any Contracting State may denounce this Convention by written notification deposited with the Secretary - General of the United Nations.

(2) Denunciation shall take effect twelve months after the date on which the notification referred to in paragraph (1) is received.

Article 12

(1) This Convention shall be signed in a single copy in English, French, Russian and Spanish, the four texts being equally authentic.

(2) Official texts shall be established by the Director - General of the United Nations Educational, Scientific and Cultural Organization and the Director General of the World Intellectual Property Organization, after consultation with the interested Governments, in the Arabic, Dutch, German, Italian and Portuguese languages.

(3) The Secretary - General of the United Natio ns shall notify the States referred to in Article 9 (1), as well as the Director - General of the United Nations Educational, Scientific and Cultural Organization, the Director General of the World Intellectual Property Organization, the Director - General of the International Labor Office and the Secretary - General of the International Telecommunication Union, of

(i) signatures to this Convention;

(ii) the deposit of instruments of ratification, acceptance or accession;

(iii) the date of entry into force of this Convention under Article 10 (1);

(iv) the deposit of any notification relating to Article 2 (2) or Article 8 (2) or (3), together with its text;

(v) the receipt of notifications of denunciation.

(4) The Secretary - General of the United Nations shall transmit two certified copies of this Convention to all States referred to in Article 9 (1).

欧洲跨境电视公约*

（《欧洲文化公约》成员国及欧盟成员国1989年5月5日于斯特拉斯堡签署，1993年5月1日生效，根据2002年3月1日生效的议定书修正）

前　言

欧洲委员会成员国及《欧洲文化公约》缔约国基于如下原则：

为了实现欧洲委员会的长期愿景，进一步加强其缔约国间的团结一致；为了保卫和实践其缔约国共同的理想和原则，即人类的尊严和平等；为了《欧洲人权公约》中第10条，即实现民主社会和人类进步的基本条件——言论和信息自由；为了重申广播政策的基础，即信息自由流动和广播独立；为了重申广播对文化进步、言论自由、机会均等、多元化的重要性；鉴于信息科技的不断发展将促进跨越国境的信息传导和交流；为了丰富高水平节目的种类和数量，从而促进欧洲的文化产出和交流，满足大众在政治、教育、文化领域的需求，巩固监管框架的基础；考虑到首届欧洲大众传媒政策部长会议宣言及其第2号决议的有关内容和规定；鉴于有必要完善现行欧洲理事会建议中有关电视广告、传媒上的男女平等、电视和无线电广播使用卫星频率，以及促进欧洲视听产品等方面的原则，一致同意以下条款：

第一章　总　则

第1条　目标和宗旨

本公约规定了需要传送的节目服务。公约的宗旨是协助在缔约国之间进

---

* 中国社会科学院法学研究所吴峻译。

行跨境播放和转播电视节目。

第2条　术语解释

为达规范之目的，对本公约所使用的术语定义如下：

“首播”指电视节目通过地面广播、电缆或卫星进行、以编码或未编码形式的首次对大众播放。传输不包括个人点播。

“转播”指广播公司面向大众接收并同时转播完整的电视节目或节目的重要部分。

“广播公司”指对面向大众播放的电视节目拥有编辑权并播放该节目、或者授权第三方完整播放该节目的自然人或法人。

“节目服务”指符合上述定义的指定广播公司提供的所有节目。

“欧洲视听作品”指欧洲籍自然人或法人控制下制作或合作制作的创作作品。

“广告”指为了获得金钱回报或为了宣传进行的公开宣传，从而促进某种服务或者产品的销售或租赁、深化一种意识或者促成广播公司或者广告客户想达到的其他目的。

“电视购物”指为了获得金钱回报而直接对大众提供商品或服务的广播，包括固定资产、权利和负债等等。

“赞助”指直接或间接对节目提供资金支持但不参与制作或广播过程的自然人或法人，从而达到宣传此人的名字、形象或者商标之目的。

第3条　适用范围

本协定适用于能够被另一或多个缔约国接收到的、无论通过电缆、地面广播或卫星。

第4条　接收和重播权

根据《欧洲人权公约》第十条，缔约国应确保言论和信息自由，应确保接收节目的自由，不限制符合本公约规定的节目重播。

第5条　首播方的责任

1. 首播方应确保所有在其管辖领域由广播公司播放的节目符合本公约的规定。

2. 为本公约之目的，本公约中的广播公司指：

——根据第三款规定被认定为设立于缔约国管辖领域的广播公司；

——符合第四款适用范围的广播公司。

3. 为本公约之目的，在下列情形下，一个广播公司可以认定是设立于缔约国境内：

a. 该广播公司的总部设在在该缔约国且其节目时间表系在该缔约国确定；

b. 如果广播公司总部在一个缔约国而其节目表在另一个缔约国确定，应根据该广播公司从事广播活动的大部分人力所在地确认所属缔约国。如果从事广播活动的大部分人力在两个国家均有分布，该广播公司总部所在地为所属国。如果从事广播活动的大部分人力均不在该两国分布，则广播公司设立于其第一次开始依法广播并保持稳定经济上联络的缔约国。

c. 如果广播公司总部在缔约国但是节目表在欧盟缔约国外确定，或者节目表在欧盟缔约国确定但总部在欧盟外，则只要该广播公司大部分广播人力处于该缔约国，即可认为属于该缔约国。

d. 如果根据欧洲议会及欧共体理事会 1997 年 6 月 19 日第 97/36/EC 号《修改欧共体理事会第 89/552/EEC 号〈关于协调成员国进行电视广播活动相关法律、行政法规或行政措施中特定规定之指令〉的指令》第二条第三款的规定，该广播公司被认定设立于欧洲共同体成员国内，该广播公司也会被认定为本公约之目的而设立于该成员国。

4. 如果广播公司不适用第三款规定的，就在下列情形下被认定位于被称为首播缔约国的缔约国管辖境内：

a. 使用该缔约国分配的频率；

b. 虽然并未使用缔约国分配的频率，但使用了属于该缔约国的卫星传输能力；

c. 虽然并未使用缔约国分配的频率及属于该缔约国的卫星传输能力，但的确使用了位于该缔约国的卫星上传服务。

5. 如果首播方不能根据第四款的规定予以认定，常务委员会须根据本公约第 21 条第 1a 款规定对该问题予以考虑。

6. 本公约不得适用于仅仅为非本公约缔约国国家提供电视播映的情形，该等播映且不会被缔约一方或多方的公众以直接或间接的方式接收。

第 6 条 信息提供

1. 广播公司的责任须在每一缔约国有权机关发放的授权或与之达成的合同中或以其他的法律措施予以清楚充分地界定。

2. 有关广播公司的信息需应首播缔约国有权机关的要求予以提供。该等信息至少须包括广播公司的名称或代码、所在地及经营状态，其法定代表的姓名，资本的结构，广播公司正在提供或拟要提供节目服务的性质、宗旨、融资方式。

第二章　节目安排事项

第 7 条　广播公司之责任

1. 涉及形式及内容的所有节目服务事项应当尊重人类的尊严及他人的基本权利。

尤其不能

a. 有伤风化，尤其不能包含色情内容；

b. 不正当地突出暴力或者可能会激起种族仇视。

2. 节目服务的所有项目如果可能不利于儿童及未成年人身体、心理或道德发展的，对其进行时间安排的时候不能因为首播及接收时间使之可能观看该等节目。

3. 广播公司须确保新闻公正地呈现事实和事件，并鼓励舆论的自由形成

第 8 条　回复权

1. 每个首播缔约国须确保每一个自然人或法人无论其国籍、居住地为何，须有机会按照第五条规定的意思就该国领土内广播公司首播的节目有机会行使答复权或寻求其他类似法律或行政救济方式。特别是，该缔约国须确保行使回复权的实际及恰当安排使得该权利可以有效行使。该权利或其他类似法律或行政救济方式的有效行使或落实须在时机和形式方面予以确保。

2. 为此目的，节目服务的名称或者负责节目服务的广播公司名称须在节目服务自身中通过适当方式在惯常间隙中予以明示。

第 9 条　公共查阅信息

每一缔约国须予以审核，并在必要时采取诸如对于公众高度关注的事件引入简报的措施，以便避免公众获知信息的权利由于该缔约国国家管辖领域内存在对该事件进行首播或转播的独家权利而受到损害。

第 9A 条　公众对于重大意义事件的了解

1. 每一缔约国都保有权利采取措施确保其管辖领域的广播公司不会对该缔约国认为具有社会重大意义之事件进行独家播送，而该等独家播送安排会剥夺该缔约国内大部分公众可能通过免费电视频道的实时报道或延后报道而对该等事件予以关注的机会。如果行使该权利，则有关缔约国可以对其认为于社会有重大意义的事件在一清单中予以列明。

2. 缔约国须通过适当方式对《欧洲人权公约》及适当情形下的国内宪法给予的保障予以尊重，该等保障使得其领域内的广播公司不再行使在修订

《修订〈欧洲跨境电视公约〉之协定》生效之日后购得的独家权利，而该等独家权利通过剥夺另一缔约国大部分公众以全部直播或部分直播或基于客观原因为公共利益而有必要或适当全部或部分予以迟延播映的免费电视形式予以关注该缔约国根据第一款规定认定的事件，且须满足下列条件：

a. 实施第一款所规定法律措施的缔约国需制定该缔约国认为对社会具有重大意义的国内或国外事件清单；

b. 该缔约国须在合理有效时间内通过清楚、透明的方式制定清单；

c. 该缔约国须认定这些是否全部或部分通过直播，或在必要或基于公共利益之客观理由的适当情形下，全部或部分迟延播放；

d. 该缔约国采取制定清单的措施须合理，并达到必要的具体程度，使得其他缔约国可以采取本款规定的措施；

e. 制定清单的缔约国须将该清单及相关法律措施通知常务委员会，其时限需由常务委员会确定；

f. 制定清单的缔约国所采取的措施须符合第三款所规定常务委员会指引中的限制，并且须得到常务委员会对该等措施的认可。

基于该款规定的措施需仅仅适用于第三款所规定由常务委员会在年度清单上所公布的事件及在修改协定生效之后所购置的独家权利。

3. 常务委员会每年须：

a. 根据第 2 款 e 项公布成员国所通知列入清单的时间及相应法律措施的合并清单；

b. 在第二款 a 至 e 项规定的要求之外，所制定的回应须经其成员四分之三多数同意方可通过，以避免在本条实施中与相对应欧洲共同体规定之间出现差异。

第 10 条　文化目标

1. 每一首播缔约国在可行及采用适当手段时须确保其管辖领域的广播公司在其进行新闻、体育赛事、竞技、广告、图文电视及电视购物之外首播时间的多数份额要为欧洲作品所保留。在考虑到广播公司对其观众的信息告知、教育、文化及娱乐责任前提下，应当给予适当的标准逐步落实该等份额。

2. 在接收缔约国及首播缔约国之间对于上一款规定产生争议的，应一方缔约国的请求，可以提交常务委员会就有关议题出具咨询意见。该等争议不得提交予第 26 条规定的仲裁程序。

3. 缔约国承诺共同寻求最合适的机制和程序以在广播公司间无歧视地对欧洲制作业的活动及发展予以扶持，尤其是在视听制作产能不发达或语言生僻的国家进行扶持。

4. 缔约国须确保其管辖领域的广播公司不在权利人同意的期间之外播映电影作品。

第 10A 条　媒体多样性

基于本公约所依据的合作及相互协作精神，缔约国须努力避免由其管辖领域的广播公司或任何其他法人或自然人进行第三条意义上的首播或转播这种节目服务以危及媒体多样性。

第三章　广告及电视

第 11 条　一般标准

1. 广告和电视购物需公平、诚信。

2. 广告及电视购物不得误导并不得损害消费者权益。

3. 针对或利用儿童进行广告及电视购物须避免任何可能伤及其权益的内容并对其特殊的倾向予以考虑。

4. 电视购物不得强令未成年人签订货物及服务的销售或租赁合同。

5. 广告商不得对节目内容发挥任何编辑类的影响。

第 12 条　期间

1. 电视购物节目、广告节目及其他形式广告的份额不得超过每天播放时间的 20%，但是第三款规定电视购物栏目除外。广告节目播映时间不得超过每天播映时间的 15%。

2. 按照时间计算的每一小时中广告节目及电视购物节目的份额不得超过 20%。

3. 用于电视购物广告节目之栏目在并非专为电视购物进行的节目服务中播音的，最低不间断时长为 15 分钟。每天最多只能有八个电视购物栏目。其总时长不得超过每天三小时。它们须以视听手段清楚标明其节目性质。

4. 为本条之目的，广告不得包括：

——广播公司就其自身节目及直接来源于该等节目的附属产品进行的宣示；

——免费进行的基于公共利益及慈善吁请的宣示。

第 13 条　形式及描述

1. 广告及电视购物须在节目服务中通过视觉或听觉手段清楚地表明其性质，与其他内容予以区分。原则上，广告及电视购物节目须予以整段播映。

2．广告及电视购物不得使用隐形手段进行。

3．不允许伪装进行广告及电视购物，尤其是不得为了广告目的在节目中展示商品或服务。

4．广告及电视购物不得主要以通常播送新闻及时事节目的人员以影像或声音的方式主导。

第 14 条　插入广告及电视购物

1．广告及电视购物须插入节目间隔之中。只要满足本条第二款之第五款的条件，广告及电视购物节目也可以插入节目进行当中，只要节目的完整性及价值和权利人的权利不受损害。

2．在自动形成的部分组成的节目或者体育节目及有类似结构的事件和表演的间隔中，广告及电视购物节目须仅仅在该等部分之间或在间隔之中方可插入。

3．诸如影片及电视电影（系列剧、连续剧、轻松娱乐节目及纪录片除外）等视听作品的传播可以在每一个完整期间为 45 分钟的节目中中断一次，但该等节目的播放时长须超过 45 分钟。如果播放时长比两个或者更多 45 分钟的节目完整期间至少多 20 分钟的话，可以再次予以中断。

4．第二款涵盖范围之外的节目被广告或电视购物节目中断的，在该节目中两个连续广告或电汇购物节目中断的间隔时间至少要有 20 分钟。

5．在任何宗教布道播音中不得插入广告及电视购物。新闻及时事节目、纪录片、宗教节目及儿童节目的播映时长少于 30 分钟的，不得为广告或电视购物所中断。如果其播映时间是 30 分钟或更长，前一款规定须适用。

第 15 条　特殊商品的广告及电视购物

1．不允许烟草商品的广告及电视购物。

2．所有种类的酒精饮料广告及电视购物须符合下列规则：

a．不得特别以未成年人为对象，在广告或电视购物中消费酒精饮料的人不得表现为未成年人；

b．不得将体育表演或驾驶与酒精消费联系在一起；

c．不得宣称酒精具有治疗作用，也不得宣称酒精具有兴奋、镇静作用或可以作为解决个人问题的手段；

d．不得鼓励对酒精的大量消耗，或者将戒酒或适量饮酒描述为负面形象；

e．不得对酒精饮料的成分予以不正当的强调。

3．不允许播出在首播缔约国只能通过医疗处方提供的药品及治疗的广告。

4. 其他所有的药品及治疗的广告须清楚地表明其性质、诚信、真实并可以予以验证，须符合保护个人免受伤害的所有要求。

5. 不允许就药品及治疗进行电视购物。

第16条　特别针对单一缔约国进行的广告及电视购物

1. 为避免扭曲竞争及危及缔约国电视体系，广告及电视购物特别通过一些频率针对首播缔约国之外单一缔约国观众的，不得规避该特别针对缔约国有关电视广告及电视购物的规则。

2. 前一款规定不适用于

a. 有关规则规定对该缔约国管辖范围内广播公司所首播广告及电视购物与另一缔约国管辖范围内广播公司、任何其他法人或自然人所首播广告及电视购物进行区别对待的；或者

b. 有关缔约国已经在该领域达成双边或多边协定。

第四章　审　　查

第17条　一般标准

1. 当节目或一系列节目整个或部分基于赞助，就须通过在节目开始或结束的部分以适当的字幕予以清楚说明。

2. 所赞助节目的内容及时间安排不得在任何情况下受到赞助商的影响，以影响广播公司在节目方面的责任及编辑独立性。

3. 所赞助节目不得鼓励赞助商商品或服务的销售、购置或租赁，尤其不得通过对该等节目中的这些商品或服务予以特别促销的说明。

第18条　禁止的赞助

1. 节目不得接受基本活动系第五条所禁止予以进行广告和电视购物的商品制造或销售或服务提供的自然人或法人的赞助。

2. 其活动包括药品制造或销售或治疗的公司可以通过推介其名称、商号、图像或公司活动的方式对节目予以赞助，但不得以任何方式提及首播缔约国规定只能通过处方提供的药品或特定治疗。

3. 禁止对新闻及时事节目予以赞助。

第四 A 章　仅仅为了自我推介或电视购物而进行的节目服务

第 18A 条　仅仅为了自我推销而进行的节目服务

1. 本公约规定须准用于仅仅为了自我推销而进行的节目服务。

2. 其他形式的广告仅在涉及第 12 条第一款及第二条限定的服务方可进行。

第 18B 条　仅仅限于电视购物而提供的节目服务

1. 本公约规定须准用于仅限于电视购物而提供的节目服务。

2. 须允许就满足第 12 条第一款规定限制的服务予以广告，第 12 条第二款并不适用。

第五章　相互协助

第 19 条　缔约国之间进行合作

1. 缔约国承诺互相提供协助，以实施本公约。

2. 为此目的：

a. 每一缔约国须制定一个或多个政府机构，并将其名称及地址在该缔约国交存其批准、接受、许可或加入文件时告知欧洲委员会秘书长；

b. 每一个制定了不止一个政府机构的缔约国须在其 a 项的通知中说明每一政府机构的职权。

3. 缔约国指定的政府机构须：

a. 提供本公约第六条第二款规定的信息；

b. 应另一缔约国所指定机构请求提供公约涵盖领域中国内法及实践做法的相关信息；

c. 只要有效并可增强为实施本公约采取措施效力的，与其他缔约国指定的政府机构合作；

d. 对另一缔约国提出因实施本公约产生的任何困难予以考虑。

第六章　常务委员会

第 20 条　常务委员会

1. 为本公约之目的，须设立常务委员会。

2. 每一缔约国可以委派一名或多名代表列席常务委员。每一代表团须有一票投票权。在其职权范围内，欧洲共同体须行使的投票权数目与其加入本公约缔约国的数目相一致；欧洲共同体不得在其有关成员国已经行使其权利的情况下行使投票权，反之亦然。

3. 第 29 条第一款规定任何并非本公约缔约国的国家可以通过观察员在常务委员会中得以代表。

4. 常务委员会可以为了履行其职责而寻求专家意见。它可以主动或应有关机构的要求邀请在本公约涵盖领域具有技术资格的任何国际或国内、政府或非政府组织在其某次会议或某次会议的部分以观察员身份出席。

5. 常务委员会须由欧洲委员会秘书长召集。其第一次会议须在本公约生效之日起的六个月内举行。之后，只要三分之一的缔约国或者欧洲委员会部长理事会要求，或者欧洲委员会秘书长根据第 23 条第二款规定主动提议，或者一方或多方缔约国根据第 21 条 c 项及第 25 条第二款的规定提出请求的，都须举行会议。

6. 大多数成员国就构成举行常务委员会会议的法定人数。

7. 满足第 9A 条第 3 款 b 项、第 23 条第三款的前提下，常务委员会的决定须以出席成员的四分之三多数通过。

8. 在符合本公约规定的前提下，常务委员会须制定其自己的《程序规则》。

第 21 条　常务委员会职能

1. 常务委员会负责对本公约进行下列适用。它可以：

a. 向缔约国提出适用本公约的建议；

b. 建议对公约作出任何必要的修改并审核根据第 23 条规定提出的修改方案；

c. 因一个或多个缔约国请求而对公约的解释所提出的问题予以审核；

d. 尽全力确保根据第 25 条提交的任何困难能够得到友好解决；

e. 向部长委员会就邀请第 29 条第一款规定之外的国家加入本公约而提出建议；

f. 就第 24A 条第二款 c 项规定的权利滥用提供意见。

2. 另外，常务委员会须：

a. 制定第 9A 条第三款 b 项所规定的指引，以便就公众了解对社会有重大意义事件的本公约规定之实施与相应的欧洲共同体规定出现不一致的情形；

b. 就缔约国按照第 9A 条第二款规定认为属于对社会有重大意义之国内

或国际事件制定其清单的措施发表意见；

c. 每年根据第 9A 条第二款 e 项发布缔约国所通知列入清单事件及相应措施的合并清单。

第 22 条　常务委员会报告

每个会议之后，常务委员会须就其讨论及决定向缔约国及欧洲委员会部长理事会提交报告。

第七章　修　　改

第 23 条　修改

1. 任何缔约国可以提出修改本公约的建议。

2. 任何修改建议须向欧洲委员会秘书长予以通知，后者须将之通告予欧洲委员会成员国、《欧洲文化公约》其他成员国、欧洲共同体及任何加入公约或根据第 30 条规定受邀加入本公约的任何非成员国。欧洲委员会秘书长须最早在就建议发出通告之日两个月后召集常务委员会会议。

3. 常务委员会须审查任何修改建议并须将经常务委员会四分之三多数通过的文本提交予部长委员会予以批准。在获批后，该等文本须提交予缔约国供其接受。

4. 任何修改须在所有缔约国将其对之接受通知之予秘书长后的第三十天开始生效。

5. 然而，部长理事会在和常务委员会协商后可以作出决定，特定修改在其提交供接受之日起的两年期间届满后生效，除非缔约国已经通知欧洲委员会秘书长其拒绝该等修改的生效。该等拒绝一旦进行了通知，该等修改在作出该等通知的公约缔约国向欧洲委员会秘书长提交接受文件后的次日生效。

6. 部长理事会已经批准了修改但并没有根据第四款或第五款的规定生效的，国家或欧洲共同体不得在不接受该等修改的同时做出接受本公约的意思表示。

第八章　违约责任

第 24 条　对本公约的违反

1. 缔约国发现违法本公约情形的，须向首播缔约国通知该等违反公约的情形，两国须尽力基于第 19、25 及 26 条的规定克服困难。

2. 对公约的违反情形具有明显、严重及重大性质，因其重大的公众关切并涉及第七条第一款或第二款、第 12 条、第 13 条第一款第一句、第 14 条或第 15 条的第一款或点三款，并且在通知后的两个星期依然存在的，接受缔约国可以临时中止对涉及节目服务的转播。

3. 在所有其他违反情形中，第四款规定的除外，接受缔约国可以在违约情形持续的情形下在发出通知后临时中止所涉节目服务达八个月。

4. 违约情形系违反第七条第三款、第八条、第九条或第十条的，不得进行临时中止转播。

第 24A 条　本公约规定权利的滥用

1. 广播公司的节目服务整个或部分针对对其享有管辖权之外缔约国（“接受缔约国”）领土且该广播公司设立之目的就是为了规避其如属于该另外缔约国管辖范围内本应适用的、本公约涵盖领域之内法律的，就构成权利滥用。

2. 缔约国一方指称该等滥用的，须适用以下程序：

a. 有关缔约国须尽力对之友好解决；

b. 三个月内无法予以友好解决的，接收缔约国须将该事项提交予常务委员会；

c. 听取有关缔约国的意见后，常务委员会须在将该事项提交之日起的六个月内作出意见，决定是否构成权利滥用，并对所涉缔约国予以相应告知。

3. 常务委员会认定构成权利滥用的，广播公司所认定须接受其管辖的缔约国须采取适当措施对该等权利滥用予以救济，并须将该等措施向常务委员会予以通告。

4. 广播公司被认定接受管辖的缔约国未能在六个月内采取第三款所规定措施的，有关缔约国可以提起公约第 26 条第二款及附件规定的仲裁程序。

5. 接收缔约国不得在仲裁程序完结之前对所涉节目服务采取任何措施。

6. 根据本条规定拟订或采取的措施须遵守《欧洲人权公约》第 10 条的规定。

第九章　争议解决

第 25 条　协商

1. 因适用本公约而产生困难的，有关缔约国须尽力予以友好解决。

2. 非所涉缔约国之一予以拒绝，常务委员会可以依各有关方决定而对该问题进行审查，以便尽快达成令人满意的解决方案。并在适当情形下就此形成咨询意见。

3. 每一所涉缔约国承诺毫不迟延地向常务委员会提供为根据前款规定行使其职能所必要的所有信息及设施。

第 26 条　仲裁

1. 如相关缔约国不能根据第 25 条的规定解决争议，他们可以基于共同协议将之提交仲裁，其程序请见本公约附件之规定。首次要求启动协商程序六个月内达成该等协议的，可以应一方缔约国的请求而将争议提交仲裁。

2. 任何缔约国都可以在任何时间宣布其认可任何其他接受同等义务的缔约国就适用本公约附件所规定仲裁程序的适用是强制性的、当然而然的并且不需要特别协议。

第十章　其他国际协定及缔约国的内国法

第 27 条　其他国际协定或安排

1. 作为欧洲共同体成员的缔约国而言，就其相互之间的关系须适用共同体规则而不适用基于本公约而制定的规则，除非并没有共同体规则能适用于所涉及的特定事项。

2. 本公约并不阻止缔约国达成国际协定，以完善并发展本公约规定或者将其适用范围予以扩张。

3. 对于双边协定，本公约不得改变缔约国基于该等协定而产生的权利和义务，而该等权利义务并不影响其他缔约国基于本公约享受其权利及履行其义务。

第 28 条　公约及缔约国内国法之间的关系

本公约并不阻止缔约国就根据第五条而认定受其管辖的广播公司进行首播节目服务适用比本公约规定更为严格、详尽的规定。

第十一章　最后条款

第 29 条　签署及生效

1. 本公约开放供欧洲委员会成员国及《欧洲文化公约》其他缔约国和欧洲共同体签署。该公约尚待批准、接受及许可。批准、接受或许可文件须提交予欧洲委员会秘书长。

2. 本公约在至少包括五个欧洲委员会成员国在内的七个国家根据前一款规定表达其接受公约意愿之日后三个月期间届满后一月的第一天开始生效。

3. 一国可以于签署之时或在本公约对该国生效之日前的任何时间宣布公约对其暂时适用。

4. 对于第一款提及的任何国家或者欧洲共同体而言，其在之后表示接受本公约的，本公约须在其提交批准、接受或许可文件之日后三个月期间届满后一月的第一天开始生效。

第 30 条　非成员国加入

1. 本公约生效后，欧洲委员会部长理事会在经过与缔约国协商之后可以通过按照《欧洲委员会规章》第 20 条 d 项规定的多数决定及有权出席部长理事会国家的一致同意而邀请任何其他国家加入本公约。

2. 对于任何加入国而言，本公约于将加入文件提交予欧洲委员会秘书长之日后三个月期间届满后一月的第一日生效。

第 31 条　适用领土

1. 任何国家在签署或提交其批准、接受、许可或加入文件时具体说明本公约须适用的领土。

2. 任何国家可以在之后通过向欧洲委员会秘书长提交声明的方式将公约的适用扩展至其声明中说明的任何其他领土。对于该等领土，公约于秘书长收到该声明之日后三个月期间届满后一月的第一日开始生效。

3. 根据前两款规定作出声明可以通过向秘书长发送通知的方式就该等声明中说明的任何领土予以撤回。该等撤回于秘书长收到该通知之日后三个月期间届满后一月的第一日生效。

第 32 条　保留

1. 签署或提交批准、接受、许可或加入文件之时，任何国家可以宣布保留在其领土上根据规定限制含有酒精饮料广告且不符合其国内法律规定的节目服务予以转播的权利。

不得进行其他保留。

2. 根据上一款规定作出的保留不得成为拒绝的对象。

3. 任何缔约国根据第一款作出保留的，可以通过向欧洲委员会秘书长发送通知的方式予以全部或部分撤销。该撤销自秘书长收到该等通知之日起开始生效。

4. 根据第一款规定作出保留的缔约国不得就所保留条款适用于任何其他缔约国而主张权利；然而，如果其保留系部分或有条件做出，它可以按照自己接受该条款的程度对其他缔约国主张该条款的适用。

第 33 条 退出

1. 任何缔约国可以在任何时间通过向欧洲委员会秘书长予以通知的方式退出本公约。

2. 该等退出须于秘书长收到该通知之日后六个月期间届满后一月的第一日生效。

第 34 条 通知

欧洲委员会秘书长须向欧洲委员会成员国、《欧洲文化公约》其他成员国、欧洲共同体及已经加入或已获邀加入本公约的任何国家通报：

a. 任何作出的签署；

b. 提交的任何批准、接受、许可或加入文件；

c. 根据第 29 条、第 30 条及第 31 条本公约生效的日期；

d. 根据第 22 条规定准备的任何报告；

e. 与本公约有关的任何其他行为、声明、通知或通告。

为以下各自合法授权签署的代表所见证，签署了本公约。

1989 年 5 月 5 日于斯特拉斯堡签署，分为英文及法文文本，两种文本有同等效力，构成唯一文本，交存于欧洲委员会档案。秘书长须将认证文本传送予每一个欧洲委员会成员国、《欧洲文化公约》其他缔约国、欧洲共同体及获邀加入本公约的任何国家。

附件

仲裁

1. 仲裁要求须通告予欧洲委员会秘书长。它须载有争议对方的名称及争议事项。秘书长应当将所收到信息通告予公约所有缔约国。

2. 在两个缔约国之间发生争议而其中之一是欧洲共同体成员国的，后者自己就是缔约国之一，仲裁请求既针对该成员国也针对共同体，后两者须共同在接到要求的一个月之内通知秘书长，说明成员国还是共同体还是两者共同成为争议一方。在上述时限内没有予以通知的，为了适用仲裁庭组成及程序规定的目的，成员国及共同体须被认为同一方当事人。同样的规则也适用于成员国及共同体共同作为争议一方的情形。在本款规定的情形下，第四款第一句所规定一月的时限之后可以延长为两个月。

3. 仲裁庭须由三个成员组成，争议每一方当事人须指定一名仲裁员；这样委任的仲裁员须经共同协议指定，而第三名仲裁员须为仲裁庭主席。后者不得为争议当事方之国民，其惯常居所也不在当事方之领土内，也不是当事方的雇员，也没有以其他身份处理该案。

4. 欧洲委员会秘书长通告要求后一个月内，如果当事人一方还没有指定仲裁员的，应另一方要求由欧洲人权法院院长在接下来的一个月期间对另一名仲裁员予以指定。院长不能指定或系争议一方国民的，由副院长或者法院最高级别的法官在有能力且并非争议一方国民的情形下予以委任。在第二名仲裁员委任之后的一个月期间内，如果仲裁庭主席未得到指定，则适用同样的程序。

5. 第三款及第四款的规定须适用以便在必要时填补任何空缺。

6. 两个或多个缔约国通过协议认定他们具有共同利益的须共同指定一名仲裁员。

7. 争议方及常务委员会须向仲裁庭提供为程序有效进行而需要的所有设施。

8. 仲裁庭须指定其自己的《程序规则》。应通过成员的多数投票而作出决定。仲裁裁决须为终局性并具有约束力。

9. 仲裁庭作出的裁决应通知予欧洲委员会秘书长，后者将之通告予本公约所有缔约国。

10. 争议每一方须承担所指定仲裁员的费用；该等当事方应平摊其他仲裁员的费用及该仲裁发生的费用。

European Convention on Trans – frontier Television

Strasbourg, 5. V. 1989

Text amended according to the provisions of the Protocol (ETS No. 171) which entered into force, on 1 March 2002.

Preamble

The member States of the Council of Europe and the other States party to the European Cultural Convention, signatory hereto,

Considering that the aim of the Council of Europe is to achieve a greater unity between its members, for the purpose of safeguarding and realising the ideals and principles which are their common heritage;

Considering that the dignity and equal worth of every human being constitute fundamental elements of those principles;

Considering that the freedom of expression and information, as embodied in Article 10 of the Convention for the Protection of Human Rights and Fundamental Freedoms, constitutes one of the essential principles of a democratic society and one of the basic conditions for its progress and for the development of every human being;

Reaffirming their commitment to the principles of the free flow of information and ideas and the independence of broadcasters, which constitute an indispensable basis for their broadcasting policy;

Affirming the importance of broadcasting for the development of culture and the free formation of opinions in conditions safeguarding pluralism and equality of opportunity among all democratic groups and political parties;

Convinced that the continued development of information and communication technology should serve to further the right, regardless of frontiers, to express, to seek, to receive and to impart information and ideas whatever their source;

Being desirous to present an increasing range of choice of programme services for the public, thereby enhancing Europe's heritage and developing its audiovisual creation, and being determined to achieve this cultural objective through efforts to increase the production and circulation of high - quality programmes, thereby responding to the public's expectations in the political, educational and cultural fields;

Recognising the need to consolidate the common broad framework of regulation;

Bearing in mind Resolution No. 2 and the Declaration of the 1st European Ministerial Conference on Mass Media Policy;

Being desirous to develop the principles embodied in the existing Council of Europe Recommendations on principles on television advertising, on equality between women and men in the media, on the use of satellite capacity for television and sound radio, and on the promotion of audiovisual production in Europe,

Have agreed as follows:

CHAPTER I – GENERAL PROVISIONS

Article 1 – Object and purpose

This Convention is concerned with programme services embodied in transmissions. The purpose is to facilitate, among the Parties, the transfrontier transmission and the retransmission of television programme services.

Article 2 – Terms employed (1)

For the purposes of this Convention:

a. "*Transmission*" means the initial emission by terrestrial transmitter, by cable, or by satellite of whatever nature, in encoded or unencoded form, of television programme services for reception by the general public. It does not include communication services operating on individual demand;

b. "*Retransmission*" signifies the fact of receiving and simultaneously transmitting, irrespective of the technical means employed, complete and unchanged television programme services, or important parts of such services, transmitted by broadcasters for reception by the general public;

c. "*Broadcaster*" means the natural or legal person who has editorial responsibility for the composition of television programme services for reception by the general public and transmits them or has them transmitted, complete and unchanged, by a third party;

d. "*Programme service*" means all the items within a single service provided by a given broadcaster within the meaning of the preceding paragraph;

e. "*European audiovisual works*" means creative works, the production or co-production of which is controlled by European natural or legal persons;

f. "*Advertising*" means any public announcement in return for payment or similar consideration or for self-promotional purposes, which is intended to promote the sale, purchase or rental of a product or service, to advance a cause or idea, or to bring about some other effect desired by the advertiser or the broadcaster itself;

g. "*Tele-shopping*" means direct offers broadcast to the public with a view to the supply of goods or services, including immovable property, rights and obligations in return for payment;

h. "*Sponsorship*" means the participation of a natural or legal person, who is not engaged in broadcasting activities or in the production of audiovisual works, in the direct or indirect financing of a programme with a view to promoting the name, trademark, images or activities of that person.

Article 3 – Field of application

This Convention shall apply to any programme service transmitted or retransmitted by entities or by technical means within the jurisdiction of a Party, whether by cable, terrestrial transmitter or satellite, and which can be received, directly or indirectly, in one or more other Parties.

Article 4 – Freedom of reception and retransmission

The Parties shall ensure freedom of expression and information in accordance with Article 10 of the Convention for the Protection of Human Rights and Fundamental Freedoms and they shall guarantee freedom of reception and shall not restrict the retransmission on their territories of programme services which comply with the terms of this Convention.

Article 5 – Duties of the transmitting Parties (1)

1. Each transmitting Party shall ensure that all programme services transmitted by broadcasters within its jurisdiction comply with the terms of this Convention.

2. For the purposes of this Convention, a broadcaster within the jurisdiction of a Party is:

- a broadcaster who is deemed to be established in that Party according to paragraph 3;
- a broadcaster to whom paragraph 4 applies.

3. For the purpose of this Convention, a broadcaster shall be deemed to be established in a Party, hereinafter referred to as "transmitting Party" in the following cases:

a. the broadcaster has its head office in that Party and the decisions on programme schedules are taken in that Party;

b. if a broadcaster has its head office in one Party but decisions on programme schedules are taken in another Party, it shall be deemed to be established in the Party where a significant part of the workforce involved in the pursuit of the television broadcasting activity operates; if a significant part of the workforce involved in the pursuit of the television broadcasting activity operates in each of those Parties, the broadcaster shall be deemed to be established in the Party where it has its head office; if a significant part of the workforce involved in the pursuit of the television broadcasting activity operates in neither of those Parties, the broadcaster shall be deemed to be established in the Party where it first began broadcasting in accordance with the system of law of that Party, provided that it maintains a stable and effective link with the economy of that Party;

c. if a broadcaster has its head office in a Party but decisions on programme schedules are taken in a State which is not Party to this Convention, or vice - versa, it shall be deemed to be established in the Party concerned, provided that a significant part of the workforce involved in the pursuit of the television broadcasting activity operates in that Party;

d. if, when applying the criteria of paragraph 3 of Article 2 of Directive 97/36/EC of the European Parliament and of the Council of 19 June 1997 amending Council Directive 89/552/EEC on the co - ordination of certain provisions laid down by law, regulation or administrative action in member States concerning the pursuit of television broadcasting activities, a broadcaster is deemed to be established in a member State of the European Community, that broadcaster shall also be deemed to be established in that State for the purposes of this Convention.

4. A broadcaster to whom the provisions of paragraph 3 are not applicable is deemed to be within the jurisdiction of a Party, so - called transmitting Party, in the following cases:

a. it uses a frequency granted by that Party;

b. although it does not use a frequency granted by a Party it does use a satellite capacity appertaining to that Party;

c. although it uses neither a frequency granted by a Party nor a satellite capacity appertaining to a Party it does use a satellite up - link situated in that Party.

5. If the transmitting Party cannot be determined according to paragraph 4, the Standing Committee shall consider this issue according to Article 21, paragraph 1a, of this Convention, in order to determine this Party.

6. This Convention shall not apply to television broadcasts intended exclusively for reception in States which are not Party to this Convention, and which are not received directly or indirectly by the public in one or more Parties.

Article 6 – Provision of information

1. The responsibilities of the broadcaster shall be clearly and adequately specified in the authorisation issued by, or contract concluded with, the competent authority of each Party, or by any other legal measure.

2. Information about the broadcaster shall be made available, upon request, by the competent authority of transmitting Party. Such information shall include, as a minimum, the name or denomination, seat and status of the broadcaster, the name of the legal representative, the composition of the capital, the nature, purpose and mode of financing of the programme service the broadcaster is providing or intends providing.

CHAPTER II – PROGRAMMING MATTERS

Article 7 – Responsibilities of the broadcaster

1. All items of programme services, as concerns their presentation and content, shall respect the dignity of the human being and the fundamental rights of others.

In particular, they shall not:

a. be indecent and in particular contain pornography;

b. give undue prominence to violence or be likely to incite to racial hatred.

2. All items of programme services which are likely to impair the physical, mental or moral development of children and adolescents shall not be scheduled when, because of the time of transmission and reception, they are likely to watch them.

3. The broadcaster shall ensure that news fairly presents facts and events and encourages the free formation of opinions.

Article 8 – Right of reply (1)

1. Each transmitting Party shall ensure that every natural or legal person, regardless of nationality or place of residence, shall have the opportunity to exercise a right of reply or to seek other comparable legal or administrative remedies relating to programmes transmitted by a broadcaster within its jurisdiction, within the meaning of Article 5. In particular, it shall ensure that timing and other arrangements for the exercise of the right of reply are such that this right can be effectively exercised. The effective exercise of this right or other comparable legal or administrative remedies shall be ensured both as regards the timing and the modalities.

2. For this purpose, the name of the programme service or of the broadcaster responsible for this programme service shall be identified in the programme service itself, at regular intervals by appropriate means.

Article 9 – Access of the public to information (1)

Each Party shall examine and, where necessary, take legal measures such as introducing the right to short reporting on events of high interest for the public to avoid the right of the public to information being undermined due to the exercise by a broadcaster within its jurisdiction of exclusive rights for the transmission or retransmission, within the meaning of Article 3, of such an event.

Article *9bis* - Access of the public to events of major importance (2)

1. Each Party retains the right to take measures to ensure that a broadcaster within its jurisdiction does not broadcast on an exclusive basis events which are regarded by that Party as being of major importance for society in such a way as to deprive a substantial proportion of the public in that Party of the possibility of following such events by live coverage or deferred coverage on free television. If it

does so, the Party concerned may have recourse to the drafting of a list of designated events which it considers to be of major importance for society.

2. Parties shall ensure by appropriate means, respecting the legal guarantees granted by the Convention for the Protection of Human Rights and Fundamental Freedoms as well as, where appropriate, the national constitution, that a broadcaster within their jurisdiction does not exercise the exclusive rights purchased by that broadcaster following the date of entry into force of the Protocol amending the European Convention on Transfrontier Television in such a way that a substantial proportion of the public in another Party is deprived of the possibility of following events which are designated by that other Party, via whole or partial live coverage or where necessary or appropriate for objective reasons in the public interest, whole or partial deferred coverage on free television as determined by that other Party under paragraph 1, respecting the following requirements:

a. the Party implementing the legal measures referred to in paragraph 1 shall draw up a list of national or non - national events which are considered by that Party as being of major importance for society;

b. the Party shall do so in a clear and transparent manner in due and effective time;

c. the Party shall determine whether these events shall be available via whole or partial live coverage, or where necessary or appropriate for objective reasons in the public interest, whole or partial deferred coverage;

d. the measures taken by the Party drawing up the list shall be proportionate and as detailed as necessary to enable other Parties to take measures referred to in this paragraph;

e. the Party drawing up the list shall notify the list and the corresponding legal measures to the Standing Committee, the time limit for which shall be fixed by the Standing Committee;

f. the measures taken by the Party drawing up the list shall be within the limitations of the guidelines of the Standing Committee referred to in paragraph 3 and the Standing Committee must have given a positive opinion on the measures.

Measures based on this paragraph shall apply only to those events published by the Standing Committee in the annual list referred to in paragraph 3 and to those exclusive rights purchased after the entry into force of the amending Protocol.

3. Once a year the Standing Committee shall:

a. publish a consolidated list of the enlisted events and corresponding legal measures notified by Parties in accordance with paragraph 2e;

b. draw up guidelines to be adopted by a majority of three quarters of the members in addition to the requirements listed up in paragraph 2a to e in order to avoid differences between the implementation of this article and that of corresponding European Community provisions.

Article 10 – Cultural objectives (1)

1. Each transmitting Party shall ensure, where practicable and by appropriate means, that a broadcaster within its jurisdiction reserves for European works a majority proportion of its transmission time, excluding the time appointed to news, sports events, games, advertising, teletext services and tele - shopping. This proportion, having regard to the broadcaster's informational, educational, cultural and entertainment responsibilities to its viewing public, should be achieved progressively, on the basis of suitable criteria.

2. In case of disagreement between a receiving Party and a transmitting Party on the application of the preceding paragraph, recourse may be had, at the request of one of the Parties, to the Standing Committee with a view to its formulating an advisory opinion on the subject. Such a disagreement shall not be submitted to the arbitration procedure provided for in Article 26.

3. The Parties undertake to look together for the most appropriate instruments and procedures to support, without discrimination between broadcasters, the activity and development of European production, particularly in countries with a low audiovisual production capacity or restricted language area.

4. The Parties shall ensure that a broadcaster within their jurisdiction does not broadcast cinematographic works outside periods agreed with the rights holders.

Article 10*bis* - Media pluralism (2)

The Parties, in the spirit of co - operation and mutual assistance which underlies this Convention, shall endeavour to avoid that programme services transmitted or retransmitted by a broadcaster or any other legal or natural persons within their jurisdiction, within the meaning of Article 3, endanger media pluralism.

CHAPTER III – ADVERTISING AND TELE-SHOPPING (3)

Article 11 – General standards (1)

1. Advertising and tele - shopping shall be fair and honest.

2. Advertising and tele - shopping shall not be misleading and shall not prejudice the interests of consumers.

3. Advertising and tele - shopping addressed to or using children shall avoid anything likely to harm their interests and shall have regard to their special susceptibilities.

4. Tele - shopping shall not exort minors to contract for the sale or rental of goods and services.

5. The advertiser shall not exercise any editorial influence over the content of programmes.

Article 12 – Duration (1)

1. The proportion of tele - shopping spots, advertising spots and other forms of advertising, with the exception of tele - shopping windows within the meaning of paragraph 3, shall not exceed 20% of the daily transmission time. The transmission time for advertising spots shall not exceed 15% of the daily transmission time.

2. The proportion of advertising spots and tele - shopping spots within a given clock hour shall not exceed 20%.

3. Windows devoted to tele - shopping programmes broadcast within programme services which are not exclusively devoted to tele - shopping shall be of a minimum uninterrupted duration of 15 minutes. The maximum number of windows per day shall be eight. Their overall duration shall not exceed three hours per day. They must be clearly identified by optical and acoustic means.

4. For the purposes of this article, advertising shall not include:

- announcements made by the broadcaster in connection with its own programmes and ancillary products directly derived from those programmes;

- announcements in the public interest and charity appeals broadcast free of charge.

Article 13 – Form and presentation (1)

1. Advertising and tele - shopping shall be clearly distinguishable as such

and recognisably separate from the other items of the programme service by optical and/or acoustic means. In principle, advertising and tele - shopping spots shall be transmitted in blocks.

2. Advertising and tele - shopping shall not use subliminal techniques.

3. Surreptitious advertising and tele - shopping shall not be allowed, in particular the presentation of products or services in programmes when it serves advertising purposes.

4. Advertising and tele - shopping shall not feature, visually or orally, persons regularly presenting news and current affairs programmes.

Article 14 – Insertion of advertising and tele – shopping (1)

1. Advertising and tele - shopping shall be inserted between programmes. Provided the conditions contained in paragraphs 2 to 5 of this article are fulfilled, advertising and tele - shopping spots may also be inserted during programmes in such a way that the integrity and value of the programme and the rights of the rights holders are not prejudiced.

2. In programmes consisting of autonomous parts, or in sports programmes and similarly structured events and performances comprising intervals, advertising and tele - shopping spots shall only be inserted between the parts or in the intervals.

3. The transmission of audiovisual works such as feature films and films made for television (excluding series, serials, light entertainment programmes and documentaries), provided their scheduled duration is more than forty - five minutes, may be interrupted once for each complete period of fourty - five minutes. A further interruption is allowed if their scheduled duration is at least twenty minutes longer than two or more complete periods of fourty - five minutes.

4. Where programmes, other than those covered by paragraph 2, are interrupted by advertising or tele - shopping spots, a period of at least twenty minutes should elapse between each successive advertising or tele - shopping break within the programme.

5. Advertising and tele - shopping shall not be inserted in any broadcast of a religious service. News and current affairs programmes, documentaries, religious programmes, and children's programmes, when their scheduled duration is less than thirty minutes, shall not be interrupted by advertising or tele - shopping. If their scheduled duration is thirty minutes or longer, the provisions of the previous paragraphs shall apply.

Article 15 – Advertising and tele – shopping of particular products (3), (1)

1. Advertising and tele - shopping for tobacco products shall not be allowed.

2. Advertising and tele - shopping for alcoholic beverages of all varieties shall comply with the following rules:

a. they shall not be addressed particularly to minors and no one associated with the consumption of alcoholic beverage in advertising or tele - shopping should seem to be a minor;

b. they shall not link the consumption of alcohol to physical performance or driving;

c. they shall not claim that alcohol has therapeutic qualities or that it is a stimulant, a sedative or a means of resolving personal problems;

d. they shall not encourage immoderate consumption of alcohol or present abstinence or moderation in a negative light;

e. they shall not place undue emphasis on the alcoholic content of beverages.

3. Advertising for medicines and medical treatment which are only available on medical prescription in the transmitting Party shall not be allowed.

4. Advertising for all other medicines and medical treatment shall be clearly distinguishable as such, honest, truthful and subject to verification and shall comply with the requirement of protection of the individual from harm.

5. Tele - shopping for medicines and medical treatment shall not be allowed.

Article 16 – Advertising and tele – shopping directed specifically at a single Party (1)

1. In order to avoid distortions in competition and endangering the television system of a Party, advertising and tele - shopping which are specifically and with some frequency directed to audiences in a single Party other than the transmitting Party shall not circumvent the television advertising and tele - shopping rules in that particular Party.

2. The provisions of the preceding paragraph shall not apply where:

a. the rules concerned establish a discrimination between advertising and tele - shopping transmitted by a broadcaster within the jurisdiction of that Party and advertising and tele - shopping transmitted by a broadcaster or any other legal or natural person within the jurisdiction of another Party, or

b. the Parties concerned have concluded bilateral or multilateral agreements in this area.

CHAPTER IV – SPONSORSHIP

Article 17 – General standards

1. When a programme or series of programmes is sponsored in whole or in part, it shall clearly be identified as such by appropriate credits at the beginning and/or end of the programme.

2. The content and scheduling of sponsored programmes may in no circumstances be influenced by the sponsor in such a way as to affect the responsibility and editorial independence of the broadcaster in respect of programmes.

3. Sponsored programmes shall not encourage the sale, purchase or rental of the products or services of the sponsor or a third party, in particular by making special promotional references to those products or services in such programmes.

Article 18 – Prohibited sponsorship (1)

1. Programmes may not be sponsored by natural or legal persons whose principal activity is the manufacture or sale of products, or the provision of services, the advertising and tele - shopping of which are prohibited by virtue of Article 15.

2. Companies whose activity includes, *inter alia*, the manufacture or sale of medicines and medical treatments may sponsor programmes by promoting the name, trademark, image or activities of the company, to the exclusion of any reference to medicines or specific medical treatment available only on medical prescription in the transmitting Party.

3. Sponsorship of news and current affairs programmes shall not be allowed.

CHAPTER IV *bis* – PROGRAMME SERVICES DEVOTED EXCLUSIVELY TO SELF – PROMOTION OR TELE – SHOPPING (4)

Article 18 *bis* – Programme services devoted exclusively to self – promotion

1. The provisions of this Convention shall apply *mutatis mutandis* to pro-

gramme services devoted exclusively to self - promotion.

2. Other forms of advertising shall be allowed on such services within the limits established by Article 12, paragraphes 1 and 2.

Article 18 *ter*: Programme services devoted exclusively to tele - shopping

1. The provisions of this Convention shall apply *mutatis mutandis* to programme services devoted exclusively to tele - shopping.

2. Advertising shall be allowed on such services within the limits established in Article 12, paragraph 1. Article 12, paragraph 2, shall not apply.

CHAPTER V – MUTUAL ASSISTANCE

Article 19 – Co – operation between the Parties

1. The Parties undertake to render each other mutual assistance in order to implement this Convention.

2. For that purpose:

a. each Contracting State shall designate one or more authorities, the name and address of each of which it shall communicate to the Secretary General of the Council of Europe at the time of deposit of its instrument of ratification, acceptance, approval or accession;

b. each Contracting State which has designated more than one authority shall specify in its communication under sub - paragraph *a*. the competence of each authority.

3. An authority designated by a Party shall:

a. furnish the information foreseen under Article 6, paragraph 2, of this Convention;

b. furnish information at the request of an authority designated by another Party on the domestic law and practices in the fields covered by this Convention;

c. co - operate with the authorities designated by the other Parties whenever useful, and notably where this would enhance the effectiveness of measures taken in implementation of this Convention;

d. consider any difficulty arising from the application of this Convention which is brought to its attention by an authority designated by another Party.

CHAPTER VI – STANDING COMMITTEE

Article 20 – Standing Committee (1)

1. For the purposes of this Convention, a Standing Committee shall be set up.

2. Each Party may be represented on the Standing Committee by one or more delegates. Each delegation shall have one vote. Within the areas of its competence, the European Community shall exercise its right to vote with a number of votes equal to the number of its member States which are Parties to this Convention; the European Community shall not exercise its right to vote in cases where the member States concerned exercise theirs, and conversely.

3. Any State referred to in Article 29, paragraph 1, which is not a Party to this Convention may be represented on the Standing Committee by an observer.

4. The Standing Committee may seek the advice of experts in order to discharge its functions. It may, on its own initiative or at the request of the body concerned, invite any international or national, governmental or non - governmental body technically qualified in the fields covered by this Convention to be represented by an observer at one or part of one of its meetings.

5. The Standing Committee shall be convened by the Secretary General of the Council of Europe. Its first meeting shall be held within six months of the date of entry into force of the Convention. It shall subsequently meet whenever one - third of the Parties or the Committee of Ministers of the Council of Europe so requests, or on the initiative of the Secretary General of the Council of Europe in accordance with the provisions of Article 23, paragraph 2, or at the request of one or more Parties in accordance with the provisions of Articles 21, sub - paragraph c, and 25, paragraph 2.

6. A majority of the Parties shall constitute a quorum for holding a meeting of the Standing Committee.

7. Subject to the provisions of Article 9*bis*, paragraph 3b, and Article 23, paragraph 3, the decisions of the Standing Committee shall be taken by a majority of three - quarters of the members present.

8. Subject to the provisions of this Convention, the Standing Committee shall draw up its own Rules of Procedure.

Article 21 – Functions of the Standing Committee (1)

1. The Standing Committee shall be responsible for following the application of this Convention. It may:

a. make recommendations to the Parties concerning the application of the Convention;

b. suggest any necessary modifications of the Convention and examine those proposed in accordance with the provisions of Article 23;

c. examine, at the request of one or more Parties, questions concerning the interpretation of the Convention;

d. use its best endeavours to secure a friendly settlement of any difficulty referred to it in accordance with the provisions of Article 25;

e. make recommendations to the Committee of Ministers concerning States other than those referred to in Article 29, paragraph 1, to be invited to accede to this Convention.

f. give opinions on abuse of rights under Article 24*bis*, paragraph 2c.

2. In addition, the Standing Committee shall:

a. draw up the guidelines referred to in Article 9*bis*, paragraph 3b, in order to avoid differences between the implementation of the rules of this Convention concerning access of the public to events of major importance for society and that of corresponding European Community provisions;

b. give an opinion on the measures taken by Parties which have drawn up a list of national or non - national events which are considered by those Parties as being of major importance for society in accordance with Article 9*bis*, paragraph 2;

c. publish once a year a consolidated list of the enlisted events and corresponding measures notified by Parties in accordance with Article 9*bis*, paragraph 2e.

Article 22 – Reports of the Standing Committee

After each meeting, the Standing Committee shall forward to the Parties and the Committee of Ministers of the Council of Europe a report on its discussions and any decisions taken.

CHAPTER VII – AMENDMENTS

Article 23 – Amendments (1)

1. Any Party may propose amendments to this Convention.

2. Any proposal for amendment shall be notified to the Secretary General of the Council of Europe who shall communicate it to the member States of the Council of Europe, to the other States party to the European Cultural Convention, to the European Community and to any non - member State which has acceded to, or has been invited to accede to this Convention in accordance with the provisions of Article 30. The Secretary General of the Council of Europe shall convene a meeting of the Standing Committee at the earliest two months following the communication of the proposal.

3. The Standing Committee shall examine any amendment proposed and shall submit the text adopted by a majority of three - quarters of the members of the Standing Committee to the Committee of Ministers for approval. After its approval, the text shall be forwarded to the Parties for acceptance.

4. Any amendment shall enter into force on the thirtieth day after all the Parties have informed the Secretary General of their acceptance thereof.

5. However, the Committee of Ministers may, after consulting the Standing Committee, decide that a particular amendment shall enter into force following the expiry of a period of two years after the date on which it has been opened to acceptance, unless a Party has notified the Secretary General of the Council of Europe of an objection to its entry into force. Should such an objection be notified, the amendment shall enter into force on the first day of the month following the date on which the Party to the Convention which has notified the objection has deposited its instrument of acceptance with the Secretary General of the Council of Europe.

6. If an amendment has been approved by the Committee of Ministers, but has not yet entered into force in accordance with paragraphs 4 or 5, a State or the European Community may not express their consent to be bound by the Convention without accepting at the same time the amendment.

CHAPTER VIII – ALLEGED VIOLATIONS OF THIS CONVENTION

Article 24 – Alleged violations of this Convention

1. When a Party finds a violation of this Convention, it shall communicate to the transmitting Party the alleged violation and the two Parties shall endeavour to overcome the difficulty on the basis of the provisions of Articles 19, 25 and 26.

2. If the alleged violation is of a manifest, serious and grave nature which raises important public issues and concerns Articles 7, paragraphs 1 or 2, 12, 13, paragraph 1, first sentence, 14 or 15, paragraphs 1 or 3, and if it persists within two weeks following the communication, the receiving Party may suspend provisionally the retransmission of the incriminated programme service.

3. In all other cases of alleged violation, with the exception of those provided for in paragraph 4, the receiving Party may suspend provisionally the retransmission of the incriminated programme service eight months following the communication, if the alleged violation persists.

4. The provisional suspension of retransmission shall not be allowed in the case of alleged violations of Articles 7, paragraph 3, 8, 9 or 10.

Article 24*bis* - Alleged abuses of rights conferred by this Convention (2)

1. When the programme service of a broadcaster is wholly or principally directed at the territory of a Party other than that which has jurisdiction over the broadcaster (the "receiving Party"), and the broadcaster has established itself with a view to evading the laws in the areas covered by the Convention which would have applied to it had it fallen within the jurisdiction of that other Party, this shall constitute an abuse of rights.

2. Where such an abuse is alleged by a Party, the following procedure shall apply:

a the Parties concerned shall endeavour to achieve a friendly settlement;

b. if they fail to do so within three months, the receiving Party shall refer the matter to the Standing Committee;

c. having heard the views of the Parties concerned, the Standing Committee shall, within six months of the date on which the matter was referred to it, give an opinion on whether an abuse of rights has been committed and shall inform the Parties concerned accordingly.

3. If the Standing Committee has concluded that an abuse of rights has occurred, the Party whose jurisdiction the broadcaster is deemed to be within shall take appropriate measures to remedy the abuse of rights and shall inform the Standing Committee of those measures.

4. If the Party whose jurisdiction the broadcaster is deemed to be within has failed to take the measures specified in paragraph 3 within six months, the arbitration procedure set out in Article 26, paragraph 2, and the appendix of the Convention shall be pursued by the Parties concerned.

5. A receiving Party shall not take any measures against the programme service concerned until the arbitration procedure has been completed.

6. Any measures proposed or taken under this article shall comply with Article 10 of the Convention for the Protection of Human Rights and Fundamental Freedoms.

CHAPTER IX – SETTLEMENT OF DISPUTES

Article 25 – Conciliation

1. In case of difficulty arising from the application of this Convention, the parties concerned shall endeavour to achieve a friendly settlement.

2. Unless one of the parties concerned objects, the Standing Committee may examine the question, by placing itself at the disposal of the parties concerned in order to reach asatisfactory solution as rapidly as possible and, where appropriate, to formulate an advisory opinion on the subject.

3. Each party concerned undertakes to accord the Standing Committee without delay all information and facilities necessary for the discharge of its functions under the preceding paragraph.

Article 26 – Arbitration

1. If the parties concerned cannot settle the dispute in accordance with the provisions of Article 25, they may, by common agreement, submit it to arbitration, the procedure of which is provided for in the appendix to this Convention. In the absence of such an agreement within six months following the first request to open

the procedure of conciliation, the dispute may be submitted to arbitration at the request of one of the parties.

2. Any Party may, at any time, declare that it recognises as compulsory, *ipso facto* and without special agreement in respect of any other Party accepting the same obligation, the application of the arbitration procedure provided for in the appendix to this Convention.

CHAPTER X – OTHER INTERNATIONAL AGREEMENTS AND THE INTERNAL LAW OF THE PARTIES

Article 27 – Other international agreements or arrangements (1)

1. In their mutual relations, Parties which are members of the European Community shall apply Community rules and shall not therefore apply the rules arising from this Convention except in so far as there is no Community rule governing the particular subject concerned.

2. Nothing in this Convention shall prevent the Parties from concluding international agreements completing or developing its provisions or extending their field of application.

3. In the case of bilateral agreements, this Convention shall not alter the rights and obligations of Parties which arise from such agreements and which do not affect the enjoyment of other Parties of their rights or the performance of their obligations under this Convention.

Article 28 – Relations between the Convention and the internal law of the Parties (1)

Nothing in this Convention shall prevent the Parties from applying stricter or more detailed rules than those provided for in this Convention to programme services transmitted by a broadcaster deemed to be within their jurisdiction, within the meaning of Article 5.

CHAPTER XI – FINAL PROVISIONS

Article 29 – Signature and entry into force (1)

1. This Convention shall be open for signature by the member States of the Council of Europe and the other States party to the European Cultural Convention, and by the European Community. It is subject to ratification, acceptance or approval. Instruments of ratification, acceptance or approval shall be deposited with the Secretary General of the Council of Europe.

2. This Convention shall enter into force on the first day of the month following the expiration of a period of three months after the date on which seven States, of which at least five member States of the Council of Europe, have expressed their consent to be bound by the Convention in accordance with the provisions of the preceding paragraph.

3. A State may, at the time of signature or at any later date prior to the entry into force of this Convention in respect of that State, declare that it shall apply the Convention provisionally.

4. In respect of any State referred to in paragraph 1, or the European Community, which subsequently express their consent to be bound by it, this Convention shall enter into force on the first day of the month following the expiration of a period of three months after the date of deposit of the instrument of ratification, acceptance or approval.

Article 30 – Accession by non – member States

1. After the entry into force of this Convention, the Committee of Ministers of the Council of Europe, after consulting the Contracting States may invite any other State to accede to this Convention by a decision taken by the majority provided for in Article 20d. of the Statute of the Council of Europe and by the unanimous vote of the representatives of the Contracting States entitled to sit on the Committee.

2. In respect of any acceding State, this Convention shall enter into force on the first day of the month following the expiration of a period of three months after the date of deposit of the instrument of accession with the Secretary General of the Council of Europe.

Article 31 – Territorial application

1. Any State may, at the time of signature or when depositing its instrument of ratification, acceptance, approval or accession, specify the territory or territories to which this Convention shall apply.

2. Any State may, at any later date, by a declaration addressed to the Secretary General of the Council of Europe, extend the application of this Convention to any other territory specified in the declaration. In respect of such territory, the Convention shall enter into force on the first day of the month following the expiration of a period of three months after the date of receipt of such declaration by the Secretary General.

3. Any declaration made under the two preceding paragraphs may, in respect of any territory specified in such declaration, be withdrawn by a notification addressed to the Secretary General. The withdrawal shall become effective on the first day of the month following the expiration of a period of six months after the date of receipt of such notification by the Secretary General.

Article 32 – Reservations (1)

1. At the time of signature or when depositing its instrument of ratification, acceptance, approval or accession any State may declare that it reserves the right of restrict the retransmission on its territory, solely to the extent that it does not comply with its domestic legislation, of programme services containing advertising for alcoholic beverages according to the rules provided for in Article 15, paragraph 2, of this Convention.

No other reservation may be made.

2. A reservation made in accordance with the preceding paragraph may not be the subject of an objection.

3. Any Contracting State which has made a reservation under paragraph 1 may wholly or partly withdraw it by means of a notification addressed to the Secretary General of the Council of Europe. The withdrawal shall take effect on the date of receipt of such notification by the Secretary General.

4. A Party which has made a reservation under paragraph 1 may not claim the application of that provision by any other Party; it may, however, if its reservation is partial or conditional, claim the application of that provision in so far as it has itself accepted it.

Article 33 – Denunciation

1. Any Party may, at any time, denounce this Convention by means of a notification addressed to the Secretary General of the Council of Europe.

2. Such denunciation shall become effective on the first day of the month following the expiration of a period of six months after the date of receipt of the notification by the Secretary General.

Article 34 – Notifications (1)

The Secretary General of the Council of Europe shall notify the member States of the Council of Europe, the other States party to the European Cultural Convention, the European Community and any State which has acceded to, or has been invited to accede to this Convention of:

a. any signature;

b. the deposit of any instrument of ratification, acceptance, approval or accession;

c. any date of entry into force of this Convention in accordance with the provisions of Articles 29, 30 and 31;

d. any report established in accordance with the provisions of Article 22;

e. any other act, declaration, notification or communication relating to this Convention.

In witness whereof the undersigned, being duly authorised thereto, have signed this Convention.

Done at Strasbourg, the 5th day of May 1989, in English and French, both texts being equally authentic, in a single copy which shall be deposited in the archives of the Council of Europe. The Secretary General of the Council of Europe shall transmit certified copies to each member State of the Council of Europe, to the other States party to the European Cultural Convention, to the European Community and to any State invited to accede to this Convention. (1)

APPENDIX

Arbitration

1. A request for arbitration shall be notified to the Secretary General of the Council of Europe. It shall include the name of the other party to the dispute and the subject matter of the dispute. The Secretary General shall communicate the in-

formation so received to all the Parties to the Convention.

2. In the event of a dispute between two Parties one of which is a member State of the European Community, the latter itself being a Party, the request for arbitration shall be addressed both to the member State and to the Community, which jointly shall notify the Secretary General, within one month of receipt of the request, whether the member State or the Community, or the member State and the Community jointly, shall be party to the dispute. In the absence of such notification within the said time - limit, the member State and the Community shall be considered as being one and the same party to the dispute for the purposes of the application of the provisions governing the constitution and procedure of the arbitration tribunal. The same shall apply when the member State and the Community jointly present themselves as party to the dispute. In cases envisaged by this paragraph, the time - limit of one month foreseen in the first sentence of paragraph 4 hereafter shall be extended to two months.

3. The arbitration tribunal shall consist of three members: each of the parties to the dispute shall appoint one arbitrator; the two arbitrators so appointed shall designate by common agreement the third arbitrator who shall be the chairman of the tribunal. The latter shall not be a national of either of the parties to the dispute, nor have his usual place of residence in the territory of either of those parties, nor be employed by either of them, nor have dealt with the case in another capacity.

4. If one of the parties has not appointed an arbitrator within one month following the communication of the request by the Secretary General of the Council of Europe, he shall be appointed at the request of the other party by the President of the European Court of Human Rights within a further one - month period. If the President of the Court is unable to act or is a national of one of the parties to the dispute, the appointment shall be made by the Vice - President of the Court or by the most senior judge to the Court who is available and is not a national of one of the parties to the dispute. The same procedure shall be observed if, within a period of one mont following the appointment of the second arbitrator, the Chairman of the arbitration tribunal is not designated.

5. The provisions of paragraphs 3 and 4 shall apply, as the case may be, in order to fill any vacancy.

6. Two or more parties which determine by agreement that they are in the

same interest shall appoint an arbitrator jointly.

7. The parties to the dispute and the Standing Committee shall provide the arbitration tribunal with all facilities necessary for the effective conduct of the proceedings.

8. The arbitration tribunal shall draw up its own Rules of Procedure. Its decisions shall be taken by majority vote of its members. Its award shall be final and binding.

9. The award of the arbitration tribunal shall be notified to the Secretary General of the Council of Europe who shall communicate it to all the Parties to this Convention.

10. Each party to the dispute shall bear the expenses of the arbitrator appointed by it; these parties shall share equally the expenses of the other arbitrator, as well as other costs entailed by the arbitration.

Notes :

(1) Text amended according to the provisions of the Protocol (ETS No. 171).

(2) Article added according to the provisions of the Protocol (ETS No. 171).

(3) Heading amended according to the provisions of the Protocol (ETS No. 171).

(4) Chapter added according to the provisions of the Protocol (ETS No. 171).

欧洲电影合作摄制公约*

(《欧洲文化公约》成员国及欧盟成员国1992年
10月2日于斯特拉斯堡签署，1994年4月1日生效)

前　　言

欧洲委员会及《欧洲文化公约》其他缔约国签署于此，考虑到欧洲委员会的宗旨就是实现其成员国更紧密的团结，以便尤其保障并促进形成其共同遗产的意识形态及原则；考虑到创作自由及表达自由构成该等原则的核心要素；考虑到在多个欧洲国家保卫文化多样性是《欧洲文化公约》的宗旨之一；考虑到应该加强电影合作摄制，以之作为以欧洲规模实现文化多样性的创作及表达的一种工具；决定发展该等原则并回顾部长理事会对电影及视听领域的建议，尤其是第R（86）3号关于促进欧洲视听摄制的建议；认可设立欧洲基金以支持创作型电影及视听作品的合作摄制及发行，即欧影，以解决鼓励欧洲电影合作摄制的关切，并承认新的推动力就这样出现以促进欧洲电影合作摄制的发展；决议基于共同行动增加摄制并界定规则使之整体适应欧洲多边电影合作摄制而达成该等文化宗旨；鉴于制定共同规则可能需要在电影合作摄制领域减少限制并鼓励欧洲合作，同意达成以下条款：

第一章　总　　则

第1条　公约宗旨

本公约各方承诺根据以下条款促进欧洲电影合作摄制的发展。

---

* 中国社会科学院法学研究所吴峻译。

第 2 条　适用范围

本公约须适用于各方在其领土上发起的多边合作领域所产生的关系。

本公约须适用于：

涉及至少设立于公约三个不同缔约方的三个合作制片商；及涉及至少设立于公约三个不同缔约方的三个合作制片商及一家或多家并不在公约缔约国设立的合作制片商。然而，非设立于公约缔约国的合作制片商总出资不得超过制片总成本的 30%。

在任何情形下，本公约仅仅在合作摄制作品满足以下第三条第三款所界定欧洲电影作品之定义的条件下予以适用。

本公约缔约国之间达成的双边协定须继续适用于双边电影合作摄制。在多边合作摄制的情形下，本公约的规定应该优先于本公约缔约国之间双边协定的有关规定。该等涉及双边合作摄制的规定须继续适用，但不得违反本公约的相关规定。

在本公约的两个缔约国之间并不存在任何适用于双边合作摄制关系的协定的，除非其中一方根据第 20 条的规定作出保留，本公约也适用于双边合作摄制。

第 3 条　公约之目的

a. “电影作品”这一术语系指任何时长介质的作品，尤其是电影故事片、动画片及纪录片作品，符合每一个相关缔约国适用于电影产业的法律规定，并是要在影院放映的；

b. “合作制片商”该术语系指在本公约缔约国设立并订立合作制片合同的电影制片公司或者制片商；

c. “欧洲电影作品”这一术语系指满足作为本公约有机组成部分之附件二所规定条件的电影作品；

d. “多边合作制片”系指一部电影作品系由上述第二条第二款所界定的至少三家合作制片商予以摄制。

第二章　适用合作制片的规则

第 4 条　融入本国影片

多边合作制片制作的欧洲电影作品属于本公约适用范围的，有权接受参与有关合作制片的本公约每个缔约国依据国内法律及行政法规而给予本国影片的优惠待遇。

合作制片商所在缔约国须按照该缔约国有效法律和行政法规规定的条件和限制及本公约规定给予每个合作制片商予以优惠待遇。

第5条　取得合作制片地位的条件

就电影作品进行任何合作制片须在有权机关之间进行协商并遵守附件一确立程序的情形下取得合作制片商所在缔约国有权机关的批准。该附件须作为本公约的有机组成部分。

须根据附件一确立的申请程序向有权机关提起。该等批准具有终局性，除非没能遵守涉及文艺、金融及技术事项方面的初始承诺。

不得授予露骨色情项目或者鼓吹暴力或公开损害人类尊严的项目合作制片的地位。

合作制片地位所赋予的优惠待遇应该由认定具有足够技术和金融实力及足够专业资格的合作制片商所享有。

每个缔约国须通过在签署之时或提存其批准、接受或加入文件之时的声明指定上述第二款规定的有权机关。该等声明可以在之后的任何日期予以修改。

第6条　每一合作制片商的出资份额

多边合作制片的情形下，最低出资份额不得少于电影作品全部制片成本的10%，最多不超过70%。最低出资份额低于20%的，有关缔约国可以采取措施，减少或拒绝对之适用本国制作扶持计划。

本公约根据第二条第四款规定替代缔约国双方双边协定的，最低出资份额不得少于电影作品全部制片成本的20%，最多不得超过80%。

第7条　合作制片商的权利

合作制片合同须向每个合作制片商保证对原片及有声负片具有共有权。合同须有条款规定，该等负片须保存在合作制片商都统一的地点，并须保证他们可以自由使用该等负片。

合作制片合同也须保证每个制片商有权获得中间片或者复制的其他任何媒介。

第8条　技术及艺术方面的参与

每个合作制片商的出资包括有效的技术及艺术参与。原则上，根据适用于缔约方的国际义务，制作商有关创意、技术及艺术人员、演职人员及设施的投入须与出资比例相符。

符合缔约国国际义务及剧本要求的前提下，参与摄制影片工作的技术及艺术团队须由合作制片的伙伴国国民组成，其后期制作通常须在这些国家进行。

第 9 条　金融合作制片

尽管有第八条的规定，符合缔约国有效法律及行政法规所规定具体条件及限制的前提下，合作制片可以根据本公约规定取得合作制片地位，但须满足以下条件：

根据合作制片合同含有一项或多项仅为金融方式的少数份额出资，但每一国的出资份额既不少于制片成本的 10%，也不多于 25%；

包括一个进行多数份额投资的合作制片商，该制片商有效进行了技术及艺术投入，并满足在其国家可被认可为本国作品的电影作品条件；

有助于促进欧洲认同；并体现在载有分配所得条款的合作制片合同中。

金融合作制片仅仅在有关机关作出个案批准的情形下方可有资格取得合作制片地位，尤其须考虑到以下第十条规定。

第 10 条　总体平衡

在缔约国电影关系之中必须保持总体的平衡，这既要考虑投资总额，也要考虑电影作品合作制片的艺术及技术参与。

缔约国一方于合理期间在其与其他缔约国一方或多方的合作制片关系中出现赤字的，为保持其文化认同，可以不对之后的合作制片予以批准，指导其与该等其他缔约方的电影关系恢复平衡。

第 11 条　入境及居留

根据有效的法律、行政法规及国际义务，每一缔约方须在入境和居留事项提供便利，并方便来自于其他缔约方参与合作制片的技术及艺术人员在其领土上取得工作许可。同样，每一缔约方须许可本公约适用范围内电影作品之制片和发行所必须设备的临时进口及再出口。

第 12 条　合作制片国家的注明

合作制片国家须在合作制片的电影作品中予以注明。

该等国家的名称应当在演职员表、所有公开及促销材料中及在电影作品播映时得到清楚表明。

第 13 条　出口

合作制片的电影作品出口到实施电影作品进口配额制国家，而合作制片方中如有一方无权将其电影作品自由输入进口国家的：

a. 该电影作品通常情况下，应计入在该作品摄制中占有多数份额的一方所在国的国家配额；

b. 合作摄制的电影作品各方来自不同国家且参与份额相同的，该作品应计入向进口国出口该作品机会最大的一国的国家配额；

c. 在上述 a、b 项均不适用时，该合作摄制电影作品应计入提供导演的一方所在国的国家配额。

第 14 条　语言

授予合作制片地位的，缔约方有权机关可以要求其境内设立的合作制片商提供该缔约方语言版本的电影作品最终版本。

第 15 条　电影节

除非合作制片商另行决定，合作摄制的电影须在份额最多合作制片商所在缔约国举办的国际电影节予以放映，或者，在进行同等份额金融投入的情形下，须在导演所在国举办的国际电影节予以放映。

第三章　最后条款

第 16 条　签字、批准、接受及许可

本公约须开放供欧洲委员会成员国及《欧洲文化公约》的其他缔约国签署，该等国家可以通过以下方式表达其愿意加入的意愿：

不经批准、接受或许可而进行签署；或者需要经过批准、接受或许可而进行签署的，在批准、接受或许可之后。

批准、接受或许可文件须交存于欧洲委员会秘书长。

第 17 条　生效

本公约在至少包括四个欧洲委员会成员国在内的五个国家已经根据第 16 条规定表达其加入公约同意意见之日起的三个月期间结束后一个月的第一天开始生效。

对于之后表达其同意加入意见的签字缔约国，本公约须从签字之日或提交批准、接受或许可文件之日起三个月期间届满后开始一个月的第一天起生效

第 18 条　非成员国家的加入

本公约生效后，欧洲委员会部长理事会可以按照《欧洲委员会贯行》第 20. d 条所规定的多数通过决定，邀请非欧洲委员会成员国的欧洲国家及欧洲经济共同体加入本公约，且须得到有权参加部长理事会所委任代表的一致同意。

对于任何加入国或欧洲经济共同体而言，在其加入之时，本公约须在向欧洲委员会秘书长提交加入文件之日后三个月期间届满之后一个月的第一日

起生效。

第 19 条　领土条款

任何国家可以在签字或者交存其批准、接受、许可或加入文件时明确本公约须适用的领土。

任何缔约国可以在之后通过向欧洲委员会秘书长提交声明的方式将本公约的适用地域扩展至声明所明确的领土范围。对于该等领土，本公约须在秘书长收到该等声明后三个月期间届满之后一个月的第一天开始生效。

根据以上两款规定作出的任何声明对于其所明确的任何领土通过向秘书长条通知的方式予以撤回。该等撤回须在秘书长收到该等声明后三个月期间届满之后一个月的第一天开始生效。

第 20 条　保留

任何国家可以在签字后提交其批准、接受、许可或加入文件时，宣布第二条第四款并不适用于其同一个或多个其他缔约方之间的双边合作制片关系。另外，该国家可以保留权利，制定一个不同于第九条第一款 a 项的最大投入份额。除此之外，不得进行其他保留。

任何缔约方根据上一款规定作出保留的可以全部或部分通过向欧洲委员会秘书长提交通知的方式全部或部分予以撤回。撤回退出须在秘书长收到该等通知之日起开始生效。

第 21 条　退出

任何缔约方可以在任何时间通过向欧洲委员会秘书长提交通知的方法退出本公约。

该等退出须在秘书长收到该等通知后三个月期间届满之后一个月的第一天开始生效。

第 22 条　通知

欧洲委员会秘书长须就以下事项通知欧洲委员会成员国、可能加入本公约或可能受邀加入本公约的任何国家和欧洲经济共同体：

任何签署；

任何批准、接受、许可或加入文件的提存；

本公约根据第 17、18 及 19 条规定生效的任何日期；

根据第五条第五款所作出的任何声明；

根据第 21 条予以通知的任何退出；

其他涉及本公约的行为、通知或通告。

为以下各自政府合法授权签署的代表所见证，签署了本公约。

于1992年10月2日签订于斯特拉斯堡。以英文和法文草就，两种语言文本均有同等效力，制成同一文本并须交存于欧洲委员会档案文档。欧洲委员会秘书长须向第16条第一款规定的国际及可能受邀加入本公约的任何国家及欧洲经济共同体提交经认证的文本。

附件一　申请程序

为利用本公约规定，设立于缔约方的合作制片商须在拍摄开始前的两个月之前提交合作制片地位的申请并须附有下列文件。在拍摄开始前至少一个月之前，该等文件须以足够的文本数量提交予有权机关，以便他们将之通告予其他缔约方的有权机关：

- 版权购买合同文本或者为对作品进行商业利用而购买版权的其他证明文件；
- 详尽的剧本；
- 所参与国家进行技术及艺术投入的清单；
- 预估的详细融资计划；
- 电影作品制片日程；
- 合作制片商之间订立的合作制片合同。该等合同须载有规定合作制片商之间进行受益或地域分配的条款。

如可能，申请及其他文件须以所提交有权机关使用的语言加以提交。

有权国内机关一旦收到申请及所附文件，须互相寄送。资金投入为少数方的缔约方之该等有权机关在收到资金投入份额最多缔约方国家的意见前不得作出批准决定。

附件二

1. 如果电影作品根据以下欧洲元素表格计算的19分可达到总分中至少达到15分，则可以被认为是第三条第三款所指的合格欧洲电影作品。

2. 对于剧本的要求，在共同进行协商后，有权机关认为作品仍然反映欧洲认同的，可以对于得分低于通常所要求15分的作品授予合作制片地位。

欧洲元素	加权点数
创意团队	
导演	3
编剧	3
作曲	1
	——
	7
饰演团队	
第一主角	3
第二主角	2
第三主角	1
	——
	6
技术团队	
摄影	1
录音	1
剪辑	1
艺术指导	1
设置或制片厂所在地	1
后期制作所在地	1
	——
	6

附记

a. 首先，第二及第三主角是根据所工作的天数来确定的。

b. 一旦涉及第八条，“艺术”系指创意及饰演团队，“技术”系指技术及工艺团队。

European Convention on Cinematographic Co – Production

Strasbourg, 2. X. 1992

Preamble

The member States of the Council of Europe and the other States party to the European Cultural Convention, signatory hereto,

Considering that the aim of the Council of Europe is to achieve a greater unity between its members in order, in particular, to safeguard and promote the ideals and principles which form their common heritage;

Considering that freedom of creation and freedom of expression constitute fundamental elements of these principles;

Considering that the defence of cultural diversity of the various European countries is one of the aims of the European Cultural Convention;

Considering that cinematographic co - production, an instrument of creation and expression of cultural diversity on a European scale, should be reinforced;

Determined to develop these principles and recalling the recommendations of the Committee of Ministers on the cinema and the audiovisual field, and particularly Recommendation No. R (86) 3 on the promotion of audiovisual production in Europe;

Acknowledging that the creation of the European Fund for the Support of Co-production and Distribution of Creative Cinematographic and Audiovisual Works, Eurimages, meets the concern encouraging European cinematographic co - production and that a new driving force has thus been given to the development of cinematographic co - productions in Europe;

Resolved to achieve this cultural objective thanks to a common effort to increase production and define the rules which adapt themselves to European multilateral cinematographic co - productions as a whole;

Considering that the adoption of common rules tends to decrease restrictions and encourage European co - operation in the field of cinematographic co - production,

Have agreed as follows:

Chapter I – General provisions

Article 1 – Aim of the Convention

The Parties to this Convention undertake to promote the development of European cinematographic co - production in accordance with the following provisions.

Article 2 – Scope

1. This Convention shall govern relations between the Parties in the field of multilateral co - productions originating in the territory of the Parties.

2. This Convention shall apply:

a. to co - productions involving at least three co - producers, established in three different Parties to the Convention; and

b. to co - productions involving at least three co - producers established in three different Parties to the Convention and one or more co - producers who are not established in such Parties. The total contribution of the co - producers who are not established in the Parties to the Convention may not, however, exceed 30% of the total cost of the production.

In all cases, this Convention shall only apply on condition that the co - produced work meets the definition of a European cinematographic work as defined in Article 3, paragraph 3, below.

3. The provisions of bilateral agreements concluded between the Parties to this Convention shall continue to apply to bilateral co - productions. In the case of multilateral co - productions, the provisions of this Convention shall override those of bilateral agreements between Parties to the Convention. The provisions concerning bilateral co - productions shall remain in force if they do not contravene the provisions of this Convention.

4. In the absence of any agreement governing bilateral co - production relations between two Parties to this Convention, the Convention shall also apply to bilateral co - productions, unless a reservation has been made by one of the Parties involved under the terms of Article 20.

Article 3 – Definitions

For the purposes of this Convention:

a. the term "*cinematographic work*" shall mean a work of any length or medium, in particular cinematographic works of fiction, cartoons and documentaries, which complies with the provisions governing the film industry in force in each of the Parties concerned and is intended to be shown in cinemas;

b. the term "*co – producers*" shall mean cinematographic production companies or producers established in the Parties to this Convention and bound by a co-production contract;

c. the term "*European cinematographic work*" shall mean a cinematographic work which meets the conditions laid down in Appendix II, which is an integral part of this Convention;

d. the term "*multilateral co – production*" shall mean a cinematographic work produced by at least three co - producers as defined in Article 2, paragraph 2, above.

Chapter II – Rules applicable to co – productions

Article 4 – Assimilation to national films

1. European cinematographic works made as multilateral co - productions and falling within the scope of this Convention shall be entitled to the benefits granted to national films by the legislative and regulatory provisions in force in each of the Parties to this Convention participating in the co - production concerned.

2. The benefits shall be granted to each co - producer by the Party in which the co - producer is established, under the conditions and limits provided for by the legislative and regulatory provisions in force in that Party and in accordance with the provisions of this Convention.

Article 5 – Conditions for obtaining co – production status

1. Any co - production of cinematographic works shall be subject to the ap-

proval of the competent authorities of the Parties in which the co - producers are established, after consultation between the competent authorities and in accordance with the procedures laid down in Appendix I. This appendix shall form an integral part of this Convention.

2. Applications for co - production status shall be submitted for approval to the competent authorities according to the application procedure laid down in Appendix I. This approval shall be final except in the case of failure to comply with the initial undertakings concerning artistic, financial and technical matters.

3. Projects of a blatantly pornographic nature or those that advocate violence or openly offend human dignity cannot be accorded co - production status.

4. The benefits provided by co - production status shall be granted to co - producers who are deemed to possess adequate technical and financial means, and sufficient professional qualifications.

5. Each Contracting State shall designate the competent authorities mentioned in paragraph 2 above by means of a declaration made at the time of signature or when depositing its instrument of ratification, acceptance, approval or accession. This declaration may be modified at any later date.

Article 6 – Proportions of contributions from each co – producer

1. In the case of multilateral co - production, the minimum contribution may not be less than 10% and the maximum contribution may not exceed 70% of the total production cost of the cinematographic work. When the minimum contribution is less than 20%, the Party concerned may take steps to reduce or bar access to national production support schemes.

2. When this Convention takes the place of a bilateral agreement between two Parties under the provisions of Article 2, paragraph 4, the minimum contribution may not be less than 20% and the largest contribution may not exceed 80% of the total production cost of the cinematographic work.

Article 7 – Rights of co – producers

1. The co - production contract must guarantee to each co - producer joint ownership of the original picture and sound negative. The contract shall include the provision that this negative shall be kept in a place mutually agreed by the co - producers, and shall guarantee them free access to it.

2. The co - production contract must also guarantee to each co - producer

the right to an internegative or to any other medium of duplication.

Article 8 – Technical and artistic participation

1. The contribution of each of the co - producers shall include effective technical and artistic participation. In principle, and in accordance with international obligations binding the Parties, the contribution of the co - producers relating to creative, technical and artistic personnel, cast and facilities, must be proportional to their investment.

2. Subject to the international obligations binding the Parties and to the demands of the screenplay, the technical and craft team involved in filming the work must be made up of nationals of the States which are partners in the co - production, and post - production shall normally be carried out in those States.

Article 9 – Financial co – productions

1. Notwithstanding the provisions of Article 8, and subject to the specific conditions and limits laid down in the laws and regulations in force in the Parties, co - productions may be granted co - production status under the provisions of this Convention if they meet the following conditions:

a. include one or more minority contributions which may be financial only, in accordance with the co - production contract, provided that each national share is neither less than 10% nor more than 25% of the production costs;

b. include a majority co - producer who makes an effective technical and artistic contribution and satisfies the conditions for the cinematographic work to be recognised as a national work in his country;

c. help to promote a European identity; and

d. are embodied in co - production contracts which include provisions for the distribution of receipts.

2. Financial co - productions shall only qualify for co - production status once the competent authorities have given their approval in each individual case, in particular taking into account the provisions of Article 10 below.

Article 10 – General balance

1. A general balance must be maintained in the cinematographic relations of the Parties, with regard both to the total amount invested and the artistic and technical participation in co - production cinematographic works.

2. A Party which, over a reasonable period, observes a deficit in its co - pro-

duction relations with one or more other Parties may, with a view to maintaining its cultural identity, withhold its approval of a subsequent co - production until balanced cinematographic relations with that or those Parties have been restored.

Article 11 – Entry and residence

In accordance with the laws and regulations and international obligations in force, each Party shall facilitate entry and residence, as well as the granting of work permits in its territory, of technical and artistic personnel from other Parties participating in a co - production. Similarly, each Party shall permit the temporary import and re - export of equipment necessary to the production and distribution of cinematographic works falling within the scope of this Convention.

Article 12 – Credits of co – producing countries

1. Co - producing countries shall be credited in co - produced cinematographic works.

2. The names of these countries shall be clearly mentioned in the credit titles, in all publicity and promotion material and when the cinematographic works are being shown.

Article 13 – Export

When a co - produced cinematographic work is exported to a country where imports of cinematographic works are subject to quotas, and one of the co - producing Parties does not have the right of free entry for his cinematographic works to the importing country:

a. the cinematographic work shall normally be added to the quota of the country which has the majority participation;

b. in the case of a cinematographic work which comprises an equal participation from different countries, the cinematographic work shall be added to the quota of the country which has the best opportunities for exporting to the importing country;

c. when the provisions of sub - paragraphs a and b above cannot be applied, the cinematographic work shall be entered in the quota of the Party which provides the director.

Article 14 – Languages

When according co - production status, the competent authority of a Party may demand from the co - producer established therein a final version of the cinematographic work in one of the languages of that Party.

Article 15 – Festivals

Unless the co - producers decide otherwise, co - produced cinematographic works shall be shown at international festivals by the Party where the majority co-producer is established, or, in the case of equal financial participation, by the Party which provides the director.

Chapter III – Final provisions

Article 16 – Signature, ratification, acceptance, approval

1. This Convention shall be open for signature by the member States of the Council of Europe and the other States party to the European Cultural Convention which may express their consent to be bound by:

a. signature without reservation as to ratification, acceptance or approval; or

b. signature subject to ratification, acceptance or approval, followed by ratification, acceptance or approval.

2. Instruments of ratification, acceptance or approval shall be deposited with the Secretary General of the Council of Europe.

Article 17 – Entry into force

1. The Convention shall enter into force on the first day of the month following the expiration of a period of three months after the date on which five States, including at least four member States of the Council of Europe, have expressed their consent to be bound by the Convention in accordance with the provisions of Article 16.

2. In respect of any signatory State which subsequently expresses its consent to be bound by it, the Convention shall enter into force on the first day of the month following the expiration of a period of three months after the date of signature or of the deposit of the instrument of ratification, acceptance or approval.

Article 18 – Accession of non – member States

1. After the entry into force of this Convention, the Committee of Ministers of the Council of Europe may invite any European State not a member of the Council of Europe as well as the European Economic Community to accede to this Convention, by a decision taken by the majority provided for in Article 20. d of the

Statute of the Council of Europe, and by the unanimous vote of the representatives of the Contracting States entitled to sit on the Committee of Ministers.

2. In respect of any acceding State or of the European Economic Community, in the event of its accession, the Convention shall enter into force on the first day of the month following the expiration of a period of three months after the date of deposit of the instrument of accession with the Secretary General of the Council of Europe.

Article 19 – Territorial clause

1. Any State may, at the time of signature or when depositing its instrument of ratification, acceptance, approval or accession, specify the territory or territories to which this Convention shall apply.

2. Any Party may, at any later date, by a declaration addressed to the Secretary General of the Council of Europe, extend the application of this Convention to any other territory specified in the declaration. In respect of such territory, the Convention shall enter into force on the first day of the month following the expiration of a period of three months after the date of receipt of such declaration by the Secretary General.

3. Any declaration made under the two preceding paragraphs may, in respect of any territory specified in such declaration, be withdrawn by a notification addressed to the Secretary General. The withdrawal shall become effective on the first day of the month following the expiration of a period of three months after the date of receipt of such notification by the Secretary General.

Article 20 – Reservations

1. Any State may, at the time of signature or when depositing its instrument of ratification, acceptance, approval or accession, declare that Article 2, paragraph 4, does not apply to its bilateral co - production relations with one or more Parties. Moreover, it may reserve the right to fix a maximum participation share different from that laid down in Article 9, paragraph 1. a. No other reservation may be made.

2. Any Party which has made a reservation under the preceding paragraph may wholly or partly withdraw it by means of a notification addressed to the Secretary General of the Council of Europe. The withdrawal shall take effect on the date of receipt of such notification by the Secretary General.

Article 21 – Denunciation

1. Any Party may, at any time, denounce this Convention by means of a notification addressed to the Secretary General of the Council of Europe.

2. Such denunciation shall become effective on the first day of the month following the expiration of a period of six months after the date of receipt of the notification by the Secretary General.

Article 22 – Notifications

The Secretary General of the Council of Europe shall notify the member States of the Council, as well as any State and the European Economic Community which may accede to this Convention or may be invited to do so, of:

a. any signature;

b. the deposit of any instrument of ratification, acceptance, approval or accession;

c. any date of entry into force of this Convention in accordance with Articles 17, 18 and 19;

d. any declaration made in accordance with Article 5, paragraph 5;

e. any denunciation notified in accordance with Article 21;

f. any other act, notification or communication relating to this Convention.

In witness whereof the undersigned, being duly authorised thereto, have signed this Convention.

Done at Strasbourg, this 2nd day of October 1992, in English and French, both texts being equally authentic, in a single copy which shall be deposited in the archives of the Council of Europe. The Secretary General of the Council of Europe shall transmit certified copies to the States mentioned in Article 16, paragraph 1, as well as to any State and to the European Economic Community which may be invited to accede to this Convention.

Appendix I – Application procedure

In order to benefit from the provisions of this Convention, the co - producers established in the Parties must, two months before shooting commences, submit an application for co - production status and attach the documents listed below. These documents must reach the competent authorities in sufficient number for them to be communicated to the authorities of the other Parties at the latest one month before shooting commences:

- a copy of the contract for the purchase of the copyright or any other proof of purchase of the copyright for the commercial exploitation of the work;
- a detailed script;
- a list of the technical and artistic contributions from each of the countries involved;
- an estimate and a detailed financing plan;
- a production schedule of the cinematographic work;
- the co - production contract made between the co - producers. This contract must include clauses providing for the distribution of receipts or territories between the co - producers.

The application and other documents shall be presented, if possible, in the language of the competent authorities to which they are submitted.

The competent national authorities shall send each other the application and attached documentation once they have been received. The competent authority of the Party with the minority financial participation shall not give its approval until the opinion of the Party with the majority financial participation has been received.

Appendix II

1. A cinematographic work qualifies as European in the sense of Article 3, paragraph 3, if it achieves at least 15 points out of a possible total of 19, according to the schedule of European elements set out below.

2. Having regard to the demands of the screenplay, the competent authorities may, after consulting together, and if they consider that the work nonetheless reflects a European identity, grant co - production status to the work with a number of points less than the normally required 15 points.

European elements	Weighting Points
Creative group	
Director	3
Script writer	3
Composer	1

European elements	Weighting Points
	——
	7
Performing group	
First role	3
Second role	2
Third role	1
	——
	6
Technical craft group	
Cameraman	1
Sound recordist	1
Editor	1
Art director	1
Studio or shooting location	1
Post – production location	1
	——
	6

N. B.

a. First, second and third roles are determined by number of days worked.

b. So far as Article 8 is concerned, "artistic" refers to the creative and performing groups, "technical" refers to the technical and craft group.

关于倡导使用多种语言、促进网络普及的建议*

（联合国教科文组织2003年10月15日通过）

序　　言

联合国教科文组织大会：

承诺全面落实《世界人权宣言》和其他国际公认的法律文书中所宣布的人权和基本自由，牢记1966年关于公民权利和政治权利以及关于经济、社会和文化权利的两个国际公约；

注意到“联合国教育、科学及文化组织在信息与传播领域以及在贯彻该组织大会通过的有关这一领域的决定和联大有关这一问题的决议的相关章节方面所起的重要作用”；

忆及教科文组织的《组织法》在前言中确认“文化之广泛传播以及为争取正义、自由与和平对人类进行之教育为维护人类尊严不可缺少之举措，亦为一切国家关切互助之精神，必须履行之神圣义务”；

还忆及《组织法》第1条规定教科文组织的宗旨与职能之一为“建议订立必要之国际协定，以便运用文字与形象促进思想之自由交流”；

坚决维护教科文组织大会第三十一届会议通过的《世界文化多样性宣言》所体现的原则，尤其是《宣言》的第5条、第6条和第8条；

参照教科文组织大会有关提倡多种语言和普及网络空间的各项决议；

相信新的信息与传播技术的发展为更好地使用文字和图像自由传播思想提供了机遇，但也对确保人人参与全球信息社会提出了挑战；

注意到全球信息网络中的语言多样性和普及使用网络空间中的信息问题

* 中国社会科学院法学研究所吴峻译。

是当今许多争论的焦点，并将对知识社会的发展起到决定性的影响；

认识到要促进普及使用信息，必须考虑知识产权方面的国际条约与协议；

认识到信息匮乏者，特别是发展中国家，必须提高获得和应用新技术的能力；

认识到基础教育和扫盲教育是普及网络空间的前提；

考虑到不同的经济发展水平会影响到网络空间的使用，必须制定特定的政策和加强互助来改变目前的不平衡现象，并营造一种相互信任与谅解的气氛；

特通过本建议书：

开发多种语言的内容和系统

1. 地方、国家、地区和国际各级的公共部门和私营部门与民间组织应努力提供必要的资金和采取必要的措施，鼓励用数字化技术制作、处理和使用教育、文化和科学方面的内容，以减少因特网上的语言障碍和促进人际交往，从而确保所有的文化都能用不同的语言，包括本土语言，来表现自己和使用网络空间。

2. 会员国和国际组织应鼓励和支持在因特网上制作有地方特色和本土色彩的内容的能力建设。

3. 会员国应就网络空间中语言生存这一重要问题制定合适的国家政策，目的是在网络空间中促进包括母语在内的语言教学。应加强和扩大对发展中国家的国际支持和援助，帮助它们开发免费使用的数字化语言教材和提高这一方面的人员的基本能力。

4. 会员国、国际组织和信息与传播技术产业应鼓励合作研制、开发和根据本地情况改造具有多种语言功能的操作系统、搜索引擎和网络浏览器，以及网上词典和术语库。应支持国际合作，共同开发供大家使用的自动翻译工具和智能语言系统，如可用多种语言进行资料检索、编写总结或摘要和语音识别的工具，同时充分尊重作者的翻译权。

5. 教科文组织应和其他国际组织合作，建立一个网上观察站，随时了解使用多种语言和多语种的资料及其应用方面的现行政策、法规、技术建议和最佳经验，包括语言电脑化方面的革新。

推动网络和服务的使用

6. 会员国和国际组织应重视和支持因特网的普及使用，使其成为促进《世界人权宣言》第19条和第27条所确认的人权的工具。

7. 会员国和国际组织应制定必要的政策，将因特网的使用作为一项公益服务加以普及，以加快提高国民和公民社会的能力的步伐，并应充分考虑农村地区的需要，鼓励在发展中国家中切实执行和支持这些政策。

8. 会员国和国际组织应特别考虑公共机构、教育机构、弱势群体和残疾人的需要，在地方、国家、地区和国际各级建立相关的机制，收取可承受的电讯和网络费用，普及因特网的使用。为此，应在这一方面建立新的鼓励机制，包括鼓励公私合营以吸引投资和减少信息与传播技术使用方面的经济障碍，如降低对信息技术设备、软件和服务征收的各项税收和关税。

9. 会员国应鼓励因特网服务商考虑以优惠价格向学校、科研机构、博物馆、档案馆和公共图书馆等公共服务机构提供网络接入服务，作为向普及使用网络空间的过渡措施。

10. 会员国应鼓励制定信息策略和模式，推动社会各阶层使用信息技术，包括设立社区项目，培养当地的信息与传播技术带头人和顾问。这些策略还应鼓励公共服务机构之间在信息与传播技术方面开展合作，以降低使用因特网的费用。

11. 应本着国际合作的精神，在协商后公平分摊费用的基础上，鼓励发展中国家中将私营的和非营利性的因特网服务商连接起来的因特网对接点与其他国家（无论是发展中国家还是工业发达国家）的对接点互相连接。

12. 地区组织和论坛应鼓励在地区之间和地区内部建立由大容量的地区骨干网络支持的网络，在公开竞争的环境中将所有国家在一个全球网络中连接起来。

13. 联合国系统内部应通力合作，交流在社会经济发展中使用信息与传播技术网络与服务的信息和经验，包括开放源码技术以及发展中国家的政策制定和能力建设。

14. 会员国和国际组织应在域名管理，包括多种语言的域名管理上，加强必要的合作。

开发公有的内容

15．会员国应承认并保障人人都有通过网络获取公有的和政府持有的信息资料的权利，包括现代民主社会的公民应该了解的信息，同时充分注意这类信息的使用中的保密性、隐私性、国家安全和知识产权等问题。国际组织应承认并宣布每个国家都有获得与本国的社会或经济状况有关的基本数据资料的权利。

16．会员国和国际组织应指定和支持公有知识信息库，供大家使用，从而营造有助于创作和扩大服务对象的学习环境。为此，必须提供充足的资金来保护公有领域的信息并将其数字化。

17．会员国和国际组织应鼓励尊重公私双方利益的合作方式，使公有的信息在不受地域、经济、社会或文化歧视的情况下得到普及使用。

18．会员国和国际组织应鼓励开放使用信息的措施，包括为信息的交流、软件的可移植性和互用性以及在全球信息网络上使用公有的信息制定统一的方法和技术标准。

19．会员国和国际组织应促进和推动信息与传播技术方面的扫盲教育，包括普及信息与传播技术和建立起对它的信任。为信息社会培养人才至关重要，应将信息与传播技术的技能培训，与开放的、综合的和跨文化的教育结合起来。这种培训不应局限于业务技能，还应包括伦理原则与价值观意识。

20．应加强联合国内部的机构间合作，以便把从各种发展项目和计划中积累起来的大量信息资源汇集成可供大家使用的知识，尤其是供发展中国家和处境不利的群体使用。

21．教科文组织应与其他有关的政府间组织密切合作，编纂一部介绍各国有关公有信息的生产和在网上传播的立法、法规和政策的汇编。

22．应当在充分尊重言论自由的前提下鼓励信息制作者、使用者和服务供应商总结和采用成功经验以及自觉遵守职业道德和公共道德。

重申公平兼顾权利拥有者与公众双方的利益

23．会员国应与有关各方密切合作，修订本国的版权法，并使其适用于网络空间，同时充分注意国际版权和相关权利的公约中规定的确保作者、著作权和相关权利拥有者与公众之间公正与公平的权益。

24. 会员国和国际组织必要时应鼓励权利拥有者和著作权保护及相关权利保护的各种限制和例外规定的合法受益者确保只有在某些特殊情况下使用这种限制和例外规定，不得违反作品的正常使用，也不得构成对权利拥有者根据知识产权组织版权条约（WCT）和知识产权组织表演和录音制品条约（WPPT）所拥有的合法权益的无理侵害。

25. 会员国和国际组织应谨慎对待技术革新及其对在国际条约和协议规定的著作权保护和相关权利保护的范围内获取和使用信息可能产生的影响。

大会建议各会员国采取法律的或其他必要的手段实施以上各项条款，并在各自的领土和管辖范围内实行本建议书所提出的各项准则与原则。

大会建议各会员国要求负责信息与传播技术的政策、策略和基础设施工作，包括在因特网上使用多种语言，开发网络和服务，扩大因特网上的公有信息以及保护知识产权的公共部门及私人机构重视本建议书。

大会要求各会员国按大会指定的日期和方式向大会报告各国为落实本建议书所采取的措施。

附录：

定义

在本建议书中，

（a）骨干网络（backbone）是把若干容量较小的网络链接起来的大容量网络。

（b）版权的限制和例外规定（Copyright limitations and exceptions）是版权法和相关权利法中对作者或其他权利拥有者利用其著作或受相关权利保护的其他作品的专有权利加以限制的规定。这种限制和例外规定的主要形式有强制许可证、法定许可证和合理使用。

（c）网络空间（cyberspace）指全球信息基础结构范围内用数字化或电子手段进行交流的虚拟世界。

（d）域名（domain name）是给因特网网址的名称，如 http：//www.unesco.org 中的“unesco.org”，便于用户查找网上资源。

（e）智能语言系统（intelligent linguistic systems）把当今电脑的快速运算、数据检索和操作能力，与更为抽象和微妙的推理能力，以及对某种语言或多种语言的人际交流中只能意会不能言传的细微差别的理解能力相结合，从而在更高的层次上模拟人类交流。

（f）因特网服务供应商（ISP）指提供因特网上网服务的供应商。

（g）互用性（interoperability）指不同商家的不同设备所用的软件和硬件能够共用数据的性能。

（h）开放源码技术（open source technology）由 Open Source Initiative（OSI）以开放源码为前提制订的一种认证标准，表明电脑程序的源代码（原始的或用编程语言写成的程序指令）供公众免费使用。

（i）点对点连接（peering）指两个或两个以上的因特网服务供应商（ISPs）之间的一种关系，它们相互之间建立直接的连接，并同意通过这一连接，而不是因特网骨干网络，相互直接转送数据包。当这种连接涉及两个以上的因特网服务供应商时，传给任何一个因特网服务供应商的所有信息将首先送到一个中央交换处，即"对接点"（peering point），然后再转送到最终目的地。

（j）可移植性（portability）指软件不需特定的机器或硬件即可在各种电脑上使用的性能。

（k）公有信息（public domain information）指可以自由利用的信息，不会侵犯任何合法权利，也不违反任何保密的义务。因此它既指因未受国家法律或国际法的保护或保护期已过而无须授权即可由任何人使用的所有著作或受相关权利保护的其他作品，也指各国政府或国际组织编制的并自愿提供的公开数据和官方信息。

（l）搜索引擎（search engine）是一种软件功能，可以按指定的关键词查找文件，并检索出包含该关键词的文件。

（m）普及使用网络空间（univers alaccessto cyber space）指所有公民以能够承受的价格公平使用信息基础设施（尤其是因特网）以及人类集体和个人的发展所必需的信息和知识。

（n）浏览器（web browser）是用于查找并显示因特网网页的应用软件。

Recommendation concerning the Promotion and Use of Multilingualism and Universal Access to Cyberspace

15 October 2003

The General Conference,

Committed to the full implementation of the human rights and fundamental freedoms proclaimed in the Universal Declaration of Human Rights and other universally recognized legal instruments, and mindful of the two International Covenants of 1966 relating respectively to civil and political rights and to economic, social and cultural rights,

Recognizing the "central and important role of the United Nations Educational, Scientific and Cultural Organization in the field of information and communication and in the implementation of the relevant decisions in this area adopted by the General Conference of that Organization and of the relevant parts of the Assembly resolutions on the subject",

Recalling that the Preamble to the Constitution of UNESCO affirms, "that the wide diffusion of culture, and the education of humanity for justice and liberty and peace are indispensable to the dignity of man and constitute a sacred duty which all the nations must fulfil in a spirit of mutual assistance and concern",

Further recalling Article I of the Constitution, which assigns to UNESCO among other purposes that of recommending "such international agreements as may be necessary to promote the free flow of ideas by word and image",

Affirming the principles embodied in the Universal Declaration on Cultural Diversity, adopted by the General Conference of UNESCO at its 31st session and particularly its Articles 5, 6 and 8,

Referring to the resolutions of the General Conference of UNESCO with regard to the promotion of multilingualism and universal access to information in cyberspace,

Convinced that the development of new information and communication technologies (ICTs) provides opportunities to improve the free flow of ideas by word and image but also presents challenges for ensuring the participation of all in the global information society,

Noting that linguistic diversity in the global information networks and universal access to information in cyberspace are at the core of contemporary debates and can be a determining factor in the development of a knowledge - based society,

Taking into account international treaties and agreements on intellectual property, in order to facilitate the promotion of universal access to information,

Acknowledging the need for capacity - building, particularly for developing countries, in acquisition and application of the new technologies for the information - poor,

Recognizing that basic education and literacy are prerequisites for universal access to cyberspace,

Considering that different levels of economic development affect prospects for access to cyberspace and that specific policies and increased solidarity are required to redress current asymmetries and create a climate of mutual trust and understanding,

Adopts the present Recommendation:

Development of multilingual content and systems

1. The public and private sectors and the civil society at local, national, regional and international levels should work to provide the necessary resources and take the necessary measures to alleviate language barriers and promote human interaction on the Internet by encouraging the creation and processing of, and access to, educational, cultural and scientific content in digital form, so as to ensure that all cultures can express themselves and have access to cyberspace in all languages, including indigenous ones.

2. Member States and international organizations should encourage and support capacity - building for the production of local and indigenous content on the Internet.

3. Member States should formulate appropriate national policies on the crucial

issue of language survival in cyberspace, designed to promote the teaching of languages, including mother tongues, in cyberspace. International support and assistance to developing countries should be strengthened and extended to facilitate the development of freely accessible materials on language education in electronic form and to the enhancement of human capital skills in this area.

4. Member States, international organizations and information and communication technology industries should encourage collaborative participatory research and development on, and local adaptation of, operating systems, search engines and web browsers with extensive multilingual capabilities, online dictionaries and terminologies. They should support international cooperative efforts with regard to automated translation services accessible to all, as well as intelligent linguistic systems such as those performing multilingual information retrieval, summarizing/abstracting and speech understanding, while fully respecting the right of translation of authors.

5. UNESCO, in cooperation with other international organizations, should establish a collaborative online observatory on existing policies, regulations, technical recommendations, and best practices relating to multilingualism and multilingual resources and applications, including innovations in language computerization.

Facilitating access to networks and services

6. Member States and international organizations should recognize and support universal access to the Internet as an instrument for promoting the realization of the human rights as defined in Articles 19 and 27 of the Universal Declaration of Human Rights.

7. Member States and international organizations should promote access to the Internet as a service of public interest through the adoption of appropriate policies in order to enhance the process of empowering citizenship and civil society, and by encouraging proper implementation of, and support to, such policies in developing countries, with due consideration of the needs of rural communities.

8. In particular, Member States and international organizations should establish mechanisms at the local, national, regional and international levels to facilitate universal access to the Internet through affordable telecommunications and Internet

costs with special consideration given to the needs of public service and educational institutions, and of disadvantaged and disabled population groups. New incentives in this area should be designed towards this end including public - private partnerships to encourage investment and the lowering of financial barriers to the use of ICT, such as taxes and customs duties on informatics equipment, software and services.

9. Member States should encourage Internet service providers (ISPs) to consider provision of concessionary rates for Internet access in public service institutions, such as schools, academic institutions, museums, archives and public libraries, as a transitional measure towards universal access to cyberspace.

10. Member States should encourage the development of information strategies and models that facilitate community access and reach out to all levels of society, including the setting up of community projects and fostering the emergence of local information and communication technology leaders and mentors. Strategies should also support cooperation on ICT among public service institutions, as a means of reducing the cost of access to Internet services.

11. Interconnection on a negotiated cost - sharing basis in the spirit of international cooperation should be encouraged between national Internet peering points combining the traffic of private and non - profit ISPs in developing countries and peering points in other countries whether developing or industrialized.

12. Regional organizations and forums should encourage the establishment of inter - and intra - regional networks powered by high - capacity regional backbones to connect each country within a global network in an open competitive environment.

13. Concerted efforts within the United Nations system should promote the sharing of information about and experience on the use of ICT - based networks and services in socio - economic development, including open source technologies, as well as policy formulation and capacity - building in developing countries.

14. Member States and international organizations should promote appropriate partnerships in the management of domain names, including multilingual domain names.

Development of public domain content

15. Member States should recognize and enact the right of universal online access to public and government - held records including information relevant for citizens in a modern democratic society, giving due account to confidentiality, privacy and national security concerns, as well as to intellectual property rights to the extent that they apply to the use of such information. International organizations should recognize and promulgate the right for each State to have access to essential data relating to its social or economic situation.

16. Member States and international organizations should identify and promote repositories of information and knowledge in the public domain and make them accessible by all, thus shaping learning environments conducive to creativity and audience development. To this end, adequate funding should be provided for the preservation and digitization of public domain information.

17. Member States and international organizations should encourage cooperative arrangements which respect both public and private interests in order to ensure universal access to information in the public domain without geographical, economic, social or cultural discrimination.

18. Member States and international organizations should encourage open access solutions including the formulation of technical and methodological standards for information exchange, portability and interoperability, as well as online accessibility of public domain information on global information networks.

19. Member States and international organizations should promote and facilitate ICT literacy, including popularizing and building trust in ICT implementation and use. The development of "human capital" for the information society, including an open, integrated and intercultural education combined with skills training in ICT, is of crucial importance. ICT training should not be limited to technical competence but should also include awareness of ethical principles and values.

20. Inter - agency cooperation within the United Nations system should be reinforced with a view to building up a universally accessible body of knowledge, particularly for the benefit of developing countries and disadvantaged communities, from the massive amount of information produced through development projects

and programmes.

21. UNESCO, in close cooperation with other intergovernmental organizations concerned, should undertake the compilation of an international inventory of legislation, regulations and policies on the generation and online dissemination of public domain information.

22. Definition and adoption of best practices and voluntary, self - regulatory, professional and ethical guidelines should be encouraged among information producers, users and service providers with due respect to freedom of expression.

Reaffirming the equitable balance between the interests of rights – holders and the public interest

23. Member States should undertake, in close cooperation with all interested parties, the updating of national copyright legislation and its adaptation to cyberspace, taking full account of the fair balance between the interests of authors, copyright and related rights - holders, and of the public embodied in international copyright and related rights conventions.

24. Member States and international organizations, when appropriate, should encourage rights - holders and the lawful beneficiaries of limitations and exceptions to copyright and related rights protection to ensure that such limitations and exceptions are applied in certain special cases that do not conflict with a normal exploitation of the work and do not unreasonably prejudice the legitimate interests of the rights - holders as required for in the WIPO Copyright Treaty (WCT) and the WIPO Performances and Phonograms Treaty (WPPT).

25. Member States and international organizations should pay careful attention to the development of technological innovations and to their potential impact on access to information in the framework of copyright and related rights protection under international treaties and agreements.

* * *

The General Conference recommends that Member States apply the above provisions by taking whatever legislative or other steps are required to give effect within their respective territories and jurisdictions to the norms and principles set forth in this recommendation.

The General Conference recommends that Member States bring this recommendation to the attention of the authorities and services responsible for public and private works on ICT policies, strategies and infrastructures, including use of multilingualism on the Internet, the development of networks and services, expansion of public domain information on the Internet and intellectual property rights issues.

The General Conference recommends that Member States should report to it, on the dates and in a manner to be determined by it, on the action they have taken to give effect to this recommendation.

Appendix

Definitions

For the purpose of this Recommendation:

(a) **Backbone** is a high - capacity network that links together other networks of lower capacity;

(b) **Copyright limitations and exceptions** are provisions in copyright and related rights laws restricting the right of the author or other rights - holders with regard to the exploitation of their work or object of related rights. The main forms of such limitations and exceptions are compulsory licenses, statutory licenses and fair use;

(c) **Cyberspace** is the virtual world for digital or electronic communication associated with the global information infrastructure;

(d) **Domain name** is the name given to an Internet address, which facilitates access to Internet resources by users (e. g. "unesco. org" in http: //www. unesco. org);

(e) **Intelligent linguistic systems** combine the rapid computational, data retrieval and manipulation power of today's computers with the more abstract and subtle reasoning skills and understanding of nuances that are implied but not necessarily explicitly stated in inter - human communication within and across languages, thus allowing the simulation of human communication to a high degree;

(f) **Internet service provider (ISP)** is a supplier of Internet access services;

(g) **Interoperability** is the ability of software and hardware on different machines from different vendors to share data;

(h) **Open source technologies** are based on the premise of open source, a certification standard issued by the Open Source Initiative (OSI) that indicates that the source code (program instructions in their original form or programming language) of a computer program is made available free of charge to the general public;

(i) **Peering** is a relationship between two or more ISPs in which the ISPs create a direct link between them and agree to forward each other's packets directly across this link instead of using the Internet backbone. When peering involves more than two ISPs, all traffic destined for any of the ISPs is first routed to a central exchange, called a peering point, and then forwarded to the final destination;

(j) **Portability** refers to the ability of software to be used on a variety of computers without necessitating a particular machine or hardware;

(k) **Public domain information** is publicly accessible information, the use of which does not infringe any legal right, or any obligation of confidentiality. It thus refers on the one hand to the realm of all works or objects of related rights, which can be exploited by everybody without any authorization, for instance because protection is not granted under national or international law, or because of the expiration of the term of protection. It refers on the other hand to public data and official information produced and voluntarily made available by governments or international organizations;

(l) **Search engine** is a software application that searches documents for specified keywords and localizes or retrieves the documents where the keywords were found;

(m) **Universal access to cyberspace** is equitable and affordable access by all citizens to information infrastructure (notably to the Internet) and to information and knowledge essential to collective and individual human development;

(n) **Web browser** is a software application used to locate and display World Wide Web pages.

Monitoring:

- Recommendation for which monitoring the Executive Board is responsible (more information)
- Timetable of the 3rd Consultation (2015):

- 2nd Consultation (2011):

Presentation of the consolidated report at the General Conference at its 36th session (Autumn 2011)

36 C/Resolution 58

Report of the CI Commission

Report of the Legal Committee (36 C/LEG/4)

Consolidated report on the implementation by Member States of the 2003 Recommendation concerning the Promotion and Use of Multilingualism and Universal Access to Cyberspace (2003) (36 C/26)

Examination of the consolidated report by the Executive Board at its 186th session (Spring 2011)

186 EX/Decision 19 (IV)

Report of the Committee on Conventions and Recommendations (186 EX/45)

Application of the 2003 Recommendation concerning the Promotion and Use of Multilinguism and Universal Access to Cyberespace (186 EX/19 Part IV)

Circular letter CL/3926 of 11 June 2010

- 1st Consultation (2007):

34 C/Resolution 49

First consolidated report to the General Conference on the measures taken by Member States for the implementation of the Recommendation concerning the Promotion and Use of Multilingualism and Universal Access to Cyberspace (34 C/23)

保护数字遗产宪章*

（联合国教科文组织2003年10月15日通过）

导　言

大会考虑到任何形式的遗产的消失都是全人类遗产的损失，忆及教科文组织的《组织法》规定，本组织应保证对图书、艺术作品及历史和科学文物等世界遗产之保存与维护，以维护、增进及传播知识；其“全民信息”计划为制定信息政策和保护有记载的知识提供了一个讨论和行动的框架；其“世界记忆”计划旨在确保世界文献遗产的保存和普遍使用，注意到信息和创造性表达方式方面的这些资源的生产、传播、使用和保存越来越多地采用数字化的形式，从而产生了一种新的遗产，即数字遗产，意识到利用这种遗产将为人类知识的创造、交流和共享提供更多的机会，认识到这种数字遗产正濒临消失的危险，为当代人和后代人保存这种遗产是全世界关注的紧迫问题，宣布下列原则并通过本宪章。

数字化遗产是共同遗产

第1条　范围

数字遗产由人类的知识和表达方式的独特资源组成。它包括以数字方式生成的或从现有的模拟资源转换成数字形式的有关文化、教育、科学和行政管理的资源及有关技术、法律、医学及其他领域的信息。那些“原生数字”资源，除了数字形式外，别无其他形式。

数字资源的形式多种多样，且日益增多，包括文字、数据库、静止的和

---

* 中国社会科学院法学研究所吴峻译。

活动的图像、声音和图表、软件和网页等。它们存在的时间一般不长，需要有意地制作、维护和管理才能保存下来。

这类资源大多具有长久的价值和意义，因而是一种应为当代人和后代人而加以保护和保存的遗产。各种语言、世界各地和人类的各种知识或表达方式都可能有这种呈增长趋势的遗产。

第2条 数字遗产的使用

保存数字遗产的目的是为了确保其始终都能被公众所使用。因此，数字遗产资料，尤其是公有的数字遗产资料的使用不应受到不合理的限制。同时，对那些敏感的信息和个人信息应加以保护，以防任何形式的侵犯。

会员国可能希望与有关组织和机构合作，创造一个有法可依和切实可行的环境，以利于最大限度地使用数字遗产。应根据有关的国际准则和协议，重申和促进在数字遗产资料的使用方面对创作者及其他权利拥有者的合法权益与公众的利益这两者的合理兼顾。

防止数字化遗产的消失

第3条 消失的危险

世界上的数字遗产面临着消失和失传的危险，造成这种状况的因素包括：能创制这种遗产的软件和硬件迅速淘汰，维护和保存这类遗产的资金、责任和方法都不确定，以及缺少相关的立法。

观念的转变落后于技术的更替。数字技术的发展日新月异，耗资巨大，各国政府和有关机构无法及时地制定出相应的保存策略。数字遗产具有经济、社会、知识和文化价值，是建设未来的重要元素，但正面临着威胁，而对这种威胁的认识尚不充分。

第4条 采取行动的必要性

如果不着手解决目前所面临的有关威胁，数字遗产将会迅速丢失，而且不可避免。会员国应鼓励采用法律、经济和技术手段来保护这种遗产，必将受益匪浅。当务之急是开展宣传工作，促使决策者和广大公众都意识到数字媒体的潜力和保存工作的实际问题。

第5条 数字遗产的持久性

数字遗产的持久性是至关重要的。要保存数字遗产，必须在数字信息从产生到使用的整个生命周期中都采取措施。数字遗产的长期保存首先需要设计出能够制作完全相同并具有稳定性的数字产品的可靠系统和程序。

必要的措施

第 6 条 制定策略和政策

应根据紧迫程度、当地的情况、现有的方法和未来的打算等因素，制定出保存数字遗产的策略和政策。这需要著作权和相关权利拥有者以及其他有关各方在制定共同标准和兼容方式及资源共享方面进行合作。

第 7 条 确定保存对象

同保存所有文献遗产一样，保存数字遗产的选择标准可因国家而异，但决定哪些数字资料应予以保存的主要标准是有关数字资料的重要性及其在文化、科学、提供证据或其他方面所具有的长远的价值。显然应优先保存“原生数字”资料。选择的决定和随后的复审应认真负责，按照已确定的原则、政策、程序和标准进行。

第 8 条 保护数字遗产

为了保护数字遗产，会员国需有必要的法律和体制框架。

作为国家遗产保护政策的一项主要内容，档案立法和图书馆、档案馆、博物馆及其他公共存放处的法定存放或自愿存放都应包括数字遗产。

在合理限制的范围内查阅合法存放的数字遗产资料应得到保证，但不得损害其正常使用。

须有确保真品的法律保障和技术保障，以防止对数字遗产的仿造或蓄意篡改。这两方面的保障都要求原样保存好有关的内容、档案功能及资料。

第 9 条 保存文化遗产

数字遗产的固有特点是不受时间、地点、文化或形式的限制。虽然它具有文化特性，但世界上任何人都可以使用。少数人群体可以对多数人群体说话，个人也可以向全球的人说话。

所有地区、国家和社区的数字遗产都应得到保存和加以利用，随着时间的推移，使所有的民族、国家、文化和语言都能得到平等与合理的反映。

职　　责

第 10 条 职能和责任

会员国可能希望指定一个或几个机构负责协调数字遗产的保存工作，并提供必要的资金。可以根据这些机构现有的职能和专长分工负责。

应采取措施：

（a）鼓励硬件和软件的开发者、数字资料的创制者、出版商、出品人、发行人以及其他私营部门的合作伙伴与国家图书馆、档案馆、博物馆和其他公共遗产组织通力合作，共同保存数字遗产；

（b）开展培训和研究，在相关的机构和专业协会之间交流经验、共享知识；

（c）鼓励公立和私立大学和研究机构确保研究资料得到保存。

第 11 条　伙伴关系与合作

保存数字遗产需要政府部门、创制者、出版商、相关企业和遗产机构进行持续不懈的努力。

在当今存在着数字鸿沟的状况下，有必要加强国际合作和互助，使所有国家都能创制、传播和保存自己的数字遗产并使其得到持续不断的利用。

鼓励企业、出版商和大众传媒促进和交流知识和专业技术。

促进制定教育和培训计划，鼓励资源共享，推广研究成果和成功经验，这些都将有助于数字保存技术的普及应用。

第 12 条　教科文组织的作用

教科文组织根据其授权和职能，有责任：

（a）在其各项计划的实施中重视本宪章提出的原则，并促进联合国系统和与保存数字遗产有关的政府间组织和非政府国际组织贯彻这些原则；

（b）成为会员国、政府间组织和非政府国际组织、公民社会及私营部门共同制定保存数字遗产的目标、政策和项目的咨询点和协商论坛；

（c）促进合作、提高认识和能力建设，及提出统一的伦理、法律和技术指导原则，以支持数字遗产保存工作；

（d）根据今后六年中实行本宪章及准则的经验，决定是否有必要为促进和保存数字遗产制定新的准则性文件。

Charter on the Preservation of Digital Heritage

15 October 2003

The General Conference,

Considering that the disappearance of heritage in whatever form constitutes an impoverishment of the heritage of all nations,

Recalling that the Constitution of UNESCO provides that the Organization will maintain, increase and diffuse knowledge, by assuring the conservation and protection of the world's inheritance of books, works of art and monuments of history and science, that its "Information for All" Programme provides a platform for discussions and action on information policies and the safeguarding of recorded knowledge, and that its "Memory of the World" Programme aims to ensure the preservation and universal accessibility of the world's documentary heritage,

Recognizing that such resources of information and creative expression are increasingly produced, distributed, accessed and maintained in digital form, creating a new legacy - the digital heritage,

Aware that access to this heritage will offer broadened opportunities for creation, communication and sharing of knowledge among all peoples,

Understanding that this digital heritage is at risk of being lost and that its preservation for the benefit of present and future generations is an urgent issue of worldwide concern,

Proclaims the following principles and adopts the present Charter.

The digital heritage as a common heritage

Article 1 – Scope

The digital heritage consists of unique resources of human knowledge and expression. It embraces cultural, educational, scientific and administrative resources, as well as technical, legal, medical and other kinds of information created digitally, or converted into digital form from existing analogue resources. Where resources are "born digital", there is no other format but the digital object.

Digital materials include texts, databases, still and moving images, audio, graphics, software and web pages, among a wide and growing range of formats. They are frequently ephemeral, and require purposeful production, maintenance and management to be retained.

Many of these resources have lasting value and significance, and therefore constitute a heritage that should be protected and preserved for current and future generations. This ever - growing heritage may exist in any language, in any part of the world, and in any area of human knowledge or expression.

Article 2 – Access to the digital heritage

The purpose of preserving the digital heritage is to ensure that it remains accessible to the public. Accordingly, access to digital heritage materials, especially those in the public domain, should be free of unreasonable restrictions. At the same time, sensitive and personal information should be protected from any form of intrusion.

Member States may wish to cooperate with relevant organizations and institutions in encouraging a legal and practical environment which will maximize accessibility of the digital heritage. A fair balance between the legitimate rights of creators and other rights holders and the interests of the public to access digital heritage materials should be reaffirmed and promoted, in accordance with international norms and agreements.

Guarding against loss of heritage

Article 3 – The threat of loss

The world's digital heritage is at risk of being lost to posterity. Contributing factors include the rapid obsolescence of the hardware and software which brings it to life, uncertainties about resources, responsibility and methods for maintenance and preservation, and the lack of supportive legislation.

Attitudinal change has fallen behind technological change. Digital evolution has been too rapid and costly for governments and institutions to develop timely and informed preservation strategies. The threat to the economic, social, intellectual and cultural potential of the heritage - the building blocks of the future - has not been fully grasped.

Article 4 – Need for action

Unless the prevailing threats are addressed, the loss of the digital heritage will be rapid and inevitable. Member States will benefit by encouraging legal, economic and technical measures to safeguard the heritage. Awareness - raising and advocacy is urgent, alerting policy - makers and sensitizing the general public to both the potential of the digital media and the practicalities of preservation.

Article 5 – Digital continuity

Continuity of the digital heritage is fundamental. To preserve digital heritage, measures will need to be taken throughout the digital information life cycle, from creation to access. Long - term preservation of digital heritage begins with the design of reliable systems and procedures which will produce authentic and stable digital objects.

Measures required

Article 6 – Developing strategies and policies

Strategies and policies to preserve the digital heritage need to be developed, taking into account the level of urgency, local circumstances, available means and future projections. The cooperation of holders of copyright and related rights, and other stakeholders, in setting common standards and compatibilities, and resource sharing, will facilitate this.

Article 7 – Selecting what should be kept

As with all documentary heritage, selection principles may vary between countries, although the main criteria for deciding what digital materials to keep would be their significance and lasting cultural, scientific, evidential or other value. "Born digital" materials should clearly be given priority. Selection decisions and any subsequent reviews need to be carried out in an accountable manner, and be based on defined principles, policies, procedures and standards.

Article 8 – Protecting the digital heritage

Member States need appropriate legal and institutional frameworks to secure the protection of their digital heritage.

As a key element of national preservation policy, archive legislation and legal or voluntary deposit in libraries, archives, museums and other public repositories should embrace the digital heritage.

Access to legally deposited digital heritage materials, within reasonable restrictions, should be assured without causing prejudice to their normal exploitation.

Legal and technical frameworks for authenticity are crucial to prevent manipulation or intentional alteration of digital heritage. Both require that the content, functionality of files and documentation be maintained to the extent necessary to secure an authentic record.

Article 9 – Preserving cultural heritage

The digital heritage is inherently unlimited by time, geography, culture or format. It is culture - specific, but potentially accessible to every person in the world. Minorities may speak to majorities, the individual to a global audience.

The digital heritage of all regions, countries and communities should be preserved and made accessible, so as to assure over time representation of all peoples, nations, cultures and languages.

Responsibilities

Article 10 – Roles and responsibilities

Member States may wish to designate one or more agencies to take coordinating responsibility for the preservation of the digital heritage, and to make available necessary resources. The sharing of tasks and responsibilities may be based on existing roles and expertise.

Measures should be taken to:

(a) urge hardware and software developers, creators, publishers, producers and distributors of digital materials as well as other private sector partners to cooperate with national libraries, archives, museums and other public heritage organizations in preserving the digital heritage;

(b) develop training and research, and share experience and knowledge among the institutions and professional associations concerned;

(c) encourage universities and other research organizations, both public and private, to ensure preservation of research data.

Article 11 – Partnerships and cooperation

Preservation of the digital heritage requires sustained efforts on the part of governments, creators, publishers, relevant industries and heritage institutions.

In the face of the current digital divide, it is necessary to reinforce international cooperation and solidarity to enable all countries to ensure creation, dissemination, preservation and continued accessibility of their digital heritage.

Industries, publishers and mass communication media are urged to promote and share knowledge and technical expertise.

The stimulation of education and training programmes, resource - sharing arrangements, and dissemination of research results and best practices will democratize access to digital preservation techniques.

Article 12 – The role of UNESCO

UNESCO, by virtue of its mandate and functions, has the responsibility to:

(a) take the principles set forth in this Charter into account in the functioning of its programmes and promote their implementation within the United Nations system and by intergovernmental and international non - governmental organizations concerned with the preservation of the digital heritage;

(b) serve as a reference point and a forum where Member States, intergovernmental and international non - governmental organizations, civil society and the private sector may join together in elaborating objectives, policies and projects in favour of the preservation of the digital heritage;

(c) foster cooperation, awareness - raising and capacity - building, and propose standard ethical, legal and technical guidelines, to support the preservation of the digital heritage;

(d) determine, on the basis of the experience gained over the next six years in implementing the present Charter and the guidelines, whether there is a need for further standard - setting instruments for the promotion and preservation of the digital heritage.

欧洲视听遗产保护公约*

（《欧洲文化公约》成员国及欧盟成员国2001年11月8日于斯特拉斯堡签署，2008年1月1日生效）

前　言

欧洲委员会成员国、《欧洲文化公约》其他缔约方及欧洲共同体作为签署方，

考虑到欧洲委员会的宗旨就是为了在其成员中促进进一步团结，特别目的就是为了确保及促进作为其共同遗产的意识形态及原则；

考虑到欧洲遗产体现了文化认同及其民族的多样性；

考虑到移动影像是欧洲文化遗产的有机组成部分，国家须确保其得到保障并保护其取得繁荣；

考虑到移动影像资料是文化表达的一种形式，是当代社会的反映，是记录日常时间的理想手段，是我们历史的基础，体现着我们的文明；

意识到移动影像资料的脆弱性及其生存并要实现薪火传承而面临的危险；

强调缔约方有责任保障、复原及提供该等遗产的重要性；

决定合作并承诺采取共同行动以保障并确保视听文化遗产的继续发展；

考虑到为保护版权及邻接权的有效国际条约；

考虑到其他国际层面在保护视听遗产领域所进行的工作，同意如下：

---

* 中国社会科学院法学研究所吴峻译。

第一章　引　　言

第 1 条　公约之宗旨

本公约宗旨是确保对欧洲视听遗产的保护及欣赏，这既将之作为艺术形式，也作为我们过去的记录，因此，为了文化、科学及研究目的，基于公共利益，采取收集、保留及提供移动影像资料的手段。

第 2 条　定义

为本公约之目的：

a. “移动影像资料”系指以任何方式在任何介质上录制的任何成套移动影像，无论其是否伴有声音、是否传递了运动的影像；

b. “电影作品”系指任何长度的移动影像资料，尤其系指故事片、动画片及纪录片，目的是在影院上映；

c. “档案机构”系指缔约方指定从事法定交存功能的任何机构；

d. “自发交存”机构系指缔约方为此目的而指定的任何机构。

第 3 条　适用范围

1. 本公约各缔约方须自其生效之时将公约规定适用于所有电影作品。

2. 通过依据本公约第 18 条而起草的协定，本公约只适用须延展至电影作品之外诸如电视制作在内的移动影像资料。

第 4 条　版权及邻接权

本公约的义务在任何情况下都不得影响有关版权及邻接权保护国际条约汇总的规定。本公约规定不得被解释为该等保护的削弱。

第二章　法定交存

第 5 条　法定交存的一般义务

1. 每一缔约方须通过法律或其他适当手段引入交存在有关缔约方领土内经制片或合作制片移动影像资料的义务，以形成其视听遗产的一部分。

2. 移动影像资料在其他某个缔约方予以法定交存的，每一缔约方资助规定对法定交存予以豁免。

第 6 条　档案机构的指定及其职能

1. 每一缔约方须指定一个或多个档案机构，其职能须确保所交存移动影像资料的保存、存档、复原及提供相关咨询。

2. 被指定机构须为公共机构或私人机构，但不得为总体上在媒体领域从事营利活动的任何自然人或法人直接或间接地予以控制。

3. 缔约方承诺监督所授予档案机构职能的履行。

第7条　技术及资金手段

每一缔约方须确保档案机构按照本公约第六条第一款的界定具有必要的手段履行其职务。

第8条　法定交存的条件

1. 每一缔约方须指定需要承担交存义务的自然人或法人。须规定该等交存的条件。尤其须确保档案机构接到原件或者可以重新达到原件质量的材料。

2. 该等材料须在最后版本首次向公众放映后最长12月内或在缔约方规定的其他合理期间内予以交存。如并未向公众放映，该时限须在制作结束之时开始。

第9条　复原交存材料

1. 每一缔约方须鼓励并促进对法定交存移动影像资料的修复，该等材料构成其视听遗产的组成部分而其物理质量已经下降。

2. 每一缔约方可以在其法律中允许为了复原的目的而对法定交存的移动影像资料进行复制。

第10条　紧急措施

每一缔约方须作出适当安排，确保构成其视听遗产组成部分的移动影像资料保存有迫在眉睫之危险的。

第三章　自发交存

第11条　促进自发交存

每一缔约方须鼓励并促进构成其视听遗产组成部分、包括附带材料在内的移动影像材料予以自发交存，该等材料并不符合本公约第五条规定的资格。

第12条　向公众提供

每一缔约方须鼓励自发交存机构通过与权力人订立合同的方式明确所交存移动影像资料可以向公众提供的条件。

第四章　档案及自发交存机构共同适用的一般规定

第13条　共同档案

1. 为更有效率地落实本公约，缔约方可以决定建立联合大会机构及自发交存机构。

2. 档案机构及自发交存机构可以是一个共同机构，但须适用针对两种职能的所有规定。

第 14 条　档案及自发交存机构的合作

每一缔约方须鼓励其档案或自发交存机构之间及与其他缔约方的机构予以合作，以促进：

a. 有关移动影像资料信息之交换；

b. 编纂欧洲视听档案；

c. 发展存储、集中、升级移动影像资料及相关信息的标准程序；

d. 发展电子信息交换的标准程序；

e. 保存播放移动影像找资料的设备。

第 15 条　交存的合同条款

每一缔约方须鼓励档案及自发交存机构与交存方订立合同，明确对于交存移动影像资料的权利和义务。除非法律有规定，该等合同可以明确因所交存资料遭受任何损失而承担责任、权利人临时或永久撤销交存、权利人向档案或自发交存机构因复原或提供其他服务而支付补偿的条件。

第五章　公约之后续事项

第 16 条　常务委员会

1. 为本公约之目的，须设立常务委员会。

2. 每一缔约方可以通过一个或多个代表列席常务委员会。每一缔约方都有权投票。作为缔约方的每一个国家都有一票投票权。对于涉及其职权方面的问题，欧洲共同体须行使投票权，其投票权数量与作为本公约缔约国之成员国的数量一致。对于其职权之外的议题，欧洲共同体不得投票。

3. 欧洲共同体或者第 19 条规定的任何非本公约缔约国国家可以通过观察员列席常务委员会。

4. 常务委员会可以由欧洲委员会秘书长召集。其第一次会议须在本公约生效六个月内召开。其后，只要三分之一的缔约方或者欧洲委员会部长理事会提出要求，或者欧洲委员会秘书长根据第 18 条第二款的规定主动要求，或者一家或多家缔约方根据第 17 条第一款 c 项规定而提出要求，就要召开会议。

5. 多数成员国就构成举行常务委员会会议的法定人数。在满足第 16 条第六款及第 18 条第三款规定的前提下，常务委员会须通过出席会议的三分之二多数作出决定。

6. 常务委员会可以为了履行其职责而寻求专家意见。它可以主动或应有关机构的要求邀请在本公约涵盖领域具有技术资格的任何国际或国内、政府或非政府组织在其某次会议或某次会议的部分以观察员身份出席。邀请该等专家的决定须由缔约方三分之二多数作出。

7. 在满足本公约规定的前提下，常务委员会须制定其自己的程序规则。

第 17 条　常务委员会的职能及其报告

1. 常务委员会须负责本公约的运作及实施。它可以：

a. 就本公约适用向有关缔约方提出建议；

b. 提出任何对本公约的必要建议，并对根据第 18 条规定提出的建议进行审查；

c. 应一个或多个缔约方的要求，对涉及本公约解释的问题予以审查。

d. 就第 19 条规定之外国家受邀加入本公约的国家向部长委员会提出建议。

2. 在每次会议后，常务委员会须向缔约方及欧洲委员会部长理事会就其讨论及所通过任何决定提交报告。

第六章　协定及修改

第 18 条　协定及修改

1. 为了在特定领域发展本公约所规定的原则，须就电影作品之外的移动影像资料达成协定。

2. 缔约国或常务委员会对第一款所规定协定提出的任何建议或者为修改该等协定而提出的任何建议须通告予欧洲委员会秘书长，并由后者转发予欧洲委员会成员国、可能成为本公约缔约国的其他国家及欧洲共同体。欧洲委员会秘书长须在该等建议通告最早两个月之后召开常务委员会会议。

3. 在秘书长根据第二款将建议转发后，常务委员会须在不迟于两个月的时间对建议进行审核。常务委员会须将经缔约方四分之三多数批准的文本提交予部长理事会以便予以通过。

4. 根据上款规定而通过对公约作出的任何修改须在所有各方已通知接受修改之后的第三十天生效。修改已得到部长理事会通过但尚未生效的，有关国家或欧洲共同体不得在没有接受修改的同时表达其加入本公约的意愿。

5. 部长理事会须对本公约协定之生效及基于常务委员会根据第三款规定提交文本而对该等协定进行修改之生效的条件。

第七章　最后条款

第19条　签署、批准、接受及许可

本公约开放供欧洲委员会成员国及《欧洲文化公约》其他缔约国和欧洲共同体签署。该公约尚待批准、接受及许可。批准、接受或许可文件须提交予欧洲委员会秘书长。

第20条　生效

1. 本公约于至少包括五个欧洲委员会成员国在内的七个国家根据第19条规定表达其接受公约意愿之日后三个月期间届满后一月的第一天生效。

2. 对于之后表示接受本公约的签署方，本公约须于其提交批准、接受或许可文件之日后三个月期间届满后一月的第一天生效。

第21条　公约与共同体法律之间的关系

作为欧洲共同体成员的缔约方而言，就其相互之间的关系须适用共同体规则二部适用基于本公约而制定的规则，除非并没有共同体规则能适用于所涉及的特定事项。

第22条　其他国家的加入

1. 本公约生效后，欧洲委员会部长理事会在经过与缔约国协商之后可以通过按照《欧洲委员会规章》第20条d项规定的多数决定及有权出席部长理事会国家的一致同意而邀请任何第19条规定之外的国家加入本公约。

2. 对于任何加入国而言，本公约于将加入文件提交予欧洲委员会秘书长之日后三个月期间届满后一个月的第一日生效。

第23条　适用领土

1. 任何国家在签署或提交其批准、接受、许可或加入文件时具体说明本公约须适用的领土。

2. 任何国家可以在之后通过向欧洲委员会秘书长提交声明的方式将公约的适用扩展至其声明中说明的任何其他领土。对于该等领土，公约于秘书长收到该声明之日后三个月期间届满后一个月的第一日生效。

3. 根据前两款规定作出声明可以通过向秘书长发送通知的方式就该等声明中说明的任何领土予以撤回。该等撤回于秘书长收到该通知之日后三个月期间届满后一个月的第一日生效。

第 24 条　保留

对本公约规定不得进行保留。

第 25 条　退出

1. 任何缔约国可以在任何时间通过向欧洲委员会秘书长予以通知的方式退出本公约。

2. 该等退出须于秘书长收到该通知之日后六个月期间届满后一个月的第一日生效。

第 26 条　通知

欧洲委员会秘书长须向欧洲委员会成员国、《欧洲文化公约》其他成员国、欧洲共同体及已经加入或已获邀加入本公约的任何国家通报：

a. 任何作出的签署；

b. 提交的任何批准、接受、许可或加入文件；

c. 本公约根据第 20 条、第 22 条及第 23 条而生效的任何日期；

d. 根据第 18 条通过任何修改或协定及其修改或协定生效的任何日期；

e. 与本公约有关的任何其他行为、声明、通知或通告。

European Convention for the Protection of the Audiovisual Heritage

Strasbourg, 8. XI. 2001

The Treaty of Lisbon amending the Treaty on European Union and the Treaty establishing the European Community entered into force on 1 December 2009. As a consequence, as from that date, any reference to the European Community shall be read as the European Union.

Preamble

The member States of the Council of Europe, the other States Parties to the European Cultural Convention and the European Community, signatory hereto,

Considering that the aim of the Council of Europe is to achieve a greater unity between its members for the purpose, in particular, of safeguarding and fostering the ideals and principles which are their common heritage;

Considering that Europe's heritage reflects the cultural identity and diversity of its peoples;

Considering that moving image material is an integral part of European cultural heritage, and that States shall ensure that it is safeguarded and protected for posterity;

Considering that moving image material is a form of cultural expression reflecting contemporary society and that it is an excellent means of recording everyday events, the basis of our history and a reflection of our civilisation;

Aware of the fragility of moving image material and the dangers which threaten its existence and its handing down to future generations;

Emphasising the importance of the Parties' responsibility to safeguard, restore and keep available this heritage;

Resolved to co - operate and undertake joint action in order to safeguard and ensure the continuation of audiovisual cultural heritage;

Taking account of the international treaties in force for the protection of copyright and neighbouring rights;

Taking account of the work carried out by other international fora in the field of the protection of the audiovisual heritage,

Have agreed as follows:

Chapter I – Introduction

Article 1 – Aim of the Convention

The aim of this Convention is to ensure the protection of the European audiovisual heritage and its appreciation both as an art form and as a record of our past by means of its collection, its preservation and the availability of moving image material for cultural, scientific and research purposes, in the public interest.

Article 2 – Definitions

For the purpose of this Convention:

a. "*moving image material*" means any set of moving images recorded by whatever means and on whatever medium, whether or not accompanied by sound, capable of conveying an impression of movement;

b. "*cinematographic work*" means moving image material of any length, in particular cinematographic works of fiction, cartoons and documentaries, which is intended to be shown in cinemas;

c. "*archive body*" refers to any institution designated by a Party to carry out the functions of legal deposit;

d. "*voluntary deposit body*" refers to any institution designated by a Party for that purpose.

Article 3 – Scope of application

1. The Parties to this Convention shall apply the provisions of the Convention to all cinematographic works as from its entry into force.

2. By protocols drawn up in accordance with Article 18 of this Convention, the application of this Convention shall be extended to moving image material other

than cinematographic works, such as television productions.

Article 4 – Copyright and neighbouring rights

The obligations of this Convention shall in no way affect the provisions in international treaties on the protection of copyright and neighbouring rights. No provision of this Convention may be interpreted as prejudicing such protection.

Chapter II – Legal deposit

Article 5 – General obligation of legal deposit

1. Each Party shall introduce, by legislative or other appropriate means, the obligation to deposit moving image material forming part of its audiovisual heritage and having been produced or co - produced in the territory of the Party concerned.

2. Each Party shall be free to provide for an exemption from legal deposit if the moving image material is legally deposited in one of the other Parties concerned.

Article 6 – Designation and tasks of archive bodies

1. Each Party shall designate one or more archive bodies, whose tasks shall be to ensure the preservation, documentation, restoration and availability for consultation of deposited moving image material.

2. The designated bodies shall be either public or private, but shall not be controlled directly or indirectly by any natural or legal person principally engaged in profit - making activities in the media sector.

3. The Parties undertake to oversee the execution of the tasks assigned to the archive bodies.

Article 7 – Technical and financial means

Each Party shall ensure that archive bodies have the necessary means for carrying out their tasks as defined in Article 6, paragraph 1, of this Convention.

Article 8 – Conditions of legal deposit

1. Each Party shall designate the natural or legal persons submitted to the obligation of deposit. It shall provide for the conditions of this deposit. It shall particularly ensure that the archive bodies receive the original or a material from which the original quality can be reconstituted.

2. The material shall be deposited within a maximum of twelve months after

the final version has been shown for the first time to the public or any other reasonable period specified by a Party. If it has not been shown to the public, the time - limit shall begin at the end of the production.

Article 9 – Restoration of deposited material

1. Each Party shall encourage and promote the restoration of legally deposited moving image material forming part of its audiovisual heritage whose physical quality has deteriorated.

2. Each Party may permit in its legislation the reproduction of legally deposited moving image material for the purpose of restoration.

Article 10 – Emergency measures

Each Party shall make appropriate arrangements to ensure the protection of moving image material forming part of its audiovisual heritage which is exposed to an imminent danger which threatens its material existence, if it is not otherwise protected under the terms of legal deposit.

Chapter III – Voluntary deposit

Article 11 – Promotion of voluntary deposit

Each Party shall encourage and promote the voluntary deposit of moving image material forming part of its audiovisual heritage, including ancillary material, which does not qualify under Article 5 of this Convention.

Article 12 – Availability to the public

Each Party shall encourage voluntary deposit bodies to specify by contract with the rights holders the conditions under which the deposited moving image material may be made available to the public.

Chapter IV – General provisions common to archive and voluntary deposit bodies

Article 13 – Joint archives

1. In order to fulfil the aims of the present Convention more effectively, the Parties may decide to establish joint archive bodies and voluntary deposit bodies.

2. The archive body and the voluntary deposit body may be one and the

same institution, on condition that the provisions specific to each function are applied.

Article 14 – Co – operation between archive and voluntary deposit bodies

Each Party shall encourage its archive or voluntary deposit bodies to co - operate with one another and with the bodies of other Parties with a view to facilitating:

a. exchange of information on moving image material;

b. the compilation of a European audiovisual filmography;

c. the development of a standard procedure for storing, pooling and updating moving image material and related information;

d. the development of a common standard for electronic information exchange;

e. the preservation of equipment for showing moving image material.

Article 15 – Contractual terms of deposit

Each Party shall encourage archive and voluntary deposit bodies to conclude contracts with the depositors specifying the rights and obligations as to the deposited moving image material. Unless regulated by law, such contracts may specify the conditions on the liability for any damage of the deposited material, its temporary or permanent withdrawal from the deposit by the rights holders, and the compensation to be paid by the rights holders for its restoration or other services of the archive or voluntary deposit bodies.

Chapter V – Follow – up of the Convention

Article 16 – Standing Committee

1. For the purposes of this Convention, a standing committee shall be set up.

2. Each Party may be represented on the standing committee by one or more delegates. Each Party has a right to vote. Each State which is a Party to this Convention shall have one vote. Concerning questions within its competence, the European Community shall exercise its right to vote and cast a number of votes equal to the number of its member States that are Parties to this Convention. The European Community shall not exercise its right to vote when a question does not fall within its competence.

3. The European Community or any State referred to in Article 19, which is not a Party to this Convention, may be represented on the standing committee by an observer.

4. The standing committee shall be convened by the Secretary General of the Council of Europe. Its first meeting shall be held within six months of the date of entry into force of the Convention. It shall subsequently meet whenever one - third of the Parties or the Committee of Ministers of the Council of Europe so requests, or on the initiative of the Secretary General of the Council of Europe in accordance with the provisions of Article 18, paragraph 2, or at the request of one or more Parties in accordance with the provisions of Articles 17, paragraph 1. c.

5. A majority of Parties shall constitute the quorum required for the adoption of decisions. Subject to the provisions of Article 16, paragraph 6, and Article 18, paragraph 3, the decisions of the Standing Committee shall be taken by a majority of two - thirds of the Parties present.

6. The Standing Committee may seek the advice of experts in order to discharge its function under this Convention. It may, on its own initiative or at the request of the body concerned, invite any international or national, governmental or non - governmental body technically qualified in the fields covered by this Convention to be represented by an observer at all or part of its meetings. The decision to invite such experts or bodies shall be taken by a majority of two - thirds of the Parties.

7. Subject to the provisions of this Convention, the Standing Committee shall draw up its own rules of procedure.

Article 17 – Functions and reports of the Standing Committee

1. The Standing Committee shall be responsible for examining the operation and implementation of this Convention. It may:

a. make recommendations to the Parties concerning the application of the Convention;

b. suggest any necessary modifications to the Convention and examine those proposed in accordance with the provisions of Article 18;

c. examine, at the request of one or more Parties, any question concerning the interpretation of the Convention;

d. make recommendations to the Committee of Ministers concerning States, other than those referred to in Article 19, to be invited to accede to this Convention.

2. After each meeting, the Standing Committee shall forward to the Parties and the Committee of Ministers of the Council of Europe a report on its discussions and any decisions taken.

Chapter VI – Protocols and amendments

Article 18 – Protocols and amendments

1. Protocols dealing with moving image material other than cinematographic works shall be concluded with a view to developing, in specific fields, the principles contained in this Convention.

2. Any proposal for a protocol referred to in paragraph 1 or any proposal for an amendment to such a protocol, or for any amendment to this Convention, presented by a Party, the Standing Committee or the Committee of Ministers shall be communicated to the Secretary General of the Council of Europe and forwarded by him to the member States of the Council of Europe, to the other States which may become Parties to this Convention and to the European Community. The Secretary General of the Council of Europe shall convene a meeting of the Standing Committee at the earliest two months following the communication of the proposal.

3. The Standing Committee shall examine the proposal not earlier than two months after it has been forwarded by the Secretary General in accordance with paragraph 2. The Standing Committee shall submit the text approved by a majority of three - quarters of the Parties to the Committee of Ministers for adoption.

4. Any amendment to the Convention adopted in accordance with the preceding paragraph shall come into force on the thirtieth day after all the Parties have informed the Secretary General of their acceptance thereof. If an amendment has been adopted by the Committee of Ministers, but has not yet entered into force, a State or the European Community may not express their consent to be bound by the Convention without accepting this amendment at the same time.

5. The Committee of Ministers shall determine the conditions for the entry into force of protocols to this Convention and amendments to such protocols based on the text submitted by the Standing Committee in accordance with paragraph 3.

Chapter VII – Final provisions

Article 19 – Signature, ratification, acceptance, approval

This Convention shall be open for signature by the member States of the Council of Europe, by the other States Parties to the European Cultural Convention and by the European Community. It is subject to ratification, acceptance or approval. Instruments of ratification, acceptance or approval shall be deposited with the Secretary General of the Council of Europe.

Article 20 – Entry into force

1. This Convention shall enter into force on the first day of the month following the expiration of a period of three months after the date on which five States, including at least four member States of the Council of Europe, have expressed their consent to be bound by the Convention, in accordance with the provisions of Article 19.

2. In respect of any signatory which subsequently expresses its consent to be bound by it, the Convention shall enter into force on the first day of the month following the expiration of a period of three months after the date of the deposit of its instrument of ratification, acceptance or approval.

Article 21 – Relations between the Convention and Community law

In their mutual relations, Parties which are members of the European Community shall apply Community rules and shall not therefore apply the rules arising from this Convention except in so far as there is no Community rule governing the particular subject concerned.

Article 22 – Accession by other States

1. After the entry into force of this Convention, the Committee of Ministers of the Council of Europe, after having consulted the Parties, may invite any State which is not referred to in Article 19 to accede to the Convention, by a decision taken by the majority provided for in Article 20. d of the Statute of the Council of Europe, and by the unanimous vote of the representatives of the Contracting States entitled to sit on the Committee of Ministers.

2. In respect of any acceding State, the Convention shall enter into force on the first day of the month following the expiration of a period of three months after

the date of deposit of the instrument of accession with the Secretary General of the Council of Europe.

Article 23 – Territorial application

1. Any State or the European Community may, at the time of signature or when depositing the instrument of ratification, acceptance, approval or accession, specify the territory or territories to which this Convention shall apply.

2. Any Party may, at any later date, by a declaration addressed to the Secretary General of the Council of Europe, extend the application of this Convention to any other territory specified in the declaration. In respect of such territory, the Convention shall enter into force on the first day of the month following the expiration of a period of three months after the date of receipt of such declaration by the Secretary General.

3. Any declaration made under the two preceding paragraphs may, in respect of any territory specified in such declaration, be withdrawn by a notification addressed to the Secretary General. The withdrawal shall become effective on the first day of the month following the expiration of a period of three months after the date of receipt of such notification by the Secretary General.

Article 24 – Reservations

No reservation may be made in respect of the provisions of this Convention.

Article 25 – Denunciation

1. Any Party may at any time denounce this Convention by means of a notification addressed to the Secretary General of the Council of Europe.

2. Such denunciation shall become effective on the first day of the month following the expiration of a period of six months after the date of receipt of the notification by the Secretary General.

Article 26 – Notifications

The Secretary General of the Council of Europe shall notify the member States of the Council of Europe, the other States which may become Parties to this Convention and the European Community:

a. any signature;

b. the deposit of any instrument of ratification, acceptance, approval or accession;

c. any date of entry into force of this Convention, in accordance with Articles 20, 22 and 23;

d. any amendment or protocol adopted in accordance with Article 18, and the date on which such an amendment or protocol enters into force;

e. any other act, notification or communication relating to this Convention.

关税和贸易总协定（第四条）

缔约国（方）在建立或维持有关电影片的国内数量限制条例时，应采取符合以下要求的放映限额办法：

（甲）放映限额可以规定在不短于1年的指定时间内，国产电影片的放映应在各国电影片商业性放映所实际使用的总时间内占一定最低比例；放映限额应以每年或其相当期间内每一电影的放映时间作为计算基础。

（乙）除根据放映限额为国产电影片保留非放映时间以外，其他放映时间，包括原为国产电影片保留后经营管理当局开放的时间在内，不得正式或实际上依照电影片的不同来源进行分配。

（丙）虽有本条（乙）项的规定，任一缔约国（方）可以符合本条（甲）项要求的放映限额办法，在实施这项办法的国家以外，对某一国家的电影片保留一最低比例的放映时间。

（丁）放映限额的限制、放宽或取消，须通过谈判确定。

General Agreement on Tariffs and Trade (Article IV)

Article IV: Special Provisions relating to Cinematograph Films

If any contracting party establishes or maintains internal quantitative regulations relating to exposed cinematograph films, such regulations shall take the form of screen quotas which shall conform to the following requirements:

(*a*) Screen quotas may require the exhibition of cinematograph films of national origin during a specified minimum proportion of the total screen time actually utilized, over a specified period of not less than one year, in the commercial exhibition of all films of whatever origin, and shall be computed on the basis of screen time per theatre per year or the equivalent thereof;

(*b*) With the exception of screen time reserved for films of national origin under a screen quota, screen time including that released by administrative action from screen time reserved for films of national origin, shall not be allocated formally or in effect among sources of supply;

(*c*) Notwithstanding the provisions of subparagraph (b) of this Article, any contracting party may maintain screen quotas conforming to the requirements of subparagraph (a) of this Article which reserve a minimum proportion of screen time for films of a specified origin other than that of the contracting party imposing such screen quotas; Provided that no such minimum proportion of screen time shall be increased above the level in effect on April 10, 1947;

(*d*) Screen quotas shall be subject to negotiation for their limitation, liberalization or elimination.

关于教育科学文化物品进口及其附件与议定书的协定*

（佛罗伦萨，1950年6月17日；议定书，内罗毕，1976年11月26日）

序　言

缔约各国考虑到思想与知识交流，以及通常情况下文明社会多样性自我表现尽可能广泛的传播，对智力发展、国际间的了解与维护世界和平至关重要；考虑到这种交流主要是通过图书、出版物与教育、科学、文化物品实现的；考虑到《联合国教科文组织组织法》敦促各国在智力活动的各个部门加强合作，包括“出版物、艺术与科学物品以及其他信息资料”的交换，并规定联合国教科文组织应通过各种大众传播手段，为增进各国人民间之相互认识和了解而协力工作，并为达此目的，建议订立必要之国际协定；承认订立一项旨在增进图书、出版物以及教育、科学和文化物品的自由流通的国际协定是达到这一目之有效手段；为此协议如下：

第一条

1. 缔约国保证不征收下列物品的关税、其他进口税或在进口时征的税：

（1）本协定附件A所列列举的图书、出版物和文件；

（2）本协定附件B、C、D和E所列举的教育、科学和文化物品，但它们应符合这些附件规定的条件，且为另一缔约国之产品；

2. 本条第1款之规定不妨碍缔约国对进口物品征收：

（1）进口时或进口后征收的任何性质的间接税或其他国内税，但这些税款数额不得超过对本国类似产品直接或间接征收的税额；

---

* 首都经济贸易大学传播学系郑文明译。

（2）关税之外的，由政府或行政当局征收的进口或进口时的费用和税款，但其数额应限于与所提供的有关服务的费用大体相当，而且不应构成对本国产品的间接保护，也不应成为对进口物品的税收性征税。

第二条

1. 缔约国保证提供进口下列物品所需的外汇和（或）许可证：

（1）教育、科研或文化公共机构用于其图书馆和收藏的图书和出版物；

（2）在本国发表的正式文件、议会文件和行政文件；

（3）联合国组织及其专门机构的图书和出版物；

（4）联合国教育、科学及文化组织收到的、并由该组织或在其监督下免费散发的、不能用于销售的图书和出版物；

（5）免费寄赠或散发的用于鼓励到进口国境外旅游的出版物；

（6）用于盲人的物品：

1）盲人使用的各种盲文版的图书、出版物和文件；

2）专门为盲人在教育、科学或文化方面的发展而设计的、由盲人组织或盲人救助机构直接进口并经进口国有关当局批准其免税接收的其他物品。

2. 实行数量限制和汇兑监督措施的缔约国，保证尽一切可能为进口其他教育、科学或文化物品，尤其是本协定各附件所列物品，提供必要的外汇和许可证。

第三条

1. 缔约国保证为进口专门在进口国有关当局批准的公开展览会上展出的、今后拟再出口的教育、科学或文化物品提供一切可能的便利，其中包括提供必要的许可证，免除关税和在进口时征收的间接税和其他国内税，但相当于所提供之有关服务的大致费用的税款除外。

2. 本条任何条款均不妨碍进口国当局为确保有关物品真正能在展览会结束时重新出口而采取必要的措施。

第四条

各缔约国保证，尽一切可能：

（1）继续共同努力，千方百计地促进教育、科学和文化物品的自由流通，取消或减少本协定未规定的对这种自由流通的限制；

（2）简化进口教育、科学和文化物品的行政手续；

（3）促使教育、科学和文化物品的报关手段快捷而又不失认真。

第五条

本协定的任何条款均不能否定缔约国有权基于直接关系国家安全、公共秩序或公共道德的动机，根据本国法律采取有关措施，禁止或限制进口某些物品，或在进口之后禁止或限制其流通。

第六条

本协定不应损害或导致修改缔约国有关保护版权或工业产权，其中包括专利和商标的法律和规章，或缔约国签署的这些方面的条约、公约、协议或声明。

第七条

缔约国保证通过谈判或调解的途径解决在解释或实施本协定时产生的任何分歧，而不影响它们过去在解决它们之间可能出现的冲突方面所已经签署的条约规定。

第八条

缔约国之间在进口物品的教育、科学或文化性质上发生争执时，有关各方可在一致同意的情况下，征求联合国教育、科学及文化组织总干事的咨询意见。

第九条

1. 本协定有具有同等效力的英文本和法文本，将签署今天的日期，并将接受联合国教育、科学及文化组织所有会员国、联合国所有成员国和联合国教育、科学及文化组织执行局专门邀请的所有非会员国的签字。

2. 本协定将提交签字国按各自宪法规定的程序予以批准。

3. 批准书将交由联合国组织秘书长存档。

第十条

自 1950 年 11 月 22 日起，第 9 条第 1 款所指国家便可加入本协定。加入本协定须向联合国组织秘书长交存一份正式文书。

第十一条

本协定自联合国组织秘书长收到十个国家的批准书或加入书之日起开始生效。

第十二条

1. 本协定生效之日已是其缔约国之国家，均应在六个月的期限内采取切实执行该协定的一切必要措施。

2. 对于在本协定生效之日后提交批准书或加入书的所有国家，这一期限为三个月，自提交批准书或加入书之日算起。

3. 在本条第 1 和第 2 款规定之期限届满后的一个月之内，本协定缔约国应向联合国教育、科学及文化组织提交关于为切实执行该协定所采取的措施的报告。

4. 联合国教育、科学及文化组织将把该报告转达给本协定所有签字国和国际贸易组织（暂为其临时委员会）。

第十三条

任何缔约国均可在签署协定时，或在交存批准书或加入书时，或在以后的任何时候，向联合国组织秘书长发出通知，声明本协定适用于其在国际上代表的某一个或数个领土。

第十四条

1. 在本协定生效满两年的期限后，任何缔约国均可以自己的名义或以其在国际上代表的任何领土的名义，向联合国组织秘书长递交书面文书，宣告废除本协定。

2. 宣告废除，在收到宣告废除的文书一年后开始生效。

第十五条

联合国组织秘书长将把第9条和第10条所述的所有批准书或加入书的交存情况，以及第8条和第14条分别规定的通知和宣告废除的情况，通知第9条第1款涉及的国家以及联合国教育、科学及文化组织和贸易组织（暂为其临时委员会）。

第十六条

应三分之一缔约国之要求，联合国教育、科学及文化组织总干事应将召开一次修订本协定的会议问题列入该组织大会下一届会议的议程。

第十七条

附件A、B、C、D和E，以及本协定所附议定书，均为本协定的组成部分。

第十八条

1. 根据《联合国宪章》第102条，本协定由联合国组织秘书长于其生效之日登记在案。

2. 经正式授权的签字人代表各自政府在本协定上签字，以昭信守。

（一）附件

A 图书、出版物和文件

1. 印刷的图书。
2. 报纸和杂志。
3. 通过除印刷以外的复制方法得到的图书和文件。
4. 在本国发表的官方文件、议会的文件和行政文件。
5. 旅游宣传画和有插图或无插图的旅游出版物（小册子、指南、时刻表、折叠式说明书和类似出版物)，其中包括由私营企业编辑的邀请公众去进口国之外旅游的出版物。

6. 邀请出国留学的出版物。

7. 手稿和打字稿。

8. 由设在进口国以外的出版社或书店经销的图书和出版物目录。

9. 由或者是为联合国组织或其某一专门机构出版的电影、录音或任何其他教育、科学或文化性质的视听材料目录。

10. 手写的、印刷的或采用印刷之外的其他复制方法复制的乐曲。

11. 地图、水文图或太空图。

12. 经进口国主管当局批准有关科学机构或教育机构免税接收的专供这些机构进行研究的建筑、工业或工程规划图和设计图及其复制品。

(本附件 A 中规定的免税不适用于下列物品)

文具;

由或为私营商业企业出版的主要以商业宣传为目的的图书、出版物和文件（但目录以及上面所提到的旅游宣传画和旅游出版物除外);

广告内容超过其版面 70% 的报纸和杂志;

广告内容超过其版面 25% 的任何其他物品（但上面所提到的书目除外)。至于旅游宣传出版物和招贴画，此百分比只涉及私营商业广告。

B 艺术品和教育、科学或文化性质的收藏品

1. 完全是手工制作的绘画，包括手工制作的复本，但不包括经过装饰的制造品。

2. 有艺术家签名和编号的完全是以手工方式在石板、木板或其他材料上雕刻而成的石版画、雕刻画和木版画。

3. 浮雕、凸起或凹陷型雕塑或雕塑艺术的原作品，但批量制作的复制品和商业性手工艺术品除外。

4. 用于公共博物馆、展览馆、或其他公共机构的经进口国的主管当局批准这些机构免税，接受的收藏品和艺术品，但条件是不得再行出售。

5. 与科学，尤其是与解剖学、动物学、植物学、矿物学、古生物学、考古学和人种学有关的无商业性目的的成套和单件收藏品。

6. 有百年以上历史的古物。

C 属于教育、科学和文化性质的视听材料

1. 教育、科学或文化性质的电影、幻灯卷片、缩微胶片和幻灯片，由各

种组织（由进口国决定，是否也包括广播机构）经进口国主管当局批准免税进口，并只能供这些组织或经上述当局批准的任何其他公立或私立的教育、科学和文化性质的机构或协会使用。

2. 新闻片，即，以复制为目的进口，内容在进口时具有时事新闻价值的新闻片（有声道或无声道），这些片子可以是已曝光和冲洗的负片或已翻印和冲洗的正片，免税进口可以每个片子两部拷贝为限。只有经进口国主管当局批准享受有关进口免税的各个组织（由进口国决定是否也包括广播机构）进口的新闻片，才能享受这一规定。

3. 教育、科学或文化性质的录音，只能用于进口国主管当局批准享受有关进口免税的教育、科学或文化性质的各个公立或私立的机构或协会（由进口国决定是否也包括广播机构）使用。

4. 联合国或其某个专门机构制作的教育、科学或文化性质的电影、幻灯卷片、缩微胶卷和录音。

D 科学仪器或设备

专供教学或纯科学研究之用的科学仪器和设备，但需符合下列规定：

（1）有关科学仪器和设备应当用于进口国主管当局批准享受有关进口免税的公共或私立的科学或教育机构，并应由这些机构监督和负责使用。

（2）进口国目前不生产具有相同科学价值的仪器和设备。

E 盲人用品

1. 供盲人使用的各种盲文图书、出版物和文件。

2. 进口国主管当局批准享受有关进口免税的盲人机构或盲人救助机构直接进口的专门为盲人在教育、科学或文化方面的发展而设计的其他物品。

（二）附加议定书

缔约国考虑到促进美利坚合众国加入教育、科学和文化物品进口协定的重要性，特协议如下：

1. 美利坚合众国有权根据第9条批准本《协定》，或根据第10条加入本《协定》，对《协定》提出内容如下文的保留意见。

2. 如果美利坚合众国在成为本《协定》的缔约国时提出了第1款中规定的保留意见，美利坚合众国则可以针对本《协定》的任何缔约国引用该保留意见的条款，任何缔约国亦可以针对美利坚合众国引用这些条款，因根据该保留意见采取的任何措施均不得有歧视性。

（保留意见的全文）

（1）如果由于某缔约国履行本《协定》所规定的义务而致使其对本《协定》所规定的某一物品的进口出现相对的增长并具有了相当的条件，已经或很可能会严重损害国内同类产品生产者，该缔约国则可以根据上述第 2 款之条款，在预防或弥补这种损害所需的范围和时间内完全或部分中止其根据本《协定》对有关的该项物品所承担的义务。

（2）在根据上述（1）款的规定采取措施之前，有关缔约国应尽早以书面形式通知联合国教育、科学及文化组织，并为该组织和本《协定》缔约国提供与其就打算采取的措施进行商谈的可能机会。

（3）在延误会造成难以弥补的损害的紧急情况下，可以不经事先磋商便根据本《议定书》（1）款之规定采取某些临时措施，但在采取有关措施之后应立即进行磋商。

Agreement on the Importation of Educational, Scientific and Cultural Materials

Florence, 17 June 1950

– Protocol, Nairobi, 26 November 1976

Preamble

The contracting States,

Considering that the free exchange of ideas and knowledge and, in general, the widest possible dissemination of the diverse forms of self - expression used by civilizations are vitally important both for intellectual progress and international understanding, and consequently for the maintenance of world peace;

Considering that this interchange is accomplished primarily by means of books, publications and educational, scientific and cultural materials;

Considering that the Constitution of the United Nations Educational, Scientific and Cultural Organization urges co - operation between nations in all branches of intellectual activity, including `the exchange of publications, objects of artistic and scientific interest and other materials of information' and provides further that the Organization shall `collaborate in the work of advancing the mutual knowledge and understanding of peoples, through all means of mass communication and to that end recommend such international agreements as may be necessary to promote the free flow of ideas by word and image' ;

Recognize that these aims will be effectively furthered by an international agreement facilitating the free flow of books, publications and educational, scientific and cultural materials; and

Have, therefore, agreed to the following provisions:

Article I

1. The contracting States undertake not to apply customs duties or other charges on, or in connection with, the importation of:

(a) Books, publications and documents, listed in Annex A to this Agreement;

(b) Educational, scientific and cultural materials, listed in Annexes B, C, D and E to this Agreement; which are the products of another contracting State, subject to the conditions laid down in those annexes.

2. The provisions of paragraph 1 of this article shall not prevent any contracting State from levying on imported materials:

(a) Internal taxes or any other internal charges of any kind, imposed at the time of importation or subsequently, not exceeding those applied directly or indirectly to like domestic products;

(b) Fees and charges, other than customs duties, imposed by governmental authorities on, or in connection with, importation, limited in amount to the approximate cost of the services rendered, and representing neither an indirect protection to domestic products nor a taxation of imports for revenue purposes.

Article II

1. The contracting States undertake to grant the necessary licences and/or foreign exchange for the importation of the following articles:

(a) Books and publications consigned to public libraries and collections and to the libraries and collections of public, educational, research or cultural institutions;

(b) Official government publications, that is, official, parliamentary and administrative documents published in their country of origin;

(c) Books and publications of the United Nations or any of its Specialized Agencies;

(d) Books and publications received by the United Nations Educational, Scientific and Cultural Organization and distributed free of charge by it or under its supervision;

(e) Articles for the blind:

(i) Books, publications and documents of all - kinds in raised characters for the blind;

(ii) Other articles specially designed for the educational, scientific or cultural advancement of the blind, which are imported directly by institutions or organizations concerned with the welfare of the blind, approved by the competent authorities of the importing country for the purpose of duty - free entry of these types of articles.

2. The contracting States which at any - time apply quantitative restrictions and exchange control measures undertake to grant, as far as possible, foreign exchange and licences necessary for the importation of other educational, scientific or cultural materials, and particularly the materials referred to in the annexes to this Agreement.

Article III

1. The contracting States undertake to give every possible facility to the importation of educational, scientific or cultural materials, which are imported exclusively for showing at a public exhibition approved by the competent authorities of the importing country and for subsequent re - exportation. These facilities shall include the granting of the necessary licences and exemption from customs duties and internal taxes and charges of all kinds payable on importation, other than fees and charges corresponding to the approximate cost of services rendered.

2. Nothing in this article shall prevent the authorities of an importing country from taking such steps as may be necessary to ensure that the materials in question shall be re - exported at the close of their exhibition.

Article IV

The contracting States undertake that they will as far as possible :

(a) Continue their common efforts to promote by every means the free circulation of educational, scientific or cultural materials, and abolish or reduce any restrictions to that free circulation which are not referred to in this agreement;

(b) Simplify the administrative procedure governing the importation of educational, scientific or cultural materials;

(c) Facilitate the expeditious and safe customs clearance of educational, scientific or cultural materials.

Article V

Nothing in this Agreement shall affect the right of contracting States to take measures, in conformity with their legislation, to prohibit or limit the importation, or the circulation after importation, of articles on grounds relating directly to national security, public order or public morals.

Article VI

This Agreement shall not modify or affect the laws and regulations of any contracting State or any of its international treaties, conventions, agreements or proclamations, with respect to copyright, trade marks or patents.

Article VII

Subject to the provisions of any previous conventions to which the contracting States may have subscribed for the settlement of disputes, the contracting States undertake to have recourse to negotiation or conciliation, with a view to settlement of any disputes regarding the interpretation or the application of this Agreement.

Article VIII

In case of a dispute between contracting States relating to the educational, scientific or cultural character of imported materials, the interested Parties may, by common agreement, refer it to the Director - General of the United Nations Educational, Scientific and Cultural Organization for an advisory opinion.

Article IX

1. This Agreement, of which the English and French texts are equally authentic, shall bear today's date and remain open for signature by all Member States of the United Nations Educational, Scientific and Cultural Organization, all Member States of the United Nations and any non - member State to which an invitation may have been addressed by the Executive Board of the United Nations Educational, Scientific and Cultural Organization.

2. The Agreement shall be ratified on behalf of the signatory States in accordance with their respective constitutional procedure.

3. The instruments of ratification shall be deposited with the Secretary General of the United Nations.

Article X

The States referred to in paragraph 1 of Article IX may accept this Agreement from 22 November 1950. Acceptance shall become effective on the deposit of a formal instrument with the Secretary - General of the United Nations.

Article XI

This Agreement shall come into force on the date on which the Secretary General of the United Nations receives instruments of ratification or acceptance from 10

States.

Article XII

1. The States Parties to this Agreement on the date of its coming into force shall each take all the necessary measures for its fully effective operation within a period of six months after that date.

2. For States which may deposit their instruments of ratification or acceptance after the date of the Agreement coming into force, these measures shall be taken within a period of three months from the date of deposit.

3. Within one month of the expiration of the periods mentioned in paragraphs 1 and 2 of this article, the contracting States to this Agreement shall submit a report to the United Nations Educational, Scientific and Cultural Organization of the measures which they have taken for such fully effective operation.

4. The United Nations Educational, Scientific and Cultural Organization shall transmit this report to all signatory States to this Agreement and to the International Trade Organization (provisionally, to its Interim Commission).

Article XIII

Any contracting State may, at the time of signature or the deposit of its instrument of ratification or acceptance, or at any time thereafter, declare by notification addressed to the Secretary - General of the United Nations that this Agreement shall extend to all or any of the territories for the conduct of whose foreign relations that contracting State is responsible.

Article XIV

1. Two years after the date of the coming into force of this Agreement, any contracting State may, on its own behalf or on behalf of any of the territories for the conduct of whose foreign relations that contracting State is responsible, denounce this Agreement by an instrument in writing deposited with the Secretary - General of the United Nations.

2. The denunciation shall take effect one year after the receipt of the instrument of denunciation.

Article XV

The Secretary - General of the United Nations shall inform the States referred to in paragraph 1 of Article IX, as well as the United Nations Educational, Scientific and Cultural Organization, and the International Trade Organization (provisionally, its Interim Commission), of the deposit of all the instruments of ratification and acceptance provided for in Articles IX and X, as well as of the notifications and denunciations provided for respectively in Articles XIII and XIV.

Article XVI

At the request of one - third of the contracting States to this Agreement, the Director - General of the United Nations Educational, Scientific and Cultural Organization shall place on the agenda of the next session of the General Conference of that Organization, the question of convoking a meeting for the revision of this Agreement.

Article XVII

Annexes A, B, C, D and E, as well as the Protocol annexed to this Agreement are hereby made an integral part of this Agreement.

Article XVIII

In accordance with Article 102 of the Charter of the United Nations, this Agreement shall be registered by the Secretary - General of the United Nations on the date of its coming into force.

IN FAITH WHEREOF the undersigned, duly authorized, have signed this Agreement on behalf of their respective governments.

Annexes

Annex A

Books, publications and documents

(i) Printed books.

(ii) Newspapers and periodicals.

(iii) Books and documents produced by duplicating processes other than printing.

(iv) Official government publications, that is, official, parliamentary and administrative documents published in their country of origin.

(v) Travel posters and travel literature (pamphlets, guides, time - tables, leaflets and similar publications), whether illustrated or not, including those published by private commercial enterprises, whose purpose is to stimulate travel outside the country of importation.

(vi) Publications whose purpose is to stimulate study outside the country of importation.

(vii) Manuscripts, including typescripts.

(viii) Catalogues of books and publications, being books and publications offered for sale by publishers or booksellers established outside the country of importation.

(ix) Catalogues of films, recordings or other visual and auditory material of an educational, scientific or cultural character, being catalogues issued by or on behalf of the United Nations or any of its Specialized Agencies.

(x) Music in manuscript or printed form, or reproduced by duplicating processes other than printing.

(xi) Geographical, hydrographical or astronomical maps and charts.

(xii) Architectural, industrial or engineering plans - and designs, and reproductions thereof, intended for study in scientific establishments or educational institutions approved by the competent authorities of the importing country for the purpose of duty - free admission of these types of articles.

The exemptions provided by Annex A shall not apply to:

(a) Stationery;

(b) Books, publications and documents (except catalogues, travel posters and travel literature referred to above) published by or for a private commercial enterprise, essentially for advertising purposes;

(c) Newspapers and periodicals in which the advertising matter is in excess of 70 per cent by space;

(d) All other items (except catalogues referred to above) in which the advertising matter is in excess of 25 per cent by space. In the case of travel posters and literature, this percentage shall apply only to private commercial advertising matter.)

Annex B

Works of art and collectors ' pieces of an educational, scientific or cultural character

(i) Paintings and drawings, including copies, executed entirely by hand, but excluding manufactured decorated wares.

(ii) Hand - printed impressions, produced from hand - engraved or hand -

etched blocks, plates or other material, and signed and numbered by the artist.

(iii) Original works of art of statuary or sculpture, whether in the round, in relief, or in intaglio, excluding mass - produced reproductions and works of conventional craftsmanship of a commercial character.

(iv) Collectors' pieces and objects of art consigned to public galleries, museums and other public institutions, approved by the competent authorities of the importing country for the purpose of duty - free entry of these types of articles, not intended for resale.

(v) Collections and collectors' pieces in such scientific fields as anatomy, zoology, botany, mineralogy, paleontology, archaeology and ethnography, not intended for resale.

(vi) Antiques, being articles in excess of 100 years of age.

Annex C

Visual and auditory materials of an educational, scientific or cultural character

(i) Films, filmstrips, microfilms and slides, of an educational, scientific or cultural character, when imported by organizations (including, at the discretion of the importing country, broadcasting organizations), approved by the competent authorities of the importing country for the purpose of duty - free admission of these types of articles, exclusively for exhibition by these organizations or by other public or private educational, scientific or cultural institutions or societies approved by the aforesaid authorities.

(ii) Newsreels (with or without sound track), depicting events of current news value at the time of importation, and imported in either negative form, exposed and developed, or positive form, printed and developed, when imported by organizations (including, at the discretion of the importing country, broadcasting organization) approved by the competent authorities of the importing country for the purpose of duty - free admission of such films, provided that free entry may be limited to two copies of each subject for copying purposes.

(iii) Sound recordings of an educational, scientific or cultural character for use exclusively in public or private educational, scientific or cultural institutions or societies (including, at the discretion of the importing country, broadcasting organizations) approved by the competent authorities of the importing country for the purpose of duty - free admission of these types of articles.

(iv) Films, filmstrips, microfilms and sound recordings of an educational, scientific or cultural character produced by the United Nations or any of its Specialized Agencies.

(v) Patterns, models and wall charts for use exclusively for demonstrating and teaching purposes in public or private educational, scientific or cultural institutions approved by the competent authorities of the importing country for the purpose of duty - free admission of these types of articles.

Annex D

Scientific instruments or apparatus

Scientific instruments or apparatus, intended exclusively for educational purposes or pure scientific research, provided:

(a) That such scientific instruments or apparatus are consigned to public or private scientific or educational institutions approved by the competent authorities of the importing country for the purpose of duty - free entry of these types of articles, and used under the control and responsibility of these institutions ;

(b) That instruments or apparatus of equivalent scientific value are not being manufactured in the country of importation.

Annex E

Articles for the blind

Books, publications and documents of all kinds in raised characters for the blind. Other articles specially designed for the educational, scientific or cultural advancement of the blind, which are imported directly by institutions or organizations concerned with the welfare of the blind, approved by the competent authorities of the importing country for the purpose of duty - free entry of these types of articles.

Protocol annexed to the Agreement on the Importation of Educational, Scientific and Cultural Materials

The contracting States,

In the interest of facilitating the participation of the United States of America in the Agreement on the Importation of Educational, Scientific and Cultural Materials, have agreed to the following:

1. The United States of America shall have the option of ratifying this Agreement, under Article IX, or of accepting it, under Article X, with the, inclusion of the reservation hereunder.

2. In the event of the United States of America becoming Party to this Agreement with the reservation provided for in the preceding paragraph 1, the provisions of that reservation may be invoked by the Government of the United States of America with regard to any of the contracting States to this Agreement, or by any contracting State with regard to the United States of America, provided that any measure imposed pursuant to such reservation shall be applied on a non - discriminatory basis.

Text of the reservation

(a) If, as a result of the obligations incurred by a contracting State under this Agreement, any product covered by this Agreement is being imported into the territory of a contracting State in such relatively increased quantities and under such conditions as to cause or threaten serious injury to the domestic industry in that territory producing like or directly competitive products, the contracting State, under the conditions provided for by paragraph 2 above, shall be free, in respect of such product and to the extent and for such time as may be necessary to prevent or remedy such injury, to suspend, in whole or in part, any obligation under this Agreement with respect to such product.

(b) Before any contracting State shall take action pursuant to the provisions of paragraph (a) above, it shall give notice in writing to the United Nations Educational, Scientific and Cultural Organization as far in advance as may be practicable and shall afford the Organization and the contracting States which are Parties to this Agreement an opportunity to consult with it in respect of the proposed action.

(c) In critical circumstances where delay would cause damage which it would be difficult to repair, action under paragraph (a) above may be taken provisionally without prior consultation, on the condition that consultation be effected immediately after taking such action.

关于禁止和防止非法进出口文化财产和非法转让其所有权的方法的公约

（联合国教科文组织1970年11月14日通过。我国1989年11月28日递交批准书）

联合国教育、科学及文化组织于1970年10月12日至11月14日在巴黎召开第十六届大会，忆及其第十四届大会通过的《国际文化合作原则宣言》所载规定的重要性，考虑到各国间为科学、文化及教育目的而进行的文化财产交流增进了对人类文明的认识、丰富了各国人民的文化生活并激发了各国之间的相互尊重和了解，

考虑到文化财产实为构成文明和民族文化的一大基本要素，只有尽可能充分掌握有关其起源、历史和传统背景的知识，才能理解其真正价值，

考虑到各国有责任保护其领土上的文化财产免受偷盗、秘密发掘和非法出口的危险，

考虑到为避免这些危险，各国必须日益认识到其尊重本国及其他所有国家的文化遗产的道义责任，

考虑到博物馆、图书馆和档案馆作为文化机构应保证根据普遍公认的道义原则汇集其收藏品，

考虑到非法进出口文化财产和非法转让其所有权阻碍了各国之间的交流，教科文组织的一部分职责就是通过向有关国家推荐这方面的各项国际公约以促进这一交流，

考虑到只有各国在国家和国际范围上进行组织，密切合作，才能有效保护文化遗产，

考虑到教科文组织大会在1964年就此通过了一项建议，

已收到关于禁止和防止非法进出口文化财产和非法转让其所有权的方法的各项进一步建议，这一问题业已作为第十九项议程项目列入本届会议议程，第十五届会议已决定就这一问题制订一项国际公约，在1970年11月14日通

过本公约。

第一条 为了达到本公约的目的，“文化财产”一词即指每个国家，根据宗教的或世俗的理由，明确指定为具有重要考古、史前史、历史、文学、艺术或科学价值的财产并属于下列各类者：

1. 动物群落、植物群落、矿物和解剖以及具有古生物学意义的物品的稀有收集品和标本；

2. 有关历史，包括科学、技术、军事及社会史、有关国家领袖、思想家、科学家、艺术家之生平以及有关国家重大事件的财产；

3. 考古发掘（包括正常的和秘密的）或考古发现的成果；

4. 业已肢解的艺术或历史古迹或考古遗址之构成部分；

5. 一百年以前的古物，如铭文、钱币和印章；

6. 具有人种学意义的文物；

7. 有艺术价值的财产，如：

（1）全部是手工完成的图画、绘画和绘图，不论其装帧框座如何，也不论所用的是何种材料（不包括工业设计图及手工装饰的工业产品）；

（2）用任何材料制成的雕塑艺术和雕刻的原作；

（3）版画、印片和平版画的原件；

（4）用任何材料组集或拼集的艺术品原件；

8. 稀有手稿和古版书籍，有特殊意义的（历史、艺术、科学、文学等）古书、文件和出版物，不论是单本的或整套的；

9. 邮票、印花税票及类似的票证，不论是单张的或成套的；

10. 档案，包括有声、照相和电影档案；

11. 一百年以前的家具物品和古乐器。

第二条

1. 本公约缔约国承认文化财产非法进出口和所有权非法转让是造成这类财产的原主国文化遗产枯竭的主要原因之一，并承认国际合作是保护各国文化财产免遭由此产生的各种危险的最有效方法之一。

2. 为此目的，缔约国承担利用现有手段，特别是通过消除其根源、制止现有做法和帮助给予必要的补偿来反对这种做法。

第三条 本公约缔约国违反本公约所列的规定而造成的文化财产之进出口或所有权转让均属非法。

第四条 本公约缔约国承认，根据本公约的宗旨，凡属以下各类财产均为每个缔约国的文化遗产的一部分：

1. 有关国家的国民的个人或集体所创造的文化财产和居住在该国领土境内的外国国民或无国籍人在该国领土内创造的对有关国家具有重要意义的文化财产；

2. 在国家领土内发现的文化财产；

3. 经此类财产原主国主管当局的同意，由考古学、人种学或自然科学团体所获得的文化财产；

4. 经由自由达成的协议实行交流的文化财产；

5. 经此类财产原主国主管当局的同意，作为赠送品而接收的或合法购置的文化财产。

第五条 为确保保护文化财产免于非法进出口和所有权的非法转让，本公约缔约国承担若尚未设立保护文化遗产的国家机构，可根据本国的情况，在其领土之内建立一个或一个以上的国家机构，配备足够人数的合格工作人员，以有效地履行下述职责：

1. 协助制订旨在切实保护文化遗产特别是防止重要文化财产的非法进出口和非法转让的法律和规章草案；

2. 根据全国受保护财产清册，制订并不断更新一份其出口将造成文化遗产的严重枯竭的重要的公共及私有文化财产的清单；

3. 促进发展或成立为保证文化财产的保存和展出所需之科学及技术机构（博物馆、图书馆、档案馆、实验室、工作室……）；

4. 组织对考古发掘的监督，确保在原地保存某些文化财产，并保护某些地区，供今后考古研究之用；

5. 为有关各方面（博物馆长、收藏家、古董商等）的利益，制订符合于本公约所规定道德原则的规章；并采取措施保证遵守这些规章；

6. 采取教育措施，鼓励并提高对各国文化遗产的尊重，并传播关于本公约规定的知识；

7. 注意对任何种类的文化财产的失踪进行适当宣传。

第六条 本公约缔约国承担：

1. 发放适当证件，出口国将在该证件中说明有关文化财产的出口已经过批准。根据规定出口的各种文化财产，均须附有此种证件；

2. 除非附有上述出口证件，禁止文化财产从本国领土出口；

3. 通过适当方法宣传这种禁止，特别要在可能出口或进口文化财产的人们中间进行宣传。

第七条 本公约缔约国承担：

1. 采取与本国立法相一致的必要措施防止本国领土内的博物馆及类似机构获取来源于另一缔约国并于本公约在有关国家生效后非法出口的文化财产。本公约对两国均已生效后，尽可能随时把自两国中的原主缔约国非法运出文化财产的建议通知该原主缔约国。

2.

（1）本公约对有关国家生效后，禁止进口从本公约另一缔约国的博物馆或宗教的或世俗的公共纪念馆或类似机构中窃取的文化财产，如果该项财产业已用文件形式列入该机构的财产清册；

（2）本公约对有关的两个国家生效后，根据两国中的原主缔约国的要求，采取适当措施收回并归还进口的此类文化财产，但要求国须向不知情的买主或对该财产具有合法权利者给予公平的赔偿。要求收回和归还失物必须通过外交部门进行，提出要求一方应提供使确定其收回或归还失物的要求的必要文件及其他证据，费用自理。各方不得对遵照本条规定而归还的文化财产征收关税或其他费用。归还和运送文化财产过程中所需的一切费用均由提出要求一方负担。

第八条 本公约缔约国对触犯上述第六条（2）和第七条（2）所列的禁止规定负有责任者予以惩处或行政制裁。

第九条 本公约的任一缔约国在其文化遗产由于考古或人种学的材料遭受掠夺而处境危殆时得向蒙受影响的其他缔约国发出呼吁。在此情况下，本公约缔约国承担参与协调一致的国际努力，以确定并实施必要的具体措施，包括对有关的特定物资的进出口及国际贸易实行管制。在尚未达成协议之前，有关各国应在可能范围内采取临时性措施，以便制止对提出要求的国家的文化遗产造成不可弥补的损失。

第十条 本公约缔约国承担：

1. 通过教育、情报和防范手段，限制非法从本公约缔约国运出的文化财产的移动，并视各国情况，责成古董商保持一份记录，载明每项文化财产的来源、提供者的姓名与住址以及每项售出的物品的名称与价格，并须把此类财产可能禁止出口的情况告知该项文化财产的购买人，违者须受刑事或行政制裁。

2. 努力通过教育手段，使公众认识到，并进一步理解文化财产的价值和偷盗、秘密发掘与非法出口对文化财产造成的威胁。

第十一条 一个国家直接或间接地由于被他国占领而被迫出口文化财产

或转让其所有权应被视为非法。

第十二条 本公约缔约国应尊重由其负责国际关系的领土内的文化财产，并应采取一切适当措施禁止并防止在这些领土内非法进出口文化财产和非法转让其所有权。

第十三条 本公约缔约国还应在符合其本国法律的情况下承担：

1．通过一切适当手段防止可能引起文化财产的非法进出口的这一类财产的所有权转让；

2．保证本国的主管机关进行合作，使非法出口的文化财产尽早归还其合法所有者；

3．受理合法所有者或其代表提出的关于找回失落的或失窃的文化财产的诉讼；

4．承认本公约缔约国有不可取消的权利规定并宣布某些文化财产是不能让与的，因而据此也不能出口，若此类财产已经出口务须促使这类财产归还给有关国家。

第十四条 为防止非法出口、履行本公约所规定的义务，本公约各缔约国应在可能范围内为其负责保护文化遗产的国家机关提供足够的预算并在必要时为此目的设立一项基金。

第十五条 在本公约对有关国家生效前，本公约之任何规定不应妨碍缔约国之间自行缔结有关归还从其原主国领土上不论以何种理由搬走之文化财产的特别协定，或制止它们继续执行业已缔结的有关协定。

第十六条 本公约缔约国应在向联合国教育、科学及文化组织大会提交的定期报告中，提供它们已经通过的立法和行政规定和它们为实施本公约所采取的其他行动以及在此领域内取得的详尽经验的资料，报告的日期及方式由大会决定。

第十七条

1．本公约缔约国可以向联合国教育、科学及文化组织请求给予技术援助，特别是有关：

（1）情报和教育；

（2）咨询和专家建议；

（3）协调和斡旋。

2．联合国教育、科学及文化组织可以主动进行有关非法转移文化财产问题的研究并出版研究报告。

3．为此，联合国教育、科学及文化组织可以请求任何非政府的主管组织予以合作。

4. 联合国教育、科学及文化组织可以主动向本公约缔约国提出有关本公约的实施的建议。

5. 经对本公约的实施有争议的两个以上的本公约缔约国的请求，联合国教科文组织得进行斡旋，使它们之间的争端得到解决。

第十八条 本公约以英文、法文、俄文和西班牙文制定，四种文本具有同等效力。

第十九条

1. 本公约须经联合国教育、科学及文化组织会员国按各国宪法程序批准或接受。

2. 批准书或接受书，应交存联合国教育、科学及文化组织总干事。

第二十条

1. 本公约应开放给非联合国教育、科学及文化组织成员但经本组织执行局邀请加入本公约的所有国家加入。

2. 加入书交存联合国教育、科学及文化组织总干事后，加入即行生效。

第二十一条 本公约在收到第三份批准书、接受书或加入书后的三个月开始生效，但这仅涉及那些在该日或该日之前业已交存其各自的批准书、接受书或加入书的国家。对于任何其他国家，本公约则在其批准书、接受书或加入书交存后三个月开始生效。

第二十二条 本公约缔约国承认，本公约不仅适用于其本国领土，而且也适用于在国际关系上由其负责的一切领土：如有必要，缔约国须在批准、接受或加入之时或以前与这些领土的政府或其他主管当局进行磋商，以便保证本公约在这些领土的适用，并将本公约适用的领土通知联合国教育、科学及文化组织总干事，该通知在收到之日起三个月生效。

第二十三条

1. 本公约之每一缔约国可以代表本国或代表由其负责国际关系的任何领土退出本公约。

2. 退约需以书面文件通知，该退约书交存联合国教育、科学及文化组织总干事处。

3. 退约在收到退约通知书后十二个月生效。

第二十四条 联合国教育、科学及文化组织总干事须将第十九条和第二十条中规定的有关批准书、接受书和加入书的交存情况以及第二十二条和第二十三条分别规定的通知和退约告知本组织会员国、第二十条中所述的非本组织会员的国家以及联合国。

第二十五条

1．本公约可经联合国教育、科学及文化组织大会予以修正。任何这样的修正只对修正公约的缔约国具有约束力。

2．如大会通过一项全面或部分地修订本公约的新公约，则除非新公约另有规定，本公约在新的修订公约生效之日起停止一切批准、接受或加入。

第二十六条 经联合国教育、科学及文化组织总干事的要求，本公约应按照《联合国宪章》第一百零二条的规定在联合国秘书处登记。

Convention on the Means of Prohibiting and Preventing the Illicit Import, Export and Transfer of Ownership of Cultural Property

Paris, 14 November 1970

The General Conference of the United Nations Educational, Scientific and Cultural Organization, meeting in Paris from 12 October to 14 November 1970, at its sixteenth session,

Recalling the importance of the provisions contained in the Declaration of the Principles of International Cultural Co - operation, adopted by the General Conference at its fourteenth session,

Considering that the interchange of cultural property among nations for scientific, cultural and educational purposes increases the knowledge of the civilization of Man, enriches the cultural life of all peoples and inspires mutual respect and appreciation among nations,

Considering that cultural property constitutes one of the basic elements of civilization and national culture, and that its true value can be appreciated only in relation to the fullest possible information regarding is origin, history and traditional setting,

Considering that it is incumbent upon every State to protect the cultural property existing within its territory against the dangers of theft, clandestine excavation, and illicit export,

Considering that, to avert these dangers, it is essential for every State to become increasingly alive to the moral obligations to respect its own cultural heritage and that of all nations,

Considering that, as cultural institutions, museums, libraries and archives should ensure that their collections are built up in accordance with universally recognized moral principles,

Considering that the illicit import, export and transfer of ownership of cultural property is an obstacle to that understanding between nations which it is part of UNESCO's mission to promote by recommending to interested States, international conventions to this end,

Considering that the protection of cultural heritage can be effective only if organized both nationally and internationally among States working in close co - operation,

Considering that the UNESCO General Conference adopted a Recommendation to this effect in 1964,

Having before it further proposals on the means of prohibiting and preventing the illicit import, export and transfer of ownership of cultural property, a question which is on the agenda for the session as item 19,

Having decided, at its fifteenth session, that this question should be made the subject of an international convention,

Adopts this Convention on the fourteenth day of November 1970.

Article 1

For the purposes of this Convention, the term `cultural property' means property which, on religious or secular grounds, is specifically designated by each State as being of importance for archaeology, prehistory, history, literature, art or science and which belongs to the following categories:

(a) Rare collections and specimens of fauna, flora, minerals and anatomy, and objects of paleontological interest;

(b) property relating to history, including the history of science and technology and military and social history, to the life of national leaders, thinkers, scientists and artist and to events of national importance;

(c) products of archaeological excavations (including regular and clandestine) or of archaeological discoveries ;

(d) elements of artistic or historical monuments or archaeological sites which have been dismembered;

(e) antiquities more than one hundred years old, such as inscriptions, coins and engraved seals;

(f) objects of ethnological interest;

(g) property of artistic interest, such as:

(i) pictures, paintings and drawings produced entirely by hand on any support and in any material (excluding industrial designs and manufactured articles decorated by hand);

(ii) original works of statuary art and sculpture in any material;

(iii) original engravings, prints and lithographs ;

(iv) original artistic assemblages and montages in any material;

(h) rare manuscripts and incunabula, old books, documents and publications of special interest (historical, artistic, scientific, literary, etc.) singly or in collections ;

(i) postage, revenue and similar stamps, singly or in collections;

(j) archives, including sound, photographic and cinematographic archives;

(k) articles of furniture more than one hundred years old and old musical instruments.

Article 2

1. The States Parties to this Convention recognize that the illicit import, export and transfer of ownership of cultural property is one of the main causes of the impoverishment of the cultural heritage of the countries of origin of such property and that international co - operation constitutes one of the most efficient means of protecting each country's cultural property against all the dangers resulting there from.

2. To this end, the States Parties undertake to oppose such practices with the means at their disposal, and particularly by removing their causes, putting a stop to current practices, and by helping to make the necessary reparations.

Article 3

The import, export or transfer of ownership of cultural property effected contrary to the provisions adopted under this Convention by the States Parties thereto, shall be illicit.

Article 4

The States Parties to this Convention recognize that for the purpose of the Convention property which belongs to the following categories forms part of the cultural heritage of each State:

(a) Cultural property created by the individual or collective genius of nationals of the State concerned, and cultural property of importance to the State concerned created within the territory of that State by foreign nationals or stateless persons resident within such territory;

(b) cultural property found within the national territory;

(c) cultural property acquired by archaeological, ethnological or natural science missions, with the consent of the competent authorities of the country of origin of such property;

(d) cultural property which has been the subject of a freely agreed exchange;

(e) cultural property received as a gift or purchased legally with the consent of the competent authorities of the country of origin of such property.

Article 5

To ensure the protection of their cultural property against illicit import, export and transfer of ownership, the States Parties to this Convention undertake, as appropriate for each country, to set up within their territories one or more national services, where such services do not already exist, for the protection of the cultural heritage, with a qualified staff sufficient in number for the effective carrying out of the following functions:

(a) contributing to the formation of draft laws and regulations designed to secure the protection of the cultural heritage and particularly prevention of the illicit import, export and transfer of ownership of important cultural property;

(b) establishing and keeping up to date, on the basis of a national inventory of protected property, a list of important public and private cultural property whose export would constitute an appreciable impoverishment of the national cultural heritage;

(c) promoting the development or the establishment of scientific and technical institutions (museums, libraries, archives, laboratories, workshops . . .) required to ensure the preservation and presentation of cultural property;

(d) organizing the supervision of archaeological excavations, ensuring the preservation in situ of certain cultural property, and protecting certain areas reserved for future archaeological research;

(e) establishing, for the benefit of those concerned (curators, collectors, antique dealers, etc.) rules in conformity with the ethical principles set forth in this Convention; and taking steps to ensure the observance of those rules;

(f) taking educational measures to stimulate and develop respect for the cultural heritage of all States, and spreading knowledge of the provisions of this Convention;

(g) seeing that appropriate publicity is given to the disappearance of any items of cultural property.

Article 6

The States Parties to this Convention undertake:

(a) To introduce an appropriate certificate in which the exporting State would specify that the export of the cultural property in question is authorized. The certificate should accompany all items of cultural property exported in accordance with the regulations ;

(b) to prohibit the exportation of cultural property from their territory unless accompanied by the above - mentioned export certificate;

(c) to publicize this prohibition by appropriate means, particularly among persons likely to export or import cultural property.

Article 7

The States Parties to this Convention undertake:

(a) To take the necessary measures, consistent with national legislation, to prevent museums and similar institutions within their territories from acquiring cultural property originating in another State Party which has been illegally exported after entry into force of this Convention, in the States concerned. Whenever possible, to inform a State of origin Party to this Convention of an offer of such cultural property illegally removed from that State after the entry into force of this Convention in both States;

(b) (i) to prohibit the import of cultural property stolen from a museum or a religious or secular public monument or similar institution in another State Party to this Convention after the entry into force of this Convention for the States concerned, provided that such property is documented as appertaining to the inventory of that institution;

(ii) at the request of the State Party of origin, to take appropriate steps to recover and return any such cultural property imported after the entry into force of this Convention in both States concerned, provided, however, that the requesting State shall pay just compensation to an innocent purchaser or to a person who has valid title to that property. Requests for recovery and return shall be made through diplomatic offices. The requesting Party shall furnish, at its expense, the documentation and other evidence necessary to establish its claim for recovery and return. The Parties shall impose no customs duties or other charges upon cultural property returned pursuant to this Article. All expenses incident to the return and delivery of the cultural property shall be borne by the requesting Party.

Article 8

The States Parties to this Convention undertake to impose penalties or admin - istrative sanctions on any person responsible for infringing the prohibitions referred to under Articles 6 (b) and 7 (b) above.

Article 9

Any State Party to this Convention whose cultural patrimony is in jeopardy from pillage of archaeological or ethnological materials may call upon other States Parties who are affected. The States Parties to this Convention undertake, in these circumstances, to participate in a concerted international effort to determine and to carry out the necessary concrete measures, including the control of exports and imports and international commerce in the specific materials concerned. Pending agreement each State concerned shall take provisional measures to the extent feasible to prevent irremediable injury to the cultural heritage of the requesting State.

Article 10

The States Parties to this Convention undertake:

(a) To restrict by education, information and vigilance, movement of cultural property illegally removed from any State Party to this Convention and, as appropriate for each country, oblige antique dealers, subject to penal or administrative sanctions, to maintain a register recording the origin of each item of cultural property, names and addresses of the supplier, description and price of each item sold and to inform the purchaser of the cultural property of the export prohibition to which such property may be subject;

(b) to endeavour by educational means to create and develop in the public mind a realization of the value of cultural property and the threat to the cultural heritage created by theft, clandestine excavations and illicit exports.

Article 11

The export and transfer of ownership of cultural property under compulsion arising directly or indirectly from the occupation of a country by a foreign power shall be regarded as illicit.

Article 12

The States Parties to this Convention shall respect the cultural heritage within the territories for the international relations of which they are responsible, and shall take all appropriate measures to prohibit and prevent the illicit import, export and transfer of ownership of cultural property in such territories.

Article 13

The States Parties to this Convention also undertake, consistent with the laws of each State:

(a) to prevent by all appropriate means transfers of ownership of cultural property likely to promote the illicit import or export of such property;

(b) to ensure that their competent services co - operate in facilitating the earliest possible restitution of illicitly exported cultural property to its rightful owner;

(c) to admit actions for recovery of lost or stolen items of cultural property brought by or on behalf of the rightful owners ;

(d) to recognize the indefeasible right of each State Party to this Convention to classify and declare certain cultural property as inalienable which should therefore ipso facto not be exported, and to facilitate recovery of such property by the State concerned in cases where it has been exported.

Article 14

In order to prevent illicit export and to meet the obligations arising from the implementation of this Convention, each State Party to the Convention should, as far as it is able, provide the national services responsible for the protection of its cultural heritage with an adequate budget and, if necessary, should set up a fund for this purpose.

Article 15

Nothing in this Convention shall prevent States Parties thereto from concluding special agreements among themselves or from continuing to implement agreements already concluded regarding the restitution of cultural property removed, whatever the reason, from its territory of origin, before the entry into force of this Convention for the States concerned.

Article 16

The States Parties to this Convention shall in their periodic reports submitted to the General Conference of the United Nations Educational, Scientific and Cultural Organization on dates and in a manner to be determined by it, give information on the legislative and administrative provisions which they have adopted and other action which they have taken for the application of this Convention, together with details of the experience acquired in this field.

Article 17

1. The States Parties to this Convention may call on the technical assistance of the United Nations Educational, Scientific and Cultural Organization, particularly as regards:

(a) Information and education;

(b) consultation and expert advice;

(c) co - ordination and good offices.

2. The United Nations Educational, Scientific and Cultural Organization may, on its own initiative conduct research and publish studies on matters relevant to the illicit movement of cultural property.

3. To this end, the United Nations Educational, Scientific and Cultural Organization may also call on the co - operation of any competent non - governmental organization.

4. The United Nations Educational, Scientific and Cultural Organization may, on its own initiative, make proposals to States Parties to this Convention for its implementation.

5. At the request of at least two States Parties to this Convention which are engaged in a dispute over its implementation, UNESCO may extend its good offices to reach a settlement between them.

Article 18

This Convention is drawn up in English, French, Russian and Spanish, the four texts being equally authoritative.

Article 19

1. This Convention shall be subject to ratification or acceptance by States members of the United Nations Educational, Scientific and Cultural Organization in accordance with their respective constitutional procedures.

2. The instruments of ratification or acceptance shall be deposited with the Director - General of the United Nations Educational, Scientific and Cultural Organi-

zation.

Article 20

1. This Convention shall be open to accession by all States not members of the United Nations Educational, Scientific and Cultural Organization which are invited to accede to it by the Executive Board of the Organization.

2. Accession shall be effected by the deposit of an instrument of accession with the Director - General of the United Nations Educational, Scientific and Cultural Organization.

Article 21

This Convention shall enter into force three months after the date of the deposit of the third instrument of ratification, acceptance or accession, but only with respect to those States which have deposited their respective instruments on or before that date. It shall enter into force with respect to any other State three months after the deposit of its instrument of ratification, acceptance or accession.

Article 22

The States Parties to this Convention recognize that the Convention is applicable not only to their metropolitan territories but also to all territories for the international relations of which they are responsible; they undertake to consult, if necessary, the governments or other competent authorities of these territories on or before ratification, acceptance or accession with a view to securing the application of the Convention to those territories, and to notify the Director - General of the United Nations Educational, Scientific and cultural Organization of the territories to which it is applied, the notification to take effect three months after the date of its receipt.

Article 23

1. Each State Party to this Convention may denounce the Convention on its own behalf or on behalf of any territory for whose international relations it is responsible.

2. The denunciation shall be notified by an instrument in writing, deposited with the Director - General of the United Nations Educational, Scientific and Cultural Organization.

3. The denunciation shall take effect twelve months after the receipt of the instrument of denunciation.

Article 24

The Director - General of the United Nations Educational, Scientific and Cultural Organization shall inform the States members of the Organization, the States not members of the Organization which are referred to in Article 20, as well as the United Nations, of the deposit of all the instruments of ratification, acceptance and accession provided for in Articles 19 and 20, and of the notifications and denunciations provided for in Articles 22 and 23 respectively.

Article 25

1. This Convention may be revised by the General Conference of the United Nations Educational, Scientific and Cultural Organization. Any such revision shall, however, bind only the States which shall become Parties to the revising convention.

2. If the General Conference should adopt a new convention revising this Convention in whole or in part, then, unless the new convention otherwise provides, this Convention shall cease to be open to ratification, acceptance or accession, as from the date on which the new revising convention enters into force.

Article 26

In conformity with Article 102 of the Charter of the United Nations, this Convention shall be registered with the Secretariat of the United Nations at the request of the Director - General of the United Nations Educational, Scientific and Cultural Organization.

阻止淫秽出版物流通协定*

（1949 年 5 月 4 日在纽约通过，1950 年 3 月 1 日生效）

第一条

每一缔约国政府都同意建立或者指定负责下列职责的政府机构：

1. 协调可以发现并阻止就淫秽读物、设计、图片或物品而违反本国法律之行为所有信息。

2. 只要其相关法律许可，提供所有可能有助于阻止进口前款规定出版物品进口或确保及加速其查封的信息；

3. 通告其各自国家涉及本协定事项的法律或者就要通过的法律。

缔约国政府须通过联合国秘书长、根据本条规定设立或指定的政府机构加强彼此了解。

第二条

根据第一条指定的政府机构须具备职权直接与其他缔约国的类似政府部门直接进行回应。

第三条

根据第一条规定所制定的政府机构须在有关内国法律许可的情形下向所有其他缔约国的类似机构通告该国就第一条规定的违反行为所作认定的详情。

第四条

非签字国也可以对本协定予以附和。他们须通过交存于联合国档案的文件将其附和公约的意愿予以通知。联合国秘书长须将经认证的该等文件之副本发送予每一个缔约国及联合国所有成员国，并同时告知交存时间。该日期之后六个月，本协定将在所有进行附和国家的领土上生效，该等国家就成为缔约国。

第五条

本协定在交存批准文件六个月后生效。

---

* 中国社会科学院法学研究所吴峻译。

如缔约国有退出的，该等退出仅对该缔约国生效。

退出须通过在联合国档案交存的任何文件予以该通知。联合国秘书长须向每一个缔约国及联合国所有成员国发送该等通知的经认证文本，并在同时告知交存日期。

该日期 12 个月之后本协定在退出国家领土上停止生效。

第六条

本协定须被批准，该等批准须在六个缔约国可以交存的时候交存于巴黎。

对于批准书的每次交存须进行官方记录，经认证的文本须通过外交渠道向缔约国予以提交。

第七条

缔约国希望在其一个或多个殖民地、属地或者具有领事管辖权的区域实施本协定的，须通过在联合国档案交存文件予以该通知。联合国秘书长须向每一个缔约国及联合国所有成员国发送该等通知的经认证文本，并在同时告知交存日期。

该日期六个月后，本协定须在批准文件交存所明确的殖民地、属地或者领事裁判区域生效。

缔约国代表其一个或多个殖民地、属地或领事裁判区推出本协定的，其生效形式和条件请见本条第一款的规定。在交存提存文件于联合国档案之日 12 个月之后生效。

本协定日期须为 1910 年 3 月 4 日，可在巴黎在 7 月 31 日由参加阻止淫秽出版物大会之国家的全权代表予以签署。

本公约对于 1910 年 5 月 4 日通过并于 1911 年 9 月 15 日生效的《阻止淫秽出版物流通协定》予以修订。修订协定于 1949 年 5 月 4 日通过，于 1950 年 3 月 1 日生效。

Agreement for the Repression of Obscene Publications

Done at: New York

Date enacted: 1949 -05 -04

In force: 1950 -03 -01

This Convention revises the Agreement for the Suppression of the Circulation of Obscene Publications adopted 1910 -05 -04, in force 1911 -09 -15. As amended by Protocol adopted 1949 -05 -04, in force 1950 -03 -01

Article 1

Each of the Contracting Governments agrees to establish or to designate an authority charged with the duty:

1. Of coordinating all information which may facilitate the discovery and suppression of acts constituting offences against their internal legislation in respect of obscene writings, designs, pictures, or objects, where the various acts constituting the offence have taken place in different countries;

2. Of furnishing all information which may be useful for the purpose of preventing the importation of publications of objects contemplated by the preceding paragraph, or of securing or expediting the seizure thereof, so far as their respective laws permit;

3. Of communicating the laws which have been or shall be introduced in their respective States with reference to the object of the present Agreement.

The Contracting Governments shall mutually make known to one another, through the Secretary - General of the United Nations, the authority established or designated in accordance with the present Article.

Article 2

The authority designated under Article 1 shall have power to correspond direct with the similar department established in each of the other Contracting States.

Article 3

The authority designated under Article 1 shall, if the internal legislation of the country concerned so permit, communicate to the similar authorities of all the other Contracting States particulars of convictions pronounced in the said country in respect of offences contemplated by Article 1.

Article 4

Non - signatory States will be permitted to adhere to the present Agreement. They shall notify their intention to that effect by means of an instrument which shall be deposited in the archives of the United Nations. The Secretary - General of the United Nations shall send a certified copy of the said instrument to each one of the Contracting States and to all the Members of the United Nations, and at the same time apprise them of the date of deposit.

Six months after that date, the Agreement will go into effect throughout the territory of the adhering State, which will thereby become a Contracting State.

Article 5

The present Agreement shall come into force six months after the date of the deposit of ratifications.

In the event of one of the Contracting States denounces it, the denunciation would only have effect in regard to that State.

The denunciation shall be notified by any instrument which shall be deposited in the archives of the United Nations. the Secretary - General of the United Nations shall send a certified copy thereof to each one of the Contracting States and to all the Members of the United Nations, and at the same time apprise them of the date of deposit.

Twelve months after this date the Agreement shall cease to be in force throughout the territory of the State which has denounced it.

Article 6

The present Agreement shall be ratified, and the ratifications shall be deposited at Paris as soon as six of the Contracting States are in a position to do so.

A procès - verbal of every deposit of ratifications shall be drawn up and a certified copy thereof shall be delivered through the diplomatic channel to each one of the Contracting States.

Article 7

Should a Contracting State wish to enforce the present Agreement in one or more of its colonies, possessions or areas under consular jurisdiction, it shall notify its intention to that effect by an instrument which shall be deposited in the archives of the United Nations. The Secretary - General of the United Nations shall send a certified copy to each of the Contracting States and to all the Members of the United Nations and the same time apprise them of the date of the deposit.

Six months after this date the Agreement shall go into effect in the colonies, possessions, or consular court districts specified in the instrument of ratification.

The denunciation of the Agreement by one of the Contracting States on behalf of one or more of its colonies, possessions or consular court districts shall be effected in the form and under the conditions set forth in the first paragraph of this Article. It shall take effect twelve months after the date of the deposit of the instrument of denunciation in the archives of the United Nations.

Article 8

The present Agreement, which shall be dated 4 March 1910, may be signed in Paris up to 31 July following, by the plenipotentiaries of the Powers represented at the Conference for the Suppression of Obscene Publications.

阻止淫秽出版物流通及买卖国际公约*

（1923年9月12日在日内瓦签订）

阿尔巴尼亚、德国、澳大利亚、比利时、巴西、英帝国（包括南非联盟、新西兰、印度及爱尔兰自由国）、保加利亚、中国、柬埔寨、哥斯达黎加、古巴、丹麦、西班牙、芬兰、法国、希腊、海地、洪都拉斯、匈牙利、意大利、日本、拉脱维亚、立陶宛、卢森堡、摩纳哥、巴拿马、荷兰、波斯、波兰（及格旦斯克）、葡萄牙、罗马尼亚、萨尔瓦多、塞尔维亚、克罗地亚及斯洛文尼亚王国、暹罗、捷克斯洛伐克、土耳其及乌拉圭：

都同样希望尽力设法阻止淫秽出版物的流通与买卖，

已经接受了法兰西共和国政府的邀请于1923年8月31日于日参加内瓦召开的国际联盟会议，审议在1910年起草的公约草案，审议各个国家提交的意见及公约最后文本的解释和签署，

为此目的委任了其全权代表，

该等全权大使已将其完全授权通告于众，形式合法有效，

并注意到本次大会的最后法案及1910年5月4日之协定，

就以下条款达成一致：

第1条

缔约方同意采取一切措施以发现、起诉并惩罚犯有任何下列违反行为的任何人，并由此同意其须为受惩罚的违法行为：

（1）目的或方式就进行贸易、分销或展览以制作、生产或持有淫秽读物、画片、印刷品、画作、印刷物品、图片、海报、徽章、相片、电影或其他淫秽物品；

（2）为上述目的而进口、携带或出口或促使进口、携带或出口任何所规定的淫秽物品或以任何方式使之流通；

---

* 中国社会科学院法学研究所吴峻译。

（3）无论公共或私人从事或参与任何所述淫秽物品的经营，或者以任何方式交易所述物品，或者将之分销或公开展览或对之进行租赁经营；

（4）以任何方式进行广告或广而告之，以帮助所述受惩罚的流通或买卖，从事任何上述行为的人，或者广告或广而告之如何或从何处可以直接或间接取得淫秽物品。

第 2 条

从事第一条规定违法行为的人员须在从事违法行为或者违法行为构成要素地的缔约国法院予以处理。他们也可以在其国籍国法院接受处理，只要该国法律允许并且处于一种该国领土，即使该等违法行为的构成元素系处于该国境外。

然而，每一个缔约方都有权根据其法律中的规则适用一审不再受理原则。

第 3 条

传送涉及本公约规定的调查请求须通过下列两种方式之一予以实施：

（1）直接在司法机关之间沟通；

（2）通过提出请求国设在被请求国的外交或领事代表提出；该等代表须直接向有关司法机关发送调查请求，或者向被请求国政府指定机构发送，并须从该等机构获得实施调查请求的书面证明。

在上述情形之一，调查请求文本须永远向被申请国的最高机关予以寄送。

（3）通过外交渠道

每一缔约方须向其他缔约方互相通报其将认可该等缔约方调查请求的上述传送方式。

涉及本条所规定方式（1）及方式（2）而产生的困难须通过外交渠道加以解决。

除非另有约定，调查请求须以被请求机关所使用的语言草就，或者使用两个国家统一的语言，或者附有经请求国外交或领事代表所认证的该两种语言之一的翻译文本，该认证也可以由被请求国翻译人员以誓言的方式予以认证。

对调查请求的执行须不得基于税收的支付或者作出任何其他性质支出的前提。

本条内容不得被解释为缔约方保证在其法院通过与其法律相悖的任何形式或方式的证明。

第 4 条

缔约方之中法律并不足够实施本公约的承诺采取或建议其各自立法机关

采取为此目的而必须的措施。

第 5 条

缔约方的法律在目前并不足够实现本公约宗旨的，对有理由相信第一条规定的淫秽物品或任何其中的物品为了第一条提及的目的而在任何处所进行制作或提存的，或者违反其规定的，同意制定规定搜查处所，并对相关物品予以查封、扣押及销毁。

第 6 条

缔约方同意，在缔约方的领土上出现违反第一条规定并且似乎违反该条规定的物品是在任何其他缔约国领土内制作或从该国进口的，根据 1910 年 5 月 4 日之协定而有该等缔约方指定的政府机构须立即向另一据信系该等物品来源国或生产国的缔约方的对应机关提交全部信息，以便使之可以采取认为合理的该等措施。

第 7 条

本公约的权威文本系以法文和英文草就，并记载今日之日期，须在 1924 年 3 月 31 日之前向大会参加国、国际联盟任何成员及任何国家开放供签署，国际联盟理事会为此目的须向该等国家寄送本公约文本。

第 8 条

本公约需要批准。批准文件须交存于国际联盟秘书长，后者须将受到该等文件的情形通知予作为本公约签署方的国际联盟成员及其他签署国。

国际联盟秘书长须立即将所交存文件经认证的援引本公约的文本传送予法兰西共和国政府。

根据《国际联盟公约》第 18 条之规定，秘书长须在其生效之日将本公约予以登记。

第 9 条

1924 年 3 月 31 日之后，本公约可以有任何列席于本次大会但并没有签署本公约的任何国家、国际联盟的任何成员国或任何国家予以附和，为此目的，国际联盟理事会须将本公约文本传送予该等国家。

附和须通过向国际联盟秘书长发送要交存秘书处存档文件的方式予以实施。秘书长须立即将该等文件的提交通告予所有作为公约签字国的国际联盟成员及其他签字国。

第 10 条

本公约的批准或符合须自然而然地无须通过特别通告就涉及同时对 1910 年 5 月 4 日协定的全盘接受，后者将和公约自身同时在国际联盟签署成员国或者国家的全部领土上生效。

第 11 条

本公约须在国际联盟秘书长收到两份批准文件交存的 30 天后生效。

第 12 条

本公约可以通过向国际联盟秘书长提交书面文件而予以退出。该退出须在秘书长收到退出文件之日一年后生效，仅仅对予以退出的国际联盟成员国或国家发生效力。国际联盟秘书长须将收到该等退出文件的情形通告作为公约签署或符合方的所有国际联盟成员国及其他签署国或附和国。对本公约予以退出自然无须设计同时退出 1910 年 5 月 4 日的协定，除非这也在通知文件中得以明确说明。

第 13 条

签署或附和本公约的任何国际联盟成员国或其他国家可以宣布其签署或符合并不涵盖其任何或所有殖民地、海外属地、受保护国或托管国，并可以在之后代表在其声明中排除的任何该等殖民地、海外属地、受保护国或托管国分别对本公约予以附和。对于任何该等殖民地、海外属地、受保护国或托管国，也可以分别予以退出，第 12 条的规定对作出任何该等退出均适用。

第 14 条

国际联盟秘书长须保存特别记录，记载本公约的签署方、批准方、附和方及退出方。该等记录须在任何时候向已经签署或附和本公约的国际联盟任何成员国或任何其他国家开放。须尽可能地对之进行经常性的公布。

第 15 条

缔约方之间就本公约适用而发生的争议，如不能直接谈判解决，须提交国际常设法院予以裁决。如争议一方或双方缔约国都不是《国际常设法院签署协定》的缔约方，经缔约方选择须提交国际常设法院或仲裁。

第 16 条

五个本公约签署方或附和方要求修改本公约的，国际联盟理事会须为此而召开大会。在任何情形下，理事会将在每个五年期结束之时考虑召开大会的必要性。

基于上述全权代表的信任，同意达成本公约。

于一九二三年九月十二日签署两份原件，一份交存于国际联盟档案，另一份仍然交存于法兰西共和国政府档案之中。

International Convention for the Suppression of the Circulation of and Traffic in Obscene Publications

concluded at Geneva on 12 September 1923

Albania, Germany, Austria, Belgium, Brazil, the British Empire (with the Union of South Africa, New Zealand, India and the Irish Free State), Bulgaria, China, Colombia, Costa Rica, Cuba, Denmark, Spain, Finland, France, Greece, Haiti, Honduras, Hungary, Italy, Japan, Latvia, Lithuania, Luxemburg, Monaco, Panama, the Netherlands, Persia, Poland (with Danzig), Portugal, Roumania, Salvador, Kingdom of the Serbs, Croats and Slovenes, Siam, Switzerland, Czechoslovakia, Turkey and Uruguay:

Being equally desirous of making as effective as possible the means of suppressing the circulation of and traffic in obscene publications,

Having accepted the invitation of the Government of the French Republic to take part in a conference, under the auspices of the League of Nations, convened in Geneva on 31 August 1923 for the examination of the Draft Convention drawn up in 1910, the examination of the observations presented by the various States and the elaboration and signature of the final text of a Convention,

Have nominated as their plenipotentiaries for this purpose,

[Names of plenipotentiaries not reproduced here.]

Who, having communicated their full powers, found in good and due form,

And having taken cognizance of the Final Act of this Conference and of the Agreement of 4 May 1910,

Have agreed upon the following provisions:

Article 1

The High Contracting Parties agree to take all measures to discover, prosecute and punish any person engaged in committing any of the following offences, and accordingly agree that it shall be a punishable offence:

(1) for purposes of or by way of trade or for distribution or public exhibition to make or produce or have in possession obscene writings, drawings, prints, paintings, printed matter, pictures, posters, emblems, photographs, cinematograph films or any other obscene objects;

(2) for the purposes abovementioned, to import, convey or export or cause to be imported, conveyed or exported any of the said obscene matters or things, or in any manner whatsoever to put them into circulation;

(3) to carry on or take part in a business, whether public or private, concerned with any of the said obscene matters or things, or to deal in the said matters or things in any manner whatsoever, or to distribute them or to exhibit them publicly or to make a business of lending them;

(4) to advertise or make known by any means whatsoever, in view of assisting in the said punishable circulation or traffic, that a person is engaged in any of the above punishable acts, or to advertise or to make known how or from whom the said obscene matters or things can be procured either directly or indirectly.

Article 2

Persons who have committed an offence falling under Article 1 shall be amenable to the courts of the Contracting Party in whose territories the offence, or any of the constitutive elements of the offence, was committed. They shall also be amenable, when the laws of the country shall permit it, to the courts of the Contracting Party whose nationals they are, if they are found in its territories, even if the constitutive elements of the offence were committed outside such territories.

Each Contracting Party shall, however, have the right to apply the maxim non bis in idem in accordance with the rules laid down in its legislation.

Article 3

The transmission of rogatory commissions relating to offences falling under the present Convention shall be effected either:

(1) By direct communication between the judicial authorities; or

(2) Through the diplomatic or consular representative of the country making the request in the country to which the request is made; this representative shall send the rogatory commission direct to the competent judicial authority or to the

authority appointed by the Government of the country to which the request is made, and shall receive direct from such authority the papers showing the execution of the rogatory commission.

In each of the above cases a copy of the rogatory commission shall always be sent to the supreme authority of the country to which application is made.

(3) Or through diplomatic channels.

Each Contracting Party shall notify to each of the other Contracting Parties the method or methods of transmission mentioned above which it will recognise for rogatory commissions of such Party.

Any difficulties which may arise in connection with transmission by methods (1) and (2) of the present Article shall be settled through diplomatic channels.

Unless otherwise agreed, the rogatory commission shall be drawn up in the language of the authority to which request is made, or in a language agreed upon by the two countries concerned, or shall be accompanied by a translation in one of these two languages certified by a diplomatic or consular agent of the country making the request or certified on his oath by a translator of the country to which request is made.

Execution of rogatory commissions shall not be subject to payment of taxes or expenses of any nature whatsoever.

Nothing in this Article shall be construed as an undertaking on the part of the Contracting Parties to adopt in their courts of law any form or methods of proof contrary to their laws.

Article 4

Those of the Contracting Parties whose legislation is not at present adequate to give effect to the present Convention undertake to take, or to propose to their respective legislatures, the measures necessary for this purpose.

Article 5

The Contracting Parties whose legislation is not at present sufficient for the purpose agree to make provision for the searching of any premises where there is reason to believe that the obscene matters or things mentioned in Article 1 or any thereof are being made or deposited for any of the purposes specified in the said Article, or in violation of its provisions, and for their seizure, detention and destruction.

Article 6

The Contracting Parties agree that, in case of any violation of the provisions of Article 1 on the territory of one of the Contracting Parties where it appears that the matter or thing in respect of which the violation of such Article has occurred was produced in or imported from the territory of any other of the Contracting Parties, the authority designated in pursuance of the Agreement of 4 May 1910 of such Contracting Party shall immediately render to the corresponding authority of the other Contracting Party, from whose country such matter or thing is believed to have come or in which it is believed to have been produced, full information so as to enable such authority to adopt such measures as shall appear to be suitable.

Article 7

The present Convention, of which the French and English texts are authoritative, shall bear this day's date, and shall be open for signature until 31 March 1924 by any State represented at the Conference, by any Member of the League of Nations, and by any State to which the Council of the League of Nations shall have communicated a copy of the Convention for this purpose.

Article 8

The present Convention is subject to ratification. The instruments of ratification shall be deposited with the Secretary - General of the League of Nations, who shall notify the receipt of them to Members of the League who are signatories of the Convention and to other signatory States.

The Secretary - General of the League of Nations shall immediately communicate a certified copy of each of the instruments deposited, with reference to this Convention, to the Government of the French Republic.

In compliance with the provisions of Article 18 of the Covenant of the League of Nations, the Secretary - General will register the present Convention upon the day of its coming into force.

Article 9

After 31 March 1924 the present Convention may be adhered to by any State represented at the Conference which has not signed the Convention, by any Member of the League of Nations, or by any State to which the Council of the League of Nations shall have communicated a copy of the Convention for this purpose.

Adhesion shall be effected by an instrument communicated to the Secretary -

General of the League of Nations to be deposited in the archives of the Secretariat.

[2] The Secretary - General shall at once notify such deposit to all Members of the League of Nations signatories of the Convention and to other signatory States.

Article 10

Ratification of or adhesion to the present Convention shall ipso facto, and without special notification, involve concomitant and full acceptance of the Agreement of 4 May 1910, which shall come into force on the same date as the Convention itself in the whole of the territory of the ratifying or adhering Member of the League or State.

pArticle 4 of the abovementioned Agreement of 4 May 1910 shall not, however, be invalidated by the preceding provision, but shall remain applicable should any State prefer to adhere to that Agreement only.

Article 11

The present Convention shall come into force on the thirtieth day after the deposit of two ratifications with the Secretary - General of the League of Nations.

Article 12

The present Convention may be denounced by an instrument in writing addressed to the Secretary - General of the League of Nations. The denunciation shall become effective one year after the date of the receipt of the instrument of denunciation by the Secretary - General, and shall operate only in respect of the Member of the League of Nations or State which makes it. The Secretary - General of the League of Nations shall notify the receipt of any such denunciation to all Members of the League of Nations signatories of or adherents to the Convention and to other signatory or adherent States. Denunciation of the present Convention shall not, ipso facto, involve the concomitant denunciation of the Agreement of 4 May 1910 unless this is expressly stated in the instrument of notification.

Article 13

Any Member of the League of Nations or State signing or adhering to the present Convention may declare that its signature or adhesion does not include any or all of its colonies, overseas possessions, protectorates or territories under its sovereignty or authority, and may subsequently adhere separately on behalf of any such colony, overseas possession, protectorate or territory so excluded in its declaration. Denunciation may also be made separately in respect of any such colony, overseas possession, protectorate or territory under its sovereignty or authority, and the provisions of Article 12 shall apply to any such denunciation.

Article 14

A special record shall be kept by the Secretary - General of the League of Nations, showing which of the parties have signed, ratified, adhered to or denounced the present Convention. This record shall be open at all times to any of the Members of the League of Nations or any State which has signed or adhered to the Convention. It shall be published as often as possible.

Article 15

Disputes between the Parties relating to the interpretation or application of this Convention shall, if they cannot be settled by direct negotiation, be referred for decision to the Permanent Court of International Justice. In case either or both of the Parties to such a dispute should not be Parties to the Protocol of Signature of the Permanent Court of International Justice, the dispute shall be referred, at the choice of the Parties, either to the Permanent Court of International Justice or to arbitration.

Article 16

Upon a request for a revision of the present Convention by five of the signatory or adherent Parties to the Convention, the Council of the League of Nations shall call a conference for that purpose. In any event, the Council will consider the desirability of calling a conference at the end of each period of five years. In faith whereof the above named Plenipotentiaries have agreed the present Convention. Done at Geneva the twelfth day of September, one thousand nine hundred and twenty - three, in two originals of which one shall remain deposited in the archives of the League of Nations and the other shall remain deposited in the archives of the Government of the French Republic.

关于文化财产国际交流的建议*

（联合国教科文组织第十九次大会 1976 年
11 月 26 日通过）

联合国教育、科学及文化组织大会，于 1976 年 10 月 26 日至 11 月 30 日在内罗毕举行第十九届会议。

忆及文化财产构成文明和民族文化的基本要素；

考虑到扩大并促进旨在对各文化领域内成就更全面的相互了解的文化交流将有助于丰富有关的文化，同时对每一文化的特点及对组成全人类文化遗产的其他民族文化的价值予以应有的认识；

考虑到文化财产的流通，如在防止对这些财产的非法贸易和损害的法律、科学及技术条件的管理下，成为促进各国间相互了解和认识的强有力手段；

考虑到文化财产的国际流通在很大程度上仍依赖于追求私利各方的活动，并因而易引向投机，使这些财产的价格上涨，使其不能为较穷的国家和机构所取得，反而鼓励非法贸易的扩散；

考虑到即使该等财产国际流通的动机是公正无私的，而所采取行动通常归为单向的提供，如短期的出借、根据中期或长期安排的存放或捐赠；

考虑到这些单向活动由于其费用及由于有关规章和惯例的复杂多样而在数量上和范围上仍为有限；

考虑到亟须通过减少或消除扩展的各种障碍以鼓励这类活动，同时促进基于相互信任的活动使所有机构能平等相待，亦至为重要；

考虑到许多文化机构，不论其资金力量如何，均拥有数件相同或相似、其特质及出处无可怀疑并经大量文献证明的文化物品，而这其中一些物品虽由于其数量多而对上述机构仅有较小或次要意义，却被其他国家的机构作为有价值的添置而受欢迎；

---

* 中国社会科学院法学研究所谢增毅译。

考虑到各文化机构间进行交流的系统政策不仅将丰富各方，而且将有助于更好地利用作为各民族遗产总体的国际社会文化遗产，通过该政策各方将出让其多余的物品以换回其所缺少的物品；

忆及该项交流政策已为作为联合国教育、科学及文化组织的工作成果而缔结的各项国际协议所推荐；

注意到在此方面上述文件的作用仍为有限，并且一般说来廉正无私文化机构间的交流实践并不广泛，而即使进行的交流活动通常也是保密的或不公开的；

考虑到因而有必要不仅同时开展单向的租借、存放或捐赠而且还要开展双边或多边交流；

收到作为本届会议日程第26项的关于文化财产国际交流的议案，其第十八届会议已决定就此问题应形成对各成员国的建议，兹于1976年11月26日通过本建议。

大会建议，各成员国应依照各自国家的宪法制度或惯例，采取为在其各自领土内实施本建议所述原则所需的任何立法或其他步骤，以适用下述规定。

大会建议，各成员国应提请适当当局及机构注意本建议。

大会建议，各成员国按照待由大会决定的日期和格式向大会递交关于其依本建议所采取行动的报告。

一、定　　义

1. 为本建议的目的：

“文化机构”应被认为指为普遍利益而设置、旨在保存、研究及宣传文化财产并使之向公众开放、为各国主管公共机构所许可或批准的任何常设机构；“文化财产”应被认为指各个国家主管机构认为具有或可能具有历史，艺术、科学或技术价值和意义的作为人类创造或自然进化表现和明证的实物，包括下列各类中的实物：

（A）动物的、植物的及地质的标本；

（B）考古实物；

（C）具有人种学意义的物品及文献；

（D）美术和工艺作品；

（E）文学、音乐、摄影及电影作品；

（F）档案及文献；

“国际交流”应被认为指国家间或不同国家的文化机构间，按有关各方间可能同意的条件，对文化财产的所有权、使用或保管的任何转让，而不问其系以对该等财产的租借、存放、买卖或捐赠的形式。

二、建议之措施

2. 考虑到所有文化财产构成人类共同文化遗产的一部分及每一国家在此方面不仅对其本国国民而且对国际社会整体负有责任，各成员国应于其权限范围内采取下述措施，以在所需的地区或地方当局的合作下，推动文化财产在不同国家的文化机构间的流通。

3. 各成员国，依照其各自国家的立法和宪法制度或惯例及特殊国情，应修改关于继承、税收及关税的现行法规或规章或通过新的立法或规章并采取一切其他必要措施，以便使之可能或易于仅为文化机构间文化财产国际交流的目的进行下述活动：

（1）文化财产永久或暂时的进口或出口及过境；

（2）公共机构或文化机构所属文化财产所有权的转让或对其限制的解除。

4. 如认为可行，各成员国应鼓励在其直接控制下或通过文化机构建立关于供国际交流的文化财产的供求档案。

5. 提供交流仅于经确定有关物品的法律地位符合国家法律并且提供机构为此目的拥有合法所有权时，方应录入档案。

6. 提供交流应包括旨在确保对有关物品的文化利用、保护及适当修复的最有利条件的完整的科学、技术及所可能要求的法律文献。

7. 交流协议应包括接受机构为妥善保护有关文化财产拟采取一切必要保护措施的说明。

8. 应考虑给予文化机构以额外的资金援助或在现有援助水平上留出一部分，以便利国际交流的进行。

9. 各成员国应特别注意对在出借期间包括运输期间文化财产易受到的风险的保险问题，并应特别研究对具有巨大价值物品的出借施行如某些国家已实行政府担保和赔偿制度的可能性。

10. 各成员国应根据其各自宪法惯例，探讨将协调文化财产国际交流所涉各项活动的任务托付于适当专门机构的可能性。

三、国际合作

11．各成员国应在所有主管机构的协助下，不论其为区域、国家或国际组织，也不论其为政府间或非政府组织，根据其宪法惯例，针对各国的文化机构和负责国家文化财产的各类行政的、学术的及科学的专业人员，在国家或区域一级发动一场广泛的信息与鼓励运动，使其注意到开展各种形式的文化财产国际交流对促进各民族间更好的相互了解所可能起的重要作用并鼓励他们参加这些交流。

12．这项运动应特别包括下列几点：

（1）应请已经缔结关于文化财产国际交流协议的文化机构公布具有一般性质的因而能用作范本的所有条款，但不公布具有专门性质，如对有关具体物品的说明、其估价或其他具体技术细节等的条款；

（2）专门的主管机构，特别是国际博物馆协会应编制或增编一部或多部述明文化财产交流的每一种可能形式并强调其特点的实用手册。这些手册应备有每一可能类型协议的示范合同，包括保险合同。在国家主管当局的协助下，手册应向各国有关的各专业组织广泛散发；

（3）为了便利对缔结交流协议的预备研究，下列各项应在各国广为散发；

（a）各国由保管文化财产的机构印制的各种出版物（书籍、期刊、博物馆及展览的图录、照片文献）；

（b）各国编制的交流供求档案；

（4）各国的文化机构应特别注意通过连续出借而非转让所有权的制度所提供的机会重新组合现已拆散的作品，使每一个持有机构能够轮流展出完整的作品。

13．如文化财产国际交流的当事方在执行此种交流中遇到技术上的困难，可征询由其经与联合国教育、科学及文化组织总干事协商后任命的一个或更多专家的意见。

四、联邦国家

14．实行联邦或非单一宪政制度的成员国可按照第十七届会议通过的《保护世界文化和自然遗产公约》第三十四条规定的原则落实本建议。

五、打击文化财产非法交易行动

15. 国际交流的开展应使各不同成员国的文化机构，能够通过获得来源合法并附以能表明其完整文化意义文献的文化财产扩大其收藏。因而，成员国应在有关国际组织的协助下采取一切必要步骤，以确保这些交流的开展同对付每一种可能形式的文化财产非法交易所采取的进一步行动同步进行。

Recommendation concerning the International Exchange of Cultural Property

26 November 1976

The General Conference of the United Nations Educational, Scientific and Cultural Organization, meeting in Nairobi from 26 October to 30 November 1976, at its nineteenth session,

Recalling that cultural property constitutes a basic element of civilization and national culture,

Considering that the extension and promotion of cultural exchanges directed towards a fuller mutual knowledge of achievements in various fields of culture, will contribute to the enrichment of the cultures involved, with due appreciation of the distinctive character of each and of the value of the cultures of other nations making up the cultural heritage of all mankind,

Considering that the circulation of cultural property, when regulated by legal, scientific and technical conditions calculated to prevent illicit trading in and damage to such property, is a powerful means of promoting mutual understanding and appreciation among nations,

Considering that the international circulation of cultural property is still largely dependent on the activities of self - seeking parties and so tends to lead to speculation which causes the price of such property to rise, making it inaccessible to poorer countries and institutions while at the same time encouraging the spread of illicit trading,

Considering that, even when the motives behind the international circulation of this property are disinterested, the action taken usually results in unilateral services, such as short - term loans, deposits under medium - or longterm arrangements, or donations,

Considering that such unilateral operations are still limited in number and restricted in range, both because of their cost and because of the variety of complexity of the relevant regulations and practices,

Considering that, while it is highly desirable to encourage such operations, by reducing or removing the obstacles to their extension, it is also vitally important to promote operations based on mutual confidence which would enable all institutions to deal with each other on an equal footing,

Considering that many cultural institutions, whatever their financial resources, possess several identical or similar specimens of cultural objects of indis - putable quality and origin which are amply documented, and that some of these items, which are of only minor or secondary importance for these institutions because of their plurality, would be welcomed as valuable accessions by institutions in other countries,

Considering that a systematic policy of exchanges among cultural institutions, by which each would part with its surplus items in return for objects that it lacked, would not only be enriching to all parties but would also lead to a better use of the international community's cultural heritage which is the sum of all the national heritages,

Recalling that this policy of exchanges has already been recommended in various international agreements concluded as a result of UNESCO's work,

Noting that, on these points, the effects of the above - mentioned instruments have remained limited, and that, generally speaking, the practice of exchanges between disinterested cultural institutions is not widespread, while such operations as do take place are frequently confidential or unpublicized,

Considering that it is consequently necessary to develop simultaneously not only the unilateral operations of loans, deposits or donations but also bio multilateral exchanges,

Having before it proposals concerning the international exchange of cultural property which appears on the agenda of the session as item 26,

Having decided, at its eighteenth session, that this question should take the form of a Recommendation to Member States,

Adopts , this twenty - sixth day of November 1976, the present Recommendation.

The General Conference recommends that Member States should apply the following provisions by taking whatever legislative or other steps may be required in conformity with the constitutional system or practice of each State, to give effect within their respective territories to the principles formulated in this Recommendation.

The General Conference recommends that Member States should bring this Recommendation to the attention of the appropriate authorities and bodies.

The General Conference recommends that Member States should submit to it, by dates and in the form to be decided upon by the Conference, reports concerning the action taken by them in pursuance of this Recommendation.

I. Definitions

1. For the purposes of this Recommendation:

"cultural institution" shall be taken to mean any permanent establishment administered in the general interest for the purpose of preserving, studying and enhancing cultural property and making it accessible to the public and which is licensed or approved by the competent public authorities of each State;

"cultural property" shall be taken to mean items which are the expression and testimony of human creation and of the evolution of nature which, in the opinion of the competent bodies in individual States, are, or may - be, of historical, artistic, scientific or technical value and interest, including items in the following categories:

(a) zoological, botanical and geological specimens ;

(b) archaeological objects;

(c) objects and documentation of ethnological interest;

(d) works of fine art and of the applied arts;

(e) literary, musical, photographic and cinematographic works ;

(f) archives and documents;

"international exchange" shall be taken to mean any transfer of ownership, use or custody of cultural property between States or cultural institutions in different countries - whether it takes the form of the loan, deposit, sale or donation of such property - carried out under such conditions as may be agreed between the parties concerned.

II. Measures recommended

2. Bearing in mind that all cultural property forms part of the common cultural heritage of mankind and that every State has a responsibility in this respect, not only towards its own nationals but also towards the international community as a whole, Member States should adopt within the sphere of their competence, the following measures to develop the circulation of cultural property among cultural institutions in different countries in co - operation with regional and local authorities as may be required.

3. Member States, in accordance with the legislation and the constitutional system or practice and the particular circumstances of their respective countries, should adapt existing statutes or regulations or adopt new legislation or regulations regarding inheritance, taxation and customs duties and take all other necessary measures in order to make it possible or easier to carry out the following operations solely for the purposes of international exchanges of cultural property between cultural institutions:

(a) definitive or temporary import or export as well as transit of cultural property;

(b) transfer of ownership or derestriction of cultural property belonging to a public body or a cultural institution.

4. Member States should foster, if they deem it advisable, the establishment either under their direct authority or through cultural institutions of files of requests for and offers of exchanges of cultural property made available for international exchange.

5. Offers of exchange should be entered in the files only when it has been established that the legal status of the items concerned conforms to national law and that the offering institution has legal title for this purpose.

6. Offers of exchanges should include full scientific, technical and, if requested, legal documentation calculated to ensure the most favourable conditions for the cultural utilization, the conservation and, where appropriate, the restoration of the items in question.

7. Exchange agreements should include an indication that the recipient institution is prepared to take all necessary measures of conservation for the proper protection of the cultural property involved.

8. Consideration should be given to the granting of additional financial assistance to cultural institutions, or to the setting aside of part of the existing levels of financial assistance, to facilitate the carrying out of international exchanges.

9. Member States should give special attention to the problem of covering the risks to which cultural property is exposed throughout the duration of loans, including the period spent in transport, and should, in particular, study the possibility of introducing government guarantee and compensation systems for the loan of objects of great value, such as those which already exist in certain countries.

10. Member States, in accordance with their constitutional practice, should examine the possibility of entrusting to appropriate specialized bodies the task of coordinating the various operations involved in the international exchange of cultural property.

III. International co – operation

11. With the assistance of all competent organizations, whether regional, national or international, intergovernmental or non - governmental, and in accordance with their constitutional practice, Member States should launch an extensive campaign of information and encouragement aimed at cultural institutions in all countries and at the professional staff of all categories - administrative, academic and scientific - who are in charge of the national cultural property, at the national or regional level, drawing their attention to the important contribution which can be made to the promotion of a better mutual understanding of all peoples by developing all forms of international circulation of cultural property and encouraging them to participate in such exchanges.

12. This campaign should cover the following points in particular:

(1) cultural institutions having already concluded agreements on the international circulation of cultural property should be invited to publicize all provisions which are of a general nature and could thus serve as a model, but not provisions of a special nature such as the description of the particular items in question, their

evaluation or other specific technical details;

(2) the competent specialized organizations, and particularly the International Council of Museums, should produce or enlarge one or more practical handbooks describing every possible form of circulation of cultural property and emphasizing their specific features. These handbooks should include model contracts, including insurance contracts, for every possible type of agreement. With the help of the competent national authorities, the handbooks should be widely distributed to all the professional organizations involved in the various countries ;

(3) in order to facilitate the preparatory studies for the conclusion of exchange agreements, the following should be widely distributed in all countries:

(a) various publications (books, periodicals, museum and exhibition catalogues, photographic documentation) produced in all countries by institutions which are custodians of cultural property;

(b) the files of exchange offers and requests compiled in each country;

(4) the attention of cultural institutions in all countries should be drawn especially to the opportunities for reassembling a presently dismembered work which would be afforded by a system of successive loans, without transfer of ownership, enabling each of the holding institutions to take its turn to display the work in its entirety.

13. Should the parties to an international exchange of cultural property encounter technical difficulties in carrying out such an exchange they may request the opinion of one or more experts nominated by them after consultation with the Director - General of UNESCO.

IV. Federal States

14. In giving effect to the present Recommendation, Member States which have a federal or non - unitary constitutional system might follow the principles set forth in Article 34 of the Convention concerning the Protection of the World Cultural and Natural Heritage, adopted by the General Conference at its seventeenth session.

V. Action against illicit trading in cultural property

15. The development of international exchanges should enable the cultural institutions of the different Member States to enlarge their collections by acquiring cultural property of lawful origin, accompanied by documentation calculated to bring out their full cultural significance. Accordingly, Member States should take all necessary steps, with the help of the international organizations concerned, to ensure that the development of such exchanges goes hand in hand with an extension of the action taken against every possible form of illicit trading in cultural property.

关于艺术家地位的建议

（联合国教科文组织 1980 年 10 月 27 日通过）

联合国教科文组织章程第一条，本组织的宗旨是通过教育、科学、文化促进国家间的合作，为和平与安全做出贡献，以促进对正义、法制、人的权利与基本自由的普遍尊重，按照《联合国宪章》这种正义、法制、人权及人的基本自由是全世界的人们，不分种族、性别、语言或宗教，所共同享有的；

《人权宣言》，尤其是第 22、23、24、25、27、28 条，详见本《建议》附录；

《联合国经济、社会及文化权利国际公约》，尤其是第 6、15 条，见本《建议》附录；从保证这些权利得到充分行使，需要采取必要措施，保护、发展和传播文化；

联合国教科文组织第 14 次大会通过的《国际文化协作原则宣言》，尤其是第三条、第四条，详见本《建议》附录；以及联合国教科文组织第 19 次大会通过的《关于全体人对文化生活的参与与贡献的建议》；

艺术最充分和最宽广的定义是而且也应该是生活的一个组成部分；认识到政府不但应当帮助创造并维持一个鼓励艺术表达自由的氛围而且应当帮助创造并维持促进艺术才能释放的物质条件；

每个艺术家都有权充分享受上述宣言、契约、建议的基本内容所包含的社会安全保障条款所提供的权利；

艺术家在社会发展和进化中发挥着重要的作用，考虑到艺术家应当被赋予同其他公民同等的在保护创造灵感和表现自由的同时，为社会发展作贡献、履行他们在社会发展中的职责的机会；

进而认识到社会文化、技术、经济、政治的发展影响着艺术家的地位，因而在考虑全世界的社会进步的情况下探讨艺术家的地位是完全必要的；

如果艺术家自己愿意，他们的权利被视为主动参与文化工作的个人并从属于劳动者的所有法律的、社会的、经济的有利条件中受益，同时考虑其艺术专业的特殊条件；

进而断言必须改善艺术家的社会保障、劳动及税赋条件，无论其为受雇还是自由职业者，同时考虑艺术家对社会发展的贡献；

保护和促进文化认同的重要性和在这一领域中保存传统艺术实践并演绎民族民间文化的艺术家的作用的重要性得到国际国内的普遍承认；

艺术的活力和生动性特别有赖于艺术家个体和群体的良好状态；

国际劳工组织（ILO）的公约和建议，尤其是罗列在本《建议》附录中的那些条约和建议，该组织总体认可了劳动者的权利因而也认可了艺术家的权利；

然而也注意到由于艺术家活动的特殊环境，国际劳工组织的某些标准允许减低，甚或明确排斥艺术家或某些类别的艺术家；因而有必要扩展这些标准的适用领域以及用其他标准来补充；

艺术家也许可以共同考虑、必要时还可以共同维护他们的共同利益，因而也许有权被视为一种职业类别，有权组成贸易联盟或者行业组织；

艺术的发展，它们受到的尊重，艺术教育的进展在很大程度上依赖于艺术家的创造；

艺术活动的复杂性，多样的表现形式，特别是为了艺术家的生活条件和才能的发展，意识到保护他们作品、表演及其作品和表演的使用中的道德权利和物质权利的重要性，意识到扩展和加强这方面保护的必要性；

尽可能地重视艺术家同人民大众这两方面在制订与实施文化政策中的意见的必要性，以及为了这一目标而给他们提供采取有效行动的方法；

当代艺术品发表在公共场合，这些都应当展示出来以使艺术家的意见受到重视；

因而虑及，在建筑师、承包商与艺术家之间应有更密切的合作，以使公共场所得到反映社会需求的美学指导，对建立公众及其环境之间新的、有意义的联系做出显著的贡献；

不同国家艺术家环境的差异性以及期待他们施展其才华的社会的差异性，重视产生他们的社会赐予其作品的迥异的意味；

仍然确信，尽管有这些差异，关注艺术家的地位使所有国家引发了共同关心的问题，相信有一个共同的愿望和灵感会被激发出来：是否能够找到一个解决办法？艺术家的地位能否得到改善？这也是本建议的旨归所在；

有大量的特别是与文学艺术财产有关的国际公约条款，尤其是《国际公约》和《保护文学艺术作品伯尔尼公约》条款，以及那些与保护表演者权利有关条款，（联合国教科文组织）大会的决议的条款，联合国教科文组织政府间会议作出的关于文化政策的建议的条款，国际劳工组织通过的条约与建议的条款，详见本《建议》附录；

在此之前，本次大会议程第31项，与艺术家地位有关的提议；

决定，在第20次大会上，这个问题应当作为给各成员国的一份建议的主题；

本《建议》在1980年10月27日通过。

大会建议各成员国采取符合各国宪法实践及所考虑的问题的性质的一切法制措施或其他可能需要的步骤，实施下列条款，在其领土上使本建议所提出的原则和措施得以生效。

对于那些联邦制或非一元宪政体制的国家，大会建议，考虑到本《建议》条款的实施是在各有立法权的邦国、国家、省、州县或其他不受联邦政体制约的领土及政治单元的行政司法管理之下采取立法措施进行的，请联邦政府将《建议》内容通知前所列举的有关当局，供其采用。

大会建议各成员国站在尽力改善艺术家地位，扶持艺术家参与文化生活及发展的立场上提请行政当局、社会团体和组织注意本《建议》。

大会建议各成员国在适当的时机与方式，将其实施本建议案的行动呈报教科文组织。

一、定　义

从本《建议》的宗旨出发：

1.“艺术家”指一切创造艺术作品或赋予艺术作品以创造性表现，或者再创作艺术作品，将他的艺术创造视为其生活的核心部分，以这种方式为文化艺术发展做出贡献，想被承认或要求被承认为艺术家的人，不管他们是否受任何雇佣关系或者协会的约束。

2.“地位”一词，一方面意味着在一个社会中，以要求艺术家（定义如前所述）执业的那个部分的重要性为基础，让艺术家得到和他们身份相称的关注；另一方面，意味着对自由与包括道德、经济和社会权利在内的权利的承认，特别关注于艺术家的应享受的收入和社会保障。

二、适用范围

本《建议》适用于第一段所定义的所有艺术家，无论行业或这些艺术家运用何种艺术形式。其中特别包括了《国际版权公约》和《保护文学艺术作品伯尔尼公约》所指的一切创造性艺术家及作者，以及《保护表演者、音像制品生产者和广播组织的罗马公约》所指的表演者和翻译者。

三、指导原则

1. 认识到艺术反映、保存、丰富了文化的体认和各种不同社会的精神遗产，构成了表现和交流的普遍形式，并且作为在民族、文化或宗教差异中的一个共性，艺术给每个人带来了属于全人类社会的理念，各成员国应当为了这些目标，保证所有的人有接触艺术的途径。

2. 为了文化的发展，为了充实闲暇文化生活，各成员国应当鼓励所有为使艺术家的行动得到突出而设计的活动，特别是包括由大众传媒和教育体系实施的活动。

3. 承认艺术在生活和个体与社会发展中的核心作用，各成员国有义务保护、维护和支持艺术家及其创作自由。为此，他们应当采取一切必要的步骤来激励艺术家的创造性和才华施展，特别是采取措施保障艺术家有更大的自由，否则艺术家无法完成使命；通过认可他们享有工作成果的权利，改善其地位。各成员国应当采取所有适当的手段，在决定有关生活质量时，尽力保障艺术家越来越多的参与。各成员国应竭尽所能表明并确证，在各国为建立一个更公正、更仁慈的社会，为共同生活在和平而精神丰富的环境而进行的全球性发展的努力之中，艺术活动发挥着重要作用。

4. 各成员国在必要时应当通过适当的立法措施保证艺术家有自由和权利建立贸易同盟和他们选择的行业组织并成为该组织的成员（如果他们愿意），应当使代表艺术家的组织有可能参与文化政策和就业（包括专业培训）政策的制订，参与艺术家工作条件的决定。

5. 总的说来，在所有适当级别的国家计划和适当级别的特别是文化领域的计划内，各成员国应当做出安排，通过密切地协调其有关文化教育和就业的政策，制订对艺术家进行帮助并给予物质、道义上支持的政策，应当保证其公正性受到公众意见认可，保证公众认为需要这样的政策。为此，教育应当适当强调对于艺术意识的鼓励，以便为公众欣赏艺术家的工作创造可能性。在版权及其邻接权立法之下，在不损害艺术家应得的权利，包括再销售权（当它不属于版权时）的前提下，艺术家应当享受公平的条件，他们的职业应当得到公众足够的注意。

6. 既然表达与交流的自由是所有艺术活动的根本前提，那么，各成员国应当注意毫不含糊地使艺术家得到符合国际国内有关人权的立法在这方面所规定的保护。

7. 从在文化以及国家全面发展中艺术活动与艺术创造的作用来看，各成员国应当创造条件使艺术家（无论是个人还是通过协会或联合会）运用他们的艺术来参与社会生活。各成员国应当同艺术家携手制定地方和国家的政策，使他们对他们自己社会以及对世界整体进步的重要贡献得到强调。

8. 各成员国应当保证所有的个人，无论其种族、肤色、性别，语言、宗教、政治的和其他方面的看法、民族和社会本原、经济地位和出生，具有同等机会去获取并提高那些全面发展和锻炼艺术才能所必需的技巧，平等就业，有同等机会不受歧视地提高业务水平。

四、艺术家的才能与培训

1. 从入学或更早的年龄开始，各成员国就应当鼓励一切趋向于加强对艺术创造的措施，鼓励艺术才能的发现与发展，应当记住，如果它是有效的，艺术创造性的激发要求采取必要的生产杰出作品的专业技能训练。为此，各成员国应当：

a）采取必要措施提供为激发艺术家的天赋和才能而设计的教育；

b）采取一切恰当措施，与艺术家协作，保证在教育中能够适当突出艺术感觉的发展，有助于培养公众接受各种形式的艺术表现；

c）尽可能采取一切恰当的措施创设或发展特殊艺术教育；

d）通过激励的方法，诸如接受入会或同意收费教育，寻求保证艺术家有机会将他们最新的知识带给他们自己的同行或给有关的行业和领域，以改进他们的技巧，建立能激励创造性的联系，接受再培训以便接触其他艺术部门和在其他艺术部门工作。为此，各成员国应当尽力提供便利，尽力使现有的条件得到必要的改进；

e）采取并发展协调的、综合性的行业指导和培训政策与培训项目，充分考虑艺术家的就业环境并使他们能够在必要时进入其他的活动部门；

f）在文化遗产的恢复、保存和使用方面激励艺术家在最广泛意义上的参与，给艺术家提供将他们的知识与艺术技巧传授给下一代的手段；

g）认识到在艺术和工艺培训中传授知识特别是不同社团入会习俗的传统方式的重要性，并采取一切适当的措施对它们加以保护和鼓励；

h）认识到艺术教育不应脱离活的艺术实践，注意这样的教育要按照在这一类型的培训中艺术机构、剧院、艺术工作室、广播电视组织等发挥作用的特定方式来调整；

i）特别注意开发妇女的创造性并特别注意鼓励在各种艺术活动部门中力求促进妇女作用的团体与组织；

j）认识到艺术生活与艺术实践还有国际这一维，要相应地给那些参与艺术活动的人提供一切便利，特别是在旅行和学习研究津贴方面的便利，以便他们建立同其他文化的活跃的、广泛的接触；

k）采取一切步骤促进艺术家在国际间的自由活动，在保证不损害国内艺术家就业与工作条件和内在才华的发展的同时，不妨碍艺术家在他们自己选择的国家进行艺术实践的自由；

l）特别是通过为他们在国内外旅游，发展地方性传统提供方便，对传统艺术家的需要给予特别的注意。

2. 在尽可能不损害艺术家和教育者的自由和独立的前提下，各成员国应当提出和支持一切革新措施来保证使艺术家在培训中意识到他们社会的文化包括传统文化与民俗文化的文化认同，从而对这一认同及其文化的认定和复苏做出贡献。

五、社会地位

各成员国应当通过把艺术活动（包括创新与研究）看作对社会的服务来促进和保护艺术家的地位。应当让他们得到使其工作全面发展所必需的评价，应当给艺术家作为主动参加文化工作的个人提供应有的经济保护。各成员国应当：

1. 允许艺术家以最适合他们各自的环境的形式得到公众的承认并建立一个制度（如果尚无这样一个制度或者设计不当），给艺术家应得的好处。

2. 务必使艺术家从国际国内有关人权立法所规定的权利和保护中受益。

3. 努力采取必要的步骤，务必使艺术家通过国际国内就业、生活与工作条件的有关立法享受与同时人群中的可比参考组同等的权利，务必使自由职业艺术家在一定限度内在收入和社会保险方面得到保护。

4. 认识到在现存公约特别是《保护文学艺术作品伯尔尼公约》、《世界版权公约》和《保护表演者、声音艺术生产者和广播组织罗马公约》等条约之下对艺术家权利进行国际保护的重要性，采取一切必要步骤去扩展那些条款的适用领域和生效范围，尤其是尚未这么做的成员国，更要考虑紧追其后的可能性。

5. 承认艺术家贸易同盟和行业组织代表其成员并保护其成员的权利，给他们机会对公共当局的措施提出恰当意见，刺激艺术活动并保证艺术活动得到保护与发展。

六、艺术家就业、工作与生活条件；专业与贸易同盟组织

1. 意识到通过给予他们克服困难所需要的道德与物质的支持来改善艺术家地位的必要性。

a）考虑一些措施，在艺术家开始他们事业之初，特别是在他们试图将全身心投入艺术的一开始，就给他们以支持；

b）促进艺术家在自己本行就业，特别是通过给艺术作品拨一部分公共经费的办法；

c）在艺术发展进程中促进艺术活动，刺激公私两方面对艺术活动成果的需求，以使艺术家增加就业机会，尤其是通过对艺术团体、委托个体艺术家或者组织地方地区性或全国性艺术活动进行补贴以及建立艺术基金的办法；

d）在不损害艺术家创造性、使命及表达与交流的自由的前提下，区分可以由艺术家来担纲的岗位，特别是：

①在国家和地方教育与社会服务系统的相应门类中，在图书馆、博物馆、研究院和其他公共机构中，给艺术家提供机会；

②促进诗人、作家参与尽力翻译外国文学。

e）鼓励发展必要的设施（博物馆、音乐厅、剧场和其他场所），以有利于扶持艺术的传播和艺术家与公众见面；

f）在公共就业服务的框架中，研究建立有效的机制支持艺术家求职的可能性和实施国际劳工组织《有偿职业介绍机构条约》（修正案 96 号，见本《建议》附录）的可能性。

2. 在鼓励艺术创造性、鼓励文化发展、鼓励就业条件的增进和改善的总政策之下，请各成员国尽可能注重实效并重视艺术家的利益，以

a）鼓励和推进参与活动的人中不同团队对艺术家所采取的标准的运用，在工作条件方面保证他们享有一切与相应团队一致的权利；

b）寻求办法将国际劳工组织所规定的关于工作与就业条件标准的立法保护扩展到艺术家；特别是与以下两方面有关的标准：

①工作时间，每周的休息和给予公假参加一切活动，对表演者来说，特别要考虑花费在旅行、排练以及公演或与观众见面的时间；

②生命、健康及工作环境的保护；

c）重视艺术家的特殊问题，在他们的工作场所方面，当管理规章涉及有利于艺术活动的艺术家工作场所变动时，在保证建筑遗产和环境的同时，强调属于安全与健康方面的规章；

d）在必要时，制定法规给予艺术家适当补偿，当理由涉及所承担的艺术活动性质或者艺术家就业状况，涉及本节的第2（b）Ⅰ段落有关事项的标准得不到遵守的时候，如果艺术家愿意的话，可以同代表艺术家及其雇主的组织商议；

e）认识到在延迟发放薪水或分享生产利润的情况下，利益分配体系可能侵害艺术家那些与他们的实际收入和社会保险有关的权利，要认识这一点并采取适当措施保障这些权利。

3. 带着给予少儿艺术家特别的重视的目标，我们提请各成员国考虑联合国关于少儿权利的声明。

4. 认识到在保护就业和工作条件保护方面由行业与贸易同盟组织所扮演的角色，提请各成员国采取必要的步骤：

a）遵守本《建议》附录所列国际劳动条约中有关结社自由、有关组织权集会权的标准，并保证这些标准得到遵守，保障这些标准及其所依据的普遍原则可以运用于艺术家；

b）鼓励在尚不存在这种组织的行业中自主建立这种组织；

c）为国内或国际的所有这类组织提供机会充分发挥作用，而不侵害结社自由的权利。

5. 提请各成员国在其特定的文化环境中，尽力为受雇佣的艺术家或自由职业艺术家提供跟那些通常是给予其他受雇佣或自主经营团体的社会保护一样的保护。法规同样应当扩展为对家庭中从属成员进行适当社会保护的措施。各成员国会发现采纳、改善或运用社会保险制度是很有益的，它应当考虑艺术活动的特殊性，即，许多艺术家就业的间断性和收入剧烈变化，但没有这一特点，艺术家创作、发表和传播其作品的自由会受到限制。因此，要求各成员国考虑采取特殊的手段对艺术家的社会保险提供财政资助，例如，求助一些新的财政参与形式，无论是公共当局或是使用或买卖艺术家作品或服务的经营企业。

6. 从总体上承认国际国内有关艺术家地位的立法滞后于科技、大众传媒发展、艺术家的作品和表演的机械化再生产手段、公共教育和明确由文化企业承担的部分的一般进展，请各成员国采取必要的适当措施：

a）保证艺术家在其作品进行传播和商业开发时获得酬劳，使艺术家保持对其作品的控制，以防止擅自开发、篡改或传播；

b）就与新的通信和再生产媒介的技术发展、文化产业发展有关的侵害，尽可能制定一个保障艺术家道德专有权和物质专利权的制度，这意味着，特别是规定表演者的权利，包括马戏和杂耍艺人、木偶表演者，在这样做的过程中，重视《罗马公约》的规定，并且，关于由有线传输与录像制品引起的问题，重视1979年的《罗马公约政府多边委员会建议》方为妥当；

c）补偿艺术家由于新的通讯和再生产媒介的技术发展、文化产业发展对他们在诸如宣传和传播作品方面的好处及由于职位的开辟而遭到的一切侵害；

d）保证那些得益于技术变化的文化产业，包括广播电视组织和机械化再生产企业，发挥他们的作用，尽力鼓励和刺激艺术创作，例如通过提供新的就业机会，通过宣传，通过作品传播，支付专利权费或通过任何其他可以肯定对艺术家公平的措施；

e）帮助艺术家和艺术家组织补救他们在求职和在新技术岗位工作中所受到的不利影响，如果存在这些影响的话。

7. a）确信艺术家收入的不稳定性和突然波动，确信艺术活动的特性，确信许多艺术行业只能在生活中相当短的时期内从业这一事实，请各成员国根据职业生涯的长短而不是根据达到某个特定的年纪为某些类别艺术家制订法规定活动补助金的权利，在其税制中考虑艺术家工作和活动的特殊条件；

b）为保持某些类别艺术家（例如芭蕾舞演员、舞蹈演员、歌唱家）的健康和延长其职业活动，请各成员国不仅在不能工作的情况下，而且为了防止疾病的目的给他们提供充分的医疗照顾，考虑研究艺术职业特别的健康问题的可能性；

c）考虑到一件艺术作品既不应当被视为消费商品也不应当被看作投资，请各成员国考虑对艺术作品和艺术表演及其创作、传播或首次出卖间接的税收的可能性，和它对艺术家和艺术发展的好处。

8. 考虑到艺术作品国际性交流的重要性日益增大，艺术家之间的交往日益增多，需要加以鼓励，各成员国个别地或集体地被提请在不损害国内文化的情况下，

a）通过灵活变通的海关管理和有关进口税特别是关于临时性进口的税收方面的特许，帮助这方面工作更加自由地开展；

b）采取措施鼓励国际旅行和艺术家之间的交流，对访问国内艺术家予以应有的关注。

七、文化政策与参与

与本《建议》第三·7和第五·5段的精神相一致，各成员国在制订和实施其文化政策时，应当努力采取妥善措施，仔细听取艺术家和代表他们的行业和贸易组织的意见，以及根据联合国教科文组织《关于广大人民群众对文化生活的参与和贡献的建议》的精神，听取广大人民群众的意见。进而，提请各成员国做出必要安排，在涉及诸如以下目标时使艺术家及其组织参与政策讨论、制定及随后的措施落实的过程：

a）加强艺术家的社会地位，例如涉及艺术家就业、工作和生活条件的措施，涉及由公共当局制订对艺术活动给予物质和道义上的支持的法规，涉及艺术家的业务培训的措施；

b）在社团中推动文化艺术，例如涉及文化发展、文化遗产包括民俗及其他传统艺术家的活动进行保护与有效展示、文化体认、环境问题及利用休闲时间的相关方面、教育中有关文化艺术的方面的措施；

c）鼓励国际文化合作，例如涉及作品的传播与翻译、作品与人员的交流、地区性的和国际性活动的组织的措施。

八、本《建议》的生效与实施

1. 各成员国应当通过与其他从事与本《建议》目标有关活动的国家、国际组织合作，特别是通过与联合国教科文组织的国家委员会、各国和国际的艺术家组织、国际劳工办公室、世界知识产权组织合作，努力扩展和完善他们自己在艺术家地位方面的行动。

2. 各成员国应当，通过最妥当的办法，支持上述代表艺术家的团体并将他们之间的业务协作纳入日程，使艺术家从本《建议》所阐述的条款中受益，使在此描述的地位获得认可。

九、关于现存的优待

有的地方艺术家的地位在某些特定方面比本《建议》规定更加优越，我们无论如何不要求降低其已经获得的优越条件，也不想直接或间接地影响它们。

附录（略）

Recommendation concerning the Status of the Artist

27 October 1980

The General Conference of the United Nations Educational, Scientific and Cultural Organization, meeting in Belgrade from 23 September to 28 October 1980 at its twenty - first session,

Recalling that, under the terms of Article I of its Constitution, the purpose of the Organization is to contribute to peace and security by promoting collaboration among the nations through education, science and culture in order to further universal respect for justice, for the rule of law and for the human rights and fundamental freedoms which are affirmed for the peoples of the world, without distinction of race, sex, language or relation, by the Charter of the United Nations,

Recalling the terms of the Universal Declaration of Human Rights, and particularly Articles 22, 23, 24, 25, 27 and 28 thereof, quoted in the annex to this Recommendation,

Recalling the terms of the United Nations International Covenant on Economic, Social and Cultural Rights, particularly its Articles 6 and 15, quoted in the annex to this Recommendation, and the need to adopt the necessary measures for the preservation, development and dissemination of culture, with a view to ensuring the full exercise of these rights,

Recalling the Declaration of the Principles of International Cultural Co - operation, adopted by the General Conference of UNESCO at its fourteenth session, particularly its Articles III and IV, which are quoted in the annex to this Recommendation, as well as the Recommendation on Participation by the People at Large in Cultural Life and their Contribution to it, adopted by the General Conference of UNESCO at its nineteenth session,

Recognizing that the arts in their fullest and broadest definition are and should be an integral part of life and that it is necessary and appropriate for governments to help create and sustain not only a climate encouraging freedom of artistic expression but also the material conditions facilitating the release of this creative talent,

Recognizing that every artist is entitled to benefit effectively from the social security and insurance provisions contained in the basic texts, Declarations, Covenant and Recommendation mentioned above,

Considering that the artist plays an important role in the life and evolution of society and that he should be given the opportunity to contribute to society's development and, as any other citizen, to exercise his responsibilities therein, while preserving his creative inspiration and freedom of expression,

Further recognizing that the cultural, technological, economic, social and political development of society influences the status of the artist and that it is consequently necessary to review his status, taking account of social progress in the world,

Affirming the right of the artist to be considered, if he so wishes, as a person actively engaged in cultural work and consequently to benefit, taking account of the particular 'conditions of his artistic profession, from all the legal, social and economic advantages pertaining to the status of workers,

Affirming further the need to improve the social security, labour and tax conditions of the artist, whether employed or self - employed, taking into account the contribution to cultural development which the artist makes,

Recalling the importance, universally acknowledged both nationally and inter-nationally, of the preservation and promotion of cultural identity and of the role in this field of artists who perpetuate the practice of traditional arts and also interpret a nation's folklore,

Recognizing that the vigour and vitality of the arts depend, inter alia, on the well - being of artists both individually and collectively,

Recalling the conventions and recommendations of the International Labour Organization (ILO) which have recognized the rights of workers in general and, hence, the rights of artists and, in particular, the conventions and recommendations listed in the appendix to this Recommendation,

Taking note, however, that some of the International Labour Organization standards allow for derogations or even expressly exclude artists, or certain categories of them, owing to the special conditions in which artistic activity takes place, and that it is consequently necessary to extend their field of application and to supplement them by other standards,

Considering further that this recognition of their status as persons actively engaged in cultural work should in no way compromise their freedom of creativity, expression and communication but should, on the contrary, confirm their dignity and integrity,

Convinced that action by the public authorities is becoming necessary and urgent in order to remedy the disquieting situation of artists in a large number of Member States, particularly with regard to human rights, economic and social circumstances and their conditions of employment, with a view to providing artists with the conditions necessary for the development and flowering of their talents and appropriate to the role that they are able to play in the planning and implementation of cultural policies and cultural development activities of communities and countries and in the improvement of the quality of life,

Considering that art plays an important part in education and that artists, by their works, may influence the conception of the world held by all people, and particularly by youth,

Considering that artists must be able collectively to consider and, if necessary, defend their common interests, and therefore must have the right to be recognized as a professional category and to constitute trade union or professional organizations,

Considering that the development of the arts, the esteem in which they are held and the promotion of arts education depend in large measure on the creativity of artists,

Aware of the complex nature of artistic activity and of the diverse forms it takes and, in particular, of the importance, for the living conditions and the development of the talents of artists, of the protection of their moral and material rights in their works, or performances, or the use made of them, and of the need to extend and reinforce such protection,

Considering the need to endeavour to take account as far as possible of the opinion both of artists and of the people at large in the formulation and implementation of cultural policies and for that purpose to provide them with the means for effective action,

Considering that contemporary artistic expression is presented in public places and that these should be laid out so as to take account of the opinions of the artists concerned, therefore that there should be close co - operation between architects, contractors and artists in order to lay down aesthetic guidelines for public places which will respond to the requirements of communication and make an effective contribution to the establishment of new and meaningful relationships between the public and its environment,

Taking into account the diversity of circumstances of artists in different countries and within the communities in which they are expected to develop their talents, and the varying significance attributed to their works by the societies in which they are produced,

Convinced, nevertheless, that despite such differences, questions of similar concern arise in all countries with regard to the status of the artist, and that a common will and inspiration are called for if a solution is to be found and if the status of the artist is to be improved, which is the intention of this Recommendation,

Taking note of the provisions of the international conventions in force relating, more particularly, to literary and artistic property, and in particular of the Universal Convention and the Berne Convention for the Protection of Literary and Artistic Works, and of those relating to the protection of the rights of performers, of the resolutions of the General Conference, of the recommendations made by UNESCO's intergovernmental conferences on cultural policies, and of the conventions and recommendations adopted by the International Labour Organization, listed in the appendix to this Recommendation,

Having before it, as item 31 of the agenda of the session, proposals concerning the status of the artist,

Having decided, at its twentieth session, that this question should be the subject of a recommendation to Member States,

Adopts this Recommendation this twenty - seventh day of October 1980:

The General Conference recommends that Member States implement the following provisions, taking whatever legislative or other steps may be required - in conformity with the constitutional practice of each State and the nature of the questions under consideration to apply the principles and norms set forth in this Recommendation within their respective territories.

For those States which have a federal or non - unitary constitutional system, the General Conference recommends that, with regard to the provisions of this Recommendation the implementation of which comes under the legal jurisdiction of individual constituent States, countries, provinces, cantons or any other territorial and political subdivisions that are not obliged by the constitutional system of the federation to take legislative measures, the federal government be invited to inform the competent authorities of such States, countries, provinces or cantons of the said provisions, with its recommendation for their adoption.

The General Conference recommends that Member States bring this Recommendation to the attention of authorities, institutions and organizations in a position to contribute to improvement of the status of the artist and to foster the participation of artists in cultural life and development.

The General Conference recommends that Member States report to it, on dates and in a manner to be determined by it, on the action they have taken to give effect to this Recommendation.

I. Definitions

For the purposes of this Recommendation:

1. `Artist' is taken to mean any person who creates or gives creative expression to, or re - creates works of art, who considers his artistic creation to be an essential part of his life, who contributes in this way to the development of art and culture and who is or asks to be recognized as an artist, whether or not he is bound by any relations of employment or association.

2. The world `status' signifies, on the one, hand, the regard accorded to artists, defined as above, in a society, on the basis of the importance attributed to the part they are called upon to play therein and, on the other hand, recognition of the liberties and rights, including moral, economic and social rights, with particular reference to income and social security, which artists should enjoy.

II. Scope of application

This Recommendation applies to all artists as defined in paragraph 1. 1, irrespective of the discipline or form of art practiced by such artists. These include inter alia all creative artists and authors within the meaning of the Universal Copyright Convention and the Berne Convention for the Protection of Literary and Artistic Works, as well as performers and interpreters within the meaning of the Rome Convention for the Protection of Performers, Producers of Phonograms and Broadcasting Organizations.

III. Guiding principles

1. Member States, recognizing that art reflects, preserves and enriches the cultural identity and spiritual heritage of the various societies, constitutes a universal form of expression and communication and, as a common denominator in ethnic, cultural or religious differences, brings home to everyone the sense of belonging to the human community, should accordingly, and for these purposes, ensure that the population as a whole has access to art.

2. Member States should encourage all activities designed to highlight the action of artists for cultural development, including in particular 'activities carried out by the mass media and the educational system, and for the employment of leisure for cultural purposes.

3. Member States, recognizing the essential role of art in the life and development of the individual and of society, accordingly have a duty to protect, defend and assist artists and their freedom of creation. For this purpose, they should take all necessary steps to stimulate artistic creativity and the flowering of talent, in particular by adopting measures to secure greater freedom for artists, without which they cannot fulfill their mission, and to improve their status by acknowledging their right to enjoy the fruits of their work. Member States should endeavour by all appropriate means to secure increased participation by artists in decisions concerning the quality of life. By all means at their disposal, Member States should demonstrate and confirm that artistic activities have a part to play in the nations'

global development effort to build a juster and more humane society and to live together in circumstances of peace and spiritual enrichment.

4. Member States should ensure, through appropriate legislative means when necessary, that artists have the freedom and the right to establish trade unions and professional organizations of their choosing and to become members of such organizations, if they so wish, and should make it possible for organizations representing artists to participate in the formulation of cultural policies and employment policies, including the professional training of artists, and in the determination of artists' conditions of work.

5. At all appropriate levels of national planning, in general, 'and of planning in the cultural field, in particular, Member States should make arrangements, by close co - ordination of their policies relating to culture, education and employment among other things, to define a policy for providing assistance and material and moral support for artists and should ensure that public opinion is informed of the justification and the need for such a policy. To that end, education should place due emphasis on the encouragement of artistic awareness, so as to create a public capable of appreciating the work of the artist. Without prejudice to the rights that should be accorded to them under copyright legislation, including resale rights (droit de suite) when this is not part of copyright, and under neighboring rights legislation, artists should enjoy equitable conditions and their profession should be given the public consideration that it merits. Their conditions of work and of employment should be such as to provide opportunities for artists who so wish to devote themselves fully to their artistic activities.

6. Since freedom of expression and communication is the essential prerequisite for all artistic activities, Member States should see that artists are unequivocally accorded the protection provided for in this respect by international and national legislation concerning human rights.

7. In view of the role of artistic activity and creation in the cultural and overall development of nations, Member States should create conditions enabling artists fully to participate, either individually or through their associations or trade unions, in the life of the communities in which they practice their art. They should associate them in the formulation of local and national cultural policies, thus stressing their important contribution in their own society as well as towards world progress

in general.

8. Member States should ensure that all individuals, irrespective of race, colour, sex, language, religion, political or other opinion, national or social origin, economic status or birth, have the same opportunities to acquire and develop the skills necessary for the complete development and exercise of their artistic talents, to obtain employment, and to exercise their profession without discrimination.

IV. The vocation and training of the artist

1. Member States should encourage, at school and from an early age, all measures tending to strengthen respect for artistic creation and the discovery and development of artistic vocations, and should bear in mind that, if it is to be effective, the stimulation of artistic creativity calls for provision of the necessary professional training of talent to produce works of outstanding quality. For this purpose, Member States should:

(a) take the necessary measures to provide an education designed to stimulate artistic talent and vocation;

(b) take all appropriate measures, in association with artists, to ensure that education gives due prominence to the development of artistic sensitivity and so contributes to the training of a public receptive to the expression of art in all its forms;

(c) take all appropriate measures, whenever possible, to institute or develop the teaching of particular artistic disciplines;

(d) seek by means of incentives, such as the granting of fellowships or paid educational leave, to ensure that artists have the opportunity to bring their knowledge up to date in their own disciplines or in related specialities and fields, to improve their technical skills, to establish contacts which will stimulate creativity, and to undergo retraining so as to have access to and work in other branches of art; for these purposes, Member States should see that appropriate facilities are provided and that those already existing are, where necessary, improved and developed;

(e) adopt and develop co - ordinated, comprehensive vocational guidance and training policies and programmes, taking into consideration the particular employment situation of artists and enabling them to enter other sectors of activity if necessary;

(f) stimulate artists' participation in the restoration, conservation and use of the cultural heritage in the widest sense of the term, and provide artists with the means of transmitting to future generations the knowledge and artistic skills which they possess;

(g) recognize the importance in arts and craft training of the traditional ways of transmitting knowledge and in particular of the initiation practices of various communities, and take all appropriate measures to protect and encourage them;

(h) recognize that art education should not be separated from the practice of living art, and see that such education is reoriented in such a way that cultural establishments, theatres, art studios, radio and television broadcasting organizations, etc., play an important part in this type of training and apprenticeship;

(i) give particular attention to the development of women's creativity and the encouragement of groups and organizations which seek to promote the role of women in the various branches of artistic activity;

(j) recognize that artistic life and the practice of the arts have an international dimension and accordingly provide those engaged in artistic activities with all the means and, in particular, travel and study grants, likely to enable them to establish lively and far-reaching contacts with other cultures;

(k) take all appropriate steps to promote the free international movement of artists, and not to hinder the freedom of artists to practice their art in the country of their choice, while ensuring that these do not prejudice the development of endogenous talents and the conditions of work and employment of national artists;

(1) give special attention to the needs of traditional artists, in particular by facilitating their travel inside and outside their own country to serve the development of local traditions.

2. As far as possible and without prejudice to the freedom and independence of both artists and educators, Member States should undertake and support initiatives to ensure that artists, during their training, are made aware of their community's cultural identity, including traditional and folk cultures, thereby contributing to the affirmation or revival of that identity and those cultures.

V. Social status

Member States should promote and protect the status of artists by considering artistic activity, including innovation and research, as a service to the community. They should make it possible for them to enjoy the esteem necessary for the full development of their work and provide the economic safeguards to which artists are entitled as people actively engaged in cultural work. Member States should:

1. Grant artists public recognition in the form best suited to their respective cultural environments and establish a system, where it does not already exist or is inadequately designed, to give artists the prestige to which they are entitled.

2. See that the artist benefits from the rights and protection provided for in international and national legislation relating to human 'rights.

3. Endeavour to take the necessary steps to see that artists enjoy the same rights as are conferred on a comparable group of the active population by national and international legislation in respect of employment and living and working conditions, and see that self - employed artists enjoy, within reasonable limits, protection as regards income and social security.

4. Recognize the importance of international protection of the rights of artists under the terms of existing conventions and in particular of the Berne Convention for the Protection of Literary and Artistic Works, the Universal Copyright Convention, and the Rome Convention for the Protection of Per - formers, Producers of Phonograms and Broadcasting Organizations, and take all necessary steps to extend the field of application, scope and effectiveness of those instruments, particularly - in the case of Member States which have not already done so - by considering the possibility of adhering to them.

5. Recognize the right of trade union and professional organizations of artists to represent and defend the interests of their members and give them the opportunity to advise the public authorities on suitable measures for stimulating artistic activity and ensuring its protection and development.

VI. Employment, working and living conditions of the artist ; professional and trade union organizations

1. Being aware of the need to improve the social recognition of artists by according them the moral and material support required to remedy their difficulties, Member States are invited to:

(a) consider measures for supporting artists at the beginning of their careers, in particular during the initial period when they are attempting to devote themselves completely to their art;

(b) promote the employment of artists in their own disciplines, particularly by devoting a proportion of public expenditure to artistic works;

(c) promote artistic activities within the context of development and stimulate public and private demand for the fruits of artistic activity in order to increase opportunities of paid work for artists, inter alia by means of subsidies to art institutions, commissions to individual artists, or the organization of artistic events at the local, regional or national levels, and by establishing art funds;

(d) identify remunerative posts which could given to artists without prejudice to their creativity, vocation and freedom of expression and communication, and in particular:

(i) give artists opportunities in the relevant categories of the educational and social services systems at national and local levels and in libraries, museums, academies and other public institutions;

(ii) increase the participation of poets and writers in the overall effort towards the translation of foreign literature;

(e) encourage the development of the necessary facilities (museums, concert halls, theatres and other forums) conducive to fostering the dissemination of the arts and the meeting of artists with the public;

(f) study the possibility of establishing, within the framework of employment policies or public employment services, effective machinery to assist artists to find jobs and that of adhering to the Fee - Charging Employment Agencies Convention (revised) (No. 96) of the International Labour Organization, which is listed in the appendix to this Recommendation.

2. Within the context of a general policy to encourage artistic creativity, cultural development and the promotion and improvement of conditions of employment, Member States are invited, wherever possible, practical and in the interest of the artist, to :

(a) encourage and facilitate the application of the standards adopted for various groups of the active population to artists, and ensure that they enjoy all the rights accorded to the corresponding groups in respect of working conditions ;

(b) seek means of extending to artists the legal protection concerning conditions of work and employment defined by the standards of the International Labour Organization, in particular the standards relating to:

(i) hours of work, weekly rest and paid leave in all fields of activities, more particularly, in the case of performers, taking into consideration the hours spent in travelling and rehearsal as well as those spent in public performance or appearances;

(ii) protection of life, health and the working environment;

(c) take into consideration the particular problems of artists, in respect of the premises where they work, while at the same time ensuring the preservation of the architectural heritage and the environment and upholding regulations pertaining to safety and health, when administering regulations relative to the alteration of artists' premises where this is in the interest of artistic activity;

(d) make provision when necessary for appropriate forms of compensation for artists, preferably in consultation with organizations representing artists and their employers, when, for reasons connected with the nature of the artistic activity undertaken or the artists' employment status, the standards relating to the matters referred to in paragraph 2 (b) (i) of this section cannot be observed;

(e) recognize that profit - sharing systems, in the form of deferred salaries or shares in the profits of production, may prejudice artists' rights vis - a - vis their real incomes and social security entitlement and take appropriate measures in such cases to preserve these rights.

3. With the object of giving specific consideration to the child artist, Member States are invited to take account of the provisions of the United Nations Declaration of the Rights of the Child.

4. Recognizing the part played by professional and trade union organizations

in the protection of employment and working conditions, Member States are invited to take appropriate steps to:

(a) observe and secure observance of the standards relating to freedom of association, to the right to organize and to collective bargaining, set forth in the international labour conventions listed in the appendix to this Recommendation and ensure that these standards and the general principles on which they are founded may apply to artists;

(b) encourage the free establishment of such organizations in disciplines where they do not yet exist;

(c) provide opportunities for all such organizations, national or international, without prejudice to the right of freedom of association, to carry out their role to the full.

5. Member States are invited to endeavour within their respective cultural environments to provide the same social protection for employed and self - employed artists as that usually granted respectively to other employed and self - employed groups. Provision should likewise be made for measures to extend appropriate social protection to dependent members of the family. The social security system which Member States may find it well to adopt, improve or supplement should take into consideration the special features of artistic activity, characterized by the intermittent nature of employment and the sharp variations in the incomes of many artists without, however, this entailing a limitation of the artist's freedom to create, publish and disseminate his work. In this context, Member States are invited to consider the adoption of special means of financing social security for artists, for example by resorting to new forms of financial participation either by the public authorities or by the business undertakings which market or which use the services or works of artists.

6. Recognizing in general that national and international legislation concerning the status of artists is lagging behind the general advances in technology, the development of the media of mass communication, the means of mechanical reproduction of works of art and of performances, the education of the public, and the decisive part played by the cultural industries, Member States are invited to take, wherever necessary, appropriate measures to:

(a) ensure that the artist is remunerated for the distribution and commercial exploitation of his work, and provide for the artist to maintain control of his work against unauthorized exploitation, modification or distribution;

(b) provide, to the extent possible, for a system guaranteeing the exclusive moral and material rights of artists in respect of any prejudice connected with the technical development of new communication and reproduction media, and of cultural industries; this means, in particular, establishing rights for performers, including circus and variety artists, and puppeteers; in doing so, it would be appropriate to take account of the provisions of the Rome Convention and, with reference to problems arising from the introduction of cable diffusion and video grams, of the Recommendation adopted by the Intergovernmental Committee of the Rome Convention in 1979;

(c) compensate any prejudice artists might suffer in consequence of the technical development of new communication and reproduction media and of cultural industries by favouring, for example, publicity for and dissemination of their works, and the creation of posts ;

(d) ensure that cultural industries benefiting from technological changes, including radio and television organizations and mechanical reproduction undertakings, play their part in the effort to encourage and stimulate artistic creation, for instance by providing new employment opportunities, by publicity, by the dissemination of works, payment of royalties or by any other means judged equitable for artists;

(e) assist artists and organizations of artists to remedy, when they exist, the prejudicial effects on their employment or work opportunities of new technologies.

7. (a) Convinced of the uncertainty of artists' incomes and their sudden fluctuations, of the special features of artistic activity and of the fact that many artistic callings can be followed only for a relatively short period of life, Member States are invited to make provision for pension rights for certain categories of artists according to length of career and not the attainment of a certain age and to take into account in their taxation system the particular conditions of artists' work and activity;

(b) in order to preserve the health and prolong the professional activity of certain categories of artists (for example ballet dancers, dancers, vocalists) Member States are invited to provide them with adequate medical care not only in the event of incapacity for work but also for the purpose of preventing illness, and to consider the possibility of research into the health problems peculiar to artistic professions;

(c) taking into account the fact that a work of art should be considered neither as a consumer good nor as an investment, Member States are invited to consider the possibility of alleviating indirect taxation on works of art and on artistic performances at the time of their creation, dissemination or first sale, and this in the interest of artists or of development of the arts.

8. In view of the growing importance of international exchanges of works of art, and contacts between artists, and the need to encourage, them, Member States separately or collectively, without prejudice to the development of national cultures, are invited to:

(a) assist freer circulation of such work by, inter alia, flexible customs arrangements and concessions in relation to import duties, particularly as regards temporary importation;

(b) take measures to encourage international travel and exchange by artists, giving due attention to visiting national artists.

VII. Cultural policies and participation

Member States should endeavour, in accordance with paragraphs 111. 7 and V. 5 of this Recommendation, to take appropriate measures to have the opinions of artists and the professional and trade union organizations representing them, as well as of the people at large, in the spirit of UNESCO's Recommendation on Participation by the People at Large in Cultural life and their Contribution to It, taken carefully into account in the formulation and execution of their cultural policies. To this end, they are invited to make the necessary arrangements for artists and their organizations to participate in discussions, decision - making processes and the subsequent implementation of measures aimed, inter alia, at:

(a) the enhancement of the status of artists in society, for example measures relating to the employment and working and living conditions of the artist, to the provision of material and moral support for artistic activities by the public authorities, and to the professional training of the artist;

(b) the promotion of culture and art within the community, for example measures relating to cultural development, to the protection and effective presentation of the cultural heritage, including folklore and the other activities of traditional artists, to cultural identity, to relevant aspects of environmental issues and the use of leisure, and to the place of culture and art in education;

(c) the encouragement of international cultural co - operation, for example measures relating to the dissemination and translation of works, to the exchange of works and of persons, and to the organization of regional or international cultural events.

VIII. Utilization and implementation of this Recommendation

1. Member States should strive to extend and supplement their own action in respect of the status of the artist by co - operating with all the national or international organizations whose activities are related to the objectives of this Recommendation, in particular with National Commissions for UNESCO, national and international artists' organizations, the International Labour Office and the World Intellectual Property Organization.

2. Member States should, by the most appropriate means, support the work of the above - mentioned bodies representing artists and enlist their professional co-operation to enable artists to benefit from the provisions set forth in this Recommendation and to obtain recognition of the status described herein.

IX. Existing advantages

Where artists enjoy, in certain respects, a status which is more favourable than that provided for in this Recommendation, its terms shall not in any case be invoked to diminish the advantages already acquired or directly or indirectly to affect them.

关于加强对翻译人员、翻译活动的法律保护和采取实际措施提升翻译人员地位的建议*

（联合国教科文组织 1976 年 11 月 22 日通过）

联合国教科文组织大会于 1976 年 10 月 26 日至 11 月 30 日召开第 19 届会议，鉴于翻译通过方便包括技术作品在内的文字及科学作品跨越语言的障碍进行传播并便于思想交流，从而促进民众之间的了解及国家之间的合作，鉴于翻译人员及翻译在国际文化、艺术及科学交流中发挥着极其重要的作用，尤其对以并不常用语言所写成或翻译的作品而言尤其如此，认识到保护翻译人员对于确保其提供高质量的翻译以有效发挥其在文化服务及发展中的作用而言必不可少，回顾到如果该等保护的规则已经规定于《世界版权公约》之中，同时《保护文字和艺术作品伯尔尼公约》及成员国的诸多法律也对该等保护作出了具体的规定，然而该等原则及规定在实践中的适用并不总是很足够，认为如果在许多国家就版权而言翻译人员或翻译享有类似赋予文字及包括技术作品在内的科学作品之作者的保护，并采取实用性措施，使得翻译人员归于作者一类并对之进行具体的规定，对于改善现有法律的有效实施而言，是非常正当的。

在其 18 届大会上决定对翻译人员的保护应该作为根据《组织法》第四条第四款的规定而向成员国提出倡议的议题，于 1976 年 11 月 22 日通过了本倡议书。大会建议成员国通过任何法律或者其他必要的措施按照宪法程序及各国体系中的实践适用下列有关保护翻译人员及翻译的条款，并在其各自领土实施本倡议书所规定的原则和标准。

大会建议各成员国使得其政府、政府部门或者负责有关翻译人员精神及

---

* 中国社会科学院法学研究所吴峻译。

物质权益及翻译保护的机构、代表或促进翻译人员权益的各种组织及协会、出版商、戏院经理人、广播电视机构及其他用户和利益攸关方关注该倡议书。

大会建议成员国以大会决定的时间和形式向教科文组织提交其采取行动实施本倡议书的报告。

一、定义及适用范围

1. 为本建议之目的：

（a）“翻译”这个术语系指将无论是否为原创作品的文字或者包括技术作品在内的科学作品从一种语言转换为另外一种语言，以在书籍、杂志、期刊或者以其他形式出版，或者为了剧院演出、或在电影、广播或电视或以其他任何媒体上予以播映；

（b）“翻译人员”这个术语系指文字或包括技术作品在内的科学作品的翻译人员；

（c）“用户”这个术语系指使用翻译的自然人或法人。

2. 本倡议书适用所有的翻译人员，无论

（a）其所适用的法律地位是；

（i）独立翻译人员；或

（ii）付薪翻译人员

（b）所翻译作品所属行业；

（c）翻译人员是兼职还是全职。

二、翻译人员的一般法律地位

3. 成员国应该就翻译人员的翻译赋予其该国为缔约国的国际版权公约及其国内法条款规定作者所享有的保护，但不得影响所翻译原创作品作者的地位。

三、确保翻译人员根据涉及版权的国际公约及国际法所给予的保护在实践中适用

4. 在翻译人员及使用者之间达成书面合同很必要。

5. 一般说来，适用翻译人员与用户之间关系的合同及在适当情形下适用

该等关系的任何法律文件，均应：

（a）无论翻译人员的法律地位如何，应予以公平报偿；

（b）如果翻译人员并非付薪工作，至少应该根据销售或使用所得的比例予以支付，该等预先支付由翻译人员持有，无论销售或使用所得为何；或者根据独立于销售的符合国内法规定或许可的其他体系计算出的数额予以补偿；或者在比例支付不能实现或者不足够的情形下，可以予以一次性的公平支付；应当在考虑有关国家法律体系及在适当情形下所翻译原创作品种类的情形下选择适当的支付方式；

（c）对翻译使用超出合同规定范围的，适当情形下给予额外支付；

（d）规定翻译人员所给予的授权仅限于明确提及的权利，该等规定也适用于可能的新版本；

（e）规定在翻译人员没有取得任何必要授权的情形下，用户负责取得该等授权；

（f）规定翻译人员确保用户无争议地享有所有被给予的授权，并保证不采取可能损害用户合法权益的任何行为，并在适当情形下遵守职业保密规定；

（g）规定在尊重所翻译原创作品作者权利的前提下，除非取得翻译人员的同意，不得对要出版的翻译文本进行任何修改；

（h）确保翻译人员及其翻译给予与作者相称的公开待遇，尤其须将翻译作者的姓名放置于所出版书籍、剧单、附带与广播或电视节目的宣示、电影演职员名单及其他推广裁量中的突出位置中；

（i）规定用户确保翻译负有符合合理预期使用国家制定的版权形式要求；

（j）规定对任何可能因翻译质量而产生的纠纷尽量通过仲裁或根据国内法律或以其他纠纷解决机制予以解决。该等纠纷解决机制既公正，又容易使用且成本较低；

（k）描述翻译人员翻译所针对及使用的语言，且不能影响第一款 a 项的规定，进一步明确规定可能会让翻译人员以同声传译的方式出现。

6. 为促进第四款、第五款及第十四款所建议措施的落实，成员国应在不影响翻译人员缔约自由的前提下，鼓励由尤其是翻译人员专业组织或代表其的其他组织或协会及用户两方面在内的有关方面达成以本倡议书建议措施为基础的示范合同或集体合同，并对由于翻译人员或翻译性质而产生任何情形予以适当变通考虑。

7. 成员国也应鼓励确保能有效代表翻译人员的措施，并鼓励翻译人员专业组织及其他能够代表翻译人员组织或协会的建立和发展，以界定专业活动应遵循的规则及职责、捍卫翻译人员的精神及物质权利并促进翻译人员及翻译人员与所翻译作品作者之间的语言、文化、科学及技术交流。为此目的，该等组织或协会可能在国内法许可的情形下采取尤其是下列具体活动：

(a) 促进采取适用于翻译的专业标准；该等标准应特别规定翻译人员有职责提供无论从语言及问题而言均为高质量的翻译，并确保翻译忠实于原作；

(b) 研究为翻译人员和用户所接受的补偿依据；

(c) 制定有助于解决因翻译质量而产生争议的法规；

(d) 就翻译人员与用户之间的谈判予以咨询，并与其他利益相关方合作，确立交易示范合同；

(e) 努力为翻译人员个人或集体作出安排，并根据国内法或者任何可能适用于该事项的集体协议使之能受益于来自于私人或公共资金的作者资助；

(f) 通过信息公告的出版、会议的组织及其他适当方式为翻译人员提供权益事项信息交流的机会；

(g) 就社会福利及税收方面，促进翻译人员享受与文字或包括科技作品在内的科学作品之作者同等的待遇；

(h) 促进建立及发展专门用于翻译人员培训的项目；

(i) 与旨在推进翻译人员权益的其他国家、地区或国际组织合作，与旨在版主进行版权保护作品权利清算的国内或地区版权信息中心合作，并和联合国教科文组织国际版权信息中心进行合作；

(j) 与用户、其代表或专业组织或协会维系紧密的接触，以便捍卫翻译人员的权益；在认定有利的情形下，与该等代表、组织或协会就集体协议进行谈判；

(k) 促进翻译职业的总体发展。

8. 然而，在不影响第七款效力的前提下，成为代表翻译人员专业组织或协会的会员不应该成为予以保护的必要条件，这是由于本倡议书的规定应该适用所有翻译人员，无论其是否为该等组织或协会的会员。

四、翻译人员的社会及财政条件

9. 作为独立翻译人员，无论是否享有版税，在实践中应该享受任何涉及退休、疾病、家庭补助等社会保险计划，并可以享受总体适用于文字或包括技术作品在内的科学作品作者的税务安排。

10. 付薪翻译人员的待遇应与其他付薪专业人员的同等标准，并且也应享受其他付薪专业人员的社会计划。在这方面，其依据的职业法律、集体合同及雇佣合同应当明确规定科技文本翻译人员的等级，以便其作为翻译人员的地位可以得到承认，尤其是对于其职业登记而言更是如此。

五、翻译人员培训及工作条件

11. 成员国原则上应当认可翻译是一项独立的行业，需要与专门的语言教学不同的专门教育，并且需要特殊训练。成员国应鼓励为翻译人员设立的写作项目，尤其要与翻译人员专业组织或协会、大学或者其他教育机构有关，并鼓励组织研讨会或讲习班。也应承认，对于翻译人员而言，能够从持续的教育安排中得益。

12. 成员国应当考虑组织建立名词术语中心，可以鼓励该中心从事以下活动：

（a）向翻译人员告知有关其在工作一般进程中所需要使用术语的目前信息予以通告。

（b）与世界名词术语中心通力合作，对国际科技术语建立标准并予以发展，以促进翻译人员完成其任务。

13. 在与专业组织或协会及其他利益相关方进行合作时，成员国应当促进不同国家翻译人员的交换，以使其对工作语言及他们所翻译作品写作的社会文化背景进行更深入的了解。

14. 为了提高翻译质量，以下原则和实际措施应当被第七款 a 项所提及的专业法律及任何翻译人员与用户间的合同予以明确承认：

（a）应当给予翻译人员一段合理的时间以便其能够完成工作；

（b）应该尽量向翻译人员提供为理解所翻译文本及准备翻译文本所必要的任何文件和信息。

（c）一般而言，翻译应该针对原创作品，只有绝对必要的情形下才进行再翻译工作；

（d）翻译人员应尽量翻译为其母语或者翻译成其熟练程度不亚于其母语的语言。

六、发展中国家

15. 本倡议书所规定的原则及规则在发展中国家可以通过任何认为必要

的方式予以变通，以帮助这些国家满足其要求，并参照于1971年在巴黎修改的《世界版权公约》为发展中国家利益所规定的特别条款及《保护文字与艺术作品伯尔尼公约》之《巴黎法案》(1971)。

七、最后条款

16. 如果翻译人员及翻译在某些方面享有比本倡议书所规定更为充分的保护，则本倡议书条款不应用来削弱其已经享有的保护。

以上系联合国教育、科学、文化组织在内罗毕召开并于1976年11月30日宣告闭幕的第19届大会所依法通过的倡议书权威文本。

Recommendation on the Legal Protection of Translators and Translations and the Practical Means to improve the Status of Translators

22 November 1976

The General Conference of the United Nations Educational, Scientific and Cultural Organization, meeting in Nairobi from 26 October to 30 November 1976, at its nineteenth session,

Considering that translation promotes understanding between peoples and co-operation among nations by facilitating the dissemination of literary and scientific works, including technical works, across linguistic frontiers and the interchange of ideas,

Noting the extremely important role played by translators and translations in international exchanges in culture, art and science, particularly in the case of works written or translated in less widely spoken languages,

Recognizing that the protection of translators is indispensable in order to ensure translations of the quality needed from them to fulfill effectively their role in the service of culture and development,

Recalling that, if the principles of this protection are already contained in the Universal Copyright Convention, while the Berne Convention for the Protection of Literary and Artistic Works and a number of national laws of Member States also contain specific provisions concerning such protection, the practical application of these principles and provisions is not always adequate,

Being of the opinion that if, in many countries with respect to copyright, translators and translations enjoy a protection which resembles the protection granted to authors and to literacy and scientific works, including technical works, the adoption of measures of an essentially practical nature, assimilating translators to authors and specific to the translating profession, is nevertheless justified to ameliorate the effective application of existing laws,

Having decided, at its eighteenth session, that the protection of translators should be the subject of a recommendation to Member States within the meaning of Article IV, paragraph 4, of the Constitution,

Adopts, this twenty - second day of November 1976, the present Recommendation.

The General Conference recommends that Member States apply the following provisions concerning the protection of translators and translations by taking whatever legislative or other steps may be required, in conformity with the constitutional provisions and institutional practice of each State, to give effect, within their respective territories, to the principles and standards set forth in this Recommendation.

The General Conference recommends that Member States bring this Recommendation to the attention of the authorities, departments or bodies responsible for matters relating to the moral and material interests of translators and to the protection of translations, of the various organizations or associations representing or promoting the interests of translators, and of publishers, managers of theatres, broadcasters and other users and interested parties.

The General Conference recommends that Member States submit to the Organization, at such times and in such form as shall be determined by the General Conference, reports on the action taken by them to give effect to this Recommendation.

I. Definitions and scope of application

1. For purposes of this Recommendation:

(a) the term 'translation' denotes the transposition of a literary or scientific work, including technical work, from one language into another language, whether or not the initial work, or the translation, is intended for publication in book, magazine, periodical, or other form, or for performance in the theatre, in a film, on radio or television, or in any other media;

(b) the term `translators' denotes translators of literary or scientific works, including technical works;

(c) the term `users' denotes the persons or legal entities for which a translation is made.

2. This Recommendation applies to all translators regardless of:

(a) the legal status applicable to them as:

(i) independent translators; or

(ii) salaried translators;

(b) the discipline to which the work translated belongs;

(c) the full - time or part - time nature of their position as translators.

II. General legal position of translators

3. Member States should accord to translators, in respect of their translations, the protection accorded to authors under the provisions. Of the international copyright conventions to which they are party and/or under their national laws, but without prejudice to the rights of the authors of the original, works translated.

III. Measures to ensure the application in practice of protection afforded translators under international conventions and in national laws relating to copyright

4. It is desirable that a written agreement be concluded between a translator and the user.

5. As a general rule, a contract governing relations between a translator and a user, as well as where appropriate any other legal instrument governing such relations, should:

(a) accord an equitable remuneration to the translator whatever his or her legal status;

(b) at least when the translator is not working as a salaried translator, remunerate him or her in proportion to the proceeds of the sale or use of the translation with payment of an advance, the said advance being retained by the translator whatever the proceeds may be; or by the payment of a sum calculated in conformity with another system of remuneration independent of sales where it is provided for or permitted by national legislation; or by the payment of an equitable lump sum which could be made where payment on a proportional basis proves insufficient or inapplicable; the appropriate method of payment should be chosen taking into account the legal system of the country concerned and where applicable the type of original work translated;

(c) make provision, when appropriate, for a supplementary payment should the use made of the translation go beyond the limitations specified in the contract;

(d) specify that the authorizations granted by the translator are limited to the rights expressly mentioned, this provision applying to possible new editions ;

(e) stipulate that in the event that the translator has not obtained any necessary authorization, it is the user who is responsible for obtaining such authorization;

(f) stipulate that the translator guarantees the user uncontested enjoyment of all the rights granted and - undertakes to refrain from any action likely to compromise the legitimate interests of the user and, when appropriate, to observe the rule of professional secrecy;

(g) stipulate that, subject to the prerogatives of the author of the original work translated, no change shall be made in the text of a translation intended for publication without seeking the prior agreement of the, translator;

(h) assure the translator and his translation similar publicity, proportionately to that which authors are generally given, in particular, the name of the author of the translation should appear in a prominent place on all published copies of the translation, on theatre bills, in announcements made in connexion with radio or television broadcasts, in the credit titles of films and in any other promotional material;

(i) provide that the user ensure that the translation bear such notices as are necessary to comply with copyright formalities in those countries where it might reasonably be expected to be used;

(j) provide for the resolution of any conflicts which may arise, particularly with respect to the quality of the translation, so far as possible, by means of arbitration or in accordance with procedures laid down by national legislation or by any other appropriate means of dispute settlement which on the one hand is such as to guarantee impartiality and on the other hand is easily accessible and inexpensive;

(k) mention the languages from and into which the translator will translate and without prejudice to the provisions of paragraph 1 (a), further specify expressly the translator's possible use as an interpreter.

6. In order to facilitate the implementation of the measures recommended in paragraphs 4, 5 and 14, Member States should, without prejudice to the translator's freedom to enter into an individual contract, encourage the parties concerned, in particular the professional organizations of translators and other organizations or associations representing them, on the one hand, and the representatives of users, on the other, to adopt model contracts or to conclude collective agreements based on the measures suggested in this Recommendation and making due allowance for all situations likely to arise by reason either of the translator or the nature of the translation.

7. Member States should also promote measures to ensure effective representation of translators and to encourage the creation and development of professional organizations of translators and other organizations or associations representing them, to define the rules and duties which should govern the exercise of the profession, to defend the moral and material interests of translators and to facilitate linguistic, cultural, scientific and technical exchanges among translators and between translators and the authors of works to be translated. To this end, such organizations or associations might undertake, where national law permits, in particular, the following specific activities:

(a) promote the adoption of standards governing the translating profession; such standards should stipulate in particular that the translator has a duty to provide a translation of high quality from both the linguistic and stylistic points of view and to guarantee that the translation will be a faithful rendering of the original;

(b) study the bases for remuneration acceptable to translators and users;

(c) set up procedures to assist in the settlement of disputes arising in connexion with the quality of translations;

(d) advise translators in their negotiations with, users and co - operate with other interested parties in establishing model contracts relating to translation;

(e) endeavour to arrange for translators individually or collectively, and in accordance with national laws or any collective agreements which may be applicable on this subject, to benefit with authors from funds received from either private or public sources;

(f) provide for exchanges of information on matters of interest to translators by the publication of information bulletins, the organization of meetings or by other appropriate means;

(g) promote the assimilation of translators, from the point of view of social benefits and taxation, to authors of literary or scientific works, including technical works;

(h) promote the establishment and development of specialized programmes for the training of translators;

(i) co - operate with other national, regional or international bodies working to promote the interests of translators, and with any national or regional copyright information centers set up to assist in the clearance of rights in works protected by copyright, as well as with the UNESCO International Copyright Information Center;

(j) maintain close contacts with users, as well as with their representatives or professional organizations or associations, in order to defend the interests of translators; and negotiate collective agreements with such representatives or organizations or associations where deemed advantageous;

(k) contribute generally to the development of the translating profession.

8. Without prejudice to paragraph 7, membership of professional organizations or associations which represent translators should not, however, be a necessary condition for protection, since the provisions of this Recommendation should apply to all translators, whether or not they are members of such organizations or associations.

IV. Social and fiscal situation of translators

9. Translators working as independent writers, whether or not they are paid by royalties, should benefit in practice from any social insurance schemes relating

to retirement, illness, family allowances, etc., and from any taxation arrangements, generally applicable to the authors of literary or scientific works, including technical works.

10. Salaried translators should be treated on the same basis as other salaried professional staff and benefit accordingly from the social schemes provided for them. In this respect, professional statutes, collective agreements and contracts of employment based thereon should mention expressly the class of translators of scientific and technical texts, so that their status' as translators may be recognized, particularly with respect to their professional classification.

V. Training and working conditions of translators

11. Member States should recognize in principle that translation is an independent discipline requiring an education distinct from exclusively language teaching and that this discipline requires special training. Member States should encourage the establishment of writing programmes for translators, especially in connexion with translators' professional organizations or associations, universities or other educational institutions, and the organization of seminars or workshops. It should also be recognized that it is useful for translators to be able to benefit from continuing education courses.

12. Member States should consider organizing terminology centers which might be encouraged to undertake the following activities:

(a) communicating to translators current information concerning terminology required by them in the general course of their work;

(b) collaborating closely with terminology centers throughout the world with a view to standardizing and developing the internationalization of scientific and technical terminology so as to facilitate the task of translators.

13. In association with professional organizations or associations and other interested parties, Member States should facilitate exchanges of translators between different countries, so as to allow them to improve their knowledge of the language from which they work and of the socio - cultural context in which the works to be translated by them are written.

14. With a view to improving the quality of translations, the following princi-

ples and practical measures should be expressly recognized in professional statutes mentioned under sub - paragraph 7 (a) and in any other written - agreements between the translators and the users:

(a) translators should be given a reasonable period of time to accomplish their work;

(b) any documents and information necessary for the understanding of the text to be translated and the drafting of the translation should, so far as possible, be made available to translators;

(c) as a general rule, a translation should be made from the original work, recourse being had to retranslation only where absolutely necessary;

(d) a translator should, as far as possible, translate into his own mother tongue or into a language of which he or she has a mastery equal to that of his or her mother tongue.

VI. Developing countries

15. The principles and norms set forth in this Recommendation may be adapted by developing countries in any way deemed necessary to help them meet their requirements, and in the light of the special provisions for the benefit of developing countries introduced in the Universal Copyright Convention as revised at Paris on 24 July 1971 and the Paris Act (1971) of the Berne Convention for the Protection of Literary and Artistic Works.

VII. Final provision

16. Where translators and translations enjoy a level of protection which is, in certain respects, more favorable than that provided for in this Recommendation, its provisions should not be invoked to diminish the protection already acquired.

The foregoing is the authentic text of the Recommendation duly adopted by the General Conference of the United Nations Educational, Scientific and Cultural Organization during its nineteenth session, which was held in Nairobi and declared, closed the thirtieth day of November 1976.

第三部分　公共文化服务

Part Ⅲ　Service for Public Culture

国际出版物交换公约*

（联合国教科文组织大会 1958 年 12 月 3 日于巴黎通过，1961 年 11 月 23 日生效）

确认出版物国际交换的重要性，基于联合国教育、科技及文化组织宪章，认可制定新的关于出版物交换国际公约的需求，特决定，在第九次会议上，这些建议应当通过一项国际公约成为国际规范的对象，1958 年 12 月 3 日，通过如下公约。

第 1 条 出版物交换

缔约国承担鼓励和促进政府机构和教育、科学和技术或者文化性质的非政府实体交换出版物，且依据本公约的规定，交换是非盈利性质的。

第 2 条 出版物交换的范围

1. 对本公约而言，第一条所指的机构和实体出于使用而非销售目的，交换下列出版物是恰当的：

（1）具有教育、法律、科学和技术、文化和信息性质的出版物，例如书籍、报纸、杂志、地图和规划、印刷品、照片、微缩复制品、音乐作品、盲文出版物和其他平面资料；

（2）1958 年 12 月 3 日联合国教育、科技及文化组织大会通过的《关于交换官方出版物和政府文件的公约》覆盖的出版物。

2. 本公约不影响依据 1958 年 12 月 3 日联合国教育、科技及文化组织大会通过的《关于交换官方出版物和政府文件的公约》进行的交换。本公约不适用于机密文件、通告和其他未公开文件。

第 3 条 交换服务

1. 缔约国可以委托国家交换服务，如果不存在这样的服务，则可委托与本公约第一条所指的机构和实体的出版物交换的发展和协调相连的，具有下

---

* 中国社会科学院国际法研究所吴晓丹译。

列作用的中央交换当局：

（1）便利国际交换，特别是恰当的时候通过传播需要交换的资料；

（2）为本国和外国机构和实体间的交换可能性提供建议和信息；

（3）恰当的时候，鼓励复印资料的交换。

2. 但是，如果国家交换服务或者本公约第一条所指的机构和实体间交换的发展和协调中央化不可行，本条第一款规定的任何和全部作用可委托其他当局。

第 4 条　传播方法

有关机构和实体可直接进行传播，亦可通过国家交换服务或交换当局。

第 5 条　运输费用

如果交换各方直接进行传播，缔约国无须承担任何费用。如果传播是通过交换当局进行的，责任缔约国应当承担相关费用，不管目的地何在。但如果是通过海上运输，包装和运输费用应由到达港的海关支付。

第 6 条　运输的费率和条件

缔约国应当采取所有必要措施，确保交换当局享受现存最有利的运输费率和条件，无论选择何种运输方式：邮递、公路、铁路、内陆或海洋、航空邮件或航空货运。

第 7 条　关税和其他

每个缔约国应当授予其交换当局根据本公约或其他执行协议进出口的关税豁免，并给予他们关税方面的最优惠待遇。

第 8 条　交换的国际协调

为协助联合国教育、科学及文化组织履行本公约授予的、关于交换的国际协调职能，缔约国应当向该组织提交有关本公约工作的年度报告和根据第 12 条加入的双边协定的副本。

第 9 条　信息和研究

联合国教育、科学及文化组织应当公布缔约国根据第八条规定提交的信息，应当筹备并公布关于本公约的研究。

第 10 条　联合国教科文组织的协助

1. 因实施本公约引发的问题，缔约国可吁请联合国教育、科技及文化组织提供技术协助。该组织应当在其日程和资源限度内，特别是为创设和组织本国交换服务提供此类协助。

2. 该组织有权主动就此事向缔约国提供建议。

第 11 条　与以往协议的关系

本公约不应当影响缔约国通过国际协议已经承担的任何义务。

第 12 条　双边协议

只要必要或可行，缔约国应当为补充本公约之目的或规范公约适用引发的任何共同关切事项的制定双边协定。

第 13 条　语言

本公约用英文、法文、俄文和西班牙文起草，且四种文本具有相同效力。

第 14 条　批准和接受

1. 本公约应当由联合国教育、科学及文化组织缔约国根据各自宪法程序规定批准或接受。

2. 批准或接受的文本应当交存联合国教育、科技及文化组织总干事。

第 15 条　加入

1. 非联合国教育、科技及文化组织的成员国可应该组织执行董事会的邀请加入本公约。

2. 加入自向联合国教育、科技及文化组织总干事交存加入文件起生效。

第 16 条　本公约的领域延伸

任何缔约国，可在批准、接受和加入时，或此后任何时间，以向联合国教育、科技及文化组织提交通知的形式，宣称本公约延伸适用任何由其负责外交关系的全部或任何领域。上述通知应当自接收之日起 12 个月后生效。

第 17 条　生效

本公约应当自收到第三份批准、接收和加入文件之日起 12 个月后生效，但仅对生效之日或之前提交相关文件的国家生效。对交存批准、接收或加入文件的国家，自交存之日起 12 个月后生效。

第 18 条　退出

1. 每个缔约国可代表本国或由其负责国际关系的领域退出本公约。

2. 退出应当提交书面通知，交存给联合国教育、科技及文化组织总干事。

3. 退出应当自收到退出文件之日起 12 个月后生效。

第 19 条　通知

联合国教育、科学及文化组织总干事应当将第十四条和第十五条规定的批准、接收和加入文件以及第十八条规定的退出通知给该组织的成员国、第十五条所指的非成员国以及联合国。

第 20 条　修订

1. 联合国教育、科技及文化组织大会可修订本公约，但该修订仅约束修订后公约的缔约国。

2. 如果大会通过了全部或部分修订本公约的新公约，除非新公约有相反规定，本公约自新修订公约生效之日起，停止接收批准、接收或加入。

第 21 条　登记

依据《联合国宪章》第 102 条，本公约应当经联合国教育、科学及文化组织总干事请求在联合国秘书处登记。

Convention concerning the International Exchange of Publications

Paris, 3 December 1958

The General Conference of the United Nations Educational, Scientific and Cultural Organization, meeting in Paris from 4 November to 5 December 1958, at its tenth session,

Convinced that development of the international exchange of publications is essential to the free exchange of ideas and knowledge among the peoples of the world,

Considering the importance accorded to the international exchange of publications by the Constitution of the United Nations Educational, Scientific and Cultural Organization,

Recognizing the need for a new international convention concerning the exchange of publications,

Having before It proposals concerning the international exchange of publications constituting item 15. 4. 1 on the agenda of the session,

Having decided, at its ninth session, that these proposals should be made the subject of international regulation by way of an international convention,

Adopts, this third day of December 1958, the present Convention.

Article 1. Exchange of publications

The Contracting States undertake to encourage and facilitate the exchange of publications between both governmental bodies and non - governmental institutions of an educational, scientific and technical, or cultural nature, which are non - profit - making in character, in accordance with the provisions of the present Convention.

Article 2. Scope of the exchange of publications

1. For the purpose of the present Convention, the following publications may

be considered appropriate articles to be exchanged, for use but not for resale, between the bodies and institutions referred to in Article 1 of the present Convention:

(a) publications of an educational, legal, scientific and technical, cultural and informational nature, such as books, newspapers and periodicals, maps and plans, prints, photographs, microcopies, musical works, Braille publications and other graphic material;

(b) publications covered by the Convention concerning the exchange of official publications and government documents between States, adopted by the General Conference of the United Nations Educational, Scientific and Cultural Organization on the third day of December 1958.

2. The present Convention in no way affects exchanges carried out under the convention concerning the exchange of official publications and government documents between States, adopted by the General Conference of the United Nations Educational, Scientific and Cultural Organization on the third day of December 1958.

3. The present Convention does not apply to confidential documents, circulars and other items which have not been made public.

Article 3. Exchange services

1. The Contracting States may entrust the national exchange service or, where no such national exchange service exists, the central exchange authority or authorities with the following functions in connexion with the development and co - ordination of the exchange of publications among bodies and institutions referred to in Article 1 of the present Convention:

(a) facilitating the international exchange of publications, in particular by transmitting, when appropriate, the material to be exchanged;

(b) supplying advice and information on exchange possibilities for bodies and institutions at home and abroad;

(c) encouraging, when appropriate, the exchange of duplicate material.

2. However, when it is deemed undesirable to centralize in the national exchange service or in central authorities the development and co - ordination of exchanges among bodies and institutions referred to in Article 1 of the present Convention, any or all of the functions enumerated in paragraph 1 of the present article may be entrusted to other authority or authorities.

Article 4. Method of transmission

The transmission may be made either directly between the bodies and institutions concerned, or through the national exchange service or exchange authorities.

Article 5. Transport charges

When transmissions are made directly between exchange partners, the Contracting States shall not be required to bear the cost thereof. If the transmission is made through the_ exchange authority or authorities, the Contracting States shall bear the cost of the transmission as far as destination, but, for transport by sea, the cost of packing and carriage shall be paid only as far as the customs office of the port of arrival.

Article 6. Rates and conditions of transport

The Contracting States shall take all the necessary measures to ensure that the exchange authorities benefit from the most favourable existing rates and transport conditions, whatever the means of transport chosen: post, road, rail, inland or sea transport, airmail or air cargo.

Article 7. Customs and other facilities

Each Contracting State shall grant its exchange authorities exemption from customs duties for both imported and exported material under the provisions of the present Convention or under any agreement in implementation thereof and shall accord them the most favourable treatment as regards customs and other facilities.

Article 8. International co – ordination of exchange

To assist the United Nations Educational, Scientific and Cultural Organization in the performance of the functions assigned to it by its Constitution concerning the international co - ordination of exchange, the Contracting States shall send to the Organization annual reports on the working of the present Convention and copies of bilateral agreements entered into in accordance with Article 12.

Article 9. Information and studies

The United Nations Educational, Scientific and Cultural Organization shall publish information received from the Contracting States in application of Article 8 and shall prepare and publish studies on the working of the present Convention.

Article 10. Assistance of UNESCO

1. The Contracting States may call upon the United Nations Educational, Scientific and Cultural Organization for technical assistance in connexion with any

problem arising out of the application of the present Convention. The Organization shall accord such assistance within the limits fixed by its programme and its resources, in particular, for the creation and organization of national exchange services.

2. The Organization is authorized to make, on its own initiative, proposals on this matter to the Contracting States.

Article 11. Relation to previous agreements

The present Convention shall not affect obligations previously entered into by the Contracting States by virtue of international agreements.

Article 12. Bilateral agreements

Whenever necessary or desirable, the Contracting States shall enter into bilateral agreements for the purpose of supplementing the present Convention and regulating matters of common concern arising out of its application.

Article 13. Languages

The present Convention is drawn up in English, French, Russian and Spanish, the four texts being equally authoritative.

Article 14. Ratification and acceptance

1. The present Convention shall be subject to ratification or acceptance by States members of the United Nations Educational, Scientific and Cultural Organization, in accordance with their respective constitutional procedures.

2. The instruments of ratification or acceptance shall be deposited with the Director - General of the United Nations Educational, Scientific and Cultural Organization.

Article 15. Accession

1. The present Convention shall be open for accession by all States not members of the Organization invited to do so by the Executive Board of the United Nations Educational, Scientific and Cultural Organization.

2. Accession shall be effected by the deposit of an instrument of accession^ with the Director - General of the United Nations Educational, Scientific and Cultural Organization.

Article 16. Territorial extension of the Convention

Any Contracting State may, at the time of ratification, acceptance or accession, or at any time thereafter, declare by notification addressed to the Director

General of the United Nations Educational, Scientific and Cultural Organization that the present Convention shall extend to all or any of the territories for whose international relations it is responsible. The said notification shall take effect twelve months after the date of its receipt.

Article 17. Entry into force

The present Convention shall enter into force twelve months after the date of the deposit of the third instrument of ratification, acceptance or accession, but only with respect to those States which have deposited their respective instruments on or before that date. It shall enter into force for each other State which deposits its instrument of ratification, acceptance or accession, twelve months after the deposit of its instrument of ratification, acceptance or accession.

Article 18. Denunciations

1. Each Contracting State may denounce the present Convention on its own behalf or on behalf of any territory for whose international relations it is responsible.

2. The denunciation shall be notified by an instrument in writing, deposited with the Director - General of the United Nations Educational, Scientific and Cultural Organization.

3. The denunciation shall take effect twelve months after the receipt of the instrument of denunciation.

Article 19. Notifications

The Director - General of the United Nations Educational, Scientific and Cultural Organization shall inform the States members of the Organization, States not members of the Organization referred to in Article 15, as well as the United Nations, of the deposit of all the instruments of ratification, acceptance and accession provided for in Articles 14 and 15 and of the notifications and denunciations provided for respectively in Articles 17 and 18.

Article 20. Revision of the Convention

1. The present Convention may be revised by the General Conference of the United Nations Educational, Scientific and Cultural Organization, any such revision, however, binding only those States which shall become parties to the revising convention.

2. Should the General Conference adopt a new convention revising the present

Convention in whole or in part, and unless the new convention otherwise provides, the present Convention shall cease to be open to ratification, acceptance or accession as from the date when the new revising convention enters into force.

Article 21. Registration

In accordance with Article 102 of the Charter of the United Nations, the present Convention shall be registered with the Secretariat of the United Nations at the request of the Director - General of the United Nations Educational, Scientific and Cultural Organization.

国家间官方出版物和政府文献交换公约*

（联合国教科文组织大会1958年12月3日于巴黎通过，1961年5月30日生效）

鉴于出版物国际交换的发展对全世界人民自由交换思想和知识的重要性，考虑到基于联合国教育、科技及文化组织宪章赋予出版物国际交换的重要性；

深知1886年3月15日在布鲁塞尔缔结的《官方文献、科学和文学出版物国际交换公约》、《及时交换公报、公共议会年报和文献的公约》以及关于出版物交换的各种区域性协议；认可制定新的关于国家间交换官方出版物和政府国际公约的需求；收到会议日程第15.4.1项关于国家间官方出版物和政府文献交换的提议；特决定，在第九次会议上，这些建议应当通过一项国际公约成为国际规范的对象；1958年12月3日，通过如下公约。

第1条 官方出版物和政府文献交换

缔约国表达了根据本公约的规定，在互惠基础上，交换官方出版物和政府文献的意愿。

第2条 官方出版物和政府文献的定义

1. 出于本公约的目的，下列被认定为官方出版物和政府文件，如果他们在任何政府当局命令下执行并承担费用：议会文献、报告、公告和其他立法文件；行政出版物和中央、联邦和地区政府机构的报告；国家书目、国家手册、法律文本、法院裁定；以及认可的其他出版物。

2. 但是，在适用本公约时，缔约国应当自由决定能够构成交换资料的官方出版物和政府文件。

3. 本公约不适用于机密文件、通告和其他不公开的文献。

第3条 双边协定

适当的时候，缔约国应当为适用本公约和规范由适用引起的共同关切之

---

* 中国社会科学院国际法研究所吴晓丹译。

目的缔结双边协定。

第 4 条　国家交换当局

1. 每个缔约国的国家交换服务，或不存在此类服务时，特此指定的中央当局应当履行交换的职能。

2. 交换当局应当在各自缔约国内执行本公约，恰当的时候，为履行第三条规定的双边协定负责。每个缔约国应当给予本国交换服务或中央交换当局履行交换职能需要的获取交换资料的权力和充足的财政支持。

第 5 条　交换出版物的清单和数目

交换的官方出版物和政府文献的清单和数目应当由缔约国交换当局协商决定。此类当局可安排修改公约规定的用于交换的官方出版物的清单和数目。

第 6 条　传播方法

传播可向交换当局或其指定的接受者直接做出。委托的方法可由交换当局协商决定。

第 7 条　费用承担

除非有相反约定，从事传播的交换当局应当承担相关费用，不管目的地何在。但如果是通过海上运输，包装和运输费用应由到达港的海关支付。

第 8 条　运输的费率和条件

缔约国应当采取所有必要措施，确保交换当局享受现存最有利的运输费率和条件，无论选择何种运输方式：邮递、公路、铁路、内陆或海洋、航空邮件或航空货运。

第 9 条　关税和其他

每个缔约国应当授予其交换当局根据本公约或其他执行协定进出口的关税豁免，并给予他们关税方面的最优惠待遇。

第 10 条　交换的国际协调

为协助联合国教育、科学及文化组织履行本公约授予的、关于交换的国际协调职能，缔约国应当向该组织提交有关本公约工作的年度报告和根据第三条加入的双边协定的副本。

第 11 条　信息和研究

联合国教育、科学及文化组织应当公布缔约国根据第十条规定提交的信息，应当筹备并公布关于本公约的研究。

第 12 条　联合国教科文组织的协助

1. 因实施本公约引发的问题，缔约国可吁请联合国教育、科技及文化组织提供技术协助。该组织应当在其日程和资源限度内，特别是为创设和组织本国交换服务提供此类协助。

2. 该组织有权主动就此事向缔约国提供建议。

第 13 条　与以往协议的关系

本公约不应当影响缔约国通过国际协议已经承担的任何义务。亦不应解释为要求重复依据有关协定的交换行为。

第 14 条　语言

本公约用英文、法文、俄文和西班牙文起草，且四种文本具有相同效力。

第 15 条　批准和接受

1. 本公约应当由联合国教育、科学及文化组织缔约国根据各自宪法程序规定批准或接受。

2. 批准或接受的文本应当交存联合国教育、科技及文化组织总干事。

第 16 条　加入

1. 所有非联合国教育、科技及文化组织的成员国可应该组织执行董事会的邀请加入本公约。

2. 自向联合国教育、科技及文化组织总干事交存加入文件起生效。

第 17 条　生效

本公约应当自收到第三份批准、接收和加入文件之日起 12 个月后生效，但仅对生效之日或之前提交相关文件的国家生效。对交存批准、接收或加入文件的国家，自交存之日起 12 个月后生效。

第 18 条　本公约的领域延伸

任何缔约国，可在批准、接受和加入时，或此后任何时间，以向联合国教育、科技及文化组织提交通知的形式，宣称本公约延伸适用任何由其负责外交关系的全部或任何领域。上述通知应当自接收之日起 12 个月后生效。

第 19 条　退出

1. 每个缔约国可代表本国或由其负责国际关系的领域退出本公约。

2. 退出应当提交书面通知，交存给联合国教育、科技及文化组织总干事。

3. 退出应当自收到退出文件之日起 12 个月后生效。

第 20 条　通知

联合国教育、科学及文化组织总干事应当将第十五条和第十六条规定的批准、接收和加入文件以及第十八条规定的退出通知给该组织的成员国、第十六条所指的非成员国以及联合国。

第 21 条　修订

1. 联合国教育、科技及文化组织大会可修订本公约，但该修订仅约束修订后公约的缔约国。

2. 如果大会通过了全部或部分修订的公约，除非新公约有相反规定，本公约自新修订公约生效之日起，停止接收批准、接收或加入。

第22条 登记

依据《联合国宪章》第102条，本公约应当经联合国教育、科学及文化组织总干事请求在联合国秘书处登记。

Convention concerning the Exchange of Official Publications and Government Documents between States

Paris, 3 December 1958

The General Conference of the United Nations Educational, Scientific and Cultural Organization, meeting in Paris from 4 November to 5 December 1958, at its tenth session,

Convinced that development of the international exchange of publications is essential to the free exchange of ideas and knowledge among the peoples of the world, Considering the importance accorded to the international exchange of publications by the Constitution of the United Nations Educational, Scientific and Cultural Organization,

Being aware of the provisions for the exchange of official publications and government documents contained in the Convention for the International Exchange of Official Documents, Scientific and Literary Publications and in the Convention for the Immediate Exchange of Official Journals, Public Parliamentary Annals and Documents, concluded in Brussels on 15 March 1886 and in various regional agreements for the exchange of publications,

Recognizing the need for a new international convention concerning the exchange of official publications and government documents between States,

Having before it proposals concerning the exchange of official publications and government documents between States constituting item 15. 4. 1 on the agenda of the session,

Having decided, at its ninth session that these proposals should be made the subject of international regulation by way of an international convention,

Adopts, this third day of December 1958, the present Convention.

Article 1. Exchange of official publications and government documents

The Contracting States express their willingness to exchange their official publications and government documents, on a reciprocal basis, in accordance with the provisions of the present Convention.

Article 2. Definition of official publications and government documents

1. For the purpose of the present Convention, the following are considered official publications and government documents when they are executed by the order and at the expense of any national governmental authority: parliamentary documents, reports and journals and other legislative papers; administrative publications and reports from central, federal and regional governmental bodies; national bibliographies, State handbooks, bodies of law, decisions of the Courts of Justice; and other publications as may be agreed.

2. However, in the application of the present Convention, the Contracting States shall be free to determine the official publications and government documents which shall constitute exchange material.

3. The present Convention does not apply to confidential documents, circulars and other items which have not been made public.

Article 3. Bilateral agreements

The Contracting States, whenever they deem it appropriate, shall enter into bilateral agreements for the purpose of implementing the present Convention and regulating matters of common concern arising out of its application.

Article 4. National exchange authorities

1. In each Contracting State, the national exchange service or, where no such service exists, the central authority or authorities designated for the purpose, shall carry out the functions of exchange.

2. The exchange authorities shall be responsible within each Contracting State for the implementation of the present Convention and of bilateral agreements as referred to in Article 3, whenever appropriate. Each Contracting State shall give its national exchange service or the central exchange authorities the powers required to obtain the material to be exchanged and sufficient financial means to carry out the functions of exchange.

Article 5. List and number of publications for exchange

The list and number of official publications and government documents for exchange shall be agreed between the exchange authorities of the Contracting States. This list and the number of official publications set forth in the Convention for exchange may be modified by arrangements between such authorities.

Article 6. Method of transmission

Transmissions may be made directly to exchange authorities or to recipients named by them. The method of listing consignments may be agreed between exchange authorities.

Article 7. Transport charges

Unless otherwise agreed, the exchange authority which undertakes the transmission shall bear the cost thereof as far as destination, but for transport by sea, the cost of packing and carriage shall be paid only as far as the customs office of the port of arrival.

Article 8. Rates and conditions of transport

The Contracting States shall take all the necessary measures to ensure that the exchange authorities benefit from the most favorable existing - rates and transport conditions, whatever the means of transport chosen: post, road, rail, inland or sea transport, airmail or air cargo.

Article 9. Customs and other facilities

Each Contracting State shall rant its exchange authorities exemption from customs duties for both imported and exported material under the provisions of the present Convention or under any agreement in implementation thereof and shall accord them the most favorable treatment as regards customs and other facilities.

Article 10. International co – ordination of exchange

To assist the United Nations Educational, Scientific and Cultural Organization in the performance of the functions concerning the international co - ordination of exchange assigned to it by its Constitution, the Contracting States shall send to the Organization annual reports on the working of the present Convention and copies of bilateral agreements entered into in accordance with Article 3.

Article 11. Information and studies

The United Nations Educational, Scientific and Cultural Organization shall publish information received from the Contracting States in conformity with Article 10 and shall prepare and publish studies on the working of the present Convention.

Article 12. Assistance of UNESCO

1. The Contracting States may call upon the United Nations Educational, Sci-

entific and Cultural Organization for technical assistance in connexion with any problem arising out of the application of the present Convention. The Organization shall accord such assistance within the limits fixed by its programme and its resources, in particular, for the creation and organization of national exchange services,

2. The Organization is authorized to make, on its own initiative, proposals on these matters to the Contracting States.

Article 13. Relation to previous agreements

The present Convention shall not affect obligations previously entered into by the Contracting States by virtue of international agreements. It shall not be construed as requiring a duplication of exchanges conducted under existing agreements.

Article 14. Languages

The present Convention is drawn up in English, French, Russian and Spanish, the four texts being equally authoritative.

Article 15. Ratification and acceptance

1. The present Convention shall be subject to - ratification or acceptance by States members of the United Nations Educational, Scientific and Cultural Organization, in accordance with their respective constitutional procedures.

2. The instruments of ratification or acceptance shall be deposited with the Director - General of the United Nations Educational, Scientific and Cultural Organization.

Article 16. Accession

1. The present Convention shall be open for accession by all States not members of the Organization invited to do so by the Executive Board of the United Nations Educational, Scientific and Cultural Organization.

2. Accession shall be effected by the deposit of an instrument of accession with the Director - General of the United Nations Educational, Scientific and Cultural Organization.

Article 17. Entry into force

The present Convention shall enter into force twelve months after the date of the deposit of the third instrument of ratification, acceptance or accession, but only with respect to those States which have deposited their respective instruments on or before that date. It shall enter into force for each other State which deposits its instrument of ratification, acceptance or accession, twelve months after the deposit of its instrument of ratification, acceptance or accession.

Article 18. Territorial extension of the Convention

Any Contracting State may, at the time of ratification, acceptance or accession, or at any time thereafter, declare by notification addressed to the Director General of the United Nations Educational, Scientific and Cultural Organization that the present Convention shall extend to all or any of the territories for whose international relations it is responsible. The said notification shall take effect twelve months after the date of its receipt.

Article 19. Denunciation

1. Each Contracting State may denounce the present Convention on its own behalf or on behalf of any territory for whose international relations it is responsible.

2. The denunciation shall be notified by an instrument in writing, deposited with the Director - General of the United Nations Educational, Scientific and Cultural Organization.

3. The denunciation shall take effect twelve months after the receipt of the instrument of denunciation.

Article 20. Notifications

The Director - General of the United Nations Educational, Scientific and Cultural Organization shall inform the States members of the Organization, States not members of the Organization referred to in Article 16, as well as the United Nations, of the deposit of all the instruments of ratification, acceptance and accession provided for in Articles 15 and 16 and of the notifications and denunciations provided for respectively in Articles 18 and 19.

Article 21. Revision of the Convention

1. The present Convention may be revised by the General Conference of the United Nations Educational, Scientific and Cultural Organization, any such revision, however, binding only those States which shall become parties to the revising convention.

2. Should the General Conference adopt a new convention revising the present Convention in whole or in part, and unless the new convention otherwise pro-

vides, the present Convention shall cease to be open to ratification, acceptance or accession as from the date when the new revising convention enters into force.

Article 22. Registration

In accordance with Article 102 of the Charter of the United Nations, the present Convention shall be registered with the Secretariat of the United Nations at the request of the Director - General of the United Nations Educational, Scientific and Cultural Organization.

关于向公众开放博物馆最有效方式的建议*

（联合国教育、科学及文化组织大会第十一次大会于1960年12月14日在巴黎通过）

联合国教育、科学及文化组织大会于1960年11月14日至12月15日在巴黎召开第十一届会议，考虑到该组织职能之一正如其组织法所规定是为了：进一步推动普及教育及传播文化；通过建立人民之间的合作促进不分种族、性别或任何经济、社会差别的教育机会均等之观念，在增进人民之间相互了解的事业中开展合作，并保存、增加和传播知识；考虑到博物馆可以有效地协助完成这些任务；考虑到各类博物馆均是欣赏与教育的根源；亦考虑到博物馆通过保护艺术品和科学资料并将其展示于众，有助于传播各种文化知识，并以此促进各国之间的了解；考虑因此应尽一切努力鼓励各阶层公众，特别是劳动阶级参观博物馆；考虑到随着世界工业体制的发展，人们享有更多的闲暇，这些闲暇应用于全民利益及其文化发展；认识到博物馆为执行其长期的教育使命，并满足劳动者的文化需要，必须考虑新的社会条件及需要；收到关于使博物馆向所有人开放最有效方法的议案，作为本届会议第17. 4. L项议程；第十届会议已决定这些议案应以项成员国建议的形式作为国际性法规的一个议题。兹于1960年12月14日通过本建议。

大会建议，各成员国应采取为在其各自领土范围内实施本建议所规定的原则和规范所可能需要的任何立法或其他步骤，以适应下列各项规定。

大会建议，各成员国应使本建议为与博物馆有关的当局和机构以及各博物馆所知晓。

大会建议，各成员国应按大会确定的日期和方式向大会报告其为实施本建议所采取的行动。

---

* 中国社会科学院国际法研究所吴晓丹译。

一、定　义

1．为本建议之目的，“博物馆”一词系指以公众利益予以管理的任何永久性机构，其目的在于通过各种方式保护、研究、增加，特别是为娱乐及教育之目的向公众展览具有文化价值的成套物品和标本；即艺术、历史、科学、技术藏品、植物园、动物园及水族馆。

二、总　则

2．各成员国应采取一切适当措施以确保其领土内博物馆向所有人开放，而不论其经济或社会地位如何。

3．为此，在选择适用措施时，应考虑到各成员国可能存在的不同的博物馆管理形式根据博物馆是否归国家所有并由国家管理，或者即使不归国家所有，是否定期或不定期得到国家资助，或者国家是否以科学、技术或行政能力参与其管理等不同情况，这些措施亦会有所不同。

三、博物馆藏品布置与参观

4．博物馆应通过清晰的陈列形式、系统的布置简介说明或标签、出版观众所须之此类说明的导游册或手册、组织适合各类观众听讲的定期导游参观等，使藏品易于为各类人所欣赏。导游员应完全称职，最好由本建议第16段所指机构之代理人名。对录音讲解设施可做谨慎使用。

5．博物馆应于每日以及于各类观众方便之时对外开放，并特别要考虑到劳动者的闲暇时间。博物馆应配备足够数量的管理人员以便实行轮班制度，使博物馆能保持连日开放，并在当地条件、风俗许可的情况下，于每晚工作时间结束后开放。各博物馆应安装必要的照明、取暖设备。

6．博物馆应易于进入并应以舒适的措施使之尽可能具有吸引力。在尊重博物馆特性及不妨碍参观藏品的前提下，最好应于博物馆范围内（在庭园、平台、适宜的地下室等）或在其周围附近，为观众提供休息厅、参观、咖啡厅及类似设施。

7．只要有可能，门票应予以免费。如果不是全部免费或者认为有必要维持少量门票费，甚至即使只是象征性的收费，各博物馆至少亦应每周或在同等时间内免费开放一天。

8. 在收门票时，对于那些国家已有正式方法可做出区别的低薪阶层及大家族之成员应予以免费。

9. 为鼓励人们定期参观应提供特殊便利，例如，在一定时期内减少定期参观费，使付款人可不限次数进入一个或一组博物馆。

10. 只要有可能，那些参加有组织的教育和文化活动，无论学生还是承认团体以及博物馆人员和本建议第17段所述协会成员都应予以免票。

四、为博物馆宣传

11. 各成员国应通过地方当局或其本身的文化关系或旅游服务等媒介，并在国家教育和国际关系的范围内，尽力鼓励人们多参观博物馆及馆内安排的展览。

12.（1）各成员国应敦促国家或地方旅游机构把鼓励人们多参观博物馆并将其部分活动及资源用于此目的作为它们的主要目标之一。

（2）应邀请博物馆经常利用这些旅游机构提供的服务并使之与博物馆自身扩大其社会和文化影响的努力相联系。

五、博物馆的社会地位及作用

13. 博物馆应成为其所在地区的知识和文化中心从而有助于社会的知识和文化生活；相应的社会应得到参与博物馆活动及发展的机会。这应特别适用于那些位于小城镇及乡村的博物馆，这些博物馆的重要性常常与其规模不成比例。

14. 博物馆与社会团体如专业组织、工会及工商企业的社会服务机构之间，应建立密切的文化关系。

15. 博物馆与广播、电视服务机构以及企事业单位之间亦应建立或增进合作，以便使博物馆展览能在最大限度的安全保障之下为成人教育及学校教育所用。

16. 对于博物馆为学校和成人教育所能做出的贡献，应予以承认并给予鼓励，这应通过设立适当的机构进一步系统化，这些机构负责在地方教育部门负责人与那些因其藏品性质而对学校特别重要的博物馆之间建立正式和定期的联系。这种合作，可采取以下形式：

（1）各博物馆可在其本身职员中配备教育专家，以便在义务部门主管的监督下利用博物馆组织以教育为目的的活动；

（2）博物馆可成立教育部门，并约请教师提供服务；

（3）为确保博物馆最充分实现教育目的，可建立地方、地区及省一级的业务部门主管与教师的联合委员会；

17. 各成员国应该（特别使通过提供法律便利条件）促进博物馆之友协会或能给予博物馆道义和物质援助的类似协会的建立和发展。这些协会应被授予为实现其目的所需的此类权力和特权。

18. 各成员国应该鼓励发展博物馆俱乐部以便鼓励年轻人参加各种博物馆活动。

Recommendation concerning the Most Effective Means of Rendering Museums Accessible to Everyone

14 December 1960

The General Conference of the United Nations Educational, Scientific and Cultural Organization, meeting in Paris from 14 November to 15 December 1960, at its eleventh session,

Considering that one of the functions of the Organization, as laid down in its Constitution, is to give fresh impulse to popular education and to the spread of culture, to collaborate in the work of advancing the mutual understanding of peoples by instituting collaboration among them to advance the ideal of equality of educational opportunity without regard to race, sex or any distinctions, economic or social, and to maintain, increase and diffuse knowledge,

Considering that museums can effectively contribute towards accomplishing these tasks,

Considering that museums of all kinds are a source of enjoyment and instruction,

Considering also that museums, by preserving works of art and scientific material and presenting them to the public, help to disseminate a knowledge of the various cultures and thus promote mutual understanding among nations,

Considering in consequence that every effort should be made to encourage all sections of the population, and especially the working classes, to visit museums,

Considering that with the progress in the industrial organization of the world, people have more leisure, and that such leisure should be used for the benefit and the cultural advancement of all, Recognizing the new social conditions and needs which the museums must take into account in order to carry out their permanent educational mission and satisfy the cultural aspirations of the workers,

Having before it proposals concerning the most effective means of rendering museums accessible to everyone, constituting item 17. 4. 1 of the agenda of the session,

Having decided at its tenth session that proposals on the question should be the subject of international regulation by way of a recommendation to Member States,

Adopt this Recommendation on the fourteenth day of December 1960.

The General Conference recommends that Member States should apply the following provisions by taking whatever legislative or other steps may be required to give effect, within their respective territories, to the principles and norms set forth in this Recommendation.

The General Conference recommends that Member States should bring this Recommendation to the knowledge of the authorities and bodies concerned with museums, and of the museums themselves.

The General Conference recommends that Member States should report to it, on dates and in a manner to be determined by it, on the action they have taken to give effect to this Recommendation.

I. Definition

1. For the purposes of this Recommendation, the term `museum' shall be taken to mean any permanent establishment administered in the general interest for the purpose of preserving, studying, enhancing by various means and, in particular, exhibiting to the public for its delectation and instruction, groups of objects and specimens of cultural value: artistic, historical, scientific and technological collections, botanical and zoological gardens and aquariums.

II. General principles

2. Member States should take all appropriate steps to ensure that the museums on their territory are accessible to all without regard to economic or social sta-

tus.

3. To that end, account should be taken, in selecting the measures to be applied, of the different forms of museum administration that may exist in individual Member States. The measures might vary, for example, according to whether museums are owned and administered by the State or whether, even if not State owned, they receive regular or occasional financial assistance from the State, or whether the State participates in their management in a scientific, technical or administrative capacity.

III. Material arrangements in and admission to museums

4. The collections should be made easy for all types of people to appreciate by a clear form of presentation, by the systematic placing of notices or labels giving concise information, by the publication of guide books and folders which provide visitors with such explanations as they require and by the organization - of regular guided visits accompanied by a commentary adapted to the, various categories of visitors; the guides should be properly qualified persons, preferably appointed through the agency of the bodies referred to in paragraph 16 of this Recommendation; discreet use may be made of apparatus for the reproduction of recorded commentaries.

5. Museums should be open every day and at hours convenient for all categories of visitors, particular account being taken of workers' leisure time. They should be provided with a sufficiently large supervisory staff to permit of a rota system so that the museum can remain open every day without interruption - subject to local conditions and customs - as well as every evening after working hours. They should be installed with the necessary equipment for lighting, heating, etc.

6. Museums should be easily accessible, and should be made as attractive as possible, with a measure of comfort. Provided that the character of the establishment is respected and that visits to the collections are not disturbed there - by, lounges, restaurants, cafes and the like should be provided for the public, preferably within the precincts of the museum (in gardens, on terraces, in. suitable basements, etc.) or in the immediate vicinity.

7. Admission should be free whenever possible. In cases where admission is

not always free and where it is considered necessary to maintain a small admission fee, even if only a token charge, admission to every museum should be free during at least one day a week, or for an equivalent period.

8. Where an admission fee is. charged, it should be waived for persons in low - income groups and for members of large families in those countries in which there exist official methods of identifying these groups.

9. Special facilities should be provided to encourage regular visits, such as, reduced subscription fees for a given period entitling the subscriber to an unlimited number of entries to a particular museum or group of museums.

10. Free admission should whenever possible be granted to organized parties - whether of school - children or adults - taking part in educational and cultural programmes, and also to members of the museum or of the associations mentioned in paragraph 17 of this Recommendation.

IV. Publicity for museums

11. Member States should, through the intermediary of either the local authorities or of their own cultural relations or tourist services, and in the context of national education and international relations, do everything in their power to encourage increased visits to museums and to exhibitions arranged therein.

12. (a) Member States should urge national or regional tourist agencies to make it one of their main objectives to encourage increased visits to museums and to devote part of their activities and resources to that end.

(b) Museums should be invited to make regular use of the services of those agencies and to associate them with their own efforts to extend their social and cultural influence.

V. Place and role of museums in the community

13. Museums should serve as intellectual and cultural centers in their own localities. They should therefore contribute to the intellectual and cultural life of the community, which in turn should be given the opportunity of taking part in the activities and development of the museums. This should apply in particular to muse-

ums situated in small towns and villages and whose importance is often out of proportion to their size.

14. Close cultural relations should be established between museums and groups in the community, such as professional organizations, trade unions, and social services in industrial and business enterprises.

15. Co - operation between museums and radio and television services and undertakings should also be established or improved so that museum exhibits can be used for the purposes of adult and school education with the maximum safety precautions.

16. The contribution which museums can make to school and adult education should be recognized and encouraged. It should furthermore be systematized by the establishment of appropriate bodies responsible for establishing official and regular liaison between local educational leaders and museums which, owing to the nature of their collections, are of particular interest to schools. This co - operation might take the following forms:

(a) Each museum might have on its staff - educational specialists, to organize,

under the curator's supervision, the use of the museum for educational purposes ;

(b) Museums might set up educational departments, which would call on the services of teachers;

(c) Joint committees of curators and teachers might be established at local, regional or provincial level to ensure that the best use is made of museums for educational purposes;

(d) Any other measures which would co - ordinate the demands of education and the resources of museums.

17. Member States should promote (in particular by granting legal facilities) the establishment and development of associations of friends of the museum or similar associations able to lend their moral and material support to museums. These associations should be granted such powers and privileges as they require to fulfill their purpose.

18. Member States should encourage the development of museum clubs to encourage young people to take part in various museum activities.

第四部分　文物与文化遗产保护

Part Ⅳ　Protection of Antique and Cultural Heritage

保护非物质文化遗产公约

（联合国教科文组织 2003 年 10 月 17 日通过。我国 2004 年 12 月 2 日递交批准书）

联合国教育、科学及文化组织（以下简称教科文组织）大会于 2003 年 9 月 29 日至 10 月 17 日在巴黎举行的第 32 届会议，参照现有的国际人权文书，尤其是 1948 年的《世界人权宣言》以及 1966 年的《经济、社会及文化权利国际公约》和《公民权利和政治权利国际公约》，考虑到 1989 年的《保护民间创作建议书》、2001 年的《教科文组织世界文化多样性宣言》和 2002 年第三次文化部长圆桌会议通过的《伊斯坦布尔宣言》强调非物质文化遗产的重要性，它是文化多样性的熔炉，又是可持续发展的保证，考虑到非物质文化遗产与物质文化遗产和自然遗产之间的内在相互依存关系，承认全球化和社会转型进程在为各群体之间开展新的对话创造条件的同时，也与不容忍现象一样，使非物质文化遗产面临损坏、消失和破坏的严重威胁，在缺乏保护资源的情况下，这种威胁尤为严重。

意识到保护人类非物质文化遗产是普遍的意愿和共同关心的事项。

承认各社区，尤其是原住民、各群体，有时是个人，在非物质文化遗产的生产、保护、延续和再创造方面发挥着重要作用，从而为丰富文化多样性和人类的创造性做出贡献。

注意到教科文组织在制定保护文化遗产的准则性文件，尤其是 1972 年的《保护世界文化和自然遗产公约》方面所做的具有深远意义的工作。

还注意到迄今尚无有约束力的保护非物质文化遗产的多边文件。

考虑到国际上现有的关于文化遗产和自然遗产的协定、建议书和决议需要有非物质文化遗产方面的新规定有效地予以充实和补充。

考虑到必须提高人们，尤其是年轻一代对非物质文化遗产及其保护的重要意义的认识。

考虑到国际社会应当本着互助合作的精神与本公约缔约国一起为保护此

类遗产做出贡献，忆及教科文组织有关非物质文化遗产的各项计划，尤其是“宣布人类口头遗产和非物质遗产代表作”计划，认为非物质文化遗产是密切人与人之间的关系以及他们之间进行交流和了解的要素，它的作用是不可估量的，于2003年10月17日通过本公约。

第一章　总　　则

第一条　本公约的宗旨

本公约的宗旨如下：

（一）保护非物质文化遗产；

（二）尊重有关社区、群体和个人的非物质文化遗产；

（三）在地方、国家和国际一级提高对非物质文化遗产及其相互欣赏的重要性的意识；

（四）开展国际合作及提供国际援助。

第二条　定义

在本公约中：

（一）“非物质文化遗产”，指被各社区、群体，有时是个人，视为其文化遗产组成部分的各种社会实践、观念表述、表现形式、知识、技能以及相关的工具、实物、手工艺品和文化场所。这种非物质文化遗产世代相传，在各社区和群体适应周围环境以及与自然和历史的互动中，被不断地再创造，为这些社区和群体提供认同感和持续感，从而增强对文化多样性和人类创造力的尊重。在本公约中，只考虑符合现有的国际人权文件，各社区、群体和个人之间相互尊重的需要和顺应可持续发展的非物质文化遗产。

（二）按上述第（一）项的定义，“非物质文化遗产”包括以下方面：

1. 口头传统和表现形式，包括作为非物质文化遗产媒介的语言；

2. 表演艺术；

3. 社会实践、仪式、节庆活动；

4. 有关自然界和宇宙的知识和实践；

5. 传统手工艺。

（三）“保护”指确保非物质文化遗产生命力的各种措施，包括这种遗产各个方面的确认、立档、研究、保存、保护、宣传、弘扬、传承（特别是通过正规和非正规教育）和振兴。

（四）“缔约国”指受本公约约束且本公约在它们之间也通用的国家。

（五）本公约经必要修改对根据第三十三条所述之条件成为其缔约方之领土也适用。在此意义上，“缔约国”亦指这些领土。

第三条 与其他国际文书的关系

本公约的任何条款均不得解释为：

（一）改变与任一非物质文化遗产直接相关的世界遗产根据 1972 年《保护世界文化和自然遗产公约》所享有的地位，或降低受其保护的程度；

（二）影响缔约国从其作为缔约方的任何有关知识产权或使用生物和生态资源的国际文书所获得的权利和所负有的义务。

第二章 公约的有关机关

第四条 缔约国大会

一、兹建立缔约国大会，下称“大会”。大会为本公约的最高权力机关。

二、大会每两年举行一次常会。如若它作出此类决定或政府间保护非物质文化遗产委员会或至少三分之一的缔约国提出要求，可举行特别会议。

三、大会应通过自己的议事规则。

第五条 政府间保护非物质文化遗产委员会

一、兹在教科文组织内设立政府间保护非物质文化遗产委员会，下称“委员会”。在本公约依照第三十四条的规定生效之后，委员会由参加大会之缔约国选出的 18 个缔约国的代表组成。

二、在本公约缔约国的数目达到 50 个之后，委员会委员国的数目将增至 24 个。

第六条 委员会委员国的选举和任期

一、委员会委员国的选举应符合公平的地理分配和轮换原则。

二、委员会委员国由本公约缔约国大会选出，任期四年。

三、但第一次选举当选的半数委员会委员国的任期为两年。这些国家在第一次选举后抽签指定。

四、大会每两年对半数委员会委员国进行换届。

五、大会还应选出填补空缺席位所需的委员会委员国。

六、委员会委员国连选连任不得超过两届。

七、委员会委员国应选派在非物质文化遗产各领域有造诣的人士为其代表。

第七条 委员会的职能

在不妨碍本公约赋予委员会的其他职权的情况下，其职能如下：

（一）宣传公约的目标，鼓励并监督其实施情况；

（二）就好的做法和保护非物质文化遗产的措施提出建议；

（三）按照第二十五条的规定，拟订利用基金资金的计划并提交大会批准；

（四）按照第二十五条的规定，努力寻求增加其资金的方式方法，并为此采取必要的措施；

（五）拟订实施公约的业务指南并提交大会批准；

（六）根据第二十九条的规定，审议缔约国的报告并将报告综述提交大会；

（七）根据委员会制定的、大会批准的客观遴选标准，审议缔约国提出的申请并就以下事项作出决定：

1. 列入第十六条、第十七条和第十八条述及的名录和提名；

2. 按照第二十二条的规定提供国际援助。

第八条 委员会的工作方法

一、委员会对大会负责。它向大会报告自己的所有活动和决定。

二、委员会以其委员的三分之二多数通过自己的议事规则。

三、委员会可设立其认为执行任务所需的临时特设咨询机构。

四、委员会可邀请在非物质文化遗产各领域确有专长的任何公营或私营机构以及任何自然人参加会议，就任何具体的问题向其请教。

第九条 咨询组织的认证

一、委员会应建议大会认证在非物质文化遗产领域确有专长的非政府组织具有向委员会提供咨询意见的能力。

二、委员会还应向大会就此认证的标准和方式提出建议。

第十条 秘书处

一、委员会由教科文组织秘书处协助。

二、秘书处起草大会和委员会文件及其会议的议程草案和确保其决定的执行。

第三章 在国家一级保护非物质文化遗产

第十一条 缔约国的作用

各缔约国应该：

（一）采取必要措施确保其领土上的非物质文化遗产受到保护；

（二）在第二条第（三）项提及的保护措施内，由各社区、群体和有关非政府组织参与，确认和确定其领土上的各种非物质文化遗产。

第十二条 清单

一、为了使其领土上的非物质文化遗产得到确认以便加以保护，各缔约国应根据自己的国情拟订一份或数份关于这类遗产的清单，并应定期加以更新。

二、各缔约国在按第二十九条的规定定期向委员会提交报告时，应提供有关这些清单的情况。

第十三条 其他保护措施

为了确保其领土上的非物质文化遗产得到保护、弘扬和展示，各缔约国应努力做到：

（一）制定一项总的政策，使非物质文化遗产在社会中发挥应有的作用，并将这种遗产的保护纳入规划工作；

（二）指定或建立一个或数个主管保护其领土上的非物质文化遗产的机构；

（三）鼓励开展有效保护非物质文化遗产，特别是濒危非物质文化遗产的科学、技术和艺术研究以及方法研究；

（四）采取适当的法律、技术、行政和财政措施，以便：

1. 促进建立或加强培训管理非物质文化遗产的机构以及通过为这种遗产提供活动和表现的场所和空间，促进这种遗产的传承；

2. 确保对非物质文化遗产的享用，同时对享用这种遗产的特殊方面的习俗做法予以尊重；

3. 建立非物质文化遗产文献机构并创造条件促进对它的利用。

第十四条 教育、宣传和能力培养

各缔约国应竭力采取种种必要的手段，以便：

（一）使非物质文化遗产在社会中得到确认、尊重和弘扬，主要通过：

1. 向公众，尤其是向青年进行宣传和传播信息的教育计划；

2. 有关社区和群体的具体的教育和培训计划；

3. 保护非物质文化遗产，尤其是管理和科研方面的能力培养活动；

4. 非正规的知识传播手段。

（二）不断向公众宣传对这种遗产造成的威胁以及根据本公约所开展的活动；

（三）促进保护表现非物质文化遗产所需的自然场所和纪念地点的教育。

第十五条 社区、群体和个人的参与

缔约国在开展保护非物质文化遗产活动时，应努力确保创造、延续和传

承这种遗产的社区、群体，有时是个人的最大限度的参与，并吸收他们积极地参与有关的管理。

第四章 在国际一级保护非物质文化遗产

第十六条 人类非物质文化遗产代表作名录

一、为了扩大非物质文化遗产的影响，提高对其重要意义的认识和从尊重文化多样性的角度促进对话，委员会应该根据有关缔约国的提名编辑、更新和公布人类非物质文化遗产代表作名录。

二、委员会拟订有关编辑、更新和公布此代表作名录的标准并提交大会批准。

第十七条 急需保护的非物质文化遗产名录

一、为了采取适当的保护措施，委员会编辑、更新和公布急需保护的非物质文化遗产名录，并根据有关缔约国的要求将此类遗产列入该名录。

二、委员会拟订有关编辑、更新和公布此名录的标准并提交大会批准。

三、委员会在极其紧急的情况（其具体标准由大会根据委员会的建议加以批准）下，可与有关缔约国协商将有关的遗产列入第一款所提之名录。

第十八条 保护非物质文化遗产的计划、项目和活动

一、在缔约国提名的基础上，委员会根据其制定的、大会批准的标准，兼顾发展中国家的特殊需要，定期遴选并宣传其认为最能体现本公约原则和目标的国家、分地区或地区保护非物质文化遗产的计划、项目和活动。

二、为此，委员会接受、审议和批准缔约国提交的关于要求国际援助拟订此类提名的申请。

三、委员会按照它确定的方式，配合这些计划、项目和活动的实施，随时推广有关经验。

第五章 国际合作与援助

第十九条 合作

一、在本公约中，国际合作主要是交流信息和经验，采取共同的行动，以及建立援助缔约国保护非物质文化遗产工作的机制。

二、在不违背国家法律规定及其习惯法和习俗的情况下，缔约国承认保护非物质文化遗产符合人类的整体利益，保证为此目的在双边、分地区、地

区和国际各级开展合作。

第二十条 国际援助的目的

可为如下目的提供国际援助：

（一）保护列入《急需保护的非物质文化遗产名录》的遗产；

（二）按照第十一条和第十二条的精神编制清单；

（三）支持在国家、分地区和地区开展的保护非物质文化遗产的计划、项目和活动；

（四）委员会认为必要的其他一切目的。

第二十一条 国际援助的形式

第七条的业务指南和第二十四条所指的协定对委员会向缔约国提供援助作了规定，可采取的形式如下：

（一）对保护这种遗产的各个方面进行研究；

（二）提供专家和专业人员；

（三）培训各类所需人员；

（四）制订准则性措施或其他措施；

（五）基础设施的建立和营运；

（六）提供设备和技能；

（七）其他财政和技术援助形式，包括在必要时提供低息贷款和捐助。

第二十二条 国际援助的条件

一、委员会确定审议国际援助申请的程序和具体规定申请的内容，包括打算采取的措施、必须开展的工作及预计的费用。

二、如遇紧急情况，委员会应对有关援助申请优先审议。

三、委员会在作出决定之前，应进行其认为必要的研究和咨询。

第二十三条 国际援助的申请

一、各缔约国可向委员会递交国际援助的申请，保护在其领土上的非物质文化遗产。

二、此类申请亦可由两个或数个缔约国共同提出。

三、申请应包含第二十二条第一款规定的所有资料和所有必要的文件。

第二十四条 受援缔约国的任务

一、根据本公约的规定，国际援助应依据受援缔约国与委员会之间签署的协定来提供。

二、受援缔约国通常应在自己力所能及的范围内分担国际所援助的保护措施的费用。

三、受援缔约国应向委员会报告关于使用所提供的保护非物质文化遗产援助的情况。

第六章　非物质文化遗产基金

第二十五条　基金的性质和资金来源

一、兹建立一项“保护非物质文化遗产基金”，下称“基金”。

二、根据教科文组织《财务条例》的规定，此项基金为信托基金。

三、基金的资金来源包括：

（一）缔约国的纳款；

（二）教科文组织大会为此所拨的资金；

（三）以下各方可能提供的捐款、赠款或遗赠：

1. 其他国家；

2. 联合国系统各组织和各署（特别是联合国开发计划署）以及其他国际组织；

3. 公营或私营机构和个人。

（四）基金的资金所得的利息；

（五）为本基金募集的资金和开展活动之所得；

（六）委员会制定的基金条例所许可的所有其他资金。

四、委员会对资金的使用视大会的方针来决定。

五、委员会可接受用于某些项目的一般或特定目的的捐款及其他形式的援助，只要这些项目已获委员会的批准。

六、对基金的捐款不得附带任何与本公约所追求之目标不相符的政治、经济或其他条件。

第二十六条　缔约国对基金的纳款

一、在不妨碍任何自愿补充捐款的情况下，本公约缔约国至少每两年向基金纳一次款，其金额由大会根据适用于所有国家的统一的纳款额百分比加以确定。缔约国大会关于此问题的决定由出席会议并参加表决，但未作本条第二款中所述声明的缔约国的多数通过。在任何情况下，此纳款都不得超过缔约国对教科文组织正常预算纳款的百分之一。

二、但是，本公约第三十二条或第三十三条中所指的任何国家均可在交存批准书、接受书、核准书或加入书时声明不受本条第一款规定的约束。

三、已作本条第二款所述声明的本公约缔约国应努力通知联合国教育、科学及文化组织总干事收回所作声明。但是，收回声明之举不得影响该国在紧接着的下一届大会开幕之日前应缴的纳款。

四、为使委员会能够有效地规划其工作，已作本条第二款所述声明的本公约缔约国至少应每两年定期纳一次款，纳款额应尽可能接近它们按本条第一款规定应交的数额。

五、凡拖欠当年和前一日历年的义务纳款或自愿捐款的本公约缔约国不能当选为委员会委员，但此项规定不适用于第一次选举。已当选为委员会委员的缔约国的任期应在本公约第六条规定的选举之时终止。

第二十七条 基金的自愿补充捐款

除了第二十六条所规定的纳款，希望提供自愿捐款的缔约国应及时通知委员会以使其能对相应的活动作出规划。

第二十八条 国际筹资运动

缔约国应尽力支持在教科文组织领导下为该基金发起的国际筹资运动。

第七章 报 告

第二十九条 缔约国的报告

缔约国应按照委员会确定的方式和周期向其报告它们为实施本公约而通过的法律、规章条例或采取的其他措施的情况。

第三十条 委员会的报告

一、委员会应在其开展的活动和第二十九条提及的缔约国报告的基础上，向每届大会提交报告。

二、该报告应提交教科文组织大会。

第八章 过渡条款

第三十一条 与宣布人类口头和非物质遗产代表作的关系

一、委员会应把在本公约生效前宣布为“人类口头和非物质遗产代表作”的遗产纳入人类非物质文化遗产代表作名录。

二、把这些遗产纳入人类非物质文化遗产代表作名录绝不是预设按第十六条第二款将确定的今后列入遗产的标准。

三、在本公约生效后，将不再宣布其他任何人类口头和非物质遗产代表作。

第九章　最后条款

第三十二条　批准、接受或核准

一、本公约须由教科文组织会员国根据各自的宪法程序予以批准、接受或核准。

二、批准书、接受书或核准书应交存教科文组织总干事。

第三十三条　加入

一、所有非教科文组织会员国的国家，经本组织大会邀请，均可加入本公约。

二、没有完全独立，但根据联合国大会第 1514（XV）号决议被联合国承认为充分享有内部自治，并且有权处理本公约范围内的事宜，包括有权就这些事宜签署协议的地区也可加入本公约。

三、加入书应交存教科文组织总干事。

第三十四条　生效

本公约在第三十份批准书、接受书、核准书或加入书交存之日起的三个月后生效，但只涉及在该日或该日之前交存批准书、接受书、核准书或加入书的国家。对其他缔约国来说，本公约则在这些国家的批准书、接受书、核准书或加入书交存之日起的三个月之后生效。

第三十五条　联邦制或非统一立宪制

对实行联邦制或非统一立宪制的缔约国实行下述规定：

（一）在联邦或中央立法机构的法律管辖下实施本公约各项条款的国家的联邦或中央政府的义务与非联邦国家的缔约国的义务相同；

（二）在构成联邦，但按照联邦立宪制无须采取立法手段的各个州、成员国、省或行政区的法律管辖下实施本公约的各项条款时，联邦政府应将这些条款连同其建议一并通知各个州、成员国、省或行政区的主管当局。

第三十六条　退出

一、各缔约国均可宣布退出本公约。

二、退约应以书面退约书的形式通知教科文组织总干事。

三、退约在接到退约书十二个月之后生效。在退约生效日之前不得影响退约国承担的财政义务。

第三十七条　保管人的职责

教科文组织总干事作为本公约的保管人，应将第三十二条和第三十三条规定交存的所有批准书、接受书、核准书或加入书和第三十六条规定的退约书的情况通告本组织各会员国、第三十三条提到的非本组织会员国的国家和联合国。

第三十八条　修订

一、任何缔约国均可书面通知总干事，对本公约提出修订建议。总干事应将此通知转发给所有缔约国。如在通知发出之日起六个月之内，至少有一半的缔约国回复赞成此要求，总干事应将此建议提交下一届大会讨论，决定是否通过。

二、对本公约的修订须经出席并参加表决的缔约国三分之二多数票通过。

三、对本公约的修订一旦通过，应提交缔约国批准、接受、核准或加入。

四、对于那些已批准、接受、核准或加入修订的缔约国来说，本公约的修订在三分之二的缔约国交存本条第三款所提及的文书之日起三个月之后生效。此后，对任何批准、接受、核准或加入修订的缔约国来说，在其交存批准书、接受书、核准书或加入书之日起三个月之后，本公约的修订即生效。

五、第三款和第四款所确定的程序对有关委员会委员国数目的第五条的修订不适用。此类修订一经通过即生效。

六、在修订依照本条第四款的规定生效之后成为本公约缔约国的国家如无表示异议，应

（一）被视为修订的本公约的缔约方；

（二）但在与不受这些修订约束的任何缔约国的关系中，仍被视为未经修订之公约的缔约方。

第三十九条　有效文本

本公约用英文、阿拉伯文、中文、西班牙文、法文和俄文拟定，六种文本具有同等效力。

第四十条　登记

根据《联合国宪章》第一百零二条的规定，本公约应按教科文组织总干事的要求交联合国秘书处登记。

Convention for the Safeguarding of the Intangible Cultural Heritage

Paris, 17 October 2003

The General Conference of the United Nations Educational, Scientific and Cultural Organization hereinafter referred to as UNESCO, meeting in Paris, from 29 September to 17 October 2003, at its 32nd session,

Referring to existing international human rights instruments, in particular to the Universal Declaration on Human Rights of 1948, the International Covenant on Economic, Social and Cultural Rights of 1966, and the International Covenant on Civil and Political Rights of 1966,

Considering the importance of the intangible cultural heritage as a mainspring of cultural diversity and a guarantee of sustainable development, as underscored in the UNESCO Recommendation on the Safeguarding of Traditional Culture and Folklore of 1989, in the UNESCO Universal Declaration on Cultural Diversity of 2001, and in the Istanbul Declaration of 2002 adopted by the Third Round Table of Ministers of Culture,

Considering the deep - seated interdependence between the intangible cultural heritage and the tangible cultural and natural heritage,

Recognizing that the processes of globalization and social transformation, alongside the conditions they create for renewed dialogue among communities, also give rise, as does the phenomenon of intolerance, to grave threats of deterioration, disappearance and destruction of the intangible cultural heritage, in particular owing to a lack of resources for safeguarding such heritage,

Being aware of the universal will and the common concern to safeguard the intangible cultural heritage of humanity,

Recognizing that communities, in particular indigenous communities, groups and, in some cases, individuals, play an important role in the production, safeguarding, maintenance and re - creation of the intangible cultural heritage, thus helping to enrich cultural diversity and human creativity,

Noting the far - reaching impact of the activities of UNESCO in establishing normative instruments for the protection of the cultural heritage, in particular the Convention for the Protection of the World Cultural and Natural Heritage of 1972,

Noting further that no binding multilateral instrument as yet exists for the safeguarding of the intangible cultural heritage,

Considering that existing international agreements, recommendations and resolutions concerning the cultural and natural heritage need to be effectively enriched and supplemented by means of new provisions relating to the intangible cultural heritage,

Considering the need to build greater awareness, especially among the younger generations, of the importance of the intangible cultural heritage and of its safeguarding,

Considering that the international community should contribute, together with the States Parties to this Convention, to the safeguarding of such heritage in a spirit of cooperation and mutual assistance,

Recalling UNESCO's programmes relating to the intangible cultural heritage, in particular the Proclamation of Masterpieces of the Oral and Intangible Heritage of Humanity,

Considering the invaluable role of the intangible cultural heritage as a factor in bringing human beings closer together and ensuring exchange and understanding among them,

Adopts this Convention on this seventeenth day of October 2003.

I. General provisions

Article 1 – Purposes of the Convention

The purposes of this Convention are:

(a) to safeguard the intangible cultural heritage;

(b) to ensure respect for the intangible cultural heritage of the communities, groups and individuals concerned;

(c) to raise awareness at the local, national and international levels of the importance of the intangible cultural heritage, and of ensuring mutual appreciation thereof;

(d) to provide for international cooperation and assistance.

Article 2 – Definitions

For the purposes of this Convention,

1. The "intangible cultural heritage" means the practices, representations, expressions, knowledge, skills - as well as the instruments, objects, artefacts and cultural spaces associated therewith - that communities, groups and, in some cases, individuals recognize as part of their cultural heritage. This intangible cultural heritage, transmitted from generation to generation, is constantly recreated by communities and groups in response to their environment, their interaction with nature and their history, and provides them with a sense of identity and continuity, thus promoting respect for cultural diversity and human creativity. For the purposes of this Convention, consideration will be given solely to such intangible cultural heritage as is compatible with existing international human rights instruments, as well as with the requirements of mutual respect among communities, groups and individuals, and of sustainable development.

2. The "intangible cultural heritage", as defined in paragraph 1 above, is manifested inter alia in the following domains:

(a) oral traditions and expressions, including language as a vehicle of the intangible cultural heritage;

(b) performing arts;

(c) social practices, rituals and festive events;

(d) knowledge and practices concerning nature and the universe;

(e) traditional craftsmanship.

3. "Safeguarding" means measures aimed at ensuring the viability of the intangible cultural heritage, including the identification, documentation, research, preservation, protection, promotion, enhancement, transmission, particularly through formal and non - formal education, as well as the revitalization of the various aspects of such heritage.

4. "States Parties" means States which are bound by this Convention and among which this Convention is in force.

5. This Convention applies mutatis mutandis to the territories referred to in Article 33 which become Parties to this Convention in accordance with the conditions set out in that Article. To that extent the expression "States Parties" also refers to such territories.

Article 3 – Relationship to other international instruments

Nothing in this Convention may be interpreted as:

(a) altering the status or diminishing the level of protection under the 1972 Convention concerning the Protection of the World Cultural and Natural Heritage of World Heritage properties with which an item of the intangible cultural heritage is directly associated; or

(b) affecting the rights and obligations of States Parties deriving from any international instrument relating to intellectual property rights or to the use of biological and ecological resources to which they are parties.

II. Organs of the Convention

Article 4 – General Assembly of the States Parties

1. A General Assembly of the States Parties is hereby established, hereinafter referred to as "the General Assembly". The General Assembly is the sovereign body of this Convention.

2. The General Assembly shall meet in ordinary session every two years. It may meet in extraordinary session if it so decides or at the request either of the Intergovernmental Committee for the Safeguarding of the Intangible Cultural Heritage or of at least one - third of the States Parties.

3. The General Assembly shall adopt its own Rules of Procedure.

Article 5 – Intergovernmental Committee for the Safeguarding of the Intangible Cultural Heritage

1. An Intergovernmental Committee for the Safeguarding of the Intangible Cultural Heritage, hereinafter referred to as "the Committee", is hereby established within UNESCO. It shall be composed of representatives of 18 States Parties, elected by the States Parties meeting in General Assembly, once this Convention enters into force in accordance with Article 34.

2. The number of States Members of the Committee shall be increased to 24

once the number of the States Parties to the Convention reaches 50.

Article 6 – Election and terms of office of States Members of the Committee

1. The election of States Members of the Committee shall obey the principles of equitable geographical representation and rotation.

2. States Members of the Committee shall be elected for a term of four years by States Parties to the Convention meeting in General Assembly.

3. However, the term of office of half of the States Members of the Committee elected at the first election is limited to two years. These States shall be chosen by lot at the first election.

4. Every two years, the General Assembly shall renew half of the States Members of the Committee.

5. It shall also elect as many States Members of the Committee as required to fill vacancies.

6. A State Member of the Committee may not be elected for two consecutive terms.

7. States Members of the Committee shall choose as their representatives persons who are qualified in the various fields of the intangible cultural heritage.

Article 7 – Functions of the Committee

Without prejudice to other prerogatives granted to it by this Convention, the functions of the Committee shall be to:

(a) promote the objectives of the Convention, and to encourage and monitor the implementation thereof;

(b) provide guidance on best practices and make recommendations on measures for the safeguarding of the intangible cultural heritage;

(c) prepare and submit to the General Assembly for approval a draft plan for the use of the resources of the Fund, in accordance with Article 25;

(d) seek means of increasing its resources, and to take the necessary measures to this end, in accordance with Article 25;

(e) prepare and submit to the General Assembly for approval operational directives for the implementation of this Convention;

(f) examine, in accordance with Article 29, the reports submitted by States Parties, and to summarize them for the General Assembly;

(g) examine requests submitted by States Parties, and to decide thereon, in accordance with objective selection criteria to be established by the Committee and approved by the General Assembly for:

(i) inscription on the lists and proposals mentioned under Articles 16, 17 and 18;

(ii) the granting of international assistance in accordance with Article 22.

Article 8 – Working methods of the Committee

1. The Committee shall be answerable to the General Assembly. It shall report to it on all its activities and decisions.

2. The Committee shall adopt its own Rules of Procedure by a two - thirds majority of its Members.

3. The Committee may establish, on a temporary basis, whatever ad hoc consultative bodies it deems necessary to carry out its task.

4. The Committee may invite to its meetings any public or private bodies, as well as private persons, with recognized competence in the various fields of the intangible cultural heritage, in order to consult them on specific matters.

Article 9 – Accreditation of advisory organizations

1. The Committee shall propose to the General Assembly the accreditation of non - governmental organizations with recognized competence in the field of the intangible cultural heritage to act in an advisory capacity to the Committee.

2. The Committee shall also propose to the General Assembly the criteria for and modalities of such accreditation.

Article 10 – The Secretariat

1. The Committee shall be assisted by the UNESCO Secretariat.

2. The Secretariat shall prepare the documentation of the General Assembly and of the Committee, as well as the draft agenda of their meetings, and shall ensure the implementation of their decisions.

III. Safeguarding of the intangible cultural heritage at the national level

Article 11 – Role of States Parties

Each State Party shall:

(a) take the necessary measures to ensure the safeguarding of the intangible cultural heritage present in its territory;

(b) among the safeguarding measures referred to in Article 2, paragraph 3, identify and define the various elements of the intangible cultural heritage present in its territory, with the participation of communities, groups and relevant non - governmental organizations.

Article 12 – Inventories

1. To ensure identification with a view to safeguarding, each State Party shall draw up, in a manner geared to its own situation, one or more inventories of the intangible cultural heritage present in its territory. These inventories shall be regularly updated.

2. When each State Party periodically submits its report to the Committee, in accordance with Article 29, it shall provide relevant information on such inventories.

Article 13 – Other measures for safeguarding

To ensure the safeguarding, development and promotion of the intangible cultural heritage present in its territory, each State Party shall endeavour to:

(a) adopt a general policy aimed at promoting the function of the intangible cultural heritage in society, and at integrating the safeguarding of such heritage into planning programmes;

(b) designate or establish one or more competent bodies for the safeguarding of the intangible cultural heritage present in its territory;

(c) foster scientific, technical and artistic studies, as well as research methodologies, with a view to effective safeguarding of the intangible cultural heritage, in particular the intangible cultural heritage in danger;

(d) adopt appropriate legal, technical, administrative and financial measures aimed at:

(i) fostering the creation or strengthening of institutions for training in the management of the intangible cultural heritage and the transmission of such heritage through forums and spaces intended for the performance or expression thereof;

(ii) ensuring access to the intangible cultural heritage while respecting customary practices governing access to specific aspects of such heritage;

(iii) establishing documentation institutions for the intangible cultural heritage and facilitating access to them.

Article 14 – Education, awareness – raising and capacity – building

Each State Party shall endeavour, by all appropriate means, to:

(a) ensure recognition of, respect for, and enhancement of the intangible cultural heritage in society, in particular through:

(i) educational, awareness - raising and information programmes, aimed at the general public, in particular young people;

(ii) specific educational and training programmes within the communities and groups concerned;

(iii) capacity - building activities for the safeguarding of the intangible cultural heritage, in particular management and scientific research; and

(iv) non - formal means of transmitting knowledge;

(b) keep the public informed of the dangers threatening such heritage, and of the activities carried out in pursuance of this Convention;

(c) promote education for the protection of natural spaces and places of memory whose existence is necessary for expressing the intangible cultural heritage.

Article 15 – Participation of communities, groups and individuals

Within the framework of its safeguarding activities of the intangible cultural heritage, each State Party shall endeavour to ensure the widest possible participation of communities, groups and, where appropriate, individuals that create, maintain and transmit such heritage, and to involve them actively in its management.

IV. Safeguarding of the intangible cultural heritage at the international level

Article 16 – Representative List of the Intangible Cultural Heritage of Humanity

1. In order to ensure better visibility of the intangible cultural heritage and awareness of its significance, and to encourage dialogue which respects cultural diversity, the Committee, upon the proposal of the States Parties concerned, shall establish, keep up to date and publish a Representative List of the Intangible Cultural Heritage of Humanity.

2. The Committee shall draw up and submit to the General Assembly for approval the criteria for the establishment, updating and publication of this Repre-

sentative List.

Article 17 – List of Intangible Cultural Heritage in Need of Urgent Safeguarding

1. With a view to taking appropriate safeguarding measures, the Committee shall establish, keep up to date and publish a List of Intangible Cultural Heritage in Need of Urgent Safeguarding, and shall inscribe such heritage on the List at the request of the State Party concerned.

2. The Committee shall draw up and submit to the General Assembly for approval the criteria for the establishment, updating and publication of this List.

3. In cases of extreme urgency - the objective criteria of which shall be approved by the General Assembly upon the proposal of the Committee - the Committee may inscribe an item of the heritage concerned on the List mentioned in paragraph 1, in consultation with the State Party concerned.

Article 18 – Programmes, projects and activities for the safeguarding of the intangible cultural heritage

1. On the basis of proposals submitted by States Parties, and in accordance with criteria to be defined by the Committee and approved by the General Assembly, the Committee shall periodically select and promote national, subregional and regional programmes, projects and activities for the safeguarding of the heritage which it considers best reflect the principles and objectives of this Convention, taking into account the special needs of developing countries.

2. To this end, it shall receive, examine and approve requests for international assistance from States Parties for the preparation of such proposals.

3. The Committee shall accompany the implementation of such projects, programmes and activities by disseminating best practices using means to be determined by it.

V. International cooperation and assistance

Article 19 – Cooperation

1. For the purposes of this Convention, international cooperation includes, inter alia, the exchange of information and experience, joint initiatives, and the establishment of a mechanism of assistance to States Parties in their efforts to safe-

guard the intangible cultural heritage.

2. Without prejudice to the provisions of their national legislation and customary law and practices, the States Parties recognize that the safeguarding of intangible cultural heritage is of general interest to humanity, and to that end undertake to cooperate at the bilateral, subregional, regional and international levels.

Article 20 – Purposes of international assistance

International assistance may be granted for the following purposes:

(a) the safeguarding of the heritage inscribed on the List of Intangible Cultural Heritage in Need of Urgent Safeguarding;

(b) the preparation of inventories in the sense of Articles 11 and 12;

(c) support for programmes, projects and activities carried out at the national, subregional and regional levels aimed at the safeguarding of the intangible cultural heritage;

(d) any other purpose the Committee may deem necessary.

Article 21 – Forms of international assistance

The assistance granted by the Committee to a State Party shall be governed by the operational directives foreseen in Article 7 and by the agreement referred to in Article 24, and may take the following forms:

(a) studies concerning various aspects of safeguarding;

(b) the provision of experts and practitioners;

(c) the training of all necessary staff;

(d) the elaboration of standard - setting and other measures;

(e) the creation and operation of infrastructures;

(f) the supply of equipment and know - how;

(g) other forms of financial and technical assistance, including, where appropriate, the granting of low - interest loans and donations.

Article 22 – Conditions governing international assistance

1. The Committee shall establish the procedure for examining requests for international assistance, and shall specify what information shall be included in the requests, such as the measures envisaged and the interventions required, together with an assessment of their cost.

2. In emergencies, requests for assistance shall be examined by the Committee as a matter of priority.

3. In order to reach a decision, the Committee shall undertake such studies and consultations as it deems necessary.

Article 23 – Requests for international assistance

1. Each State Party may submit to the Committee a request for international assistance for the safeguarding of the intangible cultural heritage present in its territory.

2. Such a request may also be jointly submitted by two or more States Parties.

3. The request shall include the information stipulated in Article 22, paragraph 1, together with the necessary documentation.

Article 24 – Role of beneficiary States Parties

1. In conformity with the provisions of this Convention, the international assistance granted shall be regulated by means of an agreement between the beneficiary State Party and the Committee.

2. As a general rule, the beneficiary State Party shall, within the limits of its resources, share the cost of the safeguarding measures for which international assistance is provided.

3. The beneficiary State Party shall submit to the Committee a report on the use made of the assistance provided for the safeguarding of the intangible cultural heritage.

VI. Intangible Cultural Heritage Fund

Article 25 – Nature and resources of the Fund

1. A "Fund for the Safeguarding of the Intangible Cultural Heritage", hereinafter referred to as "the Fund", is hereby established.

2. The Fund shall consist of funds - in - trust established in accordance with the Financial Regulations of UNESCO.

3. The resources of the Fund shall consist of:

(a) contributions made by States Parties;

(b) funds appropriated for this purpose by the General Conference of UNESCO;

(c) contributions, gifts or bequests which may be made by:

(i) other States;

(ii) organizations and programmes of the United Nations system, particularly the United Nations Development Programme, as well as other international organizations;

(iii) public or private bodies or individuals;

(d) any interest due on the resources of the Fund;

(e) funds raised through collections, and receipts from events organized for the benefit of the Fund;

(f) any other resources authorized by the Fund's regulations, to be drawn up by the Committee.

4. The use of resources by the Committee shall be decided on the basis of guidelines laid down by the General Assembly.

5. The Committee may accept contributions and other forms of assistance for general and specific purposes relating to specific projects, provided that those projects have been approved by the Committee.

6. No political, economic or other conditions which are incompatible with the objectives of this Convention may be attached to contributions made to the Fund.

Article 26 – Contributions of States Parties to the Fund

1. Without prejudice to any supplementary voluntary contribution, the States Parties to this Convention undertake to pay into the Fund, at least every two years, a contribution, the amount of which, in the form of a uniform percentage applicable to all States, shall be determined by the General Assembly. This decision of the General Assembly shall be taken by a majority of the States Parties present and voting which have not made the declaration referred to in paragraph 2 of this Article. In no case shall the contribution of the State Party exceed 1% of its contribution to the regular budget of UNESCO.

2. However, each State referred to in Article 32 or in Article 33 of this Convention may declare, at the time of the deposit of its instruments of ratification, acceptance, approval or accession, that it shall not be bound by the provisions of paragraph 1 of this Article.

3. A State Party to this Convention which has made the declaration referred to in paragraph 2 of this Article shall endeavour to withdraw the said declaration by notifying the Director - General of UNESCO. However, the withdrawal of the declaration shall not take effect in regard to the contribution due by the State until the

date on which the subsequent session of the General Assembly opens.

4. In order to enable the Committee to plan its operations effectively, the contributions of States Parties to this Convention which have made the declaration referred to in paragraph 2 of this Article shall be paid on a regular basis, at least every two years, and should be as close as possible to the contributions they would have owed if they had been bound by the provisions of paragraph 1 of this Article.

5. Any State Party to this Convention which is in arrears with the payment of its compulsory or voluntary contribution for the current year and the calendar year immediately preceding it shall not be eligible as a Member of the Committee; this provision shall not apply to the first election. The term of office of any such State which is already a Member of the Committee shall come to an end at the time of the elections provided for in Article 6 of this Convention.

Article 27 – Voluntary supplementary contributions to the Fund

States Parties wishing to provide voluntary contributions in addition to those foreseen under Article 26 shall inform the Committee, as soon as possible, so as to enable it to plan its operations accordingly.

Article 28 – International fund – raising campaigns

The States Parties shall, insofar as is possible, lend their support to international fund - raising campaigns organized for the benefit of the Fund under the auspices of UNESCO.

VII. Reports

Article 29 – Reports by the States Parties

The States Parties shall submit to the Committee, observing the forms and periodicity to be defined by the Committee, reports on the legislative, regulatory and other measures taken for the implementation of this Convention.

Article 30 – Reports by the Committee

1. On the basis of its activities and the reports by States Parties referred to in Article 29, the Committee shall submit a report to the General Assembly at each of its sessions.

2. The report shall be brought to the attention of the General Conference of UNESCO.

VIII. Transitional clause

Article 31 – Relationship to the Proclamation of Masterpieces of the Oral and Intangible Heritage of Humanity

1. The Committee shall incorporate in the Representative List of the Intangible Cultural Heritage of Humanity the items proclaimed "Masterpieces of the Oral and Intangible Heritage of Humanity" before the entry into force of this Convention.

2. The incorporation of these items in the Representative List of the Intangible Cultural Heritage of Humanity shall in no way prejudge the criteria for future inscriptions decided upon in accordance with Article 16, paragraph 2.

3. No further Proclamation will be made after the entry into force of this Convention.

IX. Final clauses

Article 32 – Ratification, acceptance or approval

1. This Convention shall be subject to ratification, acceptance or approval by States Members of UNESCO in accordance with their respective constitutional procedures.

2. The instruments of ratification, acceptance or approval shall be deposited with the Director - General of UNESCO.

Article 33 – Accession

1. This Convention shall be open to accession by all States not Members of UNESCO that are invited by the General Conference of UNESCO to accede to it.

2. This Convention shall also be open to accession by territories which enjoy full internal self - government recognized as such by the United Nations, but have not attained full independence in accordance with General Assembly resolution 1514 (XV), and which have competence over the matters governed by this Convention, including the competence to enter into treaties in respect of such matters.

3. The instrument of accession shall be deposited with the Director - General of UNESCO.

Article 34 – Entry into force

This Convention shall enter into force three months after the date of the deposit of the thirtieth instrument of ratification, acceptance, approval or accession, but only with respect to those States that have deposited their respective instruments of ratification, acceptance, approval, or accession on or before that date. It shall enter into force with respect to any other State Party three months after the deposit of its instrument of ratification, acceptance, approval or accession.

Article 35 – Federal or non – unitary constitutional systems

The following provisions shall apply to States Parties which have a federal or non - unitary constitutional system:

(a) with regard to the provisions of this Convention, the implementation of which comes under the legal jurisdiction of the federal or central legislative power, the obligations of the federal or central government shall be the same as for those States Parties which are not federal States;

(b) with regard to the provisions of this Convention, the implementation of which comes under the jurisdiction of individual constituent States, countries, provinces or cantons which are not obliged by the constitutional system of the federation to take legislative measures, the federal government shall inform the competent authorities of such States, countries, provinces or cantons of the said provisions, with its recommendation for their adoption.

Article 36 – Denunciation

1. Each State Party may denounce this Convention.

2. The denunciation shall be notified by an instrument in writing, deposited with the Director - General of UNESCO.

3. The denunciation shall take effect twelve months after the receipt of the instrument of denunciation. It shall in no way affect the financial obligations of the denouncing State Party until the date on which the withdrawal takes effect.

Article 37 – Depositary functions

The Director - General of UNESCO, as the Depositary of this Convention, shall inform the States Members of the Organization, the States not Members of the Organization referred to in Article 33, as well as the United Nations, of the deposit of all the instruments of ratification, acceptance, approval or accession provided for in Articles 32 and 33, and of the denunciations provided for in Article 36.

Article 38 – Amendments

1. A State Party may, by written communication addressed to the Director -

General, propose amendments to this Convention. The Director - General shall circulate such communication to all States Parties. If, within six months from the date of the circulation of the communication, not less than one half of the States Parties reply favourably to the request, the Director - General shall present such proposal to the next session of the General Assembly for discussion and possible adoption.

2. Amendments shall be adopted by a two - thirds majority of States Parties present and voting.

3. Once adopted, amendments to this Convention shall be submitted for ratification, acceptance, approval or accession to the States Parties.

4. Amendments shall enter into force, but solely with respect to the States Parties that have ratified, accepted, approved or acceded to them, three months after the deposit of the instruments referred to in paragraph 3 of this Article by two - thirds of the States Parties. Thereafter, for each State Party that ratifies, accepts, approves or accedes to an amendment, the said amendment shall enter into force three months after the date of deposit by that State Party of its instrument of ratification, acceptance, approval or accession.

5. The procedure set out in paragraphs 3 and 4 shall not apply to amendments to Article 5 concerning the number of States Members of the Committee. These amendments shall enter into force at the time they are adopted.

6. A State which becomes a Party to this Convention after the entry into force of amendments in conformity with paragraph 4 of this Article shall, failing an expression of different intention, be considered:

(a) as a Party to this Convention as so amended; and

(b) as a Party to the unamended Convention in relation to any State Party not bound by the amendments.

Article 39 – Authoritative texts

This Convention has been drawn up in Arabic, Chinese, English, French, Russian and Spanish, the six texts being equally authoritative.

Article 40 – Registration

In conformity with Article 102 of the Charter of the United Nations, this Convention shall be registered with the Secretariat of the United Nations at the request of the Director - General of UNESCO.

保护水下文化遗产公约*

（联合国教科文组织大会2001年11月2日通过）

联合国教育、科学和文化组织大会于2001年10月15日至11月3日在巴黎召开的第31次会议，承认水下文化遗产的重要性，是人类文化遗产不可分割的组成部分，是人民的、国家的以及他们之间的与共同遗产相关的历史上特别重要的一个因素，认识到保护和保存水下文化遗产的重要性以及所有国家为此应当承担的责任，注意到公众对水下文化遗产的日益关注和理解，确信研究、信息和教育对保护和保存水下文化遗产的重要性，确信公众在负责任的非干扰性的接触在原位的水下文化遗产的，有权享受其教育的和娱乐的益处，以及公共教育对于遗产的认知、理解和保护的价值，意识到水下文化遗产遭受未经批准的开发活动的威胁，以及采取更有力的措施以阻止这些活动的必要性，意识到针对会对水下文化遗产造成附带损害的合法活动所产生的可能的负面影响，有必要作出适当的应对，深深担忧对水下文化遗产日益频繁的商业开发，特别是某些以销售、购买或者交换水下文化遗产为目的的活动，意识到可以使用先进的技术增强对水下文化遗产的发现和接触，认为国家、国际组织、科研机构、专业组织、考古学者、潜水员以及其他利益相关团体和公众之间的合作对保护水下文化遗产尤为重要，考虑到水下文化遗产的勘测、挖掘和保护需要使用和应用特别的科学方法，使用合适的技术和设备以及高度的专业知识，所有这些都表明需要一套统一的管理标准，认识到在与国际法律和实践一致的情况下，编撰和逐步发展与保护和保存水下文化遗产相关的规则的必要性，包括1970年11月14日的联合国教科文组织《关于采取措施禁止并防止文化财产非法进出口和所有权非法转让公约》，1972年11月16日的联合国教科文组织《保护世界文化和自然遗产公约》和1982年12月10日的联合国《海洋法公约》，致力于提高国际、区域和国家

---

* 西南政法大学法学院汪梦译。

一级水下文化遗产的就地保护，或者因为科研和保护的需要，谨慎发现的有效措施，已经决定这一问题在第29届大会成为国际公约的对象，于2001年11月2日正式通过该公约。

第一条 定义

为本公约之目的：

1.（a）“水下文化遗产”是指所有的具有文化、历史或者考古特征的，部分或者全部位于水下的，周期性的或者连续的，超过100年的人类生存遗迹，例如：

（Ⅰ）遗址、结构、建筑、文物和人类遗骸，以及其考古的自然的环境；

（Ⅱ）船只、飞行器、其他运输工具或其部分，所载货物或者物品，以及其考古的和自然的环境；以及

（Ⅲ）具有史前特征的物品。

（b）铺设在海床上的管道和电缆不能视为水下文化遗产。

（c）铺设在海床上的除了管道和电缆之外的仍在使用的设备，不能视为水下文化遗产。

2.（a）“缔约国”是指同意接受本公约之约束并且本公约对其有效的国家。

（b）本公约经过修改可以适用于第26条2款（b）中所指的那些根据规定的条件成为本公约的缔约方的地区，就此，“缔约国”也指这些地区。

3.“联合国教科文组织”是指联合国教育、科学及文化组织。

4.“总干事”是指联合国教科文组织的总干事。

5.“区域”是指国家管辖范围以外的海床、洋底及其底土。

6.“水下文化遗产的活动”是指以水下文化遗产为主要对象，并可能直接地或间接地对水下文化遗产造成实质干扰或者破坏的活动。

7.“附带影响水下文化遗产的活动”是指虽然不以水下文化遗产为主要对象或对象之一，但仍旧可能对水下文化遗产造成实质干扰或者破坏的活动。

8.“国家船只和飞行器”是指由国家所有或者操作的，并且在沉没时，仅是为了政府的非商业目的而使用的军舰、其他船只或飞行器，认定为符合水下文化遗产的定义。

9.“规则”是指本公约第33条规定的有关水下文化遗产活动的规则。

第二条 目的和总则

本公约致力于确保和加强对水下文化遗产的保护。

缔约国应当在水下文化遗产的保护上通力合作。

缔约国应当根据本公约为了人类之福祉保护水下文化遗产。

缔约国应当根据本公约和国际法律，依据具体情况单独或者联合，采取一切必要的措施保护水下文化遗产，使用为此目的的最好方法是指根据自身情况和能力。

在允许或进行任何开发水下文化遗产的活动之前，就地保护遗产应当作为首选。

发现的水下文化遗产应当以确保能够长时期保护的方式存放、保存和管理。

水下文化遗产不得进行商业开发。

与国家习惯和包括联合国《海洋法公约》在内的国际法律一致，本公约内任何条款不能作出修改与主权豁免相关的国际法律和国家习惯的规则的解释，也不能改变国家对其船只和飞行器的所有权。

缔约国应当确保对海域中发现的所有人类遗骸给予适当的尊重。

除非与保护和管理水下文化遗产相违背，应当鼓励负责任的非干扰性的接触、观察和记录在原地的水下文化遗产，以便培养公众对遗产的认知、理解和保护。

依据本公约所采取的任何行动或活动不能构成对国家主权或管辖权的要求、主张或者争议的基础。

第三条 本公约与联合国《海洋法公约》的关系

本公约中的任何条款不得损害国际法律规定的国家权利、管辖和责任，包括联合国《海洋法公约》。本公约应当以与国际法律一致的方式进行解释和适用，包括联合国《海洋法公约》。

第四条 与海难救助法律和打捞法律的关系

任何适用于本公约的与水下文化遗产相关的活动不受海难救助和打捞法律规则，除非：

活动由主管机关批准，并且

完全遵守本公约，并且

确保任何发现的水下文化遗产获得最大程度的保护。

第五条 附带影响水下文化遗产的活动

每个缔约国应当根据自身情况使用最切实可行的方法保护或者减轻任何在其管辖范围内进行的水下文化遗产活动产生的附带影响可能造成的不利因素。

第六条 双边、区域或者其他多边协议

为了保护水下文化遗产，鼓励缔约国签订双边、区域或其他多边协议，

或者发展现有协议。所有这些协议应当完全符合本公约的规定，不得削弱其普适性。在这些协议中，国家可以不适用本公约，而是适用更加能够确保水下文化遗产保护的规则和制度。

这些双边、区域或其他多边协议的缔约方可以征求具有可证实的关联的国家，特别是与水下文化遗产相关的文化、历史或者考古的关联，加入该协议。

本公约不得更改在其通过之前的，缔约国缔结的有关沉船保护的其他双边、区域或多边协定中关于权利和义务的规定，特别是那些与本公约目的一致的部分。

第七条　在内水、群岛水域和领海内的水下文化遗产

缔约国行使主权时，对其主权内的内水、群岛水域和领海中的水下文化遗产的活动享有管理和授权活动的绝对权力。

在不违背有关保护水下文化遗产的其他国际协议和国际法律规则的情况下，缔约国应当规定内水、群岛水域和领海中的水下文化遗产的活动适用上述“规则”。

在群岛水域和领海内，行使主权和认可之间的一般习惯的国家和缔约国，希望在保护国家船只和飞行器的最佳可行的方法上合作的，应当向本公约告知悬旗国方，并且在可行的情况下，告知其他有可证实关联的，特别是具有文化、历史或考古关联的其他国家，尊重该认定国家对船只和飞行器的发现。

第八条　毗邻地区的水下文化遗产

在不违背和除第9、10两条之外，以及根据联合国《海洋法公约》第303条2款的规定，缔约国可以管理和授权在其毗邻地区内水下文化遗产的活动。为此，缔约国应当要求适用上述“规则”。

第九条　在专属经济区和大陆架内的报告和通知

所有缔约国都有责任按照本公约的规定保护在其专属经济区内和大陆架内的水下文化遗产。

因此：

（a）当缔约国的国民或者悬挂其国旗的船只发现或者计划进行在其专属经济区内或大陆架上的水下文化遗产活动时，应当要求国民或者船主报告此次发现或者活动；

（b）在属于另一缔约国的专属经济区内或大陆架上：

（Ⅰ）缔约国应当要求该国国民或船主就此次发现或者活动向其和另一缔约国报告；

（Ⅱ）或者，缔约国应当要求该国国民或船主报告此次发现或者活动，并且应当确保该报告快速而有效地传达至其他所有缔约国。

在存放批准、接受、核准或加入文书时，缔约国应当声明本条第 1 款（b）规定的报告的传达方式。

缔约国应当向总干事通告本条第 1 款规定的对其报告的发现或者活动。

总干事应当及时向所有缔约国传达本条第 3 款规定的向其报告的任何信息。

任何缔约国都可以向另一缔约国作出声明，有意就在该国的专属经济区内或大陆架上的水下文化遗产协商如何确保该水下文化遗产的有效保护。该声明应当以与该水下文化遗产有关的可确认的关联为基础，特别是具有文化、历史或考古的关联。

第十条 保护在专属经济区内和大陆架上的水下文化遗产

除了本条相关规定之外，不得授权在专属经济区内或大陆架上的水下文化遗产的活动。

缔约国有权根据包括联合国《海洋法公约》在内的国际法律的规定，为了保护其主权和管辖权免受侵犯，禁止或者授权在其专属经济区内或大陆架上的文化遗产活动。

当在缔约国的专属经济区内或大陆架上发现水下文化遗产，或者计划对该水下文化遗产开展活动的时候，缔约国应当：

与其他所有根据第 9 条 5 款作出意愿声明的缔约国协商如何最有效地保护水下文化遗产；

作为“协调国”协调该协商，除非其明确表示不愿意承担；在此种情况下，根据第 9 条 5 款作出意愿声明的缔约国应当指定一个协调国。

在不违背所有缔约国根据国际法律，通过采取所有可行措施来履行保护水下文化遗产的责任，为防止水下文化遗产受到包括掠夺在内的紧急危险的情况下，如若必须在协商之前防止对水下文化遗产可能造成的任何紧急损害，协调国可以根据本公约的规定采取所有可行的措施和作出任何必要的授权，无论该损害是来自于人类活动或者是包括掠夺在内的其他原因。在采取这些措施时，可以请求其他缔约国的帮助。

协调国：

应当实施包括协调国在内的协商国家同意的保护措施，除非包括协调国在内的协商国家同意由另一缔约国实施这些措施；

应当根据“规则”对这些同意的措施作出所有的必要的授权，除非包括协调国在内的协商国家同意由另一缔约国来作出这些授权；

可以对水下文化遗产开展必要的初步研究和为此作出所有的必要的授权，并且应当及时向总干事通告结果，总干事应当向其他缔约国通告这些信息。

在根据本条规定协调协商、采取措施、开展初步研究或者作出授权的时候，协调国应当代表所有缔约国的全体利益而不仅是本国利益。上述所有行动本身并不能构成主张任何包括联合国《海洋法公约》在内的国际法律没有规定的优先权或者管辖权的基础。

根据本条第2、4款的规定，在没有经过悬旗国的同意和协商国的合作的情况下，不能开展任何针对国家船只和飞行器的活动。

第十一条 “区域”内的报告和通知

根据本公约和联合国《海洋法公约》第149条的规定，缔约国有责任保护“区域”内的水下文化遗产。因此，当缔约国的国民或悬挂其国旗的船只在“区域”内发现水下文化遗产或者计划对其开展活动的时候，该缔约国应当要求该国民或船长报告此次发现或活动。

缔约国应当将报告的发现或者活动向总干事和国际海底管理局秘书长通告。

总干事应当及时将缔约国提供的这些信息通告所有缔约国。

任何缔约国可以向总干事声明有意就如何确保水下文化遗产的有效保护进行协商。该声明应当以与相关的水下文化遗产具有可确认的关联为基础，特别是文化、历史或者考古渊源国家享有的优先权。

第十二条 保护“区域”内的水下文化遗产

除了本条相关规定之外，不得授权在“区域”内的水下文化遗产进行活动。

总干事应当征求所有根据第11条第4款声明有意就如何最有效保护水下文化遗产进行协商的缔约国，指定一个缔约国为“协调国”来协调这些事项。总干事还应邀请国际海底管理局参与这些协商。

如若必须在协商之前防止对水下文化遗产可能造成的任何紧急损害，所有缔约国可以根据本公约的规定采取所有可行的措施，无论该损害是来自于人类活动或者是包括掠夺在内的其他原因。

协调国应当：

实施包括协调国在内的协商国家同意的保护措施，除非包括协调国在内的协商国家同意由另一缔约国实施这些措施；并且

根据公约对这些同意的措施作出所有的必要的授权，除非包括协调国在内的协商国家同意由另一缔约国来作出这些授权。

协调国可以对水下文化遗产开展必要的初步研究和为此作出所有的必要的授权，并且应当及时向总干事通告结果，总干事应当向其他缔约国通告这些信息。

在根据本条规定协调协商、采取措施、开展初步研究或者作出授权的时候，协调国应当代表所有的缔约国，为了全人类的利益。特别是与水下文化遗产有关的文化、历史和考古渊源国家的优先权。

在没有经过悬旗国同意的情况下，任何缔约国不得对“区域”内的国家船只或飞行器实施或者授权任何活动。

第十三条 主权豁免

享有主权豁免的军舰、其他政府船只或者军用飞行器，进行非商业目的的行动，进行他们的正常工作，并且没有对水下文化遗产开展活动，没有根据本公约第 9、10、11 和 12 条的规定报告发现水下文化遗产的义务。但是缔约国应当在不损害享有主权豁免的军舰、其他政府船只或者军用飞行器在进行非商业目的的行动时的工作或者工作能力的情况下，通过采取适当的措施来确保它们在尽可能合理和可行的情况下遵守本公约的第 9、10、11 和 12 条的规定。

第十四条 对进入领土、交易和私藏的控制

缔约国应当采取措施阻止进入领土，禁止对发现（违反本公约规定的发现）的或者非法出口的水下文化遗产进行交易或者私藏。

第十五条 缔约国管辖范围内的不使用区域

缔约国应当采取措施禁止违反本公约使用其领土进行的水下文化遗产活动，包括在其专属管辖或者控制下的海港、人工岛屿、设施和建筑。

第十六条 与国民和船只有关的措施

缔约国应当采取所有可行的措施以确保其国民和悬挂其国旗的船只不开展任何违反本公约的水下文化遗产活动。

第十七条 制裁

每个缔约国应当对违反实施本公约的措施的行为予以制裁。

对违反行为的制裁应当足够严厉以确保对公约的有效遵守，并且当违反行为发生之时能够剥夺违反者从非法活动中获得的收益以遏制违反行为。

缔约国应当合作来确保本条规定制裁得以执行。

第十八条 水下文化遗产的扣押与处置

每个缔约国应当采取措施对在其领土上的违反本公约发现的水下文化遗产予以扣押。

每个缔约国应当对根据公约扣押的水下文化遗产进行记录、保护和采取所有合理的措施使其保持稳定。

每个缔约国应当向总干事和其他对该相关水下文化遗产具有可确认的关联，特别是文化、历史或者考古关联的国家，通告根据公约扣押的水下文化遗产情况。

在考虑到保护和研究的需要；散落收藏重组的需要；向公众开放、展览和教育的需要；以及任何与该相关水下文化遗产具有可确认的关联，特别是文化、历史或考古关联的任何国家的利益的情况下，对水下文化遗产进行扣押的缔约国应当确保对其的处置符合公众利益。

第十九条 合作与信息共享

缔约国应当依据公约的规定就水下文化遗产的保护和管理进行合作和协助，包括在可行的情况下，在遗产的调查、挖掘、记录、保存、研究和展出上通力合作。

在不违反本公约目的的情况下，每个缔约国与其他缔约国就有关水下文化遗产进行信息分享，包括遗产的发现、定位、违反公约或者国际法律的遗产的挖掘或者发现、相关的科学方法和技术，以及与遗产有关的法律发展。

缔约国之间或者联合国教科文组织与缔约国之间就水下文化遗产的发现或者定位分享的信息，在不违反国内法律的情况下，一旦泄露后会对水下文化遗产带来威胁或者保存造成伤害的，应当保密并且只有缔约国主管机关才能知晓。

每个缔约国应当采取所有可行的措施，包括在可行的情况下使用适当的国际数据库，传播有关违反公约或者国际法律的对水下文化遗产的挖掘或者发现的信息。

第二十条 公众意识

每个缔约国应当采取所有可行的措施以提高公约规定的公众对水下文化遗产的价值与意义的认知，以及保护的重要性。

第二十一条 水下考古的培训

缔约国应当在提供水下考古培训、水下文化遗产保存技术，以及依照同意的条件进行与水下文化遗产有关的技术转让上进行合作。

第二十二条 主管机关

为了确保本公约的正确实施，缔约国应当成立主管机关或者合适的时候强化现有机关，旨在于进行对水下文化遗产目录的创设、维持和更新活动，进行对水下文化遗产有效的保护、保存、展出和管理和研究和教育。

缔约国应当向总干事通告主管水下文化遗产机关的名称和地址。

第二十三条 缔约国会议

总干事应当在本公约生效一年之内召开缔约国会议，之后至少每两年一次。在大多数缔约国的要求下，总干事应当召开缔约国特别会议。

缔约国会议应当确定其职能和责任。

缔约国会议应当适用自身的议事规则。

缔约国会议可以在适当考虑地理公平分配原则和男女性别平衡的基础上，成立由缔约国提名的专家组成的科学与技术咨询委员会。

科学与技术咨询委员会应当在有关规则执行的科学或者技术方面协助缔约国会。

第二十四条 公约秘书处

总干事应当负责公约秘书处的职能。

秘书处的职能应当包括：

根据第 23 条 1 款的规定组织缔约国会议；并且

协助缔约国执行缔约国会议的决定。

第二十五条 争端的和平解决

任何在两个或者以上的缔约国之间产生的有关解释或者适用公约的争端，应当通过善意的协商或者自己选择的其他和平解决机制来处理。

如果在一定合理的期限内协商没有能够解决争端，经由当事缔约国同意后，可以交由联合国教科文组织进行调解。

如果没有进行调解或者调解无效，联合国《海洋法公约》第十五部分规定的争端解决条款，在经过必要的修改后，可以适用于本公约缔约国之间的有关解释或者适用本公约出现的任何争端，无论各方是否是联合国《海洋法公约》的缔约国。

任何本公约的缔约国选择的程序，以及联合国《海洋法公约》的缔约国根据其第 287 条规定选择的程序，应当适用本条规定的争端解决，除非该缔约国当在批准、接受、核准或加入本公约之时，或者之后的任何时候，为了解决由于本公约引起的争端而根据第 287 条选择了其他的程序。

没有加入联合国《海洋法公约》的本公约的缔约国，当在批准、接受、核准或者加入本公约的时候，或者之后的任何时候，为了解决本条规定的纠纷的目的，可以通过书面声明的方式自由选择联合国《海洋法公约》第 287 条第 1 款规定的一种或多种解决方式。第 287 条应当适用于此声明，以及不包括在有效声明中的缔约国的纠纷。为了调解和仲裁的目的，根据联合国《海洋法公约》附件Ⅴ和附件Ⅶ的规定，为了解决由本公约引起的争端，该国家有权根据附件Ⅴ的第2条、附件Ⅶ的第2条列明的名单指定调解人和仲裁人。

第二十六条 批准、接受、核准或者加入

本公约由联合国教科文组织的成员国进行批准、接受或核准。

可以加入本公约包括：

非联合国教科文组织的成员，却是联合国的成员，或者属于联合国系统内的专门机构，或者属于国际原子能机构的国家，以及《国际法院规约》的缔约国和其他由联合国教科文组织大会的邀请加入本公约的国家；

为联合国承认的享有完全内部自治的，但是根据大会第1514号（ⅩⅤ）决议没有获得完全的独立的，对本公约规定的事项拥有管理权的，包括有权就这些事项加入条约的地区。

批准、接受、核准或加入本公约的文书应当由总干事保管。

第二十七条 生效

本公约自存放第26条规定的第20份文书之日起的三个月后生效，不过仅限于已经递交文书的二十个国家或地区。其他国家或者地区则是自递交文书之日起的三个月后公约生效。

第二十八条 内陆水域的声明

任何国家或地区自批准、接受、核准或者加入本公约的时候或者之后的任何时候，可以声明规则适用于内陆水域而不是海洋。

第二十九条 地理范围的限制

国家或者地区自批准、接受、核准或加入本公约的时候，可以对文书保管作出本公约不适用于其领土、内水、群岛水域或者领海的特定部分的声明，并且在声明中作出解释。在可行和尽可能的情况下，该国应当改善在其声明中指出的本公约可以适用的区域的条件，为此目的，一旦条件成熟，应当尽快撤回全部或者部分声明。

第三十条 保留

除了第29条的规定以外，不能对本公约作出保留。

第三十一条 修正案

缔约国可以以书面形式向总干事提出对本公约修正案。总干事应当将此书面文件发给所有的缔约国。如果自发送之日起的六个月内，半数以上的缔约国都回复赞成，总干事应当在下次缔约国会议的时候将此提议提交讨论和可否通过。

修正案的通过需要三分之二的绝大多数缔约国的出席和投票。

一旦通过，本公约的修正案应当由缔约国进行批准、接受、核准或者加入。

只有缔约国已经批准、接受、核准或者加入之后，修正案在三分之二的缔约国根据本条3款规定的提交文书之日起的三个月后方才生效。之后，每一个国家或者地区批准、接受、核准或者加入的，修正案应当于缔约方将其批准、接受、核准或者加入的文书上交之日起的三个月后生效。

根据本条第4款规定的国家或者地区在修正案生效之后成为本公约缔约方的，国家或者地区没有表示异议的，应当被考虑：

作为修订的公约的缔约方；并且

与不受修正案约束的缔约国相关的为修订的公约的缔约方。

第三十二条 退出

缔约国可以书面形式向总干事通告退出本公约。

自接收通知之日起的十二个月后退出生效，除非通知规定了更晚的日期。

退出不应当以任何方式影响缔约国履行本公约具体化的，独立于公约的国际法律规定的义务的责任。

第三十三条 规则

附于本公约的规则附件是公约完整的组成部分，除非另有明确规定，涉及公约的包括这些规则。

第三十四条 在联合国登记

根据《联合国宪章》第102条的规定，本公约应当按照总干事的要求在联合国秘书处进行登记。

第三十五条 官方文本

本公约的阿拉伯文、中文、英文、法文、俄文和西班牙文六种文本具有同等有效。

附件

有关水下文化遗产活动的规则

Ⅰ. 总则

规则一 通过就地对水下文化遗产进行保护应当成为首选。因此，水下文化遗产活动的批准应当与该遗产保护相一致，并且符合为了对水下文化遗产的保护、认知或者提高具有重大贡献的目的而作出批准的要求。

规则二 为了交易、投机而对水下文化遗产进行的商业开发，或者对其造成不可恢复的散落，在根本上与对水下文化遗产的保护和适当的管理相违背。水下文化遗产不得作为商品进行交易、销售和置换。

本规则不能被解释以阻止：

提供性质和目的完全符合本公约的规定的，并且经过主管机关批准的专业考古服务或者必要的附带服务；

在进行符合本公约规定的研究项目的过程中，对发现的水下文化遗产进行存储，提供这种形式的存储并不违背发现物的科学和文化的重要性或者完整性，也没有导致其不可恢复的散落；遵守了规则三十三和三十四的规定和获得主管机关的批准。

规则三 水下文化遗产的活动不应当对水下文化遗产造成超出项目目的必要性之外的不利的影响。

规则四 水下文化遗产的活动必须使用非破坏性的技术和勘测方法而不是打捞物品。如果为了科学研究或者对水下文化遗产予以最终保护的目的需要挖掘或者打捞，使用的技术和方法必须尽可能的不造成毁坏并且有助于遗址的保存。

规则五 水下文化遗产的活动应当避免对人类遗骸或者存有敬意的遗址造成不必要的干扰。

规则六 应当严格规范水下文化遗产的活动以确保文化、历史和考古信息的正确记录。

规则七 应当促进在原地的水下文化遗产对公众开放，除非这种开放不利于保护和管理。

规则八 为了推动考古学者和其他相关专家的有效交流或者使用，应当鼓励水下文化遗产的活动开展的国际合作。

Ⅱ. 项目设计

规则九 在开展任何水下文化遗产的活动之前，应当制定项目设计并且提交主管当局批准和进行相关的同行审阅。

规则十 项目设计应当包括：

对之前的或者初步的研究进行评估；

项目说明和目标；

使用的方法和采用的技术；

预计的资金；

项目完成的预期时间表；

小组组成人员以及每位成员的资历、责任和经验；

实地考查后的分析和其他活动的计划；

与主管当局密切合作的保护文物和遗址的计划；

整个项目期间的遗址管理和保护政策；

文件记录计划；安全政策；环境政策；

与博物馆、其他机构，特别是科研机构的合作安排；

报告的准备；

档案，包括取走的水下文化遗产的保存；

出版计划。

规则十一 水下文化遗产的活动的开展应当符合由主管机关批准的项目计划。

规则十二 当出现没有预料的发现或者情况改变的情况时，项目计划应当在主管机关同意后进行审核和修订。

规则十三 在出现紧急情况或者意外发现时，为了保护水下文化遗产，可以在没有项目计划的情况下开展水下文化遗产的活动，包括短期的保护措施或者活动，特别是遗址的稳定。

Ⅲ. 初步工作

规则十四 规则十（a）项规定的初步工作包括对水下文化遗产的重要性和脆弱性、会受到提出的计划破坏的周边自然环境，以及满足计划目的的数据的收集可能性的评估。

规则十五 评估也应当包括对可获得的历史和考古证据的背景研究，遗址的考古和环境特点，以及开展的活动会对水下文化遗产的长期稳定带来的任何可能的干扰的结果。

Ⅳ. 项目目标、方法和技术

规则十六 方法应当符合项目目标，采用的技术应当尽量不具有破坏性。

Ⅴ. 资金

规则十七 除对水下文化遗产的紧急保护之外，在任何活动之前，应当有足以完成项目计划的所有阶段的充足资金基础，包括对发现文物的保护、记录和保管以及报告的准备和发表。

规则十八 项目计划应当证明诸如获得资助项目完成的资金的能力。

规则十九 项目计划应当包括应急计划以确保在预计资金有任何中断的情况下，仍能够对水下文化遗产和辅助文件的保护。

Ⅵ. 项目的期限——时间表

规则二十 在任何水下文化遗产的活动之前，应当制定一份合适的时间表以确保项目计划中所有阶段的完成，包括对发现文物的保护、记录和保管以及报告准备和发表。

规则二十一 项目计划应当包括应急计划以确保项目中断或者结束的情况下，仍能够对水下文化遗产和辅助文件保护。

Ⅶ. 资格和能力

规则二十二 水下文化遗产的活动应当只能在符合项目要求的具有科学能力，合格的水下考古学者的指导、控制和在场的情况开展。

规则二十三 项目组的所有成员都应当有资质并且能够证明其在项目中的作用能力。

Ⅷ. 保护与遗址管理

规则二十四 保护计划应当在水下文化遗产的活动期间、运输中，以及长时间的为考古遗迹提供保护。保护应当符合现行的专业标准。

规则二十五 遗址管理计划应当在实地工作进行期间和结束之后，对水下文化遗产的就地保护和管理。该计划应当包括公布信息，为遗址的稳定、监控和不受干扰的保护提供合理的管理。

Ⅸ. 记录

规则二十六 记录计划应当根据现行的考古记录的专业标准，包括对水下文化遗产活动的进程报告在内的详细记录。

规则二十七 记录至少应包括遗址的全面记录，包括在水下文化遗产的活动进程中移走的或者取走的水下文化遗产的来源、实地笔记、平面图、制图、截面、照片或者其他媒介的记录。

Ⅹ. 安全

规则二十八 应当根据任何可行的法定的或者专业的要求制定足以保障

项目组和第三方的安全与健康的安全政策。

Ⅺ. 环境

规则二十九 应当制定环境政策确保海底和海洋生物不受过度地干扰。

Ⅻ. 报告

规则三十 应当依据项目计划中设定的时间表提供中期和最终报告，并且存放在相关的公共档案中。

规则三十一 报告应当包括：

目标描述；

使用的方法和技术的描述；

已获得结果的描述；

活动所有阶段的基本图形和照片记录；

对任何取走的水下文化遗产和遗址的保护和保管的建议；

对今后活动的建议。

XⅢ. 项目档案的保管

规则三十二 对项目档案的保管安排已经在任何活动开展之前达成一致，并且应当规定在项目计划之中。

规则三十三 包括了任何取走的水下文化遗产和所有辅助文件的复印件的项目档案，应当尽量完整地收藏，以便专家和公众的接触和档案的保管。为了符合水下文化遗产保护，这应当尽快完成，在任何情况下不能超过项目完成起的十年。

规则三十四 项目档案应当根据国际专业标准管理，并且经过主管机关的批准。

XⅣ. 公布

规则三十五 项目应当适时提供公众教育和项目结果的公共展示。

规则三十六 项目的最终综述应当：

在考虑到项目的复杂性和有关资料的保密或敏感性质的情况下，尽早公布；

保存在相关的公共档案中。

Convention on the Protection of the Underwater Cultural Heritage

UNESCO

Paris, 2 November 2001

The General Conference of the United Nations Educational, Scientific and Cultural

Organization, meeting in Paris from 15 October to 3 November 2001, at its 31st session,

Acknowledging the importance of underwater cultural heritage as an integral part of the cultural heritage of humanity and a particularly important element in the history of peoples, nations, and their relations with each other concerning their common heritage,

Realizing the importance of protecting and preserving the underwater cultural heritage and that responsibility therefor rests with all States,

Noting growing public interest in and public appreciation of underwater cultural heritage,

Convinced of the importance of research, information and education to the protection and preservation of underwater cultural heritage,

Convinced of the public's right to enjoy the educational and recreational benefits of responsible non - intrusive access to in situ underwater cultural heritage, and of the value of public education to contribute to awareness, appreciation and protection of that heritage,

Aware of the fact that underwater cultural heritage is threatened by unauthorized activities directed at it, and of the need for stronger measures to prevent such activities,

Conscious of the need to respond appropriately to the possible negative impact on underwater cultural heritage of legitimate activities that may incidentally affect it,

Deeply concerned by the increasing commercial exploitation of underwater cultural heritage, and in particular by certain activities aimed at the sale, acquisition or barter of underwater cultural heritage,

Aware of the availability of advanced technology that enhances discovery of and access to underwater cultural heritage,

Believing that cooperation among States, international organizations, scientific institutions, professional organizations, archaeologists, divers, other interested parties and the public at large is essential for the protection of underwater cultural heritage,

Considering that survey, excavation and protection of underwater cultural heritage necessitate the availability and application of special scientific methods and the use of suitable techniques and equipment as well as a high degree of professional specialization, all of which indicate a need for uniform governing criteria,

Realizing the need to codify and progressively develop rules relating to the protection and preservation of underwater cultural heritage in conformity with international law and practice, including the UNESCO Convention on the Means of

Prohibiting and Preventing the Illicit Import, Export and Transfer of Ownership of Cultural Property of 14 November 1970, the UNESCO Convention for the Protection of the World Cultural and Natural Heritage of 16 November 1972 and the United Nations Convention on the Law of the Sea of 10 December 1982,

Committed to improving the effectiveness of measures at international, regional and national levels for the preservation in situ or, if necessary for scientific or protective purposes, the careful recovery of underwater cultural heritage,

Having decided at its twenty - ninth session that this question should be made the subject of an international convention,

Adopts this second day of November 2001 this Convention.

Article 1 – Definitions

For the purposes of this Convention:

1. (a) "Underwater cultural heritage" means all traces of human existence having a cultural, historical or archaeological character which have been partially or totally under water, periodically or continuously, for at least 100 years such as:

(i) sites, structures, buildings, artifacts and human remains, together with their archaeological and natural context;

(ii) vessels, aircraft, other vehicles or any part thereof, their cargo or other contents, together with their archaeological and natural context; and

(iii) objects of prehistoric character.

(b) Pipelines and cables placed on the seabed shall not be considered as underwater cultural heritage.

(c) Installations other than pipelines and cables, placed on the seabed and still in use, shall not be considered as underwater cultural heritage.

2. (a) "States Parties" means States which have consented to be bound by this Convention and for which this Convention is in force.

(b) This Convention applies mutatis mutandis to those territories referred to in Article 26, paragraph 2 (b), which become Parties to this Convention in accordance with the conditions set out in that paragraph, and to that extent "States Parties" refers to those territories.

3. "UNESCO" means the United Nations Educational, Scientific and Cultural Organization.

4. "Director - General" means the Director - General of UNESCO.

5. "Area" means the seabed and ocean floor and subsoil thereof, beyond the limits of national jurisdiction.

6. "Activities directed at underwater cultural heritage" means activities having underwater cultural heritage as their primary object and which may, directly or indirectly, physically disturb or otherwise damage underwater cultural heritage.

7. "Activities incidentally affecting underwater cultural heritage" means activities which, despite not having underwater cultural heritage as their primary object or one of their objects, may physically disturb or otherwise damage underwater cultural heritage.

8. "State vessels and aircraft" means warships, and other vessels or aircraft that were owned or operated by a State and used, at the time of sinking, only for government non - commercial purposes, that are identified as such and that meet the definition of underwater cultural heritage.

9. "Rules" means the Rules concerning activities directed at underwater cultural heritage, as referred to in Article 33 of this Convention.

Article 2 - Objectives and general principles

1. This Convention aims to ensure and strengthen the protection of underwater cultural heritage.

2. States Parties shall cooperate in the protection of underwater cultural heritage.

3. States Parties shall preserve underwater cultural heritage for the benefit of humanity in conformity with the provisions of this Convention.

4. States Parties shall, individually or jointly as appropriate, take all appropriate measures in conformity with this Convention and with international law that are necessary to protect underwater cultural heritage, using for this purpose the best practicable means at their disposal and in accordance with their capabilities.

5. The preservation *in situ* of underwater cultural heritage shall be considered as the first option before allowing or engaging in any activities directed at this heritage.

6. Recovered underwater cultural heritage shall be deposited, conserved and managed in a manner that ensures its long - term preservation.

7. Underwater cultural heritage shall not be commercially exploited.

8. Consistent with State practice and international law, including the United Nations Convention on the Law of the Sea, nothing in this Convention shall be interpreted as modifying the rules of international law and State practice pertaining to sovereign immunities, nor any State's rights with respect to its State vessels and aircraft.

9. States Parties shall ensure that proper respect is given to all human remains located in maritime waters.

10. Responsible non - intrusive access to observe or document in situ underwater cultural heritage shall be encouraged to create public awareness, appreciation, and protection of the heritage except where such access is incompatible with its protection and management.

11. No act or activity undertaken on the basis of this Convention shall constitute grounds for claiming, contending or disputing any claim to national sovereignty or jurisdiction.

Article 3 - Relationship between this Convention and the United Nations Convention on the Law of the Sea

Nothing in this Convention shall prejudice the rights, jurisdiction and duties of States under international law, including the United Nations Convention on the Law of the Sea. This Convention shall be interpreted and applied in the context of and in a manner consistent with international law, including the United Nations Convention on the Law of the Sea.

Article 4 - Relationship to law of salvage and law of finds

Any activity relating to underwater cultural heritage to which this Convention applies shall not be subject to the law of salvage or law of finds, unless it:

(a) is authorized by the competent authorities, and

(b) is in full conformity with this Convention, and

(c) ensures that any recovery of the underwater cultural heritage achieves its maximum protection.

Article 5 - Activities incidentally affecting underwater cultural heritage

Each State Party shall use the best practicable means at its disposal to prevent or mitigate any adverse effects that might arise from activities under its jurisdiction incidentally affecting underwater cultural heritage.

Article 6 - Bilateral, regional or other multilateral agreements

1. States Parties are encouraged to enter into bilateral, regional or other multilateral agreements or develop existing agreements, for the preservation of underwater cultural heritage. All such agreements shall be in full conformity with the provisions of this Convention and shall not dilute its universal character. States may, in such agreements, adopt rules and regulations which would ensure better protection of underwater cultural heritage than those adopted in this Convention.

2. The Parties to such bilateral, regional or other multilateral agreements may invite States with a verifiable link, especially a cultural, historical or archaeological link, to the underwater cultural heritage concerned to join such agreements.

3. This Convention shall not alter the rights and obligations of States Parties regarding the protection of sunken vessels, arising from other bilateral, regional or other multilateral agreements concluded before its adoption, and, in particular, those that are in conformity with the purposes of this Convention.

Article 7 - Underwater cultural heritage in internal waters, archipelagic waters and territorial sea

1. States Parties, in the exercise of their sovereignty, have the exclusive right to regulate and authorize activities directed at underwater cultural heritage in their

internal waters, archipelagic waters and territorial sea.

2. Without prejudice to other international agreements and rules of international law regarding the protection of underwater cultural heritage, States Parties shall require that the Rules be applied to activities directed at underwater cultural heritage in their internal waters, archipelagic waters and territorial sea.

3. Within their archipelagic waters and territorial sea, in the exercise of their sovereignty and in recognition of general practice among States, States Parties, with a view to cooperating on the best methods of protecting State vessels and aircraft, should inform the flag State Party to this Convention and, if applicable, other States with a verifiable link, especially a cultural, historical or archaeological link, with respect to the discovery of such identifiable State vessels and aircraft.

Article 8 - Underwater cultural heritage in the contiguous zone

Without prejudice to and in addition to Articles 9 and 10, and in accordance with Article 303, paragraph 2, of the United Nations Convention on the Law of the Sea, States Parties may regulate and authorize activities directed at underwater cultural heritage within their contiguous zone. In so doing, they shall require that the Rules be applied.

Article 9 - Reporting and notification in the exclusive economic zone and on the continental shelf

1. All States Parties have a responsibility to protect underwater cultural heritage in the exclusive economic zone and on the continental shelf in conformity with this Convention. Accordingly:

(a) a State Party shall require that when its national, or a vessel flying its flag, discovers or intends to engage in activities directed at underwater cultural heritage located in its exclusive economic zone or on its continental shelf, the national or the master of the vessel shall report such discovery or activity to it;

(b) in the exclusive economic zone or on the continental shelf of another State Party:

(i) States Parties shall require the national or the master of the vessel to report such discovery or activity to them and to that other State Party;

(ii) alternatively, a State Party shall require the national or master of the vessel to report such discovery or activity to it and shall ensure the rapid and effective transmission of such reports to all other States Parties.

2. On depositing its instrument of ratification, acceptance, approval or accession, a State Party shall declare the manner in which reports will be transmitted under paragraph 1 (b) of this Article.

3. A State Party shall notify the Director - General of discoveries or activities reported to it under paragraph 1 of this Article.

4. The Director - General shall promptly make available to all States Parties any information notified to him under paragraph 3 of this Article.

5. Any State Party may declare to the State Party in whose exclusive economic zone or on whose continental shelf the underwater cultural heritage is located its interest in being consulted on how to ensure the effective protection of that underwater cultural heritage. Such declaration shall be based on a verifiable link, especially a cultural, historical or archaeological link, to the underwater cultural heritage concerned.

Article 10 – Protection of underwater cultural heritage in the exclusive economic zone and on the continental shelf

1. No authorization shall be granted for an activity directed at underwater cultural heritage located in the exclusive economic zone or on the continental shelf except in conformity with the provisions of this Article.

2. A State Party in whose exclusive economic zone or on whose continental shelf underwater cultural heritage is located has the right to prohibit or authorize any activity directed at such heritage to prevent interference with its sovereign rights or jurisdiction as provided for by international law including the United Nations Convention on the Law of the Sea.

3. Where there is a discovery of underwater cultural heritage or it is intended that activity shall be directed at underwater cultural heritage in a State Party's exclusive economic zone or on its continental shelf, that State Party shall:

(a) consult all other States Parties which have declared an interest under Article 9, paragraph 5, on how best to protect the underwater cultural heritage;

(b) coordinate such consultations as "Coordinating State", unless it expressly declares that it does not wish to do so, in which case the States Parties which have declared an interest under Article 9, paragraph 5, shall appoint a Coordinating State.

4. Without prejudice to the duty of all States Parties to protect underwater cul-

tural heritage by way of all practicable measures taken in accordance with international law to prevent immediate danger to the underwater cultural heritage, including looting, the Coordinating State may take all practicable measures, and/or issue any necessary authorizations in conformity with this Convention and, if necessary prior to consultations, to prevent any immediate danger to the underwater cultural heritage, whether arising from human activities or any other cause, including looting. In taking such measures assistance may be requested from other States Parties.

5. The Coordinating State:

(a) shall implement measures of protection which have been agreed by the consulting States, which include the Coordinating State, unless the consulting States, which include the Coordinating State, agree that another State Party shall implement those measures;

(b) shall issue all necessary authorizations for such agreed measures in conformity with the Rules, unless the consulting States, which include the Coordinating State, agree that another State Party shall issue those authorizations;

(c) may conduct any necessary preliminary research on the underwater cultural heritage and shall issue all necessary authorizations therefor, and shall promptly inform the Director - General of the results, who in turn will make such information promptly available to other States Parties.

6. In coordinating consultations, taking measures, conducting preliminary research and/or issuing authorizations pursuant to this Article, the Coordinating State shall act on behalf of the States Parties as a whole and not in its own interest. Any such action shall not in itself constitute a basis for the assertion of any preferential or jurisdictional rights not provided for in international law, including the United Nations Convention on the Law of the Sea.

7. Subject to the provisions of paragraphs 2 and 4 of this Article, no activity directed at State vessels and aircraft shall be conducted without the agreement of the flag State and the collaboration of the Coordinating State.

Article 11 - Reporting and notification in the Area

1. States Parties have a responsibility to protect underwater cultural heritage in the Area in conformity with this Convention and Article 149 of the United Nations Convention on the Law of the Sea. Accordingly when a national, or a vessel flying the flag of a State Party, discovers or intends to engage in activities directed at

underwater cultural heritage located in the Area, that State Party shall require its national, or the master of the vessel, to report such discovery or activity to it.

2. States Parties shall notify the Director - General and the Secretary - General of the International Seabed Authority of such discoveries or activities reported to them.

3. The Director - General shall promptly make available to all States Parties any such information supplied by States Parties.

4. Any State Party may declare to the Director - General its interest in being consulted on how to ensure the effective protection of that underwater cultural heritage. Such declaration shall be based on a verifiable link to the underwater cultural heritage concerned, particular regard being paid to the preferential rights of States of cultural, historical or archaeological origin.

Article 12 – Protection of underwater cultural heritage in the Area

1. No authorization shall be granted for any activity directed at underwater cultural heritage located in the Area except in conformity with the provisions of this Article.

2. The Director - General shall invite all States Parties which have declared an interest under Article 11, paragraph 4, to consult on how best to protect the underwater cultural heritage, and to appoint a State Party to coordinate such consultations as the "Coordinating State". The Director - General shall also invite the International Seabed Authority to participate in such consultations.

3. All States Parties may take all practicable measures in conformity with this Convention, if necessary prior to consultations, to prevent any immediate danger to the underwater cultural heritage, whether arising from human activity or any other cause including looting.

4. The Coordinating State shall:

(a) implement measures of protection which have been agreed by the consulting States, which include the Coordinating State, unless the consulting States, which include the Coordinating State, agree that another State Party shall implement those measures; and

(b) issue all necessary authorizations for such agreed measures, in conformity with this Convention, unless the consulting States, which include the Coordinating State, agree that another State Party shall issue those authorizations.

5. The Coordinating State may conduct any necessary preliminary research on the underwater cultural heritage and shall issue all necessary authorizations therefor, and shall promptly inform the Director - General of the results, who in turn shall make such information available to other States Parties.

6. In coordinating consultations, taking measures, conducting preliminary research, and/or issuing authorizations pursuant to this Article, the Coordinating State shall act for the benefit of humanity as a whole, on behalf of all States Parties. Particular regard shall be paid to the preferential rights of States of cultural, historical or archaeological origin in respect of the underwater cultural heritage concerned.

7. No State Party shall undertake or authorize activities directed at State vessels and aircraft in the Area without the consent of the flag State.

Article 13 - Sovereign immunity

Warships and other government ships or military aircraft with sovereign immunity, operated for non - commercial purposes, undertaking their normal mode of operations, and not engaged in activities directed at underwater cultural heritage, shall not be obliged to report discoveries of underwater cultural heritage under Articles 9, 10, 11 and 12 of this Convention. However States Parties shall ensure, by the adoption of appropriate measures not impairing the operations or operational capabilities of their warships or other government ships or military aircraft with sovereign immunity operated for non - commercial purposes, that they comply, as far as is reasonable and practicable, with Articles 9, 10, 11 and 12 of this Convention.

Article 14 - Control of entry into the territory, dealing and possession

States Parties shall take measures to prevent the entry into their territory, the dealing in, or the possession of, underwater cultural heritage illicitly exported and/or recovered, where recovery was contrary to this Convention.

Article 15 - Non – use of areas under the jurisdiction of States Parties

States Parties shall take measures to prohibit the use of their territory, including their maritime ports, as well as artificial islands, installations and structures under their exclusive jurisdiction or control, in support of any activity directed at underwater cultural heritage which is not in conformity with this Convention.

Article 16 - Measures relating to nationals and vessels

States Parties shall take all practicable measures to ensure that their nationals and vessels flying their flag do not engage in any activity directed at underwater cultural heritage in a manner not in conformity with this Convention.

Article 17 - Sanctions

1. Each State Party shall impose sanctions for violations of measures it has taken to implement this Convention.

2. Sanctions applicable in respect of violations shall be adequate in severity to be effective in securing compliance with this Convention and to discourage violations wherever they occur and shall deprive offenders of the benefit deriving from their illegal activities.

3. States Parties shall cooperate to ensure enforcement of sanctions imposed under this Article.

Article 18 - Seizure and disposition of underwater cultural heritage

1. Each State Party shall take measures providing for the seizure of underwater cultural heritage in its territory that has been recovered in a manner not in conformity with this Convention.

2. Each State Party shall record, protect and take all reasonable measures to stabilize underwater cultural heritage seized under this Convention.

3. Each State Party shall notify the Director - General and any other State with a verifiable link, especially a cultural, historical or archaeological link, to the underwater cultural heritage concerned of any seizure of underwater cultural heritage that it has made under this Convention.

4. A State Party which has seized underwater cultural heritage shall ensure that its disposition be for the public benefit, taking into account the need for conservation and research; the need for reassembly of a dispersed collection; the need for public access, exhibition and education; and the interests of any State with a verifiable link, especially a cultural, historical or archaeological link, in respect of the underwater cultural heritage concerned.

Article 19 - Cooperation and information – sharing

1. States Parties shall cooperate and assist each other in the protection and management of underwater cultural heritage under this Convention, including, where practicable, collaborating in the investigation, excavation, documentation,

conservation, study and presentation of such heritage.

2. To the extent compatible with the purposes of this Convention, each State Party undertakes to share information with other States Parties concerning underwater cultural heritage, including discovery of heritage, location of heritage, heritage excavated or recovered contrary to this Convention or otherwise in violation of international law, pertinent scientific methodology and technology, and legal developments relating to such heritage.

3. Information shared between States Parties, or between UNESCO and States Parties, regarding the discovery or location of underwater cultural heritage shall, to the extent compatible with their national legislation, be kept confidential and reserved to competent authorities of States Parties as long as the disclosure of such information might endanger or otherwise put at risk the preservation of such underwater cultural heritage.

4. Each State Party shall take all practicable measures to disseminate information, including where feasible through appropriate international databases, about underwater cultural heritage excavated or recovered contrary to this Convention or otherwise in violation of international law.

Article 20 - Public awareness

Each State Party shall take all practicable measures to raise public awareness regarding the value and significance of underwater cultural heritage and the importance of protecting it under this Convention.

Article 21 - Training in underwater archaeology

States Parties shall cooperate in the provision of training in underwater archaeology, in techniques for the conservation of underwater cultural heritage and, on agreed terms, in the transfer of technology relating to underwater cultural heritage.

Article 22 - Competent authorities

1. In order to ensure the proper implementation of this Convention, States Parties shall establish competent authorities or reinforce the existing ones where appropriate, with the aim of providing for the establishment, maintenance and updating of an inventory of underwater cultural heritage, the effective protection, conservation, presentation and management of underwater cultural heritage, as well as research and education.

2. States Parties shall communicate to the Director - General the names and

addresses of their competent authorities relating to underwater cultural heritage.

Article 23 - Meetings of States Parties

1. The Director - General shall convene a Meeting of States Parties within one year of the entry into force of this Convention and thereafter at least once every two years. At the request of a majority of States Parties, the Director - General shall convene an Extraordinary Meeting of States Parties.

2. The Meeting of States Parties shall decide on its functions and responsibilities.

3. The Meeting of States Parties shall adopt its own Rules of Procedure.

4. The Meeting of States Parties may establish a Scientific and Technical Advisory Body composed of experts nominated by the States Parties with due regard to the principle of equitable geographical distribution and the desirability of a gender balance.

5. The Scientific and Technical Advisory Body shall appropriately assist the Meeting of States Parties in questions of a scientific or technical nature regarding the implementation of the Rules.

Article 24 - Secretariat for this Convention

1. The Director - General shall be responsible for the functions of the Secretariat for this Convention.

2. The duties of the Secretariat shall include:

(a) organizing Meetings of States Parties as provided for in Article 23, paragraph 1; and

(b) assisting States Parties in implementing the decisions of the Meetings of States Parties.

Article 25 - Peaceful settlement of disputes

1. Any dispute between two or more States Parties concerning the interpretation or application of this Convention shall be subject to negotiations in good faith or other peaceful means of settlement of their own choice.

2. If those negotiations do not settle the dispute within a reasonable period of time, it may be submitted to UNESCO for mediation, by agreement between the States Parties concerned.

3. If mediation is not undertaken or if there is no settlement by mediation, the provisions relating to the settlement of disputes set out in Part XV of the United

Nations Convention on the Law of the Sea apply mutatis mutandis to any dispute between States Parties to this Convention concerning the interpretation or application of this Convention, whether or not they are also Parties to the United Nations Convention on the Law of the Sea.

4. Any procedure chosen by a State Party to this Convention and to the United Nations Convention on the Law of the Sea pursuant to Article 287 of the latter shall apply to the settlement of disputes under this Article, unless that State Party, when ratifying, accepting, approving or acceding to this Convention, or at any time thereafter, chooses another procedure pursuant to Article 287 for the purpose of the settlement of disputes arising out of this Convention.

5. A State Party to this Convention which is not a Party to the United Nations Convention on the Law of the Sea, when ratifying, accepting, approving or acceding to this Convention or at any time thereafter shall be free to choose, by means of a written declaration, one or more of the means set out in Article 287, paragraph 1, of the United Nations Convention on the Law of the Sea for the purpose of settlement of disputes under this Article. Article 287 shall apply to such a declaration, as well as to any dispute to which such State is party, which is not covered by a declaration in force. For the purpose of conciliation and arbitration, in accordance with Annexes Vand VII of the United Nations Convention on the Law of the Sea, such State shall beentitled to nominate conciliators and arbitrators to be included in the lists referred to in Annex V, Article 2, and Annex VII, Article 2, for the settlement of disputes arising out of this Convention.

Article 26 - Ratification, acceptance, approval or accession

1. This Convention shall be subject to ratification, acceptance or approval by Member States of UNESCO.

2. This Convention shall be subject to accession:

(a) by States that are not members of UNESCO but are members of the United Nations or of a specialized agency within the United Nations system or of the International Atomic Energy Agency, as well as by States Parties to the Statute of the International Court of Justice and any other State invited to accede to this Convention by the General Conference of UNESCO;

(b) by territories which enjoy full internal self - government, recognized as such by the United Nations, but have not attained full independence in accordance with General Assembly resolution 1514 (XV) and which have competence over the matters governed by this Convention, including the competence to enter into treaties in respect of those matters.

3. The instruments of ratification, acceptance, approval or accession shall be deposited with the Director - General.

Article 27 - Entry into force

This Convention shall enter into force three months after the date of the deposit of the twentieth instrument referred to in Article 26, but solely with respect to the twenty States or territories that have so deposited their instruments. It shall enter into force for each other State or territory three months after the date on which that State or territory has deposited its instrument.

Article 28 - Declaration as to inland waters

When ratifying, accepting, approving or acceding to this Convention or at any time thereafter, any State or territory may declare that the Rules shall apply to inland waters not of a maritime character.

Article 29 - Limitations to geographical scope

At the time of ratifying, accepting, approving or acceding to this Convention, a State or territory may make a declaration to the depositary that this Convention shall not be applicable to specific parts of its territory, internal waters, archipelagic waters or territorial sea, and shall identify therein the reasons for such declaration. Such State shall, to the extent practicable and as quickly as possible, promote conditions under which this Convention will apply to the areas specified in its declaration, and to that end shall also withdraw its declaration in whole or in part as soon as that has been achieved.

Article 30 - Reservations

With the exception of Article 29, no reservations may be made to this Convention.

Article 31 - Amendments

1. A State Party may, by written communication addressed to the Director - General, propose amendments to this Convention. The Director - General shall circulate such communication to all States Parties. If, within six months from the date of the circulation of the communication, not less than one half of the States Parties reply favourably to the request, the Director - General shall present such proposal

to the next Meeting of States Parties for discussion and possible adoption.

2. Amendments shall be adopted by a two - thirds majority of States Parties present and voting.

3. Once adopted, amendments to this Convention shall be subject to ratification, acceptance, approval or accession by the States Parties.

4. Amendments shall enter into force, but solely with respect to the States Parties that have ratified, accepted, approved or acceded to them, three months after the deposit of the instruments referred to in paragraph 3 of this Article by two thirds of the States Parties. Thereafter, for each State or territory that ratifies, accepts, approves or accedes to it, the amendment shall enter into force three months after the date of deposit by that Party of its instrument of ratification, acceptance, approval or accession.

5. A State or territory which becomes a Party to this Convention after the entry into force of amendments in conformity with paragraph 4 of this Article shall, failing an expression of different intention by that State or territory, be considered:

(a) as a Party to this Convention as so amended; and

(b) as a Party to the unamended Convention in relation to any State Party not bound by the amendment.

Article 32 - Denunciation

1. A State Party may, by written notification addressed to the Director - General, denounce this Convention.

2. The denunciation shall take effect twelve months after the date of receipt of the notification, unless the notification specifies a later date.

3. The denunciation shall not in any way affect the duty of any State Party to fulfil any obligation embodied in this Convention to which it would be subject under international law independently of this Convention.

Article 33 - The Rules

The Rules annexed to this Convention form an integral part of it and, unless expressly provided otherwise, a reference to this Convention includes a reference to the Rules.

Article 34 - Registration with the United Nations

In conformity with Article 102 of the Charter of the United Nations, this Convention shall be registered with the Secretariat of the United Nations at the request of the Director - General.

Article 35 – Authoritative texts

This Convention has been drawn up in Arabic, Chinese, English, French, Russian and Spanish, the six texts being equally authoritative.

Annex

Rules concerning activities directed at underwater cultural heritage

I. General principles

Rule 1. The protection of underwater cultural heritage through in situ preservation shall be considered as the first option. Accordingly, activities directed at underwater cultural heritage shall be authorized in a manner consistent with the protection of that heritage, and subject to that requirement may be authorized for the purpose of making a significant contribution to protection or knowledge or enhancement of underwater cultural heritage.

Rule 2. The commercial exploitation of underwater cultural heritage for trade or speculation or its irretrievable dispersal is fundamentally incompatible with the protection and proper management of underwater cultural heritage. Underwater cultural heritage shall not be traded, sold, bought or bartered as commercial goods. This Rule cannot be interpreted as preventing:

(a) the provision of professional archaeological services or necessary services incidental thereto whose nature and purpose are in full conformity with this Convention and are subject to the authorization of the competent authorities;

(b) the deposition of underwater cultural heritage, recovered in the course of a research project in conformity with this Convention, provided such deposition does not prejudice the scientific or cultural interest or integrity of the recovered material or result in its irretrievable dispersal; is in accordance with the provisions of Rules 33 and 34; and is subject to the authorization of the competent authorities.

Rule 3. Activities directed at underwater cultural heritage shall not adversely affect the underwater cultural heritage more than is necessary for the objectives of the project.

Rule 4. Activities directed at underwater cultural heritage must use nondestructive techniques and survey methods in preference to recovery of objects. If excavation or recovery is necessary for the purpose of scientific studies or for the ultimate protection of the underwater cultural heritage, the methods and techniques used must be as non - destructive as possible and contribute to the preservation of the remains.

Rule 5. Activities directed at underwater cultural heritage shall avoid the unnecessary disturbance of human remains or venerated sites.

Rule 6. Activities directed at underwater cultural heritage shall be strictly regulated to ensure proper recording of cultural, historical and archaeological information.

Rule 7. Public access to in situ underwater cultural heritage shall be promoted, except where such access is incompatible with protection and management.

Rule 8. International cooperation in the conduct of activities directed at underwater cultural heritage shall be encouraged in order to further the effective exchange or use of archaeologists and other relevant professionals.

II. Project design

Rule 9. Prior to any activity directed at underwater cultural heritage, a project design for the activity shall be developed and submitted to the competent authorities for authorization and appropriate peer review.

Rule 10. The project design shall include:

(a) an evaluation of previous or preliminary studies;

(b) the project statement and objectives;

(c) the methodology to be used and the techniques to be employed;

(d) the anticipated funding;

(e) an expected timetable for completion of the project;

(f) the composition of the team and the qualifications, responsibilities and experience of each team member;

(g) plans for post - fieldwork analysis and other activities;

(h) a conservation programme for artefacts and the site in close cooperation with the competent authorities;

(i) a site management and maintenance policy for the whole duration of the project;

(j) a documentation programme;

(k) a safety policy;

(l) an environmental policy;

(m) arrangements for collaboration with museums and other institutions, in particular scientific institutions;

(n) report preparation;

(o) deposition of archives, including underwater cultural heritage removed; and

(p) a programme for publication.

Rule 11. Activities directed at underwater cultural heritage shall be carried out inaccordance with the project design approved by the competent authorities.

Rule 12. Where unexpected discoveries are made or circumstances change, the project design shall be reviewed and amended with the approval of the competent authorities.

Rule 13. In cases of urgency or chance discoveries, activities directed at the underwater cultural heritage, including conservation measures or activities for a period of short duration, in particular site stabilization, may be authorized in the absence of a project design in order to protect the underwater cultural heritage.

III. Preliminary work

Rule 14. The preliminary work referred to in Rule 10 (a) shall include an assessment that evaluates the significance and vulnerability of the underwater cultural heritage and the surrounding natural environment to damage by the proposed project, and the potential to obtain data that would meet the project objectives.

Rule 15. The assessment shall also include background studies of available historical and archaeological evidence, the archaeological and environmental characteristics of the site, and the consequences of any potential intrusion for the long - term stability of the underwater cultural heritage affected by the activities.

IV. Project objective, methodology and techniques

Rule 16. The methodology shall comply with the project objectives, and the techniques employed shall be as non - intrusive as possible.

V. Funding

Rule 17. Except in cases of emergency to protect underwater cultural heritage, an adequate funding base shall be assured in advance of any activity, sufficient to complete all stages of the project design, including conservation, documentation and curation of recovered artefacts, and report preparation and dissemination.

Rule 18. The project design shall demonstrate an ability, such as by securing a bond, to fund the project through to completion.

Rule 19. The project design shall include a contingency plan that will ensure conservation of underwater cultural heritage and supporting documentation in the event of any interruption of anticipated funding.

VI. Project duration – timetable

Rule 20. An adequate timetable shall be developed to assure in advance of any activity directed at underwater cultural heritage the completion of all stages of the project design, including conservation, documentation and curation of recovered underwater cultural heritage, as well as report preparation and dissemination.

Rule 21. The project design shall include a contingency plan that will ensure conservation of underwater cultural heritage and supporting documentation in the event of any interruption or termination of the project.

VII. Competence and qualifications

Rule 22. Activities directed at underwater cultural heritage shall only be undertaken under the direction and control of, and in the regular presence of, a qualified underwater archaeologist with scientific competence appropriate to the project.

Rule 23. All persons on the project team shall be qualified and have demonstrated competence appropriate to their roles in the project.

VIII. Conservation and site management

Rule 24. The conservation programme shall provide for the treatment of the archaeological remains during the activities directed at underwater cultural heritage, during transit and in the long term. Conservation shall be carried out in accordance with current professional standards.

Rule 25. The site management programme shall provide for the protection and management in situ of underwater cultural heritage, in the course of and upon termination of fieldwork. The programme shall include public information, reasonable provision for site stabilization, monitoring, and protection against interference.

IX. Documentation

Rule 26. The documentation programme shall set out thorough documentation including a progress report of activities directed at underwater cultural heritage, in accordance with current professional standards of archaeological documentation.

Rule 27. Documentation shall include, at a minimum, a comprehensive record of the site, including the provenance of underwater cultural heritage moved or removed in the course of the activities directed at underwater cultural heritage, field notes, plans, drawings, sections, and photographs or recording in other media.

X. Safety

Rule 28. A safety policy shall be prepared that is adequate to ensure the safety and health of the project team and third parties and that is in conformity with any applicable statutory and professional requirements.

XI. Environment

Rule 29. An environmental policy shall be prepared that is adequate to ensure that the seabed and marine life are not unduly disturbed.

XII. Reporting

Rule 30. Interim and final reports shall be made available according to the timetable set out in the project design, and deposited in relevant public records.

Rule 31. Reports shall include:

(a) an account of the objectives;

(b) an account of the methods and techniques employed;

(c) an account of the results achieved;

(d) basic graphic and photographic documentation on all phases of the activity;

(e) recommendations concerning conservation and curation of the site and of any underwater cultural heritage removed; and

(f) recommendations for future activities.

XIII. Curation of project archives

Rule 32. Arrangements for curation of the project archives shall be agreed to before any activity commences, and shall be set out in the project design.

Rule 33. The project archives, including any underwater cultural heritage removed and a copy of all supporting documentation shall, as far as possible, be kept together and intact as a collection in a manner that is available for professional and public access as well as for the curation of the archives. This should be done as rapidly as possible and in any case not later than ten years from the completion of the project, in so far as may be compatible with conservation of the underwater cultural heritage.

Rule 34. The project archives shall be managed according to international professional standards, and subject to the authorization of the competent authorities.

XIV. Dissemination

Rule 35. Projects shall provide for public education and popular presentation of the project results where appropriate.

Rule 36. A final synthesis of a project shall be:

(a) made public as soon as possible, having regard to the complexity of the project and the confidential or sensitive nature of the information; and

(b) deposited in relevant public records.

保护世界文化和自然遗产公约

（联合国教科文组织大会1972年11月16日通过。我国于1985年12月12日递交批准书）

联合国教育、科学及文化组织大会于1972年10月17日至11月21日在巴黎举行的第十七次大会：

注意到文化遗产和自然遗产越来越受到破坏的威胁，一方面因年久腐变所致，另一方面，变化中的社会和经济条件使情况恶化，造成更加难以对付的损害或破坏现象；

考虑到任何文化或自然遗产的坏变或消失都构成使世界各国遗产枯竭的有害影响；

考虑到国家一级保护这类遗产的工作往往不很完善，原因在于这项工作需要大量手段，以及应予保护的财产的所在国不具备充足的经济、科学和技术力量；

回顾本组织《组织法》规定，本组织将通过确保世界遗产得到保存和保护以及建议有关国家订立必要的国际公约来维护、增进和传播知识；

考虑到现有关于文化财产和自然财产的国际公约、建议和决议表明，保护不论属于哪国人民的这类罕见且无法替代的财产，对全世界人民都很重要；

考虑到某些文化遗产和自然遗产具有突出的重要性，因而需作为全人类世界遗产的一部分加以保存；

考虑到鉴于威胁这类遗产的新危险的规模和严重性，整个国际社会有责任通过提供集体性援助来参与保护具有突出的普遍价值的文化遗产和自然遗产；这种援助尽管不能代替有关国家采取的行动，但将成为它的有效补充；

考虑到为此有必要通过采用公约形式的新规定，以便为集体保护具有突出的普遍价值的文化遗产和自然遗产建立一个依据现代科学方法组织的永久性的有效制度；

在第十六次大会上曾决定就此问题制定一项国际公约；于1972年11月

16 日通过本公约。

Ⅰ　文化遗产和自然遗产的定义

第一条　为实现本公约的宗旨，下列各项应列为“文化遗产”：

古迹：从历史、艺术或科学角度看，具有突出的普遍价值的建筑物、碑雕和碑画、具有考古性质的成分或构造物、铭文、窟洞以及景观的联合体；

建筑群：从历史、艺术或科学角度看，在建筑式样、分布均匀或与环境景色结合方面具有突出的普遍价值的单立或连接的建筑群；

遗址：从历史、审美、人种学或人类学角度看，具有突出的普遍价值的人类工程或自然与人的联合工程以及包括有考古地址的区域。

第二条　为实现本公约的宗旨，下列各项应列为“自然遗产”：

从审美或科学角度看，具有突出的普遍价值的由物质和生物结构或这类结构群组成的自然景观；

从科学或保护角度看，具有突出的普遍价值的地质和地文结构以及明确划为受到威胁的动物和植物生境区；

从科学、保存或自然美角度看，具有突出的普遍价值的天然名胜或明确划分的自然区域。

第三条　本公约缔约国均可自行确定和划分上面第一条和第二条中提及的、本国领土内的各种不同的财产。

Ⅱ　文化遗产和自然遗产的国家保护和国际保护

第四条　本公约缔约国承认，保证第一条和第二条中提及的、本国领土内的文化遗产和自然遗产的确定、保护、保存、展出和传与后代，主要是有关国家的责任。该国将为此目的竭尽全力，最大限度地利用本国资源，适当时利用所能获得的国际援助和合作，特别是财政、艺术、科学及技术方面的援助和合作。

第五条　为确保本公约各缔约国为保护、保存和展出本国领土内的文化遗产和自然遗产采取积极有效的措施，本公约各缔约国应视本国具体情况尽力做到以下几点：

1. 通过一项旨在使文化遗产和自然遗产在社会生活中起一定作用，并把遗产保护工作纳入全面规划纲要的总政策；

2. 如本国内尚未建立负责文化遗产和自然遗产的保护、保存和展出的机构，则建立一个或几个此类机构，配备适当的工作人员和为履行其职能所需的手段；

3. 发展科学和技术研究，并制订出能够抵抗威胁本国文化或自然遗产的危险的实际方法；

4. 采取为确定、保护、保存、展出和恢复这类遗产所需的适当的法律、科学、技术、行政和财政措施；

5. 促进建立或发展有关保护、保存和展出文化遗产和自然遗产的国家或地区培训中心，并鼓励这方面的科学研究。

第六条　（一）本公约缔约国，在充分尊重第一条和第二条中提及的文化遗产和自然遗产的所在国的主权，并不使国家立法规定的财产权受到损害的同时，承认这类遗产是世界遗产的一部分，因此，整个国际社会有责任进行合作，予以保护。

（二）缔约国同意，按照本公约的规定，应有关国家的要求帮助该国确定、保护、保存和展出第十一条第（二）和第（四）款中提及的文化遗产和自然遗产。

（三）本公约缔约国同意不故意采取任何可能直接或间接损害第一条和第二条中提及的位于本公约其他缔约国领土内的文化遗产和自然遗产的措施。

第七条　为实现本公约的宗旨，世界文化遗产和自然遗产的国际保护应被理解为建立一个旨在支持本公约缔约国保存和确定这类遗产的努力的国际合作和援助系统。

Ⅲ　保护世界文化遗产和自然遗产政府间委员会

第八条　（一）在联合国教育、科学及文化组织内，现建立一个保护具有突出的普遍价值的文化遗产和自然遗产的政府间委员会，称为“世界遗产委员会”。委员会由联合国教育、科学及文化组织大会常会期间召集的本公约缔约国大会选出的15个缔约国组成。委员会成员国的数目将自本公约至少在40个缔约国生效后的大会常会之日起增至21个。

（二）委员会委员的选举须保证均衡地代表世界的不同地区和不同文化。

（三）国际文物保存与修复研究中心（罗马中心）的一名代表、国际古迹遗址理事会的一名代表，以及国际自然及自然资源保护联盟的一名代表，可以咨询者身份出席委员会的会议。此外，应联合国教育、科学及文化组织大会常会期间参加大会的本公约缔约国的要求，其他具有类似目标的政府间或非政府组织的代表亦可以咨询者身份出席委员会的会议。

第九条　（一）世界遗产委员会成员国的任期自当选之应届大会常会结

束时起至应届大会后第三次常会闭幕时止。

（二）但是，第一次选举时指定的委员中，有1/3的委员的任期应于当选之应届大会后第一次常会闭幕时截止；同时指定的委员中，另有1/3的委员的任期应于当选之应届大会后第二次常会闭幕时截止。这些委员由联合国教育、科学及文化组织大会主席在第一次选举后抽签决定。

（三）委员会成员国应选派在文化或自然遗产方面有资历的人员担任代表。

第十条　（一）世界遗产委员会应通过其议事规则。

（二）委员会可随时邀请公共或私立组织或个人参加其会议，以就具体问题进行磋商。

（三）委员会可设立它认为为履行其职能所需的咨询机构。

第十一条　（一）本公约各缔约国应尽力向世界遗产委员会递交一份关于本国领土内适于列入本条第（二）款所述《世界遗产目录》的组成文化遗产和自然遗产的财产的清单。这份清单不应当看作是详尽无遗的。清单应包括有关财产的所在地及其意义的文献资料。

（二）根据缔约国按照第（一）款规定递交的清单，委员会应制订、更新和出版一份《世界遗产目录》，其中所列的均为本公约第一条和第二条确定的文化遗产和自然遗产的组成部分，也是委员会按照自己制订的标准认为是具有突出的普遍价值的财产。一份最新目录应至少每两年分发一次。

（三）把一项财产列入《世界遗产目录》需征得有关国家同意。当几个国家对某一领土的主权或管辖权均提出要求时，将该领土内的一项财产列入《目录》不得损害争端各方的权利。

（四）委员会应在必要时制订、更新和出版一份《处于危险的世界遗产目录》，其中所列财产均为载于《世界遗产目录》之中、需要采取重大活动加以保护并根据本公约要求需给予援助的财产。《处于危险的世界遗产目录》应载有这类活动的费用概算，并只可包括文化遗产和自然遗产中受到下述严重的特殊危险威胁的财产。这些危险是：蜕变加剧、大规模公共和私人工程、城市或旅游业迅速发展的项目造成的消失威胁；土地的使用变动或易主造成的破坏；未知原因造成的重大变化；随意摒弃；武装冲突的爆发或威胁；灾害和灾变；严重火灾、地震、山崩；火山爆发；水位变动、洪水和海啸等。委员会在紧急需要时可随时在《处于危险的世界遗产目录》中增列新的条目并立即予以发表。

（五）委员会应确定属于文化或自然遗产的财产可被列入本条第（二）

和第（四）款中提及的目录所依据的标准。

（六）委员会在拒绝一项要求列入本条第（二）和第（四）款中提及的目录之一的申请之前，应与有关文化或自然财产所在缔约国磋商。

（七）委员会经与有关国家商定，应协调和鼓励为拟订本条第（二）和第（四）款中提及的目录所需进行的研究。

第十二条　未被列入第十一条第（二）和第（四）款提及的两个目录的属于文化或自然遗产的财产，决非意味着在列入这些目录的目的之外的其他方面不具有突出的普遍价值。

第十三条　（一）世界遗产委员会应接收并研究本公约缔约国就已经列入或可能适于列入第十一条第（二）和第（四）款中提及的目录的本国领土内成为文化或自然遗产的财产，要求国际援助而递交的申请。这种申请的目的可以是保证这类财产得到保护、保存、展出或恢复。

（二）当初步调查表明有理由进行深入的时候，根据本条第（一）款中提出的国际援助申请还可以涉及鉴定哪些财产属于第一条和第二条所确定的文化或自然遗产。

（三）委员会应就对这些申请所需采取的行动作出决定，适当时应确定其援助的性质和程度，并授权以它的名义与有关政府作出必要的安排。

（四）委员会应制订其活动的优先顺序并在进行这项工作时应考虑到需予以保护的财产对世界文化遗产和自然遗产各具的重要性、对最能代表一种自然环境或世界各国人民的才华和历史的财产给予国际援助的必要性、所需开展工作的迫切性、受到威胁的财产所在的国家现有的资源、特别是这些国家利用本国手段保护这类财产的能力大小。

（五）委员会应制订、更新和发表已给予国际援助的财产目录。

（六）委员会应就根据本公约第十五条设立的基金的资金使用问题作出决定。委员会应设法增加这类资金，并为此目的采取一切有益的措施。

（七）委员会应与拥有与本公约目标相似的目标的国际和国家级政府组织和非政府组织合作。委员会为实施其计划和项目，可邀请这类组织，特别是国际文物保存与修复研究中心（罗马中心）、国际古迹遗址理事会和国际自然及自然资源保护联盟，并可邀请公共和私立机构及个人。

（八）委员会的决定应经出席及参加表决的委员的2/3多数通过。委员会委员的多数构成法定人数。

第十四条　（一）世界遗产委员会应由联合国教育、科学及文化组织总干事任命组成的一个秘书处协助工作。

（二）联合国教育、科学及文化组织总干事应尽可能充分利用国际文物保存与修复研究中心（罗马中心）、国际古迹遗址理事会和国际自然及自然资源保护联盟在各自职权能力范围内提供的服务，为委员会准备文件资料，制订委员会会议议程，并负责执行委员会的决定。

Ⅳ　保护世界文化遗产和自然遗产基金

第十五条　（一）设立一项保护具有突出的普遍价值的世界文化遗产和自然遗产基金，称为“世界遗产基金”。

（二）根据联合国教育、科学及文化组织《财务条例》的规定，此项基金应构成一项信托基金。

（三）基金的资金来源应包括：

1. 本公约缔约国义务捐款和自愿捐款；

2. 下列方面可能提供的捐款、赠款或遗赠：

（1）其他国家；

（2）联合国教育、科学及文化组织、联合国系统的其他组织（特别是联合国开发计划署）或其他政府间组织；

（3）公共或私立团体或个人。

3. 基金款项所得利息；

4. 募捐的资金和基金组织活动的所得收入；

5. 世界遗产委员会拟订的基金条例所认可的所有其他资金。

（四）对基金的捐款和向委员会提供的其他形式的援助只能用于委员会限定的目的。委员会可接受仅用于某个计划或项目的捐款，但以委员会业已决定实施该计划或项目为条件。对基金的捐款不得带有政治条件。

第十六条　（一）在不影响任何自愿补充捐款的情况下，本公约缔约国同意，每两年定期向世界遗产基金纳款，本公约缔约国大会应在联合国教育、科学及文化组织大会开会期间确定适用于所有缔约国的一个统一的纳款额百分比。缔约国大会关于此问题的决定，需由未作本条第（二）款中所述声明的、出席及参加表决的缔约国的多数通过。本公约缔约国的义务纳款在任何情况下都不得超过对联合国教育、科学及文化组织正常预算纳款的1%。

（二）然而，本公约第三十一条或第三十二条中提及的国家均可在交存批准书、接受书或加入书时声明不受本条第1段规定的约束。

（三）已作本条第（二）款中所述声明的本公约缔约国可随时通知联合国教育、科学及文化组织总干事收回所作声明。然而，收回声明之举在紧接的一届本公约缔约国大会之日以前不得影响该国的义务纳款。

（四）为使委员会得以有效地规划其活动，已作本条第（二）款中所述声明的本公约缔约国应至少每两年定期纳款，纳款不得少于它们如受本条第（一）款规定约束所需交纳的款额。

（五）凡拖延交付当年和前一日历年的义务纳款或自愿捐款的本公约缔约国，不能当选为世界遗产委员会成员，但此项规定不适用于第一次选举。

属于上述情况但已当选委员会成员的缔约国的任期，应在本公约第八条第（一）款规定的选举之时截止。

第十七条 本公约缔约国应考虑或鼓励设立旨在为保护本公约第一条和第二条中所确定的文化遗产和自然遗产募捐的国家、公共及私立基金会或协会。

第十八条 本公约缔约国应对在联合国教育、科学及文化组织赞助下为世界遗产基金所组织的国际募款运动给予援助。它们应为第十五条第（三）款中提及的机构为此目的所进行的募款活动提供便利。

V 国际援助的条件和安排

第十九条 凡本公约缔约国均可要求对本国领土内组成具有突出的普遍价值的文化或自然遗产的财产给予国际援助。它在递交申请时还应按照第二十一条规定提交所拥有的并有助于委员会作出决定的情报和文件资料。

第二十条 除第十三条第（二）款、第二十二条3项和第二十三条所述情况外，本公约规定提供的国际援助仅限于世界遗产委员会业已决定或可能决定列入第十一条第（二）和第（四）款中所述目录的文化遗产和自然遗产的财产。

第二十一条 （一）世界遗产委员会应制订对向它提交的国际援助申请的审议程序，并应确定申请应包括的内容，即打算开展的活动、必要的工程、工程的预计费用和紧急程度以及申请国的资源不能满足所有开支的原因所在。这类申请须尽可能附有专家报告。

（二）对因遭受灾难或自然灾害而提出的申请，由于可能需要开展紧急工作，委员会应立即给予优先审议，委员会应掌握一笔应急储备金。

（三）委员会在作出决定之前，应进行它认为必要的研究和磋商。

第二十二条 世界遗产委员会提供的援助可采取下述形式：

1. 研究在保护、保存、展出和恢复本公约第十一条第（二）和第（四）款所确定的文化遗产和自然遗产方面所产生的艺术、科学和技术性问题；

2. 提供专家、技术人员和熟练工人，以保证正确地进行已批准的工程；

3. 在各级培训文化遗产和自然遗产的鉴定、保护、保存、展出和恢复方面的工作人员和专家；

4. 提供有关国家不具备或无法获得的设备；

5. 提供可长期偿还的低息或无息贷款；

6. 在例外并具有特殊原因的情况下提供无偿补助金。

第二十三条　世界遗产委员会还可向培训文化或自然遗产的鉴定、保护、保存、展出和恢复方面的各级工作人员和专家的国家或地区中心提供国际援助。

第二十四条　在提供大规模的国际援助之前，应先进行周密的科学、经济和技术研究。这些研究应考虑采用保护、保存、展出和恢复自然遗产和文化遗产方面最先进的技术，并应与本公约的目标相一致。这些研究还应探讨合理利用有关国家现有资源的手段。

第二十五条　原则上，国际社会只担负必要工程的部分费用。除非本国资源不许可，受益于国际援助的国家承担的费用应构成用于各项计划或项目的资金的主要份额。

第二十六条　世界遗产委员会和受援国应在它们签订的协定中，确定关于获得根据本公约规定提供的国际援助的计划或项目的实施条件。接受这类国际援助的国家应负责按照协定制订的条件，对如此护卫的财产继续加以保护、保存和展出。

Ⅵ　教育计划

第二十七条　（一）本公约缔约国应通过一切适当手段，特别是教育和宣传计划，努力增强本国人民对本公约第一条和第二条中确定的文化和自然遗产的赞赏和尊重。

（二）缔约国应使公众广泛了解对这类遗产造成威胁的危险和为履行本公约进行的活动。

第二十八条　接受根据本公约提供的国际援助的缔约国应采取适当措施，使人们了解接受援助的财产的重要性和国际援助所发挥的作用。

Ⅶ　报告

第二十九条　（一）本公约缔约国在按照联合国教育、科学及文化组织大会确定的日期和方式向该组织大会递交的报告中，应提供有关它们为实施本公约所通过的立法和行政规定以及采取的其他行动的情况，并详述在这方面获得的经验。

（二）应提请世界遗产委员会注意这些报告。

（三）委员会应在联合国教育、科学及文化组织大会的每届常会上递交一份关于其活动的报告。

Ⅷ 最后条款

第三十条 本公约以阿拉伯文、英文、法文、俄文和西班牙文拟订，五种文本同一作准。

第三十一条 （一）本公约应由联合国教育、科学及文化组织会员国根据各自的宪法程序予以批准或接受。

（二）批准书或接受书应交联合国教育、科学及文化组织总干事保存。

第三十二条 （一）所有非联合国教育、科学及文化组织会员的国家，经该组织大会邀请均可加入本公约。

（二）向联合国教育、科学及文化组织总干事交存加入书后，加入方才有效。

第三十三条 本公约须在第20份批准书、接受书或加入书交存之日的3个月之后生效，但这仅涉及在该日或该日之前交存各自批准书、接受书或加入书的国家。就任何其他国家而言，本公约应在这些国家交存其批准书、接受书或加入书的3个月之后生效。

第三十四条 下述规定适用于拥有联邦制或非单一立宪制的本公约缔约国：

1. 在联邦或中央立法机构的法律管辖实施本公约规定的情况下，联邦或中央政府的义务应与非联邦国家的缔约国的义务相同；

2. 在无须按照联邦立宪制采取立法措施的联邦各个国家、地区、省或州的法律管辖实施本公约规定的情况下，联邦政府应将这些规定连同其应予通过的建议一并通知各个国家、地区、省或州的主管当局。

第三十五条 （一）本公约缔约国均可废弃本公约。

（二）废弃通告应以一份书面文件交存联合国教育、科学及文化组织的总干事。

（三）公约的废弃应在接到废约通告书12个月后生效。废弃在生效日之前不得影响退约国承担的财政义务。

第三十六条 联合国教育、科学及文化组织总干事应将第三十一条和第三十二条规定交存的所有批准书、接受书或加入书以及第三十五条规定的废弃等事项通告本组织会员国、第三十二条中提及的非本组织会员的国家以及联合国。

第三十七条　（一）本公约可由联合国教育、科学及文化组织的大会修订。但任何修订只对将成为修订公约的缔约国具有约束力。

（二）如大会通过一项全部或部分修订本公约的新公约，除非新公约另有规定，本公约应从新的修订公约生效之日起停止批准、接受或加入。

第三十八条　按照《联合国宪章》第一百零二条，本公约需应联合国教育、科学及文化组织总干事的要求在联合国秘书处登记。

Convention concerning the Protection of the World Cultural and Natural Heritage

Paris, 16 November 1972

The General Conference of the United Nations Educational, Scientific and Cultural Organization meeting in Paris from 17 October to 21 November 1972, at its seventeenth session,

Noting that the cultural heritage and the natural heritage are increasingly threatened with destruction not only by the traditional causes of decay, but also by changing social and economic conditions which aggravate the situation with even more formidable phenomena of damage or destruction,

Considering that deterioration or disappearance of any item of the cultural or natural heritage constitutes a harmful impoverishment of the heritage of all the nations of the world,

Considering that protection of this heritage at the national level often remains incomplete because of the scale of the resources which it requires and of the insufficient economic, scientific, and technological resources of the country where the property to be protected is situated,

Recalling that the Constitution of the Organization provides that it will maintain, increase, and diffuse knowledge, by assuring the conservation and protection of the world's heritage, and recommending to the nations concerned the necessary international conventions,

Considering that the existing international conventions, recommendations and resolutions concerning cultural and natural property demonstrate the importance, for all the peoples of the world, of safeguarding this unique and irreplaceable property, to whatever people it may belong,

Considering that parts of the cultural or natural heritage are of outstanding interest and therefore need to be preserved as part of the world heritage of mankind as a whole,

Considering that, in view of the magnitude and gravity of the new dangers threatening them, it is incumbent on the international community as a whole to participate in the protection of the cultural and natural heritage of outstanding universal value, by the granting of collective assistance which, although not taking the place of action by the State concerned, will serve as an efficient complement thereto,

Considering that it is essential for this purpose to adopt new provisions in the form of a convention establishing an effective system of collective protection of the cultural and natural heritage of outstanding universal value, organized on a permanent basis and in accordance with modern scientific methods,

Having decided, at its sixteenth session, that this question should be made the subject of an international convention,

Adopts this sixteenth day of November 1972 this Convention.

I. Definition of the Cultural and Natural Heritage

Article 1

For the purposes of this Convention, the following shall be considered as "cultural heritage":

monuments: architectural works, works of monumental sculpture and painting, elements or structures of an archaeological nature, inscriptions, cave dwellings and combinations of features, which are of outstanding universal value from the point of view of history, art or science;

groups of buildings: groups of separate or connected buildings which, because of their architecture, their homogeneity or their place in the landscape, are of outstanding universal value from the point of view of history, art or science;

sites: works of man or the combined works of nature and man, and areas including archaeological sites which are of outstanding universal value from the historical, aesthetic, ethnological or anthropological point of view.

Article 2

For the purposes of this Convention, the following shall be considered as "natural heritage":

natural features consisting of physical and biological formations or groups of such formations, which are of outstanding universal value from the aesthetic or scientific point of view;

geological and physiographical formations and precisely delineated areas which constitute the habitat of threatened species of animals and plants of outstanding universal value from the point of view of science or conservation;

natural sites or precisely delineated natural areas of outstanding universal value from the point of view of science, conservation or natural beauty.

Article 3

It is for each State Party to this Convention to identify and delineate the different properties situated on its territory mentioned in Articles 1 and 2 above.

II. National Protection and International Protection of the Cultural and Natural Heritage

Article 4

Each State Party to this Convention recognizes that the duty of ensuring the identification, protection, conservation, presentation and transmission to future generations of the cultural and natural heritage referred to in Articles 1 and 2 and situated on its territory, belongs primarily to that State. It will do all it can to this end, to the utmost of its own resources and, where appropriate, with any international assistance and co - operation, in particular, financial, artistic, scientific and technical, which it may be able to obtain.

Article 5

To ensure that effective and active measures are taken for the protection, conservation and presentation of the cultural and natural heritage situated on its territory, each State Party to this Convention shall endeavor, in so far as possible, and as appropriate for each country:

1. to adopt a general policy which aims to give the cultural and natural heritage a function in the life of the community and to integrate the protection of that heritage into comprehensive planning programmes;

2. to set up within its territories, where such services do not exist, one or more services for the protection, conservation and presentation of the cultural and

natural heritage with an appropriate staff and possessing the means to discharge their functions;

3. to develop scientific and technical studies and research and to work out such operating methods as will make the State capable of counteracting the dangers that threaten its cultural or natural heritage;

4. to take the appropriate legal, scientific, technical, administrative and financial measures necessary for the identification, protection, conservation, presentation and rehabilitation of this heritage; and

5. to foster the establishment or development of national or regional centres for training in the protection, conservation and presentation of the cultural and natural heritage and to encourage scientific research in this field.

Article 6

1. Whilst fully respecting the sovereignty of the States on whose territory the cultural and natural heritage mentioned in Articles 1 and 2 is situated, and without prejudice to property right provided by national legislation, the States Parties to this Convention recognize that such heritage constitutes a world heritage for whose protection it is the duty of the international community as a whole to co - operate.

2. The States Parties undertake, in accordance with the provisions of this Convention, to give their help in the identification, protection, conservation and presentation of the cultural and natural heritage referred to in paragraphs 2 and 4 of Article 11 if the States on whose territory it is situated so request.

3. Each State Party to this Convention undertakes not to take any deliberate measures which might damage directly or indirectly the cultural and natural heritage referred to in Articles 1 and 2 situated on the territory of other States Parties to this Convention.

Article 7

For the purpose of this Convention, international protection of the world cultural and natural heritage shall be understood to mean the establishment of a system of international co - operation and assistance designed to support States Parties to the Convention in their efforts to conserve and identify that heritage.

III. Intergovernmental Committee for the Protection of the World Cultural and Natural Heritage

Article 8

1. An Intergovernmental Committee for the Protection of the Cultural and Natural Heritage of Outstanding Universal Value, called "the World Heritage Committee", is hereby established within the United Nations Educational, Scientific and Cultural Organization. It shall be composed of 15 States Parties to the Convention, elected by States Parties to the Convention meeting in general assembly during the ordinary session of the General Conference of the United Nations Educational, Scientific and Cultural Organization. The number of States members of the Committee shall be increased to 21 as from the date of the ordinary session of the General Conference following the entry into force of this Convention for at least 40 States.

2. Election of members of the Committee shall ensure an equitable representation of the different regions and cultures of the world.

3. A representative of the International Centre for the Study of the Preservation and Restoration of Cultural Property (ICCROM), a representative of the International Council of Monuments and Sites (ICOMOS) and a representative of the International Union for Conservation of Nature and Natural Resources (IUCN), to whom may be added, at the request of States Parties to the Convention meeting in general assembly during the ordinary sessions of the General Conference of the United Nations Educational, Scientific and Cultural Organization, representatives of other intergovernmental or non - governmental organizations, with similar objectives, may attend the meetings of the Committee in an advisory capacity.

Article 9

1. The term of office of States members of the World Heritage Committee shall extend from the end of the ordinary session of the General Conference during which they are elected until the end of its third subsequent ordinary session.

2. The term of office of one - third of the members designated at the time of the first election shall, however, cease at the end of the first ordinary session of the General Conference following that at which they were elected; and the term of office of a further third of the members designated at the same time shall cease at

the end of the second ordinary session of the General Conference following that at which they were elected. The names of these members shall be chosen by lot by the President of the General Conference of the United Nations Educational, Scientific and Cultural Organization after the first election.

States members of the Committee shall choose as their representatives persons qualified in the field of the cultural or natural heritage.

Article 10

1. The World Heritage Committee shall adopt its Rules of Procedure.

2. The Committee may at any time invite public or private organizations or individuals to participate in its meetings for consultation on particular problems.

3. The Committee may create such consultative bodies as it deems necessary for the performance of its functions.

Article 11

1. Every State Party to this Convention shall, in so far as possible, submit to the World Heritage Committee an inventory of property forming part of the cultural and natural heritage, situated in its territory and suitable for inclusion in the list provided for in paragraph 2 of this Article. This inventory, which shall not be considered exhaustive, shall include documentation about the location of the property in question and its significance.

2. On the basis of the inventories submitted by States in accordance with paragraph 1, the Committee shall establish, keep up to date and publish, under the title of "World Heritage List," a list of properties forming part of the cultural heritage and natural heritage, as defined in Articles 1 and 2 of this Convention, which it considers as having outstanding universal value in terms of such criteria as it shall have established. An updated list shall be distributed at least every two years.

3. The inclusion of a property in the World Heritage List requires the consent of the State concerned. The inclusion of a property situated in a territory, sovereignty or jurisdiction over which is claimed by more than one State shall in no way prejudice the rights of the parties to the dispute.

4. The Committee shall establish, keep up to date and publish, whenever circumstances shall so require, under the title of "List of World Heritage in Danger", a list of the property appearing in the World Heritage List for the conservation of

which major operations are necessary and for which assistance has been requested under this Convention. This list shall contain an estimate of the cost of such operations. The list may include only such property forming part of the cultural and natural heritage as is threatened by serious and specific dangers, such as the threat of disappearance caused by accelerated deterioration, large - scale public or private projects or rapid urban or tourist development projects; destruction caused by changes in the use or ownership of the land; major alterations due to unknown causes; abandonment for any reason whatsoever; the outbreak or the threat of an armed conflict; calamities and cataclysms; serious fires, earthquakes, landslides; volcanic eruptions; changes in water level, floods and tidal waves. The Committee may at any time, in case of urgent need, make a new entry in the List of World Heritage in Danger and publicize such entry immediately.

5. The Committee shall define the criteria on the basis of which a property belonging to the cultural or natural heritage may be included in either of the lists mentioned in paragraphs 2 and 4 of this article.

6. Before refusing a request for inclusion in one of the two lists mentioned in paragraphs 2 and 4 of this article, the Committee shall consult the State Party in whose territory the cultural or natural property in question is situated.

7. The Committee shall, with the agreement of the States concerned, co - ordinate and encourage the studies and research needed for the drawing up of the lists referred to in paragraphs 2 and 4 of this article.

Article 12

The fact that a property belonging to the cultural or natural heritage has not been included in either of the two lists mentioned in paragraphs 2 and 4 of Article 11 shall in no way be construed to mean that it does not have an outstanding universal value for purposes other than those resulting from inclusion in these lists.

Article 13

1. The World Heritage Committee shall receive and study requests for international assistance formulated by States Parties to this Convention with respect to property forming part of the cultural or natural heritage, situated in their territories, and included or potentially suitable for inclusion in the lists mentioned referred to in paragraphs 2 and 4 of Article 11. The purpose of such requests may be to secure the protection, conservation, presentation or rehabilitation of such property.

2. Requests for international assistance under paragraph 1 of this article may also be concerned with identification of cultural or natural property defined in Articles 1 and 2, when preliminary investigations have shown that further inquiries would be justified.

3. The Committee shall decide on the action to be taken with regard to these requests, determine where appropriate, the nature and extent of its assistance, and authorize the conclusion, on its behalf, of the necessary arrangements with the government concerned.

4. The Committee shall determine an order of priorities for its operations. It shall in so doing bear in mind the respective importance for the world cultural and natural heritage of the property requiring protection, the need to give international assistance to the property most representative of a natural environment or of the genius and the history of the peoples of the world, the urgency of the work to be done, the resources available to the States on whose territory the threatened property is situated and in particular the extent to which they are able to safeguard such property by their own means.

5. The Committee shall draw up, keep up to date and publicize a list of property for which international assistance has been granted.

6. The Committee shall decide on the use of the resources of the Fund established under Article 15 of this Convention. It shall seek ways of increasing these resources and shall take all useful steps to this end.

7. The Committee shall co - operate with international and national governmental and non - governmental organizations having objectives similar to those of this Convention. For the implementation of its programmes and projects, the Committee may call on such organizations, particularly the International Centre for the Study of the Preservation and Restoration of cultural Property (the Rome Centre), the International Council of Monuments and Sites (ICOMOS) and the International Union for Conservation of Nature and Natural Resources (IUCN), as well as on public and private bodies and individuals.

8. Decisions of the Committee shall be taken by a majority of two - thirds of its members present and voting. A majority of the members of the Committee shall constitute a quorum.

Article 14

1. The World Heritage Committee shall be assisted by a Secretariat appointed by the Director - General of the United Nations Educational, Scientific and Cultural Organization.

2. The Director - General of the United Nations Educational, Scientific and Cultural Organization, utilizing to the fullest extent possible the services of the International Centre for the Study of the Preservation and the Restoration of Cultural Property (the Rome Centre), the International Council of Monuments and Sites (ICOMOS) and the International Union for Conservation of Nature and Natural Resources (IUCN) in their respective areas of competence and capability, shall prepare the Committee's documentation and the agenda of its meetings and shall have the responsibility for the implementation of its decisions.

IV. Fund for the Protection of the World Cultural and Natural Heritage

Article 15

1. A Fund for the Protection of the World Cultural and Natural Heritage of Outstanding Universal Value, called "the World Heritage Fund", is hereby established.

2. The Fund shall constitute a trust fund, in conformity with the provisions of the Financial Regulations of the United Nations Educational, Scientific and Cultural Organization.

3. The resources of the Fund shall consist of:

(1) compulsory and voluntary contributions made by States Parties to this Convention,

(2) Contributions, gifts or bequests which may be made by:

①other States;

②the United Nations Educational, Scientific and

Cultural Organization, other organizations of the United Nations system, particularly the United Nations Development Programme or other intergovernmental organizations;

③public or private bodies or individuals;

(3) any interest due on the resources of the Fund;

(4) funds raised by collections and receipts from events organized for the benefit of the fund; and

(5) all other resources authorized by the Fund's regulations, as drawn up by the World Heritage Committee.

4. Contributions to the Fund and other forms of assistance made available to the Committee may be used only for such purposes as the Committee shall define. The Committee may accept contributions to be used only for a certain programme or project, provided that the Committee shall have decided on the implementation of such programme or project. No political conditions may be attached to contributions made to the Fund.

Article 16

1. Without prejudice to any supplementary voluntarycontribution, the States Parties to this Convention undertake to pay regularly, every two years, to the World Heritage Fund, contributions, the amount of which, in the form of a uniform percentage applicable to all States, shall be determined by the General Assembly of States Parties to the Convention, meeting during the sessions of the General Conference of the United Nations Educational, Scientific and Cultural Organization. This decision of the General Assembly requires the majority of the States Parties present and voting, which have not made the declaration referred to in paragraph 2 of this Article. In no case shall the compulsory contribution of States Parties to the Convention exceed 1% of the contribution to the regular budget of the United Nations Educational, Scientific and Cultural Organization.

2. However, each State referred to in Article 31 or in Article 32 of this Convention may declare, at the time of the deposit of its instrument of ratification, acceptance or accession, that it shall not be bound by the provisions of paragraph 1 of this Article.

3. A State Party to the Convention which has made the declaration referred to in paragraph 2 of this Article may at any time withdraw the said declaration by notifying the Director - General of the United Nations Educational, Scientific and Cultural Organization. However, the withdrawal of the declaration shall not take effect in regard to the compulsory contribution due by the State until the date of the subsequent General Assembly of States parties to the Convention.

4. In order that the Committee may be able to plan its operations effectively, the contributions of States Parties to this Convention which have made the declaration referred to in paragraph 2 of this Article, shall be paid on a regular basis, at least every two years, and should not be less than the contributions which they should have paid if they had been bound by the provisions of paragraph 1 of this Article.

5. Any State Party to the Convention which is in arrears with the payment of its compulsory or voluntary contribution for the current year and the calendar year immediately preceding it shall not be eligible as a Member of the World Heritage Committee, although this provision shall not apply to the first election.

The terms of office of any such State which is already a member of the Committee shall terminate at the time of the elections provided for in Article 8, paragraph 1 of this Convention.

Article 17

The States Parties to this Convention shall consider or encourage the establishment of national public and private foundations or associations whose purpose is to invite donations for the protection of the cultural and natural heritage as defined in Articles 1 and 2 of this Convention.

Article 18

The States Parties to this Convention shall give their assistance to international fund - raising campaigns organized for the World Heritage Fund under the auspices of the United Nations Educational, Scientific and Cultural Organization. They shall facilitate collections made by the bodies mentioned in paragraph 3 of Article 15 for this purpose.

V. Conditions and Arrangements for International Assistance

Article 19

Any State Party to this Convention may request international assistance for property forming part of the cultural or natural heritage of outstanding universal value situated within its territory. It shall submit with its request such information and documentation provided for in Article 21 as it has in its possession and as will enable the Committee to come to a decision.

Article 20

Subject to the provisions of paragraph 2 of Article 13, sub - paragraph (c) of Article 22 and Article 23, international assistance provided for by this Convention may be granted only to property forming part of the cultural and natural heritage which the World Heritage Committee has decided, or may decide, to enter in one of the lists mentioned in paragraphs 2 and 4 of Article 11.

Article 21

1. The World Heritage Committee shall define the procedure by which requests to it for international assistance shall be considered and shall specify the content of the request, which should define the operation contemplated, the work that is necessary, the expected cost thereof, the degree of urgency and the reasons why the resources of the State requesting assistance do not allow it to meet all the expenses. Such requests must be supported by experts' reports whenever possible.

2. Requests based upon disasters or natural calamities should, by reasons of the urgent work which they may involve, be given immediate, priority consideration by the Committee, which should have a reserve fund at its disposal against such contingencies.

3. Before coming to a decision, the Committee shall carry out such studies and consultations as it deems necessary.

Article 22

. Assistance granted by the World Heritage Committee may take the following forms:

1. studies concerning the artistic, scientific and technical problems raised by the protection, conservation, presentation and rehabilitation of the cultural and natural heritage, as defined in paragraphs 2 and 4 of Article 11 of this Convention;

2. provisions of experts, technicians and skilled labour to ensure that the approved work is correctly carried out;

3. training of staff and specialists at all levels in the field of identification, protection, conservation, presentation and rehabilitation of the cultural and natural heritage;

4. supply of equipment which the State concerned does not possess or is not in a position to acquire;

5. low - interest or interest - free loans which might be repayable on a long - term basis;

6. the granting, in exceptional cases and for special reasons, of non - repayable subsidies.

Article 23

The World Heritage Committee may also provide international assistance to national or regional centres for the training of staff and specialists at all levels in the field of identification, protection, conservation, presentation and rehabilitation of the cultural and natural heritage.

Article 24

International assistance on a large scale shall be preceded by detailed scientific, economic and technical studies. These studies shall draw upon the most advanced techniques for the protection, conservation, presentation and rehabilitation of the natural and cultural heritage and shall be consistent with the objectives of this Convention. The studies shall also seek means of making rational use of the resources available in the State concerned.

Article 25

As a general rule, only part of the cost of work necessary shall be borne by the international community. The contribution of the State benefiting from international assistance shall constitute a substantial share of the resources devoted to each programme or project, unless its resources do not permit this.

Article 26

The World Heritage Committee and the recipient State shall define in the agreement they conclude the conditions in which a programme or project for which international assistance under the terms of this Convention is provided, shall be carried out. It shall be the responsibility of the State receiving such international assistance to continue to protect, conserve and present the property so safeguarded, in observance of the conditions laid down by the agreement.

VI. Educational Programmes

Article 27

1. The States Parties to this Convention shall endeavor by all appropriate

means, and in particular by educational and information programmes, to strengthen appreciation and respect by their peoples of the cultural and natural heritage defined in Articles 1 and 2 of the Convention.

2. They shall undertake to keep the public broadly informed of the dangers threatening this heritage and of the activities carried on in pursuance of this Convention.

Article 28

States Parties to this Convention which receive international assistance under the Convention shall take appropriate measures to make known the importance of the property for which assistance has been received and the role played by such assistance.

VII. Reports

Article 29

1. The States Parties to this Convention shall, in the reports which they submit to the General Conference of the United Nations Educational, Scientific and Cultural Organization on dates and in a manner to be determined by it, give information on the legislative and administrative provisions which they have adopted and other action which they have taken for the application of this Convention, together with details of the experience acquired in this field.

2. These reports shall be brought to the attention of the World Heritage Committee.

3. The Committee shall submit a report on its activities at each of the ordinary sessions of the General Conference of the United Nations Educational, Scientific and Cultural Organization.

VIII. Final Clauses

Article 30

This Convention is drawn up in Arabic, English, French, Russian and Spanish, the five texts being equally authoritative.

Article 31

1. This Convention shall be subject to ratification or acceptance by States members of the United Nations Educational, Scientific and Cultural Organization in accordance with their respective constitutional procedures.

2. The instruments of ratification or acceptance shall be deposited with the Director - General of the United Nations Educational, Scientific and Cultural Organization.

Article 32

1. This Convention shall be open to accession by all States not members of the United Nations Educational, Scientific and Cultural Organization which are invited by the General Conference of the Organization to accede to it.

2. Accession shall be effected by the deposit of an instrument of accession with the Director - General of the United Nations Educational, Scientific and Cultural Organization.

Article 33

This Convention shall enter into force three months after the date of the deposit of the twentieth instrument of ratification, acceptance or accession, but only with respect to those States which have deposited their respective instruments of ratification, acceptance or accession on or before that date. It shall enter into force with respect to any other State three months after the deposit of its instrument of ratification, acceptance or accession.

Article 34

The following provisions shall apply to those States Parties to this Convention which have a federal or non - unitary constitutional system:

1. with regard to the provisions of this Convention, the implementation of which comes under the legal jurisdiction of the federal or central legislative power, the obligations of the federal or central government shall be the same as for those States parties which are not federal States;

2. with regard to the provisions of this Convention, the implementation of which comes under the legal jurisdiction of individual constituent States, countries, provinces or cantons that are not obliged by the constitutional system of the federation to take legislative measures, the federal government shall inform the competent authorities of such States, countries, provinces or cantons of the said provi-

sions, with its recommendation for their adoption.

Article 35

1. Each State Party to this Convention may denounce the Convention.

2. The denunciation shall be notified by an instrument in writing, deposited with the Director - General of the United Nations Educational, Scientific and Cultural Organization.

3. The denunciation shall take effect twelve months after the receipt of the instrument of denunciation. It shall not affect the financial obligations of the denouncing State until the date on which the withdrawal takes effect.

Article 36

The Director - General of the United Nations Educational, Scientific and Cultural Organization shall inform the States members of the Organization, the States not members of the Organization which are referred to in Article 32, as well as the United Nations, of the deposit of all the instruments of ratification, acceptance, or accession provided for in Articles 31 and 32, and of the denunciations provided for in Article 35.

Article 37

1. This Convention may be revised by the General Conference of the United Nations Educational, Scientific and Cultural Organization. Any such revision shall, however, bind only the States which shall become Parties to the revising convention.

2. If the General Conference should adopt a new convention revising this Convention in whole or in part, then, unless the new convention otherwise provides, this Convention shall cease to be open to ratification, acceptance or accession, as from the date on which the new revising convention enters into force.

Article 38

In conformity with Article 102 of the Charter of the United Nations, this Convention shall be registered with the Secretariat of the United Nations at the request of the Director - General of the United Nations Educational, Scientific and Cultural Organization.

关于独立国家境内原住民和部落民族的第169号公约*

（国际劳工组织大会1989年6月27日通过，1991年9月5日生效）

国际劳工组织大会，国际劳工管理机构于1989年6月7日在日内瓦召开第76届大会：

注意到1957年《土著及部落民族公约》及《土著及部落民族推荐意见》中规定的标准；

回顾《国际人权宣言》、《经济、社会及文化权利国际公约》、《公民及政治权利国际公约》及多种旨在防止歧视的国际文件中的条款；

考虑到1957年后国际法的发展，及世界所有地区土著和部落民族处境的发展，适合就该议题制定新的国际标准，以消除之前标准的融合思路；

认识到该等民族在其所生活国家架构下对其自己的组织、生活方式及经济发展行使控制权并维护及发展其自我认同、语言和宗教的热望；

注意到在世界上许多地方这些民族不能像其生活国家其他民族那样同等地享有基本人权，并且其法律、价值、习惯和观念很多时候都遭到侵蚀；

呼吁关注土著及部落民族对人类文化多样性、社会和生态和谐及国际合作与理解的独到贡献；

注意到以下规定已经在联合国、联合国粮农组织、联合国教科文组织、世界卫生组织及美洲内部印第安学院之间，在适当层次并在此各自领域进行合作而形成，建议继续这种合作，促进并确保该等规定的适用，以及决定就1957年第107号《土著与部落民族公约》制定予以部分修改的建议，这被规定为会议议程第四项，以及认定该等建议须以国际公约的形式对1957年《土著与部落民族公约》进行修改；

---

* 中国社会科学院法学研究所吴峻译。

于1989年6月27日通过如下公约，本公约可以被援引为《1989年原住民与部落民族公约》。

第一部分 总体政策

第1条

1. 本公约适用于

（a）独立国家内的部落民族，其社会、经济及文化状况使其与国家其他群体区别开来，其地位系全部或部分由其自己的惯例、传统或特别法律、行政条例予以规制；

（b）独立国家内因其渊源于被征服、殖民化或确定该国家疆域之时，该国家或该国家所属更广泛地区的原住民而被认为土著民族；无论其法律地位为何，该等民族保留着其自身全部或部分的社会、经济、文化和政治体系。

2. 认定某群体是否适用本《公约》的有关规定，自己认同是否属于土著或部落民族是一项核心标准。

3. 本《公约》使用的术语“民族”不应被解释为对国际法中该术语所指向的权利造成任何影响。

第2条

1. 在有关民族参与的情形下，政府有职责着手采取协调及体系化的行动以保护该等民族的权利并保证对其完整性的尊重。

2. 该等行动应包括下列措施：

（a）确保该等民族成员平等享受国内法及行政条例赋予该等民族其他成员的权利和机会；

（b）就该等民族社会及文化认同、风俗习惯、传统及其组织，促进其社会、经济及文化权利的全面落实。

（c）协助有关民族成员消除在本国社会内土著及其他成员间存在的社会经济差距，其方式须与该等民族的渴望及生活方式相符。

第3条

1. 土著及部落民族须不受歧视、不受阻碍地享受全部人权及基本自由。本《公约》规定的适用不得在该等民族中的男女之间造成歧视。

2. 不得使用一切形式的武力和协迫，以侵犯相关人员包括本公约所规定权利在内的人权和基本自由。

第 4 条

1. 须在适当情形下采取特别措施保障有关民族人员、制度、财产、劳工、文化及环境。

2. 该等特别措施不得违反相关民族的自由意志。

3. 不受歧视地享有公民一般权利不得因该等特别措施而在任何方面受到不利影响。

第 5 条

在适用《公约》规定时，

(a) 该等民族的社会、文化、宗教及精神价值和做法须得到承认和保护，对于其作为群体及个人所遇到问题的性质，也须予以适当考虑；

(b) 该等民族价值、做法及制度的完整性得予以尊重；

(c) 在所涉及民族参与并配合的情形下，须制定旨在减缓该等民族面对生活和工作新局面时遇到困境的条款。

第 6 条

1. 适用本《公约》规定时，政府应

(a) 只要对可能直接影响有关民族的法律和行政法规予以考虑时，通过适当程序与有关民族协商，尤其要通过其代表机构进行；

(b) 确立该等民族可以自由参与的方式，至少要达到其他民族参与的程度，以便其参与负责其相关政策及项目的选举立法机关、行政机关及其他机关的所有决策层面；

(c) 确立该等民族自己的制度和动议可以充分发展的方式，在适当情形下须提供为实现此目的所必需的资源。

2. 为适用本《公约》规定而进行的协商应基于善意进行，其形式基于情形是适当的，目的是就拟采取的措施取得同意和认可。

第 7 条

1. 就影响其生活、信仰、体制、精神生活、其占据或进行他用土地的发展进程，有关民族须有权决定其优先事项，并在可能的情形下对其经济、社会及文化发展享有控制权。另外，对于可能直接影响他们的国际及地区发展计划和项目，他们须参与其指定、实施及评估。

2. 在其参与和合作下改善相关民族生活、工作条件并提高其医疗和教育水平须是其所居住地区整体经济发展计划的优先事项。有关地区发展的特殊项目之涉及也须促进该等改善。

3. 政府须确保在任何适当的情况下与相关民族合作展开研究，评估计划中的发展行为对其社会、精神、文化及环境方面的影响。该等研究的结论须被视为是实施该等行为的基本原则。

4. 政府须采取措施，与相关民族合作，保护并维护其居住地的环境。

第 8 条

1. 对相关民族使用国内法律及行政条例的，需对其风俗习惯及习惯法予以适当考虑。

2. 该等民族须风俗习惯及制度与国内法律制度界定的基本权利及国际公认的人权相符的，须有权将之保留。在任何必要的情形下，须设立程序解决适用该原则所可能产生的冲突。

3. 对本条第一款及第二款的适用不得阻止该等民族的成员行使赋予所有公民的权利及承担相应的义务。

第 9 条

1. 在与国内法律体系及国际公认人权相符的前提下，有关民族处理其成员违法行为所惯常使用的方式须得到尊重。

2. 该等民族对刑事案件的风俗习惯须为处理该等案件的国家机构和法院予以考虑。

第 10 条

1. 在对该等民族成员进行一般法律所规定的刑事处罚时，须考虑其经济、社会及文化特质。

2. 须优先考虑监禁之外的刑事处罚方式。

第 11 条

须禁止强令有关民族成员提供任何形式的个人服务，无论付费与否，但法律对所有公民都作出这种规定的情形除外。

第 12 条

须保障相关民族的权利不受侵犯并须能够为了有效保护这些权利通过其个人或代表机构发起法律程序。须采取措施以确保该等民族的成员能够在法律程序中理解或得到理解，并在必要的情形下通过提供翻译或以其他有效方式予以帮助。

第二部分 土 地

第 13 条

1. 适用本《公约》本部分之规定的，政府须对相关民族文化及精神价值与其土地或领地或在适用情形下其占有或者以其他方式所使用土地之间关系——尤其对于该等关系的总体方面——的特别重要性予以尊重。

2. 第15条及16条使用土地这一术语包括领地这一概念，涵盖有关民族占有或以其他方式使用地区的总体环境。

第14条

1. 有关民族对其传统占据土地具有的所有及占有权利须予以认可。另外，须在合适情形下采取措施确保有关民族使用并非由其独家占据土地的权利，对于这些土地他们在传统上为其基本生活及传统活动予以使用。在这方面，须尤其注意游牧民族及迁徙农民的处境。

2. 政府须采取必要的步骤以确定有关民族传统占据的土地，并确保对其所有权和占有权给予有效保护。

3. 须在全国法律体系中建立足够程序处理有关民族对其土地的主张。

第15条

1. 有关民族对于其土地所蕴涵自然资源的权利应予以特别保障。该等权利包括该等民族参与使用、管理及保护该等资源的权利。

2. 国家保留土地蕴涵矿产资源、地下资源的所有权及对其他资源权利的，政府须建立或维持相关程序，通过该等程序他们须与该等民族协商，以便在实施或允许勘探、开采土地所蕴涵该等资源的计划之前评估该等民族的利益是否受到不利影响及其影响程度。有关民族须在任何可能的情形下参与该等活动的收益，并就该等活动而蒙受的任何损失获得公平补偿。

第16条

1. 在满足本条以下各款规定的前提下，不得将有关民族迁移出其所在的土地。

2. 重新安置该等民族作为特别措施而认为是必要的情形下，仅得在取得其自主且知情情形下方得重新进行安置。不能获得该等同意的，该等重新安置仅得在遵守国内法律及行政条例所确立程序的前提下方可进行。该等程序包括适当情形下有关民族有机会得以有效代表的公开质询。

3. 可能的情况下，只要重新安置的理由不再存在，该等民族须有权返回其传统土地。

4. 不可能返回的情形下，依照协议约定或者在协议不存在的情形下通过适当程序，须尽量向该等民族提供与其之前所在土地的质量及法律状况至少同等的土地，该土地适于其目前需求及未来发展的需要。有关民族表示更愿意取得金钱或实物形式补偿的，须在适当保证的基础上予以进行该种补偿。

5．通过这种方式予以重新安置的人员须就造成的任何损失或伤害予以完全补偿。

第 17 条

1．有关民族就其成员内部转让土地权利而确立的程序须予以尊重。

2．只要考虑让有关民族能够让渡其土地或者以其他方式向其群体之外的人员转让其权利，就须与该民族协商。

3．须阻止不属于该等民族的人利用该民族风俗习惯或其成员对法律缺乏了解的状况而获得属于该民族的土地所有权、占有权及使用权。

第 18 条

就对有关民族土地进行未经授权的侵入或使用的，须确立足够的处罚措施，并且政府须采取措施阻止该等侵害。

第 19 条

就下列事项，国家农业项目须确保有关民族获得的待遇等同于对其他领域民众所享有的待遇：

（a）该等民族的地域不足于为其生存提供关键条件或不能促进其成员数目增长的，应予以提供更多土地。

（b）为促进该等民族已经生活的土地进一步发展，提供必要的手段。

第三部分　招募员工及雇佣条件

第 20 条

1．政府须在国内法律及行政条例确立的架构中与相关民族合作，制定特别措施，在一般劳工法律不能提供有效保护的前提下，对属于该等民族员工在招募及雇佣条件方面进行有效保护。

2．政府须尽一切努力阻止在该民族员工及其他员工之间产生歧视，尤其在以下方面更是如此：

（a）在工作岗位晋升措施之外进行包括熟练员工在内的员工招募；

（b）同工同酬；

（c）医疗及社会援助、职业安全及健康、所有的社会保险福利及任何其他工作相关福利、住房；

（d）结社权利及进行所有工会活动的自由，以及与雇主及雇主组织达成集体协议的权利。

3．所采取的措施须包括确保以下事项的措施：

（a）包括农业季节性、非正式及迁移性员工及其他形式员工在内的有关民族员工及被劳务承包方所雇佣的该有关民族员工，享有国内法及管理所赋予该领域其他员工的保护，并且该等有关民族的员工就其在劳工法律中的权利及可以采取的救济手段获得告知；

（b）该民族员工的工作条件不得损害其健康，尤其不得使之暴露于杀虫剂及其他有毒物质之下；

（c）该民族员工的招募体系不得是强制性的，包括不得是限制人身自由的劳役及债务劳役。

（d）在雇佣过程中，该民族员工男女机会均等及地位平等，并保护其免受性骚扰。

4. 在有关民族员工进行有偿工作的领域，应特别注意要设立足够的劳动监察服务机制，以确保符合本《公约》本部分的规定。

第四部分　职业培训、手工业及乡村行业

第21条

有关民族成员就职业培训措施而言须享有至少与其他公民同等的机会。

第22条

1. 须采取措施鼓励有关民族员工自发参与向所有员工开放的培训计划。

2. 只要目前向所有员工开放的培训计划不能满足有关民族的特殊需要，政府须在有关民族的参与下确保提供特殊的职业培训计划及设施。

3. 任何特殊职业培训计划均须基于有关民族的环境、社会及文化条件及现实需要。就此进行的任何研究须与有关民族合作进行，并就特殊配需计划的组织和运作与该等民族进行协商。可行的话，该等民族在自己决定的前提下可以逐渐承担该等特殊培训计划的组织和运作工作。

第23条

1. 对该等民族手工业、乡村行业及基于社区的工业及诸如狩猎、打鱼、诱捕及收集等设计生活必需品的经济和传统活动，须承认其作为保留该等民族文化及其经济自主与发展方面是一项重要的因素。政府须在该等民族的参与下及任何适当情形下加强及促进该等活动。

2. 应有关民族的请求，只要有可能，考虑到该等民族传统科技及文化特征，并考虑到持续性及公平发展的重要性，须提供适当的技术及金融扶持。

第五部分　社会保障及健康

第 24 条

社会保障体系须逐渐扩展至有关民族，并在适用时没有任何歧视。

第 25 条

1. 政府须确保向有关民族提供足够的医疗服务，或者向其提供资源使其能够自己负责并控制的情形下设计并提供该等服务，以便他们的生理及心理健康处于较高水平。

2. 医疗服务须尽可能以社区为基础。该等服务须通过与有关民族进行合作的方式进行规划和管理，并须考虑该等民族的经济、地理、社会及文化条件及其传统预防护理、治疗及医药手段。

3. 医疗体系须将本地社区医疗工作者的配需及招募作为优先事项，并关注基本医疗服务，并在同时保持与其他层次医疗服务的密切联系。

4. 提供该等医疗服务的，须与国家其他社会、经济和文化措施相协调。

第六部分　教育及通讯手段

第 26 条

须采取措施确保有关民族成员有机会至少能与国家其他社会成员平等地获得所有层次上的教育。

第 27 条

1. 对有关民族的教育项目和服务，须针对其特殊需要与之合作进行开发和落实，并须纳入其历史、知识、技术、价值体系及其进一步的社会、经济及文化设想。

2. 负责机构须确保对该等民族成员进行培训并使之参与教育项目的规划落实，逐渐将该等项目进行的责任在适当情形下转交给该等民族。

3. 另外，政府须承认该等民族建立其自己教育制度及设施的权利，但该等制度须符合负责机关经与该等民族协商后确定的最低标准。为此目的须提供适当的资源。

第 28 条

1. 须在可行的情形下向有关民族的儿童提供教育，使其能够以其自己或其族群普遍使用的语言阅读和书写。如不可行，负责机构须与该等民族协商，以便采取措施实现该等目标。

2. 须采取足够措施确保该等民族有机会能够熟练使用国家通用语言或者该国的一种官方语言。

3. 须采取措施保留并促进有关民族本土语言的发展和使用。

第29条

有关民族的教育目的之一就是传授一般性的指示和技能，以帮助该民族的儿童充分并平等参与到自己社区及该国社会之中。

第30条

1. 政府须采取符合有关民族传统及文化的适当措施，以便使之了解其权利和义务，尤其是劳动、经济机会、教育及医疗事项、社会福利及其基于本《公约》所享有的各项权利。

2. 如必要，须以基于本民族语言的书面翻译及大众通讯进行。

第31条

须在国内社会各阶层中间、尤其在与于有关民族发生最直接接触的阶层中采取教育措施，以消除他们可以对该等民族保有的成见。为此目的，须采取行动确保历史教科书及其他教育材料公平、准确对该等民族及文化进行介绍性的描述。

第七部分　跨境交往及合作

第32条

政府须采取适当措施，包括通过国际协定的方式促进土著及部落民族跨境的交往与合作，包括在经济、社会、文化、精神及环境领域从事的活动。

第八部分　管　理

第33条

1. 负责本《公约》涵盖事项的政府机构须确保存在该机构及其他适当机制以管理影响有关民族的项目，并须确保他们有必要的手段对赋予其职权予以正确行使。

2. 该等项目须包括：

(a) 对本《公约》所规定措施与有关民族合作进行规划、协调、执行及评价的措施；

（b）与有关民族合作，向负责机构提出立法及其他建议，对适用所采取措施进行的监督。

第九部分　一般规定

第 34 条

为落实本《公约》采取措施的性质和范围，须依照灵活的方式确定，并要考虑每一个国家的特点。

第 35 条

对本《公约》条款的适用不得对有关民族根据其他公约、示范文本、国际文件、条约或国内法律、授权、风俗习惯或协议而享有的权利及福利造成负面影响。

第十部分　最后条款

第 36 条

本公约构成对《1957 年土著及部落民族公约》的修改。

第 37 条

对本《公约》的正式批准须通告国际劳工局总干事并进行登记。

第 38 条

1. 本《公约》仅仅对已经于总干事就批准进行登记的国际劳工组织成员国予以适用。

2. 在两个成员国于总干事就批准予以登记 12 个月之后，本《公约》生效。

3. 之后，本《公约》须在任何成员国将其批准予以登记 12 个月之后对该成员国生效。

第 39 条

1. 已经批准本《公约》的成员国可以在本《公约》首次生效十年之后通过向国际劳工局总干事予以通告进行登记的方式予以退出。该等退出须在其登记一年之后方可生效。

2. 每一个批准本《公约》的成员国如果在前款规定十年期间过后的一年内行使本条规定的退出权，须在另一个十年期间适用本《公约》，并在之后可以在每一个十年期间届满后按照本条规定的条件予以退出。

第 40 条

1. 国际劳工局总干事须就国际劳工组织成员通告予其的所有批准及退出进行登记的情形向该组织的所有成员予以通报。

2. 向该组织所有成员国就其予以登记的第二次批准通告进行通报的，总干事须提请组织成员国关注《公约》生效的日期。

第 41 条

国际劳工局总干事须按照《联合国宪章》第 102 条的规定就其根据前条规定予以登记的所有批准及退出的全部详情向联合国秘书长进行通告，予以登记。

第 42 条

在该等情形下，如其认为必要，国际劳工局管理机构须向大会提交本《公约》实施情况的报告，并须审查是否有必要将《公约》全部或部分予以修改的问题纳入大会议程。

第 43 条

1. 大会通过新公约以对本《公约》全部或部分予以修改的，除非新公约另有规定：

（a）成员国对修改后的公约的批准依法构成本《公约》的自动失效，尽管以上第 39 条对新修订的公约是否生效以及何时生效做出规定；

（b）在新公约生效之日，本《公约》即停止开放接受其成员批准。

2. 本《公约》在任何情况下就其当时形式和内容对批准本《公约》但没有批准所修改公约的成员国依然有效。

第 44 条

本《公约》文本的英文及法文版本拥有同等效力。

Convention concerning Indigenous and Tribal Peoples in Independent Countries

Note: Date of coming into force: 05:09:1991.
Convention: C169
Place: Geneva
Session of the Conference: 76
Date of adoption:27:06:1989
Subject classification: Indigenous and Tribal Peoples
Subject: Indigenous and Tribal Peoples

The General Conference of the International Labour Organisation,

Having been convened at Geneva by the Governing Body of the International Labour Office, and having met in its 76th Session on 7 June 1989, and

Noting the international standards contained in the Indigenous and Tribal Populations Convention and Recommendation, 1957, and

Recalling the terms of the Universal Declaration of Human Rights, the International Covenant on Economic, Social and Cultural Rights, the International Covenant on Civil and Political Rights, and the many international instruments on the prevention of discrimination, and

Considering that the developments which have taken place in international law since 1957, as well as developments in the situation of indigenous and tribal peoples in all regions of the world, have made it appropriate to adopt new international standards on the subject with a view to removing the assimilationist orientation of the earlier standards, and

Recognising the aspirations of these peoples to exercise control over their own institutions, ways of life and economic development and to maintain and develop their identities, languages and religions, within the framework of the States in which they live, and

Noting that in many parts of the world these peoples are unable to enjoy their fundamental human rights to the same degree as the rest of the population of the States within which they live, and that their laws, values, customs and perspectives have often been eroded, and

Calling attention to the distinctive contributions of indigenous and tribal peoples to the cultural diversity and social and ecological harmony of humankind and to international co - operation and understanding, and

Noting that the following provisions have been framed with the co - operation of the United Nations, the Food and Agriculture Organisation of the United Nations, the United Nations Educational, Scientific and Cultural Organisation and the World Health Organisation, as well as of the Inter - American Indian Institute, at appropriate levels and in their respective fields, and that it is proposed to continue this co - operation in promoting and securing the application of these provisions, and

Having decided upon the adoption of certain proposals with regard to the partial revision of the Indigenous and Tribal Populations Convention, 1957 (No. 107), which is the fourth item on the agenda of the session, and

Having determined that these proposals shall take the form of an international Convention revising the Indigenous and Tribal Populations Convention, 1957;

adopts this twenty - seventh day of June of the year one thousand nine hundred and eighty - nine the following Convention, which may be cited as the Indigenous and Tribal Peoples Convention, 1989;

PART I. GENERAL POLICY

Article 1

1. This Convention applies to:

(a) tribal peoples in independent countries whose social, cultural and economic conditions distinguish them from other sections of the national community, and whose status is regulated wholly or partially by their own customs or traditions or by special laws or regulations;

(b) peoples in independent countries who are regarded as indigenous on account of their descent from the populations which inhabited the country, or a geographical region to which the country belongs, at the time of conquest or colonisation or the establishment of present state boundaries and who, irrespective of their legal status, retain some or all of their own social, economic, cultural and political institutions.

2. Self - identification as indigenous or tribal shall be regarded as a fundamental criterion for determining the groups to which the provisions of this Convention apply.

3. The use of the term *peoples* in this Convention shall not be construed as having any implications as regards the rights which may attach to the term under international law.

Article 2

1. Governments shall have the responsibility for developing, with the participation of the peoples concerned, co - ordinated and systematic action to protect the rights of these peoples and to guarantee respect for their integrity.

2. Such action shall include measures for:

(a) ensuring that members of these peoples benefit on an equal footing from the rights and opportunities which national laws and regulations grant to other members of the population;

(b) promoting the full realisation of the social, economic and cultural rights of these peoples with respect for their social and cultural identity, their customs and traditions and their institutions;

(c) assisting the members of the peoples concerned to eliminate socio - economic gaps that may exist between indigenous and other members of the national community, in a manner compatible with their aspirations and ways of life.

Article 3

1. Indigenous and tribal peoples shall enjoy the full measure of human rights and fundamental freedoms without hindrance or discrimination. The provisions of the Convention shall be applied without discrimination to male and female members of these peoples.

2. No form of force or coercion shall be used in violation of the human rights and fundamental freedoms of the peoples concerned, including the rights contained in this Convention.

Article 4

1. Special measures shall be adopted as appropriate for safeguarding the persons, institutions, property, labour, cultures and environment of the peoples concerned.

2. Such special measures shall not be contrary to the freely - expressed wishes of the peoples concerned.

3. Enjoyment of the general rights of citizenship, without discrimination, shall not be prejudiced in any way by such special measures.

Article 5

In applying the provisions of this Convention:

(a) the social, cultural, religious and spiritual values and practices of these peoples shall be recognised and protected, and due account shall be taken of the nature of the problems which face them both as groups and as individuals;

(b) the integrity of the values, practices and institutions of these peoples shall be respected;

(c) policies aimed at mitigating the difficulties experienced by these peoples in facing new conditions of life and work shall be adopted, with the participation and co - operation of the peoples affected.

Article 6

1. In applying the provisions of this Convention, governments shall:

(a) consult the peoples concerned, through appropriate procedures and in particular through their representative institutions, whenever consideration is being given to legislative or administrative measures which may affect them directly;

(b) establish means by which these peoples can freely participate, to at least the same extent as other sectors of the population, at all levels of decision - making in elective institutions and administrative and other bodies responsible for policies and programmes which concern them;

(c) establish means for the full development of these peoples' own institutions and initiatives, and in appropriate cases provide the resources necessary for this purpose.

2. The consultations carried out in application of this Convention shall be undertaken, in good faith and in a form appropriate to the circumstances, with the objective of achieving agreement or consent to the proposed measures.

Article 7

1. The peoples concerned shall have the right to decide their own priorities for the process of development as it affects their lives, beliefs, institutions and spiritual well - being and the lands they occupy or otherwise use, and to exercise control, to the extent possible, over their own economic, social and cultural development. In addition, they shall participate in the formulation, implementation and evaluation of plans and programmes for national and regional development which may affect them directly.

2. The improvement of the conditions of life and work and levels of health and education of the peoples concerned, with their participation and co - operation, shall be a matter of priority in plans for the overall economic development of areas they inhabit. Special projects for development of the areas in question shall also be so designed as to promote such improvement.

3. Governments shall ensure that, whenever appropriate, studies are carried out, in co - operation with the peoples concerned, to assess the social, spiritual, cultural and environmental impact on them of planned development activities. The results of these studies shall be considered as fundamental criteria for the implementation of these activities.

4. Governments shall take measures, in co - operation with the peoples concerned, to protect and preserve the environment of the territories they inhabit.

Article 8

1. In applying national laws and regulations to the peoples concerned, due regard shall be had to their customs or customary laws.

2. These peoples shall have the right to retain their own customs and institutions, where these are not incompatible with fundamental rights defined by the national legal system and with internationally recognised human rights. Procedures shall be established, whenever necessary, to resolve conflicts which may arise in the application of this principle.

3. The application of paragraphs 1 and 2 of this Article shall not prevent members of these peoples from exercising the rights granted to all citizens and from assuming the corresponding duties.

Article 9

1. To the extent compatible with the national legal system and internationally

recognised human rights, the methods customarily practised by the peoples concerned for dealing with offences committed by their members shall be respected.

2. The customs of these peoples in regard to penal matters shall be taken into consideration by the authorities and courts dealing with such cases.

Article 10

1. In imposing penalties laid down by general law on members of these peoples account shall be taken of their economic, social and cultural characteristics.

2. Preference shall be given to methods of punishment other than confinement in prison.

Article 11

The exaction from members of the peoples concerned of compulsory personal services in any form, whether paid or unpaid, shall be prohibited and punishable by law, except in cases prescribed by law for all citizens.

Article 12

The peoples concerned shall be safeguarded against the abuse of their rights and shall be able to take legal proceedings, either individually or through their representative bodies, for the effective protection of these rights. Measures shall be taken to ensure that members of these peoples can understand and be understood in legal proceedings, where necessary through the provision of interpretation or by other effective means.

PART II. LAND

Article 13

1. In applying the provisions of this Part of the Convention governments shall respect the special importance for the cultures and spiritual values of the peoples concerned of their relationship with the lands or territories, or both as applicable, which they occupy or otherwise use, and in particular the collective aspects of this relationship.

2. The use of the term *lands* in Articles 15 and 16 shall include the concept of territories, which covers the total environment of the areas which the peoples concerned occupy or otherwise use.

Article 14

1. The rights of ownership and possession of the peoples concerned over the

lands which they traditionally occupy shall be recognised. In addition, measures shall be taken in appropriate cases to safeguard the right of the peoples concerned to use lands not exclusively occupied by them, but to which they have traditionally had access for their subsistence and traditional activities. Particular attention shall be paid to the situation of nomadic peoples and shifting cultivators in this respect.

2. Governments shall take steps as necessary to identify the lands which the peoples concerned traditionally occupy, and to guarantee effective protection of their rights of ownership and possession.

3. Adequate procedures shall be established within the national legal system to resolve land claims by the peoples concerned.

Article 15

1. The rights of the peoples concerned to the natural resources pertaining to their lands shall be specially safeguarded. These rights include the right of these peoples to participate in the use, management and conservation of these resources.

2. In cases in which the State retains the ownership of mineral or sub - surface resources or rights to other resources pertaining to lands, governments shall establish or maintain procedures through which they shall consult these peoples, with a view to ascertaining whether and to what degree their interests would be prejudiced, before undertaking or permitting any programmes for the exploration or exploitation of such resources pertaining to their lands. The peoples concerned shall wherever possible participate in the benefits of such activities, and shall receive fair compensation for any damages which they may sustain as a result of such activities.

Article 16

1. Subject to the following paragraphs of this Article, the peoples concerned shall not be removed from the lands which they occupy.

2. Where the relocation of these peoples is considered necessary as an exceptional measure, such relocation shall take place only with their free and informed consent. Where their consent cannot be obtained, such relocation shall take place only following appropriate procedures established by national laws and regulations, including public inquiries where appropriate, which provide the opportunity for effective representation of the peoples concerned.

3. Whenever possible, these peoples shall have the right to return to their traditional lands, as soon as the grounds for relocation cease to exist.

4. When such return is not possible, as determined by agreement or, in the absence of such agreement, through appropriate procedures, these peoples shall be provided in all possible cases with lands of quality and legal status at least equal to that of the lands previously occupied by them, suitable to provide for their present needs and future development. Where the peoples concerned express a preference for compensation in money or in kind, they shall be so compensated under appropriate guarantees.

5. Persons thus relocated shall be fully compensated for any resulting loss or injury.

Article 17

1. Procedures established by the peoples concerned for the transmission of land rights among members of these peoples shall be respected.

2. The peoples concerned shall be consulted whenever consideration is being given to their capacity to alienate their lands or otherwise transmit their rights outside their own community.

3. Persons not belonging to these peoples shall be prevented from taking advantage of their customs or of lack of understanding of the laws on the part of their members to secure the ownership, possession or use of land belonging to them.

Article 18

Adequate penalties shall be established by law for unauthorised intrusion upon, or use of, the lands of the peoples concerned, and governments shall take measures to prevent such offences.

Article 19

National agrarian programmes shall secure to the peoples concerned treatment equivalent to that accorded to other sectors of the population with regard to:

(a) the provision of more land for these peoples when they have not the area necessary for providing the essentials of a normal existence, or for any possible increase in their numbers;

(b) the provision of the means required to promote the development of the lands which these peoples already possess.

PART III. RECRUITMENT AND CONDITIONS OF EMPLOYMENT

Article 20

1. Governments shall, within the framework of national laws and regulations, and in co - operation with the peoples concerned, adopt special measures to ensure the effective protection with regard to recruitment and conditions of employment of workers belonging to these peoples, to the extent that they are not effectively protected by laws applicable to workers in general.

2. Governments shall do everything possible to prevent any discrimination between workers belonging to the peoples concerned and other workers, in particular as regards:

(a) admission to employment, including skilled employment, as well as measures for promotion and advancement;

(b) equal remuneration for work of equal value;

(c) medical and social assistance, occupational safety and health, all social security benefits and any other occupationally related benefits, and housing;

(d) the right of association and freedom for all lawful trade union activities, and the right to conclude collective agreements with employers or employers' organisations.

3. The measures taken shall include measures to ensure:

(a) that workers belonging to the peoples concerned, including seasonal, casual and migrant workers in agricultural and other employment, as well as those employed by labour contractors, enjoy the protection afforded by national law and practice to other such workers in the same sectors, and that they are fully informed of their rights under labour legislation and of the means of redress available to them;

(b) that workers belonging to these peoples are not subjected to working conditions hazardous to their health, in particular through exposure to pesticides or other toxic substances;

(c) that workers belonging to these peoples are not subjected to coercive recruitment systems, including bonded labour and other forms of debt servitude;

(d) that workers belonging to these peoples enjoy equal opportunities and equal treatment in employment for men and women, and protection from sexual harassment.

4. Particular attention shall be paid to the establishment of adequate labour inspection services in areas where workers belonging to the peoples concerned undertake wage employment, in order to ensure compliance with the provisions of this Part of this Convention.

PART IV. VOCATIONAL TRAINING, HANDICRAFTS AND RURAL INDUSTRIES

Article 21

Members of the peoples concerned shall enjoy opportunities at least equal to those of other citizens in respect of vocational training measures.

Article 22

1. Measures shall be taken to promote the voluntary participation of members of the peoples concerned in vocational training programmes of general application.

2. Whenever existing programmes of vocational training of general application do not meet the special needs of the peoples concerned, governments shall, with the participation of these peoples, ensure the provision of special training programmes and facilities.

3. Any special training programmes shall be based on the economic environment, social and cultural conditions and practical needs of the peoples concerned. Any studies made in this connection shall be carried out in co - operation with these peoples, who shall be consulted on the organisation and operation of such programmes. Where feasible, these peoples shall progressively assume responsibility for the organisation and operation of such special training programmes, if they so decide.

Article 23

1. Handicrafts, rural and community - based industries, and subsistence economy and traditional activities of the peoples concerned, such as hunting, fishing, trapping and gathering, shall be recognised as important factors in the maintenance of their cultures and in their economic self - reliance and development. Gov-

ernments shall, with the participation of these people and whenever appropriate, ensure that these activities are strengthened and promoted.

2. Upon the request of the peoples concerned, appropriate technical and financial assistance shall be provided wherever possible, taking into account the traditional technologies and cultural characteristics of these peoples, as well as the importance of sustainable and equitable development.

PART V. SOCIAL SECURITY AND HEALTH

Article 24

Social security schemes shall be extended progressively to cover the peoples concerned, and applied without discrimination against them.

Article 25

1. Governments shall ensure that adequate health services are made available to the peoples concerned, or shall provide them with resources to allow them to design and deliver such services under their own responsibility and control, so that they may enjoy the highest attainable standard of physical and mental health.

2. Health services shall, to the extent possible, be community - based. These services shall be planned and administered in co - operation with the peoples concerned and take into account their economic, geographic, social and cultural conditions as well as their traditional preventive care, healing practices and medicines.

3. The health care system shall give preference to the training and employment of local community health workers, and focus on primary health care while maintaining strong links with other levels of health care services.

4. The provision of such health services shall be co - ordinated with other social, economic and cultural measures in the country.

PART VI. EDUCATION AND MEANS OF COMMUNICATION

Article 26

Measures shall be taken to ensure that members of the peoples concerned have the opportunity to acquire education at all levels on at least an equal footing with the rest of the national community.

Article 27

1. Education programmes and services for the peoples concerned shall be de-

veloped and implemented in co - operation with them to address their special needs, and shall incorporate their histories, their knowledge and technologies, their value systems and their further social, economic and cultural aspirations.

2. The competent authority shall ensure the training of members of these peoples and their involvement in the formulation and implementation of education programmes, with a view to the progressive transfer of responsibility for the conduct of these programmes to these peoples as appropriate.

3. In addition, governments shall recognise the right of these peoples to establish their own educational institutions and facilities, provided that such institutions meet minimum standards established by the competent authority in consultation with these peoples. Appropriate resources shall be provided for this purpose.

Article 28

1. Children belonging to the peoples concerned shall, wherever practicable, be taught to read and write in their own indigenous language or in the language most commonly used by the group to which they belong. When this is not practicable, the competent authorities shall undertake consultations with these peoples with a view to the adoption of measures to achieve this objective.

2. Adequate measures shall be taken to ensure that these peoples have the opportunity to attain fluency in the national language or in one of the official languages of the country.

3. Measures shall be taken to preserve and promote the development and practice of the indigenous languages of the peoples concerned.

Article 29

The imparting of general knowledge and skills that will help children belonging to the peoples concerned to participate fully and on an equal footing in their own community and in the national community shall be an aim of education for these peoples.

Article 30

1. Governments shall adopt measures appropriate to the traditions and cultures of the peoples concerned, to make known to them their rights and duties, especially in regard to labour, economic opportunities, education and health matters, social welfare and their rights deriving from this Convention.

2. If necessary, this shall be done by means of written translations and

through the use of mass communications in the languages of these peoples.

Article 31

Educational measures shall be taken among all sections of the national community, and particularly among those that are in most direct contact with the peoples concerned, with the object of eliminating prejudices that they may harbour in respect of these peoples. To this end, efforts shall be made to ensure that history textbooks and other educational materials provide a fair, accurate and informative portrayal of the societies and cultures of these peoples.

PART VII. CONTACTS AND CO – OPERATION ACROSS BORDERS

Article 32

Governments shall take appropriate measures, including by means of international agreements, to facilitate contacts and co - operation between indigenous and tribal peoples across borders, including activities in the economic, social, cultural, spiritual and environmental fields.

PART VIII. ADMINISTRATION

Article 33

1. The governmental authority responsible for the matters covered in this Convention shall ensure that agencies or other appropriate mechanisms exist to administer the programmes affecting the peoples concerned, and shall ensure that they have the means necessary for the proper fulfilment of the functions assigned to them.

2. These programmes shall include:

(a) the planning, co - ordination, execution and evaluation, in co - operation with the peoples concerned, of the measures provided for in this Convention;

(b) the proposing of legislative and other measures to the competent authorities and supervision of the application of the measures taken, in co - operation with the peoples concerned.

PART IX. GENERAL PROVISIONS

Article 34

The nature and scope of the measures to be taken to give effect to this Convention shall be determined in a flexible manner, having regard to the conditions characteristic of each country.

Article 35

The application of the provisions of this Convention shall not adversely affect rights and benefits of the peoples concerned pursuant to other Conventions and Recommendations, international instruments, treaties, or national laws, awards, custom or agreements.

PART X. FINAL PROVISIONS

Article 36

This Convention revises the Indigenous and Tribal Populations Convention, 1957.

Article 37

The formal ratifications of this Convention shall be communicated to the Director - General of the International Labour Office for registration.

Article 38

1. This Convention shall be binding only upon those Members of the International Labour Organisation whose ratifications have been registered with the Director - General.

2. It shall come into force twelve months after the date on which the ratifications of two Members have been registered with the Director - General.

3. Thereafter, this Convention shall come into force for any Member twelve months after the date on which its ratification has been registered.

Article 39

1. A Member which has ratified this Convention may denounce it after the expiration of ten years from the date on which the Convention first comes into force, by an act communicated to the Director - General of the International Labour Office

for registration. Such denunciation shall not take effect until one year after the date on which it is registered.

2. Each Member which has ratified this Convention and which does not, within the year following the expiration of the period of ten years mentioned in the preceding paragraph, exercise the right of denunciation provided for in this Article, will be bound for another period of ten years and, thereafter, may denounce this Convention at the expiration of each period of ten years under the terms provided for in this Article.

Article 40

1. The Director - General of the International Labour Office shall notify all Members of the International Labour Organisation of the registration of all ratifications and denunciations communicated to him by the Members of the Organisation.

2. When notifying the Members of the Organisation of the registration of the second ratification communicated to him, the Director - General shall draw the attention of the Members of the Organisation to the date upon which the Convention will come into force.

Article 41

The Director - General of the International Labour Office shall communicate to the Secretary - General of the United Nations for registration in accordance with Article 102 of the Charter of the United Nations full particulars of all ratifications and acts of denunciation registered by him in accordance with the provisions of the preceding Articles.

Article 42

At such times as it may consider necessary the Governing Body of the International Labour Office shall present to the General Conference a report on the working of this Convention and shall examine the desirability of placing on the agenda of the Conference the question of its revision in whole or in part.

Article 43

1. Should the Conference adopt a new Convention revising this Convention in whole or in part, then, unless the new Convention otherwise provides -

(a) the ratification by a Member of the new revising Convention shall ipso jure involve the immediate denunciation of this Convention, notwithstanding the provisions of Article 39 above, if and when the new revising Convention shall have come into force;

(b) as from the date when the new revising Convention comes into force this Convention shall cease to be open to ratification by the Members.

2. This Convention shall in any case remain in force in its actual form and content for those Members which have ratified it but have not ratified the revising Convention.

Article 44

The English and French versions of the text of this Convention are equally authoritative.

关于发生武装冲突时保护文化财产的公约及其实施条例

（美国、前苏联等国 1954 年 5 月 14 日于荷兰海牙签署。我国 2000 年 1 月 5 日递交批准书）

缔约各方认识到文化财产在最近武装冲突中遭受到严重的损失，而且由于作战技术的发展，毁灭的危险日益增加；

深信属于任何民族的文化财产遭受到损失，也就是全人类文化遗产所遭受的损失，因为每国人民对世界文化作出其自己的贡献；

考虑到文化遗产的保存对世界各国人民都是非常重要，因此，文化遗产必须获得国际性的保护；

基于在发生武装冲突时保护文化财产的原则，有如 1899 年和 1907 年海牙公约和 1935 年 4 月 15 日华盛顿条约所建立的；

认为上述保护不能成为有效，除非在平时同时采取国内措施和国际措施事先加以组织；

决心采取一切步骤来保护文化财产；

协议下列各条：

第一章　关于保护的一般规定

第一条　文化财产的定义

本条所称“文化财产”，不问其来源或所有权如何，应包括：

（甲）对各国人民的文化遗产具有重大意义的动产或不动产，例如建筑、艺术或历史上的纪念物，不论是宗教性的或者是世俗的；考古遗址；具有历史或艺术上价值的整套建筑物；艺术品；手稿、书籍和其他具有艺术、历史或考古价值的其他物品；以及科学珍藏和书籍或档案的重要珍藏或者上述各物的复制品；

（乙）其主要目的是为保存或展览（甲）款所述可以移动的文化财产的建筑物，例如博物馆、大型图书馆和档案库，以及发生武装冲突时准备用以掩护（甲）款所述可以移动的文化财产的保藏所；

（丙）用以存放大量的（甲）（乙）两款所述文化财产的中心站，称为“纪念物中心站”。

第二条　文化财产的保护

就本公约而言，文化财产的保护应包括对此项财产的保障和尊重。

第三条　文化财产的保障

缔约各国承允采用它们所认为适当的措施，以便在平时准备保障在其自己领土内的文化财产，使免受武装冲突时可以预见的后果。

第四条　对文化财产的尊重

（一）缔约各方承允尊重在其自己领土内的以及在其他缔约各方领土内的文化财产，不得为任何目的对财产及其周围环境或用以保护此项财产的设备作任何使用，如果使用的目的可能在发生武装冲突时使此项财产遭受到毁灭或损失，并不得采取针对此项财产的任何敌对行为。

（二）本条第一款所述义务只有在军事迫切需要的情况下可以放弃。

（三）缔约各方并承允设法禁止、防止及在必要时制止对文化财产以任何形式实施的盗窃、抢劫或侵占以及任何破坏行为。它们不得征用在缔约另一方领土内可以移动的文化财产。

（四）缔约各方不得对文化财产实施任何报复行为。

（五）缔约任何一方不得因缔约另一方没有适用第三条所指保障措施而规避它对缔约另一方根据本条所应负的义务。

第五条　占领

（一）缔约任何一方占领缔约另一方领土的全部或一部时，应尽可能支持被占领国国家主管当局保障并保全其文化财产。

（二）如有必要采取措施以便保全在被占领领土内由于军事行动遭受损失的文化财产而该国主管当局不能采取此项措施时，占领国应尽量同上述当局紧密合作，采取为保全所最需要的措施。

（三）被抵抗运动成员所认为合法政府的缔约任何一方政府应在可能范围内促使此项成员注意遵守本公约关于尊重文化财产各项规定的义务。

第六条　文化财产的明显标记

文化财产可以依照第十六条的规定备置一个明显的标记，以便识别。

第七条　军事措施

（一）缔约各方承允在平时将可以保证遵守本公约的各项规定列入军事条例或教程之中，并在其武装部队内培养一种尊重各国人民文化及文化财产的精神。

（二）缔约各方承允在平时在其武装部队内设计或成立服务队或专门人员，其目的在于获得对于文化财产的尊重并同负责保障文化财产的民政当局进行合作。

第二章　特别保护

第八条　特别保护的给予

（一）在特别保护之下可以有少数的保藏所，以便在发生武装冲突时掩护可以移动的文化财产，也可以有贮藏纪念物的中心站和具有重大意义的其他不可以移动的文化财产，但须具备下列条件：

（甲）此项保藏所和中心站同任何大工业中心或构成易受攻击地点例如机场、广播站、从事国防工作的设备、相当重要的港口或火车站、或主要交通线要有一定的距离；

（乙）不用于军事目的。

（二）可以构建保藏所，以提供对可移动文化财产的特别保护而不论其在何处。在可能情况下，构建的保藏所应能免遭炸弹损坏。

（三）贮藏纪念物的中心站如用于调动军事人员或物资，即使是过境性质，应视为用于军事目的。如在中心站内进行与军事行动直接有关的活动、军事人员的驻扎、或战时物资的生产，上述规定同样予以适用。

（四）经特别授权的武装保管人对第一款所述的文化财产担任保卫工作或者在此项文化财产附近驻扎通常负责维持公共秩序的警察部队均不得视为用于军事目的。

（五）本条第一款所述任何文化财产如果位于该款所规定重要军事目标附近，仍可予以特别保护，只要请求特别保护的缔约一方保证一旦发生武装冲突决不使用该目标，特别是当这一目标是个港口、火车站或机场的时候，要保证疏散同这目标一切交通往来。在此情况下，疏散工作应于平时即作准备。

（六）文化财产一经载入“受特别保护的文化财产国际登记册”后，即给予特别保护。上述记载必须根据本公约的规定并按照公约实施条例所规定的条件办理。

第九条 受特别保护文化财产的豁免权

缔约各方承允保证受特别保护的文化财产享有豁免权，从其载入国际登记册时起，不得针对此项财产作任何敌对行为，并除第八条五款所规定的情况以外，不得将此项财产或其周围用于任何军事目的。

第十条 标记和管制

在发生武装冲突时，受特别保护的文化财产应标上第十六条所描述的明显标记，并应受公约实施条例所规定的国际管制。

第十一条 豁免权的撤回

（一）缔约各方之一如对于受特别保护的文化财产的任何一项违反第九条所规定的义务时，对方可以免除自己对有关财产保证给予豁免的义务，只要上述违反义务的事实尚在继续中，但该对方应尽可能首先要求在一合理期间内终止违反义务的行为。

（二）除本条第一款所规定的情况外，对受特别保护的文化财产只有在无可避免的军事需要特别情况下，并且只有在此项需要尚继续存在时，才能撤回豁免。上述需要是否存在，只能由相当于一个师或更大单位的指挥官决定。如果情况许可，应于一个合理时间以前将撤回豁免的决定通知对方。

（三）撤回豁免的一方应尽速以书面通知公约实施条例内所规定的文化财产专员，并说明理由。

第三章 文化财产的运输

第十二条 受特别保护的运输

（一）专门从事于文化财产的迁运，不论在一国领土以内或者运到另一国领土，可以由有关缔约一方的请求，根据公约实施条例内规定的条件，在特别保护之下进行。

（二）受特别保护的运输应在上述条例所规定的国际监督之下进行，并应显示第十六条所描述的明显标记。

（三）缔约各方不得针对在特别保护之下的运输作任何敌对行为

第十三条 急迫情况下的运输

（一）如果缔约一方认为某些文化财产为安全计需要转移，而且由于情势急迫，特别是在武装冲突开始时，不能遵照第十二条所规定的程序时，运输时可以显示第十六条所描述的明显标定，但以第十二条所述关于豁免的申请尚未提出和上述申请尚未遭受拒绝为限。关于迁运的通知应尽可能向对方提出。但运输文化财产到另一国领土时，不得显示上述明显标记，除非已经明白给予豁免。

（二）缔约各方应尽可能采取必要警戒措施，以避免针对本条第一款所述备置明显标记的运输作敌对行为。

第十四条 扣押、缉捕和拿捕的豁免

（一）下列各物免受扣押、缉捕或拿捕：

（甲）享有第十二条或第十三条所规定保护的文化财产；

（乙）专门用于转运上述文化财产的交通工具。

（二）本条并不限制临检权。

第四章 人 员

第十五条 人员

在符合安全利益的情况下，从事于文化财产保护工作的人员应为此项财产的利益受到尊重，他们如果落入对方手中，只要他们负责保管的文化财产也落入对方手中，应被准许继续执行他们的任务。

第五章 明显的标记

第十六条 公约的标记

（一）公约的明显标记应如盾状，下端尖，十字交叉，蓝白相间（盾为蓝色四方形，其中一角成为盾的尖端，四方形之上为一蓝色三角形，两旁为白色三角形各一）。

（二）标记应单独使用，或者按照第十七条所规定的条件以一个三角形重复三次（下面为一个盾形）。

第十七条 标记的使用

（一）明显的标记重复三次只能用以识别下列各物：

（甲）受特别保护的不能移动的文化财产；

（乙）根据第十二条和第十三条所规定的条件而进行运输的文化财产；

（丙）根据公约实施条例所规定的条件而临时设置的保藏所。

（二）明显的标记单独使用只能用以识别下列各人或物：

（甲）不受特别保护的文化财产；

（乙）根据公约实施条例负管制职责的人员；

（丙）从事保护文化财产的人员；

（丁）公约实施条例所述的身份证。

（三）在发生武装冲突时，除本条前两款所规定者外，禁止使用明显的标记，并禁止为任何目的使用近似明显标记的任何记号。

（四）明显的标记不得置在任何不能移动的文化财产，除非同时显示经缔约一方主管当局正式填写日期并签名的授权。

第六章　公约的适用范围

第十八条　公约的适用

（一）除平时有效的规定外，本公约应适用于缔约国两方或两方以上之间可能发生经宣告的战争或任何其他武装冲突，即使一方或一方以上不承认有战争状态。

（二）公约亦应适用于对缔约一方领土的一部或全部占领，即使对于上述占领不发生武装抵抗。

（三）如果冲突的一方不是本公约的缔约一方，公约的缔约各国在其相互关系中仍受公约的约束。如果非缔约一方的国家声明接受公约的规定并且实施此项规定时，缔约各国在其与非缔约一方的关系中应更进一步受公约的约束。

第十九条　非国际性冲突

（一）如果在缔约各方之一的领土内发生非国际性冲突，冲突的各方必须适用本公约关于尊重文化财产的各规定，作为最低限度。

（二）冲突的各方应通过缔结特别协议，设法实施本公约其他规定的全部或一部。

（三）联合国教育、科学及文化组织可以向冲突的各方提供服务。

（四）上述各规定的适用不影响冲突各方的法律地位。

第七章　公约的实施

第二十条　公约实施条例

关于适用本公约的程序规定在公约实施条例内，该条例成为公约的组成部分。

第二十一条　实施保护的国家

本公约及其实施条例的适用应获得负责保障冲突各方利益的实施保护国家的合作。

第二十二条　和解程序

（一）实施保护的国家如认为有助于文化财产的利益，应在一切情况下设法斡旋，特别是当冲突的各方之间对于本公约或其实施条例各规定的适用或解释有争议时。

（二）为此，各实施保护国可以由于一方的邀请，由于联合国教育、科学及文化组织总干事的邀请，或者出于该实施保护国的主动，建议冲突各方的代表，特别是负责保护文化财产的当局举行一个会议，如果认为是适当的话，会议地点应在经适当选择的中立地区内。冲突的各方必须接受向它们提出关于举行会议的建议。实施保护国应建议，但应获得冲突各方的赞同，邀请一位属于中立国籍的人或者由联合国教育、科学及文化组织总干事提出的一人，以主席的身份参加上述会议。

第二十三条　联合国教育、科学及文化组织的协助

（一）缔约各方可以请求联合国教育、科学及文化组织在保护其文化财产的组织方面，或者在适用本公约或其实施办法时所发生的任何其他问题上给予技术上的协助。上述组织应在其计划和资力范围的限度内给予此项协助。

（二）联合国教育、科学及文化组织被授权自动向缔约各方对此提出建议。

第二十四条　特别协议

（一）缔约各方可以就它们认为适合于单独规定的一切事项缔结特别协议。

（二）不得缔结任何协议，致减弱本公约给予文化财产及从事于保护文化财产人员的保护。

第二十五条　公约的传播

缔约各方承允在平时及在发生武装冲突时尽量广泛地在其自己国内传播本公约及其实施条例的文本，特别要把对于上述公约和条例的研究列入军事训练（如果可能的话，亦列入平民训练）的计划中，使全体居民，特别是武装部队和从事保护文化财产的人员知道公约的原则。

第二十六条　译本和报告

（一）缔约各方应通过联合国教育、科学及文化组织总干事彼此交换本公约及其实施条例的正式译本。

（二）此外，缔约各方应至少四年一次向总干事报送一份报告，提供他们所认为合适的关于各自政府机关为履行本公约及其实施条例而采取、拟订或准备实行的任何措施的一切情报。

第二十七条　会议

（一）联合国教育、科学及文化组织总干事经执行局的核准可以召集缔约各方代表举行会议。如有缔约各方至少五分之一提出要求时，总干事必须召开会议。

（二）在不妨碍本公约或其实施条例所授予任何其他职权的情况下，会议的宗旨将为研究有关适用本公约及其实施条例的问题，并对此项问题提出建议。

（三）会议可以在缔约各方过半数出席并按照第三十九条规定的情况下进一步着手修改公约或其实施条例。

第二十八条　制裁

缔约各方承允在其普通刑事管辖系统内对违犯或教唆违犯本公约的任何人，不论该人属何国籍，采取一切必要步骤予以追诉并施以刑罚或纪律制裁。

最后条款

第二十九条　文字

（一）本公约用英文、法文、俄文和西班牙文写成，四种文本具有同等效力。

（二）联合国教育、科学及文化组织应安排将公约译成该组织的大会所用其他正式文字。

第三十条　签字

本公约签订日期为1954年5月14日，在1954年12月31日以前应予开放，任凭被邀出席1954年4月21日至1954年5月14日在海牙召开会议的一切国家签字。

第三十一条　批准

（一）本公约须经签字国按照各国宪法程序予以批准。

（二）批准书应向联合国教育、科学及文化组织总干事交存。

关联法规：

第三十二条　加入

本公约从生效日起应予开放，任凭第三十条所述一切国家而尚未签字者以及由联合国教育、科学及文化组织执行局邀请加入的任何其他国家加入。加入应在向联合国教育、科学及文化组织总干事交存加入书后生效。

第三十三条　生效

（一）本公约应于五份批准书交存后三个月生效。

（二）此后，公约应于缔约每一方交存其批准书或加入书后三个月对该方生效。

（三）第十八条和第十九条所指情况应于敌对行为或占领开始以前或以后使冲突的各方所交存批准书或加入书立即生效。在此情况下，联合国教育、科学及文化组织总干事应用最迅速的方法送达第三十八条所指的通知。

第三十四条　有效的实施

（一）作为公约一方的每一国家应于公约生效之日采取一切必要的措施，以保证公约能于生效后六个月期间内有效实施。

（二）上述期间对于公约生效后才交存批准书或加入书的国家而言，应为该国交存批准书或加入书以后的六个月。

第三十五条　公约地域适用的扩展

缔约任何一方可以在批准或加入时，或在此后的任何时候向联合国教育、科学及文化组织总干事提出通知，声明本公约应扩大适用于国际关系由该方负责的一切或任何领土。上述通知应于收到后三个月生效。

第三十六条　同以前各公约的关系

（一）在受1899年9月29日或1907年10月18日关于陆战法律和习惯的海牙第四公约和关于战时海军炮轰的海牙第九公约约束，同时也是本公约缔约各方的国家之间的关系上，本公约应作为上述第九公约和第四公约所附条例的补充，并在本公约及其实施条例规定使用明显的标记时，应以本公约第十六条所述的标记代替上述第九公约第五条所述的标记。

（二）在受1935年4月15日关于保护艺术和科学机关以及历史纪念物的华盛顿条约（罗埃里奇条约）约束，同时也是本公约缔约各方的国家之间的关系上，本公约应作为罗埃里奇条约的补充，并应在本公约及其实施条例规定使用明显的标记时，以本公约第十六条所述的标记代替上述条约第三条所述的明显旗帜。

第三十七条　退出

（一）缔约各方可以用其自己名义或者国际关系由其负责的任何领土的名义退出本公约。

（二）退出应以书面文件通知，交存于联合国教育、科学及文化组织总干事。

（三）退出应于收到退出书后一年生效。但是，上述期间届满时，如果退出的一方卷入到一个武装冲突之中，则在敌对行动结束以前或在文化财产返还工作完成以前（以发生在后者为准），退出不发生效力。

第三十八条 通知

联合国教育、科学及文化组织总干事应将第三十一、第三十二及第三十九条所规定的一切批准书、加入书或接受书以及第三十五、第三十七及第三十九条所规定的通知书和退出书的交存事项告知第三十条和第三十二条所指的各国及联合国。

第三十九条 公约及其实施条例的修正

（一）缔约任何一方可以提出对本公约及其实施条例的修正案。任何建议的修正案文本应交由联合国教育、科学及文化组织总干事转送缔约各方，要求各方在四个月内答复，载明它是否：

（甲）要求召开会议来考虑所提出的修正案；

（乙）赞成不必召开会议就接受所提出的修正案；

（丙）主张不必召开会议就拒绝所提出的修正案。

（二）总干事应将根据本条第一款所收到的答复转送所有缔约各方。

（三）如果所有缔约各方在规定期限内均已根据本条第一款（乙）向联合国教育、科学及文化组织总干事表示意见，赞成不必召开会议就接受修正案，则总干事应按照第三十八条通知此项决定。修正案应从通知日起经过九十天对所有缔约各国生效。

（四）如果有缔约各方三分之一以上请求，总干事应召集缔约各方开会考虑所提出的修正案。

（五）前款规定所述对公约或其实施条例的修正案只有在出席会议的缔约各方全体通过并经缔约每一方接受之后才能生效。

（六）对公约或其实施条例的修正案经第四款和第五款所述会议通过后，应于缔约各方向联合国教育、科学及文化组织总干事交存正式文件后对该方产生效力。

（七）对本公约或其实施条例的修正案生效后，只有经修正后的公约或其实施条例的文本应予开放，任凭批准或加入。

第四十条 登记

本公约应根据联合国教育、科学及文化组织总干事的请求，按照联合国宪章第一百零二条向联合国秘书处登记。

附：

关于发生武装冲突时保护文化财产公约的实施条例

第一章　管　　制

第一条　国际人名录

本公约生效时，联合国教育、科学及文化组织总干事应编制一部国际名册，包括缔约各方所推荐有资格执行文化财产专员职务的一切人士。该名册应在联合国教育、科学及文化组织总干事的倡议下，以缔约各方所提出的请求为根据而经过一定期间时加以修正。

第二条　管制的组织

缔约任何一方一旦卷入公约第十八条所适用的武装冲突时，

（甲）该方应即任命在其领土内文化财产代表一人；如该方占领另一方领土时，应任命在该领土内文化财产的特别代表一人；

（乙）代表冲突各方的实施保护国应即按照下面第三条任命驻在敌对一方的代表；

（丙）文化财产专员一人应按照第四条规定派往缔约一方。

第三条　实施保护国家代表的任命

实施保护国应从其外交或领事人员中，或者驻在国一方的同意下从其他人员中任命其代表。

第四条　专员的任命

（一）文化财产专员应经驻在国及代表敌对各方的实施保护国共同协议从国际人名录中选出。

（二）各方如从开始讨论此事起三个月内不能达成协议，它们应请求国际法院院长任命专员，该专员于驻在国同意此项任命以前不得就职。

第五条　代表的职务

实施保护国的代表应注意有无违反公约的事实，在获得驻在国同意的情况下调查违反的事实在什么环境中发生，就地提出制止此项事实的主张。如有必要时，并以此项违反的事实通知专员。代表应将其活动随时告知专员。

第六条　专员的职务

（一）文化财产专员应会同其驻在国一方代表和有关的代表们处理向他提出的与适用公约有关的一切事项。

（二）他对于本条例所规定的事项有决定权和任命权。

（三）在其驻在国一方同意的情况下，他有权命令进行调查，或自行调查。

（四）他应向冲突的各方或其实施保护国提出他所认为有利于公约实施的任何主张。

（五）他应制作关于公约实施的必要报告，并分送有关各方及其实施保护国，并应以抄本送给联合国教育、科学及文化组织总干事，总干事只可以利用报告中技术性的内容。

（六）如果没有实施保护国，由专员行使公约第二十一条及第二十二条所规定实施保护国的职务。

第七条　视察员和专家

（一）不论何时文化财产专员认为必要时，他应当根据有关代表的请求或者在同有关代表协商后，提出一位负有具体使命的文化财产视察员，视察员的提名应获得专员驻在国的同意。视察员只对专员负责。

（二）专员、代表和视察员可以获得专家的服务，专家的提名也应获得前款所述一方的同意。

第八条　管制任务的执行

文化财产专员、实施保护国的代表、视察员和专家执行任务时，在任何情况下不得超越委任的范围。他们应当特别注意其驻在国一方安全上的需要，并应当在一切情况下按照该驻在国所告知他们的军事情势上需要行事。

第九条　实施保护国的替代者

如果冲突的一方不能或不再从实施保护国的活动中获得利益时，可以邀请一个中立国家担任实施保护国的职责，以便按照上面第四条所规定的程序，指定文化财产专员。这样指定的专员如有必要可以将本条例所规定实施保护国代表的职务托付于视察员。

第十条　费用

文化财产专员、视察员和专家的报酬和费用应由驻在国开支。实施保护国代表的报酬和费用应由实施保护国与其利益受到保障的国家之间协议而定其负担。

第二章 特别保护

第十一条 临时保藏所

（一）在武装冲突时，缔约任何一方如由于不能预见的情况而设立临时保藏所，并希望予以特别保护者，应迅速将此意通知驻在该方的专员。

（二）专员如认为在当时情况下，并且由于临时保藏所中所藏文化财产的重要性，应采取此项措施时，可以准许缔约该方在保藏所上显示公约第十六条所规定的明显标志。专员应将其决定毫不迟延地通知有关实施保护国的代表，每一实施保护国的代表可以在三十天期限内命令撤除上述标记。

（三）一经上述代表表示同意或者三十天期限已过而无任何上述有关代表表示反对，而且根据专员的意见，保藏所符合于公约第八条所规定的条件时，专员应请求联合国教育、科学及文化组织总干事将该保藏所登记在受特别保护的文化财产登记册内。

第十二条 受特别保护的文化财产国际登记册

（一）应置备一本“受特别保护的文化财产国际登记册”。

（二）上述登记册应由联合国教育、科学及文化组织总干事保管。总干事应将抄本供给联合国秘书长以及缔约各方。

（三）登记册应分为若干节，缔约各方各占一节。每一节应再分成三款：保藏所、贮藏纪念物的中心站、其他不能移动的文化财产。总干事应决定每节应包含哪些细节。

第十三条 登记的申请

（一）缔约任何一方可以向联合国教育、科学及文化组织总干事提出申请，将在其领土内的某些保藏所、贮藏纪念物的中心站或其他不能移动的文化财产载入登记册。上述申请应载明此项财产的所在地，并应证明此项财产符合于公约第八条的规定。

（二）如果发生占领，占领国有权提出上述申请。

（三）联合国教育、科学及文化组织总干事应毫不迟延地将登记申请书的抄本分送缔约各方。

第十四条 异议

（一）缔约任何一方可以致函联合国教育、科学及文化组织总干事对于文化财产的登记提出异议，该函必须于总干事发出登记申请书抄本之日起四个月内送达于总干事。

（二）上述异议应载明理由，只有下列原因为有效：

（甲）此项财产不是文化财产；

（乙）此项财产不符合于公约第八条所述条件。

（三）总干事应毫不迟延地将异议书的抄本分送缔约各方，如有必要时，并应咨询纪念物、艺术和历史遗迹以及考古发掘物国际委员会，再如认为适当时，咨询任何其他有资格的组织或个人。

（四）总干事或申请登记的缔约一方可以向提出异议的缔约各方作必要的说明，其目的在使异议得以撤回。

（五）缔约一方如在平时已提出登记申请而在登记入册以前卷入武装冲突时，有关的文化财产在对任何异议可能作出或已作出确认、撤回或撤销以前，应立即由总干事暂时登记入册。

（六）如果总干事在收到异议书之日起六个月内还没有从提出异议的缔约一方收到撤回的通知，申请登记的缔约一方可以请求按照后一款规定的程序进行仲裁。

（七）关于仲裁的请求不得在总干事收到异议书以后逾一年提出。争端的双方应各指定仲裁员一人。如果对于同一登记申请提出不止一项异议时，提出异议的缔约各方应根据共同协议指定仲裁员仅一人。上述仲裁员应从本条例第一条所述国际人名录选出主任仲裁员一人。如果该两仲裁员就选择的对象不能获得协议时，应请国际法院院长指定主任仲裁员，不一定要从国际人名录选择。如上组成的仲裁庭应制定其自己的程序。对于上述仲裁庭的裁决不得上诉。

（八）发生争端时，作为争端一方的缔约每一方可以声明不愿适用前款所规定的仲裁程序。在此情况下，对于登记申请的异议应由总干事提交缔约各方。只有在参加表决的缔约各方三分之二多数决定通过时，异议才获得确认。除非联合国教育、科学及文化组织总干事认为必须根据公约第二十七条授予他的权力召集会议，表决应采取通信方式。总干事如决定以通信方式进行表决，应邀请缔约各方从邀请之日起六个月内用密封函件投票。

第十五条　登记

（一）联合国教育、科学及文化组织总干事应将申请登记的每项财产编号登记入册，但以未在第十四条第一款所规定期限内收到异议者为限。

（二）如果已有异议提出，总干事只能在异议已经撤回或者经过第十四条第七款或第八款所规定的程序异议没有获得确认的情况下将财产登记入册，但这并不影响第十四条第五款的规定。

（三）在适用第十一条第三款时，总干事应根据文化财产专员的请求将财产登记入册。

（四）总干事应毫不迟延地将在登记册内所作每项登记的经证明无误的抄本送给联合国秘书长和缔约各方，而且在申请登记的一方请求时，并应送给公约第三十条和第三十二条所述一切其他国家。登记在上述抄本发出后三十天生效。

第十六条 注销

（一）联合国教育、科学及文化组织总干事在下列情况下应注销任何财产的登记：

（甲）有关文化财产在其领土内的缔约一方请求注销时；

（乙）申请登记的缔约一方声明退出公约，而且退出业已生效时；

（丙）在第十四条和第十五条所规定特别情况下，经过第十四条第七款或第八款所述的程序异议已被确认时。

（二）总干事应毫不迟延地将注销书的经证明无误的抄本送给联合国秘书长以及曾经收到登记册登记抄本的一切国家。注销书应于上述抄本发出后三十天生效。

第三章 文化财产的运输

第十七条 获得豁免的程序

（一）公约第十二条第一款所指的请求应送达于文化财产专员，请求书应载明所根据的理由以及迁运物件的大概件数和重要性、现场、拟运往地点、所用交通工具、所经过路线、起运日期和任何其他有关的事项。

（二）专员如于听取他所认为合适的意见后认定迁运为有理由时，应就实行迁运所采取的措施同有关的实施保护国代表协商，并应于协商后将迁运事通知冲突的有关各方，通知内包括一切有用的情报。

（三）专员应指定视察员一人或数人，视察员应查明只有在请求书内载明的财产将予迁运，运输将按照业经许可的方法实行，并应出示明显的标记。视察员应随从财产到目的地。

第十八条 向国外运输

受特别保护的迁运目的地如在另一国领土内，不仅应适用公约第十二条和本条例第十七条，而且还要适用下列各规定：

（甲）文化财产留存在另一国领土时。该国即为此项财产的保管者，并应给予同它给予自己的同样重要的文化财产一样的注意；

（乙）保管国应于冲突终止时才将财产返还。返还应自请求返还之日起六个月内实行；

（丙）在进行关于迁运的各种活动时，并且在文化财产还留存于另一国领土时。该项财产免受没收，并且不得由交存国或保管国予以处置。但是如果为财产的安全认为有必要时，保管国可以在获得交存国同意的情况下，根据本条规定的条件将财产运至第三国领土；

（丁）关于特别保护的请求应表明财产运往其领土的国家接受本条的规定。

第十九条 占领领土

占领缔约另一方领土的缔约一方如将文化财产迁运到位于该领土内另一地点的保藏所而不能遵照本条例第十七条所规定的程序时，此项迁运不得视为公约第四条规定的侵占行为，前提是文化财产专员在咨询完普通保管人之后书面证明在当时环境下此项迁运确有必要。

第四章 明显标记

第二十条 标记的安放

（一）明显的标记应安放何处以及如何使其易于看到应由缔约各方的主管当局斟酌决定。标记可出示在旗帜上或臂章上。标记可以画在物件之上或者以任何其他合适的方式表示。

（二）但在发生武装冲突时以及在公约第十二条和第十三条所述情况下，标记应置在运输车辆之上，以便在白天从上空或从地面都可以清楚地看到，这一规定并不妨碍采用可能有的更完备的标志。

标记应在下列情况下从地面可以看到：

（甲）经过一定间隔时期足以清楚地显示贮藏受特别保护纪念物中心站的四周；

（乙）可以在受特别保护不能移动的文化财产的入口处看到。

第二十一条 人员的识别

（一）公约第十七条第二款乙项及丙项所述人员可以佩戴有明显标记的臂章，此项臂章由主管当局颁布并加盖印章。

（二）上述人员应携带有明显标记的特别身份证，该身份证至少应载明持有人的姓名、出生年月日、职名或等级及其职务。身份证应贴持有人的照片并有他的签名或指印或者两者具备。身份证应盖主管当局的硬印。

（三）缔约各方应以本条例所附式样作为示例，制定自己的身份证格式。缔约各方应交换所用身份证的式样。如果可能的话，身份证应制成至少两份，一份由发给的国家保存。

（四）上述人员如无正当理由不得被剥夺其身份证或佩戴臂章的权利。

Convention for the Protection of Cultural Property in the Event of Armed Conflict with Regulations for the Execution of the Convention

The Hague, 14 May 1954

The High Contracting Parties,

Recognizing that cultural property has suffered grave damage during recent armed conflicts and that, by reason of the developments in the technique of warfare, it is in increasing danger of destruction;

Being convinced that damage to cultural property belonging to any people whatsoever means damage to the cultural heritage of all mankind, since each people makes its contribution to the culture of the world;

Considering that the preservation of the cultural heritage is of great importance for all peoples of the world and that it is important that this heritage should receive international protection;

Guided by the principles concerning the protection of cultural property during armed conflict, as established in the Conventions of The Hague of 1899 and of 1907 and in the Washington Pact of 15 April, 1935;

Being of the opinion that such protection cannot be effective unless both national and international measures have been taken to organize it in time of peace;

Being determined to take all possible steps to protect cultural property;

Have agreed upon the following provisions:

Chapter I. General provisions regarding protection

Article 1. Definition of cultural property

For the purposes of the present Convention, the term 'cultural property' shall cover, irrespective of origin or ownership:

(a) movable or immovable property of great importance to the cultural heritage of every people, such as monuments of architecture, art or history, whether religious or secular; archaeological sites; groups of buildings which, as a whole, are of historical or artistic interest; works of art; manuscripts, books and other objects of artistic, historical or archaeological interest; as well as scientific collections and important collections of books or archives or of reproductions of the property defined above;

(b) buildings whose main and effective purpose is to preserve or exhibit the movable cultural property defined in sub - paragraph (a) such as museums, large libraries and depositories of archives, and refuges intended to shelter, in the event of armed conflict, the movable cultural property defined in sub - paragraph (a);

(c) centers containing a large amount of cultural property as defined in sub - paragraphs (a) and (b), to be known as 'centers containing monuments'.

Article 2. Protection of cultural property

For the purposes of the present Convention, the protection of cultural property shall comprise the safeguarding of and respect for such property.

Article 3. Safeguarding of cultural property

The High Contracting Parties undertake to prepare in time of peace for the safeguarding of cultural property situated within their own territory against the foreseeable effects of an armed conflict, by taking such measures as they consider appropriate.

Article 4. Respect for cultural property

1. The High Contracting Parties undertake to respect cultural property situated within their own territory as well as within the territory of other High Contracting Parties by refraining from any use of the property and its immediate surroundings or of the appliances in use for its protection for purposes which are likely to expose it to destruction or damage in the event of armed conflict; and by refraining from

any act of hostility, directed against such property.

2. The obligations mentioned in paragraph 1 of the present Article may be waived only in cases where military necessity imperatively requires such a waiver.

3. The High Contracting Parties further undertake to prohibit, prevent and, if necessary, put a stop to any form of theft, pillage or misappropriation of, and any acts of vandalism directed against, cultural property. They shall refrain from requisitioning movable cultural property situated in the territory of another High Contracting Party.

4. They shall refrain from any act directed by way of reprisals against cultural property.

5. No High Contracting Party may evade the obligations incumbent upon it under the present Article, in respect of another High Contracting Party, by reason of the fact that the latter has not applied the measures of safeguard referred to in Article 3.

Article 5. Occupation

1. Any High Contracting Party in occupation of the whole or part of the territory of another High Contracting Party shall as far as possible support the competent national authorities of the occupied country in safeguarding and preserving its cultural property.

2. Should it prove necessary to take measures to preserve cultural property situated in occupied territory and damaged by military operations, and should the competent national authorities be unable to take such measures, the Occupying Power shall, as far as possible, and in close co - operation with such authorities, take the most necessary measures of preservation.

3. Any High Contracting Party whose government is considered their legitimate government by members of a resistance movement, shall, if possible, draw their attention to the obligation to comply with those provisions of the Convention dealing with respect for cultural property.

Article 6. Distinctive marking of cultural property

In accordance with the provisions of Article 16, cultural property may bear a distinctive emblem so as to facilitate its recognition.

Article 7. Military measures

1. The High Contracting Parties undertake to introduce in time of peace into

their military regulations or instructions such provisions as may ensure observance of the present Convention, and to foster in the members of their armed forces a spirit of respect for the culture and cultural property of all peoples.

2. The High Contracting Parties undertake to plan or establish in peace - time, within their armed forces, services or specialist personnel whose purpose will be to secure respect for cultural property and to co - operate with the civilian authorities responsible for safeguarding it.

Chapter II. Special protection

Article 8. Granting of special protection

1. There may be placed under special protection a limited number of refuges intended to shelter movable cultural property in the event of armed conflict, of centers containing monuments and other immovable cultural property of very great importance, provided that they:

(a) are situated at an adequate distance from any large industrial center or from any important military objective constituting a vulnerable point, such as, for example, an aerodrome, broadcasting station, establishment engaged upon work of national defense, a port or railway station of relative importance or a main line of communication;

(b) are not used for military purposes.

2. A refuge for movable cultural property may also be placed under special protection, whatever its location, if it is so constructed that, in all probability, it will not be damaged by bombs.

3. A center containing monuments shall be deemed to be used for military purposes whenever it is used for the movement of military personnel or material, even in transit. The same shall apply whenever activities directly connected with military operations, the stationing of military personnel, or the production of war material are carried on within the center.

4. The guarding of cultural property mentioned in paragraph I above by armed custodians specially empowered to do so, or the presence, in the vicinity of such cultural property, of police forces normally responsible for the maintenance of public order shall not be deemed to be used for military purposes.

5. If any cultural property mentioned in paragraph 1 of the present Article is situated near an important military objective as defined in the said paragraph, it may nevertheless be placed under special protection if the High Contracting Party asking for that protection undertakes, in the event of armed conflict, to make no use of the objective and particularly, in the case of a port, railway station or aerodrome, to divert all traffic there from. In that event, such diversion shall be prepared in time of peace.

6. Special protection is granted to cultural property by its entry in the 'International Register of Cultural Property under Special Protection'. This entry shall only be made, in accordance with the provisions of the present Convention and under the conditions provided for in the Regulations for the execution of the Convention.

Article 9. Immunity of cultural property under special protection

The High Contracting Parties undertake to ensure the immunity of cultural property under special protection by refraining, from the time of entry in the International Register, from any act of hostility directed against such property and, except for the cases provided for in paragraph 5 of Article 8, from any use of such property or its surroundings for military purposes.

Article 10. Identification and control

During an armed conflict, cultural property under special protection shall be marked with the distinctive emblem described in Article 16, and shall be open to international control as provided for in the Regulations for the execution of the Convention.

Article 11. Withdrawal of immunity

1. If one of the High Contracting Parties commits, in respect of any item of cultural property under special protection, a violation of the obligations under Article 9, the opposing Party shall, so long as this violation persists, be released from the obligation to ensure the immunity of the property concerned. Nevertheless, whenever possible, the latter Party shall first request the cessation of such violation within a reasonable time.

2. Apart from the case provided for in paragraph 1 of the present Article, immunity shall be withdrawn from cultural property under special protection only in exceptional cases of unavoidable military necessity, and only for such time as that

necessity continues. Such necessity can be established only by the officer commanding a force the equivalent of a division in size or larger. Whenever circumstances permit, the opposing Party shall be notified, a reasonable time in advance, of the decision to withdraw immunity.

3. The Party withdrawing immunity shall, as soon as possible, so inform the Commissioner - General for cultural property provided for in the Regulations for the execution of the Convention, in writing, stating the reasons.

Chapter III. Transport of cultural property

Article 12. Transport under special protection

1. Transport exclusively engaged in the transfer of cultural property, whether within a territory or to another territory, may, at the request of the High Contracting Party concerned, take place under special protection in accordance with the conditions specified in the Regulations for the execution of the Convention.

2. Transport under special protection shall take place under the international supervision provided for in the aforesaid Regulations and shall display the distinctive emblem described in Article 16.

3. The High Contracting Parties shall refrain from any act of hostility directed against transport under special protection.

Article 13. Transport in urgent cases

1. If a High Contracting Party considers that the safety of certain cultural property requires its transfer and that the matter is of such urgency that the procedure laid down in Article 12 cannot be followed, especially at the beginning of an armed conflict, the transport may display the distinctive emblem described in Article 16, provided that an application for immunity referred to in Article 12 has not already been made and refused. As far as possible, notification of transfer should be made to the opposing' Parties. Nevertheless, transport conveying cultural property to the territory of another country may not display the distinctive' emblem unless immunity has been expressly granted to it.

2. The High Contracting Parties shall take, so far as possible, the necessary precautions to avoid acts of hostility directed against the transport described in paragraph 1 of the present Article and displaying the distinctive emblem.

Article 14. Immunity from seizure, capture and prize

1. Immunity from seizure, placing in prize, or capture shall be granted to:

(a) cultural property enjoying the protection provided for in Article 12 or that provided for in Article 13;

(b) the means of transport exclusively engaged in the transfer of such cultural property.

2. Nothing in the present Article shall limit the right of visit and search.

Chapter IV. Personnel

Article 15. Personnel

As far as is consistent with the interests of security, personnel engaged in the protection of cultural property shall, in the interests of such property, be respected and, if they fall into the hands of the opposing Party, shall be allowed to continue to carry out their duties whenever the cultural property for which they are responsible has also fallen into the hands of the opposing Party.

Chapter V. The distinctive emblem

Article 16. Emblem of the convention

1. The distinctive emblem of the Convention shall take the form of a shield, pointed below, persaltire blue and white (a shield consisting of a royal - blue square, one of the angles of which forms the point of the shield, and of a royal - blue triangle above the square, the space on either side being taken up by a white triangle).

2. The emblem shall be used alone, or repeated three times in a triangular formation (one shield below), under the conditions provided for in Article 17.

Article 17. Use of the emblem

1. The distinctive emblem repeated three times may be used only as a means of identification of:

(a) immovable cultural property under special protection;

(b) the transport of cultural property under the conditions provided for in Articles 12 and 13;

(c) improvised refuges, under the conditions provided for in the Regulations for the execution of the Convention.

2. The distinctive emblem may be used alone only as a means of identification of:

(a) cultural property not under special protection;

(b) the persons responsible for the duties of control in accordance with the Regulations for the execution of the Convention;

(c) the personnel engaged in the protection of cultural property;

(d) the identity cards mentioned in the Regulations for the execution of the Convention.

3. During an armed conflict, the use of the distinctive emblem in any other cases than those mentioned in the preceding paragraphs of the present Article, and the use for any purpose whatever of a sign resembling the distinctive emblem, shall be forbidden.

4. The distinctive emblem may not be placed on any immovable cultural property unless at the same time there is displayed an authorization duly dated and signed by the competent authority of the High Contracting Party.

Chapter VI. Scope of application of the Convention

Article 18. Application of the Convention

1. Apart from the provisions which shall take effect in time of peace, the present Convention shall apply in the event of declared war or of any other armed conflict which may arise between two or more of the High Contracting Parties, even if the state of war is not recognized by, one or more of them.

2. The Convention shall also apply to all cases of partial or total occupation of the territory of a High Contracting Party, even if the said occupation meets with no armed resistance.

3. If one of the Powers in conflict is not a Party to the present Convention, the Powers which are Parties thereto shall nevertheless remain bound by it in their mutual relations. They shall furthermore be bound by the Convention, in relation to the said Power, if the latter has declared, that it accepts the provisions thereof and so long as it applies them.

Article 19. Conflicts not of an international character

1. In the event of an armed conflict not of an international character occurring within the territory of one of the High Contracting Parties, each party to the conflict shall be bound to apply, as, a minimum, the provisions of the present Convention which relate to respect for cultural property.

2. The parties to the conflict shall endeavour to bring into force, by means of special agreements, all or part of the other provisions of the present Convention.

3. The United Nations Educational, Scientific and Cultural Organization may offer its services to the parties to the conflict.

4. The application of the preceding provisions shall not affect the legal status of the parties to the conflict.

Chapter VII. Execution of the Convention

Article 20. Regulations for the execution of the Convention

The procedure by which the present Convention is to be applied is defined in the Regulations for its execution, which constitute an integral part thereof.

Article 21. Protecting powers

The present Convention and the Regulations for its execution shall be applied with the co - operation of the Protecting Powers responsible for safeguarding the interests of the Parties to the conflict.

Article 22. Conciliation procedure

1. The Protecting Powers shall lend their good offices in all cases where they may deem it useful in the interests of cultural property, particularly if there is disagreement between the Parties to the conflict as to the application or interpretation of the provisions of the present Convention or the Regulations for its execution.

2. For this purpose, each of the Protecting Powers may, either at the invitation of one Party, of the Director - General of the United Nations Educational, Scientific and Cultural Organization, or on its own initiative, propose to the Parties to the conflict a meeting of their representatives, and in particular of the authorities responsible for the protection of cultural property, if considered appropriate on suitably chosen neutral territory. The Parties to the conflict shall be bound to give effect to the proposals for meeting made to them.

The Protecting Powers shall propose for approval by the Parties to the conflict a person belonging to a neutral Power or a person presented by the Director General of the United Nations Educational, Scientific and Cultural Organization, which person shall be invited to take part in such a meeting in the capacity of Chairman.

Article 23. Assistance of UNESCO

1. The High Contracting Parties may call upon the United Nations Educational, Scientific and Cultural Organization for technical assistance in organizing the protection of their cultural property, or in connexion with any other problem arising out of the application of the present Convention or the Regulations for its execution. The Organization shall accord such assistance within the limits fixed by its programme and by its resources.

2. The Organization is authorized to make, on its own initiative, proposals on this matter to the High Contracting Parties.

Article 24. Special agreements

1. The High Contracting Parties may conclude special agreements for all matters concerning which they deem it suitable to make separate provision.

2. No special agreement may be concluded which would diminish the protection afforded by the present Convention to cultural property and to the personnel engaged in its protection.

Article 25. Dissemination of the Convention

The High Contracting Parties undertake, in time of peace as in time of armed conflict, to disseminate the text of the present Convention and the Regulations for its execution as widely as possible in their respective countries. They undertake, in particular, to include the study thereof in their programmes of military and, if possible, civilian training, so that its principles are made known to the whole population, especially the armed forces and personnel engaged in the protection of cultural property.

Article 26. Translations reports

1. The High Contracting Parties shall communicate to one another, through the Director - General of the United Nations Educational, Scientific and Cultural Organization, the official translations of the present Convention and of the Regúlations for its execution.

2. Furthermore, at least once every four years, they shall forward to the Di-

rector - General a report giving whatever information they think suitable concerning any measures being taken, prepared or contemplated by their respective administrations in fulfillment of the present Convention and of the Regulations for its execution.

Article 27. Meetings

1. The Director - General of the United Nations Educational, Scientific and Cultural Organization may, with the approval of the Executive Board, convene meetings of representatives of the High Contracting Parties. He must convene such a meeting if at least one - fifth of the High Contracting Parties so request.

2. Without prejudice to any other functions which have been conferred on it by the present Convention or the Regulations for its execution, the purpose of the meeting will be to study problems concerning the application of the Convention and of the Regulations for its execution, and to formulate recommendations in respect thereof.

3. The meeting may further undertake a revision of the Convention or the Regulations for its execution if the majority of the High Contracting Parties are represented, and in accordance with the provisions of Article 39.

Article 28. Sanctions

The High Contracting Parties undertake to take, within the framework of their ordinary criminal jurisdiction, all necessary steps to prosecute and impose penal or disciplinary sanctions upon those persons, of whatever nationality, who commit or order to be committed a breach of the present Convention.

Final provisions

Article 29. Languages

1. The present Convention is drawn up in English, French, Russian and Spanish, the four texts being equally authoritative.

2. The United Nations Educational, Scientific and Cultural Organization shall arrange for translations of the Convention into the other official languages of its General Conference.

Article 30. Signature

The present Convention shall bear the date of 14 May, 1954 and, until the date of 31 December, 1954, shall remain open for signature by all States invited to the Conference which met at The Hague from 21 April, 1954 to 14 May, 1954.

Article 31. Ratification

1. The present Convention shall be subject to ratification by signatory States in accordance with their respective constitutional procedures.

2. The instruments of ratification shall be deposited with the Director - General of the United Nations Educational, Scientific and Cultural Organization.

Article 32. Accession

From the date of its entry into force, the present Convention shall be open for accession by all States mentioned in Article 30 which have not signed it, as well as any other State invited to accede by the Executive Board of the United Nations Educational, Scientific and Cultural Organization. Accession shall be effected by the deposit of an instrument of accession with the Director - General of the United Nations Educational, Scientific and Cultural Organization.

Article 33. Entry into force

1. The present Convention shall enter into force three months after five instruments of ratification have been deposited.

2. Thereafter, it shall enter into force, for each High Contracting Party, three months after the deposit of its instrument of ratification or accession.

3. The situations referred to in Articles 18 and 19 shall give immediate effect to ratifications or accessions deposited by the Parties to the conflict either before or after the beginning of hostilities or occupation. In such cases the Director - General of the United Nations Educational, Scientific and Cultural Organization shall transmit the communications referred to in Article 38 by the speediest method.

Article 34. Effective application

1. Each State Party to the Convention on the date of its entry into force shall take all necessary measures to ensure its effective application within a period of six months after such entry into force.

2. This period shall be six months from the date of deposit of the instruments of ratification or accession for any State which deposits its instrument of ratification or accession after the date of the entry into force of the Convention.

Article 35. Territorial extension of the Convention

Any High Contracting Party may, at the time of ratification or accession, or at any time thereafter, declare by notification addressed to the Director - General of the United Nations Educational, Scientific and Cultural Organization, that the present Convention shall extend to all or any of the territories for whose international relations it is responsible. The said notification shall take effect three months after the date of its receipt.

Article 36. Relation to previous conventions

1. In the relations between Powers which are bound by the Conventions of The Hague concerning the Laws and Customs of War on Land (IV) and concerning Naval Bombardment in Time of War (IX), whether those of 29 July, 1899 or those of 18 October, 1907, and which are Parties to the present Convention, this last Convention shall be supplementary to the aforementioned Convention (IX) and to the Regulations annexed to the aforementioned Convention (IV) and shall substitute for the emblem described in Article 5 of the aforementioned Convention (IX) the emblem described in Article 16 of the present Convention, in cases in which the present Convention and the Regulations for its execution provide for the use of this distinctive emblem.

2. In the relations between Powers which are bound by the Washington Pact of 15 April, 1935 for the Protection of Artistic and Scientific Institutions and of Historic Monuments (Roerich Pact) and which are Parties to the present Convention, the latter Convention shall be supplementary to the Roerich Pact and shall substitute for the distinguishing flag described in Article III of the Pact the emblem defined in Article 16 of the present Convention, in cases in which the present Convention and the Regulations for its execution provide for the use of this distinctive emblem.

Article 37. Denunciation

1. Each High Contracting Party may denounce the present Convention, on its own behalf, or on behalf of any territory for whose international relations it is responsible.

2. The denunciation shall be notified by an instrument in writing, deposited with the Director - General of the United Nations Educational, Scientific and Cultural Organization.

3. The denunciation shall take effect one year after the receipt of the instrument of denunciation. However, if, on the expiry of this period, the denouncing Party is involved in an armed conflict, the denunciation shall not take effect until the end of hostilities, or until the operations of repatriating cultural property are

completed, whichever is the later.

Article 38. Notifications

The Director - General of the United Nations Educational, Scientific and Cultural Organization shall inform the States referred to in Articles 30 and 32, as well as the United Nations, of the deposit of all the instruments of ratification, accession or acceptance provided for in Articles 31, 32 and 39 and of the notifications and denunciations provided for respectively in Articles 35, 37 and 39.

Article 39. Revision of the Convention and of the Regulations for its execution

1. Any High Contracting Party may propose amendments to the present Convention or the Regulations for its execution. The text of any proposed amendment shall be communicated to the Director - General of the United Nations Educational, Scientific and Cultural Organization who shall transmit it to each High Contracting Party with the request that such Party reply within four months stating whether it:

(a) desires that a Conference be convened to consider the proposed amendment;

(b) favours the acceptance of the proposed amendment without a Conference; or

(c) favours the rejection of the proposed amendment without a Conference.

2. The Director - General shall transmit the replies, received under paragraph 1 of the present Article, to all High Contracting Parties.

3. If all the High Contracting Parties which have, within the prescribed time - limit, stated their views to the Director - General of the United Nations Educational, Scientific and Cultural Organization, pursuant to paragraph 1 (b) of this Article, inform him that they favour acceptance of the amendment without a Conference, notification of their decision shall be made by the Director - General in accordance with Article 38. The amendment shall become effective for all the High Contracting Parties on the expiry of ninety days from the date of such notification.

4. The Director - General shall convene a Conference of the High Contracting Parties to consider the proposed amendment if requested to do so by more than one - third of the High Contracting Parties.

5. Amendments to the Convention or to the Regulations for its execution, dealt with under the provisions of the preceding paragraph, shall enter into force only after they have been unanimously adopted by the High Contracting Parties re-

presented at the Conference and accepted by each of the High Contracting Parties.

6. Acceptance by the High Contracting Parties of amendments to, the Convention or to the Regulations for its execution, which have been adopted by the Conference mentioned in paragraphs 4 and 5, shall be effected by the deposit of a formal instrument with the Director - General of the United Nations Educational, Scientific and Cultural Organization.

7. After the entry into force of amendments to the present Convention or to the Regulations for its execution, only the text of the Convention or of the Regulations for its execution thus amended shall remain open for ratification or accession.

Article 40. Registration

In accordance with Article 102 of the Charter of the United Nations, the present Convention shall be registered with the Secretariat of the United Nations at the request of the Director - General of the United Nations Educational, Scientific and Cultural Organization.

IN FAITH WHEREOF the undersigned, duly authorized, have signed the present Convention.

Regulations for the Execution of the Convention for the Protection of Cultural Property in the Event of Armed Conflict

Chapter I. Control

Article 1. International list of persons

On the entry into force of the Convention, the Director - General of the United Nations Educational, Scientific and Cultural Organization shall compile an international list consisting of all persons nominated by the High Contracting Parties as qualified to carry out the functions of Commissioner - General for Cultural Property. On the initiative of the Director - General of the United Nations Educational, Scientific and Cultural Organization, this list shall be periodically revised on the basis of requests formulated by the High Contracting Parties.

Article 2. Organization of control

As soon as any High Contracting Party is engaged in an armed conflict to which Article 18 of the Convention applies:

(a) It shall appoint a representative for cultural property situated in its territory; if it is in occupation of another territory, it shall appoint a special representative for cultural property situated in that territory;

(b) The Protecting Power acting for each of the Parties in conflict with such High Contracting Party shall appoint delegates accredited to the latter in conformity with Article 3 below;

(c) A Commissioner - General for Cultural Property shall be appointed to such High Contracting Party in accordance with Article 4.

Article 3. Appointment of delegates of Protecting Powers

The Protecting Power shall appoint its delegates from among the members of its diplomatic or consular staff or, with the approval of the Party to which they will be accredited, from among other persons.

Article 4. Appointment of Commissioner – General

1. The Commissioner - General for Cultural Property shall be chosen from the international list of persons by joint agreement between the Party to which he will be accredited and the Protecting Powers acting on behalf of the opposing Parties.

2. Should the Parties fail to reach agreement within three weeks from the beginning of their discussions on this point, they shall request the President of the International Court of Justice to appoint the Commissioner - General, who shall not take up his duties until the Party to which he is accredited has approved his appointment.

Article 5. Functions of delegates

The delegates of the Protecting Powers shall take note of violations of the Convention, investigate, with the approval of the Party to which they are accredited, the circumstances in which they have occurred, make representations locally to secure their cessation and, if necessary, notify the Commissioner - General of such violations. They shall keep him informed of their activities.

Article 6. Functions of the Commissioner – General

1. The Commissioner - General for Cultural Property shall deal with all matters

referred to him in connexion with the application of the Convention, in conjunction with the representative of the Party to which he is accredited and with the delegates concerned.

2. He shall have powers of decision and appointment in the cases specified in the present Regulations.

3. With the agreement of the Party to which he is accredited, he shall have the right to order an investigation or to, conduct it himself.

4. He shall make any representations to the Parties to the conflict or to their Protecting Powers which he deems useful for the application of the Convention.

5. He shall draw up such reports as may be necessary on the application of the Convention and communicate them to the Parties concerned and to their Protecting Powers. He shall send copies to the Director - General of the United Nations Educational, Scientific and Cultural Organization, who may make use only of their technical contents.

6. If there is no Protecting Power, the Commissioner - General shall exercise the functions of the Protecting Power as laid down in Articles 21 and 22 of the Convention.

Article 7. Inspectors and experts

1. Whenever the Commissioner - General for Cultural Property considers it necessary, either at the request of the delegates concerned or after consultation with them, he shall propose, for the approval of the Party to which he is accredited, an inspector of cultural property to be charged with a specific mission. An inspector shall be responsible only to the Commissioner - General.

2. The Commissioner - General, delegates and inspectors may have recourse to the services of experts, who will also be proposed for the approval of the Party mentioned in the preceding paragraph.

Article 8. Discharge of the mission of control

The Commissioners - General for Cultural Property, delegates of the Protecting Powers, inspectors and experts shall in no case exceed their mandates. In particular, they shall take account of the security needs of the High Contracting Party to which they are accredited and shall in all circumstances act in accordance with the requirements of the military situation as communicated to them by that High Contracting Party.

Article 9. Substitutes for Protecting Powers

If a Party to the conflict does not benefit or ceases to benefit from the activities of a Protecting Power, a neutral State may be asked to undertake those functions of a Protecting Power which concern the appointment of a Commissioner - General for Cultural Property in accordance with the procedure laid down in Article 4 above. The Commissioner - General thus appointed shall, if need be, entrust to inspectors the functions of delegates of Protecting Powers as specified in the present Regulations.

Article 10. Expenses

The remuneration and expenses of the Commissioner - General for Cultural Property, inspectors and experts shall be met by the Party to which they are accredited. Remuneration and expenses of delegates of the Protecting Powers shall be subject to agreement between those Powers and the States whose interests they are safeguarding.

Chapter II. Special protection

Article 11. Improvised refuges

1. If, during an armed conflict, any High Contracting Party is induced by unforeseen circumstances to set up an improvised refuge and desires that it should be placed under special protection, it shall communicate this fact forthwith to the Commissioner - General accredited to that Party.

2. If the Commissioner - General considers that such a measure is justified by the circumstances and by the importance of the cultural property sheltered in' this improvised refuge, he may authorize the High Contracting Party to display on such refuge the distinctive emblem defined in Article 16 of the Convention. He shall communicate his decision without delay to the delegates of the Protecting Powers who are concerned, each of whom may, within a time limit of 30 days, order the immediate withdrawal of the emblem.

3. As soon as such delegates have signified their agreement or if the time limit of 30 days has passed without any of the delegates concerned having made an objection, and if, in the view of the Commissioner - General, the refuge fulfils the conditions laid down in Article 8 of the Convention, the Commissioner - General

shall request the Director - General of the United Nations Educational, Scientific and Cultural Organization to enter the refuge in the Register of Cultural Property under Special Protection.

Article 12. International Register of Cultural Property under Special Protection

1. An `International Register of Cultural Property under Special Protection' shall be prepared.

2. The Director - General of the United Nations Educational, Scientific and Cultural Organization shall maintain this Register. He shall furnish copies to the Secretary - General of the United Nations and to the High Contracting Parties.

3. The Register shall be divided into sections, each in the name of a High Contracting Party. Each section shall be subdivided into three paragraphs, headed: Refuges, Centers containing Monuments, Other Immovable Cultural Property. The Director - General shall determine what details each section shall contain.

Article 13. Requests for registration

1. Any High Contracting Party may submit to the Director - General of the United Nations Educational, Scientific and Cultural Organization an application for the entry in the Register of certain refuges, centers containing monuments or other immovable cultural property situated within its territory. Such application shall contain a description of the location of such property and shall certify that the property complies with the provisions of Article 8 of the Convention.

2. In the event of occupation, the Occupying Power shall be competent to make such application.

3. The Director - General of the United Nations Educational, Scientific and Cultural Organization shall, without delay, send copies of applications for registration to each of the High Contracting Parties.

Article 14. Objections

1. Any High Contracting Party may, by letter addressed to the Director - General of the United Nations Educational, Scientific and Cultural Organization, lodge an objection to the registration of cultural property. This letter must be received by him within four months of the day on which he sent a copy of the application for registration.

2. Such objection shall state the reasons giving rise to it, the only, valid

grounds being that:

(a) the property is not cultural property;

(b) the property does not comply with the conditions mentioned in Article 8 of the Convention.

3. The Director - General shall send a copy of the letter of objection to the High Contracting Parties without delay. He shall, if necessary, seek the advice of the International Committee on Monuments, Artistic and Historical Sites and Archaeological Excavations and also, if he thinks fit, of any other competent organization or person.

4. The Director - General, or the High Contracting Party requesting registration, may make whatever representations they deem necessary to the High Contracting Parties which lodged the objection, with a view to causing the objection to 'be withdrawn.

5. If a High Contracting Party which has made an application for registration in time of peace becomes involved in an armed conflict before the entry has been made, the cultural property concerned shall at once be provisionally entered in the Register, by the Director - General, pending the confirmation, withdrawal or cancellation of any objection that may be, or may have been, made.

6. If, within a period of six months from the date of receipt of the letter of objection, the Director - General has not received from the High Contracting Party lodging the objection a communication stating that it has been withdrawn, the High Contracting Party applying for registration may request arbitration in accordance with the procedure in the following paragraph.

7. The request for arbitration shall not be made more than one year after the date of receipt by the Director - General of the letter of objection. Each of the two Parties to the dispute shall appoint an arbitrator. When more than one objection has been lodged against an application for registration, the High Contracting Parties which have lodged the 'objections shall, by common consent, appoint a single arbitrator. These two arbitrators shall select a chief arbitrator from the international list mentioned in Article 1 of the present Regulations. If such arbitrators cannot agree upon their choice, they shall ask the President of the International Court of Justice to appoint a chief arbitrator who need not necessarily be chosen from the international list. The arbitral tribunal thus constituted shall fix its own procedure.

There shall be no appeal from its decisions.

8. Each of the High Contracting Parties may declare, whenever a dispute to which it is a Party arises, that it does not wish to apply the arbitration procedure provided for in the preceding paragraph. In such cases, the objection to an application for registration shall be submitted by the Director - General to the High Contracting Parties. The objection will be confirmed only if the High Contracting Parties so decide by a two - third majority of the High Contracting Parties voting. The vote shall be taken by correspondence, unless the Directory - General of the United Nations Educational, Scientific and Cultural Organization deems it essential to convene a meeting under the powers conferred upon him by Article 27 of the Convention. If the Director - General decides to proceed with the vote by correspondence, he shall invite the High Contracting Parties to transmit their votes by sealed letter within six months from the day on which they were invited to do so.

Article 15. Registration

1. The Director - General of the United Nations Educational, Scientific and Cultural Organization shall cause to be entered in the Register, under a serial number, each item of property for which application for registration is made, provided that he has not received an objection within the time - limit prescribed in paragraph 1 of Article 14.

2. If an objection has been lodged, and without prejudice to the provision of paragraph 5 of Article 14, the Director - General shall enter property in the Register only if the objection has been withdrawn or has failed to be confirmed following the procedures laid down in either paragraph 7 or paragraph 8 of Article 14.

3. Whenever paragraph 3 of Article 11 applies, the Director - General shall enter property in the Register if so requested by the Commissioner - General for Cultural Property.

4. The Director - General shall send without delay to the Secretary - General of the United Nations, to the High Contracting Parties, and, at the request of the Party applying for registration, to all other States referred to in Articles 30 and 32 of the Convention, a certified copy of each entry in the Register. Entries shall become effective thirty days after dispatch of such copies.

Article 16. Cancellation

1. The Director - General of the United Nations Educational, Scientific and

Cultural Organization shall cause the registration of any property to be cancelled:

(a) at the request of the High Contracting Party within whose territory the cultural property is situated;

(b) if the High Contracting Party which requested registration has denounced the Convention, and when that denunciation has taken effect;

(c) in the special case provided for in Article 14, paragraph 5, when an objection has been confirmed following the procedures mentioned either in paragraph 7 or in paragraph 8 or Article 14.

2. The Director - General shall send without delay, to the Secretary - General of the United Nations and to all States which received a copy of the entry in the Register, a certified copy of its cancellation. Cancellation shall take effect thirty days after the dispatch of such copies.

Chapter III. Transport of cultural property

Article 17. Procedure to obtain immunity

1. The request mentioned in paragraph I of Article 12 of the Convention shall be addressed to the Commissioner - General for Cultural Property. It shall mention the reasons on which it is based and specify the approximate number and the importance of the objects to be transferred, their present location, the location now envisaged, the means of transport to be used, the route to be followed, the date proposed for the transfer, and any other relevant information.

2. If the Commissioner - General, after taking such opinions as he deems fit, considers that such transfer is justified, he shall consult those delegates of the Protecting Powers who are concerned, on the measures proposed for carrying it out. Following such consultation, he shall notify the Parties to the conflict concerned of the transfer, including in such notification all useful information.

3. The Commissioner - General shall appoint one or more inspectors, who shall satisfy themselves that only the property stated in the request is to be transferred and that the transport is to be by the approved methods and bears the distinctive emblem. The inspector or inspectors shall accompany the property to its destination.

Article 18. Transport abroad

Where the transfer under special protection is to the territory of another country, it shall be governed not only by Article 12 of the Convention and by Article 17 of the present Regulations, but by the following further provisions:

(a) while the cultural property remains on the territory of another State, that State shall be its depositary and shall extend to it as great a measure of care as that which it bestows upon its own cultural property of comparable importance;

(b) the depositary State shall return the property only on the cessation of the conflict; such return shall be effected within six months from the date on which it was requested;

(c) during the various transfer operations, and while it remains on the territory of another State, the cultural property shall be exempt from confiscation and may not be disposed of either by the depositor or by the depositary. Nevertheless, when the safety of the property requires it, the depositary may, with the assent of the depositor, have the property transported to the territory of a third country, under the conditions laid down in the present article;

(d) the request for special protection shall indicate that the State to whose territory the property is to be transferred accepts the provisions of the present Article.

Article 19. Occupied territory

Whenever a High Contracting Party occupying territory of another High Contracting Party transfers cultural property to a refuge situated elsewhere in that territory, without being able to follow the procedure provided for in Article 17 of the Regulations, the transfer in question shall not be regarded as misappropriation within the meaning of Article 4 of the Convention, provided that the Commissioner - General for Cultural Property certifies in writing, after having consulted the usual custodians, that such transfer was rendered necessary by circumstances.

Chapter IV. The distinctive emblem

Article 20. Affixing of the emblem

1. The placing of the distinctive emblem and its degree of visibility shall be left to the discretion of the competent authorities of each High Contracting Party. It may be displayed on flags or armlets; it may be painted on an object or represented

in any other appropriate form.

2. However, without prejudice to any possible fuller markings, the emblem shall, in the event of armed conflict and in the cases mentioned in Articles 12 and 13 of the Convention, be placed on the vehicles of transport so as to be clearly visible in daylight from the air as well as from the ground. The emblem shall be visible from the ground:

(a) at regular intervals sufficient to indicate clearly the perimeter of a centre containing monuments under special protection;

(b) at the entrance to other immovable cultural property under special protection.

Article 21. Identification of persons

1. The persons mentioned in Article 17, paragraph 2 (b) and (c) of the Convention may wear an armlet bearing the distinctive emblem, issued and stamped by the competent authorities.

2. Such persons shall carry a special identity card bearing the distinctive emblem. This card shall mention at least the surname and first names, the date of birth, the title or rank, and the function of the holder. The card shall bear the photograph of the holder as well as his signature or his fingerprints, or both. It shall bear the embossed stamp of the competent authorities.

3. Each High Contracting Party shall make out its own type of identity card, guided by the model annexed, by way of example, to the present Regulations. The High Contracting Parties shall transmit to each other a specimen of the model they are using. Identity cards shall be made out, if possible, at least in duplicate, one copy being kept by the issuing Power.

4. The said persons may not, without legitimate reason, be deprived of their identity card or of the right to wear the armlet.

《关于发生武装冲突时保护文化财产的公约》第二议定书

（海牙，1999 年 3 月 26 日）

缔约国意识到改善在武装冲突情况下保护文化财产的必要性和制定一项重点保护特别指定的文化财产的制度之必要性；

重申《关于在武装冲突情况下保护文化财产的公约》（海牙，1954 年 5 月 14 日）的条款的重要性，并强调有必要采取一些加强其实施的补充措施；

希望建立适当的程序使《公约》的缔约国能够更密切地参与在武装冲突的情况下对文化财产的保护；

认为在武装冲突的情况下保护文化财产的规则应当反映国际法的发展；

确认国际法公认的准则继续对本《议定书》所未能解决的问题行之有效。

达成如下协议：

第一章 引 言

第 1 条 定义

在本《议定书》的范围内：

a. “缔约国”系指签本《议定书》的缔约国；

b. “文化财产”系指《公约》第 1 条中规定的文化财产；

c. “公约”系指《关于在武装冲突情况下保护文化财产的公约》，（海牙，1954 年 5 月 14 日）；

d. “公约缔约国”系指《关于在武装冲突情况下保护文化财产的公约》的缔约国；

e. “重点保护”系指《议定书》第 10 条和第 11 条所规定的重点保护制度；

f. “军事目标”系指一种物品，由于其性质、所处地点、目的地或对其使用会给军事行动带来直接作用，该物品全部或部分被摧毁、被缴获或丧失作用也会导致明显的军事优势；

g. “非法的”系指在违反被占领土国内立法或国际法适用法规的情况下，以强迫手段或其他手段从事的非法行为；

h. “目录”系指根据本《议定书》第 27 条第 1 段 b 分段的规定所设立的《受重点保护的国际文化财产目录》；

i. “总干事”系指教科文组织总干事；

j. “教科文组织”系指联合国教育、科学及文化组织；

k. “第一项议定书”系指 1954 年 5 月 14 日在海牙通过的《关于在武装冲突情况下保护文化财产的议定书》。

第 2 条 与《公约》的关系

本《议定书》是在其缔约国的相互关系上对《公约》的补充。

第 3 条 执行范围

1. 除和平时期应执行的条款之外，在《公约》第 18 条第 1 和第 2 段、第 22 条第 1 段所确认的情况下应执行本《议定书》。

2. 当武装冲突各方中有一方不受本《议定书》的约束时，《议定书》的各缔约国在其相互关系上依然受本《议定书》之约束。在与一个不受本《议定书》约束的冲突国发生关系时，只要它接受并执行本《议定书》之规定，本《议定书》的缔约国也应受本《议定书》的约束。

第 4 条 本《议定书》第三章与《公约》及本《议定书》其他条款之间的关系

本《议定书》第三章的规定之执行不影响：

a.《公约》第一章及本《议定书》第二章各条规定的执行；

b.《公约》第二章无论是在本《议定书》的缔约国之间，还是在一个缔约国与一个根据第 3 条第 2 段规定接受并执行本《议定书》的非缔约国之间的执行，如果一项文化财产同时置于特别保护和重点保护之下，那么只执行关于重点保护的规定。

第二章　文化财产的一般性保护规定

第 5 条 文化财产的保护

根据《公约》第 3 条的规定，在和平时期为预防军事冲突对文化财产造成后果而采取的保护措施包括：编制目录，为保护文化财产而制定预防建筑物火灾或倒塌的应急措施，做好可移动文化财产的移出或有效保护的准备工作，以及确定负责文化财产保护的主管机构。

第 6 条　尊重文化财产

根据《公约》第 4 条的规定，为保证文化财产得到尊重之目的：

a. 不得援引《公约》第 4 条第 2 段所提及的关于以军事上绝对需要为由的例外规定，对某一文化财产采取敌对行动，除非：

Ⅰ. 该项文化财产所起的作用已使其变为了军事目标，并且

Ⅱ. 的确已没有其他办法能够像对该目标采取敌对行动那样获得相同的军事优势；

b. 不得援引《公约》第 4 条第 2 段关于军事上绝对需要的例外规定，将文化财产用于会使其遭损毁或破坏的目的，除非的确已没有别的办法能获得同等的军事优势；

c. 只有相当于或高于营级的军官才可做出援引军事上绝对需要的决定，在情况不允许做出其他选择时，营以下军官才可决定；

d. 在根据 a 分段规定做出攻击决定的情况下，当条件允许时，应及时向对方发出有效的警告。

第 7 条　攻击时之预防措施

在不违背国际法要求的其他注意事项的情况下，采取军事行动的各缔约国应该：

a. 采取一切可行措施，确认被攻击目标不是《公约》第 4 条所保护的文化财产；

b. 在选择攻击手段和方法时，采取各种可能的措施，以尽量避免和减少对受《公约》第 4 条保护的文化财产造成意外损失；

c. 放弃发动会对受《公约》第 4 条保护的文化财产造成意外的严重损失，而希望得到的具体和直接的军事优势又相对较小的攻击；

d. 在下列情况下取消或中止攻击：

Ⅰ. 目标是受《公约》第 4 条保护的文化财产；

Ⅱ. 可以预见，攻击会对受《公约》第 4 条保护的文化财产造成意外的严重损失，而希望得到的具体和直接的军事优势又相对较小。

第 8 条　攻击后果之预防措施

冲突各方应尽一切可能做到：

a. 把可移动的文化财产从军事目标附近移走，或对它们提供有效的就地

保护；

b. 避免将军事目标设在文化财产附近。

第 9 条　保护被占领土上的文化财产

1. 在不违背《公约》第 4 条和第 5 条之规定的情况下，部分或全部占领了另一缔约国领土的任何缔约国应在该被占领土上禁止和阻止：

a. 一切文化财产的非法出口、移动或转让；

b. 任何考古挖掘，除非它对文化财产的保护、登记或保存是绝对必要的；

c. 目的在于隐匿或毁坏文化财产所具有的文化、历史或科学见证作用的改造或改变文化财产用途的行为。

2. 对被占领土上的文化财产进行考古挖掘、改造或改变其用途，只要条件允许，都必须与该被占领土的国家当局进行密切的合作。

第三章　重点保护

第 10 条　重点保护

文化财产如果符合下述三个条件，即可置于重点保护之下：

a. 属于对全人类具有最重大意义的文化遗产；

b. 系国内有关法律和行政措施视为具有特殊的文化与历史价值并给予最高级别保护的文化财产；

c. 未被用于军事目的或用以保护军事设施，并且控制它的缔约国已声明确保它不会用于此类目的的文化财产。

第 11 条　重点保护资格的授予

1. 各缔约国应向委员会提交一份它希望授予重点保护资格的文化财产目录。

2. 管辖和控制一项文化财产的缔约国可以申请将其列入根据第 27 条第 1 段 b 分段开列的《目录》之中。该项申请应根据第 10 条规定的标准列出有关文化财产的所有情况。委员会可要求一个缔约国申请将该文化财产列入《目录》。

3. 具有必要鉴定能力的其他缔约国、国际蓝盾委员会及其他非政府组织可向委员会推荐某一具体的文化财产，在这种情况下，委员会可要求某一缔约国提出将该文化财产列入《目录》的申请。

4. 在有关文化财产处于有一个以上的国家提出主权或管辖权要求的领土

上时，申请将该文化财产列入《目录》的行为或将其列入《目录》的行为在任何情况下均不构成对冲突各方权利的损害。

5. 委员会在收到一项列入《目录》的申请之后，应即通知所有缔约国。缔约国可在60天之内向委员会提交对此项申请的反对意见。这些意见只能以第10条所列之标准作为依据，并且应具体和针对事实。委员会审议反对意见，并在做出决定之前给提出申请的缔约国以答辩的机会。在委员会收到了这种反对意见时，在不违背第26条的情况下，列入《目录》的决定应由出席并参加表决的五分之四多数委员会成员通过。

6. 委员会在对一项申请做出裁决时，应征询有关政府组织和非政府组织以及独立专家们的意见。

7. 做出授予或拒绝授予重点保护资格的决定只能以第10条所列之标准作为依据。

8. 在特殊情况下，当委员会判定申请将某一文化财产列入《目录》的有关缔约国尚不符合第10条b分段所列之标准时，只要该缔约国根据第32条规定提出国际援助的申请，委员会便可做出授予重点保护资格的决定。

9. 敌对行动一开始，作为冲突一方的缔约国便可因情况紧急，向委员会递交申请，要求对其管辖或控制之下的文化财产进行重点保护，委员会应立即将该申请转交参与冲突的各缔约国。在此情况下，委员会紧急审议有关各缔约国的反对意见。在不违背第26条之规定的情况下，委员会应尽快以五分之四多数委员通过的方式做出提供重点保护的决定。在按正常程序给以重点保护的工作未有结果之前，只要符合第10条a分段和c分段规定的标准，委员会可以授予临时性重点保护资格。

10. 文化财产自列入《目录》之时起便享受委员会给予的重点保护。

11. 总干事及时将委员会把文化财产列入《目录》的决定通知联合国秘书长及所有缔约国。

第12条　受重点保护的文化财产的豁免权

参与冲突的缔约国应确保受重点保护的文化财产的豁免权，不把这些文化财产作为进攻目标，不将这些文化财产或其周围设施用以支持军事行动。

第13条　丧失重点保护资格

1. 受重点保护的文化财产只有在下列情况下才丧失受这种保护的资格：

a. 根据第14条之规定中止或取消了该项保护资格；或者

b. 有关文化财产的使用方式已使其成为军事目标。

2. 在第1段b分段所述情况下，有关文化财产只有在下列情况下才可成为进攻目标：

a．这种进攻是唯一可以结束第1段b分段所述之该文化财产的使用方式的办法；

b．为结束该使用方式，并避免或尽量减少对该财产的损害，在选择进攻办法与方式上已采取了一切可行的预防措施；

c．除因即时合法防卫的需要，情况不允许这样做之外：

Ⅰ．进攻命令由军事行动最高指挥当局发布；

Ⅱ．已通过有效手段向对方发出了警告，命令其结束第1段b分段所述之文化财产的使用方式；并且

Ⅲ．给对方以合理的时间设法改变有关情况。

第14条 重点保护资格之中止和取消

1．当有关文化财产不再符合本《议定书》第10条规定之其中某一标准时，委员会可以中止或取消对该财产的重点保护，并将其从《目录》中删除。

2．当一种受重点保护的文化财产被用以为军事行动服务而严重违反第12条之规定时，委员会可以中止对该文化财产的重点保护。如继续违反规定，委员会可以例外地取消对其保护，并从《目录》中将其删除。

3．总干事将把委员会关于中止或取消对某项文化财产的重点保护决定及时通知联合国秘书长及本《议定书》的缔约国。

4．在做这种决定之前，委员会向缔约国提供表达自己看法的机会。

第四章 刑事责任与管辖权

第15条 严重违反本《议定书》

1．任何人不顾《公约》或本《议定书》之规定，故意做出下列行为的，就是对本《议定书》的违反：

a．将受重点保护的文化财产作为进攻目标；

b．将受重点保护的文化财产或其周围设施用以支持军事行动；

c．大量地破坏或攫取受《公约》和本《议定书》保护的文化财产；

d．将受《公约》和本《议定书》保护的文化财产作为进攻目标；

e．偷盗、掠夺或侵占受《公约》保护的文化财产，以及对它们进行破坏的行为。

2．各缔约国应采取必要措施，依据国内法对本条款所列之各种违约行为

加以指控，并通过适当刑罚制止此类行为。在这样做时，缔约国应遵守法律的一般原则和国际法，尤其是遵守把个人刑事责任扩大到直接行为者以外之其他人的规则。

第16条　管辖权

1. 在不违背第2段规定的情况下，各缔约国应采取必要的立法措施，确定自己在下列情况下对第15条所述的违约行为的管辖权：

a. 这一违约行为发生在该国的领土范围内；

b. 被推定为违约行为者是该国的国民；

c. 违反第15条第1段a分段至c分段之规定的被推定作案人就在该国领土之上。

2. 在行使管辖权方面，在不违背《公约》第28条之规定的情况下：

a. 本《议定书》不妨碍依据有关的国内或国际法承担个人的刑事责任和行使管辖权，也不影响根据国际习惯法行使管辖权；

b. 除了根据第3条第2段，本《议定书》的非缔约国可以接受并执行本《议定书》的规定这一情况外，本《议定书》非缔约国的武装力量成员和国民可不按本《议定书》的规定承担个人刑事责任，因为本《议定书》并没有规定必须确定对这些人的管辖权限，也没有规定引渡他们的义务。非缔约国的国民服役于一个本《议定书》缔约国的武装力量则不属此列。

第17条　起诉

1. 有关缔约国在发现违反第15条a分段至c分段之规定的被推定作案人在其领土上时，如不将其引渡，则应无一例外和不过分拖延地将此案送交主管当局，按照符合国内法或符合有关国际法惯例的程序提出起诉。

2. 在不违背国际法惯例的情况下，依据《公约》或本《议定书》受到司法程序审查的任何人在整个过程中依据国内法和国际法享有得到公正待遇和审判的保障，而且这种保障在任何情况下都不能低于国际法所认可的保障。

第18条　引渡

1. 第15条第1段a分段至c分段所述之违约行为，应被视为缔约国之间在本《议定书》生效之前已有的引渡条约中规定的可引渡违约行为。缔约国有义务将此类违约行为纳入它们之间今后可能达成的引渡条约之中。

2. 以现存条约为引渡条件的缔约国，如收到未与其签订有引渡条约的另一缔约国的引渡要求，其可根据自己的选择，以本《议定书》作为就第15条第1段a分段至c分段规定之违约行为进行引渡的法律依据。

3. 不以现存条约为引渡条件的缔约国，承认第15条第1段a分段至c分

段所述之违约行为属于它们之间根据被请求国法律规定的条件进行引渡的范围。

4. 如有必要，为实现缔约国之间的引渡，第15条第1段a分段至c分段所述之违约行为应视为既是在作案地也是在已根据第16条第1段确定了其管辖权的缔约国的领土上发生。

第19条　法律上的互相协助

1. 在对第15条所述之违约行为进行的调查和刑事诉讼或引渡程序中，缔约国之间应相互提供最大程度的司法协助，包括协助取得它们所掌握的、为诉讼程序所必需的证据。

2. 缔约国应按照它们之间可能业已存在的司法互助条约或协议履行第1段规定的义务，如无此类条约或协议，缔约国应依据国内法相互提供协助。

第20条　拒绝引渡的理由

1. 为引渡和相互提供司法协助之目的，第15条第1段a分段至c分段，以及第15条全部所述之违约行为不得视为政治罪行、与政治犯罪相关的罪行或有政治动机的罪行。因此，就此类违约行为提出的引渡或相互司法协助的要求不可仅以其涉及政治罪行、与政治犯罪相关的罪行或有政治动机的罪行为由而加以拒绝。

2. 如被请求的缔约国有充分理由认为，以第15条第1段a分段至c分段所述之违约行为要求引渡，或以第15条所述之违约行为要求提供相互司法协助的目的是为了因某人的种族、宗教、国籍、族裔或政治观点而对该人进行起诉和惩罚，或认为顺从这一请求将使该人的处境因上述任何一种理由受到损害，则本《议定书》的任何条款都不应被解释为规定该缔约国有进行引渡或提供相互司法协助的义务。

第21条　针对其他违约行为的措施

在不违背《公约》第28条规定的情况下，各缔约国应采取有效的立法、行政或惩罚措施，以制止故意实施的下列行为：

a. 对文化财产的违反《公约》或本《议定书》之规定的任何形式的使用；

b. 违反《公约》或本《议定书》之规定，从被占领土上非法出口、转移文化财产或转让文化财产权。

第五章　非国际性武装冲突中的文化财产保护

第 22 条　非国际性武装冲突

1. 本《议定书》适用于非国际性、发生在某一缔约国领土上的武装冲突。

2. 本《议定书》不适用于内部局势紧张和动乱，诸如骚乱、孤立零星的暴力行为或类似现象。

3. 不得援引本《议定书》任何条款损害一国主权或妨碍其政府利用合法手段行使维护、恢复国家公共秩序或捍卫国家统一及领土完整的责任。

4. 如一缔约国领土上发生了违背本《议定书》第 15 条的不具国际性质的武装冲突，本《议定书》的任何条款均无损于该缔约国的法律优先权。

5. 当一缔约国领土上发生武装冲突时，不得以任何理由以本《议定书》的任何条款为借口，直接或间接干预该冲突或该国内外事务。

6. 当本《议定书》运用于第 1 段提及的情况时，并不影响冲突各方的法律地位。

7. 教科文组织可向冲突各方提供服务。

第六章　机构问题

第 23 条　缔约国大会

1. 缔约国大会与教科文组织大会同时召开。如教科文组织总干事召集《公约》缔约国大会，《议定书》缔约国大会与之协调举行。

2. 缔约国大会通过其《议事规则》。

3. 缔约国大会拥有如下职能：

a. 根据第 24 条第 1 段的规定，选举委员会成员；

b. 批准委员会根据第 27 条第 1 段 a 分段规定制定的《指导原则》；

c. 向委员会提出“基金”的使用方针，并对之进行监督；

d. 审议委员会根据第 27 条第 1 段 d 分段规定提交的报告；

e. 审议与本《议定书》执行情况有关的各种问题，并视情况提出建议。

4. 如五分之一以上的缔约国提出要求，总干事可召开缔约国特别会议。

第 24 条　武装冲突中的文化财产保护委员会

1. 建立一个武装冲突中的文化财产保护委员会，由缔约国大会选出 12 个缔约国组成。

2. 委员会每年举行一次例行会议，并可在它认为必要时随时举行特别会议。

3. 缔约国在确定委员会的构成时，应确保世界不同地区和文化间的公平代表性。

4. 委员会成员国应挑选在文化遗产、防务问题和国际法方面具有专长的人士作为自己的代表，并通过协商，努力使整个委员会在所有这些领域都有必要的专业人才。

第25条　任期

1. 委员会成员国任期四年，并只可连任一次。

2. 除第1段的规定之外，首次选举时产生的半数成员国的任期到它们当选后召开的首届缔约国例行大会结束时为止。这半数成员国的名单由缔约国大会主席在首次选举后抽签决定。

第26条　议事规则

1. 委员会应通过其《议事规则》。

2. 委员会成员过半数即构成法定人数。委员会的决定应由参加表决的三分之二多数通过。

3. 作为冲突一方的委员会成员不参加所有涉及受该冲突影响的文化财产的有关决定的表决。

第27条　职能

1. 委员会拥有以下职能：

a. 制订执行本《议定书》的指导原则；

b. 决定对有关文化财产给予、中止或停止重点保护，建立、更新和传播《受重点保护的文化财产目录》。

c. 跟踪和监督本《议定书》的执行情况，推进应受重点保护的文化财产的确认工作。

d. 审议各缔约国提交的报告并提出看法，收集所需要的情况，并就本《议定书》的执行情况向缔约国大会提出自己的报告；

e. 受理并审议根据第32条规定提交的各种国际援助申请；

f. 决定如何使用“基金”；

g. 行使缔约国大会赋予的其他各项职能。

2. 委员会在行使其职能时，应与总干事合作。

3. 委员会应和宗旨与《公约》及其第一项《议定书》及本《议定书》类似的各种国际的及各国的政府及非政府组织进行合作。委员会可邀请某些与教科文组织有正式关系的杰出专业组织，特别是蓝盾委员会（CIBB）及其组成机构，以咨询机构身份出席委员会会议，帮助其行使职能。国际文化财产保护与修复研究中心（罗马中心）（ICCROM）和国际红十字会（CICR）的代表亦可以咨询者身份与会。

第28条　秘书处

教科文组织秘书处向委员会提供协助，为其拟定文件和会议议程，并实施其决定。

第29条　武装冲突中的文化财产保护基金

1. 建立此“基金”的目的是：

a. 为支持根据第5条、第10条b分段和第30条的规定，在和平时期开展的预防及其他有关工作提供财政和其他帮助；

b. 为支持根据第8条a分段的规定而采取的紧急、临时或其他旨在武装冲突时期保护文化财产或敌对行动一俟结束即对之进行修复的措施提供财政或其他帮助。

2. 此“基金”是根据教科文组织《财务条例》规定建立的一项信托基金。

3. “基金”的支出只能用于委员会根据第23条第3段a分段规定所确定的目的。委员会可以接受专门用于对它已决定实施的具体计划或项目的捐助。

4. “基金”的资金来源是：

a. 各缔约国的自愿捐助；

b. 来自以下各方的捐助、捐赠或遗赠：

Ⅰ. 其他国家；

Ⅱ. 教科文组织或其他联合国机构；

Ⅲ. 其他政府间组织或非政府组织；

Ⅳ. 公共或私人机构或个人。

c. “基金”所拥有资金产生的利息；

d. 为“基金”组织的募捐或其他活动所得；

e. “基金”既定方针所允许的其他各种资金来源。

第七章　信息传播和国际援助

第30条　传播

1. 缔约国应通过适宜的方法，特别是通过一些宣传教育计划，使本国全体公民更加重视和尊重文化财产。

2. 缔约国在和平时期和武装冲突时期均应尽可能广泛地传播本《议定书》。

3. 负责在武装冲突时期执行本《议定书》的军政当局应充分了解本《议定书》的内容。为此，缔约国应视情：

a. 将有关保护文化财产的方针和指令纳入它们的军事条例；

b. 与教科文组织及有关的政府组织和非政府组织合作，制订和实施和平时期的训练和教育计划；

c. 通过总干事，相互通报为实施 a 分段和 b 分段而制订的法律、行政条例和措施；

d. 尽快地通过总干事相互通报自己为执行本《议定书》所可能制订的法律和行政条例。

第 31 条　国际合作

各缔约国承诺，在本《议定书》受到严重违反时，将集体地通过委员会或单独地遵照联合国宪章与教科文组织及联合国合作采取行动。

第 32 条　国际援助

1. 缔约国可向委员会申请对受重点保护文化财产的国际援助，以及帮助其起草、制订或执行第 10 条提及的法律、行政条例和措施的援助。

2. 非本《议定书》缔约国的冲突一方，如能按第 3 条第 2 段的规定，接受并执行本《议定书》的条款，亦可请求委员会向其提供适宜的国际援助。

3. 委员会应通过有关申请国际援助的规则，并确定这种援助的形式。

4. 鼓励各缔约国通过委员会向提出申请的其他缔约国或冲突各方提供各种形式的技术援助。

第 33 条　教科文组织的协助

1. 缔约国可请求教科文组织提供技术援助，帮助其组织保护文化财产的准备工作，制订紧急情况下的预防和组织措施，建立本国的文化财产清单或解决在执行本《议定书》过程中遇到的其他各种问题。教科文组织将在其计划和能力所及的范围内提供这种协助。

2. 鼓励各缔约国以双边或多边形式提供技术援助。

3. 教科文组织有权在以上各方面主动向缔约国提出建议。

第八章　本《议定书》的实施

第 34 条　保护国

本《议定书》将在负责维护冲突各方利益的保护国的协助下执行。

第35条　调解程序

1. 每当保护国认为有必要为保护文化财产而出面斡旋，特别是如果冲突各方在执行或解释本《议定书》条款方面出现分歧时，保护国可进行斡旋。

2. 为此，各保护国可应某缔约国或总干事要求，或自行建议参与冲突的各缔约国派代表举行会议，特别是举行负责保护文化财产的有关当局会议。这种会议必要时可在非冲突一方的第三国领土上召开。参与冲突的各缔约国对向它们提出的开会建议必须作出答复。保护国或总干事将提名一位非冲突一方的第三国人士作为会议主席参加会议，并征求冲突各方同意。

第36条　无保护国情况下的调解

1. 一旦发生未指定保护国的冲突，总干事可提供斡旋或出面干预，进行其他各种形式的调解或调停，以解决分歧。

2. 委员会主席可应某一缔约国或总干事的请求，建议冲突各方派代表举行会议，特别是举行负责保护文化财产当局之间的会议。必要时，此类会议可在非冲突一方的第三国领土上召开。

第37条　翻译和报告

1. 各缔约国应将本《议定书》译为本国语言，并将正式译本提交总干事。

2. 各缔约国每四年向委员会提交一份有关本《议定书》执行情况的报告。

第38条　国家的责任

本《议定书》所有有关个人刑事责任的条款，均不影响国家在国际法方面的责任，特别是赔偿义务。

第九章　最后条款

第39条　语言

本《议定书》用英文、阿拉伯文、中文、西班牙文、法文和俄文拟定，六种文本具有同等效力。

第40条　签署

本《议定书》的拟定日期为1999年3月26日，供《海牙公约》各缔约国在1999年5月17日至12月31日期间在海牙签署。

第41条　批准、接受或赞同

1. 本《议定书》须由《海牙公约》缔约国中已在该《议定书》上签字

的国家根据本国的法定程序予以批准、接受或赞同。

2. 批准书、接受书或赞同书须提交总干事。

第 42 条 加入

1. 本《议定书》自 2000 年 1 月 1 日起，供《海牙公约》的其他缔约国加入。

2. 加入时须向总干事提交加入书。

第 43 条 生效

1. 本《议定书》将于 20 个国家递交批准书、接受书、赞同书或加入书三个月后生效。

2. 此后，本《议定书》将在每个缔约国递交批准书、接受书、赞同书或加入书三个月后对其生效。

第 44 条 武装冲突情况下的生效问题

如出现《公约》第 18 条和第 19 条所述情况，冲突各方在敌对行动开始或国家被占领之前或之后递交的对本《议定书》的批准书、接受书、赞同书或加入书将立即生效。在此种情况下，总干事将以最快方式进行第 46 条提及的情况通报。

第 45 条 退约

1. 各缔约国可退出本议定书。

2. 退约通知须以书面形式递交总干事保存。

3. 退约行为在退约书送达一年后生效。然而，在这一年到期时，如退约国正处于冲突之中，则退约行为需待冲突结束、起码是归还完文化财产后方能生效。

第 46 条 通知

总干事将把第 41 条和第 42 条提及的批准书、接受书、赞同书或加入书及第 45 条提及的退约书的交存情况通报《公约》的所有缔约国和联合国。

第 47 条 在联合国登记

根据联合国宪章第 102 条的规定，本《议定书》将应总干事要求，在联合国秘书处登记。

Second Protocol to the Convention for the Protection of Cultural Property in the Event of Armed Conflict

(the Hague, 26 March 1999)

The Parties,

Conscious of the need to improve the protection of cultural property in the event of armed conflict and to establish an enhanced system of protection for specifically designated cultural property;

Reaffirming the importance of the provisions of the Convention for the Protection of Cultural Property in the Event of Armed Conflict, done at the Hague on 14 May 1954, and emphasizing the necessity to supplement these provisions through measures to reinforce their implementation;

Desiring to provide the High Contracting Parties to the Convention with a means of being more closely involved in the protection of cultural property in the event of armed conflict by establishing appropriate procedures therefor;

Considering that the rules governing the protection of cultural property in the event of armed conflict should reflect developments in international law;

Affirming that the rules of customary international law will continue to govern questions not regulated by the provisions of this Protocol;

Have agreed as follows:

Chapter 1 Introduction

Article 1 Definitions

For the purposes of this Protocol:

a. "Party" means a State Party to this Protocol;

b. "cultural property" means cultural property as defined in Article 1 of the Convention;

c. "Convention" means the Convention for the Protection of Cultural Property in the Event of Armed Conflict, done at The Hague on 14 May 1954;

d. "High Contracting Party" means a State Party to the Convention;

e. "enhanced protection" means the system of enhanced protection established by Articles 10 and 11;

f. "military objective" means an object which by its nature, location, purpose, or use makes an effective contribution to military action and whose total or partial destruction, capture or neutralisation, in the circumstances ruling at the time, offers a definite military advantage;

g. "illicit" means under compulsion or otherwise in violation of the applicable rules of the domestic law of the occupied territory or of international law.

h. "List" means the International List of Cultural Property under Enhanced Protection established in accordance with Article 27, sub - paragraph 1 (b);

i. "Director - General" means the Director - General of UNESCO;

j. "UNESCO" means the United Nations Educational, Scientific and Cultural Organization;

k. "First Protocol" means the Protocol for the Protection of Cultural Property in the Event of Armed Conflict done at The Hague on 14 May 1954;

Article 2 Relation to the Convention

This Protocol supplements the Convention in relations between the Parties.

Article 3 Scope of application

1. In addition to the provisions which shall apply in time of peace, this Protocol shall apply in situations referred to in Article 18 paragraphs 1 and 2 of the Convention and in Article 22 paragraph 1.

2. When one of the parties to an armed conflict is not bound by this Protocol, the Parties to this Protocol shall remain bound by it in their mutual relations. They shall furthermore be bound by this Protocol in relation to a State party to the conflict which is not bound by it, if the latter accepts the provisions of this Protocol and so long as it applies them.

Article 4 Relationship between Chapter 3 and other provisions of the Convention and this Protocol

The application of the provisions of Chapter 3 of this Protocol is without prejudice to:

a. the application of the provisions of Chapter I of the Convention and of Chapter 2 of this Protocol;

b. the application of the provisions of Chapter II of the Convention save that, as between Parties to this Protocol or as between a Party and a State which accepts and applies this Protocol in accordance with Article 3 paragraph 2, where cultural property has been granted both special protection and enhanced protection, only the provisions of enhanced protection shall apply.

Chapter 2 General provisions regarding protection

Article 5 Safeguarding of cultural property

Preparatory measures taken in time of peace for the safeguarding of cultural property against the foreseeable effects of an armed conflict pursuant to Article 3 of the Convention shall include, as appropriate, the preparation of inventories, the planning of emergency measures for protection against fire or structural collapse, the preparation for the removal of movable cultural property or the provision for adequate in situ protection of such property, and the designation of competent authorities responsible for the safeguarding of cultural property.

Article 6 Respect for cultural property

With the goal of ensuring respect for cultural property in accordance with Article 4 of the Convention:

a. a waiver on the basis of imperative military necessity pursuant to Article 4 paragraph 2 of the Convention may only be invoked to direct an act of hostility against cultural property when and for as long as:

i. that cultural property has, by its function, been made into a military objective; and

ii. there is no feasible alternative available to obtain a similar military advantage to that offered by directing an act of hostility against that objective;

b. a waiver on the basis of imperative military necessity pursuant to Article 4 paragraph 2 of the Convention may only be invoked to use cultural property for purposes which are likely to expose it to destruction or damage when and for as long as no choice is possible between such use of the cultural property and another feasible method for obtaining a similar military advantage;

c. the decision to invoke imperative military necessity shall only be taken by an officer commanding a force the equivalent of a battalion in size or larger, or a force smaller in size where circumstances do not permit otherwise;

d. in case of an attack based on a decision taken in accordance with sub-paragraph (a), an effective advance warning shall be given whenever circumstances permit.

Article 7 Precautions in attack

Without prejudice to other precautions required by international humanitarian law in the conduct of military operations, each Party to the conflict shall:

a. do everything feasible to verify that the objectives to be attacked are not cultural property protected under Article 4 of the Convention;

b. take all feasible precautions in the choice of means and methods of attack with a view to avoiding, and in any event to minimizing, incidental damage to cultural property protected under Article 4 of the Convention;

c. refrain from deciding to launch any attack which may be expected to cause incidental damage to cultural property protected under Article 4 of the Convention which would be excessive in relation to the concrete and direct military advantage anticipated; and

d. cancel or suspend an attack if it becomes apparent:

i. that the objective is cultural property protected under Article 4 of the Convention;

ii. that the attack may be expected to cause incidental damage to cultural property protected under Article 4 of the Convention which would be excessive in relation to the concrete and direct military advantage anticipated.

Article 8 Precautions against the effects of hostilities

The Parties to the conflict shall, to the maximum extent feasible:

a. remove movable cultural property from the vicinity of military objectives or provide for adequate in situ protection;

b. avoid locating military objectives near cultural property.

Article 9 Protection of cultural property in occupied territory

1. Without prejudice to the provisions of Articles 4 and 5 of the Convention,

a Party in occupation of the whole or part of the territory of another Party shall prohibit and prevent in relation to the occupied territory:

a. any illicit export, other removal or transfer of ownership of cultural property;

b. any archaeological excavation, save where this is strictly required to safeguard, record or preserve cultural property;

c. any alteration to, or change of use of, cultural property which is intended to conceal or destroy cultural, historical or scientific evidence.

2. Any archaeological excavation of, alteration to, or change of use of, cultural property in occupied territory shall, unless circumstances do not permit, be carried out in close co - operation with the competent national authorities of the occupied territory.

Back to top

Chapter 3 Enhanced Protection

Article 10 Enhanced protection

Cultural property may be placed under enhanced protection provided that it meets the following three conditions:

a. it is cultural heritage of the greatest importance for humanity;

b. it is protected by adequate domestic legal and administrative measures recognising its exceptional cultural and historic value and ensuring the highest level of protection;

c. it is not used for military purposes or to shield military sites and a declaration has been made by the Party which has control over the cultural property, confirming that it will not be so used.

Article 11 The granting of enhanced protection

1. Each Party should submit to the Committee a list of cultural property for which it intends to request the granting of enhanced protection.

2. The Party which has jurisdiction or control over the cultural property may request that it be included in the List to be established in accordance with Article 27 sub - paragraph 1 (b). This request shall include all necessary information related to the criteria mentioned in Article 10. The Committee may invite a Party to request that cultural property be included in the List.

3. Other Parties, the International Committee of the Blue Shield and other non - governmental organisations with relevant expertise may recommend specific cultural property to the Committee. In such cases, the Committee may decide to invite a Party to request inclusion of that cultural property in the List.

4. Neither the request for inclusion of cultural property situated in a territory, sovereignty or jurisdiction over which is claimed by more than one State, nor its inclusion, shall in any way prejudice the rights of the parties to the dispute.

5. Upon receipt of a request for inclusion in the List, the Committee shall inform all Parties of the request. Parties may submit representations regarding such a request to the Committee within sixty days. These representations shall be made only on the basis of the criteria mentioned in Article 10. They shall be specific and related to facts. The Committee shall consider the representations, providing the Party requesting inclusion with a reasonable opportunity to respond before taking the decision. When such representations are before the Committee, decisions for inclusion in the List shall be taken, notwithstanding Article 26, by a majority of four - fifths of its members present and voting.

6. In deciding upon a request, the Committee should ask the advice of governmental and non - governmental organisations, as well as of individual experts.

7. A decision to grant or deny enhanced protection may only be made on the basis of the criteria mentioned in Article 10.

8. In exceptional cases, when the Committee has concluded that the Party requesting inclusion of cultural property in the List cannot fulfil the criteria of Article 10 sub - paragraph (b), the Committee may decide to grant enhanced protection, provided that the requesting Party submits a request for international assistance under Article 32.

9. Upon the outbreak of hostilities, a Party to the conflict may request, on an emergency basis, enhanced protection of cultural property under its jurisdiction or control by communicating this request to the Committee. The Committee shall transmit this request immediately to all Parties to the conflict. In such cases the Committee will consider representations from the Parties concerned on an expedited basis. The decision to grant provisional enhanced protection shall be taken as soon as possible and, notwithstanding Article 26, by a majority of four - fifths of its members present and voting. Provisional enhanced protection may be granted by

the Committee pending the outcome of the regular procedure for the granting of enhanced protection, provided that the provisions of Article 10 sub - paragraphs (a) and (c) are met.

10. Enhanced protection shall be granted to cultural property by the Committee from the moment of its entry in the List.

11. The Director - General shall, without delay, send to the Secretary - General of the United Nations and to all Parties notification of any decision of the Committee to include cultural property on the List.

Article 12 Immunity of cultural property under enhanced protection

The Parties to a conflict shall ensure the immunity of cultural property under enhanced protection by refraining from making such property the object of attack or from any use of the property or its immediate surroundings in support of military action.

Article 13 Loss of enhanced protection

1. Cultural property under enhanced protection shall only lose such protection:

a. if such protection is suspended or cancelled in accordance with Article 14; or

b. if, and for as long as, the property has, by its use, become a military objective.

2. In the circumstances of sub - paragraph 1 (b), such property may only be the object of attack if:

a. the attack is the only feasible means of terminating the use of the property referred to in sub - paragraph 1 (b);

b. all feasible precautions are taken in the choice of means and methods of attack, with a view to terminating such use and avoiding, or in any event minimising, damage to the cultural property;

c. unless circumstances do not permit, due to requirements of immediate self - defence:

i. the attack is ordered at the highest operational level of command;

ii. effective advance warning is issued to the opposing forces requiring the termination of the use referred to in sub - paragraph 1 (b); and

iii. Reasonable time is given to the opposing forces to redress the situation.

Article 14 Suspension and cancellation of enhanced protection

1. Where cultural property no longer meets any one of the criteria in Article 10

of this Protocol, the Committee may suspend its enhanced protection status or cancel that status by removing that cultural property from the List.

2. In the case of a serious violation of Article 12 in relation to cultural property under enhanced protection arising from its use in support of military action, the Committee may suspend its enhanced protection status. Where such violations are continuous, the Committee may exceptionally cancel the enhanced protection status by removing the cultural property from the List.

3. The Director - General shall, without delay, send to the Secretary - General of the United Nations and to all Parties to this Protocol notification of any decision of the Committee to suspend or cancel the enhanced protection of cultural property.

4. Before taking such a decision, the Committee shall afford an opportunity to the Parties to make their views known.

Chapter 4 Criminal responsibility and jurisdiction

Article 15 Serious violations of this Protocol

1. Any person commits an offence within the meaning of this Protocol if that person intentionally and in violation of the Convention or this Protocol commits any of the following acts:

a. making cultural property under enhanced protection the object of attack;

b. using cultural property under enhanced protection or its immediate surroundings in support of military action;

c. extensive destruction or appropriation of cultural property protected under the Convention and this Protocol;

d. making cultural property protected under the Convention and this Protocol the object of attack;

e. theft, pillage or misappropriation of, or acts of vandalism directed against cultural property protected under the Convention.

2. Each Party shall adopt such measures as may be necessary to establish as criminal offences under its domestic law the offences set forth in this Article and to make such offences punishable by appropriate penalties. When doing so, Parties shall comply with general principles of law and international law, including the

rules extending individual criminal responsibility to persons other than those who directly commit the act.

Article 16 Jurisdiction

1. Without prejudice to paragraph 2, each Party shall take the necessary legislative measures to establish its jurisdiction over offences set forth in Article 15 in the following cases:

a. when such an offence is committed in the territory of that State;

b. when the alleged offender is a national of that State;

c. in the case of offences set forth in Article 15 sub - paragraphs (a) to (c), when the alleged offender is present in its territory.

2. With respect to the exercise of jurisdiction and without prejudice to Article 28 of the Convention:

a. this Protocol does not preclude the incurring of individual criminal responsibility or the exercise of jurisdiction under national and international law that may be applicable, or affect the exercise of jurisdiction under customary international law;

b. except in so far as a State which is not Party to this Protocol may accept and apply its provisions in accordance with Article 3 paragraph 2, members of the armed forces and nationals of a State which is not Party to this Protocol, except for those nationals serving in the armed forces of a State which is a Party to this Protocol, do not incur individual criminal responsibility by virtue of this Protocol, nor does this Protocol impose an obligation to establish jurisdiction over such persons or to extradite them.

Article 17 Prosecution

1. The Party in whose territory the alleged offender of an offence set forth in Article 15 sub - paragraphs 1 (a) to (c) is found to be present shall, if it does not extradite that person, submit, without exception whatsoever and without undue delay, the case to its competent authorities, for the purpose of prosecution, through proceedings in accordance with its domestic law or with, if applicable, the relevant rules of international law.

2. Without prejudice to, if applicable, the relevant rules of international law, any person regarding whom proceedings are being carried out in connection with the Convention or this Protocol shall be guaranteed fair treatment and a fair trial in accordance with domestic law and international law at all stages of the proceed-

ings, and in no cases shall be provided guarantees less favorable to such person than those provided by international law.

Article 18 Extradition

1. The offences set forth in Article 15 sub - paragraphs 1 (a) to (c) shall be deemed to be included as extraditable offences in any extradition treaty existing between any of the Parties before the entry into force of this Protocol. Parties undertake to include such offences in every extradition treaty to be subsequently concluded between them.

2. When a Party which makes extradition conditional on the existence of a treaty receives a request for extradition from another Party with which it has no extradition treaty, the requested Party may, at its option, consider the present Protocol as the legal basis for extradition in respect of offences as set forth in Article 15 sub - paragraphs 1 (a) to (c).

3. Parties which do not make extradition conditional on the existence of a treaty shall recognise the offences set forth in Article 15 sub - paragraphs 1 (a) to (c) as extraditable offences between them, subject to the conditions provided by the law of the requested Party.

4. If necessary, offences set forth in Article 15 sub - paragraphs 1 (a) to (c) shall be treated, for the purposes of extradition between Parties, as if they had been committed not only in the place in which they occurred but also in the territory of the Parties that have established jurisdiction in accordance with Article 16 paragraph 1.

Article 19 Mutual legal assistance

1. Parties shall afford one another the greatest measure of assistance in connection with investigations or criminal or extradition proceedings brought in respect of the offences set forth in Article 15, including assistance in obtaining evidence at their disposal necessary for the proceedings.

2. Parties shall carry out their obligations under paragraph 1 in conformity with any treaties or other arrangements on mutual legal assistance that may exist between them. In the absence of such treaties or arrangements, Parties shall afford one another assistance in accordance with their domestic law.

Article 20 Grounds for refusal

1. For the purpose of extradition, offences set forth in Article 15 sub - para-

graphs 1 (a) to (c), and for the purpose of mutual legal assistance, offences set forth in Article 15 shall not be regarded as political offences nor as offences connected with political offences nor as offences inspired by political motives. Accordingly, a request for extradition or for mutual legal assistance based on such offences may not be refused on the sole ground that it concerns a political offence or an offence connected with a political offence or an offence inspired by political motives.

2. Nothing in this Protocol shall be interpreted as imposing an obligation to extradite or to afford mutual legal assistance if the requested Party has substantial grounds for believing that the request for extradition for offences set forth in Article 15 sub - paragraphs 1 (a) to (c) or for mutual legal assistance with respect to offences set forth in Article 15 has been made for the purpose of prosecuting or punishing a person on account of that person's race, religion, nationality, ethnic origin or political opinion or that compliance with the request would cause prejudice to that person's position for any of these reasons.

Article 21 Measures regarding other violations

Without prejudice to Article 28 of the Convention, each Party shall adopt such legislative, administrative or disciplinary measures as may be necessary to suppress the following acts when committed intentionally:

a. any use of cultural property in violation of the Convention or this Protocol;

b. any illicit export, other removal or transfer of ownership of cultural property from occupied territory in violation of the Convention or this Protocol.

Chapter 5 The protection of cultural property in armed conflicts not of an international character

Article 22 Armed conflicts not of an international character

1. This Protocol shall apply in the event of an armed conflict not of an international character, occurring within the territory of one of the Parties.

2. This Protocol shall not apply to situations of internal disturbances and tensions, such as riots, isolated and sporadic acts of violence and other acts of a similar nature.

3. Nothing in this Protocol shall be invoked for the purpose of affecting the sovereignty of a State or the responsibility of the government, by all legitimate means, to maintain or re - establish law and order in the State or to defend the national unity and territorial integrity of the State.

4. Nothing in this Protocol shall prejudice the primary jurisdiction of a Party in whose territory an armed conflict not of an international character occurs over the violations set forth in Article 15.

5. Nothing in this Protocol shall be invoked as a justification for intervening, directly or indirectly, for any reason whatever, in the armed conflict or in the internal or external affairs of the Party in the territory of which that conflict occurs.

6. The application of this Protocol to the situation referred to in paragraph 1 shall not affect the legal status of the parties to the conflict.

7. UNESCO may offer its services to the parties to the conflict.

Chapter 6 Institutional Issues

Article 23 Meeting of the Parties

1. The Meeting of the Parties shall be convened at the same time as the General Conference of UNESCO, and in co - ordination with the Meeting of the High Contracting Parties, if such a meeting has been called by the Director - General.

2. The Meeting of the Parties shall adopt its Rules of Procedure.

3. The Meeting of the Parties shall have the following functions:

(a) to elect the Members of the Committee, in accordance with Article 24 paragraph 1;

(b) to endorse the Guidelines developed by the Committee in accordance with Article 27 sub - paragraph 1 (a);

(c) to provide guidelines for, and to supervise the use of the Fund by the Committee;

(d) to consider the report submitted by the Committee in accordance with Article 27 sub - paragraph 1 (d);

(e) to discuss any problem related to the application of this Protocol, and to make recommendations, as appropriate.

4. At the request of at least one - fifth of the Parties, the Director - General

shall convene an Extraordinary Meeting of the Parties.

Article 24 Committee for the Protection of Cultural Property in the Event of Armed Conflict

1. The Committee for the Protection of Cultural Property in the Event of Armed Conflict is hereby established. It shall be composed of twelve Parties which shall be elected by the Meeting of the Parties.

2. The Committee shall meet once a year in ordinary session and in extra - ordinary sessions whenever it deems necessary.

3. In determining membership of the Committee, Parties shall seek to ensure an equitable representation of the different regions and cultures of the world.

4. Parties members of the Committee shall choose as their representatives persons qualified in the fields of cultural heritage, defence or international law, and they shall endeavour, in consultation with one another, to ensure that the Committee as a whole contains adequate expertise in all these fields.

Article 25 Term of office

1. A Party shall be elected to the Committee for four years and shall be eligible for immediate re - election only once.

2. Notwithstanding the provisions of paragraph 1, the term of office of half of the members chosen at the time of the first election shall cease at the end of the first ordinary session of the Meeting of the Parties following that at which they were elected. These members shall be chosen by lot by the President of this Meeting after the first election.

Article 26 Rules of procedure

1. The Committee shall adopt its Rules of Procedure.

2. A majority of the members shall constitute a quorum. Decisions of the Committee shall be taken by a majority of two - thirds of its members voting.

3. Members shall not participate in the voting on any decisions relating to cultural property affected by an armed conflict to which they are parties.

Article 27 Functions

1. The Committee shall have the following functions:

a. to develop Guidelines for the implementation of this Protocol;

b. to grant, suspend or cancel enhanced protection for cultural property and to establish, maintain and promote the List of Cultural Property under Enhanced

Protection;

c. to monitor and supervise the implementation of this Protocol and promote the identification of cultural property under enhanced protection;

d. to consider and comment on reports of the Parties, to seek clarifications as required, and prepare its own report on the implementation of this Protocol for the Meeting of the Parties;

e. to receive and consider requests for international assistance under Article 32;

f. to determine the use of the Fund;

g. to perform any other function which may be assigned to it by the Meeting of the Parties.

2. The functions of the Committee shall be performed in co - operation with the Director - General.

3. The Committee shall co - operate with international and national governmental and non - governmental organizations having objectives similar to those of the Convention, its First Protocol and this Protocol. To assist in the implementation of its functions, the Committee may invite to its meetings, in an advisory capacity, eminent professional organizations such as those which have formal relations with UNESCO, including the International Committee of the Blue Shield (ICBS) and its constituent bodies. Representatives of the International Centre for the Study of the Preservation and Restoration of Cultural Property (Rome Centre) (ICCROM) and of the International Committee of the Red Cross (ICRC) may also be invited to attend in an advisory capacity.

Article 28 Secretariat

The Committee shall be assisted by the Secretariat of UNESCO which shall prepare the Committee's documentation and the agenda for its meetings and shall have the responsibility for the implementation of its decisions.

Article 29 The Fund for the Protection of Cultural Property in the Event of Armed Conflict

1. A Fund is hereby established for the following purposes:

a. to provide financial or other assistance in support of preparatory or other measures to be taken in peacetime in accordance with, inter alia, Article 5, Article 10 sub - paragraph (b) and Article 30; and

b. to provide financial or other assistance in relation to emergency, provisional or other measures to be taken in order to protect cultural property during periods of armed conflict or of immediate recovery after the end of hostilities in accordance with, inter alia, Article 8 sub - paragraph (a).

2. The Fund shall constitute a trust fund, in conformity with the provisions of the financial regulations of UNESCO.

3. Disbursements from the Fund shall be used only for such purposes as the Committee shall decide in accordance with the guidelines as defined in Article 23 sub - paragraph 3 (c). The Committee may accept contributions to be used only for a certain programme or project, provided that the Committee shall have decided on the implementation of such programme or project.

4. The resources of the Fund shall consist of:

(a) voluntary contributions made by the Parties;

(b) contributions, gifts or bequests made by:

(i) other States;

(ii) UNESCO or other organizations of the United Nations system;

(iii) other intergovernmental or non - governmental organizations; and

(iv) public or private bodies or individuals;

(c) any interest accruing on the Fund;

(d) funds raised by collections and receipts from events organized for the benefit of the Fund; and

(e) all other resources authorized by the guidelines applicable to the Fund.

Chapter 7 Dissemination of Information and International Assistance

Article 30 Dissemination

1. The Parties shall endeavour by appropriate means, and in particular by educational and information programmes, to strengthen appreciation and respect for cultural property by their entire population.

2. The Parties shall disseminate this Protocol as widely as possible, both in time of peace and in time of armed conflict.

3. Any military or civilian authorities who, in time of armed conflict, assume

responsibilities with respect to the application of this Protocol, shall be fully acquainted with the text thereof. To this end the Parties shall, as appropriate:

(a) incorporate guidelines and instructions on the protection of cultural property in their military regulations;

(b) develop and implement, in cooperation with UNESCO and relevant governmental and non - governmental organizations, peacetime training and educational programmes;

(c) communicate to one another, through the Director - General, information on the laws, administrative provisions and measures taken under sub - paragraphs (a) and (b);

(d) communicate to one another, as soon as possible, through the Director - General, the laws and administrative provisions which they may adopt to ensure the application of this Protocol.

Article 31 International cooperation

In situations of serious violations of this Protocol, the Parties undertake to act, jointly through the Committee, or individually, in cooperation with UNESCO and the United Nations and in conformity with the Charter of the United Nations.

Article 32 International assistance

1. A Party may request from the Committee international assistance for cultural property under enhanced protection as well as assistance with respect to the preparation, development or implementation of the laws, administrative provisions and measures referred to in Article 10.

2. A party to the conflict, which is not a Party to this Protocol but which accepts and applies provisions in accordance with Article 3, paragraph 2, may request appropriate international assistance from the Committee.

3. The Committee shall adopt rules for the submission of requests for international assistance and shall define the forms the international assistance may take.

4. Parties are encouraged to give technical assistance of all kinds, through the Committee, to those Parties or parties to the conflict who request it.

Article 33 Assistance of UNESCO

1. A Party may call upon UNESCO for technical assistance in organizing the protection of its cultural property, such as preparatory action to safeguard cultural property, preventive and organizational measures for emergency situations and

compilation of national inventories of cultural property, or in connection with any other problem arising out of the application of this Protocol. UNESCO shall accord such assistance within the limits fixed by its programme and by its resources.

2. Parties are encouraged to provide technical assistance at bilateral or multilateral level.

3. UNESCO is authorized to make, on its own initiative, proposals on these matters to the Parties.

Chapter 8 Execution of this Protocol

Article 34 Protecting Powers

This Protocol shall be applied with the co - operation of the Protecting Powers responsible for safeguarding the interests of the Parties to the conflict.

Article 35 Conciliation procedure

1. The Protecting Powers shall lend their good offices in all cases where they may deem it useful in the interests of cultural property, particularly if there is disagreement between the Parties to the conflict as to the application or interpretation of the provisions of this Protocol.

2. For this purpose, each of the Protecting Powers may, either at the invitation of one Party, of the Director - General, or on its own initiative, propose to the Parties to the conflict a meeting of their representatives, and in particular of the authorities responsible for the protection of cultural property, if considered appropriate, on the territory of a State not party to the conflict. The Parties to the conflict shall be bound to give effect to the proposals for meeting made to them. The Protecting Powers shall propose for approval by the Parties to the conflict a person belonging to a State not party to the conflict or a person presented by the Director-General, which person shall be invited to take part in such a meeting in the capacity of Chairman.

Article 36 Conciliation in absence of Protecting Powers

1. In a conflict where no Protecting Powers are appointed the Director - General may lend good offices or act by any other form of conciliation or mediation, with a view to settling the disagreement.

2. At the invitation of one Party or of the Director - General, the Chairman of

the Committee may propose to the Parties to the conflict a meeting of their representatives, and in particular of the authorities responsible for the protection of cultural property, if considered appropriate, on the territory of a State not party to the conflict.

Article 37 Translations and reports

1. The Parties shall translate this Protocol into their official languages and shall communicate these official translations to the Director - General.

2. The Parties shall submit to the Committee, every four years, a report on the implementation of this Protocol.

Article 38 State responsibility

No provision in this Protocol relating to individual criminal responsibility shall affect the responsibility of States under international law, including the duty to provide reparation.

Chapter 9 Final Clauses

Article 39 Languages

This Protocol is drawn up in Arabic, Chinese, English, French, Russian and Spanish, the six texts being equally authentic.

Article 40 Signature

This Protocol shall bear the date of 26 March 1999. It shall be opened for signature by all High Contracting Parties at The Hague from 17 May 1999 until 31 December 1999.

Article 41 Ratification, acceptance or approval

1. This Protocol shall be subject to ratification, acceptance or approval by High Contracting Parties which have signed this Protocol, in accordance with their respective constitutional procedures.

2. The instruments of ratification, acceptance or approval shall be deposited with the Director - General.

Article 42 Accession

1. This Protocol shall be open for accession by other High Contracting Parties from 1 January 2000.

2. Accession shall be effected by the deposit of an instrument of accession

with the Director - General.

Article 43 Entry into force

1. This Protocol shall enter into force three months after twenty instruments of ratification, acceptance, approval or accession have been deposited.

2. Thereafter, it shall enter into force, for each Party, three months after the deposit of its instrument of ratification, acceptance, approval or accession.

Article 44 Entry into force in situations of armed conflict

The situations referred to in Articles 18 and 19 of the Convention shall give immediate effect to ratifications, acceptances or approvals of or accessions to this Protocol deposited by the parties to the conflict either before or after the beginning of hostilities or occupation. In such cases the Director - General shall transmit the communications referred to in Article 46 by the speediest method.

Article 45 Denunciation

1. Each Party may denounce this Protocol.

2. The denunciation shall be notified by an instrument in writing, deposited with the Director - General.

3. The denunciation shall take effect one year after the receipt of the instrument of denunciation. However, if, on the expiry of this period, the denouncing Party is involved in an armed conflict, the denunciation shall not take effect until the end of hostilities, or until the operations of repatriating cultural property are completed, whichever is the later.

Article 46 Notifications

The Director - General shall inform all High Contracting Parties as well as the United Nations, of the deposit of all the instruments of ratification, acceptance, approval or accession provided for in Articles 41 and 42 and of denunciations provided for Article 45.

Article 47 Registration with the United Nations

In conformity with Article 102 of the Charter of the United Nations, this Protocol shall be registered with the Secretariat of the United Nations at the request of the Director - General.

关于被盗或非法出口文物的公约

（本公约由国际统一私法协会于1995年6月24日签订，1998年7月1日生效。中华人民共和国政府于1997年5月7日交存加入书，同时声明如下：1. 中国加入本公约不意味着承认发生在本公约以前的任何从中国盗走和非法出口文物的行为是合法的。中国保留收回本公约生效前被盗和非法出口的文物的权利；2. 根据公约第三条第五款的规定，中国关于返还被盗文物的申请受75年的时效限制，并保留将来根据法律规定延长时效限制的权利；3. 根据公约第八条向中国提出的对文物返还或者归还的请求，可以直接向中国法院提出或者通过中国文物行政主管机关转交中国法院。本公约于1998年7月1日对中国生效。）

本公约当事国聚集在罗马，应意大利政府的邀请于1995年6月7日至24日参加有关通过“国际统一私法协会关于国际范围内归还被盗或者非法出口文物的公约草案”的外交会议；

确信保护文物遗产和文化交流对促进人民之间的理解的特殊重要性，以及传播文化对人类福祉和增进文明的特殊重要性；

深切关注在文物方面的非法交易以及由此引起的经常发生的无可挽回的损害，这些情况不仅对于这些物品本身及对于民族、部落、土著居民或者其他社团的文化遗产，并且对于全人类遗产造成了无可挽回的损害；更为关注由于对考古遗址的掠夺和由此而产生的无法弥补的考古学、历史学及科学资料的损失；

决定为了在有效地打击文物的非法交易方面做出贡献，应在缔约国之间采取重要措施，即在文物的返还和归还方面制定共同的、最低限度的法律规范，以期促进为所有各方的利益而保存和保护文物；

强调本公约旨在便利文物的返还和归还，并强调任何补救规定，如一些国家为进行有效的返还和归还所必需的补偿等规定，并不意味着应当适用于其他国家；

确认本公约未来各项规定的通过，绝不是对发生在本公约生效前的任何种类的非法交易赋予合法性的认可；

意识到本公约不会通过自身对于因非法交易而产生的问题提供一项解决办法，而是由此启动一种促进国际文化合作、维护合法交易以及国家间的文化交流协议之适当作用的进程；

认识到实施本公约应当辅之以其他有效的保护文物措施，如逐步建立和使用注册登记制度、切实保护考古遗址和技术合作等；

承认各个机构为保护文化财产所做的工作，特别是1970年联合国教科文组织关于非法贩运的公约以及在私人部门所形成的行为守则。

达成如下协议：

第一章　适用范围和定义

第一条　本公约适用于如下国际性请求：

（a）返还被盗文物；

（b）归还因违反缔约国为保护其文化遗产之目的制定的文物出口法律而被移出该国领土的文物（以下简称“非法出口文物”）。

第二条　为本公约之目的，文物系指因宗教或者世俗的原因，具有考古、史前史、历史、文学、艺术或者科学方面重要性，并属于本公约附件所列分类之一的物品。

第二章　被盗文物的返还

第三条

1. 被盗文物的占有人应归还该被盗物。

2. 为本公约之目的，凡非法发掘或者合法发掘但非法持有的文物，应当视为被盗，只要符合发掘发生地国家的法律。

3. 任何关于返还被盗文物的请求，应自请求者知道该文物的所在地及该文物占有人的身份之时起，在三年期限内提出；并在任何情况下自被盗时起五十年以内提出。

4. 但是，关于返还某一特定纪念地或者考古遗址组成部分的文物，或者属于公共收藏的文物的请求，则除请求者应自知道该文物的所在地及该文物的占有人身份之时起三年以内提出请求外，不受其他时效限制。

5. 尽管有前款的规定，任何缔约国可以声明一项请求应受75年的时效限制，或者受到该国法律所规定的更长时效的限制。在另一缔约国境内对从做出上述声明的缔约国纪念地、考古遗址或者公共收藏品中移走的文物提出返还请求，也应受上述时效的限制。

6. 前款所述声明应在签署、批准、接受、核准或者加入时做出。

7. 为本公约之目的，“公共收藏品”是由经过登记注册或者其他方式证明的文物组成，并且其所有者是下列之一：

（a）缔约国；

（b）缔约国的一个区域或者地方当局；

（c）缔约国的一个宗教机构；或

（d）为文化、教育或者科学之基本目的而在缔约国内建立的旨在服务于公共利益的机构。

8. 此外，对一缔约国境内属于一部落或者土著人社区所有的或者使用的，作为该社区传统或者祭祀用品的一部分的宗教文物或对该社区具有重要意义的文物提出返还要求，则应受适用于公共收藏品的时效限制。

第四条

1. 被要求归还被盗文物的占有人只要不知道也理应不知道该物品是被盗的，并且能证明自己在获得该物品时是慎重的，则在返还该文物时有权得到公正合理的补偿。

2. 在不损害前款所述占有人的补偿权利的情况下，只要符合提起请求的所在国法律，应做出合理的努力，促使向占有人移交文物的人或者任何此前的移交人支付此种补偿。

3. 在要求补偿时，请求人向占有人支付补偿不应损害该请求人向任何其他人获得此种补偿的权利。

4. 在确定占有人是否慎重时，应注意到获得物品的情况，包括当事各方的性质、支付的价格、占有人是否向通常可以接触到的被盗文物的登记机关进行咨询，他通常可以获得的其他有关信息和文件、占有人是否向可以接触到的机关进行咨询。或者采取一个正常人在此情况下应当采取的其他措施。

5. 占有人若以继承或者其他无偿方式从某人处获得文物，则不应享有优于此人的地位。

第三章　非法出口文物的归还

第五条

1. 缔约国可以请求另一缔约国法院或者其他主管机关命令归还从请求国领土出口的文物。

2. 为展览、研究或者修复等目的，根据请求国为保护其文化遗产之目的制定的文物出口法律而颁布的许可证，从请求国暂时出口却没有依照许可证条件予以归还的文物，应认定为已经非法出口。

3. 如果请求国证实从其境内移出文物严重地损害了下列一项或者多项利益，或者证实该文物对于请求国具有特殊的文化方面的重要性，被请求国的法院或者其他主管机关应命令归还非法出口的这一物品。上述利益系指：

（a）有关该物品或者其内容的实物保存；

（b）有关组合物品的完整性；

（c）有关诸如科学性或者历史性资料的保存；

（d）有关一部落或者土著人社区对传统或者宗教物品的使用。

4. 根据本条第 1 款做出的请求，应包括或者附有关于事实或者法律一类的资料，以有助于被请求国法院或者其他主管机关确定该请求是否符合第 1 款至第 3 款的要求。

5. 归还请求应在请求国知道文物所在地和占有人身份时起的三年之内提出。任何情况下，应自出口之日或者自根据本条第 2 款所述许可证规定该物品应被归还之日起五十年以内提出。

第六条

1. 被盗文物非法出口后获得该物品的占有人，如果在获得该物品时不知道或者理应不知道这一物品是非法出口的，则有权在归还该物时得到请求国公正、合理的补偿。

2. 在确定占有人是否已知道或者通常理应知道其文物属非法出口时，应考虑到获得物品的情况，包括缺少请求国法律所要求的出口许可证的情况。

3. 被要求归还文物的占有人经与请求国协商一致，可决定以下列方式之一代替补偿：

（a）保留对该物品的所有权；或

（b）有偿或者无偿地将所有权转让给他所选择的居住在请求国境内并提供了必要担保的人。

4. 根据本条归还文物的费用应由请求国承担，但不妨碍该国向其他人获取此种费用的权利。

5. 占有人若以继承或者其他无偿方式从某人处获得文物，则不应享有优于此人的地位。

第七条

1. 本章的规定不适用于下列情况：

（a）在要求归还文物时，该物品的出口已不再是非法的；或

（b）物品是在其创作者生前出口的，或者是在该创作者死后五十年以内出口的；

2. 尽管有前款（b）项的规定，本章的规定仍应适用于由部落或者土著人社区的成员为该社区之用而制作的文物，这种物品将要归还该社区。

第四章　一般规定

第八条

1. 第二章规定的要求和第三章规定的请求可以向文物所在地的缔约国法院或者其他主管机关提出，也可向根据其现行法律拥有管辖权的缔约国法院或者其他主管机关提出。

2. 当事人可以同意将争议提交任何法院或者其他主管机关，或者提交仲裁。

3. 即使当返还的要求或者归还的请求是向另一个缔约国法院或者其他主管机关提出的，仍可实施物品所在地缔约国法律许可的，包括保护性措施在内的任何临时性措施。

第九条

1. 本公约不妨碍缔约国适用在被盗或者非法出口文物的返还或者归还方面比本公约更为有利的规定。

2. 本条不得解释为创设了承认或者执行另一缔约国法院或者其他主管机关做出的违反本公约规定的裁决的义务。

第十条

1. 第二章的规定应仅适用于本公约对提出索还请求所在国生效后被盗的文物，但有以下条件：

（a）该物品是在本公约对一缔约国生效后从该国领土内被盗的；或者

（b）该物品在本公约对该缔约国生效后位于该国。

2．第三章的规定应仅适用于本公约对请求国生效后以及对提出索还请求所在国生效后非法出口的文物。

3．本公约不以任何方式证明发生在本公约生效以前的，或者根据本条第1款、第2款而被排除在外的任何性质的非法交易是合法的，也不限制国家或者其他人根据本公约框架外可援用的补救措施，对于本公约生效前被盗或者非法出口的文物提出返还或者归还请求的权利。

第五章　最后条款

第十一条

1．本公约在国际统一私法协会通过关于国际范围内归还被盗或者非法出口文物公约的外交会议闭幕会议上开放签署，并且至1996年6月30日之前在罗马继续向所有国家开放签字。

2．本公约须经签署国批准、接受或者核准。

3．本公约对所有自该公约开放签署之日起未能签署的国家开放供加入。

4．批准、接受、核准或者加入，须就此向保存国交存一份正式的文件。

第十二条

1．本公约应自第五份批准、接受、核准或者加入的文件交存之日后第六个月的第一天起生效。

2．在第五份批准、接受、核准或者加入的文件交存后，对于每一批准、接受、核准或者加入本公约的国家，本公约应自该国交存其批准、接受、核准或者加入的文件之日后第六个月的第一天起对其生效。

第十三条

1．本公约不影响缔约国在法律上受其约束的，并且载有本公约所调整事项的规定的任何国际文书，但该国对这种国际文书做出相反声明的情况除外。

2．任何缔约国可以与一个或者多个缔约国订立协定，以期在其相互关系中促进适用本公约。已经缔结这种协定的国家应向保存国送交一份协定文本。

3．作为经济一体化组织或者区域性机构成员的缔约国，可以声明在其相互关系中将适用该组织或者机构的内部规定，因而在这些国家之间将不适用本公约中与前述规定的适用范围相同的规定。

第十四条

1．如果缔约国拥有两个或者更多的领土单位，无论这些领土单位对本公约所处理的事项是否适用不同的法律体系，该国可以在签署或者交存其批准、接受、核准或加入的文件时，声明本公约扩展适用于其所有领土单位，或者仅适用于其中的一个或多个领土单位，并且可随时以另一声明取代此项声明。

2. 应向保存国通知这些声明，并且明确陈述本公约所适用的领土单位。

3. 如果本公约因根据本条所做的声明扩展适用于缔约国的一个或者多个领土单位，但不是其所有领土单位，则：

（a）第一条中所提及的缔约国领土，应解释为系指该国的一个领土单位的区域；

（b）缔约国或者接受请求国家的法院或者其他主管机关，应解释为系指该国的一个领土单位的法院或者其他主管机关；

（c）第八条第1款中提及的文物所在地的缔约国，应解释为系指该国内物品所在地的领土单位；

（d）第八条第3款中所提及的文物所在地的缔约国法律，应解释为系指该国的物品所在地的领土单位的法律；

（e）第九条中所提及的缔约国，应解释为系指该国的一个领土单位。

4. 如果缔约国未根据本条第1款做出声明，则本公约适用于该国的全部领土单位。

第十五条

1. 在签署时根据本公约规定做出的声明，应在批准、接受或者核准时予以确认。

2. 声明和确认声明应以书面方式正式通知保存国。

3. 声明应在本公约对有关国家生效的同时产生效力。但是，保存国在公约对有关国家生效后收到正式声明的，则此项声明应向保存国交存之日后第六个月的第一天起生效。

4. 根据本公约规定做出声明的任何国家，可以在任何时候以书面方式向保存国正式通知撤销此项声明。此种撤销应在交存通知之日后第六个月的第一天起生效。

第十六条

1. 第一缔约国在签署、批准、接受、核准或者加入时，应声明一个国家根据第八条提出对文物返还或者归还的请求，可以按照下列一种或者数种程序向其提出：

（a）直接向做出声明国家的法院或者其他主管机关提出；

（b）通过该国指定的机关接受这种请求，并且将其转交该国的法院或者主管机关；

（c）通过外交或者领事途径。

2. 每一缔约国还可以根据第二章和第三章有权命令返还或者归还文物的法院或者其他机关。

3. 根据本条第1款、第2款做出的声明，可以在任何时候以一项新的声明予以修正。

4. 本条第1款至第3款的规定不影响缔约国之间可能存在的双边或者多边的有关民事和商事司法协助的规定。

第十七条 每一缔约国应在不迟于其交存批准、接受、核准或者加入文件之日后的六个月内，以本公约使用的一种正式语言向保存国提供该国有关文物出口的法律的书面资料，这种资料应在适当的时候经常予以更新。

第十八条 除本公约有明确授权之外，不允许做出保留。

第十九条

1. 本公约对当事国生效后，该国可以随时向保存国提交退出本公约的文件。

2. 退出应自向保存国交存退出文件之日后第六个月的第一天起发生效力。当退出文件中对退出的生效规定了更长的时间时，则应自向保存国交存后至这一更长时间结束时发生效力。

3. 即使已经退出本公约，本公约仍应适用于在退出发生效力之日前提出的将文物返还的请求或者是归还文物的请求。

第二十条 国际统一私法协会主席根据五个缔约国的请求，可以定期或者随时召开特别委员会，以便审查本公约的实际运作情况。

第二十一条

1. 本公约应交意大利共和国政府保存。

2. 意大利共和国政府应：

（a）向所有签署或者加入本公约的国家和国际统一私法协会的主席通知下列事项：

（Ⅰ）每一项新的签署或者交存的批准、接受、核准或者加入的文件，并随附其日期；

（Ⅱ）根据本公约做出的每一项声明；

（Ⅲ）对声明的撤销；

（Ⅳ）本公约生效的日期；

（Ⅴ）第十二条所述协定；

（Ⅵ）交存退出本公约的文件以及此项交存的日期和退出发生效力的

日期；

（b）向所有签署、加入本公约的国家和国际统一私法协会的主席转交经审核无误的本公约文本；

（c）履行通常由保存国承担的其他职能。

下列全权代表经正式授权签署本公约，以昭信守。

本公约于1995年6月24日订于罗马，共一份，用英文和法文写成；两种文本同等作准。

附件

（a）动物群落、植物群落、矿物和解剖以及具有古生物学意义的物品的稀有收集品和标本；

（b）有关历史、包括科学、技术、军事及社会史、有关国家领袖、思想家、科学家、艺术家之生平以及有关国家重大事件的财产；

（c）考古发掘（包括正常的和秘密的）或考古发现的成果；

（d）业已肢解的艺术或历史古迹或考古遗址之构成部分；

（e）一百年以上的古物，如铭文、钱币和印章；

（f）具有人种学意义的文物；

（g）有艺术价值的财产，如：

（Ⅰ）全部是手工完成的图画、绘画和绘图，不论其装帧框座如何，也不论所用的是何种材料（不包括工业设计图及手工装饰的工业产品）；

（Ⅱ）用任何材料制成的雕塑艺术和雕刻的原作；

（Ⅲ）版画、印片和平版画的原件；

（Ⅳ）用任何材料组集或拼集的艺术品原件；

（h）稀有手稿和有特殊意义的（历史、艺术、科学、文学等）古物、古书、文件和出版物，不论是单个的或整套的；

（i）邮票、印花税票及类似的佐证，不论是单张的或整套的；

（j）档案，包括有声、照相和电影档案；

（k）一百年以上的家具物品和古乐器。

Convention on Stolen or Illegally Exported Cultural Objects

(Done at: Rome
Date enacted: 1995 -06 -24
In force: 1998 -07 -01)

The States Parties to this Convention,

Assembled in Rome at the invitation of the Government of the Italian Republic from 7 to 24 June 1995 for a Diplomatic Conference for the adoption of the draft Unidroit Convention on the International Return of Stolen or Illegally Exported Cultural Objects,

Convinced of the fundamental importance of the protection of cultural heritage and of cultural exchanges for promoting understanding between peoples, and the dissemination of culture for the well - being of humanity and the progress of civilisation,

Deeply Concerned by the illicit trade in cultural objects and the irreparable damage frequently caused by it, both to these objects themselves and to the cultural heritage of national, tribal, indigenous or other communities, and also to the heritage of all peoples, and in particular by the pillage of archaeological sites and the resulting loss of irreplaceable archaeological, historical and scientific information,

Determined to contribute effectively to the fight against illicit trade in cultural objects by taking the important step of establishing common, minimal legal rules for the restitution and return of cultural objects between Contracting States, with the objective of improving the preservation and protection of the cultural heritage in the interest of all,

Emphasising that this Convention is intended to facilitate the restitution and return of cultural objects, and that the provision of any remedies, such as compensation, needed to effect restitution and return in some States, does not imply that such remedies should be adopted in other States,

Affirming that the adoption of the provisions of this Convention for the future in no way confers any approval or legitimacy upon illegal transactions of whatever kind which may have taken place before the entry into force of the Convention,

Conscious that this Convention will not by itself provide a solution to the problems raised by illicit trade, but that it initiates a process that will enhance international cultural co - operation and maintain a proper role for legal trading and inter - State agreements for cultural exchanges,

Acknowledging that implementation of this Convention should be accompanied by other effective measures for protecting cultural objects, such as the development and use of registers, the physical protection of archaeological sites and technical co - operation,

Recognising the work of various bodies to protect cultural property, particularly the 1970 UNESCO Convention on illicit traffic and the development of codes of conduct in the private sector,

Have agreed as follows:

Chapter I – Scope of application and definition

Article 1

This Convention applies to claims of an international character for:

a. the restitution of stolen cultural objects;

b. the return of cultural objects removed from the territory of a Contracting State contrary to its law regulating the export of cultural objects for the purpose of protecting its cultural heritage (hereinafter "illegally exported cultural objects").

Article 2

For the purposes of this Convention, cultural objects are those which, on religious or secular grounds, are of importance for archaeology, prehistory, history, literature, art or science and belong to one of the categories listed in the Annex to this Convention.

Chapter II – Restitution of stolen cultural objects

Article 3

1. The possessor of a cultural object which has been stolen shall return it.

2. For the purposes of this Convention, a cultural object which has been unlawfully excavated or lawfully excavated but unlawfully retained shall be considered stolen, when consistent with the law of the State where the excavation took place.

3. Any claim for restitution shall be brought within a period of three years from the time when the claimant knew the location of the cultural object and the identity of its possessor, and in any case within a period of fifty years from the time of the theft.

4. However, a claim for restitution of a cultural object forming an integral part of an identified monument or archaeological site, or belonging to a public collection, shall not be subject to time limitations other than a period of three years from the time when the claimant knew the location of the cultural object and the identity of its possessor.

5. Notwithstanding the provisions of the preceding paragraph, any Contracting State may declare that a claim is subject to a time limitation of 75 years or such longer period as is provided in its law. A claim made in another Contracting State for restitution of a cultural object displaced from a monument, archaeological site or public collection in a Contracting State making such a declaration shall also be subject to that time limitation.

6. A declaration referred to in the preceding paragraph shall be made at the time of signature, ratification, acceptance, approval or accession.

7. For the purposes of this Convention, a "public collection," consists of a group of inventoried or otherwise identified cultural objects owned by:

(a) a Contracting State

(b) a regional or local authority of a Contracting State;

(c) a religious institution in a Contracting State; or

(d) an institution that is established for an essentially cultural, educational or scientific purpose in a Contracting State and is recognised in that State as serving the public interest.

8. In addition, a claim for restitution of a sacred or communally important cultural object belonging to and used by a tribal or indigenous community in a Contracting State as part of that community's traditional or ritual use, shall be subject to the time limitation applicable to public collections.

Article 4

1. The possessor of a stolen cultural object required to return it shall be entitled, at the time of its restitution, to payment of fair and reasonable compensation provided that the possessor neither knew nor ought reasonably to have known that the object was stolen and can prove that it exercised due diligence when acquiring the object.

2. Without prejudice to the right of the possessor to compensation referred to in the preceding paragraph, reasonable efforts shall be made to have the person who transferred the cultural object to the possessor, or any prior transferor, pay the compensation where to do so would be consistent with the law of the State in which the claim is brought.

3. Payment of compensation to the possessor by the claimant, when this is required, shall be without prejudice to the right of the claimant to recover it from any other person.

4. In determining whether the possessor exercised due diligence, regard shall be had to all the circumstances of the acquisition, including the character of the parties, the price paid, whether the possessor consulted any reasonably accessible register of stolen cultural objects, and any other relevant information and documentation which it could reasonably have obtained, and whether the possessor consulted accessible agencies or took any other step that a reasonable person would have taken in the circumstances.

5. The possessor shall not be in a more favourable position than the person from whom it acquired the cultural object by inheritance or otherwise gratuitously.

Chapter III – Return of illegaly exported cultural objects

Article 5

1. A Contracting State may request the court or other competent authority of

another Contracting State to order the return of a cultural object illegally exported from the territory of the requesting State.

2. A cultural object which has been temporarily exported from the territory of the requesting State, for purposes such as exhibition, research or restoration, under a permit issued according to its law regulating its export for the purpose of protecting its cultural heritage and not returned in accordance with the terms of that permit shall be deemed to have been illegally exported.

3. The court or other competent authority of the State addressed shall order the return of an illegally exported cultural object if the requesting State establishes that the removal of the object from its territory significantly impairs one or more of the following interests:

(a) the physical Preservation of the object or of its context;

(b) the integrity of a complex object;

(c) the preservation of information of, for example, a scientific or historical character;

(d) the traditional or ritual use of the object by a tribal or indigenous community,

or establishers that the object is of significant cultural importance for the requesting State.

4. Any request made under paragraph 1 of this article shall contain or be accompanied by such information of a factual or legal nature as may assist the court or other competent authority of the State addressed in determining whether the requirements of paragraphs 1 to 3 have been met.

5. Any request for return shall be brought within a period of three years from the time when the requesting State knew the location of the cultural object and the identity of its possessor, and in any case within a period of fifty years from the date of the export or from the date on which the object should have been returned under a permit referred to in paragraph 2 of this article.

Article 6

1. The possessor of a cultural object who acquired the object after it was illegally exported shall be entitled, at the time of its return, to payment by the requesting State of fair and reason compensation, provided that the possessor neither knew nor ought reasonably to have known at the time of acquisition that the object

had been illegally exported.

2. In determining whether the possessor knew or ought reasonably to have known that the cultural object had been illegally exported, regard shall be had to the circumstances of the acquisition, including the absence of an export certificate required under the law of the requesting State.

3. Instead of compensation, and in agreement with the requesting State, the possessor required to return the cultural object to that State may decide:

(a) to retain ownership of the object; or

(b) to transfer ownership against payment or gratuitously to a person of its choice residing in the requesting State who provides the necessary guarantees.

4. The cost of returning the cultural object in accordance with this article shall be borne by the requesting State, without prejudice to the right of that State to recover costs from any other person.

5. The possessor shall not be in a more favourable position than the person from whom it acquired the cultural object by inheritance or otherwise gratuitously.

Article 7

1. The provisions of this Chapter shall not apply where:

(a) the export of a cultural object is no longer illegal at the time at which the return is requested; or

(b) the object was exported during the lifetime of the person who created it or within a period of fifty years following the death of that person.

2. Notwithstanding the provisions of sub - paragraph (b) of the preceding paragraph, the provisions of this Chapter shall apply where a cultural object was made by a member or members of a tribal or indigenous community for traditional or ritual use by that community and the object will be returned to that community.

Chapter IV – General provisions

Article 8

1. A claim under Chapter II and a request under Chapter III may be brought before the courts or other competent authorities of the Contracting State where the cultural object is located, in addition to the courts or other competent authorities otherwise having jurisdiction under the rules in force in Contracting States.

2. The parties may agree to submit the dispute to any court or other competent authority or to arbitration.

3. Resort may be had to the provisional, including protective, measures available under the law of the Contracting State where the object is located even when the claim for restitution or request for return of the object is brought before the courts or other competent authorities of another Contracting State.

Article 9

1. Nothing in this Convention shall prevent a Contracting State from applying any rules more favourable to the restitution or the return of stolen or illegally exported cultural objects than provided for by this Convention.

2. This article shall not be interpreted as creating an obligation to recognise or enforce a decision of a court or other competent authority of another Contracting State that departs from the provisions of this Convention.

Article 10

1. The provisions of Chapter II shall apply only in respect of a cultural object that is stolen after this Convention enters into force in respect of the State where the claim is brought, provided that:

(a) the object was stolen from the territory of a Contracting State after the entry into force of this Convention for that State; or

(b) the object is located in a Contracting State after the entry into force of the Convention for that State.

2. The provisions of Chapter III shall apply only in respect of a cultural object that is illegally exported after this Convention enters into force for the requesting State as well as the State where the request is brought.

3. This Convention does not in any way legitimise any illegal transaction of whatever which has taken place before the entry into force of this Convention or which is excluded under paragraphs (1) or (2) of this article, nor limit any right of a State or other person to make a claim under remedies available outside the framework of this Convention for the restitution or return of a cultural object stolen or illegally exported before the entry into force of this Convention.

Chapter V – Final provisions

Article 11

1. This Convention is open for signature at the concluding meeting of the Diplomatic Conference for the adoption of the draft Unidroit Convention on the International Return of Stolen or Illegally Exported Cultural Objects and will remain open for signature by all States at Rome until June 1996.

2. This Convention is subject to ratification, acceptance or approval by States which have signed it.

3. This Convention is open for accession by all States which are not signatory States as from the date it is open for signature.

4. Ratification, acceptance, approval or accession is subject to the deposit of a formal instrument to that effect with the depositary.

Article 12

1. This Convention shall enter into force on the first day of the sixth month following the date of deposit of the fifth instrument of ratification, acceptance, approval or accession.

2. For each State that ratifies, accepts, approves or accedes to this Convention after the deposit of the fifth instrument of ratification, acceptance, approval or accession, this Convention shall enter into force in respect of that State on the first day of the sixth month following the date of deposit of its instrument of ratification, acceptance, approval or accession.

Article 13

1. This Convention does not affect any international instrument by which any Contracting State is legally bound and which contains provisions on matters governed by this Convention, unless a contrary declaration is made by the States bound by such instrument.

2. Any Contracting State may enter into agreements with one or more Contracting States, with a view to improving the application of this Convention in their mutual relations. The States which have concluded such an agreement shall transmit a copy to the depositary.

3. In their relations with each other, Contracting States which are Members of

organisations of economic integration or regional bodies may declare that they will apply. the internal rules of these organisations or bodies and will not therefore apply as between these States the provisions of this Convention the scope of application of which coincides with that of those rules.

Article 14

1. If a Contracting State has two or more territorial units, whether or not possessing different systems of law applicable in relation to the matters dealt with in this Convention, it may, at the time of signature or of the deposit of its instrument of ratification, acceptance, approval or accession, declare that this Convention is to extend to all its territorial units or only to one or more of them, and may substitute for its declaration another declaration at any time.

2. These declarations are to be notified to the depositary and are to state expressly the territorial units to which the Convention extends.

3. If, by virtue of a declaration under this article, this Convention extends to one or more but not all of the territorial units of a Contracting State the reference to:

(a) the territory of a Contracting State in Article 1 shall be construed as referring to the territory of a territorial unit of that State;

(b) a court or other competent authority of the Contracting State or of the State addressed shall be construed as referring to the court or other competent authority of a territorial unit of that State;

(c) the Contracting State where the cultural object is located in Article 8 (1) shall b construed as referring to the territorial unit of that State where the object is located;

(d) the law of the Contracting State where the object is located in Article 8 (3) shall be construed as referring to the law of the territorial unit of that State where the object is located; and

(e) a Contracting State in Article 9 shall be construed as referring to a territorial unit of that State.

4. If a Contracting State makes no declaration under paragraph 1 of this article, this Convention is to extend to all territorial units of that State.

Article 15

1. Declarations made under this Convention at the time of signature are sub-

ject to confirmation upon ratification, acceptance or approval.

2. Declarations and confirmations of declarations are to be in writing and to be formally notified to the depositary.

3. A declaration shall take effect simultaneously with the entry into force of this Convention in respect of the State concerned. However, a declaration of which the depositary receives formal notification after such entry into force shall take effect on the first day of the sixth month following the date of its deposit with the depositary.

4. Any State which makes a declaration. under this Convention may withdraw it at any time by a formal notification in writing addressed to the depositary. Such withdrawal shall take effect on the first day of the sixth month following the date of the deposit of the notification.

Article 16

1. Each Contracting State shall at the time of signature, ratification, acceptance, approval or accession, declare that claims for the restitution, or requests for the return, of cultural objects brought by a State under Article 8 may be submitted to it under one or more of the following procedures:

(a) directly to the courts or other competent authorities of the declaring State;

(b) through an authority or authorities designated by that State to receive such claims or requests and to forward them to the courts or other competent authorities of that State;

(c) through diplomatic or consular channels.

2. Each Contracting State may also designate the courts or other authorities competent to order the restitution or return of cultural objects under the provisions of Chapters II and III.

3. Declarations made under paragraphs 1 and 2 of this article may be modified at any time by a new declaration.

4. The provisions of paragraphs 1 to 3 of this article do not affect bilateral or multilateral agreements on judicial assistance in respect of civil and commercial matters that may exisit between Contracting States.

Article 17

Each Contracting State shall, no later than six months following the date of deposit of its instrument of ratification, acceptance, approval or accession, provide the depositary with written information in one of the official languages of the Convention concerning the legislation regulating the export of its cultural objects. This information shall be updated from time to time as appropriate.

Article 18

No reservations are permitted except those expressly authorised in this Convention.

Article 19

1. This Convention may be denounced by any State Party, at any time after the date on which it enters into force for that State, by the deposit of an instrument to that effect with the depositary.

2. A denunciation shall take effect on the first day of the sixth month following the deposit of the instrument of denunciation with the depositary. Where a longer period for the denunciation to take effect is specified in the instrument of denunciation it shall take effect upon the expiration of such longer period after its deposit with the depositary.

3. Notwithstanding such a denunciation, this Convention shall nevertheless apply to a claim for restitution or a request for return of a cultural object submitted prior to the date on which the denunciation takes effect.

Article 20

The President of the International Institute for the Unification of Private Law (Unidroit) may at regular intervals, or at any time at the request of five Contracting States, convene a special committee in order to review the practical operation of this Convention.

Article 21

1. This Convention shall be deposited with the Government of the Italian Republic.

2. The Government of the Italian Republic shall:

(a) inform all States which have signed or acceded to this Convention and the President of the International Institute for the Unification of Private Law (Unidroit) of:

(i) each new signature or deposit of an instrument of ratification, acceptance approval or accession, together with the date thereof;

(ii) each declaration made in accordance with this Convention;

(iii) the withdrawal of any declaration;

(iv) the date of entry into force of this Convention;

(v) the agreements referred to in Article 13;

(vi) the deposit of an instrument of denunciation of this Convention together with the date of its deposit and the date on which it takes effect;

(b) transmit certified true copies of this Convention to all signatory States, to all States acceding to the Convention and to the President of the International Institute for Unification of Private Law (Unidroit);

(c) perform such other functions customary for depositaries.

In witness whereof the undersigned plenipotentiaries, being duly authorised, have signed this Convention.

Done at Rome, this twenty - fourth day of June, one thousand nine hundred and ninety - five, in a single original, in the English and French languages, both texts being equally authentic.

Annex

a. Rare collections and specimens of fauna, flora, minerals and anatomy, and objects of palaeontological interest;

b. property relating to history, including the history of science and technology and military and social history, to the life of national leaders, thinkers, scientists and artists and to events of national importance;

c. products of archaeological excavations (including regular and clandestine) or of archaeological discoveries;

d. elements of artistic or historical monuments or archaeological sites which have been dismembered;

e. antiquities more than one hundred years old, such as inscriptions, coins and engraved seals;

f. objects of ethnological interest;

g. property of artistic interest, such as:

(i) pictures, paintings and drawings produced entirely by hand on any support and in any material (excluding industrial designs and manufactured articles decorated by hand);

(ii) original works of statuary art and sculpture in any material;

(iii) original engravings, prints and lithographs;

(iv) original artistic assemblages and montages in any material;

h. rare manuscripts and incunabula, old books, documents and publications of special interest (historical, artistic, scientific, literary, etc.) singly or in collections;

i. postage, revenue and similar stamps, singly or in collections;

j. archives, including sound, photographic and cinematographic archives;

k. articles of furniture more than one hundred years old and old musical instruments.

关于故意破坏文化遗产的宣言

（联合国教科文组织大会2003年10月17日通过）

联合国教育、科学及文化组织大会于2003年在巴黎举行的第三十二届会议，忆及震动了整个国际社会的摧毁巴米扬大佛的悲剧性事件，对蓄意破坏文化遗产行为呈上升趋势表示严重关注，参照教科文组织《组织法》第1（2）（c）条有关教科文组织具有通过“保证对图书、艺术作品及历史和科学文物等世界遗产之保存与维护，并建议有关国家订立必要之国际公约”，维护、增进及传播知识之职责的规定，忆及教科文组织所有保护文化遗产的公约、建议书、宣言和宪章所确定的原则，铭记文化遗产是社会、群体和个人的文化特性和社会凝聚力的重要组成部分，因此蓄意破坏文化遗产会对人的尊严和人权造成不利影响。

重申

1954年《关于在武装冲突情况下保护文化财产的海牙公约》序言中提出的一条基本原则，即“鉴于各国人民均对世界文化作出了贡献，对文化财产（不管它属于哪国人民）的损害将构成对整个人类文化遗产的破坏”，忆及1899年和1907年的《海牙公约》确定的关于在武装冲突情况下保护文化遗产的原则，特别是1907年《第四项海牙公约》第27和第56条以及后来的其他协定所确定的原则，牢记还得到相关的判例法确认的有关在和平时期及在武装冲突情况下保护文化遗产的习惯国际法条款发生了变化，还忆及与蓄意破坏文化遗产行为有关的《国际刑事法院罗马规约》第8（2）（b）（ix）条和第8（2）（e）（iv）条的规定，以及《前南斯拉夫问题国际刑事法庭规约》第3（d）条的规定（在适用时），重申本《宣言》和其他有关文化遗产的国际文书没有充分谈及的问题仍将继续遵循国际法的原则、人道的原则和受公共良心的支配，通过并庄严宣布本宣言：

I. 承认文化遗产的重要性

国际社会承认保护文化遗产的重要性，并重申要与任何形式的蓄意破坏文化遗产的行为做斗争，使文化遗产能够代代相传。

II. 适用范围

1. 本宣言针对文化遗产，包括与自然景观相关的文化遗产的蓄意破坏问题。

2. 本宣言中的“蓄意破坏”系指故意违反国际法或无理违反人道的原则和公共良心的要求，整个或部分地毁坏文化遗产，使其完整性受到破坏的行为。故意无理违反人道的原则和公共良心的要求的做法，系指国际法的基本原则目前尚未作出规定的破坏行为。

III. 反对蓄意破坏文化遗产行为的措施

1. 各国应采取一切适当措施，预防、避免、制止和打击蓄意破坏无论是何地的文化遗产的行为。

2. 各国应根据自己的经济能力，为保护文化遗产采取适当的法律、行政、教育和技术措施，并定期修订这些措施，使它们与不断变化的各国和国际文化遗产保护标准相一致。

3. 各国应采取一切适当手段，特别是通过实施教育、提高认识和宣传方面的计划，确保文化遗产受到社会的尊重。

4. 各国应：

(a) 加入（如它们尚未加入的话）1954 年《关于在武装冲突情况下保护文化财产的海牙公约》及其 1954 年和 1999 年的两项《议定书》，以及 1949 年的四项《日内瓦公约》的第一和第二项《附加议定书》；

(b) 促进制订并通过完善的法律文件，提高保护文化遗产的标准；并

(c) 促进协调实施现有的和今后将制定的有关保护文化遗产的各种文书。

IV. 在和平时期开展活动时保护文化遗产

在和平时期开展活动时，各国应当采取一切适当的措施，使自己的行为符合保护文化遗产的要求，尤其是符合 1972 年《保护世界文化和自然遗产公约》、1956 年《关于国际考古发掘原则的建议书》、1968 年《关于保护公共

或私人工程危及的文化财产的建议书》、1972 年《关于在国家一级保护文化和自然遗产的建议书》和 1976 年《关于保护历史或传统建筑群及其在现代生活中的作用的建议书》所确定的原则和宗旨。

V. 在武装冲突，包括占领的情况下保护文化遗产

在卷入国际或非国际性武装冲突，包括占领的情况下，有关各国应采取一切适当的措施，使自己的行为符合保护文化遗产的要求，符合习惯国际法以及有关在敌对时期保护这类遗产的各项国际协定和教科文组织建议书的原则和宗旨。

VI. 有关国家的责任

蓄意破坏对人类具有重要意义的文化遗产，或故意不采取适当措施禁止、防止、制止和惩罚一切蓄意破坏行为的国家，不论该遗产是否列入教科文组织或其他国际组织的保护名录，均应在国际法规定的范围内对该破坏行为承担责任。

VII. 个人的刑事责任

各国应根据国际法采取一切适当的措施，确立有关的司法管辖权，并对那些犯有或下令犯有蓄意破坏对人类具有特别重要意义之文化遗产行为的个人予以有效的刑事制裁，不论该文化遗产是否列入教科文组织或其他国际组织的保护名录。

VIII. 保护文化遗产的合作

1. 各国应相互合作并与教科文组织开展合作，保护文化遗产免遭蓄意破坏。这种合作的基本要求是：(Ⅰ) 提供和交流有可能出现的蓄意破坏文化遗产问题的有关情况的信息；(Ⅱ) 在文化遗产的确受到或即将遭到破坏的情况下进行磋商；(Ⅲ) 应有关国家的要求，在促进开展预防和打击蓄意破坏文化遗产行为的教育计划、提高认识和能力方面向它们提供援助；(Ⅳ) 应有关国家的要求，在打击蓄意破坏文化遗产的行为时，向它们提供有关的司法和行政援助。

2. 为了进行更加全面的保护，鼓励各国根据国际法采取各种适当的措施与其他有关国家进行合作，以便确立有关的司法管辖权，并对那些犯有或下令犯有上述行为（VII. 个人的刑事责任）并在该国领土被发现的个人（不论其国籍如何以及该行为在何处发生），予以有效的刑事制裁。

IX. 人权和国际人道主义法

实施本宣言，各国承认必须遵守有关将严重违反人权和国际人道主义法行为定为犯罪行为的国际规章，特别是在蓄意破坏文化遗产行为与这些违反行为有关联的情况下更应如此。

X. 公众宣传

各国应采取各种适当的措施，特别是通过组织公众宣传运动，确保在公众和目标群体中最广泛地宣传本宣言。

UNESCO Declaration concerning the Intentional Destruction of Cultural Heritage

17 October 2003

The General Conference of the United Nations Educational, Scientific and Cultural Organization meeting in Paris at its thirty - second session in 2003,

Recalling the tragic destruction of the Buddhas of Bamiyan that affected the international community as a whole,

Expressing serious concern about the growing number of acts of intentional destruction of cultural heritage,

Referring to Article 1 (2) (c) of the Constitution of UNESCO that entrusts UNESCO with the task of maintaining, increasing and diffusing knowledge by "assuring the conservation and protection of the world's inheritance of books, works of art and monuments of history and science, and recommending to the nations concerned the necessary international conventions",

Recalling the principles of all UNESCO's conventions, recommendations, declarations and charters for the protection of cultural heritage,

Mindful that cultural heritage is an important component of the cultural identity of communities, groups and individuals, and of social cohesion, so that its intentional destruction may have adverse consequences on human dignity and human rights,

Reiterating one of the fundamental principles of the Preamble of the 1954 Hague Convention for the Protection of Cultural Property in the Event of Armed Conflict providing that "damage to cultural property belonging to any people whatsoever means damage to the cultural heritage of all mankind, since each people makes its contribution to the culture of the world",

Recalling the principles concerning the protection of cultural heritage in the event of armed conflict established in the 1899 and 1907 Hague Conventions and, in particular, in Articles 27 and 56 of the Regulations of the 1907 Fourth Hague Convention, as well as other subsequent agreements,

Mindful of the development of rules of customary international law as also affirmed by the relevant case - law, related to the protection of cultural heritage in peacetime as well as in the event of armed conflict,

Also recalling Articles 8 (2) (b) (ix) and 8 (2) (e) (iv) of the Rome Statute of the International Criminal Court, and, as appropriate, Article 3 (d) of the Statute of the International Criminal Tribunal for the former Yugoslavia, related to the intentional destruction of cultural heritage,

Reaffirming that issues not fully covered by the present Declaration and other international instruments concerning cultural heritage will continue to be governed by the principles of international law, the principles of humanity and the dictates of public conscience,

Adopts and solemnly proclaims the present Declaration:

I – Recognition of the importance of cultural heritage

The international community recognizes the importance of the protection of cultural heritage and reaffirms its commitment to fight against its intentional destruction in any form so that such cultural heritage may be transmitted to the succeeding generations.

II – Scope

1. The present Declaration addresses intentional destruction of cultural heritage including cultural heritage linked to a natural site.

2. For the purposes of this Declaration "intentional destruction" means an act intended to destroy in whole or in part cultural heritage, thus compromising its integrity, in a manner which constitutes a violation of international law or an unjustifiable offence to the principles of humanity and dictates of public conscience, in the latter case in so far as such acts are not already governed by fundamental principles of international law.

III – Measures to combat intentional destruction of cultural heritage

1. States should take all appropriate measures to prevent, avoid, stop and suppress acts of intentional destruction of cultural heritage, wherever such heritage is located.

2. States should adopt the appropriate legislative, administrative, educational and technical measures, within the framework of their economic resources, to protect cultural heritage and should revise them periodically with a view to adapting them to the evolution of national and international cultural heritage protection standards.

3. States should endeavour, by all appropriate means, to ensure respect for cultural heritage in society, particularly through educational, awareness - raising and information programmes.

4. States should:

(a) become parties to the 1954 Hague Convention for the Protection of Cultural Property in the Event of Armed Conflict and its two 1954 and 1999 Protocols and the Additional Protocols I and II to the four 1949 Geneva Conventions, if they have not yet done so;

(b) promote the elaboration and the adoption of legal instruments providing a higher standard of protection of cultural heritage, and

(c) promote a coordinated application of existing and future instruments relevant to the protection of cultural heritage.

IV – Protection of cultural heritage when conducting peacetime activities

When conducting peacetime activities, States should take all appropriate measures to conduct them in such a manner as to protect cultural heritage and, in particular, in conformity with the principles and objectives of the 1972 Convention for the Protection of the World Cultural and Natural Heritage, of the 1956 Recommendation on International Principles Applicable to Archaeological Excavations, the 1968 Recommendation concerning the Preservation of Cultural Property Endangered by Public or Private Works, the 1972 Recommendation concerning the Protection, at National Level, of the Cultural and Natural Heritage and the 1976 Recommendation concerning the Safeguarding and Contemporary Role of Historic Areas.

V – Protection of cultural heritage in the event of armed conflict , including the case of occupation

When involved in an armed conflict, be it of an international or non - international character, including the case of occupation, States should take all appropriate measures to conduct their activities in such a manner as to protect cultural heritage, in conformity with customary international law and the principles and objectives of international agreements and UNESCO recommendations concerning the protection of such heritage during hostilities.

VI – State responsibility

A State that intentionally destroys or intentionally fails to take appropriate measures to prohibit, prevent, stop, and punish any intentional destruction of cultural heritage of great importance for humanity, whether or not it is inscribed on a list maintained by UNESCO or another international organization, bears the responsibility for such destruction, to the extent provided for by international law.

VII – Individual criminal responsibility

States should take all appropriate measures, in accordance with international law, to establish jurisdiction over, and provide effective criminal sanctions against, those persons who commit, or order to be committed, acts of intentional destruction of cultural heritage of great importance for humanity, whether or not it is inscribed on a list maintained by UNESCO or another international organization.

VIII – Cooperation for the protection of cultural heritage

1. States should cooperate with each other and with UNESCO to protect cul-

tural heritage from intentional destruction. Such cooperation should entail at least:

(i) provision and exchange of information regarding circumstances entailing the risk of intentional destruction of cultural heritage;

(ii) consultation in the event of actual or impending destruction of cultural heritage;

(iii) consideration of assistance to States, as requested by them, in the promotion of educational programmes, awareness - raising and capacity - building for the prevention and repression of any intentional destruction of cultural heritage;

(iv) judicial and administrative assistance, as requested by interested States, in the repression of any intentional destruction of cultural heritage.

2. For the purposes of more comprehensive protection, each State is encouraged to take all appropriate measures, in accordance with international law, to cooperate with other States concerned with a view to establishing jurisdiction over, and providing effective criminal sanctions against, those persons who have committed or have ordered to be committed acts referred to above (VII - Individual criminal responsibility) and who are found present on its territory, regardless of their nationality and the place where such act occurred.

IX – Human rights and international humanitarian law

In applying this Declaration, States recognize the need to respect international rules related to the criminalization of gross violations of human rights and international humanitarian law, in particular, when intentional destruction of cultural heritage is linked to those violations.

X – Public awareness

States should take all appropriate measures to ensure the widest possible dissemination of this Declaration to the general public and to target groups, inter alia, by organizing public awareness - raising campaigns.

关于在国家层面保护文化和自然遗产的建议*

（联合国教科文组织大会1972年11月16日通过）

联合国教育、科学与文化组织大会于1972年10月17日至21日在巴黎召开其第17次大会，鉴于社会中的生存条件在加速改变，对人的宁静与发展而言，至关重要的是为其保留生活的适当环境，使其在其中可以保持与自然及时代所留下的文明痕迹，为此目的，在社会生活中使得文化及自然遗产发挥积极功用就是适当的，并将当今时代的成就、过去的价值体系及自然之美融合进总体政策，鉴于予以融入社会及经济生活须成为地区发展及每一层次中进行国家规划的重要内容之一，鉴于当今时代特有的新现象所产生的严重危险威胁着文化及自然遗产，而后者构成人类遗产的核心特色及当今及未来文明之丰富和和谐发展的源泉之一，鉴于文化及自然遗产的每一项都是独特的，任何一个项目的消失都构成遗产的永久损失并发生不可挽回的褪色，鉴于领土存在文化及自然遗产组成部分的每个国家都有义务保护这部分的人类遗产并确保将之传与子孙，鉴于世界各国对文化及自然遗产的研究、了解和保护有助于其之间的相互理解，鉴于文化与自然遗产构成一个和谐的整体，其组成部分不可分割，鉴于文化及自然遗产保护政策的设想和制定都有共同之处，这很可能使得成员国之间进行持久性的互动，并对联合国教科文组织在该领域的活动具有决定性的效果，注意到大会已经通过了国际文件，保护文化及自然遗产，诸如《关于考古发掘应当遵循的国际原则的建议》（1956）、《保护景观和遗址的风貌与特色的建议》（1962）、《关于保护被公共或私人工程危及文化财产的建议》（1968），希望对该等国际文件中的标准和原则予以补充并将其适用予以推广，鉴于有关文化与自然遗产之保护的建议，该问题出现在大会议程第23项。本组织第16次大会已经决定将该问题作为国际规制

* 中国社会科学院法学研究所吴峻译。

的主题，并以针对成员国的建议书形式作出，于1972年11月16日通过本建议书。

I. 文化与自然遗产之定义

1. 为本倡议书之目的，以下须被认为是“文化遗产”：

纪念碑：建筑作品，包括居住洞穴与铭刻在内的纪念雕塑及画作，元素，考古、历史、艺术或科学而言的元素群或者具有特殊价值的结构；

建筑群：单独或关联建筑群体，因其建筑、一致性或者其在风景中的位置对于历史、艺术或科学而言都具有独特价值；

地址：一定地貌区域糅合了人造工程及自然景观，基于其魅力或其具有的建筑、历史、族群或人类学意义而具有特殊的价值。

2. 为本倡议书之目的，以下须被视为“自然遗产”：

由物理和生物形态或该等形态之群落所构成的自然特色，就美学或科学而言具有特殊价值；

地理及生理形态及界限清晰的区域，构成动植物类的栖息之地，就科学或保护而言具有特殊的价值或其特殊价值遭到威胁。

II. 国家政策

3. 每个国家应该根据其司法及法律要求尽可能地制定、发展并适用一项政策，其目的应该就是协调并运用所有的科学、技术、文化及其他可用资源以确保所有文化及自然遗产得到有效保护和呈现。

III. 一般原则

4. 文化及自然遗产代表着财富。其保护和呈现是其所在国家的职责，这对于其自己国名及国际社会整体而言都是如此；成员国应该采取必要的行动以履行其职责。

5. 文化或自然遗产应当被综合认为是具有一致性的整体，不仅由极具内在价值的作品构成，也包括并不醒目的项目，它们随着时间的推移取得了文化或自然价值。

6. 一般而言，这些作品及这些项目都不能从其环境予以分割。

7. 文化和自然遗产保护及呈现的终极目的就是人的发展，成员国应尽力使其该领域的工作促使文化和自然遗产不再成为国家发展的阻碍，而成为该等发展中具有决定意义的因素。

8．文化和自然遗产的保护和有效呈现应当被认为是地区发展规划及全国、地区或当地层面进行总体规划中的核心内容之一。

9．应当推进文化和自然遗产保护的积极政策并使之在社会生活中具有一席之地。成员国应当通过所有有关公共及私人服务进行一致行动，以制定并适用该等政策。与文化与自然遗产有关的防止和矫正措施应该由其他方面予以补充，其宗旨在于使得该等遗产的每一个组成部分都能够发挥功能，使其成为国家现今及以后社会、经济及文化生活的一部分，并与所涉项目之文化或自然属性相匹配。文化与自然遗产保护行为应当利用所有关涉及文化与自然遗产的保护、保持与展示研究领域中所取得的科技进步。

10．为文化与自然遗产保护和呈现，公共机构应当尽力提供越来越多的资金来源。

11．区域内一般公众应当熟悉保护措施，并应征求其建议和帮助，尤其应该涉及文化与自然遗产之对待与监督。也可以考虑私人领域提供资金支持的可能性。

IV．组织服务

12．虽然其多样性使之不可能让所有国家都采取组织的标准形式，然而应该遵从特定的共同标准。

特种公共服务项目

13．在对每个国家的适宜条件予以合理尊重的前提下，在不存在该等机构的情形下，成员国应当在其领土建立一种或多种特种公共服务项目，负责有效履行下列职责：

（a）发展并有效实施所有旨在保护和呈现该国文化与自然遗产的所示并使之在社会生活中成为积极的组成部分；主要就是编纂文化与自然遗产名录并建立适当的文件服务体系；

（b）招募并训练必要的科学、技术及行政人员，负责涉及确认、保护及融合项目并指导其实施；

（c）在各个领域专家间组织紧密的合作，研究文化与自然遗产的技术保护问题；

（d）使用或建立研究因文化与自然遗产保护所产生问题的实验室；

（e）确保所有者或租用人进行必要的复原工作并提供最优艺术及技术条件下建筑物的保养。

咨询机构

14. 特种服务项目应该与负责提供文化与自然遗产保护措施准备建议的专家机构予以合作。该等机构应该包括专家、主要保护协会代表及有关政府的代表。

不同机构间的合作

15. 处理文化及科学遗产保护与呈现的特种服务项目应该与其他公共服务项目予以联系并平等地进行工作，尤其是与那些负责区域发展规划、主要公共工程、环境及经济与社会规划部门进行联系。旅游发展计划涉及文化与自然遗产的，应该审慎计划，以便不会损害该遗产的内在属性及重要意义，并采取步骤建立有关机构之间的适当联络。

16. 只要涉及大型项目，应当在特种服务项目所有层面上展开持续性的合作，并进行适当的协调安排，以便决定可以一直做出，并考虑到涉及的种种利益。应在合作规划一开始就做出涉及研究及冲突解决机制方面的规定。

中央、联邦、地区及当地机构的职权

17. 考虑到文化与自然遗产保护与呈现所涉及的问题很难解决、需要特别指示并在有时需要做出艰难的决定这样一个事实，考虑到该领域并没有足够的专门职员，职责涉及一般意义上保护措施的设计与执行之所有事项的，应该基于适合于每个国家既有情况的审慎平衡原则而在中央或联邦及地区或当地政府机构予以划分。

V. 保护措施

18. 成员国应该尽力采取所有必要科学、技术及行政、法律及金融措施，以确保其领土内对文化与自然遗产的保护。该等措施应当根据该国的法律及组织体系予以确定。

科学和技术措施

19. 成员国应当对其文化与自然遗产作出谨慎与持久性的维护安排，以便避免不得不因为情况恶化而采用代价甚高的操作；为此，他们应该规定对其遗产组成部分通过定期检查的方式予以惯常性的监控。他们也应该仔细制定保护及呈现工作的规划项目，依据他们所能采取的科学、技术及金融手段，逐渐纳入所有文化与自然遗产。

20. 任何必须进行的工作应该在之前并在工作工程中进行与其重要性相称的充分研究。该等研究应该通过与所有有关领域专家进行合作或交由执行。

21. 成员国应当对向遭遇特别严重威胁的文化与自然遗产组成部分能够

提供额外保护的有效方法予以调查。该等方法应当考虑到所涉及彼此关联的科学、技术及艺术问题并使之可以认定将要适用的解决办法。

22. 另外，文化与自然遗产的该等组成部分应当在任何适当的情形下予以恢复至之前的用途，或者使之具有更为合理的功能，但其文化价值不能因此而受到破坏。

23. 就文化遗产进行的任何工作应该旨在保护其传统风貌、保护其不会因新建或重建而破坏与其景观之间的空间或色彩关系。

24. 时间和人类在纪念碑及其景观之间确立的和谐最为重要，一般不得受到扰乱或破坏。通过拆除其四周建筑而对纪念碑予以鼓励一般不得予以授权；也不得尝试移动纪念碑，处理问题基于紧迫性的考虑而作为例外手段适用的除外。

25. 成员国应当采取措施保护其文化与自然遗产不会因主导现代文明的科技发展而可能受到损害。该等措施应当旨在抗衡及其与车辆带来的冲击和震动。也应采取措施制止污染，防止自然灾害所带来的损害，并对文化与自然遗产遭受的损害予以修补。

26. 由于主导修复建筑群的环境在任何地方都不相同，成员国应当在适当情形下安排社会科学调查，以便准确确定有关建筑群所在社会的社会与自然需求究竟为何。任何修补操作应该特别注意能够使人在复原场景中可以工作、发展并取得自我实现。

27. 成员国应当对自然遗产项目的地理及生态进行研究，诸如公园、野生生物、避难或休闲区域或其他相同保护区域，以便评估其科学价值，认定开放参观所带来的影响并对彼此之间的关联予以监控，以避免对遗产造成严重破坏，并对动物及植物群落之管理提供足够的背景了解。

28. 成员国应当紧跟交通、通信、视听技术、自动数据处理及其他适当科技之进步及文化和休闲潮流，以便为科学研究及公共休闲提供最好的设施与服务，同时与每一区域的宗旨相符，并不会对自然资源造成破坏。

行政措施

29. 每一成员国都应该尽快制定文化与自然遗产保护名录，包括其中的项目，在并不具有特别重要的情形下，也与其环境及其性质构成不可分割的部分。

30. 通过对文化与自然遗产进行该种调查而取得的信息应当以适当的形式予以收集并进行惯常更新。

31. 为了确保文化与自然遗产在所有层面上的规划中都得到有效承认，

成员国应当准备涵盖有关文化与自然财产的地图并作出尽可能完备的文件记录。

32. 成员国应当考虑为不再提供其原定功能的历史建筑群发掘新的适当用途。

33. 应当就具有历史和艺术意义的建筑群之保护、呈现与修复制定规划。其中应当包括外围保护带，规定土地使用的条件，并说明需要保护的建筑及其保护条件。更改规划应当并入涉及有关地区的总体城镇及乡村规划政策。

34. 修复规划应当说明历史建筑拟订的用途及在修复领域及其周围城市发展之间的关联。对修复区域的制定尚在考虑之中的，应与当地政府与该领域的居民代表进行协商。

35. 任何可能导致改变保护区内建筑现存状态的工程都应取得城乡规划部门的事先授权，并征询负责文化与自然遗产保护专业人员的建议。

36. 如其居民需要，应该允许建筑群进行内部变动并安装现代服务设施，但不得对古代民居的固有特色进行剧烈改变。

37. 成员国应当基于其自然遗产名录制定短期及长期规划，以便实现满足其国家需要的保护体系。

38. 成员国应当提供咨询服务，对非政府组织、土地所有人就符合土地生产用途的保护政策提供指引。

39. 成员国应当制定政策和计划，以复原被工业或者其他形式的人类活动所破坏的自然区域。

法律措施

40. 根据其重要性，文化与自然遗产之组成部分应当根据每个国家的职权及法律程序由法律或行政法规分别或共同予以保护。

41. 保护措施应在必要时通过鼓励文化与自然遗产只保护及促进其组成部分得以呈现的新规定加以补充。为此目的，保护措施之实施应适用于文化与自然遗产组成部分之所有者的个人及公共机构。

42. 如果可能影响保护区域的面貌，没有取得专业人员许可的，不得建新建筑，并不得在保护区域之中或附近的不动产之上予以拆除、重建、改建或毁林。

43. 规划法律允许产业发展，换言之，公共及私人工程应该对现有保护法律予以考虑。负责文化与自然遗产保护的政府机构可以采取措施加快必要的保护工程，其方式就是或者向所有者提供资金支持，或者代表所有者行事，并行使其权利以完成相关工程，并可能就所有者通常支付的费用份额取得补偿。

44. 为保护不动产之需要，公共机构可以获得授权，基于国内法律的条款和条件对被保护建筑或自然区域予以征收。

45. 成员国应该建立法规以控制广告牌、霓虹标志及其他形式的广告、商业标志、搭建房屋、树立线杆、缆塔及电缆或电话线、放置电视天线、所有种类的汽车交通及停泊、放置指示牌、街道设施等，并且，一般而言，也监控作为文化与自然遗产以部分的不动产设备或坐落有关的任何物品。

46. 保护文化或自然遗产任何组成部分措施所产生的效果应具有持续性，不论所有权是否发生变化。如果被保护的建筑或自然区域被卖出，购买者应被告知其处于被保护的状态。

47. 应当根据每个国家的法律及宪法职权，任何人如故意损毁、毁坏或污损被保护纪念碑、建筑群落或地区或者具有考古、历史或艺术意义的物品，应当适用罚金或行政处罚。另外，非法挖掘所适用的设备可能会被没收。

48. 任何其他行为损害对文化或自然遗产被保护部分的保护及呈现的，应当对责任方施以罚金或行政处罚，并应该规定将受损地区根据成熟科技标准复原至原先状态。

金融措施

49. 中央及地方政府应尽力在其预算中根据形成文化或自然遗产组成部分中受保护不动产的重要性拨出特定比例的资金，以便维护、保护及呈现其为所有者的被保护不动产，以在资金方面使得不论公共机构还是私人的所有者在被保护不动产中能够进行该等工作。

50. 保护及呈现个人拥有的文化与自然遗产所发生的支出应当尽力由其所有人或用户负担。

51. 对该等指出进行的税收减让、奖项或优惠贷款可以由被保护不动产的私人所有人享有，但他们应根据被认可的标准从事其不动产保护、呈现及修复的工作。

52. 应当考虑在必要时对被保护文化与自然区域因为保护项目而承受的损失予以补偿。

53. 给予私人所有人的财务优惠待遇应该在任何适当情形下依据其对就公共利益所规定条件予以遵守的情形而定，比如是否开放公园、花园及区域，是否在自然区域、纪念碑或建筑群落中所有部分向游客开放，是否允许拍照，等等。

54. 在公共机构的预算中应该拨出特别资金，以保护大规模公共或私人工程所危及文化与自然遗产。

55. 为了增加可用的资金来源，成员国可以设立一个或多个“文化与自然会遗产基金”，将之作为合法设立的公共机构，有权接受尤其是来自于工商企业的私人馈赠、捐款及赠与。

56. 作出馈赠、捐款或赠与以收购、复原或维护文化与自然遗产特定部分的，也可以给予税收减让。

57. 为了促进自然与文化遗产修复工作，成员国可以作出特殊安排，尤其通过为装修及复原工作提供贷款，也可以通过必要的行政法规以避免在有关区域因不动产投机而导致的涨价。

58. 为避免因为须迁出翻修建筑或建筑群落而导致穷苦居民蒙受艰辛，可以规定对租金上涨予以补贴，以便使之可以继续居住。该等补贴应当是暂时性的，并基于有关方的收入而定，以便使其能够支付由于进行翻修工作而增加的生活成本。

59. 为文化与自然遗产所采取任何形式的工作，成员国可以促进对其提供资助，其方式就是发起由公共机构及私人贷款机构所支撑的“贷款基金”，负责为所有者提供偿还期长的低息贷款。

VI. 教育和文化行动

60. 所有层级的大学、教育机构及终生教育机构应当组织关于艺术史、建筑学、环境及城市规划的日常课程、授课、研讨会等。

61. 成员国应当发动教育攻势，以便引起公众对文化与自然遗产的广泛兴趣及尊重。应当持久地努力，使得公众了解为保护文化与自然遗产而正在进行或可以进行的工作，并培育对其所体现价值的欣赏与尊重。为此目的，所有信息媒介都应该在必要时予以使用。

62. 在没有忽视文化与自然遗产所体现的显著经济与社会价值的前提下，应该采取措施促进并加强该等遗产的突出文化及教育价值，从而提供保护及呈现该等遗产的终极动力。

63. 基于文化与自然遗产组成部分而进行的所有努力都应考虑到其中与人及其规模相称的、作为环境代表、建筑或城市设计的一种形式而体现其中的文化和教育价值。

64. 应该建立自发组织以鼓励国家及当地政府充分利用其保护职权向其提供的支持，并在必要时为其取得资金；该等机构应与当地历史协会、便利设施改进团体、当地发展委员会及旅游机构等等建立联系，并且也可以组织其成员参观并引导对文化与自然遗产不同项目进行的参观。

65. 可以设立信息中心、博物馆或举办展览来说明针对预定修复的文化与自然遗产组成部分正在进行的工作。

VII. 国际合作

成员国应当就文化与自然遗产之保护与呈现进行合作，并在必要的情形下向无论是政府间还是非政府国际组织寻求帮助。该等多边及双边合作应当得到仔细的协调，并应通过诸如以下形式的措施进行：

（a）所有形式及科学、技术出版物信息交换；

（b）就具体主题组织研讨会及研究会；

（c）提供研究及旅行资助，派遣科学、技术及行政人员，提供设备；

（d）通过允许年轻的研究人员及技师参与建筑项目、考古挖掘及自然区域保护，为海外科技培训提供设施；

（e）在成员国群体间进行涉及保护、挖掘、复原及修复工作的大规模项目合作，其目的就是推广经验。

Recommendation concerning the Protection, at National Level, of the Cultural and Natural Heritage

16 November 1972

The General Conference of the United Nations Educational, Scientific and Cultural Organization, meeting in Paris, at its seventeenth session, from 17 October to 21 November 1972,

Considering that, in a society where living conditions are changing at an accelerated pace, it is essential for man's equilibrium and development to preserve for him a fitting setting in which to live, where he will remain in contact with nature and the evidences of civilization bequeathed by past generations, and that, to this end, it is appropriate to give the cultural and natural heritage an active function in community life and to integrate into an overall policy the achievements of our time, the values of the past and the beauty of nature,

Considering that such integration into social and economic life must be one of the fundamental aspects of regional development and national planning at every level,

Considering that particularly serious dangers engendered by new phenomena peculiar to our times are threatening the cultural and natural heritage, which constitute an essential feature of mankind's heritage and a source of enrichment and harmonious development for present and future civilization,

Considering that each item of the cultural and natural heritage is unique and that the disappearance of any one item constitutes a definite loss and an irreversible impoverishment of that heritage.

Considering that every country in whose territory there are components of the cultural and natural heritage has an obligation to safeguard this part of mankind's heritage and to ensure that it is handed down to future generations,

Considering that the study, knowledge and protection of the cultural and natural heritage in the various countries of the world are conducive to mutual understanding among the peoples,

Considering that the cultural and natural heritage forms an harmonious whole, the components of which are indissociable,

Considering that a policy for the protection of the cultural and natural heritage, thought out and formulated in common, is likely to bring about a continuing interaction among Member States and to have a decisive effect on the activities of the United Nations Educational, Scientific and Cultural Organization in this field,

Noting that the General Conference has already adopted international instruments for the protection of the cultural and natural heritage, such as the Recommendation on International Principles Applicable to Archaeological Excavations (1956), the Recommendation concerning the Safeguarding of the Beauty and Character of Landscapes and Sites (1962) and the Recommendation concerning the Preservation of Cultural Property Endangered by Public or Private Works (1968),

Desiring to supplement and extend the application of the standards and principles laid down in such recommendations,

Having before it proposals concerning the protection of the cultural' and natural heritage, which question appears on the agenda of the session as item 23,

Having decided, at its sixteenth session, that this question should be made the subject of international regulations, to take the form of a recommendation to Member States,

Adopts this sixteenth day of November 1972, this Recommendation.

I. Definitions of the cultural and the natural heritage

1. For the purposes of this Recommendation, the following shall be considered as `cultural heritage':

monuments: architectural works, works of monumental sculpture and painting, including cave dwellings and inscriptions, and elements, groups of elements or structures of special value from the point of view of archaeology, history, art or science;

groups of buildings: groups of separate or connected buildings which, because of their architecture, their homogeneity or their place in the landscape, are of special value from the point of view of history, art or science;

sites : topographical areas, the combined works of man and of nature, which are of special value by reason of their beauty or their interest from the archaeological, historical, ethnological or anthropological points of view.

2. For the purposes of this Recommendation, the following shall be considered as `natural heritage' :

natural features consisting of physical and biological formations or groups of such formations, which are of special value from the aesthetic or scientific point of view;

geological and physiographical formations and precisely delineated areas which constitute the habitat of species of animals and plants, valuable or threatened, of special value from the point of view of science or conservation;

natural sites or precisely delineated natural areas of special value - from the point of view of science, conservation or natural beauty, or in their relation to the combined works of man and of nature.

II. National policy

3. In conformity with their jurisdictional and legislative requirements, each State should formulate, develop and apply as far as possible a policy whose principal aim should be to co - ordinate and make use of all scientific, technical, cultural and other resources available to secure the effective protection, conservation and presentation of the cultural and natural heritage.

III. General principles

4. The cultural and natural heritage represents wealth, the protection, conservation and presentation of which impose responsibilities on the States in whose territory it is situated, both vis - a - vis their own nationals and vis - a - vis the international community as a whole; Member States should take such action as may be necessary to meet these responsibilities.

5. The cultural or natural heritage should be considered in its entirety as a homogeneous whole, comprising not only works of great intrinsic value, but also more modest items that have, with the passage of time, acquired cultural or natural value.

6. None of these works and none of these items should, as a general rule, be dissociated from its environment.

7. As the ultimate purpose of protecting, conserving and presenting the cultural and natural heritage is the development of man, Member States should, as far as possible, direct their work in this field - in such a way that the cultural and natural heritage may no longer - be regarded as a check on national development but as a determining factor in such development.

8. The protection, conservation and effective presentation of the cultural and natural heritage should be considered as one of the essential aspects of regional development plans, and planning in general, at the national, regional or local level.

9. An active policy for the conservation of the cultural and natural heritage and for giving it a place in community life should be developed. Member States should arrange for concerted action by all the public and private services concerned, with a view to drawing up and applying such a policy. Preventive and corrective measures relating to the cultural and natural heritage should be supplemented by others, designed to give each of the components of this heritage a function which will make it a part of the nation's social, economic, scientific and cultural life for the present and future, compatible with the cultural or natural character of the item in question. Action for the protection of the cultural and natural heritage should take advantage of scientific and technical advances in all branches of study involved in the protection, conservation and presentation of the cultural or natural heritage.

10. Increasingly significant financial resources should, as far as possible, be made available by the public authorities for the safeguarding and presentation of the cultural and natural heritage.

11. The general public of the area should be associated with the measures to be taken for protection and conservation and should be called on for suggestions and help, with particular reference to regard for and surveillance of the cultural and

natural heritage. Consideration might also be given to the possibility of financial support from the private sector.

IV. Organization of services

12. Although their diversity makes it impossible for all Member States to adopt a standard form of organization, certain common criteria should nevertheless be observed.

Specialized public services

13. With due regard for the conditions appropriate to each country, Member States should set up in their territory, wherever they do not already exist, one or more specialized public services to be responsible for the efficient discharge of the following functions :

(a) developing and putting into effect measures of all kinds designed for the protection, conservation and presentation of the country's cultural and natural heritage and for making it an active factor in the life of the community; and primarily, compiling an inventory of the cultural and natural heritage and establishing appropriate documentation services;

(b) training and recruiting scientific, technical and administrative staff as required, to be responsible for working out identification, protection, conservation and integration programmes and directing their execution;

(c) organizing close co - operation among specialists of various disciplines to study the technical conservation problems of the cultural and natural heritage;

(d) using or creating laboratories for the study of all the scientific problems arising in connexion with the conservation of the cultural and natural heritage;

(e) ensuring that owners or tenants carry out the necessary restoration work and provide for the upkeep of the buildings in the best artistic and technical conditions.

Advisory bodies

14. The specialized services should work with bodies of experts responsible for giving advice on the preparation of measures relating to the cultural and natural heritage. Such bodies should include experts, representatives of the major preservation societies, and representatives of the administrations concerned.

Co - operation among the various bodies

15. The specialized services dealing with the protection, conservation and presentation of the cultural and natural heritage should carry out their work in liaison and on an equal footing with other public services, more particularly those responsible for regional development planning, major public works, the environment, and economic and social planning. Tourist development programmes involving the cultural and natural heritage should be carefully drawn up so as not to impair the intrinsic character and importance of that heritage, and steps should be taken to establish appropriate liaison between the authorities concerned.

16. Continuing co - operation at all levels should be organized among the specialized services whenever large - scale projects are involved, and appropriate co-ordinating arrangements made so that decisions may, be taken in concert, taking account of the various interests involved. Provision should be made for joint planning from the start of the studies and machinery developed for the settlement of conflicts.

Competence of central, federal, regional and local bodies

17. Considering the fact that the problems involved in the protection, conservation and presentation of the cultural and natural heritage are difficult to deal with, calling for special knowledge and sometimes entailing hard choices, and that there are not enough specialized staff available in this field, responsibilities in all matters concerning the devising and execution of protective measures in general should be divided among central or federal and regional or local authorities on the basis of a judicious balance adapted to the situation that exists in each State.

V. Protective measures

18. Member States should, as far as possible, take all necessary scientific, technical and administrative, legal and financial measures, to ensure the protection of the cultural and natural heritage in their territories. Such measures should be determined in accordance with the legislation and organization of the State.

Scientific and technical measures

19. Member States should arrange for careful and constant maintenance of

their cultural and natural heritage in order to avoid having to undertake the costly operations necessitated by its deterioration; for this purpose, they should provide for regular surveillance of the components of their heritage by means of periodic inspections. They should also draw up carefully planned programmes of conservation and presentation work, gradually taking in all the cultural and natural heritage, depending upon the scientific, technical and financial means at their disposal.

20. Any work required should be preceded and accompanied by such thorough studies as its importance may necessitate. Such studies should be carried out in co - operation with or by specialists in all related fields.

21. Member States should investigate effective methods of affording added protection to those components of the cultural and natural heritage that are threatened by unusually serious dangers. Such methods should take account of the interrelated scientific, technical and artistic problems involved and make it possible to determine the treatment to be applied.

22. These components of the cultural and natural heritage should, in addition, be restored, wherever appropriate, to their former use or given a new and more suitable function, provided that their cultural value is not thereby diminished.

23. Any work done on the cultural heritage should aim at preserving its traditional appearance, and protecting it from any new construction or remodeling which might impair the relations of mass or colour between it and its surroundings.

24. The harmony established by time and man between a monument and its surroundings is of the greatest importance and should not, as a general rule, be disturbed or destroyed. The isolation of a monument by demolishing its surroundings should not, as a general rule, be authorized; nor should the moving of a monument be contemplated save as an exceptional means of dealing with a problem, justified by pressing considerations.

25. Member States should take measures to protect their cultural and natural heritage against the possible harmful effects of the technological developments characteristic of modern civilization. Such measures should be designed to counter the effects of shocks and vibrations caused by machines and vehicles. Measures should also be taken to prevent pollution and guard against natural disasters and calamities, and to provide for the repair of damage to the cultural and natural heritage.

26. Since the circumstances governing the rehabilitation of groups of buildings

are not everywhere identical, Member States should provide for a social science inquiry in appropriate cases, in order to ascertain precisely what are the social and cultural needs of the community in which the group of buildings concerned is situated. Any rehabilitation operation should pay special attention to enabling man to work, to develop and to achieve fulfillment in the restored setting.

27. Member States should undertake studies and research on the geology and ecology of items of the natural heritage, such as park, wildlife, refuge or recreation areas, or other equivalent reserves, in order to appreciate their scientific value, to determine the impact of visitor use and to monitor interrelationships so as to avoid serious damage to the heritage and to provide adequate background for the management of the fauna and flora.

28. Member States should keep abreast of advances in transportation, communication, audio - visual techniques, automatic data - processing and other appropriate technology, and of cultural and recreational trends, so that the best possible facilities and services can be provided for scientific study and the enjoyment of the public, appropriate to the purpose of each area, without deterioration of the natural resources.

Administrative measures

29. Each Member State should draw up, as soon as possible, an inventory for the protection of its cultural and natural heritage, including items which, without being of outstanding importance, are inseparable from their environment and contribute to its character.

30. The information obtained by such surveys of the cultural and natural heritage should be collected in a suitable form and regularly brought up to date.

31. To ensure that the cultural and natural heritage is effectively recognized at all levels of planning, Member States should prepare maps and the fullest possible documentation covering the cultural and natural property in question.

32. Member States should give thought to finding suitable uses for groups of historic buildings no longer serving their original purpose.

33. A plan should be prepared for the protection, conservation, presentation and rehabilitation of groups of buildings of historic and artistic interest. It should include peripheral protection belts, lay down the conditions for land use, and

specify the buildings to be preserved and the conditions for their preservation. This plan should be incorporated into the overall ° town and country planning policy for the areas concerned.

34. Rehabilitation plans should specify the uses to which historic buildings are to be put, and the links there are to be between the rehabilitation area and the surrounding urban development. When the designation of a rehabilitation area is under consideration, the local authorities and representatives of the residents of the area should be consulted.

35. Any work that might result in changing the existing state of the buildings in a protected area should be subject to prior authorization by the town and country planning authorities, on the advice of the specialized services responsible for the' protection of the cultural and natural heritage.

36. Internal alterations to groups of buildings and the installation of modern conveniences should be allowed if they are needed for the well - being of their occupants and provided they do not drastically alter the real characteristic features of ancient dwellings.

37. Member States should develop short - and long - range plans, based on in - ventories of their natural heritage, to achieve a system of conservation to meet the needs of their countries.

38. Member States should provide an advisory service to guide non - governmental organizations and owners of land on national conservation policies consistent with the productive use of the land.

39. Member States should develop policies and programmes for restoration of natural areas made derelict by industry, or otherwise despoiled by man's activities.

Legal measures

40. Depending upon their importance, the components of the cultural and natural heritage should be protected, individually or collectively, by legislation or regulations in conformity with the competence and the legal procedures of each country.

41. Measures for protection should be supplemented to the extent necessary by new provisions to promote the conservation of the cultural or natural heritage and to facilitate the presentation of its components. To that end, enforcement of protective measures should apply to individual owners and to public authorities

when they are the owners of components of the cultural and natural heritage.

42. No new building should be erected, and no demolition, transformation, modification or deforestation carried out, on any property situated on or in the vicinity of a protected site, if it is likely to affect its appearance, without authorization by the specialized services.

43. Planning legislation to permit industrial development, or public and private works should take into account existing legislation on conservation, The authorities responsible for the protection of the cultural and natural heritage might take steps to expedite the necessary conservation work, either by making financial assistance available to the owner, or by acting in the owner's place and exercising their powers to have the work done, with the possibility of their obtaining reimbursement of that share of the costs which the owner would normally have paid.

44. Where required for the preservation of the property, the public authorities might be empowered to expropriate a protected building or natural site subject to the terms and conditions of domestic legislation.

45. Member States should establish regulations to control bill - posting, neon signs and other kinds of advertisement, commercial signs, camping, the erection of poles, pylons and electricity or telephone cables, the placing of television aerials, all types of vehicular traffic and parking, the placing of indicator panels, street furniture, etc., and, in general, everything connected with the equipment or occupation of property forming part of the cultural and natural heritage.

46. The effects of the measures taken to protect any element of the cultural or natural heritage should continue regardless of changes of ownership. If a protected building or natural site is sold, the purchaser should be informed that it is under protection.

47. Penalties or administrative sanctions should be applicable, in accordance with the laws and constitutional competence of each State, to anyone who willfully destroys, mutilates or defaces a protected monument, group of buildings or site, or one which is of archaeological, historical or artistic interest. In addition, equipment used in illicit excavation might be subject to confiscation.

48. Penalties or administrative sanctions should be imposed upon those responsible for any other action detrimental to the protection, conservation or presentation of a protected component of the cultural or natural heritage, and should

include provision for the restoration of an affected site to its original state in accordance with established scientific and technical standards.

Financial measures

49. Central and local authorities should, as far as possible, appropriate, in their budgets, a certain percentage of funds, proportionate to the importance of the protected property forming part of their cultural or natural heritage, for the purposes of maintaining, conserving and presenting protected property of which they are the owners, and of contributing financially to such work carried out on other protected property by the owners, whether public bodies or private persons.

50. The expenditure incurred in protecting, conserving and presenting items of the privately owned cultural and natural heritage should, so far as possible, be borne by their owners or users.

51. Tax concessions on such expenditures, or grants or loans on favourable terms, could be granted to private owners of protected properties, on condition that they carry out work for the protection, conservation, presentation and rehabilitation of their properties 'in accordance with approved standards.

52. Consideration should be given to indemnifying, if necessary, owners of protected cultural and natural areas for losses they might suffer as a consequence of protective programmes.

53. The financial advantages accorded to private owners should, where appropriate, be dependent on their observance of certain conditions laid down for the benefit of the public, such as their allowing access to parks, gardens and sites, tours through all of parts of natural sites, monuments or groups of buildings, the taking of photographs, etc.

54. Special funds should be set aside in the budgets of public authorities for the protection of the cultural and natural heritage endangered by large - scale public or private works.

55. To increase the financial resources available to them, Member States may set up one or more `Cultural and Natural Heritage Funds', as legally established public agencies, entitled to receive private gifts, donations and bequests, particularly from industrial and commercial firms.

56. Tax concessions could also be granted to those making gifts, donations or

bequests for the acquisition, restoration or maintenance of specific components of the cultural and natural heritage.

57. In order to facilitate operations for rehabilitation of the natural and cultural heritage, Member States might make special arrangements, particularly by way of loans for renovation and restoration work, and might also make the necessary regulations to avoid price rises caused by real - estate speculation in the areas under consideration.

58. To avoid hardship to the poorer inhabitants consequent on their having to move from rehabilitated buildings or groups of buildings, compensation for rises in rent might be contemplated so as to enable them to keep their accommodation. Such compensation should be temporary and determined on the basis of the income of the parties concerned, so as to enable them to meet the increased costs occasioned by the work carried out.

59. Member States might facilitate the financing of work of any description for the benefit of the cultural and natural heritage, by instituting `Loan Funds', supported by public institutions and private credit establishments, which would be responsible for granting loans to owners at low interest rates and with repayment spread out over a long period.

VI. Educational and cultural action

60. Universities, educational establishments at all levels and life - long education establishments should organize regular courses, lectures, seminars, etc., on the history of art, architecture, the environment and town planning.

61. Member States should undertake educational campaigns to arouse widespread public interest in, and respect for, the cultural and natural heritage. Continuing efforts should be made to inform the public about what is being and can be done to protect the cultural or natural heritage and to inculcate appreciation and respect for the values it enshrines. For this purpose, all media of information should be employed as required.

62. Without overlooking the great economic and social value of the cultural and natural heritage, measures should be taken to promote and reinforce the eminent cultural and educational value of that heritage, furnishing as it does the fun-

damental motive for protecting, conserving and presenting it.

63. All efforts on behalf of components of the cultural and natural heritage should take account of the cultural and educational value inherent in them as representative of an environment, a form of architecture or urban design commensurate with man and on his scale.

64. Voluntary organizations should be set up to encourage national and local authorities to make full use of their powers with regard to protection, to afford them support and, if necessary, to obtain funds for them; these bodies should keep in touch with local historical societies, amenity improvement societies, local development committees and agencies concerned with tourism, etc., and might also organize visits to, and guided tours of, different items of the cultural and natural heritage for their members.

65. Information centers, museums or exhibitions might be set up to explain the work being carried out on components of the cultural and natural heritage scheduled for rehabilitation.

VII. International co – operation

66. Member States should co - operate with regard to the protection, conservation and presentation of the cultural and natural heritage, seeking aid, if it seems desirable, from international organizations, both intergovernmental and non - governmental. Such multilateral or bilateral co - operation should be carefully co-ordinated and should take the form of measures such as the following :

(a) exchange of information and of scientific and technical publications;

(b) organization of seminars and working parties on particular subjects;

(c) provision of study and travel fellowships, and of scientific, technical and administrative staff, and equipment;

(d) provision of facilities for scientific and technical training abroad, by allowing young research workers and technicians to take part in architectural projects, archaeological excavations and the conservation of natural sites;

(e) co - ordination, within a group of Member States, of large - scale projects involving conservation, excavations, restoration and rehabilitation work, with the object of making the experience gained generally available.

关于城市历史景观的建议*

（联合国教科文组织大会2011年11月10日通过）

序　言

大会鉴于城市历史性地区属于我们共同的文化遗产中最为丰富和多样的表现形式之一，经一代又一代人的努力而形成，是人类在不同地域和不同时期辛勤劳作和不懈追求的有力见证；

同样，鉴于城市遗产属于人类的社会、文化和经济财富，反映人类丰富多样的文化、传统和实践经验在不同历史时期所蕴含的价值；

进一步考虑到城市化正以人类历史上前所未有的规模进行，并在全球范围内推动经济社会变革和发展，有必要对其在地方、国家、地区之间以及国际等各个层面上加以规范；

然而，另一方面也注意到，迅猛和常常失去控制的发展，使城市遗产支离破碎和归于湮灭，这将对世界各地的社会价值产生深刻的负面影响；

为此，考虑到，为对保护自然和文化遗产给予支持，有必要强调在地方开发和城市规划（例如，当代建筑和基础设施的开发）中引入历史性城区保护、管理和规划的策略，这将有助于维护城市的独特性；

考虑到，基于保护现有资源的可持续发展原则，对城市遗产给予积极保护并进行可持续的管理，是发展的先决条件；

* 西南政法大学法学院汪梦译。

忆及联合国教科文组织标准设定文件集，包括公约、建议和宪章①都有关于历史地区保护的内容，全部都有效；

同样注意到，由于人口变化、全球市场自由化和分散化，以及大量的旅游、遗产市场开发和气候变迁，情况已经改变；城市承受的发展压力和面临的挑战，是联合国教科文组织于1976年通过其最新的一部关于历史地区保护的建议（《关于历史地区保护及其当代作用的建议》）时，所未曾遇到的；

进一步注意到，在各地积极采取行动和召开国际会议②的共同作用下，有关文化和遗产及其管理方式的观念已发生变化，这对指导全球范围内的相关政策和实践非常有益；

期望补充和拓展现有国际机制规定的标准和原则的适用；

考虑到，联合国教科文组织第36次大会已经提出关于城市历史景观的议案，以加强对城市遗产的保护。该议案列入本次大会议程的第8.1项；

考虑到，联合国教科文组织第35次大会已经决定通过成员国共同制定一份建议的形式来解决问题；

特此决定：

1. 于2011年11月10日，通过此《关于城市历史景观的建议》；

2. 为在各成员国的领土上实施《建议》规定的原则和规则，建议各成员国采取必要立法措施；

3. 建议成员国采取必要措施，使负责保护、保存和经营管理城市历史地区及其更为广泛的地理环境的地方机构、国家机构、区域性机关、机构、单位和社会团体关注和重视本《建议》。

---

① 特别地，1972年《保护世界文化和自然遗产公约》，2005年《保护和促进文化表现形式多样性公约》，1962年《关于保护景观和遗址的风貌与特性的建议》，1968年《关于保护受到公共或者私人工程危及的文化财产的建议》，1972年《关于在国家层面保护文化和自然遗产的建议》，1976年《关于历史地区保护及其当代作用的建议》，1964年国际古迹遗址理事会《保护文物建筑及历史地段的国际宪章》（威尼斯宪章），1982年国际古迹遗址理事会与国际历史园林委员会《佛罗伦萨宪章》，1987年国际古迹遗址理事会《保护历史城镇与城区宪章》（华盛顿宪章），2005年国际古迹遗址理事会《保护历史建筑、遗址和历史地区环境的西安宣言》，以及2005年《维也纳保护具有历史意义的城市景观备忘录》。

② 特别地，1982年在墨西哥城的文化政策世界大会，1994年的世界遗产公约真实性原则奈良会议，1995年文化和发展世界委员会峰会，1996年伊斯坦布尔人居二及修订21计划大会，1998年联合国教科文组织斯德哥尔摩文化政策发展政府间大会，1998年世界银行和联合国教科文组织共同组织可持续发展文化大会——文化投资和自然捐赠，2005年维也纳世界遗产和当代建筑国际会议，2005年国际古迹遗址理事会关于遗址古迹环境的西安大会，2008年国际古迹遗址理事会关于场所精神的魁北克大会。

总　论

1. 我们的时代见证着历史上最大规模的人类迁徙。超过半数的世界人口现在居住在城市中。城市作为发展引擎和创新、创造中心愈来愈重要；他们为就业、教育提供机会并且满足人们发展需求和期望。

2. 但是，快速的和不受控制的城市化，会频繁地导致社会和空间的碎裂以及城市和周边郊区环境质量的严重恶化。值得注意的是，这可能来源于过密的建筑密度、标准化和单一的建筑群、公共空间和福利设施的减少、基础设施的缺乏、赤贫、社会隔离，以及不断增加的与气候有关的灾难的威胁。

3. 城市遗产，包括物质的和非物质的组成部分，构成了在不断变化的全球环境中促进城市宜居、推动经济发展和社会团结的关键因素。由于未来人类依赖于资源的有效规划和管理，保护城市遗产成为在可持续基础上实现城市发展和生活质量之间平衡的对策。

4. 在过去半个世纪，城市遗产保护已经成为世界范围内公共政策的重要部分。它是对保护共同价值和从历史遗产中获益的需求的回应。但是，从主要关注建筑文物向保护社会、文化和经济进程中更为广泛的城市价值转变，必须推动现有保护政策的发展完善并创新保护方法。

5. 为了支持旨在保护和提高人类环境质量的公共行动私人行为，本建议对将城市遗产保护策略更好地融入可持续发展的总体目标的客观要求作出了回应。

6. 上述“城市历史景观”的概念及其保护方法回应了城市发展进程中不同利益相关方在政策、政府管治和经营管理方面的关切。这些利益相关方包括在城市发展进程中充当不同角色的地方机构、国家机构、区域性组织、国际组织、公益团体与私人单位。

7. 本建议建立在联合国教科文组织过去已经颁布的四个有关城市遗产保护的建议的基础之上，确认在城市遗产保护的历史进程和实践中形成的相关概念和原则的重要性和有效性。此外，当代还有不少公约和宪章从不同侧面涉及文化和自然遗产的保护问题，这些公约和宪章同样构成本建议的基础。

Ⅰ. 定义

8. 城市历史景观是指经历史积淀而形成的具有文化或自然价值、特性的城市地区。这一术语的含义比“历史中心”或者“建筑物整体”的概念包含的内容更广，以囊括更为宽泛的城市背景和地理环境。

9. 广泛环境主要包括遗址的地形、地貌、水文和自然特征、历史的和当代的建造环境、地上和地下的基础设施、公共空间和公园、土地使用模式和空间构成、认知和视觉关系，以及其他城市结构因素。还包括社会和文化实践及其价值、经济进程以及与多样性和个性特征有关的遗产的非物质层面。

10. 该定义为在可持续发展的总体框架内对城市历史景观进行全面和完整的认定、评估、保护和管理提供了基础。

11. 该城市历史景观方法在于保护人类环境质量，增强城市空间的利用率和可持续使用，同时认同城市快速发展的时代特征，并促进城市在社会和功能方面的多样性。它将城市遗产保护目标与社会和经济发展相结合。为在城市发展与自然环境、当今和未来人民的发展要求与保护历史之间建立平衡的、可持续的关系，城市历史景观的保护方法应运而生。

12. 城市历史景观的方法将文化的多样性和创造力视为人类以及社会和经济发展的关键资产，为应对自然界变化和社会变迁，确保当代的介入与保护历史形成的文化遗产之间有机融合，并考虑区域环境和背景，提供解决问题的工具和手段。

13. 城市历史景观方法既尊重国家层面和国际社会的价值，又从地方传统和认识中汲取养分。

Ⅱ. 城市历史景观的挑战和机遇

14. 现有的联合国教科文组织的建议认识到当今社会中历史地区的重要作用。这些建议同时指出对于历史城市保护的特定威胁，并为应对这些挑战提供一般原则、政策和指南。

15. 城市历史景观方法反映出城市遗产保护的规范和实践在最近几十年内发生的变化，使得政策制定者和管理者能够更为有效地应对新挑战和抓住新机遇。城市历史景观方法支持社会寻求发展和改变的要求，同时也有利于保留与社区的历史、集体记忆和环境有关的特征与价值。

16. 在过去几十年中，由于世界城市人口、发展规模和速度的急剧增长，以快速变化的经济，城市及其历史地区在世界很多地方成为经济增长的中心和动力，并且在文化和社会生活中承担了新的角色。为此，他们同时承受了大量新的压力，包括：

城市化和全球化

17. 城市发展正在改变许多城市历史地区的本质。全球进程对于社会赋予城市及其环境的价值，以及他们的居民和使用者的认知和现实都产生深远影响。一方面，城市化提供的经济、社会和文化机会能够提高生活质量和加强城市的传统特征；另一方面，城市密度和发展不受管理的改变会破坏人们的空间感、城市结构的完整性以及社会认同。某些城市历史地区正在失去他们的功能性、传统作用和人口。城市历史景观方法可以协助管理和缓解这些影响。

发展

18. 经济繁荣为消除城市贫困和推动社会和人类发展提供了有效途径。更多创新的应用，例如信息技术和可持续规划、设计和建设创新，能够改善城市条件，提高生活质量。当运用城市历史景观方法合理地管理时，新的功能，例如服务和旅游，都是重要的经济首创，有利于社会福利、历史城市和其文化遗产的保护，同时确保经济和社会的多样性以及居住功能。未能抓住这些机会或者以不充分和不适当的方式利用这些机会，都将导致城市的不可持续和不宜居，对城市遗产资产造成破坏并给后代带来不可逆转的损失。

环境

19. 人类生活经常根据气候和环境变化而改变，包括那些由于灾祸导致的变化。然而，目前变化的强度和速度正在挑战我们复杂的城市环境。对环境，特别是对水和能源消耗的关切，呼唤城市生活的新方法和新模式。这种新方法和新模式要求实行对生态环境高度敏感和重视的改革，并以增强发展的可持续性和提升城市生活品质为目标。然而，上述举措必须与作为可持续发展重要资源的自然遗产和文化遗产相融合。

20. 对城市历史地区的改变同样来自于突然的灾祸和军事冲突。这些也许是短暂的，但是造成的后果可能持续很长时间。城市历史景观方法可以帮助管理和减轻这些影响。

Ⅲ. 政策

21. 反映在现有的国际建议和宪章之中的现代城市保护政策，为历史城市保护提供了舞台。然而，当前与未来面临的挑战要求确立和实施新一代公共政策，以对城市环境中的历史元素加以鉴别和保护，并保持其自然属性与文化价值之间的平衡。

22. 城市遗产的保护应当融合到总体的政策规划和实践以及与更广泛城市环境有关的规划和实践之中。政策应当为平衡短期和长期的保护以及保证可持续性提供机制。应当特别强调当代城市的发展须与城市的历史背景相和谐和融合，特别重视下述不同的利益相关人的责任：

（a）成员国应当根据城市历史景观方法将城市遗产保护策略融入到国家发展政策和计划之中。在此框架内，地方机关在制定城市发展规划时应当考虑各种地区性价值，包括景观和其他遗产价值，以及与此有关的特征；

（b）公共的和私人的利益相关人应当合作，并通过建立伙伴关系确保城市历史景观方法的成功适用；

（c）应对可持续发展问题的国际组织应当将城市历史景观方法融入到他们的政策、规划和行动之中；

（d）国内的和国际的非政府组织应当参与开发和推广运用城市历史景观方法的各种具体方式和手段，努力促进城市历史景观方法的实际应用。

23. 各级政府——地方基层的、区域的、中央/联邦的——均须意识到自己的责任，制定、宣传、执行和评估城市遗产保护政策。这些政策应当保证所有利益相关人的参与，并协调各方利益。

Ⅳ. 方法

24. 以城市历史景观为基础的方法是与地方背景相适应的一系列传统的和创新的方式方法的总称。其中一些方式方法旨在保证各利益相关方的参与并成为利益相关方参与程序的一部分。这类方法包括：

（a）市民参与方法。这类方法要求吸收跨部门的来自不同方面的利益相关方，授权他们确定其所在城市地区的关键价值，提出能够反映城市地区多样性的主张，设定保护城市遗产和促进可持续发展的目标，并就实现目标的具体方案和措施达成一致。市民参与方法作为保持城市管理活动的重要手段，应当通过尊重社区的历史、传统、价值、需要和追求，以及通过促成利益冲突各方之间的和解和妥协，来增进不同文化之间的对话。

（b）知识和规划方法。这类方法有助于保护城市遗产特性的真实性和完整性，有助于提高对文化的意义和文化多样性的认知，有助于对城市发展变化进行监控和管理，以改善城市空间和城市生活的质量。这些方法应当包括对文化和自然特征的记录和勘测。遗产、社会和环境影响评估应当用来支持和推进在可持续发展框架内的决策制定程序。

（c）管理制度。该制度应当反映地方状况，并包含旨在对具有社会、环境和文化价值的城市物质和非物质遗产进行保护和管理的立法和行政措施。必要时对相关传统或习俗性规则应予承认并强化其效力。

（d）经济方法。这一方法应当立足于传统，以提升能力和支持推陈出新的、赢利性开发为目的。除争取来自政府的资助和国际组织的全球性资助外，应当有效运用经济方法促进地方层面的私人投资。各种形式的经济合作、支持地方企业和小额贷款以及其他灵活的金融手段，对于保证城市历史景观方法在经济上具有可持续性同样至关重要。

Ⅴ. 能力建设、研究、信息和交流

25. 为了增进对历史性城市景观方法的理解和执行，能力建设应当涉及主要的利益相关人：社区、政策制定者、专家和管理者。有效的能力建设取决于这些主要利益相关人在制定和完善地方策略和目标、行动框架和资源使用方案，以及根据地方环境执行本建议时，积极开展合作。

26. 研究应当聚焦于城市生活复杂的一面，以挖掘社区的价值，促进对价值的认知，以及全面向游客展开这些价值为目标。应当鼓励学术科研机构，大学以及其他科研中心对城市历史景观方法进行研究，并在地方、国家、区域和国际等各个层次上开展合作。为对城市开发的各种建议和方案进行评估，改进保护与管理的技能和程序，必须将城市地区的现状及其发展变化情况以书面形式记录下来。

27. 鼓励使用信息和交流技术记录、阐述和展示城市地区及其组成部分的复杂性。数据的采集和分析是城市地区知识体系不可缺少的组成部分。为促进社会各个部分之间的交流，特别是为了鼓励青年和其他弱势群体的参与，加强对青年和弱势群体的研究尤为重要。

Ⅵ. 国际合作

28. 成员国、国际政府组织和非政府组织应当通过宣传世界各地的成功经验以及教训，深化公众对城市历史景观方法的认识，促进公众参与实施城市历史景观方法，以便强化知识共享和能力建设的网络。

29. 成员国应当促进地方机关间的跨国合作。

30. 应当鼓励成员国国内的国际开发和合作机构、各类非政府组织和基金会积极探索运用城市历史景观方法的各种方式和手段，并将其应用于他们与城市地区有关的辅助项目和计划。

术语定义

历史地区/城市（1976 年建议）

“历史和建筑（包括本地的）地区”是指包含考古和古生物遗址的任何建筑群、结构和空旷地，他们构成城乡环境中的人类居住地，从考古、建筑、史前史、历史、艺术和社会文化的角度看，其凝聚力和价值已经得到认可。在这些性质各异的“地区”中，可特别划分以下“各类”：史前遗址、历史城镇、老城区、老村庄、老村落以及相似的古迹群。不言而喻，后者通常应予以精心保存，维持不变。

历史城区（国际古迹遗址理事会《华盛顿宪章》）

历史城区，不论大小，其中包括城市、城镇以及历史中心或者居住区，也包括其自然和人造的环境。除了它们的历史文献作用之外，这些地区体现着传统的城市文化的价值。

城市遗产（欧盟研究报告第 16 号（2004），《通过城市间主动有效的整合实现城市历史地区的可持续发展》）

城市遗产包括下述三大主要种类：

具有突出文化价值的古迹遗产；

并无突出价值的遗产要素，但具有一致的形式而且元素丰富；

需要考虑的新城市因素（例如）：

——城市建筑形式；

——公共空间：街道、公共空地；

——城市基础设施：有形的网络和设备。

城市保护

城市保护不局限于对单一建筑的保护。它仅仅将建筑物视为城市总体环境中的一项要素。城市保护是一门内容复杂、涉及不同领域的学科。在定义上，城市保护是城市规划的中心。不过根据定义，城市保护是城市规划的核心。

建筑环境

建筑环境是指人造的（相对自然形成的）资源和基础设施，用于支持人类活动，例如建筑物、道路、公园和其他福利设施。

景观方法（国际自然保护联盟和世界自然基金会）

景观方法是一个制定景观级别保护决定的框架。景观方法帮助达成关于特别介入（例如新道路或者种植园）的可取性的决定，促进全景观范围内的规划、协商和活动的执行。

城市历史景观（见本建议第9小节的定义）

环境（国际古迹遗址理事会西安宣言）

古建筑、遗址和历史区域的周边环境是指紧靠古建筑、遗址和历史区域的和延伸的、影响其重要性和独特性或者是重要性和独特性组成部分的周围环境。

文化意义（国际古迹遗址理事会澳大利亚波拉宪章）

文化意义是指对过去、现在和将来世代的人具有美学、历史、科学、社会或者精神方面的价值。文化意义体现于地点自身，以及它的结构、环境、用途、联系、内涵、记录以及相关地点和相关物品之中。对不同的个体或者群体而言，地点可能有不同的价值。

Recommendation on the Historic Urban Landscape

UNESCO, 10 November 2011

Preamble

The General Conference,

Considering that historic urban areas are among the most abundant and diverse manifestations of our common cultural heritage, shaped by generations and constituting a key testimony to humankind's endeavours and aspirations through space and time,

Also considering that urban heritage is for humanity a social, cultural and economic asset, defined by an historic layering of values that have been produced by successive and existing cultures and an accumulation of traditions and experiences, recognized as such in their diversity,

Further considering that urbanization is proceeding on an unprecedented scale in the history of humankind, and that throughout the world this is driving socio-economic change and growth, which should be harnessed at the local, national, regional and international levels,

Recognizing, the dynamic nature of living cities,

Noting, however, that rapid and frequently uncontrolled development is transforming urban areas and their settings, which may cause fragmentation and deterioration to urban heritage with deep impacts on community values, throughout the world,

Considering, therefore, that in order to support the protection of natural and cultural heritage, emphasis needs to be put on the integration of historic urban area conservation, management and planning strategies into local development processes and urban planning, such as, contemporary architecture and infrastructure development, for which the application of a landscape approach would help maintain urban identity,

Also considering that the principle of sustainable development provides for the preservation of existing resources, the active protection of urban heritage and its sustainable management is a condition sine qua non of development,

Recalling that a corpus of UNESCO standard - setting documents, including conventions, recommendations and charters [1] exists on the subject of the conservation of historic areas, all of which remain valid,

Also noting, however, that under processes of demographic shifts, global market liberalization and decentralization, as well as mass tourism, market exploitation of heritage, and climate change, conditions have changed and cities are subject to development pressures and challenges not present at the time of adoption of the most recent UNESCO recommendation on historic areas in 1976 (Recommendation concerning the Safeguarding and Contemporary Role of Historic Areas),

Further noting the evolution of the concepts of culture and heritage and of the approaches to their management, through the combined action of local initiatives and international meetings [2], which have been useful in guiding policies and practices worldwide,

Desiring to supplement and extend the application of the standards and principles laid down in existing international instruments,

Having before it proposals concerning the historic urban landscape as an approach to urban heritage conservation, which appear on the agenda of the 36th session of the General Conference as item 8. 1,

Having decided at its 35th session that this issue should be addressed by means of a recommendation to Member States,

1. *Adopts*, this 10th day of November 2011, the present Recommendation on the Historic Urban Landscape;

2. *Recommends* that Member States adopt the appropriate legislative institutional framework and measures, with a view to applying the principles and norms set out in this Recommendation in the territories under their jurisdiction;

3. *Also recommends* that Member States bring this Recommendation to the at-

tention of the local, national and regional authorities, and of institutions, services or bodies and associations concerned with the safeguarding, conservation and management of historic urban areas and their wider geographical settings.

Introduction

1. Our time is witness to the largest human migration in history. More than half of the world's population now lives in urban areas. Urban areas are increasingly important as engines of growth and as centres of innovation and creativity; they provide opportunities for employment and education and respond to people's evolving needs and aspirations.

2. Rapid and uncontrolled urbanization, however, may frequently result in social and spatial fragmentation and in a drastic deterioration of the quality of the urban environment and of the surrounding rural areas. Notably, this may be due to excessive building density, standardized and monotonous buildings, loss of public space and amenities, inadequate infrastructure, debilitating poverty, social isolation, and an increasing risk of climate - related disasters.

3. Urban heritage, including its tangible and intangible components, constitutes a key resource in enhancing the liveability of urban areas, and fosters economic development and social cohesion in a changing global environment. As the future of humanity hinges on the effective planning and management of resources, conservation has become a strategy to achieve a balance between urban growth and quality of life on a sustainable basis.

4. In the course of the past half century, urban heritage conservation has emerged as an important sector of public policy worldwide. It is a response to the need to preserve shared values and to benefit from the legacy of history. However, the shift from an emphasis on architectural monuments primarily towards a broader recognition of the importance of the social, cultural and economic processes in the conservation of urban values, should be matched by a drive to adapt the existing policies and to create new tools to address this vision.

5. This Recommendation addresses the need to better integrate and frame urban heritage conservation strategies within the larger goals of overall sustainable development, in order to support public and private actions aimed at preserving

and enhancing the quality of the human environment. It suggests a landscape approach for identifying, conserving and managing historic areas within their broader urban contexts, by considering the interrelationships of their physical forms, their spatial organization and connection, their natural features and settings, and their social, cultural and economic values.

6. This approach addresses the policy, governance and management concerns involving a variety of stakeholders, including local, national, regional, international, public and private actors in the urban development process.

7. This Recommendation builds upon the four previous UNESCO recommendations concerning heritage preservation, and recognizes the importance and the validity of their concepts and principles in the history and practice of conservation. In addition, modern conservation conventions and charters address the many dimensions of cultural and natural heritage, and constitute the foundations of this Recommendation.

I. Definition

8. The historic urban landscape is the urban area understood as the result of a historic layering of cultural and natural values and attributes, extending beyond the notion of "historic centre" or "ensemble" to include the broader urban context and its geographical setting.

9. This wider context includes notably the site's topography, geomorphology, hydrology and natural features, its built environment, both historic and contemporary, its infrastructures above and below ground, its open spaces and gardens, its land use patterns and spatial organization, perceptions and visual relationships, as well as all other elements of the urban structure. It also includes social and cultural practices and values, economic processes and the intangible dimensions of heritage as related to diversity and identity.

10. This definition provides the basis for a comprehensive and integrated approach for the identification, assessment, conservation and management of historic urban landscapes within an overall sustainable development framework.

11. The historic urban landscape approach is aimed at preserving the quality of the human environment, enhancing the productive and sustainable use of urban spaces, while recognizing their dynamic character, and promoting social and func-

tional diversity. It integrates the goals of urban heritage conservation and those of social and economic development. It is rooted in a balanced and sustainable relationship between the urban and natural environment, between the needs of present and future generations and the legacy from the past.

12. The historic urban landscape approach considers cultural diversity and creativity as key assets for human, social and economic development, and provides tools to manage physical and social transformations and to ensure that contemporary interventions are harmoniously integrated with heritage in a historic setting and take into account regional contexts.

13. The historic urban landscape approach learns from the traditions and perceptions of local communities, while respecting the values of the national and international communities.

II. Challenges and opportunities for the historic urban landscape

14. The existing UNESCO recommendations recognize the important role of historic areas in modern societies. These recommendations also identify a number of specific threats to the conservation of historic urban areas, and provide general principles, policies and guidelines to meet such challenges.

15. The historic urban landscape approach reflects the fact that both the discipline and practice of urban heritage conservation have evolved significantly in recent decades, enabling policy - makers and managers to deal more effectively with new challenges and opportunities. The historic urban landscape approach supports communities in their quest for development and adaptation, while retaining the characteristics and values linked to their history and collective memory, and to the environment.

16. In the past decades, owing to the sharp increase in the world's urban population, the scale and speed of development, and the changing economy, urban settlements and their historic areas have become centres and drivers of economic growth in many regions of the world, and have taken on a new role in cultural and social life. As a result, they have also come under a large array of new pressures, including:

Urbanization and globalization

17. Urban growth is transforming the essence of many historic urban areas. Global processes have a deep impact on the values attributed by communities to urban areas and their settings, and on the perceptions and realities of their inhabitants and users. On the one hand, urbanization provides economic, social and cultural opportunities that can enhance the quality of life and traditional character of urban areas; on the other hand, the unmanaged changes in urban density and growth can undermine the sense of place, the integrity of the urban fabric, and the identity of communities. Some historic urban areas are losing their functionality, traditional role and populations. The historic urban landscape approach may assist in managing and mitigating such impacts.

Development

18. Many economic processes offer ways and means to alleviate urban poverty and to promote social and human development. The greater availability of innovations, such as information technology and sustainable planning, design and building practices, can improve urban areas, thus enhancing the quality of life. When properly managed through the historic urban landscape approach, new functions, such as services and tourism, are important economic initiatives that can contribute to the well - being of the communities and to the conservation of historic urban areas and their cultural heritage while ensuring economic and social diversity and the residential function. Failing to capture these opportunities leads to unsustainable and unviable cities, just as implementing them in an inadequate and inappropriate manner results in the destruction of heritage assets and irreplaceable losses for future generations.

Environment

19. Human settlements have constantly adapted to climatic and environmental changes, including those resulting from disasters. However, the intensity and

speed of present changes are challenging our complex urban environments. Concern for the environment, in particular for water and energy consumption, calls for approaches and new models for urban living, based on ecologically sensitive policies and practices aimed at strengthening sustainability and the quality of urban life. Many of these initiatives, however, should integrate natural and cultural heritage as resources for sustainable development.

20. Changes to historic urban areas can also result from sudden disasters and armed conflicts. These may be short lived but can have lasting effects. The historic urban landscape approach may assist in managing and mitigating such impacts.

III. Policies

21. Modern urban conservation policies, as reflected in existing international recommendations and charters, have set the stage for the preservation of historic urban areas. However, present and future challenges require the definition and implementation of a new generation of public policies identifying and protecting the historic layering and balance of cultural and natural values in urban environments.

22. Conservation of the urban heritage should be integrated into general policy planning and practices and those related to the broader urban context. Policies should provide mechanisms for balancing conservation and sustainability in the short and long terms. Special emphasis should be placed on the harmonious, integration of contemporary interventions into the historic urban fabric. In particular, the responsibilities of the different stakeholders are the following:

(a) Member States should integrate urban heritage conservation strategies into national development policies and agendas according to the historic urban landscape approach. Within this framework, local authorities should prepare urban development plans taking into account the area's values, including the landscape and other heritage values, and features associated therewith;

(b) Public and private stakeholders should cooperate, inter alia, through partnerships to ensure the successful application of the historic urban landscape approach;

(c) International organizations dealing with sustainable development processes should integrate the historic urban landscape approach into their strategies, plans and operations;

(d) National and international non - governmental organizations should participate in developing and disseminating tools and best practices for the implementation of the historic urban landscape approach.

23. All levels of government - local, regional, national/federal, - aware of their responsibility - should contribute to the definition, elaboration, implementation and assessment of urban heritage conservation policies. These policies should be based on a participatory approach by all stakeholders and coordinated from both the institutional and sectorial viewpoints.

IV. Tools

24. The approach based on the historic urban landscape implies the application of a range of traditional and innovative tools adapted to local contexts. Some of these tools, which need to be developed as part of the process involving the different stakeholders, might include:

(a) Civic engagement tools should involve a diverse cross - section of stakeholders, and empower them to identify key values in their urban areas, develop visions that reflect their diversity, set goals, and agree on actions to safeguard their heritage and promote sustainable development. These tools, which constitute an integral part of urban governance dynamics, should facilitate intercultural dialogue by learning from communities about their histories, traditions, values, needs and aspirations, and by facilitating mediation and negotiation between groups with conflicting interests.

(b) Knowledge and planning tools should help protect the integrity and authenticity of the attributes of urban heritage. They should also allow for the recognition of cultural significance and diversity, and provide for the monitoring and management of change to improve the quality of life and of urban space. These tools would include documentation and mapping of cultural and natural characteristics. Heritage, social and environmental impact assessments should be used to support and facilitate decision - making processes within a framework of sustainable development.

(c) Regulatory systems should reflect local conditions, and may include legislative and regulatory measures aimed at the conservation and management of the tangible and intangible attributes of the urban heritage, including their social, environmental and cultural values. Traditional and customary systems should be recognized and reinforced as necessary.

(d) Financial tools should be aimed at building capacities and supporting innovative income - generating development, rooted in tradition. In addition to government and global funds from international agencies, financial tools should be effectively employed to foster private investment at the local level. Micro - credit and other flexible financing to support local enterprise, as well as a variety of models of partnerships, are also central to making the historic urban landscape approach financially sustainable.

V. Capacity – building, research, information and communication

25. Capacity - building should involve the main stakeholders: communities, decision - makers, and professionals and managers, in order to foster understanding of the historic urban landscape approach and its implementation. Effective capacity - building hinges on an active collaboration of these main stakeholders, aimed at adapting the implementation of this Recommendation to regional contexts in order to define and refine the local strategies and objectives, action frameworks and resource mobilization schemes.

26. Research should target the complex layering of urban settlements, in order to identify values, understand their meaning for the communities, and present them to visitors in a comprehensive manner. Academic and university institutions and other centres of research should be encouraged to develop scientific research on aspects of the historic urban landscape approach, and cooperate at the local, national, regional and international level. It is essential to document the state of urban areas and their evolution, to facilitate the evaluation of proposals for change, and to improve protective and managerial skills and procedures.

27. Encourage the use of information and communication technology to document, understand and present the complex layering of urban areas and their constituent components. The collection and analysis of this data is an essential part of the knowledge of urban areas. To communicate with all sectors of society, it is particularly important to reach out to youth and all under - represented groups in order to encourage their participation.

VI. International cooperation

28. Member States and international governmental and non - governmental organizations should facilitate public understanding and involvement in the implementation of the historic urban landscape approach, by disseminating best practices and lessons learned from different parts of the world, in order to strengthen the network of knowledge - sharing and capacity - building.

29. Member States should promote multinational cooperation between local authorities.

30. International development and cooperation agencies of Member States, non - governmental organizations and foundations should be encouraged to develop methodologies which take into account the historic urban landscape approach and to harmonize them with their assistance programmes and projects pertaining to urban areas.

APPENDIX

Glossary of definitions

Historic area/city (from the 1976 Recommendation)

"Historic and architectural (including vernacular) areas" shall be taken to mean any groups of buildings, structures and open spaces including archaeological and palaeontological sites, constituting human settlements in an urban or rural environment, the cohesion and value of which, from the archaeological, architectural, prehistoric, historic, aesthetic or sociocultural point of view are recognized. Among these "areas", which are very varied in nature, it is possible to distinguish the following in particular: prehistoric sites, historic towns, old urban quarters, villages and hamlets as well as homogeneous monumental groups, it being understood that the latter should as a rule be carefully preserved unchanged.

Historic urban area (from the ICOMOS Washington Charter)

Historic urban areas, large and small, include cities, towns and historic centres or quarters, together with their natural and man - made environments. Beyond their role as historical documents, these areas embody the values of traditional urban cultures.

Urban heritage (from European Union research report No 16 (2004), Sustainable development of Urban historical areas through and active Integration within Towns - SUIT)

Urban heritage comprises three main categories:

Monumental heritage of exceptional cultural value;

Non - exceptional heritage elements but present in a coherent way with a relative abundance;

New urban elements to be considered (for instance):

o The urban built form;

o The open space: streets, public open spaces;

o Urban infrastructures: material networks and equipments.

Urban conservation

Urban conservation is not limited to the preservation of single buildings. It views architecture as but one element of the overall urban setting, making it a complex and multifaceted discipline. By definition, then, urban conservation lies at the very heart of urban planning.

Built environment

The built environment refers to human - made (versus natural) resources and infrastructure designed to support human activity, such as buildings, roads, parks, and other amenities.

Landscape approach (from the International Union for Conservation of Nature - IUCN, and the World Wildlife Fund - WWF)

The landscape approach is a framework for making landscape - level conservation decisions. The landscape approach helps to reach decisions about the advisability of particular interventions (such as a new road or plantation), and to facilitate the planning, negotiation and implementation of activities across a whole landscape.

Historic urban landscape

(see definition in paragraph 9 of the Recommendation)

Setting (from the ICOMOS Xi' an Declaration)

The setting of a heritage structure, site or area is defined as the immediate and extended environment that is part of, or contributes to, its significance and distinctive character.

Cultural significance (from the ICOMOS Australia Burra Charter)

Cultural significance means aesthetic, historic, scientific, social or spiritual value for past, present or future generations. Cultural significance is embodied in the place itself, its fabric, setting, use, associations, meanings, records, related places and related objects. Places may have a range of values for different individuals or groups.

Notes:

[1] In particular, the 1972 Convention concerning the Protection of the World Cultural and Natural Heritage, the 2005 Convention on the Protection and Promotion of the Diversity of Cultural Expressions, the 1962 Recommendation concerning the Safeguarding of the Beauty and Character of Landscapes and Sites, the 1968 Recommendation concerning the Preservation of Cultural Property Endangered by Public or Private Works, the 1972 Recommendation concerning the Protection, at National Level, of the Cultural and Natural Heritage, the 1976 Recommendation concerning the Safeguarding and Contemporary Role of Historic Areas, the 1964 ICOMOS International Charter for the Conservation and Restoration of Monuments and Sites (Venice Charter), the 1982 ICOMOS Historic Gardens (Florence Charter), and the 1987 ICOMOS Charter for the Conservation of Historic Towns and Urban Areas (Washington Charter), the 2005 ICOMOS Xi' an Declaration on the Conservation of the Setting of Heritage Structures, Sites and Areas, as well as the 2005 Vienna Memorandum on World Heritage and Contemporary Architecture - Managing the Historic Urban Landscape.

[2] In particular the 1982 World Conference on Cultural Policies in Mexico City, the 1994 Nara Meeting on Authenticity, the 1995 summit of the World Commission on Culture and Development, the 1996 HABITAT II Conference in Istanbul with ratification of Agenda 21, the 1998 UNESCO Intergovernmental Conference on Cultural Policies for Development in Stockholm, the 1998 joint World Bank - UNESCO Conference on Culture in Sustainable Development - Investing in Cultural and Natural Endowments, the 2005 International Conference on World Heritage and Contemporary Architecture in Vienna, the 2005 ICOMOS General Assembly on the Setting of Monuments and Sites in Xi' an, and the 2008 ICOMOS General Assembly on the Spirit of Place in Québec.

关于保护传统文化和民俗的建议*

（联合国教科文组织大会1989年11月15日通过）

联合国教育、科学与文化组织于1989年10月17日至11月16日在巴黎召开第25次大会：

考虑到民俗构成世界人类遗产的一部分，是把不同民族和社会群体团结到一起并彰显其文化独特性的强有力方式；

注意到民俗的社会、经济、文化和政治重要性，及其在人类历史中的作用和在当代文化中的地位；

强调作为文化遗产和活着的文化组成部分的民俗的特殊属性和重要性；

认识到传统形式的民俗，尤其是口口相传方式传承的民俗的极度脆弱性，以及民俗可能失传的风险；

强调所有国家有必要认识到民俗的作用及其面临的多方面的危险；

认为政府应当在保护民俗上起到决定性的作用并且应当尽快行动；

鉴于本组织已在第24次大会上决定，民俗的保护应当依照本组织成员国根据本组织章程第4条第4款提出的建议进行；

兹于1989年11月15日通过本建议。

大会建议，成员国应采取各自宪法或宪法实践的要求的立法措施或其他步骤实施下述有关保护民俗的规定，确保本建议规定的原则和措施在各自领土上生效。

大会建议，成员国应将本建议传达于其国内负责民俗保护的机关、部门或团体，以及与民俗相关的各类组织和机构，并鼓励它们与涉及民俗保护的相关国际组织沟通。

大会建议，成员国应以大会规定的方式、在大会规定的时间内，向本组织提交其采取措施使本建议在其国内生效的报告。

---

* 西南政法大学法学院汪梦译。

一、民俗的定义

为了本建议的目的：

民俗（或者传统和流行文化）是指以传统为基础、通过团体或个人的行为表现出来、反映社会愿望、表明社会文化特性和身份认同的、社会文化创造的统称。民俗的标准和价值，通过模仿或其他形式，以口头方式传承。民俗的表现形式有语言、文学、音乐、舞蹈、游戏、神话、仪式、习俗、手工艺品、建筑和其他艺术等。

二、民俗的识别

作为文化表现形式之一的民俗，其保护应当通过民俗所寄托并反映其社会特性的群体（家庭的、职业的、全国性的、地方性的、宗教的、民族的，等等），并为这些群体的利益而实施。为此，成员国应鼓励在国家、地方、国际等不同层面上开展适当的调查研究，以便：

（a）编撰全国范围内涉民俗组织机构名册，以使本国的民俗机构被纳入地区或全球民俗及民俗组织名录；

（b）创建识别和记录制度（收集信息、分类和抄录），或者改进和完善已存在于各种手册、信息采集指南、标准目录之中的相关制度，以对不同组织机构所采用的不同的分类体系加以协调；

（c）推动创建有关民俗的标准分类体系，以供下述目的之用：

（i）作为供全球使用的民俗要览；

（ii）对民俗全面登记注册；

（iii）为形成民俗的地方性分类，特别是为实施有关实地开展的试点项目提供指引。

三、民俗的保存

保存是指将民间传统以书面形式记录下来，其目的在于，一旦某民间传统不再在现实生活中得到应用或者发生变化，关于民间传统的书面记录可使研究人员以及传统的继受者获得了解该传统演变过程的数据。尽管现实生活中存在的活的民俗，因其具有不断演进的特点，不能总是被直接保护，但已经以物质形式固化下来的民俗应当受到有效保护。为此，成员国应当：

（a）设立若干国家民俗档案馆，以妥善保存收集到的民俗资料，并使其方便借阅；

（b）基于服务目的，设立国家民俗档案中心，在对民俗资料分类编目、通报信息以及制定民俗工作标准，包括民俗保护标准等方面行使中心职能，发挥中心作用；

（c）成立民俗博物馆或者在现有博物馆内设立民俗展区以展示传统和流行文化；

（d）在展示传统文化和流行文化时，优先考虑展示能够突出其时代特征或历史成就方面的内容（显示文化的发展环境、生活方式以及该文化所产生的作品、技能和技术）；

（e）协调信息采集与文档处理的各种方法；

（f）培训从实物保存到从事分析工作的各种民俗保存工作者，如信息采集员、档案保管员、记录员和其他专业人士；

（g）创造条件使民俗资料能够得到安全保管，制作民俗资料的副本，并向有关地方组织提供，以使文化社团能够借阅或获得相关民俗资料。

四、民俗的维护

维护是指对民俗传统和其传播人的保护。鉴于每一人群都享有拥有自身文化的权利，而人们对其群体文化的依附常常受到大众媒体营造的产业化文化影响的侵蚀，必须采取措施，在产生民俗文化的社区内外，对民间传统的地位，及其延续所需要的经济支撑给予保障。为此，成员国应当：

（a）以适当方式设计和引入民俗教学课程，使之成正式课堂教学和校外学习的内容。民俗课程教学的重点特别应当放在对最广泛意义上的民俗给予应有的尊重上。民俗课程的教学不仅要考虑乡村文化以及其他农村地区的文化，而且还应将城市地区由不同社会团体、职业群体或组织机构等创造的民间文化纳入其中，以促进人们更好地认识和理解文化的多样性、世界上的不同观点，特别是那些不为主流文化所接纳的观点；

（b）通过支持不同文化群体的成员参与民间传统的实践、以及从事民俗文化的记录、档案管理和研究等工作，保障其感受和接触自身民俗文化的权利；

（c）建立一个跨学科的、名为“国家民俗理事会”的机构或其他类似协调机构，使不同利益团体都能在该机构中有自己的代表；

(d) 为个人或机构学习、推广、培育和掌握民俗文化提供道义上或经济上的支持；

(e) 促进有关民俗保护的科学研究。

五、民俗的传播

人们应当认识到民俗作为文化认同组成部分的重要性。有必要广泛传播组成文化遗产的部分以使得民俗的价值和保护的必要性得到承认。然而，应当避免传播中的扭曲以保护传统的完整性。为了促进公平传播，成员国应当：

(a) 鼓励组织国内的、区域的和国际的诸如集市、节日、影片、展览、研讨会、专题研讨会、讨论会、培训课程、大会等活动，支持资料、论文和其他成果的传播和发表；

(b) 通过资助、在大众媒体设立民俗工作者岗位、确保大众媒体收集的民俗资料得到妥善保管和适当传播，以及在大众传媒内部设立民俗机构等方式，鼓励全国性和地方性出版社、报纸杂志社、广播电视以及其他媒体更多地登载或播出民俗方面的内容；

(c) 鼓励地区、城市以及从事民俗工作的协会或其他组织为民俗工作者设立全职岗位，以激励和协调本区域内的民俗活动；

(d) 支持现有部门或成立新的部门，以近期的实地调研为基础，制作视频电影等教育资料，并鼓励学校、民俗博物馆、国家或国际民俗节和展览会使用这些资料；

(e) 确保通过文献中心、图书馆、博物馆、档案馆，以及特定的民俗简报和期刊能够获得有关民俗的充分信息；

(f) 根据双边文化协议，促进有关民俗的个人、群体和机构间的国内的和国际的会议和交流；

(g) 鼓励国际科研机构制定职业道德规范以保证其采用正确的方法研究传统文化、尊重传统文化。

六、民俗的保护

民俗显示了个人和集体智力创造的成果。在这个意义上，民俗完全可以采用知识产权保护的原理和方式加以保护。在不损害其他相关合法权益的前提下，把民俗当作知识产权加以保护，是在一国国内外推动民俗各种表现形式不断发展、不断加强对民俗的维护以及扩大民俗传播的不可或缺的必要手段。除知识产权保护外，在民俗的文献中心和档案馆，民俗还有其他多种已经受到法律保护的权利，未来这些权利应继续得到法律的保护。为此，成员国应当：

（a）在民俗涉及知识产权的方面，要求相关机构关注世界知识产权组织以及联合国教科文组织所做的关于保护知识产权的重要工作，同时确认，知识产权保护仅仅是民俗保护的一个方面，为保护民俗，迫切需要在若干领域采取其他保护措施；

（b）考虑其他相关权利：

（ⅰ）保护身为传统传承者的举报人（保护隐私和秘密）；

（ⅱ）通过确保使收集到的民俗资料在档案馆里以正确的方式得到妥善保管，来保护资料收集人的利益；

（ⅲ）采取适当措施，保护收集到的民俗资料不被滥用，不管这种滥用是否故意或出自其他原因；

（ⅳ）确认档案馆对其收藏的民俗资料的使用负有监管责任。

七、国际合作

为了加强文化合作和交流，特别是通过人力和物质资源的共享加强合作和交流；为了执行民俗发展和振兴项目以及方便由某一成员国国籍的专业人士在另一成员国领土上进行有关民俗的研究，成员国应当：

（a）与有关民俗的国际和区域协会、机构和组织开展合作；

（b）在民俗的知识、传播和保护领域进行合作，特别通过：

（ⅰ）各种信息的交流，以及科学和技术出版物的交流；

（ⅱ）培训专业人士，提供旅行资助，派出科技人员和设备；

（ⅲ）在当代民俗的文献记载领域推广双边或者多边项目；

（ⅳ）组织专业人士间的会议、研究课程和特定主题的研讨会，特别是有关民俗数据和表现形式的分类和编目以及现代研究方法和技术方面的研讨会；

（c）密切合作以确保国际上的不同利益方（团体或者自然人、法人）享有从民俗的调查、创制、构成、表演、录制或者传播中产生的经济权利、道德权利和所谓的相邻权利；

（d）保障在其领土上开展研究的成员国有权从相关成员国获得全部有关文件、记录、视频、影像和其他资料的副本；

（e）避免可能对民俗资料造成损害、减少其价值、阻止其传播或者使用的活动，无论这些资料是否在本国国土或者其他国家的领土上被发现；

（f）采取必要措施保护民俗免受所有人类和自然的损害，包括来自于武装冲突、领土占领或者其他种类公共骚乱的威胁。

Recommendation on the Safeguarding of Traditional Culture and Folklore

15 November 1989

The General Conference of the United Nations Educational, Scientific and Cultural Organization, meeting in Paris from 17 October to 16 November 1989 at its twenty - fifth session,

Considering that folklore forms part of the universal heritage of humanity and that it is a powerful means of bringing together different peoples and social groups and of asserting their cultural identity,

Noting its social, economic, cultural and political importance, its role in the history of the people, and its place in contemporary culture,

Underlining the specific nature and importance of folklore as an integral part of cultural heritage and living culture,

Recognizing the extreme fragility of the traditional forms of folklore, particularly those aspects relating to oral tradition and the risk that they might be lost,

Stressing the need in all countries for recognition of the role of folklore and the danger it faces from multiple factors,

Judging that the governments should play a decisive role in the safeguarding of folklore and that they should act as quickly as possible,

Having decided, at its twenty - fourth session, that the safeguarding of folklore should be the subject of a recommendation to Member States within the meaning of Article IV, paragraph 4, of the Constitution,

Adopts the present Recommendation this fifteenth day of November 1989:

The General Conference recommends that Member States should apply the following provisions concerning the safeguarding of folklore by taking whatever legislative measures or other steps may be required in conformity with the constitutional practice of each State to give effect within their territories to the principles and measures defined in this Recommendation.

The General Conference recommends that Member States bring this Recommendation to the attention of the authorities, departments or bodies responsible for matters relating to the safeguarding of folklore and to the attention of the various organizations or institutions concerned with folklore, and encourage their contacts with appropriate international organizations dealing with the safeguarding of folklore.

The General Conference recommends that Member States should, at such times and in such manner as it shall determine, submit to the Organization reports on the action they have taken to give effect to this recommendation.

A. Definition of folklore

For purposes of this Recommendation:

Folklore (or traditional and popular culture) is the totality of tradition - based creations of a cultural community, expressed by a group or individuals and recognized as reflecting the expectations of a community in so far as they reflect its cultural and social identity; its standards and values are transmitted orally, by imitation or by other means. Its forms are, among others, language, literature, music, dance, games, mythology, rituals, customs, handicrafts, architecture and other arts.

B. Identification of folklore

Folklore, as a form of cultural expression, must be safeguarded by and for the group (familial, occupational, national, regional, religious, ethnic, etc.) whose identity it expresses. To this end, Member States should encourage appropriate survey research on national, regional and international levels with the aim to:

(a) develop a national inventory of institutions concerned with folklore with a view to its inclusion in regional and global registers of folklore, institutions;

(b) create identification and recording systems (collection, cataloguing, transcription) or develop those that already exist by way of handbooks, collecting guides, model catalogues, etc., in view of the need to co ordinate the classification systems used by different institutions;

(c) stimulate the creation of a standard typology of folklore by way of:

(i) a general outline of folklore for global use;

(ii) a comprehensive register of folklore; and

(iii) regional classification of folklore, especially field - work pilot projects.

C. Conservation of folklore

Conservation is concerned with documentation regarding folk traditions and its object is, in the event of the non - utilization or evolution' of such traditions, to give researchers and tradition - bearers access to data enabling them to understand the process through which tradition changes. While living folklore, owing to its evolving character, cannot always be directly protected, folklore that has been fixed in a tangible form should be effectively protected. To this end, ' Member States should:

(a) establish national archives where collected folklore can be properly stored and made available;

(b) establish a central national archive function for service purposes (central cataloguing, dissemination of information on folklore materials and standards of folklore work including the aspect of safeguarding);

(c) create museums or folklore sections at existing museums where traditional and popular culture can be exhibited;

(d) give precedence to ways of presenting traditional and popular cultures that emphasize the living or past aspects of those cultures (showing their surroundings, ways of life and the works, skills and techniques they have produced);

(e) harmonize collecting and archiving methods;

(f) train collectors, archivists, documentalists and other specialists in the conservation of folklore, from physical conservation to analytic work;

(g) provide means for making security and working copies of all folklore materials, and copies for regional institutions, thus securing the cultural community an access to the materials.

D. Preservation of folklore

Preservation is concerned with protection of folk traditions and those who are the transmitters, having regard to the fact that each people has a right to its own culture and that its adherence to that culture is often eroded by the impact of the industrialized culture purveyed by the mass media. Measures must be taken to guarantee the status of and economic support for folk traditions both in the communities which produce them beyond. To this end, Member States should:

(a) design and introduce into both formal and out - of - school curricula the teaching and study of folklore in an appropriate manner laying particular emphasis on respect for folklore in the widest sense of the term, taking into account not only village and other rural cultures but also those created in urban areas by diverse social groups, professions, institutions, etc., and thus promoting a better understanding of cultural diversity and different world views, especially those not reflected in dominant cultures;

(b) guarantee the right of access of various cultural communities to their own folklore by supporting their work in the fields of documentation, archiving, research, etc., as well as in the practice of traditions;

(c) set up on an interdisciplinary basis a National Folklore Council or similar co - ordinating body in which various interest groups will be represented;

(d) provide moral and economic support for individuals and institutions studying, making known, cultivating or holding items of folklore;

(e) promote scientific research relevant to the preservation of folklore.

E. Dissemination of folklore

The attention of people should be drawn to the importance of folklore as an ingredient of cultural identity. It is essential for the items that make up this cultural heritage to be widely disseminated so that the value of folklore and the need to preserve it can be recognized. However, distortion during dissemination should be avoided so that the integrity of the traditions can be safeguarded. To promote a fair dissemination, Member States should:

(a) encourage the organization of national, regional and international events such as fairs, festivals, films, exhibitions, seminars, symposia,. workshops, training courses, congresses, etc., and support the dissemination and publication of their materials, papers and other results;

(b) encourage a broader coverage of folklore material in national and regional press, publishing houese television, radio and other media, for instance through grants, by creating jobs for folklorists in these units, by ensuring the proper archiving and dissemination of these folklore materials collected by the mass media, and by the establishment of departments of folklore within those organizations;

(c) encourage regions, minicipalities, associations and other groups working in folklore to establish full - time jobs for folklorists to stimulate and co - ordinate folklore activities in the region;

(d) support existing units and the creation of new units for the production of educational materials, as for example video films based on recent fieldwork, and encourage their use in schools, folklore museums, national and international folklore festivals and exhibitions;

(e) ensure the availability of adequate information on folklore through documentation centers, libraries, museums, archives, as well as through special folklore bulletins and periodicals;

(f) facilitate meetings and exchanges between individuals, groups and institutions concerned with folklore, both nationally and internationally, taking into acount bilateral cultural agreements;

(g) encourage the international scientific community to adopt a code of ethics ensuring a proper approach to and respect for traditional cultures.

F. Protection of folklore

In so far as folklore constitues manifestations of intellectual creativity whether it be individual or collective, it deserves to be protected in a manner inspired by the protection provided for intellectual productions. Such protection of folklore has become indispensable as a means of promoting further development, maintenance and dissemination of those expressions, - both within and outside the country, without prejudice to related legitimate interests. Leaving aside the `intellectual property aspects' of the protection of expressions of folklore, there are various categories of rights which are already protected and should continue' to enjoy protection in the future in folklore documentation centers and archives. To this end, Member States should:

(a) regarding the `intellectual property' aspects call the attention of relevant authorities - to the important work of UNESCO and WIPO in relation to intellectual property, while recognizing that this work relates to only one aspect of folklore protection and that the need for separate action in a range of areas to safeguard folklore is urgent;

(b) regarding the other rights involved:

(i) protect the informant as the transmitter of tradition (protection of privacy and confidentiality);

(ii) protect the interest of the collector by ensuring that the materials gathered are conserved in archives in good condition and in a methodical manner;

(iii) adopt the necessary measures to safeguard the materials gathered against misuse, whether intentional or otherwise;

(iv) recognize the responsibility of archives to monitor the use made of the materials gathered.

G. International co – operation

In view of the need to intensify cultural co - operation and exchanges, in particular through the pooling of human and material resources, in order to carry out folklore development and revitalization programmes as well as research made by specialists who are the nationals of one Member State on the territory of another Member State, Member States should:

(a) co - operate with international and regional associations, institutions and organizations concerned with folklore;

(b) co - operate in the field of knowledge, dissemination and protection of folklore, in particular through:

(i) exchanges of information of every kind, exchanges of scientific and technical publications;

(ii) training of specialists, awarding of travel grants, sending of scientific and technical personnel and equipment;

(iii) the promotion of bilateral or multilateral projects in the field of the documentation of contemporary folklore;

(iv) the organization of meetings between specialists, of study courses and of working groups on particular subjects, especially on the classifying and cataloguing of folklore data and expressions and on modern methods and techniques in research;

(c) co - operate closely so as to ensure internationally that the various interested parties (communities or natural or legal persons) enjoy the economic, moral and so - called neighbouring rights resulting from the investigation, creation, composition, performance, recording and/or dissemination of folklore;

(d) guarantee Member States on whose territory research has been carried out the right to obtain from the Member States concerned, copies of all' documents, recordings, video - films, films and other material;

(e) refrain from acts likely to damage folklore materials or to diminish their value or impede their dissemination or use, whether these materials are to be found on their own territory or on the territory of other States;

(f) take necessary measures to safeguard folklore against all human and natural dangers to which it is exposed, including the risks deriving from armed conflicts, occupation of territories, or public disorders of other kinds.

关于保护和保存动态影像的建议*

（联合国教科文组织大会1980年10月27日通过）

联合国教育、科学和文化组织于1980年9月23日至10月28日在贝尔格莱德召开第21次大会：

鉴于动态影像是人们文化认同的体现。因其具有教育、文化、艺术、科学和历史价值，动态影像构成国家文化遗产的组成部分；

鉴于动态影像是一种新的文化表现形式，特别是展示了当代社会的时代特征。通过动态影像，当代文化不断发展一个重要方面得到体现；

鉴于动态影像为记录事件的来龙去脉提供了基本方式，因而从一个新的侧面，成为历史、生活方式、民族文化以及世界变化过程的重要的、常常是唯一的见证；

注意到动态影像在世界人民中作为传播和互相了解的方式发挥着日益重要的作用；

进一步注意到，通过向世界传播知识和文化，动态影像为每个人的教育和提升作出了巨大的贡献；

鉴于动态影像物质载体的性质及其载体不同的定影方法，动态影像非常脆弱，应当依照特定的技术条件保存；

进一步注意到由于磨损、事故或者未经授权的处理，许多动态影像文化遗产都已不复存在，这是对该遗产的不可逆的损害；

承认特定机构通过努力拯救面临危险的动态影像所取得的成果；

鉴于每一成员国为了子孙后代的利益，均有必要采取适当的配套措施对动态影像这一文化遗产中特别脆弱的部分予以保存和保护，使其与作为当今和后世人类财富源泉的其他形式的文化财产一样受到保存和保护；

同时鉴于为保护动态影像版权人和其他所有相关权利人的合法权益，以

---

* 西南政法大学法学院汪梦译。

及巩固和平和促进国与国之间的相互理解，各成员国在采取必要措施保护和保护动态影像时，应对公认为人类尊严所必然要求的、构成人权和基本自由核心组成部分的言论自由，表达自由和信息自由予以充分考虑；

同时承认各成员国在履行其国际法义务时，有权决定采取何种适当的保护和保存动态影像的措施；

鉴于由世界人民创造的动态图像也是全人类遗产的组成部分，因此应当推动更为密切的国际合作以保护和保存这一人类活动不可替代的记录，这尤其对那些资源有限的国家有利；

进一步鉴于，由于不断增长的国际合作，进口之动态影像在大多数国家的文化生活中发挥着重要作用；

鉴于记录一些国家历史文化，特别是曾经作为他国殖民地国家的历史文化的动态影像并不总是可以为这些国家所获得；

注意到大会过去已通过若干保护动态文化遗产的国际文件，特别是：1954 年《关于发生武装冲突时保护文化财产的公约》，1964 年《关于禁止和防止非法进出口文化财产和非法转让其所有权的方法的建议》，1970 年《关于禁止和防止非法进出口文化财产和非法转让其所有权的方法的公约》，1976 年《关于文化财产国际交流的建议》，1978 年《关于保护文化动产的建议》；

期望补充和延伸这些公约和建议规定的标准和原则；

牢记《世界版权公约》、《保护文学和艺术作品伯尔尼公约》、《保护表演者、录音制品制作者和广播组织国际公约》的有关规定；

此前已有多项关于动态影像保护和保存的动议；

已经决定（在本组织第 20 次大会上）就动态影像保护和保存问题制定一份“成员国建议”；

兹于 1980 年 10 月 27 日**通过**本建议：

大会建议成员国在遵守各国宪法制度或者实践的基础上，通过法律的或者其他任何需要的步骤适用以下条款，在其领土内使本建议规定的原则和规范产生效力。

大会建议成员国采取必要措施使其国内相关机关或者组织知晓并重视本建议。

大会建议成员国在规定的时间内依照规定的形式，提交其依据本建议采取相关行动的报告。

Ⅰ．定义

1．为本建议的目的：

(a)“动态影像”是指任何记录在载体上，无论记录的方法或者载体的性质，例如用于首次或后续定影的胶片、磁带或者光盘、不管是否有伴音、以动态效果呈现、意图向公众传播或者发行、或者为拍摄纪录片的目的而制作的系列影像，特别是指以下各类作品：

(i) 电影作品（例如故事片、短片、大众科学片、新闻和纪录片、动画和教育片）；

(ii) 由广电机构制作或者播出的电视作品；

(iii) 上述（i）和（ii）项之外的视频作品（以录像带为载体）；

(b)“预印制品”是指以获得拷贝为目的的动态影像的物质载体，包括电影影片的负片、中间负片、中间正片，以及录像带的原版母带；

(c)“放映拷贝”是指用于实际放映观看以及发行传播的动态影像的物质载体。

2. 为本建议的目的，“国内制作”是指制作人或者联合制作人中至少一人的总部或者居住地在相关国家领土范围之内的动态影像。

Ⅱ. 总则

3. 成员国应将所有国内制作的动态影像视为其本国“动态影像遗产”的组成部分。属于国外制作的动态影像，从特定国家的历史和文化看，对该国具有特别重要的意义时，同样也可以构成该国文化遗产的一部分。倘若由于技术或经济方面原因，动态影像遗产不能完整地传承于后世时，应尽可能多地将其残存部分保护和保存下来。为此，应采取适当措施确保相关所有公共机构和私人组织一起行动起来，以制定和实施一项积极的政策。

4. 应当采取适当的措施以确保对动态影像的充分的物理保护因时间和环境的作用而损坏。由于物质载体经常因不当存储而加速损坏进程，应当将动态影像保存在官方认可的电影和电视档案馆并且以最高档案标准保管。此外，为了正确保护和保存动态影像，应当特别针对开发高质量和经久耐用的载体媒介进行研究。

5. 应当采取措施防止国内制作的任何部分的损失、未经批准的处理或者物理损耗。为此，各成员国应采取适当措施确保公共或者私人非营利机构可以通过特定制度获取、保护和保存动态影像的预印制品或者存档拷贝。

6. 由公共或者私人非营利机构获取、保护和保存的动态影像作品或者信息资源应当尽可能地开放。根据《世界版权公约》、《保护文学和艺术作品伯尔尼公约》、《保护表演者、录音制品制作者和广播组织国际公约》，以及成员国国内法律的规定，对动态影像资料的使用不能侵犯制作者和发行者的合法权利或者利益。

7. 为了确保动态影像保护和保存计划切实有效并成功实施，应当推动涉及动态影像制作、发行、保护和保存的各相关方开展合作。特别应当在相关职业人员的圈子内，组织公开的信息推广和宣传活动，使其普遍认识到保护和保存动态影像对于保护国家文化遗产以及为当代社会生活留下见证所具有的重要意义。

Ⅲ. 建议的措施

8. 根据上述原则，以及通常的宪法实践，要求成员国采取所有必要的步骤，包括向官方认可的档案馆提供适当的人员、设备和资金资源，以根据下述指南有效地保护和保存动态影像遗产：

法律和行政措施

9. 为了确保属于国家文化遗产组成部分的动态影像得到系统化的保存，要求成员国采取措施，使得官方认可的档案馆能够保护和保存各国国内制作的动态影像的全部或者部分。这些措施诸如：在自愿基础上通过与动态影像合法持有人协商取得保存动态影像的权利，通过购买或者捐赠获得动态影像，以及通过法律或行政措施合理规定的强制寄存制度获得动态影像等。上述强制寄存制度应当与现行有关公共机构拥有动态影像的档案制度并存，成为其补充。成员国采取的措施应当符合其国内法和国际法关于人权和版权保护以及涉及动态影像的保护表演者、录音制品制作者和广播组织的有关规定，并考虑有关国际法文件中规定的有利于发展中国家的特殊条件。成员国建立强制寄存制度，应当规定：

（a）国内制作的动态影像，无论其载体媒介的物理性质或者制作目的，应当寄存至少一份质量最佳的完整拷贝，最好是以预印制品的形式；

（b）动态影像的预印制品，无论是否有外国合作摄制方，应由其制作者予以寄存，该制作者的定义和范围由成员国的国内立法加以规定，且其总部或居住地在该国的领土范围内；

（c）上述由制作者寄存的预印制品应当保存在官方认可的电影或电视资料档案馆内。没有官方认可的电影或电视资料档案馆的，成员国应尽一切努力建立全国性或地方性的此类机构。当此类机构尚未建成时，动态影像的预印制品应当临时贮存于拥有适当装备的场所；

（d）上述寄存的预印制品应在成员国国内法规定的最大时限内尽早

进行；

（e）任何时候如需要通过寄存的预印制品进一步复制拷贝，预印制品的寄存人可在受控的条件下获得该预印制品。寄存人获得其寄存的预印制品须以该制品不会遭受任何损害或损耗为前提；

（f）在不违反涉及版权以及保护表演者、录音制品制作者和广播组织的国际公约与国内法有关规定的前提下，上述官方认可的档案馆应当被赋予以下权利：

（i）采取一切必要的措施保护和保存动态影像，并且在可能的时候提高技术质量。在对动态影像进行复制的时候，对相关影像涉及的所有权利给予应有的尊重；

（ii）为了教学、学术或者研究的目的，允许有限观众以非营利的方式在其场所内观看发行拷贝，只要该使用不与正常的作品使用相冲突并且不对寄存的预印制品造成损害。

（g）寄存的预印制品及其复制品不能被用于其他目的，也不能改变其内容；

（h）官方认可的档案馆应当有权要求使用者为其提供的服务支付合理的报酬。

10. 应当将保护和保存所有的国内制作的动态影像作为最高目标。然而，在技术的发展使得该最高目标得以实现的时代到来之前，当因为成本或空间等方面的技术性原因，不可能把所有公共播出的动态影像都记录下来或者不可能对所有寄存的动态影像资料予以长期保存时，鼓励成员国各自确立相关指导原则，以确定哪些动态影像应当为了后代的利益予以录制和寄托保存，包括哪些动态影像属于具有非凡纪实性的“短暂的录像制品”。那些具有教育、文化、艺术、科学和历史价值、构成国家文化遗产组成部分的动态影像应当优先得到保存。为达到上述目的，而制定的任何制度都应当明智而有远见地规定，在选择受保护和保存的动态影像时，必须以最广泛基础上达成的共识为依据，并应特别重视档案专家提出的评价标准。此外，在清理档案资料时必须格外谨慎，应在经过充分的时间检验后，方可将过时和没有价值的影像资料剔除。被剔除的资料应当送还资料的寄存人。

11. 根据本建议的精神，在不妨碍动态影像跨国自由交流以及尊重所涉各种权利的前提下，应当鼓励动态影像的外国制作者以及那些负责公开发行国外制作的动态影像的人，自愿地将相关动态影像文档质量最好的一个副本交给在该影像公开发行国得到官方认可的档案馆保存，特别是在该动态影像以其公开发行国的一种或多种语言配音或加入字幕，被认为是该国动态影像遗产的组成部分，或者对于文化方面的教学或研究具有重要价值时，应当强烈敦促该动态影像的发行人本着国际合作的精神，将此类动态影像资料交付保存。官方认可的档案馆应推动所在国家建立用以规范此类寄托保存的制度，以及在尊重所涉各种权利的前提下，即使此类动态影像未在本国公开发行，只要其具有特别突出的普世性价值，也可获得并保存其副本的制度。管控和获取此类影像资料应当适用上述本建议第 9 条第（e）、（f）、（g）和（h）项的规定。

12. 倡导成员国对上述第 11 条提出的各项措施的有效性开展跟踪研究。如果在经过一段合理的试行期后发现第 11 条建议的自愿交付保存的形式，不能确保使那些以配音或增加字幕的方式改编的、具有特定国家历史或文化价值的动态影像资料得到充分保护和保存的，相关国家可通过其国内立法规定相应措施，防止此类动态影像的副本灭失，特别是因遭受破坏而灭失。在这一过程中，应当充分考虑和尊重此类影像资料所涉及的各方权利人的合法权利。

13. 进一步要求成员国在不违反有关版权以及表演者、录像制品制作者和广播组织保护的国际公约的前提下，调查研究允许官方认可的档案馆，在不与影像作品正常开发利用相冲突的条件下，基于研究和教学目的，使用其保管的影像资料的可行性。

技术措施

14. 要求成员国对在动态影像保护和保存领域有发言权的国际组织提出的有关动态影像档案贮存和处理标准方面的意见给予应有关注。

15. 进一步要求成员国作出必要安排以确保负责保护和保存动态影像遗产的机构适用下述措施：

（a）建立国家电影目录以及各类动态影像目录，对动态影像的保存、检索予以说明，并在可能时对编目制度的分类标准予以说明。公开这些目录和说明并使其可以被查阅。上述文献资料共同构成有关一国动态影像遗产的清单。

（b）在不违反相关协议的前提下，为了研究的目的，收集、保存并公开记载动态影像来源、制作、发行和放映情况的机构记录、个人文件和其他资料；

（c）保持设备，特备是那些平时用不上，但对复制和放映被保存影像资料不可缺少的设备处于良好状态。当动态影像的某一载体不能被复制和放映时，应确保该影像能够转换到另一允许复制和放映的载体上。

（d）确保适用于动态影像储存、保护、保存、修复和复制的标准被严格执行；

（e）尽快提升保护和保存动态影像的技术质量，确保影像资料能够得到长期和有效的存储与使用；当涉及资料复制的时，应当对有关影像涉及的所有权利给予应有的注意。

16. 要求成员国鼓励持有动态影像的私人机构和个人采取必要的步骤确保其影像在充分的技术条件下得到有效的保护和保存。应当鼓励这些机构和个人将在国家建立影像资料寄存制度之前制作的预印制品（如有），或其拷贝（在没有预印制品时）交由官方认可的档案馆托管。

补充措施

17. 要求成员国鼓励负责动态影像保护和保存的主管机关和其他机构组织公共宣传活动以便：

（a）增进涉及动态影像制作和发行的各方当事人对动态影像所具有的深远的教育、文化、科学和历史价值的认知，并在此基础上使其认识到，为加强对动态影像的保护和保存，他们彼此之间必须开展合作；

（b）引起公众关注动态影像在教育、文化、艺术、科学和历史方面的重要性以及为保护和保存动态影像而必需采取的各种措施。

18. 应当在国家层面上采取措施以协调动态影像保护和保存领域的研究，特别鼓励研究如何以合理成本对动态影像进行长期保护和保存的问题。有关保护和保存动态影像方法和技术方面的信息，包括相关研究的成果，应当对所有相关人员公开。

19. 应当组织制定针对动态影像保护和修复的培训计划，包括培训目前最新的方法和技术。

Ⅳ. 国际合作

20. 要求成员国共同努力以促进作为国家文化遗产组成部分的动态影像的保护和保存。该合作应当由适格的国际政府组织和非政府组织发起，并应包括下述措施：

（a）参与建设地方性或全国性基础设施的国际项目，以保护和保存不具有适当设施或者充足资源的国家的动态影像遗产；

（b）开展有关对动态影像保护和保存方法和技术方面的信息交流，特别有关最新研究成果方面的交流；

（c）组织相关领域国内和国际培训课程，特别应向发展中国家公民提供此类培训；

（d）共同为保管动态影像档案的目的拟定档案的分类标准；

（e）在不违反有关版权以及表演者、录音制品制作者和广播组织保护的国内法律和国际公约规定的前提下，授权将动态影像的拷贝租借给其他仅为教学、学术或者研究目的使用该拷贝的官方认可的档案馆，只要权利持有人同意、存在相关可以租借的档案，以及不会对相关租借出去的档案资料造成损害或者损耗。

21. 应当特别向发展中国家提供技术合作以确保或促进其动态影像遗产的充分保护和保存。

22. 当动态影像涉及一国的历史或文化，而该国没有该影像的预印制品或者放映拷贝时，为使该国获得此类动态影像，要求成员国之间通力合作。为此目的，要求成员国：

（a）在动态影像由官方认可的档案馆保存的情况下，帮助那些与此影像资料有文化和历史关联的国家从该官方认可的档案馆获得预印制品或者放映拷贝；

（b）鼓励在其领土范围内持有该动态影像的私人机构或者组织自愿将该影像的预印制品或者放映拷贝保存在该国官方认可的档案馆中。

必要时，上述（a）和（b）涉及的资料应当向请求方免费提供。在需要收取成本费时，如涉及成员国作为公共财产所持有、并且与发展中国家的文化和历史相关的动态影像的预印制品或者放映拷贝，应当以最优惠条件向这些发展中国家的官方认可的档案馆收取费用。根据本条的规定提供和获得相关影像资料时，不得违反有关版权保护的规定，以及侵犯表演者、录音制品制作者以及广播组织的合法权利。

23. 当构成一国文化或历史遗产组成部分的动态影像在该国灭失时，不论灭失的原因为何，特别是在因该国沦入殖民地或为他国占领而导致灭失的情况下，成员国应根据该国的请求，依照本组织第 20 次大会通过的相关决议的精神予以合作，帮助该国从海外重新找回失落的有关动态影像。

Recommendation for the Safeguarding and Preservation of Moving Images

27 October 1980

The General Conference of the United Nations Educational, Scientific and Cultural Organization, meeting in Belgrade from 23 September to 28 October 1980, at its twenty - first session,

Considering that moving images are an expression of the cultural identity of peoples, and because of their educational, cultural, artistic, scientific and historical value, form an integral part of a nation's cultural heritage,

Considering that moving images constitute new forms of expression, particularly characteristic of present - day society, whereby an important and ever - increasing part of contemporary culture is manifested,

Considering that moving images also provide a fundamental means of recording the unfolding of events and, as such, constitute important and often unique testimonies, of a new dimension, to the history, way of life and culture of peoples and to the evolution of the universe,

Noting that moving images have an increasingly important role to play as a means of communication and mutual understanding among all the peoples of the world,

Noting furthermore that, by disseminating knowledge and culture throughout the world, moving images contribute extensively to the education and to the enrichment of each human being,

Considering however that, due to the nature of their material embodiment and the various methods of their fixation, moving images are extremely vulnerable and should be maintained under specific technical conditions,

Noting furthermore that many elements of the moving image heritage have disappeared due to deterioration, accident or unwarranted disposal, which constitutes an irreversible impoverishment of that heritage,

Recognizing the results yielded by the efforts of specialized institutions to save moving images from the dangers to which they are exposed,

Considering that it is necessary for each State to take the appropriate complementary measures to ensure the safeguarding and preservation for posterity of this particularly fragile part of its cultural heritage, just as other forms of cultural property are safeguarded and preserved as a source of enrichment for present and future generations,

Considering at the same time that the appropriate measures to ensure the safeguarding and preservation of moving images should be taken with due regard for freedom of opinion, expression and information, recognized as an essential part of human rights and fundamental freedoms inherent in the dignity of the human being, for the need to strengthen peace and international understanding and for the legitimate position of copyright holders and of all the holders of other rights in moving images,

Recognizing also the rights of States to take appropriate measures for the safeguarding and preservation of moving images, taking into account their obligations under international law,

Considering that moving images created by the peoples of the world also form part of the heritage of mankind as a whole and consequently that closer international co - operation should be promoted to safeguard and preserve these irreplaceable records of human activity and, in particular, for the benefit of those countries with limited resources,

Considering furthermore that, due to increasing international co - operation, imported moving images have an important role in the cultural life of most countries,

Considering that important aspects of the history and culture of certain countries, and, in particular, of those previously colonized, are recorded in the form of moving images which are not always accessible to the countries concerned,

Noting that the General Conference has already adopted international instruments relating to the protection of the movable cultural heritage and, in particular, the Convention for the Protection of Cultural Property in the Event of Armed Conflict (1954), the Recommendation on the Means of Prohibiting and Preventing the Illicit Export, Import and Transfer of Ownership of Cultural Property (1964), the Convention on the Means of Prohibiting and Preventing the Illicit Import, Export and Transfer of Ownership of Cultural Property (1970), the Recommendation on the International Exchange of Cultural Property (1976) and the Recommendation on the Protection of Movable Cultural Property (1978),

Desiring to supplement and extend the application of the standards and principles laid down in these conventions and recommendations,

Bearing in mind the terms of the Universal Copyright Convention, the Berne Convention for the Protection of Literary and Artistic Works and the Convention for the Protection of Performers, Producers of Phonograms and Broadcasting Organizations,

Having before it proposals concerning the safeguarding and preservation of moving images,

Having decided, at its twentieth session, that this question should be the subject of a Recommendation to Member States,

Adopts, this twenty - seventh day of October 1980, the present Recommendation:

The General Conference recommends that Member States apply the following provisions by taking whatever legislative or other steps may be required, in conformity with the constitutional system or practice of each State, to give effect within their respective territories to the principles and norms formulated in this Recommendation.

The General Conference recommends that Member States bring this Recommendation to the attention of the appropriate authorities and bodies.

The General Conference recommends that Member States submit to it, by the dates and in the form which it shall prescribe, reports concerning the action taken by them in pursuance of this Recommendation.

I. Definitions

1. For the purposes of this Recommendation:

(a) ‘moving images’ shall be taken to mean any series of images recorded on a support (irrespective of the method of recording or of the nature of the support, such as film, tape or disc, used in their initial or subsequent fixation), with or without accompanying sound, which when projected impart an impression of motion and which are intended for communication or distribution to the public or are made for documentation purposes; they shall be taken to include inter alia items in the following categories:

(i) cinematographic productions (such as feature films, short films, popular science films, newsreels and documentaries, animated and educational films);

(ii) television productions made by or for broadcasting organizations;

(iii) videographic productions (contained in videograms) other than those referred to under (i) and (ii) above;

(b) 'pre - print material' shall be taken to mean the material support for moving images, consisting in the case of a cinematographic film of a negative, internegative or interpositive, and in the case of a videogram of a master, such pre - print material being intended for the procurement of copies;

(c) 'projection copy' shall be taken to mean the material support for moving images intended for actual viewing and/or the communication of the images.

2. For the purpose of this Recommendation, 'national production' shall be taken to mean moving images, the maker or at least one of the co - makers of which has his headquarters or habitual residence within the territory of the State concerned.

II. General principles

3. All moving images of national production should be considered by Member States as an integral part of their 'moving image heritage'. Moving images of original foreign production may also form part of the cultural heritage of a country when they are of particular national importance from the point of view of the culture or history of the country concerned. Should it not be possible for this heritage to be handed down in its entirety to future generations for technical or financial reasons, as large a proportion as possible should be safeguarded and preserved. The necessary arrangements should be made to ensure that concerted action is taken by all the public and private bodies concerned in order to elaborate and ap-

ply an active policy to this end.

4. The appropriate measures should be taken to ensure that the moving image heritage is afforded adequate physical protection from the depredations wrought by time and by the environment. Since poor storage conditions accelerate the deterioration process to which the material supports are continuously subject and may even lead to their total destruction, moving images should be preserved in officially recognized film and television archives and processed according to the highest archival standards. Furthermore, research should be specifically directed towards the development of high quality and lasting support media for the proper safeguarding and preservation of moving images.

5. Measures should be taken to prevent the loss, unwarranted disposal or deterioration of any item of the national production. Means should therefore be instituted in each country whereby pre - print material or archival quality copies of moving images may be systematically acquired, safeguarded and preserved in public or private non - profit - making institutions.

6. Access should be made available as far as possible to the works and information sources represented by moving images which are acquired, safeguarded and preserved by public and private non - profit - making institutions. Their utilizations should not prejudice either the legitimate rights or the interests of those involved in the making and exploitation thereof, in accordance with the provisions of the Universal Copyright Convention, the Berne Convention for the Protection of Literary and Artistic Works and the Convention for the Protection of Performers, Producers of Phonograms and Broadcasting Organizations, and national legislation.

7. In order to ensure that a truly effective safeguarding and preservation programme is successfully undertaken, the co - operation of all those involved in the making, distribution, safeguarding and preservation of moving images should be obtained. Public information activities should therefore be organized in particular with a view to instilling in the professional circles concerned a general awareness of the significance of moving images for a country's heritage and the consequent need to safeguard and preserve them as testimonies to the life of contemporary society.

III. Measures recommended

8. In accordance with the principles set out above, and in conformity with their normal constitutional practice, Member States are invited to take all the necessary steps, including the provision to officially recognized archives of appropriate resources in terms of staff, equipment and funds, to safeguard and preserve effectively their moving image heritage in accordance with the following guidelines:

Legal and administrative measures

9. To ensure that moving images forming part of the cultural heritage of countries are systematically preserved, Member States are invited to take measures whereby officially recognized archives are able to acquire for safeguarding and preservation any part or all of their country's national production. Such measures may include, for example, voluntary arrangements with the holders of rights for the deposit of moving images, acquisition of moving images by purchase or donation or the institution of mandatory deposit systems through appropriate legislation or administrative measures. Such systems should complement and coexist with existing archival arrangements relating to publicly owned moving images. Measures taken should be consistent with the provisions of national legislation and international instruments concerning the protection of human rights, copyright and the protection of performers, producers of phonograms and broadcasting organizations relating to moving images, and should take into account the special conditions provided in favour of developing countries in certain of these instruments. When mandatory deposit systems are adopted, they should provide that:

(a) moving images of national production, whatever the physical characteristics of their support medium or the purpose for which they were created, should be deposited in at least one complete copy of the highest archival quality, preferably in the form of pre - print material;

(b) the material should be deposited by the maker - as defined by national legislation - having his headquarters or habitual residence within the territory of the State concerned, irrespective of any co - production arrangement made with a foreign maker;

(c) the material deposited should be preserved in officially recognized film or television archives; where they do not exist, every effort should be made to establish such institutions at the national and/or regional level; pending the establishment of officially recognized archives, the material should be provisionally stored in appropriately equipped premises;

(d) the deposit should be made as soon as possible within a maximum time-limit fixed by national regulations;

(e) the depositor should have controlled access to the deposited material whenever further printing is required, on condition that such access does not cause any damage to or deterioration of the material deposited;

(f) the officially recognized archives should be entitled, subject to the relevant provisions of international conventions and of national legislation governing copyright and the protection of performers, producers of phonograms and broadcasting organizations, to:

(i) take all the necessary measures in order to safeguard and preserve the moving image heritage, and, where possible, to enhance the technical quality; where the reproduction of moving images is involved, due regard should be given to all the rights in the images concerned;

(ii) permit the viewing on their premises of a projection copy on a non-profi-making basis by a limited number of viewers for purposes of teaching, scholarship or research, provided that such use does not conflict with the normal exploitation of the work and on condition that no deterioration of or damage to the material deposited is thereby caused;

(g) the material deposited and the copies made there from should not be used for any other purposes, nor should their contents be modified;

(h) officially recognized archives should be entitled to request users to make a reasonable contribution to the cost of the services provided.

10. The safeguarding and preservation of all moving images of national production should be regarded as the highest objective. However, until such time as developments in technology make this feasible everywhere, in those cases where it is not possible, for technical reasons of cost or space, to record all publicly broadcast moving images or to safeguard and preserve on a long - term basis all the material deposited, each Member State is invited to establish the principles for deter-

mining which images should be recorded and/or deposited for posterity, including ' ephemeral recordings ' having an exceptional documentary character. Those moving images which, because of their educational, cultural, artistic, scientific and historical value, form part of a nation ' s cultural heritage should be retained on a priority basis. Any system introduced to this end should foresee that selection should be based on the broadest possible consensus of informed opinion and should take particular account of the appraisal criteria established by the archival profession. Furthermore, due care should be taken to prevent the elimination of material until sufficient time has elapsed to allow for the necessary perspective. Material eliminated in this way should be returned to the depositor.

11. Foreign producers, and those responsible for the public distribution of moving images made abroad, should be encouraged, in accordance with the spirit of this Recommendation and without prejudice to the free movement of moving images across national borders, to deposit voluntarily in the officially recognized archives of the countries in which they are publicly distributed a copy of moving images of the highest archival quality, subject to all the rights therein. In particular, those responsible for the distribution of moving images, dubbed or subtitled in the language or languages of the country in which they are publicly distributed, which are regarded as an integral part of the moving image heritage of the country concerned or which are of significant value for the cultural needs of teaching or research, should be urged to deposit the material relating to these images in the spirit of international co - operation. Officially recognized archives should seek establishment of such deposit systems, and furthermore, the acquisition, subject to all the rights therein, of copies of moving images which are of exceptional universal value, even if they have not been publicly distributed in the country concerned. Control of and access to such material should be governed by the provisions of paragraph 9 (e), (f), (g) and (h) above.

12. Member States are invited to conduct follow - up studies on the effectiveness of the measures proposed in paragraph 11. If, following a reasonable trial period, the suggested form of voluntary deposit fails to ensure the adequate safeguarding and preservation of adapted moving images that are of particular national importance from the standpoint of the culture or history of a State, it would be for the State concerned, under the provisions of its national legislation, to define such

measures as would prevent the disappearance, particularly through destruction, of copies of adapted moving images, due regard being given to the rights of all those holding legitimate rights in such moving images of particular national importance.

13. Member States are invited furthermore to investigate the feasibility of permitting - taking due account of international conventions concerning copyright and the protection of performers, producers of phonograms and broadcasting organizations - officially recognized archives to utilize the deposited material for research and recognized teaching purposes provided that such utilization does not conflict with the normal exploitation of the works.

Technical measures

14. Member States are invited to play due attention to the archival standards concerning storage and treatment of moving images recommended by the international organizations competent in the field of the safeguarding and preservation of moving images.

15. Furthermore, Member States are invited to make the necessary arrangements to ensure that the institutions responsible for safeguarding and preserving the moving image heritage take the following measures:

(a) establish and make available national filmographies and catalogues of all categories of moving images and descriptions of their holdings, seeking, where possible, the standardization of cataloguing systems; these documentary materials would together form an inventory of the country's moving image heritage;

(b) collect, preserve and make available for research purposes institutional records, personal papers and other material that document the origin, production, distribution and projection of moving images, subject to the agreement of those concerned,

(c) maintain in good condition the equipment, some of which may no longer be in general use but which may be necessary for the reproduction and projection of material preserved or, should that not prove possible, ensure that the moving images concerned are transferred onto another material support permitting their reproduction and projection;

(d) ensure that the standards applicable to the storage, safeguarding, preservation, restoration and duplication of moving images are rigorously applied;

(e) as far as possible, improve the technical quality of the moving images to be safeguarded and preserved, ensuring that they are in a condition conducive to their long - term and effective storage and use; when treatment involves the reproduction of material, due regard should be given to all the rights in the images concerned.

16. Member States are invited to encourage private bodies and individuals holding moving images to take the necessary steps to ensure the safeguarding and preservation of these images under adequate technical conditions. These bodies and individuals should be encouraged to entrust to officially recognized archives the pre - print material if available or, in default thereof, copies of moving images made before the introduction of the deposit system.

Supplementary measures

17. Member States are invited to encourage the competent authorities and other bodies concerned with the safeguarding and preservation of moving images to undertake public information activities in order to:

(a) promote among all those involved in the making and distribution of moving images an appreciation of the lasting value of such images from the educational, cultural, artistic, scientific and historical points of view and an awareness of the consequent need to collaborate in their safeguarding and preservation;

(b) draw the attention of the public at large to the educational, cultural, artistic, scientific and historical importance of moving images and to the measures necessary for their safeguarding and preservation.

18. Measures should be taken at the national level in order to co - ordinate research in fields related to the safeguarding and preservation of moving images and to encourage research specifically directed towards their long - term preservation at a reasonable cost. Information on methods and techniques for safeguarding and preserving moving images, including the results of relevant research, should be disseminated to all concerned.

19. Training programmes in the safeguarding and restoration of moving images should be organized, covering the most recent methods and techniques.

IV. International co – operation

20. Member States are invited to associate their efforts in order to promote the safeguarding and preservation of moving images which form part of the cultural heritage of nations. Such co - operation should be stimulated by the competent international governmental and non - governmental organizations and should comprise the following measures:

(a) participation in international programmes for the establishment of the necessary infrastructure, at the regional or national level, to safeguard and preserve the moving image heritage of countries which do not possess appropriate facilities or adequate resources;

(b) exchange of information on methods and techniques for the safeguarding and preservation of moving images and, in particular, on the findings of recent research;

(c) organization of national or international training courses in related fields in particular for nationals of developing countries;

(d) joint action for the standardization of cataloguing methods specifically intended for archival holdings of moving images;

(e) authorization, subject to the relevant provisions of international conventions and of national legislation governing copyright and the protection of performers, producers of phonograms and broadcasting organizations, of the lending of copies of moving images to other officially recognized archives exclusively for purposes of teaching, scholarship or research, provided that the consent of the holders of rights and the archives concerned is obtained to such lending and that no deterioration of or damage to the material lent is thereby caused.

21. Technical co - operation should be provided in particular to developing countries, in order to ensure or facilitate the adequate safeguarding and preservation of their moving image heritage.

22. Member States are invited to co - operate for the purpose of enabling any State to gain access to moving images that relate to its history or culture and of which it does not hold either preprint material or projection copies. To this end each Member State is invited:

(a) to facilitate, in the case of moving images on deposit in officially recognized archives and which relate to the history or culture of another country, the acquisition by the officially recognized archives of that country of either pre - print material or a projection copy thereof;

(b) to encourage private bodies or institutions within its territory which hold such moving images to deposit on a voluntary basis either pre - print material or a projection copy thereof with the officially recognized archives of the country concerned.

Where necessary, the material supplied in accordance with (a) and (b) above should be made available against reimbursement of the cost by the requesting body. However, in view of the cost involved, pre - print material or projection copies of moving images held by Member States as public property and which relate to the history and culture of developing countries should be made available to the officially recognized archives of those countries under especially favourable conditions. Any material provided in accordance with this paragraph should be made available subject to any copyright and any rights of performers, producers of phonograms or broadcasting organizations which may exist therein.

23. When moving images forming part of a country ' s cultural or historical heritage have been lost by that country, whatever the circumstances, and in particular as a consequence of colonial or foreign occupation, Member States are invited, in connection with requests for such images, to co - operate in the spirit of resolution 5/10. 1/1, III, adopted by the General Conference at its twentieth session.

关于保护文化动产的建议*

（联合国教科文组织大会1978年11月28日通过）

联合国教育、科学及文化组织大会，在巴黎于1978年10月24日至11月28日举行第二十届会议；

注意到公众对文化财产的强烈兴趣，正在世界范围内体现为众多博物馆及类似机构的创建，展览数目日益增多，收藏品、纪念物和考古遗址吸引了日益增长的旅游者，以及文化交流的加强；

考虑到此为非常积极的发展，应受到鼓励，特别是通过适用1976年大会于其第十九届会议上通过的《关于文化财产国际交流的建议》中所提出的各项措施；

考虑到公众要求了解、欣赏任何发源地文化遗产财富的日益增长的愿望，却加剧了文化财产由于特别易于接触或保护不当、运输中的内在风险以及在一些国家重新兴起的私自发掘、盗窃、非法贩运及野蛮破坏行为所正经受的各种风险；

注意到因为这种风险的加剧，而且由于市场上文化物品价值的增长，在没有充分政府担保制度的国家，综合保险费用超出了大多数博物馆能力所及，并且显然阻碍了组织国际展览及不同国家间进行其他交流；

考虑到代表不同文化的可移动文化财产构成人类共同遗产的一部分，因而每一国家在保护这些文化财产上对国际社会整体负有道义责任；

考虑到各国应相应地加强并普遍实施确保对可移动文化财产有效保护的风险预防和控制措施，并与此同时降低对所产生风险进行保险的费用；

希望补充并扩展大会在这方面所确定的规范和原则的适用范围，特别是《武装冲突情况下保护文化财产公约》（1954年）、《关于适用于考古发掘的国际原则的建议》（1956年）、《关于使博物馆向所有人开放最有效方法的建

---

* 郑州大学法学院杨会永译。

议》（1960 年）、《关于禁止和防止非法进出口文化财产和非法转让其所有权的方法的建议》（1964 年）、《关于禁止和防止非法进出口文化财产和非法转让其所有权的方法的公约》（1970 年）、《关于在国家一级保护文化和自然遗产的建议》（1972 年）、《保护世界文化和自然遗产公约》（1972 年）以及《关于文化财产国际交流的建议》（1976）中所确定的事项；

收到关于保护可移动文化财产的建议；

大会第十九届会议已决定就此问题形成对各成员国的建议；

于 1978 年 11 月 28 日通过本建议。

大会建议各成员国按照每一国家的宪法制度或惯例，采取为在其各自领土内实施本建议所述原则与规范所必需的任何立法或其他步骤，以适用下述规定。

大会建议各成员国提请相关主管机构及组织注意本建议。

大会建议各成员国按照大会决定的日期和格式，向大会递交关于其依本建议所采取行动的报告。

一、定　　义

1. 为本建议的目的：

1.1“可移动文化财产”应被认为指作为人类创造或自然进化的表现和明证并具有考古、历史、艺术、科学或技术价值和意义的一切可移动物品，包括下列各类中的物品：

（1）于陆地和水下所进行考古勘探和发掘获取的物品；

（2）古物，如工具、陶器、铭文、钱币、印章、珍宝、武器及墓葬遗物，包括木乃伊；

（3）从历史纪念物上割裂的块片；

（4）具有人类学和人种学价值的材料；

（5）有关历史，包括科学与技术历史和军事及社会历史、有关人民及国家领导人、思想家、科学家及艺术家生活及有关国家重大事件的物品；

（6）具有艺术意义的物品，如：用手工于任何载体和以任何材料做成的绘画与绘图（不包括工业设计图及用手工装饰的工业产品），作为原始创造力媒介的原版、招贴、照片；用任何材料组集或拼集的艺术品原件，任何材料的雕塑艺术品和雕刻品，玻璃、陶瓷、金属、木材等质地的实用艺术品；

（7）具有特殊意义的手稿和古版本书、古籍抄本、书籍、文件或出版物；

(8) 具有集币章（徽章和钱币）和集邮意义的物品；

(9) 档案，包括文字记录、地图及其他制图材料、照片、摄影电影胶片、录音及可机读的记录；

(10) 家具、挂毡、地毡、服饰及乐器物品；

(11) 动物、植物及地质的标本；

1.2 “保护”应被认为指以下所述风险的预防和保险措施：

(1) “风险的预防”系指为在某种综合保护体系内护卫可移动文化财产免受该等财产所可能遭受的任何风险，包括起因于武装冲突、骚乱或其他公共秩序混乱的风险所需的一切措施；

(2) “风险的保险”系指在由于任何风险，包括产生自武装冲突、骚乱或其他公共秩序混乱的风险而造成的可移动文化财产的损坏、退化、变形或丢失情况下的赔偿担保，而不问此种保险的实现系通过政府担保与赔偿制度，或是通过由国家以可减或超额损失的安排部分承担风险，或是通过商业或国家保险，或是通过互助保险安排。

2. 每一成员国应制定其认为最合适的标准，以确定其领土内由于其考古、历史、艺术、科学或技术价值而应给予本建议所述保护的可移动文化财产项目。

二、总　　则

3. 上述定义之可移动文化财产包括属于国家或公共机构的或者属于私人机构或个人的物品。由于所有这些财产均构成各有关国家文化遗产的要素，对于诸如损坏、退化和丢失的各种风险的预防和保险，虽然采取的解决方法可能各不相同，但应被视为一个整体。

4. 威胁可移动文化遗产日益增长的危险，应促使所有对保护该遗产负有责任者，尽其所能，发挥作用，包括：负责保护文化遗产的国家和地方机构工作人员，博物馆馆长及类似机构的管理者，私人物主及宗教建筑物的负责人，艺术品和古董商人、保安专家，以及负责打击犯罪的人员、海关官员及有关的其他公共机构。

5. 公众的合作对于实现真正有效的保护至为重要。负责信息情报和教学的公共与私人机构应努力灌输对文化遗产重要性、其遭受危险及保护该遗产的必要性的一般认识。

6. 文化财产由于不良的存放、展览、运输及环境（不利的光线、温度、湿度、空气污染）条件而易退化，长此以往，可能具有比意外损坏或偶然破坏行为更为严重的后果。因此，应保持适宜的环境条件，以便确保文化财产的物质安全。负有责任的专家应在目录中列入物品物理状况的数据及关于必要环境条件的建议。

7. 风险的预防还要求发展保护技术和修复工厂，以及在博物馆和收藏有可移动文化财产的其他机构内安装有效保护系统。每一成员国应努力确保根据当地情况采取最适合的措施。

8. 有关艺术品和其他文化财产的犯罪在一些国家正日益增加，最为常见的是同跨境欺诈性转移相联系。盗窃和抢劫是经系统组织的并且是大规模的。野蛮破坏行为也在日益增加。为了与这些形式的犯罪活动作斗争，不论其为有组织的或是个人的行动，需要有严格的管制措施。由于赝品能够用于真品的盗窃或假冒调换，亦必须采取措施以防止其流通。

9. 保护及风险预防比发生损坏或丢失时的赔偿更为重要，因为其根本的目的是为保护文化遗产而不是用一笔钱款来取代不可替代的物品。

10. 因为在运输和临时展览中由于环境变化、操作不当、包装不正确或其他不利条件而产生的风险会有相当可观的增加，对损坏或丢失予以适当保险是重要的。风险保险的费用应通过博物馆和其他类似机构对保险合同的合理管理，或借助于全部或部分政府担保而予以降低。

三、建议之措施

11. 根据前文所规定的原则与规范，各成员国应按照其立法和宪法制度采取一切必要步骤，以有效地保护可移动文化财产，并特别是在运输的情况下，应确保适用必要的谨慎和保护措施，并对所产生风险予以保险。

风险预防措施

博物馆和其他类似机构

12. 各成员国应采取一切必要措施，以确保对博物馆和其他类似机构中的文化财产的适当保护。特别是，他们应：

12.1 鼓励按照专门为此目的制定的方法（标准卡片、照片，并且如可能应使用彩色照片，及可能的微缩胶卷），尽可能详细地对文化财产系统编目和分类。这样的目录在需要确定文化财产损坏和退化时是有用的。借助于这样的文献，可以在采取一切应有预防措施的情况下，向负责打击盗窃、非法贸易及赝品流通的国家和国际机构提供必要的情报；

12.2 视情鼓励利用当代技术提供的谨慎方法对文化财产进行标准化鉴定；

12.3 敦促博物馆及类似机构通过包括切实可行的安全措施和技术设施的综合系统加强风险预防，并确保所有文化财产的保存、展览、运输，以保护其免受可能致使其损坏或毁坏的所有因素，特别是包括热度、亮度、湿度、污染、各种化学和生物药剂、振荡和震动影响；

12.4 向其所负责的博物馆及类似机构提供必要的为执行上述第12.3项所规定措施所必需的资金；

12.5 采取必要措施以确保与保护可移动文化财产相联系的所有任务，都按照最适合于特定文化财产的传统工艺和最先进的科学方法和技术而予执行；为此目的，应建立专业资格培训与审查的适当制度，以便保证所有涉及人员均具备所要求的能力。这方面的设施应加强，或如需要应予建立。如若适当，出于经济性的考虑，建议设立地区性保护和修复中心；

12.6 对辅助人员（包括保安人员）予以适当培训，并拟订此等人员的行动守则，规定其履行其职责的准则；

12.7 鼓励对保护、保存及保安人员的常规培训；

12.8 确保博物馆和类似机构的工作人员亦接受必要培训，以使其能够于发生灾祸时在由主管公共机构所实施营救活动中予以有效合作；

12.9 鼓励向负有保护文化财产责任者公布并传播关于可移动文化财产的保护、保存及保安各方面的最新科学与技术情报；如有必要，则以保密形式进行；

12.10 颁布博物馆及公共和私人收藏保安设备操作标准并鼓励其适用。

13. 应竭尽全力避免屈从于勒索要求，以阻止为此目的进行的对可移动文化财产的盗窃或非法侵占行为。有关人员或机构应研究将该政策公之于众的方式和方法。

私人收藏

14. 各成员国还应根据其立法和宪法制度通过下述各项措施，促进对属于私人机构或个人的收藏的保护：

14.1 邀请物主编制其收藏的目录，向负责保护文化遗产的官方机构递送目录，并视情况需要向主管的官方博物馆研究员、技术人员开放，以便于就保护措施进行研究并提出建议；

14.2 如若适当，向物主提供激励措施，如协助保护列于目录中的物品或适当的财政措施；

14. 3 研究对向博物馆或类似机构捐献或遗赠文化财产者给以财政惠益的可能性；

14. 4 委托一个官方机构（负责博物馆或警察的部门）组织，就包括防火的保安设施和其他保护措施，向私人物主提供咨询服务。

位于宗教建筑物和考古遗址内的可移动文化财产

15. 为确保位于宗教建筑物和考古遗址内的可移动财产得到适当保存和保护以免遭盗窃和劫掠，各成员国应鼓励建造储藏设施并适用专门保安措施。这些措施应同财产的价值及其所受风险的程度相称。如若适当，各政府应为此提供技术和资金援助。鉴于位于宗教建筑物内可移动文化财产的特殊意义，各成员国及主管当局应于财产所在地方对此等财产提供适当保护和介绍。

国际交流

16. 可移动文化财产在运输和临时展览期间，特别易遭受因操作不当、包装不正确、临时存放中的不良条件或气候变化以及接待安排不适当所产生的损坏风险，需要有特别保护措施。在国际交流的情况下，各成员国应：

16. 1 采取必要措施以确保对运输和展览期间的适当保护与爱护条件，以及就适当的风险保险作出规定并在有关各方间就此达成协议。文化财产经由其领土转运的国家的政府，如经请求，应提供协助；

16. 2 鼓励有关机构：

（1）确保文化财产按照最高的标准予以运输、包装及操作。为此而采取的措施可能包括由专家确定最适合的包装方式及运输方法和运输时间；建议如若适当，出借文化财产的博物馆主管研究员于运输期间护送这些财产并检查其状况；负责物品运输和包装的机构应附上一份述明对象物理形状的列表；接受机构应根据清单核对物品；

（2）采取适当措施以防止由于展览场所的临时或长期拥挤而可能产生的任何直接或间接损坏；

（3）视需要同意拟用于测量、记录和调整湿度的方法，以将相对湿度保持在规定限度内，并同意为保护易受光照影响的物品而采取的措施（日光曝晒、所用电灯类型、以勒克斯为单位计算的照明度最高标准、用以测量并控制该标准的方法）；

16. 3 简化关于文化财产合法流动的行政手续，并安排对装载文化财产板条箱及其他包装形式的适当识别；

16. 4 采取措施以保护运输途中或为文化交流目的临时进口的文化财产，特别是方便其在合适的地点办理迅速清关手续。该地点应靠近并如有可能在该办理清关手续机构的地点，并确保在采取一切所需预防措施情况下进行清况；

16.5 如有必要随时指示其外交和领事代表，采取有效措施加快海关程序办理，确保处于运输中的文化财产得到保护。

教育与宣传

17. 为确保全体人民认识到文化财产的价值及其保护的必要性，特别是考虑到文化认同的保护，成员国应当鼓励主管机构在国家、区域或地方层面采取以下措施：

17.1 利用任何可行的教育和信息资源，帮助儿童、青年和成年人获取有关可移动文化财产的知识，并培养其尊重文化财产的精神；

17.2 使用任何可行的方法吸引一般公众关注：

（1）文化财产的价值和重要性，但不应突出其纯粹的商业价值；

（2）参与由主管机构举办的文化财产保护活动的机会。

控制措施

18. 为防止盗窃、非法贸易、野蛮破坏行为以及使用赝品的违法行为，成员国应当根据情况需要，建立或加强专门负责预防和打击上述违法行为的执法机构。

19. 成员国应当根据情况需要采取以下必要措施：

19.1 在其刑事、民事、行政或其他法律制度中，针对盗窃、抢劫、收买或非法占有以及故意破坏可移动文化财产的行为，规定制裁或其他适当手段；该制裁或手段应当考虑违法行为的严重性；

19.2 确保负责防范打击涉及可移动文化财产违法行为的执法机构和部门之间能够进行良好协作，并且建立一个含赝品信息在内的此类违法信息的快速传递系统，能够在政府部门和博物馆管理者以及艺术品和古董商人等各类相关者之间传递信息；

19.3 确保可移动文化财产所需要的适当保护条件，采取措施避免那些经常出现并导致文化财产退化的管理疏忽和放任行为。

20. 成员国也应当鼓励私人收藏者以及艺术品和古董商人向第19.2项提及的政府部门传递任何赝品信息。

完善风险保险的财政措施

政府担保

21. 成员国应当：

21.1 对可移动文化财产在运输和临时展览期间遭受的各类风险给予特别

关注；

21.2 特别考虑以法律、法令或其他形式，建立某些国家已经存在的政府担保制度，或者由国家或其他团体以可减或超额损失的安排部分承担风险的制度；

21.3 在前述制度框架下并依上述形式，如果在博物馆或类似机构展览的文化物品遭受损坏、退化、变形或丢失，应对文化物品的出借人予以赔偿。前述制度应当明确规定赔偿支付的条件和程序。

22. 涉及政府担保的规定不应适用于因商业目的而成为交易标的的文化财产。

博物馆和类似机构层面的措施

23. 成员国还应当敦促博物馆和其他类似机构实施风险管理原则，处理决策、分类、评估、控制和财政中的各类风险。

24. 所有采取保险机制的博物馆和其他类似机构所实施的风险管理活动，应当包括制定内部程序手册、定期调查各类风险和可能的最大损失、分析保险合同和费率、市场研究以及竞标程序。该风险管理应当委托专人或专门机构实施。

四、国际合作

25. 成员国应当：

25.1 就风险预防和风险保险问题协调相关政府间和非政府组织；

25.2 加强负责打击盗窃和非法交易文化财产以及发现赝品的政府部门之间的国际合作，并且特别敦促这些政府部门通过专门机制，相互快速传递有关违法活动的各种有用信息；

25.3 在必要的情况下就法律援助和违法预防方面的合作问题缔结国际协议；

25.4 参与组织可移动文化财产保护和修复以及风险管理的国际培训课程，并确保相关专业人员定期参加此类课程；

25.5 与专业国际组织合作颁布本建议涉及领域的伦理和技术标准，鼓励科学技术信息的交流，尤其是有关可移动文化财产保护和保存方面创新信息的交流。

Recommendation for the Protection of Movable Cultural Property

28 November 1978

The General Conference of the United Nations Educational, Scientific and Cultural Organization, meeting in Paris from 24 October to 28 November 1978, at its twentieth session,

Noting the great interest in cultural property now finding expression throughout the world in the creation of numerous museums and similar institutions, the growing number of exhibitions, the constantly increasing flow of visitors to collections, monuments and archaeological sites, and the intensification of cultural exchanges,

Considering that this is a very positive development which should be encouraged, in particular by applying the measures advocated in the Recommendation concerning the International Exchange of Cultural Property adopted by the General Conference at its nineteenth session in 1976,

Considering that the growing desire of the public to know and appreciate the wealth of the cultural heritage, of whatever origin, has nevertheless led to an increase in all the dangers to which cultural property is exposed as a result of particularly easy access or inadequate protection, the risks inherent in transport, and the recrudescence, in some countries, of clandestine excavations, thefts, illicit traffic and acts of vandalism,

Noting that because of this aggravation of the risks, but also as a consequence of the increase in the market value of cultural items, the cost of comprehensive insurance in countries where there is no adequate system of governmental guarantees is beyond the means of most museums and is a definite impediment to the organization of international exhibitions and other exchanges between different countries,

Considering that movable cultural property representing the different cultures forms part of the common heritage of mankind and that every State is therefore morally responsible to the international community as a whole for its safeguarding,

Considering that States should accordingly intensify and give general effect to such measures for the prevention and management of risks as will ensure the effective protection of movable cultural property and, at the same time, reduce the cost of covering the risks incurred,

Wishing to supplement and extend the scope of the norms and principles laid down in this respect by the General Conference, in particular in the Convention for the Protection of Cultural Property in the Event of Armed Conflict (1954), the Recommendation on International Principles Applicable to Archaeological Excavations (1956), the Recommendation on the Most Effective Means of Rendering Museums Accessible to Everyone (1960), the Recommendation on the Means of Prohibiting and Preventing the Illicit Export, Import and Transfer of Ownership of Cultural Property (1964), the Convention on the Means of Prohibiting and Preventing the Illicit Import, Export and Transfer of Ownership of Cultural Property (1970), the Recommendation concerning the Protection, at National Level, of the Cultural and Natural Heritage (1972), the Convention concerning the Protection of the World Cultural and Natural Heritage (1972) and the Recommendation concerning the International Exchange of Cultural Property (1976),

Having before it proposals concerning the protection of movable cultural property,

Having decided, at its nineteenth session, that this question should take the form of a recommendation to Member States,

Adopts, this twenty - eighth day of November 1978, the present Recommendation.

The General Conference recommends that Member States apply the following provisions by taking whatever legislative or other steps may be required, in conformity with the constitutional system or practice of each State, to give effect within their respective territories to the principles and norms formulated in this Recommendation.

The General Conference recommends that Member States bring this Recommendation to the attention of the appropriate authorities and bodies.

The General Conference recommends that Member States submit to it, by dates and in the. form to be decided upon by the Conference, reports concerning the action taken by them in pursuance of this Recommendation.

I. DEFINITIONS

1. For the purposes of this Recommendation:

(a) "movable cultural property" shall be taken to mean all movable objects which are the expression and testimony of human creation or of the evolution of nature and which are of archaeological, historical, artistic, scientific or technical value and interest, including items in the following categories:

(i) products of archaeological exploration and excavations conducted on land and under water;

(ii) antiquities such as tools, pottery, inscriptions, coins, seals, jewellery, weapons and funerary remains, including mummies;

(iii) items resulting from the dismemberment of historical monuments;

(iv) material of anthropological and ethnological interest;

(v) items relating to history, including the history of science and technology and military and social history, to the life of peoples and national leaders, thinkers, scientists and artists and to events of national importance;

(vi) items of artistic interest, such as: paintings and drawings, produced entirely by hand on any support and in any material (excluding industrial designs and manufactured articles decorated by hand); original prints, and posters and photographs, as the media for original creativity; original artistic assemblages and montages in any material; works of statuary art and sculpture in any material; works of applied art in such materials as glass, ceramics, metal, wood, etc.;

(vii) manuscripts and incunabula, codices, books, documents or publications of special interest;

(viii) items of numismatic (medals and coins) and philatelic interest;

(ix) archives, including textual records, maps and other cartographic materials, photographs, cinematographic films, sound recordings and machine - readable records;

(x) items of furniture, tapestries, carpets, dress and musical instruments;

(xi) zoological, botanical and geological specimens;

(b) "protection" shall be taken to mean the prevention and coverage of risks as defined below:

(i) "prevention of risks" means all the measures required, within a comprehensive protection system, to safeguard movable cultural property from every risk to which such property may be exposed, including those resulting from armed conflict, riots or other public disorders;

(ii) "risk coverage" means the guarantee of indemnification in the case of damage to, deterioration, alteration or loss of movable cultural property resulting from any risk whatsoever, including risks incurred as a result of armed conflict, riots or other public disorders whether such coverage is effected through a system of governmental guarantees and indemnities, through the partial assumption of the risks by the State under a deductible or excess loss arrangement, through commercial or national insurance or through mutual insurance arrangements.

2. Each Member State should adopt whatever criteria it deems most suitable for defining the items of movable cultural property within its territory which should be given the protection envisaged in this Recommendation by reason of their archaeological, historical, artistic, scientific or technical value.

II. GENERAL PRINCIPLES

3. The movable cultural property thus defined includes objects belonging either to the State or public bodies or to private bodies or individuals. Since all this property constitutes an important element of the cultural heritage of the nations concerned, the prevention and coverage of the various risks, such as damage, deterioration and loss, should be considered as a whole, even though the solutions adopted may vary from case to case.

4. The growing perils which threaten the movable cultural heritage should incite all those responsible for protecting it, in whatever capacity, to play their part: staff of national and local administrations in charge of safeguarding cultural property, administrators and curators of museums and similar institutions, private owners and those responsible for religious buildings, art and antique dealers, security ex-

perts, services responsible for the suppression of crime, customs officials and the other public authorities involved.

5. The co - operation of the public is essential for truly effective protection. The public and private bodies responsible for information and teaching should strive to instil general awareness of the importance of cultural property, the dangers to which it is exposed, and the need to safeguard it.

6. Cultural property is liable to deterioration as a result of poor conditions of storage, exhibition, transport and environment (unfavourable lighting, temperature or humidity, atmospheric pollution), which in the long run may have more serious effects than accidental damage or occasional vandalism. Suitable environmental conditions should consequently be maintained in order to ensure the material security of cultural property. The responsible specialists should include in the inventories data on the physical state of the objects and recommendations concerning the requisite environmental conditions.

7. The prevention of risks also calls for the development of conservation techniques and restoration workshops and the installation of effective protection systems in museums and other institutions possessing collections of movable cultural property. Each Member State should endeavour to ensure that the most suitable measures are taken in accordance with local circumstances.

8. Offences concerning works of art and other cultural property are increasing in some countries, most frequently being linked to fraudulent transfers across frontiers. Thefts and plunder are organized systematically and on a large scale. Acts of vandalism are also increasing. To combat these forms of criminal activity, be they of an organized nature or the action of individuals, strict control measures are necessary. Since fakes can be used for theft or the fraudulent transformation of authentic objects, measures must also be taken to prevent their circulation.

9. Protection and the prevention of risks are much more important than compensation in the event of damage or loss, since the essential purpose is to preserve the cultural heritage, not to replace by sums of money objects which are irreplaceable.

10. Because of the considerable increase in the risks resulting during transport and temporary exhibition, from environmental changes, inept handling, faulty packaging or other unfavourable conditions, adequate coverage against damage or loss is essential. The cost of risk coverage should be reduced through the rational

management by museums and similar institutions of insurance contracts or by means of full or partial governmental guarantees.

III. MEASURES RECOMMENDED

11. In accordance with the principles and norms set out above Member States should take all necessary steps, in conformity with their legislation and constitutional system, to protect movable cultural property effectively and, in the case of transport in particular, should ensure the application of the necessary measures of care and conservation and the coverage of the risks incurred.

Measures for the prevention of risks

Museums and other similar institutions

12. Member States should take all necessary steps to ensure adequate protection for cultural property in museums and similar institutions. In particular, they should:

(a) encourage the systematic inventorying and cataloguing of cultural property, with the fullest possible details and in accordance with methods specially developed for the purpose (standardized fiches, photographs - and also, if possible, colour photographs - and, as appropriate, microfilms). Such an inventory is useful when it is desired to determine damage or deterioration to cultural property. With such documentation the necessary information can be given, with all due precautions, to the national and international authorities responsible for combating thefts, illicit trading and the circulation of fakes;

(b) encourage, as appropriate, the standardized identification of movable cultural property using unobtrusive means offered by contemporary technology;

(c) urge the museums and similar institutions to reinforce the prevention of risks by a comprehensive system of practical security measures and technical installations and to ensure that all cultural property is kept, exhibited and transported in such a way as to protect it from all elements likely to damage or destroy it, including in particular heat, light, humidity, pollution, the various chemical and biological agents, vibration and shock;

(d) provide the museums and similar institutions for which they are responsible with the necessary funds for implementing the measures set out in subparagraph (c) above;

(e) take the necessary steps to ensure that all the tasks associated with the conservation of movable cultural property are carried out in accordance with the traditional techniques best suited to the particular cultural property and the most advanced scientific methods and technology; for this purpose, a suitable system for training and the vetting of professional qualifications should be established, in order to ensure that all those involved possess the required level of competence. The facilities for this should be strengthened or, if necessary, established. If appropriate, for the sake of economy, the establishment of regional conservation and restoration centres is recommended;

(f) provide suitable training for supporting staff (including security staff) and draw up guidelines for such staff, laying down standards for the performance of their duties;

(g) encourage regular training for protection, conservation and security staff;

(h) ensure that the staff of museums and similar institutions also receive the necessary training to enable them, in the event of disasters, to co - operate effectively in the rescue operations carried out by the competent public services:

(i) encourage the publication and dissemination to those responsible, if necessary in confidential form, of the latest technical and scientific information on all aspects of the protection, conservation and security of movable cultural property;

(j) issue performance standards for all security equipment for museums and public and private collections and encourage their application.

13. No effort should be spared to avoid giving in to ransom demands, so as to discourage the theft or illegal appropriation of movable cultural property carried out for that purpose. The persons or institutions concerned should consider ways and means of making this policy known.

Private collections

14. Member States should also, in conformity with their legislation and constitutional system, facilitate the protection of collections belonging to private bodies or individuals by:

(a) inviting the owners to make inventories of their collections, to communicate the inventories to the official services responsible for the protection of the cultural heritage and, if the situation requires, to grant access to the competent official curators and technicians in order to study and advise on safeguarding measures;

(b) if appropriate, providing for incentives to the owners, such as assistance for the conservation of items listed in the inventories or appropriate fiscal measures;

(c) studying the possibility of granting fiscal benefits to those who donate or bequeath cultural property to museums or similar institutions;

(d) entrusting an official body (the department responsible for museums or the police) with the organization of an advisory service for private owners on security installations and other protective measures, including fire protection.

Movable cultural property situated in religious buildings and archaeological sites

15. To ensure that movable cultural property situated in religious buildings and archaeological sites is suitably preserved and protected against theft and plunder, Member States should encourage the construction of installations for storing it and the application of special security measures. Such measures should be in proportion to the value of the property and the extent of the risks to which it is exposed. If appropriate, governments should provide technical and financial assistance for this purpose. In view of the special significance of movable cultural property situated in religious buildings, Member States and the competent authorities should endeavour to provide for the proper protection and presentation of such property where it is located.

International exchanges

16. Since movable cultural property is particularly exposed, during transport and temporary exhibition, to risks of damage which can arise from inept handling, faulty packaging, poor conditions during temporary storage or climatic changes, as well as inadequate reception arrangements, special measures of protection are required. In the case of international exchanges Member States should:

(a) take the necessary measures to ensure that appropriate conditions of protection and care during transport and exhibition as well as adequate coverage of risks are specified and agreed on between the parties concerned. Governments through whose territory the cultural property will transit should provide assistance, if so requested;

(b) encourage the institutions concerned to:

(i) ensure that cultural property is transported, packed and handled in accordance with the highest standards. The measures to be taken to this effect could include the determination by experts of the most appropriate form of packaging, as well as the type and timing of transport; it is recommended that, where appropriate, the responsible curator of the lending museum accompany the property during transport and certify its conditions; the institutions responsible for the shipping and packing of the objects should attach a list describing their physical appearance, and the receiving institutions should check the objects against those lists;

(ii) take appropriate measures to prevent any direct or indirect damage which might arise from the temporary or permanent overcrowding of the exhibition premises;

(iii) agree, where necessary, on the methods to be used for measuring, recording and regulating the degree of humidity in order to maintain the relative humidity within definite limits, and on the measures to be taken to protect light - sensitive objects (exposure to daylight, type of lamp to be used, maximum level of illumination in lux, methods used to measure and control this level);

(c) simplify the administrative formalities relating to the lawful movement of cultural property and arrange for appropriate identification of crates and other forms of packaging containing cultural property;

(d) take steps to protect cultural property in transit or temporarily imported for the purpose of cultural exchanges, and in particular facilitate rapid customs clearance in suitable premises, which should be situated close to, and if possible on, the premises of the institution concerned, and ensure that clearance is effected with all the desirable precautions; and

(e) whenever necessary, give instructions to their diplomatic and consular representatives to enable them to take effective action to accelerate customs procedures and ensure the protection of cultural property during transport.

Education and information

17. To ensure that the population as a whole becomes aware of the value of cultural property and of the need to protect it, particularly with a view to the preservation of their cultural identity, Member States should encourage the competent authorities at national, regional or local level to:

(a) provide children, young people and adults with the means of acquiring knowledge and respect for movable cultural property, using all available educational and information resources for that purpose;

(b) draw the attention of the public at large by every possible means to:

(i) the significance and importance of cultural property, but without stressing the purely commercial value of that property;

(ii) the opportunities available to them for participating in the activities undertaken by the competent authorities in order to protect such property.

Control measures

18. To combat thefts, illegal excavations, vandalism and the use of fakes, Member States should, where the situation demands, establish or strengthen services specifically responsible for the prevention and suppression of these offences.

19. Member States should, where the situation calls for it, take the necessary measures to:

(a) provide for sanctions or any appropriate measures, whether under the penal or civil code or administrative or other measures, in the case of the theft, pillage, receiving or illegal appropriation of movable cultural property, and of damage intentionally caused to such property; these sanctions or measures should take into account the gravity of the offence;

(b) ensure better co - ordination between all services and sectors working for the prevention of offences concerning movable cultural property and organize a system of rapid dissemination of information on such offences, including information on fakes, among official bodies and the various sectors concerned, such as museum curators and art and antique dealers;

(c) ensure proper conditions for the safeguarding of movable cultural property by taking steps to counter the neglect and abandon to which it is very often exposed and which is conducive to its deterioration.

20. Member States should also encourage private collectors and art and antique dealers to transmit all information concerning fakes to the official bodies mentioned in paragraph 19 (b).

Measures to improve the financing of risk coverage

Governmental guarantees

21. Member States should:

(a) give special attention to the problem of covering adequately the risks to which movable cultural property is exposed during transport and temporary exhibitions;

(b) in particular, consider instituting in any legislative, statutory or other form, a system of governmental guarantees such as those which exist in certain countries, or a system of partial assumption of the risks by the State or any community concerned with a view to covering an insurance franchise deductible or an excess of loss;

(c) within the framework of such systems and in the forms mentioned above, provide for compensation to lenders in the event of damage to, or the deterioration, alteration or loss of cultural objects loaned for the purpose of exhibition in museums or similar institutions. The provisions instituting these systems should specify the conditions and procedures governing the payment of such compensation.

22. The provisions concerning governmental guarantees should not apply to cultural property which is the object of transactions for commercial purposes.

Measures at the level of museums and similar institutions

23. Member States should also urge museums and other similar institutions to apply the principles of risk management, comprising the determination, classification, assessment, control and financing of risks of all kinds.

24. The risk management programme of all institutions which have taken out insurance should include the internal drafting of a procedures manual, periodic surveys on types of risks and the probable maximum loss, analysis of contracts and rates, market studies and a competitive bidding procedure. A person or body should be specifically entrusted with risk management

IV. INTERNATIONAL CO – OPERATION

25. Member States should:

(a) collaborate with intergovernmental and non - governmental organizations competent in regard to the prevention and coverage of risks;

(b) strengthen at international level co - operation between official bodies responsible for the suppression of thefts and illicit trading in cultural property and for the discovery of fakes, and, in particular, urge these bodies to circulate rapidly among themselves, through machinery provided for this purpose, all useful information on illegal activities;

(c) if necessary conclude international agreements for co - operation in regard to legal aid and the prevention of offences;

(d) take part in the organization of international training courses in the conservation and restoration of movable cultural property, and in risk management, and ensure that they are regularly attended by their specialized staff;

(e) establish, in collaboration with the specialized international organizations, ethical and technical standards in the fields covered by the present Recommendation and encourage the exchange of scientific and technical information, particularly on innovations relating to the protection and conservation of movable cultural property.

关于历史地区保护及其当代作用的建议*

（联合国教科文组织大会1976年11月26日通过）

联合国教育、科学及文化组织大会于1976年11月26日至30日在内罗毕召开第19届会议。

考虑到历史遗址是各地人类日常环境的组成部分，代表着其形成史在今天鲜活的表现形式，为生活背景提供了必要的多样性，得以与社会多样性相匹配，这样他们就富有价值，并丰富了其他的人类维度；

考虑到历史遗址在代代延续的过程中为文化、宗教及社会活动的丰富和多样性提供了最为直观的证据，其保护和融入现代社会生活是城镇规划和土地发展的基本元素；

考虑到面对教条化和非人性的危险，这种世代存续而来的鲜活证据对于人类及能从中找到生活方式表达及其认同的国家而言，至关重要；

注意到全世界都存在以扩张或现代化的名义无视其摧毁的对象而予以拆毁，并进行非理性及不合理的建筑，从而导致了历史遗址的严重损失；

考虑到历史遗址是非移动遗产，其破坏即使不会引起经济损失，却可能常常引起社会动荡；

考虑到这种情形意味着每一个公民及公共机构都须在力所能及的范围承担责任和义务；

考虑到为了从其所面临着日趋破败甚至是完全被摧毁的风险中将该等不可替代的财富抢救出来，每一个国家都亟须采取体系化并且富有成效的政策，作为国家、地区或地方规划的一部分对历史遗址及其景观予以保护并使之重新焕发新颜；

注意到在许多情形下，不存在能够有效及灵活地涉及建筑遗产及其与在城市、领土、地区或地方规划相协调的法律；

---

* 中国社会科学院法学研究所吴峻译。

注意到大会已经通过了国际文件，保护文化及自然遗产，诸如《关于考古发掘应当遵循的国际原则的建议》（1956）、《保护景观以及遗址风貌与特色的建议》（1962）《关于保护被公共或私人工程危及的文化财产的建议》，（1968）《关于在国家层面保护文化和自然遗产的建议》（1972）；

希望对该等国际文件中的标准和原则予以补充并将其推广适用；

鉴于有关历史遗址现代功能之保护的建议，该问题出现在大会议程第27项；

在其19届大会已经决定该问题须以针对成员国的建议书形式作出；

于1976年11月26日通过本建议书。

大会建议成员国通过国内法或其他某种形式的措施适用上述规定，以在其管辖范围的领土之上落实本建议书规定的原则和规则。

大会建议成员国将该建议书作为值得关注的对象介绍给予保护历史遗迹及其环境有关的全国、地区及地方政府机构、机构、服务机构或组织及协会。

大会建议成员国依照其决定的日期及时间向其报告他们就该建议书所采取的行动。

I. 定义

1. 为本建议书之目的，

（a）“历史及建筑（包括民间建筑）遗址”系指任何建筑群、结构及开放空间，包括考古及古生物遗址，在城市或农村环境中构成人类居住之地，从考古、建筑、史前、历史、美学或者社会文化上而言承认其内在的一致性及价值。这些“遗址”多种多样，可能从以下“具体”予以区分：史前遗址、历史小城、老城区、小村中及同类型的碑林，通常理解一般应该对后者进行谨慎地保护，不得改变。

（b）“环境”系指自然或人造系统，影响着该等地区被认知的静态或动态的方式，或者直接与之发生空间上的联系或者进行社会、经济或文化的联系。

（c）“保护”系指历史或传统遗址及其环境的确认、保护、保留、复原、修缮、维护及重新使用。

II. 一般原则

2. 历史遗址及其景观应被视作不可替代的共同遗产之组成部分。其所在国家的政府及其公民应认识到他们有责任区保护该等遗产并将之融入我们现今时代的社会生活之中。全国、地区或地方政府机构应根据每个成员国有关权力分配的条件，对其基于所有公民及国际社会的利益而履行该等职责的行为而负责。

3. 须将每个历史遗址及其景观全部视为一致性的整体，其平衡及具体性质依照其组成部分的结合情形而定，这些组成部分既包括建筑、空间组织架构及环境，也包括人类的活动。无论如何不起眼，包括人类活动的所有有效因素也对整个而言有着相当的意义，不得被忽视。

4. 历史遗址及其景观应得到积极保护，免于遭到所有形式的破坏，尤其不遭受不当使用、不必要附加及损害其原本风貌的误导性或鲁莽改变，且并不会因任何形式的污染而受到损坏。所采取的任何复原工作须基于科学原则进行。同样的，尤其应通过将组成建筑群落各种部分之间的连接和对照及使得每个建筑群落都特色独具，从而产生和谐及美感。

5. 基于现代城市化的背景，在历史遗迹遭受直接损毁的风险之外，导致了建筑数量及密度有相当程度的增加，新近开发的区域能够破坏邻近历史区域的环境及特色。建筑及城市规划者应当谨慎地确保纪念碑及历史遗址景观不会遭到破坏，且历史遗迹能够和谐地融入当代生活中去。

6. 在日渐普及的建筑技巧及形式可能在世界各地造成一种格式化环境的这种危险时刻，对历史遗迹予以保留，可以对保留及发展每个国家的文化及社会价值大有裨益。这有助于世界文化遗产中建筑丰富多样。

III. 全国、地区及地方政策

7. 在每一个成员国应制定全国、地区及地方政策，符合每个国家就权力分配所规定的条件，以便全国、地区及地方政府机构可以采取法律、技术、经济及社会措施，以保护历史遗址及其景观并使之适应当代生活的要求。制定的政策应该影响全国、地区及地方层级上的规划，并为所有层级上的城市规划及地区和当地发展规划提供指引，且源自其中的活动构成制定宗旨及项目、职责分配及操作行为的核心组成部分。应当在进行保护的时候寻求个人及私人组织的合作。

IV. 保护措施

8. 对历史遗址及其景观进行的保护应当符合以上原则、采用以下方法、根据法律及宪法规定以及每一国家之组织及经济结构确定的具体措施。

法律及行政措施

9. 保护历史遗址及其景观适用的总体政策应该基于每一个国家整体都有

效的原则。成员国应调整目前的规定或者在必要时制定新的法律和行政法规，以确保在考虑本章及下列各章规定条款的情形下对历史遗址及其景观的保护。他们应当鼓励调整或制定地区或地方措施以确保该等保护。也应该对涉及城市及地区规划和住房政策的法律进行审核，以协调并使之符合涉及建筑遗产保护的法律。

10. 要确立保护历史遗址体系的规定，应该规定涉及确立必要规划和文件及下列具体事项的一般原则：适用于被保护区域及其景观的一般条件及限制；对于为保留及提供公共服务之目的而规划的项目及操作；须进行的维护及对需要负责方的指定；适用城镇规划、重新开发及农村土地管理的土地；指定负责授权在保护区域进行任何复原、改动、新建或拆除行动的政府机构；保护项目融资及执行的方式。

11. 保护规划及文件应该界定：需要保护的地域及项目；适用的特定条件及限制；在维护、复原及改善工作中须遵守的标准；适用于确立城乡生活所必需的供应体系及服务的一般条件；适用于新建的条件。

12. 旨在阻止保护地区内土地出现投机性增值，从而可能不利于基于社会整体利益，该等法律也应该原则上包括为此规划的保护及修复，也要防止对保护法律的违反。该等规定可以涉及城镇规划措施，以便可以对建筑用地价格进行影响，例如建立相邻关系或小规模的开发规划，向公共机构授予优先权利，在所有者未能进行行动的时候为了保护、修复或自动干预而进行的强制购买，并且可以规定有效的惩罚措施，例如终止操作、强制复原和/或适当罚款。

13. 公共机关及个人须有义务遵守保护措施。然而，应该提供就独断或不公决定提起异议的机制。

14. 涉及建立公共及私人机构并涉及公共及私人项目的规定应该适应适用于历史遗址及其景观保护的行政条例。

15. 尤其是对于设计贫民区物业、小区及修建补贴住房的规定应该予以规划或修改，以使之符合保护政策并有助于其实现。领受任何补贴之清单应进行相应的规定和调整，旨在促进补贴住房及对老建筑进行修复而进行公共建设的情形下尤是如此。所有的拆建在任何情形下仅仅涉及不具备历史或建筑价值的建筑，所涉补贴应予以审慎监督。另外，为建设补贴住房的资金中一定比例应分配用于对老建筑进行的修复。

16. 保护措施的法律后果在涉及建筑和土地而言应该予以公开并应该被具有适当职权的官方机构所记录。

17．在适当考虑每一国家特定条件及在全国、地区和当地政府机构间职责分配的情形下，以下原则应当是保护机制操作的依据：

（a）应当在所有相关全国、地区及当地公共服务或个人组织之间确保建立永久协调的负责机构；

（b）一旦特别是由下列人士组成的所有多领域小组完成了先期科学研究，应予以制定保护规划及文件：

包括艺术史学家；建筑师及城市规划人员在内的保护与复原专家；

社会学家及经济学家；

生态学家及地貌建筑家；

公共卫生及社会福利专家；

及更为广泛意义上涉及历史遗址之保护与发展领域的所有专家；

（c）政府机构应当牵头出具意见并组织有关公众予以参与；

（d）保护规划及文件应当得到法律指定机构的批准；

（e）负责在全国、地区及当地所有层面上实施保护规定及行政法规的公共机构应当配备必要的职员及足够的技术、行政资源和资金。

技术、经济及社会措施

18．历史遗址及其景观保护名录应当在全国、地区或当地层面上予以指定。其中须说明优先项目，以便有限保护资源可以予以审慎而明智的分配。任何保护措施无论具有什么性质，只要需要作为紧急事项予以考虑，就应该马上实施，而不是去等待保护规划和文件已经准备妥当。

19．应当对区域整体进行调查，包括对其空间发展进行的分析。其中应涉及考古、历史、建筑、技术及经济数据。应该起草分析文件，以便认定哪些建筑或建筑群须予以特别保护、在特定条件下进行保护或者在特别及详细记录的情形下予以拆除。这会使得政府机构停止与该建议相悖的任何工作。另外，基于相同目的，应该制定公共及私人开放空间及其植被景观的清单。

20．在建筑调查之外，通过社会、经济、文化及科技数据及架构和更广泛的乡村或地区背景下的调查也是必要的。如可能，应当包括对年龄结构数据及对经济、社会及文化活动、生活方式及社会关系、土地租赁问题、乡村基础设施、公路体系现状、通信网络及被保护区域及周边区域互动联系进行的研究。有关政府机构应当对该等研究高度重视，并应铭记：有效的保护规划不可能在缺乏这些基础的情形下出台。

21．在上述调查完结后，在制定保护规划及细则之前，原则上应该进行项目操作，其中应该对城镇规划、建筑、经济及社会因素、还有城市及乡村结构可以吸收与其具体特征相匹配功能之能力予以适当考虑。项目操作应当旨在将居住密度保持在应该达到的水平，并且应该规定在进行过程予以临时安置及不能返回其原有居所的居民提供永久性住所的同时，还应当规定在不同阶段应该进行的工作。项目操作应当在所涉社区及群体充分参与的情形下进行。由于历史遗址及其景观的社会、经济及物质条件可能会随着时间的流逝而发生变化，调查及分析就应该持续进行。因此，制定保护规划及其实施需要在现有研究的基础上进行，而不是在对规划进程进行细化时予以推迟。

22. 一旦制定了保护规划及细则并得到有关公共机构的批准，就需要通过其规划者或者其授权予以执行。

23. 在留有若干不同时期的历史遗址中，所进行的保护工作应当考虑所有该等时期的特色。

24. 存在保护规划的，城市发展或贫民窟清除项目中，拆除没有建筑或历史意义之建筑的，结构上对之进行保留系为不合理的，对无价值的延伸部分及额外楼层进行拆除的，有时甚至拆除破坏遗址一致性的新近建筑的，仅得在获得规划区的授权后方可进行。

25. 保护规划没有涵盖城市发展或贫民区清除项目的，尊重相邻建筑的同时，还须尊重具有建筑或历史价值的建筑及其他元素。该等元素可能会因该等项目而遭受不利影响的，应在拆除之前起草上所述保护规划。

26. 有必要进行持续监督以确保该等操作不至于导致过高利润，也不会使之满足与规划相左的其他目的。

27. 通常适用于火灾及自然灾害的安全标准应该在任何影响历史遗址的城市发展或贫民区清除项目中得以遵守，但是须与保护文化遗产所适用的标准相匹配。发生冲突的，应寻求特别解决方案，在所有涉及服务之间予以协调，在不损害文化遗产的同时实现最大程度的安全。

28. 尤其应该注意新建筑的监管和监督，以确保其建筑与历史建筑群的空间组织及设置和谐相处。为此目的，在进行任何新建之前应该进行城市背景分析，这不但界定了建筑群的一般特色，而且还分析了其主导特色，即高度、色彩、材料及形式的和谐，门面及顶部监护的一致性，建筑数量及容积之间的关系，其一般比例及其位置。尤其应该注意土地的大小，因为对土地进行任何形式的重新组织可能会导致体积的改变，这可能损害整体的和谐。

29. 除非在非常情况及出于不可避免的原因，通过拆毁其周遭建筑而使得纪念碑趋于孤立，或者移除一座纪念碑，一般不会予以授权的。

30. 应当保护历史遗址及其景观，使之不会因杆、缆塔、电线或电话线及电视天线及大型广告标志的设立而被撕裂。在已经设立的情形下，应当采取适当措施将之移除。公告牌、霓虹灯及其他形式的广告、商业标志、街道及家具应当进行最大限度审慎的规划和监督，以使其和谐融入整体。应当采取特殊措施以阻止任何形式的破坏。

31. 有关成员国及群体应当禁止在历史遗迹及其景观附近建立有害工业，并采取预防措施消除车辆噪音、冲击及震动的破坏性影响，使这些区域免于遭受特定技术发展所带来日益严重的环境破坏——尤其是各种形式的污染。应当进一步制定规定，防止过度旅游带来的危害。

32. 就大多数历史群落中汽车交通及建筑规模与其建筑质量之间的矛盾，成员国应当鼓励并协助当地政府机构寻求解决方式。为解决这一冲突并鼓励步行，应该仔细考虑在边缘甚至是中心停车区提供空间和入口，并且考虑确立分流机制，以促进步行交通、享有服务及公共交通的发展。许多诸如将电线或其他电缆埋于地下的修复操作如单一进行时就过于昂贵，可以轻易而又经济地通过道路交通的发展而予以协调。

33. 保护及复原应当伴有重新使用的活动。因此，对于在特定行业及手艺业中保持目前的适当功能并确立新的功能而言，它都是至关重要的。新的功能如果可行，长远来看，应与将要引入城市、地区或国家的经济和社会背景相匹配。保护行为的成本估算不仅应基于建筑的文化价值，也要涉及其通过应用而带有的价值。

如果不对该等价值大小进行考虑，就不能正确看待保护产生的社会问题。该等功能应该回应居民的社会、文化及经济需要，同时又不会损害所涉地区的特定性质。文化重新利用政策应使得历史遗址成为文化活动中心，并使之在周围社会文化发展中扮演核心角色。

34. 在乡村地区，对所有引起动荡的工作及所有经济和社会结构的改变，应予以仔细监控，以便保留历史乡村社区在其自然条件下的完整性。

35. 保护活动应将公共机构的贡献与个人或共同所有人及居民和用户各自或共同作出的贡献联系在一起。应鼓励后者提出建议，并使之一般承担积极的角色。因此，在社会与个人间进行不断的合作，这应该在所有层面予以建立，并尤其通过下列方式进行：信息适应所涉人员的种类；调查适应所询问的人员；建立附属于规划小组的顾问群体；在负责决策、管理及组织涉及保护规划行动或创设公共公司，以在规划实施中承担角色的组织发挥咨询功能时，应当有所有者、居民及用户的代表。

36. 应当鼓励组成自发保护团体及非盈利协会，并建立荣誉或资金奖励，以便对保护工作中各个层面的杰出工作予以认可。

37. 应当通过在中央、地区和当地政府机构中进行充分的预算拨付，以确保存在必要资金以满足保护历史遗址及其景观规划中公共投资的水平。所有该等资金应当由被授权在国家、区域或当地层面协调所有形式资金扶持并根据总体行动规划予以拨付的公共、私人或半公共机构予以管理。

38. 下列所描述的公共协助方式应当基于的原则就是：只要适当及必须，有关政府机构采取的措施应当考虑到复原所发生的“额外支出”，即与新市场或建筑物租赁价值相比而言，所有者所承担的额外支出。

39. 一般而言，该等公共资金应当主要用于保护包括低租金住房建筑在内的现存建筑，不得用于兴建新建筑，除非后者并不对现存建筑的使用及功能构成负面影响。

40. 对于奖项、补贴、优惠利率贷款或者税收减让，应当向私人所有者及承担保护规划所规定工作并须满足该等规划规定标准之用户予以提供。该等税收减让、奖项及贷款可以首先主要向生活住宅和商业地产的所有者群体或者用户进行提供，因为合作行动比单个行动要经济得多。向私人所有者及用户提供的金融减让，在适当情形下，应当依赖于要求遵守基于公共利益而规定特定条件、确保诸如允许参观建筑物公园、花园或遗址、进行拍照等建筑物的一致性。

41. 应当在公共及私人机构中的预算中单列特别资金，用于大规模公共工程及污染所危及的历史建筑群保护。公共机构也应当单列特别资金，用于自然灾害所造成损害的修复。

42. 另外，所有职权涉及公共工程的政府部门及机构对其项目和预算的安排应为了通过融资工作促进历史建筑群的再次利用，这既符合其自身宗旨，也合乎保护规划之目的。

43. 为增加其资金来源，成员国应当鼓励设立公共及/或私人金融机构，以保护历史遗址及其景观。该等机构应当具有公司的地位，有权接受个人、基金会及工商业企业的捐款。可以向捐款人提供特别税收减让。

44. 为保护历史遗址及其景观通过设立贷款公司而执行任何形式的融资工作，可以通过公共机构及私人贷款机构加以促进，该等机构将负责向所有者提供优惠税率的长期贷款。

45. 成员国及其他层面上的有关政府可以建立周转资金，其特别宗旨就是促使愿意保护历史建筑及其特色的所有者可以继续居住于中，这就促进建立负责购买及在复原后适当情形下出卖建筑物的非盈利组织。

46. 极其重要的是，保护措施不应导致社会结构的断裂。为了使得出于装修而须迁出建筑物或建筑群落那些最贫穷居民免于困苦局面，对上涨租金予以补贴可以使其能保有其家庭、商业办公场所及作坊，也保有其传统的生存方式及职业，尤其对于乡村手工业、小农经营、捕鱼业等更是如此。这种补贴与收入有关，将帮助有关人支付由于工程之进行而上涨的租金。

V. 研究教育及信息

47. 为了提高熟练工人和必要手艺人的工作水平，为了鼓励整个民众认识到保护工作的必要性并参与其中，以下措施应当由成员国根据其法律及宪法职权予以施行。

48. 有关成员国及组织应当鼓励对下列事项的系统研究：历史遗址及其环境的城镇规划问题；所有层面上进行保护和规划的相关性；历史遗址保留方式；材料改变；在保护工作中应用新技术；保护必需的工艺技术。

49. 针对上述问题进行并包括实践培训期间的特定教育应当予以引入并发展。另外，关键要鼓励对历史遗址及其周围任何开放空间进行保护的熟练工人和工艺人员予以培训。另外，有必要对这种工艺自身予以鼓励，它们因工业化而危在旦夕。有关机构需要在这个议题上与诸如罗马的文化财产保护复原研究中心、纪念碑及遗址国际理事会（ICOMOS）及国际博物馆理事会（ICOM）之类的国际组织进行合作。

50. 基于历史遗址保护领域的当地发展需要，对行政职员予以教育，应当在适当及必需的情形下予以融资，并由适当政府机构根据长期计划予以引导。

51. 对保护工作必要性的认识应当在学校教育、校外教育及大学教育中予以强化，并使用诸如书籍、报纸、电视、广播、电影及巡回展览的信息媒介进行。历史遗址及其景观保护的有效政策不但在美学意义上、也在社会及经济意义上具有优势，对此应该提供清楚及全面的信息。该等信息应在专门的私人及政府组织和一般公众之间广为传播，以便他们可以知道其环境通过这种方式得到改善的原因和方式。

52. 历史遗址研究应当纳入所有层面的教育之中，尤其是历史教育，以便在年轻人的头脑中培育出对过去作品的理解和尊重，并在现代生活中对该等遗产的作用予以证明。这种教育应该广泛使用视听媒介及对历史建筑群落进行参观的方式。

53. 应当推进对教师进行更新教育、对导游进行指引和训练，以便向年轻人及愿意了解历史遗址的成年人提供帮助。

Ⅵ. 国际合作

54. 成员国应当就历史遗址及其景观保护进行合作并在必要的情形下向政府间及非政府国际组织（尤其是联合国教科文组织的 ICOM－ICOMOS 文件中心）寻求帮助。该等多边及双边合作应当得到仔细的协调，并应通过诸如以下形式的措施进行：

（a）所有形式的信息及科学、技术出版物信息予以交换；

（b）就具体主题组织研讨会及研究会；

（c）提供研究及旅行资助，派遣科学、技术及行政人员，提供设备；

（d）联合抗击所有形式的污染；

（e）实施大规模的历史遗址保护、复原及修复项目并公布所取得的经验。在边疆地区，历史遗址及其景观发展与保护的任务对边疆两侧成员国共同产生了影响，他们应该就其政策及活动予以协调，以确保文化遗产的使用和保护是基于可行的最好方式进行；

（f）邻国基于地区历史及文化发展特点，为了对共同拥有利益的区域进行保护，提供相互协助。

55. 为符合本倡议书之精神与原则，成员国不得采取任何行动毁损或者改变其领土内历史街区、城镇及遗址的特色。

Recommendation concerning the Safeguarding and Contemporary Role of Historic Areas

26 November 1976

The General Conference of the United Nations Educational, Scientific and Cultural Organization, meeting in Nairobi at its nineteenth session, from 26 October to 30 November 1976,

Considering that historic areas are part of the daily environment of human beings everywhere, that they represent the living presence of the past which formed them, that they provide the variety in life's background needed to match the diversity of society, and that by so doing they gain in value and acquire an additional human dimension,

Considering that historic areas afford down the ages the most tangible evidence of the wealth and diversity of cultural, religious and social activities and that their safeguarding and their integration into the life of contemporary society is a basic factor in town - planning and land development,

Considering that in face of the dangers of stereotyping and depersonalization, this living evidence of days gone by is of vital importance for humanity and for nations who find in it both the expression of their way of life and one of the corner - stones of their identity,

Noting that throughout the world, under the pretext of expansion or modernization, demolition ignorant of what it is demolishing and irrational and inappropriate reconstruction work is causing serious damage to this historic heritage,

Considering that historic areas are an immovable heritage whose destruction may often lead to social disturbance, even where it does not lead to economic loss,

Considering that this situation entails responsibilities for every citizen and lays on public authorities obligations which they alone are capable of fulfilling,

Considering that in order to save these irreplaceable assets from the dangers of deterioration or even total destruction to which they are thus exposed, it is for each State to adopt, as a matter of urgency, comprehensive and energetic policies for the protection and revitalization of historic areas and their surroundings as part of national, regional or local planning,

Noting the absence in many cases of a legislation effective and flexible enough concerning the architectural heritage and its interconnexion with town-planning, territorial, regional or local planning,

Noting that the General Conference has already adopted international instruments for the protection of the cultural and natural heritage such as the Recommendation on International Principles Applicable to Archaeological Excavations (1956), the Recommendation Concerning the Safeguarding of the Beauty and Character of Landscapes and Sites (1962), the Recommendation Concerning the. Preservation of Cultural Property En - dangered by Public or Private Works (1968), and the Recommendation Concerning the Protection, at National Level, of the Cultural and Natural Heritage (1972),

Desiring to supplement and extend the application of the standards and principles laid down in these international instruments,

Having before it proposals concerning the safeguarding and contemporary role of historic areas, which question appears on the agenda of the session as item 27,

Having decided at its eighteenth session that this question should take the form of a Recommendation to Member States,

Adopts, this twenty - sixth day of November 1976, the present Recommendation.

The General Conference recommends that Member States apply the above provisions by adopting, as a national law or in some other form, measures with a view to giving effect to the principles and norms set out in this Recommendation in the territories under their jurisdiction.

The General Conference recommends that Member States bring this Recommendation to the attention of the national, regional and local authorities and of institutions, services or bodies and associations concerned with the safeguarding of historic areas and their environment.

The General Conference recommends that Member States report to it, at the dates and in the form determined by it, on action taken by them on this Recommendation.

I. Definitions

1. For the purposes of the present recommendation:

(a) `Historic and architectural (including vernacular) areas' shall be taken to mean any groups of buildings, structures and open spaces including ar - chaeological and palaeontological sites, constituting human settlements in an urban or rural environment, the cohesion and value of which, from the archaeological, architectural, prehistoric, historic, aesthetic or sociocultural point of view are recognized. Among these `areas', which are very varied in nature, it is possible to distinguish the following 'in particular : prehistoric sites, historic towns, old urban quarters, villages and hamlets as well as homogeneous monumental groups, it being understood that the latter should as a rule be carefully preserved unchanged.

(b) The `environment' shall be taken to mean the natural or man - made setting which influences the static or dynamic way these areas are perceived or which is directly linked to them in space or by social, economic or cultural ties.

(c) `Safeguarding' shall be taken to mean the identification, protection, con - servation, restoration, renovation, maintenance and revitalization of historic or traditional areas and their environment.

II. General principles

2. Historic areas and their surroundings should be regarded as forming an irreplaceable universal heritage. The governments and the citizens of the States in whose territory they are situated should deem it their duty to safeguard this heritage and integrate it into the social life of our. times. The national, regional or local authorities should be answerable for their performance of this duty in the interests of all citizens and of the international community, in accordance with the conditions of each Member State as regards the allocation of powers.

3. Every historic area and its surroundings should be considered in their totality as a coherent whole whose balance and specific nature depend on the fusion of the parts of which it is composed and which include human activities as much as the buildings, the spatial organization and the surroundings. All valid elements, including human activities, however modest, thus have a significance in relation to the whole which must not be disregarded.

4. Historic areas and their surroundings should be actively protected, against damage of all kinds, particularly that resulting from unsuitable use, unnecessary additions and misguided or insensitive changes such as will impair their authenticity, and from damage due to any form of pollution. Any restoration work undertaken should be based on scientific principles. Similarly, great at tention should be paid to the harmony and aesthetic feeling produced by the linking or the contrasting of the various parts which make up the groups of buildings and which give to each group its particular character.

5. In the conditions of modern urbanization, which leads to a considerable increase in the scale and density of buildings, apart from the danger of direct destruction of historic areas, there is a real danger that newly developed areas can ruin the environment and character of adjoining historic areas. Architects and town - planners should be careful to ensure that views from and to monuments and historic areas are not spoilt and that historic areas are integrated harmoniously into contemporary life.

6. At a time when there is a danger that a growing universality of building techniques and architectural forms may create a uniform environment throughout the world, the preservation of historic areas can make an outstanding contribution to maintaining and developing the cultural and social values of each nation. This can contribute to the architectural enrichment of the cultural heritage of the world.

III. National, regional and local policy

7. In each Member State a national, regional and local policy should be drawn up, in conformity with the conditions of each State as regards the allocation of powers, so that legal, technical, economic and social measures may be taken by the national, regional or local authorities with a view to safeguarding historic areas

and their surroundings and adapting them to the requirements of modern life. The policy thus laid down should influence planning at national, regional or local level and provide guidelines for town - planning and regional and rural development planning at all levels, the activities stemming from it forming an essential component in the formulation of aims and programmes, the assignment of responsibilities and the conduct of operations. The co - operation of individuals and private associations should be sought in implementing the safeguarding policy.

IV. Safeguarding measures

8. Historic areas and their surroundings should be safeguarded in conformity with the principles stated above and with the methods set out below, the specific measures being determined according to the legislative and constitutional competence and the organizational and economic structure of each State.

Legal and administrative measures

9. The application of an overall policy for safeguarding historic areas and their surroundings should be based on principles which are valid for the whole of each country. Member States should adapt the existing provisions, or, where necessary, enact new laws and regulations, so as to secure the protection of historic areas and their surroundings taking into account the provisions contained in this chapter and in the following chapters. They should encourage the adaptation or the adoption of regional or local measures to ensure such protection. Laws concerning town and regional planning and housing policy should also be reviewed so as to co - ordinate and bring them into line with the laws concerning the safeguarding of the architectural heritage.

10. The provisions establishing a system for safeguarding historic areas should set out the general principles relating to the establishment of the necessary plans and documents and, in particular: the general conditions and restrictions applicable to the protected areas and their surroundings ; a statement as to the programmes and operations to be planned for the purpose of conservation and provision of public services; maintenance to be carried out and the designation of those

to be responsible for it; the fields to which town - planning, redevelopment and rural land management are applicable; the designation of the body responsible for authorizing any restoration, modification, new construction or demolition within the protected perimeter; the means by which the safeguarding programmes are to be financed and carried out.

11. Safeguarding plans and documents should define: the areas and items to be protected; the specific conditions and restrictions applicable to them; the standards to be observed in the work of maintenance, restoration and improvements ; the general conditions governing the establishment of the supply systems and services needed in urban or rural life; the conditions governing new constructions.

12. These laws should also in principle include provisions designed to prevent any infringement of the preservation laws, as well as any speculative rise in property values within the protected areas which could compromise protection and restoration planned in the interests of the community as a whole. These provisions could involve town - planning measures affording a means of influencing the price of building land, such as the establishment of neighborhood or smaller development plans, granting the right of pre - emption to a public body, compulsory purchase in the interests of safeguarding or rehabilitation or automatic intervention in the case of failure to act on the part of the owners, and could provide for effective penalties such as the suspension of operations, compulsory restoration and/or a suitable fine.

13. Public authorities as well as individuals must be obliged to comply with the measures for safeguarding. However, machinery for appeal against arbitrary or unjust decisions should be provided.

14. The provisions concerning the setting up of public and private bodies and concerning public and private work projects should be adapted to the regulations governing the safeguarding of historic areas and their surroundings.

15. In particular, provisions concerning slum property and blocks and the construction of subsidized housing should be planned or amended both to fit in with the safeguarding policy and to contribute to it. The schedule of any subsidies paid should be drawn up and adjusted accordingly, in particular in order to facilitate the development of subsidized housing and public construction by rehabilitating old buildings. All demolition should in any case only concern buildings with

no historic or architectural value and the subsidies involved should be carefully controlled. Further, a proportion of the funds earmarked for the construction of subsidized housing should be allocated to the rehabilitation of old buildings.

16. The legal consequences of the protection measures as far as buildings and land are concerned should be made public and should be recorded by a competent official body.

17. Making due allowance for the conditions specific to each country and the allocation of responsibilities within the various national, regional and local authorities, the following principles should underlie the operation of the safeguarding machinery:

(a) there should be an authority responsible for ensuring the permanent co - ordination of all those concerned, e. g. national, regional and local public services or groups of individuals;

(b) safeguarding plans and documents should be drawn up, once all the necessary advance scientific studies have been carried out, by multidisciplinary teams composed, in particular, of:

specialists in conservation and restoration, including art historians; architects and town - planners;

sociologists and economists;

ecologists and landscape architects ;

specialists in public health and social welfare;

and, more generally, all specialists in disciplines involved in the protection and enhancement of historic areas ;

(c) the authorities should take the lead in sounding the opinions and organizing the participation of the public concerned;

(d) the safeguarding plans and documents should be approved by the body designated by law;

(e) the public authorities reponsible for giving effect to the. safeguarding pro - visions and regulations at all levels, national, regional and local, should be provided with the necessary staff and given adequate technical, administrative and financial resources.

Technical, economic and social measures

18. A list of historic areas and their surroundings to be protected should be

drawn up' at national, regional or local level. It should indicate priorities so that the limited resources available for protection may be allocated judiciously. Any protection measures, of whatever nature, that need to be taken as a matter of urgency should be taken without waiting for the safeguarding plans and documents to be prepared.

19. A survey of the area as a whole, including an analysis of its spatial evolution, should be made. It should cover archaeological, historical, architectural, technical and economic data. An analytical document should be drawn up so as to determine which buildings or groups of buildings are to be protected with great care, conserved under certain conditions, or, in quite exceptional and thoroughly documented circumstances, destroyed. This would enable the authorities to call a halt to any work incompatible with this recommendation. Additionally, an inventory of public and private open spaces and their vegetation should be drawn up for the same purposes.

20. In addition to this architectural survey, thorough surveys of social, economic, cultural and technical data and structures and of the wider urban or regional context are necessary. Studies should include, if possible, demographic data and an analysis of economic, social and cultural activities, ways of life and social relationships, land - tenure problems, the urban infrastructure, the state of the road system, communication networks and the reciprocal links between protected areas and surrounding zones. The authorities concerned should attach the greatest importance to these studies and should bear in mind that valid safeguarding plans cannot be prepared without them.

21. After the survey described above has been completed and before the safeguarding plans and specifications are drawn up, there should in principle be a programming operation in which due account is taken both of town - planning, architectural, economic and social considerations and of the ability of the urban and rural fabric to assimilate functions that are compatible with its specific character. The programming operation should aim at bringing the density of settlement to the desired level and should provide for the work to be carried out in stages as well as for the temporary accommodation needed while it is proceeding, and premises for the permanent rehousing of those inhabitants who cannot return to their previous dwellings. This programming operation should be undertaken with the closest pos-

sible participation of the communities and groups of people concerned. Because the social, economic and physical context of historic areas and their surroundings may be expected to change over time, survey and analysis should be a continuing process. It is accordingly essential that the preparation of safeguarding plans and their execution be undertaken on the basis of studies available, rather than being postponed while the planning process is refined.

22. Once the safeguarding plans and specifications have been drawn up and approved by the competent public authority, it would be desirable for them to be executed either by their authors or under their authority.

23. In historic areas containing features from several different periods, preservation should be carried out taking into account the manifestations of all such periods.

24. Where safeguarding plans exist urban development or slum clearance programmes consisting of the demolition of buildings of no architectural or historic interest and which are structurally too unsound to be kept, the removal of extensions and additional storeys of no value, and sometimes even the demolition of recent buildings which break the unity of the area, may only be authorized in conformity with the plan.

25. Urban development or slum clearance programmes for areas not covered by safeguarding plans should respect buildings and other elements of architectural or historic value as well as accompanying buildings. If such elements are likely to be adversely affected by the programme, safeguarding plans as indicated above should be drawn up in advance of demolition.

26. Constant supervision is necessary to ensure that these operations are not conducive to excessive profits nor serve other purposes contrary to the objectives of the plan.

27. The usual security standards applicable to fire and natural catastrophes should be observed in any urban development or slum clearance programme affecting a historic area, provided that this be compatible with the criteria applicable to the preservation of the cultural heritage. If conflict does occur, special solutions should be sought, with the collaboration of all the services concerned, so as to provide the maximum security, while not impairing the cultural heritage.

28. Particular care should be devoted to regulations for and control over new

buildings so as to ensure that their architecture adapts harmoniously to the spatial organization and setting of the groups of historic buildings. To this end, an analysis of the urban context should precede any new construction not only so as to define the general character of the group of buildings but also to analyse its dominant features, e. g. the harmony of heights, colours, materials and forms, constants in the way the facades and roofs are built, the relationship between the volume of buildings and the spatial volume, as well as their average proportions and their position. Particular attention should be given to the size of the lots since there is a danger that any reorganization of the lots may cause a change of mass which could be deleterious to the harmony of the whole.

29. The isolation of a monument through the demolition of its surroundings should not generally be authorized, neither should a monument be moved unless in exceptional circumstances and for unavoidable reasons.

30. Historic areas and their surroundings should be protected from the disfigurement caused by the erection of poles, pylons and electricity or telephone cables and the placing of television aerials and large - scale advertising signs. Where these already exist appropriate measures should be taken for their removal. Bill - posting, neon signs and other kinds of advertisement, commercial signs, street pavements and furniture, should be planned with the greatest care and controlled so that they fit harmoniously into the whole. Special efforts should be made to prevent all forms of vandalism.

31. Member States and groups concerned should protect historic areas and their surroundings against the increasingly serious environmental damage caused by certain technological developments - in particular the various forms of pollution - by banning harmful industries in the proximity of these areas and by taking preventive measures to counter the destructive effects of noise, shocks and vibrations caused by machines and vehicles. Provision should further be made for measures to counter the harm resulting from overexploitation by tourism.

32. Member States should encourage and assist local authorities to seek solutions to the conflict existing in most historic groupings between motor traffic on the one hand and the scale of the buildings and their architectural qualities on the other. To solve the conflict and to encourage pedestrian traffic, careful attention should be paid to the placing of, and access to, peripheral and even central car

parks and routing systems established which will facilitate pedestrian traffic, service access and public transport alike. Many rehabilitation operations such as putting electricity and other cables underground, too expensive if carried out singly, could then be co - ordinated easily and economically with the development of the road system.

33. Protection and restoration should be accompanied by revitalization activities. It would thus be essential to maintain appropriate existing functions, in particular trades and crafts, and establish new ones, which, if they are to be viable, in the long term, should be compatible with. the economic and social context of the town, region or country where they are introduced. The cost of safeguarding operations should be evaluated not only in terms of the cultural value of the buildings but also in relation to the value they acquire through the use made of them. The social problems of safeguarding cannot be seen correctly unless reference is made to both these value scales. These functions should answer the social, cultural and economic needs of the inhabitants without harming the specific nature of the area concerned. A cultural revitalization policy should make historic areas centers of cultural activities and give them a central role to play in the cultural development of the communities around them.

34. In rural areas all works which cause disturbances and all changes of economic and social structure should be carefully controlled so as to preserve the integrity of historic rural communities within their natural setting.

35. Safeguarding activities should couple the public authorities' contribution with the contribution made by the individual or collective owners and the inhabitants and users, separately or together, who should be encouraged to put forward suggestions and generally play an active part. Constant co - operation between the community and the individual should thus be established at all levels particularly through methods such as: information adapted to the types of persons concerned; surveys adapted to the persons questioned; establishment of advisory groups attached to planning teams; representation of owners, inhabitants and users in an advisory function on bodies responsible for decision - making, management and. the organization of operations connected with plans for safeguarding, or the creation of public corporations to play a part in the plan's implementation.

36. The formation of voluntary conservation groups and non - profit - making

associations and the establishment of honorary or financial rewards should be encouraged so that specially meritorious work in all aspects of safeguarding may be recognized.

37. Availability of the necessary funds for the level of public investment provided for in the plans for the safeguarding of historic areas and their surroundings should be ensured by including adequate appropriations in the budgets of the central, regional and local authorities. All these funds should be centrally managed by public, private or semi - public bodies entrusted with the co - ordination of all forms of financial aid at national, regional or local level and with the channelling of them according to an overall plan of action.

38. Public assistance in the forms described below should be based on the principle that, wherever this is appropriate and necessary, the measures taken by the authorities concerned should take into account the `extra cost' of restoration, i. e. the additional cost imposed on the owner as compared with the new market or rental value of the building.

39. In general, such public funds should be used primarily to conserve existing buildings including especially buildings for low rental housing and should not be allocated to the construction of new buildings unless the latter do not prejudice the use and functions of existing buildings.

40. Grants, subsidies, loans at favourable rates, or tax concessions should be made available to private owners and to users carrying out work provided for by the safeguarding plans and in conformity with the standards laid down in those plans. These tax concessions, grants - and loans could be made first and foremost to groups of owners or users of living accommodation and commercial property, since joint operations are more economical than individual action. The financial concessions granted to private owners and users should, where appropriate, be dependent on covenants requiring the observance of certain conditions laid down in the public interest, and ensuring the integrity of the buildings such as allowing the buildings to be visited and allowing access to parks, gardens or sites, the taking of photographs, etc.

41. Special funds should be set aside in the budgets of public and private bodies for the protection of groups of historic buildings endangered by large scale public works and pollution. Public authorities should also set aside special funds

for the repair of damage caused by natural disasters.

42. In addition, all government departments and agencies active in the field of public works should arrange their programmes and budgets so as to contribute to the rehabilitation of groups of historic buildings by financing work, which is both in conformity with their own aims and the aims of the safeguarding plan.

43. To increase the financial resources - available to them, Member States should encourage the setting up of public and/or private financing agencies for the safeguarding of historic areas and their surroundings. These agencies should have corporate status and be empowered to receive gifts from individuals, foundations and industrial and commercial concerns. Special tax concessions may be granted to donors.

44. The financing of work of any description carried out for the safeguarding of historic areas and their surroundings by setting up a loans corporation, could be facilitated by public institutions and private credit establishments, which would be responsible for making loans to owners at reduced rates of interest with repayment spread out over a long period.

45. Member States and other levels of government concerned could facilitate the creation of non - profit - making associations responsible for buying and, where appropriate after restoration, selling buildings by using revolving funds established for the special purpose of enabling owners of historic buildings who wish to safeguard them and preserve their character to continue to reside there.

46. It is most important that safeguarding measures should not lead to a break in the social fabric. To avoid hardship to the poorest inhabitants consequent on their having to move from buildings or groups of buildings due for renovation, compensation for rises in rent could enable them to keep their homes, commercial premises and workshops and their traditional living patterns and occupations, especially rural crafts, small - scale agriculture, fishing, etc. This compensation, which would be income - related, would help those concerned to pay the increased rentals resulting from the work carried out.

V. Research education and information

47. In order to raise the standard of work of the skilled workers and craftsmen required and to encourage the whole population to realize the need for safeguard-

ing and to take part in it, the following measures should be taken by Member States, in accordance with their legal and constitutional competence.

48. Member States and groups concerned should encourage the systematic study of, and research on: town - planning aspects of historic areas and their environment; the interconnexions between safeguarding and planning at all levels; methods of conservation applicable to historic areas; the alteration of materials ; the application of modern techniques to conservation work; the crafts techniques indispensable for safeguarding.

49. Specific education concerning the above questions and including practical training periods should be introduced and developed. In addition, it is essential to encourage the training of skilled workers and craftsmen specializing in the safeguarding of historic areas, including any open spaces surrounding them. Furthermore, it is necessary to encourage the crafts themselves, which are jeopardized by the processes of industrialization. It is desirable that the institutions concerned co - operate in this matter with specialized international agencies such as the Center for the Study of the Preservation and Restoration of Cultural Property, in Rome, the International Council of Monuments and Sites (ICOMOS) and the International Council of Museums (ICOM).

50. The education of administrative staff for the needs of local development in the field of safeguarding of historic areas should be financed where applicable and needed and directed by the appropriate authorities according to a long - term programme.

51. Awareness of the need for safeguarding work should be encouraged by education in school, out of school and at university and by using information media such as books, the press, television, radio, cinema and travelling exhibitions. Clear, comprehensive information should be provided as to the advantages - not only aesthetic, but also social and economic - to be reaped from a well - conducted policy for the safeguarding of historic areas and their surroundings. Such information should be widely circulated among specialized private and government bodies and the general public so that they may - know why and how their surroundings can be improved in this way.

52. The study of historic areas should be included in education at all levels, especially in history teaching, so as to inculcate in young minds an understanding

of and respect for the works of the past and to demonstrate the role of this heritage in modern life. Education of this kind should make wide use of audio - visual media and of visits to groups of historic buildings.

53. Refresher courses for teachers and guides and the training of instructors should be facilitated so as to aid, groups of young people and adults wishing to learn about historic areas.

VI. International co – operation

54. Member States should co - operate with regard to the safeguarding of historic areas and their surroundings, seeking aid, if it seems desirable, from international organizations, both intergovernmental and non - governmental, in particular that of the UNESCO - ICOM - ICOMOS Documentation Centre. Such multilateral or bilateral cooperation should be carefully co - ordinated and should take the form of measures such as the following:

(a) exchange of information in all forms and of scientific and technical publications;

(b) organization of seminars and working parties on particular subjects;

(c) provision of study and travel fellowships, and the dispatch of scientific, technical and administrative staff, and equipment;

(d) joint action to combat pollution of all kinds;

(e) implementation of large - scale conservation, restoration and rehabilitation projects for historic areas and publication of the experience acquired. In frontier areas where the task of developing and safeguarding historic areas and their surroundings gives rise to problems jointly affecting Member States on either side of the frontier, they should co - ordinate their policies and activities to ensure that the, - cultural heritage is used and protected in the best possible way;

(f) mutual assistance between neighboring countries for the preservation of areas of common interest characteristic of the historic and cultural development of the region.

55. In conformity with the spirit and the principles of this recommendation, a Member State should not take any action to demolish or 'change the character of the historic quarters, towns and sites, situated in territories occupied by that State.

关于保护景观以及遗址风貌与特色的建议*

（联合国教科文大会 1962 年 12 月 11 日通过）

联合国教育、科学及文化组织大会于 1962 年 11 月 9 日至 12 月 12 日在巴黎召开第十二次大会。

考虑到人类在各个时期不时使构成其自然环境组成部分的景观和遗址的风貌与特征遭到损坏，从而使得全世界各个地区的文化、艺术甚至极其重要的遗产濒于枯竭；

考虑到因原始土地的开发，城市中心盲目的发展以及工商业与装备的巨大工程和庞大规划的实施，使现代文明加速了这种趋势，尽管其进程到上个世纪已相对减弱；

考虑到这种现象影响到不论其为自然的或人工的景观和遗址的艺术价值，以及野生生物的文化和科学价值；

考虑到由于景观和遗址的风貌与特征，保护景观和遗址正如本建议所述，对人类生活必不可少；对人类而言，它们代表了一种强而有力的物质、道德和精神的再生影响，同时正如无数众所周知的事例所证明的，也有利于人类的文化和艺术生活；

进一步考虑到景观和遗址是许多国家经济和社会生活中的一个重要因素，而且大大有助于保障其居民的健康；

然而，也认识到应适当考虑社会生活及其演变以及技术进步的迅速发展之需要；

因此，考虑到只要尚有这样做的可能，为保护各地的景观和遗址的风貌与特征，亟待紧急考虑和采取必要的措施；

鉴于此前已收到关于保护景观和遗址的风貌与特征的若干提议，并且该

---

* 郑州大学法学院杨会永译。

问题已列为本次大会的第17.4.2项议程；

考虑到第十一次大会已决定以成员国建议的形式制定一份国际法文件将上述提议的内容纳入其中，

特于1962年12月11日通过本建议。

大会建议各成员国应通过其国内法律或其他方式制定使本建议所体现的准则和原则在其所管辖的领土上生效的措施，以适用以下规定。

大会建议各成员国应将本建议提请与保护景观和遗址以及区域发展有关的部门和机构的注意，也提请受委托保护自然和发展旅游业的机构以及青年组织的注意。

大会建议各成员国应按规定的日期和形式向大会提交有关本建议执行情况的报告。

一、定　义

1. 为本建议之目的，保护景观和遗址的风貌与特征系指保存并在可能的情况下修复无论是自然的或人工的，具有文化或艺术价值，或构成典型自然环境的自然、乡村及城市景观和遗址的任何部分。

2. 本建议的规定也拟作为保护自然的补充措施。

二、总　则

3. 为保护景观和遗址所进行的研究和采取的措施应适用于一国之全部领土范围，并不应局限于某些选定的景观和遗址。

4. 在选择将采取的措施时，应适当考虑有关景观与遗址的相关意义。这些措施可根据景观与遗址的特征、大小、位置以及它们所面临威胁的性质而有所区别。

5. 保护不应只局限于自然景观与遗址，而应扩展到那些全部或部分由人工形成的景观与遗址。因此，应制定特别规定确保对那些通常受威胁最大、特别是因建筑施工和土地买卖而受到威胁的某些城市中的景观和遗址进行保护。对进入古迹应采取特别保护措施。

6. 为保护景观和遗址所采取的措施应既是预防性的，又是补救性的。

7. 预防性措施应旨在保护遗址免受可能威胁它们的危险。这些措施尤其应包括对可能损坏景观和遗址的工程和活动进行监督，例如：

（1）建造各种公共或私人建筑，其设计应符合建筑本身的某些艺术要求，并且在避免简单模仿某些传统的和独特的形式的同时，应与它将保护的一般环境相协调；

（2）修建道路；

（3）高、低压电线、电力生产和输送工厂和设施、飞机场、广播电台和电视台等；

（4）加油站；

（5）广告招牌以及灯光招牌；

（6）砍伐森林，包括破坏构成景观风貌的树木，尤其是主干道或林荫道两旁成行的树木；

（7）空气和水的污染；

（8）采矿、采石及其废弃物的处理；

（9）喷泉管道、灌溉工程、水坝、隧道、沟渠、治理河流工程等；

（10）宿营地；

（11）废弃物和垃圾以及家庭、商业和工业废物的倾倒。

8. 在保护景观和遗址的风貌与特征时，也应考虑到因某些工作和现代生活的某些活动而引起的噪音所造成的危害。

9. 除为公共或社会利益之迫切需要外，对可能损坏以其他方式列入保护目录或受到保护的地区内的景观和遗址的活动应施以制裁。

10. 补救性措施应旨在修缮对景观和遗址所造成的损坏，并尽可能使其恢复至原状。

11. 为促进各国负责保护景观和遗址的各种公共服务机构的工作，应建立科学研究机构，以便与主管当局合作，收集和编纂适用于这方面的法律和规定。这些规定和研究机构所从事的工作成果应定期实时刊登于专门的行政刊物上。

三、保护措施

12. 景观和遗址的保护应通过使用以下方法得以确保：

（1）由主管当局进行全面监督；

（2）将责任列入城市发展规划以及区域、乡村和城市的各级规划；

（3）“通过分区”列出大面积景观区保护目录；

（4）列出零散的遗址保护目录；

（5）建立和维护自然保护区与国家公园；

（6）由社区购买遗址。

全面监督

13. 对全国范围内可能损坏景观和遗址的工程和活动，应实行全面监督。

城市规划与乡村规划方案

14. 城市规划与乡村规划方案应包括，明确那些应强制执行的义务规定，以确保位于所涉及地区内的甚至未列入保护目录的景观和遗址得到保护。政府实施的强制征收活动，以及在已列入保护目录的遗址中实施公共工程，应征得主管当局的同意。

15. 城市和乡村规划方案应根据轻重缓急予以制定，特别是对处在迅速发展过程中的城市或地区，为保护该城市或地区的艺术或优美特征制定此种方案是合理的。

“通过分区”列出大面积景观区保护目录

16. 大面积景观区“通过分区”列入保护目录。

17. 在一个已列入保护目录的区域内，当艺术特征为头等重要时，列入保护目录应包括：地块控制；遵循美学要求，包括材料的使用、颜色以及高度标准；采取预防措施以消除因筑坝和采石所造成的动土影响；制定管理树木砍伐的法规等。

18. “通过分区”列出的目录应予以公布，并应制订和公布为保护已列入目录的景观所应遵守的一般规则。

19. 一般来说，“通过分区”列出保护目录，不应涉及赔偿金的支付。

列出零散遗址保护目录

20. 对无论位于自然中还是位于城市内的零散小遗址，连同某个具有特殊意义的景观的各个部分，均应列入保护目录。对景色优美的地区，以及著名古迹周围的地区和建筑物，也应列入保护目录。凡列入保护目录的每一个遗址、地区和建筑物都须经过特别行政决定，并及时通知其所有者。

21. 列入保护目录即意味着未经主管当局的许可，所有者不得擅自损毁该遗址、改变其环境或风貌等。

22. 主管当局发布上述许可时，应同时满足遗址保护所必需的全部条件。然而，正常的农耕活动，以及正常的建筑物维护工程，不需经主管当局的许可。

23. 政府实施的强制征收活动，以及在已列入保护目录的遗址中实施公共工程，应征得主管当局的同意。任何人不得根据法令，获得可能改变已列入保护目录的遗址的特性或风貌的权利。遗址所有者也不得未经主管当局的同意，被授予习惯性权利。

24. 任何情况下绝对禁止对列入保护目录遗址的土地、空气或水的污染，矿石开采同样应经主管当局的特别许可。

25. 在已列入保护目录地区及其紧邻周边环境中，禁止任何形式的广告；或者仅限于在经负责保护该遗址的主管当局同意的特别位置发布广告。

26. 原则上，在列入保护目录遗址上的宿营申请应予拒绝，或者仅在经主管当局确定的固定区域内许可宿营，并予以监督。

27. 当所有者因其遗址被列入保护目录而遭受直接、明确的损害时，其有权获得赔偿。

自然保护区和国家公园

28. 如果情况允许，成员国应当将受保护的遗址和分区与供公众教育和娱乐的国家公园或自然保护区进行整合。该自然保护区和国家公园应形成一系列旨在研究景观的形成与修复以及自然保护的实验性分区。

由社区购买遗址

29. 成员国应当鼓励具保护意愿的景观或遗址所在地区的社区出资收购该景观或遗址。如有必要，可以采取强制征收方法予以收购。

四、保护措施的应用

30. 每一成员国制定的景观和遗址保护的基本规范和原则应具有法律效力，应在法律授权的框架内委托主管当局采取措施予以落实。

31. 成员国应当组建专业的行政性或咨询性机构。

32. 行政机构应是经授权实施保护性措施的专门中央或地方部门。为此，该部门应当履行以下职务：研究保护和编制保护目录时遇到的问题；实施现场勘查；制定所需采取的保护措施，以及监督该措施的执行。同时，该机构应有权提出相关措施的建议，以降低因实施某种工程或修复因该工程遭受的损坏而带来的风险。

33. 咨询机构应由国家、地区或地方层面的委员会组成，负责研究与保护相关的问题，并就此问题向中央、地区当局或者当地社区提出意见。委员会的意见在任何环节都应能及时获取，特别是在涉及公共利益的大规模工程的初步规划阶段，例如修建高速公路、安装水处理技术或新型工业设施等。

34. 成员国应推动国家和地方非政府组织的建立与运作，其职能之一是与第 31、32、33 款提及的机构开展合作，尤其是将威胁景观和遗址的风险因素告知公众，并向主管部门发布警示。

35. 违反景观和遗址保护规则的行为应被要求支付赔偿金，或履行尽可能恢复至遗址原状的义务。

36. 对故意破坏受保护景观和遗址的违法行为，应处以行政或刑事制裁。

五、公众教育

37. 应在校内和校外开展教育活动，以唤起和增进公众对景观和遗址的尊重，并公开宣传相关保护法律和措施。

38. 校内开展教育活动的教师应经过中级和高等教育机构开办的专业课程的专门培训。

39. 成员国也应推动现有博物馆的工作，以加强其所已经开展的教育活动；并考虑建立专门博物馆或在现有博物馆设置专门部门的可能性，研究和展示特定地区的自然和文化特色。

40. 新闻媒体、保护景观和遗址及保护自然的私人团体、旅游行业相关组织以及青年或大众教育组织，负有开展校外公众教育的任务。

41. 成员国应推动公众教育，促进有志于本项任务的协会、团体和组织的工作，通过提供物质帮助，并使他们和教育工作者能够利用电影、广播电视节目等宣传媒体，为其提供常设性、临时性或流动展览物品、适合广泛传播且已规划教育路线的宣传册和书籍。可通过期刊、杂志以及地方定期出版物进行广泛宣传。

42. 设置国家和国际性的景观和遗址保护“节日”，组织竞赛和类似的重大活动，有助于鼓励人们欣赏自然或人造景观和遗址，以引导公众认识到这一事实，即保护景观和遗址的风貌和特性对社区而言是极其重要的。

Recommendation concerning the Safeguarding of Beauty and Character of Landscapes and Sites

11 December 1962

The General Conference of the United Nations Educational, Scientific and Cultural Organization, meeting in Paris from 9 November to 12 December 1962, in its twelfth session:

Considering that at all periods men have sometimes subjected the beauty and character of landscapes and sites forming part of their natural environment to damage which has impoverished the cultural, aesthetic and even vital heritage of whole regions in all parts of the world,

Considering that by the cultivation of virgin land, the sometimes ill - regulated development of urban centers, the carrying out of extensive works and vast plans for industrial and commercial development and equipment. modern civilizations have accelerated this trend whose progress was relatively slow up to the last century,

Considering that this phenomenon affects the aesthetic value of landscapes and sites, natural or man - made, and the cultural and scientific importance of wild life,

Considering that, on account of their beauty and character, the safeguarding of landscapes and sites, as defined in this recommendation, is necessary to the life of men for whom they represent a powerful physical, moral and spiritual regenerating influence, while at the same time contributing to the artistic and cultural life of peoples, as innumerable and universally known examples bear witness,

Considering furthermore that landscapes and sites are an important factor in the economic and social life of many countries, and are largely instrumental in ensuring the health of their inhabitants,

Recognizing, however, that due account should be taken of the needs of com - munity life, its evolution and the rapid development of technical progress,

Considering, therefore, that it is highly desirable and urgent to consider and adopt the necessary steps with a view to safeguarding the beauty and character of landscapes and sites everywhere, whenever it is still possible to do so,

Having before it proposals concerning the safeguarding of the beauty and character of landscapes and sites, this question forming item 17. 4. 2 of the session's agenda,

Having decided at its eleventh session that proposals on this item should be the subject of an international instrument in the form of a recommendation to Member States,

Adopts, on this eleventh day of December 1962, this recommendation.

The General Conference recommends that Member States should apply the following provisions by adopting, in the form of a national law or in some other way, measures designed to give effect in the territories under their jurisdiction to the norms and principles embodied in this recommendation.

The General Conference recommends that Member States should bring this recommendation to the attention of the authorities and bodies concerned with the protection of landscapes and sites and with regional development, and of bodies entrusted with the protection of nature and the development of the tourist trade, together with youth organizations.

The General Conference recommends that Member States should, on dates and in a form to be determined, submit to it reports concerning the implementation of this recommendation.

I. Definition

1. For the purpose of this recommendation, the safeguarding of the beauty and character of landscapes and sites is taken to mean the preservation and, where possible, the restoration of the aspect of natural, rural and urban landscapes and sites, whether natural or man - made, which have a cultural or aesthetic interest or form typical natural surroundings.

2. The provisions of this recommendation are also intended to supplement' measures for the protection of nature.

II. General principles

3. The studies and measures to be adopted with a view to the safeguarding of landscapes and sites should extend to the whole territory of a State, and should not be confined to certain selected landscapes or sites.

4. In choosing the measures to be adopted, due account should be taken of the relative significance of the landscapes and sites concerned. These measures might vary in accordance with the character and size of the landscapes and sites, their location and the nature of the dangers with which they are threatened.

5. Protection should not be limited to natural landscapes and sites, but should also extend to landscapes and sites whose formation is due wholly or in part to the work of man. Thus, special provisions should be made to ensure the safeguarding of certain urban landscapes and sites which are, in general, the most threatened, especially by building operations and land speculation. Special protection should be accorded to the approaches to monuments.

6. Measures taken for the safeguarding of landscapes and sites should be both preventive and corrective.

7. Preventive measures should be aimed at protecting sites from dangers which may threaten them. These measures should include, in particular, the supervision of works and activities likely to damage landscapes and sites, for example :

(a) The construction of all types of public and private buildings. These should be designed so as to meet certain aesthetic requirements in respect of the building itself and, while avoiding a facile imitation of certain traditional and picturesque forms, should be in harmony with the general atmosphere which it is desired to safeguard;

(b) The construction of roads;

(c) High or low tension electric lines, power production and transmission plant and equipment, aerodromes, broadcasting and television stations, etc.;

(d) Petrol filling stations;

(e) Advertising hoardings and illuminated signs;

(f) Deforestation, including the destruction of trees contributing to the beauty of the landscape, particularly those lining thoroughfares or avenues;

(g) Pollution of the air and water;

(h) Working of mines and quarries and the disposal of their waste products;

(i) Piping of spring water, irrigation works, dams, channels, aqueducts, river regulation works, etc.; Camping;

(j) Dumping of worn - out material and waste, and domestic, commercial or industrial scrap.

8. In safeguarding the beauty and character of landscapes and sites, allowance should also be made for the dangers resulting from certain forms of work and certain activities of present - day life, by reason of the noise which they occasion.

9. Activities likely to mar landscapes or sites in areas that are scheduled or protected in some other way should be sanctioned only if the public or social welfare imperatively requires it.

10. Corrective measures should be aimed at repairing the damage caused to landscapes and sites and, as far as possible., restoring them to their original condition.

11. In order to facilitate the task of the various public services responsible for the safeguarding of landscapes and sites in each State, scientific research institutes should be set up to co - operate with the competent authorities with a view to the alignment and codification of the laws and regulations applicable in this matter. These provisions and the results of the work carried out by the research institutes should be published in a single administrative publication brought periodically up to date.

III. Protective measures

12. The safeguarding of landscapes and sites should be ensured by use of the following methods:

(a) General supervision by the responsible authorities ;

(b) Insertion of obligations into urban development plans and planning at all levels: regional, rural and urban;

(c) Scheduling of extensive landscapes `by zones';

(d) Scheduling of isolated sites;

(e) Creation and maintenance of natural reserves and national parks;

(f) Acquisition of sites by communities.

General supervision

13. General supervision should be exercised over works and activities likely to damage landscapes and sites throughout the whole territory of the State.

Town planning and rural planning schemes

14. Urban and rural planning schemes should embody provisions defining the obligations which should be imposed to ensure the safeguarding of landscapes and sites, even unscheduled ones, situated on the territory affected. Expropriation by the authorities, together with the carrying out of public works in a scheduled site, should be subject to the agreement of the authorities

15. Urban and rural planning schemes should be drawn up in order of urgency, specifically for towns or regions in process of rapid development, where the protection of the aesthetic or picturesque character of the town or region justifies the establishment of such schemes.

Scheduling of extensive landscapes by zones´

16. Extensive landscapes should be scheduled `by zones'.

17. When, in a scheduled zone, the aesthetic character is of prime importance, scheduling `by zones' should involve control of plots and observation of certain general requirements of an aesthetic order covering the use of materials, and their colour, height standards, precautions to be taken to conceal disturbances of the soil resulting from the construction of dams and the operation of quarries, and regulations governing the cutting down of trees, etc.

18. Scheduling `by zones' should be publicized, and general rules to be observed for the safeguarding of scheduled landscapes should be enacted and made public.

19. Scheduling `by zones' should not, as a rule, involve payment of compensation.

Scheduling of isolated sites

20. Isolated small sites, whether natural or urban, together with portions of a landscape of particular interest, should be scheduled. Areas which provide a fine view, and areas and buildings surrounding an outstanding monument should also

be scheduled. Each of these scheduled sites, areas and buildings should be the subject of a special administrative decision of which the owner should be duly notified.

21. Scheduling should mean that the owner is prohibited from destroying the site, or altering its condition or aspect, without permission from the authorities responsible for its protection.

22. When such permission is granted, it should be accompanied by all the conditions necessary to the safeguarding of the site. No permission should be needed, however, for normal agricultural activities, nor for normal maintenance work on buildings.

23. Expropriation by the authorities, together with the carrying out of public works in a scheduled site, should be subject to the agreement of the authorities responsible for its protection. No - one should be able to acquire, by prescription, within a scheduled site, rights likely to change the character or aspect of the site. No conventionary rights should be granted by the owner without the agreement of the responsible authorities.

24. Scheduling should involve a prohibition on the pollution of the ground, air or water in any way whatsoever, while the extraction of minerals should likewise be 'subject to special permission.

25. All advertising should be forbidden in a scheduled area and its immediate surroundings, or be limited to special emplacements to be decided by the authorities responsible for the protection of the site.

26. Permission to camp in a scheduled site should, in principle, be refused, or granted only within an area fixed by the responsible authorities and subject to their inspection.

27. Scheduling of a site may entitle the owner to compensation in cases of direct and definite prejudice resulting there from.

Natural reserves and national parks

28. When conditions are suitable, Member States should incorporate in the zones and sites to be protected, national parks intended for the education and recreation of the public, or natural reserves, strict or special. Such natural reserves and national parks should form a group of experimental zones intended also for research into the formation and restoration of the landscape and the protection of nature.

Acquisition of sites by communities

29. Member States should encourage the acquisition by communities of areas forming part of a landscape or site which it is desired to protect. When necessary, it should be possible to effect such acquisition by expropriation.

IV. Application of protective measures

30. The fundamental norms and principles governing the protection of land - scapes and sites in each Member State should have the force of law, and the measures for their application should be entrusted' to the responsible authorities within the framework of the powers conferred on them by law.

31. Member States should set up specialized bodies of an administrative or advisory nature.

32. The administrative bodies should be specialized central or regional departments entrusted with carrying out protective measures. Accordingly, those departments should be in a position to study problems of protection and scheduling, to undertake surveys on the spot, to prepare decisions to be taken and to supervise their implementation. They should likewise be entrusted with proposing measures designed to reduce the dangers which may be involved in carrying out certain types of work or repairing damage caused by such work.

33. The advisory bodies should consist of commissions at national, regional or local level, entrusted with the task of studying questions relating to protection and giving their opinion on those questions to the central or regional authorities or to the local communities concerned. The opinion of these commissions should be sought in all cases and in good time, particularly at the stage of preliminary planning, in the case of large - scale works of public interest, such as the building of highways, the setting up of hydro - technical or new industrial installations, etc.

34. Member States should facilitate the formation and operation of national and local non - governmental bodies, one of whose functions would be to collaborate with the bodies mentioned in paragraphs 31, 32 and 33, particularly by informing the public and warning the appropriate departments of dangers threatening landscapes and sites.

35. Violation of the rules governing the protection of landscapes and sites

should involve payment of damages or the obligation to restore the site to its former condition, as far as possible.

36. Administrative or criminal prosecutions should be provided for in the case of deliberate damage to protected landscapes and sites.

V. Education of the public

37. Educational action should be taken in school and out of school with a view to arousing and developing public respect for landscapes and sites and publicizing the regulations laid down to ensure their protection.

38. Teachers to be entrusted with this task in schools should undergo special training in the form of specialized courses in institutions of secondary and higher education.

39. Member States should also facilitate the work of existing museums, with a view to intensifying the educational action they have already undertaken to this end, and should consider the possibility of establishing special museums, - or specialized departments in existing museums, for the study and display of the natural and cultural features of particular regions.

40. The education of the public outside schools should be the task of the press; of private associations for the protection of landscapes and sites or for the protection of nature, of bodies concerned with - the tourist trade and of youth or popular education organizations.

41. Member States should facilitate the education of the public and promote the work of associations, bodies and organizations devoted to this task by the supply of material assistance - and by making available to them and to educationists in general appropriate publicity media such as films, radio and television programmes, material for permanent, temporary or mobile exhibitions. pamphlets and books suitable for wide distribution and planned on educational lines. Wide publicity could be provided through journals and magazines and regional periodicals.

42. National and international `days', competitions and similar occasions should be devoted to encouraging the appreciation of natural or man - made landscapes and sites in order to direct public attention to the fact that the protection of their beauty and character is of prime importance to the community.

关于保护被公共或私人工程危及的文化财产的建议*

（联合国教科文大会1968年11月19日通过）

联合国教育、科学及文化组织大会于1968年10月15日至11月20日在巴黎举行第十五次大会。

考虑到当代文明及其未来发展除了有赖于其他因素外，还有赖于全世界人民的文化传统、创造力以及社会与经济的发展；

考虑到文化财产是昔日不同传统和精神成就的产物和见证，因此，它是全世界人民民族特征的重要组成部分；

考虑到根据文化财产的历史和艺术价值尽量予以保护的必要性，以使有关文化财产的意义和信息成为人们据此可以了解自身尊严的精神生活的一部分；

考虑到根据联合国教育、科学及文化组织1966年11月4日第十四次大会通过的《国际文化合作原则宣言》的精神，保护文化遗产并对人们开放，构成鼓励各国人民互相了解的方法，从而有利于和平事业；

考虑到各国人民的福祉特别有赖于一个有利的、起促进作用的环境，而对历史上各个时期的文化财产的保护则直接有利于这一环境的形成和维护；

另一方面，认识到世界文明的趋向，即工业化在人类发展及其精神的和民族的成就方面发挥着重要作用；

但也考虑到由于工业的发展和城市化的趋势，那些远古的、史前的及历史的古迹遗址以及诸多具有艺术、历史或科学价值的现代建筑，正日益受到公共和私人工程的威胁；

考虑到除促进社会和经济发展外，各国政府也有责任尽力确保人类文化遗产的保护和保存；

---

* 郑州大学法学院杨会永译。

考虑到协调文化遗产的保护和社会经济的发展所带来的变化刻不容缓，因此，应努力以宽厚的理解精神并根据可靠的规划来满足这两方面的要求；

同样也考虑到适当保护并对人们开放文化财产，非常有利于拥有这些人类瑰宝的国家和地区，通过发展民族和国际旅游业促进其社会和经济的发展；

最后考虑到保护文化财产的最可靠的保障，在于人类本身对它们的尊重和感情，并且相信通过各成员国采取适当的措施可极大地加强这种感情。

已收到关于保护受到公共或私人工程危害的文化财产的若干提案，并将其列为本次大会第十六项议程；

第十三次大会已决定以成员国建议的形式制定一份国际文件，将上述提案的内容纳入该文件，

特于 1968 年 11 月 19 日通过本建议。

大会建议各国成员应采取为在其各自领土内实施本建议所规定的原则和规范所可能需要的任何立法或其他措施，以适用下述各项规定。

大会建议各成员国应把本建议提请负责公共或私人工程的当局或行政部门以及负责保存与保护古迹和历史、艺术、考古和科学遗址的机构的注意和重视。大会也建议应同样把此建议通知制定教育和旅游发展规划的机构。

大会建议各成员国应按照由大会确定的日期和方式，向大会递交关于其实施本建议所采取行动的报告。

一、定　义

1. 为本建议之目的，“文化财产”一词适用于：

1.1 不可移动之物体，无论宗教的或世俗的，诸如考古、历史或科学遗址、建筑或其他具有历史、科学、艺术或建筑价值的特征，包括传统建筑群、城乡建筑区内的历史住宅区以及仍以有效形式存在的早期文化的民族建筑。它既适用于地下发现的考古或历史遗存，又适用于地上现存的不可移动的遗址。文化财产一词也包括此类财产周围的环境。

1.2 具有文化价值的可移动财产，包括存在于或发掘于不可移动财产中的物品，以及埋藏于地下可能会在考古或历史遗址或其他地方发现的物品。

2. “文化财产”一词不仅包括已经确定的和列入目录的建筑、考古及历史遗址和建筑，而且也包括未列入目录的或尚未分类的古代遗迹，以及具有艺术或历史价值的近代遗址和建筑。

二、总　　则

3. 保护文化财产的措施应广泛适用于一个成员国的全部领土，而不应只局限于某些古迹和遗址。

4. 重要的文化财产的保护清单均应予以维护，而无论其已列入保护目录或尚未列入保护目录。若无此种清单，应优先在文化财产受到公共或私人工程威胁的地区，对此类财产进行全面调查，以建立此种清单。

5. 根据以下要求采取措施时，应充分考虑有关文化财产的相对价值：

5.1 保护整个遗址、建筑或其他形式的不可移动文化财产免受私人或公共工程的影响；

5.2 如果发现有文化财产的地区将由于公共或私人工程而遭到改变，并且所涉及的全部或部分文化财产将予以保存或搬迁，则应对该文化财产进行抢救或拯救。

6. 抢救措施应根据文化财产的特点、大小和位置以及它所受到的危害的性质而有所不同。

7. 保护或抢救文化财产的措施应具有预防性和补救性。

8. 预防性和补救性措施应旨在保护或抢救可能受公共或私人工程损坏或毁坏的文化财产，如：

（1）城市扩建和更新工程；尽管这些工程也许会保留列入目录的古迹，但是有时会迁移一些不甚重要的建筑，结果却破坏了历史关系和历史居住区的环境；

（2）在一些地区所进行的类似工程；该地区的传统建筑群作为一个整体具有文化价值，但由于缺乏一个已列入目录的古迹而有被毁坏的危险；

（3）对单个历史建筑物的不适当的修改和修缮；

（4）修建或改建对遗址、具有历史意义的重要建筑物或建筑群构成特别威胁的高速公路；

（5）修建灌溉、水力发电站或防洪大坝；

（6）铺设管道以及动力线和输电线；

（7）农田耕作，包括深耕、排水和灌溉，土地的清理和平整以及植树造林；

（8）因工业的发展以及工业化社会的技术进步所需的工程，如机场、采矿和采石以及河道和港口的疏浚和拓展。

9. 为保持历史的联系和延续性，各成员国应对受到公共和私人工程危害的文化遗产“就地保护”所需的措施给予适当的优先考虑。当经济或社会形势需要必须迁移、放弃或毁掉文化财产时，抢救或拯救行动毫无例外应包括对所涉及的文化遗产进行仔细研究并制备详细记录。

10. 为相关的抢救行动——尤其在不可移动文化财产的全部或大部分已被遗弃或毁掉时——所进行的具有科学或历史价值的研究结果，应予以公布，或以其他方式提供给人们，供今后研究之用。

11. 为了免遭公共或私人工程毁坏而迁移的重要建筑和其他古迹，应安置在与其原来的位置、自然、历史或艺术相联系的及相似的地点或环境中。

12. 重要的可移动文化财产，包括从考古发掘中发现的、从抢救行动中获得的具有代表性的样品，应为研究之目的而予以保存，或放在诸如博物馆（包括遗址博物馆）或大学等机构中展览。

三、保护和抢救措施

13. 对受到公共或私人工程威胁的文化财产的保护或抢救应通过采取以下措施得到保障，具体措施将成员国的立法和组织机构来决定：

（1）立法；

（2）财政；

（3）行政措施；

（4）保护和抢救文化财产的程序；

（5）处罚；

（6）修缮；

（7）奖励；

（8）咨询；

（9）教育计划。

立法

14. 各成员国应根据本建议所述准则和原则，制定或维护确保受到公共或私人工程危害的文化财产的保护或抢救所需的国家和地方立法措施。

财政

15. 各成员国应保证有足够的预算用于保护或抢救受到公共或私人工程危害的文化财产。尽管法律制度和传统的差异以及财力的不同有碍于采取统一措施，但以下各点应予以考虑：

15.1 负责保护文化财产的国家或地方当局应有足够的预算对受到公共或私人工程危害文化财产进行保护或抢救；或者；

15.2 保护或抢救受到公共或私人工程危害的文化财产的费用，包括初步的考古研究费用，应作为建设预算的一部分；或者；

15.3 应提供结合上述第15.1款和第15.2款所述两种方法的可行性。

16. 如果由于所需工程巨大并且复杂而引起的特殊开支，应有可能通过立法、特别补助、国家古迹资助或其他适当途径得到额外资金。负责保护文化财产的行政部门，应被授权管理或使用这笔用于保护或抢救受到公共或私人工程危害的文化财产的预算外捐款。

17. 各成员国应通过以下方法，鼓励重要的历史或艺术建筑（包括构成传统建筑群一部分的建筑）所有者，或城乡建筑区内具有历史意义的街区的居民，保护其文化财产特征及其美学特点，否则它们将受到公共或私人工程的危害：

17.1 优惠的税率；或者

17.2 通过适当的立法编制一项预算，以赠款、贷款或其他方式帮助地方当局、团体和具有艺术、考古、科学或历史重要性建筑（包括传统建筑群）的私人所有者，维护这些建筑或使之适应当代社会所需的作用；

17.3 提供结合上述第17.1款和第17.2款所述两种方法的可能性；

18. 如果文化财产尚未被列入保护目录或相反已得到保护，其所有者应有可能向有关当局要求此种帮助。

19. 国家或地方当局以及私人所有者在为保护受到公共或私人工程危害的文化财产编制预算时，应考虑到文化财产的内在价值及其因对游客的吸引力而可能产生的经济收益。

行政措施

20. 保护或抢救受到公共或私人工程危害的文化财产的责任，应委托给适当的官方机构。若已经存在保护文化财产的官方机构或行政部门，就应赋予它们保护文化财产免受公共或私人工程危害的责任。若不存在这种行政部门，就应该设立特别机构或行政部门，以保护受公共或私人工程危害的文化财产。尽管宪法规定和传统的差异有碍于采取统一体系，但某些共同的原则，应予以采纳：

20.1 应设立一个协调或咨询机构，由负责保护文化财产、负责公共和私人工程、负责城市规划部门的代表以及研究和教育机构的代表组成。这些代表应能就保护受到公共或私人工程危害的文化财产，特别是就公共或私人工程的需求与保护抢救文化财产之间的利益冲突方面提出建议；

20.2 省、市或其他形式的地方政府也应设有负责保护或抢救受到公共或私人工程危害的文化财产的行政部门。这些行政部门应能根据自己的职能和需要，请求国家行政部门或其他有关机构的帮助；

20.3 负责保护文化财产的行政部门应配备足够的保护或抢救受到公共或私人工程危害的文化财产所需的专家，如建筑师、城市规划师、考古学家、历史学家、督导员以及其他专家和技师；

20.4 应采取行政措施，协调不同的负责保护文化财产的行政部门，与负责公共和私人工程以及其他负责保护或抢救文化财产免受公共或私人工程危害的行政部门之间的工作；

20.5 应采取行政措施，在所有存在需要被保护以免受公共和私人工程危害的历史住宅区、遗址和遗迹的地区，无论是已列入目录还是未列入目录，都要建立一个负责城市发展规划的行政机构或委员会；

21. 在对任何被确认为具有文化意义或可能包含考古或历史价值物品的建造地点进行初步调查阶段，首先应在区域或市级层面设计若干不同方案，以备决策考虑。备选方案的选择应在综合比较分析的基础之上做出，以便能够采取从经济和保护或抢救文化财产角度考虑都是最优的解决方案；

保护和抢救文化财产的程序

22. 在任何可能危害文化财产的公共或私人工程实施之前，应做好充分的调查，以确定：

22.1 可采取对重要文化财产的就地保护措施；

22.2 抢救行为的工作量，例如拟发掘的考古遗址的选择、建筑物的迁移以及可移动文化财产的抢救等；

23. 保护或抢救文化财产的措施应当在公共或私人工程实施之前做好。在应受所有国家法律保护的具有考古或文化价值的地区，诸如历史古城、村落、遗址和城区等，新的建设工程的启动应以实施初步考古发掘为前提条件。如有必要，应推迟工期以确保采取充分措施保护或抢救相关文化财产。

24. 重要考古遗迹，特别是像很难发现的史前遗迹、城乡建筑区内具有历史意义的街区、传统建筑群、早期文化的民族建筑以及其他不可移动文化财产，应当通过分区规划或列入保护目录的方法予以保护，否则它们将受到公共或私人工程的危害：

24.1 考古保护区应予分区规划或列入保护目录，如有必要，可收购不可移动文化财产，以便能够彻底发掘或就地保存发现的废墟；

24.2 对城乡中心内具有历史意义的街区、传统建筑群，应进行分区并采取适当管制措施，以保留其周围环境和特征，例如对具有历史或艺术价值的建筑物的修缮程度施加控制，以及控制可引进的新建筑物的类型和设计。对于城市改造的良好设计规划方案来说，保护名胜古迹应是一个绝对条件，尤其是对历史城镇或街区的城市而言。类似的管制措施应当涵盖列入保护目录的遗迹或遗址的周边区域和周围环境，以保护其关联性和特征。应适当允许将一般管制措施调整适用于新的建设活动；当新的建设物被划入历史功能分区后，应中止执行该管制措施。利用海报和灯光等进行一般性商业广告应予禁止，但是应允许商业机构使用精心设计的标志展示其业务。

25. 成员国应当明确，在公共或私人工程实施过程中发现考古遗迹者有义务尽可能早地将其报告给主管部门。相关主管部门应当进行仔细勘察，如果该遗址很重要，应延缓建设，以便进行彻底的发掘，对因工程迟延而遭受的损失应予适当补助或赔偿。

26. 成员国应当规定收购条款，由国家或地方政府以及其他相关团体购买那些受公共或私人工程危害的重要文化财产。如有必要，可通过强制征收的方式进行收购。

27. 成员国应当采取措施，确保因故意或过失而妨碍保护或抢救受公共或私人工程危害文化财产的违法行为，受到其刑法的严厉制裁，处以罚金或监禁，或者二者并处。此外，下列措施亦可采用：

27.1 如有可能，由破坏者对其所损坏的遗址或建筑物承担修复费用；

27.2 在偶然性考古发现中，如果不可移动文化财产受到损坏、破坏或放任不管，应向国家支付赔偿金；对被隐匿起来的可移动物品，应予没收而无需赔偿。

修缮

28. 成员国应当根据文化财产本身性质之所许，采取必要措施确保修缮、修复或重建遭受公共或私人工程损坏的文化财产。成员国也应预知要求地方当局和重要文化财产的私人所有者实施修缮或修复活动的可能性，必要时可给予技术和财政上的支持。

奖励

29. 成员国应鼓励个人、团体和市政当局参加保护或抢救受公共或私人工程危害的文化财产的活动。有效措施包括：

29.1 向进行报告或返还被隐匿的考古发现物品的个人给予特别奖励；

29.2 向个人授予荣誉证书、奖章或其他形式的奖励，即便他们隶属于在保护或抢救受公共或私人工程危害的文化财产方面作出杰出贡献的政府部门、团体、机构或市政当局。

咨询

30．成员国应当为缺乏必需经验的个人、团体或市政当局或其工作人员，提供技术建议或进行监督，以维持保护或抢救受公共或私人工程危害的文化财产的适当标准。

教育计划

31．本着国际合作的精神，成员国应采取措施激励和增强国民对昔日本国和他国传统文化遗产的兴趣和尊重，以保护或抢救受公共或私人工程危害的文化财产。

32．专业出版物、报纸上的文章以及广播电视应揭露那些设计拙劣的公共或私人工程对文化财产所造成威胁的本质，并宣传文化财产得以成功保护或抢救的典型案例。

33．教育机构、历史文化团体、与旅游产业相关的公共组织以及大众教育团体应当展开活动，宣传短视的公共或私人工程对文化财产所造成的威胁，并强调文化财产保护工程有助于增进国家间的交流。

34．博物馆、教育机构以及其他感兴趣的组织应当筹备专题展览，展示不受控制的公共或私人工程对文化财产所造成的威胁，以及针对已经遭受危害的文化财产所曾经采取的保护或抢救措施。

Recommendation concerning the Preservation of Cultural Property Endangered by Public or Private Works

19 November 1968

The General Conference of the United Nations Educational, Scientific and Cultural Organization, meeting in Paris from 15 October to 20 November 1968, at its fifteenth session,

Considering that contemporary civilization and its future evolution rest upon, among other elements, the cultural traditions of the peoples of the world, their creative force and their social and economic development,

Considering that cultural property is the product and witness of the different traditions and of the spiritual achievements of the past and thus is an essential element in the personality of the peoples of the world,

Considering that it is indispensable to preserve it as much as possible, according to its historical and artistic importance, so that the significance and message of cultural property become a part of the spirit of peoples who thereby may gain consciousness of their own dignity,

Considering that preserving cultural property and rendering it accessible constitute, in the spirit of the Declaration of the Principles of International Cultural Co - operation adopted on 4 November 1966 in the course of its fourteenth session, means of encouraging mutual understanding among peoples and thereby serve the cause of peace,

Considering also that the well - being of all peoples depends, inter alia, upon the existence of a favourable and stimulating environment and that the preservation of cultural property of all periods of history contributes directly to such an environment,

Recognizing, on the other hand, the role that industrialization, towards which world civilization is moving, plays in the development of peoples and their spiritual and national fulfilment,

Considering, however, that the prehistoric, protohistoric and historic monuments and remains, as well as numerous recent structures having artistic, historic or scientific importance are increasingly threatened by public and private works resulting from industrial development and urbanization,

Considering that it is the duty of governments to ensure the protection and the preservation of the cultural heritage of mankind, as much as to promote social and economic development,

Considering in consequence that it is urgent to harmonize the preservation of the cultural heritage with the changes which follow from social and economic development, making serious efforts to meet both requirements in a broad spirit of understanding, and with reference to appropriate planning,

Considering equally that adequate preservation and accessibility of cultural property constitute a major contribution to the social and economic development of countries and regions which possess such treasures of mankind by means of promoting national and international tourism,

Considering finally that the surest guarantee for the preservation of cultural property rests in the respect and the attachment felt for it by the people themselves, and persuaded that such feelings may be greatly strengthened by adequate measures carried out by Member States,

Having before it proposals concerning the preservation of cultural property endangered by public or private works, which constitute item 16 on the agenda of the session,

Having decided at its thirteenth session that proposals on this item should be the subject of an international instrument in the form of a recommendation to Member States,

Adopts on this nineteenth day of November 1968 this recommendation.

The General Conference recommends that Member States should apply the following provisions by taking whatever legislative or other steps may be required to give effect within their respective territories to the norms and principles set forth in this recommendation.

The General Conference recommends that Member States should bring this recommendation to the attention of the authorities or services responsible for public or private works as well as to the bodies responsible for the conservation and the protection of monuments and historic, artistic, archaeological and scientific sites. It recommends that authorities and bodies which plan programmes for education and the development of tourism be equally informed.

The General Conference recommends that Member States should report to it, on the dates and in a manner to be determined by it, on the action they have taken to give effect to this recommendation.

I. Definition

1. For the purpose of this recommendation, the term 'cultural property' applies to:

(a) Immovables, such as archaeological and historic or scientific sites, structures or other features of historic, scientific, artistic or architectural value, whether religious or secular, including - groups of traditional structures, historic quarters in urban or rural built - up areas and the ethnological structures of previous cultures still extant in valid form. It applies to such immovables constituting ruins existing above the earth as well as to archaeological or historic remains found within the earth. The term cultural property also includes the setting of such property;

(b) Movable property of cultural importance including that existing in or recovered from immovable property and that concealed in the earth, which - may be found' in archaeological or historical sites or elsewhere.

2. The term 'cultural property' includes not only the established and scheduled architectural, archaeological and historic sites and structure, but also the unscheduled or unclassified vestiges of the past as well as artistically or historically important recent sites and structures.

II. General principles

3. Measures to preserve cultural property should extend to the whole territory of the State and should not be confined to certain monuments and sites.

4. Protective inventories of important cultural property, whether scheduled or

unscheduled, should be maintained. Where such inventories do not exist, priority should be given in their establishment to the thorough survey of cultural property in areas where such property is endangered by public or private works.

5. Due account should be taken of the relative significance of the cultural property concerned when determining measures required for the:

(a) Preservation of an, entire site, structure, or other forms of immovable cultural property from the effects of private or public works;

(b) Salvage or rescue of cultural property if the area in which it is found is to be transformed by public or private works, and the whole or a part of the property in question is to be preserved and removed.

6. Measures should vary according to the character, size and location of the cultural property and the nature of the dangers with which it is threatened.

7. Measures for the preservation or salvage of cultural property should be preventive and corrective.

8. Preventive and corrective measures should be aimed at protecting or saving cultural property from public or private works likely to damage and destroy it, such as:

(a) Urban expansion and renewal projects, although they may retain scheduled monuments while
. sometimes removing less important structures, with the result that historical relations and the setting of historic quarters are destroyed;

(b) Similar projects in areas where groups of traditional structures having cultural value as a whole risk being destroyed for the lack of a scheduled individual monument;

(c) Injudicious modifications and repair of individual historic buildings;

(d) The construction or alteration of highways which are a particular danger to sites or to historically important structures or groups of structures;

(e) The construction of dams for irrigation, hydro - electric power or flood control;

(f) The construction of pipelines and of power and transmission lines of electricity;

(g) Farming operations including deep ploughing, drainage and irrigation operations, the clearing and levelling of land and afforestation;

(h) Works required by the growth of industry and the technological progress of industrialized societies such as airfields, mining and quarrying operations and dredging and reclamation of channels and harbours.

9. Member States should give due priority to measures required for the preservation in situ of cultural property endangered by public or private works in order to preserve historical associations and continuity. When overriding economic or social conditions require that cultural property be transferred, abandoned or destroyed, the salvage or rescue operations should always include careful study of the cultural property involved and the preparations of detailedrecords.

10. The results of studies having scientific or historic value carried out in connexion with salvage operations, particularly when all or much of the immovable cultural property has been abandoned or destroyed, should be published or otherwise made available for future research.

11. Important structures and other monuments which have been transferred in order to save them from destruction by public or private works should be placed on a site or in a setting which resembles their former position and natural, historic or artistic associations.

12. Important movable cultural property, including representative samples of objects recovered from archaeological excavations, obtained from salvage operations should be preserved for study or placed on exhibition in institutions such as museums, including site museums, or universities.

III. Preservation and salvage measures

13. The preservation or salvage of cultural property endangered by public or private works should be ensured through the means mentioned below, the precise measures to be determined by the legislation and organizational system of the State:

(a) Legislation;

(b) Finance;

(c) Administrative measures;

(d) Procedures to preserve and to salvage cultural property;

(e) Penalties;

(f) Repairs;

(g) Awards;

(h) Advice;

(i) Educational programmes.

Legislation

14. Member States should enact or maintain on the national as well as on the local level the legislative measures necessary to ensure the preservation or salvage of cultural property endangered by public or private works in accordance with the norms and principles embodied in this recommendation.

Finance

15. Member States should ensure that adequate budgets are available for the preservation or salvage of cultural property endangered by public or private works, Although differences in legal systems and traditions as well as disparity in resources preclude the adoption of uniform measures, the following should be considered:

(a) The national or local authorities responsible for the safeguarding of cultural property should have adequate budgets to undertake the preservation or salvage of cultural property endangered by public or private works; or

(b) The costs of preserving or salvaging cultural property endangered by public or private works, including preliminary archaeological research, should form part of the budget of construction costs; or

(c) The possibility of combining the two methods mentioned in sub - paragraphs (a) and (b) above should be provided for.

16. In the event of unusual costs due to the size and complexity of the operations required, there should be possibilities of obtaining additional funds through enabling legislation, special subventions, a national fund for monuments or other appropriate means. The services responsible for the safeguarding of cultural property should be empowered to administer or to utilize these extra - budgetary contributions required for the preservation or salvage of cultural property endangered by public or private works.

17. Member States should encourage proprietors of artistically or historically important structures, including structures forming part of a traditional group, or residents in a historic quarter in urban or rural built - up areas to preserve the char-

acter and aesthetic qualities of their cultural property which would otherwise be endangered by public or private works, through:

(a) Favourable tax rates ; or

(b) The establishment, through appropriate legislation, of a budget to assist, by grants, loans or other measures, local authorities, institutions and private owners of artistically, architecturally, scientifically or historically important structures including groups of traditional structures to maintain or to adapt them suitably for functions which would meet the needs of contemporary society; or

(c) The possibility of combining the two methods mentioned in sub - paragraphs (a) and (b) above should be provided for.

18. If the cultural property is not scheduled or otherwise protected it should be possible for the owner to request such assistance from the appropriate authorities.

19. National or local authorities, as well as private owners, when budgeting for the preservation of cultural property endangered by public or private works, should take into account the intrinsic value of cultural property and also the contribution it can make to the economy as a tourist attraction.

Administrative measures

20. Responsibility for the preservation or salvage of cultural property endangered by public or private works should be entrusted to appropriate official bodies. Whenever official bodies or services already exist for the protection of cultural property, these bodies or services should be given responsibility for the preservation of cultural property against the dangers caused by public or private works. If such services do not exist, special bodies or services should be created for the purpose of the preservation of cultural property endangered by public or private works; and although differences of constitutional provisions and traditions preclude the adoption of a uniform system, certain common principles should be adopted.

(a) There should be a co - ordinating or consultative body, composed of representatives of the authorities responsible for the safeguarding of cultural property, for public and private works, for town planning, and of research and educational institutions, which should be competent to advise on the preservation of cultural property endangered by public or private works and, in particular, on conflicts of interest between requirements for public or private works and the preservation or salvage of cultural property.

(b) Provincial, municipal or other forms of local government should also have services responsible for the preservation or salvage of cultural property endangered by public or private works. These services should be able to call upon the assistance of national services or other appropriate bodies in accordance with their capabilities and requirements.

(c) The services responsible for the safeguarding of cultural property should be adequately staffed with the specialists required for the preservation or salvage of cultural property endangered by public or private works, such as architects, urbanists, archaeologists, historians, inspectors and other specialists and technicians.

(d) Administrative measures should be taken to co - ordinate the work of the different services responsible for the safeguarding of cultural property with that of other services responsible for public and private works and that of any other department or service whose responsibilities touch upon the problem of the preservation or salvage of cultural property endangered by public or private works.

(e) Administrative measures should be taken to establish an authority or commission in charge of urban development programmes in all communities having scheduled or unscheduled historic quarters, sites and monuments which need to be preserved against public and private construction.

21. At the preliminary survey stage of any project involving construction in a locality recognized as being of cultural interest or likely to contain objects of archaeological or historical importance, several variants of the project should be prepared, at regional or municipal level, before a decision is taken. The choice between these variants should be made on the basis of a comprehensive comparative analysis, in order that the most advantageous solution, both economically and from the point of view of preserving or salvaging cultural property, may be adopted.

Procedures to preserve and to salvage cultural property

22. Thorough surveys should be carried out well in advance of any public or private works which might endanger cultural property to determine:

(a) The measures to be taken to preserve important cultural property in situ;

(b) The amount of salvage operations which would be required such as the selection of archaeological sites to be excavated, structures to be transferred and movable cultural property salvaged, etc.

23. Measures for the preservation or salvage of cultural property should be carried out well in advanceof public or private works. In areas of archaeological or cultural importance, such as historictowns, villages, sites and districts, which should be protected by the legislation of every country, the starting of new work should be made conditional upon the execution of preliminary archaeological excavations. If necessary, work should be delayed to ensure that adequate measures are taken for the preservation or salvage of the cultural property concerned.

24. Important archaeological sites, and, in particular, prehistoric sites as they are difficult to recognize, historic quarters in urban or rural areas, groups of traditional structures, ethnological structures of previous cultures and other immovable cultural property which would otherwise be endangered by public or private works should be protected by zoning or scheduling:

(a) Archaeological reserves should be zoned or scheduled and, if necessary, immovable property purchased, to permit thorough excavation or the preservation of the ruins found at the site.

(b) Historic quarters in urban or rural centres and groups of traditional structures should be zoned and appropriate regulations adopted to preserve their setting and character, such as the imposition of controls on the degree to which historically or artistically important structures can be renovated and the type and design of new structures which can be introduced. The preservation of monuments should be an absolute requirement of any well - designed plan for urban redevelopment especially in historic cities or districts. Similar regulations should cover the area surrounding a scheduled monument or site and its setting to preserve its association and character. Due allowance should be made for the modification of ordinary regulations applicable to new construction; these should be placed in abeyance when new structures are introduced into an historical zone. Ordinary types of commercial advertising by means of posters and illuminated announcements should be forbidden, but commercial establishments could be allowed to indicate their presence by means of judiciously presented signs.

25. Member States should make it obligatory for persons finding archaeological remains in the course of public or private works to declare them at the earliest

possible moment to the competent service. Careful examination should be carried out by the service concerned and, if the site is important, construction should be deferred to permit thorough excavation, due allowance or compensation being made for the delays incurred.

26. Member States should have provisions for the acquisition, through purchase, by national or local governments and other appropriate bodies of important cultural property endangered by public or private works. When necessary, it should be possible to effect such acquisition through expropriation.

27. Member States should take steps to ensure that offences, through intent or negligence, against the preservation or salvage of cultural property endangered by public or private works are severely punished by their Penal Code, which should provide for fines or imprisonment or both. In addition, the following measures could be applied:

(a) Whenever possible, restoration of the site or structure at the expense of those responsible for the damage to it;

(b) In the case of a chance archaeological find, payment of damages to the State when immovable cultural property has been damaged, destroyed or neglected; confiscation without compensation when a movable object has been concealed.

Repairs

28. Member States should, when the nature of the property so allows, adopt the necessary measures to ensure the repair, restoration or reconstruction of cultural property damaged by public orprivate works. They should also foresee the possibility of requiring local authorities and private owners of important cultural property to carry out repairs or restorations, with technical and financial assistance if necessary.

Awards

29. Member States should encourage individuals, associations and municipalities to take part in programmes for the preservation or salvage of cultural property endangered by public or private works. Measures to that effect could include:

(a) Ex gratia payments to individuals reporting or surrendering hidden archaeological finds;

(b) Awards of certificates, medals or other forms of recognition to individuals, even if they belong to government service, associations, institutions or municipalities which have carried out outstanding projects for the preservation or salvage of cultural property endangered by public or private works.

Advice

30. Member States should provide individuals, associations or municipalities lacking the required experience or staff with technical advice or supervision to maintain adequate standards for the preservation or salvage of cultural property endangered by public or private works.

Educational programmes

31. In a spirit of international collaboration, Member States should take steps to stimulate and develop among their nationals interest in, and respect for, the cultural heritage of the past of their own and other traditions in order to preserve or to salvage cultural property endangered by public or private works.

32. Specialized publications, articles in the press and radio and television broadcasts should publicize the nature of the dangers to cultural property arising from ill - conceived public or private works as well as cases where cultural property has been successfully preserved or salvaged.

33. Educational institutions, historical and cultural associations, public bodies concerned with the tourist industry and associations for popular education should have programmes to publicize the dangers to cultural property arising from short - sighted public or private works, and to underline the fact that projects to preserve cultural property contribute to international understanding.

34. Museums and educational institutions and other interested organizations should prepare special exhibitions on the dangers to cultural property arising from uncontrolled public or private works and on the measures which have been used to preserve or to salvage cultural property which has been endangered.

关于考古挖掘应当遵循的国际原则的建议*

（联合国教科文组织大会1956年12月5日通过）

联合国教育、科学与文化组织于1956年11月5日至12月5日在印度首都新德里召开第九届大会。

认为保存历史遗物和作品最可靠的保证在于各民族自己对这些历史遗物和作品的尊重与热爱之情感中，并笃信这种情感可以通过由成员国发展科学和国际关系的愿望所激发而采取的适当措施而得到大大加强；

确信对历史作品的沉思与研究所激发的感情可以大大促进各国之间的相互了解，因此促成关涉该作品的国际合作并使用一切方法促进其社会使命的完成，乃极为必需；

考虑到虽然每一个成员国更直接关心在其领土上的考古发现，但作为整体的国际社会因这些发现而受益良多。

考虑到人类历史包含着对各不同文明的认识，因此，为了大多数人的利益有必要对一切考古遗存加以研究，并尽可能予以保存和妥善保管。

确信负责保护考古遗产的各国当局应遵循由经验证明并由各国考古机构付诸实践的某些共同原则，乃极为必需。

认为尽管对考古发掘的管理权限首先并且主要属各国国内，但该原则应同一种被广泛理解并自由接受的国际合作原则相一致。

收到关于适用于考古发掘的国际原则的议案，作为本届会议第9．4．3项议程。决定在第八届会议上向成员国建议在国际范围内修订这些议案。

1956年12月5日通过如下建议：

大会建议，成员国应采取任何立法或必要措施，在本国范围内，应用下列条款以实施本建议所提供的原则和标准。

大会建议，成员国应使本建议为与考古发掘和博物馆有关的部门和组织

---

* 首都经济贸易大学传播学系郑文明译。

所知晓。

大会建议，成员国应按照由大会确定的日期和方式向大会报告其为实施本建议所采取的行动。

Ⅰ. 定义

考古发掘

1. 为本建议之目的，考古发掘系指旨在发现具有考古特征的实物的任何研究，不论这种研究是涉及挖掘土地还是对地面的系统勘探，也不论这种研究是在一成员国内陆或领海水域地层上或地层下进行。

受保护的财产

2. 本建议的规定适用于从历史或艺术和建筑观点看对其保护符合公众利益的任何遗存，每一成员国自由制定最适当准则以评价在其领土上所发现实物的公众利益。特别是，本建议的规定应适用于在最广义上具有考古意义的任何纪念物和可移动或不可移动的实物。

3. 为评估考古遗存的公众利益所制定的准则，可能会视其为保存该财产问题还是发掘者或发现者有义务申报其发现的问题而有所不同。

（A）在前一情况下，基于保存源于一定日期前的所有实物的准则应予放弃，而代之以将保护扩展于属于特定时期或达到法律所确定最低年限的所有实物的准则。

（B）在后一种情况下，每一成员国应适用更广泛的准则，责成发掘者或发现者申报其所发现的具有考古特征的任何可移动或不可移动实物。

Ⅱ. 总则

考古遗产的保护

4. 每一成员国应充分考虑有关发掘引起的问题并遵照本建议的规定以确保对其考古遗产的保护。

5. 每一成员国特别应当：

（A）使考古勘探和发掘受到主管部门的事先授权的限制；

（B）使发现考古遗存的任何人负有义务尽早向主管部门申报这些遗存；

（C）对破坏上述规定的行为施以惩罚；

（D）对未申报物品予以没收充公；

（E）确定地下考古层的法律地位并对国家所有权得到确认的上述地下层在其立法中特别提及；

（F）考虑将考古遗产中的珍贵部分列为历史遗物。

保护机构：考古发掘

6. 尽管传统差异和财力不均使各成员国在负责发掘的管理机构中不可能采取统一的组织体制，不过所有成员国的考古机构仍可适用某些共同原则：

（A）考古机构应尽可能是中央国家部门—或者至少应当是由法律授权的在需要时可使用必要手段实施紧急措施的组织。除考古工作的一般管理外，该机构还应该在发掘人员技术培训方面同研究所及大学进行合作。该机构还应编制可移动或不可移动历史遗物的包括地图在内的总文献目录，并为各个重要博物馆或陶瓷或肖像收藏等，编制附加文献目录。

（B）尤其应采取措施以保证资金的正常供给，以便：（1）以令人满意的方式管理这些机构；（2）执行同本国考古资源相称的工作计划，包括科学出版；（3）对偶然发现实行控制；（4）对发掘遗址和历史遗物予以维修。

7. 每一成员国应对所发现考古遗存及实物的修复，实施有效监管。

8. 迁移任何需就地保存的历史遗物，应取得主管部门的事先批准。

9. 每一成员国应考虑使不同时期的一定数量考古遗址部分或整体地维持不动，以便可以利用改进的技术和更先进的考古知识进行发掘。在每个正在发掘的较大规模遗址上，只要地面天然状态允许，可以保留几处明确界定的“见证”区不进行发掘，以供最终证实该遗址的地层情况和考古结构。

中央和地方收藏机构的创设

10. 鉴于考古学是一门比较科学，在建立和筹办博物馆以及储备藏品时，应考虑到尽可能为考古比较工作提供便利的需要。为此目的，可以创设中央和地方收藏机构，或在特殊情况下创设尤为重要的考古遗址—优先于小规模零星收藏的地方收藏机构，对少数人开放。这些机构应永久性地对确保展品之保存所需的行政配套和科研人员拥有支配权。

11. 在重要的考古遗址上，应建立具有教育性质的小型展览馆—可能的话建立博物馆—以向参观者宣传该考古遗存的意义。

公众教育

12. 主管部门应提出教育议案以便通过历史教学、学生参加某些发掘、在报刊上报道由知名专家所提供的考古情报、组织导游、展览和关于发掘方法及所取得成果的讲演、清楚展示经勘探的考古遗址及发现的纪念物、出版价廉而简明的书面专题材料和指南，来唤起和推动对于历史遗存的尊重和热爱。为了鼓励公众参观这些遗址，各成员国应作出一切必要安排为公众参观这些遗址提供便利。

Ⅲ. 关于发掘和国际合作的规则

授予外国人的发掘权

13. 在其领土上进行发掘的每一成员国应制定发掘特许授予的一般规则、发掘者应遵守的规则、特别是关于国家有关部门所行监督、特许的期限、特许撤销的理由、工作的中止或特许权从经授权的发掘者向国家考古机构转移等总的规则。

14. 适用于外国发掘者的规则适用于本国公民。因此，特许证书应省略不必要的特别规定。

国际合作

15. 为了考古学和国际合作的更高利益，各成员国应通过制定开明政策以鼓励考古发掘。成员国可以允许有资格的个人或学术团体，不论其国籍如何，在平等基础上申请发掘特许权。各成员国应鼓励由其本国科学家和来自外国研究所的考古学家组成的联合团队或由国际团队进行发掘。

16. 当特许权授予外国团队时，

颁发特许证的国家如果任命代理人，应尽可能指定一位有能力帮助该团队并善于与其合作的考古学家。

17. 当成员国无法为外国考古发掘组织提供必要资源时，正从事考古发掘的其他成员国，经主持人同意，应为成员国派送考古学家到发掘点提供便利。

18. 因缺乏技术和其他资源而无法完成科学考古发掘工作的成员国可以请求外国专家或外国团队参与。

相互担保

19. 考古发掘许可只应授予拥有有资质考古学家的机构或个人，他们能提供不允怀疑的科学、道德、金钱保障，以确保任何考古发掘都能按许可证的约定和在规定的期间内完成。

20. 另一方面，当进行发掘的特许权授予外国考古学家时，该许可应保证他们有足够的工作期限，以及为其工作提供方便，并提供其在诸如因公认正当原因被迫中断工作情况下免于被无故取消许可证方面充分的安全保障。

考古遗存的保存

21. 特许权证书应规定发掘者在工作过程中及工作完成时的义务。该证书应特别规定对遗址的保卫、维持和修复及在工作过程中和完成工作时对出土实物和历史遗物的保全。特许权证书还应说明，如果发掘者的义务经证明为过重的话，发掘者在履行其义务过程中可期望从特许权授予国得到某种帮助。

接近发掘遗址

22. 在考古工作报告公开以前，如经发掘主持人同意，甚至在发掘过程中，应允许任何国籍的有资格的专家参观遗址。这种特权在任何情况下均不应危害发掘者对其发掘物进行科学研究的权利。

发掘物的分配

23.（A）每一成员国都应明确规定适用于其领土上的关于处置发掘物的原则。

（B）发掘物应首先用于发掘地所在国博物馆建立代表该国文明、历史、艺术及建筑的整套收藏方面。

（C）特许权授予机构把通过原始材料分配以提升考古研究水平作为主要目标。在科研报告公开后，特许权授予机构可以考虑将若干发掘物分配给已授权的发掘者，这些发掘是指发掘物的复制品，或在更广泛的意义上是指因与同一发掘活动中的其他发掘物相同而可以被转让的发掘物或发掘物群。发掘物返还给发掘者常常要受到某种规定的限制，即发掘物应在规定的期限内，被分配给向公众开放的科研机构，附加条件是如果这些规定未能得到执行或停止执行、转让的发掘物将返还给特许权授予机构。

（D）如果授予国由于缺乏文献资料、科研设备或受到研究方法的限制，无法展开对这些发掘物的研究，经公共或私人科研机构请求，应允许这些发掘物暂时出口，但易碎或具有国家重要性的除外。

（E）各成员国应考虑将本国收藏中不需要的物品让与或存放于外国博物馆或用以同外国博物馆交换。

科研权利；发掘者的权利与义务

24.（A）特许权授予国应为发掘者在合理期限内对其掘获物的科研权利提供保障。

（B）授予国应要求发掘者在特许权证书规定的期限内，或在合理期限内，公开其考古工作成果。提交初步报告的期限不应超过两年。主管考古部门应保证，未经发掘者书面同意，在五年时间内不公布整套发掘物或相关科学文献。受相同条款约束，上述部门还应防止对尚未公开的考古资料进行照相或其他形式的复制。为了能在双方国家同时公开初步报告，如确有此需要，发掘者应按照要求向上述部门提交其报告副本。

（C）以非广泛使用的语言发表的关于考古研究的科学出版物应配有译成

较广泛使用语言的内容概要，如有可能，也应配有目录和插图说明。

关于考古发掘的文献

25. 遵照第24条所作规定，国家考古机构应尽可能备妥关于考古资料的文献及保存收藏品，以供发掘者及有资质专家，特别是被授予某一特定遗址特许权，或希望获得一项特许权者检查和研究。

区域性会议和科研讨论

26. 为了便于研究共同关心的问题，各成员国可以不时地召集由有关国家考古机构代表参加的区域性会议。同样，每一成员国也可以鼓励在其陆地上工作的发掘者举行科研讨论会。

Ⅳ. 文物贸易

27. 为了共同考古遗产的更高利益，每一成员国应考虑制定管理文物贸易的规则，以确保文物贸易不致鼓励考古资料走私或对遗址保护及为公开展览的文物资料收藏产生不利影响。

28. 为实现其科学和教育目的，外国博物馆应能够获得免于源地国任何法律限制的文物。

Ⅴ. 制止私自发掘和考古发掘物非法出口

保护考古遗址免于私自发掘和损害

29. 每一成员国应采取一切必要措施以防止私自发掘和对上述第2条和第3条所规定历史遗物的损害，并防止由此获得的物品的出口。

制止措施的国际合作

30. 应采取一切必要措施，以便接受考古实物的博物馆确保无任何理由相信这些实物是以私自发掘、盗窃或源地国主管部门视为非法的任何其他方法而取得的。任何可疑的出让物及与此有关的一切细节应提请有关机构注意。当考古实物已经为博物馆所取得时，应尽速公布，使之能够得以鉴别并表明其取得方式的充分细节。

实物返还源地国

31. 发掘机构和博物馆应互相协助，以确保或便于返还由私自发掘或盗窃所获实物及一切违反源地国立法而出口的实物。希望每一成员国应采取必要步骤以保证此种返还。在第23条（C）、（D）和（E）项所述暂时出口情况下，如果实物未在规定期限内返还，上述原则应予适用。

Ⅵ. 被占领土内的发掘

32. 在武装冲突情况下，占领另一国领土的任何成员国不应在被占领土上进行考古发掘。遇有偶然发现，特别是军事工程中的偶然发现，占领国应采取一切可能措施保护这些发现物。这些发现物应于敌对行动结束时，连同与此有关的一切文献一并移交给此前所占领土的主管部门。

Ⅶ. 双边协议

33. 一俟有必要或需要，各成员国应缔结双边协议，以处理适用本建议所产生的共同关心事项。

Recommendation on International Principles Applicable to Archaeological Excavation

5 December 1956

The General Conference of the United Nations Educational, Scientific and Cultural Organization, meeting at New Delhi, from 5 November to 5 December 1956, at its ninth session,

Being of the opinion that the surest guarantee for the preservation of monuments and works of the past rests in the respect and affection felt for them by. the peoples themselves, and persuaded that such feelings may be greatly strengthened by adequate measures inspired by the wish of Member States to develop science and international relations,

Convinced that the feelings aroused by the contemplation and study of works of the past do much to foster mutual understanding between nations, and that it is therefore highly desirable to secure international co - operation with regard to them and to further, in every possible way, the fulfillment of their social mission,

Considering that, while individual States are more directly concerned with the archaeological discoveries made on their territory, the international community as a whole is nevertheless the richer for such discoveries,

Considering that the history of man implies the knowledge of all different civilizations; and that it is therefore necessary, in the general interest, that all archaeological remains be studied and, where possible, preserved and taken into safe keeping, '

Convinced that it is highly desirable that the national authorities responsible for the protection of the archaeological heritage should be guided by certain common principles which have been tested by experience and put into practice by national archaeological services,

Being of the opinion that, though the regulation of excavations is first and foremost for the domestic jurisdiction of each State, this principle should be brought into harmony with that of a liberally understood and freely accepted international co - operation,

Having before it proposals concerning international principles applicable to archaeological excavations, which constitute item 9. 4. 3 on the agenda of the session,

Having decided, at its eighth session, that these proposals should be regulated at the international level by way of a recommendation to Member States,

Adopts, this fifth day of December 1956, the following Recommendation:

The General Conference recommends that Member States should apply the following provisions by taking whatever legislative or other steps may be required to give effect, within their respective territories, to the principles and norms formulated in the present Recommendation.

The General Conference recommends that Member States should bring the present Recommendation to the knowledge of authorities and organizations concerned with archaeological excavations and museums.

The General Conference recommends that Member States should report to it, on dates and in a manner to be determined by it, on the action which they have taken to give effect to the present Recommendation.

I. Definitions

Archaeological excavations

1. For the purpose of the present Recommendation, by archaeological excavations is meant any research aimed at the discovery of objects of archaeological character, whether such research involves digging of the ground or systematic exploration of its surface or is carried out on the bed or in the sub - soil of inland or territorial waters of a Member State.

Property protected

2. The provisions of the present Recommendation apply to any remains, whose preservation is in the public interest from the point of view of history or art and architecture, each Member State being free to adopt the most appropriate crite-

rion for assessing the public interest of objects found on its territory. In particular, the provisions of the present Recommendation should apply to any monuments and movable or immovable objects of archaeological interest considered in the widest sense.

3. The criterion adopted for assessing the public interest of archaeological remains might vary according to whether it is a question of the preservation of such property, or of the excavator's or finder's obligation to declare his discoveries.

(a) In the former case, the criterion based on preserving all objects originating before a certain date should be abandoned, and replaced by one whereby protection is extended to all objects belonging to a given period or of a minimum age fixed by law.

(b) In the latter case, each Member State should adopt far wider criteria, compelling the excavator or finder to declare any object, of archaeological character, whether - movable or immovable, which he may discover.

II. General principles

Protection of the archaeological heritage

4. Each Member State should ensure the protection of its archaeological heritage, taking fully into account problems arising in connexion with excavations, and in conformity with the provisions of the present Recommendation.

5. Each Member State should in particular:

(a) Make archaeological explorations and excavations subject to prior authorization by the competent authority;

(b) Oblige any person finding archaeological remains to declare them at the earliest possible date to the competent authority;

(c) Impose penalties for the infringement of these regulations;

(d) Make undeclared objects subject to confiscation;

(e) Define the legal status of the archaeological sub - soil and, where State ownership of the said sub - soil is recognized, specifically mention the fact in its legislation;

(f) Consider classifying as historical monuments the essential elements of its archaeological heritage.

Protecting body: archaeological excavations

6. Although differences of tradition and unequal financial resources make it impossible for all Member States to adopt a uniform system of organization in the administrative services responsible for excavations, certain common principles should nevertheless apply to all national archaeological services

(a) The archaeological service should, so far as possible, be a central State administration - or at any rate an organization provided by law with the necessary means for carrying out any emergency measures that may be required. In addition to the general administration of archaeological work, this service should co - operate with research institutes and universities in the technical training of excavators. This body should also set up a central documentation, including maps, of its movable and immovable monuments and additional documentation for every important museum or ceramic or iconographic collection, etc.

(b) Steps should be taken to ensure in particular the regular provision of funds:

(i) to administer the services in a satisfactory manner;

(ii) to carry out a programme of work proportionate to the archaeological resources of the country, including scientific publications ;

(iii) to exercise control over accidental discoveries;

(iv) to provide for the upkeep of excavation sites and monuments.

7. Careful supervision should be exercised by each Member State over the restoration of archaeological remains and objects discovered.

8. Prior approval should be obtained from the competent authority for the removal of any monuments, which ought to be preserved in situ.

9. Each Member State should consider maintaining untouched, partially or totally, a certain number of archaeological sites of different periods in order that their excavation may benefit from improved techniques and more advanced archaeological knowledge. On each of the larger sites now being excavated, in so far as the nature of the land permits, well defined `witness' areas might be left unexcavated in several places in order to allow for eventual verification of the stratigraphy and archaeological composition of the site.

Formation of central and regional collections

10. In as much as archaeology is a comparative science, account should be

taken, in the setting up and organizing of museums and reserve collections, of the need for facilitating the work of comparison as much as possible. For this purpose, central and regional collections might be formed or, in exceptional cases, local collections on particularly important archaeological sites - in preference to small scattered collections, accessible to comparatively few people. These establishments should command, on a permanent basis, the administrative facilities and scientific staff necessary to ensure the preservation of the exhibits.

11. On important archaeological sites, a small exhibit of an educational nature - possibly a museum - should be set up to convey to visitors the interest of the archaeological remains.

Education of the public

12. The competent authority should initiate educational measures in order to arouse and develop respect and affection for the remains of the past by the teaching of history, the participation of students in certain excavations, the publication in the press of archaeological information supplied by recognized specialists, the organization of guided tours, exhibitions and lectures dealing with methods of excavation and results achieved, the clear display of archaeological sites explored and monuments discovered, and the publication of cheap and simply written monographs and guides. In order to encourage the public to visit these sites, Member States should make all necessary arrangements to facilitate access to them.

III. Regulations governing excavations and international collaboration

Authority to excavate granted to foreigners

13. Each Member State on whose territory excavations are to take place should lay down general rules governing the granting of excavation con - cessions, the conditions to be observed by the excavator, in particular as concerns the supervision exercised by the national authorities, the period of the concession, the reasons which may justify its withdrawal, the suspension of work, or its transfer from the authorized excavator to the national archaeological service.

14. The conditions imposed upon a foreign excavator should be those applicable to nationals. Consequently, the deed of concession should omit special stipulations which are not imperative.

International collaboration

15. In the higher interest of archaeology and of international collaboration, Member, States should encourage excavations by a liberal policy. They might allow qualified individuals or learned bodies, irrespective of nationality, to apply on an equal footing for the concession to excavate. Member States should encourage excavations carried out by joint missions of scientists from their own country and of archaeologists representing foreign institutions, or by international missions.

16. When a concession is granted to a foreign mission, the representative of the conceding State - if such be appointed - should, as far as possible, also be an archaeologist capable of helping the mission and collaborating with it.

17. Member States which lack the necessary resources for the organization of archaeological excavations in foreign countries should be accorded facilities for sending archaeologists to sites being worked by other Member States, with the consent of the director of excavations.

18. A Member State whose technical or other resources are insufficient for the scientific carrying out of an excavation should be able to call on the participation of foreign experts or on a foreign mission to undertake it.

Reciprocal guarantees

19. Authority to carry out excavations should be granted only to institutions represented by qualified archaeologists or to persons offering such unimpeachable scientific, moral and financial guarantees as to ensure that any excavations will be completed in accordance with the terms of the deed of concession and within the period laid down.

20. On the other hand, when authority to carry out excavations is granted to foreign archaeologists, it should guarantee them a period of work long enough, and conditions of security sufficient to facilitate their task and protect them from unjustified cancellation of the concession in the event, for instance, of their being obliged, for reasons recognized as valid, to interrupt their work for a given period of time.

Preservation of archaeological remains

21. The deed of concession should define the obligations of the excavator during and on completion of his work. The deed should, in particular, provide for guarding, maintenance and restoration of the site together with the conservation,

during and on completion of his work, of objects and monuments uncovered. The deed should moreover indicate what help if any the excavator might expect from the conceding State in the discharge of his obligations should these prove too onerous.

Access to excavation sites

22. Qualified experts of any nationality should be allowed to visit a site before a report of the work is published and with the consent of the director of excavations, even during the work. This privilege should in no case jeopardize the excavator's scientific rights in his finds.

Assignment of finds

23. (a) Each Member State should clearly define the principles which hold good on its territory in regard to the disposal of finds from excavations.

(b) Finds should be used, in the first place, for building up, in the museums of the country in which excavations are carried out, complete collections fully representative of that country's civilization, history, art and architecture.

(c) With the main object of promoting archaeological studies through the distribution of original material, the conceding authority, after scientific publication, might consider allocating to the approved excavator a number of finds from his excavation, consisting of duplicates or, in a more general sense, of objects or groups of objects which can be released in view of their similarity to other objects from the same excavation. The return to the excavator' of objects resulting from excavations should always be subject to the condition that they be allocated within a specified period of time to scientific centers open to the public, with the proviso that if these conditions are not put into effect, or cease to be carried out, the released objects will be returned to the conceding authority.

(d) Temporary export of finds, excluding objects which are exceptionally fragile or of national importance, should be authorized on requests emanating from a scientific institution of public or private character if the study of these finds in the conceding State is not possible because of lack of bibliographical or scientific facilities, or is impeded by difficulties of access.

(e) Each Member State should consider ceding to, exchanging with, or depositing in foreign museums objects, which are not required in the national collections.

Scientific rights; rights and obligations of the excavator

24. (a) The conceding State should guarantee to the excavator scientific rights in his finds for a reasonable period.

(b) The conceding State should require the excavator to publish the results of his work within the period stipulated in the deed, or, failing such stipulations, within a reasonable period. This period should not exceed two years for the preliminary report. For a period of five years following the discovery, the competent archaeological authorities should undertake not to release the complete collection of finds, nor the relative scientific documentation, for detailed study, without the written authority of the excavator. Subject to the same conditions, these authorities should also prevent photographic or other reproduction of archaeological material still unpublished. In order to allow, should it be so desired, for simultaneous publication of the preliminary report in both countries, the excavator should, on demand, submit a copy of his text to these authorities.

(c) Scientific publications dealing with archaeological research and issued in a language which is not widely used should include a summary and, if possible, a list of contents and captions of illustrations translated into some more widely known language.

Documentation on excavations

25. Subject to the provisions set out in paragraph 24, the national archaeological services should, as far as possible, make their documentation and reserve collections of archaeological material readily available for inspection and study to excavators and qualified experts, especially those who have been granted a concession for a particular site or who wish to obtain one.

Regional meetings and scientific discussions

26. In order to facilitate the study of problems of common interest, Member States might, from time to time, convene regional meetings attended by representatives of the archaeological services of interested States. Similarly, each Member State might encourage excavators working on its soil to meet for scientific discussions.

IV. Trade in antiquities

27. In the higher interests of the common archaeological heritage, each Mem-

ber State should consider the adoption of regulations to govern the trade in antiquities so as to ensure that this trade does not encourage smuggling of archaeological material or affect adversely the protection of sites and the collecting of material for public exhibit.

28. Foreign museums should, in order to fulfill their scientific and educational aims, be able to acquire objects which have been released from any restrictions due to the laws in force in the country of origin.

V. Repression of clandestine excavations and of the illicit export of archaeological finds

Protection of archaeological sites against clandestine excavations and damage

29. Each Member State should take all necessary measures to prevent clandestine excavations and damage to monuments defined in paragraphs 2 and 3 above, and also to prevent the export of objects thus obtained.

International co - operation in repressive measures

30. All necessary measures should be taken in order that museums to which archaeological objects are offered ascertain that there is no reason to believe that these objects have been procured by clandestine excavation, theft or any other method regarded as illicit by the competent authorities of the country of origin. Any suspicious offer and all details appertaining thereto should be brought to the attention of the services concerned. When archaeological objects have been acquired by museums, adequate details allowing them to be identified and indicating the manner of their acquisition should be published as soon as possible.

Return of objects to their country of origin

31. Excavation services and museums should lend one another assistance in order to ensure or facilitate the recovery of objects derived from clandestine excavations or theft, and of all objects exported in infringement of the legislation of the country of origin. It is desirable that each Member State should take the necessary measures to ensure this recovery. These principles should be applied in the event of temporary exports as mentioned in paragraph 23 (c), (d) and (e) above, if the objects are not returned within the stipulated period.

VI. Excavations in occupied territory

32. In the event of armed conflict, any Member State occupying the territory of another State should refrain from carrying out archaeological excavations in the occupied territory. In the event of chance finds being made, particularly during military works, the occupying Power should take all possible measures to protect these finds, which should be handed over, on the termination of hostilities, to the competent authorities of the territory previously occupied, together with all documentation relating thereto.

VII. Bilateral agreements

33. Member States should, whenever necessary or desirable, conclude bilateral agreements to deal with matters of common interest arising out of the application of the present Recommendation.

欧洲区域或少数民族语言宪章*

（欧洲理事会1992年11月5日于斯特拉斯堡通过）

前　言

欧洲理事会成员国签署。

鉴于欧洲理事会的宗旨在于加强成员国间的团结，特别是为了保护和实现作为他们共同遗产的理想和原则；

鉴于欧洲历史地区或少数民族语言的保护，其中一些有濒临灭绝的危险，为欧洲文化财富和传统的维持和发展作出贡献；

鉴于根据联合国《公民权利和政治权利国际公约》的原则和欧洲理事会《保护人权和基本自由公约》的精神，在私人和公共生活中使用区域或少数民族语言是不可剥夺的权利；

考虑到欧洲安全和合作委员会的工作，特别是1975年的赫尔辛基最终决定和1990年的哥本哈根会议文件；

强调跨文化主义与多语言主义的价值，以及考虑到区域或少数民族语言的保护和鼓励不应当损害官方语言和学习它们的需要；

认识到在欧洲不同国家和地区保护推广区域或少数民族语言，就对建设根植于在国家主权和领土完整框架内的民主和文化多元化原则的欧洲具有重要贡献；

考虑到欧洲国家不同地区的历史传统和特殊情况，

同意下述：

---

* 西南政法大学法学院汪梦译。

第一章 总 则

第一条 定义

为了本宪章的目的：

a.“区域或少数民族语言”是指：

i. 在一国某一特定区域内，由该国国民组成的、数量小于该国其余人口的群体所使用的传统语言；

ii 与该国的官方语言不同；

不包括该国官方语言的方言或者移民的语言；

b.“使用区域或少数民族语言的区域”是指能够证明采用本宪章规定的不同的保护和推广措施是合法的，使用该语言作为表达方式的一定数量的人居住的地理地区；

c.“非区域语言”是指由国家国民使用的，与由该国其余的人口使用的不同的语言，虽然传统上在该国区域内使用，但是不能与其特定地区产生联系。

第二条 承诺

1. 成员国承诺第二章的规定适用于所有在其领土内使用的第1条规定的区域或少数民族语言。

2. 针对正式批准时规定的每种语言，根据第3条接受或者核准，成员国承诺适用至少本宪章第三章规定的35款或者项的条款，包括至少从第8、12条选择的三种和第9、10、11、13条中每一条选择的一种。

第三条 具体协议

1. 每个成员国应当在其批准文书上明确接受或核准每种区域或少数民族语言，或者在其领土内的全部或者部分没有广泛使用的官方语言，应当根据第2条2款的规定进行选择。

2. 在随后的任何时间，任何国家可以通知秘书长其接受没有在批准文书上明确的本宪章其他条款所规定的义务，接受或者核准，或者针对其他区域或少数民族语言以及在其领土内的全部或者部分没有广泛使用的官方语言适用本条1款。

3. 上述条款提及的承诺应当视为批准、接受或者核准的组成部分，自通告之日起具有同等效力。

第四条 现有的保护体制

1. 本宪章的任何规定不应当被作出限制或者保留《欧洲人权公约》保障的任何权利的解释。

2. 本宪章的条款不应当影响任何对有关区域或少数民族语言状况、在一国生活的少数民族人群的法律机制、双边或者多边国际协议中有利的规定。

第五条 现有义务

本宪章的任何规定不能作为代表任何与联合国宪章的目的或者其国际法律、包括国家主权和领土完整原则相违背的任何行动的权利。

第六条 告知

国家应当确保相关的机关、组织和个人被告知本宪章规定的权利和义务。

第二章 第二条一款涉及的目标和原则

第七条 目标和原则

1. 针对在领土范围内使用的区域或少数民族语言，以及每种语言的现状，国家应当将其政策、法律和实践建立在下述目标和原则之上：

a. 认可区域或少数民族语言是文化财富的体系；

b. 尊重每种区域或少数民族语言所在的地理地区，以确保现有的或者新的行政机构不会成为推广该区域或少数民族语言的障碍；

c. 为了保护区域或少数民族语言需要坚决的行动；

d. 促进和鼓励区域或少数民族语言在口头、书面以及私人和公共生活中的使用；

e. 在本宪章涉及的领域内，维持和发展使用区域或少数民族语言的群体与在该国使用相同或者相似方式的语言的其他群体之间的联系，以及与该国使用不同语言的其他群体建立文化联系；

f. 在所有适当的阶段，为区域或少数民族语言的教学和研究提供合适的方法和方式；

g. 为生活在使用区域或少数民族语言的地区不会使用该种语言而希望学习的人提供便利；

h. 推动在大学或者同等机构内对区域或少数民族语言的学习和研究；

i. 在本宪章涉及范围内，推动两个或者多个使用相同或者类似的区域或少数民族语言的国家进行适当形式的跨国交流。

2. 成员国承诺，如若尚未完成，则要消除任何与区域或少数民族语言使用有关的非正当区分、排除、限制或者偏袒，以及清除任何打击或者威胁该语言使用的维护和发展的意图。采取有利于区域或少数民族语言的特殊措施，旨在促进这些语言使用者与其他人口之间的平等，或者考虑到他们特殊的情况，不能视为对更为广泛使用的语言的使用者的歧视行为。

3. 在国家提供的教育和培训目标和鼓励大众传播依此目标之中，成员国通过适当的措施促进国家内所有语言群体的相互理解，特别地，对有关区域或少数民族语言的尊重、理解和宽容。

4. 在确定有关区域或少数民族语言的政策时，成员国应当考虑到使用这些语言的群体表达的需求和愿望。如有必要，鼓励成立机构就所有关于区域或少数民族语言的方面向机关提供咨询。

5. 成员国应当将修正过的上述 1－4 款规定的原则适用于非区域语言。但是，就这些语言而言，采取使得本宪章有效的措施的性质和范围应当以灵活的方式决定，注意尊重使用这些语言的群体的传统和特征，其需求和希望。

第三章　根据第二条二款规定承诺推广区域或少数民族语言在公共生活中使用的措施

第八条　教育

1. 就教育而言，在这些语言使用的地区内，根据每种语言的情况，在不违背国家官方语言教学下，成员国：

a：

i. 保证相关区域或少数民族语言的学前教育；

ii. 保证实质性的相关区域或少数民族语言的学前教育；

iii. 至少为那些提出要求的家庭的学生或者数量足够的学生采取上述 i 和 ii 的措施；

iv. 如果公共机构在学前教育方面没有适用直接主管权，支持和鼓励采取上述 i 至 iii 措施；

b：

i. 保证相关区域或少数民族语言的初级教育；

ii. 保证实质性的相关区域或者少数民族语言的初级教育；

iii. 有关区域或少数民族语言的教学成为初级教育课程的组成部分；

iv. 至少为那些提出要求的家庭的学生或者数量足够的学生适用上述 i 和 ii 的措施

c：

i. 保证相关区域或少数民族语言的中级教育；

ii. 保证实质性的相关区域或者少数民族语言的中级教育；

iii. 有关区域或少数民族语言的教学成为中级教育课程的组成部分；

iv. 至少为那些提出要求的家庭的学生或者数量足够的学生适用上述 i 和 ii 的措施

d：

i. 保证相关区域或少数民族语言的技术和职业教育；

ii. 保证实质性的相关区域或者少数民族语言的技术和职业教育；

iii. 有关区域或少数民族语言的教学成为技术和职业教育课程的组成部分；

iv. 至少为那些提出要求的家庭的学生或者数量足够的学生适用上述 i 和 ii 的措施

e：

i. 保证可以相关区域或少数民族语言接受大学或者更高层次的教育；

ii. 将为学习这些语言提供设施作为大学或者更高层次教育的对象；

iii. 如果因为国家有关更高层次教育机构的作用，上述 i 和 ii 款不能适用，鼓励和允许大学或者其他形式的更高层次教育提供区域或少数民族语言教育或者将为学习这些语言提供设施作为大学或者更高层次教育的对象；

f：

i. 安排提供主要或者全部以区域或者少数民族语言教学的成年和继续教育课程；

ii. 提供作为成年和继续教育对象的这些语言；

iii. 如果公共机构在成年教育方面没有作为成年和继续教育对象的直接主管权，支持和鼓励提供这些语言教育；

g. 安排确保反映区域或少数民族语言的历史和文化的教学；

h. 为要求执行成员国认可的上述 a 至 g 的教师提供基本的和进一步的培训；

i. 成立监督机构负责监管措施的执行、成立或者发展区域或少数民族语言教学的完成的进度，以及起草调查结果的定期报告并且向公众公布。

2. 针对教育和不是区域或少数民族语言传统使用的地区，如果区域或少数民族语言使用者的数量达标，成员国应当允许在所有适当的教育阶段鼓励或者提供区域或少数民族语言的教学。

第九条 司法机关

1. 成员国承诺，就使用区域或少数民族语言的居民数量证明下述特定措施正当的司法辖区而言，根据每种语言的情况，本款规定的设施的使用不会阻碍正常司法程序进行的在法官认为：

a. 在刑事程序中：

i. 在一方的请求下，法庭应当使用区域或少数民族语言进行审判程序；

ii. 保障被告使用其区域或少数民族语言的权利；

iii. 无论是书面或者口头的请求和证据不应当仅仅因为是以区域或少数民族语言形成的而不被采纳；

iv. 在请求的情况下，法律程序中提供使用区域或少数民族语言的文件，如有必要使用的翻译人员和翻译不能对使用者收取额外的费用；

b. 民事程序：

i. 在一方的请求下，法庭应当使用区域或少数民族语言进行审判程序；

ii. 当诉讼当事人需要亲自出庭的时候，在不产生额外费用的情况下，允许其使用其区域或少数民族语言；

iii. 允许文件和证据使用区域或少数民族语言，

如有必要可以使用翻译人员和翻译。

c. 有关行政事务的法庭程序：

i. 在一方的请求下，法庭应当使用区域或少数民族语言进行审判程序；

ii. 当诉讼当事人需要亲自出庭的时候，在不产生额外费用的情况下，允许其使用其区域或少数民族语言；

iii. 允许文件和证据使用区域或少数民族语言，

如有必要可以使用翻译人员和翻译。

d. 采取步骤确保上述 b 款的 i 和 iii，c 款的适用以及必须使用的翻译人员和翻译不会对当事人产生额外的费用。

2. 成员国承诺：

a. 不能仅仅因为在其国内的法律文件是使用区域或少数民族语言起草的而拒绝承认其有效性；

b. 不能仅仅因为在其国内的、双方之间的法律文件是使用区域或少数民族语言起草的而拒绝承认其有效性，并且可以向并非这些语言使用者的有利害关系的第三方行使权力，只要该第三方经由行使权力的个人知道了文件的内容；

c. 不能仅仅因为在其国内的、双方之间的法律文件是使用区域或少数民族语言起草的而拒绝承认其有效性。

3. 成员国承诺，除非已经提供的，区域或少数民族语言使用者可以获取使用这些语言的国内最重要的法律条文和与这些使用者有特殊关系的条文。

第十条 行政机关和公共部门

1. 成员国承诺，在使用区域或少数民族语言的居民数量证明下述特定措施正当的国家的行政辖区而言，根据每种语言的情况，在尽可能合理的情况下：

a：

i. 确保行政机关使用区域或少数民族语言；

ii. 确保这些行政机关的官员就区域或少数民族语言的公共使用联系这些使用语言的人；

iii. 确保区域或少数民族语言的使用者提交的书面或者口头申请，收到以这些语言作出的回复；

iv. 确保区域或少数民族语言的使用者可以通过这些语言提交书面或者口头申请；

v. 确保区域或少数民族语言使用者可以使用这些语言有效地上交文件；

b. 为使用区域或少数民族语言的人口提供广泛使用这些语言的行政文本和表格或者双语版本；

c. 允许行政机关使用区域或少数民族语言起草文件。

2. 成员国承诺，在使用区域或少数民族语言的居民数量证明下述特定措施正当时，地方和区域机关应当允许或者鼓励：

a. 在地方和区域机关的体系内使用区域或少数民族语言；

b. 区域或少数民族语言使用者以这些语言提交书面或者口头申请的可能性；

c. 使用相关的区域或少数民族语言发布区域机关的官方文件；

d. 使用相关的区域或少数民族语言发布当地机关的官方文件；

e. 在不排除该国官方语言使用的情况下，由区域机关在会议讨论中使用区域或少数民族语言；

f. 在不排除该国官方语言使用的情况下，由地方机关在会议讨论中使用区域或少数民族语言；

g. 必要的时候，使用或者批准，使用官方语言填写的名称结合使用区域或少数民族语言填写的传统和正确的地名名称形式。

3. 针对由行政机关或者其他人自己提供的公共服务，成员国承诺，在区域或少数民族语言使用的范围内，根据每种语言的情况，尽可能合理的情况下：

a. 确保在提供服务的时候使用区域或少数民族语言；

b. 允许区域或少数民族语言的使用者提交请求并且收到以这些语言作出的回复；

c. 允许区域或少数民族语言的使用者以这些语言提交请求。

4. 为了核准的1、2、3款的规定生效，成员国承诺采取下述一种或者多种措施：

a. 需要的情况下进行翻译或者说明；

b. 如有必要，雇佣和培训需要的官员或者其他公共部门职员；

c. 尽快遵从具有区域或少数民族语言知识的，在该语言使用地区任命的公共部门的职员的要求。

5. 成员国承诺，在相关人的请求下允许使用或者批准区域或少数民族语言的姓氏。

第十一条　媒体

1. 成员国承诺，针对在区域或少数民族语言使用的地方的语言使用者，根据每种语言的情况，直接或者间接在此领域有权力或者发挥影响的公共主管机关应当尊重媒体独立和自治原则：

a. 执行公共服务任务的广播和电视：

i. 确保至少成立一家使用区域或少数民族语言的广播电台和一个电视频道；

ii. 鼓励和促进成立至少一家使用区域或少数民族语言的广播电台和一个电视频道；

iii. 为广播电视使用区域或少数民族语言播送节目提供充分准备；

b：

i. 鼓励和促进成立至少一家使用区域或少数民族语言的广播电台；

ii. 鼓励和促进使用区域或少数民族语言的电台广播常态化；

c：

i. 鼓励和促进成立至少一家使用区域或少数民族语言的电视频道；

ii. 鼓励和促进使用区域或少数民族语言的电视播放常态化；

d. 鼓励和促进使用区域或少数民族语言的音频和视听作品的制作和发行；

e：

i. 鼓励和促进成立和维持至少一家使用区域或少数民族语言的报纸；

ii. 鼓励和促进使用区域或少数民族语言的报纸文章发行的常态化

f：

i. 当法律规定对媒体的总体经济资助的情况下，支付使用区域或少数民族语言的媒体的额外费用；

ii. 对使用区域或少数民族语言的视频作品适用现有的经济资助措施；

g. 支持对使用区域或少数民族语言的记者和其他工作人员的培训。

2. 成员国承诺，保障从使用与区域或少数民族语言相同或者相似的语言的邻国直接接收广播和电视内容的自由，不反对使用该语言的邻国重播广播和电视内容。进一步，确保使用与区域或少数民族语言相同或者相似的语言的书面报刊信息的自由表达和流通。上述权利的行使附带有责任和义务，受制于法律规定的和民主社会要求的手续、条件、限制或者刑罚，国家安全、领土完整或者公共安全、防止骚乱和犯罪、保护健康或者道德、保护名誉权和其他权利、防止秘密信息的泄露、维持司法权的公正和权威。

3. 成员国承诺，根据保障媒体自由和多元化的法律，成立能够代表或者关注区域或少数民族语言的使用者的权益保护的机构。

第十二条　文化活动和设施

1. 就文化活动和设施而言——特别是图书馆、视频图书馆、文化中心、博物馆、档案馆、研究机构、剧院、电影院、文学作品、影视作品、方言形式的文化表达、节日和文化产业，特别是新技术的使用——成员国承诺，在区域或少数民族语言使用的范围内以及直接或者间接在此领域有权力或者发挥作用的公共主管机关：

a. 鼓励针对区域或少数民族语言的表达形式和主动性，促进接触这些语言创作的作品的不同方式；

b. 通过帮助和发展翻译、配音、后期合成和字幕方式，促进接触使用区域或少数民族语言创作的作品的其他语言的不同方式；

c. 通过帮助和发展翻译、配音、后期合成和字幕方式，促进接触其他语言创作的作品的区域或少数民族语言的不同方式；

d. 确保负责组织或者支持不同种类的文化活动的机构能够为将知识、区域或少数民族语言的使用和文化融入他们发起或者提供支撑的任务提供适当的补贴；

e. 推广能够确保负责组织或者支持文化活动的机构拥有可以自由支配的、熟悉相关区域或少数民族语言以及其他人口语言的员工的措施；

f. 鼓励区域或少数民族语言的使用者的代表直接参与到提供设施和规划文化活动之中；

g. 鼓励或者促进成立一家或者多家负责收集、保存副本、展示或者发表使用区域或少数民族语言创作的作品的机构；

h. 如有必要，建立、促进或者资助翻译和术语研究项目，特别是维持和发展适当的使用区域或少数民族语言的行政、商业、经济、社会、技术和法律术语。

2. 针对传统使用区域或少数民族语言之外的地区，成员国承诺，如果区域或少数民族语言的使用者的数量达标，允许根据上述条款鼓励或者提供适当的文化活动设施。

3. 成员国承诺，为地区或少数民族语言及其影响下的文化制定相应对外文化政策。

第十三条　经济和社会生活

1. 针对经济和社会活动，成员国承诺，在其全国：

a. 取消其法律条款中与经济或社会生活相关的，任何没有正当理由禁止或者限制区域或少数民族语言的使用的规定，特别是雇佣合同，以及技术文件中关于为产品或者安装使用的说明；

b. 禁止公司内部条例和私人文件中的任何条款中加入排除或者限制区域或少数民族语言的使用，至少在相同语言使用者之间；

c. 反对用来阻止与经济或社会活动相关的区域或少数民族语言使用的实践；

d. 促进或者鼓励通过没有特别规定在上述条款中的对区域或少数民族语言的使用。

2. 针对经济和社会活动，成员国承诺，只要在区域或少数民族语言使用的范围内公共机关有权，在尽可能合理的情况下：

a. 通过与商业习惯一致的程序，在其金融和银行条例规定中加入允许使用区域或少数民族语言填写支付指令（支票、汇票等）和其他商业文件，或者适当的情况下，确保这些条款的执行；

b. 在其直接管控的经济和社会部门（公共部门），组织活动或者推广区域或少数民族语言的使用；

c. 确保社会福利设施，例如医院、养老院，提供接收和治疗使用区域或少数民族语言的，因为生病、年老或者其他原因需要照顾的个人使用其语言的可能性；

d. 通过适当的方式确保安全说明同时使用区域或少数民族语言书写；

e. 安排由公共主管机关提供的有关消费者权利的信息使用区域或少数民族语言。

第十四条　跨国交流

成员国承诺：

a. 适用现有的约束使用相同或者相似形式的相同语言的国家的双边和多边协议，或者如有必要，寻求签订这种协议，以便促进国家中相同语言的使用者在文化、教育、信息、职业培训和终身教育领域的联系；

b. 为了区域或少数民族语言的利益，促进或者推广跨国界合作，特别是以相同或者相似形式使用相同语言的地方的区域或者地方机构。

第四章　宪章的适用

第十五条　定期报告

1. 成员国应当向欧洲理事会秘书长定期提交，依照部长委员会规定的形式，根据本宪章第二章关于他们的政策、适用第三章他们核准的条款所采取的措施的报告。首次报告应当根据成员国自身的情况下在本宪章生效的一年之内提交，其他的报告应当在首次报告之后的每三年提交一次。

2. 成员国应当公开他们的报告。

第十六条　审查报告

1. 根据第 15 条向欧洲理事会秘书长提交的报告应当由第 17 条规定的专家委员会审查。

2. 在成员国依法成立的机构或者协会可以请求专家委员会关注有关本宪章第三章规定的成员国承诺的事项。在咨询过相关成员国之后，专家委员会可以考虑下述第 3 款规定的报告准备信息。这些机构或者协会可以进一步提交有关第二章规定的成员国采取的政策的陈述。

3. 根据第 1 款规定的保护和第 2 款涉及的信息，专家委员会应当向部长委员会准备报告。该报告应当包括成员国被要求作出的评论并由部长委员会公之于众。

4. 第 3 款规定的报告应当包含，特别是专家委员会为准备后者机构向要求的一个或者多个成员国作出的建议，向部长委员会提出的提议。

5. 欧洲理事会秘书长应当每两年向议会众议院提交关于本宪章适用的详细报告。

第十七条　专家委员会

1. 专家委员会应当包括每个成员国的一名成员，由部长委员会从成员国提名的正直和与本宪章规定事务适格的个人名单中任命。

2. 委员会成员的任期 6 年，可以连任。在任期内不能履职的成员应当根据第 1 款规定的程序替换，该替换的成员应当完成上任的任期。

3. 专家委员会应当通过程序规则。其秘书应当由欧洲理事会秘书长提供。

第五章　最后规定

第十八条

本宪章公开由欧洲理事会成员国签署。可以批准、接受或者核准。批准、接受或者核准的文书应当由欧洲理事会秘书长保管。

第十九条

1. 本宪章应当自欧洲理事会的五个已经表达同意受到本宪章第 18 条约束的成员国的表达之日起的三个月期满后的第一天生效。

2. 至于任何其他此后表达同意受到约束的成员国，本宪章应当自批准、接受或者核准的文书保管之日起的三个月期满后的第一天生效。

第二十条

1. 自本宪章生效之后，欧洲理事会部长委员会可以邀请任何不是欧洲理事会成员的国家加入本宪章。

2. 对于任何加入的国家，本宪章应当自文书交由欧洲理事会秘书长保管之日起的三个月期满后的第一天生效。

第二十一条

1. 任何国家可以在签署或者保管批准、接受、核准或者加入文书的时候，对本宪章第 7 条 2 至 5 款的规定予以一个或者多个保留。其他条款不得进行保留。

2. 任何根据上述条款作出保留的签约国，可以通过向欧洲理事会秘书长提交通知的方式部分或者全部撤回。撤回自秘书长收到该通知之日起生效。

第二十二条

1. 任何成员国可以通过向欧洲理事会秘书长提交通知的方式在任何时间退出本宪章。

2. 该退出自秘书长收到通知之日起的 6 个月期满后的第一天生效。

第二十三条

欧洲理事会秘书长应当通知理事会成员国和其他任何加入本宪章的国家：

签署；

a. 任何批准、接受、核准或者加入文书的保管；

b. 本宪章根据第 19、20 条生效的日期；

c. 接收的第 3 条 2 款规定的适用的通知；

d. 与本宪章有关的其他行动、通知或者交流；

e. 为此，授权签署本宪章。

European Charter for Regional or Minority Languages

Strasbourg, 5. XI. 1992

Preamble

The member States of the Council of Europe signatory hereto,

Considering that the aim of the Council of Europe is to achieve a greater unity between its members, particularly for the purpose of safeguarding and realising the ideals and principles which are their common heritage;

Considering that the protection of the historical regional or minority languages of Europe, some of which are in danger of eventual extinction, contributes to the maintenance and development of Europe's cultural wealth and traditions;

Considering that the right to use a regional or minority language in private and public life is an inalienable right conforming to the principles embodied in the United Nations International Covenant on Civil and Political Rights, and according to the spirit of the Council of Europe Convention for the Protection of Human Rights and Fundamental Freedoms;

Having regard to the work carried out within the CSCE and in particular to the Helsinki Final Act of 1975 and the document of the Copenhagen Meeting of 1990;

Stressing the value of interculturalism and multilingualism and considering that the protection and encouragement of regional or minority languages should not be to the detriment of the official languages and the need to learn them;

Realising that the protection and promotion of regional or minority languages in the different countries and regions of Europe represent an important contribution to the building of a Europe based on the principles of democracy and cultural diversity within the framework of national sovereignty and territorial integrity;

Taking into consideration the specific conditions and historical traditions in the different regions of the European States,

Have agreed as follows:

Part I - General provisions

Article 1 - Definitions

For the purposes of this Charter:

a. "regional or minority languages" means languages that are:

i. traditionally used within a given territory of a State by nationals of that State who form a group numerically smaller than the rest of the State's population; and ii. different from the official language(s) of that State;

ii does not include either dialects of the official language(s) of the State or the languages of migrants;

b. "territory in which the regional or minority language is used" means the geographical area in which the said language is the mode of expression of a number of people justifying the adoption of the various protective and promotional measures provided for in this Charter;

c. "non - territorial languages" means languages used by nationals of the State which differ from the language or languages used by the rest of the State's population but which, although traditionally used within the territory of the State, cannot be identified with a particular area thereof;

Article 2 - Undertakings

1. Each Party undertakes to apply the provisions of Part II to all the regional or minority languages spoken within its territory and which comply with the definition in Article 1;

2. In respect of each language specified at the time of ratification, acceptance or approval, in accordance with Article 3, each Party undertakes to apply a minimum of thirty - five paragraphs or sub - paragraphs chosen from among the provisions of Part III of the Charter, including at least three chosen from each of the Articles 8 and 12 and one from each of the Articles 9, 10, 11 and 13;

Article 3 - Practical arrangements

1. Each Contracting State shall specify in its instrument of ratification, accept-

ance or approval, each regional or minority language, or official language which is less widely used on the whole or part of its territory, to which the paragraphs chosen in accordance with Article 2, paragraph 2, shall apply;

2. Any Party may, at any subsequent time, notify the Secretary General that it accepts the obligations arising out of the provisions of any other paragraph of the Charter not already specified in its instrument of ratification, acceptance or approval, or that it will apply paragraph 1 of the present article to other regional or minority languages, or to other official languages which are less widely used on the whole or part of its territory;

3. The undertakings referred to in the foregoing paragraph shall be deemed to form an integral part of the ratification, acceptance or approval and will have the same effect as from their date of notification;

Article 4 - Existing regimes of protection

1. Nothing in this Charter shall be construed as limiting or derogating from any of the rights guaranteed by the European Convention on Human Rights;

2. The provisions of this Charter shall not affect any more favourable provisions concerning the status of regional or minority languages, or the legal regime of persons belonging to minorities which may exist in a Party or are provided for by relevant bilateral or multilateral international agreements;

Article 5 - Existing obligations

Nothing in this Charter may be interpreted as implying any right to engage in any activity or perform any action in contravention of the purposes of the Charter of the United Nations or other obligations under international law, including the principle of the sovereignty and territorial integrity of States;

Article 6 - Information

The Parties undertake to see to it that the authorities, organisations and persons concerned are informed of the rights and duties established by this Charter;

Part II - Objectives and principles pursued in accordance withArticle 2, paragraph 1

Article 7 - Objectives and principles

1. In respect of regional or minority languages, within the territories in which

such languages are used and according to the situation of each language, the Parties shall base their policies, legislation and practice on the following objectives and principles:

a. the recognition of the regional or minority languages as an expression of cultural wealth;

b. the respect of the geographical area of each regional or minority language in order to ensure that existing or new administrative divisions do not constitute an obstacle to the promotion of the regional or minority language in question;

c. the need for resolute action to promote regional or minority languages in order to safeguard them;

d. the facilitation and/or encouragement of the use of regional or minority languages, in speech and writing, in public and private life;

e. the maintenance and development of links, in the fields covered by this Charter, between groups using a regional or minority language and other groups in the State employing a language used in identical or similar form, as well as the establishment of cultural relations with other groups in the State using different languages;

f. the provision of appropriate forms and means for the teaching and study of regional or minority languages at all appropriate stages;

g. the provision of facilities enabling non - speakers of a regional or minority language living in the area where it is used to learn it if they so desire;

h. the promotion of study and research on regional or minority languages at universities or equivalent institutions;

i. the promotion of appropriate types of transnational exchanges, in the fields covered by this Charter, for regional or minority languages used in identical or similar form in two or more States;

2. The Parties undertake to eliminate, if they have not yet done so, any unjustified distinction, exclusion, restriction or preference relating to the use of a regional or minority language and intended to discourage or endanger the maintenance or development of it. The adoption of special measures in favour of regional or minority languages aimed at promoting equality between the users of these languages and the rest of the population or which take due account of their specific conditions is not considered to be an act of discrimination against the users of

more widely - used languages;

3. The Parties undertake to promote, by appropriate measures, mutual understanding between all the linguistic groups of the country and in particular the inclusion of respect, understanding and tolerance in relation to regional or minority languages among the objectives of education and training provided within their countries and encouragement of the mass media to pursue the same objective;

4. In determining their policy with regard to regional or minority languages, the Parties shall take into consideration the needs and wishes expressed by the groups which use such languages. They are encouraged to establish bodies, if necessary, for the purpose of advising the authorities on all matters pertaining to regional or minority languages;

5. The Parties undertake to apply, mutatis mutandis, the principles listed in paragraphs 1 to 4 above to non - territorial languages. However, as far as these languages are concerned, the nature and scope of the measures to be taken to give effect to this Charter shall be determined in a flexible manner, bearing in mind the needs and wishes, and respecting the traditions and characteristics, of the groups which use the languages concerned;

Part III - Measures to promote the use of regional or minority languages in public life in accordance with the undertakings entered into under Article 2, paragraph 2

Article 8 - Education

1. With regard to education, the Parties undertake, within the territory in which such languages are used, according to the situation of each of these languages, and without prejudice to the teaching of the official language(s) of the State:

a;

i. to make available pre - school education in the relevant regional or minority languages; or

ii. to make available a substantial part of pre - school education in the relevant regional or minority languages; or

iii. to apply one of the measures provided for under i and ii above at least to those pupils whose families so request and whose number is considered sufficient; or

iv. if the public authorities have no direct competence in the field of pre - school education, to favour and/or encourage the application of the measures referred to under i to iii above;

b;

i. to make available primary education in the relevant regional or minority languages; or

ii. to make available a substantial part of primary education in the relevant regional or minority languages; or

iii. to provide, within primary education, for the teaching of the relevant regional or minority languages as an integral part of the curriculum; or

iv. to apply one of the measures provided for under i to iii above at least to those pupils whose families so request and whose number is considered sufficient;

c;

i. to make available secondary education in the relevant regional or minority languages; or

ii. to make available a substantial part of secondary education in the relevant regional or minority languages; or

iii. to provide, within secondary education, for the teaching of the relevant regional or minority languages as an integral part of the curriculum; or

iv. to apply one of the measures provided for under i to iii above at least to those pupils who, or where appropriate whose families, so wish in a number considered sufficient;

d;

i. to make available technical and vocational education in the relevant regional or minority languages; or

ii. to make available a substantial part of technical and vocational education in the relevant regional or minority languages; or

iii. to provide, within technical and vocational education, for the teaching of the relevant regional or minority languages as an integral part of the curriculum; or

iv. to apply one of the measures provided for under i to iii above at least to those pupils who, or where appropriate whose families, so wish in a number considered sufficient;

e;

i. to make available university and other higher education in regional or minority languages; or

ii. to provide facilities for the study of these languages as university and higher education subjects; or

iii. if, by reason of the role of the State in relation to higher education institutions, sub - paragraphs i and ii cannot be applied, to encourage and/or allow the provision of university or other forms of higher education in regional or minority languages or of facilities for the study of these languages as university or higher education subjects;

f;

i. to arrange for the provision of adult and continuing education courses which are taught mainly or wholly in the regional or minority languages; or

ii. to offer such languages as subjects of adult and continuing education; or

iii. if the public authorities have no direct competence in the field of adult education, to favour and/or encourage the offering of such languages as subjects of adult and continuing education;

g. to make arrangements to ensure the teaching of the history and the culture which is reflected by the regional or minority language;

h. to provide the basic and further training of the teachers required to implement those of paragraphs a to g accepted by the Party;

i. to set up a supervisory body or bodies responsible for monitoring the measures taken and progress achieved in establishing or developing the teaching of regional or minority languages and for drawing up periodic reports of their findings, which will be made public;

2. With regard to education and in respect of territories other than those in which the regional or minority languages are traditionally used, the Parties undertake, if the number of users of a regional or minority language justifies it, to allow, encourage or provide teaching in or of the regional or minority language at all the appropriate stages of education;

Article 9 – Judicial authorities

1. The Parties undertake, in respect of those judicial districts in which the number of residents using the regional or minority languages justifies the measures specified below, according to the situation of each of these languages and on condition that the use of the

facilities afforded by the present paragraph is not considered by the judge to hamper the proper administration of justice:

a. in criminal proceedings:

i. to provide that the courts, at the request of one of the parties, shall conduct the proceedings in the regional or minority languages; and/or

ii. to guarantee the accused the right to use his/her regional or minority language; and/or

iii. to provide that requests and evidence, whether written or oral, shall not be considered inadmissible solely because they are formulated in a regional or minority language; and/or

iv. to produce, on request, documents connected with legal proceedings in the relevant regional or minority language, if necessary by the use of interpreters and translations involving no extra expense for the persons concerned;

b. in civil proceedings:

i. to provide that the courts, at the request of one of the parties, shall conduct the proceedings in the regional or minority languages; and/or

ii. to allow, whenever a litigant has to appear in person before a court, that he or she may use his or her regional or minority language without thereby incurring additional expense; and/or

iii. to allow documents and evidence to be produced in the regional or minority languages,

if necessary by the use of interpreters and translations;

c. in proceedings before courts concerning administrative matters:

i. to provide that the courts, at the request of one of the parties, shall conduct the proceedings in the regional or minority languages; and/or

ii. to allow, whenever a litigant has to appear in person before a court, that he or she may use his or her regional or minority language without thereby incurring additional expense; and/or

iii. to allow documents and evidence to be produced in the regional or minority languages,

if necessary by the use of interpreters and translations;

d. to take steps to ensure that the application of sub - paragraphs i and iii of paragraphs b and c above and any necessary use of interpreters and translations does not involve extra expense for the persons concerned;

2. The Parties undertake:

a. not to deny the validity of legal documents drawn up within the State solely because they are drafted in a regional or minority language; or

b. not to deny the validity, as between the parties, of legal documents drawn up within the country solely because they are drafted in a regional or minority language, and to provide that they can be invoked against interested third parties who are not users of these languages on condition that the contents of the document are made known to them by the person(s) who invoke(s) it; or

c. not to deny the validity, as between the parties, of legal documents drawn up within the country solely because they are drafted in a regional or minority language;

3. The Parties undertake to make available in the regional or minority languages the most important national statutory texts and those relating particularly to users of these languages, unless they are otherwise provided;

Article 10 – Administrative authorities and public services

1. Within the administrative districts of the State in which the number of residents who are users of regional or minority languages justifies the measures specified below and according to the situation of each language, the Parties undertake, as far as this is reasonably possible:

a;

i. to ensure that the administrative authorities use the regional or minority languages; or

ii. to ensure that such of their officers as are in contact with the public use the regional or minority languages in their relations with persons applying to them in these languages; or

iii. to ensure that users of regional or minority languages may submit oral or written applications and receive a reply in these languages; or

iv. to ensure that users of regional or minority languages may submit oral or written applications in these languages; or

v. to ensure that users of regional or minority languages may validly submit a document in these languages;

b. to make available widely used administrative texts and forms for the population in the regional or minority languages or in bilingual versions;

c. to allow the administrative authorities to draft documents in a regional or minority language;

2. In respect of the local and regional authorities on whose territory the number of residents who are users of regional or minority languages is such as to justify the measures specified below, the Parties undertake to allow and/or encourage:

a. the use of regional or minority languages within the framework of the regional or local authority;

b. the possibility for users of regional or minority languages to submit oral or written applications in these languages;

c. the publication by regional authorities of their official documents also in the relevant regional or minority languages;

d. the publication by local authorities of their official documents also in the relevant regional or minority languages;

e. the use by regional authorities of regional or minority languages in debates in their assemblies, without excluding, however, the use of the official language(s) of the State;

f. the use by local authorities of regional or minority languages in debates in their assemblies, without excluding, however, the use of the official language(s) of the State;

g. the use or adoption, if necessary in conjunction with the name in the official language (s), of traditional and correct forms of place - names in regional or minority languages;

3. With regard to public services provided by the administrative authorities or other persons acting on their behalf, the Parties undertake, within the territory in which regional or minority languages are used, in accordance with the situation of each language and as far as this is reasonably possible:

a. to ensure that the regional or minority languages are used in the provision of the service; or

b. to allow users of regional or minority languages to submit a request and receive a reply in these languages; or

c. to allow users of regional or minority languages to submit a request in these languages;

4. With a view to putting into effect those provisions of paragraphs 1, 2 and 3 accepted by them, the Parties undertake to take one or more of the following measures:

a. translation or interpretation as may be required;

b. recruitment and, where necessary, training of the officials and other public service employees required;

c. compliance as far as possible with requests from public service employees having a knowledge of a regional or minority language to be appointed in the territory in which that language is used;

5. The Parties undertake to allow the use or adoption of family names in the regional or minority languages, at the request of those concerned;

Article 11 - Media

1. The Parties undertake, for the users of the regional or minority languages within the territories in which those languages are spoken, according to the situation of each language, to the extent that the public authorities, directly or indirectly, are competent, have power or play a role in this field, and respecting the principle of the independence and autonomy of the media:

a. to the extent that radio and television carry out a public service mission:

i. to ensure the creation of at least one radio station and one television channel in the regional or minority languages; or

ii. to encourage and/or facilitate the creation of at least one radio station and one television channel in the regional or minority languages; or

iii. to make adequate provision so that broadcasters offer programmes in the regional or minority languages;

b;

i. to encourage and/or facilitate the creation of at least one radio station in the regional or minority languages; or

ii. to encourage and/or facilitate the broadcasting of radio programmes in the regional or minority languages on a regular basis;

c;

i. to encourage and/or facilitate the creation of at least one television channel in the regional or minority languages; or

ii. to encourage and/or facilitate the broadcasting of television programmes in the regional or minority languages on a regular basis;

d. to encourage and/or facilitate the production and distribution of audio and audiovisual works in the regional or minority languages;

e;

i. to encourage and/or facilitate the creation and/or maintenance of at least one newspaper in the regional or minority languages; or

ii. to encourage and/or facilitate the publication of newspaper Articles in the regional or minority languages on a regular basis;

f;

i. to cover the additional costs of those media which use regional or minority languages, wherever the law provides for financial assistance in general for the media; or

ii. to apply existing measures for financial assistance also to audiovisual productions in the regional or minority languages;

g. to support the training of journalists and other staff for media using regional or minority languages;

2. The Parties undertake to guarantee freedom of direct reception of radio and television broadcasts from neighbouring countries in a language used in identical or similar form to a regional or minority language, and not to oppose the retransmission of radio and television broadcasts from neighbouring countries in such a language. They further undertake to ensure that no restrictions will be placed on the freedom of expression and free circulation of information in the written press in a language used in identical or similar form to a regional or minority language. The exercise of the above - mentioned freedoms, since it carries with it duties and responsibilities, may be subject to such formalities, conditions, restrictions or penalties as are prescribed by law and are necessary in a democratic society, in the interests of national security, territorial integrity or public safety, for the prevention of disorder or crime, for the protection of health or morals, for the protection of the reputation or rights of others, for preventing disclosure of information received in confidence, or for maintaining the authority and impartiality of the judiciary;

3. The Parties undertake to ensure that the interests of the users of regional or minority languages are represented or taken into account within such bodies as may be established in accordance with the law with responsibility for guaranteeing the freedom and pluralism of the media;

Article 12 – Cultural activities and facilities

1. With regard to cultural activities and facilities – especially libraries, video

libraries, cultural centres, museums, archives, academies, theatres and cinemas, as well as literary work and film production, vernacular forms of cultural expression,

festivals and the culture industries, including inter alia the use of new technologies – the Parties undertake, within the territory in which such languages are used and to the extent that the public authorities are competent, have power or play a role in this field:

a. to encourage types of expression and initiative specific to regional or minority languages and foster the different means of access to works produced in these languages;

b. to foster the different means of access in other languages to works produced in regional or minority languages by aiding and developing translation, dubbing, post - synchronisation and subtitling activities;

c. to foster access in regional or minority languages to works produced in other languages by aiding and developing translation, dubbing, post - synchronisation and subtitling activities;

d. to ensure that the bodies responsible for organising or supporting cultural activities of various kinds make appropriate allowance for incorporating the knowledge and use of regional or minority languages and cultures in the undertakings which they initiate or for which they provide backing;

e. to promote measures to ensure that the bodies responsible for organising or supporting cultural activities have at their disposal staff who have a full command of the regional or minority language concerned, as well as of the language(s) of the rest of the population;

f. to encourage direct participation by representatives of the users of a given regional or minority language in providing facilities and planning cultural activities;

g. to encourage and/or facilitate the creation of a body or bodies responsible for collecting, keeping a copy of and presenting or publishing works produced in the regional or minority languages;

h. if necessary, to create and/or promote and finance translation and terminological research services, particularly with a view to maintaining and developing appropriate administrative, commercial, economic, social, technical or legal terminology in each regional or minority language;

2. In respect of territories other than those in which the regional or minority languages are traditionally used, the Parties undertake, if the number of users of a regional or minority language justifies it, to allow, encourage and/or provide appropriate cultural activities and facilities in accordance with the preceding paragraph;

3. The Parties undertake to make appropriate provision, in pursuing their cultural policy abroad, for regional or minority languages and the cultures they reflect;

Article 13 - Economic and social life

1. With regard to economic and social activities, the Parties undertake, within the whole country:

a. to eliminate from their legislation any provision prohibiting or limiting without justifiable reasons the use of regional or minority languages in documents relating to economic or social life, particularly contracts of employment, and in technical documents such as instructions for the use of products or installations;

b. to prohibit the insertion in internal regulations of companies and private documents of any clauses excluding or restricting the use of regional or minority languages, at least between users of the same language;

c. to oppose practices designed to discourage the use of regional or minority languages in connection with economic or social activities;

d. to facilitate and/or encourage the use of regional or minority languages by means other than those specified in the above sub - paragraphs;

2. With regard to economic and social activities, the Parties undertake, in so far as the public authorities are competent, within the territory in which the regional or minority languages are used, and as far as this is reasonably possible:

a. to include in their financial and banking regulations provisions which allow, by means of procedures compatible with commercial practice, the use of regional or minority languages in drawing up payment orders (cheques, drafts, etc.) or other financial documents, or, where appropriate, to ensure the implementation of such provisions;

b. in the economic and social sectors directly under their control (public sector), to organise activities to promote the use of regional or minority languages;

c. to ensure that social care facilities such as hospitals, retirement homes and hostels offer the possibility of receiving and treating in their own language persons using a regional or minority language who are in need of care on grounds of ill - health, old age or for other reasons;

d. to ensure by appropriate means that safety instructions are also drawn up in regional or minority languages;

e. to arrange for information provided by the competent public authorities concerning the rights of consumers to be made available in regional or minority languages;

Article 14 - Transfrontier exchanges

The Parties undertake:

a. to apply existing bilateral and multilateral agreements which bind them with the States in which the same language is used in identical or similar form, or if necessary to seek to conclude such agreements, in such a way as to foster contacts between the users of the same language in the States concerned in the fields of culture, education, information, vocational training and permanent education;

b. for the benefit of regional or minority languages, to facilitate and/ or promote co - operation across borders, in particular between regional or local authorities in whose territory the same language is used in identical or similar form;

Part IV - Application of the Charter

Article 15 - Periodical reports

1. The Parties shall present periodically to the Secretary General of the Council of Europe, in a form to be prescribed by the Committee of Ministers, a report on their policy pursued in accordance with Part II of this Charter and on the measures taken in application of those provisions of Part III which they have accepted. The first report shall be presented within the year following the entry into force of the Charter with respect to the Party concerned, the other reports at three - yearly intervals after the first report;

2. The Parties shall make their reports public;

Article 16 - Examination of the reports

1. The reports presented to the Secretary General of the Council of Europe under Article 15 shall be examined by a committee of experts constituted in accordance with Article 17;

2. Bodies or associations legally established in a Party may draw the attention of the committee of experts to matters relating to the undertakings entered into by that Party under Part III of this Charter. After consulting the Party concerned, the committee of experts may take account of this information in the preparation of the report specified in paragraph 3 below. These bodies or associations can furthermore submit statements concerning the policy pursued by a Party in accordance with Part II;

3. On the basis of the reports specified in paragraph 1 and the information mentioned in paragraph 2, the committee of experts shall prepare a report for the Committee of Ministers. This report shall be accompanied by the comments which the Parties have been requested to make and may be made public by the Committee of Ministers;

4. The report specified in paragraph 3 shall contain in particular the proposals of the committee of experts to the Committee of Ministers for the preparation of such recommendations of the latter body to one or more of the Parties as may be required;

5. The Secretary General of the Council of Europe shall make a two - yearly detailed report to the Parliamentary Assembly on the application of the Charter;

Article 17 – Committee of experts

1. The committee of experts shall be composed of one member per Party, appointed by the Committee of Ministers from a list of individuals of the highest integrity and recognised competence in the matters dealt with in the Charter, who shall be nominated by the Party concerned;

2. Members of the committee shall be appointed for a period of six years and shall be eligible for reappointment. A member who is unable to complete a term of office shall be replaced in accordance with the procedure laid down in paragraph 1, and the replacing member shall complete his predecessor's term of office;

3. The committee of experts shall adopt rules of procedure. Its secretarial services shall be provided by the Secretary General of the Council of Europe;

Part V – Final provisions

Article 18

This Charter shall be open for signature by the member States of the Council of Europe. It is subject to ratification, acceptance or approval. Instruments of ratification, acceptance or approval shall be deposited with the Secretary General of the Council of Europe;

Article 19

1. This Charter shall enter into force on the first day of the month following the expiration of a period of three months after the date on which five member States of the Council of Europe have expressed their consent to be bound by the Charter in accordance with the provisions of Article 18;

2. In respect of any member State which subsequently expresses its consent to be bound by it, the Charter shall enter into force on the first day of the month following the expiration of a period of three months after the date of the deposit of the instrument of ratification, acceptance or approval;

Article 20

1. After the entry into force of this Charter, the Committee of Ministers of the Council of Europe may invite any State not a member of the Council of Europe to accede to this Charter;

2. In respect of any acceding State, the Charter shall enter into force on the first day of the month following the expiration of a period of three months after the date of deposit of the instrument of accession with the Secretary General of the Council of Europe;

Article 21

1. Any State may, at the time of signature or when depositing its instrument of ratification, acceptance, approval or accession, make one or more reservations to paragraphs 2 to 5 of Article 7 of this Charter. No other reservation may be made;

2. Any Contracting State which has made a reservation under the preceding paragraph may wholly or partly withdraw it by means of a notification addressed to the Secretary General of the Council of Europe. The withdrawal shall take effect on the date of receipt of such notification by the Secretary General;

Article 22

1. Any Party may at any time denounce this Charter by means of a notification addressed to the Secretary General of the Council of Europe;

2. Such denunciation shall become effective on the first day of the month following the expiration of a period of six months after the date of receipt of the notification by the Secretary General;

Article 23

The Secretary General of the Council of Europe shall notify the member States of the Council and any State which has acceded to this Charter of:

a. any signature;

b. the deposit of any instrument of ratification, acceptance, approval or accession;

c. any date of entry into force of this Charter in accordance with Articles 19 and 20;

d. any notification received in application of the provisions of Article 3, paragraph 2;

e. any other act, notification or communication relating to this Charter;

In witness whereof the undersigned, being duly authorised thereto, have signed this Charter.

欧洲理事会文化遗产社会价值框架公约*

（欧洲理事会于2005年10月27日通过）

前言

欧洲理事会成员国于此签署本公约。

鉴于欧洲理事会的目标之一是促成成员之间更加团结，以保障和促进他们共同遗产中根植于尊重人权、民主和法治的理念和原则；

认识到有必要将人们和人类价值置于广泛及跨学科概念而言的文化遗产之中心地位；

在一个不断发展的社会中，强调文化遗产的价值和潜力被广泛地用作可持续发展和提高生活质量的资源；

认识到在尊重他人的权利和自由的同时，人人都有从事其选择的文化遗产的权利，是《联合国世界人权宣言》（1948）和《经济、社会和文化权利国际公约》（1966）所保护的自由参与文化生活的权利的一个方面；

确信需要全社会人人都参与到界定和管理文化遗产的持续进程之中；

确信平等对待所有文化遗产和促进文化和宗教之间对话的遗产政策和教育倡议的原则的正确性；

参考欧洲理事会的各种文书，特别是《欧洲文化公约》（1954）、《保护欧洲建筑遗产公约》（1985）、《保护考古遗产欧洲公约》（1992年修订）、《欧洲景观公约》（2000）；

确信为了将这些原则付诸实施的动态进程中的通力合作，建立一个泛欧洲框架的重要性；

同意如下：

---

* 西南政法大学法学院汪梦译。

第一章　目的、定义和原则

第一条　公约的目的

公约的缔约国同意：

a. 认识到与文化遗产有关的权利，是《世界人权宣言》中所规定的参与文化生活的权利中固有组成部分；

b. 认识到针对文化遗产的个人和集体的责任；

c. 强调文化遗产的保护和可持续使用以人类发展和生活质量为其目标；

d. 就以下事项，采取必要的步骤适用本公约的条款：

文化遗产在建设一个和平及民主社会、可持续发展进程以及推广文化多样性中的作用；

于所有相关的公共、机构和私人参与者之间实现权能协同增效。

第二条　定义

为本公约的目的，

a. 文化遗产是从过去继承的一类资源，人们独立拥有并认为其反映和表达了他们不断变化的价值观、信仰、知识和传统。它包括随着时间的推移人和不同场所之间相互作用所形成环境的所有方面；

b. 遗产界包括重视文化遗产具体方面的人，他们希望在公共行动框架内保存该文化遗产并相传后代；

第三条　欧洲的共同遗产

缔约国同意增进对欧洲共同遗产的认识，包括：

a. 欧洲的所有形式的文化遗产，一起构成对回忆、认知、认同、凝聚力和创造力的共享的渊源，并且

b. 通过进步和过去的冲突而获得的经验而产生的理念、原则和价值，促进建立在尊重人权、民主和法治基础上的和平和稳定的社会的发展。

第四条　与文化遗产有关的权利和义务

缔约国认识到：

a. 人人都有单独或者集体享有享受文化遗产的权利以及为丰富文化遗产作出贡献的权利；

b. 人人都有单独或者集体承担如同自身遗产一样尊重其他文化遗产的义务，包括欧洲共同遗产的义务；

c. 文化遗产权的行使仅受到在民主社会中为保护公共利益和他人权利和

自由的必要的限制。

第五条 文化遗产法律和政策

缔约国承诺：

a. 认识到文化遗产的因素与公共利益的关联性以及其对于社会的重要性；

b. 通过文化遗产的确定、研究、解释、保护、保存和展示来增强其价值；

c. 根据每个缔约国的自身情况，确保存在行使第四条所规定文化遗产权的法律条款；

d. 形成支持参与文化遗产活动的经济和社会氛围；

e. 促使文化遗产保护成为可持续发展、文化多样性和现代创造力这些相辅相成目标的中心要素；

f. 无论来源，认可其管辖地域中文化遗产之价值；

g. 形成促进本公约条款的执行的统一策略。

第六条 公约的效力

本公约的任何条款不应当解释为：

a. 限制或者削弱由国际文书、特别是《世界人权宣言》和《保护人权与基本自由公约》所保障的人权和基本自由；

b. 损害其他国内或者国际法律文书对文化遗产和环境更有利的规定；

c. 产生强制执行的权利。

第二章 文化遗产对社会和人类发展的贡献

第七条 文化遗产和对话

缔约国通过公共机关和其他适格机构承诺：

a. 鼓励对展示文化遗产的道德标准和方法进行反思，并尊重多样性的解释；

b. 制定协商程序，以平等地处理不同团体对同一文化遗产所持价值观所产生相互矛盾的情况；

c. 获得文化遗产知识，通过增强彼此信任和相互理解，使之成为解决和防止冲突的和平共存的资源；

d. 将这些方法融入终身教育和培训的所有方面。

第八条 环境、遗产和生活质量

缔约国承诺使用文化环境的所有遗产方面，以便：

a. 丰富经济、政治、社会和文化发展进程和土地利用规划，运用文化遗产影响评估以及必要时适用缓解策略；

b. 推广有关文化、生物、地理和景观多样性政策的完整措施，以达成这些要素之间的平衡；

c. 通过促使生活在该地区的人们形成责任共担的意识来加强社会凝聚力；

d. 在不威胁环境文化价值的情况下，促进实现当前对环境进行附加的质量目标。

第九条 文化遗产的可持续使用

为了维持文化遗产，缔约国承诺：

a. 通过确保有关改变的决定应包括涉及的文化价值的解释，以促进尊重文化遗产的完整性；

b. 界定和推广可持续管理的原则以及鼓励维持；

c. 确保所有普通技术规制均考虑到文化遗产的特殊保存要求；

d. 促进基于传统的材料、技术和技巧的使用，开发它们为现代应用的潜能；

e. 通过个人、公司和机构的专业资格和认证系统来促进高质量工作。

第十条 文化遗产和经济活动

为了充分利用作为可持续经济发展的要素之一的文化遗产的潜力，缔约国承诺：

a. 提升对文化遗产经济潜能的认识和使用程序；

b. 当制定经济政策时考虑到文化遗产的特殊性质和利益；

c. 确保这些政策尊重文化遗产的完整性不损害其固有的价值。

第三章 文化遗产和公共参与的共同义务

第十一条 文化遗产公共义务的构成

在管理文化遗产时，缔约国承诺：

a. 推广所有级别的公共机关的所有部门采用的完整的和信息完善的方法；

b. 制定可以使得公共机关、专家、所有者、投资者、公司、非政府组织和市民社会联合行动的法律、经济和专业框架；

c. 采用使得公共机关可以与其他相关人共同合作的创新方法；

d. 尊重和鼓励完善公共机关职能的主动志愿行动；

e. 鼓励与遗产保存有关的非政府组织所采取的公共利益的行动。

第十二条 文化遗产的接触和民主参与

缔约国承诺：

a. 鼓励所有人参与到：

文化遗产的确定、研究、解释、保护、保存和展示的进程中对文化遗产所代表的机遇与挑战所进行的公共反思和讨论；

b. 考虑到每一个遗产群体与其所认同文化遗产间的关联；

c. 认识到非营利机构作为活动参与者和文化遗产政策建设性的批评者的作用；

d. 采取步骤促进特别是年轻人和弱势群体对遗产的接触，以便使之更加认识到文化遗产的价值、保持和保存遗产的需要以及可从其获得的益处。

第十三条 文化遗产和知识

缔约国承诺：

a. 促使文化遗产涵盖在所有级别的教育之中，其自身并不必须成为学习科目，但是可以作为其他科目学习的丰富的渊源；

b. 增强文化遗产教育与职业培训之间的联系；

c. 鼓励文化遗产、遗产群体、环境和它们内在关系的跨学科研究；

d. 鼓励教育系统内部和外部持之以恒的专业培训和知识、技能的交流。

第十四条 文化遗产和信息社会

缔约国承诺形成数字技术的使用以增强对文化遗产的接触和从其获得的益处，通过以下方式实现：

a. 鼓励为促进内容质量以及尝试确保信息社会语言和文化多样化而采取的主动行动；

b. 在打击文化财产的非法交易的同时，支持对文化遗产研究、保存、增强和安全的国际的兼容标准；

c. 在保护知识产权的同时，试图消除特别是为学习目的而接触有关文化遗产的信息的障碍；

d. 认识到有关遗产的数字内容的创制不应破坏对现存遗产的保存。

第四章 监督和合作

第十五条 缔约国的承诺

缔约国承诺：

a. 经由欧洲理事会，在与本公约设立的原则一致的情况下发展覆盖有关文化遗产的法律、政策和实践的监督功能；

b. 为向公众开放的、促进评估每一个缔约国如何完成本公约规定的义务的信息共享系统保存、开发和提供数据。

第十六条　监督机制

a. 部长委员会根据《欧洲理事会规约》第十七条的规定，应当任命适格的委员会或者指定现有的委员会以监督公约的适用，使其获得为其行动职责制定规则的授权；

b. 任命的委员会应当：

必要的时候设立程序规则；

管理第十五条规定的信息共享系统，提供概述，说明本公约所规定每项义务得以遵守的方法；

根据一个或者多个缔约国的要求，考虑到欧洲理事会所有法律文书的情况下，就有关公约解释的任何问题给出建设性意见；

在一个或者多个缔约国的倡议下，承担公约执行任何方面进行评估的工作；

通过与其他委员会的合作以及参与到欧洲理事会的其他行动中，促进本公约的跨部门的适用；

就其活动报告部长委员会。

专家和观察员可以参与到委员会的工作中。

第十七条　后续活动的合作

缔约国承诺之间通力合作，采取下列方式，通过欧洲理事会落实本公约的目的和原则，特别是促进对欧洲共同遗产的认知：

a. 设立监督程序以解决确定的优先事项的合作策略；

b. 促进多边和跨边界活动，发展地区合作网络以便执行这些策略；

c. 交流、发展、编制和确保优秀实践的传播；

d. 告知公众本公约的目的和执行。

任一缔约国可以通过相互协议为促进国际合作提供经济支持。

第五章　最后条款

第十八条　签署和生效

a. 本公约应当向欧洲理事会成员国开放签署。

b. 应当接受批准、接受或者核准。批准、接受或者核准的文书应当由欧洲理事会秘书长保管。

c. 本公约应当自欧洲理事会的十个成员国根据上述条款的规定已经表达同意接受本公约约束之日起三个月届满后的第一天生效。

d. 任何在此之后表达同意接受公约约束的签署国，本公约应当自批准、接受或者核准文书保管之日起三个月届满后的第一天生效。

第十九条　加入

a. 自本公约生效之后，欧洲理事会的部长委员会可以邀请任何不是欧洲理事会和欧洲联盟成员国的国家经过由《欧洲理事会规约》第二十条d款规定的多数作出的决定，以及由有权参加部长委员会的缔约国的代表的全票通过，加入公约。

b. 任何加入国家或者加入欧洲联盟的成员国，本公约应当自欧洲理事会秘书长保存加入文书之日起三个月届满后的第一天生效。

第二十条　领土适用

a. 任何国家可以在签署之时或者保存其批准、接受、核准或者加入的文书之时，明确本公约应当适用的领土范围。

b. 任何国家可以在之后的任何时间，通过向欧洲理事会秘书长作出声明，延伸本公约适用于其声明中明确的任何领土。对此延伸适用，本公约应当自秘书长接收到该声明之日起三个月届满后的第一天生效。

c. 任何根据上述条款作出的明确适用领土的声明可以通过向秘书长作出通知而撤回。该撤回应当自秘书长接收到该通知之日起六个月届满后的第一天生效。

第二十一条　退出

a. 任何缔约国可以在任何时候通过向欧洲理事会秘书长作出通知的方式退出本公约。

b. 该退出应当自秘书长接收到通知之日起六个月届满后的第一天生效。

第二十二条　修订

a. 任一缔约国和第十六条规定的委员会可以就本公约提出修订。

b. 任何修订的提议应当通知欧洲理事会秘书长，他应当通知欧洲理事会的成员国、其他缔约国、任何根据第十九条的规定邀请加入本公约的非成员国和欧洲联盟。

c. 委员会应当检查提出的任何修订并且向部长委员会提交由缔约国代表的四分之三多数通过的文本以正式通过。在部长委员会根据《欧洲理事会规约》第二十条的规定的多数通过以及有权参加部长委员会的缔约国的全票通过之后，该文本应当提交缔约国接受。

d. 任何接受该修订的缔约国，修订应当自欧洲理事会的十个成员国已经通知秘书长接受修订之日起三个月届满后的第一天生效。在此之后接受修订的缔约国，该修订应当自该国已经通知秘书长接受修订之日起三个月届满后的第一天生效。

第二十三条 通知

就下列事项，欧洲理事会秘书长应当通知欧洲理事会的成员国、任何已经加入或者邀请加入本公约的国家，以及已经加入或者邀请加入的欧洲联盟：

a. 签署；

b. 任何批准、接受、核准或者加入文书的保管；

c. 第十八条、十九条和二十条规定的本公约生效日期；

d. 第二十二条规定的针对本公约提出的修订以及其生效日期；

e. 与本公约有关的任何其他行动、声明、通知或者通告。

为此，签署方见证并或合法授权签署本公约。

Council of Europe Framework Convention on the Value of Cultural Heritage for Society

Faro, 27. X. 2005

Preamble

The member States of the Council of Europe, Signatories hereto,

Considering that one of the aims of the Council of Europe is to achieve greater unity between its members for the purpose of safeguarding and fostering the ideals and principles, founded upon respect for human rights, democracy and the rule of law, which are their common heritage;

Recognising the need to put people and human values at the centre of an enlarged and cross - disciplinary concept of cultural heritage;

Emphasising the value and potential of cultural heritage wisely used as a resource for sustainable development and quality of life in a constantly evolving society;

Recognising that every person has a right to engage with the cultural heritage of their choice, while respecting the rights and freedoms of others, as an aspect of the right freely to participate in cultural life enshrined in the United Nations Universal Declaration of Human Rights (1948) and guaranteed by the International Covenant on Economic, Social and Cultural Rights (1966);

Convinced of the need to involve everyone in society in the ongoing process of defining and managing cultural heritage;

Convinced of the soundness of the principle of heritage policies and educational initiatives which treat all cultural heritages equitably and so promote dialogue among cultures and religions;

Referring to the various instruments of the Council of Europe, in particular the European Cultural Convention (1954), the Convention for the Protection of the Architectural Heritage of Europe (1985), the European Convention on the Protection of the Archaeological Heritage (1992, revised) and the European Landscape Convention (2000);

Convinced of the importance of creating a pan - European framework for co - operation in the dynamic process of putting these principles into effect;

Have agreed as follows:

Section I – Aims, definitions and principles

Article 1 – Aims of the Convention

The Parties to this Convention agree to:

a. recognise that rights relating to cultural heritage are inherent in the right to participate in cultural life, as defined in the Universal Declaration of Human Rights;

b. recognise individual and collective responsibility towards cultural heritage;

c. emphasise that the conservation of cultural heritage and its sustainable use have human development and quality of life as their goal;

d. take the necessary steps to apply the provisions of this Convention concerning:

- the role of cultural heritage in the construction of a peaceful and democratic society, and in the processes of sustainable development and the promotion of cultural diversity;
- greater synergy of competencies among all the public, institutional and private actors concerned.

Article 2 – Definitions

For the purposes of this Convention,

a. cultural heritage is a group of resources inherited from the past which people identify, independently of ownership, as a reflection and expression of their constantly evolving values, beliefs, knowledge and traditions. It includes all aspects of the environment resulting from the interaction between people and places through time;

b. a heritage community consists of people who value specific aspects of cultural heritage which they wish, within the framework of public action, to sustain and transmit to future generations.

Article 3 – The common heritage of Europe

The Parties agree to promote an understanding of the common heritage of Europe, which consists of:

a. all forms of cultural heritage in Europe which together constitute a shared source of remembrance, understanding, identity, cohesion and creativity, and

b. the ideals, principles and values, derived from the experience gained through progress and past conflicts, which foster the development of a peaceful and stable society, founded on respect for human rights, democracy and the rule of law.

Article 4 – Rights and responsibilities relating to cultural heritage

The Parties recognise that:

a. everyone, alone or collectively, has the right to benefit from the cultural heritage and to contribute towards its enrichment;

b. everyone, alone or collectively, has the responsibility to respect the cultural heritage of others as much as their own heritage, and consequently the common heritage of Europe;

c. exercise of the right to cultural heritage may be subject only to those restrictions which are necessary in a democratic society for the protection of the public interest and the rights and freedoms of others.

Article 5 – Cultural heritage law and policies

The Parties undertake to:

a. recognise the public interest associated with elements of the cultural heritage in accordance with their importance to society;

b. enhance the value of the cultural heritage through its identification, study, interpretation, protection, conservation and presentation;

c. ensure, in the specific context of each Party, that legislative provisions exist for exercising the right to cultural heritage as defined in Article 4;

d. foster an economic and social climate which supports participation in cultural heritage activities;

e. promote cultural heritage protection as a central factor in the mutually supporting objectives of sustainable development, cultural diversity and contemporary creativity;

f. recognise the value of cultural heritage situated on territories under their jurisdiction, regardless of its origin;

g. formulate integrated strategies to facilitate the implementation of the provisions of this Convention.

Article 6 – Effects of the Convention

No provision of this Convention shall be interpreted so as to:

a. limit or undermine the human rights and fundamental freedoms which may be safeguarded by international instruments, in particular, the Universal Declaration of Human Rights and the Convention for the Protection of Human Rights and Fundamental Freedoms;

b. affect more favourable provisions concerning cultural heritage and environment contained in other national or international legal instruments;

c. create enforceable rights.

Section II – Contribution of cultural heritage to society and human development

Article 7 – Cultural heritage and dialogue

The Parties undertake, through the public authorities and other competent bodies, to:

a. encourage reflection on the ethics and methods of presentation of the cultural heritage, as well as respect for diversity of interpretations;

b. establish processes for conciliation to deal equitably with situations where contradictory values are placed on the same cultural heritage by different communities;

c. develop knowledge of cultural heritage as a resource to facilitate peaceful co - existence by promoting trust and mutual understanding with a view to resolution and prevention of conflicts;

d. integrate these approaches into all aspects of lifelong education and training.

Article 8 – Environment, heritage and quality of life

The Parties undertake to utilise all heritage aspects of the cultural environment to:

a. enrich the processes of economic, political, social and cultural development and land - use planning, resorting to cultural heritage impact assessments and adopting mitigation strategies where necessary;

b. promote an integrated approach to policies concerning cultural, biological, geological and landscape diversity to achieve a balance between these elements;

c. reinforce social cohesion by fostering a sense of shared responsibility towards the places in which people live;

d. promote the objective of quality in contemporary additions to the environment without endangering its cultural values.

Article 9 – Sustainable use of the cultural heritage

To sustain the cultural heritage, the Parties undertake to:

a. promote respect for the integrity of the cultural heritage by ensuring that decisions about change include an understanding of the cultural values involved;

b. define and promote principles for sustainable management, and to encourage maintenance;

c. ensure that all general technical regulations take account of the specific conservation requirements of cultural heritage;

d. promote the use of materials, techniques and skills based on tradition, and explore their potential for contemporary applications;

e. promote high - quality work through systems of professional qualifications and accreditation for individuals, businesses and institutions.

Article 10 – Cultural heritage and economic activity

In order to make full use of the potential of the cultural heritage as a factor in sustainable economic development, the Parties undertake to:

a. raise awareness and utilise the economic potential of the cultural heritage;

b. take into account the specific character and interests of the cultural heritage when devising economic policies; and

c. ensure that these policies respect the integrity of the cultural heritage without compromising its inherent values.

Section III – Shared responsibility for cultural heritage and public participation

Article 11 – The organisation of public responsibilities for cultural heritage

In the management of the cultural heritage, the Parties undertake to:

a. promote an integrated and well - informed approach by public authorities in all sectors and at all levels;

b. develop the legal, financial and professional frameworks which make possible joint action by public authorities, experts, owners, investors, businesses, non - governmental organisations and civil society;

c. develop innovative ways for public authorities to co - operate with other actors;

d. respect and encourage voluntary initiatives which complement the roles of public authorities;

e. encourage non - governmental organisations concerned with heritage conservation to act in the public interest.

Article 12 – Access to cultural heritage and democratic participation

The Parties undertake to:

a. encourage everyone to participate in:

- the process of identification, study, interpretation, protection, conservation and presentation of the cultural heritage ;
- public reflection and debate on the opportunities and challenges which the cultural heritage represents;

b. take into consideration the value attached by each heritage community to the cultural heritage with which it identifies;

c. recognise the role of voluntary organisations both as partners in activities and as constructive critics of cultural heritage policies;

d. take steps to improve access to the heritage, especially among young people and the disadvantaged, in order to raise awareness about its value, the need to maintain and preserve it, and the benefits which may be derived from it.

Article 13 – Cultural heritage and knowledge

The Parties undertake to:

a. facilitate the inclusion of the cultural heritage dimension at all levels of education, not necessarily as a subject of study in its own right, but as a fertile source for studies in other subjects;

b. strengthen the link between cultural heritage education and vocational training;

c. encourage interdisciplinary research on cultural heritage, heritage communities, the environment and their inter - relationship;

d. encourage continuous professional training and the exchange of knowledge and skills, both within and outside the educational system.

Article 14 – Cultural heritage and the information society

The Parties undertake to develop the use of digital technology to enhance access to cultural heritage and the benefits which derive from it, by:

a. encouraging initiatives which promote the quality of contents and endeavour to secure diversity of languages and cultures in the information society;

b. supporting internationally compatible standards for the study, conservation, enhancement and security of cultural heritage, whilst combating illicit trafficking in cultural property;

c. seeking to resolve obstacles to access to information relating to cultural heritage, particularly for educational purposes, whilst protecting intellectual property rights;

d. recognising that the creation of digital contents related to the heritage should not prejudice the conservation of the existing heritage.

Section IV – Monitoring and co – operation

Article 15 – Undertakings of the Parties

The Parties undertake to:

a. develop, through the Council of Europe, a monitoring function covering legislations, policies and practices concerning cultural heritage, consistent with the principles established by this Convention;

b. maintain, develop and contribute data to a shared information system, accessible to the public, which facilitates assessment of how each Party fulfils its commitments under this Convention.

Article 16 – Monitoring mechanism

a. The Committee of Ministers, pursuant to Article 17 of the Statute of the Council of Europe, shall nominate an appropriate committee or specify an existing committee to monitor the application of the Convention, which will be authorised to make rules for the conduct of its business;

b. The nominated committee shall:

- establish rules of procedure as necessary;
- manage the shared information system referred to in Article 15, maintaining an overview of the means by which each commitment under this Convention is met;
- at the request of one or more Parties, give an advisory opinion on any question relating to the interpretation of the Convention, taking into consideration all Council of Europe legal instruments;
- on the initiative of one or more Parties, undertake an evaluation of any aspect of their implementation of the Convention;
- foster the trans - sectoral application of this Convention by collaborating with other committees and participating in other initiatives of the Council of Europe;
- report to the Committee of Ministers on its activities.

The committee may involve experts and observers in its work.

Article 17 – Co – operation in follow – up activities

The Parties undertake to co - operate with each other and through the Council of Europe in pursuing the aims and principles of this Convention, and especially in promoting recognition of the common heritage of Europe, by:

a. putting in place collaborative strategies to address priorities identified through the monitoring process;

b. fostering multilateral and transfrontier activities, and developing networks for regional co - operation in order to implement these strategies;

c. exchanging, developing, codifying and assuring the dissemination of good practices;

d. informing the public about the aims and implementation of this Convention.

Any Parties may, by mutual agreement, make financial arrangements to facilitate international co - operation.

Section V – Final clauses

Article 18 – Signature and entry into force

a. This Convention shall be open for signature by the member States of the Council of Europe.

b. It shall be subject to ratification, acceptance or approval. Instruments of ratification, acceptance or approval shall be deposited with the Secretary General of the Council of Europe.

c. This Convention shall enter into force on the first day of the month following the expiration of a period of three months after the date on which ten member States of the Council of Europe have expressed their consent to be bound by the Convention in accordance with the provisions of the preceding paragraph.

d. In respect of any signatory State which subsequently expresses its consent to be bound by it, this Convention shall enter into force on the first day of the month following the expiration of a period of three months after the date of deposit of the instrument of ratification, acceptance or approval.

Article 19 – Accession

a. After the entry into force of this Convention, the Committee of Ministers of the Council of Europe may invite any State not a member of the Council of Europe, and the European Community, to accede to the Convention by a decision taken by the majority provided for in Article 20. d of the Statute of the Council of Europe and by the unanimous vote of the representatives of the Contracting States entitled to sit on the Committee of Ministers.

b. In respect of any acceding State, or the European Community in the event of its accession, this Convention shall enter into force on the first day of the month following the expiration of a period of three months after the date of deposit of the instrument of accession with the Secretary General of the Council of Europe.

Article 20 – Territorial application

a. Any State may, at the time of signature or when depositing its instrument of ratification, acceptance, approval or accession, specify the territory or territories to which this Convention shall apply.

b. Any State may, at any later date, by a declaration addressed to the Secretary General of the Council of Europe, extend the application of this Convention to any other territory specified in the declaration. In respect of such territory, the Convention shall enter into force on the first day of the month following the expiration of a period of three months after the date of receipt of such declaration by the Secretary General.

c. Any declaration made under the two preceding paragraphs may, in respect of any territory specified in such declaration, be withdrawn by a notification addressed to the Secretary General. The withdrawal shall become effective on the first day of the month following the expiration of a period of six months after the date of receipt of such notification by the Secretary General.

Article 21 – Denunciation

a. Any Party may, at any time, denounce this Convention by means of a notification addressed to the Secretary General of the Council of Europe.

b. Such denunciation shall become effective on the first day of the month following the expiration of a period of six months after the date of receipt of the notification by the Secretary General.

Article 22 – Amendments

a. Any Party, and the committee mentioned in Article 16, may propose amendments to this Convention.

b. Any proposal for amendment shall be notified to the Secretary General of the Council of Europe, who shall communicate it to the member States of the Council of Europe, to the other Parties, and to any non - member State and the European Community invited to accede to this Convention in accordance with the provisions of Article 19.

c. The committee shall examine any amendment proposed and submit the text adopted by a majority of three - quarters of the Parties' representatives to the Committee of Ministers for adoption. Following its adoption by the Committee of Ministers by the majority provided for in Article 20. of the Statute of the Council of Europe, and by the unanimous vote of the States Parties entitled to hold seats in the Committee of Ministers, the text shall be forwarded to the Parties for acceptance.

d. Any amendment shall enter into force in respect of the Parties which have accepted it, on the first day of the month following the expiry of a period of three months after the date on which ten member States of the Council of Europe have informed the Secretary General of their acceptance. In respect of any Party which subsequently accepts it, such amendment shall enter into force on the first day of the month following the expiry of a period of three months after the date on which the said Party has informed the Secretary General of its acceptance.

Article 23 – Notifications

The Secretary General of the Council of Europe shall notify the member States of the Council of Europe, any State which has acceded or been invited to accede to this Convention, and the European Community having acceded or been invited to accede, of:

a. any signature;

b. the deposit of any instrument of ratification, acceptance, approval or accession;

c. any date of entry into force of this Convention in accordance with the provisions of Articles 18, 19 and 20;

d. any amendment proposed to this Convention in accordance with the provisions of Article 22, as well as its date of entry into force;

e. any other act, declaration, notification or communication relating to this Convention.

In witness whereof the undersigned, being duly authorised thereto, have signed this Convention.

第五部分　著作权保护

Part V　Protection of Copyrights

视听表演北京条约

（世界知识产权组织外交会议
2012年6月24日于北京通过）

目　录

序　　言

缔约各方出于以尽可能有效和一致的方式发展和维护保护表演者对其视听表演的权利的愿望；

回顾《建立世界知识产权组织（WIPO）公约》大会 2007 年所通过的旨在确保发展方面的考虑构成本组织工作的组成部分的发展议程各项建议的重要性；

承认有必要采用新的国际规则，以提供解决由经济、社会、文化和技术发展所提出的问题的适当方法；

承认信息与通信技术的发展和交汇对视听表演的制作与使用的深刻影响；

承认有必要保持表演者对其视听表演的权利与广大公众的利益，尤其是教育、研究和获得信息的利益之间的平衡；

承认 1996 年 12 月 20 日在日内瓦签订的《世界知识产权组织表演和录音制品条约》（WPPT）对表演者的保护不延伸到其以视听录制品录制的表演方面；

提及关于版权和邻接权若干问题的外交会议于 1996 年 12 月 20 日通过的《关于视听表演的决议》；

达成协议如下：

第 1 条　与其他公约和条约的关系

（1）本条约的任何内容均不得减损缔约方相互之间依照《世界知识产权

组织表演和录音制品条约》或依照1961年10月26日在罗马签订的《保护表演者、录音制品制作者和广播组织国际公约》已承担的现有义务。

（2）依本条约给予的保护不得触动或以任何方式影响对文学和艺术作品版权的保护。因此，本条约的任何内容均不得被解释为损害此种保护。

（3）除《世界知识产权组织表演和录音制品条约》之外，本条约不得与任何其他条约有任何关联，亦不得损害任何其他条约所规定的任何权利和义务。[1]、[2]

第2条　定义

在本条约中：

（a）“表演者”系指演员、歌唱家、音乐家、舞蹈家以及对文学或艺术作品或民间文学艺术表达进行表演、歌唱、演说、朗诵、演奏、表现或以其他方式进行表演的其他人员；[3]

（b）“视听录制品”系指活动图像的体现物，不论是否伴有声音或声音表现物，从中通过某种装置可感觉、复制或传播该活动图像；[4]

（c）“广播”系指以无线方式的传送，使公众能接收声音或图像，或图像和声音，或图像和声音的表现物；通过卫星进行的此种传送亦为“广播”；传送密码信号，只要广播组织或经其同意向公众提供了解码的手段，即为“广播”；

（d）“向公众传播”表演系指通过除广播以外的任何媒体向公众传送未录制的表演或以视听录制品录制的表演。在第11条中，“向公众传播”包括使公众能听到或看到，或能听到并看到以视听录制品形式录制的表演。

第3条　保护的受益人

（1）缔约各方应将本条约规定的保护给予系其他缔约方国民的表演者。

（2）非缔约方国民但在一个缔约方境内有惯常居所的表演者，在本条约中视同该缔约方的国民。

第4条　国民待遇

（1）在本条约所专门授予的专有权以及本条约第11条所规定的获得合理报酬的权利方面，每一缔约方均应将其给予本国国民的待遇给予其他缔约方的国民。

（2）在本条约第11条第（1）款和第11条第（2）款授予的权利方面，缔约方应有权将其依本条第（1）款给予另一缔约方国民的保护限制在其本国国民在该另一缔约方享有的那些权利的范围和期限之内。

（3）如果另一缔约方使用了本条约第11条第（3）款允许的保留，本条第（1）款规定的义务对缔约方不再适用；如果某一缔约方作出了此种保留，本条第（1）款规定的义务也不适用于该缔约方。

第5条　精神权利

（1）不依赖于表演者的经济权利，甚至在这些权利转让之后，表演者仍应对于其现场表演或以视听录制品录制的表演有权：

（i）要求承认其系表演的表演者，除非因使用表演的方式而决定可省略不提其系表演者；以及

（ii）反对任何对其表演进行的将有损其声誉的歪曲、篡改或其他修改，但同时应对视听录制品的特点予以适当考虑。

（2）根据本条第（1）款授予表演者的权利在其死亡后应继续保留，至少到其经济权利期满为止，并可由被要求提供保护的缔约方立法所授权的个人或机构行使。但批准或加入本条约时其立法尚未规定在表演者死亡后保护上款所述全部权利的国家，则可规定其中部分权利在表演者死亡后不再保留。

（3）为保障本条所授予的权利而采取的补救方法应由被要求提供保护的缔约方立法规定。[5]

第6条　表演者对其尚未录制的表演的经济权利

表演者应享有专有权，对于其表演授权：

（i）广播和向公众传播其尚未录制的表演，除非该表演本身已属广播表演；和

（ii）录制其尚未录制的表演。

第7条　复制权

表演者应享有授权以任何方式或形式对其以视听录制品录制的表演直接或间接地进行复制的专有权。[6]

第8条　发行权

（1）表演者应享有授权通过销售或其他所有权转让形式向公众提供其以视听录制品录制的表演的原件或复制品的专有权。

（2）对于已录制表演的原件或复制品经表演者授权被首次销售或其他所有权转让之后适用本条第（1）款中权利的用尽所依据的条件（如有此种条件），本条约的任何内容均不得影响缔约各方确定该条件的自由。[7]

第9条　出租权

（1）表演者应享有授权按缔约各方国内法中的规定将其以视听录制品录制的表演的原件和复制品向公众进行商业性出租的专有权，即使该原件或复制品已由表演者发行或经表演者授权发行。

（2）除非商业性出租已导致此种录制品的广泛复制，从而严重损害表演者的专有复制权，否则缔约方被免除第（1）款规定的义务。[8]

第 10 条　提供已录制表演的权利

表演者应享有专有权，以授权通过有线或无线的方式向公众提供其以视听录制品录制的表演，使该表演可为公众中的成员在其个人选定的地点和时间获得。

第 11 条　广播和向公众传播的权利

（1）表演者应享有授权广播和向公众传播其以视听录制品录制的表演的专有权。

（2）缔约各方可以在向世界知识产权组织总干事交存的通知书中声明，它们将规定一项对于以视听录制品录制的表演直接或间接地用于广播或向公众传播获得合理报酬的权利，以代替本条第（1）款中规定的授权的权利。缔约各方还可以声明，它们将在立法中对行使该项获得合理报酬的权利规定条件。

（3）任何缔约方均可声明其将仅对某些使用情形适用本条第（1）款或第（2）款的规定，或声明其将以某种其他方式对其适用加以限制，或声明其将根本不适用第（1）款和第（2）款的规定。

第 12 条　权利的转让

（1）缔约方可以在其国内法中规定，表演者一旦同意将其表演录制于视听录制品中，本条约第 7 条至第 11 条所规定的进行授权的专有权应归该视听录制品的制作者所有，或应由其行使，或应向其转让，但表演者与视听录制品制作者之间按国内法的规定订立任何相反合同者除外。

（2）缔约方可以要求，对于依照其国内法的规定制作的视听录制品，此种同意或合同应采用书面形式，并应由合同当事人双方或由经其正式授权的代表签字。

（3）不依赖于上述专有权转让规定，国内法或者具有个人性质、集体性质或其他性质的协议可以规定，表演者有权依照本条约的规定，包括第 10 条和第 11 条的规定，因表演的任何使用而获得使用费或合理报酬。

第 13 条　限制与例外

（1）缔约各方可以在其国内立法中，对给予表演者的保护规定与其国内立法给予文学和艺术作品的版权保护相同种类的限制或例外。

（2）缔约各方应使本条约中所规定权利的任何限制或例外仅限于某些不与表演的正常利用相抵触、也不致不合理地损害表演者合法利益的特殊情况。[9]

第 14 条　保护期

依本条约给予表演者的保护期，应自表演录制之年年终算起，至少持续到 50 年期满为止。

第 15 条　关于技术措施的义务

缔约各方应规定适当的法律保护和有效的法律补救办法，制止规避由表演者为行使本条约所规定的权利而使用并限制对其表演实施未经该有关表演者许可的或法律不允许的行为的有效技术措施。[10]、[11]

第 16 条　关于权利管理信息的义务

（1）缔约各方应规定适当和有效的法律补救办法，制止任何人明知，或就民事补救而言，有合理根据知道其行为会诱使、促成、便利或包庇对本条约所规定的任何权利的侵犯，而故意实施以下活动：

（i）未经许可去除或改变任何权利管理的电子信息；

（ii）未经许可发行、为发行目的进口、广播、向公众传播或提供明知未经许可而被去除或改变权利管理电子信息的表演或以视听录制品录制的表演的复制品。

（2）本条中的用语“权利管理信息”系指识别表演者、表演者的表演或对表演拥有任何权利的所有人的信息，或有关使用表演的条款和条件的信息，以及代表此种信息的任何数字或代码，各该项信息均附于以视听录制品录制的表演上。[12]

第 17 条　手续

享有和行使本条约所规定的权利无须履行任何手续。

第 18 条　保留和通知

（1）除第 11 条第（3）款的规定外，本条约不允许有任何保留。

（2）依第 11 条第（2）款或第 19 条第（2）款所作的任何通知，可以在批准书或加入书中提出，通知的生效日期应与本条约对作出通知的国家或政府间组织生效的日期相同。任何此种通知亦可随后提出，但在此情况下，通知应于世界知识产权组织总干事收到通知三个月后或通知中指明的任何更晚的日期生效。

第 19 条　时间上的适用范围

（1）缔约各方应对本条约生效之时存在的已录制的表演，以及本条约对缔约各方生效之后进行的所有表演，给予本条约所规定的保护。

（2）尽管有本条第（1）款的规定，缔约方仍可以在向世界知识产权组织总干事交存的通知书中声明，对于本条约对每一缔约方生效之时存在的已录制的表演，将不适用本条约第 7 条至第 11 条的规定，或不适用其中的任何一条或多条规定。对于此种缔约方，其他缔约方可以使所述各条的适用仅限于本条约对该缔约方生效之后进行的表演。

（3）本条约规定的保护不得损害本条约对每一缔约方生效之前实施的任何行为、订立的任何协议或取得的任何权利。

（4）缔约各方可以在其立法中制定过渡性条款，规定凡在本条约生效之前就某一表演从事合法活动的人，可以在本条约对相应缔约方生效之后，就该同一表演从事与第 5 条和第 7 条至第 11 条所规定的权利范围相符的活动。

第 20 条　关于权利行使的条款

（1）缔约各方承诺根据其法律制度采取必要的措施，以确保本条约的适用。

（2）缔约各方应确保依照其法律可以提供执法程序，以便能采取制止对本条约所规定权利的任何侵权行为的有效行动，包括防止侵权的即时补救和为遏制进一步侵权的补救。

第 21 条　大会

（1）（a）缔约方应设大会。

（b）每一缔约方应有一名代表出席大会，该代表可由副代表、顾问和专家协助。

（c）各代表团的费用应由指派它的缔约方负担。大会可以要求世界知识产权组织（以下称为“WIPO”）提供财政援助，以便利按照联合国大会既定惯例认为是发展中国家或市场经济转型期国家的缔约方代表团参加。

（2）（a）大会应处理涉及维护和发展本条约及适用和实施本条约的事项。

（b）大会应履行依第 23 条第（2）款向其指定的关于接纳某些政府间组织成为本条约缔约方的职能。

（c）大会应对召开任何修订本条约的外交会议作出决定，并给予世界知识产权组织总干事筹备此种外交会议的必要指示。

（3）（a）凡属国家的每一缔约方应有一票，并应只能以其自己的名义表决。

（b）凡属政府间组织的缔约方可以代替其成员国参加表决，其票数与其属本条约缔约方的成员国数目相等。如果此种政府间组织的任何一个成员国行使其表决权，则该组织不得参加表决，反之亦然。

（4）大会应由总干事召集，如无例外情况，应与世界知识产权组织大会同时同地举行。

（5）大会应努力通过协商一致作出决定，并应制定自己的议事规则，包括召集特别会议、法定人数的要求，以及按本条约的规定，作出各类决定所需的多数等规则。

第22条　国际局

与本条约有关的行政工作应由世界知识产权组织国际局履行。

第23条　成为本条约缔约方的资格

（1）世界知识产权组织的任何成员国均可以成为本条约的缔约方。

（2）如果任何政府间组织声明其对于本条约涵盖的事项具有权限和具有约束其所有成员国的立法，并声明其根据其内部程序被正式授权要求成为本条约的缔约方，大会可以决定接纳该政府间组织成为本条约的缔约方。

（3）欧洲联盟在通过本条约的外交会议上作出上款提及的声明后，可以成为本条约的缔约方。

第24条　本条约规定的权利和义务

除本条约有任何相反的具体规定以外，每一缔约方均应享有本条约规定的一切权利并承担本条约规定的一切义务。

第25条　本条约的签署

本条约通过后即在世界知识产权组织总部开放以供任何有资格的有关方签署，期限一年。

第26条　本条约的生效

本条约应在第23条所指的三十个有资格的有关方交存批准书或加入书三个月之后生效。

第27条　成为本条约缔约方的生效日期

本条约应自下列日期起具有约束力：

（i）对第26条提到的三十个有资格的有关方，自本条约生效之日起；

（ii）对第23条提到的每一个其他有资格的有关方，自其向世界知识产权组织总干事交存批准书或加入书之日满三个月起。

第28条　退约

本条约的任何缔约方均可退出本条约，退约应通知世界知识产权组织总干事。任何退约应于世界知识产权组织总干事收到通知之日起一年后生效。

第29条　本条约的语言

（1）本条约的签字原件为一份，以中文、阿拉伯文、英文、法文、俄文和西班牙文签署，各该文种的文本具有同等效力。

（2）除本条第（1）款提到的语文外，任何其他语文的正式文本须由世界知识产权组织总干事应有关方请求，在与所有有关方磋商之后制定。在本款中，“有关方”系指涉及其正式语文或正式语文之一的世界知识产权组织任何成员国，并且如果涉及其正式语文之一，亦指欧洲联盟和可以成为本条约缔约方的任何其他政府间组织。

第30条　保存人

世界知识产权组织总干事为本条约的保存人。

注释：

［1］关于第1条第（1）款的议定声明：各方达成共识，本条约的任何内容均不得影响《世界知识产权组织表演和录音制品条约》（WPPT）所规定的任何权利或义务或其解释；另外，各方达成共识，第3款不对本条约缔约方增加批准或加入《世界知识产权组织表演和录音制品条约》或遵守其任何规定的任何义务。

［2］关于第1条第（3）款的议定声明：各方达成共识，系世界贸易组织成员的缔约方承认《与贸易有关的知识产权协定》（《TRIPS协定》）的各项原则与目标，并达成共识：本条约的任何内容均不影响《TRIPS协定》的规定，包括但不限于涉及反竞争行为的规定。

［3］关于第2条（a）款的议定声明：各方达成共识，表演者的定义涵盖凡对表演过程中创作的或首次录制的文学或艺术作品进行表演的人。

［4］关于第2条（b）款的议定声明：特此确认，载于第2条（b）款的“视听录制品”的定义，不损害《世界知识产权组织表演和录音制品条约》的第2条（c）款。

［5］关于第5条的议定声明：为本条约的目的，并在不损害任何其他条约的前提下，会议达成共识：鉴于视听录制品及其制作和发行的特点，在正常利用表演的过程中以及在经表演者授权的使用过程中对该表演所作的修改，诸如使用现有或新的媒体或格式进行编辑、压缩、配音或格式化编排，将不足以构成第5条第（1）款第（ii）项意义下的修改。只有在客观上对表演者的声誉造成重大损害的改动才涉及第5条第（1）款第（ii）项所规定的权利。会议还达成共识：纯粹使用新的或改进的技术或媒体，其本身不足以构成第5条第（1）款第（ii）项意义下的修改。

［6］关于第7条的议定声明：第7条所规定的复制权及其通过第13条所允许的例外，完全适用于数字环境，尤其是以数字形式使用表演的情况。各方达成共识，在电子媒体中以数字形式存储受保护的表演，构成该条意义下的复制。

［7］关于第8条和第9条的议定声明：这些条款中的用语“原件和复制品”，受各该条中发行权和出租权的约束，专指可以作为有形物品投放流通的固定的复制品。

［8］关于第13条的议定声明：关于《世界知识产权组织版权条约》（WCT）第10条（涉及限制与例外）的议定声明，亦可比照适用于本条约的第13条（涉及限制和例外）。

［9］与第 13 条相关的关于第 15 条的议定声明：各方达成共识，本条任何规定均不阻止缔约方采取有效而必要的措施，以确保当视听表演已采用技术措施而受益人有权合法使用该表演时，例如在权利人未对某一具体表演采取能让受益人享受国内法所规定的例外与限制的适当和有效措施的情况下，受益人能享受其国内法中根据第 13 条作出的例外或限制规定。此外，在不损害录有表演的视听作品的法律保护的情况下，各方达成共识，第 15 条规定的义务不适用于不受或不再受履行本条约的国内立法保护的表演。

［10］关于第 15 条的议定声明："表演者使用的技术措施"一语，与《世界知识产权组织表演和录音制品条约》的情况一样，应作广义的理解，亦指代表表演者实施行为的人，包括其代理人、被许可人或受让人，包括制作者、服务提供者和经适当许可使用表演进行传播或广播的人。

［11］关于第 16 条的议定声明：关于《世界知识产权组织版权条约》第 12 条（涉及关于权利管理信息的义务）的议定声明，亦可比照适用于本条约的第 16 条（涉及关于权利管理信息的义务）。

Beijing Treaty on Audiovisual Performance

adopted by the Diplomatic Conference on the
Protection of Audiovisual Performances in
Beijing, on June 24, 2012

Preamble

The Contracting Parties,

Desiring to develop and maintain the protection of the rights of performers in their audiovisual performances in a manner as effective and uniform as possible,

Recalling the importance of the Development Agenda recommendations, adopted in 2007 by the General Assembly of the Convention Establishing the World Intellectual Property Organization (WIPO), which aim to ensure that development considerations form an integral part of the Organization's work,

Recognizing the need to introduce new international rules in order to provide adequate solutions to the questions raised by economic, social, cultural and technological developments,

Recognizing the profound impact of the development and convergence of information and communication technologies on the production and use of audiovisual performances,

Recognizing the need to maintain a balance between the rights of performers in their audiovisual performances and the larger public interest, particularly education, research and access to information,

Recognizing that the WIPO Performances and Phonograms Treaty (WPPT) done in Geneva on December 20, 1996, does not extend protection to performers in respect of their performances fixed in audiovisual fixations,

Referring to the Resolution concerning Audiovisual Performances adopted by the Diplomatic Conference on Certain Copyright and Neighboring Rights Questions on December 20, 1996,

Have agreed as follows:

Article 1 Relation to Other Conventions and Treaties

(1) Nothing in this Treaty shall derogate from existing obligations that Contracting Parties have to each other under the WPPT or the International Convention for the Protection of Performers, Producers of Phonograms and Broadcasting Organizations done in Rome on October 26, 1961.

(2) Protection granted under this Treaty shall leave intact and shall in no way affect the protection of copyright in literary and artistic works. Consequently, no provision of this Treaty may be interpreted as prejudicing such protection.

(3) This Treaty shall not have any connection with treaties other than the WPPT, nor shall it prejudice any rights and obligations under any other treaties[1], [2].

Article 2 Definitions

For the purposes of this Treaty:

(a) "performers" are actors, singers, musicians, dancers, and other persons who act, sing, deliver, declaim, play in, interpret, or otherwise perform literary or artistic works or expressions of folklore[3];

(b) "audiovisual fixation" means the embodiment of moving images, whether or not accompanied by sounds or by the representations thereof, from which they can be perceived, reproduced or communicated through a device[4];

(c) "broadcasting" means the transmission by wireless means for public reception of sounds or of images or of images and sounds or of the representations there of; such transmission by satellite is also "broadcasting"; transmission of encrypted signals is "broadcasting" where the means for decrypting are provided to the public by the broadcasting organization or with its consent;

(d) "communication to the public" of a performance means the transmission to the public by any medium, otherwise than by broadcasting, of an unfixed performance, or of a performance fixed in an audiovisual fixation. For the purposes of Article 11, "communication to the public" includes making a performance fixed in an audiovisual fixation audible or visible or audible and visible to the public.

Article 3 Beneficiaries of Protection

(1) Contracting Parties shall accord the protection granted under this Treaty to

performers who are nationals of other Contracting Parties.

(2) Performers who are not nationals of one of the Contracting Parties but who have their habitual residence in one of them shall, for the purposes of this Treaty, be assimilated to nationals of that Contracting Party.

Article 4 National Treatment

(1) Each Contracting Party shall accord to nationals of other Contracting Parties the treatment it accords to its own nationals with regard to the exclusive rights specifically granted in this Treaty and the right to equitable remuneration provided for in Article 11 of this Treaty.

(2) A Contracting Party shall be entitled to limit the extent and term of the protection accorded to nationals of another Contracting Party under paragraph (1), with respect to the rights granted in Article 11 (1) and 11 (2) of this Treaty, to those rights that its own nationals enjoy in that other Contracting Party.

(3) The obligation provided for in paragraph (1) does not apply to a Contracting Party to the extent that another Contracting Party makes use of the reservations permitted by Article 11 (3) of this Treaty, nor does it apply to a Contracting Party, to the extent that it has made such reservation.

Article 5 Moral Rights

(1) Independently of a performer's economic rights, and even after the transfer of those rights, the performer shall, as regards his live performances or performances fixed in audiovisual fixations, have the right:

(i) to claim to be identified as the performer of his performances, except where omission is dictated by the manner of the use of the performance; and

(ii) to object to any distortion, mutilation or other modification of his performances that would be prejudicial to his reputation, taking due account of the nature of audiovisual fixations.

(2) The rights granted to a performer in accordance with paragraph (1) shall, after his death, be maintained, at least until the expiry of the economic rights, and shall be exercisable by the persons or institutions authorized by the legislation of the Contracting Party where protection is claimed. However, those Contracting Parties whose legislation, at the moment of their ratification of or accession to this Treaty, does not provide for protection after the death of the performer of all rights set out in the preceding paragraph may provide that some of these rights will, after

his death, cease to be maintained.

(3) The means of redress for safeguarding the rights granted under this Article shall be governed by the legislation of the Contracting Party where protection is claimed[5].

Article 6 Economic Rights of Performers in their Unfixed Performances

Performers shall enjoy the exclusive right of authorizing, as regards their performances:

(i) the broadcasting and communication to the public of their unfixed performances except where the performance is already a broadcast performance; and

(ii) the fixation of their unfixed performances.

Article 7 Right of Reproduction

Performers shall enjoy the exclusive right of authorizing the direct or indirect reproduction of their performances fixed in audiovisual fixations, in any manner or form[6].

Article 8 Right of Distribution

(1) Performers shall enjoy the exclusive right of authorizing the making available to the public of the original and copies of their performances fixed in audiovisual fixations through sale or other transfer of ownership.

(2) Nothing in this Treaty shall affect the freedom of Contracting Parties to determine the conditions, if any, under which the exhaustion of the right in paragraph (1) applies after the first sale or other transfer of ownership of the original or a copy of the fixed performance with the authorization of the performer[7].

Article 9 Right of Rental

(1) Performers shall enjoy the exclusive right of authorizing the commercial rental to the public of the original and copies of their performances fixed in audiovisual fixations as determined in the national law of Contracting Parties, even after distribution of them by, or pursuant to, authorization by the performer.

(2) Contracting Parties are exempt from the obligation of paragraph (1) unless the commercial rental has led to widespread copying of such fixations materially impairing the exclusive right of reproduction of performers[7].

Article 10 Right of Making Available of Fixed Performances

Performers shall enjoy the exclusive right of authorizing the making available to the public of their performances fixed in audiovisual fixations, by wire or wireless means, in such a way that members of the public may access them from a place and at a time individually chosen by them.

Article 11 Right of Broadcasting and Communication to the Public

(1) Performers shall enjoy the exclusive right of authorizing the broadcasting and communication to the public of their performances fixed in audiovisual fixations.

(2) Contracting Parties may in a notification deposited with the Director General of WIPO declare that, instead of the right of authorization provided for in paragraph (1), they will establish a right to equitable remuneration for the direct or indirect use of performances fixed in audiovisual fixations for broadcasting or for communication to the public. Contracting Parties may also declare that they will set conditions in their legislation for the exercise of the right to equitable remuneration.

(3) Any Contracting Party may declare that it will apply the provisions of paragraphs (1) or (2) only in respect of certain uses, or that it will limit their application in some other way, or that it will not apply the provisions of paragraphs (1) and (2) at all.

Article 12 Transfer of Rights

(1) A Contracting Party may provide in its national law that once a performer has consented to fixation of his or her performance in an audiovisual fixation, the exclusive rights of authorization provided for in Articles 7 to 11 of this Treaty shall be owned or exercised by or transferred to the producer of such audiovisual fixation subject to any contract to the contrary between the performer and the producer of the audiovisual fixation as determined by the national law.

(2) A Contracting Party may require with respect to audiovisual fixations produced under its national law that such consent or contract be in writing and signed by both parties to the contract or by their duly authorized representatives.

(3) Independent of the transfer of exclusive rights described above, national laws or individual, collective or other agreements may provide the performer with the right to receive royalties or equitable remuneration for any use of the performance, as provided for under this Treaty including as regards Articles 10 and 11.

Article 13 Limitations and Exceptions

(1) Contracting Parties may, in their national legislation, provide for the same kinds of limitations or exceptions with regard to the protection of performers as

they provide for, in their national legislation, in connection with the protection of copyright in literary and artistic works.

(2) Contracting Parties shall confine any limitations of or exceptions to rights provided for in this Treaty to certain special cases which do not conflict with a normal exploitation of the performance and do not unreasonably prejudice the legitimate interests of the performer[8].

Article 14 Term of Protection

The term of protection to be granted to performers under this Treaty shall last, at least, until the end of a period of 50 years computed from the end of the year in which the performance was fixed.

Article 15 Obligations concerning Technological Measures

Contracting Parties shall provide adequate legal protection and effective legal remedies against the circumvention of effective technological measures that are used by performers in connection with the exercise of their rights under this Treaty and that restrict acts, in respect of their performances, which are not authorized by the performers concerned or permitted by law[9], [10].

Article 16 Obligations concerning Rights Management Information

(1) Contracting Parties shall provide adequate and effective legal remedies against any person knowingly performing any of the following acts knowing, or with respect to civil remedies having reasonable grounds to know, that it will induce, enable, facilitate, or conceal an infringement of any right covered by this Treaty:

(i) to remove or alter any electronic rights management information without authority;

(ii) to distribute, import for distribution, broadcast, communicate or make available to the public, without authority, performances or copies of performances fixed in audiovisual fixations knowing that electronic rights management information has been removed or altered without authority.

(2) As used in this Article, "rights management information" means information which identifies the performer, the performance of the performer, or the owner of any right in the performance, or information about the terms and conditions of use of the performance, and any numbers or codes that represent such information, when any of these items of information is attached to a performance fixed in

an audiovisual fixation[11].

Article 17 Formalities

The enjoyment and exercise of the rights provided for in this Treaty shall not be subject to any formality.

Article 18 Reservations and Notifications

(1) Subject to provisions of Article 11 (3), no reservations to this Treaty shall be permitted.

(2) Any notification under Article 11 (2) or 19 (2) may be made in instruments of ratification or accession, and the effective date of the notification shall be the same as the date of entry into force of this Treaty with respect to the Contracting Party having made the notification. Any such notification may also be made later, in which case the notification shall have effect three months after its receipt by the Director General of WIPO or at any later date indicated in the notification.

Article 19 Application in Time

(1) Contracting Parties shall accord the protection granted under this Treaty to fixed performances that exist at the moment of the entry into force of this Treaty and to all performances that occur after the entry into force of this Treaty for each Contracting Party.

(2) Notwithstanding the provisions of paragraph (1), a Contracting Party may declare in a notification deposited with the Director General of WIPO that it will not apply the provisions of Articles 7 to 11 of this Treaty, or any one or more of those, to fixed performances that existed at the moment of the entry into force of this Treaty for each Contracting Party. In respect of such Contracting Party, other Contracting Parties may limit the application of the said Articles to performances that occurred after the entry into force of this Treaty for that Contracting Party.

(3) The protection provided for in this Treaty shall be without prejudice to any acts committed, agreements concluded or rights acquired before the entry into force of this Treaty for each Contracting Party.

(4) Contracting Parties may in their legislation establish transitional provisions under which any person who, prior to the entry into force of this Treaty, engaged in lawful acts with respect to a performance, may undertake with respect to the same performance acts within the scope of the rights provided for in Articles 5 and 7 to 11 after the entry into force of this Treaty for the respective Contracting Par-

ties.

Article 20 Provisions on Enforcement of Rights

(1) Contracting Parties undertake to adopt, in accordance with their legal systems, the measures necessary to ensure the application of this Treaty.

(2) Contracting Parties shall ensure that enforcement procedures are available under their law so as to permit effective action against any act of infringement of rights covered by this Treaty, including expeditious remedies to prevent infringements and remedies which constitute a deterrent to further infringements.

Article 21 Assembly

(1)

(a) The Contracting Parties shall have an Assembly.

(b) Each Contracting Party shall be represented in the Assembly by one delegate who may be assisted by alternate delegates, advisors and experts.

(c) The expenses of each delegation shall be borne by the Contracting Party that has appointed the delegation. The Assembly may ask WIPO to grant financial assistance to facilitate the participation of delegations of Contracting Parties that are regarded as developing countries in conformity with the established practice of the General Assembly of the United Nations or that are countries in transition to a market economy.

(2)

(a) The Assembly shall deal with matters concerning the maintenance and development of this Treaty and the application and operation of this Treaty.

(b) The Assembly shall perform the function allocated to it under Article 23 (2) in respect of the admission of certain intergovernmental organizations to become party to this Treaty.

(c) The Assembly shall decide the convocation of any diplomatic conference for the revision of this Treaty and give the necessary instructions to the Director General of WIPO for the preparation of such diplomatic conference.

(3)

(a) Each Contracting Party that is a State shall have one vote and shall vote only in its own name.

(b) Any Contracting Party that is an intergovernmental organization may participate in the vote, in place of its Member States, with a number of votes equal to the number of its Member States which are party to this Treaty. No such intergovernmental organization shall participate in the vote if any one of its Member States exercises its right to vote and vice versa.

(4) The Assembly shall meet upon convocation by the Director General and, in the absence of exceptional circumstances, during the same period and at the same place as the General Assembly of WIPO.

(5) The Assembly shall endeavor to take its decisions by consensus and shall establish its own rules of procedure, including the convocation of extraordinary sessions, the requirements of a quorum and, subject to the provisions of this Treaty, the required majority for various kinds of decisions.

Article 22 International Bureau

The International Bureau of WIPO shall perform the administrative tasks concerning the Treaty.

Article 23 Eligibility for Becoming Party to the Treaty

(1) Any Member State of WIPO may become party to this Treaty.

(2) The Assembly may decide to admit any intergovernmental organization to become party to this Treaty which declares that it is competent in respect of, and has its own legislation binding on all its Member States on, matters covered by this Treaty and that it has been duly authorized, in accordance with its internal procedures, to become party to this Treaty.

(3) The European Union, having made the declaration referred to in the preceding paragraph in the Diplomatic Conference that has adopted this Treaty, may become party to this Treaty.

Article 24 Rights and Obligations under the Treaty

Subject to any specific provisions to the contrary in this Treaty, each Contracting Party shall enjoy all of the rights and assume all of the obligations under this Treaty.

Article 25 Signature of the Treaty

This Treaty shall be open for signature at the headquarters of WIPO by any eligible party for one year after its adoption.

Article 26 Entry into Force of the Treaty

This Treaty shall enter into force three months after 30 eligible parties referred to in Article 23 have deposited their instruments of ratification or accession.

Article 27 Effective Date of Becoming Party to the Treaty

This Treaty shall bind:

(i) the 30 eligible parties referred to in Article 26, from the date on which this Treaty has entered into force;

(ii) each other eligible party referred to in Article 23, from the expiration of three months from the date on which it has deposited its instrument of ratification or accession with the Director General of WIPO.

Article 28 Denunciation of the Treaty

This Treaty may be denounced by any Contracting Party by notification addressed to the Director General of WIPO. Any denunciation shall take effect one year from the date on which the Director General of WIPO received the notification.

Article 29 Languages of the Treaty

(1) This Treaty is signed in a single original in English, Arabic, Chinese, French, Russian and Spanish languages, the versions in all these languages being equally authentic.

(2) An official text in any language other than those referred to in paragraph (1) shall be established by the Director General of WIPO on the request of an interested party, after consultation with all the interested parties. For the purposes of this paragraph, "interested party" means any Member State of WIPO whose official language, or one of whose official languages, is involved and the European Union, and any other intergovernmental organization that may become party to this Treaty, if one of its official languages is involved.

Article 30 Depositary

The Director General of WIPO is the depositary of this Treaty.

---

[1] **Agreed statement concerning Article 1:** It is understood that nothing in this Treaty affects any rights or obligations under the WIPO Performances and Phonograms Treaty (WPPT) or their interpretation and it is further understood that paragraph 3 does not create any obligations for a Contracting Party to this Treaty to ratify or accede to the WPPT or to comply with any of its provisions.

[2] **Agreed statement concerning Article 1 (3):** It is understood that Contracting Parties who are members of the World Trade Organization (WTO) acknowledge all the principles and objectives of the Agreement on Trade - Related Aspects of Intellectual Property Rights (TRIPS Agreement) and understand that nothing in this Treaty affects the provisions of the TRIPS Agreement, including, but not limited to, the provisions relating to anti - competitive practices.

[3] **Agreed statement concerning Article 2 (a)**: It is understood that the definition of "performers" includes those who perform a literary or artistic work that is created or first fixed in the course of a performance.

[4] **Agreed statement concerning Article 2 (b)**: It is hereby confirmed that the definition of "audiovisual fixation" contained in Article 2 (b) is without prejudice to Article 2 (c) of the WPPT.

[5] **Agreed statement concerning Article 5**: For the purposes of this Treaty and without prejudice to any other treaty, it is understood that, considering the nature of audiovisual fixations and their production and distribution, modifications of a performance that are made in the normal course of exploitation of the performance, such as editing, compression, dubbing, or formatting, in existing or new media or formats, and that are made in the course of a use authorized by the performer, would not in themselves amount to modifications within the meaning of Article 5 (1) (ii). Rights under Article 5 (1) (ii) are concerned only with changes that are objectively prejudicial to the performer's reputation in a substantial way. It is also understood that the mere use of new or changed technology or media, as such, does not amount to modification within the meaning of Article 5 (1) (ii).

[6] **Agreed statement concerning Article 7**: The reproduction right, as set out in Article 7, and the exceptions permitted thereunder through Article 13, fully apply in the digital environment, in particular to the use of performances in digital form. It is understood that the storage of a protected performance in digital form in an electronic medium constitutes a reproduction within the meaning of this Article.

[7] **Agreed statement concerning Articles 8 and 9**: As used in these Articles, the expression "original and copies," being subject to the right of distribution and the right of rental under the said Articles, refers exclusively to fixed copies that can be put into circulation as tangible objects.

[8] **Agreed statement concerning Article 13**: The Agreed statement concerning Article 10 (on Limitations and Exceptions) of the WIPO Copyright Treaty (WCT) is applicable mutatis mutandis also to Article 13 (on Limitations and Exceptions) of the Treaty.

[9] **Agreed statement concerning Article 15 as it relates to Article 13**: It is understood that nothing in this Article prevents a Contracting Party from adopting effective and necessary measures to ensure that a beneficiary may enjoy limitations and exceptions provided in that Contracting Party's national law, in accordance with Article 13, where technological measures have been applied to an audiovisual performance and the beneficiary has legal access to that performance, in circumstances such as where appropriate and effective measures have not been taken by rights holders in relation to that performance to enable the beneficiary to enjoy the limitations and exceptions under that Contracting Party's national law. Without prejudice to the legal protection of an audiovisual work in which a performance is fixed, it is further understood that the obligations under Article 15 are not applicable to performances unprotected or no longer protected under the national law giving effect to this Treaty.

[10] **Agreed statement concerning Article 15**: The expression "technological measures used by performers" should, as this is the case regarding the WPPT, be construed broadly, referring also to those acting on behalf of performers, including their representatives, licensees or assignees, including producers, service providers, and persons engaged in communication or broadcasting using performances on the basis of due authorization.

[11] **Agreed statement concerning Article 16**: The Agreed statement concerning Article 12 (on Obligations concerning Rights Management Information) of the WCT is applicable *mutatis mutandis* also to Article 16 (on Obligations concerning Rights Management Information) of the Treaty.

与贸易有关的知识产权协议

（1993 年 12 月 15 日）

各成员方本着减少国际贸易中的扭曲及障碍的愿望，考虑到有必要促进对知识产权有效和充分的保护，以及确保实施保护产权的措施及程序本身不致成为合法贸易的障碍；

认识到为此目的，有必要制定关于下列新规则及规范：

（1）1994 关贸总协定基本原则及有关的国际知识产权协议和公约的适用性；

（2）关于与贸易有关的知识产权的效力、范围和使用的适当标准及原则的规定；

（3）关于在考虑到各国法律体系差异的同时，使用有效并适当的方法，实施与贸易有关的知识产权的规定；

（4）关于采取多边性的防止和解决各国间争端的有效并迅捷的程序的规定；

（5）旨在使谈判结果有最广泛的参加者的过渡安排；

认识到建立应付国际仿冒商品贸易的原则、规则及规范的多边框架的必要性；

认识到知识产权为私有权；

认识到保护知识产权的国家体制基本的公共政策目标，包括发展和技术方面的目标；

还认识到最不发达国家成员方为建立一个稳固可行的技术基础而在国内实施法律和条例方面对最大限度的灵活性具有特殊需要；

强调通过多边程序为解决与贸易有关的知识财产问题争端作出更加有力的承诺以缓解紧张局势的重要性；

希望在世界贸易组织及世界知识产权组织（本协议中称“WIPO”之间以及其他有关国际组织之间）建立一种相互支持的关系。

协议如下：

第一部分　总则和基本原则

第 1 条　义务的性质和范围

1. 各成员方应使本协议的规定生效。各成员方可以，但不应受强制地，在其本国法律中实行比本协议所要求的更加广泛的保护，只要这种保护不与本协议条款相抵触。各成员方应在各自的法律体系及惯例范围内自由确定实施本协议各条款的适当方法。

2. 本协议所称的"知识产权"一词系指第二部分第 1 至第 7 节所列举所有种类的知识财产。

3. 各成员方应给予其他成员方国民以本协议所规定的待遇。就相关的知识产权而言，如果所有世界贸易组织成员方已是这些公约的成员方，则其他成员方国民应被理解为符合 1967《巴黎公约》、1971《伯尔尼公约》、《罗马公约》及《有关集成电路知识产权条约》所规定的受保护资格标准的自然人或法人。任何利用由《罗马公约》第 5 条第 3 款或第 6 条第 2 款所提供之可能性的成员方应如那些条款所预见的那样，向与贸易有关的知识产权理事会作出通报。

第 2 条　知识产权公约

1. 关于本协议第二、第三及第四部分，各成员方应遵守《巴黎公约》(1967) 第 1 条至第 12 条以及第 19 条规定。

2. 本协议第一至第四部分的所有规定均不得减损各成员方按照《巴黎公约》、《伯尔尼公约》、《罗马公约》和《有关集成电路知识产权条约》而可能相互承担的现行义务。

第 3 条　国民待遇

1. 在服从分别在 1967《巴黎公约》、1971《伯尔尼公约》、《罗马公约》或《有关集成电路知识产权条约》中已作的例外规定的条件下，在保护知识产权方面，每一成员方应给予其他成员方的待遇其优惠不得少于它给予自己国民的优惠。对于录音及广播机构的表演者、制作者，本项义务只对本协议中规定的权利适用。任何利用由 1971《伯尔尼公约》第 6 条或《罗马公约》第 16 条第 1 款第（2）子款所规定之可能性的成员方均应向与贸易有关的知识产权理事会作出在那些条款中预知的通报。

2. 第 1 款所允许的与司法及行政程序有关的例外，包括在一成员方司法管辖权范围内指定服务地址或委任代理人，只有在为确保与本协议规定不一致的法律、规章得到遵守所必要的，并且此种作法不以一种可能对贸易构成变相限制的方式被采用的条件下，各成员方方可利用。

第4条　最惠国待遇

在知识产权的保护方面，由一成员方授予任一其他国家国民的任何利益、优惠、特权或豁免均应立即无条件地给予所有其他成员方的国民。一成员方给予的下列利益、优惠、特权或豁免，免除此项义务：

（1）得自国际司法协助协定或一种一般性的并非专门限于保护知识产权的法律实施的；

（2）按照认可所给予的待遇，只起在另一国所给予的待遇的作用，而不起国民待遇作用的1971《伯尔尼公约》或《罗马公约》的规定授予的；

（3）有关本协议未作规定的录音与广播组织的表演者及制作者权利的；

（4）得自世界贸易组织协定生效之前已生效的与知识产权保护有关的国际协定的，条件是此类协定已通报与贸易有关的知识产权理事会，并且不得构成一种对其他各成员方国民随意的或不公正的歧视。

第5条　关于保护的获得或保持的多边协定

第3条和第4条规定的义务，不适用于在世界知识产权组织主持下达成的有关知识产权获得或保持的多边协定规定的程序。

第6条　失效

就本协议下争端的解决而言，按照第3条及第4条，本协议中的任何条款均不得用以提出知识产权失效问题。

第7条　目标

知识产权的保护和实施应当对促进技术革新以及技术转让和传播作出贡献，对技术知识的生产者和使用者的共同利益作出贡献，并应当以一种有助于社会和经济福利以及有助于权利与义务平衡的方式进行。

第8条　原则

1. 各成员方在制订或修正其法律和规章时，可采取必要措施以保护公众健康和营养，并促进对其社会经济和技术发展至关重要部门的公众利益，只要该措施符合本协议规定。

2. 可能需要采取与本协议的规定相一致的适当的措施，以防止知识产权所有者滥用知识产权或借以对贸易进行不合理限制或实行对国际间的技术转让产生不利影响的做法。

第二部分　关于知识产权的效力、范围及使用的标准

第1节　版权及相关权利

第9条　与《伯尔尼公约》的关系

1. 各成员方应遵守1971《伯尔尼公约》第1至第21条及其附件的规定。然而，各成员方根据本协议对公约第6条附则授予的权利或由其引申出的权利没有权利和义务。

2. 对版权的保护可延伸到公式，但不得延伸到思想、程序、操作方法或数学上的概念等。

第10条　计算机程序和数据汇编

1. 计算机程序，无论是信源代码还是目标代码均应根据1971《伯尔尼公约》的规定作为文献著作而受到保护。

2. 不论是机读的还是其他形式的数据或其他材料的汇编，其内容的选择和安排如构成了智力创造即应作为智力创造加以保护。这种不得延及数据或材料本身的保护不应妨碍任何存在于数据或材料本身的版权。

第11条　出租权

至少在计算机程序和电影艺术作品方面，一成员方应给予作者及其权利继承人以授权或禁止将其拥有版权的作品原著或复制品向公众作商业性出租的权利。除非此类出租已导致了对该作品的广泛复制，而这种复制严重损害了该成员方给予作者及其权利继承人的独家再版权，否则在电影艺术作品方面一成员方可免除此项义务。在计算机程序方面，当程序本身不是出租的主要对象时，此项义务不适用于出租。

第12条　保护期

电影艺术作品或实用艺术作品以外作品的保护期，应以不同于自然人的寿命计算，此期限应为自授权出版的日历年年终起算的不少于50年，或者若作品在创作后50年内未被授权出版，则应为自创作年年终起算的50年。

第13条　限制和例外

各成员方应将对独占权的限制和例外规定限于某些特殊情况，而不影响作品的正常利用，也不无理妨碍权利所有者的合法利益。

第14条　对录音（音响录音制品）的保护

1. 在表演者的表演在录制品上的录制方面，表演者应能阻止下列未经其

许可的行为：录制和翻录其尚未录制的表演；表演者也应能阻止下列未经其许可的行为：将其现场表演作无线电广播和向公众传播。

2. 录音制品制作者应享有授权或禁止直接或间接翻制其录音制品的权利。

3. 广播机构应有权禁止下列未经其许可的行为：录制、翻录、以无线广播手段转播，以及向公众传播同一录音制品的电视广播。若各成员方未向广播机构授予此种权利，则应依照《伯尔尼公约》（1971），向广播内容的版权所有者提供阻止上述行为的可能性。

4. 第11条关于计算机程序的规定经对细节作必要修改后，应适用于录音制品的制作者及经一成员方法律确认的录音制品的任何其他版权所有者。若一成员方在1994年4月15日实行了在出租录音制品方面向版权所有者提供合理补偿的制度，则它可在录音制品的商业性出租未对版权所有者的独占翻录权造成重大损害的条件下，维持该项制度。

5. 录音制品制作者和表演者根据本协议可以获得的保护期至少应持续到从录音制品被制作或演出进行的日历年年终起算的50年期结束时。按照第3款给予的保护期至少应从广播播出的日历年年终起算持续20年。

6. 有关按第2款及第3款授予的权利，任何成员方可在《罗马公约》允许的范围内对按第2款及第3款授予的权利规定条件、限制、例外及保留。

但是，1971《伯尔尼公约》第18条的规定经对细节作必要修改后，也应适用于录音制品表演者和制作者的权利。

第2节　商　　标

第15条　保护事项

1. 任何能够将一个企业的商品和服务与另一企业的商品和服务区别开来的标志或标志组合，均应能够构成商标。此种标志，尤其是包含有个人姓名的词、字母、数目字、图形要素和色彩组合以及诸如此类的标志组合，应有资格注册为商标。若标志没有固有的能够区别有关商品及服务的特征，则各成员方可将其通过使用而得到的独特性作为或给予注册的依据。各成员方可要求标志在视觉上是可以感知的，以此作为注册的一项条件。

2. 第1款不得理解为阻止一成员以其他理由拒绝商标注册，只要这些理由不减损《巴黎公约》（1967）的规定。

3. 各成员方可将使用作为给予注册的依据。然而，商标的实际使用不应是提出注册申请的一项条件。申请不得仅由在自申请之日起的3年期期满之前未如所计划那样地加以使用而遭拒绝。

4．商标所适用的商品或服务的性质在任何情况下，均不得构成对商标注册的障碍。

5．各成员方应在每一商标注册之前或之后立即将其公布，并应为请求取消注册提供合理机会。此外，各成员方可为反对一个商标的注册提供机会。

第 16 条　授予权利

1．已注册商标所有者应拥有阻止所有未经其同意的第三方在贸易中使用与已注册商标相同或相似的商品或服务的，其使用有可能招致混淆的相同或相似的标志。在对相同商品或服务使用相同标志的情况下，应推定存在混淆之可能。上述权利不应妨碍任何现行的优先权，也不应影响各成员方以使用为条件获得注册权的可能性。

2．1967《巴黎公约》第 6 条附则经对细节作必要修改后应适用于服务。在确定一个商标是否为知名商标时，各成员方应考虑到有关部分的公众对该商标的了解，包括由于该商标的推行而在有关成员方得到的了解。

3．1967《巴黎公约》第 6 条附则经对细节作必要修改后应适用于与已注册商标的商品和服务不相似的商品或服务，条件是该商标与该商品和服务有关的使用会表明该商品或服务与已注册商标所有者之间的联系，而且已注册商标所有者的利益有可能为此种使用所破坏。

第 17 条　例外

各成员方可对商标所赋予的权利作些有限的例外规定，诸如公正使用说明性术语，条件是此种例外要考虑到商标所有者和第三方的合法利益。

第 18 条　保护期

商标首次注册及每次续期注册的期限不得少于 7 年。商标注册允许无限期地续期。

第 19 条　使用规定

1．如果注册的保持要求以商标付诸使用为条件，则除非商标所有者提出了此类使用存在障碍的充分理由，否则注册只有在商标至少连续三年以上未予使用的情况下方可取消。

2．当商标由其他人的使用是处在该商标所有者的控制之下时，这种使用应按是为保持注册目的之使用而予以承认。

第 20 条　其他要求

商标在贸易当中的使用不得受到一些特殊要求不正当的妨碍，比如与另一商标一道使用，以特殊形式使用，或以有害于该商标将一个企业的商品或服务与其他企业的商品或服务区分开来的能力之方式使用等。这并不排除规定识别生产某种商品或服务的企业的商标与识别该企业同类特殊商品或服务的商标一道但不连在一起使用的要求。

第21条 许可与转让

各成员方可以确定商标许可与转让的条件，同时，不言而喻，强制性的商标许可是不应允许的，已注册商标的所有者有权将商标所属企业与商标一同转让或只转让商标不转让企业。

第3节 地理标志

第22条 对地理标志的保护

1. 本协议所称的地理标志是识别一种原产于一成员方境内或境内某一区域或某一地区的商品的标志，而该商品特定的质量、声誉或其他特性基本上可归因于它的地理来源。

2. 在地理标志方面，各成员方应向各利益方提供法律手段以阻止：

（1）使用任何手段，在商品的设计和外观上，以在商品地理标志上误导公众的方式标志或暗示该商品原产于并非其真正原产地的某个地理区域；

（2）作任何在1967《巴黎公约》第10条附则意义内构成一种不公平竞争行为的使用。

3. 若某种商品不产自于某个地理标志所指的地域，而其商标又包含了该地理标志或由其组成，如果该商品商标中的该标志具有在商品原产地方面误导公众的性质，则成员方在其法律许可的条件下或应利益方之请求应拒绝或注销该商标的注册。

4. 上述第1、2、3款规定的保护应适用于下述地理标志：该地理标志虽然所表示的商品原产地域、地区或所在地字面上无误，但却向公众错误地表明商品是原产于另一地域。

第23条 对葡萄酒和烈性酒地理标志的额外保护

1. 每一成员方应为各利益方提供法律手段，以阻止不产自于某一地理标志所指地方的葡萄酒或烈性酒使用该地理标志，即使在标明了商品真正原产地或在翻译中使用了该地理标志或伴以“种类”、“类型”、“风味”、“仿制”等字样的情况下也不例外。

2. 对于不产自于由某一地理标志所指的原产地而又含有该产地地理标志的葡萄酒或烈性酒，如果一成员方的立法允许或应某一利益方之请求，应拒绝或注销其商标注册。

3. 如果不同的葡萄酒使用了同名的地理标志，则根据上述第22条第4

款规定，每一种标志均受到保护。每一成员方应确定使同名地理标志能够相互区别开来的现实条件，同时应考虑到确保有关的生产者受到公正待遇并不致使消费者产生误解混淆。

4. 为了便于对葡萄酒地理标志进行保护，应在与贸易有关的知识产权理事会内就建立对参加体系的那些成员方有资格受到保护的葡萄酒地理标志进行通报与注册的多边体系进行谈判。

第 24 条　国际谈判与例外

1. 成员方同意进行旨在加强第 23 条规定的对独特地理标志的保护的谈判。成员方不得援用下述第 4 至 8 款的规定，拒绝进行谈判或缔结双边或多边协定。在此类谈判中，成员方应愿意考虑这些规定对关于其使用是此类谈判之议题的独特地理标志的连续适用性。

2. 与贸易有关的知识产权理事会应对本节规定之适用情况实行审查，首次此类审查应在世界贸易组织协定生效 2 年之内进行。任何影响履行该规定义务的事项均可提请理事会注意。应一成员方之请求，理事会应就经有关成员方之间双边磋商或多组双边磋商仍无法找到令人满意的解决办法的问题，同任何一个或多个成员方进行磋商。理事会应采取可能被一致认为有助于本节之实施及促进本节目标之实现的行动。

3. 在实施本节规定时，成员方不得在世界贸易组织协定生效日即将来临之际减少对该成员方境内的地理标志的保护。

4. 本节中无任何规定要求一成员方阻止其国民或居民继续或类似地使用另一成员方与商品或服务有关的用以区别葡萄酒或烈性酒的特殊地理标志。这些国民或居民在该成员方境内：

（1）在 1994 年 4 月 15 日之前至少已有 10 年；

（2）在上述日期之前已诚实守信地连续使用了标示相同或相关商品或服务的地理标志。

5. 若一商标已被诚实守信地使用或注册：

（1）在如第六部分中所确定的这些规定在那一成员方适用之日以前；

（2）在该地理标志在其原产国获得保护之前，通过诚实守信的使用而获得一商标的权利，则为实施本节而采取的措施就不得以该商标同某一地理标志相同或类似为由而损害其注册的合格性和合法性，或使用该商标的权利。

6. 本节中无任何规定要求一成员方适用其关于任何其他成员方的商品和服务的地理标志的规定，这些商品或服务的相关标志与作为那一成员方境内此类商品或服务的普通名称在一般用语中是惯用的名词完全相同。本节中无任何规定要求一成员方适用其关于任何其他成员方的葡萄制品的地理标志的规定，这些葡萄制品与在世界贸易组织协定生效之日存在于该成员方境内的葡萄品种的惯用名称完全相同。

7. 一成员方可以规定，任何根据本节所提出的有关商标使用或注册的请求必须在对该受保护标志的非法使用被公布后5年之内提出，或在商标在那一成员方境内注册之日以后提出，条件是在注册之日商标已被公告。如果该日期早于非法使用被公布的日期，则条件就应是地理标志未被欺诈地使用或注册。

8. 本节规定丝毫不得妨碍任何个人在贸易中使用其姓名或其前任者姓名的权利，若该姓名的使用导致公众的误解则除外。

第4节　工业设计

第25条　保护的要求

1. 成员方应为新的或原始的独立创造的工业设计提供保护。成员方可以规定设计如果与已知的设计或已知的设计要点的组合没有重大区别，则不视其为新的或原始的。成员方可以规定此类保护不应延伸至实质上是由技术或功能上的考虑所要求的设计。

2. 每一成员方应保证对于获取对纺织品设计保护的规定不得无理损害寻求和获得此类保护的机会，特别是在费用、检查或发表方面。各成员方可自行通过工业设计法或版权法履行该项义务。

第26条　保护

1. 受保护工业设计的所有者应有权阻止未经所有者同意的第三方为商业目的生产、销售或进口含有或体现为是受保护设计的复制品或实为复制品的设计的物品。

2. 成员方可以对工业设计的保护规定有限的例外，条件是这种例外没有无理地与对受保护工业设计的正常利用相冲突，且没有无理损害受保护设计所有者的合法利益，同时考虑到第三方的合法利益。

3. 有效保护期限至少为10年。

第5节　专　　利

第27条　可取得专利的事项

1. 根据下述第2、3款的规定，所有技术领域内的任何发明，无论是产品还是工艺，均可取得专利，只要它们是新的、包含一个发明性的步骤，工业上能够适用。根据第65条第4款、第70条第8款和本条第3款的规定，专利的取得和专利权的享受应不分发明地点、技术领域以及产品是进口的还是当地生产的。

2. 若阻止某项发明在境内的商业利用对保护公共秩序或公共道德，包括保护人类、动物或植物的生命或健康或避免对环境造成严重污染是必要的，则成员方可拒绝给予该项发明以专利权，条件是，不是仅因为其国内法禁止这种利用而作出此种拒绝行为。

3. 以下情况，成员方也可不授予专利：

（1）对人类或动物的医学治疗的诊断、治疗和外科手术方法；

（2）微生物以外的动植物，非生物和微生物生产方法以外的动物或植物的实为生物的生产方法。然而，成员方应或以专利形式，或以一种特殊有效的体系，或以综合形式，对植物种类提供保护。应在世界贸易组织协定生效4年之后对本子款的规定进行审查。

第28条　授予的权利

1. 一项专利应授予其所有者以下独占权：

（1）若一项专利的标的事项是一种产品，则专利所有者有权阻止未得到专利所有者同意的第三方制造、使用、出卖、销售、或为这些目的而进口被授予专利的产品；

（2）若专利的标的事项是一种方法，则专利所有者有权阻止未得到专利所有者同意的第三方使用该方法，或使用、出卖、销售或至少是为这些目的而进口直接以此方法获得的产品。

2. 专利所有者还应有权转让或通过继承转让该项专利，及签订专利权使用契约。

第29条　专利申请者的条件

1. 成员方应要求专利申请者用足够清晰与完整的方式披露其发明，以便于为熟悉该门技术者所运用，并要求申请者在申请之日指明发明者已知的运用该项发明的最佳方式，若是要求取得优先权，则需在优先权申请之日指明。

2. 成员方可要求专利申请者提供关于该申请者在国外相同的申请与授予情况的信息。

第30条　授予权利的例外

成员方可对专利授予的独占权规定有限的例外，条件是该例外规定没有无理地与专利的正常利用相冲突，也未损害专利所有者的合法利益，同时考虑到第三者的合法利益。

第 31 条　未经权利人授权的其他使用

若一成员方的法律允许未经权利人授权而对专利的标的事项作其他使用，包括政府或经政府许可的第三者的使用，则应遵守以下规定：

（1）此类使用的授权应根据专利本身的条件来考虑。

（2）只有在拟议中的使用者在此类使用前已作出以合理的商业条件获得权利人授权的努力，而该项努力在一段合理时间内又未获成功时，方可允许此类使用。在发生全国性紧急状态或其他极端紧急状态或为公共的非商业性目的而使用的情况下，成员方可放弃上述要求。即使是在发生全国性紧急状态或其他极端紧急状态的情况下，仍应合理地尽早通报权利人。至于公共的非商业性使用，若政府或订约人在未查专利状况的情况下得知或有根据得知，一项有效的专利正在或将要被政府使用或为政府而使用，则应及时通知权利人。

（3）此类使用的范围和期限应限制在被授权的意图之内；至于半导体技术，只应用于公共的非商业性目的，或用于抵消在司法或行政程序后被确定的反竞争的做法。

（4）此类使用应是非独占性的。

（5）此类使用应是不可转让的，除非是同享有此类使用的那部分企业或信誉一道转让。

（6）任何此类使用之授权，均应主要是为授权此类使用的成员方国内市场供应之目的。

（7）在被授权人的合法利益受到充分保护的条件下，当导致此类使用授权的情况下不复存在和可能不再产生时，有义务将其终止；应有动机的请求，主管当局应有权对上述情况的继续存在进行检查。

（8）考虑到授权的经济价值，应视具体情况向权利人支付充分的补偿金。

（9）任何与此类使用之授权有关的决定，其法律效力应接受该成员方境内更高当局的司法审查或其他独立审查。

（10）任何与为此类使用而提供的补偿金有关的决定，应接受成员方境内更高当局的司法审查或其他独立审查。

（11）若是为抵消在司法或行政程序后被确定为反竞争做法而允许此类使用，则成员方没有义务适用上述第（2）和第（6）子款规定的条件；在决定此种情况中补偿金的数额时，可以考虑纠正反竞争做法的需要；若导致此项授权的条件可能重新出现，则主管当局应有权拒绝终止授权。

（12）若此类使用被授权允许利用一项不侵犯另一项专利（第一项专利）就不能加以利用的专利（第二项专利），则下列附加条件应适用：

①第二项专利中要求予以承认的发明，应包括比第一项专利中要求予以承认的发明经济意义更大的重要的技术进步；

②第一项专利的所有者应有权以合理的条件享有使用第二项专利中要求予以承认之发明的相互特许权；

③除非同第二项专利一道转让，否则第一项专利所授权的使用应是不可转让的。

第32条　撤销、收回

应提供对撤销或收回专利的决定进行司法审查的机会。

第33条　保护的期限

有效的保护期限自登记之日起不得少于20年。

第34条　工艺专利的举证责任

1. 在第28条第1款第（2）子款所述及关于侵犯所有者权利的民事诉讼中，若一项专利的标的事项是获取某种产品的工艺，则司法当局应有权令被告证明获取相同产品的工艺不同于取得专利的工艺。因此，各成员方应规定在下列情况中至少一种情况下，任何未经专利所有者同意而生产的相同产品若无相反的证据，应被视为是以取得专利的工艺获取的：

（1）如果以该项取得专利的工艺获取的产品是新的；

（2）如果该相同产品极有可能是以该工艺生产的，而专利所有者又不能通过合理的努力确定实际使用的工艺。

2. 只要上述第（1）或第（2）子款所述及的条件得到满足，任何成员方均应有权规定上述第1款所指明的举证责任应由有嫌疑的侵权者承担。

3. 在举出相反证据时，应考虑被告保护其生产和商业秘密的合法权益。

第6节　集成电路的外观设计

第35条　与有关集成电路的知识产权条约的关系

各成员方同意按有关集成电路的知识产权条约中第2条至第7条（第6条中第3款除外）、第12条和第16条第3款规定，对集成电路的外观设计提供保护，此外还服从以下规定。

第36条　保护范围

根据下述第37条第1款的规定，成员方应认为下列未经权利所有人授权的行为是非法的：进口、销售或为商业目的分售受保护的外观设计、含有受保护设计的集成电路或仅在继续含有非法复制的外观设计的范围内含有这种集成电路的产品。

第 37 条　不需要权利人授权的行为

1. 尽管有上述第 36 条的规定，但若从事或指令从事上条中所述及的关于含有非法复制的外观设计的集成电路或含有此种集成电路的任何产品的任何行为的人，在获取该集成电路或含有此种集成电路的产品时，未得知且没有合理的根据得知它含有非法复制的外观设计，则成员方不应认为这种行为是非法的。成员方应规定，该行为人在接到关于复制该设计是非法行为的充分警告之后，仍可从事与在此之前的存货和订单有关的任何行为，但有责任向权利人支付一笔与对自由商谈而取得的通过关于该设计的专利使用权所应付费用相当的合理的专利权税。

2. 若对该外观设计的专利权使用授权是非自愿的或者被政府使用或为政府而使用是未经权利人授权的，则上述第 31 条第（1）－（11）子款规定的条件在对细节作必要修改后应适用。

第 38 条　保护的期限

1. 在要求将登记作为保护条件的成员方，对外观设计的保护期限自填写登记申请表之日或自在世界上任何地方首次进行商业开发之日计起，应不少于 10 年时间。

2. 在不要求将登记作为保护条件的成员方，对外观设计的保护期限自在世界上任何地方首次进行商业开发之日计起，应不少于 10 年时间。

3. 尽管有上述第 1、第 2 款规定，成员方仍可规定在外观设计被发明 15 年后保护应自动消失。

第 7 节　对未泄露之信息的保护

第 39 条

1. 在确保有效的保护以对付 1967《巴黎公约》第 10 条附则所述及的不公平竞争的过程中，各成员方应对下述第 2 款所规定的未泄露之信息和下述第 3 款所规定的提交给政府或政府机构的数据提供保护。

2. 自然人和法人应有可能阻止由其合法掌握的信息在未得到其同意的情况下，被以违反诚信商业作法的方式泄露、获得或使用，只要此信息：

（1）在作为一个实体或其组成部分的精确形状及组合不为正规地处理此种信息的那部分人所共知或不易被其得到的意义上说是秘密的；

（2）由于是秘密的而具有商业价值；

（3）被其合法的掌握者根据情况采取了合理的保密措施。

3. 成员方当被要求呈交本公开的试验或其他所获得需要付出相当劳动的

数据以作为同意使用新型化学物质生产的药品或农用化学品在市场上销售的一项条件时，应保护该数据免受不公平的商业利用。此外，成员方应保护该数据免于泄露，除非是出于保护公共利益的需要，或采取了保证该数据免受不公平商业利用的措施。

第 8 节　在契约性专利权使用中对反竞争性行为的控制

第 40 条

1．各成员方一致认为，与限制竞争的知识产权有关的一些专利权使用作法或条件对贸易可能产生不利影响，可能妨碍技术的转让和传播。

2．本协议中无任何规定阻止成员方在其立法中详细载明在特定情况下可能构成对有关市场中的竞争具有不利影响的知识产权滥用的专利权使用作法或条件。如上述所规定，一成员方可按照本协议的其他规定，根据国内有关法律和规定采取适当措施阻止或控制此种作法。这些措施可能包括例如独占性回授条件、阻止否认合法性的条件和强制性的一揽子许可证交易。

3．若一成员方有理由认为是另一成员方国民或居民的知识产权所有者正在从事违反该成员方关于本节主题事项的法律规章的活动，并希望使该另一成员方遵守此类法规，则在不妨碍两个成员方中任何一方依法采取任何行动和作出最终决定的充分自由的条件下，该另一成员方在接到该成员方的请求后，应与之进行磋商。被请求的成员方对与提出请求的成员方进行磋商应给予充分的同情的考虑，为此提供充分的机会，并应在服从国内法和令双方满意的关于提出请求的成员方保护资料机密性的协议之最后决定的条件下，通过提供与该问题有关的可以公开利用的非机密性资料和可供该成员方利用的其他资料进行合作。

4．其国民或居民正在另一成员方接受关于所断言的违反该成员方关于本节主题事项的法律规章的诉讼的成员方，根据请求，应由另一成员方给予按照与上述第 3 款相同的条件进行磋商的机会。

第三部分　知识产权的实施

第 1 节　一般义务

第 41 条

1．成员方应保证由本部分所具体规定的实施程序根据国内法是有效的，以便允许对任何对本协议所涉及的知识产权的侵犯行为采取有效行动，包括及时地阻止侵权的补救措施和对进一步侵权构成一种威慑的补救措施。在运用这些程序时，应避免对合法贸易构成障碍，并规定防止其滥用的保障措施。

2. 知识产权的实施程序应公平合理，不应不必要地烦琐、消耗资财，也不应有不合理的时限及毫无道理的拖延。

3. 对一案件案情实质的裁决最好应以书面形式作出并陈述理由。至少应使诉讼各方没有不适当延迟地获知裁决结果。对该案件案情实质的判定应只以各方被提供机会了解的证据为依据。

4. 诉讼各方应有机会让司法当局对最终行政决定及根据一成员方法律中关于一案件重要程度的司法规定对至少是对一案件案情实质最初司法裁决的法律方面进行审查。然而，没有义务为对刑事案件中的判定无罪进行审查提供机会。

5. 显然，本部分未规定任何关于设置与实施大多数法律不同的实施知识产权的司法制度的义务，也不影响成员方实施其大多数法律的能力。本部分也未规定任何关于在实施知识产权和实施大多数法律之间进行资源分配的义务。

第 2 节　民事和行政程序及补救

第 42 条　公平合理的程序

成员方应使权利所有人可以利用关于本协议所涉及的任何知识产权之实施的民事司法程序。被告应有权及时获得内容充实的书面通知，其中包括控告的依据。应允许成员方由独立的法律辩护人充当其代表。关于强制性的亲自出庭，程序中不应规定过多烦琐的要求。该程序所涉及的各方应有充分的权利证实其要求，并提出所有相关的证据。该程序应规定一种识别和保护机密性资料的方法，除非该规定与现行的宪法要求相抵触。

第 43 条　证据

1. 若一当事方已提交了足以支持其要求的合理有效的证据，并具体指明了由对方掌握的与证实其要求有关的证据，则司法当局应有权决定按照在此类案件中确保对机密性资料保护的条件，令对方出示该证据。

2. 若诉讼一当事方有意地并无正当理由地拒绝有关方面使用或在合理期限内未提供必要的资料，或严重地妨碍与某一强制行动有关的程序，则一成员方可授权司法当局根据呈交上来的信息，包括因被拒绝使用信息而受到不利影响的一方呈交的申诉和事实陈述，作出或是肯定的或是否定的最初和最终裁决。这一切须在向各方提供机会听到断言或证据的情况下进行。

第 44 条　禁令

1. 司法当局应有权命令一当事方停止侵权行为，特别是在涉及对知识产权有侵权行为的进口货物结关之后，立即阻止这些货物进入其司法管辖区内的商业渠道。各成员方对涉及由个人在得知或有合理的根据得知经营受保护产品会构成对知识产权的侵犯之前获得或订购的该产品不必提供此项授权。

2. 尽管有本部分的其他规定，若第二部分中专门阐述的关于未经权利人授权的政府使用或由政府授权的第三方的使用的各项规定得到遵守，则各成员方可将针对此类使用的可资利用的补救措施限制在依据第 31 条第（8）子款的补偿金支付上。在其他情况下，本部分的补救措施应适用，或者若这些补救措施与成员方的法律不符，则应适用宣告性判决和适当的补偿金。

第 45 条　损害

1. 司法当局有权令故意从事侵权活动或有合理的根据知道是在从事侵权活动的侵权人就因侵权人对权利所有人知识产权的侵犯而对权利所有人造成的损害向其支付适当的补偿。

2. 司法当局有权令侵权人向权利所有人支付费用，可能包括聘请律师的有关费用。在有关案件中，即使侵权人并非故意地从事侵权活动或有合理的根据知道其正在从事侵权活动，成员方仍可授权司法当局下令追偿利润和/或支付预先确定的损失。

第 46 条　其他补救

为了对侵权行为造成有效的威慑，司法当局有权令其发现正在授权的货物避免对权利所有人造成损害的方式不作任何补偿地在商业渠道以外予以处置，或者在不与现行法律要求相抵触的情况下予以销毁。司法当局还有权令在侵权物品生产中主要使用的材料和工具以减少进一步侵权危险的方式不作任何补偿地在商业渠道以外予以处置。在考虑此类请求时，应考虑侵权的严重程度与被决定的补救两者相称的必要性以及第三者的利益。对于仿冒商标产品，除例外情况，仅仅除去非法所贴商标还不足以允许将该产品放行到商业渠道之中。

第 47 条　告知权

成员方可规定，司法当局有权令侵权人将与侵权产品或服务的生产、销售有牵连的第三方的身份及其销售渠道告知权利所有人，除非这种授权与侵权的危害程度不成比例。

第 48 条　被告的赔偿

1. 司法当局有权令应其请求而采取措施并滥用实施程序的申诉方受到错

误命令或抑制的被告方因此种滥用而遭受的损害向其提供补偿。司法当局还应有权令申诉方支付被告的费用，可能包括聘请律师的有关费用。

2. 关于与知识产权的保护或实施有关的任何法律的实施，若政府机构和政府官员在实施法律过程中有诚意地采取了行动或打算采取行动，则应仅免除其对适当补救措施的责任。

第49条　行政程序

在能够决定以任何民事补救作为关于一案件案情实质的行政程序之结果的范围内，此类程序应遵守与本节中所规定的那些原则大体相等的原则。

第3节　临时措施

第50条

1. 司法当局应有权决定及时、有效的临时措施：

（1）阻止任何对知识产权侵权行为的发生，特别是阻止包括刚刚结关的进口商品在内的侵权商品进入其司法管辖区内的商业渠道；

（2）保护关于被断言的侵权行为的有关证据。

2. 在适当的情况下，特别是在任何延迟可能会给权利人带来不可弥补的损害或证据极有毁灭危险的情况下，司法当局有权采取适当的措施。

3. 司法当局有权要求申诉人提供合理有效的证据，以便司法当局充分肯定地确认申诉人就是权利人，申诉人的权利正在受到侵犯，或者这种侵犯即将发生。同时司法当局应要求申诉人提供足以保护被告和防止滥用的保证金或同等的担保。

4. 若临时措施已经采取，应在实施措施后最短时间内通知受影响的成员方。应被告知请求，应对这些措施进行重新审查，包括听取被告陈述，以便在关于措施的通报发出后的合理时间内决定这些措施是否应加以修正、撤销或确认。

5. 将要实施临时措施令的司法当局可以要求申诉人提供为鉴别相关产品所必需的其他资料。

6. 在成员方法律允许的情况下，导致对案件案情实质作出裁决的合理诉讼时间，由发布措施令的司法当局决定。在没有此种决定的情况下，该合理时间为不超过20个工作日或者31天，以长者为准。若此类诉讼在该合理时间内没有开始，则在不妨碍上述第4款规定的同时，按照上述第1、第2款所采取的临时措施，应根据被告的请求予以撤销或使其停止生效。

7. 若临时措施被撤销，或由于申诉人的任何作为或疏忽而失效，或随后发现对知识产权的侵犯或侵犯的威胁并不存在，则应被告知请求，司法当局应有权令申诉人就这些措施对被告造成的任何损害向被告提供适当的赔偿。

8. 在能够决定以任何临时措施作为行政程序之结果的范围内，此类程序应遵守与本节中所规定的那些原则大体相等的原则。

第 4 节　与边境措施相关的特殊要求

第 51 条　海关当局的中止放行

成员方应依照以下规定采纳程序，使有确凿根据怀疑仿冒商标商品或盗版商品的进口可能发生的权利人能够以书面形式向主管的行政或司法当局提出由海关当局中止放行该货物进入自由流通的申请。在本节的要求得到满足的条件下，成员方可使对含有其他侵犯知识产权行为货物的申请能够被提出。成员方还可规定关于海关当局中止放行从其境内出口的侵权货物的相应程序。

第 52 条　申请

应要求任何启动上述第 51 条程序的权利人提供适当的证据，以使主管当局确信，根据进口国的法律，确有对权利人知识产权无可争辩的侵犯，并提供对该货物充分详细的描述，以使海关当局可以迅速地对其加以识别。主管当局应在一个合理的时间内通知申请人是否接受其请求，若主管当局决定受理，应通知申诉人海关当局采取行动的时间。

第 53 条　保证金或同等担保

1. 主管当局应有权要求申请人提供一笔足以保护被告和有关当局并阻止滥用的保证金或同等担保。该保证金或同等担保不应无理地阻碍对这些程序的援用。

2. 假如根据本节关于申请的规定，对涉及工业设计、专利、外观设计或未泄露信息的货物进入自由流通的放行已由海关当局根据非由司法或其他独立机构作出的裁决中止，下述第 55 条规定的期限已到期而仍未获得主管当局暂时放行的许可，而且假如关于进口的所有其他条件均得到了遵从，则该货物的所有人、进口商或收货人在提交了一笔其数额足以保护权利人不受侵权损害的保证金的条件下，应有权使该货物放行。保证金的支付不应妨碍向权利人作其他有效的补偿。显然，如果权利人在一段合理的时间内没有寻求起诉权，则保证金应予免除。

第 54 条　中止通知

根据上述第 51 条的规定，货物放行一旦被中止，应立即通知进口商和申请人。

第 55 条　中止的持续期限

若在申请人被送达中止通知后不超过 10 个工作日之内，海关当局仍未接到关于被告以外的一方已开始将会导致对案件的案情实质作出裁决的诉讼，或者主管当局已采取延长对货物放行中止的临时措施的通知，则只要进口或出口的所有其他条件均已得到了遵从，该货物便应予放行。在适当的情况下，上述期限可再延长 10 个工作日。若导致对一案件案情实质作出裁决的诉讼已经开始，则应被告之请求，应进行审查，包括听取被告的陈述，以便决定在一段合理的时间内这些措施是否应加以修正、撤销或确认。尽管有上述规定，或货物的放行已经被中止，或根据临时司法措施继续被中止，则第 50 条第 6 款的规定应适用。

第 56 条　对商品进口商和货主的补偿

有关当局应有权令申请人就因错误扣押货物或扣押根据上述第 55 条规定应予放行的货物而对进口商、收货人和货主所造成的损害向其支付适当的赔偿。

第 57 条　资料和调查权

在不妨碍对机密资料进行保护的同时，成员方应授权主管当局给予权利人使被海关当局扣押的货物接受检查以证实权利人要求的充分机会。有关当局也应有权给予进口商使任何此类货物接受检查的同等机会。若对案件的案情实质已作出了积极的裁决，成员方可以授权主管当局将有关发货人、进口商和收货人的姓名和地址以及有关货物的数量通知权利人。

第 58 条　依职权之行为

若成员方要求主管当局主动采取行动，中止放行其已获得无可争辩的证据证明知识产权正在受到侵犯的货物，则：

（1）主管当局在任何时候均可从权利人处寻求任何有助于其行使权力的资料；

（2）应迅速地将该中止通知进口商和权利人。若进口商已就中止一事向主管当局呈交了上诉，则中止应按上述第 55 条规定的经对细节作了必要修改的条件进行；

（3）若政府机构和政府官员有诚意地采取了行动或者打算采取行动，则成员方仅应免除其对适当补救措施所应承担的责任。

第 59 条　补救

在不妨碍权利人其他行动权和被告向司法当局寻求审查权利的同时，主管当局根据上述第 40 条的规定，应有权下令销毁或处理侵权货物，对于仿冒商标的货物，当局应不允许侵权货物原封不动地再出口，若使其按照不同的海关程序办理，例外情况除外。

第60条　少量进口

对于旅游者和私人行李中携带的或少量寄存的非商业性质的少量货物，成员方可免除上述条款的适用。

第5节　刑事程序

第61条

成员方应规定刑事程序和惩罚，至少适用于具有商业规模的故意的商标仿冒和盗版案件。可资利用的补救措施应包括足以构成一种威慑的与对相应程度的刑事犯罪适用的处罚水平相同的监禁和/或罚款措施。在适当的案件中，可资利用的补救措施还包括对侵犯货物及在从事此种违法行为时主要使用的材料和工具予以扣押、没收和销毁。成员方可规定适用于其他侵犯知识产权案件的刑事程序和惩罚，特别是对于故意和具有商业规模的侵权案件。

第四部分　知识产权的取得和保持及相关程序

第62条

1. 成员方可要求遵循合理的程序和手续，以此作为第二部分第2至第6节所规定的知识产权的取得和保持的一项条件。此类程序和手续应符合本协议的规定。

2. 若知识产权的取得以知识产权被授予或登记为准，则成员方应确保在符合取得知识产权的实质性条件的情况下，有关授予或登记的程序允许在一段合理时间内授予或登记权利，以避免保护期限被不适当地缩短。

3. 1967年《巴黎公约》第4条应在对细节作必要修改之后适用于服务标记。

4. 有关知识产权之取得和保持的程序、有关行政撤销的程序（若成员方的法律规定了这样的程序），有关诸如抗辩、撤销和废除等的程序，应服从第41条第2款和第3款规定的总原则。

5. 上述第4款所涉及的任何程序中的最终行政决定应接受司法当局或准司法当局的审查。然而，在抗辩和行政撤销不成功的情况下，假若此类程序的基础可能成为程序无效的原因，则没有任何义务为对裁决进行此类审查提供机会。

第五部分　争端的预防和解决

第 63 条　透明度

1. 由一成员方制度实施的关于本协议主题事项（知识产权的效力、范围、取得、实施和防止滥用问题）的法律和规章、对一般申请的最终司法裁决和行政裁决，应以该国官方语言，以使各成员方政府和权利人能够熟悉的方式予以公布；若此种公布不可行，则应使之可以公开利用。正在实施中的一成员方的政府或一政府机构与另一成员方政府或一政府机构之间关于本协议主题事项的各项协议也应予以公布。

2. 成员方应将上述第 1 款所述及的法律和规章通报与贸易有关的知识产权理事会，以协助理事会对本协议的执行情况进行检查。理事会应努力去最大限度地减轻成员方在履行该项义务方面的负担。若与世界知识产权组织就建立一份含有这些法律和规章的共同登记簿一事进行的磋商取得成功，理事会便可决定免除直接向理事会通报此类法律和规章的义务。理事会在这方面还应考虑采取本协议从 1967《巴黎公约》第 6 条的各项规定派生出来的各项义务所要求的与通报有关的任何行动。

3. 应另一成员方的书面请求，每一成员方应准备提供上述第 1 款所述及的资料。一成员方在有理由相信知识产权领域中某个特定的司法裁决、行政裁决或双边协议影响到其由本协议所规定的权利时，也可以书面形式要求向其提供或充分详尽地告知该特定的司法裁决、行政裁决或双边协议。

4. 上述第 1 至第 3 款中无任何规定要求成员方泄露将会妨碍法律实施、或违背公共利益、或损害特定的国营或私营企业合法商业利益的资料。

第 64 条　争端解决

1. 由争端解决谅解所详细阐释并运用的 1994 关贸总协定第 22 条和第 23 条的各项规定应运用于本协议下的争端磋商与解决，本协议中另有规定者除外。

2. 在自世界贸易组织协定生效之日起的 5 年之内，1994 关贸总协定第 23 条第 1 款第（2）和第（3）子款不应适用于本协议下的争端解决。

3. 在第 2 款所述及的期限内，与贸易有关的知识产权理事会应检查根据本协议提出的由 1994 关贸总协定第 23 条第 1 款第（2）和第（3）子款所规定的那种类型控诉的规模和形式，并向部长级会议提交建议请其批准。部长级会议关于批准此类建议或延长第 2 款中所述及时限的任何决定，只应以全体一致的方式作出，被批准的建议应对所有成员方生效，无须进一步的正式接受程序。

第六部分　过渡期安排

第 65 条　过渡期安排

1. 根据下述第 2、第 3 和第 4 款的规定，成员方无义务在世界贸易组织协定生效之日后一般 1 年期满之前适用于本协议的规定。

2. 发展中国家成员方有权将第 1 款中所确定的本协议除第 3、第 4 和第 5 条以外的各项规定的适用日期推迟 4 年时间。

3. 处于由中央计划经济向市场、私营企业经济转换进程中的和正在进行知识产权制度结构改革并在制定和实施知识产权法方面面临特殊困难的任何其他成员方，也可从上述第 2 款所述及的期限推迟中获益。

4. 一发展中国家成员方如果按本协议有义务在上述第 2 款所规定的本协议对该成员方适用之日将对产品专利的保护扩大到在其境内无法加以保护的技术领域，则可将第二部分第 5 节关于产品专利的规定对此类技术领域的适用再推迟 5 年时间。

5. 利用上述第 1、第 2、第 3 和第 4 款所规定过渡期的成员方，应保证在该时期内其法律、规章和做法中的任何变更不导致它们与本协议规定相一致的程度降低。

第 66 条　最不发达国家成员方

1. 鉴于最不发达国家成员方的特殊需要和要求，其经济、财政和行政的压力，以及其对创造一个可行的技术基础的灵活性的需要，不应要求这些成员方在自上述第 65 条第 1 款所规定的适用日期起的 10 年内适用本协议，第 3、第 4 和第 5 条除外。应最不发达国家无可非议的请求，与贸易有关的知识产权理事会应将此期限予以延长。

2. 发达国家缔约方应给境内的企业和机构提供奖励，以促进和鼓励对最不发达国家成员方转让技术，使其能够建立一个稳固可行的技术基础。

第 67 条　技术合作

为便于本协议的实施，发达国家成员方应根据请求和双边达成的条件，向发展中国家和最不发达国家成员方提供对其有利的技术和金融合作。此类合作应包括协助制定对有关知识产权保护、实施及阻止滥用的法律和规章，还应包括对设方和加强与这些事项有关的国内机关和机构包括人员培训提供支持。

第七部分　机构安排和最后条款

第 68 条　与贸易有关的知识产权理事会

与贸易有关的知识产权理事会应对本协议的执行情况，尤其是成员方履行本协议所规定义务的情况进行监督，并应为成员方提供与贸易有关的知识产权事宜进行磋商的机会。理事会应履行成员方指定给它的其他职责，并尤其应在争端解决程序方面对成员方提出的请求提供帮助。在行使职能时，与贸易有关的知识产权理事会可与它认为合适的方面进行磋商，并从那里寻找资料。在与世界知识产权组织进行磋商时，理事会应谋求在其第一次会议的 1 年内作出与该组织所属各机构进行合作的适当安排。

第 69 条　国际合作

成员方同意相互进行合作，以消除侵犯知识产权商品的国际贸易。为此，它们应在其行政范围内设立和通报联络站，并随时交流关于侵权商品贸易的情报。它们尤其应促进海关当局之间在仿冒商标商品和盗版商品贸易方面的情报交流与合作。

第 70 条　对现有标的事项的保护

1. 对于某个成员方在本协议对其适用之日以前发生的行为，本协议不规定该成员方承担任何义务。

2. 本协议另有规定者除外，对于在本协议对有关成员方适用之日已存在的，及在该日期在该成员方受到保护的或在本协议规定的期限内达到或以后将要达到保护标准的所有标的事项，本协议规定义务。与本款和下述第 3、第 4 款有关的关于现有著作的版权义务仅应根据 1971《伯尔尼公约》第 18 条来决定，关于现有唱片的唱片制作商和表演者的权利仅应根据 1971《伯尔尼公约》第 18 条来决定，该条的适用办法由本协议第 14 条第 6 款作了具体规定。

3. 对于在本协议适用之日处于无专利权状态的标的事项，没有对其恢复保护的义务。

4. 关于在按照与本协议相一致立法的条件已构成侵权的、并在有关成员方接受世界贸易组织协定之日以前已开始的或已对其进行了大量投资的体现受保护标的事项的特定对象方面的任何行为，任何成员方可为在本协议对那一成员方生效之日以后此类行为继续发生的情况下，权利人可以利用的补救措施规定一个限度。然而，在此情况下，该成员方至少应规定支付合理的补偿。

5. 成员方没有义务在本协议对其适用之日以前适用关于购买的原物或复制品的第 11 条和第 14 条第 4 款规定。

6. 不应要求成员方将第 31 条或第 27 条第 1 款关于对技术领域专利权的享用应一视同仁的规定适用于本协议生效之日以前未经权利人许可而经政府授权的使用。

7. 在以登记为保护条件的知识产权方面，对于在本协议对有关成员方适用之日仍未得到批准的保护申请，应允许对其作正式修改，以要求根据本协议的规定加强保护。此类修改不得包括新事项。

8. 若世界贸易组织协定生效之日已到而一成员方仍未能对药品和农用化学品提供与其根据第 27 条所承担义务相当的有效的专利保护，则该成员方应：

（1）尽管有第五部分的规定，仍自建立世界贸易组织协定生效之日起，规定一种使关于此类发明的专利申请得以提出的方式；

（2）自本协议适用之日起，将本协议所规定的授予专利权标准适用于这些申请，视这些标准已由成员方在申请提出之日，或若优先权有效并已被提出权利要求，则在优先权申请之日予以适用。

（3）自专利被批准时起，并在自依照本协议第 33 条的申请提出之日计起的专利期的其余部分，对符合上述第（2）子款保护标准的申请提供专利保护。

9. 若按第 8 款第（1）子款，一项产品是一成员方内的专利申请对象，则尽管有第五部分的规定，应自在那一成员方获准进行市场销售之时计起给予其独占的市场销售权 5 年，或直到一项产品专利在那一成员方被批准或拒绝之时，以时间较短者为准，条件是在世界贸易组织协定生效之后，在另一成员方那项产品的专利申请已被提出，专利已被批准，并获准在该另一成员方进行市场销售。

第 71 条　审查和修正

1. 与贸易有关的知识产权理事会应在上述第 65 条第 2 款所述及的过渡期期满之后，对本协议的履行情况进行审查。理事会应参考在履行中获得的经验在过渡期期满之日 2 年后对本协议的履行情况进行审查，并在此后每隔两年审查一次。理事会也可根据可能成为对本协议进行修改或修正之理由的任何有关的新情况进行审查。

2. 仅为适应在已生效的其他国际协议中已达到的和根据那些国际协议为世界贸易组织所有成员方所接受的对知识产权更高的保护程度而提出的修正案可提交部长级会议，以便其根据与贸易有关的知识产权理事会一致同意的建议采取与世界贸易组织协定第10条第6款相符的行动。

第72条　保留

未经其他成员方的同意，不得对本协议的任何条款作出保留。

第73条　保障的例外规定

本协议中的任何内容均不应解释为：

（1）要求一成员方提供他认为其泄露违背其根本安全利益的任何资料。

（2）阻止任一成员方采取他认为是对保护其根本安全利益所必需的行动：

①与裂变物质或从中获取裂变物质的物质有关的；

②与枪支、弹药和战争工具走私有关的，以及与直接或间接为供给军方之目的而从事的其他货物和物资的走私有关的；

③在战时或在国际关系中出现其他紧急情况时采取的。

（3）阻止任何成员方为根据《联合国宪章》所承担的维持国际和平与安全的义务而采取的行动。

Agreement on Trade Related Aspects of Intellectual Property Rights

PART I GENERAL PROVISIONS AND BASIC PRINCIPLES

PART II STANDARDS CONCERNING THE AVAILABILITY, SCOPE AND USE OF INTELLECTUAL PROPERTY RIGHTS

1. Copyright and Related Rights
2. Trademarks
3. Geographical Indications
4. Industrial Designs
5. Patents
6. Layout - Designs (Topographies) of Integrated Circuits
7. Protection of Undisclosed Information
8. Control of Anti - Competitive Practices in Contractual Licences

PART III ENFORCEMENT OF INTELLECTUAL PROPERTY RIGHTS

1. General Obligations
2. Civil and Administrative Procedures and Remedies
3. Provisional Measures
4. Special Requirements Related to Border Measures
5. Criminal Procedures

PART IV ACQUISITION AND MAINTENANCE OF INTELLECTUAL PROPERTY RIGHTS AND RELATED *INTERPARTES* PROCEDURES

PART V DISPUTE PREVENTION AND SETTLEMENT

PART VI TRANSITIONAL ARRANGEMENTS

PART VII INSTITUTIONAL ARRANGEMENTS; FINAL PROVISIONS

Members,

Desiring to reduce distortions and impediments to international trade, and taking into account the need to promote effective and adequate protection of intellectual property rights, and to ensure that measures and procedures to enforce intellectual property rights do not themselves become barriers to legitimate trade;

Recognizing, to this end, the need for new rules and disciplines concerning:

(a) the applicability of the basic principles of GATT 1994 and of relevant international intellectual property agreements or conventions;

(b) the provision of adequate standards and principles concerning the availability, scope and use of trade - related intellectual property rights;

(c) the provision of effective and appropriate means for the enforcement of trade - related intellectual property rights, taking into account differences in national legal systems;

(d) the provision of effective and expeditious procedures for the multilateral prevention and settlement of disputes between governments; and

(e) transitional arrangements aiming at the fullest participation in the results of the negotiations;

Recognizing the need for a multilateral framework of principles, rules and disciplines dealing with international trade in counterfeit goods;

Recognizing that intellectual property rights are private rights;

Recognizing the underlying public policy objectives of national systems for the protection of intellectual property, including developmental and technological objectives;

Recognizing also the special needs of the least - developed country Members in respect of maximum flexibility in the domestic implementation of laws and regulations in order to enable them to create a sound and viable technological base;

Emphasizing the importance of reducing tensions by reaching strengthened commitments to resolve disputes on trade - related intellectual property issues through multilateral procedures;

Desiring to establish a mutually supportive relationship between the WTO and the World Intellectual Property Organization (referred to in this Agreement as "WIPO") as well as other relevant international organizations;

Hereby agree as follows:

PART I GENERAL PROVISIONS AND BASIC PRINCIPLES

Article 1 Nature and Scope of Obligations

1. Members shall give effect to the provisions of this Agreement. Members may, but shall not be obliged to, implement in their law more extensive protection than is required by this Agreement, provided that such protection does not contravene the provisions of this Agreement. Members shall be free to determine the appropriate method of implementing the provisions of this Agreement within their own legal system and practice.

2. For the purposes of this Agreement, the term "intellectual property" refers to all categories of intellectual property that are the subject of Sections 1 through 7 of Part II.

3. Members shall accord the treatment provided for in this Agreement to the nationals of other Members.[①] In respect of the relevant intellectual property right, the nationals of other Members shall be understood as those natural or legal persons that would meet the criteria for eligibility for protection provided for in the Paris Convention (1967), the Berne Convention (1971), the Rome Convention and the Treaty on Intellectual Property in Respect of Integrated Circuits, were all Members of the WTO members of those conventions.[②] Any Member availing itself of the possibilities provided in paragraph 3 of Article 5 or paragraph 2 of Article 6 of the Rome Convention shall make a notification as foreseen in those provisions to the Council for Trade - Related Aspects of Intellectual Property Rights (the

---

① When "nationals" are referred to in this Agreement, they shall be deemed, in the case of a separate customs territory Member of the WTO, to mean persons, natural or legal, who are domiciled or who have a real and effective industrial or commercial establishment in that customs territory.

② In this Agreement, "Paris Convention" refers to the Paris Convention for the Protection of Industrial Property; "Paris Convention (1967)" refers to the Stockholm Act of this Convention of 14 July 1967. "Berne Convention" refers to the Berne Convention for the Protection of Literary and Artistic Works; "Berne Convention (1971)" refers to the Paris Act of this Convention of 24 July 1971. "Rome Convention" refers to the International Convention for the Protection of Performers, Producers of Phonograms and Broadcasting Organizations, adopted at Rome on 26 October 1961. "Treaty on Intellectual Property in Respect of Integrated Circuits" (IPIC Treaty) refers to the Treaty on Intellectual Property in Respect of Integrated Circuits, adopted at Washington on 26 May 1989. "WTO Agreement" refers to the Agreement Establishing the WTO.

"Council for TRIPS").

Article 2 Intellectual Property Conventions

1. In respect of Parts II, III and IV of this Agreement, Members shall comply with Articles 1 through 12, and Article 19, of the Paris Convention (1967).

2. Nothing in Parts I to IV of this Agreement shall derogate from existing obligations that Members may have to each other under the Paris Convention, the Berne Convention, the Rome Convention and the Treaty on Intellectual Property in Respect of Integrated Circuits.

Article 3 National Treatment

1. Each Member shall accord to the nationals of other Members treatment no less favourable than that it accords to its own nationals with regard to the protection ① of intellectual property, subject to the exceptions already provided in, respectively, the Paris Convention (1967), the Berne Convention (1971), the Rome Convention or the Treaty on Intellectual Property in Respect of Integrated Circuits. In respect of performers, producers of phonograms and broadcasting organizations, this obligation only applies in respect of the rights provided under this Agreement. Any Member availing itself of the possibilities provided in Article 6 of the Berne Convention (1971) or paragraph 1 (b) of Article 16 of the Rome Convention shall make a notification as foreseen in those provisions to the Council for TRIPS.

2. Members may avail themselves of the exceptions permitted under paragraph 1 in relation to judicial and administrative procedures, including the designation of an address for service or the appointment of an agent within the jurisdiction of a Member, only where such exceptions are necessary to secure compliance with laws and regulations which are not inconsistent with the provisions of this Agreement and where such practices are not applied in a manner which would constitute a disguised restriction on trade.

Article 4 Most-Favoured-Nation Treatment

With regard to the protection of intellectual property, any advantage, favour, privilege or immunity granted by a Member to the nationals of any other country shall be accorded immediately and unconditionally to the nationals of all other

---

① For the purposes of Articles 3 and 4, "protection" shall include matters affecting the availability, acquisition, scope, maintenance and enforcement of intellectual property rights as well as those matters affecting the use of intellectual property rights specifically addressed in this Agreement.

Members. Exempted from this obligation are any advantage, favour, privilege or immunity accorded by a Member:

(a) deriving from international agreements on judicial assistance or law enforcement of a general nature and not particularly confined to the protection of intellectual property;

(b) granted in accordance with the provisions of the Berne Convention (1971) or the Rome Convention authorizing that the treatment accorded be a function not of national treatment but of the treatment accorded in another country;

(c) in respect of the rights of performers, producers of phonograms and broadcasting organizations not provided under this Agreement;

(d) deriving from international agreements related to the protection of intellectual property which entered into force prior to the entry into force of the WTO Agreement, provided that such agreements are notified to the Council for TRIPS and do not constitute an arbitrary or unjustifiable discrimination against nationals of other Members.

Article 5 Multilateral Agreements on Acquisition or Maintenance of Protection

The obligations under Articles 3 and 4 do not apply to procedures provided in multilateral agreements concluded under the auspices of WIPO relating to the acquisition or maintenance of intellectual property rights.

Article 6 Exhaustion

For the purposes of dispute settlement under this Agreement, subject to the provisions of Articles 3 and 4 nothing in this Agreement shall be used to address the issue of the exhaustion of intellectual property rights.

Article 7 Objectives

The protection and enforcement of intellectual property rights should contribute to the promotion of technological innovation and to the transfer and dissemination of technology, to the mutual advantage of producers and users of technological knowledge and in a manner conducive to social and economic welfare, and to a balance of rights and obligations.

Article 8 Principles

1. Members may, in formulating or amending their laws and regulations, adopt measures necessary to protect public health and nutrition, and to promote the

public interest in sectors of vital importance to their socio - economic and technological development, provided that such measures are consistent with the provisions of this Agreement.

2. Appropriate measures, provided that they are consistent with the provisions of this Agreement, may be needed to prevent the abuse of intellectual property rights by right holders or the resort to practices which unreasonably restrain trade or adversely affect the international transfer of technology.

PART II STANDARDS CONCERNING THE AVAILABILITY, SCOPE AND USE OF INTELLECTUAL PROPERTY RIGHTS

SECTION 1: COPYRIGHT AND RELATED RIGHTS

Article 9 Relation to the Berne Convention

1. Members shall comply with Articles 1 through 21 of the Berne Convention (1971) and the Appendix thereto. However, Members shall not have rights or obligations under this Agreement in respect of the rights conferred under Article 6bis of that Convention or of the rights derived therefrom.

2. Copyright protection shall extend to expressions and not to ideas, procedures, methods of operation or mathematical concepts as such.

Article 10 Computer Programs and Compilations of Data

1. Computer programs, whether in source or object code, shall be protected as literary works under the Berne Convention (1971).

2. Compilations of data or other material, whether in machine readable or other form, which by reason of the selection or arrangement of their contents constitute intellectual creations shall be protected as such. Such protection, which shall not extend to the data or material itself, shall be without prejudice to any copyright subsisting in the data or material itself.

Article 11 Rental Rights

In respect of at least computer programs and cinematographic works, a Member shall provide authors and their successors in title the right to authorize or to prohibit the commercial rental to the public of originals or copies of their copyright works. A Member shall be excepted from this obligation in respect of cinematographic works unless such rental has led to widespread copying of such works which is materially impairing the exclusive right of reproduction conferred in that Member on authors and their successors in title. In respect of computer programs, this obligation does not apply to rentals where the program itself is not the essential object of the rental.

Article 12 Term of Protection

Whenever the term of protection of a work, other than a photographic work or a work of applied art, is calculated on a basis other than the life of a natural person, such term shall be no less than 50 years from the end of the calendar year of authorized publication, or, failing such authorized publication within 50 years from the making of the work, 50 years from the end of the calendar year of making.

Article 13 Limitations and Exceptions

Members shall confine limitations or exceptions to exclusive rights to certain special cases which do not conflict with a normal exploitation of the work and do not unreasonably prejudice the legitimate interests of the right holder.

Article 14 Protection of Performers, Producers of Phonograms (Sound Recordings) and Broadcasting Organizations

1. In respect of a fixation of their performance on a phonogram, performers shall have the possibility of preventing the following acts when undertaken without their authorization: the fixation of their unfixed performance and the reproduction of such fixation. Performers shall also have the possibility of preventing the following acts when undertaken without their authorization: the broadcasting by wireless means and the communication to the public of their live performance.

2. Producers of phonograms shall enjoy the right to authorize or prohibit the direct or indirect reproduction of their phonograms.

3. Broadcasting organizations shall have the right to prohibit the following acts when undertaken without their authorization: the fixation, the reproduction of fixations, and the rebroadcasting by wireless means of broadcasts, as well as the communication to the public of television broadcasts of the same. Where Members do not grant such rights to broadcasting organizations, they shall provide owners of copyright in the subject matter of broadcasts with the possibility of preventing

the above acts, subject to the provisions of the Berne Convention (1971).

4. The provisions of Article 11 in respect of computer programs shall apply *mutatis mutandis* to producers of phonograms and any other right holders in phonograms as determined in a Member's law. If on 15 April 1994 a Member has in force a system of equitable remuneration of right holders in respect of the rental of phonograms, it may maintain such system provided that the commercial rental of phonograms is not giving rise to the material impairment of the exclusive rights of reproduction of right holders.

5. The term of the protection available under this Agreement to performers and producers of phonograms shall last at least until the end of a period of 50 years computed from the end of the calendar year in which the fixation was made or the performance took place. The term of protection granted pursuant to paragraph 3 shall last for at least 20 years from the end of the calendar year in which the broadcast took place.

6. Any Member may, in relation to the rights conferred under paragraphs 1, 2 and 3, provide for conditions, limitations, exceptions and reservations to the extent permitted by the Rome Convention. However, the provisions of Article 18 of the Berne Convention (1971) shall also apply, *mutatis mutandis*, to the rights of performers and producers of phonograms in phonograms.

SECTION 2: TRADEMARKS

Article 15 Protectable Subject Matter

1. Any sign, or any combination of signs, capable of distinguishing the goods or services of one undertaking from those of other undertakings, shall be capable of constituting a trademark. Such signs, in particular words including personal names, letters, numerals, figurative elements and combinations of colours as well as any combination of such signs, shall be eligible for registration as trademarks. Where signs are not inherently capable of distinguishing the relevant goods or services, Members may make registrability depend on distinctiveness acquired through use. Members may require, as a condition of registration, that signs be visually perceptible.

2. Paragraph 1 shall not be understood to prevent a Member from denying registration of a trademark on other grounds, provided that they do not derogate

from the provisions of the Paris Convention (1967).

3. Members may make registrability depend on use. However, actual use of a trademark shall not be a condition for filing an application for registration. An application shall not be refused solely on the ground that intended use has not taken place before the expiry of a period of three years from the date of application.

4. The nature of the goods or services to which a trademark is to be applied shall in no case form an obstacle to registration of the trademark.

5. Members shall publish each trademark either before it is registered or promptly after it is registered and shall afford a reasonable opportunity for petitions to cancel the registration. In addition, Members may afford an opportunity for the registration of a trademark to be opposed.

Article 16 Rights Conferred

1. The owner of a registered trademark shall have the exclusive right to prevent all third parties not having the owner's consent from using in the course of trade identical or similar signs for goods or services which are identical or similar to those in respect of which the trademark is registered where such use would result in a likelihood of confusion. In case of the use of an identical sign for identical goods or services, a likelihood of confusion shall be presumed. The rights described above shall not prejudice any existing prior rights, nor shall they affect the possibility of Members making rights available on the basis of use.

2. Article 6*bis* of the Paris Convention (1967) shall apply, *mutatis mutandis*, to services. In determining whether a trademark is well - known, Members shall take account of the knowledge of the trademark in the relevant sector of the public, including knowledge in the Member concerned which has been obtained as a result of the promotion of the trademark.

3. Article 6*bis* of the Paris Convention (1967) shall apply, *mutatis mutandis*, to goods or services which are not similar to those in respect of which a trademark is registered, provided that use of that trademark in relation to those goods or services would indicate a connection between those goods or services and the owner of the registered trademark and provided that the interests of the owner of the registered trademark are likely to be damaged by such use.

Article 17 Exceptions

Members may provide limited exceptions to the rights conferred by a trademark, such as fair use of descriptive terms, provided that such exceptions take account of the legitimate interests of the owner of the trademark and of third parties.

Article 18 Term of Protection

Initial registration, and each renewal of registration, of a trademark shall be for a term of no less than seven years. The registration of a trademark shall be renewable indefinitely.

Article 19 Requirement of Use

1. If use is required to maintain a registration, the registration may be cancelled only after an uninterrupted period of at least three years of non - use, unless valid reasons based on the existence of obstacles to such use are shown by the trademark owner. Circumstances arising independently of the will of the owner of the trademark which constitute an obstacle to the use of the trademark, such as import restrictions on or other government requirements for goods or services protected by the trademark, shall be recognized as valid reasons for non - use.

2. When subject to the control of its owner, use of a trademark by another person shall be recognized as use of the trademark for the purpose of maintaining the registration.

Article 20 Other Requirements

The use of a trademark in the course of trade shall not be unjustifiably encumbered by special requirements, such as use with another trademark, use in a special form or use in a manner detrimental to its capability to distinguish the goods or services of one undertaking from those of other undertakings. This will not preclude a requirement prescribing the use of the trademark identifying the undertaking producing the goods or services along with, but without linking it to, the trademark distinguishing the specific goods or services in question of that undertaking.

Article 21 Licensing and Assignment

Members may determine conditions on the licensing and assignment of trademarks, it being understood that the compulsory licensing of trademarks shall not be permitted and that the owner of a registered trademark shall have the right to assign the trademark with or without the transfer of the business to which the trademark belongs.

SECTION 3: GEOGRAPHICAL INDICATIONS

Article 22 Protection of Geographical Indications

1. Geographical indications are, for the purposes of this Agreement, indications which identify a good as originating in the territory of a Member, or a region or locality in that territory, where a given quality, reputation or other characteristic of the good is essentially attributable to its geographical origin.

2. In respect of geographical indications, Members shall provide the legal means for interested parties to prevent:

(a) the use of any means in the designation or presentation of a good that indicates or suggests that the good in question originates in a geographical area other than the true place of origin in a manner which misleads the public as to the geographical origin of the good;

(b) any use which constitutes an act of unfair competition within the meaning of Article 10*bis* of the Paris Convention (1967).

3. A Member shall, *ex officio* if its legislation so permits or at the request of an interested party, refuse or invalidate the registration of a trademark which contains or consists of a geographical indication with respect to goods not originating in the territory indicated, if use of the indication in the trademark for such goods in that Member is of such a nature as to mislead the public as to the true place of origin.

4. The protection under paragraphs 1, 2 and 3 shall be applicable against a geographical indication which, although literally true as to the territory, region or locality in which the goods originate, falsely represents to the public that the goods originate in another territory.

Article 23 Additional Protection for Geographical Indications for Wines and Spirits

1. Each Member shall provide the legal means for interested parties to prevent use of a geographical indication identifying wines for wines not originating in the place indicated by the geographical indication in question or identifying spirits for spirits not originating in the place indicated by the geographical indication in question, even where the true origin of the goods is indicated or the geographical indication is used in translation or accompanied by expressions such as "kind",

“type”, “style”, “imitation” or the like. [1]

2. The registration of a trademark for wines which contains or consists of a geographical indication identifying wines or for spirits which contains or consists of a geographical indication identifying spirits shall be refused or invalidated, *ex officio* if a Member's legislation so permits or at the request of an interested party, with respect to such wines or spirits not having this origin.

3. In the case of homonymous geographical indications for wines, protection shall be accorded to each indication, subject to the provisions of paragraph 4 of Article 22. Each Member shall determine the practical conditions under which the homonymous indications in question will be differentiated from each other, taking into account the need to ensure equitable treatment of the producers concerned and that consumers are not misled.

4. In order to facilitate the protection of geographical indications for wines, negotiations shall be undertaken in the Council for TRIPS concerning the establishment of a multilateral system of notification and registration of geographical indications for wines eligible for protection in those Members participating in the system.

Article 24 International Negotiations; Exceptions

1. Members agree to enter into negotiations aimed at increasing the protection of individual geographical indications under Article 23. The provisions of paragraphs 4 through 8 below shall not be used by a Member to refuse to conduct negotiations or to conclude bilateral or multilateral agreements. In the context of such negotiations, Members shall be willing to consider the continued applicability of these provisions to individual geographical indications whose use was the subject of such negotiations.

2. The Council for TRIPS shall keep under review the application of the provisions of this Section; the first such review shall take place within two years of the entry into force of the WTO Agreement. Any matter affecting the compliance with the obligations under these provisions may be drawn to the attention of the Council, which, at the request of a Member, shall consult with any Member or Members in respect of such matter in respect of which it has not been possible to find a satisfactory solution through bilateral or plurilateral consultations between the

---

① Notwithstanding the first sentence of Article 42, Members may, with respect to these obligations, instead provide for enforcement by administrative action.

Members concerned. The Council shall take such action as may be agreed to facilitate the operation and further the objectives of this Section.

3. In implementing this Section, a Member shall not diminish the protection of geographical indications that existed in that Member immediately prior to the date of entry into force of the WTO Agreement.

4. Nothing in this Section shall require a Member to prevent continued and similar use of a particular geographical indication of another Member identifying wines or spirits in connection with goods or services by any of its nationals or domiciliaries who have used that geographical indication in a continuous manner with regard to the same or related goods or services in the territory of that Member either (*a*) for at least 10 years preceding 15 April 1994 or (*b*) in good faith preceding that date.

5. Where a trademark has been applied for or registered in good faith, or where rights to a trademark have been acquired through use in good faith either:

(a) before the date of application of these provisions in that Member as defined in Part VI; or

(b) before the geographical indication is protected in its country of origin;

measures adopted to implement this Section shall not prejudice eligibility for or the validity of the registration of a trademark, or the right to use a trademark, on the basis that such a trademark is identical with, or similar to, a geographical indication.

6. Nothing in this Section shall require a Member to apply its provisions in respect of a geographical indication of any other Member with respect to goods or services for which the relevant indication is identical with the term customary in common language as the common name for such goods or services in the territory of that Member. Nothing in this Section shall require a Member to apply its provisions in respect of a geographical indication of any other Member with respect to products of the vine for which the relevant indication is identical with the customary name of a grape variety existing in the territory of that Member as of the date of entry into force of the WTO Agreement.

7. A Member may provide that any request made under this Section in connection with the use or registration of a trademark must be presented within five years after the adverse use of the protected indication has become generally known

in that Member or after the date of registration of the trademark in that Member provided that the trademark has been published by that date, if such date is earlier than the date on which the adverse use became generally known in that Member, provided that the geographical indication is not used or registered in bad faith.

8. The provisions of this Section shall in no way prejudice the right of any person to use, in the course of trade, that person's name or the name of that person's predecessor in business, except where such name is used in such a manner as to mislead the public.

9. There shall be no obligation under this Agreement to protect geographical indications which are not or cease to be protected in their country of origin, or which have fallen into disuse in that country.

SECTION 4: INDUSTRIAL DESIGNS

Article 25 Requirements for Protection

1. Members shall provide for the protection of independently created industrial designs that are new or original. Members may provide that designs are not new or original if they do not significantly differ from known designs or combinations of known design features. Members may provide that such protection shall not extend to designs dictated essentially by technical or functional considerations.

2. Each Member shall ensure that requirements for securing protection for textile designs, in particular in regard to any cost, examination or publication, do not unreasonably impair the opportunity to seek and obtain such protection. Members shall be free to meet this obligation through industrial design law or through copyright law.

Article 26 Protection

1. The owner of a protected industrial design shall have the right to prevent third parties not having the owner's consent from making, selling or importing articles bearing or embodying a design which is a copy, or substantially a copy, of the protected design, when such acts are undertaken for commercial purposes.

2. Members may provide limited exceptions to the protection of industrial designs, provided that such exceptions do not unreasonably conflict with the normal exploitation of protected industrial designs and do not unreasonably prejudice the legitimate interests of the owner of the protected design, taking account of the le-

gitimate interests of third parties.

3. The duration of protection available shall amount to at least 10 years.

SECTION 5: PATENTS

Article 27 Patentable Subject Matter

1. Subject to the provisions of paragraphs 2 and 3, patents shall be available for any inventions, whether products or processes, in all fields of technology, provided that they are new, involve an inventive step and are capable of industrial application. ① Subject to paragraph 4 of Article 65, paragraph 8 of Article 70 and paragraph 3 of this Article, patents shall be available and patent rights enjoyable without discrimination as to the place of invention, the field of technology and whether products are imported or locally produced.

2. Members may exclude from patentability inventions, the prevention within their territory of the commercial exploitation of which is necessary to protect *ordre public* or morality, including to protect human, animal or plant life or health or to a-void serious prejudice to the environment, provided that such exclusion is not made merely because the exploitation is prohibited by their law.

3. Members may also exclude from patentability:

(a) diagnostic, therapeutic and surgical methods for the treatment of humans or animals;

(b) plants and animals other than micro - organisms, and essentially biological processes for the production of plants or animals other than non - biological and microbiological processes. However, Members shall provide for the protection of plant varieties either by patents or by an effective *sui generis* system or by any combination thereof. The provisions of this subparagraph shall be reviewed four years after the date of entry into force of the WTO Agreement.

Article 28 Rights Conferred

1. A patent shall confer on its owner the following exclusive rights:

(a) where the subject matter of a patent is a product, to prevent third parties not having the owner's consent from the acts of: making, using, offering for sale,

---

① For the purposes of this Article, the terms "inventive step" and "capable of industrial application" may be deemed by a Member to be synonymous with the terms "non - obvious" and "useful" respectively.

selling, or importing [1] for these purposes that product;

(b) where the subject matter of a patent is a process, to prevent third parties not having the owner's consent from the act of using the process, and from the acts of: using, offering for sale, selling, or importing for these purposes at least the product obtained directly by that process.

2. Patent owners shall also have the right to assign, or transfer by succession, the patent and to conclude licensing contracts.

Article 29 Conditions on Patent Applicants

1. Members shall require that an applicant for a patent shall disclose the invention in a manner sufficiently clear and complete for the invention to be carried out by a person skilled in the art and may require the applicant to indicate the best mode for carrying out the invention known to the inventor at the filing date or, where priority is claimed, at the priority date of the application.

2. Members may require an applicant for a patent to provide information concerning the applicant's corresponding foreign applications and grants.

Article 30 Exceptions to Rights Conferred

Members may provide limited exceptions to the exclusive rights conferred by a patent, provided that such exceptions do not unreasonably conflict with a normal exploitation of the patent and do not unreasonably prejudice the legitimate interests of the patent owner, taking account of the legitimate interests of third parties.

Article 31 Other Use Without Authorization of the Right Holder

Where the law of a Member allows for other use [2] of the subject matter of a patent without the authorization of the right holder, including use by the government or third parties authorized by the government, the following provisions shall be respected:

(a) authorization of such use shall be considered on its individual merits;

(b) such use may only be permitted if, prior to such use, the proposed user has made efforts to obtain authorization from the right holder on reasonable commercial terms and conditions and that such efforts have not been successful within a reasonable period of time. This requirement may be waived by a Member in the

---

① This right, like all other rights conferred under this Agreement in respect of the use, sale, importation or other distribution of goods, is subject to the provisions of Article 6.

② "Other use" refers to use other than that allowed under Article 30.

case of a national emergency or other circumstances of extreme urgency or in cases of public non - commercial use. In situations of national emergency or other circumstances of extreme urgency, the right holder shall, nevertheless, be notified as soon as reasonably practicable. In the case of public non - commercial use, where the government or contractor, without making a patent search, knows or has demonstrable grounds to know that a valid patent is or will be used by or for the government, the right holder shall be informed promptly;

(c) the scope and duration of such use shall be limited to the purpose for which it was authorized, and in the case of semi - conductor technology shall only be for public non - commercial use or to remedy a practice determined after judicial or administrative process to be anti - competitive;

(d) such use shall be non - exclusive;

(e) such use shall be non - assignable, except with that part of the enterprise or goodwill which enjoys such use;

(f) any such use shall be authorized predominantly for the supply of the domestic market of the Member authorizing such use;

(g) authorization for such use shall be liable, subject to adequate protection of the legitimate interests of the persons so authorized, to be terminated if and when the circumstances which led to it cease to exist and are unlikely to recur. The competent authority shall have the authority to review, upon motivated request, the continued existence of these circumstances;

(h) the right holder shall be paid adequate remuneration in the circumstances of each case, taking into account the economic value of the authorization;

(i) the legal validity of any decision relating to the authorization of such use shall be subject to judicial review or other independent review by a distinct higher authority in that Member;

(j) any decision relating to the remuneration provided in respect of such use shall be subject to judicial review or other independent review by a distinct higher authority in that Member;

(k) Members are not obliged to apply the conditions set forth in subparagraphs (b) and (f) where such use is permitted to remedy a practice determined after judicial or administrative process to be anti - competitive. The need to correct anti - competitive practices may be taken into account in determining the amount of remuneration in such cases. Competent authorities shall have the authority to refuse termination of authorization if and when the conditions which led to such authorization are likely to recur;

(l) where such use is authorized to permit the exploitation of a patent ("the second patent") which cannot be exploited without infringing another patent ("the first patent"), the following additional conditions shall apply:

(i) the invention claimed in the second patent shall involve an important technical advance of considerable economic significance in relation to the invention claimed in the first patent;

(ii) the owner of the first patent shall be entitled to a cross - licence on reasonable terms to use the invention claimed in the second patent; and

(iii) the use authorized in respect of the first patent shall be non - assignable except with the assignment of the second patent.

Article 32 Revocation/Forfeiture

An opportunity for judicial review of any decision to revoke or forfeit a patent shall be available.

Article 33 Term of Protection

The term of protection available shall not end before the expiration of a period of twenty years counted from the filing date. [①]

Article 34 Process Patents: Burden of Proof

1. For the purposes of civil proceedings in respect of the infringement of the rights of the owner referred to in paragraph 1 (b) of Article 28, if the subject matter of a patent is a process for obtaining a product, the judicial authorities shall have the authority to order the defendant to prove that the process to obtain an identical product is different from the patented process. Therefore, Members shall provide, in at least one of the following circumstances, that any identical product when produced without the consent of the patent owner shall, in the absence of proof to the contrary, be deemed to have been obtained by the patented process:

(a) if the product obtained by the patented process is new;

(b) if there is a substantial likelihood that the identical product was made by the process and the owner of the patent has been unable through reasonable ef-

---

① It is understood that those Members which do not have a system of original grant may provide that the term of protection shall be computed from the filing date in the system of original grant.

forts to determine the process actually used.

2. Any Member shall be free to provide that the burden of proof indicated in paragraph 1 shall be on the alleged infringer only if the condition referred to in subparagraph (a) is fulfilled or only if the condition referred to in subparagraph (b) is fulfilled.

3. In the adduction of proof to the contrary, the legitimate interests of defendants in protecting their manufacturing and business secrets shall be taken into account.

SECTION 6: LAYOUT – DESIGNS (TOPOGRAPHIES) OF INTEGRATED CIRCUITS

Article 35 Relation to the IPIC Treaty

Members agree to provide protection to the layout - designs (topographies) of integrated circuits (referred to in this Agreement as "layout - designs") in accordance with Articles 2 through 7 (other than paragraph 3 of Article 6), Article 12 and paragraph 3 of Article 16 of the Treaty on Intellectual Property in Respect of Integrated Circuits and, in addition, to comply with the following provisions.

Article 36 Scope of the Protection

Subject to the provisions of paragraph 1 of Article 37, Members shall consider unlawful the following acts if performed without the authorization of the right holder: [①] importing, selling, or otherwise distributing for commercial purposes a protected layout - design, an integrated circuit in which a protected layout - design is incorporated, or an article incorporating such an integrated circuit only in so far as it continues to contain an unlawfully reproduced layout - design.

Article 37 Acts Not Requiring the Authorization of the Right Holder

1. Notwithstanding Article 36, no Member shall consider unlawful the performance of any of the acts referred to in that Article in respect of an integrated circuit incorporating an unlawfully reproduced layout - design or any article incorporating such an integrated circuit where the person performing or ordering such acts did not know and had no reasonable ground to know, when acquiring the integrated circuit or article incorporating such an integrated circuit, that it incorporat-

---

① The term "right holder" in this Section shall be understood as having the same meaning as the term "holder of the right" in the IPIC Treaty.

ed an unlawfully reproduced layout - design. Members shall provide that, after the time that such person has received sufficient notice that the layout - design was unlawfully reproduced, that person may perform any of the acts with respect to the stock on hand or ordered before such time, but shall be liable to pay to the right holder a sum equivalent to a reasonable royalty such as would be payable under a freely negotiated licence in respect of such a layout - design.

2. The conditions set out in subparagraphs (a) through (k) of Article 31 shall apply *mutatis mutandis* in the event of any non - voluntary licensing of a layout - design or of its use by or for the government without the authorization of the right holder.

Article 38 Term of Protection

1. In Members requiring registration as a condition of protection, the term of protection of layout - designs shall not end before the expiration of a period of 10 years counted from the date of filing an application for registration or from the first commercial exploitation wherever in the world it occurs.

2. In Members not requiring registration as a condition for protection, layout-designs shall be protected for a term of no less than 10 years from the date of the first commercial exploitation wherever in the world it occurs.

3. Notwithstanding paragraphs 1 and 2, a Member may provide that protection shall lapse 15 years after the creation of the layout - design.

SECTION 7: PROTECTION OF UNDISCLOSED INFORMATION

Article 39

1. In the course of ensuring effective protection against unfair competition as provided in Article 10*bis* of the Paris Convention (1967), Members shall protect undisclosed information in accordance with paragraph 2 and data submitted to governments or governmental agencies in accordance with paragraph 3.

2. Natural and legal persons shall have the possibility of preventing information lawfully within their control from being disclosed to, acquired by, or used by others without their consent in a manner contrary to honest commercial practices ①

① For the purpose of this provision, "a manner contrary to honest commercial practices" shall mean at least practices such as breach of contract, breach of confidence and inducement to breach, and includes the acquisition of undisclosed information by third parties who knew, or were grossly negligent in failing to know, that such practices were involved in the acquisition.

so long as such information:

(a) is secret in the sense that it is not, as a body or in the precise configuration and assembly of its components, generally known among or readily accessible to persons within the circles that normally deal with the kind of information in question;

(b) has commercial value because it is secret; and

(c) has been subject to reasonable steps under the circumstances, by the person lawfully in control of the information, to keep it secret.

3. Members, when requiring, as a condition of approving the marketing of pharmaceutical or of agricultural chemical products which utilize new chemical entities, the submission of undisclosed test or other data, the origination of which involves a considerable effort, shall protect such data against unfair commercial use. In addition, Members shall protect such data against disclosure, except where necessary to protect the public, or unless steps are taken to ensure that the data are protected against unfair commercial use.

SECTION 8: CONTROL OF ANTI – COMPETITIVE PRACTICES IN CONTRACTUAL LICENCES

Article 40

1. Members agree that some licensing practices or conditions pertaining to intellectual property rights which restrain competition may have adverse effects on trade and may impede the transfer and dissemination of technology.

2. Nothing in this Agreement shall prevent Members from specifying in their legislation licensing practices or conditions that may in particular cases constitute an abuse of intellectual property rights having an adverse effect on competition in the relevant market. As provided above, a Member may adopt, consistently with the other provisions of this Agreement, appropriate measures to prevent or control such practices, which may include for example exclusive grantback conditions, conditions preventing challenges to validity and coercive package licensing, in the light of the relevant laws and regulations of that Member.

3. Each Member shall enter, upon request, into consultations with any other Member which has cause to believe that an intellectual property right owner that is a national or domiciliary of the Member to which the request for consultations has

been addressed is undertaking practices in violation of the requesting Member's laws and regulations on the subject matter of this Section, and which wishes to secure compliance with such legislation, without prejudice to any action under the law and to the full freedom of an ultimate decision of either Member. The Member addressed shall accord full and sympathetic consideration to, and shall afford adequate opportunity for, consultations with the requesting Member, and shall cooperate through supply of publicly available non - confidential information of relevance to the matter in question and of other information available to the Member, subject to domestic law and to the conclusion of mutually satisfactory agreements concerning the safeguarding of its confidentiality by the requesting Member.

4. A Member whose nationals or domiciliaries are subject to proceedings in another Member concerning alleged violation of that other Member's laws and regulations on the subject matter of this Section shall, upon request, be granted an opportunity for consultations by the other Member under the same conditions as those foreseen in paragraph 3.

PART III ENFORCEMENT OF INTELLECTUAL PROPERTY RIGHTS

SECTION 1: GENERAL OBLIGATIONS

Article 41

1. Members shall ensure that enforcement procedures as specified in this Part are available under their law so as to permit effective action against any act of infringement of intellectual property rights covered by this Agreement, including expeditious remedies to prevent infringements and remedies which constitute a deterrent to further infringements. These procedures shall be applied in such a manner as to avoid the creation of barriers to legitimate trade and to provide for safeguards against their abuse.

2. Procedures concerning the enforcement of intellectual property rights shall be fair and equitable. They shall not be unnecessarily complicated or costly, or entail unreasonable time - limits or unwarranted delays.

3. Decisions on the merits of a case shall preferably be in writing and rea-

soned. They shall be made available at least to the parties to the proceeding without undue delay. Decisions on the merits of a case shall be based only on evidence in respect of which parties were offered the opportunity to be heard.

4. Parties to a proceeding shall have an opportunity for review by a judicial authority of final administrative decisions and, subject to jurisdictional provisions in a Member's law concerning the importance of a case, of at least the legal aspects of initial judicial decisions on the merits of a case. However, there shall be no obligation to provide an opportunity for review of acquittals in criminal cases.

5. It is understood that this Part does not create any obligation to put in place a judicial system for the enforcement of intellectual property rights distinct from that for the enforcement of law in general, nor does it affect the capacity of Members to enforce their law in general. Nothing in this Part creates any obligation with respect to the distribution of resources as between enforcement of intellectual property rights and the enforcement of law in general.

SECTION 2: CIVIL AND ADMINISTRATIVE PROCEDURES AND REMEDIES

Article 42 Fair and Equitable Procedures

Members shall make available to right holders ① civil judicial procedures concerning the enforcement of any intellectual property right covered by this Agreement. Defendants shall have the right to written notice which is timely and contains sufficient detail, including the basis of the claims. Parties shall be allowed to be represented by independent legal counsel, and procedures shall not impose overly burdensome requirements concerning mandatory personal appearances. All parties to such procedures shall be duly entitled to substantiate their claims and to present all relevant evidence. The procedure shall provide a means to identify and protect confidential information, unless this would be contrary to existing constitutional requirements.

Article 43 Evidence

1. The judicial authorities shall have the authority, where a party has presented reasonably available evidence sufficient to support its claims and has specified

① For the purpose of this Part, the term "right holder" includes federations and associations having legal standing to assert such rights.

evidence relevant to substantiation of its claims which lies in the control of the opposing party, to order that this evidence be produced by the opposing party, subject in appropriate cases to conditions which ensure the protection of confidential information.

2. In cases in which a party to a proceeding voluntarily and without good reason refuses access to, or otherwise does not provide necessary information within a reasonable period, or significantly impedes a procedure relating to an enforcement action, a Member may accord judicial authorities the authority to make preliminary and final determinations, affirmative or negative, on the basis of the information presented to them, including the complaint or the allegation presented by the party adversely affected by the denial of access to information, subject to providing the parties an opportunity to be heard on the allegations or evidence.

Article 44 Injunctions

1. The judicial authorities shall have the authority to order a party to desist from an infringement, *inter alia* to prevent the entry into the channels of commerce in their jurisdiction of imported goods that involve the infringement of an intellectual property right, immediately after customs clearance of such goods. Members are not obliged to accord such authority in respect of protected subject matter acquired or ordered by a person prior to knowing or having reasonable grounds to know that dealing in such subject matter would entail the infringement of an intellectual property right.

2. Notwithstanding the other provisions of this Part and provided that the provisions of Part II specifically addressing use by governments, or by third parties authorized by a government, without the authorization of the right holder are complied with, Members may limit the remedies available against such use to payment of remuneration in accordance with subparagraph (h) of Article 31. In other cases, the remedies under this Part shall apply or, where these remedies are inconsistent with a Member's law, declaratory judgments and adequate compensation shall be available.

Article 45 Damages

1. The judicial authorities shall have the authority to order the infringer to pay the right holder damages adequate to compensate for the injury the right holder has suffered because of an infringement of that person's intellectual property right by

an infringer who knowingly, or with reasonable grounds to know, engaged in infringing activity.

2. The judicial authorities shall also have the authority to order the infringer to pay the right holder expenses, which may include appropriate attorney's fees. In appropriate cases, Members may authorize the judicial authorities to order recovery of profits and/or payment of pre - established damages even where the infringer did not knowingly, or with reasonable grounds to know, engage in infringing activity.

Article 46 Other Remedies

In order to create an effective deterrent to infringement, the judicial authorities shall have the authority to order that goods that they have found to be infringing be, without compensation of any sort, disposed of outside the channels of commerce in such a manner as to avoid any harm caused to the right holder, or, unless this would be contrary to existing constitutional requirements, destroyed. The judicial authorities shall also have the authority to order that materials and implements the predominant use of which has been in the creation of the infringing goods be, without compensation of any sort, disposed of outside the channels of commerce in such a manner as to minimize the risks of further infringements. In considering such requests, the need for proportionality between the seriousness of the infringement and the remedies ordered as well as the interests of third parties shall be taken into account. In regard to counterfeit trademark goods, the simple removal of the trademark unlawfully affixed shall not be sufficient, other than in exceptional cases, to permit release of the goods into the channels of commerce.

Article 47 Right of Information

Members may provide that the judicial authorities shall have the authority, unless this would be out of proportion to the seriousness of the infringement, to order the infringer to inform the right holder of the identity of third persons involved in the production and distribution of the infringing goods or services and of their channels of distribution.

Article 48 Indemnification of the Defendant

1. The judicial authorities shall have the authority to order a party at whose request measures were taken and who has abused enforcement procedures to provide to a party wrongfully enjoined or restrained adequate compensation for the in-

jury suffered because of such abuse. The judicial authorities shall also have the authority to order the applicant to pay the defendant expenses, which may include appropriate attorney's fees.

2. In respect of the administration of any law pertaining to the protection or enforcement of intellectual property rights, Members shall only exempt both public authorities and officials from liability to appropriate remedial measures where actions are taken or intended in good faith in the course of the administration of that law.

Article 49 Administrative ProceduresV

To the extent that any civil remedy can be ordered as a result of administrative procedures on the merits of a case, such procedures shall conform to principles equivalent in substance to those set forth in this Section.

SECTION 3: PROVISIONAL MEASURES

Article 50

1. The judicial authorities shall have the authority to order prompt and effective provisional measures:

(a) to prevent an infringement of any intellectual property right from occurring, and in particular to prevent the entry into the channels of commerce in their jurisdiction of goods, including imported goods immediately after customs clearance;

(b) to preserve relevant evidence in regard to the alleged infringement.

2. The judicial authorities shall have the authority to adopt provisional measures *inaudita altera parte* where appropriate, in particular where any delay is likely to cause irreparable harm to the right holder, or where there is a demonstrable risk of evidence being destroyed.

3. The judicial authorities shall have the authority to require the applicant to provide any reasonably available evidence in order to satisfy themselves with a sufficient degree of certainty that the applicant is the right holder and that the applicant' s right is being infringed or that such infringement is imminent, and to order the applicant to provide a security or equivalent assurance sufficient to protect the defendant and to prevent abuse.

4. Where provisional measures have been adopted *inaudita altera parte*, the parties affected shall be given notice, without delay after the execution of the measures at the latest. A review, including a right to be heard, shall take place upon request of the

defendant with a view to deciding, within a reasonable period after the notification of the measures, whether these measures shall be modified, revoked or confirmed.

5. The applicant may be required to supply other information necessary for the identification of the goods concerned by the authority that will execute the provisional measures.

6. Without prejudice to paragraph 4, provisional measures taken on the basis of paragraphs 1 and 2 shall, upon request by the defendant, be revoked or otherwise cease to have effect, if proceedings leading to a decision on the merits of the case are not initiated within a reasonable period, to be determined by the judicial authority ordering the measures where a Member's law so permits or, in the absence of such a determination, not to exceed 20 working days or 31 calendar days, whichever is the longer.

7. Where the provisional measures are revoked or where they lapse due to any act or omission by the applicant, or where it is subsequently found that there has been no infringement or threat of infringement of an intellectual property right, the judicial authorities shall have the authority to order the applicant, upon request of the defendant, to provide the defendant appropriate compensation for any injury caused by these measures.

8. To the extent that any provisional measure can be ordered as a result of administrative procedures, such procedures shall conform to principles equivalent in substance to those set forth in this Section.

SECTION 4: SPECIAL REQUIREMENTS RELATED TO BORDER MEASURES ①

Article 51 Suspension of Release by Customs Authorities

Members shall, in conformity with the provisions set out below, adopt procedures ② to enable a right holder, who has valid grounds for suspecting that the im-

① Where a Member has dismantled substantially all controls over movement of goods across its border with another Member with which it forms part of a customs union, it shall not be required to apply the provisions of this Section at that border.

② It is understood that there shall be no obligation to apply such procedures to imports of goods put on the market in another country by or with the consent of the right holder, or to goods in transit.

portation of counterfeit trademark or pirated copyright goods [①] may take place, to lodge an application in writing with competent authorities, administrative or judicial, for the suspension by the customs authorities of the release into free circulation of such goods. Members may enable such an application to be made in respect of goods which involve other infringements of intellectual property rights, provided that the requirements of this Section are met. Members may also provide for corresponding procedures concerning the suspension by the customs authorities of the release of infringing goods destined for exportation from their territories.

Article 52 Application

Any right holder initiating the procedures under Article 51 shall be required to provide adequate evidence to satisfy the competent authorities that, under the laws of the country of importation, there is *prima facie* an infringement of the right holder's intellectual property right and to supply a sufficiently detailed description of the goods to make them readily recognizable by the customs authorities. The competent authorities shall inform the applicant within a reasonable period whether they have accepted the application and, where determined by the competent authorities, the period for which the customs authorities will take action.

Article 53 Security or Equivalent Assurance

1. The competent authorities shall have the authority to require an applicant to provide a security or equivalent assurance sufficient to protect the defendant and the competent authorities and to prevent abuse. Such security or equivalent assurance shall not unreasonably deter recourse to these procedures.

2. Where pursuant to an application under this Section the release of goods involving industrial designs, patents, layout - designs or undisclosed information into free circulation has been suspended by customs authorities on the basis of a decision other than by a judicial or other independent authority, and the period

---

① For the purposes of this Agreement:

(a) "counterfeit trademark goods" shall mean any goods, including packaging, bearing without authorization a trademark which is identical to the trademark validly registered in respect of such goods, or which cannot be distinguished in its essential aspects from such a trademark, and which thereby infringes the rights of the owner of the trademark in question under the law of the country of importation;

(b) "pirated copyright goods" shall mean any goods which are copies made without the consent of the right holder or person duly authorized by the right holder in the country of production and which are made directly or indirectly from an article where the making of that copy would have constituted an infringement of a copyright or a related right under the law of the country of importation.

provided for in Article 55 has expired without the granting of provisional relief by the duly empowered authority, and provided that all other conditions for importation have been complied with, the owner, importer, or consignee of such goods shall be entitled to their release on the posting of a security in an amount sufficient to protect the right holder for any infringement. Payment of such security shall not prejudice any other remedy available to the right holder, it being understood that the security shall be released if the right holder fails to pursue the right of action within a reasonable period of time.

Article 54 Notice of Suspension

The importer and the applicant shall be promptly notified of the suspension of the release of goods according to Article 51.

Article 55 Duration of Suspension

If, within a period not exceeding 10 working days after the applicant has been served notice of the suspension, the customs authorities have not been informed that proceedings leading to a decision on the merits of the case have been initiated by a party other than the defendant, or that the duly empowered authority has taken provisional measures prolonging the suspension of the release of the goods, the goods shall be released, provided that all other conditions for importation or exportation have been complied with; in appropriate cases, this time - limit may be extended by another 10 working days. If proceedings leading to a decision on the merits of the case have been initiated, a review, including a right to be heard, shall take place upon request of the defendant with a view to deciding, within a reasonable period, whether these measures shall be modified, revoked or confirmed. Notwithstanding the above, where the suspension of the release of goods is carried out or continued in accordance with a provisional judicial measure, the provisions of paragraph 6 of Article 50 shall apply.

Article 56 Indemnification of the Importer and of the Owner of the Goods

Relevant authorities shall have the authority to order the applicant to pay the importer, the consignee and the owner of the goods appropriate compensation for any injury caused to them through the wrongful detention of goods or through the detention of goods released pursuant to Article 55.

Article 57 Right of Inspection and Information

Without prejudice to the protection of confidential information, Members shall provide the competent authorities the authority to give the right holder sufficient opportunity to have any goods detained by the customs authorities inspected in order to substantiate the right holder's claims. The competent authorities shall also have authority to give the importer an equivalent opportunity to have any such goods inspected. Where a positive determination has been made on the merits of a case, Members may provide the competent authorities the authority to inform the right holder of the names and addresses of the consignor, the importer and the consignee and of the quantity of the goods in question.

Article 58 Ex Officio Action

Where Members require competent authorities to act upon their own initiative and to suspend the release of goods in respect of which they have acquired *prima facie* evidence that an intellectual property right is being infringed:

(a) the competent authorities may at any time seek from the right holder any information that may assist them to exercise these powers;

(b) the importer and the right holder shall be promptly notified of the suspension. Where the importer has lodged an appeal against the suspension with the competent authorities, the suspension shall be subject to the conditions, *mutatis mutandis*, set out at Article 55;

(c) Members shall only exempt both public authorities and officials from liability to appropriate remedial measures where actions are taken or intended in good faith.

Article 59 Remedies

Without prejudice to other rights of action open to the right holder and subject to the right of the defendant to seek review by a judicial authority, competent authorities shall have the authority to order the destruction or disposal of infringing goods in accordance with the principles set out in Article 46. In regard to counterfeit trademark goods, the authorities shall not allow the re - exportation of the infringing goods in an unaltered state or subject them to a different customs procedure, other than in exceptional circumstances.

Article 60 De Minimis Imports

Members may exclude from the application of the above provisions small quantities of goods of a non - commercial nature contained in travellers' personal luggage or sent in small consignments.

SECTION 5: CRIMINAL PROCEDURES

Article 61

Members shall provide for criminal procedures and penalties to be applied at least in cases of wilful trademark counterfeiting or copyright piracy on a commercial scale. Remedies available shall include imprisonment and/or monetary fines sufficient to provide a deterrent, consistently with the level of penalties applied for crimes of a corresponding gravity. In appropriate cases, remedies available shall also include the seizure, forfeiture and destruction of the infringing goods and of any materials and implements the predominant use of which has been in the commission of the offence. Members may provide for criminal procedures and penalties to be applied in other cases of infringement of intellectual property rights, in particular where they are committed wilfully and on a commercial scale.

PART IV ACQUISITION AND MAINTENANCE OF INTELLECTUAL PROPERTY RIGHTS AND RELATEDINTER-*PARTES* PROCEDURES

Article 62

1. Members may require, as a condition of the acquisition or maintenance of the intellectual property rights provided for under Sections 2 through 6 of Part II, compliance with reasonable procedures and formalities. Such procedures and formalities shall be consistent with the provisions of this Agreement.

2. Where the acquisition of an intellectual property right is subject to the right being granted or registered, Members shall ensure that the procedures for grant or registration, subject to compliance with the substantive conditions for acquisition of the right, permit the granting or registration of the right within a reasonable period of time so as to avoid unwarranted curtailment of the period of protection.

3. Article 4 of the Paris Convention (1967) shall apply *mutatis mutandis* to service marks.

4. Procedures concerning the acquisition or maintenance of intellectual property rights and, where a Member's law provides for such procedures, administrative

revocation and *inter partes* procedures such as opposition, revocation and cancellation, shall be governed by the general principles set out in paragraphs 2 and 3 of Article 41.

5. Final administrative decisions in any of the procedures referred to under paragraph 4 shall be subject to review by a judicial or quasi - judicial authority. However, there shall be no obligation to provide an opportunity for such review of decisions in cases of unsuccessful opposition or administrative revocation, provided that the grounds for such procedures can be the subject of invalidation procedures.

PART V DISPUTE PREVENTION AND SETTLEMENT

Article 63 Transparency

1. Laws and regulations, and final judicial decisions and administrative rulings of general application, made effective by a Member pertaining to the subject matter of this Agreement (the availability, scope, acquisition, enforcement and prevention of the abuse of intellectual property rights) shall be published, or where such publication is not practicable made publicly available, in a national language, in such a manner as to enable governments and right holders to become acquainted with them. Agreements concerning the subject matter of this Agreement which are in force between the government or a governmental agency of a Member and the government or a governmental agency of another Member shall also be published.

2. Members shall notify the laws and regulations referred to in paragraph 1 to the Council for TRIPS in order to assist that Council in its review of the operation of this Agreement. The Council shall attempt to minimize the burden on Members in carrying out this obligation and may decide to waive the obligation to notify such laws and regulations directly to the Council if consultations with WIPO on the establishment of a common register containing these laws and regulations are successful. The Council shall also consider in this connection any action required regarding notifications pursuant to the obligations under this Agreement stemming from the provisions of Article 6*ter* of the Paris Convention (1967).

3. Each Member shall be prepared to supply, in response to a written request

from another Member, information of the sort referred to in paragraph 1. A Member, having reason to believe that a specific judicial decision or administrative ruling or bilateral agreement in the area of intellectual property rights affects its rights under this Agreement, may also request in writing to be given access to or be informed in sufficient detail of such specific judicial decisions or administrative rulings or bilateral agreements.

4. Nothing in paragraphs 1, 2 and 3 shall require Members to disclose confidential information which would impede law enforcement or otherwise be contrary to the public interest or would prejudice the legitimate commercial interests of particular enterprises, public or private.

Article 64 Dispute Settlement

1. The provisions of Articles XXII and XXIII of GATT 1994 as elaborated and applied by the Dispute Settlement Understanding shall apply to consultations and the settlement of disputes under this Agreement except as otherwise specifically provided herein.

2. Subparagraphs 1 (b) and 1 (c) of Article XXIII of GATT 1994 shall not apply to the settlement of disputes under this Agreement for a period of five years from the date of entry into force of the WTO Agreement.

3. During the time period referred to in paragraph 2, the Council for TRIPS shall examine the scope and modalities for complaints of the type provided for under subparagraphs 1 (b) and 1 (c) of Article XXIII of GATT 1994 made pursuant to this Agreement, and submit its recommendations to the Ministerial Conference for approval. Any decision of the Ministerial Conference to approve such recommendations or to extend the period in paragraph 2 shall be made only by consensus, and approved recommendations shall be effective for all Members without further formal acceptance process.

PART VI TRANSITIONAL ARRANGEMENTS

Article 65 Transitional Arrangements

1. Subject to the provisions of paragraphs 2, 3 and 4, no Member shall be obliged to apply the provisions of this Agreement before the expiry of a general period of one year following the date of entry into force of the WTO Agreement.

2. A developing country Member is entitled to delay for a further period of four years the date of application, as defined in paragraph 1, of the provisions of this Agreement other than Articles 3, 4 and 5.

3. Any other Member which is in the process of transformation from a centrally - planned into a market, free - enterprise economy and which is undertaking structural reform of its intellectual property system and facing special problems in the preparation and implementation of intellectual property laws and regulations, may also benefit from a period of delay as foreseen in paragraph 2.

4. To the extent that a developing country Member is obliged by this Agreement to extend product patent protection to areas of technology not so protectable in its territory on the general date of application of this Agreement for that Member, as defined in paragraph 2, it may delay the application of the provisions on product patents of Section 5 of Part II to such areas of technology for an additional period of five years.

5. A Member availing itself of a transitional period under paragraphs 1, 2, 3 or 4 shall ensure that any changes in its laws, regulations and practice made during that period do not result in a lesser degree of consistency with the provisions of this Agreement.

Article 66 Least – Developed Country Members

1. In view of the special needs and requirements of least - developed country Members, their economic, financial and administrative constraints, and their need for flexibility to create a viable technological base, such Members shall not be required to apply the provisions of this Agreement, other than Articles 3, 4 and 5, for a period of 10 years from the date of application as defined under paragraph 1 of Article 65. The Council for TRIPS shall, upon duly motivated request by a least - developed country Member, accord extensions of this period.

2. Developed country Members shall provide incentives to enterprises and institutions in their territories for the purpose of promoting and encouraging technology transfer to least - developed country Members in order to enable them to create a sound and viable technological base.

Article 67 Technical Cooperation

In order to facilitate the implementation of this Agreement, developed country Members shall provide, on request and on mutually agreed terms and conditions, technical and financial cooperation in favour of developing and least - developed country Members. Such cooperation shall include assistance in the preparation of laws and regulations on the protection and enforcement of intellectual property rights as well as on the prevention of their abuse, and shall include support regarding the establishment or reinforcement of domestic offices and agencies relevant to these matters, including the training of personnel.

PART VII INSTITUTIONAL ARRANGEMENTS; FINAL PROVISIONS

Article 68 Council for Trade – Related Aspects of Intellectual Property Rights

The Council for TRIPS shall monitor the operation of this Agreement and, in particular, Members' compliance with their obligations hereunder, and shall afford Members the opportunity of consulting on matters relating to the trade - related aspects of intellectual property rights. It shall carry out such other responsibilities as assigned to it by the Members, and it shall, in particular, provide any assistance requested by them in the context of dispute settlement procedures. In carrying out its functions, the Council for TRIPS may consult with and seek information from any source it deems appropriate. In consultation with WIPO, the Council shall seek to establish, within one year of its first meeting, appropriate arrangements for cooperation with bodies of that Organization.

Article 69 International Cooperation

Members agree to cooperate with each other with a view to eliminating international trade in goods infringing intellectual property rights. For this purpose, they shall establish and notify contact points in their administrations and be ready to exchange information on trade in infringing goods. They shall, in particular, promote the exchange of information and cooperation between customs authorities with regard to trade in counterfeit trademark goods and pirated copyright goods.

Article 70 Protection of Existing Subject Matter

1. This Agreement does not give rise to obligations in respect of acts which occurred before the date of application of the Agreement for the Member in question.

2. Except as otherwise provided for in this Agreement, this Agreement gives

rise to obligations in respect of all subject matter existing at the date of application of this Agreement for the Member in question, and which is protected in that Member on the said date, or which meets or comes subsequently to meet the criteria for protection under the terms of this Agreement. In respect of this paragraph and paragraphs 3 and 4, copyright obligations with respect to existing works shall be solely determined under Article 18 of the Berne Convention (1971), and obligations with respect to the rights of producers of phonograms and performers in existing phonograms shall be determined solely under Article 18 of the Berne Convention (1971) as made applicable under paragraph 6 of Article 14 of this Agreement.

3. There shall be no obligation to restore protection to subject matter which on the date of application of this Agreement for the Member in question has fallen into the public domain.

4. In respect of any acts in respect of specific objects embodying protected subject matter which become infringing under the terms of legislation in conformity with this Agreement, and which were commenced, or in respect of which a significant investment was made, before the date of acceptance of the WTO Agreement by that Member, any Member may provide for a limitation of the remedies available to the right holder as to the continued performance of such acts after the date of application of this Agreement for that Member. In such cases the Member shall, however, at least provide for the payment of equitable remuneration.

5. A Member is not obliged to apply the provisions of Article 11 and of paragraph 4 of Article 14 with respect to originals or copies purchased prior to the date of application of this Agreement for that Member.

6. Members shall not be required to apply Article 31, or the requirement in paragraph 1 of Article 27 that patent rights shall be enjoyable without discrimination as to the field of technology, to use without the authorization of the right holder where authorization for such use was granted by the government before the date this Agreement became known.

7. In the case of intellectual property rights for which protection is conditional upon registration, applications for protection which are pending on the date of application of this Agreement for the Member in question shall be permitted to be amended to claim any enhanced protection provided under the provisions of this A-

greement. Such amendments shall not include new matter.

8. Where a Member does not make available as of the date of entry into force of the WTO Agreement patent protection for pharmaceutical and agricultural chemical products commensurate with its obligations under Article 27, that Member shall:

(a) notwithstanding the provisions of Part VI, provide as from the date of entry into force of the WTO Agreement a means by which applications for patents for such inventions can be filed;

(b) apply to these applications, as of the date of application of this Agreement, the criteria for patentability as laid down in this Agreement as if those criteria were being applied on the date of filing in that Member or, where priority is available and claimed, the priority date of the application; and

(c) provide patent protection in accordance with this Agreement as from the grant of the patent and for the remainder of the patent term, counted from the filing date in accordance with Article 33 of this Agreement, for those of these applications that meet the criteria for protection referred to in subparagraph (b).

9. Where a product is the subject of a patent application in a Member in accordance with paragraph 8 (a), exclusive marketing rights shall be granted, notwithstanding the provisions of Part VI, for a period of five years after obtaining marketing approval in that Member or until a product patent is granted or rejected in that Member, whichever period is shorter, provided that, subsequent to the entry into force of the WTO Agreement, a patent application has been filed and a patent granted for that product in another Member and marketing approval obtained in such other Member.

Article 71 Review and Amendment

1. The Council for TRIPS shall review the implementation of this Agreement after the expiration of the transitional period referred to in paragraph 2 of Article 65. The Council shall, having regard to the experience gained in its implementation, review it two years after that date, and at identical intervals thereafter. The Council may also undertake reviews in the light of any relevant new developments which might warrant modification or amendment of this Agreement.

2. Amendments merely serving the purpose of adjusting to higher levels of protection of intellectual property rights achieved, and in force, in other multilater-

al agreements and accepted under those agreements by all Members of the WTO may be referred to the Ministerial Conference for action in accordance with paragraph 6 of Article X of the WTO Agreement on the basis of a consensus proposal from the Council for TRIPS.

Article 72 Reservations

Reservations may not be entered in respect of any of the provisions of this Agreement without the consent of the other Members.

Article 73 Security Exceptions

Nothing in this Agreement shall be construed:

(a) to require a Member to furnish any information the disclosure of which it considers contrary to its essential security interests; or

(b) to prevent a Member from taking any action which it considers necessary for the protection of its essential security interests;

(i) relating to fissionable materials or the materials from which they are derived;

(ii) relating to the traffic in arms, ammunition and implements of war and to such traffic in other goods and materials as is carried on directly or indirectly for the purpose of supplying a military establishment;

(iii) taken in time of war or other emergency in international relations; or

(c) to prevent a Member from taking any action in pursuance of its obligations under the United Nations Charter for the maintenance of international peace and security.

世界版权公约

（联合国教科文组织1971年7月24日巴黎修订本，我国于1992年7月1日加入）

缔约各国，

鉴于希望在所有国家保证对文学、科学、艺术作品的版权进行保护；

确信适用于世界各国并以公约形式确定下来的版权保护制度有利而无损于现行各种国际制度，并将确保尊重个人权利，促进文学、科学和艺术的发展；

相信这种国际版权保护制度将会促进人类精神产品的广泛传播和增进各国的相互了解；

决定修订1952年9月6日于日内瓦签订的《世界版权公约》（下称“1952年公约”），

为此特协议如下：

第一条

缔约各国议定，要充分有效地保护文学、科学、艺术作品——包括文字、音乐、戏剧、电影作品，绘画、雕刻，雕塑——之作者及其他版权所有者的权利。

第二条

（一）任何缔约国国民出版的作品及在该国首先出版的作品，在其他各缔约国中，均享有同那一国家给予其本国国民于本国首先出版之作品的同等保护，也享有本公约特许之保护。

（二）任何缔约国国民未出版的作品，在其他各缔约国中，享有同该国给予其国民未出版之作品的同等保护，也享有本公约特许之保护。

（三）为实施本公约，任何缔约国可依本国法律将寄居该国的任何人看作本国之国民。

第三条

（一）依本国法律要求履行手续——如缴送样本、注册登记、刊载启事、办理证书、偿付费用或在该国国内制作出版等——作为版权保护条件的各缔约国，对根据本公约加以保护的一切作品，和在该国领土以外出版而其作者又非本国国民的作品，应视为符合上述要求，只要这些作品是作者或版权所有者授权出版的，并且，自初版之日起，在所有各册的版权栏内，标有的C符号，注明版权所有者之姓名、初版年份等。

（二）本条（第一）款之规定，不得妨碍缔约各国对本国初版或其国民于任何地方出版的作品为取得和享有版权而提出履行手续或其他条件的要求。

（三）本条（第一）款之规定，不得妨碍缔约各国规定，凡要求版权司法保护者，必须在起诉时履行程序性要求，如起诉人须通过本国辩护人出庭，或由起诉人将有关争讼之作品呈交法院或行政当局备案，或兼呈两处备案。如果上述程序性要求未能履行，版权效力不受影响的话，那么，对要求版权司法保护的本国国民不做这种要求时，也不应将这种要求强加于另一缔约国之国民。

（四）缔约各国应有法律措施保护其他各缔约国国民尚未出版之作品，而无须履行手续。

（五）如果某缔约国准予有一个以上的版权保护期限，而第一个期限比第四条中规定的最短期限之一为长，那么对于第二个或其后的版权期限，不应要求该国执行本条第（一）款的规定。

第四条

（一）根据第二条和本条规定，某作品的版权保护期限，应由该作品向其要求版权保护的缔约国的法律来规定。

（二）甲、受本公约保护的作品，其保护期限不得短于作者有生之年及其死后的二十五年。但是，如果本公约在某缔约国生效之日，该国已将某些类别作品的保护期限规定为自该作品初版以后的某一段时间之内，那么该缔约国有权保持其规定，并可将这些规定扩大应用于其他类别的作品。对所有这类作品，其版权保护期限自初版日起，不得少于二十五年。

乙、任何缔约国若在本公约于该国生效日尚未根据作者有生之年确定保护期限，则有权根据情况，从作品初版之日或从出版前的登记日起计算版权保护期限，只要根据情况或从作品初版之日，或从出版前的登记日算起，版权保护期限不少于二十五年。

丙、如果某缔约国的法律准许有两个或两个以上的连续保护期限，则第一个保护期限不得短于本款甲、乙两项所详尽规定的最低期限之一。

（三）本条第（二）款之规定不得应用于摄影作品或实用美术作品。但是，如果某些缔约国对摄影作品或作为艺术品保护的实用美术作品给予保护时，则对上述两类作品中的任何一件，其保护期限不得少于十年。

（四）甲、根据作者所属缔约国家的法律而未出版的作品，或根据首先出版某作品的缔约国家的法律已出版的作品，缔约国家均不得给予该作品以比其所属之同类作品规定的保护期限更长的保护期。

乙、为实施本款甲项，如果某缔约国之法律准予有两个或两个以上的连续保护期限，那么该国的保护期限应视为所有期限之总和。但是，如果某一明文规定的作品在第二或其后的期限内，因某种原因被上述国家取消了版权保护，则其他各缔约国亦不得在第二或其后的期限中保护之。

（五）为实施本条第（四）款，如果某缔约国国民的作品首次出版是在非缔约国家之内，那么，这些作品应按作者所属的缔约国首先出版该作品来处理。

（六）为实施本条第（四）款，某作品若在两个或两个以上缔约国家同时出版，该作品应视为在保护期限最短的缔约国内首先出版。任何作品如在初版三十日内，在两个或两个以上缔约国出版，则应视为在上述缔约国内同时出版。

第四条之二

（一）本公约第一条所述之权利，须包含保证作者经济利益的各种基本权利，包括作者的准予以任何方式复制、上演及广播等项专利权。本条之规定可扩大应用于受本公约保护的一切作品，无论它们是原著形式还是从原著演绎而来的任何形式。

（二）但是，任何缔约国依本国法律，可以对本条第（一）款所述之权利做出符合本公约精神和内容的例外规定。凡法律允许做出例外规定的任何缔约国，必须对已做出例外规定的各项权利给予合理的有效的保护。

第五条

（一）本公约第一条所述各项权利，应包括作者翻译、出版受授权他人翻译、出版受本公约保护的作品的专利权。

（二）然而，各缔约国根据本国法律，可以对作品的翻译权利加以限制；但必须遵照如下规定：

甲、若某著作首次出版七年之后，其翻译权所有人自己没有，也未授权他人将该著作以某缔约国的通用语言翻译出版，那么，该缔约国的任何人可向主管当局申请并获得非专利权许可证，将该著作以通用语言翻译出版。

乙、申请者应按有关缔约国之例行规定，证明他曾要求翻译出版该作品，但遭翻译权所有人拒绝；或者他曾一再努力但无法找到版权所有人。若前版缔约国通用语译本均已绝版，则根据同样条件也可颁发许可证。

丙、如果翻译权所有人无法找到，那么许可证申请人应将申请书递交作品上写明的出版者；若翻译权所有人国籍业已弄清，则应将申请书递交翻译权所有人的祖国的外交或领事代表，或呈交该国政府指定的机构。递交申请书不满两个月时，不得颁发许可证。

丁、颁发许可证的缔约国的法律应做出相应规定，以保证翻译权所有人得到合理而且符合国际标准的报酬，保证这种报酬的支付与转递，保证准确地翻译该作品。

戊、凡经出版的各册译本，均应刊印原著名称及作者姓名。只有在申请许可证的缔约国内出版译作时，该许可证方得有效。此种翻译出版物可以向另一缔约国出口和销售，只要该国通用语言与所译作品的语言一致，只要该国的法律对此种许可做出了规定，而且对进口和销售不予禁止。如无上面的条件，在某缔约国进口和销售上述译本将受该国之法律和条约的限制。许可证不得由持证人转让。

己、如果作者已停止发行某作品之各种版本，则不得颁发此作品之翻译许可证。

第五条之二

（一）根据联合国大会确认之惯例，如果某缔约国被视为发展中国家，则该国可向联合国教育、科学及文化组织总干事（下称总干事）呈交报告书备案；在批准、接受或参加本公约时，或在此之后，该国可以引用第五条之三和之四中任何一条或全部例外规定。

（二）任何这种报告书自本公约生效日起十年有效，或是在该报告书备案时的十年期限之所余时间内有效；如果在有关的十年限期期满之前三到十五个月之中，该缔约国将续订报告书呈交总干事备案，那么原报告书可以全部或部分修订，从而获得新的十年一度的有效期。根据本条规定，初次报告书也可在新的十年阶段当中提出。

（三）按本条第（一）款之规定，如某缔约国不再视为发展中国家，那么尽管有本条第（二）款之规定，该缔约国仍无权修改根据本条第（一）和第（二）款之规定提交的报告书。不管该缔约国是否撤回其报告书，在当前十年期限或该国已不再视为发展中国家的三年期限期满之后——不论哪个后到期，该缔约国都不得引用第五条之三和之四之例外规定。

（四）根据第五条之三和之四的例外规定，凡已出版的著作的各册，在该著作根据本条规定提交的报告书有效期满后，仍可继续发行，直至其库存全部售完为止。

（五）如果任何一个缔约国依照第十三条关于应用本公约于一特定国家或领土的规定已呈交报告书，而该特定国家和领土的情况又可视为与本条第（一）款所述之缔约国情况相似，则该国亦可依照本条关于此类国家和领土之规定呈交和修改其报告书。在上述报告书有效期内，上述有关国家和领土亦可应用本公约第五条之三和之四的规定。由上述有关国家和领土向缔约国呈送的出版物应视为第五条之三和之四所述之出口出版物。

第五条之三

（一）甲、凡适用第五条之二第（一）款之任何缔约国均可依该国法律规定的三年或三年以上的期限取代第五条第（二）款规定之七年期限；然而，某一作品译成的文字如在一个或若干发达国家内并非通用，而上述国家又是本公约或仅是 1952 年公约的缔约国，那么其有限期应为一年而不是三年。

乙、按参加本公约或仅参加 1952 年公约的发达国家所达成的一致协议，如同一语言在其诸国内广泛运用，而某作品又译成上述语言，那么凡适用于第五条之二第（一）款之缔约国可将该协议规定的另一期限代替本款甲项规定之三年期限，其时间不得短于一年。然而，此项不适用于英、法、西班牙三种语言通用的地方。任何此类协议之报告书均应呈交总干事。

丙、如果申请人按照有关缔约国之例行规定，证明他已提出过申请，要求翻译权所有者予以承认，但被拒绝；或经本人一再努力，仍不能找到版权所有者，他就可以获得许可证。提出上述要求的同时，他应告诉联合国教育、科学及文化组织设立的国际版权情报中心，或出版者主要营业地点所在的缔约国政府提交总干事的报告书中所指定的任何国家或地区的情报中心。

丁、如无法找到翻译权所有者，则许可证申请人应将其申请书航空挂号邮给在出版物上署名的出版者，并同时邮给按本款丙项提及的任何国家或地区的情报中心。如无上述地方可递交，他应将其申请书送交联合国教育、科学及文化组织设立的国际版权情报中心。

（二）甲、根据本条规定，半年之后才能颁发三年后可得之许可证；九个月之后才能颁发一年后可得以许可证。上述六、九个月之期限应按第（一）款丙项之规定，从提出许可证申请之日算起，如翻译权所有者身份、地址不详，则按第（一）款丁项之规定从要求获得许可证的申请书发出之日算起。

乙、翻译权所有者本人、或授权他人在上述六个月或九个月内已将译著出版，则不得再颁发许可证。

（三）根据本条之规定，凡为教学、学习或研究之目的者，应一律颁发许可证。

（四）甲、按本条规定颁发的一切许可证，仅在申请者所在的缔约国内有效，其出版物不得出口。

乙、根据本条颁发的许可证出版的任何出版物应用适当的语言刊印启事申明其出版物仅在颁发许可证的缔约国内销售有效。如果该著作刊印了第三条第（一）款特别规定之启事，那么其译本各册均应刊印与之相同的启事。

丙、某缔约国政府机构或民众团体根据本条规定已颁发版权许可证，并将某作品译成除英、法、西班牙语之外的一种文字，该政府机构或民众团体向另一国递送根据上述许可证而准备好的某译著样本，则本款甲项有关禁止出口书的规定，不适用于下列情况：

（1）如果收件者是颁发许可证的缔约国的个别国民或是此类个别国民组成的组织；

（2）寄送出的上述样本仅为教学、学习和研究之用；

（3）样本的寄送及其后分发给收件人均不为营利之目的；

（4）如接受上述样本的国家已与该缔约国达成协议同意接受、销售或同意二者皆可；而达成上述协议的任何一方政府已将该协议呈报总干事。

（五）应在国家一级做出相应规定，以保证：

甲、在颁发上述许可证时应给予合理的报酬，其报酬标准与上述两国个人间自由商谈版权许可证时通常规定的版税相同。

乙、报酬的支付与转递；如果该国货币流通条例有碍其报酬的支付与转递，主管当局应竭尽全力采用国际措施，以保证用国际可兑现货币或与之等值货币进行转递。

（六）如果某作品的译本一旦由翻译权所有者本人或授权他人在某缔约国内出版发行，其文字与该国已特许的版本一样，其内容又大体相同，其价格与该国通常出版的同类著作相当，则凡据本条规定缔约国颁发之许可证应停止生效。但在上述许可证失效之前出版的该译著各册均可继续发行，直至库存全部售完为止。

（七）凡以插图为主的作品，只要具备第五条之四的规定，均可颁发翻译其文字说明、复制其插图的许可证。

（八）甲、总部设在第五条之二适用的某一缔约国的广播组织根据下列诸条件提出申请，则受本公约保护用铅印或类似形式复制出版的作品的翻译许可证也可颁发给该组织：

（1）译本是根据该缔约国法律规定出版并获得的版本译成的；

（2）译本仅供以教学或向职业专家传播专门技术和科研成果为目的的广播使用；

（3）译文专为第（2）条之目的使用，是通过对缔约国本土内听众的合法广播进行的，其中包括特为上述广播之目的而通过录音或录像方式合法录制的广播；

（4）译本的录音或录像只能在其总部设在颁发许可证的缔约国的广播组织间交换；

（5）译本的一切使用方式均无营利的目的。

乙、如果完全符合上述甲项的标准和条件，则任何专门为系统性教育活动而准备和出版的视听材料的任何课文的翻译许可证亦可发给某广播组织。

丙、根据本款甲、乙两项，本条其他规定均适用于许可证的颁发与使用。

（九）根据本条规定，依据本条颁发的任何许可证应受第五条各项规定的约束；即使按第五条第（二）款之规定七年期限已满，上述许可证也应继续受第五条和本条规定的约束。然而，上述期限到期后，许可证持有者有权提出申请仅服从第五条规定的新许可证来代替上述许可证。

第五条之四

（一）凡适合第五条之二第（一）款规定的任何缔约国均可采纳下述规定：

甲、在（1）由本条第（三）款所述的文学、科学或艺术作品的特定版本首先出版日算起，在第丙项规定的有关期限到期之后，或（2）在依缔约国国家法律规定的任何更长的期限之后，如果复制权所有者本人没有，也未授权他人将上述出版物在该国一般民众中销售，或未为系统教育活动之目的以与在该国中同类作品的一般索价相近的合理价格销售，那么该国的任何国民均可向主管当局申请获得非专利权许可证，用上述规定之价格或更低的价格出版上述版本为其系统教育活动使用。上述国民，须根据有关缔约国例行规定，证明他提出过申请要求版权所有者予以承认，但被拒绝；或经其本人一再努力，仍未找到版权所有者，才能获得许可证。在他提出要求同时，他得向联合国教育、科学及文化组织设立的国际版权情报中心或向在第丁项提及的任何国家或地区性的情报中心提出报告。

乙、在六个月内，如果经版权所有者许可的上述版本的出版物已不再在有关国家向一般公众出售，或已不再为系统教育活动之目的而以与同类作品在该国内的一般索价相近的合理价格销售，则根据同样条件亦可颁发许可证。

丙、本款甲项规定的期限应为五年，其例外规定如下：（1）自然和物理科学（包括数学）及技术著作，其期限为三年；

（2）小说、诗歌、戏剧、音乐作品和艺术方面读物，其期限为七年。

丁、如果找不到复制权所有者，许可证申请者应将其申请样本航空挂号邮给在其作品上署名的出版者，和在出版者的主要营业地点所在的国家呈交给总干事报告书中明确指定的任何国家或地区性情报中心。如无任何上述报告书，他应向联合国教育、科学及文化组织设立的国际版权情报中心呈交一份报告书。在自发出申请报告书之日起的三个月之内不得颁发许可证。

戊、根据本条规定，在下述情况下，不得颁发三年后可获得的许可证：

（1）在从本款甲项提及的提出版权许可要求之日起六个月内，或如果复制权所有者身份、地址不明，从本款丁项提及的许可证申请书发出之日起六个月内；

（2）在此期间，如果本款甲项提及的任何出版物已开始发行。

己、作者姓名及其作品特定版本的书名应刊印在复制出版物的一切版本上。许可证仅在申请许可证的缔约国内有效，其复制出版物不得出口，许可证持有者不得转让其许可证。

庚、国家法律应做出相应规定，以保证准确复制上述特定版本。

辛、根据本条规定，凡属下述情况，不应颁发复制出版翻译作品的许可证：

（1）译本不是翻译权所有者本人翻译出版的也不是他授权别人翻译出版的；

（2）译本不是用有权颁发许可证的缔约国的通用语言出版的。

（二）第（一）款之例外规定应受下述补充规定之约束：

甲、按照本条规定颁发的版权许可证准予出版的版本，须以适当的语言刊登启事申明其出版物能在申请版权许可证的缔约国内销售。如果需要刊印第三条第（一）款规定之特别启事，则该版之一切本册均应刊印同类启事。

乙、应在国家一级做出相应规定，以保证：

（1）在颁发许可证时给予合理的报酬，其报酬标准与上述两国个人间自由商谈版权许可证时通常规定的版税同；

（2）报酬的支付与转递；如果该国货币流通条例妨碍报酬的支付与转递，则主管当局应竭尽全力采用国际措施，以保证用国际上可兑现的货币或与之等值的货币进行转递。

丙、无论何时，如复制权所有者本人或授权他人以与该缔约国出售同类作品通常索取的合理价格在该国中向公众或为系统教育活动之目的出售某作品之版本各册，如果该版本与根据许可证复制的出版物的版本语言相同，内容大体一致，则根据本条规定，任何许可证应予停止生效；但许可证失效前已经出版的所有各册仍可继续出售，直至库存全部售完为止。

丁、如作者已将正在发行的该版本全部各册收回，则不得再颁发许可证。

（三）甲、本条所适用的文学、科学或艺术作品，应限于以印刷或类似的复制形式出版的作品，但本款乙项的规定例外。

乙、本条规定亦适用于以录音、录像的形式复制已经合法录制的内有受保护作品的视听材料，只要这些视听材料是专门为系统教育活动而准备和出版的；本条规定也适用于上述视听材料中的课文的翻译，只要这些译文是以缔约国的通用语文、而且是根据该缔约国颁发的许可证翻译的。

第六条

本公约所用“出版”一词，系指：对某些作品以一定的方式进行复制，并在公众中发行，以供阅读或观赏。

第七条

本公约在其有效日期内，将不适用于参加本公约的缔约国的那些具有永久性的公有作品或其版权。

第八条

（一）本公约将由总干事备案，其修订日期为 1971 年 7 月 24 日。本公约对 1952 年公约的所有签字国保留其签字日期为自上述日期起的一百二十天以内。本公约须经各签字国批准或接受。

（二）未在本公约签字的国家均可参加。

（三）批准、接受或参加本公约须向总干事呈交有关证书方能有效。

第九条

（一）本公约将于呈交十二份批准、接受或参加证书之后三个月生效。

（二）再则，本公约将于每一有关国家在其呈交批准、接受或参加证书三个月后生效。

（三）参加本公约的任何国家，如未参加 1952 年公约，也将被视为参加该项公约；但是，如呈交其参加证书在本公约生效之前，该国可申请加入 1952 年公约，其生效条件与本公约同。在本公约生效后，任何国家均不可单独加入 1952 年公约。

（四）本公约签字国与只参加1952年公约的签字国之间的关系，均服从1952年公约的规定。但是，只参加1952年公约的任何国家，可向总干事呈交一份通知书，宣布承认1971年公约适用于该国的作品和在该国首次出版的本公约签字国的作品。

第十条

（一）每一缔约国须根据其宪法采取必要措施确保本公约的实施。

（二）不言而喻，本公约在任何一缔约国生效时，该国应依照其本国法律使本公约各条款生效。

第十一条

（一）设立一“政府间委员会”，其职责如下：

甲、研究世界版权公约的实施事宜；

乙、做好定期修改本公约的准备工作；

丙、与“联合国教育、科学及文化组织”、“国际保护文学艺术作品联盟”、“美洲国家组织”等各有关国际组织合作，研究有关国际版权保护的一切问题；

丁、向世界版权公约参加国通报“政府间委员会”的各项活动。

（二）该委员会将由参加本公约或只参加1952年公约的十八个国家的代表组成。

（三）该委员会的选举应根据各个国家地理位置、人口、语言和发展水平适当考虑其利益均衡情况。

（四）联合国教科文组织总干事、世界知识产权组织总干事、美洲国家组织秘书长或他们的代表可以顾问身份参加该委员会的各种会议。

第十二条

政府间委员会认为必要，或应本公约至少十个缔约国要求，得召集会议对本公约进行修改。

第十三条

（一）任何缔约国，在其呈递批准、接受或参加证书时，或在其后的任何时间内，可通知总干事，宣布本公约适用于由它对其国际关系负责的所有或其中任何一个国家或领土；因之，本公约于第九条规定的三个月期限满期后，将在通知中所提到的国家或领土内实施。倘无此类通知，本公约将不适用于此类国家或领土。

（二）但是，本条款不得理解为某一缔约国承认或默许另一缔约国根据本条条款使本公约对其有约束力的有关国家或领土的现实状况。

第十四条

（一）任何缔约国可以自己的名义、或代表根据第九条规定发出的通知中所涉及的所有或其中任何一个国家或领土，通知废除本公约。废除本公约应以通知方式函寄总干事。此类废除函件也同样适用于1952年公约。

（二）此类废除只在相应的缔约国或其所代表的国家或领土内有效。此类废除事项于收到通知之日起一年后生效。

第十五条

如两个或数个缔约国对本公约的解释和实施发生争执，会谈或其他方法均不能使有关国家取得一致意见时，得提交国际法庭裁决。

第十六条

（一）本公约将印成英语、法语、西班牙语三种文本，此三种文本将同样签字并具同等效力。

（二）总干事经和有关政府协商，将确定阿拉伯语、德语、意大利语和葡萄牙语的正式文本。

（三）某个或数个缔约国有权与总干事协商责成总干事确定他们选择的文字作为其他文本。

（四）所有此类文本均为本公约签字文本的附件。

第十七条

（一）本公约绝不影响伯尔尼保护文学艺术作品公约的条款或由该公约所设联盟的会员资格。

（二）为实施前节条文，本条后面已附一声明。对于1951年1月1日伯尔尼公约负有义务的各个国家或以后某个时期可能成为负有义务的国家，此声明是本公约不可分割的组成部分。在本公约上签字的此类国家也将认为是在该声明上签了字，而此类国家的批准、接受或参加，如对本公约一样，也包括该声明。

第十八条

本公约将不废除美洲各共和国中仅限两国或数国之间已经实行或可能实行的双边或多边版权公约或协定。无论是在现有上述此类公约和协定的条款与本公约的各项条款间，或是本公约的各项条款与本公约生效之后美洲两个或数个共和国还可能构成的新的公约或协定的条款出现分歧时，应以最近构成的公约或协议为准。在本公约生效前，某一缔约国依据现有公约或协定所获之版权不应受到影响。

第十九条

本公约将不废除在两个或数个缔约国之间行之有效的双边或多边公约或

协定。一旦此类现行公约或协定的条款与本公约的条款出现分歧时，将以本公约各项条款为准。在本公约生效前，任何缔约国依据现行公约或协定所获之版权将不受影响，本条的规定将不影响第十七条、第十八条各款的实行。

第二十条

不得对本公约持任何保留意见。

第二十一条

（一）总干事应及时将本公约的正式文本送交各有关国家并送交联合国秘书长注册。

（二）总干事还应通知是已递交批准、接受或参加本公约证书的各有关国家本公约的生效日期、根据本公约发出的通知及根据第十四条做出的废除通知。

有关第十七条的附加声明

国际保护文学艺术作品联盟（以下称“伯尔尼联盟”）的会员国和本公约的签字国为了在本联盟基础上加强其相互关系，并避免伯尔尼公约和世界版权公约在并存情况下可能出现的任何冲突，认识到某些国家按照其文化、社会、经济发展阶段而调整其版权保护水平的临时需要，经共同商定，兹接受以下声明的各项内容：

甲、除本条乙项规定外，根据伯尔尼公约，对于1951年1月1日已经退出伯尔尼联盟的国家，籍属该国的作品将不在伯尔尼联盟国家中受世界版权公约的保护。

乙、鉴于某一缔约国按联合国大会惯例被视为发展中的国家，并在该国退出伯尔尼联盟时，将一份大意为自称是发展中国家的报告书呈交联合国教科文组织总干事，只要该国可能运用本公约第五条之二的例外规定，则本声明甲项之规定不应适用。

丙、只要是涉及保护某些按伯尔尼公约规定以伯尔尼联盟之一成员国为其国籍的作品的版权，世界版权公约均不应适用于伯尔尼联盟各国的关系上。

有关第十一条的决议

修订世界版权公约会议，考虑了本决议为其附件的公约第十一条规定的政府间委员会问题，特做决议如下：

（一）起初，委员会应包括依据1952年公约第十一条及其附加决议而设立的政府间委员会的十二个成员国；除此以外，还包括以下国家的代表：阿尔及利亚、澳大利亚、日本、墨西哥、塞内加尔和南斯拉夫。

（二）继本公约生效后召开的本委员会第一次例会之前，如果任何非

1952年公约缔约国尚未加入本公约，则本委员会应根据第十一条第（二）款和第（三）款之规定在其第一次例会上选择其他缔约国来取代上述国家。

（三）本公约一经生效，依据本决议第（一）款规定成立的本委员会应被认为按本公约第十一条规定组成。

（四）本公约生效后一年内，本委员会应举行一次会议。此后本委员会应至少每两年举行一次例会。

（五）本委员会应选举主席一人副主席两人。并应按照下列原则设立自己的议事规则：

甲、本委员会之成员国任期通常应为六年，在原有任期中，每两年有三分之一成员国离任，也可理解为：首批三分之一成员国的任期，应在继本公约生效后召开的第二次例会后结束，下一批三分之一成员国的任期应在第三次例会后结束，最后一批三分之一成员国的任期应在第四次例会后结束。

乙、本委员会递补空缺职位的议事规则，成员国离任的顺序安排，连任资格的确定和选举程序的原则应是：既考虑到本公约第十一条第（三）款提出的问题，又能平衡成员国连任和成员国代表资格轮换的需要。

本委员会希望由联合国教科文组织提供其秘书处人员。

Universal Copyright Convention

as revised at Paris on 24 July 1971,
with Appendix Declaration relating to Article XVII and
Resolution concerning Article XI 1971
Paris, 24 July 1971
- Protocol 1, Paris, 24 July 1971
- Protocol 2, Paris, 24 July 1971

The Contracting States,

Moved by the desire to ensure in all countries copyright protection of literary, scientific and artistic works,

Convinced that a system of copyright protection appropriate to all nations of the world and expressed in a universal convention, additional to, and without impairing international systems already in force, will, ensure respect for the rights of the individual and encourage the development of literature, the sciences and the arts,

Persuaded that such a universal copyright system will facilitate a wider dissemination of works of the human mind and increase international under - standing,

Have resolved to revise the Universal Copyright Convention as signed at Geneva on 6 September 1952 (hereinafter called `the 1952 Convention'), and consequently,

Have agreed as follows:

Article I

Each Contracting State undertakes to provide for the adequate and effective protection of the rights of authors and other copyright proprietors in literary, scientific and artistic works, including writings, musical, dramatic and cinematographic works, and paintings, engravings and sculpture.

Article II

1. Published works of nationals of any Contracting State and works first pub-

lished in that State shall enjoy in each other Contracting State the same protection as that other State accords to works of its nationals first published in its own territory, as well as the protection specially granted by this Convention.

2. Unpublished works of nationals of each Contracting State shall enjoy in each other Contracting State the same protection as that other State accords to unpublished works of its own nationals, as well as the protection specially granted by this Convention.

3. For the purpose of this Convention any Contracting State may, by domestic legislation, assimilate to its own nationals any person domiciled in that State.

Article III

1. Any Contracting 'State which, under its domestic law, requires as a condition of copyright, compliance with formalities such as deposit, registration, notice, notarial certificates, payment of fees or manufacture or publication in that Contracting State, shall regard these requirements as satisfied with respect to all works protected in accordance with this Convention and first published outside its territory and the author of which is not one of its nationals, if from the time of the first publication all the copies of the work published with the authority of the author or other copyright proprietor bear the symbol accompanied by the name of the copyright proprietor and the year of first publication placed in such manner and location as to give reasonable notice of claim of copyright.

2. The provisions of paragraph 1 shall not preclude any Contracting State from requiring formalities or other conditions for the acquisition and enjoyment of copyright in respect of works first published in its territory or works of its nationals wherever published.

3. The provisions of paragraph 1 shall not preclude any Contracting State from providing that a person seeking judicial relief must, in bringing the action, comply with procedural requirements, such as that the complainant must appear through domestic counsel or that the complainant must deposit with the court or an administrative office, or both, a copy of the work involved in the litigation; provided that failure to comply with such requirements shall not affect the validity of the copyright, nor shall any such requirement be imposed upon a national of another Contracting State if such requirement is not imposed on nationals of the State in which protection is claimed.

4. In each Contracting State there shall be legal means of protecting without formalities the unpublished works of nationals of other Contracting States.

5. If a Contracting State grants protection for more than one term of copyright and the first term is for a period longer than one of the minimum periods prescribed in Article IV, such State shall not be required to comply with the provisions of paragraph 1 of this Article in respect of the second or any subsequent term of copyright.

Article IV

1. The duration of protection of a work shall be governed, in accordance with the provisions of Article II and this Article, by the law of the Contracting State in which protection is claimed.

2. (a) The term of protection for works protected under this Convention shall not be less than the life of the author and twenty - five years after his death. However, any Contracting State which, on the effective date of this Convention in that State, has limited this term for certain classes of works to a period computed from the first publication of the work, shall be entitled to maintain these exceptions and to extend them to other classes of works. For all these classes the term of protection shall not be less than twenty - five years from the date of first publication.

(b) Any Contracting State which, upon the effective date of this Convention in that State, does not compute the term of protection upon the basis of the life of the author, shall be entitled to compute the term of protection from the date of the first publication of the work or from its registration prior to publication, as the case may be, provided the term of protection shall not be less than twenty - five years from the date of first publication or from its registration prior to publication, as the case may be.

(c) If the legislation of a Contracting State grants two or more successive terms of protection, the duration of the first term shall not be less than one of the minimum periods specified in sub - paragraphs (a) and (b).

3. The provisions of paragraph 2 shall not apply to photographic works or to works of applied art; provided, however, that the term of protection in those Contracting States which protect photographic works, or works of applied art in so far as they are protected as artistic works, shall not be less than ten years for each of said classes of works.

4. (a) No Contracting State shall be obliged to grant protection to a work for a period longer than that fixed for the class of works to which the work in question belongs, in the case of unpublished works by the law of the Contracting State of which the author is a national, and in the case of published works by the law of the Contracting State in which the work has been first published.

(b) For the purposes of the application of sub - paragraph (a), if the law of any Contracting State grants two or more successive terms of protection, the period of protection of that State shall be considered to be the aggregate of those terms. However, if a specified work is not protected by such State during the second or any subsequent term for any reason, the other Contracting States shall not be obliged to protect it during the second or any subsequent term.

5. For the purposes of the application of paragraph 4, the work of a national of a Contracting State, first published in a non - Contracting State, shall be treated as though first published in the Contracting State of which the author is a national.

6. For the purposes of the application of paragraph 4, in case of simultaneous publication in two or more Contracting States, the work shall be treated as though first published in the State which affords the shortest term; any work published in two or more Contracting States within thirty days of its first publication shall be considered as having been published simultaneously in said Contracting States.

Article IV bis

1. The rights referred to in Article I shall include the basic rights ensuring the author's economic interests, including the exclusive - right to authorize reproduction by any means, public performance and broadcasting. The provisions of this Article shall extend to works protected under this Convention either in their original form or in any form recognizably derived from the original.

2. However, any Contracting State may, by its domestic legislation, make exceptions that do not conflict with the spirit and provisions of this Convention, to the rights mentioned in paragraph 1 of this Article. Any State whose legislation so provides, shall nevertheless accord a reasonable degree of effective protection to each of the rights to which exception has been made.

Article V

1. The rights referred to in Article I shall include the exclusive right of the au-

thor to make, publish and authorize the making and publication of translations of works protected under this Convention.

2. However, any Contracting State may, by its domestic legislation, restrict the right of translation of writings, but only subject to the following provisions :

(a) If, after the expiration of a period of seven years from the date of the first publication of a writing, a translation of such writing has not been published in a language in general use in the Contracting State, by the owner of the right of translation or with his authorization, any national of such Contracting State may obtain a non - exclusive licence from the competent authority thereof to translate the work into that language and publish the work so translated.

(b) Such national shall in accordance with the procedure of the State concerned, establish either that he has requested, and been denied, authorization by the proprietor of the right to make and publish the translation, or that, after due diligence on his part, he was unable to find the owner of the right. A licence may also be granted on the same conditions if all previous editions of a translation in a language in general use in the Contracting State are out of print.

(c) If the owner of the right of translation cannot be found, then the applicant for a licence shall send copies of his application to the publisher whose name appears on the work and, if the nationality of the owner of the right of translation is known, to the diplomatic or consular representative of the State of which such owner is a national, or to the organization which may have been designated by the government of that State. The licence shall not be granted before the expiration of a period of two months from the date of the dispatch of the copies of the application.

(d) Due provision shall be made by domestic legislation to ensure to the owner of the right of translation a compensation which is just and conforms to international standards, to ensure payment and transmittal of such compensation, and to ensure a correct translation of the work.

(e) The original title and the name of the author of the work shall be printed on all copies of the published translation. The' licence shall be valid only for publication of the translation in the territory of the Contracting State where it has been applied for. Copies so published may be imported and sold in another Contracting State if a language in general use in such other State is the same language as that into which the work has been so translated, and if the domestic law in such other State makes provision for such licences and does not prohibit such importation and sale. Where the foregoing conditions do not exist, the importation and sale of such copies in a Contracting State shall be governed by its domestic law and its agreements. The licence shall not be transferred by the licensee.

(f) The licence shall not be granted when the author has withdrawn from . circulation all copies of the work.

Article V_{bis}

1. Any Contracting State regarded as a developing country in conformity with the established practice of the General Assembly of the United Nations may, by a notification deposited with the Director - General of the United Nations Educational, Scientific and Cultural Organization (hereinafter called `the Director - General') at the time of this ratification, acceptance or accession or thereafter, avail itself of any or all of the exceptions provided for in Articles Vter and Vquater.

2. Any such notification shall be effective for ten years from the date of coming into force of this Convention, or for such part of that ten - year period as remains at the date of deposit of the notification, and may be renewed in whole or in part for further periods of ten years each if, not more than fifteen or less than three months before the expiration of the relevant ten - year period, the Contracting State deposits a further notification with the Director - General. Initial notifications may also be made during these further periods of ten years in accordance with the provisions of this Article.

3. Notwithstanding the provisions of paragraph 2, a Contracting State that has ceased to be regarded as a developing country as referred to in paragraph 1 shall no longer be entitled to renew its notification made under the provisions of paragraph 1 or 2, and whether or not it formally withdraws the notification such State shall be precluded from availing itself of the exceptions provided for in Articles Vter and Vquater at the end of the current ten - year period, or at the end of three years after it has ceased to be regarded as a developing country, whichever period expires later.

4. Any copies of a work already made under the exceptions provided for in Articles Vter and Vquater may continue to be distributed after the expiration of the period for which notifications under this Article were effective until their stock is

exhausted.

5. Any Contracting State that has deposited a notification in accordance with Article XIII with respect to the application of this Convention to a particular country or territory, the situation of which can be regarded as analogous to that of the States referred to in paragraph 1 of this Article, may also deposit notifications and renew them in accordance with the provisions of this Article with respect to any such country or territory. During the effective period of such notifications, the provisions of Articles Vter and Vquater may be applied with respect to such country or territory. The sending of copies from the country or territory to the Contracting State shall be considered as export within the meaning of Articles Vter and Vquater.

Article V ter

1. (a) Any Contracting State to which Article Vbis (1) applies may substitute for the period of seven years provided for in Article V (2) a period of three years or any longer period prescribed by its legislation. However, in the case of a translation into a language not in general use in one or more developed countries that are party to this Convention or only the 1952 Convention, the period shall be one year instead of three.

(b) A Contracting State to which Article Vbis (1) applies may, with the unanimous agreement of the developed countries party to this Convention or only the 1952 Convention and in which the same language is in general use, substitute, in the case of translation into that language, for the period of three years provided for in sub - paragraph (a) another period as determined by such agreement but not shorter than one year. However, this sub - paragraph shall not apply where the language in question is English, French or Spanish. Notification of any such agreement shall be made to the Director - General.

(c) The licence may only be granted if the applicant, in accordance with the procedure of the State concerned, establishes either that he has requested, and been denied, authorization by the owner of the right of translation, or that, after due diligence on his part, he was unable to find the owner of the right. At the same time as he makes his request he shall inform either the International Copyright Information Center established by the United Nations Educational, Scientific and Cultural Organization or any national or regional information centre which may have been designated in a notification to that effect deposited with the Director - General by the government of the State in which the publisher is believed to have his principal place of business.

(d) If the owner of the right of translation cannot be found, the applicant for a licence shall send, by registered airmail, copies of this application to the publisher whose name appears on the work and to any national or regional information center as mentioned in sub - paragraph (c). If no such center is notified he shall also send a copy to the international copyright information center established by the United Nations Educational, Scientific and Cultural Organization.

2. (a) Licences obtainable after three years shall not be granted under this Article until a further period of six months has elapsed and licences obtainable after one year until a further period of nine months has elapsed. The further period shall begin either from the date of the request for permission to translate mentioned in paragraph 1 (c) or, if the identity or address of the owner of the right of translation is not known, from the date of dispatch of the copies of the application for a licence mentioned in paragraph 1 (d).

(b) Licences shall not be granted if a translation has been published by the owner of the right of translation or with his authorization during the said period of six or nine months.

3. Any licence under this Article shall be granted only for the purpose of teaching, scholarship or research.

4. (a) Any licence granted under this Article shall not extend to the export of copies and shall be valid only for publication in the territory of the Contracting State where it has been applied for.

(b) Any copy published in accordance with a licence granted under this Article shall bear a notice in the appropriate language stating that the copy is available for distribution only in the Contracting State granting the licence. If the writing bears the notice specified in Article III (1) the copies shall bear the same notice.

(c) The prohibition of export provided for in sub - paragraph (a) shall not apply where a governmental or other public entity of a State which has granted a licence under this Article to translate a work into a language other than English, French or Spanish sends copies of a translation prepared under such licence to another country if:

(i) the recipients are individuals who are nationals of the Contracting State granting the licence, or organizations grouping such individuals;

(ii) the copies are to be used only for the purpose of teaching, scholarship or research;

(iii) the sending of the copies and their subsequent distribution to recipients is without the object of commercial purpose; and

(iv) the country to which the copies have been sent has agreed with the Contracting State to allow the receipt, distribution or both and the

Director - General has been notified of such agreement by any one of the governments which have concluded it.

5. Due provision shall be made at the national level to ensure:

a) that the licence provides for just compensation that is consistent with standards of royalties normally operating in the case of licences freely negotiated between persons in the two countries concerned; and

(b) payment and transmittal of the compensation; however, should national currency regulations intervene, the competent authority shall make all efforts, by the use of international machinery, to ensure transmittal in internationally convertible currency or its equivalent.

6. Any licence granted by a Contracting State under this Article shall terminate if a translation of the work in the same language with substantially the same content as the edition in respect of which the licence was granted is published in the said State by the owner of the right of translation or with his authorization, at a price reasonably related to that normally charged in the same State for comparable works. Any copies already made before the licence is terminated may continue to be distributed until their stock is exhausted.

7. For works which are composed mainly of illustrations a licence to translate the text and to reproduce the illustrations may be granted only if the conditions of Article Vquater are also fulfilled.

8. (a) A licence to translate a work protected under this Convention, published in printed or analogous forms of reproduction, may also be granted to a broadcasting organization having its headquarters in a Contracting State to which Article Vbis (1) applies, upon an application made in that State by the said organization under the following conditions:

(i) the translation is made from a copy made and acquired in accordance with the laws of the Contracting State;

(ii) the translation is for use only in broadcasts intended exclusively for teaching or for the dissemination of the results of specialized technical or scientific research to experts in a particular profession;

(iii) the translation is used exclusively for the purposes set out in condition (ii), through broadcasts lawfully made which are intended for recipients on the territory of the Contracting State, including broadcasts made through the medium of sound or visual recordings lawfully and exclusively made for the purpose of such broadcasts;

(iv) sound or visual recordings of the translation may be exchanged only between broadcasting organizations having their headquarters in the Contracting State granting the licence; and

(v) all uses made of the translation are without any commercial purpose.

(b) Provided all of the criteria and conditions set out in sub - paragraph (a) are met, a licence may also be granted to a broadcasting organization to translate any text incorporated in an audio - visual fixation which was itself prepared and published for the sole purpose of being used in connexion with systematic instructional activities.

(c) Subject to sub - paragraphs (a) and (b), the other provisions of this Article shall apply to the grant and exercise of the licence.

9. Subject to the provisions of this Article, any licence granted under this Article shall be governed by the provisions of Article V, and shall continue to be governed by the provisions of Article V and of this Article, even after the seven - year period provided for in Article V (2) has expired. However, after the said period has expired, the licensee shall be free to request that the said licence be replaced by a new licence governed exclusively by the provisions of Article V.

Article V_{quater}

1. Any Contracting State to which Article Vbis (1) applies may adopt the following provisions:

(a) If, after the expiration of (i) the relevant period specified in sub - paragraph (c) commencing from the date of first publication of a particular edition of a literary, scientific or artistic work referred to in paragraph 3, or (ii) any longer period determined by national legislation of the State; copies of such edition have not been distributed in that State to the general public or in connexion with systematic instructional activities at a price reasonably related to that normally charged in the State for comparable works, by the owner of the right of reproduction or with his authorization, any national of such State may obtain a non - exclusive licence from the competent authority to publish such edition at that or a lower price for use in connexion with systematic instructional activities. The licence may only be granted if such national, in accordance with the procedure of the State concerned, establishes either that he has requested, and been denied, authorization by the proprietor of the right to publish such work, or that, after due diligence on his part, he was unable to find the owner of the right. At the same time as he makes his request he shall inform either the international copyright information center established by the United Nations Educational, Scientific and Cultural Organization or any national or regional information center referred to in sub - paragraph (d).

(b) A licence may also be granted on the same conditions if, for a period of six months, no authorized copies of the edition in question have been on sale in the State concerned to the general public or in connexion with systematic instructional activities at a price reasonably related to that normally charged in the State for comparable works.

(c) The period referred to in sub - paragraph (a) shall be five years except that:

(i) for works of the natural and physical sciences, including mathematics, and of technology, the period shall be three years;

(ii) for works of fiction, poetry, drama and music, and for art books, the period shall be seven years.

(d) If the owner of the right of reproduction cannot be found, the applicant for a licence shall send, by registered air mail, copies of his application to the publisher whose name appears on the work and to any national or regional information centre identified as such in a notification deposited with the Director - General by the State in which the publisher is believed to have his principal place of business. In the absence of any such notification, he shall also send a copy to the international copyright information center established by the United Nations Educational, Scientific and Cultural Organization. The licence shall not be granted before the expiration of a period of three months from the date of dispatch of the copies of the application.

(e) Licences obtainable after three years shall not be granted under this Article:

(i) until a period of six months has elapsed from the date of the request for permission referred to in sub - paragraph (a) or, if the identity or address of the owner of the right of reproduction is unknown, from the date of the dispatch of the copies of the application for a licence referred to in sub - paragraph (d);

(ii) if any such distribution of copies of the edition as is mentioned in sub - paragraph (a) has taken place during that period.

(f) The name of the author and the title of the particular edition of the work shall be printed on all copies of the published reproduction. The licence shall not extend to the export of copies and shall be valid only for publication in the territory of the Contracting State where it has been applied for. The licence shall not be transferable by the licensee.

(g) Due provision shall be made by domestic legislation to ensure an accurate reproduction of the particular edition in question.

(h) A licence to reproduce and publish a translation of a work shall not be granted under this Article in the following cases:

(i) where the translation was not published by the owner of the right of translation or with his authorization;

(ii) where the translation is not in a language in general use in the State with power to grant the licence.

2. The exceptions provided for in paragraph 1 are subject to the following additional provisions:

(a) Any copy published in accordance with a licence granted under this Article shall bear a notice in the appropriate language stating that the copy is available for distribution only in the Contracting State to which the said licence applies. If the edition bears the notice specified in Article III (1), the copies shall bear the same notice.

(b) Due provision shall be made at the national level to ensure:

(i) that the licence provides for just compensation that is consistent with standards of royalties normally operating in the case of licences freely negotiated between persons in the two countries concerned; and

(ii) payment and transmittal of the compensation; however, should national currency regulations intervene, the competent authority shall make all efforts, by the use of international machinery, to ensure transmittal in internationally convertible currency or its equivalent.

(c) Whenever copies of an edition of a work are distributed in the Contracting State to the general public or in connexion with systematic instructional activities, by the owner of the right of reproduction or with his authorization, at a price reasonably related to that normally charged in the, State for comparable works, any licence granted under this Article shall terminate if such edition is in the same language and is substantially the same in content as the edition published under the licence. Any copies already made before the licence is terminated may continue to be distributed until their stock is exhausted.

(d) No licence shall be granted when the author has withdrawn from circulation all copies of the edition in question.

3. (a) Subject to sub - paragraph (b), the literary, scientific or artistic works to which this Article applies shall be limited to works published in printed or analogous forms of reproduction.

(b) The provisions of this Article shall also apply to reproduction in audio - visual form of lawfully made audio - visual fixations including any protected works incorporated therein and to the translation of any incorporated text into a language in general use in the State with power to grant the licence; always provided that the audio - visual fixations in question were prepared and published for the sole purpose of being used in connexion with systematic instructional activities.

Article VI

`Publication', as used in this Convention, means the reproduction in tangible form and the general distribution to the public of copies of a work from which it can be read or otherwise visually perceived.

Article VII

This Convention shall not apply to works or rights in works which, at the effective date of this Convention in a Contracting State where protection is claimed, are permanently in the public domain in the said Contracting State.

Article VIII

1. This Convention, which shall bear the date of 24 July 1971, shall be deposited with the Director - General and shall remain open for signature by all States

party to the 1952 Convention for a period of 120 days after the date of this Convention. It shall be subject to ratification or acceptance by the signatory States.

2. Any State which has not signed this Convention may accede thereto.

3. Ratification, acceptance or accession shall be effected by the deposit of an instrument to that effect with the Director - General.

Article IX

1. This Convention shall come into force three months after the deposit of twelve instruments of ratification, acceptance or accession.

2. Subsequently, this Convention shall come into force in respect of each State three months after that State has deposited its instrument of ratification, acceptance or accession.

3. Accession to this Convention by a State not party to the 1952 Convention shall also constitute accession to that Convention; however, if its instrument of accession is deposited before this Convention comes into force, such State may make its accession to the 1952 Convention conditional upon the coming into force of this Convention. After the coming into force of this Convention, no State may accede solely to the 1952 Convention.

4. Relations between States party to this Convention and States that are party only to the 1952 Convention, shall be governed by the 1952 Convention. However, any State party only to the 1952 Convention may, by a notification deposited with the Director - General, declare that it will admit the application of the 1971 Convention to works of its nationals or works first published in its territory by all States party to this Convention. '

Article X

1. Each Contracting State undertakes to adopt, in accordance with its Constitution, such measures as are necessary to ensure the application of this Convention.

2. It is understood that at the date this Convention comes into force in respect of any State, that State must be in a position under its domestic law to give effect to the terms of this Convention.

Article XI

1. An Intergovernmental Committee is hereby established with the following duties :

(a) to study the problems concerning the application and operation of the Universal Copyright Convention;

(b) to make preparation for periodic revisions of this Convention;

(c) to study any other problems concerning the international protection of copyright, in co - operation with the various interested international organizations, such as the United Nations Educational, Scientific and Cultural Organization, the International Union for the Protection of Literary and Artistic Works and the Organization of American States;

(d) to inform States party to the Universal Copyright Convention as to its activities.

2. The Committee shall consist of the representatives of eighteen States party to this Convention or only to the 1952 Convention.

3. The Committee shall be selected with due consideration to a fair balance of national interests on the basis of geographical location, population, languages and stage of development.

4. The Director - General of the United Nations Educational, Scientific and Cultural Organization, the Director - General of the World Intellectual Property Organization and the Secretary - General of the Organization of American States, or their representatives, may attend meetings of the Committee in an advisory capacity.

Article XII

The Intergovernmental Committee shall convene a conference for revision whenever it deems necessary, or at the request of at least ten States party to this Convention.

Article XIII

1. Any Contracting State may, at the time of deposit of its instrument of ratification, acceptance or accession, or at any time thereafter, declare by notification addressed to the Director - General that this Convention shall apply to all or any of the countries or territories for the international relations of which it is responsible and this Convention shall thereupon apply to the countries or territories named in such notification after the expiration of the term of three months provided for in Article IX. In the absence of such notification, this Convention shall not apply to any such country or territory.

2. However, nothing in this Article shall be understood as implying the recognition or tacit acceptance by a Contracting State of the factual situation concerning a country or territory to which this Convention is made applicable by another Contracting State in accordance with the provisions of this Article.

Article XIV

1. Any Contracting State may denounce this Convention in its own name or on behalf of all or any of the countries or territories with respect to which a notification has been given under Article XIII. The denunciation shall be made by notification addressed to the Director - General. Such denunciation shall also constitute denunciation of the 1952 Convention.

2. Such denunciation shall operate only in respect of the State or of the country or territory on whose behalf it was made and shall not take effect until twelve months after the date of receipt of the notification.

Article XV

A dispute between two or more Contracting States concerning the interpretation or application of this Convention, not settled by negotiation, shall, unless the States concerned agree on some other method of settlement, be brought before the International Court of Justice for determination by it.

Article XVI

1. This Convention shall be established in English, French and Spanish. The three texts shall be signed and shall be equally authoritative.

2. Official texts of this Convention shall be established by the Director - General, after consultation with the governments concerned, in Arabic, German, Italian and Portuguese.

3. Any Contracting State or group of Contracting States shall be entitled to have established by the Director - General other texts in the language of its choice by arrangement with the Director - General.

4. All such texts shall be annexed to the signed texts of this Convention.

Article XVII

1. This Convention shall not in any way affect the provisions of the Berne Convention for the Protection of Literary and Artistic Works or membership in the Union created by that Convention.

2. In application of the foregoing paragraph, a declaration has been annexed

to the present Article. This declaration is an integral part of this Convention for the States bound. by the Berne Convention on 1 January 1951, or which have or may become bound to it at a later date. The signature of this Convention by such States shall also constitute signature of the said declaration, and ratification, acceptance or accession by such States shall include the declaration, as well as this Convention.

Article XVIII

This Convention shall not abrogate multilateral or bilateral copyright conventions or arrangements that are or may be in effect exclusively between two or more American Republics. In the event of any difference either between the provisions of such existing conventions or arrangements and the provisions of this Convention, or between the provisions of this Convention and those of any new convention or arrangement which may be formulated between two or more American Republics after this Convention comes into force, the convention or arrangement most recently formulated shall prevail between the parties thereto. Rights in works acquired in any Contracting State under existing conventions or arrangements before the date this Convention comes into force in such` State shall not be affected.

Article XIX

This Convention shall not abrogate multilateral or bilateral conventions or arrangements in effect between two or more Contracting States. In the event of any difference between the provisions of such existing conventions or arrangements and the provisions of this Convention, the provisions of this Convention shall prevail. Rights in works acquired in any Contracting State under existing conventions or arrangements before the date on which this Convention comes into force in such State shall not be affected. Nothing in this Article shall affect the provisions of Articles XVII and XVIII.

Article XX

Reservations to this Convention shall not be permitted.

Article XXI

1. The Director - General shall send duly certified copies of this Convention to the States interested and to the Secretary - General of the United Nations for registration by him.

2. He shall also inform all interested States of the ratifications, acceptances

and accessions which have been deposited, the date on which this Convention comes into force, the notifications under this Convention and denunciations under Article XIV.

Appendix declaration relating to Article XVII.

The States which are members of the International Union for the Protection of Literary and Artistic Works (hereinafter called `the Berne Union') and which - are signatories to this Convention,

Desiring to reinforce their mutual relations on the basis of the said Union and to avoid any conflict which might result from the co - existence of the Berne Convention and the Universal Copyright Convention,

Recognizing the temporary need of some States to adjust their level of copyright protection in accordance with their stage of cultural, social and economic development,

Have, by common agreement, accepted the terms of the following declaration:

(a) Except as provided by paragraph (b), works which, according to the Berne Convention, have as their country of origin a country which has withdrawn from the Berne Union after 1 January 1951, shall not be protected by the Universal Copyright Convention in the countries of the Berne Union;

(b) Where a Contracting State is regarded as a developing country in conformity with the established practice of the General Assembly of the United Nations, and has deposited with the Director - General of the United Nations Educational, Scientific and Cultural Organization, at the time of its withdrawal from the Berne Union, a notification to the effect that it regards itself as a developing country, the provisions of paragraph (a) shall not be applicable as long as such State may avail itself of the exceptions provided for by this Convention in accordance with Article Vbis;

(c) The Universal Copyright Convention shall not be applicable to the relationships among countries of the Berne Union in so far as it relates to the protection of works having as their country of origin, within the meaning of the Berne Convention, a country of the Berne Union.

Resolution concerning Article XI

The Conference for Revision of the Universal Copyright Convention,

Having considered the problems relating to the Intergovernmental Committee provided for in Article XI of this Convention, to which this resolution is annexed,

Resolves that:

1. At its inception, the Committee shall include representatives of the twelve States members of the Intergovernmental Committee established under Article XI of the 1952 Convention and the resolution annexed to it, and, in addition, representatives of the following States: Algeria, Australia, Japan, Mexico, Senegal and Yugoslavia.

2. Any States that are not party to the 1952 Convention and have not acceded to this Convention before the first ordinary session of the Committee following the entry into force of this Convention shall be replaced by other States to be selected by the Committee at its first ordinary session in conformity with the provisions of Article XI (2) and (3).

3. As soon as this Convention comes into force the Committee as provided for in paragraph 1 shall be deemed to be constituted in accordance with Article XI of this Convention.

4. A session of the Committee shall take place within one year after the coming into force of this Convention; thereafter the Committee shall meet in ordinary session at intervals of not more than two years.

5. The Committee shall elect its Chairman and' - two Vice - Chairmen. It shall establish its Rules of Procedure having regard to the following principles:

(a) The normal duration of the term of office of the members represented on the Committee shall be six years with one - third retiring every two years, it being however understood that, of the original terms of office, one - third shall expire at the end of the Committee's second ordinary session which will follow the entry into force of this Convention, a further third at the end of its third ordinary session, and the remaining third at the end of its fourth ordinary session.

(b) The rules governing the procedure whereby the Committee shall fill vacancies, the order in which terms of membership expire, eligibility for re - election, and election procedures, shall be based upon a balancing of the needs for continuity of membership and rotation of representation, as well as the considerations set out in Article XI (3).

Expresses the wish that the United Nations Educational, Scientific and Cultural Organization provide its Secretariat.

保护文学和艺术作品伯尔尼公约

(1886年9月9日通过，
1896年5月4日于巴黎补充，
1908年11月13日于柏林修订，
1914年3月20日于伯尔尼补充，
1928年6月2日于罗马修订，
1948年6月26日于布鲁塞尔修订，
1967年7月14日于斯德哥尔摩修订，
1971年7月24日于巴黎修订。)
颁布日期1971年7月24日
实施日期1971年9月28日
(1886年9月9日)

公　约

本联盟各成员国，受到尽可能有效地和尽可能一致地保护作者对其文学艺术作品所享权利的共同愿望的鼓舞；

承认一九六七年在斯德哥尔摩举行的修订会议工作的重要性。

决定修订斯德哥尔摩会议通过的文本，但不更动该文本第一至二十条和第二十二至二十六条。

下列签字的全权代表经交验全权证书认为妥善后，兹协议如下：

第一条　适用本公约的国家组成保护作者对其文学艺术作品所享权利的联盟。

第二条

一、“文学艺术作品”一词包括科学和文学艺术领域内的一切作品，不论其表现方式或形式如何，诸如书籍、小册子及其他著作；讲课、演讲、讲道及其他同类性质作品；戏剧或音乐戏剧作品；舞蹈艺术作品及哑剧作品；配词或未配词的乐曲；电影作品或以与电影摄影术类似的方法创作的作品；图画、油画、建筑、雕塑、雕刻及版画；摄影作品以及与摄影术类似的方法创作的作品；实用美术作品；插图、地图；与地理、地形、建筑或科学有关的设计图、草图及造型作品。

二、但本联盟各成员国法律有权规定仅保护表现于一定物质形式的文学艺术作品或其中之一种或数种。

三、翻译作品、改编作品、改编乐曲以及某件文字或艺术作品的其他改变应得到与原著同等的保护，而不损害原著作者的权利。

四、本联盟成员国得以立法确定对立法、行政或司法性质的官方文件及这些文件的正式译本的保护。

五、文字或艺术作品的汇集本，诸如百科全书和选集，由于对其内容的选择和整理而成为智力创作品，应得到与此类作品同等的保护，而不损害作者对这种汇集本内各件作品的权利。

六、上述作品得在本联盟所有成员国内享受保护。此种保护应为作者及其权利继受人的利益而行使。

七、考虑到本公约第七条第四款的规定，本联盟成员国得以立法规定涉及实用美术作品及工业设计和模型的法律的适用范围，并规定此类作品，设计和模型的保护条件。在起源国单独作为设计和模型受到保护的作品，在本联盟其他成员国可能只得到该国为设计和模型所提供的专门保护。但如在该国并不给予这类专门保护，则这些作品将作为艺术品得到保护。

八、本公约所提供的保护不得适用于日常新闻或纯属报刊消息性质的社会新闻。

第二条之二

一、本联盟成员国有权以立法规定把政治演讲和诉讼过程中发表的言论部分或全部排除于上条提供的保护之外。

二、本联盟成员国同样有权以立法规定对讲演、发言或其他同类性质作品进行报刊转载、无线或有线广播以及构成本公约第十一条之二第一款所指的公共传播对象的条件，如果上述报道之目的证明此种使用为正当的话。

三、但作者享有将上两款所提作品收编成汇集本的专有权。

第三条

一、根据本公约：

a）为本联盟任何一成员国公民的作者，其作品无论是否发表，应受到保护。

b）非为本联盟任何一成员国公民的作者，其作品首次在本联盟一成员国出版或在本联盟一成员国和一非本联盟成员国内同时出版的，应受到保护；

二、非本联盟任何一成员国公民但在一成员国国内有经常居所的作者，在适用本公约时，与该国公民作者同等对待。

三、“已发表作品”应理解为在其作者同意下出版的著作，不论其复制件的制作方式如何，但考虑到这部著作的性质，复制件的发行在数量和方式上需要满足公众的合理需要。戏剧、音乐戏剧或电影作品的上演，音乐作品的演奏，文学作品的当众朗诵，文学或艺术作品的广播或转播，美术作品的展出及建筑作品的建造不是发表。

四、在首次发表后三十天内在两个或两个以上国家出版的任何作品视为同时在几国发表。

第四条　即使第三条规定之条件未具备；下述作者根据本公约也应受到保护：

a）其电影作品的制片人在本联盟某一成员国有所在地或经常居所的；

b）建造在本联盟某一成员国内的建筑物或设置在本联盟某一成员国内房屋中的绘画和造型艺术品的。

第五条

一、根据本公约得到保护作品的作者，在除作品起源国外的本联盟各成员国，就其作品享受各该国法律现今给予或今后将给予其国民的权利，以及本公约特别授予的权利。

二、享受和行使这类权利不需履行任何手续，也不管作品起源国是否存在有关保护的规定。因此，除本公约条款外，只有向之提出保护要求的国家的法律方得规定保护范围及向作者提供的保护其权利的补救方法。

三、起源国的保护由该国本国法律作出规定。即使作者并非作品起源国的国民，但他就其作品根据本公约受到保护，他在该国仍享有同该国公民作者相同的权利。

四、起源国指的是：

a）对于首次在本联盟一成员国发表的作品，应以该国家为起源国；对于在给予不同保护期的本联盟数成员国同时发表的作品，起源国为立法给予最短保护期的国家；

b）对于在非本联盟成员国和本联盟某一成员国同时发表的作品，应视后者为起源国；

c）对于未发表的作品或首次在非本联盟成员国发表而未同时在本联盟成员国发表的作品，则以作者为其公民的本联盟成员国为起源国，然而

i）对于其制片人于本联盟某一成员国有所在地或经常居所的电影作品，则以该国为起源国；

ii）对于建立在本联盟某一成员国内的建筑物或设置在本联盟某一成员国内房屋中的绘画和造型艺术作品，应以该国为起源国。

第六条

一、凡任何非本联盟成员国未能充分保护本联盟某一成员国国民为作者的作品时，后一国可对在作品首次发表时系前一国国民而又在任何一联盟成员国内无经常居所之作者的作品的保护加以限制。如首次发表作品国利用这种权利，则本联盟其他成员国对受此特殊待遇的作品无义务给予比首次发表作品国所给予的更广泛的保护。

二、根据前款规定所确定的任何限制均不应损害在此种限制实施之前作者就在本联盟任何一成员国发表的作品已经获得的权利。

三、根据本条对作品权利的保护施加限制的本联盟成员国应以书面声明通知世界知识产权组织总干事（以下称总干事），指出保护受到限制的国家以及为这些国家公民的作者的权利所受的各种限制。总干事应立即向本联盟所有成员通报该项声明。

第六条之二

一、不受作者财产权的影响，甚至在上述财产权转让之后，作者仍保有主张对其作品的著作者身份的权利，并享有反对对上述作品进行任何歪曲或割裂或有损于作者声誉的其他损害的权利。

二、根据前款给予作者的权利，在其死后至少应保留到财产权期满为止，并由向之提出保护要求的国家本国法所授权的人或机构行使。但在批准或加入本条约时其法律未包括保护作者死后保护前款承认之权利的各国，有权规定这些权利中某些权利在作者死后无效。

三、为保障本条所承认的权利而采取的补救方法由向之提出保护要求的国家的法律规定。

第七条

一、本公约给予保护的期限为作者终生及其死后五十年。

二、但对于电影作品，本联盟成员国有权规定，保护期限自作品在作者同意下公映后五十年届满，如自作品摄制完成后五十年内尚未公映，则自作品摄制完成后五十年届满。

三、对于不具名作品和具笔名作品，本公约给予的保护期为自其合法向公众发表之日起五十年。但如作者采用的笔名不致引起对其身份发生任何怀疑时，该保护期则为第一款所规定的期限。如不具名作品或具笔名作品的作者在上述期间内披露其身份，则适用第一款所规定的保护期限。本联盟成员国没有义务保护不具名作品或具笔名作品，如果有充分理由假定其作者已死去五十年。

四、本联盟成员国有权以法律规定摄影作品及作为艺术品加以保护的实用美术作品的保护期限；但这一期限不应少于自该作品完成时算起二十五年。

五、作者死后的保护期和上述第二、三及四款所规定的期限应从作者死亡日或上述款项提及事情发生日起算，但这种期限只能从死亡后或所述事件发生后次年的一月一日开始计算。

六、本联盟成员国有权规定比前述各款规定期限为长的保护期。

七、受本公约罗马文本约束并在本文件签署时有效的本国法律中规定了比前述各款规定期限为短的保护期的本联盟成员国，有权在加入或批准本文件时保留这种期限。

八、在一切情况下，期限由向之提出保护要求的国家的法律加以规定；但除该国法律另有规定外，这个期限不得超过作品起源国规定的期限。

第七条之二 前条规定同样适用于作品的版权属于合著者共有的场合，但作者死后的保护期应从最后死亡的作者死亡之日起算。

第八条 受本公约保护的文学艺术作品的作者，在对原著享有权利的整个保护期内，享有翻译和授权翻译其作品的专有权。

第九条

一、受本公约保护的文学艺术作品的作者，享有批准以任何方式和采取任何形式复制这些作品的专有权。

二、本联盟成员国法律有权允许在某些特殊情况下复制上述作品，只要这种复制不致损害作品的正常使用也不致无故危害作者的合法利益。

三、所有录音或录像均应视为本公约所指的复制。

第十条

一、从一部合法向公众发表的作品中摘出引文，包括以报刊摘要形式摘引报纸期刊的文章，只要符合善良习惯，并在为达到正当目的所需要范围内，就属合法。

二、通过出版物、无线电广播或录音录像使用文学艺术作品作为教学解说的权利，只要是在为达到正当目的所需要的范围内使用，并且符合正当习惯，即可由本联盟成员国法律以及成员国之间现已签订或将要签订的特别协议加以规定。

三、根据本条前两款使用作品时，应指明出处，如原出处有作者姓名，也应同时说明。

第十条之二

一、对在报纸或期刊上已发表的经济、政治和宗教问题的时事性文章，或无线电已转播的同样性质的作品，本联盟成员国法律有权准许在报刊上转载，或向公众作无线或有线广播，如果对这种转载、广播或转播的权利未作直接保留的话。但任何时候均应明确指出出处；不履行该项义务的后果由向之提出保护要求的国家以法律规定。

二、本联盟成员国法律也有权规定，在何种条件下，对在时事事件过程中出现或公开的文学和艺术作品，在为报道目的正当需要范围内，可予以复制，或者以摄影或电影手段或通过无线电或有线广播向公众作时事新闻报道。

第十一条

一、戏剧作品、音乐戏剧作品或音乐作品的作者享有下述专有权：1. 许可公开演奏和公演其作品，包括用各种手段和方式的公开演奏和公演；2. 许可用各种手段公开播送其作品的表演和演奏。

二、戏剧作品或音乐戏剧作品的作者，在对其原著权利的整个期间内，对其作品的翻译享有同样的专有权。

第十一条之二

一、文学和艺术作品的作者享有下述专有权：

1. 许可以无线电广播其作品或以任何其他无线播送符合、声音或图像方法向公众发表其作品；2. 许可由原广播机构以外的另一机构通过有线广播或无线广播向公众发表作品；3. 许可通过扩音器或其他任何传送符号、声音或图像的类似工具向公众传送广播作品。

二、本联盟成员国的法律得规定行使上面第一款所指的权利的条件，但这些条件的效力只限于作出这些规定的国家。在任何情况下，这些条件均不应有损于作者的人身非财产权利，也不应有损于作者获得公正报酬的权利，该报酬在无友好协议的情况下应由主管当局规定之。

三、除另有规定外，根据本条第一款给予的许可，不包括利用录音或录像工具录制广播作品的许可。但本联盟成员国法律有权为某一广播机构使用其自己设备并为其自己播送之用而进行短期录制制定规章。本联盟成员国法律也可以批准由于这些录制品具有的特殊文献性质而交付官方档案馆保存。

第十一条之三

（一）文学作品作者享有下述专有权：（1）许可公开朗诵其作品，包括用各种手段或方式公开朗诵其作品，以及（2）许可用各种手段公开播送其作品的朗诵。

（二）文学作品作者在对其原著享有权利的整个期限内，对其作品的翻译也享有同样权利。

第十二条 文学和艺术作品的作者享有批准对其作品进行改编、整理和其他改变的专有权。

第十三条

一、本联盟每一成员国得就乐曲作者及允许歌词与乐曲一道录音的歌词作者对允许录制上述乐曲及乐曲连同歌词（如有歌词时）的专有权的保留及条件为本国作出规定；但这类保留及条件之效力严格限于对此作出规定的国家范围内，而且在任何情况下均不应损害作者获得在没有友好协议情况下由主管当局规定的公正报酬的权利。

二、根据1928年6月2日在罗马和1948年6月26日在布鲁塞尔签订的本公约文本**第十三条第三款**，在本联盟任何一成员国内录制的乐曲录音，自本条约文本在该国生效之日起两年内，可以不经乐曲作者同意在该国进行复制。

三、根据本条第一、二款制作的录音品，如未经利益关系人批准而输入认定此种录音属于违法行为的国家的，可在该国予以没收。

第十四条

一、文学和艺术作品的作者享有下述专有权：（一）许可把这类作品改编或复制成电影以及发行经改编或复制的作品；（二）许可公开演出演奏以及向公众作有线广播经改编或复制的作品。

二、根据文学或艺术作品制作的电影作品以任何其他形式进行改编，在不损害其作者批准权的情况下，仍须经原著作者批准。

三、第十三条第一款的规定不应适用。

第十四条之二

一、在不损害可能已经过改编或翻印的所有作品的版权的情况下，电影作品将作为原作品受到保护。电影作品版权所有者享有原作品作者的权利，包括前一条规定的权利。

二、a）向之提出保护要求的国家的法律有权决定电影作品版权的所有者。

b）然而，在其法律承认参加电影作品制作的作者应属于版权所有者的本联盟成员国内，这些作者，如果曾承担参加此项工作的义务，除非有相反或特别的规定，无权反对对电影作品的复制、发行、公开演出演奏、向公众有线广播、无线电广播、向公众发表、配制解说和配音。

c）为适用上面 b 项规定，上述义务是否应以书面合同或相当的书面文书规定的问题，由影片制片人所在地或居住地的本联盟成员国的法律加以规定。但向之提出保护要求的本联盟成员国有权规定这一义务应以书面合同或相当的书面文书予以确定。运用这一权利的国家应以书面声明通知总干事，并由后者将这一声明通知本联盟其他成员国。

d）“相反或特别的规定”是指附加于上述义务的限制性条件。

三、除非国内法另有规定，本条第二款 b 项之规定不适用于为电影作品创作的剧本、台词和音乐作品的作者，也不适用于电影作品的主要导演。但其法律并未规定对电影导演适用上述第二款 b 项的本联盟成员国，应以书面声明通知总干事，总干事应将此声明转达本联盟所有成员国。

第十四条之三

一、对于作家和作曲家的艺术原著和原稿，作者或作者死后由国家法律授权的人或机构，享有从作者第一次转让作品之后对作品的每次销售中分取盈利的不可剥夺的权利。

二、只有在作者国籍所属国法律允许的情况下，才可对本联盟某一成员国要求上款所规定的保护，而且保护的程度应限于向之提出保护要求的国家的法律所规定的程度。

三、征税的程序和税额由各国法律决定。

第十五条

一、只要受本公约保护的文学或艺术作品的作者以通常方式在该作品上署名，在没有相反证据的情况下，即视为该作品的作者，并有权在本联盟的成员国中对侵犯其权利的人提起诉讼。即使作者采用的是笔名，只要根据该笔名即能确定作者身份，本款也同样适用。

二、以通常方式在电影作品上署名的自然人或法人，除非有相反的证据，即假定为该作品的制片人。

三、对于不具名作品和上述第一款所述作品以外的笔名作品，如果出版者的名字出现在作品上，在没有相反证据的情况下，该出版者即视为作者的代表，并以此资格有权维护和行使作者的权利。当作者披露其身份并证实其为作者时，本款的规定即停止适用。

四、a）对作者的身份不明但有充分理由假定该作者是本联盟某一成员国国民的未发表作品，该国法律有权指定主管当局代表该作者并据此维护和行使作者在本联盟各成员国内的权利。

b）根据本规定而指定主管当局的本联盟成员国应以书面声明将此事通知总干事，声明中应写明被指定当局的全部有关情况。总干事应将此声明立即通知本联盟其他所有成员国。

第十六条

一、对于侵犯版权的一切作品，给予原著法律保护的本联盟任何成员国都可以予以没收。

二、上款规定同样适用于从不保护或停止保护某一作品的国家所进口的复制品。

三、没收应按各国法律实行。

第十七条　本公约的规定绝不妨碍本联盟每一成员国政府以立法或行政程序行使允许、监督或禁止任何作品或其制品的发行、演出或展出的权利，如果有关当局认为有必要对这些作品行使这种权利的话。

第十八条

一、本公约适用于在本公约开始生效时尚未因保护期满而在其起源国成为公共财产的所有作品。

二、但是，如果作品因原来给予的保护期满而在向之提出保护要求的国家成为公共财产，则该作品不再重新受该国保护。

三、本原则应当遵照本联盟成员国之间现在或将来缔结的专门条约的规定实行。在没有这种规定的情况下，各国可在本国范围内自行决定实行本原则的条件。

四、新加入本联盟时以及因适用第七条或放弃保留而扩大保护范围时，以上规定也同样适用。

第十九条　本公约的规定不妨碍要求本联盟某一成员国法律可能提供的更广泛的保护。

第二十条　本联盟各成员国政府有权在它们之间签订特别协议，以给予作者比本公约所规定的更多的权利，或者包括不违反本公约的其他条款。凡符合上述条件的现有协议的条款仍然适用。

第二十一条

一、有关发展中国家的特别条款载于附件。

二、在遵守第二十八条第一款 b 项规定的情况下，附件构成本文件的组成部分。

第二十二条

一、a）本联盟设一大会，由本联盟中受第二十二条至二十六条约束的成员国组成。

b）每一国家政府应有一名代表，辅以若干副代表、顾问及专家。

c）各代表团的费用由派遣国政府负担。

二、a）大会：

①处理有关维持及发展本联盟以及执行本公约的一切问题；

②适当考虑本联盟中不受第二十二至二十六条约束的成员国的意见，向成立世界知识产权组织（以下称“产权组织”）公约中提到的国际知识产权局（以下称“国际局”）发布有关筹备修订会议的指示；

③审查和批准本组织总干事有关本联盟的报告及活动，并就本联盟主管范围内的问题向他发布一切必要的指示；

④选举大会执行委员会委员；

⑤审查和批准执委员报告及活动，并向它发布指示；

⑥制订计划，通过本联盟三年期预算和批准财政决算；

⑦通过本联盟财务条例；

⑧设立为实现本联盟目标而需要的专家委员会和工作组；

⑨决定哪些非本联盟成员国和政府间的及非政府间的国际性组织以观察员身份参加它的会议；

⑩通过对第二十二条至第二十六条的修改；

⑪采取旨在达到本联盟目标的其他适当行动；

⑫行使本公约规定的其他所有职权；

⑬行使它所接受的成立产权组织公约所赋予它的权利。

b）就与产权组织管理的其他联盟的利益也有关的问题，大会在作决议时应考虑产权组织协调委员会的意见。

三、a）大会每一成员国有一票。

b）大会成员国的半数构成法定人数。

c）尽管有 b 项的规定，但在某一次会议上，出席国家不足半数但相当于或多于大会会员国三分之一，则大会可作出决议；但除有关大会议事规则之决议外，大会的决议须具备下列条件方能生效：国际局将上述决议通知未出席大会的成员国，请它们在上述通知发出时起三个月内用书面投票表示同意或反对或弃权。如果在期满时，用这样方式投票或弃权的国家数目达到会议法定人数所欠缺的数目，同时已获得必要的多数，上述决议即可生效。

d）在遵守第二十六条第二款规定的情况下，大会的决议以投票数三分之二的多数通过。

e）弃权不计入投票数。

f）一名代表只能代表一国，也只能以该国名义投票。

g）作为大会成员国的本联盟成员国以观察员身份参加会议。

四、a）大会每三年召开一次例会，由总干事召集，除特殊情况外，与产权组织的大会在同时同地举行。

b）大会特别会议在执行委员会的要求下或大会成员国四分之一的要求下由总干事召集。

五、大会通过其议事规则。

第二十三条

一、大会设执行委员会。

二、a）执委会由大会在其成员国中选出的国家组成。此外，产权组织总部所在地国在遵守第二十五条第七款 b 项规定的条件下，在执委会中有一当然席位。

b）执委会各成员国政府有一名代表，并辅以若干副代表、顾问和专家。

c）各代表团的费用由派遣国政府负担。

三、执委会成员国数目有大会成员国数目的四分之一。在计算席位数目时，以四相除剩下的余数不计算在内。

四、在选举执委会成员国时，大会要考虑到按地区公平分配和保证使与本联盟缔结特别协议的国家参加执委会的必要性。

五、a）执委会成员国的任期自它们当选的该届大会闭会时起至大会下届例会闭会时止。

b）执委会的成员国得连选连任，但其数目最多不得超过三分之二。

c）大会应制定执委会成员国选举和连选的细则。

六、a）执行委员会：

①拟订大会议事日程草案；

②向大会提交有关总干事草拟的本联盟的计划草案和三年期预算草案的建议；

③在计划和三年期预算的范围内，通过总干事草拟的年度计划和预算；

④向大会提交总干事的定期报告和财务决算年度报告，并附以必要的意见；

⑤根据大会决议并考虑到大会两届例会之间出现的情况，采取一切必要措施以保证总干事执行本联盟的计划；

⑥履行本公约赋予它的其他一切职能。

b）就与产权组织管理的其他联盟的利益也有关系的问题，执行委员会在作决定时应考虑产权组织协调委员会的意见。

七、a）执委会在总干事的召集下，每年举行一次例会，尽可能与产权组织协调委员会在同一时期和同一地点举行。

b）执委会在总干事召集下，或是由他倡议，或是应执委会主席或四分之一成员国的要求，可举行非常会议。

八、a）执委会每一成员国有一票表决权。

b）执委会成员国半数构成法定人数。

c）决定以所投票数中的简单多数票通过。

d）弃权不计入投票数。

e）一名代表只代表一国，并只能以该国名义投票。

九、非执委会成员国的本联盟成员国将以观察员身份参加其会议。

十、执行委员会通过其议事规则。

第二十四条

一、a）本联盟的行政任务由国际局执行，该局接替与保护工业产权国际公约设立的联盟局合并的本联盟局的工作。

b）国际局特别应担任本联盟不同机构的秘书处工作。

c）产权组织总干事是本联盟最高官员并代表本联盟。

二、国际局汇集并出版有关保护版权的资料，本联盟每一成员国应及时将有关保护版权的所有新法令及官方文本送交国际局。

三、国际局出版一种月刊。

四、国际局应本联盟成员国的请求，向它们提供有关保护版权问题的资料。

五、国际局从事各项研究工作并提供有利于版权保护的服务。

六、总干事及由他指派的任何工作人员得出席大会、执委会、其他各种专家委员会或工作组的会议，但无表决权。总干事或他指派的一位工作人员行使这些机构的秘书职务。

七、a）国际局根据大会指示并与执委会合作，筹备修订除第二十二条至第二十六条外的公约条款的会议。

b）国际局得就筹备修订会议与政府间和非政府间的国际组织协商。

c）总干事和他指定的人员可参加这些会议的工作，但无表决权。

八、国际局执行交付给它的其他任务。

第二十五条

一、a）本联盟设立一项预算。

b）本联盟的预算包括本联盟本身的收入及支出，它向各联盟共同开支预算的摊款，以及按规定交给产权组织会议预算支配的款项。

c）不专归本联盟的而同时又属于产权组织管理的另一个或其他几个联盟所有的开支，被认为是各联盟的共同开支。本联盟在共同开支中所占份额视这些开支与它的权益而定。

二、在制定本联盟的预算时，须适当考虑与产权组织管理的其他联盟的预算相协调。

三、本联盟预算由下列经费资助：

①联盟成员国的会费；

②因国际局提供与本联盟有关的服务而收的费用；

③销售与本联盟有关的国际局的出版物所得的款项及转让这些出版物的版权所得的版税；

④捐款、遗赠及补助金；

⑤租金、利息及其他杂项收入。

四、a）为确定成员国在预算中应缴的会费，本联盟每个成员国分别归入一定等级并根据下列所定数量单位缴纳每年的会费：

第一级……………………… 二十五个单位
第二级………………………… 二十个单位
第三级………………………… 十五个单位
第四级…………………………… 十个单位
第五级…………………………… 五个单位
第六级…………………………… 三个单位
第七级…………………………… 一个单位

b）除以前已经指明者外，每个国家在交存其批准书或加入书时，须说明它希望被列入哪一级别。任何国家也可以改变级别。如果某一成员国选择了较低的等级，它应在大会下一届会议上对此声明，这一变动自该届会议后的那一日历年开始时生效。

c）每个国家的年度会费金额在所有国家每年向本联盟预算交付的会费总数中所占比例，同它的单位数在全部交费国家的单位总数中所占比例相同。

d）会费应于每年一月一日交付。

e）逾期未交纳会费的国家，如拖欠总数相当于或超过前两整年内它应缴纳的会费数，则不得在它为其成员的本联盟一切机构中行使表决权。但如：本联盟任何机构确认这种拖欠是由非常的及不可避免的情况造成的，则仍可允许该国继续行使其表决权。

f）如在新的会计年度开始前预算尚未通过，则可按照财务条例规定的制度，以前一年度的水平实行预算。

五、因国际局提供与本联盟有关的服务应交费用的金额由总干事加以规定，并由他向大会和执委会就此提出报告。

六、a）本联盟拥有一笔由每一会员国一次付款组成的周转基金。如基金不足，由大会决定增加。

b）每个国家首次缴纳上述基金的金额或负担增加该基金的份额应与基金建立或决定增加基金的当年该国缴纳会费数成比例。

c）付款的比例及条件由大会根据总干事的提议并征求产权组织协调委员会意见后决定。

七、a）产权组织与该组织总部所在地国签订的关于总部的协定应规定，如周转基金不足，可由该国垫款。垫款数和提供垫款的条件由该国和产权组织每次以具体协定加以规定。该国在其承担垫款义务期间，在执委会中占有一当然席位。

b）a 项所指国家和产权组织均有权以书面通知废除提供垫款的义务。这种废除自通知提出那一年底起三年后生效。

八、账目核查工作，根据财务条例规定的条件，由本联盟一个或几个成员国进行，或由大会指派并经它们同意的外部审计员进行。

第二十六条

一、所有大会成员国、执委会或总干事均可提出修改第二十二，二十三，二十四，二十五条及本条的建议。这些建议要在提交大会审查前至少六个月由总干事通知大会成员国。

二、对第一款所指各条的修正案应由大会通过。通过需要投票数的四分之三；但对第二十二条及本款的任何修改需经投票数的五分之四通过。

三、对第一款所提各条的任何修正案，至少要在总干事收到在修正案通过时为大会成员国的四分之三国家关于它们根据各自的宪法程序批准修正案的书面通知一个月后才能生效。以此种方式通过的对上述各条的修正案对修正案生效时为大会成员国的所有国家或在该日期之后成为大会成员国的国家具有约束力；但任何增加本联盟成员国财务义务的修正案只对已通知批准该修正案的国家有约束力。

第二十七条

一、本公约可进行修订，以便使之得到改进，从而使本联盟体制臻于完备。

二、为此目的，可相继在本联盟成员国内举行各该国代表的会议。

三、在遵守第二十六条有关修改第二十二至二十六条的规定的情况下，所有对本公约文本的修订，包括附件的修订，均需已投票数全体一致通过。

第二十八条

一、a）凡签署本公约文本的任何本联盟成员国均可批准本公约文本，如尚未签署，则可加入本公约文本。批准书或加入书交总干事保存。

b）本联盟任何成员国在其批准书或加入书中均可声明其批准或加入不适用于第一至第二十一条及附件；但如该国已根据附件第六条第一款作出声明，则它在上述文件中只能声明其批准或加入不适用于第一至第二十条。

c）凡根据 b 项已声明其批准或加入对该项所提各条不发生效力的本联盟任何成员国可在其后任何时候声明将其批准或加入的效力扩大到这些规定。这一声明交总干事保存。

二、a）第一至二十一条及附件在具备下述两条件三个月后生效：

①至少有五个本联盟成员国批准或加入本公约文本而未按照第一款 b 项作过声明；

②西班牙、美利坚合众国、法国和大不列颠及北爱尔兰联合王国已受到 1971 年 7 月 24 日在巴黎修订过的世界版权公约的约束。

b）对于交存批准书或加入书但未按第一款 b 项作过声明的各国，a 项规定的生效不应早于上述生效后三个月。

c）对于 b 项对之不适用的已批准或加入本公约文本的而又未按照第一款 b 项作过声明的本联盟任何成员国，第一至二十一条及附件在总干事通知交存该文件之日起三个月后生效，除非交存文件中注明更晚的日期。在后一情况下，第一至二十一条及附件则在注明的日期对该国生效。

d）a 和 c 项的规定不意味着附件第五条的适用。

三、对不管是否按照第一款 b 项作过声明而批准或加入本公约文本的任何本联盟成员国，第二十二至三十八条在总干事通知已交存批准书或加入书之日起三个月后生效，除非在交存文件中注明更晚的日期。在后一情况下，第二十二至三十八条则按注明的日期对该国生效。

第二十九条

一、任何非本联盟成员国可加入本公约文本并因之成为本公约的当事国一方和本联盟成员国。加入书交总干事保存。

二、a）在遵守b项规定的情况下，对任何非本联盟成员国，本公约在总干事发生其加入书交存的通知之日起三个月后生效，除非交存文件注明更晚的日期。在后一情况下，本公约则在注明的日期对该国生效。

b）如依a项规定的生效先于第二十八条第二款a项规定的第一至第二十一条和附件的生效，则在此间隔期间，上述国家将受被第一至第二十一条及附件所取代的本公约布鲁塞尔文本第一至二十条的约束。

第二十九条之二

不受本公约斯德哥尔摩文本第二十二至三十八条约束的任何国家，为能适用成立产权组织公约的第十四条第二款，其对该文本的批准或加入即意味着批准或加入斯德哥尔摩文本，但应受本文本第二十八条第一款b项的限制。

第三十条

一、除本条第二款，第二十八条第一款b项、第三十三条第二款以及附件允许的例外以外，批准或加入就当然意味着接受本公约的一切条款并享有本公约规定的一切利益。

二、a）凡批准或加入本公约文本的本联盟任何成员国，除附件第五条第二款规定者外，可保持它原来作出的保留的效力，条件是在交存其批准书或加入书时对此作出声明。

b）任何非本联盟成员国在加入本公约文本并在不违背附件第五条第二款的情况下，可以声明它准备以1896年在巴黎经过修订的本联盟1886年公约第五条的规定至少临时代替本公约文本有关翻译权的第八条，条件是这些规定指的仅为译成该国通用语文的翻译。在不违背附件第一条第六款b项的情况下，对于使用这一保留条件的国家为其起源国的作品的翻译权，本联盟任何成员国有权实行与后一国提供的相等的保护。

c）任何国家可随时通知总干事，收回这类保留。

第三十一条

一、任何国家可在其批准书或加入书中声明，或在以后随时书面通知总干事，本公约适用于其对外关系由该国负责的全部领域或声明或通知中指明的若干部分领域。

二、任何已作出此项声明或通知的国家可在任何时候通知总干事本公约不再适用于这些领域的全部或部分。

三、a）按照第一款作出的任何声明同载有该声明的文件中的批准书或加入书同日生效，根据该款作出的通知在总干事发出通知三个月后生效。

b）按照第二款作出的通知在总干事收到该通知十二个月后生效。

四、本条不得解释为包含本联盟某一成员国对另一成员国根据按第一款作出的声明在某一领域适用本公约的事实情势表示明示或默示的承认。

第三十二条

一、本文本在本联盟各成员国之间的关系方面和在它适用的范围内代替1886年9月9日的伯尔尼公约及其以后的修订文本。在未批准或未加入本文本的本联盟成员国关系中，以前生效的各文本全部或在本文本依前句的规定未代替的限度内保持其适用性。

二、成为本文本当事国的非本联盟成员国，在符合第三款规定的条件下，对于不受本文本约束的或虽受其约束但已作过第二十八条第一款b项规定的声明的本联盟任何成员国，适用此条例。上述国家承认，在同它们的关系上，本联盟该成员国。

①适用它成为其当事国的最新的本公约文本的规定，并且

②在符合附件第一条第六款规定的情况下，有权使保护与本文本规定的水平相适应。

三、在批准或加入本文本时作出附件所允许的某种保留的国家，在它与非本文本当事国的本联盟成员国的关系上，得适用附件中包含保留条款的规定，但以这些国家认可上述保留的适用为条件。

第三十三条

一、两个或两个以上本联盟成员国在解释或适用本公约方面发生争议，经谈判不能解决时，如果有关国家不能就其他解决办法达成协议，则其中任何一方均可根据国际法院规约的规定通过起诉将争端提交国际法院。起诉国应将交法院审理的争议通知国际局；国际局应将此事告知本联盟其他成员国。

二、任何国家在签署本文本或交存其批准书或加入书时，可声明它不受第一款规定的约束。在有关该国和本联盟其他任何成员国间的任何争端方面，第一款的规定不适用。

三、任何作了符合第二款规定的声明的国家，可随时通知总干事撤回其声明。

第三十四条

一、除第二十九条之二的情况外，任何国家在第一至二十一条及附件生效后，不得加入也不得批准本公约以前的各文本。

二、在第一至二十一条及附件生效后，任何国家不得根据附在斯德哥尔摩文本后的有关发展中国家的议定书第五条发表声明。

第三十五条

一、本公约无限期有效。

二、任何国家可通知总干事废除本文本。对本文本的废除即是废除以前的所有文本，废除只对该国有效，而对本联盟其他成员国，本公约继续有效并继续执行。

三、废除自总干事收到废除通知之日起算一年后生效。

四、一国自成为本联盟成员国之日起算未满五年者，不得行使本条规定之废除权。

第三十六条

一、本公约各参加国承担义务根据其宪法采取必要措施以保证本公约的执行。

二、不言而喻，一国在交存其批准书或加入书时，应能按照其本国法律执行本公约的规定。

第三十七条

一、a）本文本在不违背第二款指出的情况下，以英法两种文字签署一份，并交总干事保存。

b）总干事在与有关政府协商后，制订阿拉伯文、西班牙文、意大利文、德文与葡萄牙文的正式文本以及大会指定的其他文本。

c）在对不同文本的解释发生争议时，以法文本为准。

二、本文本开放供签字到 1972 年 1 月 31 日为止，在此日期以前，第一款 a 项提到的文本交存法兰西共和国政府。

三、总干事应将经过签字并经核实的本文本的两份副本转送本联盟各成员国政府，并可根据请求，转送任何其他国家的政府。

四、总干事并将本文本向联合国组织秘书处登记。

五、总干事将下列情况通知本联盟所有成员国政府：签字情况，批准书或加入书的交存，包括在这些文件中的或依据第二十八条第一款 c 项、第三十条第二款 a、b 项和第三十三条第二款而作出的声明的交存，本文本任何规定生效的情况，废除的通知和根据第三十条第二款 c 项、第三十一条第一款和第二款、第三十三条第三款和第三十八条第一款的通知以及附件中规定的通知。

第三十八条

一、凡未批准或未加入本文本以及不受斯德哥尔摩文本第二十二至二十六条约束的本联盟成员国，如它们愿意，均可在1975年4月26日前，行使上述各条规定的权利，有如受它们约束一样。任何希望行使上述权利之国家应为此目的向总干事交存一份书面通知，该通知自其签署之日起生效。直到上述期限届满为止，这些国家应视为大会成员国。

二、在本联盟成员国尚未全部成为产权组织成员国之前，产权组织国际局同时作为本联盟局进行工作，总干事即该局局长。

三、在本联盟所有成员国已成为产权组织成员国时，本联盟局的权利、义务和财产即归属产权组织国际局。

附件：

关于发展中国家特别规定

第一条

（一）根据联合国大会的惯例被视为发展中国家的任何缔约国，凡已批准或加入由本附件作为其组成部分的本公约文本，但由于其经济情况及社会或文化需要而又不能在当前采取恰当安排以确保对本文本规定的全部权利进行保护的，可在其交存批准书或加入书的同时，或依据附件第五条第一款c项规定，在以后任何日期，在向总干事提交的通知中声明，将利用附件第二条或第三条所规定的优惠，或这两条所规定的权益。它可以按照附件第五条第一款a项规定作出声明，以代替利用附件第二条所规定的优惠。

（二）a）按照第一款规定并在第一到二十一条及本附件依第二十八条第二款规定生效之日起算十年期满以前作出的任何此类声明，直到这一期限届满前均属有效。有关国家在该十年期限届满十五个月至三个月时间内得向总干事提交通知将此种声明全部或部分地每次续展十年。

b）按照第一款规定并在第一至二十一条及本附件依第二十八条第二款规定生效之日起算十年期满以后作出的任何声明，直到现行十年期满前均属有效。该种声明得按照a项第二句的规定予以延期。

（三）任何不再被视为第一款所指的发展中国家的本联盟成员国，无权继续第二款所规定的声明，也不管它收回其声明与否，该类国家在现行十年期满时，或在停止被视为发展中国家三年后（以后到期的期限为准）不能再利用第一款所指的优惠。

（四）根据第一款或第二款规定作出的声明有效期满时，依本附件规定已许可印制的并尚有存货的作品，可以继续发行至售完为止。

（五）受本文本规定约束并根据第三十一条第一款就使该文本适用其情况可能类似本条第一款所指国家情况的特殊领域作出声明或通知的任何国家，可就此领域作出第一款所指的声明或第二款所指的延期通知。只要这种声明或通知有效，本附件的规定就适用于它所指的领土。

（六）a）一国利用第一款所指的优惠这一事实，不应使另一国给予起源国为前一国家的作品低于根据第一至二十条所应给予的保护。

b）第三十条第二款 b 项第二句的规定的对等权利，在根据附件第一条第三款实施的期限满期前，不得用于其起源国为根据附件第五条第一款 a 项而作出声明的国家的作品。

第二条

（一）任何声明利用本条规定的优惠的国家，就有关以印刷形式或其他任何类似的复制形式出版的作品而言，均有权以主管当局根据附件第四条在下款所述情况下发给的非专有和不可转让的许可证的制度来代替第八条规定的专有翻译权。

（二）a）在遵守第三款的情况下，当一部作品自其初次出版起算三年或有关国家本国法规定的更长期限届满尚未以该国通行文字由翻译权所有者或在其授权下出版译本时，该国任何国民都有权得到用该国通行文字翻译该作品并以印刷形式或其他任何类似的复制形式出版该译文的许可证。

b）如果以有关文字出版的译文的所有版本均已售完，也可根据本条发给许可证。

（三）a）当作品译成在一个或若干发达的本联盟成员国中不通行的文字的情况下，则用一年期限来代替第二款 a 项规定的三年期限。

b）在通行同一种文字的发达的本联盟成员国的一致协议下，如果要译成这种文字，第一款所提到的任何国家均得以该协议规定的更短期限来代替第二款 a 项规定的三年期限，但不得少于一年。尽管如此，如涉及的文字为英文、西班牙文或法文，上一句规定即不适用。所有这方面的协议应由签订国政府通知总干事。

（四）本条规定的许可证，如果经过三年才能取得的，则需再过六个月才能发给；如果经一年才能取得的，则需再过九个月才能发给，并且，上述六个月或九个月期限：

①自申请人履行附件第四条第一款规定的手续之日起算；

②如翻译权所有者的身份或住址不详，则自申请人根据附件第四条第二

款的规定向发给许可证的主管部门提交的申请书副本寄出之日起算。

b）如果在6个月或9个月的期限内，由翻译权所有者或经其授权用申请使用的文字将译本出版，则不得根据本条发给任何许可证。

（五）本条所指的任何许可证之发给只限于学校、大学教育或研究之用。

（六）如果翻译权所有者或经其授权出版的一部译作的价格同在有关国家内同类著作通行的价格类似，这本译作的文字和基本内容又同根据许可证批准出版的译文的文字和内容一样，则应撤销缔约国根据本条发给的许可证。在撤销许可证前业已出版的份数可一直发行到售完为止。

（七）对主要是图画组成的作品，其文字翻译与图画复制出版的许可证只有在附件第三条规定的条件得到履行的情况下才能发给。

（八）在作者停止其作品全部份数的发行时，则不得根据本条发给任何许可证。

（九）a）对翻译一部以印刷形式或其他任何类似的复制形式出版的作品发给的许可证：也可根据广播机构向第一款所指国家主管当局提出的要求，发给设置在该国内的广播机构，但必须符合全部下列条件：

①译文的根据必须是依该国法律制作和获得的样本；

②译文只能用于教学广播或向特定专业的专家传播科技情报成果的广播；

③专门为②小项所指目的的译文，需用于合法的和对该国领土上的收听者的广播中，其中包括合法的和专为此项广播而录制的录音和录像；

④所有对译文的使用均无任何营利性质。

b）对广播机构根据依本款发给的许可证而制作的译文的录音或录像，在a项规定的保留和条件下，并按与上述广播机构所订合同，也可以为在其当局发给该许可证的国家设有所在地的另一广播机构所使用。

c）只要a项列举的所有准则和条件得到遵守，也可以向广播机构颁发翻译专为学校和大学使用而制作与出版的视听教材中所有课文的许可证。

d）在不违背a到c项的情况下，本条前几款的规定也适用于根据本款发给的任何许可证和对许可证的作用。

第三条

（一）任何声明利用本条规定的优惠的国家，均有权以主管当局在下述条件下并根据附件第四条发给的非专有和不可转让的许可证制度来代替第九条规定的专有复制权。

（二）a）对于根据第七款而对之适用本条的作品，当

①第三款规定的自这一作品特定版首次出版时起草的期限满期后，或

②由第一款所指的国家本国法律规定的并自同一日期起草的更长的期限满期后，若该版的印制件尚未以与同类著作在该国通行的价格相似的价格由复制权所有者或在他授权下在该国出售，从而，未能满足广大公众或学校及大学教学之需要，则该国任何国民均可取得以同等价格或更低价格复制和出版该版本的许可证，以满足学校及大学教学之需要。

b）根据本条规定之条件，又可对复制及出版符合 a 项规定发行的版本发给许可证，如果在适用期限满期后，该版本被批准的印制件在有关国家已脱销六个月，而无法以与该国同类著作通行价格相似的价格满足广大公众或学校及大学教学的需要。

（三）第二款 a 项①小项所指的期限为五年。但

①对有关精密科学和自然科学以及技术的作品，则为三年；

②对属于想象领域的作品，如小说、诗歌、戏剧和音乐作品以及艺术书籍，则为七年。

（四）a）在三年期满后取得许可证的情况下，须再经过六个月期限满期后才能根据本条发给许可证：

①自申请人履行附件第四条第一款规定的手续之日起算；

②如复制权所有者的身份或住址不详，则自申请人按附件第四条第二款的规定将许可证申请书副本寄给主管当局之日起算。

b）在其他情况下如适用附件第四条第二款时，许可证不得在寄出申请书副本后三个月期满以前发给。

c）如在 a 项和 b 项规定的六个月或三个月期间，已实现第二款 a 项提到的销售则不得根据本条发给任何许可证。

d）在作者已停止发行为进行复制及出版而申请许可证的作品版本的全部份数时，不得发给许可证。

（五）为复制和出版一本作品的译本的许可证，在下述情况下不得根据本条发给：

①所涉及的译本并非由翻译权所有者或在其授权下出版的；

②译本所用的不是向之申请许可证的国家通行的语文的。

（六）如某一作品的版本的印制件以同该国同类著作的通行价格相似的价格，为满足广大公众或学校及大学教学需要，而在第一款所指的国内由复制权所有者或经其授权出售，而该版本的文字和基本内容又同根据许可证批准出版的版本的文字和内容相同，则应撤销根据本条发给的任何许可证。在撤销许可证前业已发行的所有份数可一直发行到售完止。

（七）a）除b项规定的情况外，本条适用的作品只能是以印刷的形式或任何其他类似的复制形式出版的作品。

b）本条同样适用于对包括被保护作品的合法制作的录像或录音的复制以及对附在其上的用向之申请许可证国通行语文印行的译文的复制，条件是所涉及的录像或录音的制作和出版需以学校和大学使用为唯一目的。

第四条

（一）附件第二条或第三条所指的任何许可证只有在下述情况下才能发给：申请人按照有关国家的现行规定，证明已向权利所有者视不同情况提出翻译和出版译本，或复制和出版版本的要求，而又未能得到批准，或经过相当努力仍未能找到权利所有者。在向权利所有者提出这一申请的同时，申请人还必须把这一申请通知第二款提及的国内或国际情报中心。

（二）如申请人无法找到权利所有者，即应将其向发给许可证提及的主管当局提交的申请书副本挂号寄给该作品上列有名称的出版者和据信为出版商主要业务中心所在国的政府为此目的向总干事递交的通知所指定的任何国内或国际情报中心。

（三）在根据附件第二条和第三条发给的许可证出版的译本或复制本的所有印制件上都应列出作者姓名。在所有印制件上应有作品名称。如系译本，原著作名称在任何情况下应列于所有印制件上。

（四）a）任何根据附件第二条或第三条发给的许可证不得扩大到印制件的出口，它只适用于在发给许可证的国家领域内出版的译本或复制本。

b）为施行a项规定，凡从任何一领土向根据附件第一条第五款规定代表该领土作过声明的国家运寄印制件应视作出口。

c）当根据附件第二条就译成英文、西班牙文或法文以外语文的译本发给许可证的一国政府机构或其他公共机构将根据该许可证出版的译本的印制件寄到另一国时，这一寄送不视为a项所禁止的出口，但需符合以下所有条件：

①收件人需是发给许可证的主管当局所属国的国民或由这些国民组成的组织；

②印制件只供学校、大学或科学研究使用；

③寄往收件人的印制件及其进一步分发均无任何营利性质；而且

④印制件寄往国与其主管当局发给批准接收或分发或两者同时批准的许可证的国家已订有协议，并且后者已将该协议通知总干事。

（五）任何根据按附件第二条或第三条发给的许可证出版的印制件均须载有适当语文的通知，说明该印制件只能在该许可证适用的国家或领土内发行。

（六）a）以国内程序采取适当措施，以使

①许可证规定根据不同情况向翻译权或复制权所有者支付公平的报酬，其数额相当于两国有关方面在通过谈判给予许可证情况下正常支付的版税费率；而且

②保证这笔报酬的支付和转汇；如果存在着国家对外汇的管制，则主管当局将求助于国际机构，以便尽一切努力保证使这笔报酬转换为国际上可兑换的货币或其等价物。

b）将以国内立法程序采取适当措施以便按照不同情况保证作品翻译和复制的准确性。

第五条

（一）a）任何有权声明将利用附件第二条规定的优惠的国家，在批准或加入本文本时，可不作这一声明，而代之以：

①按照第三十条第二款 a 项有关翻译权的规定作一声明，如果它是第三十条第二款 a 项对之适用的国家的话；

②按照第三十条第二款 b 项第一句的规定作一声明，如果它是第三十条第二款 a 项对之不适用的国家，甚至并不是本联盟成员国的话。

b）在一国已不再被视为是附件第一条第一款所指的发展中国家的情况下，根据本款所作的声明继续有效，直至按照附件第一条第三款规定的实施期限满期之日为止。

c）任何按照本款作出声明的国家不得进一步利用附件第二条规定的优惠，即使它将收回该项声明。

（二）除第三款的情况外，任何已利用附件第二条规定的优惠的国家不得再根据第一款作出声明。

（三）不再被视为附件第一条第一款所指的发展中国家的任何国家，在根据附件第一条第三款的实施期限满期前最迟两年，可以按照第三十条第二款 b 项第一句作出声明，即使它并不是本联盟成员国。这一声明将在根据附件第一条第三款的实施期限满期之日生效。

第六条

（一）本联盟任何成员国，自本文本生效之日起和在受到第一至二十一条和附件的约束以前的任何时候都可以声明：

①对于如果受第一至二十一条和本附件约束，即有权利用第一条第一款提到的优惠的国家而言，可声明它将对其起源国为如下国家的作品适用附件

第二条或第三条或同时适用两条的规定。这一国家在适用下面②小项时，同意把上述两条适用于这类作品或受第一至二十一条及本附件约束；这一声明可以援引附件第五条而不是第二条；

②可声明它同意将本附件适用于其起源国为根据上述①小项而作过声明或根据附件第一条而提出过通知的国家的作品。

（二）任何按第一款的声明均应以书面形式作出并交存总干事。声明自交存之日起生效。

Berne Convention for the Protection of Literary and Artistic Works

Paris Act of July 24, 1971, as amended on September 28,
1979 Berne Convention for the Protection of
Literary and Artistic Works of September 9, 1886,
completed at PARIS on May 4, 1896,
revised at BERLIN on November 13, 1908,
completed at BERNE on March 20, 1914,
revised at ROME on June 2, 1928,
at BRUSSELS on June 26, 1948,
at STOCKHOLM on July 14, 1967, and
at PARIS on July 24, 1971,
and amended on September 28, 1979

The countries of the Union, being equally animated by the desire to protect, in as effective and uniform a manner as possible, the rights of authors in their literary and artistic works,

Recognizing the importance of the work of the Revision Conference held at Stockholm in 1967,

Have resolved to revise the Act adopted by the Stockholm Conference, while maintaining without change Articles 1 to 20 and 22 to 26 of that Act.

Consequently, the undersigned Plenipotentiaries, having presented their full powers, recognized as in good and due form, have agreed as follows:

Article 1

[*Establishment of a Union*] 1

1 Each Article and the Appendix have been given titles to facilitate their identification. There are no titles in the signed (English) text.

The countries to which this Convention applies constitute a Union for the protection of the rights of authors in their literary and artistic works.

Article 2

[*Protected Works*: 1. "Literary and artistic works"; 2. Possible requirement of fixation; 3. Derivative works; 4. Official texts; 5. Collections; 6. Obligation to protect; beneficiaries of protection; 7. Works of applied art and industrial designs; 8. News]

(1) The expression "literary and artistic works" shall include every production in the literary, scientific and artistic domain, whatever may be the mode or form of its expression, such as books, pamphlets and other writings; lectures, addresses, sermons and other works of the same nature; dramatic or dramatico - musical works; choreographic works and entertainments in dumb show; musical compositions with or without words; cinematographic works to which are assimilated works expressed by a process analogous to cinematography; works of drawing, painting, architecture, sculpture, engraving and lithography; photographic works to which are assimilated works expressed by a process analogous to photography; works of applied art; illustrations, maps, plans, sketches and three - dimensional works relative to geography, topography, architecture or science.

(2) It shall, however, be a matter for legislation in the countries of the Union to prescribe that works in general or any specified categories of works shall not be protected unless they have been fixed in some material form.

(3) Translations, adaptations, arrangements of music and other alterations of a literary or artistic work shall be protected as original works without prejudice to the copyright in the original work.

(4) It shall be a matter for legislation in the countries of the Union to determine the protection to be granted to official texts of a legislative, administrative and legal nature, and to official translations of such texts.

(5) Collections of literary or artistic works such as encyclopaedias and anthologies which, by reason of the selection and arrangement of their contents, constitute intellectual creations shall be protected as such, without prejudice to the copyright in each of the works forming part of such collections.

(6) The works mentioned in this Article shall enjoy protection in all countries of the Union. This protection shall operate for the benefit of the author and his

successors in title.

(7) Subject to the provisions of Article 7 (4) of this Convention, it shall be a matter for legislation in the countries of the Union to determine the extent of the application of their laws to works of applied art and industrial designs and models, as well as the conditions under which such works, designs and models shall be protected. Works protected in the country of origin solely as designs and models shall be entitled in another country of the Union only to such special protection as is granted in that country to designs and models; however, if no such special protection is granted in that country, such works shall be protected as artistic works.

(8) The protection of this Convention shall not apply to news of the day or to miscellaneous facts having the character of mere items of press information.

Article 2_{bis}

[*Possible Limitation of Protection of Certain Works*: 1. Certain speeches; 2. Certain uses of lectures and addresses; 3. Right to make collections of such works]

(1) It shall be a matter for legislation in the countries of the Union to exclude, wholly or in part, from the protection provided by the preceding Article political speeches and speeches delivered in the course of legal proceedings.

(2) It shall also be a matter for legislation in the countries of the Union to determine the conditions under which lectures, addresses and other works of the same nature which are delivered in public may be reproduced by the press, broadcast, communicated to the public by wire and made the subject of public communication as envisaged in Article 11bis (1) of this Convention, when such use is justified by the informatory purpose.

(3) Nevertheless, the author shall enjoy the exclusive right of making a collection of his works mentioned in the preceding paragraphs.

Article 3

[*Criteria of Eligibility for Protection*: 1. Nationality of author; place of publication of work; 2. Residence of author; 3. "Published" works; 4. "Simultaneously published" works]

(1) The protection of this Convention shall apply to:

(a) authors who are nationals of one of the countries of the Union, for their works, whether published or not;

(b) authors who are not nationals of one of the countries of the Union, for their works first published in one of those countries, or simultaneously in a country outside the Union and in a country of the Union.

(2) Authors who are not nationals of one of the countries of the Union but who have their habitual residence in one of them shall, for the purposes of this Convention, be assimilated to nationals of that country.

(3) The expression "published works" means works published with the consent of their authors, whatever may be the means of manufacture of the copies, provided that the availability of such copies has been such as to satisfy the reasonable requirements of the public, having regard to the nature of the work. The performance of a dramatic, dramatico - musical, cinematographic or musical work, the public recitation of a literary work, the communication by wire or the broadcasting of literary or artistic works, the exhibition of a work of art and the construction of a work of architecture shall not constitute publication.

(4) A work shall be considered as having been published simultaneously in several countries if it has been published in two or more countries within thirty days of its first publication.

Article 4

[*Criteria of Eligibility for Protection of Cinematographic Works, Works of Architecture and Certain Artistic Works*]

The protection of this Convention shall apply, even if the conditions of Article 3 are not fulfilled, to:

(a) authors of cinematographic works the maker of which has his headquarters or habitual residence in one of the countries of the Union;

(b) authors of works of architecture erected in a country of the Union or of other artistic works incorporated in a building or other structure located in a country of the Union.

Article 5

[*Rights Guaranteed*: 1. and 2. Outside the country of origin; 3. In the country of origin; 4. "Country of origin"]

(1) Authors shall enjoy, in respect of works for which they are protected under this Convention, in countries of the Union other than the country of origin, the rights which their respective laws do now or may hereafter grant to their nationals, as well as the rights specially granted by this Convention.

(2) The enjoyment and the exercise of these rights shall not be subject to any formality; such enjoyment and such exercise shall be independent of the existence of protection in the country of origin of the work. Consequently, apart from the provisions of this Convention, the extent of protection, as well as the means of redress afforded to the author to protect his rights, shall be governed exclusively by the laws of the country where protection is claimed.

(3) Protection in the country of origin is governed by domestic law. However, when the author is not a national of the country of origin of the work for which he is protected under this Convention, he shall enjoy in that country the same rights as national authors.

(4) The country of origin shall be considered to be:

(a) in the case of works first published in a country of the Union, that country; in the case of works published simultaneously in several countries of the Union which grant different terms of protection, the country whose legislation grants the shortest term of protection;

(b) in the case of works published simultaneously in a country outside the Union and in a country of the Union, the latter country;

(c) in the case of unpublished works or of works first published in a country outside the Union, without simultaneous publication in a country of the Union, the country of the Union of which the author is a national, provided that:

(i) when these are cinematographic works the maker of which has his headquarters or his habitual residence in a country of the Union, the country of origin shall be that country, and

(ii) when these are works of architecture erected in a country of the Union or other artistic works incorporated in a building or other structure located in a country of the Union, the country of origin shall be that country.

Article 6

[*Possible Restriction of Protection in Respect of Certain Works of Nationals of Certain Countries Outside the Union*: 1. In the country of the first publication and in other countries; 2. No retroactivity; 3. Notice]

(1) Where any country outside the Union fails to protect in an adequate manner the works of authors who are nationals of one of the countries of the Union, the latter country may restrict the protection given to the works of authors who are,

at the date of the first publication thereof, nationals of the other country and are not habitually resident in one of the countries of the Union. If the country of first publication avails itself of this right, the other countries of the Union shall not be required to grant to works thus subjected to special treatment a wider protection than that granted to them in the country of first publication.

(2) No restrictions introduced by virtue of the preceding paragraph shall affect the rights which an author may have acquired in respect of a work published in a country of the Union before such restrictions were put into force.

(3) The countries of the Union which restrict the grant of copyright in accordance with this Article shall give notice thereof to the Director General of the World Intellectual Property Organization (hereinafter designated as "the Director General") by a written declaration specifying the countries in regard to which protection is restricted, and the restrictions to which rights of authors who are nationals of those countries are subjected. The Director General shall immediately communicate this declaration to all the countries of the Union.

Article 6bis

[*Moral Rights*: 1. To claim authorship; to object to certain modifications and other derogatory actions; 2. After the author's death; 3. Means of redress]

(1) Independently of the author's economic rights, and even after the transfer of the said rights, the author shall have the right to claim authorship of the work and to object to any distortion, mutilation or other modification of, or other derogatory action in relation to, the said work, which would be prejudicial to his honor or reputation.

(2) The rights granted to the author in accordance with the preceding paragraph shall, after his death, be maintained, at least until the expiry of the economic rights, and shall be exercisable by the persons or institutions authorized by the legislation of the country where protection is claimed. However, those countries whose legislation, at the moment of their ratification of or accession to this Act, does not provide for the protection after the death of the author of all the rights set out in the preceding paragraph may provide that some of these rights may, after his death, cease to be maintained.

(3) The means of redress for safeguarding the rights granted by this Article shall be governed by the legislation of the country where protection is claimed.

Article 7

[*Term of Protection*: 1. Generally; 2. For cinematographic works; 3. For anonymous and pseudonymous works; 4. For photographic works and works of applied art; 5. Starting date of computation; 6. Longer terms; 7. Shorter terms; 8. Applicable law; "comparison" of terms]

(1) The term of protection granted by this Convention shall be the life of the author and fifty years after his death.

(2) However, in the case of cinematographic works, the countries of the Union may provide that the term of protection shall expire fifty years after the work has been made available to the public with the consent of the author, or, failing such an event within fifty years from the making of such a work, fifty years after the making.

(3) In the case of anonymous or pseudonymous works, the term of protection granted by this Convention shall expire fifty years after the work has been lawfully made available to the public. However, when the pseudonym adopted by the author leaves no doubt as to his identity, the term of protection shall be that provided in paragraph (1). If the author of an anonymous or pseudonymous work discloses his identity during the above - mentioned period, the term of protection applicable shall be that provided in paragraph (1). The countries of the Union shall not be required to protect anonymous or pseudonymous works in respect of which it is reasonable to presume that their author has been dead for fifty years.

(4) It shall be a matter for legislation in the countries of the Union to determine the term of protection of photographic works and that of works of applied art in so far as they are protected as artistic works; however, this term shall last at least until the end of a period of twenty - five years from the making of such a work.

(5) The term of protection subsequent to the death of the author and the terms provided by paragraph (2), paragraph (3) and paragraph (4) shall run from the date of death or of the event referred to in those paragraphs, but such terms shall always be deemed to begin on the first of January of the year following the death or such event.

(6) The countries of the Union may grant a term of protection in excess of those provided by the preceding paragraphs.

(7) Those countries of the Union bound by the Rome Act of this Convention

which grant, in their national legislation in force at the time of signature of the present Act, shorter terms of protection than those provided for in the preceding paragraphs shall have the right to maintain such terms when ratifying or acceding to the present Act.

(8) In any case, the term shall be governed by the legislation of the country where protection is claimed; however, unless the legislation of that country otherwise provides, the term shall not exceed the term fixed in the country of origin of the work.

Article 7 $_{bis}$

[*Term of Protection for Works of Joint Authorship*]

The provisions of the preceding Article shall also apply in the case of a work of joint authorship, provided that the terms measured from the death of the author shall be calculated from the death of the last surviving author.

Article 8

[*Right of Translation*]

Authors of literary and artistic works protected by this Convention shall enjoy the exclusive right of making and of authorizing the translation of their works throughout the term of protection of their rights in the original works.

Article 9

[*Right of Reproduction*: 1. Generally; 2. Possible exceptions; 3. Sound and visual recordings]

(1) Authors of literary and artistic works protected by this Convention shall have the exclusive right of authorizing the reproduction of these works, in any manner or form.

(2) It shall be a matter for legislation in the countries of the Union to permit the reproduction of such works in certain special cases, provided that such reproduction does not conflict with a normal exploitation of the work and does not unreasonably prejudice the legitimate interests of the author.

(3) Any sound or visual recording shall be considered as a reproduction for the purposes of this Convention.

Article 10

[*Certain Free Uses of Works*: 1. Quotations; 2. Illustrations for teaching; 3. Indication of source and author]

(1) It shall be permissible to make quotations from a work which has already been lawfully made available to the public, provided that their making is compatible with fair practice, and their extent does not exceed that justified by the purpose, including quotations from newspaper articles and periodicals in the form of press summaries.

(2) It shall be a matter for legislation in the countries of the Union, and for special agreements existing or to be concluded between them, to permit the utilization, to the extent justified by the purpose, of literary or artistic works by way of illustration in publications, broadcasts or sound or visual recordings for teaching, provided such utilization is compatible with fair practice.

(3) Where use is made of works in accordance with the preceding paragraphs of this Article, mention shall be made of the source, and of the name of the author if it appears thereon.

Article 10bis

[*Further Possible Free Uses of Works*: 1. Of certain articles and broadcast works; 2. Of works seen or heard in connection with current events]

(1) It shall be a matter for legislation in the countries of the Union to permit the reproduction by the press, the broadcasting or the communication to the public by wire of articles published in newspapers or periodicals on current economic, political or religious topics, and of broadcast works of the same character, in cases in which the reproduction, broadcasting or such communication thereof is not expressly reserved. Nevertheless, the source must always be clearly indicated; the legal consequences of a breach of this obligation shall be determined by the legislation of the country where protection is claimed.

(2) It shall also be a matter for legislation in the countries of the Union to determine the conditions under which, for the purpose of reporting current events by means of photography, cinematography, broadcasting or communication to the public by wire, literary or artistic works seen or heard in the course of the event may, to the extent justified by the informatory purpose, be reproduced and made available to the public.

Article 11

[*Certain Rights in Dramatic and Musical Works*: 1. Right of public performance and of communication to the public of a performance; 2. In respect of translations]

(1) Authors of dramatic, dramatico - musical and musical works shall enjoy the exclusive right of authorizing:

(i) the public performance of their works, including such public performance by any means or process;

(ii) any communication to the public of the performance of their works.

(2) Authors of dramatic or dramatico - musical works shall enjoy, during the full term of their rights in the original works, the same rights with respect to translations thereof.

Article 11 bis

[*Broadcasting and Related Rights*: 1. Broadcasting and other wireless communications, public communication of broadcast by wire or rebroadcast, public communication of broadcast by loudspeaker or analogous instruments; 2. Compulsory licenses; 3. Recording; ephemeral recordings]

(1) Authors of literary and artistic works shall enjoy the exclusive right of authorizing:

(i) the broadcasting of their works or the communication thereof to the public by any other means of wireless diffusion of signs, sounds or images;

(ii) any communication to the public by wire or by rebroadcasting of the broadcast of the work, when this communication is made by an organization other than the original one;

(iii) the public communication by loudspeaker or any other analogous instrument transmitting, by signs, sounds or images, the broadcast of the work.

(2) It shall be a matter for legislation in the countries of the Union to determine the conditions under which the rights mentioned in the paragraph 1 may be exercised, but these conditions shall apply only in the countries where they have been prescribed. They shall not in any circumstances be prejudicial to the moral rights of the author, nor to his right to obtain equitable remuneration which, in the absence of agreement, shall be fixed by competent authority.

(3) In the absence of any contrary stipulation, permission granted in accordance with paragraph (1) of this Article shall not imply permission to record, by means of instruments recording sounds or images, the work broadcast. It shall, however, be a matter for legislation in the countries of the Union to determine the regulations for ephemeral recordings made by a broadcasting organization by

means of its own facilities and used for its own broadcasts. The preservation of these recordings in official archives may, on the ground of their exceptional documentary character, be authorized by such legislation.

Article 11 ter

[*Certain Rights in Literary Works*: 1. Right of public recitation and of communication to the public of a recitation; 2. In respect of translations]

(1) Authors of literary works shall enjoy the exclusive right of authorizing:

(i) the public recitation of their works, including such public recitation by any means or process;

(ii) any communication to the public of the recitation of their works.

(2) Authors of literary works shall enjoy, during the full term of their rights in the original works, the same rights with respect to translations thereof.

Article 12

[*Right of Adaptation, Arrangement and Other Alteration*]

Authors of literary or artistic works shall enjoy the exclusive right of authorizing adaptations, arrangements and other alterations of their works.

Article 13

[*Possible Limitation of the Right of Recording of Musical Works and Any Words Pertaining Thereto*: 1. *Compulsory licenses*; 2. *Transitory measures*; 3. Seizure on importation of copies made without the author's permission]

(1) Each country of the Union may impose for itself reservations and conditions on the exclusive right granted to the author of a musical work and to the author of any words, the recording of which together with the musical work has already been authorized by the latter, to authorize the sound recording of that musical work, together with such words, if any; but all such reservations and conditions shall apply only in the countries which have imposed them and shall not, in any circumstances, be prejudicial to the rights of these authors to obtain equitable remuneration which, in the absence of agreement, shall be fixed by competent authority.

(2) Recordings of musical works made in a country of the Union in accordance with Article 13 (3) of the Conventions signed at Rome on June 2, 1928, and at Brussels on June 26, 1948, may be reproduced in that country without the permission of the author of the musical work until a date two years after that country be-

comes bound by this Act.

(3) Recordings made in accordance with paragraph (1) and paragraph (2) of this Article and imported without permission from the parties concerned into a country where they are treated as infringing recordings shall be liable to seizure.

Article 14

[*Cinematographic and Related Rights*: 1. Cinematographic adaptation and reproduction; distribution; public performance and public communication by wire of works thus adapted or reproduced; 2. Adaptation of cinematographic productions; 3. No compulsory licenses]

(1) Authors of literary or artistic works shall have the exclusive right of authorizing:

(i) the cinematographic adaptation and reproduction of these works, and the distribution of the works thus adapted or reproduced;

(ii) the public performance and communication to the public by wire of the works thus adapted or reproduced.

(2) The adaptation into any other artistic form of a cinematographic production derived from literary or artistic works shall, without prejudice to the authorization of the author of the cinematographic production, remain subject to the authorization of the authors of the original works.

(3) The provisions of Article 13 (1) shall not apply.

Article 14 bis

[*Special Provisions Concerning Cinematographic Works*: 1. Assimilation to "original" works; 2. Ownership; limitation of certain rights of certain contributors; 3. Certain other contributors]

(1) Without prejudice to the copyright in any work which may have been adapted or reproduced, a cinematographic work shall be protected as an original work. The owner of copyright in a cinematographic work shall enjoy the same rights as the author of an original work, including the rights referred to in the preceding Article.

(2)

(a) Ownership of copyright in a cinematographic work shall be a matter for legislation in the country where protection is claimed.

(b) However, in the countries of the Union which, by legislation, include among the owners of copyright in a cinematographic work authors who have brought contributions to the making of the work, such authors, if they have undertaken to bring such contributions, may not, in the absence of any contrary or special stipulation, object to the reproduction, distribution, public performance, communication to the public by wire, broadcasting or any other communication to the public, or to the subtitling or dubbing of texts, of the work.

(c) The question whether or not the form of the undertaking referred to above should, for the application of the preceding subparagraph (b), be in a written agreement or a written act of the same effect shall be a matter for the legislation of the country where the maker of the cinematographic work has his headquarters or habitual residence. However, it shall be a matter for the legislation of the country of the Union where protection is claimed to provide that the said undertaking shall be in a written agreement or a written act of the same effect. The countries whose legislation so provides shall notify the Director General by means of a written declaration, which will be immediately communicated by him to all the other countries of the Union.

(d) By "contrary or special stipulation" is meant any restrictive condition which is relevant to the aforesaid undertaking.

(3) Unless the national legislation provides to the contrary, the provisions of paragraph (2) (b) above shall not be applicable to authors of scenarios, dialogues and musical works created for the making of the cinematographic work, or to the principal director thereof. However, those countries of the Union whose legislation does not contain rules providing for the application of the said paragraph (2) (b) to such director shall notify the Director General by means of a written declaration, which will be immediately communicated by him to all the other countries of the Union.

Article 14ter

[*"Droit de suite" in Works of Art and Manuscripts*: 1. Right to an interest in resales; 2. Applicable law; 3. Procedure]

(1) The author, or after his death the persons or institutions authorized by national legislation, shall, with respect to original works of art and original manuscripts of writers and composers, enjoy the inalienable right to an interest in any sale of the work subsequent to the first transfer by the author of the work.

(2) The protection provided by the preceding paragraph may be claimed in a country of the Union only if legislation in the country to which the author belongs so permits, and to the extent permitted by the country where this protection is claimed.

(3) The procedure for collection and the amounts shall be matters for determination by national legislation.

Article 15

[*Right to Enforce Protected Rights*: 1. Where author's name is indicated or where pseudonym leaves no doubt as to author's identity; 2. In the case of cinematographic works; 3. In the case of anonymous and pseudonymous works; 4. In the case of certain unpublished works of unknown authorship]

(1) In order that the author of a literary or artistic work protected by this Convention shall, in the absence of proof to the contrary, be regarded as such, and consequently be entitled to institute infringement proceedings in the countries of the Union, it shall be sufficient for his name to appear on the work in the usual manner. This paragraph shall be applicable even if this name is a pseudonym, where the pseudonym adopted by the author leaves no doubt as to his identity.

(2) The person or body corporate whose name appears on a cinematographic work in the usual manner shall, in the absence of proof to the contrary, be presumed to be the maker of the said work.

(3) In the case of anonymous and pseudonymous works, other than those referred to in paragraph (1) above, the publisher whose name appears on the work shall, in the absence of proof to the contrary, be deemed to represent the author, and in this capacity he shall be entitled to protect and enforce the author's rights. The provisions of this paragraph shall cease to apply when the author reveals his identity and establishes his claim to authorship of the work.

(4) (a) In the case of unpublished works where the identity of the author is unknown, but where there is every ground to presume that he is a national of a country of the Union, it shall be a matter for legislation in that country to designate the competent authority which shall represent the author and shall be entitled to protect and enforce his rights in the countries of the Union.

(b) Countries of the Union which make such designation under the terms of this provision shall notify the Director General by means of a written declaration giving full information concerning the authority thus designated. The Director General shall at once communicate this declaration to all other countries of the Union.

Article 16

[*Infringing Copies*: 1. *Seizure*; 2. Seizure on importation; 3. Applicable law]

(1) Infringing copies of a work shall be liable to seizure in any country of the Union where the work enjoys legal protection.

(2) The provisions of the preceding paragraph shall also apply to reproductions coming from a country where the work is not protected, or has ceased to be protected.

(3) The seizure shall take place in accordance with the legislation of each country.

Article 17

[*Possibility of Control of Circulation, Presentation and Exhibition of Works*]

The provisions of this Convention cannot in any way affect the right of the Government of each country of the Union to permit, to control, or to prohibit, by legislation or regulation, the circulation, presentation, or exhibition of any work or production in regard to which the competent authority may find it necessary to exercise that right.

Article 18

[*Works Existing on Convention's Entry Into Force*: 1. Protectable where protection not yet expired in country of origin; 2. Non - protectable where protection already expired in country where it is claimed; 3. Application of these principles; 4. Special cases]

(1) This Convention shall apply to all works which, at the moment of its coming into force, have not yet fallen into the public domain in the country of origin through the expiry of the term of protection.

(2) If, however, through the expiry of the term of protection which was previously granted, a work has fallen into the public domain of the country where protection is claimed, that work shall not be protected anew.

(3) The application of this principle shall be subject to any provisions contained in special conventions to that effect existing or to be concluded between countries of the Union. In the absence of such provisions, the respective countries shall determine, each in so far as it is concerned, the conditions of application of

this principle.

(4) The preceding provisions shall also apply in the case of new accessions to the Union and to cases in which protection is extended by the application of Article 7 or by the abandonment of reservations.

Article 19

[*Protection Greater than Resulting from Convention*]

The provisions of this Convention shall not preclude the making of a claim to the benefit of any greater protection which may be granted by legislation in a country of the Union.

Article 20

[*Special Agreements Among Countries of the Union*]

The Governments of the countries of the Union reserve the right to enter into special agreements among themselves, in so far as such agreements grant to authors more extensive rights than those granted by the Convention, or contain other provisions not contrary to this Convention. The provisions of existing agreements which satisfy these conditions shall remain applicable.

Article 21

[*Special Provisions Regarding Developing Countries*: 1. Reference to Appendix; 2. Appendix part of Act]

(1) Special provisions regarding developing countries are included in the Appendix.

(2) Subject to the provisions of Article 28 (1) (b), the Appendix forms an integral part of this Act.

Article 22

[*Assembly*: 1. Constitution and composition; 2. Tasks; 3. Quorum, voting, observers; 4. Convocation; 5. Rules of procedure]

(1) (a) The Union shall have an Assembly consisting of those countries of the Union which are bound by Article 22 to Article 26.

(b) The Government of each country shall be represented by one delegate, who may be assisted by alternate delegates, advisors, and experts.

(c) The expenses of each delegation shall be borne by the Government which has appointed it.

(2) (a) The Assembly shall:

(i) deal with all matters concerning the maintenance and development of the Union and the implementation of this Convention;

(ii) give directions concerning the preparation for conferences of revision to the International Bureau of Intellectual Property (hereinafter designated as "the International Bureau") referred to in the Convention Establishing the World Intellectual Property Organization (hereinafter designated as "the Organization"), due account being taken of any comments made by those countries of the Union which are not bound by Article 22 to Article 26;

(iii) review and approve the reports and activities of the Director General of the Organization concerning the Union, and give him all necessary instructions concerning matters within the competence of the Union;

(iv) elect the members of the Executive Committee of the Assembly;

(v) review and approve the reports and activities of its Executive Committee, and give instructions to such Committee;

(vi) determine the program and adopt the biennial budget of the Union, and approve its final accounts;

(vii) adopt the financial regulations of the Union;

(viii) establish such committees of experts and working groups as may be necessary for the work of the Union;

(ix) determine which countries not members of the Union and which intergovernmental and international non - governmental organizations shall be admitted to its meetings as observers;

(x) adopt amendments to Article 22 to Article 26;

(xi) take any other appropriate action designed to further the objectives of the Union;

(xii) exercise such other functions as are appropriate under this Convention;

(xiii) subject to its acceptance, exercise such rights as are given to it in the Convention establishing the Organization.

(b) With respect to matters which are of interest also to other Unions administered by the Organization, the Assembly shall make its decisions after having heard the advice of the Coordination Committee of the Organization.

(3) (a) Each country member of the Assembly shall have one vote.

(b) One - half of the countries members of the Assembly shall constitute a quorum.

(c) Notwithstanding the provisions of subparagraph (b), if, in any session, the number of countries represented is less than one - half but equal to or more than one - third of the countries members of the Assembly, the Assembly may make decisions but, with the exception of decisions concerning its own procedure, all such decisions shall take effect only if the following conditions are fulfilled. The International Bureau shall communicate the said decisions to the countries members of the Assembly which were not represented and shall invite them to express in writing their vote or abstention within a period of three months from the date of the communication. If, at the expiration of this period, the number of countries having thus expressed their vote or abstention attains the number of countries which was lacking for attaining the quorum in the session itself, such decisions shall take effect provided that at the same time the required majority still obtains.

(d) Subject to the provisions of Article 26 (2), the decisions of the Assembly shall require two - thirds of the votes cast.

(e) Abstentions shall not be considered as votes.

(f) A delegate may represent, and vote in the name of, one country only.

(g) Countries of the Union not members of the Assembly shall be admitted to its meetings as observers.

(4) (a) The Assembly shall meet once in every second calendar year in ordinary session upon convocation by the Director General and, in the absence of exceptional circumstances, during the same period and at the same place as the General Assembly of the Organization.

(b) The Assembly shall meet in extraordinary session upon convocation by the Director General, at the request of the Executive Committee or at the request of one - fourth of the countries members of the Assembly.

(5) The Assembly shall adopt its own rules of procedure.

Article 23

[*Executive Committee*: 1. Constitution; 2. Composition; 3. Number of members; 4. Geographical distribution; special agreements; 5. Term, limits of re - eligibility, rules of election; 6. Tasks; 7. Convocation; 8. Quorum, voting; 9. Observers; 10. Rules of procedure]

(1) The Assembly shall have an Executive Committee.

(2) (a) The Executive Committee shall consist of countries elected by the Assembly from among countries members of the Assembly. Furthermore, the country on whose territory the Organization has its headquarters shall, subject to the provisions of Article 25 (7) (b), have an ex officio seat on the Committee.

(b) The Government of each country member of the Executive Committee shall be represented by one delegate, who may be assisted by alternate delegates, advisors, and experts.

(c) The expenses of each delegation shall be borne by the Government which has appointed it.

(3) The number of countries members of the Executive Committee shall correspond to one - fourth of the number of countries members of the Assembly. In establishing the number of seats to be filled, remainders after division by four shall be disregarded.

(4) In electing the members of the Executive Committee, the Assembly shall have due regard to an equitable geographical distribution and to the need for countries party to the Special Agreements which might be established in relation with the Union to be among the countries constituting the Executive Committee.

(5) (a) Each member of the Executive Committee shall serve from the close of the session of the Assembly which elected it to the close of the next ordinary session of the Assembly.

(b) Members of the Executive Committee may be re - elected, but not more than two - thirds of them.

(c) The Assembly shall establish the details of the rules governing the election and possible re - election of the members of the Executive Committee.

(6) (a) The Executive Committee shall:

(i) repare the draft agenda of the Assembly;

(ii) submit proposals to the Assembly respecting the draft program and biennial budget of the Union prepared by the Director General;

(iii) [*deleted*]

(iv) submit, with appropriate comments, to the Assembly the periodical reports of the Director General and the yearly audit reports on the accounts;

(v) in accordance with the decisions of the Assembly and having regard to circumstances arising between two ordinary sessions of the Assembly, take all necessary measures to ensure the execution of the program of the Union by the Director General;

(vi) perform such other functions as are allocated to it under this Convention.

(b) With respect to matters which are of interest also to other Unions administered by the Organization, the Executive Committee shall make its decisions after having heard the advice of the Coordination Committee of the Organization.

(7) (a) The Executive Committee shall meet once a year in ordinary session upon convocation by the Director General, preferably during the same period and at the same place as the Coordination Committee of the Organization.

(b) The Executive Committee shall meet in extraordinary session upon convocation by the Director General, either on his own initiative, or at the request of its Chairman or one - fourth of its members.

(8) (a) Each country member of the Executive Committee shall have one vote.

(b) One - half of the members of the Executive Committee shall constitute a quorum.

(c) Decisions shall be made by a simple majority of the votes cast.

(d) Abstentions shall not be considered as votes.

(e) A delegate may represent, and vote in the name of, one country only.

(9) Countries of the Union not members of the Executive Committee shall be admitted to its meetings as observers.

(10) The Executive Committee shall adopt its own rules of procedure.

Article 24

[*International Bureau*: 1. Tasks in general, Director General; 2. General information; 3. Periodical; 4. Information to countries; 5. Studies and services; 6. Participation in meetings; 7. Conferences of revision; 8. Other tasks]

(1) (a) The administrative tasks with respect to the Union shall be performed by the International Bureau, which is a continuation of the Bureau of the Union united with the Bureau of the Union established by the International Convention for the Protection of Industrial Property.

(b) In particular, the International Bureau shall provide the secretariat of the various organs of the Union.

(c) The Director General of the Organization shall be the chief executive of the Union and shall represent the Union.

(2) The International Bureau shall assemble and publish information concerning the protection of copyright. Each country of the Union shall promptly communicate to the International Bureau all new laws and official texts concerning the protection of copyright.

(3) The International Bureau shall publish a monthly periodical.

(4) The International Bureau shall, on request, furnish information to any country of the Union on matters concerning the protection of copyright.

(5) The International Bureau shall conduct studies, and shall provide services, designed to facilitate the protection of copyright.

(6) The Director General and any staff member designated by him shall participate, without the right to vote, in all meetings of the Assembly, the Executive Committee and any other committee of experts or working group. The Director General, or a staff member designated by him, shall be ex officio secretary of these bodies.

(7) (a) The International Bureau shall, in accordance with the directions of the Assembly and in cooperation with the Executive Committee, make the preparations for the conferences of revision of the provisions of the Convention other than Article 22 to Article 26.

(b) The International Bureau may consult with intergovernmental and international non - governmental organizations concerning preparations for conferences of revision.

(c) The Director General and persons designated by him shall take part, without the right to vote, in the discussions at these conferences.

(8) The International Bureau shall carry out any other tasks assigned to it.

Article 25

[*Finances*: 1. Budget; 2. Coordination with other Unions; 3. Resources; 4. Contributions; possible extension of previous budget; 5. Fees and charges; 6. Working capital fund; 7. Advances by host Government; 8. Auditing of accounts]

(1) (a) The Union shall have a budget.

(b) The budget of the Union shall include the income and expenses proper to the Union, its contribution to the budget of expenses common to the Unions, and, where applicable, the sum made available to the budget of the Conference of the Organization.

(c) Expenses not attributable exclusively to the Union but also to one or more other Unions administered by the Organization shall be considered as expenses common to the Unions. The share of the Union in such common expenses shall be in proportion to the interest the Union has in them.

(2) The budget of the Union shall be established with due regard to the requirements of coordination with the budgets of the other Unions administered by the Organization.

(3) The budget of the Union shall be financed from the following sources:

(i) contributions of the countries of the Union;

(ii) fees and charges due for services performed by the International Bureau in relation to the Union;

(iii) sale of, or royalties on, the publications of the International Bureau concerning the Union;

(iv) gifts, bequests, and subventions;

(v) rents, interests, and other miscellaneous income.

(4) (a) For the purpose of establishing its contribution towards the budget, each country of the Union shall belong to a class, and shall pay its annual contributions on the basis of a number of units fixed as follows:

Class I ………………………………………… 25

Class II ………………………………………… 20

Class III ………………………………………… 15

Class IV ………………………………………… 10

Class V ………………………………………… 5

Class VI ………………………………………… 3

Class VII ………………………………………… 1

(b) Unless it has already done so, each country shall indicate, concurrently with depositing its instrument of ratification or accession, the class to which it wishes to belong. Any country may change class. If it chooses a lower class, the country must announce it to the Assembly at one of its ordinary sessions. Any such change shall take effect at the beginning of the calendar year following the session.

(c) The annual contribution of each country shall be an amount in the same proportion to the total sum to be contributed to the annual budget of the Union by all countries as the number of its units is to the total of the units of all contributing countries.

(d) Contributions shall become due on the first of January of each year.

(e) A country which is in arrears in the payment of its contributions shall have no vote in any of the organs of the Union of which it is a member if the amount of its arrears equals or exceeds the amount of the contributions due from it for the preceding two full years. However, any organ of the Union may allow such a country to continue to exercise its vote in that organ if, and as long as, it is satisfied that the delay in payment is due to exceptional and unavoidable circumstances.

(f) If the budget is not adopted before the beginning of a new financial period, it shall be at the same level as the budget of the previous year, in accordance with the financial regulations.

(5) The amount of the fees and charges due for services rendered by the International Bureau in relation to the Union shall be established, and shall be reported to the Assembly and the Executive Committee, by the Director General.

(6) (a) The Union shall have a working capital fund which shall be constituted by a single payment made by each country of the Union. If the fund becomes insufficient, an increase shall be decided by the Assembly.

(b) The amount of the initial payment of each country to the said fund or of its participation in the increase thereof shall be a proportion of the contribution of that country for the year in which the fund is established or the increase decided.

(c) The proportion and the terms of payment shall be fixed by the Assembly on the proposal of the Director General and after it has heard the advice of the Coordination Committee of the Organization.

(7) (a) In the headquarters agreement concluded with the country on the territory of which the Organization has its headquarters, it shall be provided that, whenever the working capital fund is insufficient, such country shall grant advances. The amount of these advances and the conditions on which they are granted shall be the subject of separate agreements, in each case, between such country and the Organization. As long as it remains under the obligation to grant advances, such country shall have an ex officio seat on the Executive Committee.

(b) The country referred to in subparagraph (a) and the Organization shall each have the right to denounce the obligation to grant advances, by written notification. Denunciation shall take effect three years after the end of the year in which it has been notified.

(8) The auditing of the accounts shall be effected by one or more of the countries of the Union or by external auditors, as provided in the financial regulations. They shall be designated, with their agreement, by the Assembly.

Article 26

[*Amendments*: 1. Provisions susceptible of amendment by the Assembly; proposals; 2. Adoption; 3. Entry into force]

(1) Proposals for the amendment of Article 22, Article 23, Article 24, Article 25, and the present Article, may be initiated by any country member of the Assembly, by the Executive Committee, or by the Director General. Such proposals shall be communicated by the Director General to the member countries of the Assembly at least six months in advance of their consideration by the Assembly.

(2) Amendments to the Articles referred to in paragraph (1) shall be adopted by the Assembly. Adoption shall require three - fourths of the votes cast, provided that any amendment of Article 22, and of the present paragraph, shall require four - fifths of the votes cast.

(3) Any amendment to the Articles referred to in paragraph (1) shall enter into force one month after written notifications of acceptance, effected in accordance with their respective constitutional processes, have been received by the Director General from three - fourths of the countries members of the Assembly at the time it adopted the amendment. Any amendment to the said Articles thus accepted shall bind all the countries which are members of the Assembly at the time the amendment enters into force, or which become members thereof at a subsequent date, provided that any amendment increasing the financial obligations of countries of the Union shall bind only those countries which have notified their acceptance of such amendment.

Article 27

[*Revision*: 1. Objective; 2. Conferences; 3. Adoption]

(1) This Convention shall be submitted to revision with a view to the introduction of amendments designed to improve the system of the Union.

(2) For this purpose, conferences shall be held successively in one of the countries of the Union among the delegates of the said countries.

(3) Subject to the provisions of Article 26 which apply to the amendment of Article 22 to Article 26, any revision of this Act, including the Appendix, shall require the unanimity of the votes cast.

Article 28

[*Acceptance and Entry Into Force of Act for Countries of the Union*: 1. Ratification, accession; possibility of excluding certain provisions; withdrawal of exclusion; 2. Entry into force of Articles 1 to 21 and Appendix; 3. Entry into force of Articles 22 to 38]

(1) (a) Any country of the Union which has signed this Act may ratify it, and, if it has not signed it, may accede to it. Instruments of ratification or accession shall be deposited with the Director General.

(b) Any country of the Union may declare in its instrument of ratification or accession that its ratification or accession shall not apply to Article 1 to Article 21 and the Appendix, provided that, if such country has previously made a declaration under Article VI (1) of the Appendix, then it may declare in the said instrument only that its ratification or accession shall not apply to Article 1 to Article 20.

(c) Any country of the Union which, in accordance with subparagraph (b), has excluded provisions therein referred to from the effects of its ratification or accession may at any later time declare that it extends the effects of its ratification or accession to those provisions. Such declaration shall be deposited with the Director General.

(2) (a) Article 1 to Article 21 and the Appendix shall enter into force three months after both of the following two conditions are fulfilled:

(i) at least five countries of the Union have ratified or acceded to this Act without making a declaration under paragraph (1) (b),

(ii) France, Spain, the United Kingdom of Great Britain and Northern Ireland, and the United States of America, have become bound by the Universal Copyright Convention as revised at Paris on July 24, 1971.

(b) The entry into force referred to in subparagraph (a) shall apply to those countries of the Union which, at least three months before the said entry into force, have deposited instruments of ratification or accession not containing a declaration under paragraph (1) (b).

(c) With respect to any country of the Union not covered by subparagraph (b) and which ratifies or accedes to this Act without making a declaration under paragraph (1) (b), Article 1 to Article 21 and the Appendix shall enter into force three months after the date on which the Director General has notified the deposit of the relevant instrument of ratification or accession, unless a subsequent date has been indicated in the instrument deposited. In the latter case, Article 1 to Article 21 and the Appendix shall enter into force with respect to that country on the date thus indicated.

(d) The provisions of subparagraph (a) to subparagraph (c) do not affect the application of Article VI of the Appendix.

(3) With respect to any country of the Union which ratifies or accedes to this Act with or without a declaration made under paragraph (1) (b), Article 22 to Article 38 shall enter into force three months after the date on which the Director General has notified the deposit of the relevant instrument of ratification or accession, unless a subsequent date has been indicated in the instrument deposited. In the latter case, Article 22 to Article 38 shall enter into force with respect to that country on the date thus indicated.

Article 29

[*Acceptance and Entry Into Force for Countries Outside the Union*: 1. Accession; 2. Entry into force]

(1) Any country outside the Union may accede to this Act and thereby become party to this Convention and a member of the Union. Instruments of accession shall be deposited with the Director General.

(2)

(a) Subject to subparagraph (b), this Convention shall enter into force with respect to any country outside the Union three months after the date on which the Director General has notified the deposit of its instrument of accession, unless a subsequent date has been indicated in the instrument deposited. In the latter case, this Convention shall enter into force with respect to that country on the date thus indicated.

(b) If the entry into force according to subparagraph (a) precedes the entry into force of Articles 1 to 21 and the Appendix according to Article 28 (2) (a), the said country shall, in the meantime, be bound, instead of by Articles 1 to 21 and the Appendix, by Articles 1 to 20 of the Brussels Act of this Convention.

Article 29 bis

[*Effect of Acceptance of Act for the Purposes of Article* 14 (2) *of the WIPO Con-*

vention]

Ratification of or accession to this Act by any country not bound by Articles 22 to 38 of the Stockholm Act of this Convention shall, for the sole purposes of Article 14 (2) of the Convention establishing the Organization, amount to ratification of or accession to the said Stockholm Act with the limitation set forth in Article 28 (1) (b) (i) thereof.

Article 30

[*Reservations*: 1. Limits of possibility of making reservations; 2. Earlier reservations; reservation as to the right of translation; withdrawal of reservation]

(1) Subject to the exceptions permitted by paragraph (2) of this Article, by Article 28 (1) (b), by Article 33 (2), and by the Appendix, ratification or accession shall automatically entail acceptance of all the provisions and admission to all the advantages of this Convention.

(2)

(a) Any country of the Union ratifying or acceding to this Act may, subject to Article V (2) of the Appendix, retain the benefit of the reservations it has previously formulated on condition that it makes a declaration to that effect at the time of the deposit of its instrument of ratification or accession.

(b) Any country outside the Union may declare, in acceding to this Convention and subject to Article V (2) of the Appendix, that it intends to substitute, temporarily at least, for Article 8 of this Act concerning the right of translation, the provisions of Article 5 of the Union Convention of 1886, as completed at Paris in 1896, on the clear understanding that the said provisions are applicable only to translations into a language in general use in the said country. Subject to Article I (6) (b) of the Appendix, any country has the right to apply, in relation to the right of translation of works whose country of origin is a country availing itself of such a reservation, a protection which is equivalent to the protection granted by the latter country.

(c) Any country may withdraw such reservations at any time by notification addressed to the Director General.

Article 31

[*Applicability to Certain Territories*: 1. Declaration; 2. Withdrawal of declaration; 3. Effective date; 4. Acceptance of factual situations not implied]

(1) Any country may declare in its instrument of ratification or accession, or may inform the Director General by written notification at any time thereafter, that this Convention shall be applicable to all or part of those territories, designated in the declaration or notification, for the external relations of which it is responsible.

(2) Any country which has made such a declaration or given such a notification may, at any time, notify the Director General that this Convention shall cease to be applicable to all or part of such territories.

(3)

(a) Any declaration made under paragraph (1) shall take effect on the same date as the ratification or accession in which it was included, and any notification given under that paragraph shall take effect three months after its notification by the Director General.

(b) Any notification given under paragraph (2) shall take effect twelve months after its receipt by the Director General.

(4) This Article shall in no way be understood as implying the recognition or tacit acceptance by a country of the Union of the factual situation concerning a territory to which this Convention is made applicable by another country of the Union by virtue of a declaration under paragraph (1).

Article 32

[*Applicability of this Act and of Earlier Acts*: 1. As between countries already members of the Union; 2. As between a country becoming a member of the Union and other countries members of the Union; 3. Applicability of the Appendix in Certain Relations]

(1) This Act shall, as regards relations between the countries of the Union, and to the extent that it applies, replace the Berne Convention of September 9, 1886, and the subsequent Acts of revision. The Acts previously in force shall continue to be applicable, in their entirety or to the extent that this Act does not replace them by virtue of the preceding sentence, in relations with countries of the Union which do not ratify or accede to this Act.

(2) Countries outside the Union which become party to this Act shall, subject to paragraph (3), apply it with respect to any country of the Union not bound by this Act or which, although bound by this Act, has made a declaration pursuant to Article 28 (1) (b). Such countries recognize that the said country of the Union,

in its relations with them:

(i) may apply the provisions of the most recent Act by which it is bound, and

(ii) subject to Article I (6) of the Appendix, has the right to adapt the protection to the level provided for by this Act. (3) Any country which has availed itself of any of the faculties provided for in the Appendix may apply the provisions of the Appendix relating to the faculty or faculties of which it has availed itself in its relations with any other country of the Union which is not bound by this Act, provided that the latter country has accepted the application of the said provisions.

Article 33

[*Disputes*: 1. Jurisdiction of the International Court of Justice; 2. Reservation as to such jurisdiction; 3. Withdrawal of reservation]

(1) Any dispute between two or more countries of the Union concerning the interpretation or application of this Convention, not settled by negotiation, may, by any one of the countries concerned, be brought before the International Court of Justice by application in conformity with the Statute of the Court, unless the countries concerned agree on some other method of settlement. The country bringing the dispute before the Court shall inform the International Bureau; the International Bureau shall bring the matter to the attention of the other countries of the Union.

(2) Each country may, at the time it signs this Act or deposits its instrument of ratification or accession, declare that it does not consider itself bound by the provisions of paragraph (1). With regard to any dispute between such country and any other country of the Union, the provisions of paragraph (1) shall not apply.

(3) Any country having made a declaration in accordance with the provisions of paragraph (2) may, at any time, withdraw its declaration by notification addressed to the Director General.

Article 34

[*Closing of Certain Earlier Provisions*: 1. Of earlier Acts; 2. Of the Protocol to the Stockholm Act]

(1) Subject to Article 29_{bis} no country may ratify or accede to earlier Acts of this Convention once Articles 1 to 21 and the Appendix have entered into force.

(2) Once Articles 1 to 21 and the Appendix have entered into force, no country may make a declaration under Article 5 of the Protocol Regarding Developing

Countries attached to the Stockholm Act.

Article 35

[*Duration of the Convention*; *Denunciation*: 1. Unlimited duration; 2. Possibility of denunciation; 3. Effective date of denunciation; 4. Moratorium on denunciation]

(1) This Convention shall remain in force without limitation as to time.

(2) Any country may denounce this Act by notification addressed to the Director General. Such denunciation shall constitute also denunciation of all earlier Acts and shall affect only the country making it, the Convention remaining in full force and effect as regards the other countries of the Union.

(3) Denunciation shall take effect one year after the day on which the Director General has received the notification.

(4) The right of denunciation provided by this Article shall not be exercised by any country before the expiration of five years from the date upon which it becomes a member of the Union.

Article 36

[*Application of the Convention*: 1. Obligation to adopt the necessary measures; 2. Time from which obligation exists]

(1) Any country party to this Convention undertakes to adopt, in accordance with its constitution, the measures necessary to ensure the application of this Convention.

(2) It is understood that, at the time a country becomes bound by this Convention, it will be in a position under its domestic law to give effect to the provisions of this Convention.

Article 37

[*Final Clauses*: 1. Languages of the Act; 2. Signature; 3. Certified copies; 4. Registration; 5. Notifications]

(1)

(a) This Act shall be signed in a single copy in the French and English languages and, subject to paragraph (2), shall be deposited with the Director General.

(b) Official texts shall be established by the Director General, after consultation with the interested Governments, in the Arabic, German, Italian, Portuguese and Spanish languages, and such other languages as the Assembly may designate.

(c) In case of differences of opinion on the interpretation of the various texts, the French text shall prevail.

(2) This Act shall remain open for signature until January 31, 1972. Until that date, the copy referred to in paragraph (1) (a) shall be deposited with the Government of the French Republic.

(3) The Director General shall certify and transmit two copies of the signed text of this Act to the Governments of all countries of the Union and, on request, to the Government of any other country.

(4) The Director General shall register this Act with the Secretariat of the United Nations.

(5) The Director General shall notify the Governments of all countries of the Union of signatures, deposits of instruments of ratification or accession and any declarations included in such instruments or made pursuant to Articles 28 (1) (c), 30 (2) (a) and (b), and 33 (2), entry into force of any provisions of this Act, notifications of denunciation, and notifications pursuant to Articles 30 (2) (c), 31 (1) and (2), 33 (3), and 38 (1), as well as the Appendix.

Article 38

[*Transitory Provisions*: 1. Exercise of the "five - year privilege"; 2. Bureau of the Union, Director of the Bureau; 3. Succession of Bureau of the Union]

(1) Countries of the Union which have not ratified or acceded to this Act and which are not bound by Articles 22 to 26 of the Stockholm Act of this Convention may, until April 26, 1975, exercise, if they so desire, the rights provided under the said Articles as if they were bound by them. Any country desiring to exercise such rights shall give written notification to this effect to the Director General; this notification shall be effective on the date of its receipt. Such countries shall be deemed to be members of the Assembly until the said date.

(2) As long as all the countries of the Union have not become Members of the Organization, the International Bureau of the Organization shall also function as the Bureau of the Union, and the Director General as the Director of the said Bureau.

(3) Once all the countries of the Union have become Members of the Organization, the rights, obligations, and property, of the Bureau of the Union shall devolve on the International Bureau of the Organization.

APPENDIX

[SPECIAL PROVISIONS REGARDING DEVELOPING COUNTRIES]

Article I

[*Faculties Open to Developing Countries*: 1. Availability of certain faculties; declaration: 2. Duration of effect of declaration, 3. Cessation of developing country status; 4. Existing stocks of copies; 5. Declarations concerning certain territories; 6. Limits of reciprocity]

(1) Any country regarded as a developing country in conformity with the established practice of the General Assembly of the United Nations which ratifies or accedes to this Act, of which this Appendix forms an integral part, and which, having regard to its economic situation and its social or cultural needs, does not consider itself immediately in a position to make provision for the protection of all the rights as provided for in this Act, may, by a notification deposited with the Director General at the time of depositing its instrument of ratification or accession or, subject to Article V (1) (c), at any time thereafter, declare that it will avail itself of the faculty provided for in Article II, or of the faculty provided for in Article III, or of both of those faculties. It may, instead of availing itself of the faculty provided for in Article II, make a declaration according to Article V (1) (a).

(2)

(a) Any declaration under paragraph (1) notified before the expiration of the period of ten years from the entry into force of Articles 1 to 21 and this Appendix according to Article 28 (2) shall be effective until the expiration of the said period. Any such declaration may be renewed in whole or in part for periods of ten years each by a notification deposited with the Director General not more than fifteen months and not less than three months before the expiration of the ten - year period then running.

(b) Any declaration under paragraph (1) notified after the expiration of the period of ten years from the entry into force of Articles 1 to 21 and this Appendix according to Article 28 (2) shall be effective until the expiration of the ten - year period then running. Any such declaration may be renewed as provided for in the second sentence of subparagraph (a).

(3) Any country of the Union which has ceased to be regarded as a developing country as referred to in paragraph (1) shall no longer be entitled to renew its declaration as provided in paragraph (2), and, whether or not it formally withdraws its declaration, such country shall be precluded from availing itself of the faculties referred to in paragraph (1) from the expiration of the ten - year period then running or from the expiration of a period of three years after it has ceased to be regarded as a developing country, whichever period expires later.

(4) Where, at the time when the declaration made under paragraph (1) or (2) ceases to be effective, there are copies in stock which were made under a license granted by virtue of this Appendix, such copies may continue to be distributed until their stock is exhausted.

(5) Any country which is bound by the provisions of this Act and which has deposited a declaration or a notification in accordance with Article 31 (1) with respect to the application of this Act to a particular territory, the situation of which can be regarded as analogous to that of the countries referred to in paragraph (1), may, in respect of such territory, make the declaration referred to in paragraph (1) and the notification of renewal referred to in paragraph (2). As long as such declaration or notification remains in effect, the provisions of this Appendix shall be applicable to the territory in respect of which it was made.

(6)

(a) The fact that a country avails itself of any of the faculties referred to in paragraph (1) does not permit another country to give less protection to works of which the country of origin is the former country than it is obliged to grant under Articles 1 to 20.

(b) The right to apply reciprocal treatment provided for in Article 30 (2) (b), second sentence, shall not, until the date on which the period applicable under Article I (3) expires, be exercised in respect of works the country of origin of which is a country which has made a declaration according to Article V (1) (a).

Article II

[*Limitations on the Right of Translation*: 1. Licenses grantable by competent authority; 2. to 4. Conditions allowing the grant of such licenses; 5. Purposes for which licenses may be granted; 6. Termination of licenses; 7. Works composed mainly of illustrations; 8. Works withdrawn from circulation; 9. Licenses for broadcasting organizations]

(1) Any country which has declared that it will avail itself of the faculty provided for in this Article shall be entitled, so far as works published in printed or analogous forms of reproduction are concerned, to substitute for the exclusive right of translation provided for in Article 8 a system of non - exclusive and nontransferable licenses, granted by the competent authority under the following conditions and subject to Article IV.

(2)

(a) Subject to paragraph (3), if, after the expiration of a period of three years, or of any longer period determined by the national legislation of the said country, commencing on the date of the first publication of the work, a translation of such work has not been published in a language in general use in that country by the owner of the right of translation, or with his authorization, any national of such country may obtain a license to make a translation of the work in the said language and publish the translation in printed or analogous forms of reproduction.

(b) A license under the conditions provided for in this Article may also be granted if all the editions of the translation published in the language concerned are out of print.

(3)

(a) In the case of translations into a language which is not in general use in one or more developed countries which are members of the Union, a period of one year shall be substituted for the period of three years referred to in paragraph (2) (a).

(b) Any country referred to in paragraph (1) may, with the unanimous agreement of the developed countries which are members of the Union and in which the same language is in general use, substitute, in the case of translations into that language, for the period of three years referred to in paragraph (2) (a) a shorter period as determined by such agreement but not less than one year. However, the provisions of the foregoing sentence shall not apply where the language in question is English, French or Spanish. The Director General shall be notified of any such agreement by the Governments which have concluded it.

(4)

(a) No license obtainable after three years shall be granted under this Article until a further period of six months has elapsed, and no license obtainable after one year shall be granted under this Article until a further period of nine months has elapsed

(i) from the date on which the applicant complies with the requirements mentioned in Article IV (1), or (ii) where the identity or the address of the owner of the right of translation is unknown, from the date on which the applicant sends, as provided for in Article IV (2), copies of his application submitted to the authority competent to grant the license.

(b) If, during the said period of six or nine months, a translation in the language in respect of which the application was made is published by the owner of the right of translation or with his authorization, no license under this Article shall be granted.

(5) Any license under this Article shall be granted only for the purpose of teaching, scholarship or research.

(6) If a translation of a work is published by the owner of the right of translation or with his authorization at a price reasonably related to that normally charged in the country for comparable works, any license granted under this Article shall terminate if such translation is in the same language and with substantially the same content as the translation published under the license. Any copies already made before the license terminates may continue to be distributed until their stock is exhausted.

(7) For works which are composed mainly of illustrations, a license to make and publish a translation of the text and to reproduce and publish the illustrations may be granted only if the conditions of Article III are also fulfilled.

(8) No license shall be granted under this Article when the author has withdrawn from circulation all copies of his work.

(9)

(a) A license to make a translation of a work which has been published in printed or analogous forms of reproduction may also be granted to any broadcasting organization having its headquarters in a country referred to in paragraph (1), upon an application made to the competent authority of that country by the said organization, provided that all of the following conditions are met:

(i) the translation is made from a copy made and acquired in accordance with the laws of the said country;

(ii) the translation is only for use in broadcasts intended exclusively for teaching or for the dissemination of the results of specialized technical or scientific research to experts in a particular profession;

(iii) the translation is used exclusively for the purposes referred to in condition (ii) through broadcasts made lawfully and intended for recipients on the territory of the said country, including broadcasts made through the medium of sound or visual recordings lawfully and exclusively made for the purpose of such broadcasts;

(iv) all uses made of the translation are without any commercial purpose.

(b) Sound or visual recordings of a translation which was made by a broadcasting organization under a license granted by virtue of this paragraph may, for the purposes and subject to the conditions referred to in subparagraph (a) and with the agreement of that organization, also be used by any other broadcasting organization having its headquarters in the country whose competent authority granted the license in question.

(c) Provided that all of the criteria and conditions set out in subparagraph (a) are met, a license may also be granted to a broadcasting organization to translate any text incorporated in an audio - visual fixation where such fixation was itself prepared and published for the sole purpose of being used in connection with systematic instructional activities.

(d) Subject to subparagraphs (a) to (c), the provisions of the preceding paragraphs shall apply to the grant and exercise of any license granted under this paragraph.

Article III

[*Limitation on the Right of Reproduction*: 1. Licenses grantable by competent authority; 2. to 5. Conditions allowing the grant of such licenses; 6. Termination of licenses; 7. Works to which this Article applies]

(1) Any country which has declared that it will avail itself of the faculty provided for in this Article shall be entitled to substitute for the exclusive right of reproduction provided for in Article 9 a system of nonexclusive and non - transferable licenses, granted by the competent authority under the following conditions

and subject to Article IV.

(2)

(a) If, in relation to a work to which this Article applies by virtue of paragraph (7), after the expiration of

(i) the relevant period specified in paragraph (3), commencing on the date of first publication of a particular edition of the work, or

(ii) any longer period determined by national legislation of the country referred to in paragraph (1), commencing on the same date, copies of such edition have not been distributed in that country to the general public or in connection with systematic instructional activities, by the owner of the right of reproduction or with his authorization, at a price reasonably related to that normally charged in the country for comparable works, any national of such country may obtain a license to reproduce and publish such edition at that or a lower price for use in connection with systematic instructional activities.

(b) A license to reproduce and publish an edition which has been distributed as described in subparagraph (a) may also be granted under the conditions provided for in this Article if, after the expiration of the applicable period, no authorized copies of that edition have been on sale for a period of six months in the country concerned to the general public or in connection with systematic instructional activities at a price reasonably related to that normally charged in the country for comparable works.

(3) The period referred to in paragraph (2) (a) (i) shall be five years, except that

(i) for works of the natural and physical sciences, including mathematics, and of technology, the period shall be three years;

(ii) for works of fiction, poetry, drama and music, and for art books, the period shall be seven years.

(4)

(a) No license obtainable after three years shall be granted under this Article until a period of six months has elapsed

(i) from the date on which the applicant complies with the requirements mentioned in

Article IV (1), or

(ii) where the identity or the address of the owner of the right of reproduction is unknown, from the date on which the applicant sends, as provided for in Article IV (2), copies of his application submitted to the authority competent to grant the license.

(b) Where licenses are obtainable after other periods and Article IV (2) is applicable, no license shall be granted until a period of three months has elapsed from the date of the dispatch of the copies of the application.

(c) If, during the period of six or three months referred to in subparagraphs (a) and (b), a distribution as described in paragraph (2) (a) has taken place, no license shall be granted under this Article.

(d) No license shall be granted if the author has withdrawn from circulation all copies of the edition for the reproduction and publication of which the license has been applied for.

(5) A license to reproduce and publish a translation of a work shall not be granted under this Article in the following cases:

(i) where the translation was not published by the owner of the right of translation or with his authorization, or

(ii) where the translation is not in a language in general use in the country in which the license is applied for.

(6) If copies of an edition of a work are distributed in the country referred to in paragraph (1) to the general public or in connection with systematic instructional activities, by the owner of the right of reproduction or with his authorization, at a price reasonably related to that normally charged in the country for comparable works, any license granted under this Article shall terminate if such edition is in the same language and with substantially the same content as the edition which was published under the said license. Any copies already made before the license terminates may continue to be distributed until their stock is exhausted.

(7)

(a) Subject to subparagraph (b), the works to which this Article applies shall be limited to works published in printed or analogous forms of reproduction.

(b) This Article shall also apply to the reproduction in audio - visual form of lawfully made audiovisual fixations including any protected works incorporated therein and to the translation of any incorporated text into a language in general use in the country in which the license is applied for, always provided that the audio - visual fixations in question were prepared and published for the sole purpose of being used in connection with systematic instructional activities.

Article IV

[*Provisions Common to Licenses Under Articles II and III*: 1 and 2. Procedure; 3. Indication of author and title of work; 4. Exportation of copies; 5. Notice; 6. Compensation]

(1) A license under Article II or Article III may be granted only if the applicant, in accordance with the procedure of the country concerned, establishes either that he has requested, and has been denied, authorization by the owner of the right to make and publish the translation or to reproduce and publish the edition, as the case may be, or that, after due diligence on his part, he was unable to find the owner of the right. At the same time as making the request, the applicant shall inform any national or international information center referred to in paragraph (2).

(2) If the owner of the right cannot be found, the applicant for a license shall send, by registered airmail, copies of his application, submitted to the authority competent to grant the license, to the publisher whose name appears on the work and to any national or international information center which may have been designated, in a notification to that effect deposited with the Director General, by the Government of the country in which the publisher is believed to have his principal place of business.

(3) The name of the author shall be indicated on all copies of the translation or reproduction published under a license granted under Article II or Article III. The title of the work shall appear on all such copies. In the case of a translation, the original title of the work shall appear in any case on all the said copies.

(4)

(a) No license granted under Article II or Article III shall extend to the export of copies, and any such license shall be valid only for publication of the translation or of the reproduction, as the case may be, in the territory of the country in which it has been applied for.

(b) For the purposes of subparagraph (a), the notion of export shall include the sending of copies from any territory to the country which, in respect of that territory, has made a declaration under Article I (5).

(c) Where a governmental or other public entity of a country which has granted a license to make a translation under Article II into a language other than English, French or Spanish sends copies of atranslation published under such license to another country, such sending of copies shall not, for thepurposes of subparagraph (a), be considered to constitute export if all of the following conditions are met:

(i) the recipients are individuals who are nationals of the country whose competent authority has granted the license, or organizations grouping such individuals;

(ii) the copies are to be used only for the purpose of teaching, scholarship or research;

(iii) the sending of the copies and their subsequent distribution to recipients is without any commercial purpose; and

(iv) the country to which the copies have been sent has agreed with the country whose competent authority has granted the license to allow the receipt, or distribution, or both, and the Director General has been notified of the agreement by the Government of the country in which the license has been granted.

(5) All copies published under a license granted by virtue of Article II or Article III shall bear a notice in the appropriate language stating that the copies are available for distribution only in the country or territory to which the said license applies.

(6)

(a) Due provision shall be made at the national level to ensure

(i) that the license provides, in favour of the owner of the right of translation or of reproduction, as the case may be, for just compensation that is consistent with standards of royalties normally operating on licenses freely negotiated between persons in the two countries concerned, and

(ii) payment and transmittal of the compensation: should national currency regulations intervene, the competent authority shall make all efforts, by the use of international machinery, to ensure transmittal in internationally convertible currency or its equivalent.

(b) Due provision shall be made by national legislation to ensure a correct translation of the work, or an accurate reproduction of the particular edition, as the case may be.

Article V

[*Alternative Possibility for Limitation of the Right of Translation*: 1. Regime provided for under the 1886 and 1896 Acts; 2. No possibility of change to regime under Article II; 3. Time limit for choosing the alternative possibility]

(1)

(a) Any country entitled to make a declaration that it will avail itself of the faculty provided for in Article II may, instead, at the time of ratifying or acceding to this Act:

(i) if it is a country to which Article 30 (2) (a) applies, make a declaration under that provision as far as the right of translation is concerned;

(ii) if it is a country to which Article 30 (2) (a) does not apply, and even if it is not a country outside the Union, make a declaration as provided for in Article 30 (2) (b), first sentence.

(b) In the case of a country which ceases to be regarded as a developing country as referred to in Article I (1), a declaration made according to this paragraph shall be effective until the date on which the period applicable under Article I (3) expires.

(c) Any country which has made a declaration according to this paragraph may not subsequently avail itself of the faculty provided for in Article II even if it withdraws the said declaration.

(2) Subject to paragraph (3), any country which has availed itself of the faculty provided for in Article II

may not subsequently make a declaration according to paragraph (1).

(3) Any country which has ceased to be regarded as a developing country as referred to in Article I (1) may, not later than two years prior to the expiration of the period applicable under Article I (3), make a declaration to the effect provided for in Article 30 (2) (b), first sentence, notwithstanding the fact that it is not a country outside the Union. Such declaration shall take effect at the date on which the period applicable under Article I (3) expires.

Article VI

[*Possibilities of applying, or admitting the application of, certain provisions of the Appendix before becoming bound by it*: 1. Declaration; 2. Depository and effective date of declaration]

(1) Any country of the Union may declare, as from the date of this Act, and at any time before becoming bound by Articles 1 to 21 and this Appendix:

(i) if it is a country which, were it bound by Articles 1 to 21 and this Appendix, would be entitled to avail itself of the faculties referred to in Article I (1), that it will apply the provisions of Article II or of Article III or of both to works whose country of origin is a country which, pursuant to (ii) below, admits the application of those Articles to such works, or which is bound by Articles 1 to 21 and this Appendix; such declaration may, instead of referring to Article II, refer to Article V;

(ii) that it admits the application of this Appendix to works of which it is the country of origin by countries which have made a declaration under (i) above or a notification under Article I.

(2) Any declaration made under paragraph (1) shall be in writing and shall be deposited with the Director General. The declaration shall become effective from the date of its deposit.

保护录音制品制作者防止未经许可复制其录音制品公约

（1971年10月29日签订，我国于1992年11月7日加入）

缔约各国：

担心普遍和不断增加的对录音制品的未经许可的复制以及由此给作者、表演者和录音制品制作者利益带来的损害，

相信保护录音制品制作者，防止此种行为，还将有利于其表演和作品录制在录音制品上的表演者和作者；

承认联合国教育科学文化组织和世界知识产权组织在这方面所做工作的价值；

期望毫不影响已经生效的国际协定，特别是毫不妨碍保护表演者、广播组织和录音制品制作者的1961年10月26日罗马公约得到更广泛的承认，达成协议如下：

第一条

在本公约中：

(a)“录音制品”指任何仅听觉可感知的对表演的声音或其他声音的固定；

(b)“录音制品制作者”指首次将表演的声音或其他声音固定下来的自然人或法人；

(c)“复制品”指一件含有直接或间接从录音制品获取的声音的物品，该物品载有固定在该录音制品上的声音的全部或主要部分；

(d)“公开发行”指将录音制品的复制品直接或间接提供给公众或任何一部分公众的行为。

第二条

各缔约国应当保护是其他缔约国国民的录音制品制作者，防止未经录音制品制作者同意而制作复制品和防止此类复制品的进口，只要任何此种制作

或进口的目的是为了公开发行；以及防止公开发行此类复制品。

第三条

执行本公约的方式应当由各缔约国国内法律规定并应当包括以下一种或多种：通过授予版权或其他专项权利的方式保护；通过有关不正当竞争的法律保护；通过刑事制裁的方式保护。

第四条

给予保护的期限应当由各缔约国国内法律规定。但是，如果国内法律规定一具体保护期，此保护期不应短于自录音制品载有的声音首次被固定之年年底起，或从录音制品首次出版之年年底起二十年。

第五条

如果一缔约国依照其国内法律要求以履行手续作为保护录音制品制作者的条件，只要公开发行的经授权的录音制品的所有复制品或其包装物载有○P标记并伴有首次出版年份，而且标记的部位足以使人注意到保护的要求，则应当认为符合手续；如果复制品或其包装物上未（通过载有其姓名、商标或其他适当标志）注明制作者、他的合法继承人或专有许可证持有人，则标记还应当包括制作者和他的合法继承人或专有许可证持有人的姓名。

第六条

任何通过版权或其他专项权利的方式或通过刑事制裁的方式提供保护的缔约国，可以在其国内法律中为录音制品制作者的保护规定与允许对文学和艺术作品作者的保护所作的相同的限制。但是，只有符合所有下列条件，才允许颁发强制许可证：

（a）复制品仅用于教学和科学研究的目的；

（b）许可证仅适用于在颁发许可证的主管当局管辖的领土内进行的复制，不适用于复制品的出口；

（c）根据许可证制作复制品，应支付由上述主管当局考虑要制作的复制品的数量和其他因素而确定的合理报酬。

第七条

（1）本公约的解释不得限制或妨碍任何国内法律或国际协定给予作者、表演者、录音制品制作者或广播组织的其他保护。

（2）如果被固定在录音制品上的表演的表演者享受保护，保护程度以及享受此种保护的条件，应当由各缔约国国内法律确定。

（3）不得要求缔约国将本公约的条款适用于本公约在该国生效之前已经固定的任何录音制品。

（4）任何在1971年10月29日仅根据首次固定地为录音制品制作者提供保护的缔约国，可以向世界知识产权组织总干事递交通知书，声明其将适用这个标准而不是制作者国籍标准。

第八条

（1）世界知识产权组织国际局应当汇集和出版与保护录音制品有关的信息资料。各缔约国应当将所有这方面的新法律和官方文件及时传送国际局。

（2）国际局应当应要求向任何缔约国提供有关本公约的资料，应当为促进本公约规定的保护开展研究和提供服务。

（3）国际局应当与联合国教育科学文化组织和国际劳工组织合作，在各自的职权范围内履行本条第（1）、（2）款所列的职能。

第九条

（1）本公约应当向联合国秘书长交存。在1972年4月30日之前，联合国和任何联合国专门机构、国际原子能机构或国际法院规约的任何成员国均可在本公约上签字。

（2）本公约须经签字国批准或接受；本条第（1）款提到的任何国家均可加入本公约。

（3）批准、接受或加入书应当向联合国秘书长交存。

（4）不言而喻，一个国家受本公约约束时，便能够根据其国内法律使本公约条款付诸实施。

第十条

不允许对本公约作出保留。

第十一条

（1）本公约应当于第五份批准、接受或加入书交存三个月后生效。

（2）对于在第五份批准、接受或加入书交存之后批准、接受或加入的国家，本公约应当于世界知识产权组织总干事根据第十三条第（4）款通知有关各国已收到该国证书之日起三个月后在该国生效。

（3）在批准、接受或加入时，或在此后任何时间，任何国家可在致联合国秘书长的通知书中声明本公约适于它负责其国际关系的所有领土或其中任何一领土。此通知书应当于收到之日起三个月后生效。

（4）但是，上款不得理解为一缔约国承认或默认另一缔约国根据上款规定使本公约对之适用的某一领土的现实状况。

第十二条

（1）任何缔约国可以以自己的名义或代表第十一条第（3）款所指的任

何领土，通过致联合国秘书长的书面通知退出本公约。

（2）此种退出应当于联合国秘书长收到通知书之日起十二个月后生效。

第十三条

（1）本公约应当以一份英文、法文、俄文和西班牙文合一的文本签署，四种文字具有同等效力。

（2）阿拉伯文、荷兰文、德文、意大利文和葡萄牙文的正式文本应当由世界知识产权组织总干事和有关政府协商后制定。

（3）联合国秘书长应当通知世界知识产权组织总干事、联合国教育科学文化组织总干事和国际劳工局局长：

（a）本公约的签署；

（b）批准、接受或加入书的交存；

（c）本公约生效的日期；

（d）任何根据第十一条第（3）款通知的声明；

（e）收到的退出公约通知书。

（4）世界知识产权组织总干事应当将根据上款规定收到的通知书以及根据第七条第（4）款作出的声明通知第九条第（1）款提到的国家。他还应当将此种声明通知联合国教育科学文化组织总干事和国际劳工局局长。

（5）联合国秘书长应当将本公约的两份经核证无误的副本送往第九条第（1）款提到的国家。

Convention for the Protection of Producers of Phonograms against Unauthorized Duplication of Their Phonograms

of October 29, 1971

The Contracting States,

concerned at the widespread and increasing unauthorized duplication of phonograms and the damage this is occasioning to the interests of authors, performers and producers of phonograms;

convinced that the protection of producers of phonograms against such acts will also benefit the performers whose performances, and the authors whose works, are recorded on the said phonograms;

recognizing the value of the work undertaken in this field by the United Nations Educational, Scientific and Cultural Organization and the World Intellectual Property Organization;

anxious not to impair in any way international agreements already in force and in particular in no way to prejudice wider acceptance of the Rome Convention of October 26, 1961, which affords protection to performers and to broadcasting organizations as well as to producers of phonograms;

have agreed as follows:

Article 1

[*Definitions* *]

For the purposes of this Convention:

(*a*) "phonogram" means any exclusively aural fixation of sounds of a performance or of other sounds;

---

* Articles have been given titles to facilitate their identification. There are no titles in the signed text.

(*b*) "producer of phonograms" means the person who, or the legal entity which, first fixes the sounds of a performance or other sounds;

(*c*) "duplicate" means an article which contains sounds taken directly or indirectly from a phonogram and which embodies all or a substantial part of the sounds fixed in that phonogram;

(*d*) "distribution to the public" means any act by which duplicates of a phonogram are offered, directly or indirectly, to the general public or any section thereof.

Article 2

[*Obligations of Contracting States*; *Whom they must protect and against what*]

Each Contracting State shall protect producers of phonograms who are nationals of other Contracting States against the making of duplicates without the consent of the producer and against the importation of such duplicates, provided that any such making or importation is for the purpose of distribution to the public, and against the distribution of such duplicates to the public.

Article 3

[*Means of Implementation by Contracting States*]

The means by which this Convention is implemented shall be a matter for the domestic law of each Contracting State and shall include one or more of the following: protection by means of the grant of a copyright or other specific right; protection by means of the law relating to unfair competition; protection by means of penal sanctions.

Article 4

[*Term of Protection*]

The duration of the protection given shall be a matter for the domestic law of each Contracting State. However, if the domestic law prescribes a specific duration for the protection, that duration shall not be less than twenty years from the end either of the year in which the sounds embodied in the phonogram were first fixed or of the year in which the phonogram was first published.

Article 5

[*Formalities*]

If, as a condition of protecting the producers of phonograms, a Contracting State, under its domestic law, requires compliance with formalities, these shall be considered as fulfilled if all the authorized duplicates of the phonogram distributed to the public or their containers bear a notice consisting of the symbol (P), accompanied by the year date of the first publication, placed in such manner as to give reasonable notice of claim of protection; and, if the duplicates or their containers do not identify the producer, his successor in title or the exclusive licensee (by carrying his name, trademark or other appropriate designation), the notice shall also include the name of the producer, his successor in title or the exclusive licensee.

Article 6

[*Limitations on Protection*]

Any Contracting State which affords protection by means of copyright or other specific right, or protection by means of penal sanctions, may in its domestic law provide, with regard to the protection of producers of phonograms, the same kinds of limitations as are permitted with respect to the protection of authors of literary and artistic works. However, no compulsory licenses may be permitted unless all of the following conditions are met:

(*a*) the duplication is for use solely for the purpose of teaching or scientific research;

(*b*) the license shall be valid for duplication only within the territory of the Contracting State whose competent authority has granted the license and shall not extend to the export of duplicates;

(*c*) the duplication made under the license gives rise to an equitable remuneration fixed by the said authority taking into account, inter alia, the number of duplicates which will be made.

Article 7

[*Savings*: 1. *Safeguard of Copyright and Neighboring Rights*; 2. *Protection for Performers*; 3. *Non – Retroactivity*; 4. *Substitution of the Criterion of Fixation*]

(1) This Convention shall in no way be interpreted to limit or prejudice the protection otherwise secured to authors, to performers, to producers of phonograms or to broadcasting organizations under any domestic law or international agreement.

(2) It shall be a matter for the domestic law of each Contracting State to determine the extent, if any, to which performers whose performances are fixed in a

phonogram are entitled to enjoy protection and the conditions for enjoying any such protection.

(3) No Contracting State shall be required to apply the provisions of this Convention to any phonogram fixed before this Convention entered into force with respect to that State.

(4) Any Contracting State which, on October 29, 1971, affords protection to producers of phonograms solely on the basis of the place of first fixation may, by a notification deposited with the Director General of the World Intellectual Property Organization, declare that it will apply this criterion instead of the criterion of the nationality of the producer.

Article 8

[*Secretariat*]

(1) The International Bureau of the World Intellectual Property Organization shall assemble and publish information concerning the protection of phonograms. Each Contracting State shall promptly communicate to the International Bureau all new laws and official texts on this subject.

(2) The International Bureau shall, on request, furnish information to any Contracting State on matters concerning this Convention, and shall conduct studies and provide services designed to facilitate the protection provided for therein.

(3) The International Bureau shall exercise the functions enumerated in paragraph (1) and paragraph (2) above in cooperation, for matters within their respective competence, with the United Nations Educational, Scientific and Cultural Organization and the International Labour Office.

Article 9

[*Joining the Convention*: 1. *Signature and Deposit*; 2 *and* 3. *Ratification and Accession*; 4. *States' Obligations as to their Domestic Law*]

(1) This Convention shall be deposited with the Secretary - General of the United Nations. It shall be open until April 30, 1972, for signature by any State that is a member of the United Nations, any of the Specialized Agencies brought into relationship with the United Nations, or the International Atomic Energy Agency, or is a party to the Statute of the International Court of Justice.

(2) This Convention shall be subject to ratification or acceptance by the signatory States. It shall be open for accession by any State referred to in paragraph (1)

of this Article.

(3) Instruments of ratification, acceptance or accession shall be deposited with the Secretary - General of the United Nations.

(4) It is understood that, at the time a State becomes bound by this Convention, it will be in a position in accordance with its domestic law to give effect to the provisions of the Convention.

Article 10

[*Reservations*]

No reservations to this Convention are permitted.

Article 11

[*Entry into Force and Applicability*: 1 *and* 2. *Entry into Force of the Convention*; 3 *and* 4. *Applicability of the Convention to Certain Territories*]

(1) This Convention shall enter into force three months after deposit of the fifth instrument of ratification, acceptance or accession.

(2) For each State ratifying, accepting or acceding to this Convention after the deposit of the fifth instrument of ratification, acceptance or accession, the Convention shall enter into force three months after the date on which the Director General of the World Intellectual Property Organization informs the States, in accordance with Article 13, paragraph (4), of the deposit of its instrument.

(3) Any State may, at the time of ratification, acceptance or accession or at any later date, declare by notification addressed to the Secretary - General of the United Nations that this Convention shall apply to all or any one of the territories for whose international affairs it is responsible. This notification will take effect three months after the date on which it is received.

(4) However, the preceding paragraph may in no way be understood as implying the recognition or tacit acceptance by a Contracting State of the factual situation concerning a territory to which this Convention is made applicable by another Contracting State by virtue of the said paragraph.

Article 12

[*Denunciation of the Convention*]

(1) Any Contracting State may denounce this Convention, on its own behalf or on behalf of any of the territories referred to in Article 11, paragraph (3), by written notification addressed to the Secretary - General of the United Nations.

(2) Denunciation shall take effect twelve months after the date on which the Secretary - General of the United Nations has received the notification.

Article 13

[*Languages and Notifications*]

(1) This Convention shall be signed in a single copy in English, French, Russian and Spanish, the four texts being equally authentic.

(2) Official texts shall be established by the Director General of the World Intellectual Property Organization, after consultation with the interested Governments, in the Arabic, Dutch, German, Italian and Portuguese languages.

(3) The Secretary - General of the United Nations shall notify the Director General of the World Intellectual Property Organization, the Director - General of the United Nations Educational, Scientific and Cultural Organization and the Director - General of the International Labour Office of:

(*a*) signatures to this Convention;

(*b*) the deposit of instruments of ratification, acceptance or accession;

(*c*) the date of entry into force of this Convention;

(*d*) any declaration notified pursuant to Article 11, paragraph (3);

(*e*) the receipt of notifications of denunciation.

(4) The Director General of the World Intellectual Property Organization shall inform the States referred to in Article 9, paragraph (1), of the notifications received pursuant to the preceding paragraph and of any declarations made under Article 7, paragraph (4). He shall also notify the Director - General of the United Nations Educational, Scientific and Cultural Organization and the Director - General of the International Labour Office of such declarations.

(5) The Secretary - General of the United Nations shall transmit two certified copies of this Convention to the States referred to in Article 9, paragraph (1).

世界知识产权组织表演和录音制品条约

（世界知识产权组织外交会议
1996 年 12 月 20 日于日内瓦通过）

序　　言

缔约各方，

出于以尽可能有效和一致的方式发展和维护保护表演者和录音制品制作者权利的愿望；

承认有必要采用新的国际规则，以提供解决由经济、社会、文化和技术发展所提出的问题的适当方法；

承认信息与通信技术的发展和交汇对表演和录音制品的制作与使用的深刻影响；

承认有必要保持表演者和录音制品制作者的权利与广大公众的利益尤其是教育、研究和获得信息的利益之间的平衡。

达成协议如下：

第一章　总　　则

第 1 条　与其他公约的关系

（1）本条约的任何内容均不得减损缔约方相互之间依照于 1961 年 10 月 26 日在罗马签订的《保护表演者、录音制品制作者和广播组织国际公约》（以下简称“《罗马公约》”）已承担的现有义务。

（2）依本条约授予的保护不得触动或以任何方式影响对文学和艺术作品

版权的保护。因此，本条约的任何内容均不得被解释为损害此种保护。[①]

（3）本条约不得与任何其他条约有任何关联，亦不得损害依任何其他条约的任何权利和义务。

第2条　定义

在本条约中：

（a）“表演者”指演员、歌唱家、音乐家、舞蹈家以及表演、歌唱、演说、朗诵、演奏、表现，或以其他方式表演文学或艺术作品或民间文学艺术作品的其他人员；

（b）“录音制品”系指除以电影作品或其他音像作品所含的录制形式之外，对表演的声音、或其他声音、或声音表现物所进行的录制；[②]

（c）“录制”系指对声音或声音表现物的体现，从中通过某种装置可感觉、复制或传播该声音；

（d）“录音制品制作者”系指对首次将表演的声音、或其他声音、或声音表现物录制下来提出动议并负有责任的自然人或法人；

（e）“发行”录制的表演或录音制品系指经权利持有人同意并在以合理的数量向公众提供复制品的条件下，将录制的表演或录音制品的复制品提供给公众；[③]

（f）“广播”系指以无线方式的播送，使公众能接收声音、或图像和声音、或图像和声音表现物；通过卫星进行的此种播送亦为“广播”；播送密码信号，如果广播组织或经其同意向公众提供了解码的手段，则是“广播”；

（g）“向公众传播”表演或录音制品系指通过除广播以外的任何媒体向公众播送表演的声音或以录音制品录制的声音或声音表现物。在第15条中，“向公众传播”包括使公众能听到以录音制品录制的声音或声音表现物。

第3条　依本条约受保护的受益人

（1）缔约各方应将依本条约规定的保护给予系其他缔约方国民的表演者

---

① 关于第（2）款的议定声明：不言而喻，第1条第（2）款澄清本条约规定的对录音制品的权利与以录音制品体现的作品的版权之间的关系。在需要以录音制品体现的作品的作者与对录音制品持有权利的表演者或制作者许可的情况下，获得作者许可的需要并非因同时还需获得表演者或制作者的许可而不复存在，反之亦然。

此外，不言而喻，第1条第（2）款的任何内容均不阻止缔约方对表演者或录音制品制作者规定的专有权超出依照本条约需要规定的专有权。

② 关于第2条（b）项的议定声明：不言而喻，第2条（b）项规定的录音制品的定义并不表明对录音制品的权利因将录音制品包含在电影作品或其他音像作品中而受到任何影响。

③ 关于第2条（e）项，第8、9、12和13条的议定声明：这些条款中的用语“复制品”和“原件和复制品”，受各该条中发行权和出租权的约束，专指可作为有形物品投放流通的固定的复制品。

和录音制品制作者。

（2）其他缔约方的国民应被理解为符合《罗马公约》规定的标准、有资格受到保护的表演者或录音制品制作者，如同本条约的全体缔约方均假设为该公约缔约国的情形。对于这些资格标准，缔约各方应适用于本条约第 2 条中的有关定义。[①]

（3）任何利用《罗马公约》第 5 条第（3）款所规定的可能性、或为该公约第 5 条的目的利用《罗马公约》第 17 条所规定的可能性的缔约方，应向世界知识产权组织（WIPO）总干事做出那些条款所预先规定的通知。[②]

第 4 条 国民待遇

（1）在本条约所专门授予的专有权以及本条约第 15 条所规定的获得合理报酬的权利方面，每个缔约方均应将其给予本国国民的待遇给予第 3 条第（2）款所定义的其他缔约方的国民。

（2）本条第（1）款规定的义务不适用于另一缔约方使用了本条约第 15 条第（3）款允许的保留的情况。

第二章 表演者的权利

第 5 条 表演者的精神权利

（1）不依赖于表演者的经济权利，甚至在这些权利转让之后，表演者仍应对于其现场有声表演或以录音制品录制的表演有权要求承认其系表演的表演者，除非使用表演的方式决定可省略不提其系表演者；并有权反对任何对其表演进行将有损其名声的歪曲、篡改或其他修改。

（2）根据本条第（1）款授予表演者的权利在其死后应继续保留，至少到其经济权利期满为止，并应可由被要求提供保护的缔约方立法所授权的个人或机构行使。但批准或加入本条约时其立法尚未规定在表演者死后保护上款所述之全部权利的国家，则可规定其中部分权利在表演者死后不再保留。

（3）为保联本条所授予的权利而采取的补救办法应由被要求提供保护的缔约方立法规定。

---

① 关于第 3 条第（2）款的议定声明：为了适用第 3 条第（2）款，不言而喻，录制系指制作完成原始带（“母带”）。

② 关于第 3 条的议定声明：不言而喻，《罗马公约》第 5 条（a）项和第 16 条（a）项第（Ⅳ）目中所指的“另一缔约国的国民”，在适用于本条约时，对于系本条约缔约方的政府间组织，指系该组织成员的国家之一的国民。

第6条　表演者对其尚未录制的表演的经济权利

表演者应享有专有权，对于其表演授权：

（Ⅰ）广播和向公众传播其尚未录制的表演，除非该表演本身已属广播表演；和

（Ⅱ）录制其尚未录制的表演。

第7条　复制权

表演者应享有授权以任何方式或形式对其以录音制品录制的表演直接或间接地进行复制的专有权。①

第8条　发行权

（1）表演者应享有授权通过销售或其他所有权转让形式各公众提供其以录音制品录制的表演的原件或复制品的专有权。

（2）对于在已录制的表演的原件或复制品经表演者授权被首次销售或其他所有权转让之后适用本条第（1）款中权利的用尽所依据的条件（如有此种条件），本条约的任何内容均不得影响缔约各方确定该条件的自由。②

第9条　出租权

（1）表演者应按缔约各方国内法中的规定享有授权将其以录音制品录制的表演的原件和复制品向公众进行商业性出租的专有权，即使该原件或复制品已由表演者发行或根据表演者的授权发行。

（2）尽管有本条第（1）款的规定，任何缔约方如在1994年4月15日已有且现仍实行表演者出租其以录音制品录制的表演的复制品获得公平报酬的制度，只要录音制品的商业性出租没有引起对表演者复制专有权的严重损害，即可保留这一制度。③

第10条　提供已录制表演的权利

表演者应享有专有权，以授权通过有线或无线的方式向公众提供其以录音制品录制的表演，使该表演可为公众中的成员在其个人选定的地点和时间获得。

---

①　关于第7、11和16条的议定声明：第7条和第11条所规定的复制权及其中通过第16条允许的例外，完全适用于数字环境，尤其是以数字形式使用表演和录音制品的情况。不言而喻，在电子媒体中以数字形式存储受保护的表演或录音制品，构成这些条款意义下的复制。

②　关于第2条（e），第8、9、12和13条的议定声明：这些条款中的用语“复制品”和“原件和复制品”，受各该条中发行权和出租权的约束，专指可作为有形物品投放流通的固定的复制品。

③　关于第2条（e）项，第8、9、12和13条的议定声明：这些条款中的用语“复制品”和“原件和复制品”，受各该条中发行权和出租权的约束，专指可作为有形物品投放流通的固定的复制品。

第三章　录音制品制作者的权利

第11条　复制权

录音制品制作者应享有授权以任何方式或形式对其录音制品直接或间接地进行复制的专有权。①

第12条　发行权

（1）录音制品制作者应享有授权通过销售或其他所有权转让形式向公众提供其录音制品的原件或复制品的专有权。

（2）对于在录音制品的原件或复制品经录音制品制作者授权被首次销售或其他所有权转让之后适用本条第（1）款中权利的用尽所依据的条件（如有此种条件），本条约任何内容均不得影响缔约各方确定该条件的自由。②

第13条　出租权

（1）录音制品制作者应享有授权对其录音制品的原件和复制品向公众进行商业性出租的专有权，即使该原件或复制品已由录音制品制作者发行或根据录音制品制作者的授权发行。

（2）尽管有本条第（1）款的规定，任何缔约方如在1994年4月15日已有且现仍实行录音制品制作者出租其录音制品的复制品获得公平报酬的制度，只要录音制品的商业性出租没有引起对录音制品制作者复制专有权的严重损害，即可保留这一制度。③

第14条　提供录音制品的权利

录音制品制作者应享有专有权，以授权通过有线或无线的方式向公众提供其录音制品，使该录音制品可为公众中的成员在其个人选定的地点和时间获得。

第四章　共同条款

第15条　因广播和向公众传播获得报酬的权利

---

① 关于第7、11和16条的议定声明：第7条和第11条所规定的复制权及其中通过第16条允许的例外，完全适用于数字环境，尤其是以数字形式使用表演和录音制品的情况。不言而喻，在电子媒体中以数字形式存储受保护的表演或录音制品，构成这些条款意义下的复制。

② 关于第2条（e）项，第8、9、12和13条的议定声明：这些条款中的用语“复制品”和“原件和复制品”，受各该条中发行权和出租权的约束，专指可作为有形物品投放流通的固定的复制品。

③ 关于第2条（e）项，第8、9、12和13条的议定声明：这些条款中的用语“复制品”和“原件和复制品”，受各该条中发行权和出租权的约束，专指可作为有形物品投放流通的固定的复制品。

（1）对于将为商业目的发行的录音制品直接或间接地用于广播或用于对公众的任何传播，表演者和录音制品制作者应享有获得一次性合理报酬的权利。

（2）缔约各方可在其国内立法中规定，该一次性合理报酬应由表演者、或由录音制品制作者或由二者向用户索取。缔约各方可制定国内立法，对表演者和录音制品制作者之间如未达成协议，表演者和录音制品制作者应如何分配该一次性合理报酬所依据的条件作出规定。

（3）任何缔约方均可在向世界知识产权组织总干事交存的通知书中，声明其将仅对某些使用适用本条第（1）款的规定，或声明其将以某种其他方式对其适用加以限制，或声明其将根本不适用这些规定。

（4）在本条中，以有线或无线的方式向公众中的成员在其他选定的地点和时间获得的录音制品应被认为仿佛其原本即为商业目的而发行。[①][②]

第16条　限制与例外

（1）缔约各方在其国内立法中，可在对表演者和录音制品制作者的保护方面规定与其国内立法中对文学和艺术作品的版权保护所规定的相同种类的限制或例外。

（2）缔约各方应将对本条约所规定权利的任何限制或例外限于某些不与录音制品的正常利用相抵触、也不无理地损害表演者或录音制品制作者合法利益的特殊情况。[③][④]

第17条　保护期

（1）依本条约授予表演者的保护期，应自表演以录音制品录制之年年终

---

① 关于第15条的议定声明：不言而喻，第15条并非表示完全解决表演者和录音制品制作者在数字时代应享有的广播和向公众传播的权利的水平。各代表团未能就关于需在若干情况下规定专有权的几个方面或关于需在没有保留可能情况下规定权利的不同提案达成协商一致，因此将此议题留待以后解决。

② 关于第15条的议定声明：不言而喻，第15条不妨碍将本条授予的权利提供给民间文学艺术作品的表演者和录制民间文学艺术作品录音制品的制作者，只要这些录音制品未被以获得商业利润为目的而发行。

③ 关于第7、11和16条的议定声明：第7条和第11条所规定的复制权及其中通过第16条允许的例外，完全适用于数字环境，尤其是以数字形式使用表演和录音制品的情况。不言而喻，在电子媒体中以数字形式存储受保护的表演或录音制品，构成这些条款意义下的复制。

④ 关于第16条的议定声明：关于《世界知识产权组织版权条约》第10条（涉及限制与例外）的议定声明，亦可比照适用于《世界知识产权组织表演和录音制品条约》的第16条（涉及限制与例外）。〔关于WCT第10条的议定声明原文如下：不言而喻，第10条的规定允许缔约各方将其国内法中依《伯尔尼公约》被认为可接受的限制与例外继续适用并适当地延伸到数字环境中。同样，这些规定应被理解为允许缔约方制定对数字网络环境适宜的新的例外与限制。

"另外，不言而喻，第10条第（2）款既不缩小也不扩大由《伯尔尼公约》所允许的限制与例外的可适用性范围。"〕

算起，至少持续到50年期满为止。

（2）依本条约授予录音制品制作者的保护期，应自该录音制品发行之年年终算起，至少持续到50年期满为止；或如果录音制品自录制完成起50年内未被发行，则保护期应自录制完成之年年终起至少持续50年。

第18条　关于技术措施的义务

缔约各方应规定适当的法律保护和有效的法律补救办法，制止规避由表演者或录音制品制作者为行使本条约所规定的权利而使用的、对就其表演或录音制品进行未经该有关表演者或录音制品制作者许可、或未由法律准许的行为加以约束的有效技术措施。

第19条　关于权利管理信息的义务

（1）缔约各方应规定适当和有效的法律补救办法，制止任何人明知、或就民事补救而言有合理根据知道其行为会诱使、促成、便利或包庇对本条约所涵盖的任何权利的侵犯而故意从事以下行为：

（Ⅰ）未经许可去除或改变任何权利管理的电子信息；

（Ⅱ）未经许可发行、为发行目的进口、广播、向公众传播或提供明知已被未经许可去除或改变权利管理电子信息的表演、录制的表演或录音制品的复制品。

（2）本条中的用语“权利管理信息”系指识别表演者、表演者的表演、录音制品制作者、录音制品、对表演或录音制品拥有任何权利的所有人的信息，或有关使用表演或录音制品的条款和条件的信息，和代表此种信息的任何数字或代码，各该项信息均附于录制的表演或录音制品的每件复制品上或在录制的表演或录音制品向公众提供时出现。①

第20条　手续

享有和行使本条约所规定的权利无须履行任何手续。

第21条　保留

除第15条第（3）款的规定外，不允许对本条约有任何保留。

第22条　适用的时限

（1）缔约各方应将《伯尔尼公约》第18条的规定比照适用于本条约所

---

① 关于第19条的议定声明：关于《世界知识产权组织版权条约》第12条（涉及关于权利管理信息的义务）的议定声明，亦可比照适用于《世界知识产权组织表演和录音制品条约》的第19条涉及关于权利管理信息的义务。〔关于WCT第12条的议定声明原文如下：“不言而喻，‘对本条约或《伯尔尼公约》所涵盖的任何权利的侵犯’的提法既包括专有权，也包括获得报酬的权利。”

“此外，不言而喻，缔约各方不会依赖本条来制定或实施要求履行为《伯尔尼公约》或本条约所不允许的手续的权利管理制度，从而阻止商品的自由流通或妨碍享有依本条约规定的权利。”〕

规定的表演者和录音制品制作者的权利。

(2) 尽管有本条第 (1) 款的规定，缔约方可将对本条约第 5 条的适用限制于在本条约对该缔约方生效之后进行的表演。

第 23 条　关于权利行使的条款

(1) 缔约各方承诺根据其法律制度采取必要的措施，以确保本条约的适用。

(2) 缔约各方应确保依照其法律可以提供执法程序，以便能采取制止对本条约所涵盖权利的任何侵犯行为的有效行动，包括防止侵权的快速补救和为遏制进一步侵权的补救。

第五章　行政条款和最后条款

第 24 条　大会

(1) (a) 缔约方应设大会。

(b) 每一缔约方应有一名代表，该代表可由副代表、顾问和专家协助。

(c) 各代表团的费用应由指派它的缔约方负担。大会可要求世界知识产权组织（以下称为“本组织”）提供财政援助，以便利按照联合国大会既定惯例认为是发展中国家或向市场经济转轨的国家的缔约方代表团参加。

(2) (a) 大会应处理涉及维护和发展本条约及适用和实施本条约的事项。

(b) 大会应履行依第 26 条第 (2) 款向其指定的关于接纳某些政府间组织成为本条约缔约方的职能。

(c) 大会应对召开任何修订本条约的外交会议作出决定，并给予本组织总干事筹备此种外交会议的必要指示。

(3) (a) 凡属国家的每一缔约方应有一票，并应只能以其自己的名义表决。

(b) 凡属政府间组织的缔约方可代替其成员参加表决，其票数与其属本条约缔约方的成员国数目相等。如果此种政府间组织的任何一个成员国行使其表决权，则该组织不得参加表决，反之亦然。

(4) 大会应每两年召开一次例会，由本组织总干事召集。

(5) 大会应制定其本身的议事规则，其中包括特别会议的召集、法定人数的要求及在不违反本条约规定的前提下作出各种决定所需的多数。

第 25 条　国际局

本组织的国际局应履行与本条约有关的行政工作。

第 26 条　成为本条约缔约方的资格

（1）本组织的任何成员国均可成为本条约的缔约方。

（2）如果任何政府间组织声明其对于本条约涵盖的事项具有权限和具有约束其所有成员国的立法，并声明其根据其内部程序被正式授权要求成为本条约的缔约方，大会可决定接纳该政府间组织成为本条约的缔约方。

（3）欧洲共同体在通过本条约的外交会议上做出上款提及的声明后，可成为本条约的缔约方。

第 27 条　本条约规定的权利和义务

除本条约有任何相反的具体规定以外，每一缔约方均应享有本条约规定的一切权利并承担本条约规定的一切义务。

第 28 条　本条约的签署

本条约应在 1997 年 12 月 31 日以前开放供本组织的任何成员国和欧洲共同体签署。

第 29 条　本条约的生效

本条约应于 30 个国家向本组织总干事交存批准书或加入书三个月之后生效。

第 30 条　成为本条约缔约方的生效日期

本条约应自下列日期起具有约束力：

（Ⅰ）对第 29 条提到的 30 个国家，自本条约生效之日起；

（Ⅱ）对其他各国，自该国向本组织总干事交存文书之日满三个月起；

（Ⅲ）对欧洲共同体，如果其在本条约根据第 29 条生效后交存批准书或加入书，则自交存此种文书后满三个月起，或如果其在本条约生效前交存批准书或加入书，则自本条约生效后满三个月起；

（Ⅳ）对被接纳成为本条约缔约方的任何其他政府间组织，自该组织交存加入书后满三个月起。

第 31 条　退约

本条约的任何缔约方均可退出本条约，退约应通知本组织总干事。任何退约应于本组织总干事收到通知之日起一年后生效。

第 32 条　本条约的语文

（1）本条约的签字原件应为一份，以英文、阿拉伯文、中文、法文、俄文和西班牙文签署，各该文种的文本具有同等效力。

（2）除本条第（1）款提到的语文外，任何其他语文的正式文本须由总干事应有关当事方请求，在与所有有关当事方磋商之后制定。在本款中，“有关当事方”系指涉及其正式语文或正式语文之一的本组织任何成员国，并且如果涉及其正式语文之一，亦指欧洲共同体和可成为本条约缔约方的任何其他政府间组织。

第 33 条　保存人

本组织总干事为本条约的保存人。

WIPO Performances and Phonograms Treaty

adopted in Geneva on December 20, 1996

Preamble

The Contracting Parties,

Desiring to develop and maintain the protection of the rights of performers and producers of phonograms in a manner as effective and uniform as possible,

Recognizing the need to introduce new international rules in order to provide adequate solutions to the questions raised by economic, social, cultural and technological developments,

Recognizing the profound impact of the development and convergence of information and communication technologies on the production and use of performances and phonograms,

Recognizing the need to maintain a balance between the rights of performers and producers of phonograms and the larger public interest, particularly education, research and access to information,

Have agreed as follows:

CHAPTER I General Provisions

Article 1 Relation to Other Conventions

(1) Nothing in this Treaty shall derogate from existing obligations that Contracting Parties have to each other under the International Convention for the Protection of Performers, Producers of Phonograms and Broadcasting Organizations

done in Rome, October 26, 1961 (hereinafter the "Rome Convention").

(2) Protection granted under this Treaty shall leave intact and shall in no way affect the protection of copyright in literary and artistic works. Consequently, no provision of this Treaty may be interpreted as prejudicing such protection. 1

(3) This Treaty shall not have any connection with, nor shall it prejudice any rights and obligations under, any other treaties.

Article 2 Definitions

For the purposes of this Treaty:

(a) "performers" are actors, singers, musicians, dancers, and other persons who act, sing, deliver, declaim, play in, interpret, or otherwise perform literary or artistic works or expressions of folklore;

(b) "phonogram" means the fixation of the sounds of a performance or of other sounds, or of a representation of sounds, other than in the form of a fixation incorporated in a cinematographic or other audiovisual work; 2

(c) "fixation" means the embodiment of sounds, or of the representations thereof, from which they can be perceived, reproduced or communicated through a device;

(d) "producer of a phonogram" means the person, or the legal entity, who or which takes the initiative and has the responsibility for the first fixation of the sounds of a performance or other sounds, or the representations of sounds;

(e) "publication" of a fixed performance or a phonogram means the offering of copies of the fixed performance or the phonogram to the public, with the consent of the rightholder, and provided that copies are offered to the public in reasonable quantity; 3

(f) "broadcasting" means the transmission by wireless means for public reception of sounds or of images and sounds or of the representations thereof; such transmission by satellite is also "broadcasting"; transmission of encrypted signals is "broadcasting" where the means for decrypting are provided to the public by the broadcasting organization or with its consent;

(g) "communication to the public" of a performance or a phonogram means the transmission to the public by any medium, otherwise than by broadcasting, of sounds of a performance or the sounds or the representations of sounds fixed in a phonogram. For the purposes of Article 15, "communication to the public" includes making the sounds or representations of sounds fixed in a phonogram audible to the public.

Article 3 Beneficiaries of Protection under this Treaty4

(1) Contracting Parties shall accord the protection provided under this Treaty to the performers and producers of phonograms who are nationals of other Contracting Parties.

(2) The nationals of other Contracting Parties shall be understood to be those performers or producers of phonograms who would meet the criteria for eligibility for protection provided under the Rome Convention, were all the Contracting Parties to this Treaty Contracting States of that Convention. In respect of these criteria of eligibility, Contracting Parties shall apply the relevant definitions in Article 2 of this Treaty. 5

(3) Any Contracting Party availing itself of the possibilities provided in Article 5 (3) of the Rome Convention or, for the purposes of Article 5 of the same Convention, Article 17 thereof shall make a notification as foreseen in those provisions to the Director General of the World Intellectual Property Organization (WIPO).

Article 4 National Treatment

(1) Each Contracting Party shall accord to nationals of other Contracting Parties, as defined in Article 3 (2), the treatment it accords to its own nationals with regard to the exclusive rights specifically granted in this Treaty, and to the right to equitable remuneration provided for in Article 15 of this Treaty.

(2) The obligation provided for in paragraph (1) does not apply to the extent that another Contracting Party makes use of the reservations permitted by Article 15 (3) of this Treaty.

CHAPTER II Rights of Performers

Article 5 Moral Rights of Performers

(1) Independently of a performer's economic rights, and even after the transfer of those rights, the performer shall, as regards his live aural performances or performances fixed in phonograms, have the right to claim to be identified as the performer of his performances, except where omission is dictated by the manner of the use of the performance, and to object to any distortion, mutilation or other modification of his performances that would be prejudicial to his reputation.

(2) The rights granted to a performer in accordance with paragraph (1) shall, after his death, be maintained, at least until the expiry of the economic rights, and shall be exercisable by the persons or institutions authorized by the legislation of the Contracting Party where protection is claimed. However, those Contracting Parties whose legislation, at the moment of their ratification of or accession to this Treaty, does not provide for protection after the death of the performer of all rights set out in the preceding paragraph may provide that some of these rights will, after his death, cease to be maintained.

(3) The means of redress for safeguarding the rights granted under this Article shall be governed by the legislation of the Contracting Party where protection is claimed.

Article 6 Economic Rights of Performers in their Unfixed Performances

Performers shall enjoy the exclusive right of authorizing, as regards their performances:

(i) the broadcasting and communication to the public of their unfixed performances except where the performance is already a broadcast performance; and

(ii) the fixation of their unfixed performances.

Article 7 Right of Reproduction

Performers shall enjoy the exclusive right of authorizing the direct or indirect reproduction of their performances fixed in phonograms, in any manner or form. 6

Article 8 Right of Distribution

(1) Performers shall enjoy the exclusive right of authorizing the making available to the public of the original and copies of their performances fixed in phonograms through sale or other transfer of ownership.

(2) Nothing in this Treaty shall affect the freedom of Contracting Parties to determine the conditions, if any, under which the exhaustion of the right in paragraph (1) applies after the first sale or other transfer of ownership of the original or a copy of the fixed performance with the authorization of the performer. 3

Article 9 Right of Rental

(1) Performers shall enjoy the exclusive right of authorizing the commercial rental to the public of the original and copies of their performances fixed in phonograms as determined in the national law of Contracting Parties, even after distribution of them by, or pursuant to, authorization by the performer.

(2) Notwithstanding the provisions of paragraph (1), a Contracting Party that, on April 15, 1994, had and continues to have in force a system of equitable remuneration of performers for the rental of copies of their performances fixed in phonograms, may maintain that system provided that the commercial rental of phonograms is not giving rise to the material impairment of the exclusive right of reproduction of performers. 3

Article 10 Right of Making Available of Fixed Performances

Performers shall enjoy the exclusive right of authorizing the making available to the public of their performances fixed in phonograms, by wire or wireless means, in such a way that members of the public may access them from a place and at a time individually chosen by them.

CHAPTER III Rights of Producers of Phonograms

Article 11 Right of Reproduction

Producers of phonograms shall enjoy the exclusive right of authorizing the direct or indirect reproduction of their phonograms, in any manner or form. 6

Article 12 Right of Distribution

(1) Producers of phonograms shall enjoy the exclusive right of authorizing the making available to the public of the original and copies of their phonograms through sale or other transfer of ownership.

(2) Nothing in this Treaty shall affect the freedom of Contracting Parties to determine the conditions, if any, under which the exhaustion of the right in paragraph (1) applies after the first sale or other transfer of ownership of the original or a copy of the phonogram with the authorization of the producer of the phonogram. 3

Article 13 Right of Rental

(1) Producers of phonograms shall enjoy the exclusive right of authorizing the commercial rental to the public of the original and copies of their phonograms, even after distribution of them, by or pursuant to, authorization by the producer.

(2) Notwithstanding the provisions of paragraph (1), a Contracting Party that, on April 15, 1994, had and continues to have in force a system of equitable remuneration of producers of phonograms for the rental of copies of their phonograms, may maintain that system provided that the commercial rental of phonograms is not

giving rise to the material impairment of the exclusive rights of reproduction of producers of phonograms. 3

Article 14 Right of Making Available of Phonograms

Producers of phonograms shall enjoy the exclusive right of authorizing the making available to the public of their phonograms, by wire or wireless means, in such a way that members of the public may access them from a place and at a time individually chosen by them.

CHAPTER IV Common Provisions

Article 15 Right to Remuneration for Broadcasting and Communication to the Public

(1) Performers and producers of phonograms shall enjoy the right to a single equitable remuneration for the direct or indirect use of phonograms published for commercial purposes for broadcasting or for any communication to the public.

(2) Contracting Parties may establish in their national legislation that the single equitable remuneration shall be claimed from the user by the performer or by the producer of a phonogram or by both. Contracting Parties may enact national legislation that, in the absence of an agreement between the performer and the producer of a phonogram, sets the terms according to which performers and producers of phonograms shall share the single equitable remuneration.

(3) Any Contracting Party may, in a notification deposited with the Director General of WIPO, declare that it will apply the provisions of paragraph (1) only in respect of certain uses, or that it will limit their application in some other way, or that it will not apply these provisions at all.

(4) For the purposes of this Article, phonograms made available to the public by wire or wireless means in such a way that members of the public may access them from a place and at a time individually chosen by them shall be considered as if they had been published for commercial purposes. 7, 8

Article 16 Limitations and Exceptions

(1) Contracting Parties may, in their national legislation, provide for the same kinds of limitations or exceptions with regard to the protection of performers and producers of phonograms as they provide for, in their national legislation, in con-

nection with the protection of copyright in literary and artistic works.

(2) Contracting Parties shall confine any limitations of or exceptions to rights provided for in this Treaty to certain special cases which do not conflict with a normal exploitation of the performance or phonogram and do not unreasonably prejudice the legitimate interests of the performer or of the producer of the phonogram. 6, 9

Article 17 Term of Protection

(1) The term of protection to be granted to performers under this Treaty shall last, at least, until the end of a period of 50 years computed from the end of the year in which the performance was fixed in a phonogram.

(2) The term of protection to be granted to producers of phonograms under this Treaty shall last, at least, until the end of a period of 50 years computed from the end of the year in which the phonogram was published, or failing such publication within 50 years from fixation of the phonogram, 50 years from the end of the year in which the fixation was made.

Article 18 Obligations concerning Technological Measures

Contracting Parties shall provide adequate legal protection and effective legal remedies against the circumvention of effective technological measures that are used by performers or producers of phonograms in connection with the exercise of their rights under this Treaty and that restrict acts, in respect of their performances or phonograms, which are not authorized by the performers or the producers of phonograms concerned or permitted by law.

Article 19 Obligations concerning Rights Management Information

(1) Contracting Parties shall provide adequate and effective legal remedies against any person knowingly performing any of the following acts knowing, or with respect to civil remedies having reasonable grounds to know, that it will induce, enable, facilitate or conceal an infringement of any right covered by this Treaty:

(i) to remove or alter any electronic rights management information without authority;

(ii) to distribute, import for distribution, broadcast, communicate or make available to the public, without authority, performances, copies of fixed performances or phonograms knowing that electronic rights management information has been removed or altered without authority.

(2) As used in this Article, "rights management information" means informa-

tion which identifies the performer, the performance of the performer, the producer of the phonogram, the phonogram, the owner of any right in the performance or phonogram, or information about the terms and conditions of use of the performance or phonogram, and any numbers or codes that represent such information, when any of these items of information is attached to a copy of a fixed performance or a phonogram or appears in connection with the communication or making available of a fixed performance or a phonogram to the public. 10

Article 20 Formalities

The enjoyment and exercise of the rights provided for in this Treaty shall not be subject to any formality.

Article 21 Reservations

Subject to the provisions of Article 15 (3), no reservations to this Treaty shall be permitted.

Article 22 Application in Time

(1) Contracting Parties shall apply the provisions of Article 18 of the Berne Convention, mutatis *mutandis*, to the rights of performers and producers of phonograms provided for in this Treaty.

(2) Notwithstanding paragraph (1), a Contracting Party may limit the application of Article 5 of this Treaty to performances which occurred after the entry into force of this Treaty for that Party.

Article 23 Provisions on Enforcement of Rights

(1) Contracting Parties undertake to adopt, in accordance with their legal systems, the measures necessary to ensure the application of this Treaty.

(2) Contracting Parties shall ensure that enforcement procedures are available under their law so as to permit effective action against any act of infringement of rights covered by this Treaty, including expeditious remedies to prevent infringements and remedies which constitute a deterrent to further infringements.

CHAPTER V Administrative and Final Clauses

Article 24 Assembly

(1)

(a) The Contracting Parties shall have an Assembly.

(b) Each Contracting Party shall be represented by one delegate who may be assisted by alternate delegates, advisors and experts.

(c) The expenses of each delegation shall be borne by the Contracting Party that has appointed the delegation. The Assembly may ask WIPO to grant financial assistance to facilitate the participation of delegations of Contracting Parties that are regarded as developing countries in conformity with the established practice of the General Assembly of the United Nations or that are countries in transition to a market economy.

(2)

(a) The Assembly shall deal with matters concerning the maintenance and development of this Treaty and the application and operation of this Treaty.

(b) The Assembly shall perform the function allocated to it under Article 26 (2) in respect of the admission of certain intergovernmental organizations to become party to this Treaty.

(c) The Assembly shall decide the convocation of any diplomatic conference for the revision of this Treaty and give the necessary instructions to the Director General of WIPO for the preparation of such diplomatic conference.

(3)

(a) Each Contracting Party that is a State shall have one vote and shall vote only in its own name.

(b) Any Contracting Party that is an intergovernmental organization may participate in the vote, in place of its Member States, with a number of votes equal to the number of its Member States which are party to this Treaty. No such intergovernmental organization shall participate in the vote if any one of its Member States exercises its right to vote and vice versa.

(4) The Assembly shall meet in ordinary session once every two years upon convocation by the Director General of WIPO.

(5) The Assembly shall establish its own rules of procedure, including the convocation of extraordinary sessions, the requirements of a quorum and, subject to the provisions of this Treaty, the required majority for various kinds of decisions.

Article 25 International Bureau

The International Bureau of WIPO shall perform the administrative tasks concerning the Treaty.

Article 26 Eligibility for Becoming Party to the Treaty

(1) Any Member State of WIPO may become party to this Treaty.

(2) The Assembly may decide to admit any intergovernmental organization to become party to this Treaty which declares that it is competent in respect of, and has its own legislation binding on all its Member States on, matters covered by this Treaty and that it has been duly authorized, in accordance with its internal procedures, to become party to this Treaty.

(3) The European Community, having made the declaration referred to in the preceding paragraph in the Diplomatic Conference that has adopted this Treaty, may become party to this Treaty.

Article 27 Rights and Obligations under the Treaty

Subject to any specific provisions to the contrary in this Treaty, each Contracting Party shall enjoy all of the rights and assume all of the obligations under this Treaty.

Article 28 Signature of the Treaty

This Treaty shall be open for signature until December 31, 1997, by any Member State of WIPO and by the European Community.

Article 29 Entry into Force of the Treaty

This Treaty shall enter into force three months after 30 instruments of ratification or accession by States have been deposited with the Director General of WIPO.

Article 30 Effective Date of Becoming Party to the Treaty

This Treaty shall bind:

(i) the 30 States referred to in Article 29, from the date on which this Treaty has entered into force;

(ii) each other State from the expiration of three months from the date on which the State has deposited its instrument with the Director General of WIPO;

(iii) the European Community, from the expiration of three months after the deposit of its instrument of ratification or accession if such instrument has been deposited after the entry into force of this Treaty according to Article 29, or, three months after the entry into force of this Treaty if such instrument has been deposited before the entry into force of this Treaty;

(iv) any other intergovernmental organization that is admitted to become party to this Treaty, from the expiration of three months after the deposit of its instrument of accession.

Article 31 Denunciation of the Treaty

This Treaty may be denounced by any Contracting Party by notification addressed to the Director General of WIPO. Any denunciation shall take effect one year from the date on which the Director General of WIPO received the notification.

Article 32 Languages of the Treaty

(1) This Treaty is signed in a single original in English, Arabic, Chinese, French, Russian and Spanish languages, the versions in all these languages being equally authentic.

(2) An official text in any language other than those referred to in paragraph (1) shall be established by the Director General of WIPO on the request of an interested party, after consultation with all the interested parties. For the purposes of this paragraph, "interested party" means any Member State of WIPO whose official language, or one of whose official languages, is involved and the European Community, and any other intergovernmental organization that may become party to this Treaty, if one of its official languages is involved.

Article 33 Depositary

The Director General of WIPO is the depositary of this Treaty.

1 Agreed statement concerning Article 1 (2): It is understood that Article 1 (2) clarifies the relationship between rights in phonograms under this Treaty and copyright in works embodied in the phonograms. In cases where authorization is needed from both the author of a work embodied in the phonogram and a performer or producer owning rights in the phonogram, the need for the authorization of the author does not cease to exist because the authorization of the performer or producer is also required, and vice versa.

It is further understood that nothing in Article 1 (2) precludes a Contracting Party from providing exclusive rights to a performer or producer of phonograms beyond those required to be provided under this Treaty.

2 Agreed statement concerning Article 2 (*b*): It is understood that the definition of phonogram provided in Article 2 (*b*) does not suggest that rights in the phonogram are in any way affected through their incorporation into a cinemato-

graphic or other audiovisual work.

3 Agreed statement concerning Articles 2 (*e*), 8, 9, 12, and 13: As used in these Articles, the expressions "copies" and "original and copies," being subject to the right of distribution and the right of rental under the said Articles, refer exclusively to fixed copies that can be put into circulation as tangible objects.

4 Agreed statement concerning Article 3: It is understood that the reference in Articles 5 (*a*) and 16 (*a*) (iv) of the Rome Convention to "national of another Contracting State" will, when applied to this Treaty, mean, in regard to an intergovernmental organization that is a Contracting Party to this Treaty, a national of one of the countries that is a member of that organization.

5 Agreed statement concerning Article 3 (2): For the application of Article 3 (2), it is understood that fixation means the finalization of the master tape ("bande-mère").

6 Agreed statement concerning Articles 7, 11 and 16: The reproduction right, as set out in Articles 7 and 11, and the exceptions permitted there under through Article 16, fully apply in the digital environment, in particular to the use of performances and phonograms in digital form. It is understood that the storage of a protected performance or phonogram in digital form in an electronic medium constitutes a reproduction within the meaning of these Articles.

7 Agreed statement concerning Article 15: It is understood that Article 15 does not represent a complete resolution of the level of rights of broadcasting and communication to the public that should be enjoyed by performers and phonogram producers in the digital age. Delegations were unable to achieve consensus on differing proposals for aspects of exclusivity to be provided in certain circumstances or for rights to be provided without the possibility of reservations, and have therefore left the issue to future resolution.

8 Agreed statement concerning Article 15: It is understood that Article 15 does not prevent the granting of the right conferred by this Article to performers of folklore and producers of phonograms recording folklore where such phonograms have not been published for commercial gain.

9 Agreed statement concerning Article 16: The agreed statement concerning Article 10 (on Limitations and Exceptions) of the WIPO Copyright Treaty is applicable mutatis *mutandis* also to Article 16 (on Limitations and Exceptions) of the WI-

PO Performances and Phonograms Treaty.

[The text of the agreed statement concerning Article 10 of the WCT reads as follows: "It is understood that the provisions of Article 10 permit Contracting Parties to carry forward and appropriately extend into the digital environment limitations and exceptions in their national laws which have been considered acceptable under the Berne Convention. Similarly, these provisions should be understood to permit Contracting Parties to devise new exceptions and limitations that are appropriate in the digital network environment."

"It is also understood that Article 10 (2) neither reduces nor extends the scope of applicability of the limitations and exceptions permitted by the Berne Convention."]

10 Agreed statement concerning Article 19: The agreed statement concerning Article 12 (on Obligations concerning Rights Management Information) of the WIPO Copyright Treaty is applicable *mutatis mutandis* also to Article 19 (on Obligations concerning Rights Management Information) of the WIPO Performances and Phonograms Treaty.

[The text of the agreed statement concerning Article 12 of the WCT reads as follows: "It is understood that the reference to 'infringement of any right covered by this Treaty or the Berne Convention' includes both exclusive rights and rights of remuneration."

"It is further understood that Contracting Parties will not rely on this Article to devise or implement rights management systems that would have the effect of imposing formalities which are not permitted under the Berne Convention or this Treaty, prohibiting the free morvement of goods or impeding the enjoyment of rights under this Treaty."]

世界知识产权组织版权条约

（本条约于 1996 年 12 月 20 日由关于版权和邻接权若干问题外交会议在日内瓦通过）

序　　言

缔约各方，出于以尽可能有效和一致的方式发展和维护保护作者对其文学和艺术作品之权利的愿望，承认有必要采用新的国际规则并澄清对某些现有规则的解释，以提供解决由经济、社会、文化和技术发展新形势所提出的问题的适当办法，承认信息与通信技术的发展和交汇对文学和艺术作品的创作与使用的深刻影响，强调版权保护作为文学和艺术创作促进因素的重要意义，承认有必要按《伯尔尼公约》所反映的保持作者的权利与广大公众的利益尤其是教育、研究和获得信息的利益之间的平衡，达成协议如下：

第一条　与《伯尔尼公约》的关系

（1）对于属《保护文学和艺术作品伯尔尼公约》所建联盟之成员国的缔约方而言，本条约系该公约第 20 条意义下的专门协定。本条约不得与除《伯尔尼公约》以外的条约有任何关联，亦不得损害依任何其他条约的任何权利和义务。

（2）本条约的任何内容均不得减损缔约方相互之间依照《保护文学和艺术作品伯尔尼公约》已承担的现有义务。

（3）“《伯尔尼公约》”以下系指《保护文学和艺术作品伯尔尼公约》1971 年 7 月 24 日的巴黎文本。

（4）缔约各方应遵守《伯尔尼公约》第一至第二十一条和附件的规定①

① 关于第一条第（4）款的议定声明：《伯尔尼公约》第九条所规定的复制权及其所允许的例外，完全适用于数字环境，尤其是以数字形式使用作品的情况。不言而喻，在电子媒体中以数字形式存储受保护的作品，构成《伯尔尼公约》第九条意义下的复制。

第二条 版权保护的范围

版权保护延及表达，而不延及思想、过程、操作方法或数学概念本身。

第三条 对《伯尔尼公约》第二至第六条的适用

缔约各方对于本条约所规定的保护应比照适用《伯尔尼公约》第二至第六条的规定。①

第四条 计算机程序

计算机程序作为《伯尔尼公约》第二条意义下的文学作品受到保护，此种保护适用于各计算机程序，而无论其表达方式或表达形式如何。②

第五条 数据汇编（数据库）

数据或其他资料的汇编，无论采用任何形式，只要由于其内容的选择或排列构成智力创作，其本身即受到保护。这种保护不延及数据或资料本身，亦不损害汇编中的数据或资料已存在的任何版权。③

第六条 发行权

（1）文学和艺术作品的作者应享有授权通过销售或其他所有权转让形式向公众提供其作品原件和复制品的专有权。

（2）对于在作品的原件或复制品经作者授权被首次销售或其他所有权转让之后适用本条第（1）款中权利的用尽所依据的条件（如有此种条件），本条约的任何内容均不得影响缔约各方确定该条件的自由。④

第七条 出租权

（1）（i）计算机程序、

（ii）电影作品、和

（iii）按缔约各方国内法的规定，以录音制品体现的作品的作者，应享有授权将其作品的原件或复制品向公众进行商业性出租的专有权。

---

① 关于第三条的议定声明：不言而喻，在适用本条约第三条时，《伯尔尼公约》第二至第六条中的“本联盟成员国”，在把《伯尔尼公约》的这些条款适用于本条约所规定的保护中，将被视为如同系指本条约的缔约方，另外，不言而喻，《伯尔尼公约》这些条款中的“非本联盟成员国”，在同样的情况下，应被视为如同系指非本条约缔约方的国家，《伯尔尼公约》第二条第（8）款、第二条之二第（2）款、第三、四和五条中的“本公约”，将被视为如同系指《伯尔尼公约》和本条约。最后，不言而喻，《伯尔尼公约》第三至第六条中所指的“本联盟成员国之一的国民”，在把这些条款适用于本条约时，对于系本条约缔约方的政府间组织，指系该组织成员的国家之一的国民。

② 关于第四条的议定声明：按第二条的解释，依本条约第四条规定的计算机程序保护的范围，与《伯尔尼公约》第二条的规定一致，并与TRIPS协定的有关规定相同。

③ 关于第五条的议定声明：按第二条的解释，依本条约第五条规定的数据汇编（数据库）保护的范围，与《伯尔尼公约》第二条的规定一致，并与TRIPS协定的有关规定相同。

④ 关于第六和第七条的议定声明：该两条中的用语“复制品”和“原件和复制品”，受该两条中发行权和出租权的约束，专指可作为有形物品投放流通的固定的复制品。

（2）本条第（1）款不得适用于：

（i）程序本身并非出租主要对象的计算机程序；和

（ii）电影作品，除非此种商业性出租已导致对此种作品的广泛复制，从而严重地损害了复制专有权。

（3）尽管有本条第（1）款的规定，任何缔约方如在1994年4月15日已有且现仍实行作者出租其以录音制品体现的作品的复制品获得公平报酬的制度，只要以录音制品体现的作品的商业性出租没有引起对作者复制专有权的严重损害，即可保留这一制度。①②

第八条　向公众传播的权利

在不损害《伯尔尼公约》第十一条第（1）款第（ii）目、第十一条之二第（1）款第（i）和（ii）目、第十一条之三第（1）款第（ii）目、第十四条第（1）款第（ii）目和第十四条之二第（1）款的规定的情况下，文学和艺术作品的作者应享有专有权，以授权将其作品以有线或无线方式向公众传播，包括将其作品向公众提供，使公众中的成员在其个人选定的地点和时间可获得这些作品。③

第九条　摄影作品的保护期限

对于摄影作品，缔约各方不得适用《伯尔尼公约》第七条第（4）款的规定。

第十条　限制与例外

（1）缔约各方在某些不与作品的正常利用相抵触、也不无理地损害作者合法利益的特殊情况下，可在其国内立法中对依本条约授予文学和艺术作品作者的权利规定限制或例外。

（2）缔约各方在适用《伯尔尼公约》时，应将对该公约所规定权利的任何限制或例外限于某些不与作品的正常利用相抵触、也不无理地损害作者合

---

① 关于第六和第七条的议定声明：该两条中的用语“复制品”和“原件和复制品”，受该两条中发行权和出租权的约束，专指可作为有形物品投放流通的固定的复制品。

② 关于第七条的议定声明：不言而喻，第七条第（1）款规定的义务不要求缔约方对依照该缔约方法律未授予其对录音制品权利的作者规定商业性出租的专有权。这一义务应被理解为与TRIPS协定第十四条第（4）款相一致。

③ 关于第七条的议定声明：不言而喻，仅仅为促成或进行传播提供实物设施不致构成本条约或《伯尔尼公约》意义下的传播。并且，第八条中的任何内容均不得理解为阻止缔约方适用第十一条之二第（2）款。

法利益的特殊情况。[①]

第十一条 关于技术措施的义务

缔约各方应规定适当的法律保护和有效的法律补救办法，制止规避由作者为行使本条约所规定的权利而使用的、对就其作品进行未经该有关作者许可或未由法律准许的行为加以约束的有效技术措施。

第十二条 关于权利管理信息的义务

（1）缔约各方应规定适当和有效的法律补救办法，制止任何人明知、或就民事补救而言有合理根据知道其行为会诱使、促成、便利或包庇对本条约或《伯尔尼公约》所涵盖的任何权利的侵犯而故意从事以下行为：

（i）未经许可去除或改变任何权利管理的电子信息；

（ii）未经许可发行、为发行目的进口、广播、或向公众传播明知已被未经许可去除或改变权利管理电子信息的作品或作品的复制品。

（2）本条中的用语“权利管理信息”系指识别作品、作品的作者、对作品拥有任何权利的所有人的信息，或有关作品使用的条款和条件的信息，和代表此种信息的任何数字或代码，各该项信息均附于作品的每件复制品上或在作品向公众进行传播时出现。[②]

第十三条 适用的时限

缔约各方应将《伯尔尼公约》第十八条的规定适用于本条约所规定的一切保护。

第十四条 关于权利行使的条款

（1）缔约各方承诺根据其法律制度采取必要的措施，以确保本条约的适用。

（2）缔约各方应确保依照其法律可以提供执法程序，以便能采取制止对本条约所涵盖权利的任何侵犯行为的有效行动，包括防止侵权的快速补救和为遏制进一步侵权的补救。

---

① 关于第十条的议定声明：不言而喻，第十条的规定允许缔约各方将其国内法中依《伯尔尼公约》被认为可接受的限制与例外继续适用并适当地延伸到数字环境中。同样，这些规定应被理解为允许缔约方制定对数字网络环境适宜的新的例外与限制。

另外，不言而喻，第十条第（2）款既不缩小也不扩大由《伯尔尼公约》所允许的限制与例外的可适用性范围。

② 关于第十二条的议定声明：不言而喻，“对本条约或《伯尔尼公约》所涵盖的任何权利的侵犯”的提法既包括专有权，也包括获得报酬的权利。

此外，不言而喻，缔约各方不会依赖本条来制定或实施要求履行为《伯尔尼公约》或本条约所不允许的手续的权利管理制度，从而阻止商品的自由流通或妨碍享有依本条约规定的权利。

第十五条　大会

（1）（a）缔约方应设大会。

（b）每一缔约方应有一名代表，该代表可由副代表、顾问和专家协助。

（c）各代表团的费用应由指派它的缔约方负担。大会可要求世界知识产权组织（以下称为“本组织”）提供财政援助，以便利按照联合国大会既定惯例认为是发展中国家或向市场经济转轨的国家的缔约方代表团参加。

（2）（a）大会应处理涉及维护和发展本条约及适用和实施本条约的事项。

（b）大会应履行依第十七条第（2）款向其指定的关于接纳某些政府间组织成为本条约缔约方的职能。

（c）大会应对召开任何修订本条约的外交会议作出决定，并给予本组织总干事筹备此种外交会议的必要指示。

（3）（a）凡属国家的每一缔约方应有一票，并应只能以其自己的名义表决。

（b）凡属政府间组织的缔约方可代替其成员国参加表决，其票数与其属本条约缔约方的成员国数目相等。如果此种政府间组织的任何一个成员国行使其表决权，则该组织不得参加表决，反之亦然。

（4）大会应每两年召开一次例会，由本组织总干事召集。

（5）大会应制定其本身的议事规则，其中包括特别会议的召集、法定人数的要求及在不违反本条约规定的前提下作出各种决定所需的多数。

第十六条　国际局

本组织的国际局应履行与本条约有关的行政工作。

第十七条　成为本条约缔约方的资格

（1）本组织的任何成员国均可成为本条约的缔约方。

（2）如果任何政府间组织声明其对于本条约涵盖的事项具有权限和具有约束其所有成员国的立法，并声明其根据其内部程序被正式授权要求成为本条约的缔约方，大会可决定接纳该政府间组织成为本条约的缔约方。

（3）欧洲共同体在通过本条约的外交会议上做出上款提及的声明后，可成为本条约的缔约方。

第十八条　本条约规定的权利和义务

除本条约有任何相反的具体规定以外，每一缔约方均应享有本条约规定的一切权利并承担本条约规定的一切义务。

第十九条　本条约的签署

本条约应在 1997 年 12 月 31 日以前开放供本组织的任何成员国和欧洲共

同体签署。

第二十条 本条约的生效

本条约应于30个国家向本组织总干事交存批准书或加入书三个月之后生效。

第二十一条 成为本条约缔约方的生效日期

本条约应自下列日期起具有约束力：

（i）对第二十条提到的30个国家，自本条约生效之日起；

（ii）对其他各国，自该国向本组织总干事交存文书之日满三个月起；

（iii）对欧洲共同体，如果其在本条约根据第二十条生效后交存批准书或加入书，则自交存此种文书后满三个月起；或如果其在本条约生效前交存批准书或加入书，则自本条约生效后满三个月起；

（iv）对被接纳成为本条约缔约方的任何其他政府间组织，自该组织交存加入书后满三个月起。

第二十二条 本条约不得有保留

本条约不允许有任何保留。

第二十三条 退约

本条约的任何缔约方均可退出本条约，退约应通知本组织总干事。任何退约应于本组织总干事收到通知之日起一年后生效。

第二十四条 本条约的语文

（1）本条约的签字原件应为一份，以英文、阿拉伯文、中文、法文、俄文和西班牙文签署，各该文种的文本具有同等效力。

（2）除本条第（1）款提到的语文外，任何其他语文的正式文本须由总干事应有关当事方请求，在与所有有关当事方磋商之后制定。在本款中，“有关当事方”系指涉及其正式语文或正式语文之一的本组织任何成员国，并且如果涉及其正式语文之一，亦指欧洲共同体和可成为本条约缔约方的任何其他政府间组织。

第二十五条 保存人

本组织总干事为本条约的保存人。

WIPO Copyright Treaty

adopted in Geneva on December 20, 1996

Preamble

The Contracting Parties,

Desiring to develop and maintain the protection of the rights of authors in their literary and artistic works in a manner as effective and uniform as possible,

Recognizing the need to introduce new international rules and clarify the interpretation of certain existing rules in order to provide adequate solutions to the questions raised by new economic, social, cultural and technological developments,

Recognizing the profound impact of the development and convergence of information and communication technologies on the creation and use of literary and artistic works,

Emphasizing the outstanding significance of copyright protection as an incentive for literary and artistic creation,

Recognizing the need to maintain a balance between the rights of authors and the larger public interest, particularly education, research and access to information, as reflected in the Berne Convention,

Have agreed as follows:

Article 1 Relation to the Berne Convention

(1) This Treaty is a special agreement within the meaning of Article 20 of the Berne Convention for the Protection of Literary and Artistic Works, as regards Contracting Parties that are countries of the Union established by that Convention. This Treaty shall not have any connection with treaties other than the Berne Convention, nor shall it prejudice any rights and obligations under any other treaties.

(2) Nothing in this Treaty shall derogate from existing obligations that Contracting Parties have to each other under the Berne Convention for the Protection of Literary and Artistic Works.

(3) Hereinafter, "Berne Convention" shall refer to the Paris Act of July 24, 1971 of the Berne Convention for the Protection of Literary and Artistic Works.

(4) Contracting Parties shall comply with Articles 1 to 21 and the Appendix of the Berne Convention.[1]

Article 2 Scope of Copyright Protection

Copyright protection extends to expressions and not to ideas, procedures, methods of operation or mathematical concepts as such.

Article 3 Application of Articles 2 to 6 of the Berne Convention

Contracting Parties shall apply *mutatis mutandis* the provisions of Articles 2 to 6 of the Berne Convention in respect of the protection provided for in this Treaty.[2]

Article 4 Computer Programs

Computer programs are protected as literary works within the meaning of Article 2 of the Berne Convention. Such protection applies to computer programs, whatever may be the mode or form of their expression.[3]

Article 5 Compilations of Data (Databases)

Compilations of data or other material, in any form, which by reason of the selection or arrangement of their contents constitute intellectual creations, are protected as such. This protection does not extend to the data or the material itself and is without prejudice to any copyright subsisting in the data or material contained in the compilation.[4]

Article 6 Right of Distribution

(1) Authors of literary and artistic works shall enjoy the exclusive right of authorizing the making available to the public of the original and copies of their works through sale or other transfer of ownership.

(2) Nothing in this Treaty shall affect the freedom of Contracting Parties to determine the conditions, if any, under which the exhaustion of the right in paragraph (1) applies after the first sale or other transfer of ownership of the original or a copy of the work with the authorization of the author.[5]

Article 7 Right of Rental

(1) Authors of

(i) computer programs;

(ii) cinematographic works; and

(iii) works embodied in phonograms, as determined in the national law of Contracting Parties,

shall enjoy the exclusive right of authorizing commercial rental to the public of the originals or copies of their works.

(2) Paragraph (1) shall not apply

(i) in the case of computer programs, where the program itself is not the essential object of the rental; and

(ii) in the case of cinematographic works, unless such commercial rental has led to widespread copying of such works materially impairing the exclusive right of reproduction.

(3) Notwithstanding the provisions of paragraph (1), a Contracting Party that, on April 15, 1994, had and continues to have in force a system of equitable remuneration of authors for the rental of copies of their works embodied in phonograms may maintain that system provided that the commercial rental of works embodied in phonograms is not giving rise to the material impairment of the exclusive right of reproduction of authors.[5 6]

Article 8 Right of Communication to the Public

Without prejudice to the provisions of Articles 11 (1) (ii), 11*bis* (1) (i) and (ii), 11*ter* (1) (ii), 14 (1) (ii) and 14*bis* (1) of the Berne Convention, authors of literary and artistic works shall enjoy the exclusive right of authorizing any communication to the public of their works, by wire or wireless means, including the making available to the public of their works in such a way that members of the public may access these works from a place and at a time individually chosen by them.[7]

Article 9 Duration of the Protection of Photographic Works

In respect of photographic works, the Contracting Parties shall not apply the provisions of Article 7 (4) of the Berne Convention.

Article 10 Limitations and Exceptions

(1) Contracting Parties may, in their national legislation, provide for limitations of or exceptions to the rights granted to authors of literary and artistic works under this Treaty in certain special cases that do not conflict with a normal exploitation of the work and do not unreasonably prejudice the legitimate interests of the

author.

(2) Contracting Parties shall, when applying the Berne Convention, confine any limitations of or exceptions to rights provided for therein to certain special cases that do not conflict with a normal exploitation of the work and do not unreasonably prejudice the legitimate interests of the author.[8]

Article 11 Obligations concerning Technological Measures

Contracting Parties shall provide adequate legal protection and effective legal remedies against the circumvention of effective technological measures that are used by authors in connection with the exercise of their rights under this Treaty or the Berne Convention and that restrict acts, in respect of their works, which are not authorized by the authors concerned or permitted by law.

Article 12 Obligations concerning Rights Management Information

(1) Contracting Parties shall provide adequate and effective legal remedies against any person knowingly performing any of the following acts knowing, or with respect to civil remedies having reasonable grounds to know, that it will induce, enable, facilitate or conceal an infringement of any right covered by this Treaty or the Berne Convention:

(i) to remove or alter any electronic rights management information without authority;

(ii) to distribute, import for distribution, broadcast or communicate to the public, without authority, works or copies of works knowing that electronic rights management information has been removed or altered without authority.

(2) As used in this Article, "rights management information" means information which identifies the work, the author of the work, the owner of any right in the work, or information about the terms and conditions of use of the work, and any numbers or codes that represent such information, when any of these items of information is attached to a copy of a work or appears in connection with the communication of a work to the public.[9]

Article 13 Application in Time

Contracting Parties shall apply the provisions of Article 18 of the Berne Convention to all protection provided for in this Treaty.

Article 14 Provisions on Enforcement of Rights

(1) Contracting Parties undertake to adopt, in accordance with their legal sys-

tems, the measures necessary to ensure the application of this Treaty.

(2) Contracting Parties shall ensure that enforcement procedures are available under their law so as to permit effective action against any act of infringement of rights covered by this Treaty, including expeditious remedies to prevent infringements and remedies which constitute a deterrent to further infringements.

Article 15 Assembly

(1)

(a) The Contracting Parties shall have an Assembly.

(b) Each Contracting Party shall be represented by one delegate who may be assisted by alternate delegates, advisors and experts.

(c) The expenses of each delegation shall be borne by the Contracting Party that has appointed the delegation. The Assembly may ask the World Intellectual Property Organization (hereinafter referred to as "WIPO") to grant financial assistance to facilitate the participation of delegations of Contracting Parties that are regarded as developing countries in conformity with the established practice of the General Assembly of the United Nations or that are countries in transition to a market economy.

(2)

(a) The Assembly shall deal with matters concerning the maintenance and development of this Treaty and the application and operation of this Treaty.

(b) The Assembly shall perform the function allocated to it under Article 17 (2) in respect of the admission of certain intergovernmental organizations to become party to this Treaty.

(c) The Assembly shall decide the convocation of any diplomatic conference for the revision of this Treaty and give the necessary instructions to the Director General of WIPO for the preparation of such diplomatic conference.

(3)

(a) Each Contracting Party that is a State shall have one vote and shall vote only in its own name.

(b) Any Contracting Party that is an intergovernmental organization may participate in the vote, in place of its Member States, with a number of votes equal to the number of its Member States which are party to this Treaty. No such intergovernmental organization shall participate in the vote if any one of its Member States exercises its right to vote and *vice versa*.

(4) The Assembly shall meet in ordinary session once every two years upon convocation by the Director General of WIPO.

(5) The Assembly shall establish its own rules of procedure, including the convocation of extraordinary sessions, the requirements of a quorum and, subject to the provisions of this Treaty, the required majority for various kinds of decisions.

Article 16 International Bureau

The International Bureau of WIPO shall perform the administrative tasks concerning the Treaty.

Article 17 Eligibility for Becoming Party to the Treaty

(1) Any Member State of WIPO may become party to this Treaty.

(2) The Assembly may decide to admit any intergovernmental organization to become party to this Treaty which declares that it is competent in respect of, and has its own legislation binding on all its Member States on, matters covered by this Treaty and that it has been duly authorized, in accordance with its internal procedures, to become party to this Treaty.

(3) The European Community, having made the declaration referred to in the preceding paragraph in the Diplomatic Conference that has adopted this Treaty, may become party to this Treaty.

Article 18 Rights and Obligations under the Treaty

Subject to any specific provisions to the contrary in this Treaty, each Contracting Party shall enjoy all of the rights and assume all of the obligations under this Treaty.

Article 19 Signature of the Treaty

This Treaty shall be open for signature until December 31, 1997, by any Member State of WIPO and by the European Community.

Article 20 Entry into Force of the Treaty

This Treaty shall enter into force three months after 30 instruments of ratification or accession by States have been deposited with the Director General of WIPO.

Article 21 Effective Date of Becoming Party to the Treaty

This Treaty shall bind:

(i) the 30 States referred to in Article 20, from the date on which this Treaty has entered into force;

(ii) each other State from the expiration of three months from the date on which the State has deposited its instrument with the Director General of WIPO;

(iii) the European Community, from the expiration of three months after the deposit of its instrument of ratification or accession if such instrument has been deposited after the entry into force of this Treaty according to Article 20, or, three months after the entry into force of this Treaty if such instrument has been deposited before the entry into force of this Treaty;

(iv) any other intergovernmental organization that is admitted to become party to this Treaty, from the expiration of three months after the deposit of its instrument of accession.

Article 22 No Reservations to the Treaty

No reservation to this Treaty shall be admitted.

Article 23 Denunciation of the Treaty

This Treaty may be denounced by any Contracting Party by notification addressed to the Director General of WIPO. Any denunciation shall take effect one year from the date on which the Director General of WIPO received the notification.

Article 24 Languages of the Treaty

(1) This Treaty is signed in a single original in English, Arabic, Chinese, French, Russian and Spanish languages, the versions in all these languages being equally authentic.

(2) An official text in any language other than those referred to in paragraph (1) shall be established by the Director General of WIPO on the request of an interested party, after consultation with all the interested parties. For the purposes of this paragraph, "interested party" means any Member State of WIPO whose official language, or one of whose official languages, is involved and the European Community, and any other intergovernmental organization that may become party to this Treaty, if one of its official languages is involved.

Article 25 Depositary

The Director General of WIPO is the depositary of this Treaty.

1 Agreed statements concerning Article 1 (4): The reproduction right, as set out in Article 9 of the Berne Convention, and the exceptions permitted there

under, fully apply in the digital environment, in particular to the use of works in digital form. It is understood that the storage of a protected work in digital form in an electronic medium constitutes a reproduction within the meaning of Article 9 of the Berne Convention.

2 Agreed statements concerning Article 3 : It is understood that in applying Article 3 of this Treaty, the expression "country of the Union" in Articles 2 to 6 of the Berne Convention will be read as if it were a reference to a Contracting Party to this Treaty, in the application of those Berne Articles in respect of protection provided for in this Treaty. It is also understood that the expression "country outside the Union" in those Articles in the Berne Convention will, in the same circumstances, be read as if it were a reference to a country that is not a Contracting Party to this Treaty, and that "this Convention" in Articles 2 (8), 2*bis* (2), 3, 4 and 5 of the Berne Convention will be read as if it were a reference to the Berne Convention and this Treaty. Finally, it is understood that a reference in Articles 3 to 6 of the Berne Convention to a "national of one of the countries of the Union" will, when these Articles are applied to this Treaty, mean, in regard to an intergovernmental organization that is a Contracting Party to this Treaty, a national of one of the countries that is member of that organization.

3 Agreed statements concerning Article 4: The scope of protection for computer programs under Article 4 of this Treaty, read with Article 2, is consistent with Article 2 of the Berne Convention and on a par with the relevant provisions of the TRIPS Agreement.

4 Agreed statements concerning Article 5: The scope of protection for compilations of data (databases) under Article 5 of this Treaty, read with Article 2, is consistent with Article 2 of the Berne Convention and on a par with the relevant provisions of the TRIPS Agreement.

5 Agreed statements concerning Articles 6 and 7: As used in these Articles, the expressions "copies" and "original and copies," being subject to the right of distribution and the right of rental under the said Articles, refer exclusively to fixed copies that can be put into circulation as tangible objects.

6 Agreed statements concerning Article 7: It is understood that the obligation under Article 7 (1) does not require a Contracting Party to provide an exclusive right of commercial rental to authors who, under that Contracting Party's law,

are not granted rights in respect of phonograms. It is understood that this obligation is consistent with Article 14 (4) of the TRIPS Agreement.

7 **Agreed statements concerning Article 8**: It is understood that the mere provision of physical facilities for enabling or making a communication does not in itself amount to communication within the meaning of this Treaty or the Berne Convention. It is further understood that nothing in Article 8 precludes a Contracting Party from applying Article 11*bis* (2).

8 **Agreed statement concerning Article 10**: It is understood that the provisions of Article 10 permit Contracting Parties to carry forward and appropriately extend into the digital environment limitations and exceptions in their national laws which have been considered acceptable under the Berne Convention. Similarly, these provisions should be understood to permit Contracting Parties to devise new exceptions and limitations that are appropriate in the digital network environment.

It is also understood that Article 10 (2) neither reduces nor extends the scope of applicability of the limitations and exceptions permitted by the Berne Convention.

9 **Agreed statements concerning Article 12**: It is understood that the reference to "infringement of any right covered by this Treaty or the Berne Convention" includes both exclusive rights and rights of remuneration.

It is further understood that Contracting Parties will not rely on this Article to devise or implement rights management systems that would have the effect of imposing formalities which are not permitted under the Berne Convention or this Treaty, prohibiting the free movement of goods or impeding the enjoyment of rights under this Treaty.

避免对版权使用费双重征税的多边公约

（1979年12月13日于马德里）

缔约各国，

考虑到对版权使用费双重征税有损于作者的利益，从而严重阻碍有版权作品的传播，而此类传播正是各国人民发展文化、科学和教育的基本因素之一；

鉴于通过双边协定和国内措施防止双重征税的行动业已取得令人鼓舞的成果，其有益作用已得到普遍承认，相信缔结一项专门针对版权使用费的多边公约可发展此种成果；

认为尊重各国合法利益，尤其是尊重某些国家以尽可能广泛地接触人类智力作品作为不断发展本国文化、科学和教育必不可少条件的特定需要，此类问题必须解决；

期望找到有效措施，旨在尽可能避免对版权使用费双重征税，如果双重征税业已存在，则消除此种征税或降低其作用；

达成协议如下：

第一章　定　　义

第一条　版权使用费

1. 为本公约之目的，并受本条第、三款规定之约束，版权使用费系指根据首先应当支付这些使用费的缔约国国内版权法的规定，为使用或有权使用多边版权公约所规定的文学、艺术或科学作品的版权所产生的任何款项，包括对法定或强制许可证或对“延续权”所支付的款项。

2. 但是，本公约不得用来包括根据首先应当支付版权使用费的缔约国国内版权法的规定，因利用电影作品或利用类似电影摄影方法生产的作品而应当支付的使用费，如果上述使用费应付给此类作品的制作者或他们的继承人或权利继承人。

3. 除涉及“延续权”而支付的款项外，在本公约中，下列款项不得视为版权使用费：因购买、租用、借用或以任何其他形式转让文学、艺术或科学作品的物质产品权利而支付之款项，即使此种款项的金额系参照应付版权使用费而确定，或版权使用费系全部或部分按上述款项金额所确定。当作品的物质产品权利作为转让使用该作品的版权的附属物而转让时，只有作为酬谢此种作品所有权的款项才是本公约所称之版权使用费。

4. 在涉及“延续权”而支付款项的情况下，以及在本条第三款所述转让作品的物质产品权利的各种情况下，无论该项转让是否免费，因清偿或偿付保险费、运输或仓储费用、代理人佣金或任何其他劳务费用以及因该物质产品的移动而直接或间接产生的款项，包括关税和其他有关课税以及特殊税捐，均不得视为本公约所称之版权使用费。

第二条　版权使用费受益人

为本公约之目的，“版权使用费受益人”是指全部或部分地收取此种使用费的受益者，而不论他是作为作者或其继承人或其权利继承上收取该使用费，还是应用关于版权使用费双重征税双边协定规定的任何其他有关标准收取使用费。

第三条　受益人居住国

1. 为本约之目的，版权使用费受益人为其居民的国家应视为受益人居住国。

2. 因其户籍、住所，实际营业场所或根据关于版权使用费双重征税问题双边协定的任何其他标准而在某个国家负有纳税义务的人，应被视为该国居民。但此项条件不包括仅因其在该国有收入来源或因在该国拥有资本而负有纳税义务的任何人。

第四条　版权使用费起源国

为本公约之目的，当使用或有权使用某一文学、艺术或科学作品的版权时，某个具有下列情况的国家，应视为版权使用费起源国：

（a）此种版权使用费首先应当由该国或该国行政下属机关或地方当局支付；

（b）此种版权使用费首先应当由该国居民支付，除非此种版权使用费系来源于该居民通过在其他国家某个常设机构或固定基地所进行的活动；

（c）应当支付此种版权使用费的人虽然并非该国居民，但此种版权使用费系来源于此人通过在该国的常设机构或固定基地所进行的活动。

第二章　防止版权使用费双重征税行动的指导原则

第五条　国家的财政主权与权利平等

采取防止版权使用费双重征税的行动应当遵照本公约第八条的规定执行，并对版权使用费来源国和受益人居住国的财政主权，以及对它们就这些使用费进行征税的平等权利给予应有的尊重。

第六条　财政上的非歧视原则

防止对版权使用费双重征税的措施不得因国籍、种族、性别、语言或宗教的不同而产生课税歧视。

第七条　情报交换

在为执行本公约所必需的范围内，缔约各国主管当局将互相交换情报，其交换方式和条件应以双边协定的方法确定。

第三章　防止版权使用费双重征税行动指导原则的实施

第八条　实施办法

1. 各缔约国承诺，将根据本国宪法和上述指导原则，竭尽一切可能努力避免对版权使用费双重征税，如果业已存在双重征税，则消除此种征税或降低其作用。此种行动应通过双边协定的方法或国内措施的方式实施。

2. 本条第一款所称双边协定包括处理一般双重征税问题的双边协定或仅限于处理版权使用费双重征税问题的双边协定。对于后一种双边协定本公约附有一份可供选择的、包括若干备选条款的范本，此项范本并非本公约不可分割的部分。在尊重本公约规定的同时，缔约各国可根据其具体情况，依他们认为最满意的准则缔结双边协定。缔约各国实施早先签订的双边协定不受本公约的影响。

3. 如系采取国内措施，虽有本公约第一条的规定，各缔约国可参照本国版权立法来规定版权使用费的定义。

第四章　一般性条款

第九条　外交或领事团成员

本公约的规定不影响缔约各国外交或领事团成员以及他们的家属的财政

特权，不论此种财政特权系根据国际法的一般规则所享有，还是由专门的公约条款所确定。

第十条　情报资料

1. 联合国教育科学文化组织秘书处和世界知识产权组织国际局应收集和出版涉及版权使用费征税问题的规范性的情报资料。

2. 各缔约国应当尽快地向联合国教育科学文化组织秘书处和世界知识产权组织国际局交送有关版权使用费征税问题的任何新法律的文本以及这一方面的所有官方文件，包括任何专门的双边协定文本或任何处理一般双重征税双边协定中有关版权使用费双重征税问题的条款文本。

3. 联合国教育科学文化组织秘书处和世界知识产权组织国际局，根据任一缔约国的请求，应向其提供与本公约各项问题有关的情报资料；为促进本公约的实施，上述两组织还应当开展研究工作和提供各种服务。

第五章　最后条款

第十一条　批准、接受、加入

1. 本公约应交存联合国组织秘书长。本公约在一九八〇年十月三十一日以前向联合国会员国、与联合国建立关系的任何专门机构或国际原子能机构的成员国、或国际法庭规约成员国开放供签署。

2. 本公约须经签署国批准或接受。本条第一款所述任何国家均可加入本公约。

3. 批准书、接受书或加入书应交联合国秘书长保存。

4. 不言而喻，当一个国家成为本公约成员国时，它将根据其国内法律使本公约所有条款生效。

第十二条　保留

缔约各国，不论在签署本公约时，还是在批准、接受或加入本公约时，对于实施第一条至第四条、第九条和第十七条的条款可以提出保留。但不得对本公约作其他保留。

第十三条　生效

1. 本公约应当于第十份批准书、接受书或加入书交存三个月后生效。

2. 对于在第十份批准书、接受书或加入书交存之后批准、接受或加入本公约的每一国家，本公约应于该国证书递交三个月后生效。

第十四条 退出公约

1. 任何缔约国可以书面通知联合国秘书长退出本公约。

2. 此种退出应于联合国秘书长收到通知之日十二个月后生效。

第十五条 修订

1. 本公约生效五年之后，任何缔约国可以通知联合国秘书长要求召开会议修订本公约。联合国秘书长应将此要求通知所有缔约国。如在联合国秘书长发出通知之日起六个月之内，有不少于三分之一的缔约国通知他同意此种要求，但以发出此种通知的国家不少于五个为条件，则秘书长应通知联合国教育科学文化组织总干事和世界知识产权组织总干事，他们应召集审查条约的会议，以便将旨在改进防止对版权使用费双重征税行动的修正案加进本公约。

2. 本公约的任何修订需经参加审查会议的三分之二的国家投赞成票，而此一多数应包括在召开审查会议时本公约成员国的三分之二。

3. 在全部或部分修订本公约的新公约生效以后参加公约的国家，如果没有表示不同意向，则应当认为该国：

（a）是修订后的公约的成员国；

（b）在同任何不受修订后的公约约束的本公约成员国的关系方面，是本公约的成员国。

4. 对于尚未成为修订后公约的缔约各国之间的关系或涉及本公约与它们之间的关系，本公约应当继续有效。

第十六条 公约的语文和通知

1. 本公约应在一份具有阿拉伯文、英文、法文、俄文和西班牙文五种文字的统一文本上签署，五种文字具有同等效力。

2. 德文、意大利文、葡萄牙文的正式文本应由联合国教育科学文化组织总干事和世界知识产权组织总干事与有关政府协商后确定。

3. 联合国秘书长应将下述事项通知第十一条第一款所述国家，以及联合国教育科学文化组织总干事和世界知识产权组织总干事：

（a）本公约的签署情况，连同所附文件全文；

（b）批准书、接受书和加入书的交存情况、连同所附文件全文；

（c）依照第十三条第一款本公约生效的日期；

（d）收到的退出公约通知书；

（e）根据第十五条递交给他的请求书，以及从缔约国收到的关于修改本公约的任何函电。

4. 联合国秘书长应将两份经核证的本公约副本送给第十一条第一款所述所有国家。

第十七条 解释和争议的解决办法

1. 如两个或两个以上的缔约国对本公约的解释或适用事项发生争议，而通过谈判不能解决，应将争议提交国际法庭裁决，除非有关国家商定采取其他解决办法。

2. 任何国家在签署本公约或在交存批准书、接受书或加入书时，可宣布它不受上款规定的约束。如该国与任何其他缔约国发生争议时，第一款的规定将不适用。

3. 根据第二款发表过声明的任何国家可随时通知联合国秘书长收回该项声明。

为此，下列签字者经正式授权签署本公约，以资证明。

Multilateral Convention for the Avoidance of Double Taxation of Copyright

Madrid, 13 December 1979

The Contracting States,

Considering that the double taxation of copyright royalties is prejudicial to the interests of authors and thus constitutes a serious impediment to the dissemination of copyrighted works, which is one of the basic factors in the development of the culture, science and education of all peoples,

Believing that the encouraging results already achieved by action against double taxation, through bilateral agreements and domestic measures, whose beneficial effects are generally recognized, can be improved by the conclusion of a multilateral convention specific to copyright royalties,

Being of the opinion that these problems must be solved while respecting the legitimate interests of States and particularly the needs specific to those where the widest possible access to works of the human mind is an essential condition to their continuing development in the fields of culture, science and education,

Seeking to find effective measures designed to avoid double taxation of copyright royalties where possible and, should it subsist, to eliminate it or to reduce its effect,

Have agreed on the following provisions

Chapter I: Definitions

Article 1: Copyright royalties

1. For the purposes of this Convention and subject to the provisions of paragraphs 2 and 3 of this Article, copyright royalties are payments of any kind made

on the basis of the domestic copyright laws of the Contracting State in which these royalties - are originally due, for the use of, or the right to use, a copyright in a literary, artistic or scientific work, as defined in the multilateral copyright conventions, including such payments made in respect of legal or compulsory licences or in respect of the `droit de suite'.

2. This Convention shall not, however, be taken to cover royalties due in respect of the exploitation of cinematographic works or works produced by a process analogous to cinematography as defined in the domestic copyright laws of the Contracting State in which these royalties are originally due when the said royalties are due to the producers of such works or their heirs or successors - in - title.

3. With the exception of payments made in respect of the `droit de suite' the following shall not be considered as copyright royalties for the purposes of this Convention.: payments for the purchase, rental, loan or any other transfers of a right in the material base of a literary, artistic or scientific work, even if the amount of this payment is fixed in the light of the copyright royalties due or if the latter are determined, in - whole or in part, by that of the said payment. When a right in the material base of work is transferred as an accessory to the transfer of the entitlement to use a copyright in the work, only the payments in return for this entitlement are copyright royalties for the purposes of this Convention.

4. In the case of payments made in respect of the `droit de suite' and in all cases of the transfer of a right in the material base of a work referred to, in paragraph 3 of this Article and independently of the fact that the transfer in question is or is not free of charge, any payment made in settlement of or as a reimbursement for an insurance premium, transport or warehousing costs, agent's commission or any other remuneration for a service, and any other expenses incurred, directly or indirectly, by the removal of the material base in question, including customs duties and other related taxes and special levies, shall not be a copyright royalty for the purposes of this Convention.

Article 2: Beneficiary of copyright royalties

For the purposes of this Convention, the `beneficiary' of copyright royalties is the beneficial owner thereof to whom all or a part of such royalties is paid, whether he collects them as author, or heir or successor - in - title of the author, or whether he collects them in application of any other relevant criterion as agreed to in a bilateral agreement concerning double taxation of copyright royalties.

Article 3: State of residence of the beneficiary

1. For the purposes of this Convention, the State of which the beneficiary of the copyright royalties is a resident shall be deemed to be the State of residence of the beneficiary.

2. A person shall be deemed to be a resident of a State if he is liable to tax therein by reason of his domicile, residence, place of effective management or any other relevant criterion as agreed to in a bilateral agreement concerning double taxation of copyright royalties. But this term does not include any person who is liable to tax in that State in respect only of income from sources in that State as capital he possesses there.

Article 4: State of source of royalty

For the purposes of this Convention, a State shall be deemed to be the State of source of copyright royalties when such royalties for the use of, or the right to use, a copyright in a literary, artistic or scientific work are originally due:

(a) by that State or by a political or administrative subdivision or local authority of that State;

(b) by a resident of that State except where they result from an activity carried on by him in another State through a permanent establishment or from a fixed base;

(c) by a non - resident of that State, where they result from an activity carried on by him through a permanent establishment or from a fixed base.

Chapter II: Guiding principles for action against double taxation of copyright royalties

Article 5: Fiscal sovereignty and equality of rights of States

Action against double taxation of copyright royalties shall be carried out, in accordance with the provisions of Article 8 of this Convention, with due respect for the fiscal sovereignty of the State of source and the State of residence, and due respect for the equality of their right to tax these royalties.

Article 6: Fiscal non – discrimination

The measures against double taxation of copyright royalties shall not give rise to any tax discrimination based on nationality, race, sex, language or religion.

Article 7: Exchange of information

In so far as it is necessary for the implementation of this Convention, the competent authorities of the Contracting States will exchange reciprocally information in the form and under the conditions which shall be laid down by means of bilateral agreement.

Chapter III: Implementation of the guiding principles for the action against double taxation of copyright royalties

Article 8: Means of implementation

1. Each Contracting State undertakes to make every possible effort, in accordance with its Constitution and the guiding principles set out above, to avoid double taxation of copyright royalties, where possible, and, should it subsist, to eliminate it or to reduce its effect. This action shall be carried out by means of bilateral agreements or by way of domestic measures.

2. The bilateral agreements referred to in paragraph 1 of this Article include those which deal with double taxation in general or those which are limited to double taxation of copyright royalties. An optional model of a bilateral agreement of the latter category, comprising several alternatives, is attached to this Convention of which it does not form an integral part. The Contracting States, while respecting the provisions of this Convention, may conclude bilateral agreements based on the norms that are most acceptable to them in each particular case. The application of bilateral agreements concluded earlier by the Contracting States is in no way affected by this Convention.

3. In case of adoption of domestic measures, each Contracting State may, notwithstanding the provisions of Article 1 of this Convention, define copyright royalties by reference to its own copyright legislation.

Chapter IV: General provisions

Article 9: Members of diplomatic or consular missions

The provisions of this Convention do not affect the fiscal privileges of members of diplomatic or consular missions of the Contracting States, as well as of their families, either under the general rules of international law or under the provisions of special conventions.

Article 10: Information

1. The Secretariat of the United Nations Educational, Scientific and Cultural Organization and the International Bureau of the World Intellectual Property Organization shall assemble and publish relevant normative information concerning taxation of copyright royalties.

2. Each Contracting State shall communicate, as soon as possible, to the Secretariat of the United Nations Educational, Scientific and Cultural Organization and to the International Bureau of the World Intellectual Property Organization, the text of any new law, as well as all official texts concerning the taxation of copyright royalties, including the text of any specific bilateral agreement on the relevant provisions on the said subject contained in any bilateral agreement dealing with double taxation in general.

3. The Secretariat of the United Nations Educational, Scientific and Cultural Organization and the International Bureau of the World Intellectual Property Organization shall furnish to any Contracting State, upon its request, information on questions relating to this Convention; they shall also carry out studies and provide services in order to facilitate the application of this Convention.

Chapter V: Final clauses

Article 11: Ratification, acceptance, accession

1. This Convention shall be deposited with the Secretary - General of the United Nations Organization. It shall remain open until October 31, 1980, for signature by any State that is a member of the United Nations, any of the Specialized Agencies brought into relationship with the United Nations or the International Atomic Energy Agency, or is a party to the Statute of the International Court of Justice.

2. This Convention shall be subject to ratification or acceptance by the signatory States. It shall be open for accession by any State referred to in paragraph 1 of this Article.

3. Instruments of ratification, acceptance or assession shall be deposited with the Secretary - General of the United Nations.

4. It is understood that, at the time a State becomes bound by this Convention, it will be in a position in accordance with its domestic law to give effect to the provisions of this Convention.

Article 12: Reservations

The Contracting States may, either at the time of signature of this Convention or at the time of ratification, acceptance or accession, make reservations as regards the conditions of application of the provisions contained in Articles 1 to 4, 9 and 17. No other reservation to the Convention shall be permitted.

Article 13: Entry into force

1. This Convention shall enter into force three months after the deposit of the tenth instrument of ratification, acceptance or accession.

2. For each State ratifying, accepting, or acceding to this Convention after the deposit of the tenth instrument of ratification, acceptance or accession, this Convention shall enter into force three months after the deposit of its instrument.

Article 14: Denunciation

1. Any Contracting State may denounce this Convention by a written notification addressed to the Secretary - General of the United Nations.

2. Such denunciation shall take effect twelve months after the date of receipt of the notification by the Secretary - General of the United Nations.

Article 15: Revision

1. After this Convention has been in force for five years, any Contracting State may, by notification addressed to the Secretary - General of the United Nations, request that a conference be convened for the purpose of revising the Convention. The Secretary - General shall notify all Contracting States of this request. If, within a period of six months following the date of notification by the Secretary - General of the United Nations, not less than one - third of the Contracting States, provided the number is not less than five, notify him of their concurrence with the request, the Secretary - General shall inform the Director - General of the United Nations Educational, Scientific and Cultural Organization and the Director General of the World Intellectual Property Organization, who shall convene a revision conference with a view to introducing into this Convention amendments de-

signed to improve action against double taxation of copyright royalties.

2. The adoption of any revision of this Convention shall require an affirmative vote by two - thirds of the States attending the revision conference, provided that this majority includes two - thirds of the States which, at the time of the revision conference, are parties to the Convention.

3. Any State which becomes a party to the Convention after the entry into force of a new Convention wholly or partially revising this Convention shall, failing an expression of a different intention by that State, be considered as:

(a) a party to the revised convention;

(b) a party to this Convention in relation to any State which is a party to the present Convention but is not bound by the revised convention.

4. This Convention shall remain in force as regards relations between or with the Contracting States, which have not become parties to the revised convention.

Article 16: Languages of the convention and notifications

1. This Convention shall be signed in a single copy in Arabic, English, French, Russian and Spanish, the five texts being equally authoritative.

2. Official texts shall be established by the Director General of the United Nations Educational, Scientific and Cultural Organization and the Director General of the World Intellectual Property Organization, after consultation with the interested Governments concerned, in the German, Italian and Portuguese languages.

3. The Secretary - General of the United Nations shall notify the States referred to in Article 11, paragraph 1, as well as the Director - General of the United Nations Educational, Scientific and Cultural Organization and the Director General of the World Intellectual Property Organization of

(a) signature of this Convention, together with any accompanying text;

(b) the deposit of instruments of ratification, acceptance of accession, together with any accompanying text;

(c) the date of entry into force of this Convention under Article 13, paragraph 1;

(d) the receipt of notifications of denunciation;

(e) the requests communicated to him in accordance with Article 15, as well as any communication received from the Contracting States concerning the revision of this Convention.

4. The Secretary - General of the United Nations shall transmit two certified

copies of this Convention to all States referred to in Article 11, paragraph 1.

Article 17: Interpretation and settlement of disputes

1. A dispute between two or more Contracting States concerning the interpretation or in the matter of application of this Convention, not settled by negotiation, shall, unless the States concerned agree on some other method of settlement, be brought before the International Court of Justice for determination by it.

2. Any State may, at the time of signing this Convention or depositing its instrument of ratification, acceptance or accession, declare that it does not consider itself bound by the provisions of paragraph 1. In the event of a dispute between that State and any other Contracting State, the provisions of paragraph I shall not apply.

3. Any State that has made a declaration in accordance with paragraph 2 may at any time withdraw it by notification addressed to the Secretary General of the United Nations.

保护表演者、音像制品制作者和广播组织国际公约

（1961年10月26日于罗马签订）

缔约各国，出于保护表演者、录音制品制作者和广播组织的权利的愿望，达成如下协议：

第一条 本公约给予之保护将不更动也决不影响文学和艺术作品的版权保护。因此，本公约的条款不得作妨碍此种保护的解释。

第二条

（一）在本公约中，国民待遇指被要求给予保护的缔约国的国内法律给予

（甲）其节目在该国境内表演、广播或首次录制的身为该国国民的表演者的待遇；

（乙）其录音制品在该国境内首次录制或首次发行的身为该国国民的录音制品制作者的待遇；

（丙）其广播节目从设在该国领土上的发射台发射的总部设在该国境内的广播组织的待遇。

（二）国民待遇应服从本公约具体给予的保护和具体规定的限制。

第三条 在本公约中：

（甲）“表演者”是指演员、歌唱家、音乐家、舞蹈家和表演、歌唱、演说、朗诵、演奏或以别的方式表演文学或艺术作品的其他人员；

（乙）“录音制品”是指任何对表演的声音和其他声音的专门录音；

（丙）“录音制品制作者”是指首次将表演的声音或其他声音录制下来的自然人或法人；

（丁）“发行”是指向公众提供适当数量的某种唱片的复制品；

（戊）“复制”是指制作一件或多件某种录音的复版；

（己）“广播”是指供公众接收的声音或图像和声音的无线电传播；

（庚）“转播”是指一个广播组织的广播节目被另一个广播组织同时广播。

第四条 只要符合下列条件之一，缔约各国应当给予表演者以国民待遇：

（甲）表演是在另一缔约国进行的；

（乙）表演已被录制在受本公约第五条保护的录音制品上；

（丙）表演未被录制成录音制品，但在受本公约第六条保护的广播节目中播放。

第五条

（一）只要符合下列条件之一，缔约各国应当给予录音制品制作者以国民待遇：

（甲）录音制品制作者是另一个缔约国的国民（国民标准）；

（乙）首次录音是在另一个缔约国制作的（录制标准）；

（丙）录音制品是在另一个缔约国首次发行的（发行标准）。

（二）如果某种录音制品是在某一非缔约国首次发行的，但在首次发行后三十天内也在某一缔约国发行（同时发行），则该录音制品应当认为是在该缔约国首次发行。

（三）任何缔约国，通过向联合国秘书长递交通知书的办法，可以声明它将不执行发行标准，或者不执行录制标准。此类通知书可以在批准、接受或参加本公约的时候递交，也可以在此后任何时间递交。在后一种情况下，通知书应当于递交六个月之后生效。

第六条

（一）只要符合下列两项条件之一，缔约各国就应当给予广播组织以国民待遇：

（甲）该广播组织的总部设在另一缔约国；

（乙）广播节目是由设在另一缔约国的发射台播放的。

（二）任何缔约国，通过向联合国秘书长递交通知书的办法，可以声明它只保护其总部设在另一个缔约国并从设在该同一缔约国的发射台播放的广播组织的广播节目。此种通知书可以在批准、接受或参加本公约的时候递交，或在此后任何时间递交。在后一种情况下，通知书应当于递交六个月之后生效。

第七条

（一）本公约为表演者提供的保护应当包括防止可能发生的下列情况：

（甲）未经他们同意，广播和向公众传播他们的表演。但是如该表演本身就是广播演出或出自录音、录像者例外；

（乙）未经他们同意，录制他们未曾录制过的表演；

（丙）未经他们同意，复制他们的表演的录音或录像：

（1）如果录音、录像的原版是未经他们同意录制的；

（2）如果制作复制品的目的超出表演者同意的范围；

（3）如果录音、录像的原版是根据第十五条的规定录制的，而制作复制品的目的与此条规定的目的不同。

（二）（1）如果广播是经演员同意的，则防止转播，防止为广播目的的录音、录像，以及防止为广播目的的此类录音、录像的复制，应当由要求其保护的缔约国的国内法律规定。

（2）广播组织使用为广播目的而制作的录音录像的期限和条件，应当根据要求其保护的缔约的国内法律确定。

（3）但是，本款第（1）和（2）小款中提到的国内法律不得用来使表演者失去通过合同控制他们与广播组织之间的关系的能力。

第八条　如果若干表演者参加同一项表演，任何缔约国均可根据本国法律和规章，明确指出表演者在行使权利方面确定代表的方式。

第九条　任何缔约国均可根据国内法律和规章，将本公约提供的保护扩大到不是表演文学或艺术作品的艺人。

第十条　录音制品制作者应当有权授权或禁止直接或间接复制他们的录音制品。

第十一条　对于录音制品，如果某缔约国根据其国内法律要求履行手续作为保护录音制品制作者或表演者或二者的权利的条件，那么只要已经发行的录音制品的所有供销售的复制品上或其包装物上载有包括符号（P）和首次发行年份的标记，并且标记的方式足以使人注意到对保护的要求，就应当认为符合手续；如果复制品或其包装物上没有注明制作者或制作者的许可证持有者（载明姓名、商标或其他适当的标志），则标记还应当包括制作者权利所有者的姓名；此外，如果复制品或其包装物上没有注明主要表演者，则标记还应当包括在制作这些录音的国家内拥有此种表演者权利的人的姓名。

第十二条　如果某种为商业目的发行的录音制品或此类唱片的复制品直接用于广播或任何向公众的传播，使用者则应当付一笔总的合理的报酬给表演者，或录音制品制作者，或给二者。如有关各方之间没有协议，国内法律可以提出分享这些报酬的条件。

第十三条　广播组织应当有权授权或禁止：

（甲）转播他们的广播节目；

（乙）录制他们的广播节目；

（丙）复制：

（1）未经他们同意而制作他们的广播节目的录音或录像；

（2）根据第十五条的规定而制作他们的广播节目的录音和录像，但复制的目的不符合该条规定的目的。

（丁）向公众传播电视节目，如果此类传播是在收门票的公共场所进行的。行使这种权利的条件由被要求保护的缔约国的国内法律确定。

第十四条　本公约所给予的保护期限至少应当为二十年，其计算始于：

（甲）对录音制品和录制在录音制品上的节目——录制年份的年底；

（乙）对未被录制成录音制品的节目——表演年份的年底；

（丙）对广播节目——开始广播的年份的年底。

第十五条

（一）任何缔约国可以依其国内法律与规章，在涉及下列情况时，对本公约规定的保护做出例外规定：

（甲）私人使用；

（乙）在时事报道中少量引用；

（丙）某广播组织为了自己的广播节目利用自己的设备暂时录制；

（丁）仅用于教学和科学研究之目的。

（二）尽管有本条第一款，任何缔约国对于表演者、录音制品制作者和广播组织的保护，可以在其国内法律与规章中做出像它在国内法律和规章中做出的对文学和艺术作品的版权保护的同样的限制。但是，只有在不违背本公约的范围内才能颁发强迫许可证。

第十六条

（一）任何国家一旦成为本公约的成员，就应当履行本公约的所有义务，同时享受本公约的所有权益。但是，任何国家可以在任何时候在递交联合国秘书长的通知书中声明：

（甲）关于第十二条：

（1）它将不执行该条规定；

（2）它将在某些使用方面不执行该条规定；

（3）对其制作者不是另一缔约国国民的录音制品，它将不执行该条规定；

（4）对其制作者是另一缔约国国民的录音制品，它将根据该缔约国给予发表声明的国家的国民首次录制的录音制品的保护范围与期限，对此条规定的保护范围与期限做出相应限制；但是，录音制品制作者为其国民的缔约国，对同一个或同一伙受益人不像发表声明的国家那样给予保护的事实，不能认为是保护范围的不同。

（乙）关于第十三条，它将不执行该条（丁）款；如果某个缔约国发表此种声明，其他缔约国对其总部设在上述缔约国的广播组织则没有义务给予第十三条（丁）款提到的权利。

（二）如果本条第一款提到的通知书是在批准、接受或参加证书递交之日以后发布。

第十七条 任何在1961年10月26日仅根据录制标准给予录音制品制作者以保护的国家，可以在批准、接受或参加本公约时通过向联合国秘书长递交通知书声明，为了第五条的目的，它仅执行录制标准；为了第十六条第一款（甲）目第（3）和第（4）小节的目的，他将执行录制标准以代替国民标准。

第十八条 任何根据第五条第三款、第六条第二款、第十六条第一款或第十七条递交了通知书的国家，通过向联合国秘书长递交另外一份通知书，可以缩小第一次通知书的范围或撤回该通知书。

第十九条 不管本公约有什么规定，一旦表演者同意将其表演录像或录音录像，第七条就不再适用。

第二十条

（一）本公约不得影响任何缔约国当本公约在该国生效之前已经获得的权利。

（二）任何缔约国无须一定将本公约的条款运用于本公约在该国生效之前已经进行的表演和已经广播的节目，以及已经录制的录音制品。

第二十一条 本公约规定的保护不得影响表演者、录音制品制作者和广播组织另外取得的任何保护。

第二十二条 缔约各国保留互相之间签订特别协定的权利，只要此类协定给予表演者、录音制品制作者和广播组织的权利比本公约给予的权利更广泛，或包含其他不与本公约相反的条款。

第二十三条 本公约应当送交联合国秘书长。凡被邀请参加国际保护表演者、录音制品制作者和广播组织外交会议的任何世界版权公约的成员国或保护文学艺术作品国际联盟的成员国，1962年6月30日前均可在本公约上签字。

第二十四条

（一）本公约须经签字国批准或接受。

（二）第二十三条提到的被邀请参加会议的任何国家和任何联合国成员国，只要它们参加了世界版权公约或保护文学艺术作品国际联盟，均可参加本公约。

（三）批准、接受或参加本公约须向联合国秘书长递交有关证书后方能生效。

第二十五条

（一）本公约应当于第六份批准、接受或参加证书递交三个月之后生效。

（二）此后，本公约应当于各个有关国家递交批准、接受或参加证书三个月之后在该国生效。

第二十六条

（一）各缔约国保证根据本国宪法采取必要措施保障本公约的实施。

（二）各国在递交批准、接受或参加证书时，它就必须处于根据其国内法律使本公约所有条款生效的地位。

第二十七条

（一）任何国家在批准、接受或参加本公约时，或在此后任何时间，可以在致联合国秘书长的通知书中，声明本公约将适用于由它对其国际关系负责的所有或其中任何一个领地，只要世界版权公约或保护文学艺术作品国际公约适用于这个或这些领地。此通知书应当从收到之日起三个月后生效。

（二）第五条第三款、第六条第二款、第十六条第二款和第十七、十八条所提到的通知书，可以适用于本条第一款提到的所有或其中任何一个领地。

第二十八条

（一）任何缔约国可以用自己的名义或代表第二十七条中提到的所有或其中任何一个领地，通知退出本公约。

（二）退出本公约必须通过向联合国秘书长递交通知书方能生效，而且应当于通知书收到之日后十二个月生效。

（三）本公约在某缔约国生效未满五年，该缔约国不得行使通知退出的权利。

（四）当某缔约国既不是世界版权公约的成员也不是保护文学艺术作品国际联盟的成员时，它就不再是本公约的成员。

（五）当世界版权公约或保护文学艺术作品的国际公约不适用于第二十七条中提到的领地时，本公约就不再适用于该领地。

第二十九条

（一）本公约生效五年之后，任何缔约国可以通知联合国秘书长要求召开会议修改本公约。联合国秘书长应当将此要求通知所有缔约国。如果联合国秘书长发出通知后六个月之内，有不少于半数的缔约国通知他同意此种要求，则秘书长应当通知国际劳工组织总干事、联合国教育科学文化组织总干事和保护文学艺术作品国际联盟国际局主任，他们应当与第三十二条提到的政府间委员会合作召集修改公约的会议。

（二）本公约的任何修改需要参加修改会议的三分之二的国家投赞成票通过，但是这个多数要包括在召开修改会议时本公约的三分之二的成员国。

（三）一旦通过了一个全部或部分地修订本公约的公约，除修订的公约内另有规定外，则：

（甲）从修订的公约生效之日起，应当停止批准、接受或参加本公约；

（乙）对于尚未成为修订公约的缔约国的各国，涉及它们之间的关系或涉及本公约与它们之间的关系，本公约应当继续有效。

第三十条　如两个或数个缔约国对本公约的解释或实施发生争执而又不能通过谈判解决时，此争执应当根据争执诸方中任何一方的要求，提交国际法庭裁决，除非他们同意采取另外的办法解决。

第三十一条　在不妨碍第五条第三款、第六条第二款、第十六条第一款和第十七条的规定的情况下，不得对本公约作保留。

第三十二条

（一）特设立一个政府间委员会，其职责如下：

（甲）研究本公约的运用和执行的有关事宜；

（乙）为可能修订本公约收集建议和准备文件资料。

（二）委员会由缔约国的代表组成，代表的选择应当考虑地区的合理分配；委员会成员的数目，如果缔约国是十二个或少于十二个，则为六名，如果缔约国是十三个至十八个，则为九名，如缔约国超过十八个，则为十二名。

（三）委员会应当于公约生效后十二个月选举产生，选举由国际劳工组织总干事、联合国教育科学文化组织总干事和保护文学艺术作品国际联盟国际局主任根据大多数缔约国事先通过的规则来组织，每个缔约国均为一票。

（四）委员会选举主席和官员，制订自己的议事程序规则。这些规则应当特别规定保证在各成员国之间用轮换的办法进行委员会未来的活动和对成员的选择。

（五）由其总干事或主任指定的国际劳工组织、联合国教育科学文化组织和保护文学艺术作品国际联盟国际局的官员组成委员会的秘书处。

（六）只要委员会大多数成员认为有必要，委员会应随时召开，会议轮流在国际劳工组织总部、联合国教育科学文化组织总部和保护文学艺术作品国际联盟国际局总部举行。

（七）委员会成员的费用应当由各自的政府负担。

第三十三条

（一）本公约用英文、法文和西班牙文制订，三种文本具有同等效力。

（二）此外，本公约的正式文本还将用德文、意大利文和葡萄牙文制订。

第三十四条

（一）联合国秘书长应当通知第二十三条提到的会议的应邀参加国家和所有联合国成员国，以及国际劳工组织总干事、联合国教育科学文化组织总干事和保护文学艺术作品国际联盟国际局主任以下事项：

（甲）每份批准、接受或参加证书的递交；

（乙）公约生效的日期；

（丙）公约规定的所有通知、声明或信件；

（丁）出现第二十八条第四、五款提到的任何情况。

（二）联合国秘书长还应当将根据第二十九条向他提出的要求以及从缔约国收到的任何涉及修改本公约的信件通知国际劳工组织总干事、联合国教育科学文化组织总干事和保护文学艺术作品国际联盟国际局主任。

Rome Convention for the Protection of Performers, Producers of Phonograms and Broadcasting Organizations

Done at Rome on October 26, 1961

The Contracting States, moved by the desire to protect the rights of performers, producers of phonograms, and broadcasting organisations,

Have agreed as follows:

Article 1

[Safeguard of Copyright Proper *]

* Articles have been given titles to facilitate their identification. There are no titles in the signed text.

Protection granted under this Convention shall leave intact and shall in no way affect the protection of copyright in literary and artistic works. Consequently, no provision of this Convention may be interpreted as prejudicing such protection.

Article 2

[Protection given by the Convention. Definition of National Treatment]

1. For the purposes of this Convention, national treatment shall mean the treatment accorded by the domestic law of the Contracting State in which protection is claimed:

(a) to performers who are its nationals, as regards performances taking place, broadcast, or first fixed, on its territory;

(b) to producers of phonograms who are its nationals, as regards phonograms first fixed or first published on its territory;

(c) to broadcasting organisations which have their headquarters on its territory, as regards broadcasts transmitted from transmitters situated on its territory.

2. National treatment shall be subject to the protection specifically guaranteed,

and the limitations specifically provided for, in this Convention.

Article 3

[Definitions: (a) Performers; (b) Phonogram; (c) Producers of Phonograms; (d) Publication; (e) Reproduction; (f) Broadcasting; (g) Rebroadcasting]

For the purposes of this Convention:

(a) 'performers' means actors, singers, musicians, dancers, and other persons who act, sing, deliver, declaim, play in, or otherwise perform literary or artistic works;

(b) 'phonogram' means any exclusively aural fixation of sounds of a performance or of other sounds;

(c) 'producer of phonograms' means the person who, or the legal entity which, first fixes the sounds of a performance or other sounds;

(d) 'publication' means the offering of copies of a phonogram to the public in reasonable quantity;

(e) 'reproduction' means the making of a copy or copies of a fixation;

(f) 'broadcasting' means the transmission by wireless means for public reception of sounds or of images and sounds;

(g) 'rebroadcasting' means the simultaneous broadcasting by one broadcasting organisation of the broadcast of another broadcasting organisation.

Article 4

[Performances Protected. Points of Attachment for Performers]

Each Contracting State shall grant national treatment to performers if any of the following conditions is met:

(a) the performance takes place in another Contracting State;

(b) the performance is incorporated in a phonogram which is protected under Article 5 of this Convention;

(c) the performance, not being fixed on a phonogram, is carried by a broadcast which is protected by Article 6 of this Convention.

Article 5

[Protected Phonograms: 1. Points of Attachment for Producers of Phonograms; 2. Simultaneous Publication; 3. Power to exclude certain Criteria]

1. Each Contracting State shall grant national treatment to producers of phonograms if any of the following conditions is met:

(a) the producer of the phonogram is a national of another Contracting State (criterion of nationality);

(b) the first fixation of the sound was made in another Contracting State (criterion of fixation);

(c) the phonogram was first published in another Contracting State (criterion of publication).

2. If a phonogram was first published in a non - contracting State but if it was also published, within thirty days of its first publication, in a Contracting State (simultaneous publication), it shall be considered as first published in the Contracting State.

3. By means of a notification deposited with the Secretary - General of the United Nations, any Contracting State may declare that it will not apply the criterion of publication or, alternatively, the criterion of fixation. Such notification may be deposited at the time of ratification, acceptance or accession, or at any time thereafter; in the last case, it shall become effective six months after it has been deposited.

Article 6

[Protected Broadcasts: 1. Points of Attachment for Broadcasting Organizations; 2. Power to Reserve]

1. Each Contracting State shall grant national treatment to broadcasting organisations if either of the following conditions is met:

(a) the headquarters of the broadcasting organisation is situated in another Contracting State;

(b) the broadcast was transmitted from a transmitter situated in another Contracting State.

2. By means of a notification deposited with the Secretary - General of the United Nations, any Contracting State may declare that it will protect broadcasts only if the headquarters of the broadcasting organisation is situated in another Contracting State and the broadcast was transmitted from a transmitter situated in the same Contracting State. Such notification may be deposited at the time of ratification, acceptance or accession, or at any time thereafter; in the last case, it shall become effective six months after it has been deposited.

Article 7

[Minimum Protection for Performers: 1. Particular Rights; 2. Relations between Performers and Broadcasting Organizations]

1. The protection provided for performers by this Convention shall include the possibility of preventing:

(a) the broadcasting and the communication to the public, without their consent, of their performance, except where the performance used in the broadcasting or the public communication is itself already a broadcast performance or is made from a fixation;

(b) the fixation, without their consent, of their unfixed performance;

(c) the reproduction, without their consent, of a fixation of their performance:

(i)

if the original fixation itself was made without their consent;

(ii)

if the reproduction is made for purposes different from those for which the performers gave their consent;

(iii)

if the original fixation was made in accordance with the provisions of Article 15, and the reproduction is made for purposes different from those referred to in those provisions.

2.

(1) If broadcasting was consented to by the performers, it shall be a matter for the domestic law of the Contracting State where protection is claimed to regulate the protection against rebroadcasting, fixation for broadcasting purposes and the reproduction of such fixation for broadcasting purposes.

(2) The terms and conditions governing the use by broadcasting organisations of fixations made for broadcasting purposes shall be determined in accordance with the domestic law of the Contracting State where protection is claimed.

(3) However, the domestic law referred to in sub - paragraphs (1) and (2) of this paragraph shall not operate to deprive performers of the ability to control, by contract, their relations with broadcasting organisations.

Article 8

[Performers acting jointly]

Any Contracting State may, by its domestic laws and regulations, specify the manner in which performers will be represented in connexion with the exercise of their rights if several of them participate in the same performance.

Article 9

[Variety and Circus Artists]

Any Contracting State may, by its domestic laws and regulations, extend the protection provided for in this Convention to artists who do not perform literary or artistic works.

Article 10

[Right of Reproduction for Phonogram Producers]

Producers of phonograms shall enjoy the right to authorise or prohibit the direct or indirect reproduction of their phonograms.

Article 11

[Formalities for Phonograms]

If, as a condition of protecting the rights of producers of phonograms, or of performers, or both, in relation to phonograms, a Contracting State, under its domestic law, requires compliance with formalities, these shall be considered as fulfilled if all the copies in commerce of the published phonogram or their containers bear a notice consisting of the symbol (P), accompanied by the year date of the first publication, placed in such a manner as to give reasonable notice of claim of protection; and if the copies or their containers do not identify the producer or the licensee of the producer (by carrying his name, trade mark or other appropriate designation), the notice shall also include the name of the owner of the rights of the producer; and, furthermore, if the copies or their containers do not identify the principal performers, the notice shall also include the name of the person who, in the country in which the fixation was effected, owns the rights of such performers.

Article 12

[Secondary Uses of Phonograms]

If a phonogram published for commercial purposes, or a reproduction of such phonogram, is used directly for broadcasting or for any communication to the public, a single equitable remuneration shall be paid by the user to the performers, or to the producers of the phonograms, or to both. Domestic law may, in the absence of agreement between these parties, lay down the conditions as to the sharing of this remuneration.

Article 13

[Minimum Rights for Broadcasting Organizations]

Broadcasting organisations shall enjoy the right to authorise or prohibit:

(a) the rebroadcasting of their broadcasts;

(b) the fixation of their broadcasts;

(c) the reproduction:

(i)

of fixations, made without their consent, of their broadcasts;

(ii)

of fixations, made in accordance with the provisions of Article 15, of their broadcasts, if the reproduction is made for purposes different from those referred to in those provisions;

(d) the communication to the public of their television broadcasts if such communication is made in places accessible to the public against payment of an entrance fee; it shall be a matter for the domestic law of the State where protection of this right is claimed to determine the conditions under which it may be exercised.

Article 14

[Minimum Duration of Protection]

The term of protection to be granted under this Convention shall last at least until the end of a period of twenty years computed from the end of the year in which:

(a) the fixation was made - for phonograms and for performances incorporated therein;

(b) the performance took place - for performances not incorporated in phonograms;

(c) the broadcast took place - for broadcasts.

Article 15

[Permitted Exceptions: 1. Specific Limitations; 2. Equivalents with copyright]

1. Any Contracting State may, in its domestic laws and regulations, provide

for exceptions to the protection guaranteed by this Convention as regards:

(a) private use;

(b) use of short excerpts in connexion with the reporting of current events;

(c) ephemeral fixation by a broadcasting organisation by means of its own facilities and for its own broadcasts;

(d) use solely for the purposes of teaching or scientific research.

2. Irrespective of paragraph 1 of this Article, any Contracting State may, in its domestic laws and regulations, provide for the same kinds of limitations with regard to the protection of performers, producers of phonograms and broadcasting organisations, as it provides for, in its domestic laws and regulations, in connexion with the protection of copyright in literary and artistic works. However, compulsory licences may be provided for only to the extent to which they are compatible with this Convention.

Article 16

[Reservations]

1. Any State, upon becoming party to this Convention, shall be bound by all the obligations and shall enjoy all the benefits thereof. However, a State may at any time, in a notification deposited with the Secretary - General of the United Nations, declare that:

(a) as regards Article 12:

(i)

it will not apply the provisions of that Article;

(ii)

it will not apply the provisions of that Article in respect of certain uses;

(iii)

as regards phonograms the producer of which is not a national of another Contracting State, it will not apply that Article;

(iv)

as regards phonograms the producer of which is a national of another Contracting State, it will limit the protection provided for by that Article to the extent to which, and to the term for which, the latter State grants protection to phonograms first fixed by a national of the State making the declaration; however, the fact that the Contracting State of which the producer is a national does not grant the protection to the same beneficiary or beneficiaries as the State making the declaration shall not be considered as a difference in the extent of the protection;

(b) as regards Article 13, it will not apply item 13 (d); if a Contracting State makes such a declaration, the other Contracting States shall not be obliged to grant the right referred to in Article 13 (d), to broadcasting organisations whose headquarters are in that State.

2. If the notification referred to in paragraph 1 of this Article is made after the date of the deposit of the instrument of ratification, acceptance or accession, the declaration will become effective six months after it has been deposited.

Article 17

[Certain countries applying only the fixation´criterion]

Any State which, on October 26, 1961, grants protection to producers of phonograms solely on the basis of the criterion of fixation may, by a notification deposited with the Secretary - General of the United Nations at the time of ratification, acceptance or accession, declare that it will apply, for the purposes of Article 5, the criterion of fixation alone and, for the purposes of paragraph 16. 1 (a) (iii) and 16. 1 (a) (iv), the criterion of fixation instead of the criterion of nationality.

Article 18

[Withdrawal of reservations]

Any State which has deposited a notification under Article 5. 3, Article 6. 2, Article 16. 1 or Article 17, may, by a further notification deposited with the Secretary - General of the United Nations, reduce its scope or withdraw it.

Article 19

[Performers´Rights in Films]

Notwithstanding anything in this Convention, once a performer has consented to the incorporation of his performance in a visual or audio - visual fixation, Article 7 shall have no further application.

Article 20

[Non – retroactivity]

1. This Convention shall not prejudice rights acquired in any Contracting State before the date of coming into force of this Convention for that State.

2. No Contracting State shall be bound to apply the provisions of this Con-

vention to performances or broadcasts which took place, or to phonograms which were fixed, before the date of coming into force of this Convention for that State.

Article 21

[Protection by other means]

The protection provided for in this Convention shall not prejudice any protection otherwise secured to performers, producers of phonograms and broadcasting organisations.

Article 22

[Special agreements]

Contracting States reserve the right to enter into special agreements among themselves in so far as such agreements grant to performers, producers of phonograms or broadcasting organisations more extensive rights than those granted by this Convention or contain other provisions not contrary to this Convention.

Article 23

[Signature and deposit]

This Convention shall be deposited with the Secretary - General of the United Nations. It shall be open until June 30, 1962, for signature by any State invited to the Diplomatic Conference on the International Protection of Performers, Producers of Phonograms and Broadcasting Organisations which is a party to the Universal Copyright Convention or a member of the International Union for the Protection of Literary and Artistic Works.

Article 24

[Becoming Party to the Convention]

1. This Convention shall be subject to ratification or acceptance by the signatory States.

2. This Convention shall be open for accession by any State invited to the Conference referred to in Article 23, and by any State Member of the United Nations, provided that in either case such State is a party to the Universal Copyright Convention or a member of the International Union for the Protection of Literary and Artistic Works.

3. Ratification, acceptance or accession shall be effected by the deposit of an instrument to that effect with the Secretary - General of the United Nations.

Article 25

[Entry into force]

1. This Convention shall come into force three months after the date of deposit of the sixth instrument of ratification, acceptance or accession.

2. Subsequently, this Convention shall come into force in respect of each State three months after the date of deposit of its instrument of ratification, acceptance or accession.

Article 26

[Implementation of the Convention by the Provision of Domestic Law]

1. Each Contracting State undertakes to adopt, in accordance with its Constitution, the measures necessary to ensure the application of this Convention.

2. At the time of deposit of its instrument of ratification, acceptance or accession, each State must be in a position under its domestic law to give effect to the terms of this Convention.

Article 27

[Applicability of the Convention to Certain Territories]

1. Any State may, at the time of ratification, acceptance or accession, or at any time thereafter, declare by notification addressed to the Secretary - General of the United Nations that this Convention shall extend to all or any of the territories for whose international relations it is responsible, provided that the Universal Copyright Convention or the International Convention for the Protection of Literary and Artistic Works applies to the territory or territories concerned. This notification shall take effect three months after the date of its receipt.

2. The notifications referred to in Article 5. 3, Article 6. 2, Article 16. 1 and Articles 17 and 18, may be extended to cover all or any of the territories referred to in paragraph 1 of this Article.

Article 28

[Denunciation of the Convention]

1. Any Contracting State may denounce this Convention, on its own behalf or on behalf of all or any of the territories referred to in Article 27.

2. The denunciation shall be effected by a notification addressed to the Secretary - General of the United Nations and shall take effect twelve months after the date of receipt of the notification.

3. The right of denunciation shall not be exercised by a Contracting State before the expiry of a period of five years from the date on which the Convention came into force with respect to that State.

4. A Contracting State shall cease to be a party to this Convention from that time when it is neither a party to the Universal Copyright Convention nor a member of the International Union for the Protection of Literary and Artistic Works.

5. This Convention shall cease to apply to any territory referred to in Article 27 from that time when neither the Universal Copyright Convention nor the International Convention for the Protection of Literary and Artistic Works applies to that territory.

Article 29

[Revision of the Convention]

1. After this Convention has been in force for five years, any Contracting State may, by notification addressed to the Secretary - General of the United Nations, request that a conference be convened for the purpose of revising the Convention. The Secretary - General shall notify all Contracting States of this request. If, within a period of six months following the date of notification by the Secretary-General of the United Nations, not less than one half of the Contracting States notify him of their concurrence with the request, the Secretary - General shall inform the Director - General of the International Labour Office, the Director - General of the United Nations Educational, Scientific and Cultural Organization and the Director of the Bureau of the International Union for the Protection of Literary and Artistic Works, who shall convene a revision conference in co - operation with the Intergovernmental Committee provided for in Article 32.

2. The adoption of any revision of this Convention shall require an affirmative vote by two - thirds of the States attending the revision conference, provided that this majority includes two - thirds of the States which, at the time of the revision conference, are parties to the Convention.

3. In the event of adoption of a Convention revising this Convention in whole or in part, and unless the revising Convention provides otherwise:

(a) this Convention shall cease to be open to ratification, acceptance or accession as from the date of entry into force of the revising Convention;

(b) this Convention shall remain in force as regards relations between or with

Contracting States which have not become parties to the revising Convention.

Article 30

[Settlement of disputes]

Any dispute which may arise between two or more Contracting States concerning the interpretation or application of this Convention and which is not settled by negotiation shall, at the request of any one of the parties to the dispute, be referred to the International Court of Justice for decision, unless they agree to another mode of settlement.

Article 31

[Limits on Reservations]

Without prejudice to the provisions of Article 5. 3, Article 6. 2, Article 16. 1 and Article 17, no reservation may be made to this Convention.

Article 32

[Intergovernmental Committee]

1. An Intergovernmental Committee is hereby established with the following duties:

(a) to study questions concerning the application and operation of this Convention; and

(b) to collect proposals and to prepare documentation for possible revision of this Convention.

2. The Committee shall consist of representatives of the Contracting States, chosen with due regard to equitable geographical distribution. The number of members shall be six if there are twelve Contracting States or less, nine if there are thirteen to eighteen Contracting States and twelve if there are more than eighteen Contracting States.

3. The Committee shall be constituted twelve months after the Convention comes into force by an election organised among the Contracting States, each of which shall have one vote, by the Director - General of the International Labour Office, the Director - General of the United Nations Educational, Scientific and Cultural Organization and the Director of the Bureau of the International Union for the Protection of Literary and Artistic Works, in accordance with rules previously approved by a majority of all Contracting States.

4. The Committee shall elect its Chairman and officers. It shall establish its

own rules of procedure. These rules shall in particular provide for the future operation of the Committee and for a method of selecting its members for the future in such a way as to ensure rotation among the various Contracting States.

5. Officials of the International Labour Office, the United Nations Educational, Scientific and Cultural Organization and the Bureau of the International Union for the Protection of Literary and Artistic Works, designated by the Directors - General and the Director thereof, shall constitute the Secretariat of the Committee.

6. Meetings of the Committee, which shall be convened whenever a majority of its members deems it necessary, shall be held successively at the headquarters of the International Labour Office, the United Nations Educational, Scientific and Cultural Organization and the Bureau of the International Union for the Protection of Literary and Artistic Works.

7. Expenses of members of the Committee shall be borne by their respective Governments.

Article 33

[Languages]

1. The present Convention is drawn up in English, French and Spanish, the three texts being equally authentic.

2. In addition, official texts of the present Convention shall be drawn up in German, Italian and Portuguese.

Article 34

[Notifications]

1. The Secretary - General of the United Nations shall notify the States invited to the Conference referred to in Article 23 and every State Member of the United Nations, as well as the Director - General of the International Labour Office, the Director - General of the United Nations Educational, Scientific and Cultural Organization and the Director of the Bureau of the International Union for the Protection of Literary and Artistic Works:

(a) of the deposit of each instrument of ratification, acceptance or accession;

(b) of the date of entry into force of the Convention;

(c) of all notifications, declarations or communications provided for in this Convention;

(d) if any of the situations referred to in paragraphs 28. 4 and 28. 5 arise.

2. The Secretary - General of the United Nations shall also notify the Director - General of the International Labour Office, the Director - General of the United Nations Educational, Scientific and Cultural Organization and the Director of the Bureau of the International Union for the Protection of Literary and Artistic Works of the requests communicated to him in accordance with Article 29, as well as of any communication received from the Contracting States concerning the revision of the Convention.

图书在版编目（CIP）数据

国际文化法文件汇编/中共中央宣传部政策法规研究室，中国社会科学院法学研究所编.
-北京：学习出版社，2013.12
ISBN 978-7-5147-0414-3

Ⅰ.①国… Ⅱ.①中…②中… Ⅲ.①文化宣传-行政法-汇编-世界
Ⅳ.①D912.109

中国版本图书馆 CIP 数据核字（2013）第 274358 号

国际文化法文件汇编

GUOJI WENHUAFA WENJIAN HUIBIAN

中共中央宣传部政策法规研究室
中国社会科学院法学研究所 编

责任编辑：夏 静
技术编辑：周媛卿
封面设计：杨 洪

出版发行：学习出版社
北京市崇外大街 11 号新成文化大厦 B 座 11 层（100062）
010-66063020 010-66061634 010-66061646
网 址：http://www.xuexiph.cn
经 销：新华书店
印 刷：北京联兴盛业印刷股份有限公司

开 本：710 毫米×1000 毫米 1/16
印 张：70.5
字 数：1228 千字
版次印次：2014 年 3 月第 1 版 2014 年 3 月第 1 次印刷

书 号：ISBN 978-7-5147-0414-3
定 价：126.00 元